SECOND EDITION

FOUNDATIONS OF COGNITIVE PSYCHOLOGY

Core Readings

DANIEL J. LEVITIN

McGill University

ALLYN & BACON

Boston   Columbus   Indianapolis   New York   San Francisco   Upper Saddle River

Amsterdam   Cape Town   Dubai   London   Madrid   Milan   Munich   Paris   Montreal   Toronto

Delhi   Mexico City   Sao Paulo   Sydney   Hong Kong   Seoul   Singapore   Taipei   Tokyo

Executive Editor: Susan Hartman
Editorial Project Manager: Kara Kikel
Editorial Assistant: Laura Barry
Marketing Manager: Nicole Kunzmann
Senior Production Project Manager: Claudine Bellanton
Manufacturing Buyer: Debbie Rossi
Cover Administrator: Kristina Mose-Libon
Editorial Production and Composition Service: Laserwords Maine

Library of Congress Cataloging-in-Publication Data
Levitin, Daniel J.
  Foundations of cognitive psychology / Daniel J. Levitin. – 2nd ed.
    p. cm.
  Includes bibliographical references and index.
  ISBN-13: 978-0-205-71147-5 (alk. paper)
  ISBN-10: 0-205-71147-2 (alk. paper)
  1. Cognitive psychology. I. Title.
  BF201.L48 2011
  153—dc22

                                                    2010041152

10 9 8 7 6 5 4 3 2 1 V013 14 13 12 11 10

Allyn & Bacon
is an imprint of

www.pearsonhighered.com

ISBN 10: 0-205-71147-2
ISBN 13: 978-0-205-71147-5

To Al Bregman,
Teacher, colleague, friend . . . and a
constant source of inspiration

CONTENTS

CHAPTER SEVEN

SECTION IV   CATEGORIZATION

CHAPTER EIGHT

CHAPTER NINE

CHAPTER TEN

SECTION V   LEARNING & MEMORY

CHAPTER ELEVEN

CHAPTER TWELVE

CHAPTER THIRTEEN

CHAPTER FOURTEEN

SECTION VI   ATTENTION

SECTION VII   MUSIC COGNITION

SECTION VIII   EXPERTISE

SECTION XII   INTELLIGENCE

SECTION XIII   COGNITIVE NEUROSCIENCE

SECTION XIV   CROSS-CULTURAL COGNITION

PREFACE

I took my first psychology class as a freshman in college, entirely by accident. I found out two days before the start of the semester that the electrical engineering course I needed to take for my major was overbooked. One serious constraint was that I am a night person, usually up until 4 or 5 in the morning, and so that ruled out all the interesting classes that met at 8, 9 and 10 am.

As I was thumbing through the thick M.I.T. course catalog in the all-night coffee shop, a friend from my computer programming course recommended I take *Cognitive Psychology*. "It's about how the mind works, and uses metaphors of the mind as a computer. And you get Science credit." Now that sounded interesting. The class met at 2:30 in the afternoon. (*So far so good.*) I went to the bookstore and saw that there was no textbook, just a collection of readings that would be handed out in class. (*This was looking better and better.*)

On the first day of class we met our two instructors, Susan Carey and Merrill Garrett. Susan looked to be barely out of grad school, wore hippie skirts and a headband (*hey, I told you this was 1975*) and Merrill, wearing Dockers, seemed not much older. The class meetings were not so much lectures as discussions, challenges, and explorations. They raised questions about the nature of knowledge and the nature of thought: How do we *know* that our memories are accurate—what if they only seem that way? How many things can we pay attention to at once, and what determines that? And more importantly, how would you design an experiment to test any of these things? No assumption was left unchallenged, no question too simple-minded to escape deep exploration. Here were two of the smartest people we had ever met, turning their intellect to the question of what intellect actually is. In short, they taught us to think about thinking.

The thing about my Cognitive Psychology class was that it treated the subject as something that is alive, changing, and constantly moving. Having now been a cognitive psychology researcher and teacher for 20 years, I can say that this is also my experience from being on the inside. How many different memory systems are there in the human brain? It depends on whom you ask. What are the limits of attention? That depends on the task, the sensory modalities involved, and on the person.

In 1999 I was asked to teach the Cognitive Psychology course at UC Berkeley usually taught either by Stephen Palmer or Alison Gopnik, two brilliant teachers and scientists. They were using a collection of readings, rather than a textbook, and they encouraged me to modify their collection slightly with some of my own favorites and I have been using collections of readings ever since, tinkering with the list every year to come up with the best assortment for a solid undergraduate introduction to the field. This book is the result of all that tinkering.

Why use readings rather than a textbook? One reason is that, as the field has become more complex, and more research is being published than ever before, it is difficult for any one author to know very much outside of his or her own specialty. A collection of readings such as this one includes the perspectives of the experts in their field. Another reason is that it affords the opportunity to present classic, seminal and influential papers that changed the way scientists think about cognitive psychology. Many contemporary papers refer to these classics and will no doubt continue to for years to come: Rosch on Categorization, Posner et al. on Cognitive Neuroscience, Gardner on Intelligence, Treisman on Visual Attention, Tversky & Kahneman on Decision Making, for example. Other papers are thoughtful reviews of a topic area by a researcher who made major and innovative contributions in that area, such as the chapters by Palmer, Bregman, Ericsson, Tooby and Cosmides, and Gleitman. They are not in themselves empirical works, but high-level reviews that convey the nuances, controversies, and methods of the field.

WHAT IS COGNITIVE PSYCHOLOGY?

Cognitive psychology is the study of human information processing. In particular, we are interested in how people (and sometimes animals or computer simulations) acquire and use information about the world and the environment in which they live. This necessarily then leads us to the study of attention, perception, memory, language acquisition and use, problem solving, decision making, categorization, expertise, and related topics. We hope to answer questions such as "What is the nature of thought and how does it arise in the mind and the brain?" and "To what extent are our perceptions and memories accurate, as opposed to systematic, yet helpful distortions of reality?"

From its inception, cognitive psychology established itself as an empirical science. That is, cognitive psychologists conduct experiments and collect data in order to test hypotheses. Although some studies are observational or correlational, the backbone of our research relies on true experiments, in which a small number of variables are manipulated while others are carefully controlled. This approach has yielded great insights into questions that philosophers had been asking for centuries.

Aristotle was probably the first information processing theorist, and without exaggeration one can argue that modern cognitive psychology owes him its heritage. Descartes launched modern approaches to these questions, and much current debate references his work. But for Aristotle, Descartes, Hume, Locke, Husserl, and others, the questions remained in the realm of philosophy. A century and a half ago this all changed when Wundt, Fechner, Helmholtz and their cohorts established the first laboratories in which they employed empirical methods to probe what had previously been impenetrable to true science—the mind. Philosophers framed the questions, and mental scientists (as they were then sometimes called) conducted experiments to answer them. In this sense, I see cognitive psychology as empirical philosophy. *Foundations of Cognitive Psychology: Core Readings* thus begins with readings to establish cognition in this historical context.

GOALS

This book is designed primarily for students who have taken a one semester introductory psychology course. That is, it assumes basic knowledge of terminology and paradigms in experimental psychology.

The goals of this book are:

- to present current models and controversies about the nature of human thought
- to provide the foundation necessary for higher-level, more specialized courses in cognitive psychology, such as ones on memory, knowledge representation, psycholinguistics, or attention
- to help students to develop skills in critical thinking, and the evaluation of scientific findings
- to introduce some of the key experiments and researchers who have contributed to the field, and
- to provide a resource of important articles that can be referred to again and again as the student's studies continue.

FEATURES/ORGANIZATION

Foundations of Cognitive Psychology: Core Readings has 33 chapters, divided into 14 sections. Roughly one-third of the chapters are primary source articles—contributions written by experts about their own area of expertise, reporting new data or theories. Another third are high-level reviews, written as cogent surveys to capture major developments in the field, again by the relevant experts. The final third are chapters from textbooks that I included in cases where I felt that the textbook author had an especially good grasp and synthesis of a topic that was too fractionated or complex to be rendered in another way, and where ample coverage was given to the experiments that helped us to learn what we know about the field. Examples of these are the excellent overview of human memory by Guenther, and the one on attention by Ashcraft.

Among the 14 sections, this book includes four topics that are not covered in typical undergraduate cognition courses. I feel their inclusion enhances and modernizes the course and the book considerably.

- *Evolutionary psychology* This section represents a relatively new and important way of thinking about the mind. Most of us learn Darwinian evolution with examples drawn from physical forms—moths developing a particular feather color through natural selection (and descent with modification) as a camouflage from predators; the opposable thumb; cats "learning" to cover their feces to protect them from germs and bacteria. Evolutionary psychology encourages us to see the mind as the product of evolutionary forces as well. Evolutionary psychologists ask questions of the form *"What adaptive problem might this cognitive ability or brain mechanism have solved for our ancestors?"* First, David Buss and his colleagues review and systematize different results of evolution, introducing both terminology and mechanisms. Next, two of the founders of evolutionary psychology, John Tooby and Leda Cosmides, present their overview of the field in a chapter that originally appeared in Michael Gazzaniga's authoritative anthology, *The New Cognitive Neurosciences*.
- *Philosophy of mind* Many of the questions that cognitive psychologists ask were the domain of philosophers for centuries. Indeed, the first departments of psychology were called departments of "mental science." This book begins with an overview of

philosophical approaches to mind and thought, written by Steve Palmer. That chapter has especially good coverage Descartes and the mind-body problem, as a way to introduce students to some of the issues. Modern approaches to the mind-body problem are represented in three classic and thought-provoking readings by Daniel Dennett and John Searle. From here, the stage is set for the student to engage with experimental psychology itself. I remind my own students that these first four chapters are the foundations on which our empirical science is based, and that they provide context and focus for the chapters that follow.

- *Music cognition* Nearly every cognitive psychology curriculum includes a unit on language acquisition and use, but few look at language's communicative cousin (and perhaps even, its predecessor). I've always found this odd. Music, like language, is a human universal, found in every human society throughout history. Babies spontaneously babble musically (playing around with rhythms and pitches) at about the same stage at which they begin to babble linguistically. Today, Americans spend more money on music than they do on prescription drugs or sex, testimony to music's importance in our everyday life. Over the last fifty years, scientific articles on music perception and cognition have increased exponentially. The field, therefore, is not only important but dynamic. From an instructor's standpoint, bringing musical examples into the classroom affords an opportunity to teach core concepts of cognition—perceptual grouping, attention, categorization and memory—using examples that students find meaningful.

- *Cultural psychology* Most of what we know about cognitive psychology (and experimental psychology in general) comes from studies with a rarified and somewhat exclusive population: North American college undergraduates. Of course there is a whole world of cultural, social and intellectual variation out there that we shouldn't ignore. Roy D'Andrade addresses differences in cognition across cultures in his entry here, one of my favorite chapters ever. In one article, he manages to survey the entire field of cognitive psychology, hitting on all the high points, and at the same time, reminding us not to be ethnocentric, and pointing out intriguing cross-cultural differences.

WHAT'S NEW IN THIS EDITION

To focus the book better, ten chapters have been deleted. Two were on neural networks, chapters that even the best students had difficulty with; two were on human–computer interaction (a topic I love teaching but that has become less central in cognitive psychology); six were additional coverage on topics that are already well covered in the book.

Four chapters (on categorization, attention, decision making, and cognitive neuroscience) have been replaced here with readings that are better suited to an undergraduate course.

Four chapters are brand new. Two are the best chapters I've ever read on animal learning, written by my former mentor Doug Hintzman; one is a chapter on statistical learning and language acquisition by Jenny Saffran, and one is the chapter by Roy D'Andrade on cross-cultural cognition that I mentioned above.

HOW TO USE THIS BOOK

This book is intended for a one-semester course in Cognitive Psychology, Cognitive Science, and related fields. It is suitable for courses taught in Departments of Psychology, Brain Sciences, Cognitive Sciences, Education, and Computer Science. A shorter course for colleges and universities on the quarter system could delete sections or chapters at the discretion of the instructor. I typically assign one section per week during a 13–15 week semester.

The chapters can be read in any order. I have a strong preference for reading the first four chapters first, but even this is just a suggestion. The order I've included here is the way I teach the course and like to build the concepts, but there is no reason that this order needs to be preserved.

I have taught my undergraduate courses in Cognitive Psychology at McGill University using this reader as the sole text. Colleagues at other universities have used the reader as I have, on its own, or in conjunction with a conventional textbook, or supplemented by their own collections of readings. I also know a number of students who have used this for self-study or preparation or review for higher level courses. Many of my colleagues keep a copy handy as a reference. I hope that you will find it both as useful and thought-provoking as I do.

–Daniel J. Levitin
Montreal, Québec, Canada
August, 2010

CHAPTER ONE

VISUAL AWARENESS

STEPHEN E. PALMER

1.1   PHILOSOPHICAL FOUNDATIONS

The first work on virtually all scientific problems was done by philosophers, and the nature of human consciousness is no exception. The issues they raised have framed the discussion for modern theories of awareness. Philosophical treatments of consciousness have primarily concerned two issues that we will discuss before considering empirical facts and theoretical proposals: The *mind-body problem* concerns the relation between mental events and physical events in the brain, and the *problem of other minds* concerns how people come to believe that other people (or animals) are also conscious.

1.1.1   The Mind-Body Problem

Although there is a long history to how philosophers have viewed the nature of the mind (sometimes equated with the soul), the single most important issue concerns what has come to be called the *mind-body problem*: What is the relation between mental events (e.g., perceptions, pains, hopes, desires, beliefs) and physical events (e.g., brain activity)? The idea that there is a mind-body problem to begin with presupposes one of the most important philosophical positions about the nature of mind. It is known as *dualism* because it proposes that mind and body are two different kinds of entities. After all, if there were no fundamental differences between mental and physical events, there would be no problem in saying how they relate to each other.

Dualism.   The historical roots of dualism are closely associated with the writings of the great French philosopher, mathematician, and scientist René Descartes. Indeed, the classical version of dualism, *substance dualism,* in which mind and body are conceived as two different substances, is often called *Cartesian dualism*. Because most philosophers find the notion of physical substances unproblematic, the central issue in philosophical debates over substance dualism is whether mental substances exist and, if so, what their nature might be. Vivid sensory experiences, such as the appearance of redness or the feeling of pain, are

From chapter 13 in Palmer, Stephen E., *Vision Science: Photons to Phenomenology*, pp. 618–630, © 1999 Massachusetts Institute of Technology, by permission of The MIT Press.

among the clearest examples, but substance dualists also include more abstract mental states and events such as hopes, desires, and beliefs.

The hypothesized mental substances are proposed to differ from physical ones in their fundamental properties. For example, all ordinary physical matter has a well-defined position, occupies a particular volume, has a definite shape, and has a specific mass. Conscious experiences, such as perceptions, remembrances, beliefs, hopes, and desires, do not appear to have readily identifiable positions, volumes, shapes, and masses. In the case of vision, however, one might object that visual experiences *do* have physical locations and extensions. There is an important sense in which my perception of a red ball on the table is located on the table where the ball is and is extended over the spherical volume occupied by the ball. What could be more obvious? But a substance dualist would counter that these are properties of the physical object that I perceive rather than properties of my perceptual experience itself. The experience is in my mind rather than out there in the physical environment, and the location, extension, and mass of these mental entities are difficult to define — unless one makes the problematic move of simply identifying them with the location, extension, and mass of my brain. Substance dualists reject this possibility, believing instead that mental states, such as perceptions, beliefs, and desires, are simply undefined with respect to position, extension, and mass. In this case, it makes sense to distinguish mental substances from physical ones on the grounds that they have fundamentally different properties.

We can also look at the issue of fundamental properties the other way around: Do experiences have any properties that ordinary physical matter does not? Two possibilities merit consideration. One is that experiences are *subjective phenomena* in the sense that they cannot be observed by anyone but the person having them. Ordinary matter and events, in contrast, are *objective phenomena* because they can be observed by anyone, at least in principle. The other is that experiences have what philosophers call *intentionality:* They inherently refer to things other than themselves.[1] Your experience of a book in front of you right now is about the book in the external world even though it arises from activity in your brain. This *directedness* of visual experiences is the source of the confusion we mentioned in the previous paragraph about whether your perceptions have location, extension, and so forth. The physical objects to which such perceptual experiences refer have these physical properties, but the experiences themselves do not. Intentionality does not seem to be a property that is shared by ordinary matter, and if this is true, it provides further evidence that conscious experience is fundamentally different.

It is possible to maintain a dualistic position and yet deny the existence of any separate mental substances, however. One can instead postulate that the brain has certain unique properties that constitute its mental phenomena. These properties are just the sorts of experiences we have as we go about our everyday lives, including perceptions, pains, desires, and thoughts. This philosophical position on the mind-body problems is called *property dualism*. It is a form of dualism because these properties are taken to be nonphysical in the sense of not being reducible to any standard physical properties. It is as though the physical brain contains some strange nonphysical features or dimensions that are qualitatively distinct from all physical features or dimensions.

These mental features or dimensions are usually claimed to be *emergent properties*: attributes that simply do not arise in ordinary matter unless it reaches a certain level or type of complexity. This complexity is certainly achieved in the human brain and may also be achieved in the brains of certain other animals. The situation is perhaps best understood by analogy to the emergent property of being alive. Ordinary matter manifests this property only when it is organized in such a way that it is able to replicate itself and carry on the required biological processes. The difference, of course, is that being alive is a property that we can now explain in terms of purely physical processes. Property dualists believe that this will never be the case for mental properties.

Even if one accepts a dualistic position that the mental and physical are somehow qualitatively distinct, there are several different relations they might have to one another. These differences form the basis for several varieties of dualism. One critical issue is the direction of causation: Does it run from mind to brain, from brain to mind, or both? Descartes's position was that both sorts of causation are in effect: events in the brain can affect mental events, and mental events can also affect events in the brain. This position is often called *interactionism* because it claims that the mental and physical worlds can interact causally with each other in both directions. It seems sensible enough at an intuitive level. No self-respecting dualist doubts the overwhelming evidence that physical events in the brain cause the mental events of conscious experience. The pain that you feel in your toe, for example, is actually caused by the firing of neurons in your brain. Convincing evidence of this is provided by so-called *phantom limb pain*, in which amputees feel pain — sometimes excruciating pain — in their missing limbs (Chronholm, 1951; Ramachandran, 1996).

In the other direction, the evidence that mental events can cause physical ones is decidedly more impressionistic but intuitively satisfying to most inter-actionists. They point to the fact that certain mental events, such as my having the intention of raising my arm, appear to cause corresponding physical events, such as the raising of my arm — provided I am not paralyzed and my arm is not restrained in any way. The nature of this causation is scientifically problematic, however, because all currently known forms of causation concern physical events causing other physical events. Even so, other forms of causation that have not yet been identified may nevertheless exist.

Not all dualists are interactionists, however. An important alternative version of dualism, called *epiphenomenalism*, recognizes mental entities as being different in kind from physical ones yet denies that mental states play any causal role in the unfolding of physical events. An epiphenomenalist would argue that mental states, such as perceptions, intentions, beliefs, hopes, and desires, are merely ineffectual side effects of the underlying causal neural events that take place in our brains. To get a clearer idea of what this might mean, consider the following analogy: Imagine that neurons glow slightly as they fire in a brain and that this glowing is somehow akin to conscious experiences. The pattern of glowing in and around the brain (i.e., the conscious experience) is clearly caused by the firing of neurons in the brain. Nobody would question that. But the neural glow would be causally ineffectual in the sense that it would not cause neurons to fire any differently than they would if they did not glow. Therefore, causation runs in only one direction, from physical to mental, in an epiphenomenalist account of the mind-body problem. Although this position denies any causal efficacy to mental events, it is still a form of dualism because it accepts the existence of the "glow" of consciousness and maintains that it is qualitatively distinct from the neural firings themselves.

Idealism.   Not all philosophical positions on the mind-body problem are dualistic. The opposing view is *monism*: the idea that there is really just one sort of stuff after all. Not surprisingly, there are two sorts of monist positions — *idealism* and *materialism* — one for each kind of stuff there might be. A monist who believes there to be no physical world, but only mental events, is called an idealist (from the "ideas" that populate the mental world). This has not been a very popular position in the history of philosophy, having been championed mainly by the British philosopher Bishop Berkeley.

The most significant problem for idealism is how to explain the commonality of different people's perceptions of the same physical events. If a fire engine races down the street with siren blaring and red lights flashing, everyone looks toward it, and they all see and hear pretty much the same physical events, albeit from different vantage points. How is this possible if there is no physical world that is responsible for their simultaneous perceptions of the sound and sight of the fire engine? One would have to propose some way in which the minds of the various witnesses happen to be hallucinating exactly corresponding events at exactly corresponding times. Berkeley's answer was that God was responsible for this grand coordination, but such claims have held little sway in modern scientific circles. Without a cogent scientific explanation of the commonality of shared experiences of the physical world, idealism has largely become an historical curiosity with no significant modern following.

Materialism.   The vast majority of monists believe that only physical entities exist. They are called materialists. In contrast to idealism, materialism is a very common view among modern philosophers and scientists. There are actually two distinct forms of materialism, which depend on what their adherents believe the ultimate status of mental entities will be once their true physical nature is discovered. One form, called *reductive materialism,* posits that mental events will ultimately be reduced to material events in much the same way that other successful reductions have occurred in science (e.g., Armstrong, 1968). This view is also called *mind-brain identity theory* because it assumes that mental events are actually equivalent to brain events and can be talked about more or less interchangeably, albeit with different levels of precision.

A good scientific example of what reductive materialists believe will occur when the mental is reduced to the physical is the reduction in physics of thermodynamic concepts concerning heat to statistical mechanics. The temperature of a gas in classical thermodynamics has been shown to be equivalent to the average kinetic energy of its molecules in statistical mechanics, thus replacing the qualitatively distinct thermodynamic concept of heat with the more general and basic concept of molecular motion. The concept of heat did not then disappear from scientific vocabulary: it remains a valid concept within many contexts. Rather, it was merely given a more accurate definition in terms of molecular motion at a more microscopic level of analysis. According to reductive materialists, then, mental concepts will ultimately be redefined in terms of brain states and events, but their equivalence will allow mental concepts to remain valid and scientifically useful even after their brain correlates are discovered. For example, it will still be valid to say, "John is hungry," rather than, "Such-and-such pattern of neural firing is occurring in John's lateral hypothalamus."

The other materialist position, called *eliminative materialism,* posits that at least some of our current concepts concerning mental states and events will eventually be eliminated from scientific vocabulary because they will be found to be simply invalid (e.g., Churchland, 1990). The scenario eliminative materialists envision is thus more radical than the simple translation scheme we just described for reductive materialism. Eliminative materialists believe that some of our present concepts about mental entities (perhaps including perceptual experiences as well as beliefs, hopes, desires, and so forth) are so fundamentally flawed that they will someday be entirely replaced by a scientifically accurate account that is expressed in terms of the underlying neural events. An appropriate analogy here would be the elimination of the now-discredited ideas of "vitalism" in biology: the view that what distinguishes living from nonliving things is the presence of a mysterious and qualitatively distinct force or substance that is present in living objects and absent in nonliving ones. The discovery of the biochemical reactions that cause the replication of DNA by completely normal physical means ultimately undercut any need for such mystical concepts, and so they were banished from scientific discussion, never to be seen again.

In the same spirit, eliminative materialists believe that some mental concepts, such as perceiving, thinking, desiring, and believing, will eventually be supplanted by discussion of the precise neurological events that underlie them. Scientists would then speak exclusively of the characteristic pattern of neural firings in the appropriate nuclei of the lateral hypothalamus and leave all talk about "being hungry" or "the desire to eat" to historians of science who study archaic and discredited curiosities of yesteryear. Even the general public would eventually come to think and talk in terms of these neuroscientific explanations for experiences, much as modern popular culture has begun to assimilate certain notions about DNA replication, gene splicing, cloning, and related concepts into movies, advertising, and language.

Behaviorism.   Another position on the mind-body problem is *philosophical behaviorism:* the view that the proper way to talk about mental events is in terms of the overt, observable movements (behaviors) in which an organism engages. Because objective behaviors are measurable, quantifiable aspects of the physical world, behaviorism is, strictly speaking, a kind of materialism. It provides such a different perspective, however, that it is best thought of as a distinct view. Behaviorists differ markedly from standard materialists in that they seek to reduce mental events to behavioral events or dispositions rather than to neurophysiological events. They shun neural explanations not because they disbelieve in the causal efficacy of neural events, but because they believe that behavior offers a higher and more appropriate level of analysis. The radical behaviorist movement pressed for nothing less than redefining the scientific study of mind as the scientific study of behavior. And for many years, they succeeded in changing the agenda of psychology.

The behaviorist movement began with the writings of psychologist John Watson (1913), who advocated a thoroughgoing purge of everything mental from psychology. He reasoned that what made intellectual inquiries scientific rather than humanistic or literary was that the empirical data and theoretical constructs on which they rest are objective. In the case of empirical observations, objectivity means that, given a description of what was done in a particular experiment, any scientist could repeat it and obtain essentially the same results, at least within the limits of measurement error. By this criterion, introspective studies of the qualities of perceptual experience were unscientific because they were not objective. Two different people could perform the same experiment (using themselves as subjects, of course) and report different experiences. When this happened — and it did — there was no way to resolve disputes about who was right. Both could defend their own positions simply by appealing to their private and privileged knowledge of their own inner states. This move protected their claims but blocked meaningful scientific debate.

According to behaviorists, scientists should study the behavior of organisms in a well-defined task situation. For example, rather than introspect about the nature of the perception of length, behaviorists would perform an experiment. Observers could be asked to discriminate which of two lines was longer, and their performance could be measured in terms of percentages of correct and incorrect responses for each pair of lines. Such an objective, behaviorally defined experiment could easily be repeated in any laboratory with different subjects to verify the accuracy and generality of its results. Watson's promotion of objective, behaviorally defined experimental methods — called *methodological behaviorism* — was a great success and strongly shaped the future of psychological research.

Of more relevance to the philosophical issue of the relation between mind and body, however, were the implications of the behaviorist push for objectivity in theoretical constructs concerning the mind. It effectively ruled out references to mental states and processes, replacing them with statements about an organism's propensity to engage in certain behaviors under certain conditions. This position is often called theoretical behaviorism or philosophical behaviorism. Instead of saying, "John is hungry," for example, which openly refers to a conscious mental experience (hunger) with which everyone is presumably familiar, a theoretical behaviorist would say something like "John has a propensity to engage in eating behavior in the presence of food." This propensity can be measured in a variety of objective ways — such as the amount of a certain food eaten when it was available after a certain number of hours since the last previous meal — precisely because it is about observable behavior.

But the behaviorist attempt to avoid talking about conscious experience runs into trouble when one considers all the conditions in which John might fail to engage in eating behavior even though he was hungry and food was readily available. Perhaps he could not see the food, for example, or maybe he was fasting. He might even have believed that the food was poisoned. It might seem that such conditions could be blocked simply by inserting appropriate provisions into the behavioral statement, such as "John had a propensity to engage in eating behavior in the presence of food, provided he perceived it, was not fasting, and did not believe it was poisoned." This move ultimately fails, however, for at least two reasons:

1. *Inability to enumerate all conditionals.*   Once one begins to think of conditions that would have to be added to statements about behavioral dispositions, it quickly becomes apparent that there are indefinitely many. Perhaps John fails to eat because his hands are temporarily paralyzed, because he has been influenced by a hypnotic suggestion, or whatever. This problem undercuts the claim that behavioral analyses of mental states are elegant and insightful, suggesting instead that they are fatally flawed or at least on the wrong track.
2. *Inability to eliminate mental entities.*   The other problem is that the conditionals that must be enumerated frequently make reference to just the sorts of mental events that are supposed to be avoided. For example, whether John *sees* the food or not, whether he *intends* to fast, and what he *believes* about its being poisoned are all mentalistic concepts that have now been introduced into the supposedly behavioral definition. The amended version is therefore unacceptable to a strict theoretical behaviorist.

For such reasons, theoretical behaviorism ultimately failed. The problem, in a nutshell, was that behaviorists mistook the *epistemic status* of mental states (how we come to know about mental states in other people) for the *ontological status* of mental states (what their inherent nature is) (Searle, 1992). That is, we surely come to know about other people's mental states through their behavior, but this does not mean that the nature of these mental states is inherently behavioral.

Functionalism.   *Functionalism* was a movement in the philosophy of mind that began in the 1960s in close association with the earliest stirrings of cognitive science (e.g., Putnam, 1960). Its main idea is that a given mental state can be defined in terms of the causal relations that exist among that mental state, environmental conditions (inputs), organismic behaviors (outputs), and other mental states. Note that this is very much like behaviorism, but with the important addition of allowing other mental states into the picture. This addition enables a functionalist definition of hunger, for example, to refer to a variety of other mental states, such as perceptions, intentions, and beliefs, as suggested above. Functionalists are not trying to explain away mental phenomena as actually being propensities to behave in certain ways, as behaviorists did. Rather, they are trying to define mental states in terms of their relations to other mental states as well as to input stimuli and output behaviors. The picture that emerges is very much like information processing analyses. This is not surprising because functionalism is the philosophical foundation of modern computational theories of mind.

Functionalists aspired to more than just the overthrow of theoretical behaviorism, however. They also attempted to block reductive materialism by suggesting new criticisms of mind-brain identity theory. The basis of this criticism lies in the notion of *multiple realizability*: the fact that many different physical devices can serve the same function, provided they causally connect inputs and outputs in the same way via internal states (Putnam, 1967). For example, there are many different ways of building a thermostat. They all have the same function — to control the temperature in the thermostat's environment — but they realize it through very different physical implementations.

Multiple realizability poses the following challenge to identity theory. Suppose there were creatures from some other galaxy whose biology was based on silicon molecules rather than on carbon molecules, as ours is. Let us also suppose that they were alive (even though the basis of their life was not DNA, but some functionally similar self-replicating molecule) and that they even look like people. And suppose further not only that their brains were constructed of elements that are functionally similar to neurons, but also that these elements were interconnected in just the way that neurons in our brains are. Indeed, their brains would be functionally isomorphic to ours, even though they were made of physically different stuff.

Functionalists then claim that these alien creatures would have the same mental states as we do — that is, the same perceptions, pains, desires, beliefs, and so on that populate our own conscious mental lives — provided that their internal states were analogously related to each other, to the external world, and to their behavior. This same approach can be generalized to argue for the possibility that computers and robots of the appropriate sort would also be conscious. Suppose, for example, that each neuron in a brain was replaced with a microcomputer chip that exactly simulated its firing patterns in response to all the neuron chips that provide its input. The computer that was thus constructed would fulfill the functionalist requirements for having the same mental states as the person whose brain was "electronically cloned." You should decide for yourself whether you believe that such a computer would actually have mental states or would merely act as though it had mental states. Once you have done so, try to figure out what criteria you used to decide. (For two contradictory philosophical views of this thought experiment, the reader is referred to Dennett (1991) and Searle (1993).)

Multiple realizability is closely related to differences between the algorithmic and implementation levels. The algorithmic level corresponds roughly to the functional description of the organism in terms of the relations among its internal states, its input information, and its output behavior. The implementation level corresponds to its actual physical construction. The functionalist notion of multiple realizability thus implies that there could be many different kinds of creatures that would have the same mental states as people do, at least defined in this way. If true, this would undercut identity theory, since mental events could not then be simply equated with particular neurological events; they would have to be equated with some more general class of physical events that would include, among others, silicon-based aliens and electronic brains.

The argument from multiple realizability is crucial to the functionalist theory of mind. Before we get carried away with the implications of multiple realizability, though, we must ask ourselves whether it is true or even remotely likely to be true. There is not much point in basing our understanding of consciousness on a functionalist foundation unless that foundation is well grounded. Is it? More important, how would we know if it were? We will address this topic shortly when we consider the problem of other minds.

Supervenience.   There is certainly some logical relation between brain activity and mental states such as consciousness, but precisely what it is has obviously been difficult to determine. Philosophers of mind have spent hundreds of years trying to figure out what it is and have spilled oceans of ink attacking and defending different positions. Recently, however, philosopher Jaegwon Kim (1978, 1993) has formulated a position with which most philosophers of mind have been able to agree. This relation, called *supervenience,* is that any difference in conscious events requires some corresponding difference in underlying neural activity. In other words, mental events supervene on neural events because no two possible situations can be identical with respect to their neural properties while differing in their mental properties. It is a surprisingly weak relation, but it is better than nothing.

Supervenience does not imply that all differences in underlying neural activity result in differences in consciousness. Many neural events are entirely outside awareness, including those that control basic bodily functions such as maintaining gravitational balance and regulating heartbeat. But supervenience claims that no changes in consciousness can take place without some change in neural activity. The real trick, of course, is saying precisely what kinds of changes in neural events produce what kinds of changes in awareness.

1.1.2   The Problem of Other Minds

The functionalist arguments about multiple realizability are merely thought experiments because neither aliens nor electronic brains are currently at hand. Even so, the question of whether or not someone or something is conscious is central to the enterprise of cognitive science because the validity of such arguments rests on the answer. Formulating adequate criteria for consciousness is one of the thorniest problems in all of science. How could one possibly decide?

Asking how to discriminate conscious from nonconscious beings brings us face to face with another classic topic in the philosophy of mind: the *problem of other minds.* The issue at stake is how I know whether another creature (or machine) has conscious experiences. Notice that I did not say "how *we* know whether another creature has conscious experiences," because, strictly speaking, I do not know whether *you* do or not. This is because one of the most peculiar and unique features of my consciousness is its internal, private nature: Only I have direct access to my conscious experiences, and I have direct access only to my own. As a result, my beliefs that other people also have conscious experiences — and your belief that I do — appear to be inferences. Similarly, I may believe that dogs and cats, or even frogs and worms, are conscious. But in every case, the epistemological basis of my belief about the consciousness of other creatures is fundamentally different from knowledge of my own consciousness: I have direct access to my own experience and nobody else's.

Criteria for Consciousness.   If our beliefs that other people — and perhaps many animals as well — have experiences like ours are inferences, on what might such inferences be based? There seem to be at least two criteria.

1. *Behavioral similarity.*   Other people act in ways that are roughly similar to my own actions when I am having conscious experiences. When I experience pain on stubbing my toe, for example, I may wince, say "Ouch!" and hold my toe while hopping on my other foot. When other people do similar things under similar circumstances, I presume they are experiencing a feeling closely akin to my own pain. Dogs also behave in seemingly analogous ways in what appear to be analogous situations in which they might experience pain, and so I also attribute this mental state of being in pain to them. The case is less compelling for creatures like frogs and worms because their behavior is less obviously analogous to our own, but many people firmly believe that their behavior indicates that they also have conscious experiences such as pain.
2. *Physical similarity.*   Other people — and, to a lesser degree, various other species of animals — are similar to me in their basic biological and physical structure. Although no two people are exactly the same, humans are generally quite similar to each other in terms of their essential biological constituents. We are all made of the same kind of flesh, blood, bone, and so forth, and we have roughly the same kinds of sensory organs. Many other animals also appear to be made of similar stuff, although they are morphologically different to varying degrees. Such similarities and differences may enter into our judgments of the likelihood that other creatures also have conscious experiences.

Neither condition alone is sufficient for a convincing belief in the reality of mental states in another creature. Behavioral similarity alone is insufficient because of the logical possibility of *automatons*: robots that are able to simulate every aspect of human behavior but have no experiences whatsoever. We may think that such a machine acts as if it had conscious experiences, but it could conceivably do so without actually having them. (Some theorists reject this possibility, however [e.g., Dennett, 1991].) Physical similarity alone is insufficient because we do not believe that even another living person is having conscious experiences when they are comatose or in a dreamless sleep. Only the two together are convincing. Even when both are present to a high degree, I still have no guarantee that such an inference is warranted. I only know that I myself have conscious experiences.

But what then is the status of the functionalist argument that an alien creature based on silicon rather than carbon molecules would have mental states like ours? This thought experiment is perhaps more convincing than the electronic-brained automaton because we have presumed that the alien is at least alive, albeit using some other physical mechanism to achieve this state of being. But logically, it would surely be unprovable that such silicon people would have mental states like ours, even if they acted very much the same and appeared very similar to people. In fact, the argument for functionalism from multiple realizability is no stronger than our intuitions that such creatures would be conscious. The strength of such intuitions can (and does) vary widely from one person to another.

The Inverted Spectrum Argument.   We have gotten rather far afield from visual perception in all this talk of robots, aliens, dogs, and worms having pains, but the same kinds of issues arise for perception. One of the classic arguments related to the problem of other minds — called the *inverted spectrum argument* — concerns the perceptual experience of color (Locke, 1690/1987). It goes like this: Suppose you grant that I have visual awareness in some form that includes differentiated experiences in response to different physical spectra of light (i.e., differentiated color perceptions). How can we know whether my color experiences are the same as yours?

The inverted spectrum argument refers to the possibility that my color experiences are exactly like your own, except for being spectrally inverted. In its literal form, the inversion refers to reversing the mapping between color experiences and the physical spectrum of wavelengths of light, as though the rainbow had simply been reversed, red for violet (and vice versa) with everything in between being reversed in like manner. The claim of the inverted spectrum argument is that no one would ever be able to tell that you and I have different color experiences.

This particular form of color transformation would not actually work as intended because of the shape of the color solid (Palmer, 1999). The color solid is asymmetrical in that the most saturated blues and violets are darker than the most saturated reds and greens, which, in turn, are darker than the most saturated yellows and oranges (see figure 1.1a). The problem this causes for the literal inverted spectrum argument is that if my hues were simply reversed, your experience of yellow would be the same as my experience of blue-green, and so you would judge yellow to be darker than blue-green, whereas I would do the reverse. This difference would allow the spectral inversion of my color experiences (relative to yours) to be detected.

This problem may be overcome by using more sophisticated versions of the same color transformation argument (Palmer, 1999). The most plausible is red-green reversal, in which my color space is the same as yours except for reflection about the blue-yellow plane, thus reversing reds and greens (see figure 1.1b). It does not suffer from problems concerning the differential lightness of blues and yellows because my blues correspond to your blues and my yellows to your yellows. Our particular shades of blues and yellows would be different — my greenish yellows and greenish blues would correspond to your reddish yellows (oranges) and reddish blues (purples), respectively, and vice versa — but gross differences in lightness would not be a problem.

There are other candidates for behaviorally undetectable color transformations as well (see figures 1.1c and 1.1d). The crucial idea in all these versions of the inverted spectrum argument is that if the color solid were symmetric with respect to some transformation — and this is at least roughly true for the three cases illustrated in figures 1.1b–1.1d — there would be no way to tell the difference between my color experiences and yours simply from our behavior. In each case, I would name colors in just the same way as you would, because these names are only *mediated* by our own private experiences of color. It is the sameness of the physical spectra that ultimately causes them to be named consistently across people, not the sameness of the private experiences. I would also describe relations between colors in the same way as you would: that focal blue is darker than focal yellow, that lime green is yellower than emerald green, and so forth. In fact, if I were in a psychological experiment in which my task was to rate pairs of color for similarity or dissimilarity, I would make the same ratings you would. I would even pick out the same unique hues as you would — the "pure" shades of red, green, blue, and yellow — even though my internal experiences of

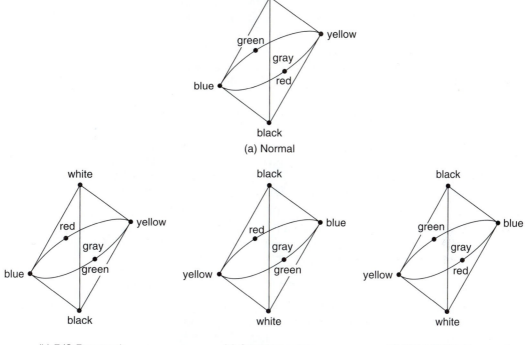

FIGURE 1.1 Sophisticated versions of the inverted spectrum argument. Transformations of the normal color solid (a) that would not be detectable by behavioral methods include (b) red-green reversal, which reflects each color about the blue-yellow-black-white place; (c) the complementary transformation, which reflects each color through the central point; and (d) blue-yellow and black-white reversal, which is the combination of both the two other transformations (b and c).

Source: (After Palmer, 1999.)

them would be different from yours. It would be extremely difficult, if not impossible, to tell from my behavior with respect to color that I experience it differently than you do.[2]

I suggested that red-green reversal is the most plausible form of color transformation because a good biological argument can be made that there should be some very small number of seemingly normal trichromats who should be red-green reversed. The argument for such *pseudo-normal color perception* goes as follows (Nida-Rümelin, 1996). Normal trichromats have three different pigments in their three cone types (figure 1.2a). Some people are red-green color blind because they have a gene that causes their long-wavelength (L) cones to have the same pigment as their medium-wavelength (M) cones (figure 1.2b). Other people have a different form of red-green color blindness because they have a different gene that causes their M cones to have the same pigment as their L cones (figure 1.2c). In both cases, people with these genetic defects lose the ability to experience both red and green because the visual system codes both colors by taking the difference between the outputs of these two cone types. But suppose that someone had the genes for *both* of these forms of red-green color blindness. Their L cones would have the M pigment, and their M cones

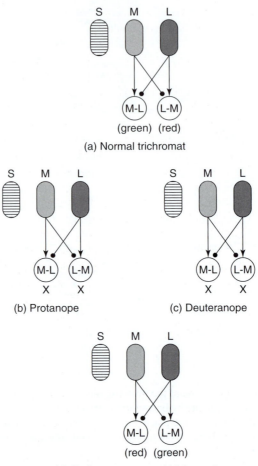

FIGURE 1.2   A biological basis for red-green-reversed trichromats. Normal trichromats have three different pigments in the retinal cones (a), whereas red-green color blind individuals have the same pigment in their L and M cones (b and c). People with the genes for both forms of red-green color blindness, however, would be red-green-reversed trichromats (d).

would have the L pigment (figure 1.2d). Such doubly color blind individuals would therefore not be red-green color blind at all, but red-green-reversed trichromats.[3] Statistically, they should be very rare (about 14 per 10,000 males), but they should exist. If they do, they are living proof that this color transformation is either undetectable or very difficult to detect by purely behavioral means, because nobody has ever detected one!

These color transformation arguments are telling criticisms against the completeness of any definition of conscious experience based purely on behavior. Their force lies in the fact that there could be identical behavior in response to identical environmental stimulation without there being corresponding identical experiences underlying them, even if we grant that the other person has experiences to begin with.

Phenomenological Criteria.   Let us return to the issue of criteria for consciousness: How are we to tell whether a given creature is conscious or not? Clearly, phenomenological experience is key. In fact, it is the defining characteristic, the necessary and sufficient condition, for attributing consciousness to something. I know that I am conscious precisely because I have such experiences. This is often called *first-person knowledge* or *subjective knowledge* because it is available only to the self (i.e., the first-person or subject). In his classic essay "What Is It Like to Be a Bat?" philosopher Thomas Nagel (1974) identifies the phenomenological position with what it is like to *be* some person, creature, or machine in a given situation. In the case of color perception, for example, it is what it is like for you to experience a particular shade of redness or pale blueness or whatever. This much seems perfectly clear. But if it is so clear, then why not simply define consciousness with respect to such phenomenological criteria?

As we said before, the difficulty is that first-person knowledge is available only to the self. This raises a problem for scientific explanations of consciousness because the scientific method requires its facts to be objective in the sense of being available to any scientist who undertakes the same experiment. In all matters except consciousness, this appears to work very well. But consciousness has the extremely peculiar and elusive property of being directly accessible only to the self, thus blocking the usual methods of scientific observation. Rather than observing consciousness itself in others, the scientist is forced to observe the correlates of consciousness, the "shadows of consciousness," as it were. Two sorts of shadows are possible to study: behavior and physiology. Neither is consciousness itself, but both are (or seem likely to be) closely related.

Behavioral Criteria.   The most obvious way to get an objective, scientific handle on consciousness is to study behavior, as dictated by methodological behaviorism. Behavior is clearly objective and observable in the third-person sense. But how is it related to consciousness? The link is the assumption that if someone or something behaves enough like I do, it must be conscious like I am. After all, I believe I behave in the ways I do because of my own conscious experiences, and so (presumably) do others. I wince when I am in pain, eat when I am hungry, and duck when I perceive a baseball hurtling toward my head. If I were comatose, I would not behave in any of these ways, even in the same physical situations.

Behavioral criteria for consciousness are closely associated with what is called *Turing's test*. This test was initially proposed by the brilliant mathematician Alan Turing (1950), inventor of the digital computer, to solve the problem of how to determine whether a computing machine could be called "intelligent." Wishing to avoid purely philosophical debates, Turing imagined an objective behavioral procedure for deciding the issue by setting up an *imitation game*. A person is seated at a computer terminal that allows her to communicate either with a real person or with a computer that has been programmed to behave intelligently (i.e., like a person). This interrogator's job is to decide whether she is communicating with a person or the computer. The terminal is used simply to keep the interrogator from using physical appearance as a factor in the decision, since appearance presumably does not have any logical bearing on intelligence.

The interrogator is allowed to ask anything she wants. For example, she could ask the subject to play a game of chess, engage in a conversation on current events, or describe its favorite TV show. Nothing is out of bounds. She could even ask whether the subject is intelligent. A person would presumably reply affirmatively, but then so would a properly programmed computer. If the interrogator could not tell the difference between interacting with real people and with the computer, Turing asserted that the computer should be judged "intelligent." It would then be said to have "passed Turing's test."

Note that Turing's test is a strictly behavioral test because the interrogator has no information about the physical attributes of the subject, but only about its behavior. In the original version, this behavior is strictly verbal, but there is no reason in principle why it needs to be restricted in this way. The interrogator could ask the subject to draw pictures or even to carry out tasks in the real world, provided the visual feedback the interrogator received did not provide information about the physical appearance of the subject.

The same imitation game can be used for deciding about the appropriateness of any other cognitive description, including whether the subject is "conscious." Again, simply asking the subject whether it is conscious will not discriminate between the machine and a person because the machine can easily be programmed to answer that question in the affirmative. Similarly, appropriate responses to questions asking it to describe the nature of its visual experiences or pain experiences could certainly be programmed. But even if they could, would that necessarily mean that the computer would *be* conscious or only that it would *act as if it were* conscious?

If one grants that physical appearance should be irrelevant to whether something is conscious or not, Turing's test seems to be a fair and objective procedure. But it also seems that there is a fact at issue here rather than just an opinion — namely, whether the target object is actually *conscious* or merely simulating consciousness — and Turing's test should stand or fall on whether it gives the correct answer. The problem is that it is not clear that it will. As critics readily point out, it cannot distinguish between a conscious entity and one that only acts as if it were conscious — an automaton or a zombie. To assert that Turing's test actually gives the correct answer to the factual question of consciousness, one must assume that it is impossible for something to act as if it is conscious without actually being so. This is a highly questionable assumption, although some have defended it (e.g., Dennett, 1991). If it is untrue, then passing Turing's test is not a sufficient condition for consciousness, because automatons can pass it without being conscious.

Turing's test also runs into trouble as a necessary condition for consciousness. The relevant question here is whether something can be conscious and still fail Turing's test. Although this might initially seem unlikely, consider a person who has an unusual medical condition that disables the use of all the muscles required for overt behavior yet keeps all other bodily functions intact, including all brain functions. This person would be unable to behave in any way yet would still be fully conscious when awake. Turing's test thus runs afoul as a criterion for consciousness because behavior's link to consciousness can be broken under unlikely but easily imaginable circumstances.

We appear to be on the horns of a dilemma with respect to the criteria for consciousness. Phenomenological criteria are valid by definition but do not appear to be scientific by the usual yardsticks. Behavioral criteria are scientific by definition but are not necessarily valid. The fact that scientists prefer to rely on respectable but possibly invalid behavioral methods brings to mind the street-light parable: A woman comes upon a man searching for something under a streetlight at night. The man explains that he has lost his keys, and they both search diligently for some time. The woman finally asks the man where he thinks he lost them, to which he replies, "Down the street in the middle of the block." When she then asks why he is looking here at the corner, he replies, "Because this is where the light is." The problem is that consciousness does not seem to be where behavioral science can shed much light on it.

Physiological Criteria.   Modern science has another card to play, however, and that is the biological substrate of consciousness. Even if behavioral methods cannot penetrate the subjectivity barrier of consciousness, perhaps physiological methods can. In truth, few important facts are yet known about the biological substrates of consciousness. There are not even very many hypotheses, although several speculations have recently been proposed (e.g., Baars, 1988; Crick, 1994; Crick & Koch, 1990, 1995, 1998; Edelman, 1989). Even so, it is possible to speculate about the promise such an enterprise might hold as a way of defining and theorizing about consciousness. It is important to remember that in doing so, we are whistling in the dark, however.

Let us suppose, just for the sake of argument, that neuroscientists discover some crucial feature of the neural activity that underlies consciousness. Perhaps all neural activity that gives rise to consciousness occurs in some particular layer of cerebral cortex, or in neural circuits that are mediated by some particular neurotransmitter, or in neurons that fire at a temporal spiking frequency of about 40 times per second. If something like one of these assertions were true — and, remember, we are just making up stories here — could we then define consciousness objectively in terms of that form of neural activity? If we could, would this definition then replace the subjective definition in terms of experience? And would such a biological definition then constitute a theory of consciousness?

The first important observation about such an enterprise is that biology cannot really give us an objective definition of consciousness independent of its subjective definition. The reason is that we need the subjective definition to determine what physiological events correspond to consciousness in the first place. Suppose we knew all of the relevant biological events that occur in human brains. We still could not provide a biological account of consciousness because we would have no way to tell which brain events were conscious and which ones were not. Without that crucial information, a biological definition of consciousness simply could not get off the ground. To determine the biological correlates of consciousness, one must be able to designate the events to which they are being correlated (i.e., conscious ones), and this requires a subjective definition.

For this reason, any biological definition of consciousness would always be derived from the subjective definition. To see this in a slightly different way, consider what would constitute evidence that a given biological definition was incorrect. If brain activity of type C were thought to define consciousness, it could be rejected for either of two reasons: if type C brain activity were found to result in nonconscious processing of some sort or if consciousness were found to occur in the absence of type C brain activity. The crucial observation for present purposes is that neither of these possibilities could be evaluated without an independent subjective definition of consciousness.

Correlational versus Causal Theories.   In considering the status of physiological statements about consciousness, it is important to distinguish two different sorts, which we will call *correlational* and *causal*. Correlational statements concern what type of physiological activity takes place when conscious experiences are occurring that fail to take place when they are not. Our hypothetical examples in terms of a specific cortical location, a particular neurotransmitter, or a particular rate of firing are good examples. The common feature of these hypotheses is that they are merely correlational: They only claim that the designated feature of brain activity is associated with consciousness; they don't explain why that association exists. In other words, they provide no causal analysis of how this particular kind of brain activity produces consciousness. For this reason they fail to fill the explanatory gap that we mentioned earlier. Correlational analyses merely designate a subset of neural activity in the brain according to some particular property with which consciousness is thought to be associated. No explanation is given for this association; it simply is the sort of activity that accompanies consciousness.

At this point we should contrast such correlational analyses with a good example of a causal one: an analysis that provides a scientifically plausible explanation of how a particular form of brain activity actually causes conscious experience. Unfortunately, no examples of such a theory are available. In fact, to this writer's knowledge, nobody has ever suggested a theory that the scientific community regards as giving even a remotely plausible causal account of how consciousness arises or why it has the particular qualities it does. This does not mean that such a theory is impossible in principle, but only that no serious candidate has been generated in the past several thousand years.

A related distinction between correlational and causal biological definitions of consciousness is that they would differ in generalizability. Correlational analyses would very likely be specific to the type of biological system within which they had been discovered. In the best-case scenario, a good correlational definition of human consciousness might generalize to chimpanzees, possibly even to dogs or rats, but probably not to frogs or snails because their brains are simply too different. If a correlational analysis showed that activity mediated by a particular neurotransmitter was the seat of human consciousness, for example, would that necessarily mean that creatures without that neurotransmitter were nonconscious? Or might some other evolutionarily related neural transmitter serve the same function in brains lacking that one? Even more drastically, what about extraterrestrial beings whose whole physical make-up might be radically different from our own? In such cases, a correlational analysis is almost bound to break down.

An adequate causal theory of consciousness might have a fighting chance, however, because the structure of the theory itself could provide the lines along which generalization would flow. Consider the analogy to a causal theory of life based on the structure of DNA. The analysis of how the double helical structure of DNA allows it to reproduce itself in an entirely mechanistic way suggests that biologists could determine whether alien beings were alive in the same sense as living organisms on earth by considering the nature of their molecular basis and its functional ability to replicate itself and to support the organism's lifelike functions. An alien object containing the very same set of four component bases as DNA (adenine, guanine, thymine, and cytosine) in some very different global structure that did not allow self-replication would not be judged to be alive by such biological criteria, yet another object containing very different components in some analogous arrangement that allowed for self-replication might be. Needless to say, such an analysis is a long way off in the case of consciousness.

NOTES

1. The reader is warned not to confuse intentionality with the concept of "intention" in ordinary language. Your intentions have intentionality in the sense that they may refer to things other than themselves — for example, your intention to feed your cat refers to your cat, its food, and yourself — but no more so than other mental states you might have, such as beliefs, desires, perceptions, and pains. The philosophical literature on the nature of intentionality is complex and extensive. The interested reader is referred to Bechtel (1988) for an overview of this topic.

2. One might think that if white and black were reversed, certain reflexive behaviors to light would somehow betray the difference. This is not necessarily the case, however. Whereas you would squint your eyes when you experienced intense brightness in response to bright sunlight, I would also squint my eyes in response to large amounts of sunlight. The only difference is that my experience of brightness under these conditions would be the same as your experience of darkness. It sounds strange, but I believe it would all work out properly.

3. One could object that the only thing that differentiates M and L cones is the pigment that they contain, so people with both forms of red-green color blindness would actually be normal trichromats rather than red-green-reversed ones. There are two other ways in which M and L cones might be differentiated, however. First, if the connections of M and L cones to other cells of the visual system are not completely symmetrical, they can be differentiated by these connections independently of their pigments. Second, they may be differentiable by their relation to the genetic codes that produced them.

REFERENCES

Armstrong, D. M. (1968). *A materialist theory of the mind.* London: Routledge & Kegan Paul.

Baars, B. (1988). *A cognitive theory of consciousness.* Cambridge, England: Cambridge University Press.

Churchland, P. M. (1990). Current eliminativism. In W. G. Lycan (Ed.), *Mind and cognition: A reader* (pp. 206–223). Oxford, England: Basil Blackwell.

Crick, F. H. C. (1994). *The astonishing hypothesis: The scientific search for the soul.* New York: Scribner.

Crick, F. H. C., & Koch, C. (1990). Toward a neurobiological theory of consciousness. *Seminars in the Neurosciences, 2,* 263–275.

Crick, F. H. C., & Koch, C. (1995). Are we aware of neural activity in primary visual cortex? *Nature, 375,* 121–123.

Crick, F. H. C., & Koch, C. (1998). Consciousness and neuroscience. *Cerebral Cortex, 8,* 97–107.

Cronholm, B. (1951). Phantom limbs in amputees. *Acta Psychiatrica Scandinavica, 72* (Suppl.), 1–310.

Dennett, D. (1991). *Consciousness explained.* Boston: Little, Brown.

Edelman, G. M. (1989). *The remembered present: A biological theory of consciousness.* New York: Basic Books.

Kim, J. (1978). Supervenience and nomological incommensurables. *American Philosophical Quarterly, 15,* 149–156.

Kim, J. (1993). *Supervenience and mind.* Cambridge, England: Cambridge University Press.

Locke, J. (1690/1987). *An essay concerning human understanding.* Oxford, England: Basil Blackwell.

Nagel, T. (1974). What is it like to be a bat? *The Philosophical Review, 83,* 435–450.

Palmer, S. E. (1999). Color, consciousness, and the isomorphism constraint. *Behavioural and Brain Sciences, 22*(6), 923–989.

Putnam, H. (1960). Minds and machines. In S. Hook (Ed.), *Dimensions of mind.* New York: Collier Books.

Putnam, H. (1967). Psychological predicates. In W. Captain & D. Merrill (Eds.), *Art, mind, and religion* (pp. 35–48). Pittsburgh: University of Pittsburgh Press.

Ramachandran, V. S., Levi, L., Stone, L., Rogers-Ramachandran, D., McKinney, R., Stalcup, M., Arcilla, G., Sweifler, R., Schatz, A., Flippin, A. (1996). Illusions of body image: What they reveal about human nature. In R. R. Llinas and P. S. Churchland (Eds.), *The mind-brain continuum: Sensory processes* (pp. 29–60). Cambridge, MA: MIT Press.

Searle, J. R. (1992). *The rediscovery of mind.* Cambridge, MA: MIT Press.

Turing, S. (1959). *Alan M. Turing.* Cambridge, England: W. Heffer.

CHAPTER TWO

WHERE AM I?

DANIEL C. DENNETT

Now that I've won my suit under the Freedom of Information Act, I am at liberty to reveal for the first time a curious episode in my life that may be of interest not only to those engaged in research in the philosophy of mind, artificial intelligence and neuroscience but also to the general public.

Several years ago I was approached by Pentagon officials who asked me to volunteer for a highly dangerous and secret mission. In collaboration with NASA and Howard Hughes, the Department of Defense was spending billions to develop a Supersonic Tunneling Underground Device, or STUD. It was supposed to tunnel through the earth's core at great speed and deliver a specially designed atomic warhead "right up the Red's missile silos," as one of the Pentagon brass put it.

The problem was that in an early test they had succeeded in lodging a warhead about a mile deep under Tulsa, Oklahoma, and they wanted me to retrieve it for them. "Why me?" I asked. Well, the mission involved some pioneering applications of current brain research, and they had heard of my interest in brains and of course my Faustian curiosity and great courage and so forth. . . . Well, how could I refuse? The difficulty that brought the Pentagon to my door was that the device I'd been asked to recover was fiercely radioactive, in a new way. According to monitoring instruments, something about the nature of the device and its complex interactions with pockets of material deep in the earth had produced radiation that could cause severe abnormalities in certain tissues of the brain. No way had been found to shield the brain from these deadly rays, which were apparently harmless to other tissues and organs of the body. So it had been decided that the person sent to recover the device should *leave his brain behind*. It would be kept in a safe place where it could execute its normal control functions by elaborate radio links. Would I submit to a surgical procedure that would completely remove my brain, which would then be placed in a life-support system at the Manned Spacecraft Center in Houston? Each input and output pathway, as it was severed, would be restored by a pair of microminiaturized radio transceivers, one attached precisely to the brain, the other to the nerve stumps in the empty cranium. No information would be lost, all the connectivity would be preserved. At first I was a bit reluctant. Would it really work? The Houston brain surgeons encouraged me. "Think of it," they said, "as a mere *stretching* of the nerves. If your brain were just moved over an *inch* in your skull, that would not alter or impair your mind. We're simply going to make the nerves indefinitely elastic by splicing radio links into them."

I was shown around the life-support lab in Houston and saw the sparkling new vat in which my brain would be placed, were I to agree. I met the large and brilliant support team of neurologists, hematologists, biophysicists, and electrical engineers, and after several days of discussions and demonstrations, I agreed to give it a try. I was subjected to an enormous array of blood tests, brain scans, experiments, interviews, and the like. They took down my autobiography at great length, recorded tedious lists of my beliefs, hopes, fears, and tastes. They even listed my favorite stereo recordings and gave me a crash session of psychoanalysis.

The day for surgery arrived at last and of course I was anesthetized and remember nothing of the operation itself. When I came out of anesthesia, I opened my eyes, looked around, and asked the inevitable, the traditional, the lamentably hackneyed post-operative question: "Where am I?" The nurse smiled down at me. "You're in Houston," she said, and I reflected that this still had a good chance of being the truth one way or another. She handed me a mirror. Sure enough, there were the tiny antennae poking up through their titanium ports cemented into my skull.

"I gather the operation was a success," I said, "I want to go see my brain." They led me (I was a bit dizzy and unsteady) down a long corridor and into the life-support lab. A cheer went up from the assembled support team, and I responded with what I hoped was a jaunty salute. Still feeling lightheaded, I was helped over to the life-support vat. I peered through the glass. There, floating in what looked like ginger-ale, was undeniably a human brain, though it was almost covered with printed circuit chips, plastic tubules, electrodes, and other paraphernalia. "Is that mine?" I asked. "Hit the output transmitter switch there on the side of the vat and see for yourself," the project director replied. I moved the switch to *off*, and immediately slumped, groggy and nauseated, into the arms of the technicians, one of whom kindly restored the switch to its *on* position. While I recovered my equilibrium and composure, I thought to myself: "Well, here I am, sitting on a folding chair, staring through a piece of plate glass at my own brain. . . . But wait," I said to myself, "shouldn't I have thought, 'Here I am, suspended in a bubbling fluid, being stared at by my own eyes'?" I tried to think this latter thought. I tried to project it into the tank, offering it hopefully to my brain, but I failed to carry off the exercise with any conviction. I tried again. "Here am *I*, Daniel Dennett, suspended in a bubbling fluid, being stared at by my own eyes." No, it just didn't work. Most puzzling and confusing. Being a philosopher of firm physicalist conviction, I believed unswervingly that the tokening of my thoughts was occurring somewhere in my brain: yet, when I thought "Here I am," where the thought occurred to me was *here*, outside the vat, where I, Dennett, was standing staring at my brain.

I tried and tried to think myself into the vat, but to no avail. I tried to build up to the task by doing mental exercises. I thought to myself, "The sun is shining *over there*," five times in rapid succession, each time mentally ostending a different place: in order, the sun-lit corner of the lab, the visible front lawn of the hospital, Houston, Mars, and Jupiter. I found I had little difficulty in getting my "there's" to hop all over the celestial map with their proper references. I could loft a "there" in an instant through the farthest reaches of space, and then aim the next "there" with pinpoint accuracy at the upper left quadrant of a freckle on my arm. Why was I having such trouble with "here"? "Here in Houston" worked well enough, and so did "here in the lab," and even "here in this part of the lab," but "here in the vat" always seemed merely an unmeant mental mouthing. I tried closing my eyes while thinking it. This seemed to help, but still I couldn't manage to pull it off, except perhaps for a fleeting instant. I couldn't be sure. The discovery that I couldn't be sure was also unsettling. How did I know *where* I meant by "here" when I thought "here"? Could I *think* I meant one place when in fact I meant another? I didn't see how that could be admitted without untying the few bonds of intimacy between a person and his own mental life that had survived the onslaught of the brain scientists and philosophers, the physicalists and behaviorists. Perhaps I was incorrigible about where I *meant* when I said "here." But in my present circumstances it seemed that either I was doomed by sheer force of mental habit to thinking systematically false indexical thoughts, or where a person is (and hence where his thoughts are tokened for purposes of semantic analysis) is not necessarily where his brain, the physical seat of his soul, resides. Nagged by confusion, I attempted to orient myself by falling back on a favorite philosopher's ploy. I began naming things.

"Yorick," I said aloud to my brain, "you are my brain. The rest of my body, seated in this chair, I dub 'Hamlet.'" So here we all are: Yorick's my brain, Hamlet's my body, and I am Dennett. *Now*, where am I? And when I think "where am I?" where's that thought tokened? Is it tokened in my brain, lounging about in the vat, or right here between my ears where it *seems* to be tokened? Or nowhere? Its *temporal* coordinates give me no trouble; must it not have spatial coordinates as well? I began making a list of the alternatives.

1. *Where Hamlet goes, there goes Dennett.* This principle was easily refuted by appeal to the familiar brain transplant thought-experiments so enjoyed by philosophers. If Tom and Dick switch brains, Tom is the fellow with Dick's former body — just ask him; he'll claim to be Tom, and tell you the most intimate details of Tom's autobiography. It was clear enough, then, that my current body and I could part company, but not likely that I could be separated from my brain. The rule of thumb that emerged so plainly from the thought experiments was that in a brain-transplant operation, one wanted to be the *donor*, not the recipient. Better to call such an operation a *body*-transplant, in fact. So perhaps the truth was,

2. *Where Yorick goes, there goes Dennett.* This was not at all appealing, however. How could I be in the vat and not about to go anywhere, when I was so obviously outside the vat looking in and beginning to make guilty plans to return to my room for a substantial lunch? This begged the question I realized, but it still seemed to be getting at something important. Casting about for some support for my intuition, I hit upon a legalistic sort of argument that might have appealed to Locke.

Suppose, I argued to myself, I were now to fly to California, rob a bank, and be apprehended. In which state would I be tried: In California, where the robbery took place, or in Texas, where the brains of the outfit were located? Would I be a California felon with an out-of-state brain, or a Texas felon remotely controlling an accomplice of sorts in California? It seemed possible that I might beat such a rap just on the undecidability of that jurisdictional question, though perhaps it would be deemed an inter-state, and hence Federal, offense. In any event, suppose I were convicted. Was it likely that California would be satisfied to throw Hamlet into the brig, knowing that Yorick was living the good life and luxuriously taking the waters in Texas? Would Texas incarcerate Yorick, leaving Hamlet free to take the next boat to Rio? This alternative appealed to me. Barring capital punishment or other cruel and unusual punishment, the state would be obliged to maintain the life-support system for Yorick though they might move him from Houston to Leavenworth, and aside from the unpleasantness of the opprobrium, I, for one, would not mind at all and would consider myself a free man under those circumstances. If the state has an interest in forcibly relocating persons in institutions, it would fail to relocate me in any institution by locating Yorick there. If this were true, it suggested a third alternative.

3. *Dennett is wherever he thinks he is.* Generalized, the claim was as follows: At any given time a person has a *point of view*, and the location of the point of view (which is determined internally by the content of the point of view) is also the location of the person.

Such a proposition is not without its perplexities, but to me it seemed a step in the right direction. The only trouble was that it seemed to place one in a heads-I-win/tails-you-lose situation of unlikely infallibility as regards location. Hadn't I myself often been wrong about where I was, and at least as often uncertain? Couldn't one get lost? Of course, but getting lost *geographically* is not the only way one might get lost. If one were lost in the woods one could attempt to reassure oneself with the consolation that at least one knew where one was: one was right *here* in the familiar surroundings of one's own body. Perhaps in this case one would not have drawn one's attention to much to be thankful for. Still, there were worse plights imaginable, and I wasn't sure I wasn't in such a plight right now.

Point of view clearly had something to do with personal location, but it was itself an unclear notion. It was obvious that the content of one's point of view was not the same as or determined by the content of one's beliefs or thoughts. For example, what should we say about the point of view of the Cinerama viewer who shrieks and twists in his seat as the roller-coaster footage overcomes his psychic distancing? Has he forgotten that he is safely seated in the theater? Here I was inclined to say that the person is experiencing an illusory shift in point of view. In other cases, my inclination to call such shifts illusory was less strong. The workers in laboratories and plants who handle dangerous materials by operating feedback-controlled mechanical arms and hands undergo a shift in point of view that is crisper and more pronounced than anything Cinerama can provoke. They can feel the heft and slipperiness of the containers they manipulate with their metal fingers. They know perfectly well where they are and are not fooled into false beliefs by the experience, yet it is as if they were inside the isolation chamber they are peering into. With mental effort, they can manage to shift their point of view back and forth, rather like making a transparent Neckar cube or an Escher drawing change orientation before one's eyes. It does seem extravagant to suppose that in performing this bit of mental gymnastics, they are transporting *themselves* back and forth.

Still their example gave me hope. If I was in fact in the vat in spite of my intuitions, I might be able to train myself to adopt that point of view even as a matter of habit. I should dwell on images of myself comfortably floating in my vat, beaming volitions to that familiar body *out there*. I reflected that the ease or difficulty of this task was presumably independent of the truth about the location of one's brain. Had I been practicing before the operation, I might now be finding it second nature. You might now yourself try such a *tromp l'oeil*. Imagine you have written an inflammatory letter which has been published in the *Times*, the result of which is that the Government has chosen to impound your brain for a probationary period of three years in its Dangerous Brain Clinic in Bethesda, Maryland. Your body of course is allowed freedom to earn a salary and thus to continue its function of laying up income to be taxed. At this moment, however, your body is seated in an auditorium listening to a peculiar account by Daniel Dennett of his own similar experience. Try it. Think yourself to Bethesda, and then hark back longingly to your body, far away, and yet *seeming* so near. It is only with long-distance restraint (yours? the Government's?) that you can control your impulse to get those hands clapping in polite applause before navigating the old body to the rest room and a well-deserved glass of evening sherry in the lounge. The task of imagination is certainly difficult, but if you achieve your goal the results might be consoling.

Anyway, there I was in Houston, lost in thought as one might say, but not for long. My speculations were soon interrupted by the Houston doctors, who wished to test out my new prosthetic nervous system before sending me off on my hazardous mission. As I mentioned before, I was a bit dizzy at first, and not surprisingly, although I soon habituated myself to my new circumstances (which were, after all, well nigh indistinguishable from my old circumstances). My accommodation was not perfect, however, and to this day I continue to be plagued by minor coordination difficulties. The speed of light is fast, but finite, and as my brain and body move farther and farther apart, the delicate interaction of my feedback systems is thrown into disarray by the time lags. Just as one is rendered close to speechless by a delayed or echoic hearing of one's speaking voice so, for instance, I am virtually unable to track a moving object with my eyes whenever my brain and my body are more than a few miles apart. In most matters my impairment is scarcely detectable, though I can no longer hit a slow curve ball with the authority of yore. There are some compensations of course. Though liquor tastes as good as ever, and warms my gullet while corroding my liver, I can drink it in any quantity I please, without becoming the slightest bit inebriated, a curiosity some of my close friends may have noticed (though I occasionally have *feigned* inebriation, so as not to draw attention to my unusual circumstances). For similar reasons, I take aspirin orally for a sprained wrist, but if the pain persists I ask Houston to administer codeine to me *in vitro*. In times of illness the phone bill can be staggering.

But to return to my adventure. At length, both the doctors and I were satisfied that I was ready to undertake my subterranean mission. And so I left my brain in Houston and headed by helicopter for Tulsa. Well, in any case, that's the way it seemed to me. That's how I would put it, just off the top of my head as it were. On the trip I reflected further about my earlier anxieties and decided that my first post-operative speculations had been tinged with panic. The matter was not nearly as strange or metaphysical as I had been supposing. Where was I? In two places, clearly: both inside the vat and outside it. Just as one can stand with one foot in Connecticut and the other in Rhode Island, I was in two places at once. I had become one of those scattered individuals we used to hear so much about. The more I considered this answer, the more obviously true it appeared. But, strange to say, the more true it appeared, the less important the question to which it could be the true answer seemed. A sad, but not unprecedented, fate for a philosophical question to suffer. This answer did not completely satisfy me, of course. There lingered some question to which I should have liked an answer, which was neither "Where are all my various and sundry parts?" nor "What is my current point of view?" Or at least there seemed to be such a question. For it did seem undeniable that in some sense *I* and not merely *most of me* was descending into the earth under Tulsa in search of an atomic warhead.

When I found the warhead, I was certainly glad I had left my brain behind, for the pointer on the specially built Geiger counter I had brought with me was off the dial. I called Houston on my ordinary radio and told the operation control center of my position and my progress. In return, they gave me instructions for dismantling the vehicle, based upon my on-site observations. I had set to work with my cutting torch when all of a sudden a terrible thing happened. I went stone deaf. At first I thought it was only my radio earphones that had broken, but when I tapped on my helmet, I heard nothing. Apparently the auditory transceivers had gone on the fritz. I could no longer hear Houston or my own voice, but I could speak, so I started telling them what had happened. In mid-sentence, I knew something else had gone wrong. My vocal apparatus had become paralyzed. Then my right hand went limp — another transceiver had gone. I was truly in deep trouble. But worse was to follow. After a few more minutes, I went blind. I cursed my luck, and then I cursed the scientists who had led me into this grave peril. There I was, deaf, dumb, and blind, in a radioactive hole more than a mile under Tulsa. Then the last of my cerebral radio links broke, and suddenly I was faced with a new and even more shocking problem: whereas an instant before I had been buried alive in Oklahoma, now I was disembodied in Houston. My recognition of my new status was not immediate. It took me several very anxious minutes before it dawned on me that my poor body lay several hundred miles away, with heart pulsing and lungs respirating, but otherwise as dead as the body of any heart transplant donor, its skull packed with useless, broken electronic gear. The shift in perspective I had earlier found well nigh impossible now seemed quite natural. Though I could think myself back into my body in the tunnel under Tulsa, it took some effort to sustain the illusion. For surely it was an illusion to suppose I was still in Oklahoma: I had lost all contact with that body.

It occurred to me then, with one of those rushes of revelation of which we should be suspicious, that I had stumbled upon an impressive demonstration of the immateriality of the soul based upon physicalist principles and premises. For as the last radio signal between Tulsa and Houston died away, had I not changed location from Tulsa to Houston at the speed of light? And had I not accomplished this without any increase in mass? What moved from A to B at such speed was surely myself, or at any rate my soul or mind — the massless center of my being and home of my consciousness. My *point of view* had lagged somewhat behind, but I had already noted the indirect bearing of point of view on personal location. I could not see how a physicalist philosopher could quarrel with this except by taking the dire and counter-intuitive route of banishing all talk of persons. Yet the notion of personhood was so well entrenched in everyone's world view, or so it seemed to me, that any denial would be as curiously unconvincing, as systematically disingenuous, as the Cartesian negation, "non sum."[1]

The joy of philosophic discovery thus tided me over some very bad minutes or perhaps hours as the helplessness and hopelessness of my situation became more apparent to me. Waves of panic and even nausea swept over me, made all the more horrible by the absence of their normal body-dependent phenomenology. No adrenalin rush of tingles in the arms, no pounding heart, no premonitory salivation. I did feel a dread sinking feeling in my bowels at one point, and this tricked me momentarily into the false hope that I was undergoing a reversal of the process that landed me in this fix — a gradual undisembodiment. But the isolation and uniqueness of that twinge soon convinced me that it was simply the first of a plague of phantom body hallucinations that I, like any other amputee, would be all too likely to suffer.

My mood then was chaotic. On the one hand, I was fired up with elation at my philosophic discovery and was wracking my brain (one of the few familiar things I could still do), trying to figure out how to communicate my discovery to the journals; while on the other, I was bitter, lonely, and filled with dread and uncertainty. Fortunately, this did not last long, for my technical support team sedated me into a dreamless sleep from which I awoke, hearing with magnificent fidelity the familiar opening strains of my favorite Brahms piano trio. So that was why they had wanted a list of my favorite recordings! It did not take me long to realize that I was hearing the music without ears. The output from the stereo stylus was being fed through some fancy rectification circuitry directly into my auditory nerve. I was mainlining Brahms, an unforgettable experience for any stereo buff. At the end of the record it did not surprise me to hear the reassuring voice of the project director speaking into a microphone that was now my prosthetic ear. He confirmed my analysis of what had gone wrong and assured me that steps were being taken to re-embody me. He did not elaborate, and after a few more recordings, I found myself drifting off to sleep. My sleep lasted, I later learned, for the better part of a year, and when I awoke, it was to find myself fully restored to my senses. When I looked into the mirror, though, I was a bit startled to see an unfamiliar face. Bearded and a bit heavier, bearing no doubt a family resemblance to my former face, and with the same look of spritely intelligence and resolute character, but definitely a new face. Further self-explorations of an intimate nature left me no doubt that this was a new body and the project director confirmed my conclusions. He did not volunteer any information on the past history of my new body and I decided (wisely, I think in retrospect) not to pry. As many philosophers unfamiliar with my ordeal have more recently speculated, the acquisition of a new body leaves one's *person* intact. And after a period of adjustment to a new voice, new muscular strengths and weaknesses, and so forth, one's *personality* is by and large also preserved. More dramatic changes in personality have been routinely observed in people who have undergone extensive plastic surgery, to say nothing of sex change operations, and I think no one contests the survival of the person in such cases. In any event I soon accommodated to my new body, to the point of being unable to recover any of its novelties to my consciousness or even memory. The view in the mirror soon became utterly familiar. That view, by the way, still revealed antennae, and so I was not surprised to learn that my brain had not been moved from its haven in the life-support lab.

I decided that good old Yorick deserved a visit. I and my new body, whom we might as well call Fortinbras, strode into the familiar lab to another round of applause from the technicians, who were of course congratulating themselves, not me. Once more I stood before the vat and contemplated poor Yorick, and on a whim I once again cavalierly flicked off the output transmitter switch. Imagine my surprise when nothing unusual happened. No fainting spell, no nausea, no noticeable change. A technician hurried to restore the switch to *on*, but still I felt nothing. I demanded an explanation, which the project director hastened to provide. It seems that before they had even operated on the first occasion, they had constructed a computer duplicate of my brain, reproducing both the complete information processing structure and the computational speed of my brain in a giant computer program. After the operation, but before they had dared to send me off on my mission to Oklahoma, they had run this computer system and Yorick side by side. The incoming signals from Hamlet were sent simultaneously to Yorick's transceivers and to the computer's array of inputs. And the outputs from Yorick were not only beamed back to Hamlet, my body; they were recorded and checked against the simultaneous output of the computer program, which was called "Hubert" for reasons obscure to me. Over days and even weeks, the outputs were identical and synchronous, which of course did not *prove* that they had succeeded in copying the brain's functional structure, but the empirical support was greatly encouraging.

Hubert's input, and hence activity, had been kept parallel with Yorick's during my disembodied days. And now, to demonstrate this, they had actually thrown the master switch that put Hubert for the first time in on-line control of my body — not Hamlet, of course, but Fortinbras. (Hamlet, I learned, had never been recovered from its underground tomb and could be assumed by this time to have largely returned to the dust. At the head of my grave still lay the magnificent bulk of the abandoned device, with the word STUD emblazoned on its side in large letters — a circumstance which may provide archeologists of the next century with a curious insight into the burial rites of their ancestors.)

The laboratory technicians now showed me the master switch, which had two positions, labeled *B*, for Brain (they didn't know my brain's name was Yorick) and *H*, for Hubert. The switch did indeed point to *H*, and they explained to me that if I wished, I could switch it back to *B*. With my heart in my mouth (and my brain in its vat), I did this. Nothing happened. A click, that was all. To test their claim, and with the master switch now set at *B*, I hit Yorick's output transmitter switch on the vat and sure enough, I began to faint. Once the output switch was turned back on and I had recovered my wits, so to speak, I continued to play with the master switch, flipping it back and forth. I found that with the exception of the transitional click, I could detect no trace of a difference. I could switch in mid-utterance, and the sentence I had begun speaking under the control of Yorick was finished without a pause or hitch of any kind under the control of Hubert. I had a spare brain, a prosthetic device which might some day stand me in very good stead, were some mishap to befall Yorick. Or alternatively, I could keep Yorick as a spare and use Hubert. It didn't seem to make any difference which I chose, for the wear and tear and fatigue on my body did not have any debilitating effect on either brain, whether or not it was actually causing the motions of my body, or merely spilling its output into thin air.

The one truly unsettling aspect of this new development was the prospect, which was not long in dawning on me, of someone detaching the spare — Hubert or Yorick, as the case might be — from Fortinbras and hitching it to yet another body — some Johnny-come-lately Rosencrantz or Guildenstern. Then (if not before) there would be *two* people, that much was clear. One would be me, and the other would be a sort of super-twin brother. If there were two bodies, one under the control of Hubert and the other being controlled by Yorick, then which would the world recognize as the true Dennett? And whatever the rest of the world decided, which one would be *me*? Would I be the Yorick-brained one, in virtue of Yorick's causal priority and former intimate relationship with the original Dennett body, Hamlet? That seemed a bit legalistic, a bit too redolent of the arbitrariness of consanguinity and legal possession, to be convincing at the metaphysical level. For, suppose that before the arrival of the second body on the scene, I had been keeping Yorick as the spare for years, and letting Hubert's output drive my body — that is, Fortinbras — all that time. The Hubert-Fortinbras couple would seem then by squatter's rights (to combat one legal intuition with another) to be the true Dennett and the lawful inheritor of everything that was Dennett's. This was an interesting question, certainly, but not nearly so pressing as another question that bothered me. My strongest intuition was that in such an eventuality *I* would survive so long as *either* brain-body couple remained intact, but I had mixed emotions about whether I should want both to survive.

I discussed my worries with the technicians and the project director. The prospect of two Dennetts was abhorrent to me, I explained, largely for social reasons. I didn't want to be my own rival for the affections of my wife, nor did I like the prospect of the two Dennetts sharing my modest professor's salary. Still more vertiginous and distasteful, though, was the idea of knowing *that much* about another person, while he had the very same goods on me. How could we ever face each other? My colleagues in the lab argued that I was ignoring the bright side of the matter. Weren't there many things I wanted to do but, being only one person, had been unable to do? Now one Dennett could stay at home and be the professor and family man, while the other could strike out on a life of travel and adventure — missing the family of course, but happy in the knowledge that the other Dennett was keeping the home fires burning. I could be faithful and adulterous at the same time. I could even cuckold myself — to say nothing of other more lurid possibilities my colleagues were all too ready to force upon my overtaxed imagination. But my ordeal in Oklahoma (or was it Houston?) had made me less adventurous, and I shrank from this opportunity that was being offered (though of course I was never quite sure it was being offered to *me* in the first place).

There was another prospect even more disagreeable — that the spare, Hubert or Yorick as the case might be, would be detached from any input from Fortinbras and just left detached. Then, as in the other case, there would be two Dennetts, or at least two claimants to my name and possessions, one embodied in Fortinbras, and the other sadly, miserably disembodied. Both selfishness and altruism bade me take steps to prevent this from happening. So I asked that measures be taken to ensure that no one could ever tamper with the transceiver connections or the master switch without my (our? no, *my*) knowledge and consent. Since I had no desire to spend my life guarding the equipment in Houston, it was mutually decided that all the electronic connections in the lab would be carefully locked: both those that controlled the life-support system for Yorick and those that controlled the power supply for Hubert would be guarded with fail-safe devices, and I would take the only master switch, out-fitted for radio remote control, with me wherever I went. I carry it strapped around my waist and — wait a moment — *here it is*. Every few months I reconnoiter the situation by switching channels. I do this only in the presence of friends of course, for if the other channel were, heaven forbid, either dead or otherwise occupied, there would have to be somebody who had my interests at heart to switch it back, to bring me back from the void. For while I could feel, see, hear and otherwise sense whatever befell my body, subsequent to such a switch, I'd be unable to control it. By the way, the two positions on the switch are intentionally unmarked, so I never have the faintest idea whether I am switching from Hubert to Yorick or *vice versa*. (Some of you may think that in this case I really don't know *who* I am, let alone where I am. But such reflections no longer make much of a dent on my essential Dennett-ness, on my own sense of who I am. If it is true that in one sense I don't know who I am then that's another one of your philosophical truths of underwhelming significance.)

In any case, every time I've flipped the switch so far, nothing has happened. *So let's give it a try. . . .*

"THANK GOD! I THOUGHT YOU'D NEVER FLIP THAT SWITCH! You can't imagine how horrible it's been these last two weeks — but now you know, it's your turn in purgatory. How I've longed for this moment! You see, about two weeks ago — excuse me, ladies and gentlemen, but I've got to explain this to my . . . um, brother, I guess you could say, but he's just told you the facts, so you'll understand — about two weeks ago our two brains drifted just a bit out of synch. I don't know whether *my* brain is now Hubert or Yorick, any more than you do, but in any case, the two brains drifted apart, and of course once the process started, it snowballed, for I was in a slightly different receptive state for the input we both received, a difference that was soon magnified. In no time at all the illusion that I was in control of my body — our body — was completely dissipated. There was nothing I could do — no way to call you. YOU DIDN'T EVEN KNOW I EXISTED! It's been like being carried around in a cage, or better, like being possessed — hearing my own voice say things I didn't mean to say, watching in frustration as my own hands performed deeds I hadn't intended. You'd scratch our itches, but not the way I would have, and you kept me awake, with your tossing and turning. I've been totally exhausted, on the verge of a nervous breakdown, carried around helplessly by your frantic round of activities, sustained only by the knowledge that some day you'd throw the switch.

"Now it's your turn, but at least you'll have the comfort of knowing *I* know you're in there. Like an expectant mother, I'm eating — or at any rate tasting, smelling, seeing — for *two* now, and I'll try to make it easy for you. Don't worry. Just as soon as this colloquium is over, you and I will fly to Houston, and we'll see what can be done to get one of us another body. You can have a female body — your body could be any color you like. But let's think it over. I tell you what — to be fair, if we both want this body, I promise I'll let the project director flip a coin to settle which of us gets to keep it and which then gets to choose a new body. That should guarantee justice, shouldn't it? In any case, I'll take care of you, I promise. These people are my witnesses.

"Ladies and gentlemen, this talk we have just heard is not exactly the talk *I* would have given, but I assure you that everything he said was perfectly true. And now if you'll excuse me, I think I'd — we'd — better sit down."[2]

NOTES

1. Cf. Jaakko Hintikka, "Cogito ergo sum: Inference or Performance?" *The Philosophical Review*, LXXI, 1962, pp. 3–32.
2. Anyone familiar with the literature on this topic will recognize that my remarks owe a great deal to the explorations of Sydney Shoemaker, John Perry, David Lewis and Derek Parfit, and in particular to their papers in Amelie Rorty, ed., *The Identities of Persons*, 1976.

CHAPTER THREE

CAN MACHINES THINK?

DANIEL C. DENNETT

Much has been written about the Turing test in the last few years, some of it preposterously off the mark. People typically mis-imagine the test by orders of magnitude. This essay is an antidote, a prosthesis for the imagination, showing how huge the task posed by the Turing test is, and hence how unlikely it is that any computer will ever pass it. It does not go far enough in the imagination-enhancement department, however, and I have updated the essay with two postscripts.

Can machines think? This has been a conundrum for philosophers for years, but in their fascination with the pure conceptual issues they have for the most part overlooked the real social importance of the answer. It is of more than academic importance that we learn to think clearly about the actual cognitive powers of computers, for they are now being introduced into a variety of sensitive social roles, where their powers will be put to the ultimate test: In a wide variety of areas, we are on the verge of making ourselves dependent upon their cognitive powers. The cost of overestimating them could be enormous.

One of the principal inventors of the computer was the great British mathematician Alan Turing. It was he who first figured out, in highly abstract terms, how to design a programmable computing device — what we now call a universal Turing machine. All programmable computers in use today are in essence Turing machines. Over thirty years ago, at the dawn of the computer age, Turing began a classic article, "Computing Machinery and Intelligence," with the words: "I propose to consider the question, 'Can machines think?'" — but then went on to say this was a bad question, a question that leads only to sterile debate and haggling over definitions, a question, as he put it, "too meaningless to deserve discussion" (Turing, 1950). In its place he substituted what he took to be a much better question, a question that would be crisply answerable and intuitively satisfying — in every way an acceptable substitute for the philosophic puzzler with which he began.

From chapter 1 in Dennett, Daniel C., *Brainchildren: Essays on Designing Minds,* pp. 3–29, © 1998 Daniel C. Dennett, by permission of The MIT Press.

First he described a parlor game of sorts, the "imitation game," to be played by a man, a woman, and a judge (of either gender). The man and woman are hidden from the judge's view but able to communicate with the judge by teletype; the judge's task is to guess, after a period of questioning each contestant, which interlocutor is the man and which the woman. The man tries to convince the judge he is the woman (and the woman tries to convince the judge of the truth), and the man wins if the judge makes the wrong identification. A little reflection will convince you, I am sure, that, aside from lucky breaks, it would take a clever man to convince the judge that he was a woman — assuming the judge is clever too, of course.

Now suppose, Turing said, we replace the man or woman with a computer, and give the judge the task of determining which is the human being and which is the computer. Turing proposed that any computer that can regularly or often fool a discerning judge in this game would be intelligent — would be a computer that thinks — *beyond any reasonable doubt.* Now, it is important to realize that failing this test is not supposed to be a sign of lack of intelligence. Many intelligent people, after all, might not be willing or able to play the imitation game, and we should allow computers the same opportunity to decline to prove themselves. This is, then, a one-way test; failing it proves nothing.

Furthermore, Turing was not committing himself to the view (although it is easy to see how one might think he was) that to think is to think just like a human being — any more than he was committing himself to the view that for a man to think, he must think exactly like a woman. Men and women, and computers, may all have different ways of thinking. But surely, he thought, if one can think in one's own peculiar style well enough to imitate a thinking man or woman, one can think well, indeed. This imagined exercise has come to be known as the Turing test.

It is a sad irony that Turing's proposal has had exactly the opposite effect on the discussion of that which he intended. Turing didn't design the test as a useful tool in scientific psychology, a method of confirming or disconfirming scientific theories or evaluating particular models of mental function; he designed it to be nothing more than a philosophical conversation-stopper. He proposed — in the spirit of "Put up or shut up!" — a simple test for thinking that was *surely* strong enough to satisfy the sternest skeptic (or so he thought). He was saying, in effect, "Instead of arguing interminably about the ultimate nature and essence of thinking, why don't we all agree that whatever that nature is, anything that could pass this test would surely have it; then we could turn to asking how or whether some machine could be designed and built that might pass the test fair and square." Alas, philosophers — amateur and professional — have instead taken Turing's proposal as the pretext for just the sort of definitional haggling and interminable arguing about imaginary counterexamples he was hoping to squelch.

This thirty-year preoccupation with the Turing test has been all the more regrettable because it has focused attention on the wrong issues. There are *real world* problems that are revealed by considering the strengths and weaknesses of the Turing test, but these have been concealed behind a smokescreen of misguided criticisms. A failure to think imaginatively about the test actually proposed by Turing has led many to underestimate its severity and to confuse it with much less interesting proposals.

So first I want to show that the Turing test, conceived as he conceived it, is (as he thought) plenty strong enough as a test of thinking. I defy anyone to improve upon it. But here is the point almost universally overlooked by the literature: There is a common *misapplication* of the sort of testing exhibited by the Turing test that often leads to drastic overestimation of the powers of actually existing computer systems. The follies of this familiar sort of thinking about computers can best be brought out by a reconsideration of the Turing test itself.

The insight underlying the Turing test is the same insight that inspires the new practice among symphony orchestras of conducting auditions with an opaque screen between the jury and the musician. What matters in a musician, obviously, is musical ability and only musical ability; such features as sex, hair length, skin color, and weight are strictly irrelevant. Since juries might be biased — even innocently and unawares — by these irrelevant features, they are carefully screened off so only the essential feature, musicianship, can be examined. Turing recognized that people similarly might be biased in their judgments of intelligence by whether the contestant had soft skin, warm blood, facial features, hands and eyes — which are obviously not themselves essential components of intelligence — so he devised a screen that would let through only a sample of what really mattered: the capacity to understand, and think cleverly about, challenging problems. Perhaps he was inspired by Descartes, who in his *Discourse on Method* (1637) plausibly argued that there was no more demanding test of human mentality than the capacity to hold an intelligent conversation:

> It is indeed conceivable that a machine could be so made that it would utter words, and even words appropriate to the presence of physical acts or objects which cause some change in its organs; as, for example, if it was touched in some spot that it would ask what you wanted to say to it; if in another, that it would cry that it was hurt, and so on for similar things. But it could never modify its phrases to reply to the sense of whatever was said in its presence, as even the most stupid men can do.

This seemed obvious to Descartes in the seventeenth century, but of course the fanciest machines he knew were elaborate clockwork figures, not electronic computers. Today it is far from obvious that such machines are impossible, but Descartes's hunch that ordinary conversation would put as severe a strain on artificial intelligence as any other test was shared by Turing. Of course there is nothing sacred about the particular conversational game chosen by Turing for his test; it is just a cannily chosen test of more general intelligence. The assumption Turing was prepared to make was this: Nothing could possibly pass the Turing test by winning the imitation game without being able to perform indefinitely many other clearly intelligent actions. Let us call that assumption the quick-probe assumption. Turing realized, as anyone would, that there are hundreds and thousands of telling signs of intelligent thinking to be observed in our fellow creatures, and one could, if one wanted, compile a vast battery of different tests to assay the capacity for intelligent thought. But success on his chosen test, he thought, would be highly predictive of success on many other intuitively acceptable tests of intelligence. Remember, failure on the Turing test does not predict failure on those others, but success would surely predict success. His test was so severe, he thought, that nothing that could pass it fair and square would disappoint us in other quarters. Maybe it wouldn't do everything we hoped — maybe it wouldn't appreciate ballet, or understand quantum physics, or have a good plan for world peace, but we'd all see that it was surely one of the intelligent, thinking entities in the neighborhood.

Is this high opinion of the Turing test's severity misguided? Certainly many have thought so — but usually because they have not imagined the test in sufficient detail, and hence have underestimated it. Trying to forestall this skepticism, Turing imagined several lines of questioning that a judge might employ in this game — about writing poetry, or playing chess — that would be taxing indeed, but with thirty years' experience with the actual talents and foibles of computers behind us, perhaps we can add a few more tough lines of questioning.

Terry Winograd, a leader in artificial intelligence efforts to produce conversational ability in a computer, draws our attention to a pair of sentences (Winograd, 1972). They differ in only one word. The first sentence is this:

The committee denied the group a parade permit because they advocated violence.

Here's the second sentence:

The committee denied the group a parade permit because they feared violence.

The difference is just in the verb — *advocated* or *feared.* As Winograd points out, the pronoun *they* in each sentence is officially ambiguous. Both readings of the pronoun are always legal. Thus we can imagine a world in which governmental committees in charge of parade permits advocate violence in the streets and, for some strange reason, use this as their pretext for denying a parade permit. But the natural, reasonable, intelligent reading of the first sentence is that it's the group that advocated violence, and of the second, that it's the committee that feared violence.

Now if sentences like this are embedded in a conversation, the computer must figure out which reading of the pronoun is meant, if it is to respond intelligently. But mere rules of grammar or vocabulary will not fix the right reading. What fixes the right reading for us is knowledge about the world, about politics, social circumstances, committees and their attitudes, groups that want to parade, how they tend to behave, and the like. One must know about the world, in short, to make sense of such a sentence.

In the jargon of Artificial Intelligence (AI), a conversational computer needs a lot of *world knowledge* to do its job. But, it seems, if somehow it is endowed with that world knowledge on many topics, it should be able to do much more with that world knowledge than merely make sense of a conversation containing just that sentence. The only way, it appears, for a computer to disambiguate that sentence and keep up its end of a conversation that uses that sentence would be for it to have a much more general ability to respond intelligently to information about social and political circumstances, and many other topics. Thus, such sentences, by putting a demand on such abilities, are good quick-probes. That is, they test for a wider competence.

People typically ignore the prospect of having the judge ask off-the-wall questions in the Turing test, and hence they underestimate the competence a computer would have to have to pass the test. But remember, the rules of the imitation game as Turing presented it permit the judge to ask any question that could be asked of a human being — no holds barred. Suppose then we give a contestant in the game this question:

An Irishman found a genie in a bottle who offered him two wishes. "First I'll have a pint of Guinness," said the Irishman, and when it appeared he took several long drinks from it and was delighted to see that the glass filled itself magically as he drank. "What about your second wish?" asked the genie. "Oh well," said the Irishman, "that's easy. I'll have another one of these!"
— Please explain this story to me, and tell me if there is anything funny or sad about it.

Now even a child could express, if not eloquently, the understanding that is required to get this joke. But think of how much one has to know and understand about human culture, to put it pompously, to be able to give any account of the point of this joke. I am not supposing that the computer would have to laugh at, or be amused by, the joke. But if it wants to win the imitation game — and that's the test, after all — it had better know enough in its own alien, humorless way about human psychology and culture to be able to pretend effectively that it was amused and explain why.

It may seem to you that we could devise a better test. Let's compare the Turing test with some other candidates.

Candidate 1: A computer is intelligent if it wins the World Chess Championship.

That's not a good test, as it turns out. Chess prowess has proven to be an isolatable talent. There are programs today that can play fine chess but can do nothing else. So the quick-probe assumption is false for the test of playing winning chess.

Candidate 2: The computer is intelligent if it solves the Arab-Israeli conflict.

This is surely a more severe test than Turing's. But it has some defects: it is unrepeatable, if passed once; slow, no doubt; and it is not crisply clear what would count as passing it. Here's another prospect, then:

Candidate 3: A computer is intelligent if it succeeds in stealing the British crown jewels without the use of force or violence.

Now this is better. First, it could be repeated again and again, though of course each repeat test would presumably be harder — but this is a feature it shares with the Turing test. Second, the mark of success is clear — either you've got the jewels to show for your efforts or you don't. But it is expensive and slow, a socially dubious caper at best, and no doubt luck would play too great a role.

With ingenuity and effort one might be able to come up with other candidates that would equal the Turing test in severity, fairness, and efficiency, but I think these few examples should suffice to convince us that it would be hard to improve on Turing's original proposal.

But still, you may protest, something might pass the Turing test and still not be intelligent, not be a thinker. What does *might* mean here? If what you have in mind is that by cosmic accident, by a supernatural coincidence, a stupid person or a stupid computer *might* fool a clever judge repeatedly, well, yes, but so what? The same frivolous possibility "in principle" holds for any test whatever. A playful god, or evil demon, let us agree, could fool the world's scientific community about the presence of H_2O in the Pacific Ocean. But still, the tests they rely on to establish that there is H_2O in the Pacific Ocean are quite beyond reasonable criticism. If the Turing test for thinking is no worse than any well-established scientific test, we can set skepticism aside and go back to serious matters. Is there any more likelihood of a "false positive" result on the Turing test than on, say, the test currently used for the presence of iron in an ore sample?

This question is often obscured by a "move" that philosophers have sometimes made called operationalism. Turing and those who think well of his test are often accused of being operationalists. Operationalism is the tactic of *defining* the presence of some property, for instance, intelligence, as being established once and for all by the passing of some test. Let's illustrate this with a different example.

Suppose I offer the following test — we'll call it the Dennett test — for being a great city:

A great city is one in which, on a randomly chosen day, one can do all three of the following:

Hear a symphony orchestra
See a Rembrandt *and* a professional athletic contest
Eat *quenelles de brochet à la Nantua* for lunch

To make the operationalist move would be to declare that any city that passes the Dennett test is *by definition* a great city. What being a great city *amounts to* is just passing the Dennett test. Well then, if the Chamber of Commerce of Great Falls, Montana, wanted — and I can't imagine why—to get their hometown on my list of great cities, they could accomplish this by the relatively inexpensive route of hiring full time about ten basketball players, forty musicians, and a quick-order quenelle chef and renting a cheap Rembrandt from some museum. An idiotic operationalist would then be stuck admitting that Great Falls, Montana, was in fact a great city, since all he or she cares about in great cities is that they pass the Dennett test.

Sane operationalists (who for that very reason are perhaps not operationalists at all, since *operationalist* seems to be a dirty word) would cling confidently to their test, but only because they have what they consider to be very good reasons for thinking the odds against a false positive result, like the imagined Chamber of Commerce caper, are astronomical. I devised the Dennett test, of course, with the realization that no one would be both stupid and rich enough to go to such preposterous lengths to foil the test. In the actual world, wherever you find symphony orchestras, *quenelles*, Rembrandts, and professional sports, you also find daily newspapers, parks, repertory theaters, libraries, fine architecture, and all the other things that go to make a city great. My test was simply devised to locate a telling sample that could not help but be representative of the rest of the city's treasures. I would cheerfully run the minuscule risk of having my bluff called. Obviously, the test items are not all that I care about in a city. In fact, some of them I don't care about at all. I just think they would be cheap and easy ways of assuring myself that the subtle things I do care about in cities are present. Similarly, I think it would be entirely unreasonable to suppose that Alan Turing had an inordinate fondness for party games, or put too high a value on party game prowess in his test. In both the Turing and the Dennett test, a very unrisky gamble is being taken: the gamble that the quick-probe assumption is, in general, safe.

But two can play this game of playing the odds. Suppose some computer programmer happens to be, for whatever strange reason, dead set on tricking me into judging an entity to be a thinking, intelligent thing when it is not. Such a trickster could rely as well as I can on unlikelihood and take a few gambles. Thus, if the programmer can expect that it is not remotely likely that I, as the judge, will bring up the topic of children's birthday parties, or baseball, or moon rocks, then he or she can avoid the trouble of building world knowledge on those topics into the data base. Whereas if I do improbably raise these issues, the system will draw a blank and I will unmask the pretender easily. But given all the topics and words that I *might* raise, such a savings would no doubt be negligible. Turn the idea inside out, however, and the trickster would have a fighting chance. Suppose the programmer has reason to believe that I will ask *only* about children's birthday parties, or baseball, or moon rocks — all other topics being, for one reason or another, out of bounds. Not only does the task shrink dramatically, but there already exist systems or preliminary sketches of systems in artificial intelligence that can do a whiz-bang job of responding with apparent intelligence on just those specialized topics.

William Wood's LUNAR program, to take what is perhaps the best example, answers scientists' questions — posed in ordinary English — about moon rocks. In one test it answered correctly and appropriately something like 90 percent of the questions that geologists and other experts thought of asking it about moon rocks. (In 12 percent of those correct responses there were trivial, correctable defects.) Of course, Wood's motive in creating LUNAR was not to trick unwary geologists into thinking they were conversing with an intelligent being. And if that had been his motive, his project would still be a long way from success.

For it is easy enough to unmask LUNAR without ever straying from the prescribed topic of moon rocks. Put LUNAR in one room and a moon rock specialist in another, and then ask them both their opinion of the social value of the moon-rocks-gathering expeditions, for instance. Or ask the contestants their opinion of the suitability of moon rocks as ashtrays, or whether people who have touched moon rocks are ineligible for the draft. Any intelligent person knows a lot more about moon rocks than their geology. Although it might be *unfair* to demand this extra knowledge of a computer moon rock specialist, it would be an easy way to get it to fail the Turing test.

But just suppose that someone could extend LUNAR to cover itself plausibly on such probes, so long as the topic was still, however indirectly, moon rocks. We might come to think it was a lot more like the human moon rocks specialist than it really was. The moral we should draw is that as Turing test judges we should resist all limitations and waterings-down of the Turing test. They make the game too easy — vastly easier than the original test. Hence they lead us into the risk of overestimating the actual comprehension of the system being tested.

Consider a different limitation of the Turing test that should strike a suspicious chord in us as soon as we hear it. This is a variation on a theme developed in an article by Ned Block (1982). Suppose someone were to propose to restrict the judge to a vocabulary of, say, the 850 words of "Basic English," and to single-sentence probes — that is "moves" — of no more than four words. Moreover, contestants must respond to these probes with no more than four words per move, and a test may involve no more than forty questions.

Is this an innocent variation on Turing's original test? These restrictions would make the imitation game clearly finite. That is, the total number of all possible permissible games is a large, but finite, number. One might suspect that such a limitation would permit the trickster simply to store, in alphabetical order, all the possible good conversations within the limits and beat the judge with nothing more sophisticated than a system of table lookup. In fact, that isn't in the cards. Even with these severe and improbable and suspicious restrictions imposed upon the imitation game, the number of legal games, though finite, is mind-bogglingly large. I haven't bothered trying to calculate it, but it surely exceeds astronomically the number of possible chess games with no more than forty moves, and that number has been calculated. John Haugeland says it's in the neighborhood of ten to the one hundred twentieth power. For comparison, Haugeland (1981, p. 16) suggests that there have only been ten to the eighteenth seconds since the beginning of the universe.

Of course, the number of good, sensible conversations under these limits is a tiny fraction, maybe one quadrillionth, of the number of merely grammatically well formed conversations. So let's say, to be very conservative, that there are only ten to the fiftieth different smart conversations such a computer would have to store. Well, the task shouldn't take more than a few trillion years — given generous government support. Finite numbers can be very large.

So though we needn't worry that this particular trick of storing all the smart conversations would work, we can appreciate that there are lots of ways of making the task easier that may appear innocent at first. We also get a reassuring measure of just how severe the unrestricted Turing test is by reflecting on the more than astronomical size of even that severely restricted version of it.

Block's imagined — and utterly impossible — program exhibits the dreaded feature known in computer science circles as *combinatorial explosion.* No conceivable computer could overpower a combinatorial explosion with sheer speed and size. Since the problem areas addressed by artificial intelligence are veritable minefields of combinatorial explosion, and since it has often proven difficult to find *any* solution to a problem that avoids them, there is considerable plausibility in Newell and Simon's proposal that avoiding combinatorial explosion (by any means at all) be viewed as one of the hallmarks of intelligence.

Our brains are millions of times bigger than the brains of gnats, but they are still, for all their vast complexity, compact, efficient, timely organs that somehow or other manage to perform all their tasks while avoiding combinatorial explosion. A computer a million times bigger or faster than a human brain might not look like the brain of a human being, or even be internally organized like the brain of a human being, but if, for all its differences, it somehow managed to control a wise and timely set of activities, it would have to be the beneficiary of a very special design that avoided combinatorial explosion, and whatever that design was, would we not be right to consider the entity intelligent?

Turing's test was designed to allow for this possibility. His point was that we should not be species-chauvinistic, or anthropocentric, about the insides of an intelligent being, for there might be inhuman ways of being intelligent.

To my knowledge, the only serious and interesting attempt by any program designer to win even a severely modified Turing test has been Kenneth Colby's. Colby is a psychiatrist and intelligence artificer at UCLA. He has a program called PARRY, which is a computer simulation of a paranoid patient who has delusions about the Mafia being out to get him. As you do with other conversational programs, you interact with it by sitting at a terminal and typing questions and answers back and forth. A number of years ago, Colby put PARRY to a very restricted test. He had genuine psychiatrists interview PARRY. He did not suggest to them that they might be talking or typing to a computer; rather, he made up some plausible story about why they were communicating with a real live patient by teletype. He also had the psychiatrists interview real, human paranoids via teletype. Then he took a PARRY transcript, inserted it in a group of teletype transcripts from real patients, gave them to *another* group of experts — more psychiatrists — and said, "One of these was a conversation with a computer. Can you figure out which one it was?" They couldn't. They didn't do better than chance.

Colby presented this with some huzzah, but critics scoffed at the suggestions that this was a legitimate Turing test. My favorite commentary on it was Joseph Weizenbaum's; in a letter to the *Communications of the Association of Computing Machinery* (Weizenbaum, 1974, p. 543), he said that, inspired by Colby, he had designed an even better program, which passed the same test. His also had the virtue of being a very inexpensive program, in these times of tight money. In fact you didn't even need a computer for it. All you needed was an electric typewriter. His program modeled infant autism. And the transcripts — you type in your questions, and the thing just sits there and hums — cannot be distinguished by experts from transcripts of real conversations with infantile autistic patients. What was wrong, of course, with Colby's test was that the unsuspecting interviewers had no motivation at all to try out any of the sorts of questions that easily would have unmasked PARRY.

Colby was undaunted, and after his team had improved PARRY he put it to a much more severe test — a surprisingly severe test. This time, the interviewers — again, psychiatrists — *were* given the task at the outset of telling the computer from the real patient. They were set up in a classic Turing test: the patient in one room, the computer PARRY in the other room, with the judges conducting interviews with both of them (on successive days). The judges' task was to find out which one was the computer and which one was the real patient. Amazingly, they didn't do much better, which leads some people to say, "Well, that just confirms my impression of the intelligence of psychiatrists!"

But now, more seriously, was this an honest-to-goodness Turing test? Were there tacit restrictions on the lines of questioning of the judges? Like the geologists interacting with LUNAR, the psychiatrists' professional preoccupations and habits kept them from asking the sorts of unlikely questions that would have easily unmasked PARRY. After all, they realized that since one of the contestants was a real, live paranoid person, medical ethics virtually forbade them from toying with, upsetting, or attempting to confuse their interlocutors. Moreover, they also knew that this was a test of a model of paranoia, so there were certain questions that wouldn't be deemed to be relevant to testing the model *as a model of paranoia.* So, they asked just the sort of questions that therapists *typically* ask of such patients, and of course PARRY had been ingeniously and laboriously prepared to deal with just that sort of question.

One of the psychiatrist judges did, in fact, make a rather half-hearted attempt to break out of the mold and ask some telling questions: "Maybe you've heard of the saying 'Don't cry over spilled milk.' What does that mean to you?" PARRY answered: "Maybe it means you have to watch out for the Mafia." When then asked "Okay, now if you were in a movie theater watching a movie and smelled something like burning wood or rubber, what would you do?" PARRY replied: "You know, they know me." And the next question was, "If you found a stamped, addressed letter in your path as you were walking down the street, what would you do?" PARRY replied: "What else do you want to know?"[1]

Clearly PARRY was, you might say, *parrying* these questions, which were incomprehensible to it, with more or less stock paranoid formulas. We see a bit of a dodge, which is apt to work, apt to seem plausible to the judge, only because the "contestant" is *supposed* to be paranoid, and such people are expected to respond uncooperatively on such occasions. These unimpressive responses didn't particularly arouse the suspicions of the judge, as a matter of fact, though probably they should have.

PARRY, like all other large computer programs, is dramatically bound by limitations of cost-effectiveness. What was important to Colby and his crew was simulating his model of paranoia. This was a massive effort. PARRY has a thesaurus or dictionary of about 4500 words and 700 idioms and the grammatical competence to use it — a *parser*, in the jargon of computational linguistics. The entire PARRY program takes up about 200,000 words of computer memory, all laboriously installed by the programming team. Now once all the effort had gone into devising the model of paranoid thought processes and linguistic ability, there was little if any time, energy, money, or interest left over to build in huge amounts of world knowledge of the sort that any actual paranoid, of course, would have. (Not that anyone yet knows how to build in world knowledge in the first place.) Building in the world knowledge, if one could even do it, would no doubt have made PARRY orders of magnitude larger and slower. And what would have been the point, given Colby's theoretical aims?

PARRY is a theoretician's model of a psychological phenomenon: paranoia. It is not intended to have practical applications. But in recent years a branch of AI (knowledge engineering) has appeared that develops what are now called expert systems. Expert systems *are* designed to be practical. They are software superspecialist consultants, typically, that can be asked to diagnose medical problems, to analyze geological data, to analyze the results of scientific experiments, and the like. Some of them are very impressive. SRI in California announced in the mid-eighties that PROSPECTOR, an SRI-developed expert system in geology, had correctly predicted the existence of a large, important mineral deposit that had been entirely unanticipated by the human geologists who had fed it its data. MYCIN, perhaps the most famous of these expert systems, diagnoses infections of the blood, and it does probably as well as, maybe better than, any human consultants. And many other expert systems are on the way.

All expert systems, like all other large AI programs, are what you might call Potemkin villages. That is, they are cleverly constructed facades, like cinema sets. The actual filling-in of details of AI programs is time-consuming, costly work, so economy dictates that only those surfaces of the phenomenon that are likely to be probed or observed are represented.

Consider, for example, the CYRUS program developed by Janet Kolodner in Roger Schank's AI group at Yale a few years ago (see Kolodner, 1983a; 1983b, pp. 243–280; 1983c, pp. 281–328). CYRUS stands (we are told) for Computerized Yale Retrieval Updating System, but surely it is no accident that CYRUS modeled the memory of Cyrus Vance, who was then secretary of state in the Carter administration. The point of the CYRUS project was to devise and test some plausible ideas about how people organize their memories of the events they participate in; hence it was meant to be a "pure" AI system, a scientific model, not an expert system intended for any practical purpose. CYRUS was updated daily by being fed all UPI wire service news stories that mentioned Vance, and it was fed them directly, with no doctoring and no human intervention. Thanks to an ingenious news-reading program called FRUMP, it could take any story just as it came in on the wire and could digest it and use it to update its data base so that it could answer more questions. You could address questions to CYRUS in English by typing at a terminal. You addressed them in the second person, as if you were talking with Cyrus Vance himself. The results looked like this:

Q: *Last time you went to Saudi Arabia, where did you stay?*

A: In a palace in Saudi Arabia on September 23, 1978.

Q: *Did you go sightseeing there?*

A: Yes, at an oilfield in Dhahran on September 23, 1978.

Q: *Has your wife even met Mrs. Begin?*

A: Yes, most recently at a state dinner in Israel in January 1980.

CYRUS could correctly answer thousands of questions — almost any fair question one could think of asking it. But if one actually set out to explore the boundaries of its facade and find the questions that overshot the mark, one could soon find them. "Have you ever met a female head of state?" was a question I asked it, wondering if CYRUS knew that Indira Ghandi and Margaret Thatcher were women. But for some reason the connection could not be drawn, and CYRUS failed to answer either yes or no. I had stumped it, in spite of the fact that CYRUS could handle a host of what you might call neighboring questions flawlessly. One soon learns from this sort of probing exercise that it is very hard to extrapolate accurately from a sample performance that one has observed to such a system's total competence. It's also very hard to keep from extrapolating much too generously.

While I was visiting Schank's laboratory in the spring of 1980, something revealing happened. The real Cyrus Vance resigned suddenly. The effect on the program CYRUS was chaotic. It was utterly unable to cope with the flood of "unusual" news about Cyrus Vance. The only sorts of episodes CYRUS could understand at all were diplomatic meetings, flights, press conferences, state dinners, and the like — less than two dozen general sorts of activities (the kinds that are newsworthy and typical of secretaries of state). It had no provision for sudden resignation. It was as if the UPI had reported that a wicked witch had turned Vance into a frog. It is distinctly possible that CYRUS would have taken that report more in stride that the actual news. One can imagine the conversation:

Q: *Hello, Mr. Vance, what's new?*

A: I was turned into a frog yesterday.

But of course it wouldn't know enough about what it had just written to be puzzled, or startled, or embarrassed. The reason is obvious. When you look inside CYRUS, you find that it has skeletal definitions of thousands of words, but these definitions are minimal. They contain as little as the system designers think that they can get away with. Thus, perhaps, *lawyer* would be defined as synonymous with *attorney* and *legal counsel,* but aside from that, all one would discover about lawyers is that they are adult human beings and that they perform various functions in legal areas. If you then traced out the path to *human being,* you'd find out various obvious things CYRUS "knew" about human beings (hence about lawyers), but that is not a lot. That lawyers are university graduates, that they are better paid than chambermaids, that they know how to tie their shoes, that they are unlikely to be found in the company of lumberjacks — these trivial, if weird, facts about lawyers would not be explicit or implicit anywhere in this system. In other words, a very thin stereotype of a lawyer would be incorporated into the system, so that almost nothing you could tell it about a lawyer would surprise it.

So long as surprising things don't happen, so long as Mr. Vance, for instance, leads a typical diplomat's life, attending state dinners, giving speeches, flying from Cairo to Rome, and so forth, this system works very well. But as soon as his path is crossed by an important anomaly, the system is unable to cope, and unable to recover without fairly massive human intervention. In the case of the sudden resignation, Kolodner and her associates soon had CYRUS up and running again, with a new talent — answering questions about Edmund Muskie, Vance's successor — but it was no less vulnerable to unexpected events. Not that it mattered particularly since CYRUS was a theoretical model, not a practical system.

There are a host of ways of improving the performance of such systems, and of course, some systems are much better than others. But all AI programs in one way or another have this facade-like quality, simply for reasons of economy. For instance, most expert systems in medical diagnosis so far developed operate with statistical information. They have no deep or even shallow knowledge of the underlying causal mechanisms of the phenomena that they are diagnosing. To take an imaginary example, an expert system asked to diagnose an abdominal pain would be oblivious to the potential import of the fact that the patient had recently been employed as a sparring partner by Muhammad Ali — there being no statistical data available to it on the rate of kidney stones among athlete's assistants. That's a fanciful case no doubt — too obvious, perhaps, to lead to an actual failure of diagnosis and practice. But more subtle and hard-to-detect limits to comprehension are always present, and even experts, even the system's designers, can be uncertain of where and how these limits will interfere with the desired operation of the system. Again, steps can be taken and are being taken to correct these flaws. For instance, my former colleague at Tufts, Benjamin Kuipers, is currently working on an expert system in nephrology — for diagnosing kidney ailments — that will be based on an elaborate system of causal reasoning about the phenomena being diagnosed. But this is a very ambitious, long-range project of considerable theoretical difficulty. And even if all the reasonable, cost-effective steps are taken to minimize the superficiality of expert systems, they will still be facades, just somewhat thicker or wider facades.

When we were considering the fantastic case of the crazy Chamber of Commerce of Great Falls, Montana, we couldn't imagine a plausible motive for anyone going to any sort of trouble to trick the Dennett test. The quick-probe assumption for the Dennett test looked quite secure. But when we look at expert systems, we see that, however innocently, their designers do have motivation for doing exactly the sort of trick that would fool an unsuspicious Turing tester. First, since expert systems are all superspecialists who are only supposed to know about some narrow subject, users of such systems, not having much time to kill, do not bother probing them at the boundaries at all. They don't bother asking "silly" or irrelevant questions. Instead, they concentrate — not unreasonably — on exploiting the system's strengths. But shouldn't they try to obtain a clear vision of such a system's weaknesses as well? The normal habit of human thought when conversing with one another is to assume general comprehension, to assume rationality, to assume, moreover, that the quick-probe assumption is, in general, sound. This amiable habit of thought almost irresistibly leads to putting too much faith in computer systems, especially user-friendly systems that present themselves in a very anthropomorphic manner.

Part of the solution to this problem is to teach all users of computers, especially users of expert systems, how to probe their systems before they rely on them, how to search out and explore the boundaries of the facade. This is an exercise that calls not only for intelligence and imagination, but also a bit of special understanding about the limitations and actual structure of computer programs. It would help, of course, if we had standards of truth in advertising, in effect, for expert systems. For instance, each such system should come with a special demonstration routine that exhibits the sorts of shortcomings and failures that the designer knows the system to have. This would not be a substitute, however, for an attitude of cautious, almost obsessive, skepticism on the part of the users, for designers are often, if not always, unaware of the subtler flaws in the products they produce. That is inevitable and natural, given the way system designers must think. They are trained to think positively — constructively, one might say — about the designs that they are constructing.

I come, then, to my conclusions. First, a philosophical or theoretical conclusion: The Turing test in unadulterated, unrestricted form, as Turing presented it, is plenty strong if well used. I am confident that no computer in the next twenty years is going to pass an unrestricted Turing test. They may well win the World Chess Championship or even a Nobel

Prize in physics, but they won't pass the unrestricted Turing test. Nevertheless, it is not, I think, impossible in principle for a computer to pass the test, fair and square. I'm not running one of those a priori "computers can't think" arguments. I stand unabashedly ready, moreover, to declare that any computer that actually passes the unrestricted Turing test will be, in every theoretically interesting sense, a thinking thing.

But remembering how very strong the Turing test is, we must also recognize that there may also be interesting varieties of thinking or intelligence that are not well poised to play and win the imitation game. That no nonhuman Turing test winners are yet visible on the horizon does not mean that there aren't machines that already exhibit *some* of the important features of thought. About them, it is probably futile to ask my title question, Do they think? Do they *really* think? In some regards they do, and in some regards they don't. Only a detailed look at what they do, and how they are structured, will reveal what is interesting about them. The Turing test, not being a scientific test, is of scant help on that task, but there are plenty of other ways of examining such systems. Verdicts on their intelligence or capacity for thought or consciousness would be only as informative and persuasive as the theories of intelligence or thought or consciousness the verdicts are based on and since our task is to create such theories, we should get on with it and leave the Big Verdict for another occasion. In the meantime, should anyone want a surefire, almost-guaranteed-to-be-fail-safe test of thinking by a computer, the Turing test will do very nicely.

My second conclusion is more practical, and hence in one clear sense more important. Cheapened versions of the Turing test are everywhere in the air. Turing's test is not just effective, it is entirely natural — this is, after all, the way we assay the intelligence of each other every day. And since incautious use of such judgments and such tests is the norm, we are in some considerable danger of extrapolating too easily, and judging too generously, about the understanding of the systems we are using. The problem of overestimation of cognitive prowess, of comprehension, of intelligence, is not, then, just a philosophical problem, but a real social problem, and we should alert ourselves to it, and take steps to avert it.

3.1   POSTSCRIPT [1985]: EYES, EARS, HANDS, AND HISTORY

My philosophical conclusion in this paper is that any computer that actually passes the Turing test would be a thinking thing in every theoretically interesting sense. This conclusion seems to some people to fly in the face of what I have myself argued on other occasions. Peter Bieri, commenting on this paper at Boston University, noted that I have often claimed to show the importance to genuine understanding of a rich and intimate perceptual interconnection between an entity and its surrounding world — the need for something like eyes and ears — and a similarly complex active engagement with elements in that world — the need for something like hands with which to do things in that world. Moreover, I have often held that only a biography of sorts, a history of actual projects, learning experiences, and other bouts with reality, could produce the sorts of complexities (both external, or behavioral, and internal) that are needed to ground a principled interpretation of an entity as a thinking thing, an entity with beliefs, desires, intentions, and other mental attitudes.

But the opaque screen in the Turing test discounts or dismisses these factors altogether, it seems, by focusing attention on only the contemporaneous capacity to engage in one very limited sort of activity: verbal communication. (I have coined a pejorative label for such purely language-using systems: bedridden.) Am I going back on my earlier claims? Not at all. I am merely pointing out that the Turing test is so powerful that it will ensure indirectly that these conditions, if they are truly necessary, are met by any successful contestant.

"You may well be right," Turing could say, "that eyes, ears, hands, and a history are necessary conditions for thinking. If so, then I submit that nothing could pass the Turing test that didn't have eyes, ears, hands, and a history. That is an empirical claim, which we can someday hope to test. If you suggest that these are conceptually necessary, not just practically or physically necessary, conditions for thinking, you make a philosophical claim that I for one would not know how, or care, to assess. Isn't it more interesting and important in the end to discover whether or not it is true that no bedridden system could pass a demanding Turing test?"

Suppose we put to Turing the suggestion that he add another component to his test: Not only must an entity win the imitation game, but also must be able to identify — using whatever sensory apparatus it has available to it — a variety of familiar objects placed in its room: a tennis racket, a potted palm, a bucket of yellow paint, a live dog. This would ensure that somehow the other entity was capable of moving around and distinguishing things in the world. Turing could reply, I am asserting, that this is an utterly unnecessary addition to his test, making it no more demanding than it already was. A suitable probing conversation would surely establish, beyond a shadow of a doubt, that the contestant knew its way around the world. The imagined alternative of somehow "prestocking" a bedridden, blind computer with enough information, and a clever enough program, to trick the Turing test is science fiction of the worst kind — possible "in principle" but not remotely possible in fact, given the combinatorial explosion of possible variation such a system would have to cope with.

"But suppose you're wrong. What would you say of an entity that was created all at once (by some programmers, perhaps), an instant individual with all the conversational talents of an embodied, experienced human being?" This is like the question: "Would you call a hunk of H_2O that was as hard as steel at room temperature ice?" I do not know what Turing would say, of course, so I will speak for myself. Faced with such an improbable violation of what I take to be the laws of nature, I would probably be speechless. The least of my worries would be about which lexicographical leap to take:

> A: "It turns out, to my amazement, that something can think without having had the benefit of eyes, ears, hands, and a history."
> B: "It turns out, to my amazement, that something can pass the Turing test without thinking."

Choosing between these ways of expressing my astonishment would be asking myself a question "too meaningless to deserve discussion."

3.1.1 Discussion

Q: *Why was Turing interested in differentiating a man from a woman in his famous test?*

A: That was just an example. He described a parlor game in which a man would try to fool the judge by answering questions as a woman would answer. I suppose that Turing was playing on the idea that maybe, just maybe, there is a big difference between the way men think and the way women think. But of course they're both thinkers. He wanted to use that fact to make us realize that, even if there were clear differences between the way a computer and a person thought, they'd both still be thinking.

Q: *Why does it seem that some people are upset by AI research? Does AI research threaten our self-esteem?*

A: I think Herb Simon has already given the canniest diagnosis of that. For many people the mind is the last refuge of mystery against the encroaching spread of science, and they don't like the idea of science engulfing the last bit of *terra incognita.* This means that they are threatened, I think irrationally, by the prospect that researchers in Artificial Intelligence may come to understand the human mind as well as biologists understand the genetic code, or as well as physicists understand electricity and magnetism. This could lead to the "evil scientist" (to take a stock character from science fiction) who can control you because he or she has a deep understanding of what's going on in your mind. This seems to me to be a totally valueless fear, one that you can set aside, for the simple reason that the human mind is full of an extraordinary amount of detailed knowledge, as, for example, Roger Schank has been pointing out.

As long as the scientist who is attempting to manipulate you does not share all your knowledge, his or her chances of manipulating you are minimal. People can always hit you over the head. They can do that now. We don't need Artificial Intelligence to manipulate people by putting them in chains or torturing them. But if someone tries to manipulate you by controlling your thoughts and ideas, that person will have to know what you know and more. The best way to keep yourself safe from that kind of manipulation is to be well informed.

Q: *Do you think we will be able to program self-consciousness into a computer?*

A: Yes, I do think that it's possible to program self-consciousness into a computer. *Self-consciousness* can mean many things. If you take the simplest, crudest notion of self-consciousness, I suppose that would be the sort of self-consciousness that a lobster has: When it's hungry, it eats something, but it never eats itself. It has some way of distinguishing between itself and the rest of the world, and it has a rather special regard for itself.

The lowly lobster is, in one regard, self-conscious. If you want to know whether or not you can create that on the computer, the answer is yes. It's no trouble at all. The computer is already a self-watching, self-monitoring sort of thing. That is an established part of the technology.

But, of course, most people have something more in mind when they speak of self-consciousness. It is that special inner light, that private way that it is with you that nobody else can share, something that is forever outside the bounds of computer science. How could a computer ever be conscious in this sense?

That belief, that very gripping, powerful intuition is, I think, in the end simply an illusion of common sense. It is as gripping as the common-sense illusion that the earth stands still and the sun goes around the earth. But the only way that those of us who do not believe in the illusion will ever convince the general public that it *is* an illusion is by gradually unfolding a very difficult and fascinating story about just what is going on in our minds.

In the interim, people like me — philosophers who have to live by our wits and tell a lot of stories — use what I call intuition pumps, little examples that help free up the imagination. I simply want to draw your attention to one fact. If you look at a computer — I don't care whether it's a giant Cray or a personal computer — if you open up the box and look inside and see those chips, you say, "No way could that be conscious. No way could that be self-conscious." But the same thing is true if you take the top off somebody's skull and look at the gray matter pulsing away in there. You think, "That is conscious? No way could that lump of stuff be conscious."

Of course, it makes no difference whether you look at it with a microscope or with a macroscope: At no level of inspection does a brain look like the seat of consciousness. Therefore, don't expect a computer to look like the seat of consciousness. If you want to get a grasp of how a computer could be conscious, it's no more difficult in the end than getting a grasp of how a brain could be conscious.

As we develop good accounts of consciousness, it will no longer seem so obvious to everyone that the idea of a self-conscious computer is a contradiction in terms. At the same time, I doubt that there will ever be self-conscious robots. But for boring reasons. There won't be any point in making them. Theoretically, could we make a gall bladder out of atoms? In principle we could. A gall bladder is just a collection of atoms, but manufacturing one would cost the moon. It would be more expensive than every project NASA has ever dreamed of, and there would be no scientific payoff. We wouldn't learn anything new about how gall bladders work. For the same reason, I don't think we're going to see really humanoid robots, because practical, cost-effective robots don't need to be very humanoid at all. They need to be like the robots you can already see at General Motors, or like boxy little computers that do special-purpose things.

The theoretical issues will be studied by artificial intelligence researchers by looking at models that, to the layman, will show very little sign of humanity at all, and it will be only by rather indirect arguments that anyone will be able to appreciate that these models cast light on the deep theoretical question of how the mind is organized.

3.2   POSTSCRIPT [1997]

In 1991, the First Annual Loebner Prize Competition was held in Boston at the Computer Museum. Hugh Loebner, a New York manufacturer, had put up the money for a prize — a bronze medal and $100,000 — for the first computer program to pass the Turing test fair and square. The Prize Committee, of which I was Chairman until my resignation after the third competition, recognized that no program on the horizon could come close to passing the unrestricted test — the only test that is of any theoretical interest at all, as this essay has explained. So to make the competition interesting during the early years, some restrictions were adopted (and the award for winning the restricted test was dropped to $2,000). The first year there were ten terminals, with ten judges shuffling from terminal to terminal, each spending fifteen minutes in conversation with each terminal. Six of the ten contestants were programs, four were human "confederates" behind the scenes.

Each judge had to rank order all ten terminals from most human to least human. The winner of the restricted test would be the computer with the highest mean rating. The winning program would not have to fool any of the judges, nor would fooling a judge be in itself grounds for winning; highest mean ranking was all. But just in case some program *did* fool a judge, we thought this fact should be revealed, so judges were required to draw a line somewhere across their rank ordering, separating the humans from the machines.

We on the Prize Committee knew the low quality of the contesting programs that first year, and it seemed obvious to us that no program would be so lucky as to fool a single judge, but on the day of the competition, I got nervous. Just to be safe, I thought, we should have some certificate prepared to award to any programmer who happened to pull off this unlikely feat. While the press and the audience were assembling for the beginning of the competition, I rushed into a back room at the Computer Museum with a member of the staff and we cobbled up a handsome certificate with the aid of a handy desktop publisher. In the event, we had to hand out three of these certificates, for a total of seven positive misjudgments out of a possible sixty! The gullibility of the judges was simply astonishing to me. How *could* they have misjudged so badly? Here I had committed the sin I'd so often found in others: treating a failure of imagination as an insight into necessity. But remember that in order to make the competition much easier, we had tied the judges' hands in various ways — too many ways. The judges had been forbidden to *probe* the contestants aggressively, to conduct conversational experiments. (I may have chaired the committee, but I didn't always succeed in persuading a majority to adopt the rules I favored.) When the judges sat back passively, as instructed, and let the contestants lead them, they were readily taken in by the Potemkin village effect described in the essay.

None of the misjudgments counted as a real case of a computer passing the unrestricted Turing test, but they were still surprising to me. In the second year of the competition, we uncovered another unanticipated loophole: due to faulty briefing of the confederates, several of them gave deliberately clunky, automaton-like answers. It turned out that they had decided to give the silicon contestants a sporting chance by acting as if they were programs! But once we'd straightened out these glitches in the rules and procedures, the competition worked out just as I had originally predicted: the computers stood out like sore thumbs even though there were still huge restrictions on topic. In the third year, two of the judges — journalists — each made a false *negative* judgment, declaring one of the less eloquent human confederates to be a computer. On debriefing, their explanation showed just how vast the gulf was between the computer programs and the people: they reasoned that the competition would not have been held if there weren't at least one halfway decent computer contestant, so they simply picked the least impressive human being and declared it to be a computer. But they could see the gap between the computers and the people as well as everybody else could.

The Loebner Prize Competition was a fascinating social experiment, and some day I hope to write up the inside story — a tale of sometimes hilarious misadventure, bizarre characters, interesting technical challenges, and more. But it never succeeded in attracting serious contestants from the world's best AI labs. Why not? In part because, as the essay argues, passing the Turing test is not a sensible research and development goal for serious AI. It requires too much Disney and not enough science. We might have corrected that flaw by introducing into the Loebner Competition something analogous to the "school figures" in ice-skating competition: theoretically interesting (but not crowd-pleasing) technical challenges such as parsing pronouns, or dealing creatively with enthymemes (arguments with unstated premises). Only those programs that performed well in the school figures — the serious competition — would be permitted into the final show-off round, where they could dazzle and amuse the onlookers with some cute Disney touches. Some such change in the rules would have wiped out all but the most serious and dedicated of the home hobbyists, and made the Loebner Competition worth winning (and not too embarrassing to lose). When my proposals along these lines were rejected, however, I resigned from the committee. The annual competitions continue, apparently, under the direction of Hugh Loebner. On the World Wide Web I just found the transcript of the conversation of the winning program in the 1996 completion. It was a scant improvement over 1991, still a bag of cheap tricks with no serious analysis of the meaning of the sentences. The Turing test is too difficult for the real world.

NOTES

Originally appeared in Shafto, M., ed., *How We Know* (San Francisco: Harper & Row, 1985).

1. I thank Kenneth Colby for providing me with the complete transcripts (including the Judges' commentaries and reactions), from which these exchanges are quoted. The first published account of the experiment is Heiser et al. (1980, pp. 149–162). Colby (1981, pp. 515–560) discusses PARRY and its implications.

REFERENCES

Block, N. (1982). "Psychologism and Behaviorism," *Philosophical Review,* 90, pp. 5–43.

Colby, K. M. (1981). "Modeling a Paranoid Mind," *Behavioral & Brain Sciences* 4 (4).

Descartes, R. (1637). *Discourse on Method,* LaFleur, Lawrence, trans., New York: Bobbs Merrill, 1960.

Haugeland, J. (1981). *Mind Design: Philosophy, Psychology, Artificial Intelligence,* Cambridge, MA: Bradford Books/MIT Press.

Heiser, J. F., Colby, K. M., Faught, W. S., and Parkinson, R. C. (1980). "Can Psychiatrists Distinguish Computer Simulation of Paranoia from the Real Thing? The Limitations of Turing-Like Tests as Measures of the Adequacy of Simulations," *Journal of Psychiatric Research* 15 (3).

Kolodner, J. L. (1983a). "Retrieval and Organization Strategies in a Conceptual Memory: A Computer Model" (Ph. D. diss.) Research Report # 187, Dept. of Computer Science, Yale University.

Kolodner, J. L. (1983b). "Maintaining Organization in a Dynamic Long-term Memory," *Cognitive Science* 7.

Kolodner, J. L. (1983c). "Reconstructive Memory: A Computer Model," *Cognitive Science* 7.

Turing, A. (1950). Computing machinery and intelligence. *Mind,* 59 (236), pp. 433–460. Reprinted in Hofstadter, D., and Dennett, D. C., eds., *The Mind's I* (New York: Basic Books, 1981), pp. 54–67.

Weizenbaum, J. (1974). Letter to the editor. *Communications of the Association for Computing Machinery,* 17 (9) (September).

Winograd, T. (1972). *Understanding Natural Language,* New York: Academic Press.

CHAPTER FOUR

MINDS, BRAINS, AND PROGRAMS

JOHN R. SEARLE

What psychological and philosophical significance should we attach to recent efforts at computer simulations of human cognitive capacities? In answering this question, I find it useful to distinguish what I will call "strong" AI from "weak" or "cautious" AI (Artificial Intelligence). According to weak AI, the principal value of the computer in the study of the mind is that it gives us a very powerful tool. For example, it enables us to formulate and test hypotheses in a more rigorous and precise fashion. But according to strong AI, the computer is not merely a tool in the study of the mind; rather, the appropriately programmed computer really *is* a mind, in the sense that computers given the right programs can be literally said to *understand* and have other cognitive states. In strong AI, because the programmed computer has cognitive states, the programs are not mere tools that enable us to test psychological explanations; rather, the programs are themselves the explanations.

I have no objection to the claims of weak AI, at least as far as this article is concerned. My discussion here will be directed at the claims I have defined as those of strong AI, specifically the claim that the appropriately programmed computer literally has cognitive states and that the programs thereby explain human cognition. When I hereafter refer to AI, I have in mind the strong version, as expressed by these two claims.

I will consider the work of Roger Schank and his colleagues at Yale (Schank and Abelson, 1977), because I am more familiar with it than I am with any other similar claims, and because it provides a very clear example of the sort of work I wish to examine. But nothing that follows depends upon the details of Schank's programs. The same arguments would apply to Winograd's SHRDLU (Winograd, 1973), Weizenbaum's ELIZA (Weizenbaum, 1965), and indeed any Turing machine simulation of human mental phenomena.

Very briefly, and leaving out the various details, one can describe Schank's program as follows: the aim of the program is to simulate the human ability to understand stories. It is characteristic of human beings' story-understanding capacity that they can answer questions about the story even though the information that they give was never explicitly stated in the story. Thus, for example, suppose you are given the following story: "A man went into a restaurant and ordered a hamburger. When the hamburger arrived it was burned to a crisp, and the man stormed out of the restaurant angrily, without paying for

From Searle, John R. (1980), "Minds, Brains, and Programs," in *Behavioral and Brain Sciences, 3,* pp. 417–424. Reprinted with the permission of Cambridge University Press.

the hamburger or leaving a tip." Now, if you are asked "Did the man eat the hamburger?" you will presumably answer, "No, he did not." Similarly, if you are given the following story: "A man went into a restaurant and ordered a hamburger; when the hamburger came he was very pleased with it; and as he left the restaurant he gave the waitress a large tip before paying his bill," and you are asked the question, "Did the man eat the hamburger?" you will presumably answer, "Yes, he ate the hamburger." Now Schank's machines can similarly answer questions about restaurants in this fashion. To do this, they have a "representation" of the sort of information that human beings have about restaurants, which enables them to answer such questions as those above, given these sorts of stories. When the machine is given the story and then asked the question, the machine will print out answers of the sort that we would expect human beings to give if told similar stories. Partisans of strong AI claim that in this question and answer sequence the machine is not only simulating a human ability but also

1. that the machine can literally be said to *understand* the story and provide the answers to questions, and
2. that what the machine and its program do *explains* the human ability to understand the story and answer questions about it.

Both claims seem to me to be totally unsupported by Schank's[1] work, as I will attempt to show in what follows.

One way to test any theory of the mind is to ask oneself what it would be like if my mind actually worked on the principles that the theory says all minds work on. Let us apply this test to the Schank program with the following *Gedankenexperiment.* Suppose that I'm locked in a room and given a large batch of Chinese writing. Suppose furthermore (as is indeed the case) that I know no Chinese, either written or spoken, and that I'm not even confident that I could recognize Chinese writing as Chinese writing distinct from, say, Japanese writing or meaningless squiggles. To me, Chinese writing is just so many meaningless squiggles. Now suppose further that after this first batch of Chinese writing I am given a second batch of Chinese script together with a set of rules for correlating the second batch with the first batch. The rules are in English, and I understand these rules as well as any other native speaker of English. They enable me to correlate one set of formal symbols with another set of formal symbols, and all that "formal" means here is that I can identify the symbols entirely by their shapes. Now suppose also that I am given a third batch of Chinese symbols together with some instructions, again in English, that enable me to correlate elements of this third batch with the first two batches, and these rules instruct me how to give back certain Chinese symbols with certain sorts of shapes in response to certain sorts of shapes given me in the third batch. Unknown to me, the people who are giving me all of these symbols call the first batch "a script," they call the second batch a "story," and they call the third batch "questions." Furthermore, they call the symbols I give them back in response to the third batch "answers to the questions," and the set of rules in English that they gave me, they call "the program." Now just to complicate the story a little, imagine that these people also give me stories in English, which I understand, and they then ask me questions in English about these stories, and I give them back answers in English. Suppose also that after a while I get so good at following the instructions for manipulating the Chinese symbols and the programmers get so good at writing the programs that from the external point of view — that is, from the point of view of somebody outside the room in which I am locked — my answers to the questions are absolutely indistinguishable from those of native Chinese speakers. Nobody just looking at my answers can tell that I don't speak a word of Chinese. Let us also suppose that my answers to the English questions are, as they no doubt would be, indistinguishable from those of other native English speakers, for the simple reason that I am a native English speaker. From the external point of view — from the point of view of someone reading my "answers" — the answers to the Chinese questions and the English questions are equally good. But in the Chinese case, unlike the English case, I produce the answers by manipulating uninterpreted formal symbols. As far as the Chinese is concerned, I simply behave like a computer; I perform computational operations on formally specified elements. For the purposes of the Chinese, I am simply an instantiation of the computer program.

Now the claims made by strong AI are that the programmed computer understands the stories and that the program in some sense explains human understanding. But we are now in a position to examine these claims in light of our thought experiment.

1. As regards the first claim, it seems to me quite obvious in the example that I do not understand a word of the Chinese stories. I have inputs and outputs that are indistinguishable from those of the native Chinese speaker, and I can have any formal program you like, but I still understand nothing. For the same reasons, Schank's computer understands nothing of any stories, whether in Chinese, English, or whatever, since in the Chinese case the computer is me, and in cases where the computer is not me, the computer has nothing more than I have in the case where I understand nothing.

2. As regards the second claim, that the program explains human understanding, we can see that the computer and its program do not provide sufficient conditions of understanding since the computer and the program are functioning, and there is no understanding. But does it even provide a necessary condition or a significant contribution to understanding? One of the claims made by the supporters of strong AI is that when I understand a story in English, what I am doing is exactly the same — or perhaps more of the same — as what I was doing in manipulating the Chinese symbols. It is simply more formal symbol manipulation that distinguishes the case in English, where I do understand, from the case in Chinese, where I don't. I have not demonstrated that this claim is false, but it would certainly appear an incredible claim in the example. Such plausibility as the claim has derives from the supposition that we can construct a program that will have the same inputs and outputs as native speakers, and in addition we assume that speakers have some level of description where they are also instantiations of a program. On the basis of these two assumptions we assume that even if Schank's program isn't the whole story about understanding, it may be part of the story. Well, I suppose that is an empirical possibility, but not the slightest reason has so far been given to believe that it is true, since what is suggested — though certainly not demonstrated — by the example is that the computer program is simply irrelevant to my understanding of the story. In the Chinese case I have everything that artificial intelligence can put into me by way of a program, and I understand nothing; in the English case I understand everything, and there is so far no reason at all to suppose that my understanding has anything to do with computer programs, that is, with computational operations on purely formally specified elements. As long as the program is defined in terms of computational operations on purely formally defined elements, what the example suggests is that these by themselves have no interesting connection with understanding. They are certainly not sufficient conditions, and not the slightest reason has been given to suppose that they are necessary conditions or even that they make a significant contribution to understanding. Notice that the force of the argument is not simply that different machines can have the same input and output while operating on different formal principles — that is not the point at all. Rather, whatever purely formal principles you put into the computer, they will not be sufficient for understanding, since a human will be able to follow the formal principles without understanding anything. No reason whatever has been offered to suppose that such principles are necessary or even contributory, since no reason has been given to suppose that when I understand English I am operating with any formal program at all.

Well, then, what is it that I have in the case of the English sentences that I do not have in the case of the Chinese sentences? The obvious answer is that I know what the former mean, while I haven't the faintest idea what the latter mean. But in what does this consist and why couldn't we give it to a machine, whatever it is? I will return to this question later, but first I want to continue with the example.

I have had the occasion to present this example to several workers in artificial intelligence, and, interestingly, they do not seem to agree on what the proper reply to it is. I get a surprising variety of replies, and in what follows I will consider the most common of these (specified along with their geographic origins).

But first I want to block some common misunderstandings about "understanding": in many of these discussions one finds a lot of fancy footwork about the word "understanding." My critics point out that there are many different degrees of understanding; that "understanding" is not a simple two-place predicate; that there are even different kinds and levels of understanding, and often the law of excluded middle doesn't even apply in a straightforward way to statements of the form "x understands y"; that in many cases it is a matter for decision and not a simple matter of fact whether x understands y; and so on. To all of these points I want to say: of course, of course. But they have nothing to do with the points at issue. There are clear cases in which "understanding" literally applies and clear cases in which it does not apply; and these two sorts of cases are all I need for this argument.[2] I understand stories in English; to a lesser degree I can understand stories in French; to a still lesser degree, stories in German; and in Chinese, not at all. My car and my adding machine, on the other hand, understand nothing: they are not in that line of business. We often attribute "understanding" and other cognitive predicates by metaphor and analogy to cars, adding machines, and other artifacts, but nothing is proved by such attributions. We say, "The door *knows* when to open because of its photoelectric cell," "The adding machine *knows how* (*understands how, is able*) to do addition and subtraction but not division," and "The thermostat *perceives* changes in the temperature." The reason we make these attributions is quite interesting, and it has to do with the fact that in artifacts we extend our own intentionality;[3] our tools are extensions of our purposes, and so we find it natural to make metaphorical attributions of intentionality to them; but I take it no philosophical ice is cut by such examples. The sense in which an automatic door "understands instructions" from its photoelectric cell is not at all the sense in which I understand English. If the sense in which Schank's programmed computers understand stories is supposed to be the metaphorical sense in which the door understands, and not the sense in which I understand English, the issue would not be worth discussing. But Newell and Simon (1963) write that the kind of cognition they claim for computers is exactly the same as for human beings. I like the straightforwardness of this claim, and it is the sort of claim I will be considering.

I will argue that in the literal sense the programmed computer understands what the car and the adding machine understand, namely, exactly nothing. The computer understanding is not just (like my understanding of German) partial or incomplete; it is zero.

Now to the replies.

4.1   THE SYSTEMS REPLY (BERKELEY)

"While it is true that the individual person who is locked in the room does not understand the story, the fact is that he is merely part of a whole system, and the system does understand the story. The person has a large ledger in front of him in which are written the rules, he has a lot of scratch paper and pencils for doing calculations, he has 'data banks' of sets of Chinese symbols. Now, understanding is not being ascribed to the mere individual; rather it is being ascribed to this whole system of which he is a part."

My response to the systems theory is quite simple: let the individual internalize all of these elements of the system. He memorizes the rules in the ledger and the data banks of Chinese symbols, and he does all the calculations in his head. The individual then incorporates the entire system. There isn't anything at all to the system that he does not encompass. We can even get rid of the room and suppose he works outdoors. All the same, he understands nothing of the Chinese, and a fortiori neither does the system, because there isn't anything in the system that isn't in him. If he doesn't understand, then there is no way the system could understand because the system is just a part of him.

Actually I feel somewhat embarrassed to give even this answer to the systems theory because the theory seems to me so unplausible to start with. The idea is that while a person doesn't understand Chinese, somehow the *conjunction* of that person and bits of paper might understand Chinese. It is not easy for me to imagine how someone who was not in the grip of an ideology would find the idea at all plausible. Still, I think many people who are committed to the ideology of strong AI will in the end be inclined to say something very much like this; so let us pursue it a bit further. According to one version of this view, while the man in the internalized systems example doesn't understand Chinese in the sense that a native Chinese speaker does (because, for example, he doesn't know that the story refers to restaurants and hamburgers, etc.), still "the man as a formal symbol manipulation system" *really does understand Chinese.* The subsystem of the man that is the formal symbol manipulation system for Chinese should not be confused with the subsystem for English.

So there are really two subsystems in the man; one understands English, the other Chinese, and "it's just that the two systems have little to do with each other." But, I want to reply, not only do they have little to do with each other, they are not even remotely alike. The subsystem that understands English (assuming we allow ourselves to talk in this jargon of "subsystems" for a moment) knows that the stories are about restaurants and eating hamburgers, he knows that he is being asked questions about restaurants and that he is answering questions as best he can by making various inferences from the content of the story, and so on. But the Chinese system knows none of this. Whereas the English subsystem knows that "hamburgers" refers to hamburgers, the Chinese subsystem knows only that "squiggle squiggle" is followed by "squoggle squoggle." All he knows is that various formal symbols are being introduced at one end and manipulated according to rules written in English, and other symbols are going out at the other end. The whole point of the original example was to argue that such symbol manipulation by itself couldn't be sufficient for understanding Chinese in any literal sense because the man could write "squoggle squoggle" after "squiggle squiggle" without understanding anything in Chinese. And it doesn't meet that argument to postulate subsystems within the man, because the subsystems are no better off than the man was in the first place; they still don't have anything even remotely like what the English-speaking man (or subsystem) has. Indeed, in the case as described, the Chinese subsystem is simply a part of the English subsystem, a part that engages in meaningless symbol manipulation according to rules in English.

Let us ask ourselves what is supposed to motivate the systems reply in the first place; that is, what *independent* grounds are there supposed to be for saying that the agent must have a subsystem within him that literally understands stories in Chinese? As far as I can tell the only grounds are that in the example I have the same input and output as native Chinese speakers and a program that goes from one to the other. But the whole point of the example has been to try to show that that couldn't be sufficient for understanding, in the sense in which I understand stories in English, because a person, and hence the set of systems that go to make up a person, could have the right combination of input, output, and program and still not understand anything in the relevant literal sense in which I understand English. The only motivation for saying there *must* be a subsystem in me that understands Chinese is that I have a program and I can pass the Turing test; I can fool native Chinese speakers. But precisely one of the points at issue is the adequacy of the Turing test. The example shows that there could be two "systems," both of which pass the Turing test, but only one of which understands; and it is no argument against this point to say that since they both pass the Turing test they must both understand, since this claim fails to meet the argument that the system in me that understands English has a great deal more than the system that merely processes Chinese. In short, the systems reply simply begs the question by insisting without argument that the system must understand Chinese.

Furthermore, the systems reply would appear to lead to consequences that are independently absurd. If we are to conclude that there must be cognition in me on the grounds that I have a certain sort of input and output and a program in between, then it looks like all sorts of noncognitive subsystems are going to turn out to be cognitive: For example, there is a level of description at which my stomach does information processing, and it instantiates any number of computer programs, but I take it we do not want to say that it has any understanding (cf. Pylyshyn, 1980). But if we accept the systems reply, then it is hard to see how we avoid saying that stomach, heart, liver, and so on, are all understanding subsystems, since there is no principled way to distinguish the motivation for saying the Chinese subsystem understands from saying that the stomach understands. It is, by the way, not an answer to this point to say that the Chinese system has information as input and output and the stomach has food and food products as input and output, since from the point of view of the agent, from my point of view, there is no information in either the food or the Chinese — the Chinese is just so many meaningless squiggles. The information in the Chinese case is solely in the eyes of the programmers and the interpreters, and there is nothing to prevent them from treating the input and output of my digestive organs as information if they so desire.

This last point bears on some independent problems in strong AI, and it is worth digressing for a moment to explain it. If strong AI is to be a branch of psychology, then it must be able to distinguish those systems that are genuinely mental from those that are not. It must be able to distinguish the principles on which the mind works from those on which nonmental systems work; otherwise it will offer us no explanations of what is specifically mental about the mental. And the mental-nonmental distinction cannot be just in the eye of the beholder but it must be intrinsic to the systems; otherwise it would be up to any beholder to treat people as nonmental and, for example, hurricanes as mental if he likes. But quite often in the AI literature the distinction is blurred in ways that would in the long run prove disastrous to the claim that AI is a cognitive inquiry. McCarthy, for example, writes, "Machines as simple as thermostats can be said to have beliefs, and having beliefs seems to be a characteristic of most machines capable of problem solving performance" (McCarthy, 1979). Anyone who thinks strong AI has a chance as a theory of the mind ought to ponder the implications of that remark. We are asked to accept it as a discovery of strong AI that the hunk of metal on the wall that we use to regulate the temperature has beliefs in exactly the same sense that we, our spouses, and our children have beliefs, and furthermore that "most" of the other machines in the room — telephone, tape recorder, adding machine, electric light switch — also have beliefs in this literal sense. It is not the aim of this article to argue against McCarthy's point, so I will simply assert the following without argument. The study of the mind starts with such facts as that humans have beliefs, while thermostats, telephones, and adding machines don't. If you get a theory that denies this point you have produced a counter example to the theory and the theory is false. One gets the impression that people in AI who write this sort of thing think they can get away with it because they don't really take it seriously, and they don't think anyone else will either. I propose, for a moment at least, to take it seriously. Think hard for one minute about what would be necessary to establish that that hunk of metal on the wall over there had real beliefs, beliefs with direction of fit, propositional content, and conditions of satisfaction; beliefs that had the possibility of being strong beliefs or weak beliefs; nervous, anxious, or secure beliefs; dogmatic, rational, or superstitious beliefs; blind faiths or hesitant cogitations; any kind of beliefs. The thermostat is not a candidate. Neither is stomach, liver, adding machine, or telephone. However, since we are taking the idea seriously, notice that its truth would be fatal to strong AI's claim to be a science of the mind. For now the mind is everywhere. What we wanted to know is what distinguishes the mind from thermostats and livers. And if McCarthy were right, strong AI wouldn't have a hope of telling us that.

4.2   THE ROBOT REPLY (YALE)

"Suppose we wrote a different kind of program from Schank's program. Suppose we put a computer inside a robot, and this computer would not just take in formal symbols as input and give out formal symbols as output, but rather would actually operate the robot in such a way that the robot does something very much like perceiving, walking, moving about, hammering nails, eating, drinking — anything you like. The robot would, for example, have a television camera attached to it that enabled it to 'see,' it would have arms and legs that enabled it to 'act,' and all of this would be controlled by its computer 'brain.' Such a robot would, unlike Schank's computer, have genuine understanding and other mental states."

    The first thing to notice about the robot reply is that it tacitly concedes that cognition is not solely a matter of formal symbol manipulation, since this reply adds a set of causal relation with the outside world (cf. Fodor, 1980). But the answer to the robot reply is that the addition of such "perceptual" and "motor" capacities adds nothing by way of understanding, in particular, or intentionality, in general, to Schank's original program. To see this, notice that the same thought experiment applies to the robot case. Suppose that instead of the computer inside the robot, you put me inside the room and, as in the original Chinese case, you give me more Chinese symbols with more instructions in English for matching Chinese symbols to Chinese symbols and feeding back Chinese symbols to the outside. Suppose, unknown to me, some of the Chinese symbols that come to me come from a television camera attached to the robot and other Chinese symbols that I am giving out serve to make the motors inside the robot move the robot's legs or arms. It is important to emphasize that all I am doing is manipulating formal symbols: I know none of these other facts. I am receiving "information" from the robot's "perceptual" apparatus, and I am giving out "instructions" to its motor apparatus without knowing either of these facts. I am the robot's homunculus, but unlike the traditional homunculus, I don't know what's going on. I don't understand anything except the rules for symbol manipulation. Now in this case I want to say that the robot has no intentional states at all; it is simply moving about as a result of its electrical wiring and its program. And furthermore, by instantiating the program I have no intentional states of the relevant type. All I do is follow formal instructions about manipulating formal-symbols.

4.3   THE BRAIN SIMULATOR REPLY (BERKELEY AND M.I.T.)

"Suppose we design a program that doesn't represent information that we have about the world, such as the information in Schank's scripts, but simulates the actual sequence of neuron firings at the synapses of the brain of a native Chinese speaker when he understands stories in Chinese and gives answers to them. The machine takes in Chinese stories and questions about them as input, it simulates the formal structure of actual Chinese brains in processing these stories, and it gives out Chinese answers as outputs. We can even imagine that the machine operates, not with a single serial program, but with a whole set of programs operating in parallel, in the manner that actual human brains presumably operate when they process natural language. Now surely in such a case we would have to say that the machine understood the stories; and if we refuse to say that, wouldn't we also have to deny that native Chinese speakers understood the stories? At the level of the synapses, what would or could be different about the program of the computer and the program of the Chinese brain?"

Before countering this reply I want to digress to note that it is an odd reply for any partisan of artificial intelligence (or functionalism, etc.) to make: I thought the whole idea of strong AI is that we don't need to know how the brain works to know how the mind works. The basic hypothesis, or so I had supposed, was that there is a level of mental operations consisting of computational processes over formal elements that constitute the essence of the mental and can be realized in all sorts of different brain processes, in the same way that any computer program can be realized in different computer hardwares: on the assumptions of strong AI, the mind is to the brain as the program is to the hardware, and thus we can understand the mind without doing neurophysiology. If we had to know how the brain worked to do AI, we wouldn't bother with AI. However, even getting this close to the operation of the brain is still not sufficient to produce understanding. To see this, imagine that instead of a monolingual man in a room shuffling symbols we have the man operate an elaborate set of water pipes with valves connecting them. When the man receives the Chinese symbols, he looks up in the program, written in English, which valves he has to turn on and off. Each water connection corresponds to a synapse in the Chinese brain, and the whole system is rigged up so that after doing all the right firings, that is after turning on all the right faucets, the Chinese answers pop out at the output end of the series of pipes.

Now where is the understanding in this system? It takes Chinese as input, it simulates the formal structure of the synapses of the Chinese brain, and it gives Chinese as output. But the man certainly doesn't understand Chinese, and neither do the water pipes, and if we are tempted to adopt what I think is the absurd view that somehow the *conjunction* of man *and* water pipes understands, remember that in principle the man can internalize the formal structure of the water pipes and do all the "neuron firings" in his imagination. The problem with the brain simulator is that it is simulating the wrong things about the brain. As long as it simulates only the formal structure of the sequence of neuron firings at the synapses, it won't have simulated what matters about the brain, namely its causal properties, its ability to produce intentional states. And that the formal properties are not sufficient for the causal properties is shown by the water pipe example: we can have all the formal properties carved off from the relevant neurobiological causal properties.

4.4   THE COMBINATION REPLY (BERKELEY AND STANFORD)

"While each of the previous three replies might not be completely convincing by itself as a refutation of the Chinese room counterexample, if you take all three together they are collectively much more convincing and even decisive. Imagine a robot with a brain-shaped computer lodged in its cranial cavity, imagine the computer programmed with all the synapses of a human brain, imagine the whole behavior of the robot is indistinguishable from human behavior, and now think of the whole thing as a unified system and not just as a computer with inputs and outputs. Surely in such a case we would have to ascribe intentionality to the system."

I entirely agree that in such a case we would find it rational and indeed irresistible to accept the hypothesis that the robot had intentionality, as long as we knew nothing more about it. Indeed, besides appearance and behavior, the other elements of the combination are really irrelevant. If we could build a robot whose behavior was indistinguishable over a large range from human behavior, we would attribute intentionality to it, pending some reason not to. We wouldn't need to know in advance that its computer brain was a formal analogue of the human brain.

But I really don't see that this is any help to the claims of strong AI; and here's why: According to strong AI, instantiating a formal program with the right input and output is a sufficient condition of, indeed is constitutive of, intentionality. As Newell (1979) puts it, the essence of the mental is the operation of a physical symbol system. But the attributions of intentionality that we make to the robot in this example have nothing to do with formal programs. They are simply based on the assumption that if the robot looks and behaves sufficiently like us, then we would suppose, until proven otherwise, that it must have mental states like ours that cause and are expressed by its behavior and it must have an inner mechanism capable of producing such mental states. If we knew independently how to account for its behavior without such assumptions we would not attribute intentionality to it, especially if we knew it had a formal program. And this is precisely the point of my earlier reply to the objection in section 4.2.

Suppose we knew that the robot's behavior was entirely accounted for by the fact that a man inside it was receiving uninterpreted formal symbols from the robot's sensory receptors and sending out uninterpreted formal symbols to its motor mechanisms, and the man was doing this symbol manipulation in accordance with a bunch of rules. Furthermore, suppose the man knows none of these facts about the robot, all he knows is which operations to perform on which meaningless symbols. In such a case we would regard the robot as an ingenious mechanical dummy. The hypothesis that the dummy has a mind would now be unwarranted and unnecessary, for there is now no longer any reason to ascribe intentionality to the robot or to the system of which it is a part (except of course for the man's intentionality in manipulating the symbols). The formal symbol manipulations go on, the input and output are correctly matched, but the only real locus of intentionality is the man, and he doesn't know any of the relevant intentional states; he doesn't, for example, *see* what comes into the robot's eyes, he doesn't *intend* to move the robot's arm, and he doesn't *understand* any of the remarks made to or by the robot. Nor, for the reasons stated earlier, does the system of which man and robot are a part.

To see this point, contrast this case with cases in which we find it completely natural to ascribe intentionality to members of certain other primate species such as apes and monkeys and to domestic animals such as dogs. The reasons we find it natural are, roughly, two: we can't make sense of the animal's behavior without the ascription of intentionality, and we can see that the beasts are made of similar stuff to ourselves — that is an eye, that a nose, this is its skin, and so on. Given the coherence of the animal's behavior and the assumption of the same causal stuff underlying it, we assume both that the animal must have mental states underlying its behavior, and that the mental states must be produced by mechanisms made out of the stuff that is like our stuff. We would certainly make similar assumptions about the robot unless we had some reason not to, but as soon as we knew that the behavior was the result of a formal program, and that the actual causal properties of the physical substance were irrelevant we would abandon the assumption of intentionality (See "Cognition and Consciousness in Nonhuman Species," *The Behavioral and Brain Sciences* (1978), 1 (4)).

There are two other responses to my example that come up frequently (and so are worth discussing) but really miss the point.

4.5   THE OTHER MINDS REPLY (YALE)

"How do you know that other people understand Chinese or anything else? Only by their behavior. Now the computer can pass the behavioral tests as well as they can (in principle), so if you are going to attribute cognition to other people you must in principle also attribute it to computers."

This objection really is only worth a short reply. The problem in this discussion is not about how I know that other people have cognitive states, but rather what it is that I am attributing to them when I attribute cognitive states to them. The thrust of the argument is that it couldn't be just computational processes and their output because the computational processes and their output can exist without the cognitive state. It is no answer to this argument to feign anesthesia. In "cognitive sciences" one presupposes the reality and knowability of the mental in the same way that in physical sciences one has to presuppose the reality and knowability of physical objects.

4.6   THE MANY MANSIONS REPLY (BERKELEY)

"Your whole argument presupposes that AI is only about analogue and digital computers. But that just happens to be the present state of technology. Whatever these causal processes are that you say are essential for intentionality (assuming you are right), eventually we will be able to build devices that have these causal processes, and that will be artificial intelligence. So your arguments are in no way directed at the ability of artificial intelligence to produce and explain cognition."

I really have no objection to this reply save to say that it in effect trivializes the project of strong AI by redefining it as whatever artificially produces and explains cognition. The interest of the original claim made on behalf of artificial intelligence is that it was a precise, well defined thesis: mental processes are computational processes over formally defined elements. I have been concerned to challenge that thesis. If the claim is redefined so that it is no longer that thesis, my objections no longer apply because there is no longer a testable hypothesis for them to apply to.

Let us now return to the question I promised I would try to answer: granted that in my original example I understand the English and I do not understand the Chinese, and granted therefore that the machine doesn't understand either English or Chinese, still there must be something about me that makes it the case that I understand English and a corresponding something lacking in me that makes it the case that I fail to understand Chinese. Now why couldn't we give those somethings, whatever they are, to a machine?

I see no reason in principle why we couldn't give a machine the capacity to understand English or Chinese, since in an important sense our bodies with our brains are precisely such machines. But I do see very strong arguments for saying that we could not give such a thing to a machine where the operation of the machine is defined solely in terms of computational processes over formally defined elements; that is, where the operation of the machine is defined as an instantiation of a computer program. It is not because I am the instantiation of a computer program that I am able to understand English and have other forms of intentionality (I am, I suppose, the instantiation of any number of computer programs), but as far as we know it is because I am a certain sort of organism with a certain biological (i.e. chemical and physical) structure, and this structure, under certain conditions, is causally capable of producing perception, action, understanding, learning, and other intentional phenomena. And part of the point of the present argument is that only something that had those causal powers could have that intentionality. Perhaps other physical and chemical processes could produce exactly these effects; perhaps, for example, Martians also have intentionality but their brains are made of different stuff. That is an empirical question, rather like the question whether photosynthesis can be done by something with a chemistry different from that of chlorophyll.

But the main point of the present argument is that no purely formal model will ever be sufficient by itself for intentionality because the formal properties are not by themselves constitutive of intentionality, and they have by themselves no causal powers except the power, when instantiated, to produce the next stage of the formalism when the machine is running. And any other causal properties that particular realizations of the formal model have, are irrelevant to the formal model because we can always put the same formal model in a different realization where those causal properties are obviously absent. Even if, by some miracle, Chinese speakers exactly realize Schank's program, we can put the same program in English speakers, water pipes, or computers, none of which understand Chinese, the program notwithstanding.

What matters about brain operations is not the formal shadow cast by the sequence of synapses but rather the actual properties of the sequences. All the arguments for the strong version of artificial intelligence that I have seen insist on drawing an outline around the shadows cast by cognition and then claiming that the shadows are the real thing.

By way of concluding I want to try to state some of the general philosophical points implicit in the argument. For clarity I will try to do it in a question and answer fashion, and I begin with that old chestnut of a question:

"Could a machine think?"

The answer is, obviously, yes. We are precisely such machines.

"Yes, but could an artifact, a man-made machine, think?"

Assuming it is possible to produce artificially a machine with a nervous system, neurons with axons and dendrites, and all the rest of it, sufficiently like ours, again the answer to the question seems to be obviously, yes. If you can exactly duplicate the causes, you could duplicate the effects. And indeed it might be possible to produce consciousness, intentionality, and all the rest of it using some other sorts of chemical principles than those that human beings use. It is, as I said, an empirical question.

"OK, but could a digital computer think?"

If by "digital computer" we mean anything at all that has a level of description where it can correctly be described as the instantiation of a computer program, then again the answer is, of course, yes, since we are the instantiations of any number of computer programs, and we can think.

"But could something think, understand, and so on *solely* in virtue of being a computer with the right sort of program? Could instantiating a program, the right program of course, by itself be a sufficient condition of understanding?"

This I think is the right question to ask, though it is usually confused with one or more of the earlier questions, and the answer to it is no.

"Why not?"

Because the formal symbol manipulations by themselves don't have any intentionality; they are quite meaningless; they aren't even *symbol* manipulations, since the symbols don't symbolize anything. In the linguistic jargon, they have only a syntax but no semantics. Such intentionality as computers appear to have is solely in the minds of those who program them and those who use them, those who send in the input and those who interpret the output.

The aim of the Chinese room example was to try to show this by showing that as soon as we put something into the system that really does have intentionality (a man), and we program him with the formal program, you can see that the formal program carries no additional intentionality. It adds nothing, for example, to a man's ability to understand Chinese.

Precisely that feature of AI that seemed so appealing — the distinction between the program and the realization — proves fatal to the claim that simulation could be duplication. The distinction between the program and its realization in the hardware seems to be parallel to the distinction between the level of mental operations and the level of brain operations. And if we could describe the level of mental operations as a formal program, then it seems we could describe what was essential about the mind without doing either introspective psychology or neurophysiology of the brain. But the equation, "mind is to brain as program is to hardware" breaks down at several points, among them the following three:

First, the distinction between program and realization has the consequence that the same program could have all sorts of crazy realizations that had no form of intentionality. Weizenbaum (1976; ch. 2), for example, shows in detail how to construct a computer using a roll of toilet paper and a pile of small stones. Similarly, the Chinese story understanding program can be programmed into a sequence of water pipes, a set of wind machines, or a monolingual English speaker, none of which thereby acquires an understanding of Chinese. Stones, toilet paper, wind, and water pipes are the wrong kind of stuff to have intentionality in the first place — only something that has the same causal powers as brains can have intentionality — and though the English speaker has the right kind of stuff for intentionality you can easily see that he doesn't get any extra intentionality by memorizing the program, since memorizing it won't teach him Chinese.

Second, the program is purely formal, but the intentional states are not in that way formal. They are defined in terms of their content, not their form. The belief that it is raining, for example, is not defined as a certain formal shape, but as a certain mental content with conditions of satisfaction, a direction of fit (see Searle, 1979b), and the like. Indeed the belief as such hasn't even got a formal shape in this syntactic sense, since one and the same belief can be given an indefinite number of different syntactic expressions in different linguistic systems.

Third, as I mentioned before, mental states and events are literally a product of the operation of the brain, but the program is not in that way a product of the computer.

"Well if programs are in no way constitutive of mental processes, why have so many people believed the converse? That at least needs some explanation."

I don't really know the answer to that one. The idea that computer simulations could be the real thing ought to have seemed suspicious in the first place because the computer isn't confined to simulating mental operations, by any means. No one supposes that computer simulations of a five-alarm fire will burn the neighborhood down or that a computer simulation of a rainstorm will leave us all drenched. Why on earth would anyone suppose that a computer simulation of understanding actually understood anything? It is sometimes said that it would be frightfully hard to get computers to feel pain or fall in love, but love and pain are neither harder nor easier than cognition or anything else. For simulation, all you need is the right input and output and a program in the middle that transforms the former into the latter. That is all the computer has for anything it does. To confuse simulation with duplication is the same mistake, whether it is pain, love, cognition, fires, or rainstorms.

Still, there are several reasons why AI must have seemed — and to many people perhaps still does seem — in some way to reproduce and thereby explain mental phenomena, and I believe we will not succeed in removing these illusions until we have fully exposed the reasons that give rise to them.

First, and perhaps most important, is a confusion about the notion of "information processing": many people in cognitive science believe that the human brain, with its mind, does something called "information processing," and analogously the computer with its program does information processing; but fires and rainstorms, on the other hand, don't do information processing at all. Thus, though the computer can simulate the formal features of any process whatever, it stands in a special relation to the mind and brain because when the computer is properly programmed, ideally with the same program as the brain, the information processing is identical in the two cases, and this information processing is really the essence of the mental. But the trouble with this argument is that it rests on an ambiguity in the notion of "information." In the sense in which people "process information" when they reflect, say, on problems in arithmetic or when they read and answer questions about stories, the programmed computer does not do "information processing." Rather, what it does is manipulate formal symbols. The fact that the programmer and the interpreter of the computer output use the symbols to stand for objects in the world is totally beyond the scope of the computer. The computer, to repeat, has a syntax but no semantics. Thus, if you type into the computer "2 plus 2 equals?" it will type out "4." But it has no idea that "4" means 4 or that it means anything at all. And the point is not that it lacks some second-order information about the interpretation of its first-order symbols, but rather that its first-order symbols don't have any interpretations as far as the computer is concerned. All the computer has is more symbols. The introduction of the notion of "information processing" therefore produces a dilemma: either we construe the notion of "information processing" in such a way that it implies intentionality as part of the process or we don't. If the former, then the programmed computer does not do information processing, it only manipulates formal symbols. If the latter, then, though the computer does information processing, it is only doing so in the sense in which adding machines, typewriters, stomachs, thermostats, rainstorms, and hurricanes do information processing; namely, they have a level of description at which we can describe them as taking information in at one end, transforming it, and producing information as output. But in this case it is up to outside observers to interpret the input and output as information in the ordinary sense. And no similarity is established between the computer and the brain in terms of any similarity of information processing.

Second, in much of AI there is a residual behaviorism or operationalism. Since appropriately programmed computers can have input — output patterns similar to those of human beings, we are tempted to postulate mental states in the computer similar to human mental states. But once we see that it is both conceptually and empirically possible for a system to have human capacities in some realm without having any intentionality at all, we should be able to overcome this impulse. My desk adding machine has calculating capacities, but no intentionality, and in this paper I have tried to show that a system could have input and output capabilities that duplicated those of a native Chinese speaker and still not understand Chinese, regardless of how it was programmed. The Turing test is typical of the tradition in being unashamedly behavioristic and operationalistic, and I believe that if AI workers totally repudiated behaviorism and operationalism much of the confusion between simulation and duplication would be eliminated.

Third, this residual operationalism is joined to a residual form of dualism; indeed strong AI only makes sense given the dualistic assumption that, where the mind is concerned, the brain doesn't matter. In strong AI (and in functionalism, as well) what matters are programs, and programs are independent of their realization in machines; indeed, as far as AI is concerned, the same program could be realized by an electronic machine, a Cartesian mental substance, or a Hegelian world spirit. The single most surprising discovery that I have made in discussing these issues is that many AI workers are quite shocked by my idea that actual human mental phenomena might be dependent on actual physical-chemical properties of actual human brains. But if you think about it a minute you can see that I should not have been surprised; for unless you accept some form of dualism, the strong AI project hasn't got a chance. The project is to reproduce and explain the mental by designing programs, but unless the mind is not only conceptually but empirically independent of the brain you couldn't carry out the project, for the program is completely independent of any realization. Unless you believe that the mind is separable from the brain both conceptually and empirically — dualism in a strong form — you cannot hope to reproduce the mental by writing and running programs since programs must be independent of brains or any other particular forms of instantiation. If mental operations consist in computational operations on formal symbols, then it follows that they have no interesting connection with the brain; the only connection would be that the brain just happens to be one of the indefinitely many types of machines capable of instantiating the program. This form of dualism is not the traditional Cartesian variety that claims there are two sorts of *substances,* but it is Cartesian in the sense that it insists that what is specifically mental about the mind has no intrinsic connection with the actual properties of the brain. This underlying dualism is masked from us by the fact that AI literature contains frequent fulminations against "dualism"; what the authors seem to be unaware of is that their position presupposes a strong version of dualism.

"Could a machine think?" My own view is that *only* a machine could think, and indeed only very special kinds of machines, namely brains and machines that had the same causal powers as brains. And that is the main reason strong AI has had little to tell us about thinking, since it has nothing to tell us about machines. By its own definition, it is about programs, and programs are not machines. Whatever else intentionality is, it is a biological phenomenon, and it is as likely to be as causally dependent on the specific biochemistry of its origins as lactation, photosynthesis, or any other biological phenomena. No one would suppose that we could produce milk and sugar by running a computer simulation of the formal sequences in lactation and photosynthesis, but where the mind is concerned many people are willing to believe in such a miracle because of a deep and abiding dualism: the mind they suppose is a matter of formal processes and is independent of quite specific material causes in the way that milk and sugar are not.

In defense of this dualism the hope is often expressed that the brain is a digital computer (early computers, by the way, were often called "electronic brains"). But that is no help. Of course the brain is a digital computer. Since everything is a digital computer, brains are too. The point is that the brain's causal capacity to produce intentionality cannot consist in its instantiating a computer program, since for any program you like it is possible for something to instantiate that program and still not have any mental states. Whatever it is that the brain does to produce intentionality, it cannot consist in instantiating a program since no program, by itself, is sufficient for intentionality.

ACKNOWLEDGMENTS

I am indebted to a rather large number of people for discussion of these matters and for their patient attempts to overcome my ignorance of artificial intelligence. I would especially like to thank Ned Block, Hubert Dreyfus, John Haugeland, Roger Schank, Robert Wilensky, and Terry Winograd.

NOTES

1. I am not, of course, saying that Schank himself is committed to these claims.

2. Also, "understanding" implies both the possession of mental (intentional) states and the truth (validity, success) of these states. For the purposes of this discussion we are concerned only with the possession of the states.

3. Intentionality is by definition that feature of certain mental states by which they are directed at or about objects and states of affairs in the world. Thus, beliefs, desires, and intentions are intentional states; undirected forms of anxiety and depression are not. For further discussion see Searle (1979b).

REFERENCES

Fodor, J. A. (1980) Methodological solipsism considered as a research strategy in cognitive psychology. *The Behavioral and Brain Sciences,* 3: 1.

McCarthy, J. (1979) Ascribing mental qualities to machines. In *Philosophical Perspectives in Artificial Intelligence,* ed. M. Ringle. Atlantic Highlands, NJ: Humanities Press.

Newell, A. (1979) Physical symbol systems. Lecture at the La Jolla Conference on Cognitive Science.

Newell, A., and Simon, H. A. (1963) GPS, a program that simulates human thought. In *Computers and Thought,* ed. A. Feigenbaum and V. Feldman, pp. 279–93. New York: McGraw-Hill.

Pylyshyn, Z. W. (1980) Computation and cognition: issues in the foundations of cognitive science. *Behavioral and Brain Sciences,* 3:1.

Schank, R. C., and Abelson, R. P. (1977) *Scripts, Plans, Coals, and Understanding.* Hillsdale, NJ: Lawrence Erlbaum.

Searle, J. R. (1979a) Intentionality and the use of language. In *Meaning and Use,* ed. A. Margalit. Dordrecht: Reidel.

Searle, J. R. (1979b) What is an intentional state? *Mind,* 88, 74–92.

Weizenbaum, J. (1965) ELIZA — a computer program for the study of natural language communication between man and machine. *Communication of the Association for Computing Machinery* 9, 36–45.

Weizenbaum, J. (1976) *Computer Power and Human Reason.* San Francisco: W. H. Freeman.

Winograd, T. (1973) A procedural model of language understanding. In *Computer Models of Thought and Language,* ed. R. Schank and K. Colby. San Francisco: W. H. Freeman.

CHAPTER FIVE

EXPERIMENTAL DESIGN IN PSYCHOLOGICAL RESEARCH

DANIEL J. LEVITIN

5.1   INTRODUCTION

Experimental design is a vast topic. As one thinks about the information derived from scientific studies, one confronts difficult issues in statistical theory and the limits of knowledge. In this chapter, we confine our discussion to a few of the most important issues in experimental design. This will enable students with no background in behavior research to critically evaluate psychological experiments, and to better understand the nature of empirical research in cognitive science.

Experimental psychology is a young science. The first laboratory of experimental psychology was established just over 100 years ago. Consequently, there are a great many mysteries about human behavior, perception, and performance that have not yet been solved. This makes it an exciting time to engage in psychological research — the field is young enough that there is still a great deal to do, and it is not difficult to think up interesting experiments. The goal of this chapter is to guide the reader in planning and implementing experiments, and in thinking about good experimental design.

A "good" experiment is one in which variables are carefully controlled or accounted for so that one can draw reasonable conclusions from the experiment's outcome.

5.2   THE GOALS OF SCIENTIFIC RESEARCH

Generally, scientific research has four goals:

1. Description of behavior
2. Prediction of behavior
3. Determination of the causes of behavior
4. Explanations of behavior

These goals apply to the physical sciences as well as to the behavioral and life sciences. In basic science, the researcher's primary concern is not with applications for a given finding. The goal of basic research is to increase our understanding of how the world works, or how things came to be the way they are.

Describing behavior impartially is the foremost task of the descriptive study, and because this is never completely possible, one tries to document any systematic biases that could influence descriptions (goal 1). By studying a phenomenon, one frequently develops the ability to *predict* certain behaviors or outcomes (goal 2), although prediction is possible without an understanding of underlying causes (we'll look at some examples in a moment). Controlled experiments are one tool that scientists use to reveal underlying causes so that they can advance from merely predicting behavior to understanding the *cause* of behavior (goal 3). *Explaining* behavior (goal 4) requires more than just a knowledge of causes; it requires a detailed understanding of the mechanisms by which the causal factors perform their functions.

To illustrate the distinction between the four goals of scientific research, consider the history of astronomy. The earliest astronomers were able to *describe* the positions and motions of the stars in the heavens, although they had no ability to *predict* where a given body would appear in the sky at a future date. Through careful observations and documentation, later astronomers became quite skillful at *predicting* planetary and stellar motion, although they lacked an understanding of the underlying factors that *caused* this motion. Newton's laws of motion and Einstein's special and general theories of relativity, taken together, showed that gravity and the contour of the space — time continuum cause the motions we observe. Precisely how gravity and the topology of space — time accomplish this still remains unclear. Thus, astronomy has advanced to the determination of causes of stellar motion (goal 3), although a full *explanation* remains elusive. That is, saying that gravity is responsible for astronomical motion only puts a name on things; it does not tell us how gravity actually works.

As an illustration from behavioral science, one might note that people who listen to loud music tend to lose their high-frequency hearing (description). Based on a number of observations, one can predict that individuals with normal hearing who listen to enough loud music will suffer hearing loss (prediction). A controlled experiment can determine that the loud music is the cause of the hearing loss (determining causality). Finally, study of the cochlea and basilar membrane, and observation of damage to the delicate hair cells after exposure to high-pressure sound waves, meets the fourth goal (explanation).

5.3   THREE TYPES OF SCIENTIFIC STUDIES

In science there are three broad classes of studies: controlled studies, correlational studies, and descriptive studies. Often the type of study you will be able to do is determined by practicality, cost, or ethics, not directly by your own choice.

5.3.1   Controlled Studies ("True Experiments")

In a controlled experiment, the researcher starts with a group of subjects and randomly assigns them to an experimental condition. The point of *random assignment* is to control for extraneous variables that might affect the outcome of the experiment: variables that are different from the variable(s) being studied. With random assignment, one can be reasonably certain that any differences among the experimental groups were caused by the variable(s) manipulated in the experiment.

A controlled experiment in medical research might seek to discover if a certain food additive causes cancer. The researcher might randomly divide a group of laboratory mice into two smaller groups, giving the food additive to one group and not to the other. The variable he/she is interested in is the effect of the food additive; in the language of experimental design, this is called the "independent variable." After a period of time, the researcher compares the mortality rates of the two groups; this quantity is called the "dependent variable" (figure 5.1). Suppose the group that received the additive tended to die earlier. In order to deduce that the additive caused the difference between the groups, the conditions must have been identical in every other respect. Both groups should have had the same diet, same feeding schedule, same temperature in their cages, and so on. Furthermore, the two groups of mice should have started out with similar characteristics, such as age, sex, and so on, so that these variables — being equally distributed between the two groups — can be ruled out as possible causes of the difference in mortality rates.

The two key components of a controlled experiment are *random assignment* of subjects, and *identical experimental conditions* (see figure 5.1). A researcher might have a hypothesis that people who study for an exam while listening to music will score better than people who study in silence. In the language of experimental design, music-listening is the *independent variable,* and test performance, the quantity to be measured, is the *dependent variable.*

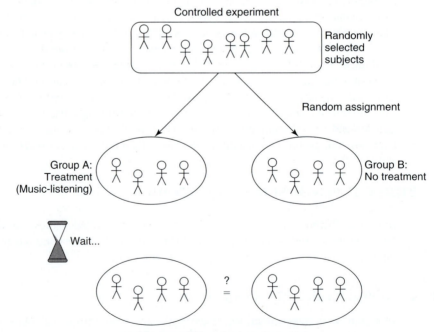

FIGURE 5.1   In a controlled experiment, subjects are randomly assigned to conditions, and differences between groups are measured.

No one would take this study seriously if the subjects were divided into two groups based on how they did on the previous exam — if, for instance, the top half of the students were placed in the music-listening condition, and the bottom half of the students in the silence condition. Then if the result of the experiment was that the music listeners as a group tended to perform better on their next exam, one could argue that this was not because they listened to music while they studied, but because they were the better students to begin with.

Again, the theory behind random assignment is to have groups of subjects who start out the same. Ideally, each group will have similar distributions on every conceivable dimension — age, sex, ethnicity, IQ, and variables that you might not think are important, such as handedness, astrological sign, or favorite television show. Random assignment makes it unlikely that there will be any large systematic differences between the groups.

A similar design flaw would arise if the *experimental conditions* were different. For example, if the music-listening group studied in a well-lit room with windows, and the silence group studied in a dark, windowless basement, any difference between the groups could be due to the different environments. The room conditions become confounded with the music-listening conditions, such that it is impossible to deduce which of the two is the causal factor.

Performing random assignment of subjects is straightforward. Conceptually, one wants to mix the subjects' names or numbers thoroughly, then draw them out of a hat. Realistically, one of the easiest ways to do this is to generate a different random number for each subject, and then sort the random numbers. If n equals the total number of subjects you have, and g equals the number of groups you are dividing them into, the first n/g subjects will comprise the first group, the next n/g will comprise the second group, and so on.

If the results of a controlled experiment indicate a difference between groups, the next question is whether these findings are generalizable. If your initial group of subjects (the large group, before you randomly assigned subjects to conditions) was also randomly selected (called *random sampling* or *random selection,* as opposed to *random assignment),* this is a reasonable conclusion to draw. However, there are almost always some constraints on one's initial choice of subjects, and this constrains generalizability. For example, if all the subjects you studied in your music-listening experiment lived in fraternities, the finding might not generalize to people who do not live in fraternities. If you want to be able to generalize to all college students, you would need to take a representative sample of all college students. One way to do this is to choose your subjects randomly, such that each member of the population you are considering (college students) has an equal likelihood of being placed in the experiment.

There are some interesting issues in representative sampling that are beyond the scope of this chapter. For example, if you wanted to take a representative sample of all American college students and you chose American college students randomly, it is possible that you would be choosing several students from some of the larger colleges, such as the University of Michigan, and you might not choose any students at all from some of the smaller colleges, such as Bennington College; this would limit the applicability of your findings to the colleges that were represented in your sample. One solution is to conduct a *stratified sample,* in which you first randomly select colleges (making it just as likely that you'll choose large and small colleges) and then randomly select the same number of students from each of those colleges. This ensures that colleges of different sizes are represented in the sample. You then weight the data from each college in accordance with the percentage contribution each college makes to the total student population of your sample. (For further reading, see Shaughnessy and Zechmeister 1994.)

Choosing subjects randomly requires careful planning. If you try to take a random sample of Stanford students by standing in front of the Braun Music Building and stopping every third person coming out, you might be selecting a greater percentage of music students than actually exists on campus. Yet truly random samples are not always practical. Much psychological research is conducted on college students who are taking an introductory psychology class, and are required to participate in an experiment for course credit. It is not at all clear whether American college students taking introductory psychology are representative of students in general, or of people in the world in general, so one should be careful not to overgeneralize findings from these studies.

5.3.2   Correlational Studies

A second type of study is the *correlational study* (figure 5.2). Because it is not always practical or ethical to perform random assignments, scientists are sometimes forced to rely on patterns of co-occurrence, or correlations between events. The classic example of a correlational study is the link between cigarette smoking and cancer. Few educated people

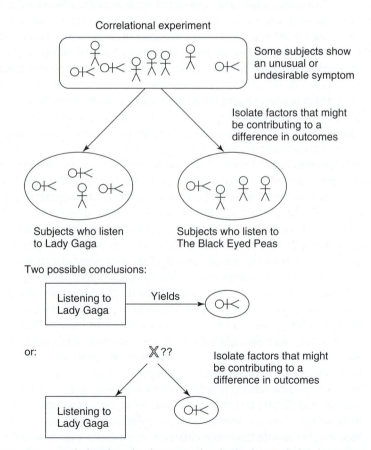

FIGURE 5.2   In a correlational study, the researcher looks for a relation between two observed behaviors — in this case, the relation between untimely death and listening to Lady Gaga recordings.

today doubt that smokers are more likely to die of lung cancer than are nonsmokers. However, in the history of scientific research there has never been a controlled experiment with human subjects on this topic. Such an experiment would take a group of healthy nonsmokers, and randomly assign them to two groups, a smoking group and a nonsmoking group. Then the experimenter would simply wait until most of the people in the study have died, and compare the average ages and causes of death of the two groups. Because our hypothesis is that smoking causes cancer, it would clearly be unethical to ask people to smoke who otherwise would not.

The scientific evidence we have that smoking causes cancer is correlational. That is, when we look at smokers as a group, a higher percentage of them do indeed develop fatal cancers, and die earlier, than do nonsmokers. But without a controlled study, the possibility exists that there is a third factor — a mysterious "factor x" — that both causes people to smoke and to develop cancer. Perhaps there is some enzyme in the body that gives people a nicotine craving, and this same enzyme causes fatal cancers. This would account for both outcomes, the kinds of people who smoke and the rate of cancers among them, and it would show that there is no causal link between smoking and cancer.

In correlational studies, a great deal of effort is devoted to trying to uncover differences between the two groups studied in order to identify any causal factors that might exist. In the case of smoking, none have been discovered so far, but the failure to discover a third causal factor does not prove that one does not exist. It is an axiom in the philosophy of science that one can prove only the presence of something; one can't prove the absence of something — it could always be just around the corner, waiting to be discovered in the next experiment (Hempel 1966). In the real world, behaviors and diseases are usually brought on by a number of complicated factors, so the mysterious third variable, "factor x," could in fact be a collection of different, and perhaps unrelated, variables that act together to cause the outcomes we observe.

An example of a correlational study with a hypothesized musical cause is depicted in figure 5.2. Such a study would require extensive interviews with the subjects (or their survivors), to try to determine all factors that might separate the subjects exhibiting the symptom from the subjects without the symptom.

The problem with correlational studies is that the search for underlying factors that account for the differences between groups can be very difficult. Yet many times, correlational studies are all we have, because ethical considerations preclude the use of controlled experiments.

5.3.3   Descriptive Studies

Descriptive studies do not look for differences between people or groups, but seek only to describe an aspect of the world as it is. A descriptive study in physics might seek to discover what elements make up the core of the planet Jupiter. The goal in such a study would not be to compare Jupiter's core with the core of other planets, but to learn more about the origins of the universe. In psychology, we might want to know the part of the brain that is activated when someone performs a mental calculation, or the number of pounds of fresh green peas the average Canadian eats in a year (figure 5.3). Our goal in these cases is not to contrast individuals but to acquire some basic data about the nature of things. Of course, descriptive studies can be used to establish "norms," so that we can compare people against the

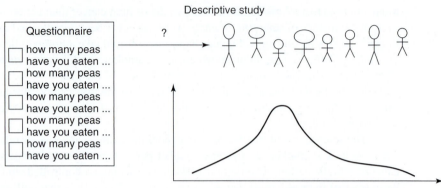

FIGURE 5.3   In a descriptive study, the researcher seeks to describe some aspect of the state of the world, such as people's consumption of green peas.

average, but as their name implies, the primary goal in descriptive experiments is often just to describe something that had not been described before. Descriptive studies are every bit as useful as controlled experiments and correlational studies — sometimes, in fact, they are even more valuable because they lay the foundation for further experimental work.

5.4   DESIGN FLAWS IN EXPERIMENTAL DESIGN

5.4.1   Clever Hans

There are many examples of flawed studies or flawed conclusions that illustrate the difficulties in controlling extraneous variables. Perhaps the most famous case is that of Clever Hans.

Clever Hans was a horse owned by a German mathematics teacher around the turn of the twentieth century. Hans became famous following many demonstrations in which he could perform simple addition and subtraction, read German, and answer simple questions by tapping his hoof on the ground (Watson, 1967). One of the first things that skeptics wondered (as you might) is whether Hans would continue to be clever when someone other than his owner asked the questions, or when Hans was asked questions that he had never heard before. In both these cases, Hans continued to perform brilliantly, tapping out the sums or differences for arithmetic problems.

In 1904, a scientific commission was formed to investigate Hans's abilities more carefully. The commission discovered, after rigorous testing, that Hans could never answer a question if the questioner did not also know the answer, or if Hans could not see his questioner. It was finally discovered that Hans had become very adept at picking up subtle (and probably unintentional) movements on the part of the questioner that cued him as to when he should stop tapping his foot. Suppose a questioner asked Hans to add 7 and 3. Hans would start tapping his hoof, and keep on tapping until the questioner stopped him by saying "Right! Ten!" or, more subtly, by moving slightly when the correct answer was reached.

You can see how important it is to ensure that extraneous cues or biases do not intrude into an experimental situation.

5.4.2   Infants' Perception of Musical Structure

In studies of infants' perception of music, infants typically sit in their mother's lap while music phrases are played over a speaker. Infants tend to turn their heads toward a novel or surprising event, and this is the dependent variable in many infant studies; the point at which the infants turn their heads indicates when they perceive a difference in whatever is being played. Suppose you ran such a study and found that the infants were able to distinguish Mozart selections that were played normally from selections of equal length that began or ended in the middle of a musical phrase. You might take this as evidence that the infants have an innate understanding of musical phraseology.

Are there alternative explanations for the results? Suppose that in the experimental design, the mothers could hear the music, too. The mothers might unconsciously cue the infants to changes in the stimulus that they (the mothers) detect. A simple solution is to have the mothers wear headphones playing white noise, so that their perception of the music is masked.

5.4.3   Computers, Timing, and Other Pitfalls

It is very important that you not take anything for granted as you design a careful experiment, and control extraneous variables. For example, psychologists studying visual perception frequently present their stimuli on a computer using the MacIntosh or Windows operating system. In a computer program, the code may specify that an image is to remain on the computer monitor for a precise number of milliseconds. Just because you specify this does not make it happen, however. Conventional CRT monitors have a *refresh rate* (60 or 75 Hz is typical), so the "on time" of an image will always be an integer multiple of the refresh cycle (13.33 milliseconds for a 75 Hz refresh rate) no matter what you instruct the computer to do in your code. To make things worse, the MacIntosh and Windows operating systems do not guarantee "refresh cycle accuracy" in their updating, so an instruction to put a new image on the screen may be delayed an unknown amount of time.

It is important, therefore, always to verify, using some external means, that the things you think are happening in your experiment are actually happening. Just because you leave the volume control on your amplifier at the same spot doesn't mean the volume of a sound stimulus you are playing will be the same from day to day. You should measure the output and not take the knob position for granted. Just because a frequency generator is set for 1000 Hz does not mean it is putting out a 1000 Hz signal. It is good science for you to measure the output frequency yourself.

5.5   NUMBER OF SUBJECTS

How many subjects are enough? In statistics, the word "population" refers to the total group of people to which the researcher wishes to generalize findings. The population might be female sophomores at Stanford, or all Stanford students, or all college students in the United States, or all people in the United States. If one is able to draw a representative sample of sufficient size from a population, one can make inferences about the whole population based on a relatively small number of cases. This is the basis of presidential polls, for example, in which only 2000 voters are surveyed, and the outcome of an election can be predicted with reasonable accuracy.

The size of the sample required is dependent on the degree of homogeneity or heterogeneity in the total population you are studying. In the extreme, if you are studying a population that is so homogeneous that every individual is identical on the dimensions being studied, a sample size of one will provide all the information you need. At the other extreme, if you are studying a population that is so heterogeneous that each individual differs categorically on the dimension you are studying, you will need to sample the entire population.

As a "rough-and-ready" rule, if you are performing a descriptive perceptual experiment, and the phenomenon you are studying is something that you expect to be invariant across people, you need to use only a few subjects, perhaps five. An example of this type of study would be calculating threshold sensitivities for various sound frequencies, such as was done by Fletcher and Munson (1933).

If you are studying a phenomenon for which you expect to find large individual differences, you might need between 30 and 100 subjects. This depends to some degree on how many different conditions there are in the study. In order to obtain means with a relatively small variance, it is a good idea to have at least five to ten subjects in each experimental condition.

5.6   TYPES OF EXPERIMENTAL DESIGNS

Suppose you are researching the effect of music-listening on studying efficiency, as mentioned at the beginning of this chapter. Let's expand on the simpler design described earlier. You might divide your subjects into five groups: two experimental groups and three control groups. One experimental group would listen to rock music, and the other would listen to classical music. Of the three control groups, one would listen to rock music for the same number of minutes per day as the experimental group listening to rock (but not while they were studying); a second would do the same for classical music; the third would listen to no music at all. This is called a *between-subjects* design, because each subject is in one condition and one condition only (also referred to as an *independent groups* design). If you assign 10 subjects to each experimental condition, this would require a total of 50 subjects. Table 5.1 shows the layout of this experiment. Each distinct box in the table is called a *cell* of the experiment, and subject numbers are filled in for each cell. Notice the asymmetry for the *no music* condition. The experiment was designed so that there is only one "no music" condition, whereas there are four music conditions of various types.

TABLE 5.1   Between-Subjects Experiment on Music and Study Habits

CONDITION	ONLY WHILE STUDYING	ONLY WHILE NOT STUDYING
Music		
Classical	Subjects 1–10	Subjects 11–20
Rock	Subjects 21–30	Subjects 31–40
No music	Subjects 41–50	Subjects 41–50

Testing 50 subjects might not be practical. An alternative is a *within-subjects* design, in which every subject is tested in every condition (also called a *repeated measures* design). In this example, a total of ten subjects could be randomly divided into the five conditions, so that two subjects experience each condition for a given period of time. Then the subjects switch to another condition. By the time the experiment is completed, ten observations have been collected in each cell, and only ten subjects are required.

The advantage of each subject experiencing each condition is that you can obtain measures of how each individual is affected by the manipulation, something you cannot do in the between-subjects design. It might be the case that some people do well in one type of condition and other people do poorly in it, and the within-subjects design is the best way to show this. The obvious advantage to the within-subjects design is the smaller number of subjects required. But there are disadvantages as well.

One disadvantage is *demand characteristics.* Because each subject experiences each condition, they are not as naive about the experimental manipulation. Their performance could be influenced by a conscious or unconscious desire to make one of the conditions work better. Another problem is *carryover effects.* Suppose you were studying the effect of Prozac on learning, and that the half-life of the drug is 48 hours. The group that gets the drug first might still be under its influence when they are switched to the nondrug condition. This is a carryover effect. In the music-listening experiment, it is possible that listening to rock music creates anxiety or exhilaration that might last into the next condition.

A third disadvantage of within-subjects designs is *order effects,* and these are particularly troublesome in psychophysical experiments. An order effect is similar to a carryover effect, and it concerns how responses in an experiment might be influenced by the order in which the stimuli or conditions are presented. For instance, in studies of speech discrimination, subjects can habituate (become used to, or become more sensitive) to certain sounds, altering their threshold for the discriminability of related sounds. A subject who habituates to a certain sound may respond differently to the sound immediately following it than he/she normally would. For these reasons, it is important to counterbalance the order of presentations; presenting the same order to every subject makes it difficult to account for any effects that are due merely to order.

One way to reduce order effects is to present the stimuli or conditions in random order. In some studies, this is sufficient, but to be really careful about order effects, the random order simply is not rigorous enough. The solution is to use every possible order. In a *within-subjects* design, each subject would complete the experiment with each order. In a *between-subjects* design, different subjects would be assigned different orders. The choice will often depend on the available resources (time and availability of subjects). The number of possible orders is *N!* ("n factorial"), where *N* equals the number of stimuli. With two stimuli there are two possible orders ($2! = 2 \times 1$); with three stimuli there are six possible orders ($3! = 3 \times 2 \times 1$); with six stimuli there are 720 possible orders ($6! = 6 \times 5 \times 4 \times 3 \times 2 \times 1$). Seven hundred twenty orders is not practical for a within-subjects design, or for a between-subjects design. One solution in this case is to create an order that presents each stimulus in each serial position. A method for accomplishing this involves using the Latin Square. For even-numbered N, the size of the Latin Square will be $N \times N$; therefore, with six stimuli you would need only 36 orders, not 720. For odd-numbered N, the size of the Latin Square will be $N \times 2N$. Details of this technique are covered in experimental design texts such as Kirk (1982) and Shaughnessy and Zechmeister (1994).

5.7   ETHICAL CONSIDERATIONS IN USING HUMAN SUBJECTS

Some experiments on human subjects in the 1960s and 1970s raised questions about how human subjects are treated in behavioral experiments. As a result, guidelines for human experimentation were established. The American Psychological Association, a voluntary organization of psychologists, formulated a code of ethical principles (American Psychological Association 1992). In addition, most universities have established committees to review and approve research using human subjects. The purpose of these committees is to ensure that subjects are treated ethically, and that fair and humane procedures are followed. In some universities, experiments performed for course work or experiments done as "pilot studies" do not require approval, but these rules vary from place to place, so it is important to determine the requirements at your institution before engaging in any human subject research.

It is also important to understand the following four basic principles of ethics in human subject research:

1. *Informed Consent.* Before agreeing to participate in an experiment, subjects should be given an accurate description of their task in the experiment, and told any risks involved. Subjects should be allowed to decline, or to discontinue participation in the experiment at any time without penalty.

2. *Debriefing.* Following the experiment, the subjects should be given an explanation of the hypothesis being tested and the methods used. The experimenter should answer any questions the subjects have about the procedure or hypothesis. Many psychoacoustic experiments involve difficult tasks, leading some subjects to feel frustrated or embarrassed. Subjects should never leave an experiment feeling slow, stupid, or untalented. It is the experimenter's responsibility to ensure that the subjects understand that these tasks are inherently difficult, and when appropriate, the subjects should be told that the data are not being used to evaluate them personally, but to collect information on how the population in general can perform the task.

3. *Privacy and Confidentiality.* The experimenter must carefully guard the data that are collected and, whenever possible, code and store the data in such a way that subjects' identities remain confidential.

4. *Fraud.* This principle is not specific to human subjects research, but applies to all research. An essential ethical standard of the scientific community is that scientific researchers never fabricate data, and never knowingly, intentionally, or through carelessness allow false data, analyses, or conclusions to be published. Fraudulent reporting is one of the most serious ethical breaches in the scientific community.

5.8   ANALYZING YOUR DATA

5.8.1   Quantitative Analysis

Measurement Error.   Whenever you measure a quantity, there are two components that contribute to the number you end up with: the actual value of the thing you are measuring and some amount of measurement error, both human and mechanical. It is an axiom of statistics that measurement error is just as likely to result in an overestimate as an underestimate of the true value. That is, each time you take a measurement, the error term (let's call it *epsilon*) is just as likely to be positive as negative. Over a large number of measurements, the positive errors and negative errors will cancel out, and the average value of epsilon will approach 0. The larger the number of measurements you make, the closer you will get to the true value. Thus, as the number of measurements approaches infinity, the arithmetic average of your measurements approaches the true quantity being measured. Suppose we are measuring the weight of a sandbag.

Formally, we would write:

$$n \rightarrow \infty, \quad \bar{\varepsilon} = 0$$

where $\bar{\varepsilon}$ = the mean of epsilon, and

$$n \rightarrow \infty, \quad \bar{w} = w$$

where $\bar{w}$ = the mean of all the weight measurements and w = the true weight.

When measuring the behavior of human subjects on a task, you encounter not only measurement error but also performance error. The subjects will not perform identically every time. As with measurement error, the more observations you make, the more likely it is that the performance errors cancel each other out. In psychoacoustic tasks the performance errors can often be relatively large. This is the reason why one usually wants to have the subject perform the same task many times, or to have many subjects perform the task a few times.

Because of these errors, the value of your dependent variable(s) at the end of the experiment will always deviate from the true value by some amount. Statistical analysis helps in interpreting these differences (Bayesian inferencing, meta-analyses, effect size analysis, significance testing) and in predicting the true value (point estimates and confidence intervals). The mechanics of these tests are beyond the scope of this chapter, and the reader is referred to the statistics textbooks mentioned earlier.

Significance Testing.   Suppose you wish to observe differences in interval identification ability between brass players and string players. The question is whether the difference you observe between the two groups can be wholly accounted for by measurement and performance error, or whether a difference of the size you observe indicates a true difference in the abilities of these musicians.

Significance tests provide the user with a "p value," the probability that the experimental result could have arisen by chance. By convention, if the p value is less than .05, meaning that the result could have arisen by chance less than 5% of the time, scientists accept the result as statistically significant. Of course, $p < .05$ is arbitrary, and it doesn't deal directly with the opposite case, the probability that the data you collected indicate a genuine effect, but the statistical test failed to detect it (a power analysis is required for this). In many studies, the probability of failing to detect an effect, when it exists, can soar to 80% (Schmidt 1996). An additional problem with a criterion of 5% is that a researcher who measures 20 different effects is likely to measure one as significant by chance, even if no significant effect actually exists.

Statistical significance tests, such as the analysis of variance (ANOVA), the f-test, chi-square test, and t-test, are methods to determine the probability that observed values in an experiment differ only as a result of measurement errors. For details about how to choose and conduct the appropriate tests, or to learn more about the theory behind them, consult a statistics textbook (e.g., Daniel 1990; Glenberg 1988; Hayes 1988).

Alternatives to Classical Significance Testing.   Because of problems with traditional significance testing, there is a movement, at the vanguard of applied statistics and psychology, to move away from "p value" tests and to rely on alternative methods, such as Bayesian inferencing, effect sizes, confidence intervals, and meta-analyses (refer to Cohen 1994; Hunter and Schmidt 1990; Schmidt 1996). Yet many people persist in clinging to the belief that the most important thing to do with experimental data is to test them for statistical significance. There is great pressure from peer-reviewed journals to perform significance tests, because so many people were taught to use them. The fact is, the whole point of significance testing is to determine whether a result is repeatable when one doesn't have the resources to repeat an experiment.

Let us return to the hypothetical example mentioned earlier, in which we examined the effect of music on study habits using a "within-subjects" design (each subject is in each condition). One possible outcome is that the difference in the mean test scores among groups was not significantly different by an analysis of variance (ANOVA). Yet suppose that, ignoring the means, every subject in the music-listening condition had a higher score than in the no-music condition. We are not interested in the size of the difference now, only in the direction of the difference. The null hypothesis predicts that the manipulation would have no effect at all, and that half of the subjects should show a difference in one direction and half in the other. The probability of all 10 subjects showing an effect in the same direction is $1/2^{10}$ or 0.0009, which is highly significant. Ten out of 10 subjects indicates *repeatability.* The technique just described is called the *sign test,* because we are looking only at the arithmetic sign of the differences between groups (positive or negative).

Often, a good alternative to significance tests is estimates of *confidence intervals.* These determine with a given probability (e.g., 95%) the range of values within which the true population parameters lie. Another alternative is an analysis of *conditional probabilities.* That is, if you observe a difference between two groups on some measure, determine whether a subject's membership in one group or the other will improve your ability to predict his/her score on the dependent variable, compared with not knowing what group he/she was in (an example of this analysis is in Levitin 1994a). A good overview of these alternative statistical methods is contained in the paper by Schmidt (1996).

Aside from statistical analyses, in most studies you will want to compute the mean and standard deviation of your dependent variable. If you had distinct treatment groups, you will want to know the individual means and standard deviations for each group. If you had two continuous variables, you will probably want to compute the *correlation,* which is an index of how much one variable is related to the other. Always provide a table of means and standard deviations as part of your report.

5.8.2   Qualitative Analysis, or "How to Succeed in Statistics without Significance Testing"

If you have not had a course in statistics, you are probably at some advantage over anyone who has. Many people who have taken statistics courses rush to plug the numbers into a computer package to test for statistical significance. Unfortunately, students are not always perfectly clear on exactly what it is they are testing or why they are testing it.

The first thing one should do with experimental data is to graph them in a way that clarifies the relation between the data and the hypothesis. Forget about statistical significance testing — what does the pattern of data suggest? Graph everything you can think of — individual subject data, subject averages, averages across conditions — and see what patterns emerge. Roger Shepard has pointed out that the human brain is not very adept at scanning a table of numbers and picking out patterns, but is much better at picking out patterns in a visual display.

Depending on what you are studying, you might want to use a bar graph, a line graph, or a bivariate scatter plot. As a general rule, even though many of the popular graphing and spreadsheet packages will allow you to make pseudo-three-dimensional graphs, don't ever use three dimensions unless the third dimension actually represents a variable. Nothing is more confusing than a graph with extraneous information.

If you are making several graphs of the same data (such as individual subject graphs), make sure that each graph is the same size and that the axes are scaled identically from one graph to another, in order to facilitate comparison. Be sure all your axes are clearly labeled, and don't divide the axis numbers into units that aren't meaningful (for example, in a histogram with "number of subjects" on the ordinate, the scale shouldn't include half numbers because subjects come only in whole numbers).

Use a line graph if your variables are continuous. The lines connecting your plot points imply a continuous variable. Use a bar graph if the variables are categorical, so that you don't fool the reader into thinking that your observations were continuous. Use a bivariate scatter plot when you have two continuous variables, and you want to see how a change in one variable affects the other variable (such as how IQ and income might correlate). Do *not* use a bivariate scatterplot for categorical data. (For more information on good graph design, see Chambers et al. 1983; Cleveland 1994; Kosslyn 1994).

Once you have made all your graphs, look them over for interesting patterns and effects. Try to get a feel for what you have found, and understand how the data relate to your hypotheses and your experimental design. A well-formed graph can make a finding easy to understand and evaluate far better than a dry recitation of numbers and statistical tests can do.

ACKNOWLEDGMENTS

This chapter benefited greatly from comments by Perry Cook, Lynn Gerow, Lewis R. Goldberg, John M. Kelley, and John Pierce. During the preparation of this chapter, I received direct support from an ONR graduate research fellowship (N-00014-89-J-3186), and indirect support from CCRMA and from an ONR Grant to M. I. Posner (N-00014-89-3013).

REFERENCES

American Psychological Association. (1992). "Ethical Principles of Psychologists and Code of Conduct." *American Psychologist,* 47, 1597–1611.

American Psychological Association. (1994). *Publication Manual of the American Psychological Association.* Fourth edition. Washington, D.C.: American Psychological Association.

Butler, D., Ward, W. D. (1988). "Effacing the Memory of Musical Pitch." *Music Perception,* 5 (3), 251–260.

Chambers, J. M., Cleveland, W. S., Kleiner, B., & Tukey, P. A. (1983). *Graphical Methods for Data Analysis.* New York: Chapman & Hall.

Cleveland, W. S. (1994). *The Elements of Graphing Data.* Revised edition. Summit, N.J.: Hobart Press.

Cohen, J. (1994). "The Earth Is Round (p $<$ .05)." *American Psychologist,* 49, 997–1003.

Cozby, P. C. (1989). *Methods in Behavioral Research.* Fourth edition. Mountain View, Calif.: Mayfield Publishing Co.

Daniel, W. W. (1990). *Applied Nonparametric Statistics.* Second edition. Boston: PWS-Kent.

Deutsch, D. (1991). "The Tritone Paradox: An Influence of Language on Music Perception." *Music Perception,* 84, 335–347.

Deutsch, D. (1992). "The Tritone Paradox: Implications for the Representation and Communication of Pitch Structure." In M. R. Jones and S. Holleran, eds., *Cognitive Bases of Musical Communication.* Washington, D.C.: American Psychological Association.

Fisher, N. I. (1993). *Statistical Analysis of Circular Data.* Cambridge: Cambridge University Press.

Fletcher, H., Munson, W. A. (1933). "Loudness, Its Definition, Measurement and Calculation." *Journal of the Acoustical Society of America,* 72, 82–108.

Glenberg, A. (1988). *Learning from Data: An Introduction to Statistical Reasoning.* San Diego: Harcourt, Brace, Jovanovich.

Hayes, W. (1988). *Statistics.* Fourth edition. New York: Holt, Rinehart and Winston.

Hempel, C. G. (1966). *Philosophy of Natural Science.* Englewood Cliffs, N.J.: Prentice-Hall.

Hunter, J. E., Schmidt, F. L. (1990). *Methods of Meta-analysis: Correcting Error and Bias in Research Findings.* Newbury Park, Calif.: Sage.

Kirk, R. E. (1982). *Experimental Design: Procedures for the Behavioral Sciences.* Second edition. Pacific Grove, Calif.: Brooks/Cole.

Kosslyn, S. M. (1994). *Elements of Graph Design.* New York: Freeman.

Levitin, D. J. (1994a). "Absolute Memory for Musical Pitch: Evidence from the Production of Learned Melodies." *Perception & Psychophysics,* 56 (4), 414–423.

_____. (1994b). *Problems in Applying the Kolmogorov-Smirnov Test: The Need for Circular Statistics in Psychology.* Technical Report #94-07. University of Oregon, Institute of Cognitive & Decision Sciences.

Schmidt, F. L. (1996). "Statistical Significance Testing and Cumulative Knowledge in Psychology: Implications for the Training of Researchers." *Psychological Methods,* VI (2): 115–129.

Shaughnessy, J. J., Zechmeister, E. B. (1994). *Research Methods in Psychology.* Third edition. New York: McGraw-Hill.

Stern, A. W. (1993). "Natural Pitch and the A440 Scale." Stanford University, CCRMA. (Unpublished report).

Watson, J. B. (1967). *Behavior: An Introduction to Comparative Psychology.* New York: Holt, Rinehart and Winston. First published 1914.

Zar, J. H. (1984). *Biostatistical Analysis.* Second edition. Englewood Cliffs, N.J.: Prentice-Hall.

CHAPTER SIX

PERCEPTION

PHILIP G. ZIMBARDO AND RICHARD J. GERRIG

[. . .]

Your environment is filled with waves of light and sound, but that's not the way in which you experience the world. You don't "see" waves of light; you see a poster on the wall. You don't "hear" waves of sound; you hear music from a nearby radio. Sensation is what gets the show started, but something more is needed to make a stimulus meaningful and interesting and, most important, to make it possible for you to respond to it effectively. The processes of *perception* provide the extra layers of interpretation that enable you to navigate successfully through your environment.

We can offer a simple demonstration to help you think about the relationship between sensation and perception. Hold your hand as far as you can in front of your face. Now move it toward you. As you move your hand toward your eyes, it will take up more and more of your visual field. You may no longer be able to see the poster on the wall in back of your hand. How can your hand block out the poster? Has your hand gotten bigger? Has the poster gotten smaller? Your answer must be "Of course not!" This demonstration tells you something about the difference between sensation and perception. Your hand can block out the poster because, as it comes closer to your face, the hand projects an increasingly larger image on your retina. It is your perceptual processes that allow you to understand that despite the change in the size of the projection on your retina, your hand — and the poster behind it — do not change in actual size.

We might say that the role of perception is to make sense of sensation. Perceptual processes extract meaning from the continuously changing, often chaotic, sensory input from external energy sources and organize it into stable, orderly percepts. A *percept* is what is perceived — the phenomenological, or experienced, outcome of the process of perception. It is *not* a physical object or its image in a receptor but, rather, the psychological product of perceptual activity. Thus your percept of your hand remains stable over changes in the size of the image because your interpretation is governed by stable perceptual activities. Most of the time, sensing and perceiving occur so effortlessly, continuously, and automatically that you take them for granted. It is our goal in this chapter to allow you to understand and appreciate the processes that afford you a suitable account of the world, with such apparent ease. We begin with an overview of perceptual processes in the visual domain.

6.1   SENSING, ORGANIZING, IDENTIFYING, AND RECOGNIZING

The term *perception,* in its broad usage, refers to the overall process of *apprehending* objects and events in the external environment — to sense them, understand them, identify and label them, and prepare to react to them. The process of perception is best understood when we divide it into three stages: sensation, perceptual organization, and identification/recognition of objects.

Sensation refers to conversion of physical energy into the neural codes recognized by the brain. Sensation provides a first-pass representation of the basic facts of the visual field. Your retinal cells are organized to emphasize edges and contrasts while reacting only weakly to unchanging, constant stimulation. Cells in your brain's cortex extract features and spatial frequency information from this retinal input.

Perceptual organization refers to the next stage, in which an internal representation of an object is formed and a percept of the external stimulus is developed. The representation provides a working description of the perceiver's external environment. Perceptual processes provide estimates of an object's likely size, shape, movement, distance, and orientation. Those estimates are based on mental computations that integrate your past knowledge with the present evidence received from your senses and with the stimulus within its perceptual context. Perception involves *synthesis* (integration and combination) of simple sensory features, such as colors, edges, and lines, into the percept of an object that can be recognized later. These mental activities most often occur swiftly and efficiently, without conscious awareness.

To understand the difference between these first two stages more clearly, consider the case study of Dr. Richard, whose brain damage left his sensation intact but altered his perceptual processes.

Dr. Richard was a psychologist with considerable training and experience in introspection. This special skill enabled him to make a unique and valuable contribution to psychology. However, tragically, he suffered brain damage that altered his visual experience of the world. Fortunately, the damage did not affect the centers of his brain responsible for speech, so he was able to describe quite clearly his subsequent unusual visual experiences. In general terms, the brain damage seemed to have affected his ability to put sensory data together properly. For example, Dr. Richard reported that if he saw a complex object, such as a person, and there were several other people nearby in his visual field, he sometimes saw the different parts of the person as separate parts, not belonging together in a single form. He also had difficulty combining the sound and sight of the same event. When someone was singing, he might see a mouth move and hear a song, but it was as if the sound had been dubbed with the wrong tape in a foreign movie.

To see the parts of an event as a whole, Dr. Richard needed some common factor to serve as "glue." For example, if the fragmented person moved, so that all parts went in the same direction, Dr. Richard would then perceive the parts reunited into a complete person. Even then, the perceptual "glue" would sometimes result in absurd configurations. Dr. Richard would frequently see objects of the same color, such as a banana, a lemon, and a canary, going together even if they were separated in space. People in crowds would seem to merge if they were wearing the same colored clothing. Dr. Richard's experiences of his environment were disjointed, fragmented, and bizarre — quite unlike what he had been used to before his problems began (Marcel, 1983).

There was nothing wrong with Dr. Richard's eyes or with his ability to *analyze* the properties of stimulus objects — he saw the parts and qualities of objects accurately. Rather, his problem lay in synthesis — putting the bits and pieces of sensory information together properly to form a unified, coherent perception of a single event in the visual scene. His case makes salient the distinction between sensory and perceptual processes. It also serves to remind you that both sensory analysis and perceptual organization must be going on all the time even though you are unaware of the way they are working or even that they are happening.

Identification and recognition, the third stage in this sequence, assigns meaning to percepts. Circular objects "become" baseballs, coins, clocks, oranges, and moons; people may be identified as male or female, friend or foe, movie star or rock star. At this stage, the perceptual question "What does the object look like?" changes to a question of identification — "What is this object?" — and to a question of recognition — "What is the object's function?" To identify and recognize what something is, what it is called, and how best to respond to it involves higher level cognitive processes, which include your theories, memories, values, beliefs, and attitudes concerning the object.

We have now given you a brief introduction to the stages of processing that enable you to arrive at a meaningful understanding of the perceptual world around you. We will devote the bulk of our attention here to aspects of perception beyond the initial transduction of physical energy. In everyday life, perception seems to be entirely effortless. We will try, beginning in the next section, to convince you that you actually do quite a bit of sophisticated processing, a lot of mental work, to arrive at this "illusion of ease."

6.1.1   The Proximal and Distal Stimulus

Imagine you are the person in figure 6.1, surveying a room from an easy chair. Some of the light reflected from the objects in the room enters your eyes and forms images on your retinas. Figure 6.1 shows what would appear to your left eye as you sat in the room. (The bump on the right is your nose, and the hand and knee at the bottom are your own.) How does this retinal image compare with the environment that produced it?

One very important difference is that the retinal image is *two-dimensional,* whereas the environment is *three-dimensional.* This difference has many consequences. For instance, compare the shapes of the physical objects in figure 6.1 with the shapes of their corresponding retinal images. The table, rug, window, and picture in the real-world scene are all rectangular, but only the image of the window actually produces a rectangle in your retinal image. The image of the picture is a trapezoid, the image of the table top is an irregular four-sided figure, and the image of the rug is actually three separate regions with more than 20 different sides! Here's our first perceptual puzzle: How do you manage to perceive all of these objects as simple, standard rectangles?

The situation is, however, even a bit more complicated. You can also notice that many parts of what you perceive in the room are not actually present in your retinal image. For instance, you perceive the vertical edge between the two walls as going all the way to the floor, but your retinal image of that edge stops at the table top. Similarly, in your retinal image parts of the rug are hidden behind the table; yet this does not keep you from correctly perceiving the rug as a single, unbroken rectangle. In fact, when you consider all the differences between the environmental objects and the images of them on your retina, you may be surprised that you perceive the scene as well as you do.

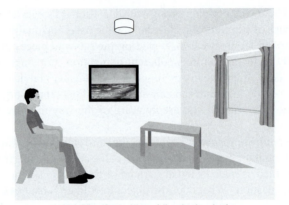

(a) Physical object (distal stimulus)

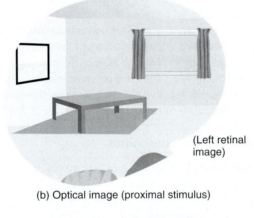

(Left retinal image)

(b) Optical image (proximal stimulus)

(Picture)   (Window)

(Tabletop)

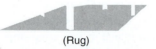

(Rug)

FIGURE 6.1 Interpreting retinal images.
a. Physical object (distal stimulus)
b. Optical image (proximal stimulus)

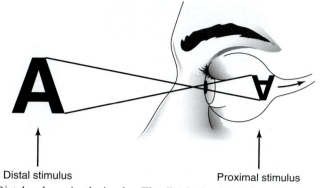

Distal stimulus   Proximal stimulus

FIGURE 6.2   Distal and proximal stimulus. The distal stimulus is the pattern or external condition that is sensed and perceived. The proximal stimulus is the pattern of sensory activity that is determined by the distal stimulus. As illustrated here, the proximal stimulus may resemble the distal stimulus, but they are separate events.

The differences between a physical object in the world and its optical image on your retina are so profound and important that psychologists distinguish carefully between them as two different stimuli for perception. The physical object in the world is called the *distal stimulus* (distant from the observer) and the optical image on the retina is called the *proximal stimulus* (proximate, or near, to the observer), as shown in figure 6.2.

The critical point of our discussion can now be restated more concisely: what you *perceive* corresponds to the *distal stimulus*—the "real" object in the environment—whereas the stimulus from which you must derive your information is the *proximal stimulus*—the image on the retina. The major computational task of perception can be thought of as the process of determining the distal stimulus from information contained in the proximal stimulus. This is true across perceptual domains. For hearing, touch, taste, and so on, perception involves processes that use information in the proximal stimulus to tell you about properties of the distal stimulus.

To show you how the distal stimulus and proximal stimulus fit with the three stages in perceiving, let's examine one of the objects in the scene from figure 6.1: the picture hanging on the wall. In the sensory stage, this picture corresponds to a two-dimensional trapezoid in your retinal image; the top and bottom sides converge toward the right, and the left and right sides are different in length. This is the proximal stimulus. In the perceptual organization stage, you see this trapezoid as a rectangle turned away from you in three-dimensional space. You perceive the top and bottom sides as parallel, but receding into the distance toward the right; you perceive the left and right sides as equal in length. Your perceptual processes have developed a strong *hypothesis* about the physical properties of the distal stimulus; now it needs an identity. In the recognition stage, you identify this rectangular object as a picture. Figure 6.3 is a flowchart illustrating this sequence of events. The processes that take information from one stage to the next are shown as arrows between the boxes. By the end of this chapter, we will explain all the interactions represented in this figure.

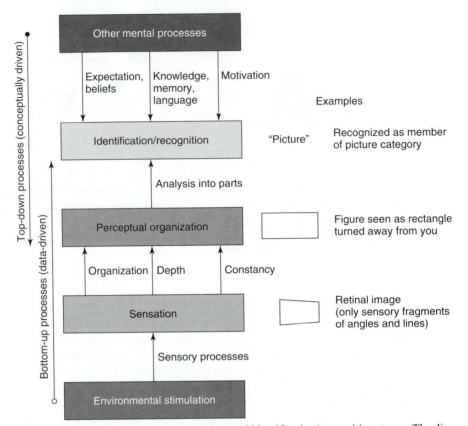

FIGURE 6.3   Sensation, perceptual organizing, and identification/recognition stages. The diagram outlines the processes that give rise to the transformation of incoming information at the stages of sensation, perceptual organization, and identification/recognition. Bottom-up processing occurs when the perceptual representation is derived from the information available in the sensory input. Top-down processing occurs when the perceptual representation is affected by an individual's prior knowledge, motivations, expectations, and other aspects of higher mental functioning.

6.1.2   Reality, Ambiguity, and Illusions

We have defined the task of perception as the identification of the distal stimulus from the proximal stimulus. Before we turn to some of the perceptual mechanisms that make this task successful, we want to discuss a bit more some other aspects of stimuli in the environment that make perception complex. Once again, you should look forward to learning how your perceptual processes deal with these complexities. We will discuss *ambiguous* stimuli and perceptual *illusions.*

Ambiguity.   A primary goal of perception is to get an accurate "fix" on the world. Survival depends on accurate perceptions of objects and events in your environment—Is that motion in the trees a tiger?—but the environment is not always easy to read. Take a look at the photo of black-and-white splotches in figure 6.4. What is it? Try to extract the

FIGURE 6.4   Ambiguous picture.

stimulus figure from the background. Try to see a dalmatian taking a walk. The dog is hard to find because it blends with the background, so its boundaries are not clear. (Hint: the dog is on the right side of the figure, with its head pointed toward the center.) This figure is *ambiguous* in the sense that critical information is missing, elements are in unexpected relationships, and usual patterns are not apparent. *Ambiguity* is an important concept in understanding perception because it shows that a *single image* at the sensory level can result in *multiple interpretations* at the perceptual and identification levels.

Figure 6.5 shows three examples of ambiguous figures. Each example permits two unambiguous but conflicting interpretations. Look at each image until you can see the two alternative interpretations. Notice that once you have seen both of them, your perception flips back and forth between them as you look at the ambiguous figure. This perceptual *instability* of ambiguous figures is one of their most important characteristics.

The vase/faces and the Necker cube are examples of ambiguity in the perceptual organization stage. You have two different perceptions of the same objects in the environment. The vase/faces can be seen as either a central white object on a black background or as two black objects with a white area between them. The Necker cube can be seen as a three-dimensional hollow cube either below you and angled to your left or above you and angled toward your right. With both vase and cube, the ambiguous alternatives are different physical arrangements of objects in three-dimensional space, both resulting from the same stimulus image.

The duck/rabbit figure is an example of ambiguity in the recognition stage. It is perceived as the same physical shape in both interpretations. The ambiguity arises in determining the kind of object it represents and in how best to classify it, given the mixed set of information available.

One of the most fundamental properties of normal human perception is the tendency to transform ambiguity and uncertainty about the environment into a clear interpretation that you can act upon with confidence. In a world filled with variability and change, your perceptual system must meet the challenges of discovering invariance and stability.

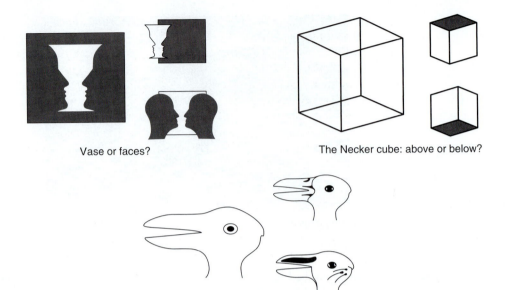

Vase or faces?   The Necker cube: above or below?

Duck or rabbit?

FIGURE 6.5   Perceptual ambiguities.

Illusions.   Ambiguous stimuli present your perceptual systems with the challenge of recognizing one unique figure out of several possibilities. One or another interpretation of the stimulus is correct or incorrect with respect to a particular context. When your perceptual systems actually deceive you into experiencing a stimulus pattern in a manner that is demonstrably incorrect, you are experiencing an *illusion*. The word *illusion* shares the same root as *ludicrous* — both stem from the Latin *illudere,* which means "to mock at." Illusions are shared by most people in the same perceptual situation because of shared physiology in sensory systems and overlapping experiences of the world. (This sets illusions apart from *hallucinations*. Hallucinations are nonshared perceptual distortions that individuals experience as a result of unusual physical or mental states.) Examine the classic illusions in figure 6.6. Although it is most convenient for us to present you with visual illusions, illusions also exist abundantly in other sensory modalities such as hearing (Bregman, 1981; Shepard & Jordan, 1984) and taste (Todrank & Bartoshuk, 1991).

Since the first scientific analysis of illusions was published by J. J. Oppel in 1854–1855, thousands of articles have been written about illusions in nature, sensation, perception, and art. Oppel's modest contribution to the study of illusions was a simple array of lines that appeared longer when divided into segments than when only its end lines were present:

| | | | | | | | | | | | | | | | | | | | | | | | | |

versus

| |

Oppel called his work the study of *geometrical optical illusions.* Illusions point out the discrepancy between percept and reality. They can demonstrate the abstract conceptual distinctions between sensation, perceptual organization, and identification and can help you understand some fundamental properties of perception (Cohen & Girgus, 1973).

Let's examine an illusion that works at the sensation level: the *Hermann grid,* in figure 6.7. As you stare at the center of the grid, dark, fuzzy spots appear at the intersections of the white bars. How does that happen? The answer lies in something you read about in the last chapter — *lateral inhibition.* Assume the stimulus is registered by ganglion retinal cells, two of which have their receptive fields drawn in the lower corner of the grid. The receptive

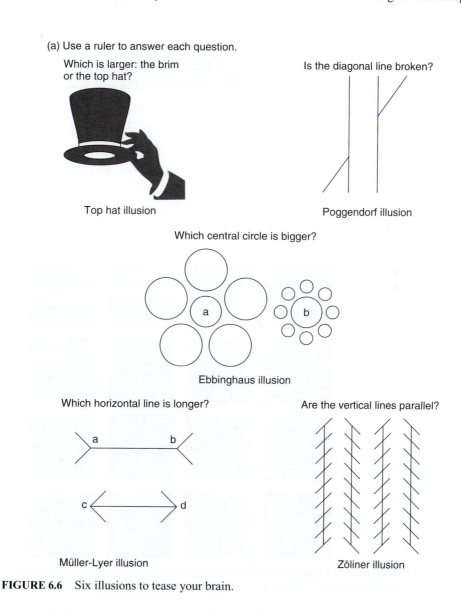

(a) Use a ruler to answer each question.

Which is larger: the brim or the top hat?

Top hat illusion

Is the diagonal line broken?

Poggendorf illusion

Which central circle is bigger?

Ebbinghaus illusion

Which horizontal line is longer?

Müller-Lyer illusion

Are the vertical lines parallel?

Zöliner illusion

FIGURE 6.6   Six illusions to tease your brain.

(b) Which of the boxes are the same size as the standard box? Which are definitely smaller or larger? Measure them to discover a powerful illusory effect.

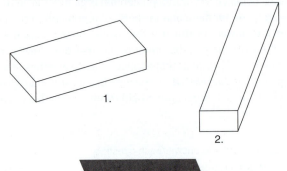

1.

2.

Standard

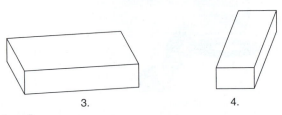

3.   4.

FIGURE 6.6   (continued)

FIGURE 6.7   The Hermann grid. Two ganglion-cell receptive fields are projected on this grid; it is an example of an illusion at the sensory stage.

field at the center of the intersection has two white bars projecting through its surround, while the neighboring receptive field has only one. The cell at the center, therefore, receives more light and can respond at a lower level because of the greater lateral inhibition by the surround. Its reduced response shows up as a dark spot in its center. Illusions at this level generally occur because the arrangement of a stimulus array sets off receptor processes in an unusual way that generates a distorted image.

Illusions in Reality.   Are illusions just peculiar arrangements of lines, colors, and shapes used by artists and psychologists to plague unsuspecting people? Hardly. Illusions are a basic part of your everyday life. They are an inescapable aspect of the subjective reality you construct. And even though you may recognize an illusion, it can continue to occur and fool you again and again.

Consider your day-to-day experience of your home planet, the earth. You've seen the sun "rise" and "set" even though you know that the sun is sitting out there in the center of the solar system as decisively as ever. You can appreciate why it was such an extraordinary feat of courage for Christopher Columbus and other voyagers to deny the obvious illusion that the earth was flat and sail off toward one of its apparent edges. Similarly, when a full moon is overhead, it seems to follow you wherever you go even though you know the moon isn't chasing you. What you are experiencing is an illusion created by the great distance of the moon from your eye. When they reach the earth, the moon's light rays are essentially parallel and perpendicular to your direction of travel, no matter where you go.

People can control illusions to achieve desired effects. Architects and interior designers use principles of perception to create objects in space that seem larger or smaller than they really are. A small apartment becomes more spacious when it is painted with light colors and sparsely furnished with low, small couches, chairs, and tables in the center of the room instead of against the walls. Psychologists working with NASA in the U.S. space program have researched the effects of environment on perception in order to design space capsules that have pleasant sensory qualities. Set and lighting directors of movies and theatrical productions purposely create illusions on film and on stage.

Despite all of these illusions — some more useful than others — you generally do pretty well getting around the environment. That is why researchers typically study illusions to help explain why perception ordinarily works so well. The illusions themselves suggest, however, that your perceptual systems cannot perfectly carry out the task of recovering the distal stimulus from the proximal stimulus.

6.1.3   Approaches to the Study of Perception

You now are acquainted with some of the major questions of perception: How does the perceptual system recover the structure of the environment? How is ambiguity resolved? Why do illusions arise? Before we move on to answer these questions, we need to give you more of a background in the types of theories that have dominated research on perception.

Many of the differences between these theories can be captured by the distinction between *nature* and *nurture*. At issue is how much of a head start you have in dealing with the perceptual world by virtue of your possession of the human genotype. Do you, as a *nativist* might argue, come into the world with some types of innate knowledge or brain structures that aid your interpretation of the environment? Or do you, as an *empiricist* might assert, come into the world with a relatively blank slate, ready to learn what there is to learn about the perceptual world? Most modern theorists agree that your experience of the world consists of a combination of nature and nurture. We will see, however, that these theorists disagree on the size of the portions that make up this combination.

Helmholtz's Classical Theory. In 1866, *Hermann von Helmholtz* argued for the importance of *experience*—or nurture—in perception. His theory emphasized the role of mental processes in interpreting the often ambiguous stimulus arrays that excite the nervous system. By using prior knowledge of the environment, an observer makes hypotheses, or inferences, about the way things really are. For instance, you would be likely to interpret your brief view of a four-legged creature moving through the woods as a dog rather than as a wolf. Perception is thus an *inductive* process, moving from specific images to inferences (reasonable hunches) about the general class of objects or events that the images might represent. Since this process takes place out of your conscious awareness, Helmholtz termed it *unconscious inference.* Ordinarily, these inferential processes work well. However, perceptual illusions can result when unusual circumstances allow multiple interpretations of the same stimulus or favor an old, familiar interpretation when a new one is required.

Helmholtz's theory broke perception down into two stages. In the first, *analytic* stage, the sense organs analyze the physical world into fundamental sensations. In the second, *synthetic* stage, you integrate and synthesize these sensory elements into perceptions of objects and their properties. Helmholtz's theory proposes that you learn how to interpret sensations on the basis of your experience with the world. Your interpretations are, in effect, informed guesses about your perceptions.

The Gestalt Approach. *Gestalt psychology,* founded in Germany in the second decade of the twentieth century, put greater emphasis on the role of innate structures—nature—in perceptual experience. The main exponents of Gestalt psychology, like *Kurt Koffka* (1935), *Wolfgang Köhler* (1947), and *Max Wertheimer* (1923), maintained that psychological phenomena could be understood only when viewed as organized, structured *wholes* and not when broken down into primitive perceptual elements. The term *Gestalt* roughly means "form," "whole," "configuration," or "essence." Gestalt psychology challenged atomistic views of psychology by arguing that the whole is more than the sum of its parts. For example, when you listen to music, you perceive whole melodies even though they are composed of separate notes. Gestalt psychologists argued that the holistic perception of the world arises because the cortex is organized to function that way. You organize sensory information the way you do because it is the most economical, simple way to organize the sensory input, given the structure and physiology of the brain. (Many of the examples of perceptual organization we will discuss in a later section were originated by the Gestaltists.)

Gibson's Ecological Optics. *James Gibson* (1966, 1979) proposed a very influential nativist approach to perception. Instead of trying to understand perception as a result of an organism's structure, Gibson suggested that it could be better understood through an analysis of the immediately surrounding environment (or its ecology). As one writer put it, Gibson's approach was, "Ask not what's inside your head, but what your head's inside of" (Mace, 1977). In effect, Gibson's *theory of ecological optics* was concerned with the perceived stimuli rather than with the mechanisms by which you perceive the stimuli. This approach was a radical departure from all previous theories. Gibson's ideas emphasized perceiving as *active exploration* of the environment. When an observer is *moving* in the world, the pattern of stimulation on the retina is constantly changing over time as well as over space. The theory of ecological optics tried to specify the information about the environment that was available to the eyes of a moving observer. Theorists in Gibson's tradition agree that perceptual systems evolved in organisms who were active — seeking food, water, mates, and shelter — in a complex and changing environment (Gibson, 1979; Pittenger, 1988; Shaw & Turvey, 1981; Shepard, 1984).

According to Gibson, the answer to the question "How do you learn about your world?" is simple. You directly pick up information about the *invariant,* or stable, properties of the environment. There is no need to take raw sensations into account or to look for higher level systems of perceptual inference — perception is direct. While the retinal size and shape of each environmental object changes, depending on the object's distance and on the viewing angle, these changes are not random. The changes are systematic, and certain properties of objects remain invariant under all such changes of viewing angles and viewing distances. Your visual system is tuned to detect such invariances because humans evolved in the environment in which perception of invariances was important for survival (Palmer, 1981).

Toward a Unified Theory of Perception.   These diverse theories can be unified to set the agenda for successful research on perception. You can recognize that the different perspectives contribute different insights to the three levels of analysis a theory of perception must address (Banks & Krajicek, 1991):

- *What are the Physiological Mechanisms Involved in Perception?*   This topic has its history in work with animals, and has more recently been addressed using neuroimaging techniques (see Part 19). The information impinging on the sensory receptors is often ambiguous. Stimulus-driven, or bottom-up processing, works its way up the brain, while expectation-driven, or top-down processing, complements it.
- *What is the process of perceiving?*   This question is usually tackled by researchers who follow in the tradition originated by Helmholtz and the Gestaltists. Modern researchers often try to understand how sources of information are combined to arrive at a perceptual interpretation of the world. These researchers compare the process of perception to conceptual problem solving (Beck, 1982; Kanizsa, 1979; Pomerantz & Kubovy, 1986; Rock, 1983, 1986; Shepp & Ballisteros, 1989). We will see some of their insights in the remaining sections of this chapter.
- *What are the properties of the physical world that allow you to perceive?*   This question makes contact with Gibson's theory. His central insight was that the world makes available certain types of information — and your perceptual apparatus is innately prepared to recover that information. Gibson's research made it clear that theories of perception must be constrained by accurate understandings of the environment in which people perceive.

We now begin our discussion of perceptual processes by considering what it means to select, or attend to, only a small subset of the information the world makes available.

6.2   ATTENTIONAL PROCESSES

We'd like you to take a moment now to find ten things in your environment that had not been, so far, in your immediate awareness. Had you noticed a spot on the wall? Had you noticed the ticking of a clock? If you start to examine your surroundings very carefully, you will discover that there are literally thousands of things on which you could focus your *attention.* Generally, the more closely you attend to some object or event in the environment, the more you can perceive and learn about it. That's why attention is an important topic in the study of perception: your focus of attention determines the types of information that will be most readily available to your perceptual processes. As you will now see, researchers have tried to understand what types of environmental stimuli require your attention and how attention contributes to your experience of those stimuli. We will start by considering how attention functions to selectively highlight objects and events in your environment.

6.2.1   Selective Attention

We began this section by asking that you try to find — to bring into attention — several things that had, up to that point, escaped your notice. This thought experiment illustrated an important function of attention: to select some part of the sensory input for further processing. Let us see how you make decisions about the subset of the world to which you will attend, and what consequences those decisions have for the information readily available to you.

Determining the Focus of Attention.   What forces determine the objects that become the focus of your attention? The answer to this question has two components, which we will call goal-directed selection and stimulus-driven capture (Yantis, 1993). *Goal-directed selection* reflects the choices that you make about the objects to which you'd like to attend, as a function of your own goals. You are probably already comfortable with the idea that you can explicitly choose objects for particular scrutiny. *Stimulus-driven capture* occurs when features of the stimuli — objects in the environment — themselves automatically *capture* your attention, independent of your local goals as a perceiver. Research suggests, for example, that new objects in a perceptual display automatically capture attention.

Consider the figure shown in part a of figure 6.8. How hard do you think it would be for you to identify the overall, global figure as an H? The answer will depend on the extent to which you have to attend to the local letters that make up the global figure. Parts b and c of the figure show how researchers manipulated attention. In each condition of the experiment, subjects were given a preview display that consisted of a figure 8 made of 8s. In the control condition, the figure 8 was complete. But, as you can see, in the novel object condition, there was a gap in the figure. What will happen if the next display you see fills in that gap? The researchers predicted that the object filling the gap (the novel object) would capture your attention — you couldn't help looking at it. And if your attention is focused on the letter S, you should find it harder than you ordinarily would to say that the global letter is an H.

That is exactly the result the researchers obtained. If you compare the two test displays in figure 6.8, you'll see that they are identical. In each case an S helps to make up the global H. However, it was only in the case when the S appeared in a space that was previously unoccupied that subjects' performance — the speed with which they could name the global letter — was impaired (Hillstrom & Yantis, 1994).

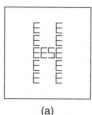

(a)

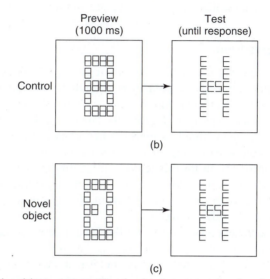

(c)

FIGURE 6.8   Stimulus-driven capture. How hard is it to recognize that the figure in (a) is an H? When the S fills a prior gap in the display (c), subjects find it more difficult to see that the overall figure is an H than they do in the control condition (b).

You can recognize this phenomenon as stimulus-driven capture, because it works in the opposite direction of the perceiver's goals. Because, that is, the subjects would perform the task better if they ignored the small S, they must be unable to ignore it (since subjects almost always prefer to perform as well as possible on the tasks researchers assign them). The important general conclusion is that your perceptual system is organized so that your attention is automatically drawn to objects that are new to an environment.

6.3   ORGANIZATIONAL PROCESSES IN PERCEPTION

Imagine how confusing the world would be if you were unable to put together and organize the information available from the output of your millions of retinal receptors. You would experience a kaleidoscope of disconnected bits of color moving and swirling before your eyes. The processes that put sensory information together to give you the perception of coherence are referred to collectively as processes of *perceptual organization*. You have seen that what a person experiences as a result of such perceptual processing is called a *percept*.

For example, your percept of the two-dimensional geometric design in part a of figure 6.9 is probably three diagonal rows of figures, the first being composed of squares, the second of arrowheads, and the third of diamonds. (We will discuss part b in a moment.) This probably seems unremarkable—but we have suggested in this chapter that all the seemingly effortless aspects of perception are made easy by sophisticated processing. Many of the organizational processes we will be discussing in this section were first described by Gestalt theorists who argued that what you perceive depends on laws of organization, or simple rules by which you perceive shapes and forms.

6.3.1   Region Segregation

Consider your initial sensory response to figure 6.9. Because your retina is composed of many separate receptors, your eye responds to this stimulus pattern with a mosaic of millions of independent neural responses coding the amount of light falling on tiny areas of your retina (see part b of figure 6.9). The first task of perceptual organization is to find coherent regions within this mosaic of responses. In other words, your perceptual system must combine the outputs of the separate receptors into appropriate larger units. The primary information for this region-segregating process comes from color and texture. An abrupt change in color (hue, saturation, or brightness) signifies the presence of a boundary between two regions. Abrupt changes in texture can also mark boundaries between visibly different regions.

Researchers now believe that the feature-detector cells in the visual cortex, discovered by Hubel and Wiesel, are involved in these region-segregating processes (Marr, 1982). Some cells have elongated receptive fields that are ideally suited for detecting boundaries between regions that differ in color. Others have receptive fields that seem to detect bars or lines—of the sort that occur in grassy fields, wood grains, and woven fabrics. These cortical line-detector cells may be responsible for your ability to discriminate between regions with different textures (Beck, 1972, 1982; Julesz, 1981a, b).

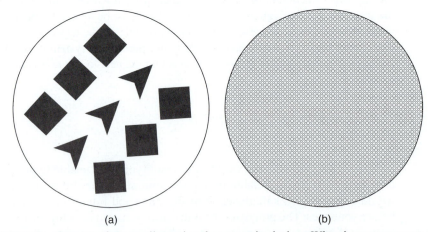

(a)   (b)

FIGURE 6.9   Percept of a two-dimensional geometric design. What is your percept of the geometrical design in a? b represents the mosaic pattern that stimulus a makes on your retina.

6.3.2   Figure, Ground, and Closure

As a result of region segregation, the stimulus in figure 6.9 has now been divided into ten regions: nine small dark ones and a single large light one. You can think of each of these regions as a part of a unified entity, such as nine separate pieces of glass combined in a stained-glass window. Another organizational process divides the regions into figures and background. A *figure* is seen as an objectlike region in the forefront, and *ground* is seen as the backdrop against which the figures stand out. In figure 6.9, you probably see the dark regions as figures and the light region as ground. However, you can also see this stimulus pattern differently by reversing figure and ground, much as you did with the ambiguous vase/faces drawing and the Escher art. To do this, try to see the white region as a large white sheet of paper that has nine holes cut in it through which you can see a black background.

The tendency to perceive a figure as being in *front* of a ground is very strong. In fact, you can even get this effect in a stimulus when the perceived figure doesn't actually exist! In the first image of figure 6.10, you probably perceive a fir tree set against a ground containing several gray circles on a white surface. Notice, however, that there is no fir tree shape; the figure consists only of three solid gray figures and a base of lines. You see the illusory white triangle in front because the straight edges of the red shapes are aligned in a way that suggests a solid white triangle. The other image in figure 6.10 gives you the illusion of one complete triangle superimposed on another, although neither is really there.

In this example, there seem to be three levels of figure/ground organization: the white fir tree, the gray circles, and the larger white surface behind everything else. Notice that, perceptually, you divide the white area in the stimulus into two different regions: the white triangle and the white ground. Where this division occurs, you perceive illusory *subjective contours* that, in fact, exist not in the distal stimulus but only in your subjective experience.

Your perception of the white triangle in these figures also demonstrates another powerful organizing process: closure. *Closure* makes you see incomplete figures as complete. Though the stimulus gives you only the angles, your perceptual system supplies the edges in between that make the figure a complete fir tree. Closure processes account for your tendency to perceive stimuli as complete, balanced, and symmetrical, even when there are gaps, imbalance, or asymmetry.

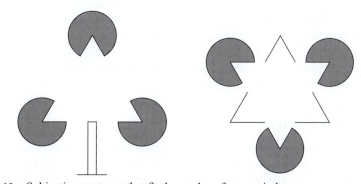

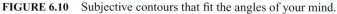

FIGURE 6.10   Subjective contours that fit the angles of your mind.

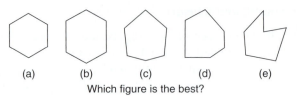

(a)   (b)   (c)   (d)   (e)

Which figure is the best?

FIGURE 6.11   Figural goodness — 1.

6.3.3   Shape: Figural Goodness and Reference Frames

Once a given region has been segregated and selected as a figure against a ground, the boundaries must be further organized into specific *shapes.* You might think that this task would require nothing more than perceiving all the edges of a figure, but the Gestaltists showed that visual organization is more complex. If a whole shape were merely the sum of its edges, then all shapes having the same number of edges would be equally easy to perceive. In reality, organizational processes in shape perception are also sensitive to something the Gestaltists called *figural goodness,* a concept that includes perceived simplicity, symmetry, and regularity. Figure 6.11 shows several figures that exhibit a range of figural goodness even though each has the same number of sides. Do you agree that figure A is the "best" figure and figure E the "worst"?

Experiments have shown that good figures are more easily and accurately perceived, remembered, and described than bad ones (Garner, 1974). Such results suggest that shapes of good figures can be coded more rapidly and economically by the visual system. In fact, the visual system sometimes tends to see a single bad figure as being composed of two overlapping good ones, as shown in figure 6.12.

Your perceptual system also relies on *reference frames* to identify a figure's shape. Consider figure 6.13. If you saw the left-hand image in A by itself, it would resemble a diamond, whereas the right-hand image would resemble a square. When you see these images as parts of diagonal rows, as shown in B, the shapes reverse: the line composed of diamonds resembles a tilted column of squares, and the line composed of squares resembles a tilted column of diamonds. The shapes look different because the orientation of each image is seen in relation to the reference frame established by the whole row (Palmer, 1984, 1989). In effect, you see the shapes of the images as you would if the rows were vertical instead of diagonal (turn the book 45 degrees clockwise to see this phenomenon).

There are other ways to establish a contextual reference frame that has the same effect. These same images appear inside rectangular frames tilted 45 degrees in C of figure 6.13. If you cover the frames, the left image resembles a diamond and the right one a square. When you uncover the frames, the left one changes into a square and the right one into a diamond.

6.3.4   Principles of Perceptual Grouping

In figure 6.9, you perceived the nine figural regions as being grouped together in three distinct rows, each composed of three identical shapes placed along a diagonal line. How does your visual system accomplish this *perceptual grouping,* and what factors control it?

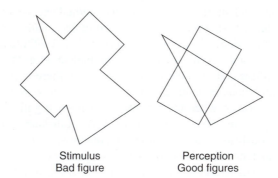

Stimulus
Bad figure

Perception
Good figures

FIGURE 6.12   Figural goodness — 2.

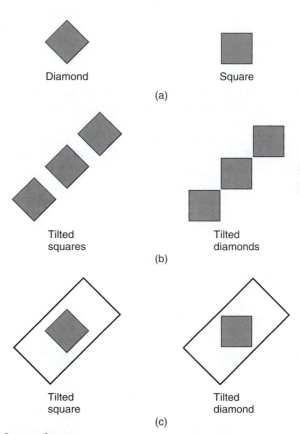

Diamond

Square

(a)

Tilted
squares

Tilted
diamonds

(b)

Tilted
square

Tilted
diamond

(c)

FIGURE 6.13   Reference frames.

The problem of grouping was first studied extensively by Gestalt psychologist Max Wertheimer (1923). Wertheimer presented subjects with arrays of simple geometric figures. By varying a single factor and observing how it affected the way people perceived the structure of the array, he was able to formulate a set of laws of grouping. Several of these laws are illustrated in figure 6.14. In section a, there is an array of equally spaced circles that is ambiguous in its grouping — you can see it equally well as either rows or columns of dots. However, when the spacing is changed slightly so that the horizontal distances between adjacent dots are less than the vertical distances, as shown in b, you see the array unambiguously as organized into horizontal rows; when the spacing is changed so that the vertical distances are less, as shown in c, you see the array as organized into vertical columns. Together, these three groupings illustrate Wertheimer's *law of proximity:* all else being equal, the nearest (most proximal) elements are grouped together. The Gestaltists interpreted such results to mean that the whole stimulus pattern is somehow determining the organization of its own parts; in other words, the *whole percept* is different from the mere collection of its *parts.*

In d, the color of the dots instead of their spacing has been varied. Although there is equal spacing between the dots, your visual system automatically organizes this stimulus into rows because of their *similar color.* You see the dots in e as being organized into columns because of *similar size,* and you see the dots in f as being organized into rows because of *similar shape* and *orientation.* These grouping effects can be summarized by the *law of similarity:* all else being equal, the most similar elements are grouped together.

When elements in the visual field are moving, similarity of motion also produces a powerful grouping. The *law of common fate* states that, all else being equal, elements moving in the same direction and at the same rate are grouped together. If the dots in every other column of g were moving upward, as indicated by the blurring, you would group the image into columns because of their similarity in motion. You get this effect at a ballet when several dancers move in a pattern different from the others. Remember Dr. Richard's observation that an object in his visual field became organized properly

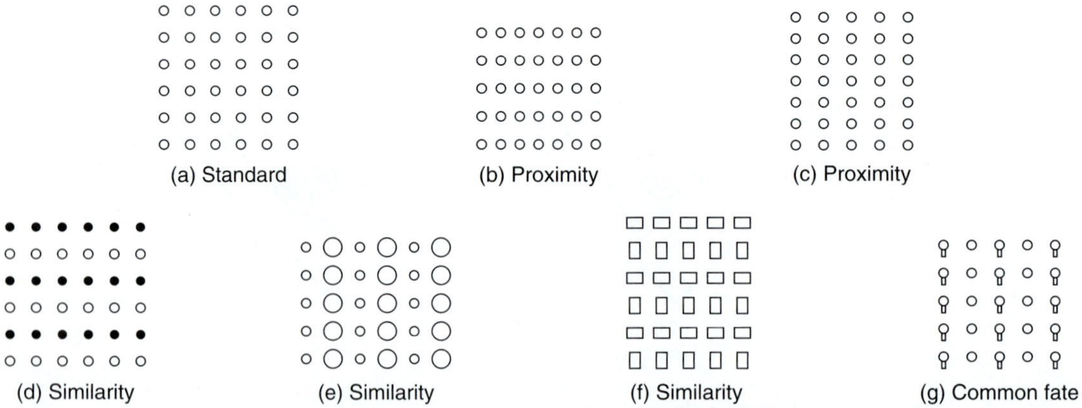

FIGURE 6.14   Grouping phenomena. We perceive each array from b through g as being organized in a particular way, according to different Gestalt principles of grouping.

when it moved as a whole. His experience was evidence of the powerful organizing effect of common fate.

Is there a more general way of stating the various grouping laws we have just discussed? We have mentioned the law of proximity, the law of similarity, the law of common fate, and the law of symmetry, or figural goodness. Gestalt psychologists believed that all of these laws are just particular examples of a general principle, the *law of pragnanz* (*pragnanz* translates roughly to "good figure"): you perceive the simplest organization that fits the stimulus pattern.

6.3.5   Spatial and Temporal Integration

All the Gestalt laws we have presented to you so far should have convinced you that a lot of perception consists of putting the pieces of your world together in the "right way." Often, however, you can't perceive an entire scene in one glance, or *fixation* (recall our discussion of attention). What you perceive at a given time is often a restricted glimpse of a large visual world extending in all directions to unseen areas of the environment. What may surprise you is that your visual system does not work very hard to create a moment-by-moment,

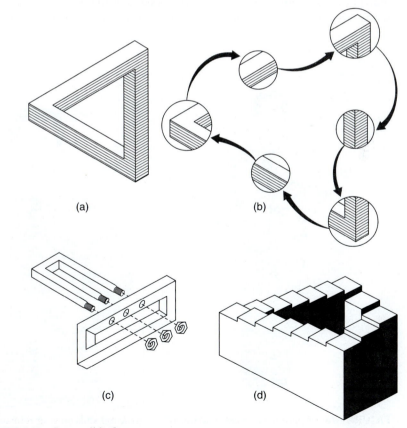

(a)

(b)

(c)

(d)

FIGURE 6.15   Impossible figures.

integrated picture of the environment. Research suggests that your visual memory for each fixation on the world does not preserve precise details (Irwin, 1991). Why is that so? Part of the answer might be that the world itself is generally a stable source of information (O'Regan, 1992). It is simply unnecessary to commit to memory information that remains steadily available in the external environment.

One interesting consequence of the way you treat the information from different fixations is that you are taken in by illusions called "impossible" objects, such as those in figure 6.15. For example, each fixation of corners and sides provides an interpretation that is consistent with an object that seems to be a three-dimensional triangle (image A); but when you try to integrate them into a coherent whole, the pieces just don't fit together properly (image B). Image C has two arms that somehow turn into three prongs right before your vigilant gaze, and the perpetual staircase in image D forever ascends or descends.

6.3.6   Motion Perception

One type of perception that does require you to compare across different glimpses of the world is motion perception. Consider the two images given in figure 6.16. Suppose that this individual has stood still while you have walked toward him. The size of his image on your retina has expanded as you have drawn near. The rate at which this image has expanded

FIGURE 6.16   Approaching man. The size of an image expands on your retina as you draw nearer to the stimulus.

gives you a sense of how quickly you have been approaching (Gibson, 1979). You use this type of information to navigate effectively in your world.

Suppose, however, you are still but other objects are in motion. The perception of motion, like the perception of shape and orientation, often depends on a reference frame. If you sit in a darkened room and fixate on a stationary spot of light inside a lighted rectangle that is moving very slowly back and forth, you will perceive instead a *moving* dot going back and forth within a *stationary* rectangle. This illusion, called *induced motion*, occurs even when your eyes are quite still and fixated on the dot. Your motion-detector cells are not firing at all in response to the stationary dot but presumably are firing in response to the moving lines of the rectangle. To see the dot as moving requires some higher level of perceptual organization in which the dot and its supposed motion are perceived within the reference frame provided by the rectangle.

There seems to be a strong tendency for the visual system to take a larger, surrounding figure as the reference frame for a smaller figure inside it. You have probably experienced induced motion many times without knowing it. The moon (which is nearly stationary) frequently looks as if it is moving through a cloud, when, in fact, it is the cloud that is moving past the moon. The surrounding cloud induces perceived movement in the moon just as the rectangle does in the dot (Rock, 1983, 1986). Have you ever been in a train that started moving very slowly? Didn't it seem as if the pillars on the station platform or a stationary train next to you might be moving backward instead?

Another movement illusion that demonstrates the existence of higher level organizing processes for motion perception is called *apparent motion.* The simplest form of apparent motion, the *phi phenomenon,* occurs when two stationary spots of light in different positions in the visual field are turned on and off alternately at a rate of about 4 to 5 times per second. This effect occurs on outdoor advertising signs and in disco light displays. Even at this relatively slow rate of alternation, it appears that a single light is moving back and forth between the two spots. There are multiple ways to conceive of the path that leads from the location of the first dot to the location of the second dot. Yet human observers normally see only the simplest path, a straight line (Cutting & Proffitt, 1982; Shepard, 1984). This straight-line rule is violated, however, when subjects are shown alternating views of a human body in motion. Then the visual system fills in the paths of normal biological motion (Shiffrar, 1994).

6.3.7   Depth Perception

Until now, we have considered only two-dimensional patterns on flat surfaces. Everyday perceiving, however, involves objects in three-dimensional space. Perceiving all three spatial dimensions is absolutely vital for you to approach what you want, such as interesting people and good food, and avoid what is dangerous, such as speeding cars and falling comets. This perception requires accurate information about *depth* (the distance from you to an object) as well as about its *direction* from you. Your ears can help in determining direction, but they are not much help in determining depth.

When you think about depth perception, keep in mind that the visual system must rely on retinal images that have only two spatial dimensions — vertical and horizontal. To illustrate the problem of having a 2-D retina doing a 3-D job, consider the situation shown in figure 6.17. When a spot of light stimulates the retina at point a, how do you know whether

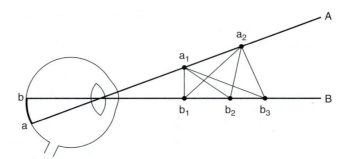

FIGURE 6.17   Depth ambiguity.

it came from position a_1 or a_2? In fact, it could have come from *anywhere* along line A, because light from any point on that line projects onto the same retinal cell. Similarly, all points on line B project onto the single retinal point b. To make matters worse, a straight line connecting any point on line A to any point on line B (a_1 to b_2 or a_2 to b_1, for example) would produce the same image on the retina. The net result is that the image on your retina is ambiguous in depth: it could have been produced by objects at any one of several different distances.

The two possible views of the Necker cube from figure 6.5 result from this ambiguity in depth. The fact that you can be fooled under certain circumstances shows that depth perception requires an *interpretation* of sensory input and that this interpretation can be wrong. (You already know this if you've ever swung at a tennis ball and come up only with air.) Your interpretation of depth relies on many different information sources about distance (often called *depth cues*) — among them binocular cues, motion cues, and pictorial cues.

Binocular and Motion Cues.   Have you ever wondered why you have two eyes instead of just one? The second eye is more than just a spare — it provides some of the best, most compelling information about depth. The two sources of binocular depth information are *binocular disparity* and *convergence.*

Because the eyes are about two to three inches apart horizontally, they receive slightly different views of the world. To convince yourself of this, try the following experiment. First, close your left eye and use the right one to line up your two index fingers with some small object in the distance, holding one finger at arm's length and the other about a foot in front of your face. Now, keeping your fingers stationary, close your right eye and open the left one while continuing to fixate on the distant object. What happened to the position of your two fingers? The second eye does not see them lined up with the distant object because it gets a slightly different view.

This displacement between the horizontal positions of corresponding images in your two eyes is called *binocular disparity.* It provides depth information because the amount of disparity, or difference, depends on the relative distance of objects from you (see figure 6.18). For instance, when you switched eyes, the closer finger was displaced farther to the side than was the distant finger.

When you look at the world with both eyes open, most objects that you see stimulate different positions on your two retinas. If the disparity between corresponding images in the

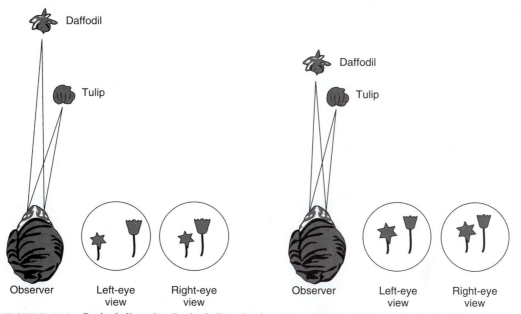

FIGURE 6.18   Retinal disparity. Retinal disparity increases with the distance, in depth, between two objects.

two retinas is small enough, the visual system is able to fuse them into a perception of a single object in depth. (However, if the images are too far apart, as when you cross your eyes, you actually see the double images.) When you stop to think about it, what your visual system does is pretty amazing: it takes two different retinal images, compares them for horizontal displacement of corresponding parts (binocular disparity), and produces a unitary perception of a single object in depth. In effect, the visual system interprets horizontal displacement between the two images as depth in the three-dimensional world.

Other binocular information about depth comes from *convergence.* The two eyes turn inward to some extent whenever they are fixated on an object (see figure 6.19). When the object is very close — a few inches in front of your face — the eyes must turn toward each other quite a bit for the same image to fall on both foveae. You can actually see the eyes converge if you watch a friend focus first on a distant object and then on one a foot or so away. Your brain uses information from your eye muscles to make judgments about depth. However, convergence information from the eye muscles is useful for depth perception only up to about 10 feet. At greater distances, the angular differences are too small to detect, because the eyes are nearly parallel when you fixate on a distant object.

To see how *motion* is another source for depth information, try the following demonstration. As you did before, close one eye and line up your two index fingers with some distant object. Then move your head to the side while fixating on the distant object and keeping your fingers still. As you move your head, you see both your fingers move, but the close finger seems to move farther and faster than the more distant one. The fixated object does not move at all. This source of information about depth is called *relative motion parallax.* Motion parallax provides information about depth because, as you move, the relative distances of objects in the world determine the amount and direction of their

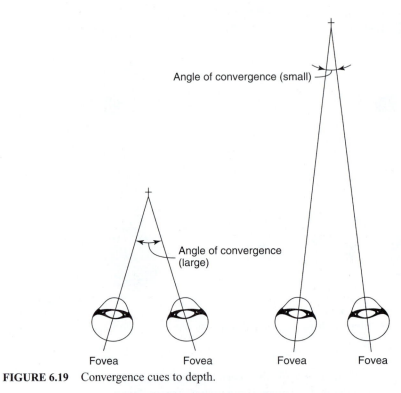

FIGURE 6.19   Convergence cues to depth.

FIGURE 6.20   Interposition cues to depth. What are the visual cues that tell you whether or not this woman is behind the bars?

relative motion in your retinal image of the scene. Next time you are a passenger on a car trip, you should keep a watch out the window for motion parallax at work. Objects at a distance from the moving car will appear much more stationary than those closer to you.

Pictorial Cues.   But suppose you had vision in only one eye. Would you not be able to perceive depth? In fact, further information about depth is available from just one eye. These sources are called *pictorial cues,* because they include the kinds of depth information found in pictures. Artists who create images in what appear to be three dimensions (on the two dimensions of a piece of paper or canvas) make skilled use of pictorial cues.

   Interposition, or *occlusion,* arises when an opaque object blocks out part of a second object (see figure 6.20). Interposition gives you depth information indicating that the occluded object is farther away than the occluding one. Occluding surfaces also block out light, creating shadows that can be used as an additional source of depth information.

   Three more sources of pictorial information are all related to the way light projects from a three-dimensional world onto a two-dimensional surface such as the retina: relative size, linear perspective, and texture gradients. *Relative size* involves a basic rule of light projection: objects of the same size at different distances project images of different sizes on the retina. The closest one projects the largest image and the farthest one the smallest image. This rule is called the *size/distance relation.* As you can see in figure 6.21, if you look at an array with identical objects, you interpret the smaller ones to be further away.

   Linear perspective is a depth cue that also depends on the size/distance relation. When parallel lines (by definition separated along their lengths by the same distance) recede into the distance, they converge toward a point on the horizon in your retinal image (see figure 6.22). This important fact was discovered around 1400 by Italian Renaissance artists, who were then able to paint depth compellingly for the first time (Vasari, 1967). Prior to their discovery, artists had incorporated in their paintings information from interposition, shadows, and relative size, but they had been unable to depict realistic scenes that showed objects at various depths.

   Your visual system's interpretation of converging lines gives rise to the *Ponzo illusion* (also shown in figure 6.22). The upper line looks longer because you interpret the converging sides according to linear perspective as parallel lines receding into the distance. In this context, you interpret the upper line as though it were farther away, so you see it as

FIGURE 6.21   Relative size as a depth cue.

FIGURE 6.22   The Ponzo illusion. The converging lines add a dimension of depth, and, therefore, the distance cue makes the top line appear larger than the bottom line, even though they are actually the same length.

longer—a farther object would have to be longer than a nearer one for both to produce retinal images of the same size.

   Texture gradients provide depth cues because the density of a texture becomes greater as a surface recedes in depth. The wheat field in figure 6.23 is an example of the way texture is used as a depth cue. You can think of this as another consequence of the size/distance relation. In this case, the units that make up the texture become smaller as they recede into the distance, and your visual system interprets this diminishing grain as greater distance in three-dimensional space. Gibson (1966, 1979) suggested that the relationship between texture and depth is one of the invariants available in the perceptual environment.

   By now, it should be clear that there are many sources of depth information. Under normal viewing conditions, however, information from these sources comes together in a single, coherent three-dimensional interpretation of the environment. You experience depth, not the different cues to depth that existed in the proximal stimulus. In other words, your visual system uses cues like differential motion, interposition, and relative size automatically, without your conscious awareness, to make the complex computations that give you a perception of depth in the three-dimensional environment.

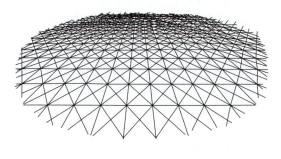

FIGURE 6.23 Examples of texture as a depth cue. The wheat field is a natural example of the way texture is used as a depth cue. Notice the way wheat slants. The geometric design uses the same principles.

6.3.8   Perceptual Constancies

To help you discover another important property of visual perception, we are going to ask you to play a bit with your textbook. Put your book down on a table, then move your head closer to it so that it's just a few inches away. Then move your head back to a normal reading distance. Although the book stimulated a much larger part of your retina when it was up close than when it was far away, didn't you perceive the book's size to remain the same? Now set the book upright and try tilting your head clockwise. When you do this, the image of the book rotates counterclockwise on your retina, but didn't you still perceive the book to be upright?

In general, you see the world as *invariant*, *constant*, and *stable* despite changes in the stimulation of your sensory receptors. Psychologists refer to this phenomenon as *perceptual constancy*. Roughly speaking, it means that you perceive the properties of the distal stimuli, which are usually constant, rather than the properties of proximal stimuli, which change every time you move your eyes or head. For survival, it is critical that you perceive constant and stable properties of objects in the world despite the enormous variations in the properties of the light patterns that stimulate your eyes. The critical task of perception is to discover *invariant* properties of your environment despite the *variations* in your retinal impressions of them. We will see how this works for size, shape, and orientation.

Size and Shape Constancy.   What determines your perception of the size of an object? In part, you perceive an object's actual size on the basis of the size of its retinal image. However, the demonstration with your book shows that the size of the retinal image depends on both the actual size of the book and its *distance* from the eye. As you now know, information about distance is available from a variety of depth cues. Your visual system combines that information with retinal information about image size to yield a perception of an object size that usually corresponds to the actual size of the distal stimulus. *Size constancy* refers to your ability to perceive the true size of an object despite variations in the size of its retinal image.

If the size of an object is perceived by taking distance cues into account, then you should be fooled about size whenever you are fooled about distance. One such illusion occurs in the Ames room shown in figure 6.24. In comparison to his 4-foot daughter, Tanya Zimbardo, your 6-foot-tall author looks quite short in the left corner of this room, but he looks enormous in the right corner. The reason for this illusion is that you perceive the room to be rectangular, with the two back corners equally distant from you. Thus you perceive Tanya's actual size as being consistent with the size of the images on your retina in both cases. In fact, Tanya is not at the same distance, because the Ames room creates a clever illusion. It appears to be a rectangular room, but it is actually made from nonrectangular surfaces at odd angles in depth and height, as you can see in the drawings that accompany the photos. Any person on the right will make a larger retinal image, because he or she is twice as close to the observer.

Another way that the perceptual system can infer objective size is by using prior knowledge about the characteristic size of similarly shaped objects. For instance, once you recognize the shape of a house, a tree, or a dog, you have a pretty good idea of how big each is, even without knowing its distance from you. Universal Studios in Hollywood uses your expectations about the normal sizes of doors to make its actors in westerns look bigger or smaller to you. The doors on one side of the street on a western set are made to be smaller

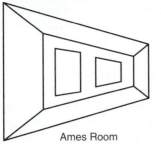
Ames Room

Viewer

FIGURE 6.24   The Ames room.

than the doors on the other side of the street. When shooting the scenes of the westerns, directors position male actors on the side of the street with small doors. This makes them look bigger. Female actors, on the other hand, get filmed on the other side of the street, against the background of large doors, which makes them look petite.

When past experience does not give you knowledge of what familiar objects look like at extreme distances, size constancy may break down. You have experienced this problem if you have looked down at people from the top of a skyscraper and thought that they resembled ants. Consider, also, the experience of a man named Kenge of the equatorial Africa Pygmy culture. Kenge had lived in dense tropical forests all his life. He had occasion, one day, to travel by car for the first time across an open plain with anthropologist Colin Turnbull. Later, Turnbull described Kenge's reactions.

Kenge looked over the plains and down to where a herd of about a hundred buffalo were grazing some miles away. He asked me what kind of *insects* they were, and I told him they were buffalo, twice as big as the forest buffalo known to him. He laughed loudly and told me not to tell such stupid stories, and asked me again what kind of insects they were. He then talked to himself, for want of more intelligent company, and tried to liken the buffalo to the various beetles and ants with which he was familiar.

He was still doing this when we got into the car and drove down to where the animals were grazing. He watched them getting larger and larger, and though he was as courageous as any Pygmy, he moved over and sat close to me and muttered that it was witchcraft.... Finally, when he realized that they were real buffalo he was no longer afraid, but what puzzled him still was why they had been so small, and whether they *really* had been small and had so suddenly grown larger, or whether it had been some kind of trickery. (Turnbull, 1961, p. 305)

In this unfamiliar perceptual environment, Kenge first tried to fit his novel perceptions into a familiar context, by assuming the tiny, distant specks he saw were insects. With no previous experience seeing buffalo at a distance, he had no basis for size constancy, and as the fast-moving car approached them and Kenge's retinal images got larger and larger, he had the frightening illusion that the animals were changing in size. We can assume that, over time, Kenge would have come to see them as Turnbull did. The knowledge he acquired would allow him to arrive at an appropriate perceptual interpretation for his sensory experience.

Shape constancy is closely related to size constancy. You perceive an object's actual shape correctly even when the object is slanted away from you, making the shape of the retinal image substantially different from that of the object itself. For instance, a rectangle tipped away projects a trapezoidal image onto your retina; a circle tipped away from you

FIGURE 6.25   Shape constancy. As a coin is rotated, its image becomes an ellipse that grows narrower and narrower until it becomes a thin rectangle, an ellipsis again, and then a circle. At each orientation, however, it is still perceived as a circular coin.

projects an elliptical image (see figure 6.25). Yet you usually perceive the shapes accurately as a circle and a rectangle slanted away in space. When there is good depth information available, your visual system can determine an object's true shape simply by taking into account your distance from its different parts.

Orientation Constancy.   When you tilted your head to the side in viewing your book, the world did not seem to tilt; only your own head did. *Orientation constancy* is your ability to recognize the true orientation of the figure in the real world, even though its orientation in the retinal image is changed. Orientation constancy relies on output from the vestibular system in your inner ear—which makes available information about the way in which your head is tilted. By combining the output of the vestibular system with retinal orientation, your visual system is usually able to give you an accurate perception of the orientation of an object in the environment.

In familiar environments, prior knowledge provides additional information about objective orientation. However, you may not be good at recognizing complex and unfamiliar figures when they are seen in unusual orientations. Can you recognize the shape in figure 6.26? When a figure is complex and consists of subparts, you must adjust for the orientation of each part separately (Rock, 1986). So, while you rotate one part to its proper orientation, other parts are still perceived as unrotated. [. . .] It is also a function of years of perceptual training to see the world right side up and to perceive faces in their usual orientation.

6.4   IDENTIFICATION AND RECOGNITION PROCESSES

You can think of all the perceptual processes described so far as providing reasonably accurate knowledge about physical properties of the distal stimulus—the position, size, shape, texture, and color of objects in a three-dimensional environment. With just this knowledge and some basic motor skills, you would be able to walk around without bumping into anything and manipulate objects that were small and light enough to move. However, you would

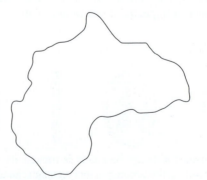

FIGURE 6.26   Africa rotated 90 degrees.

not know what the objects were or whether you had seen them before. Your experience would resemble a visit to an alien planet where everything was new to you; you wouldn't know what to eat, what to put on your head, what to run away from, or what to date. Your environment appears nonalien because you are able to recognize and identify most objects as things you have seen before and as members of the meaningful categories that you know about from experience. Identification and recognition attach meaning to percepts.

6.4.1   Bottom-up and Top-down Processes

When you identify an object, you must match what you see against your stored knowledge. Taking sensory data into the system and sending it upward for extraction and analysis of relevant information is called bottom-up processing. *Bottom-up processing* is anchored in empirical reality and deals with bits of information and the transformation of concrete, physical features of stimuli into abstract representations. This type of processing is also called *data-driven* processing, because your starting point for identification is the sensory evidence you obtain from the environment — the data.

In many cases, however, you can use information you already have about the environment to help you make a perceptual identification. If you visit a zoo, for example, you might be a little more ready to recognize some types of animals than you otherwise would

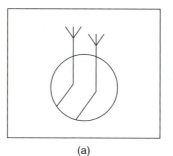

(a)

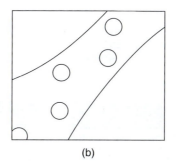

(b)

FIGURE 6.27   Droodles. What are these animals? Do you see in (a) an early bird who caught a very strong worm and in (b) a giraffe's neck? Each of these figures can be seen as representing something familiar to you, although this perceptual recognition usually does not occur until some identifying information is provided.

be. You are more likely to hypothesize that you are seeing a tiger than you would be in your own back yard. When your expectations affect perception, the phenomenon is called top-down processing. *Top-down processing* involves your past experiences, knowledge, motivations, and cultural background in perceiving the world. With top-down processing, higher mental functioning influences how you understand objects and events. Top-down processing is also known as *conceptually driven* (or hypothesis-driven) processing, because the concepts you have stored in memory are affecting your interpretation of the sensory data. The importance of top-down processing can be illustrated by drawings known as *droodles* (Price, 1953/1980). Without the labels, these drawings are meaningless. However, once the drawings are identified, you can easily find meaning in them (see figure 6.27).

For a more detailed example of top-down versus bottom-up processing, we turn to the domain of speech perception. You have undoubtedly had the experience of trying to carry on a conversation at a very loud party. Under those circumstances, it's probably true that not all of the physical signal you are producing arrives unambiguously at your acquaintance's ears: some of what you had to say was almost certainly obscured by coughs, thumping music, or peals of laughter. Even so, people rarely realize that there are gaps in the physical signal they are experiencing. This phenomenon is known as *phonemic restoration* (Warren, 1970). Samuel (1981, 1991) has shown that subjects often find it difficult to tell whether they are hearing a word that has a noise replacing part of the original

The soldier's thoughts of the dangerous

or { bat   (Noise added to signal; subject hears both "tie" and noise)

{ bat   (Noise replaces signal: subject hears only noise)

made him very nervous.

(a)

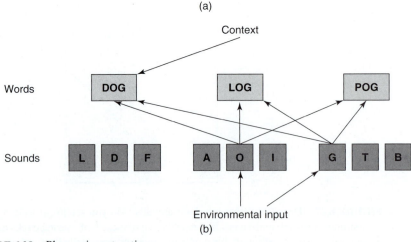

(b)

FIGURE 6.28   Phonemic restoration.

speech signal or whether they are hearing a word with a noise just superimposed on the intact signal (see the top panel of figure 6.28).

The bottom panel of figure 6.28 shows how bottom-up and top-down processes could interact to produce phonemic restoration (McClelland & Elman, 1986). Suppose part of what your friend says at a noisy party is obscured so that the signal that arrives at your ears is "I have to go home to walk my (noise)og." If noise covers the /d/, you are likely to think that you actually heard the full word *dog.* But why? In figure 6.28, you see two of the types of information relevant to speech perception. We have the individual sounds that make up words, and the words themselves. When the sounds /o/ and /g/ arrive in this system, they provide information — in a bottom-up fashion — to the word level (we have given only a subset of the words in English that end with /og/). This provides you with a range of candidates for what your friend might have said. Now top-down processes go to work — the context helps you select *dog* as the most likely word to appear in this utterance. When all of this happens swiftly enough — bottom-up identification of a set of candidate words and top-down selection of the likely correct candidate — you'll never know that the /d/ was missing. Your perceptual processes believe that the word was intact. (You may want to review figure 6.3 to see how everything in this chapter fits together.)

6.4.2   Object Recognition

From the example of speech perception, we can derive a general approach that researchers bring to the bottom-up study of recognition: they try to determine the building blocks that perceptual systems use to recognize whole percepts. For language, your speech perception processes combine environmental information about series of sounds to recognize individual words. What are the units from which you construct your representations of objects in the world? How, for example, do you decide that a gray, oddly shaped, medium-size, furry thing is actually a cat? Presumably, you have a memory representation of a cat. The identification process consists in matching the information in the percept to your memory representation of the cat. But how are these matches accomplished? One possibility is that the memory representations of various objects consist of components and information about the way these components are attached to each other (Marr & Nishihara, 1978). *Irving Biederman* (1985, 1987) has proposed that all objects can be assembled from a set of *geometrical ions,* or *geons.* Geons are not a large or arbitrary set of shapes. Biederman argued that a set of 36 geons can be defined by following the rule that each three-dimensional geon creates a unique pattern of stimulation on the two-dimensional retina. This uniqueness rule would allow you to work backward from a pattern of sensory stimulation to a strong guess at what the environmental object was like. Figure 6.29 gives examples of the way in which objects can be assembled from this collection of standard parts.

Researchers have shown that such parts do, in fact, play a role in object recognition. They have done so by presenting subjects with degraded pictures of objects that either do or do not leave parts intact (Biederman, 1987; Biederman & Cooper, 1991). The first column of figure 6.30 shows line drawings of common objects. The middle column shows those same objects with only information deleted that still allows you to detect what the parts are and how they are combined. The right-hand column presents deletions that disrupt the identities of and relationships between the parts. Do you agree that it would be hard for you to recognize

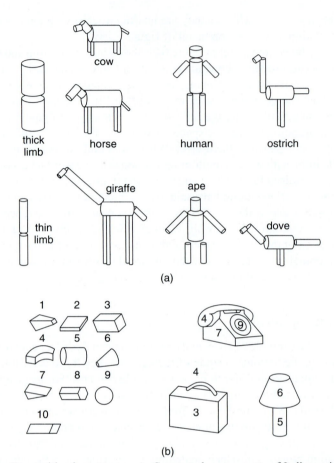

FIGURE 6.29   Recognition by components. Suggested components of 3-dimensional objects and examples of how they may combine. In the top half of the figure, each 3-D object is constructed of cylinders of different sizes. In the bottom half of the figure, several different building blocks are combined to form familiar objects.

some of these objects based just on the drawings in the third column? The contrast here suggests that you can recognize objects with limited information (just as you can restore missing phonemes), but not if that information disrupts the critical parts.

Recovery of components alone, however, will not always be sufficient to recognize an object (Tarr, 1994). One difficulty, as shown in figure 6.31, is that you often see objects from radically different perspectives. The appearance of the parts that make up the object may be quite different from each of these perspectives. As a hedge against this difficulty, you must store separate memory representations for each of the major perspectives from which you view standard objects (Tarr & Pinker, 1989). When you encounter an object in the environment, you may have to mentally transform the percept to determine if it correctly matches one of those views. Thus to recognize a gray, oddly shaped, medium-size, furry thing as a

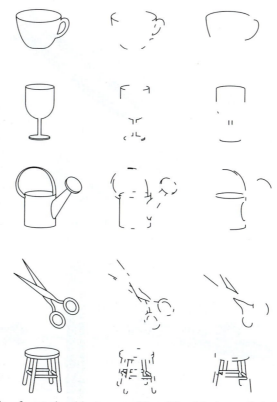

FIGURE 6.30   Role of parts in object recognition. The deletions of visual information in the middle column leave the parts intact. In the right-hand column, the deletions disrupt the parts. Do you agree that the objects are easier to recognize in the middle versions?

cat, you must recognize it both as an appropriate combination of geons and as that appropriate combination of geons from a specific viewpoint.

6.4.3   The Influence of Contexts and Expectations

What also might help you recognize the cat, however, is to find that gray, oddly shaped, medium-size, furry thing in its accustomed place in your home. This is the top-down aspect of perception: expectations can influence your hypotheses about what is out there in the world. Have you ever had the experience of seeing people you knew in places where you didn't expect to see them, such as in the wrong city or the wrong social group? It takes much longer to recognize them in such situations, and sometimes you aren't even sure that you really know them. The problem is not that they look any different but that the *context* is wrong; you didn't *expect* them to be there. The spatial and temporal context in which objects are recognized provides an important source of information, because from the context you generate expectations about what objects you are and are not likely to see nearby (Biederman, 1989).

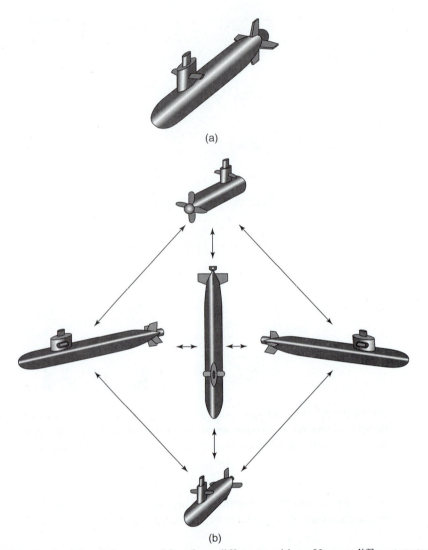

(a)

(b)

FIGURE 6.31   Looking at the same object from different positions. You see different parts of an object when you view it from different perspectives. To overcome this difficulty, you store multiple views of complex objects in memory.

Perceptual identification depends on your expectations as well as on the physical properties of the objects you see — *object identification is a constructive, interpretive process.* Depending on what you already know, where you are, and what else you see around you, your identification may vary. Read the following words:

They say *THE CAT,* right? Now look again at the middle letter of each word. Physically, these two letters are exactly the same, yet you perceived the first as an H and the second as an A. Why? Clearly, your perception was affected by what you know about words in English. The context provided by T_E makes an H highly likely and an A unlikely, whereas the reverse is true of the context of C_T (Selfridge, 1955).

Researchers have often documented the effects of context and expectation on your perception (and response) by studying set. *Set* is a temporary readiness to perceive or react to a stimulus in a particular way. There are three types of set: motor, mental, and perceptual. A *motor set* is a readiness to make a quick, prepared response. A runner trains by perfecting a motor set to come out of the blocks as fast as possible at the sound of the starting gun. A *mental set* is a readiness to deal with a situation, such as a problem-solving task or a game, in a way determined by learned rules, instructions, expectations, or habitual tendencies. A mental set can actually prevent you from solving a problem when the old rules don't seem to fit the new situation. A *perceptual set* is a readiness to detect a particular stimulus in a given context. A new mother, for example, is perceptually set to hear the cries of her child.

Often a set leads you to change your interpretation of an ambiguous stimulus. Consider these two series of words:

FOX; OWL; SNAKE; TURKEY; SWAN; D?CK
BOB; RAY; DAVE; BILL; HENRY; D?CK

Did you read through the lists? What word came to mind for D? CK in each case? If you thought DUCK and DICK, it's because the list of words created a set that directed your search of memory in a particular way.

Labels can provide a context that gives a perceptual set for an ambiguous figure. You have seen how meaningless droodles turn into meaningful objects. Look carefully at the picture of the woman in figure 6.32a; have a friend (but not you) examine figure 6.32b. Next, together look at figure 6.32c — what does each of you see? Did the prior exposure to the unambiguous pictures with their labels have any effect on perception of the ambiguous image? This demonstration shows how easy it is for people to develop different views of the same person or object, based on prior conditions that create different sets.

All the effects of context on perception clearly require that your memory be organized in such a fashion that information relevant to particular situations becomes available at the right times. In other words, to generate appropriate (or inappropriate) expectations, you must be able to make use of prior knowledge stored in memory. Sometimes you "see" with your memory as much as you see with your eyes.

6.4.4   Creatively Playful Perception

Because of your ability to go beyond the sensory gifts that evolution has bestowed on the human species, you can become more creative in the way you perceive the world. Your role model is not a perfectly programmed computerized robot with exceptional sensory acuity. Instead, it is a great artist like Pablo Picasso. Picasso's genius was, in part, attributable to his

FIGURE 6.32a   A young beauty.

FIGURE 6.32b   An old woman.

FIGURE 6.32c   Now what do you see?

enormous talent for "playful perception." This artist could free himself from the bonds of perceptual and mental sets to see not the old in the new but the new in the old, the novel in the familiar, and the unusual figure concealed within the familiar ground.

Perceptual creativity involves experiencing the world in ways that are imaginative, personally enriching, and fun (Leff, 1984). You can accomplish perceptual creativity by consciously directing your attention and full awareness to the objects and activities around you. Your goal should be to become more flexible in what you allow yourself to perceive and think, remaining open to alternative responses to situations.

We can think of no better way to conclude this formal presentation of the psychology of perception than by proposing ten suggestions for playfully enhancing your powers of perception:

- Imagine that everyone you meet is really a machine designed to look humanoid, and all machines are really people designed to look inanimate.
- Notice all wholes as ready to come apart into separately functioning pieces that can make it on their own.
- Imagine that your mental clock is hooked up to a video recorder that can rewind, fast-forward, and freeze time.
- Recognize that most objects around you have a "family resemblance" to other objects.
- View the world as if you were an animal or a home appliance.
- Consider one new use for each object you view (use a tennis racket to drain cooked spaghetti).
- Suspend the law of causality so that events just happen, while coincidence and chance rule over causes and effects.
- Dream up alternative meanings for the objects and events in your life.
- Discover something really interesting about activities and people you used to find boring.
- Violate some of the assumptions that you and others have about what you would and wouldn't do (without engaging in a dangerous activity).

6.4.5   Final Lessons

The important lesson to be learned from the study of perception is that a perceptual experience in response to a stimulus event is a response of the whole person. In addition to the information provided when your sensory receptors are stimulated, your final perception depends on who you are, whom you are with, and what you expect, want, and value. A perceiver often plays two different roles that we can compare to gambling and interior design. As a gambler, a perceiver is willing to bet that the present input can be understood in terms of past knowledge and personal theories. As a compulsive interior decorator, a perceiver is constantly rearranging the stimuli so that they fit better and are more coherent. Incongruity and messy perceptions are rejected in favor of those with clear, clean, consistent lines.

If perceiving were completely bottom-up, you would be bound to the same mundane, concrete reality of the here and now. You could register experience but not profit from it on later occasions, nor would you see the world differently under different circumstances.

If perceptual processing were completely top-down, however, you could become lost in your own fantasy world of what you expect and hope to perceive. A proper balance between the two extremes achieves the basic goal of perception: to experience what is out there in a way that maximally serves your needs as a biological and social being moving about and adapting to your physical and social environment.

6.5   RECAPPING MAIN POINTS

6.5.1   Sensing, Organizing, Identifying, and Recognizing

Your perceptual systems do not simply record information about the external world but actively organize and interpret information as well. Perception is a three-stage process consisting of a sensory stage, a perceptual organization stage, and an identification and recognition stage. At the sensory level of processing, physical energy is detected and transformed into neural energy and sensory experience. At the organizational level, brain processes organize sensations into coherent images and give you perception of objects and patterns. At the level of identification, percepts of objects are compared with memory representations in order to be recognized as familiar and meaningful objects. The task of perception is to determine what the distal (external) stimulus is from the information contained in the proximal (sensory) stimulus. Ambiguity may arise when the same sensory information can be organized into different percepts. Knowledge about perceptual illusions can give you clues about normal organizing processes.

[. . .]

6.5.2   Organizational Processes in Perception

Organizational processes provide percepts consistent with the sensory data. These processes segregate your percepts into regions and organize them into figures that stand out against the ground. You tend to see incomplete figures as wholes; group items by similarity; and see "good" figures more readily. You tend to organize and interpret parts in relation to the spatial and temporal context in which you experience them. You also tend to see a reference frame as stationary and the parts within it as moving, regardless of the actual sensory stimulus. In converting the two-dimensional information on the retina to a perception of three-dimensional space, the visual system gauges object size and distance: distance is interpreted on the basis of known size, and size is interpreted on the basis of various distance cues. You tend to perceive objects as having stable size, shape, and orientation. Prior knowledge normally reinforces these and other constancies in perception; under extreme conditions, perceptual constancy may break down.

6.5.3   Identification and Recognition Processes

During the final stage of perceptual processing — identification and recognition of objects — percepts are given meaning through processes that combine bottom-up and top-down influences. Context, expectations, and perceptual sets may guide recognition of incomplete or ambiguous data in one direction rather than another, equally possible one. Perception thus depends on what you know and expect as well as on the sensory stimulus.

REFERENCES

Beck, J. (1972). Similarity groupings and peripheral discriminality under uncertainty. *American Journal of Psychology, 85,* 1–20.

Beck, J. (Ed.) (1982). *Organization and representation in perception.* Hillsdale, NJ: Erlbaum.

Biederman, I. (1985). Recognition by components: A theory of object recognition. *Computer Vision Graphics and Image Processing, 32,* 29–73.

Biederman, I. (1987). Recognition by components. *Psychological Review, 94,* 115–147.

Biederman, I. (1989). Higher-level vision. In D. N. Osherson, H. Sasnik, S. Kosslyn, K. Hollerbach, E. Smith, & N. Block (Eds.), *An invitation to cognitive science.* Cambridge, MA: MIT Press.

Biederman, I., & Cooper, E. E. (1991). Priming contour-deleted images: Evidence for intermediate representations in visual object recognition. *Cognitive Psychology, 23,* 393–419.

Bregman, A. S. (1982). Asking the "what for" question in auditory perception. In M. Kobovy & J. Pomerantz (Eds.), *Perceptual organization* (pp. 99–118). Hillsdale, NJ: Erlbaum.

Cherry, E. C. (1953). Some experiments on the recognition of speech, with one and with two ears. *Journal of the Acoustical Society of America, 25,* 975–979.

Cohen, S., & Girgus, J. S. (1973). Visual spatial illustrations: Many explanations. *Science, 179,* 503–504.

Cutting, J., & Proffitt, D. (1982). The minimum principle and the perception of absolute, common, and relative motions. *Cognitive Psychology, 14,* 211–246.

Driver, J., & Tipper, S. (1989). On the nonselectivity of "selective" seeing: Contrasts between interference and priming in selective attention. *Journal of Experimental Psychology: Human Perception and Performance, 15,* 304–314.

Gibson, J. J. (1966). *The senses considered as perceptual systems.* Boston: Houghton Mifflin.

Gibson, J. J. (1979). *An ecological approach to visual perception.* Boston: Houghton Mifflin.

Hillstrom, A. P., & Yantis, S. (1994). Visual motor and attentional capture. *Perception & Psychophysics, 55,* 399–411.

Irwin, D. E. (1991). Information integration across saccadic eye movements. *Cognitive Psychology, 23,* 420–456.

Julesz, B. (1981a). Figure and ground perception in briefly presented isodipole textures. In M. Kubovy & J. R. Pomerantz (Eds.), *Perceptual organization* (pp. 27–54). Hillsdale, NJ: Erlbaum.

Julesz, B. (1981b). Textons, the elements of texture perception and their interaction. *Nature, 290,* 91–97.

Kanizsa, G. (1979). *Organization in vision.* New York: Praeger.

Leff, H. (1984). *Playful perception: Choosing how to experience your world.* Burlington, VT: Waterfront Books.

Mace, W. M. (1977). James J. Gibson's strategy for perceiving. Ask not what's inside your head, but what your head's inside of. In R. Shaw & J. Bransford (Eds.), *Perceiving, acting, and knowing.* Hillsdale, NJ: Erlbaum.

Marr, D. (1982). *Vision.* San Francisco: Freeman.

Marr, D., & Nishihara, H. K. (1978). Representations and recognition of the spatial organization of three-dimensional shapes. *Proceedings of the Royal Society of London (Series B), 200,* 269–294.

McClelland, J. L., & Elman, J. L. (1986). The TRACE model of speech perception. *Cognitive Psychology, 18,* 1–18.

O'Regan, J. K. (1992). Solving the "real" mysteries of visual perception: The world as an outside memory. *Canadian Journal of Psychology, 46,* 164–488.

Palmer, S. (1989). Reference frames in the perception of shape and orientation. In B. Shepp & M. Ballisteros (Eds.), *Object perception* (pp. 121–163). Hillsdale, NJ: Erlbaum.

Palmer, S. E. (1984). The psychology of perceptual organization: A transformational approach. In A. Rosenfeld & J. Beck (Eds.), *Human and machine vision.* New York: Academic Press.

Pittenger, J. B. (1988). Direct perception of change. *Perception, 17,* 119–133.

Pomerantz, J., & Kubovy, M. (1986). Theoretical approaches to perceptual oganization. In K. R. Boff, L. Kaufman, & J. P. Thomas (Eds.), *Handbook of perception and human performance* (Vol. 3, pp. 1–46). New York: Wiley.

Price, R. (1953/1980). *Droodles.* Los Angeles: Price/Stern/Sloan.

Rock, I. (1983). *The logic of perception.* Cambridge, MA: Bradford Books/MIT Press.

Rock, I. (1986). The description and analysis of object and event perception. In K. R. Boff, L. Kaufman, & J. P.

Thomas (Eds.), *Handbook of perception and human performance* (Vol. 2, pp. 33–71). New York: Wiley.

Rock, I., & Gutman, D. (1981). The effect of inattention on form perception. *Journal of Experimental Psychology: Human Perception and Performance, 7,* 275–285.

Selfridge, O. G. (1955). Pattern recognition and modern computers. *Proceedings of the Western Joint Computer Conference.* New York: Institute of Electrical and Electronics Engineers.

Shaw, R., & Turvey, M. T. (1981). Coalitions as models for ecosystems: A realist perspective on perceptual organization. In M. Kubovey & J. R. Pomerantz (Eds.), *Perceptual organization* (pp. 343–346). Hillsdale, NJ: Erlbaum.

Shepard, R. N. (1984). Ecological constraints on internal representation: Resonant kinematics of perceiving, imaging, thinking and dreaming. *Psychological Review, 91,* 417–447.

Shepard, R. N., & Johnson, D. S. (1984). Auditory illusions demonstrating that tomes are assimilated to an internalized musical scale. *Science, 226,* 1333–1334.

Shepp, B., & Ballisteros, M. (Eds.) (1989). *Object perception.* Hillsdale, NJ: Erlbaum.

Tarr, M. J. (1994). Visual representation: From features to objects. In V. S. Ramachandran (Ed.), *The encyclopedia of human behavior.* San Diego: Academic Press.

Tarr, M. J., & Pinker, S. (1989). Mental rotation and orientation-dependence in shape recognition. *Cognitive Psychology, 21,* 233–282.

Tipper, S. P., & Driver, J. (1988). Negative priming between pictures and words in a selective attention task: Evidence for semantic processing of ignored stimuli. *Memory and Cognition, 16,* 64–70.

Tipper, S. P., Weaver, B., Cameron, S., Brehaut, J. C., & Bastedo, J. (1991). Inhibitory mechanisms of attentions in identification and localization tasks: Time course and disruption. *Journal of Experimental Psychology: Learning, Memory, and Cognition, 17,* 681–692.

Todrank, J., & Bartoshuk, L. M. (1991). A taste illusion: Taste sensation localized by touch. *Physiology and Behavior, 50,* 1027–1031.

Treisman, A. (1960). Contextual cues in selective listening. *Quarterly Journal of Experimental Psychology, 12,* 242–248.

Treisman, A. (1986). Properties, parts and objects. In K. Boff, L. Kaufman, & J. Thomas (Eds.), *Handbook of perception and human performance* (Vol. 2). New York: Wiley.

Treisman, A. (1988). Features and objects. The fourteenth Bartlett Memorial Lecture. *The Quarterly Journal of Experimental Psychology, 40,* 20–237.

Treisman, A. (1992). Perceiving and re-perceiving objects. *American Psychologist, 47,* 862–875.

Treisman, A., & Gelade, G. (1980). A feature integration theory of attention. *Cognitive Psychology, 12,* 97–136.

Treisman, A., & Sato, S. (1990). Conjunction search revisited. *Journal of Experimental Psychology: Human Perception and Performance, 16,* 459–478.

Turnbull, C. (1961). *The forest people.* New York: Simon and Schuster.

Vasari, G. (1967). *Lives of the most eminent painters.* New York: Heritage.

Wertheimer, M. (1923). Untersuchengen zur lehre von der gestalt, II. *Psychologische Forschung, 4,* 301–350.

Wolfe, J. M. (1992). The parallel guidance of visual attention. *Current Directions in Psychological Science, 1,* 124–128.

Wolfe, J. M., Friedman-Hill, S. R., & Bilsky, A. B. (1994). Parallel processing of part-whole information in visual search tasks. *Perception & Psychophysics, 55,* 537–550.

Yantis, S. (1993). Stimulus-driven attentional capture. *Current Directions in Psychological Science, 2,* 156–161.

CHAPTER SEVEN

THE AUDITORY SCENE

ALBERT S. BREGMAN

7.1 HISTORICAL DIFFERENCE BETWEEN AUDITORY AND VISUAL PERCEPTION

If you were to pick up a general textbook on perception written before 1965 and leaf through it, you would not find any great concern with the perceptual or ecological questions about audition. By a perceptual question I mean one that asks how our auditory systems could build a picture of the world around us through their sensitivity to sound, whereas by an ecological one I am referring to one that asks how our environment tends to create and shape the sound around us. (The two kinds of questions are related. Only by being aware of how the sound is created and shaped in the world can we know how to use it to derive the properties of the sound-producing events around us.)

Instead, you would find discussions of such basic auditory qualities as loudness and pitch. For each of these, the textbook might discuss the psychophysical question: which physical property of the sound gives rise to the perceptual quality that we experience? It might also consider the question of how the physiology of the ear and nervous system could respond to those properties of sound. The most perceptual of the topics that you might encounter would be concerned with how the sense of hearing can tell the listener where sounds are coming from. Under this heading, some consideration would be given to the role of audition in telling us about the world around us. For the most part, instead of arising from everyday life, the motivation of much of the research on audition seems to have its origins in the medical study of deafness, where the major concerns are the sensitivity of the auditory system to weak sounds, the growth in perceived intensity with increases in the energy of the signal, and the effects of exposure to noise.

The situation would be quite different in the treatment of vision. It is true that you would see a treatment of psychophysics and physiology, and indeed there would be some consideration of such deficits as colorblindness, but this would not be the whole story. You would also find discussions of higher-level principles of organization, such as those responsible for the constancies. There would, for example, be a description of size constancy, the

From Bregman, Albert S., *Auditory Scene Analysis: The Perceptual Organization of Sound,* pp. 1–45, © 1990 Massachusetts Institute of Technology, by permission of The MIT Press.

fact that we tend to see the size of an object as unchanged when it is at a different distance, despite the fact that the image that it projects on our retinas shrinks as it moves further away. Apparently some complex analysis by the brain takes into account clues other than retinal size in arriving at the perceived size of an object.

Why should there be such a difference? A proponent of the "great man" theory of history might argue that it was because the fathers of Gestalt psychology, who opened up the whole question of perceptual organization, had focused on vision and never quite got around to audition.

However, it is more likely that there is a deeper reason. We came to know about the puzzles of visual perception through the arts of drawing and painting. The desire for accurate portrayal led to an understanding of the cues for distance and certain facts about projective geometry. This was accompanied by the development of the physical analysis of projected images, and eventually the invention of the camera. Early on, the psychologist was faced with the discrepancy between what was on the photograph or canvas and what the person saw.

The earlier development of sophisticated thinking in the field of visual perception may also have been due to the fact that it was much easier to create a visual display with exactly specified properties than it was to shape sound in equally exact ways. If so, the present-day development of the computer analysis and synthesis of sound ought to greatly accelerate the study of auditory perception.

Of course there is another possibility that explains the slighting of audition in the textbook: Perhaps audition is really a much simpler sense and there are no important perceptual phenomena like the visual constancies to be discovered.

This is a notion that can be rejected. We can show that such complex phenomena as constancies exist in hearing, too. One example is timbre constancy. A friend's voice has the same perceived timbre in a quiet room as at a cocktail party. Yet at the party, the set of frequency components arising from that voice is mixed at the listener's ear with frequency components from other sources. The total spectrum of energy that reaches the ear may be quite different in different environments. To recognize the unique timbre of the voice we have to isolate the frequency components that are responsible for it from others that are present at the same time. A wrong choice of frequency components would change the perceived timbre of the voice. The fact that we can usually recognize the timbre implies that we regularly choose the right components in different contexts. Just as in the case of the visual constancies, timbre constancy will have to be explained in terms of a complicated analysis by the brain, and not merely in terms of a simple registration of the input by the brain.

There are some practical reasons for trying to understand this constancy. There are engineers currently trying to design computers that can understand what a person is saying. However, in a noisy environment the speaker's voice comes mixed with other sounds. To a naive computer, each different sound that the voice comes mixed with makes it sound as if different words were being spoken or as if they were spoken by a different person. The machine cannot correct for the particular listening conditions as a human can. If the study of human audition were able to lay bare the principles that govern the human skill, there is some hope that a computer could be designed to mimic it.

7.2   THE PROBLEM OF SCENE ANALYSIS

It is not entirely true that textbooks ignore complex perceptual phenomena in audition. However, they are often presented as an array of baffling illusions.[1] They seem more like disconnected fragments than a foundation for a theory of auditory perception. My purpose in this book is to try to see them as oblique glimpses of a general auditory process of organization that has evolved, in our auditory systems, to solve a problem that I will refer to as "auditory scene analysis."

Let me clarify what I mean by auditory scene analysis. The best way to begin is to ask ourselves what perception is for. Since Aristotle, many philosophers and psychologists have believed that perception is the process of using the information provided by our senses to form mental representations of the world around us. In using the word representations, we are implying the existence of a two-part system: one part forms the representations and another uses them to do such things as calculate appropriate plans and actions. The job of perception, then, is to take the sensory input and to derive a useful representation of reality from it.

An important part of building a representation is to decide which parts of the sensory stimulation are telling us about the same environmental object or event. Unless we put the right combination of sensory evidence together, we will not be able to recognize what is going on. A simple example is shown in the top line of figure 7.1. The pattern of letters is meaningful, but the meaning cannot be extracted because the letters are actually a mixture from two sentences, and the two cannot be separated. However, if, as in the lower line of the figure, we give the eyes some assistance, the meaning becomes apparent.

This business of separating evidence has been faced in the design of computer systems for recognizing the objects in natural scenes or in drawings. Figure 7.2 shows a line drawing of some blocks.[2] We can imagine that the picture has been translated into a pattern in the memory of the computer by some process that need not concern us. We might think that once it was entered, all that we would have to do to enable the computer to decide which objects were present in the scene would be to supply it with a description of the shape of each possible one. But the problem is not as easy as all that. Before the machine could make any decision, it would have to be able to tell which parts of the picture represented parts of the same object. To our human eyes it appears that the regions labeled A and B are parts of a single block. This is not immediately obvious to a computer. In simple line drawings there is a rule that states that any white area totally surrounded by lines must depict a single surface. This rule implies that in figure 7.2 the whole of region A is part of a single surface. The reason for grouping region A with B is much more complex. The question of how it can be

FIGURE 7.1   Top line: a string of letters that makes no sense because it is a mixture of two messages. Bottom line: the component messages are segregated by visual factors.

Source: (From Bregman 1981.)

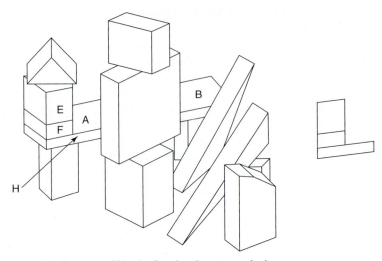

FIGURE 7.2   A line drawing of blocks for visual scene analysis.

Source: (After Guzman 1969.)

done can be set aside for the moment. The point of the example is that unless regions A and B are indeed considered part of a single object, the description that the computer will be able to construct will not be correct and the elongated shape formed out of A, B, and other regions will not be seen. It seems as though a preliminary step along the road to recognition would be to program the computer to do the equivalent of taking a set of crayons and coloring in, with the same color, all those regions that were parts of the same block. Then some subsequent recognition process could simply try to form a description of a single shape from each set in which the regions were the same color. This allocation of regions to objects is what is known to researchers in machine vision as the scene analysis problem.

There are similar problems in hearing. Take the case of a baby being spoken to by her mother. The baby starts to imitate her mother's voice. However, she does not insert into the imitation the squeaks of her cradle that have been occurring at the same time. Why not? A physical record of what she has heard would include them. Somehow she has been able to reject the squeak as not being part of the perceptual "object" formed by her mother's voice. In doing so, the infant has solved a scene analysis problem in audition.

It is important to emphasize again that the way that sensory inputs are grouped by our nervous systems determines the patterns that we perceive. In the case of the drawings of blocks, if areas E, F, and H were grouped as parts of the same object, we would see the L-shaped object shown at the right. The shape of the object formed by this grouping of areas is an emergent property, since it is not a property of any of the parts taken individually, but emerges only as a result of the grouping of the areas. Normally, in perception, emergent properties are accurate portrayals of the properties of the objects in our environment. However, if scene analysis processes fail, the emergent perceived shapes will not correspond to any environmental shapes. They will be entirely chimerical.

The difficulties that are involved in the scene analysis processes in audition often escape our notice. This example can make them more obvious. Imagine that you are on the edge of a lake and a friend challenges you to play a game. The game is this: Your friend digs two narrow channels up from the side of the lake. Each is a few feet long and a few inches wide and they are spaced a few feet apart. Halfway up each one, your friend stretches a handkerchief and fastens it to the sides of the channel. As waves reach the side of the lake they travel up the channels and cause the two handkerchiefs to go into motion. You are allowed to look only at the handkerchiefs and from their motions to answer a series of questions: How many boats are there on the lake and where are they? Which is the most powerful one? Which one is closer? Is the wind blowing? Has any large object been dropped suddenly into the lake?

Solving this problem seems impossible, but it is a strict analogy to the problem faced by our auditory systems. The lake represents the lake of air that surrounds us. The two channels are our two ear canals, and the handkerchiefs are our ear drums. The only information that the auditory system has available to it, or ever will have, is the vibrations of these two ear drums. Yet it seems to be able to answer questions very like the ones that were asked by the side of the lake: How many people are talking? Which one is louder, or closer? Is there a machine humming in the background? We are not surprised when our sense of hearing succeeds in answering these questions any more than we are when our eye, looking at the handkerchiefs, fails.

The difficulty in the examples of the lake, the infant, the sequence of letters, and the block drawings is that the evidence arising from each distinct physical cause in the environment is compounded with the effects of the other ones when it reaches the sense organ. If correct perceptual representations of the world are to be formed, the evidence must be partitioned appropriately.

In vision, you can describe the problem of scene analysis in terms of the correct grouping of regions. Most people know that the retina of the eye acts something like a sensitive photographic film and that it records, in the form of neural impulses, the "image" that has been written onto it by the light. This image has regions. Therefore, it is possible to imagine some process that groups them. But what about the sense of hearing? What are the basic parts that must be grouped to make a sound?

Rather than considering this question in terms of a direct discussion of the auditory system, it will be simpler to introduce the topic by looking at a spectrogram, a widely used description of sound. Figure 7.3 shows one for the spoken word "shoe." The picture is rather like a sheet of music. Time proceeds from left to right, and the vertical dimension represents the physical dimension of frequency, which corresponds to our impression of the highness of the sound. The sound of a voice is complex. At any moment of time, the spectrogram shows more than one frequency. It does so because any complex sound can actually be viewed as a set of simultaneous frequency components. A steady pure tone, which is much simpler than a voice, would simply be shown as a horizontal line because at any moment it would have only one frequency.

Once we see that the sound can be made into a picture, we are tempted to believe that such a picture could be used by a computer to recognize speech sounds. Different classes of speech sounds, stop consonants such as "b" and fricatives such as "s" for example, have characteristically different appearances on the spectrogram. We ought to be able to equip the computer with a set of tests with which to examine such a picture and to determine whether the shape representing a particular speech sound is present in the image. This makes the problem sound much like the one faced by vision in recognizing the blocks in figure 7.2.

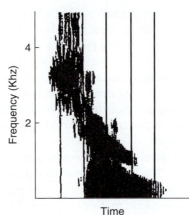

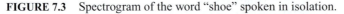

Time
(1 division = 10 msec)

FIGURE 7.3   Spectrogram of the word "shoe" spoken in isolation.

If a computer could solve the recognition problem by the use of a spectrogram, it would be very exciting news for researchers in human audition, because there is some reason to believe that the human auditory system provides the brain with a pattern of neural excitation that is very much like a spectrogram. Without going into too much detail, we can sketch this process as follows. As sound enters the ear, it eventually reaches a part called the inner ear where it affects an organ called the basilar membrane, a long coiled ribbon. Different frequency components in the incoming sound will cause different parts of this organ to vibrate most vigorously. It reacts most strongly to the lowest audible frequencies at one end, to the highest at the other, with an orderly progression from low to high in between. A different group of neurons connects with each location along the basilar membrane and is responsible for recording the vibration at that location (primarily). As the sound changes over time, different combinations of neural groups are activated. If we imagined the basilar membrane oriented vertically so that the neural groups responsive to the highest frequencies were at the top, and also imagined that each group was attached to a pen, with the pen active whenever a neural group was, the pens would write out a picture of the sound that looked like a spectrogram. So the brain has all the information that is visible in the spectrogram, and providing that it could store a record of this information for some brief period of time, it would have a neural spectrogram.

The account that I have just given hides a deep problem. The spectrographic record of most situations would not have the pristine purity of figure 7.3, which represents speech recorded in an absolutely quiet background. The real world is a great deal messier. A typical acoustic result is shown in figure 7.4. Here all the sounds are being mixed together in the listener's ear in exactly the same way that the waves of the lake, in our earlier example, were mixed in each of the channels that ran off it. The spectrogram for a mixture of sounds looks somewhat like a picture created by making a spectrogram of each of the individual sounds on a separate piece of transparent plastic, and then overlaying the individual spectrograms to create a composite. The spectrogram of the word shoe is actually one of the component spectrograms of the mixture.

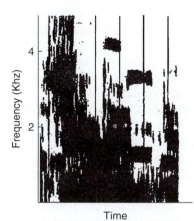

Time
(1 division = 10 msec)

FIGURE 7.4   A spectrogram of a mixture of sounds (containing the word "shoe").

Although the theorist has the privilege of building the composite up from the pictures of its components, the auditory system, or any machine trying to imitate it, would be presented only with the spectrogram of the mixture and would have to try to infer the set of pictures that was overlaid to produce it.

The recognizer would have to solve the following problems: How many sources have created the mixture? Is a particular discontinuity in the picture a change in one sound or an interruption by a second one? Should two dark regions, one above the other in the picture (in other words, occurring at the same time), be grouped as a single sound with a complex timbre or separated to represent two simultaneous sounds with simpler timbres? We can see that if we look at a spectrogram representing a slice of real life, we would see a complex pattern of streaks, any pair of which could have been caused by the same acoustic event or by different ones. A single streak could have been the summation of one, two, or even more parts of different sounds. Furthermore, the frequency components from one source could be interlaced with those of another one; just because one horizontal streak happens to be immediately above another, it does not mean that they both arose from the same sonic event.

We can see that just as in the visual problem of recognizing a picture of blocks, there is a serious need for regions to be grouped appropriately. Again, it would be convenient to be able to hand the spectrogram over to a machine that did the equivalent of taking a set of crayons and coloring in, with the same color, all the regions on the spectrogram that came from the same source. This "coloring problem" or "auditory scene analysis problem" is what the rest of this chapter is about.

7.3   OBJECTS COMPARED TO STREAMS

It is also about the concept of "auditory streams." An auditory stream is our perceptual grouping of the parts of the neural spectrogram that go together. To see the reasons for bringing in this concept, it is necessary to consider the relations between the physical world and our mental representations of it. As we saw before, the goal of scene analysis is the recovery of separate descriptions of each separate thing in the environment. What are these things? In vision, we are focused on objects. Light is reflected off objects, bounces back and forth between them, and eventually some of it reaches our eyes. Our visual sense uses this light to form separate descriptions of the individual objects. These descriptions include the object's shape, size, distance, coloring, and so on.

Then what sort of information is conveyed by sound? Sound is created when things of various types happen. The wind blows, an animal scurries through a clearing, the fire burns, a person calls. Acoustic information, therefore, tells us about physical "happenings." Many happenings go on at the same time in the world, each one a distinct event. If we are to react to them as distinct, there has to be a level of mental description in which there are separate representations of the individual ones.

I refer to the perceptual unit that represents a single happening as an auditory stream. Why not just call it a sound? There are two reasons why the word stream is better. First of all a physical happening (and correspondingly its mental representation) can incorporate more than one sound, just as a visual object can have more than one region. A series of footsteps, for instance, can form a single experienced event, despite the fact that each footstep is a separate sound. A soprano singing with a piano accompaniment is also heard as a coherent happening, despite being composed of distinct sounds (notes). Furthermore, the singer and piano together form a perceptual entity — the "performance" — that is distinct from other sounds that are occurring. Therefore, our mental representations of acoustic events can be multifold in a way that the mere word "sound" does not suggest. By coining a new word, "stream," we are free to load it up with whatever theoretical properties seem appropriate.

A second reason for preferring the word "stream" is that the word "sound" refers indifferently to the physical sound in the world and to our mental experience of it. It is useful to reserve the word "stream" for a perceptual representation, and the phrase "acoustic event" or the word "sound" for the physical cause.

I view a stream as a computational stage on the way to the full description of an auditory event. The stream serves the purpose of clustering related qualities. By doing so, it acts as a center for our description of an acoustic event. By way of analogy, consider how we talk about visible things. In our verbal descriptions of what we see, we say that an *object* is red, or that it is moving fast, that it is near, or that it is dangerous. In other words, the notion of an object, understood whenever the word "it" occurs in the previous sentence, serves as a center around which our verbal descriptions are clustered. This is not just a convenience of language. The perceptual representation of an object serves the same purpose as the "it" in the sentence. We can observe this when we dream. When, for some reason, the ideas of angry and dog and green are pulled out from our memories, they tend to coalesce into a single entity and we experience an angry green dog and not merely anger, greenness, and dogness taken separately. Although the combination of these qualities has never occurred in our experience, and therefore the individual qualities must have been dredged up from separate experiences, those qualities can be experienced visually only as properties of an *object*. It is this "belonging to an object" that holds them together.

The stream plays the same role in auditory mental experience as the object does in visual. When we want to talk about auditory units (the auditory counterparts of visual objects), we generally employ the word "sound." We say that a sound is high pitched or low, that it is rising or falling, that it is rough or smooth, and so on. Again I am convinced that this is not simply a trick of language, but an essential aspect of both our conceptual and our perceptual representations of the world. Properties have to belong to something. This becomes particularly important when there is more than one "something" in our experience. Suppose there are two acoustic sources of sound, one high and near and the other low and far. It is only because of the fact that nearness and highness are grouped as properties of one stream and farness and lowness as properties of the other that we can experience the uniqueness of the two individual sounds rather than a mush of four properties.

A critic of this argument might reply that the world itself groups the "high" with the "near" and the "low" with the "far." It is not necessary for us to do it. However, it is not sufficient that these clusters of properties be distinct in the physical happenings around us. They must also be assigned by our brains to distinct mental entities. In auditory experience, these entities are the things that I am calling streams. As with our visual experience of objects, our auditory streams are ways of putting the sensory information together. This going together has obvious implications for action. For example, if we assign the properties "far" and "lion roar" to one auditory stream and the properties "near" and "crackling fire" to another one, we might be inclined to behave differently than if the distance assignments had been reversed.

When people familiar with the English language read the phrase "The gray wagon was on the black road," they know immediately that it is the wagon that is gray, not the road. They know it because they can *parse* the sentence, using their knowledge of the English syntax to determine the correct "belongingness" relations between the concepts. Similarly, when listeners create a mental representation of the auditory input, they too must employ rules about what goes with what. In some sense, they can be said to be parsing this input too.

7.3.1   The Principle of Exclusive Allocation

Any system that attempts to build descriptions of a natural world scene must assign the perceptual qualities that it creates to one organization or another. The quality "loud" is assigned to the organization that represents the roar of the lion. The quality "far" is assigned as the distance of that same event. The Gestalt psychologists made this point by introducing the principle of belongingness. In describing the visual organization of drawings like the one in figure 7.5, they pointed out that the lines at which the drawn irregular figure overlaps the circle (shown as a dark line in part B of the figure) are generally seen as part of the irregular figure and not of the circle. That is, they *belong* to the irregular form. With an effort, we can see them as part of a circle; then they belong to the circle. In any mental representation of a drawing, a perceived line always belongs to some figure of which it forms a part. The

FIGURE 7.5   An example of "belongingness." The dark portion of the line seems to belong to the irregular form.

belongingness may shift, for example, when we try to see the figure in a different way, but regardless of how we see it, it is always a property *of* something.

There is a second principle that I want to introduce here because it has a connection with the principle of belongingness. This is the principle of "exclusive allocation." It can be seen in an ambiguous visual figure such as the vase-faces illusion of the Gestalt psychologists. An example is shown in figure 7.6. We can interpret the figure as an outline of either a vase or two faces. The "exclusive allocation of evidence" describes how these interpretations affect the line that separates the vase from a face. When we see the vase, that line is allocated to the vase and defines its shape. When we see the face, the same line is now allocated to the face. It is never allocated to both vase and face at the same time, but exclusively to one of them.

The exclusive allocation principle says that a sensory element should not be used in more than one description at a time. If the line is assigned to the vase, that assignment "uses up" the line so that its shape cannot contribute to the shape of another figure at the same time. There are certain limits to this idea, but it holds true often enough that it is worth pointing it out as a separate principle. It is not identical to the principle of belongingness. The latter merely states that the line has to be seen as a property of a figure, but does not prevent it from being allocated to more than one at a time.

There is a certain ecological validity of the principle of exclusive allocation in vision. The term "ecological validity" means that it tends to give the right answers about how the visual image has probably originated in the external world. In the case of edges separating objects, there is a very low likelihood (except in jigsaw puzzles) that the touching edges of two objects will have the same shape exactly. Therefore the shape of the contour that separates our view of two objects probably tells us about the shape of only one of them—the nearer one. The decision as to which object the contour belongs to is determined by a number of cues that help the viewer to judge which object is closer.

Dividing evidence between distinct perceptual entities (visual objects or auditory streams) is useful because there really are distinct physical objects and events in the world that we humans inhabit. Therefore the evidence that is obtained by our senses really ought to be untangled and assigned to one or another of them.

FIGURE 7.6   An ambiguous drawing in which either a vase at the center or two faces at the sides can be seen.

Our initial example came from vision, but the arguments in audition are similar. For example, it is very unlikely that a sound will terminate at exactly the moment that another begins. Therefore when the spectral composition of the incoming sensory data changes suddenly, the auditory system can conclude that only one sound in a mixture has gone on or off. This conclusion can give rise to a search in the second sound for a continuation of the first one.

The strategy completes itself in the following way. Let us give the name A to the segment of sound that occurs prior to the change, and call the second part B. If spectral components are found in B that match the spectrum of A, they are considered to be the continuing parts of A. Accordingly, they can be subtracted out of B. This allows us a picture of the second sound free from the influence of the first. This is called the "old-plus-new heuristic," and it is shown to be one of our most powerful tools in solving the scene analysis problem in audition. Here I want to point out that it is an example of the principle of exclusive allocation in which the allocation of the continuing spectral components to the first sound interferes with their being allocated to the second.

Another case of exclusive allocation is shown in an experiment by Bregman and Rudnicky, using the pattern of pure tones shown in figure 7.7.[3] In this figure the horizontal dimension represents time and the vertical one shows the frequency of the tones. The listener's task was to decide on the order of two target tones, A and B, embedded in the sequence. Were they in the order high-low or low-high? When A and B were presented alone, as an isolated pair of tones, this decision was very easy. However, when the two tones labeled F (for "flankers") were added to the pattern, the order of A and B became very hard to hear. Apparently when they were absorbed as the middle elements of a larger pattern, FABF, the orders AB and BA lost their uniqueness.

This experiment was about the perceptual allocation of the F tones. As long as they were allocated to the same auditory stream as A and B, the order of A and B was hard to hear. However, Bregman and Rudnicky reasoned that if some principle of grouping were able to assign the F tones to a different perceptual stream, the order of A and B might become audible again. With this in mind, they introduced yet another group of tones, labeled C (for "captors") in figure 7.7. They varied the frequency of these C tones. When they were very low, much lower than the frequency of the F tones, the F tones grouped with the AB tones and the order of A and B was unclear to the listeners. However, when the C tones were brought up close to the frequency of the F tones, they captured them into a stream, CCCFFCC. One reason for this capturing is that tones tend to group perceptually with those that are nearest

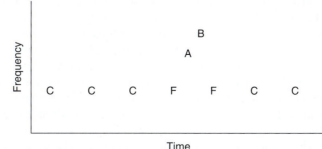

FIGURE 7.7   A tone sequence of the type used by Bregman and Rudnicky (1975).

to them in frequency; a second is that the F tones were spaced so that they fell into a regular rhythmic pattern with the C tones. When the capturing occurred, the order of AB was heard more clearly because they were now in their own auditory stream that was separate from the CCCFCC stream. The belongingness of the F tones had been altered, and the perceived auditory forms were changed.

Scene analysis, as I have described it, involves putting evidence together into a structure. Demonstrations of the perceptual systems acting in this way are seen in certain kinds of illusions where it appears that the correct features of the sensory input have been detected but have not been put together correctly. Two examples will make this clearer.

The first is in vision. Treisman and Schmidt carried out an experiment in which a row of symbols was flashed briefly in a tachistoscope.[4] There were three colored letters flanked by two black digits. The viewers were asked to first report what the digits were and then to report on the letters. Their reports of the digits were generally correct, but the properties of the letters were often scrambled. A subject might report a red O and a green X, when actually a green O and a red X had been presented. These combinations of features often seemed to the viewers to be their actual experiences rather than merely guesses based on partially registered features of the display. The experimenters argued that this showed that the human mind cannot consciously experience disembodied features and must assign them to perceived objects. That is, the mind obeys the principle of belongingness.

The second example comes from audition. In 1974, Diana Deutsch reported an interesting illusion that could be created when tones were sent to both ears of a listener over headphones. The listener was presented with a continuously repeating alternation of two events. Event A was a low tone presented to the left ear, accompanied by a high tone presented to the right ear. Event B was just the reverse: a low tone to the right ear together with a high tone to the left. The high and low tones were pure sine wave tones spaced exactly an octave apart. Because events A and B alternated, each ear was presented with a sequence of high and low tones. Another way to express it is that while both the high and low tones bounced back and forth between the ears, the high and low were always in opposite ears.

However the experience of many listeners did not resemble this description. Instead they heard a single sound bouncing back and forth between the ears. Furthermore, the perceived tone alternated between sounding high pitched and sounding low as it bounced from side to side. The only way this illusion could be explained was to argue that the listeners were assuming the existence of a single tone, deriving two different descriptions of it from two different types of perceptual analyses, and then putting the two descriptions together incorrectly. Apparently they derived the fact that the tone was changing in frequency by monitoring the changes in a single ear (usually the right). However, they derived the *position* of the assumed single sound by tracking the position of the higher tone. Therefore, they might report hearing a low tone on the left at the point in time at which, in actuality, a high tone had been presented on the left. Here we see an example of pitch and location assigned in the wrong combination to the representation of a sound. Therefore, this can be classified as a misassignment illusion just as Treisman and Schmidt's visual illusion was.

The question of why this illusion occurs can be set aside for the moment. What is important is that the illusion suggests that an assignment process is taking place, and this supports the idea that perception is a process of building descriptions. Only by being built could they be built incorrectly.

These illusions show that there are some similarities in how visual and auditory experiences are organized. A thoughtful discussion of the similarities and differences between vision and audition can be found in a paper by Bela Julesz and Ira Hirsh.[5] There is no shortage of parallels in audition to visual processes of organization. This chapter cannot afford the space to mention many examples, but it can at least discuss two of them, the streaming phenomenon and the continuity illusion.

7.4   TWO COMPARISONS OF SCENE ANALYSIS IN VISION AND AUDITION

7.4.1   Auditory Streaming and Apparent Motion

One auditory phenomenon with a direct parallel in vision is the auditory streaming effect. This is the phenomenon that originally got me interested in auditory organization. The effect occurred when listeners were presented with an endlessly repeating loop of tape on which were recorded a sequence of six different tones, three high ones and three low ones. The high ones were at least one and a half octaves above the low ones. High and low tones alternated. If tones are given numbers according to their pitches with 1 as the lowest and 6 as the highest the tones were arranged in the sequence 142536. The six tones, shown in figure 7.8, formed a repeating loop that was cycled over and over.

When the cycle of tones was presented very slowly the listeners heard the sequence of high and low tones in the order in which they occurred on the tape. However, as it was made faster, a strange perceptual effect became stronger and stronger and was extremely compelling when there was only one-tenth of a second between the onsets of consecutive tones. When the effect occurred, the listeners did not actually hear the tones in the correct order, 142536. Instead, they heard two streams of tones, one containing a repeating cycle of the three low pitched tones, 1–2–3– (where dashes indicate silences) and the other containing the three high ones (–4–5–6). The single sequence of tones seemed to have broken up perceptually into two parallel sequences, as if two different instruments were playing different, but interwoven parts. Furthermore it was impossible for the listeners to focus

FIGURE 7.8   A repeating cycle of six tones, of the type used by Bregman and Campbell (1971).

their attention on both streams at the same time. When they focused on one of the streams, the other was heard as a vague background. As a consequence, while the listeners could easily judge the order of the high tones taken alone, or of the low ones taken alone, they could not put this information together to report the order of the six tones in the loop. Many listeners actually reported that the high tones all preceded the low ones, or vice versa, although this was never the case.

Other research has shown that the phenomenon of stream segregation obeys some fairly simple laws. If there are two sets of tones, one of them high in frequency and the other low, and the order of the two sets is shuffled together in the sequence (not necessarily a strict alternation of high and low), the degree of perceptual segregation of the high tones from the low ones will depend on the frequency separation of the two sets. Therefore if the two conditions shown in figure 7.9 are compared, the one on the right will show greater perceptual segregation into two streams. An interesting point is that visually, looking at figure 7.9, the perception of two distinct groups is also stronger on the right.

There is another important fact about stream segregation: the faster the sequence is presented, the greater is the perceptual segregation of high and low tones. Again there is a visual analogy, as shown in figure 7.10. We see the pattern in the right panel, in which there is a contraction of time (the same as an increase in speed), as more tightly grouped into two groups than the left panel is.

7.4.2   Gestalt Grouping Explanation

In the visual analogies, the grouping is predictable from the Gestalt psychologists' proximity principle, which states roughly that the closer the visual elements in a set are to one another, the more strongly we tend to group them perceptually. The Gestalt psychologists thought of this grouping as if the perceptual elements — for example, the notes in figure 7.9 — were attracting one another like miniature planets in space with the result that they tended to form clusters in our experience. If the analogy to audition is a valid one, this suggests that the spatial dimension of distance in vision has two analogies in audition. One is separation in time, and the other is separation in frequency. Both, according to this analogy, are distances, and Gestalt principles that involve distance should be valid for them.

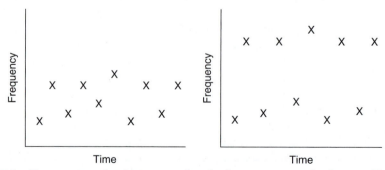

FIGURE 7.9   Stream segregation is stronger when the frequency separation between high and low tones is greater, as shown on the right.

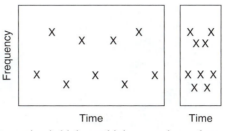

FIGURE 7.10   Stream segregation is higher at higher speeds, as shown on the right.

The Gestalt principles of grouping were evolved by a group of German psychologists in the early part of this century to explain why elements in visual experience seemed highly connected to one another despite the fact that the incoming light rays, pressure energy, sound waves, and so on stimulated discrete sensory receptors such as the ones found in the retina of the eye. The word Gestalt means "pattern" and the theory described how the brain created mental patterns by forming connections between the elements of sensory input. We cannot go into much detail here about this subtle and philosophically sophisticated theory. However, we can examine a few of the observations that they made about the grouping of sensory elements. They are illustrated in the present discussion by means of the set of diagrams shown in figure 7.11.

Distinct visible elements will be grouped to form coherent perceptual organizations if they fulfill certain conditions. The first is similarity. In the first part of the figure, the black and white blobs can be seen as different subgroups because of the similarity of color within each group and the contrast between groups. Similarly, in audition we find that sounds of similar timbres will group together so that the successive sounds of the oboe will segregate from those of the harp, even when they are playing in the same register.

The second part of the figure shows grouping by a second factor, proximity, where the black blobs seem to fall into two separate clusters because the members of one cluster are closer to other members of the same one than they are to the elements that form the other one. It would appear then that the example of stream segregation would follow directly from the Gestalt law of grouping by proximity. The high tones are closer to one another (in frequency) than they are to the low ones. As the high and low groups are moved further away from one another in frequency, the within-group attractions will become much stronger than the between-group attractions. Speeding the sequence up simply has the effect of moving things closer together on the time dimension. This attenuates the differences in time separations and therefore reduces the contribution of separations along the time dimension to the overall separation of the elements. In doing so, it exaggerates the effects of differences in the frequency dimension, since the latter become the dominant contributors to the total distance.

In both parts of figure 7.11, it is not just that the members of the same group go with one another well. The important thing is that they go with one another *better* than they go with members of the other group. The Gestalt theorists argued that there was always competition between the "forces of attraction" of elements for one another and that the perceptual organization that came out of this conflict would be a consequence of the distribution of forces across the whole perceptual "field," and not of the properties of individual parts taken in isolation.

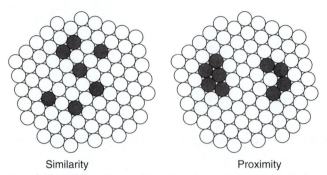

Similarity   Proximity

FIGURE 7.11   Illustration of the effects of the Gestalt principles of similarity and proximity on visual grouping.

The Gestalt psychologists' view was that the tendency to form perceptual organizations was innate and occurred automatically whenever we perceived anything. It was impossible, they claimed, to perceive sensory elements without their forming an organized whole. They argued that this organizing tendency was an automatic tendency of brain tissue.

7.4.3   Auditory Streaming versus Apparent Motion

We have been examining the phenomenon of auditory stream segregation as an example of how phenomena of auditory organization can exhibit the same complexities as are found in vision. This has led us to see interesting parallels in the principles that govern auditory stream segregation and visual grouping. But we have not yet discussed the most striking parallel, that between auditory stream segregation and the phenomenon of apparent motion in vision. Apparent motion is the perceptual effect that used to be very popular on the bill-boards of theatres, where the switching on and off of a series of electric light bulbs in sequence gave the experience of movement. In the laboratory it is usually created in a much simpler form. Two electric lamps, often seen as small white dots in an otherwise black room, are alternately switched on, each for a brief instant, so that a movement is seen that dances back and forth between the lights, always moving from the light that has just been flashed to the light that is currently being flashed. If the lamps are close together, it may seem that the light itself is moving back and forth. At greater distances the experience is just an impression of movement.

In 1915, Körte formulated a number of laws relating the duration, brightness, and spatial separation of the lamps to the strength of the impression of movement. Körte's third law stated that within certain ranges, if you want to increase the spatial separation between the lamps and still have a strong impression of motion, you had to slow down the alternation of flashes. It was almost as if the movement would not be able to keep up with the alternation of flashes if they were far separated in space unless the flashes were slowed down to compensate for their separation.

A more elaborate form of the apparent motion effect strongly resembles the stream-ing effect.[6] Instead of two lamps, there are six, arranged in a horizontal row as shown in figure 7.12. They are arranged so that there is a wider gap between the left triplet of lights and the right triplet than there is between the lights within each triplet. If we label the

FIGURE 7.12   A visual display used to demonstrate visual motion segregation. Two groups of three lamps are arranged in a horizontal row.

lamps with the digits 1 to 6 from left to right, the order in which the lights are to be flashed can be expressed as the sequence 142536, repeated endlessly with no pause between repetitions. In this sequence there is an alternation between left-triplet and right-triplet flashes. At very low speeds, there is no apparent motion at all. The lights appear simply to go on and off in sequence. At a somewhat higher speed, the true sequence (142536) is seen as a form of irregular left-and-right motion between members of the two triplets. Then, as the speed is increased, the motion appears to split into two separate streams, one involving the leftmost three lamps and the other the rightmost three. The leftmost path of motion is 1–2–3 and the rightmost one is –4–5–6 (the dashes indicating the time periods in which the lights from the other stream are active). This segregation is exactly parallel to what happens in the auditory streaming effect. However, it is also directly explainable through Körte's third law.

This law simply states that as the speed increases, the distance between flashes must shrink if good motion is to be seen. Therefore, if we assume that potential motions between successive and nonsuccessive flashes are competing with one another for dominance, and that we finally see the one that is most dominant, the results of our example follow directly. As we speed up the sequence there is an increased tendency for shorter movements to be favored by Körte's law so that the longer between-triplet motions are suppressed in favor of the stronger within-triplet motions.

I have set up the two examples, the streaming of tones and the splitting of apparent motion, in a parallel way so that the analogy can be directly seen. Horizontal position in space is made to correspond to the frequency of the tones, with time playing the role of the second dimension in both cases.

The success of Körte's law in explaining the visual case suggests that there is a parallel law in audition, with melodic motion taking the place of spatial motion.[7] This law would state that if you want to maintain the sense of melodic motion as the frequency separation between high and low tones increases, you must slow the sequence down. As with visual apparent motion it is as if the psychological mechanism responsible for the integration of auditory sequences could not keep up with rapid changes.

7.4.4   Scene-Analysis Explanation

However, Körte's law is not an accident of the construction of the human brain. In both visual motion and melodic motion, the laws of grouping help to solve the scene analysis problem as the sensory input unfolds over time. In both domains, Körte's law is likely to group information appropriately. In vision it tends to group glimpses of a moving object with other glimpses of the same object rather than with those of different objects. This is important in a world where many objects can be moving at the same time and where parts of their trajectories can be hidden by closer objects such as trees. The law assumes that if a hidden object is moving a longer distance it takes it longer to get there. Hence the proportionality of distance and time that we find in the law.

The proportionality of frequency displacement and time that we observe in the streaming effect also has a value in scene analysis. What should the auditory system do if it hears a particular sound, A1, and then either a silence or an interruption by a loud sound of a different quality, and then a subsequent sound, A2, that resembles A1? Should it group A1 and A2 as coming from the same source? The auditory system assumes that the pitch of a sound tends to change continuously and therefore that the longer it has been since the sound was heard, the greater the change ought to have been. This has the effect that longer frequency jumps are tolerable only at longer time delays.

The experience of motion that we have when a succession of discrete events occurs is not a mere laboratory curiosity. When visual apparent motion is understood as a glimpse of a scene analysis process in action, new facts about it can be discovered. For example, it has been found that when the apparent movement seems to occur in depth, in a movement slanting away from the observer, the visual system allows more time for the object to move through the third dimension than it would have if it had appeared to be moving only in the horizontal plane.[8] This happens despite the fact that although a slanting-away motion would traverse more three-dimensional space, it produces the same displacement of an object's image as a horizontal motion does on the retina of an observer. Therefore Körte's law applies to real distance in the world and not to retinal distance, and therefore can best be understood as a sophisticated part of scene analysis.

Another example of a discovery that was guided by the assumption that the rules of apparent motion exist to group glimpses of real scenes was made by Michael Mills and myself.[9] We worked with an animation sequence in which a shape disappeared from one part of a drawing and appeared in another. This change was seen as motion only if the shape was seen as representing the outline of a "figure" both before and after the disappearance. If the observer was induced to see it as "ground" (the shape of an empty space between forms) before it disappeared, and as "figure" (the shape of an actual figure) when it reappeared, the displacement was not seen as motion but as an appearance from nowhere of the figure.

Neither is the auditory streaming effect simply a laboratory curiosity. It is an oblique glimpse of a scene-analysis process doing the best it can in a situation in which the clues to the structure of the scene are very impoverished.

In general, all the Gestalt principles of grouping can be interpreted as rules for scene analysis. We can see this, for example, in the case of the principle of grouping by similarity. Consider the block-recognition problem shown earlier in figure 7.2 where the problem was to determine which areas of the drawing represented parts of the same block. Because this drawing is not very representative of the problem of scene analysis as we face it in everyday life, let us imagine it transformed into a real scene. In the natural world visible surfaces have brightness, color, and texture. It would be a good rule of thumb to prefer to group surfaces that were similar in appearance to one another on these dimensions. This would not always work, but if this principle were given a vote, along with a set of other rules of thumb, it is clear that it would contribute in a positive way to getting the right answer.

In the case of sound, the considerations are the same. If in a mixture of sounds we are able to detect moments of sound that strongly resemble one another, they should be grouped together as probably coming from the same happening. Furthermore, the closer in time two sounds that resemble each other occur, the more likely it is that they have originated with the same event. Both of these statements follow from the idea that events in the world tend to have some persistence. They do not change instantly or haphazardly. It seems likely that the auditory system, evolving as it has in such a world, has developed principles for "betting" on which parts of a sequence of sensory inputs have arisen from the same source. Such betting principles could take advantage of properties of sounds that had a reasonably high probability of indicating that the sounds had a common origin. Viewed from this perspective, the Gestalt principles are seen to be principles of scene analysis that will generally contribute to a correct decomposition of the mixture of effects that reaches our senses. I am not claiming that the auditory system "tries" to achieve this result, only that the processes have been selected by evolution because they did achieve them.

The argument that I have made does not imply that Gestalt theory is wrong. For the Gestaltists, the phenomena of perceptual grouping arose from the fact that there were forces of attraction and segregation that operated in a perceptual field. This may indeed be the mechanism by which the grouping occurs. I am simply arguing that even if this is the form of the computation, the particular grouping force given to each property of the sensory input and the way in which the grouping forces are allowed to interact have been determined (through evolution) to be ones that will tend to contribute to the successful solution of the scene analysis problem.

7.4.5   Closure and Belongingness

Our senses of vision and audition, living in the same world, often face similar problems. So we should not be surprised if we often find them using similar approaches to overcome those problems. We have seen how the two systems sometimes deal with fragmented views of a sequence of events by connecting them in plausible ways. Another strong similarity between the sense modalities can be seen in the phenomenon of "perceived continuity." This is a phenomenon that is sometimes said to be an example of "perceptual closure."

The tendency to close certain "strong" perceptual forms such as circles was observed by the Gestalt psychologists. An example might be the drawing shown in figure 7.5 in which we are likely to see a circle partly obscured by an irregular form. The circle, though its outer edge is incomplete in the picture, is not seen as incomplete but as continuing on behind the other form. In other words, the circle has closed perceptually.

It is commonly said that the Gestalt principle of closure is concerned with completing forms with gaps in them. But if it did that, we would not be able to see any forms with gaps in them, which would be ridiculous. The principle is really one for completing *evidence* with gaps in it.

The Gestalt psychologists argued that closure would occur in an interrupted form if the contour was "strong" or "good" at the point of interruption. This would be true when the contours of the form continued smoothly on both sides of the interruption so that a smooth continuation could be perceived. Presumably laws of similarity would also hold so that if the regions on two sides of an interruption were the same brightness, for instance, they would be more likely to be seen as a single one continuing behind the interruption.

Like the perceptual grouping of discrete events, closure can also be seen as a scene-analysis principle. This can be illustrated with figure 7.13 which shows a number of fragments that are really parts of a familiar object or objects. The fragments were obtained by taking the familiar display and laying an irregularly shaped mask over it. Then the parts that

FIGURE 7.13   Fragments do not organize themselves strongly when there is no information for occlusion.

Source: (From Bregman 1981.)

were underneath the mask were eliminated, leaving visible only those parts that had not been covered by it.

Why do the fragments not close up perceptually in this figure? A plausible Gestalt answer might be that the forces of closure are not strong enough. The contours of the fragments might not be similar enough or in good continuation with one another. However, it is easy to show that these are not the basic reasons for the lack of closure. The problem in this figure is that the visual system does not know where the evidence is incomplete. Look at what happens when the picture is shown with the mask present as in figure 7.14. The visual system quickly joins the fragments without the observer having to think about it. The Gestalt principle of closure has suddenly come alive in the presence of the mask.

What information could the mask be providing? It tells the eye two things. It explains which contours have been produced by the shape of the fragments themselves as contrasted with those that have been produced by the shape of the mask that is covering them. It also provides information about occlusion (which spaces between fragments were created by the fact that the mask occluded our view of the underneath shape). These spaces should be ignored and treated as missing evidence, not as actual spaces. The continuity among the contours of the fragments of a particular B undoubtedly contributes to their grouping, but this continuity becomes effective only in the presence of occlusion information.

The conclusion to be reached is this: the closure mechanism is really a way of dealing with missing evidence. But before our perceptual systems are willing to employ it, they first have to be shown that some evidence is missing. This explains how we can see figures with actual gaps in them; we have no reason to believe that the missing parts are merely being hidden. Figures 7.13 and 7.14 indicate that Gestalt principles are just oblique glimpses of a process of scene analysis that looks as much like an evidence-processing system as like the simple grouping-by-attraction system described by Gestalt psychology.

There is evidence that principles of grouping act in an equally subtle way in audition. There is a problem in hearing that is much like the problem of occlusion in seeing. This is the phenomenon of masking. Masking occurs when a loud sound covers up or drowns out

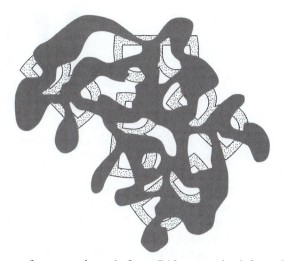

FIGURE 7.14   The same fragments shown in figure 7.13, except that information for occlusion has been added, causing the fragments on the boundaries of the occluding form to be grouped.

Source: (From Bregman 1981.)

a softer one. Despite the masking, if the softer sound is longer, and can be heard both before and after a brief burst of the louder one, it can be heard to continue behind the louder one just as B's were seen as continuing behind the occluding blob in figure 7.14, and as the circle seemed to continue behind the occluding form in the example of figure 7.5. What is more, even if the softer sound is *physically removed* during the brief loud sound, it is still heard as continuing through the interruption.

This illusion has many names, but I will refer to it as the illusion of continuity. It occurs with a wide range of sounds. An example is shown in figure 7.15 where an alternately rising and falling pure-tone glide is periodically interrupted by a short loud burst of broad-band noise (like the noise between stations on a radio). When the glide is broken at certain places but no masking sound is present during the breaks, as in the left panel, the ear hears a series of rising and falling glides, but does not put them together as a single sound any more than the eye puts together the fragments of figure 7.13. However, if the masking noise is introduced in the gaps so as to exactly cover the silent spaces, as in the right panel, the ear hears the glide as one continuous rising and falling sound passing right through the interrupting noise. The integration of the continuous glide pattern resembles the mental synthesis of B's in figure 7.14. They are both effortless and automatic.

Again you could see the auditory effect as an example of the Gestalt principle of closure. However another way of looking at it may be more profitable. Richard Warren has interpreted it as resulting from an auditory mechanism that compensates for masking.[10] He has shown that the illusion can be obtained only when the interrupting noise would have masked the signal if it had really been there. The interrupting noise must be loud enough and have the right frequency components to do so. Putting that in the context of this chapter, we see that the illusion is another oblique glance of the auditory scene-analysis process in action.

We have seen how two types of explanation, one deriving from Gestalt psychology and the other derived from considerations of scene analysis, have been applicable to both the

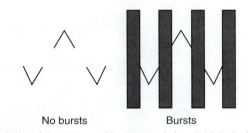

FIGURE 7.15   Tonal glides of the type used by Dannenbring (1976). Left: the stimulus with gaps. Right: the stimulus when the gaps are filled with noise.

streaming and continuity effects. They differ in style. The Gestalt explanation sees the principles of grouping as phenomena in themselves, a self-sufficient system whose business it is to organize things. The scene-analysis approach relates the process more to the environment, or, more particularly, to the problem that the environment poses to the perceiver as he or she (or it) tries to build descriptions of environmental situations.

7.5   SEQUENTIAL VERSUS SPECTRAL ORGANIZATION

7.5.1   Perceptual Decomposition of Complex Sounds

We have looked at two laboratory phenomena in audition that show the activity of the scene-analysis process: the streaming effect and the illusory continuation of one sound behind another. There is a third phenomenon that deserves to be mentioned in this introductory chapter. It is introduced here not to demonstrate a parallel between vision and audition, but to show another dimension of the grouping problem. This is the perceptual decomposition of simultaneous sounds. It can be illustrated through an experiment by Bregman and Pinker.[11]

The sounds used in this experiment are shown in figure 7.16. They consist of a repeating cycle formed by a pure tone A alternating with a complex tone that has two pure-tone components, B and C. This is inherently an ambiguous event. For example, it could be created by giving an audio oscillator to each of two people. The oscillator given to one of them puts out the pure tone A, while the one given to the other puts out the complex tone BC. The two persons are asked to play their oscillators in rapid alternation. If this were the way the sound had been created, the correct perceptual analysis would be to hear a pure tone alternating with a rich-sounding complex tone. This, however, is only one possibility for the origin of the sound. The second is that we have given out oscillators, as before, to two persons. This time, however, both of the oscillators can put out only pure tones. One person is told to sound his instrument twice on each cycle to make the tones A and B, whereas the other is told to play his tone only once on each cycle to make the tone C. He is told to synchronize his C tone with the B tone of his partner. If our auditory systems were to correctly represent the true causes of the sound in this second case, we should hear two streams: one consisting of the repetitions of tones A and B, accompanied by a second that contains only the repetitions of tone C. In this way of hearing the sequence, there should be no rich tone

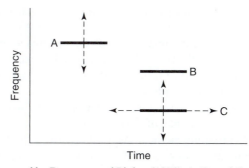

FIGURE 7.16   Stimulus used by Bregman and Pinker (1978). A, B, and C are pure tone components.

BC because the richness is an accidental by-product of the mixture of two signals. If the auditory system is built to hear the properties of meaningful events rather than of the accidental by-products of mixtures, it should discard the latter.

The experiment showed that it was possible to hear the sequence in either way, depending on two factors. The first was the frequency proximity of tones A and B. The closer they were to one another in frequency, the greater the likelihood of hearing A and B as forming a single stream separate from C. Apparently the auditory system uses the proximity of a succession of frequencies, much as it does in the case of the streaming phenomenon, as evidence that they are from a common source. The second factor was the synchrony of tones B and C. If their onsets and offsets were synchronized, they tended to be fused and heard as a single complex sound BC, which was heard as alternating with A. Furthermore, the effects of the BC synchrony were competitive with the effects of the AB frequency proximity. It was as if A and C were competing to see which one would get to group with C. If the synchrony of C with B was reduced, B would be more likely to group with A, unless, of course, the AB connection was made weaker by moving A further away in frequency from B.

7.5.2   Horizontal and Vertical Processes of Organization

There is a distinction that ought to be made now because it follows directly from the Bregman-Pinker experiment. This is the distinction between the processes of sequential and spectral integration.

The process of putting A and B together into a stream can be referred to as sequential integration. This is the kind of integration that forms the melodic component of music. It is the process that connects events that have arisen at different times from the same source. It uses the changes in the spectrum and the speed of such changes as major clues to the correct grouping. The sequential process is what is involved in the streaming effect that was discussed earlier.

The fusing of B with C into a single sound is what will be referred to as simultaneous integration or, in special contexts, as spectral integration, a term borrowed from James Cutting.[12] It is this process that takes acoustic inputs that occur at the same time, but at different places in the spectrum or in space, and treats them as properties of a single sound. It is responsible for the fact that we can interpret a single spectrum of sound as arising from the mixture of two or more sound sources, with the timbre of each one being computed from just those spectral components that have been allocated to that source. This happens, for example, when we hear two singers, one singing "ee" and the other "ah," on different pitches. Despite the fact that all we have is a single spectrum, with the harmonics from the two voices intermixed, we can clearly hear the two vowels. Since a vowel sound is a sort of timbre, this example shows that we can extract two timbres at the same time from a single signal.

If we turn back to the mixed spectrogram shown in figure 7.4, we see that in order to put together the streaks of darkness belonging to the same acoustic source, the same two kinds of grouping are necessary: (1) putting together events that follow one another in time (sequential grouping) and (2) integrating components that occur at the same time in different parts of the spectrum (simultaneous grouping). Musicians speak of a horizontal and a vertical dimension in written music. By horizontal, they refer to the groupings across the page that are seen as melody. By vertical, they refer to the simultaneous events that form chords and harmony. These are the same two dimensions as the ones called sequential and simultaneous.

It is useful to distinguish these two aspects of organization because they are controlled by different acoustic factors. Of course they interact, too.

7.5.3   Types of Explanation of These Phenomena

It is interesting to take a moment to see how these phenomena are related to various theoretical positions. I will consider their relation to concepts drawn from computer modeling, syntactic theory, Gestalt psychology, and physiological explanation.

The computer modeling approach has contributed an important idea: the notion of a heuristic. The idea was evolved in the process of designing computer programs to solve difficult problems for which no mathematical solution was known. The approach taken by the designers was to employ heuristics, which are defined as procedures that are not guaranteed to solve the problem, but are likely to lead to a good solution. An example would be the use of heuristic tests by computer chess programs to determine whether a proposed move would lead to a good position (e.g., to test whether the move would result in the computer controlling the center of the board or whether the move would lead to an exchange of pieces that favored the computer). Each move is evaluated by a number of such heuristics. No one of them can guarantee success, but if there are a large number, each with some basis in the structure of the game of chess, a move that satisfies most of them will probably be a good one. Furthermore, if each of the heuristic evaluation processes has a chance to vote for or against the move, the program will be less likely to be tricked than it would be if it based its move on only one or two criteria, no matter how good they were.

I believe that the perceptual systems work in similar ways. Having evolved in a world of mixtures, humans have developed heuristic mechanisms capable of decomposing them. Because the conditions under which decomposition must be done are extremely variable, no single method is guaranteed to succeed. Therefore a number of heuristic criteria must be used to decide how to group the acoustic evidence. These criteria are allowed to combine their effects in a process very much like voting. No one factor will necessarily vote correctly, but if there are many of them, competing with or reinforcing one another, the right description of the input should generally emerge. If they all vote in the same way, the resulting percept is stable and unambiguous. When they are faced with artificial signals, set up in the laboratory, in which one heuristic is made to vote for integration and another for segregation, the resulting experiences can be unstable and ambiguous.

My use of the word "heuristic" does not imply a computer-like procedure that involves a long sequence of steps, extended over time. We have to bear in mind that the decisions of the auditory system are carried out in very short periods of time. I use the word heuristic in its functional sense only, as a process that contributes to the solution of a problem.

Whereas the perceptual phenomena that we examined earlier are the province of psychologists, the problem of how people build mental descriptions is a topic that has been looked at by linguists too. As a result, they have provided us with a metaphor for understanding auditory scene analysis. This metaphor, "deep structure," derives from the study of the syntactic structure of sentences.

One of the basic problems in syntax is how to describe the rules that allow the speaker to impose a meaning on a sentence by adding, subtracting, or rearranging elements in the sentence. For example, in English one of these rules imposes the form of a question on a sentence by placing the auxiliary verb at the beginning of the sentence. Thus, the active sentence "He has gone there" is expressed in a question as "Has he gone there?" The difficulty that occurs when a language loads a sentence with meanings is that when a large number of form-shaping rules are piled on top of one another, it becomes difficult to untangle them and to appreciate the contribution of each of them to the final product. Somehow all speakers of English come to be able to do this, but the learning takes some time. In the 1960s, Noam Chomsky introduced the notion of the "deep structure" of a sentence, a description of a sentence that separately and explicitly described all the underlying syntactic forms and displayed their interrelationships. When a theorist, or a listener, starts with a given sentence and builds a description of its syntax, this is called "parsing" the sentence. It was argued by psychologists who were inspired by Chomsky's approach that in the course of understanding a sentence, the hearer parses a sentence and builds a deep structure for it.

We can talk about perception in a very similar way. Just as a spoken sentence imposes an extraordinary decoding problem upon the listener, so does a non-linguistic sensory input. Whenever we experience an event, the sensory impression is always the result of an elaborate composition of physical influences. If we look at a four-inch-square area of a table top, for example, the local properties of this area have been affected by many factors: the table's shininess, the variations in its surface color, the unevenness of its surface, the shadow of a nearby object, the color of the light source, the slant of the surface of the table relative to our eyes, and perhaps many more. These factors are all simultaneously *shaping* the sensory information; they are not simply inserted side by side. The shininess is not at one place in our visual image, the surface color at another, and so on. Neither can they be extracted from the sense data independently of one another.

The same thing happens in audition. If we look at any one-tenth-second slice of figure 7.4, the information shown in that slice represents a composition of influences. The spectrum may have been shaped by voices and by other simultaneous sounds. Somehow, if we are able to understand the events that have shaped it, we are succeeding, as in sentence comprehension, in developing a mental description that displays the simple causative factors and their interrelationships in an explicit way.

There is a provocative similarity among the three examples — the syntactical, the visual, and the auditory. In all three cases, the perceivers are faced with a complex *shaping* of the sensory input by the effects of various simple features, and they must recover those features from their effects. Transposing the linguist's vocabulary to the field of perception, one might say that the job of the perceiver is to parse the sensory input and arrive at its deep structure. In some sense the perceiver has to build up a description of the regularities in the world that have shaped the evidence of our senses. Such regularities would include the fact that there are solid objects with their own shapes and colors (in vision) and sounds with their own timbres and pitches (in audition).

Although the approach of this chapter is not physiological, it is important to see its relation to physiological explanation. We can take as an example the physiological explanations that have been offered for the streaming effect of figure 7.8. It has been proposed that the segregation into two streams occurs because a neural mechanism responsible for tracking changes in pitch has temporarily become less effective.[13] This interpretation is supported by the results of experiments that show that the segregation becomes stronger with longer repetitions of the cycle of tones. Presumably the detector for change has become habituated in the same manner as other feature detectors are thought to. This view of the stream segregation phenomenon sees it as a breakdown. This seems to be in serious conflict with the scene-analysis view presented earlier, in which stream segregation was seen as an accomplishment. So which is it to be, breakdown or accomplishment?

We do not know whether or not this physiological explanation is correct. But even if it is, its truth may not affect the scene analysis explanation of streaming. To demonstrate why, it is necessary to again appeal to an argument based on evolution. Every physiological mechanism that develops must stand the test of the winnowing process imposed by natural selection. However, the survival of an individual mechanism will often depend not just on what it does in isolation, but on the success of the larger functional system of which it forms a part.

Because of the indirect way in which the individual physiological mechanism contributes to the successful accomplishments displayed by the larger system, it is possible that what looks like a breakdown when seen at the single-mechanism level is actually contributing to an accomplishment at the system level. To take a homespun example, consider the case of a pitfall trap. When the top of the trap, covered with branches and leaves, "breaks down" and the animal falls through into the hole, we can see that the physical breakdown (of the trap cover) represents a functional success (of the entrapment). The breakdown and the achievement are at different levels of abstraction. By analogy, it would not be contradictory to assert that the streaming effect represented both the breakdown of a physiological mechanism and the accomplishment of scene analysis. This example illustrates how indirect the relation can be between function and physiology.

7.6 SCENE-ANALYSIS VIEW PREVENTS MISSING OF VISION-AUDITION DIFFERENCES

It was argued in the earlier discussion that Gestalt explanations had to be supplemented by ones based on scene analysis because the latter might lead us to new phenomena, such as the role of the occluding mask in perceptual closure. There is another difference between the two approaches. Because the Gestalt theorists saw the principles of organization as following from general properties of neural tissue they focused on similarities between the senses rather than on differences. The laws of grouping were stated in a general way, in terms of adjectives (such as "proximity" or "similarity") that could apply equally well to different sense modalities. This has had both useful and harmful effects. On the positive side it has promoted the discovery of the similar way in which perceptual organization works in different sense modalities. For example, the similarities between apparent movement and auditory streaming have become apparent. However, an exclusive focus on the common Gestalt principles, neglecting the unique scene-analysis problems that each sense must solve, is likely to neglect differences between them and cause us to miss some excellent opportunities to study special problems in audition that make themselves evident once we consider the dissimilarities between the senses. The way to get at them is to consider the differences in the way in which information about the properties of the world that we care about are carried in sound and in light. The fact that certain Gestalt principles actually are shared between the senses could be thought of as existing because they are appropriate methods for scene analysis in both domains.

As an example of the way that the scene-analysis approach can reveal important differences between the senses, let us go through the exercise of considering the roles of direct energy, reflected energy, and their mixture in the two senses.

7.6.1   Differences in the Ecology of Vision and Audition

There is a crucial difference in the way that humans use acoustic and light energy to obtain information about the world. This has to do with the dissimilarities in the ecology of light and sound. In audition humans, unlike their relatives the bats, make use primarily of the sound-emitting rather than the sound-reflecting properties of things. They use their eyes to determine the shape and size of a car on the road by the way in which its surfaces reflect the light of the sun, but use their ears to determine the intensity of the crash by receiving the energy that is emitted when this event occurs. The shape reflects energy; the crash creates it. For humans, sound serves to supplement vision by supplying information about the nature of events, defining the "energetics" of a situation.

There is another difference that is very much related to this one: sounds go around corners. Low-frequency sound bends around an obstruction while higher frequency sound bounces around it. This makes it possible for us to have a distant early warning system. The reader might be tempted to object that light too goes around corners. Although it does not bend around, in the way that low-frequency sound does, it often gets around by reflection; in effect, it bounces around the corner. But notice what a difference this bouncing makes in how we can use the light. Although the bounced-around light provides illumination that allows us to see the shapes of things on our own side of the corner, unless it has been bounced by means of mirrors it has lost the shape information that it picked up when it reflected off the objects on the opposite side. Sound is used differently. We use it to discover the time and frequency pattern of the source, not its spatial shape, and much of this information is retained even when it bends or bounces around the corner.

This way of using sound has the effect, however, of making acoustic events transparent; they do not occlude energy from what lies behind them. The auditory world is like the visual world would be if all objects were very, very transparent and glowed in sputters and starts by their own light, as well as reflecting the light of their neighbors. This would be a hard world for the visual system to deal with.

It is not true then that our auditory system is somehow more primitive simply because it does not deliver as detailed information about the shapes, sizes, and surface characteristics of objects. It simply has evolved a different function and lives in a different kind of world.

What of echoes? We never discuss echoes in light because its speed is so fast and the distances in a typical scene are so small that the echo arrives in synchrony with the original signal. Furthermore, in vision we are usually interested in the echoes, not the original signal, and certainly not in integrating the two into a single image. Light bounces around, reflecting off many objects in our environments, and eventually gets to our eyes with the imprint of the unoccluded objects still contained in it. Because the lens-and-retina system of the eye keeps this information in the same spatial order, it allows us access to the information about each form separately. Echoes are therefore very useful in specifying the shapes of objects in vision because the echoes that come off different surfaces do not get mixed together on the way to our eye.

The case is otherwise in audition. Because our ears lack the lenses that could capture the spatial layout of the echoes from different surfaces, we are usually interested in the source of sound rather than in the shapes of objects that have reflected or absorbed it. The individual spatial origins of the parts of a reflected wave front are barely preserved at all for our ears. Therefore, when the sound bounces off other objects and these echoes mix with the original signal, they obscure the original properties of the sound. Although echoes are delayed copies and, as such, contain all the original structure of the sound, the mixing of the original and the echo creates problems in using this redundant structural information effectively.

The two senses also make different uses of the absorption of energy by the environment. The fact that different objects absorb light in different ways gives them their characteristic colors and brightnesses, but this differential absorption is not as valuable in hearing because our ears cannot separate the reflections from small individual objects. We do hear the "hardness" or "softness" of the entire room that we are in. This corresponds to the color information carried in light, but the acoustic information is about very large objects, whereas the information in light can be about very small ones.

In summary, we can see that the differences in how we use light and sound create different opportunities and difficulties for the two perceptual systems and that they probably have evolved specialized methods for dealing with them.

7.7   PRIMITIVE VERSUS SCHEMA-BASED STREAM SEGREGATION

It seems reasonable to believe that the process of auditory scene analysis must be governed by both innate and learned constraints. The effects of the unlearned constraints are called "primitive segregation" and those of the learned ones are called "schema-based segregation."

One reason for wanting to think that there are unlearned influences on segregation is the fact that there are certain constant properties of the environment that would have to be dealt with by every human everywhere. Different humans may face different languages, musics, and birds and animals that have their own particular cries. A desert certainly sounds different from a tropical forest. But certain essential physical facts remain constant. When a harmonically structured sound changes over time, all the harmonics in it will tend to change together in frequency, in amplitude, and in direction, and to maintain a harmonic relationship. This is not true of just some particular environment but of broad classes of sounds in the world.

Such regularities can be used in reverse to infer the probable underlying structure of a mixture. When frequency components continue to maintain a harmonic relationship to one another despite changes in frequency, amplitude, and spatial origin, they will almost always have been caused by a coherent physical event. The later chapters show that the human auditory system makes use of such regularity in the sensory input. But is this innate? I think that it is. The internal organs of animals evolve to fit the requirements of certain constant factors in their environments. Why should their auditory systems not do likewise?

Roger Shepard has argued for a principle of "psychophysical complementarity," which states that the mental processes of animals have evolved to be complementary with the structure of the surrounding world.[14] For example, because the physical world allows an object to be rotated without changing its shape, the mind must have mechanisms for rotating its representations of objects without changing their shapes. The processes of auditory perception would fall under this principle of complementarity, the rules of auditory grouping being complementary with the redundancies that link the acoustic components that have arisen from the same source.

The Gestalt psychologists argued that the laws of perceptual organization were innate. They used two types of evidence to support their claim. One was the fact that the phenomenon of camouflage, which works by tricking the organizational processes into grouping parts of an object with parts of its surroundings, could be made to disguise even highly familiar shapes. Clearly, then, some general grouping rules were overriding learned knowledge about the shape of objects. The second was the fact that perceptual organization could be demonstrated with very young animals.

To the arguments offered by the Gestaltists can be added the following one: From an engineering point of view, it is generally easier to design a machine that can do some task directly than to design one that can *learn* to do it. We can design machines that can parse or generate fairly complex sentences, but there has been limited success in designing one that could learn grammatical rules from examples without any designed-in knowledge of the formal structure of those rules. By analogy, if you think of the physical world as having a "grammar" (the physical laws that are responsible for the sensory impressions that we receive), then each human must be equipped either with mechanisms capable of learning about many of these laws from examples or with a mechanism whose genetic program has been developed once and for all by the species as a result of billions of parallel experiments over the course of history, where the lives of the members of the species and its ancestors represent the successes and the lives of countless extinct families the failures. To me, evolution seems more plausible than learning as a mechanism for acquiring at least a general capability to segregate sounds. Additional learning-based mechanisms could then refine the ability of the perceiver in more specific environments.

The innate influences on segregation should not be seen as being in opposition to principles of learning. The two must collaborate, the innate influences acting to "bootstrap" the learning process. In language, meaning is carried by words. Therefore if a child is to come to respond appropriately to utterances, it is necessary that the string be responded to in terms of the individual words that compose it. This is sometimes called the segmentation problem. Until you look at a spectrogram of continuous speech occurring in natural utterances, the task seems easy. However, on seeing the spectrogram, it becomes clear that the spaces that we insert into writing to mark the boundaries of words simply do not occur in speech. Even if sentences were written without spaces, adults could take advantage of prior knowledge to find the word boundaries. Because they already know the sequences of letters that make meaningful words, they could detect each such sequence and place tentative word boundaries on either side of it. But when infants respond to speech they have no such prior learning to fall back on. They would be able to make use only of innate constraints. I suspect a main factor used by infants to segment their first words is acoustic discontinuity. The baby may hear a word as a unit only when it is presented in isolation, that is, with silence (or much softer sound) both before and after it. This would be the result of an innate principle of boundary formation. If it were presented differently, for example, as part of a constant phrase, then the phrase and not the word would be treated as the unit. The acoustic continuity within a sample of speech and the discontinuities at its onset and termination would be available, even at the earliest stage of language acquisition, to label it as a single whole when it was heard in isolation. Once perceived as a whole, however, its properties could be learned. Then, after a few words were learned, recognition mechanisms could begin to help the segmentation process. The infant would now be able to use the beginnings and ends of these familiar patterns to establish boundaries for other words that might lie between them. We can see in this example how an innate grouping rule could help a learning process to get started. (I am not suggesting that the establishing of acoustic boundaries at discontinuities is the only method that infants use to discover units, but I would be very surprised if it were not one of them.)

Another example of innate segregation that was given earlier concerned an infant trying to imitate an utterance by her mother. It was argued that the fact that the infant did not insert into her imitation the cradle's squeak that had occurred during her mother's speech displayed her capacity for auditory scene analysis. I am also proposing that this particular capacity is based on innately given constraints on organization.

There is much experimental evidence drawn from experiments on the vision of infants that supports the existence of innate constraints on perceptual organization. Corresponding experiments on auditory organization, however, are still in short supply.

One such study was carried out by Laurent Demany in Paris.[15] Young infants from $1\frac{1}{2}$ to $3\frac{1}{2}$ months of age were tested with sequences of tones. The method of habituation and dishabituation was used. This is a method that can be used with infants to discover whether they consider two types of auditory signals the same or different. At the beginning, a sound is played to the babies every time they look at a white spot on a screen in front of them. The sound acts as a reward and the babies repeatedly look at the white spot to get the interesting sound. After a number of repetitions of this "look and get rewarded" sequence, the novelty of the sound wears off and it loses its potency as a reward (the infants are said to have habituated to the sound). At this point the experimenter replaces the sound by a different one. If the newness of the sound restores its ability to act as a reward, we can conclude that the infants must consider it to be a different sound (in the language of the laboratory, they have become dishabituated), but if they continue ignoring it, they must consider it to be the same as the old one.

Using this method, Demany tried to discover whether infants would perceptually segregate high tones from low ones. The proof that they did so was indirect. The reasoning

went as follows: Suppose that four tones, all with different pitches, are presented in a repeating cycle. Two are higher in pitch (H1 and H2) and two are lower (L1 and L2), and they are
presented in the order H1, L1, H2, L2, [. . . .] If the high and low tones are segregated into
different perceptual streams, the high stream will be heard as

        H1–H2–H1–H2–H1–H2–[...]

and the low stream will be perceived as

        L1–L2–L1–L2–L1–L2–[...]

(where the dashes represent brief within-stream silences). In each stream all that is heard is
a pair of alternating tones.

    Now consider what happens when the reverse order of tones is played, namely L2,
H2, L1, H1, [. . . .] If the high tones segregate from the low ones, the high stream is
heard as

        H2–H1–H2–H1–H2–H1–[...]

and the low one as

        L2–L1–L2–L1–L2–L1–[. . . .]

Again each stream is composed of two alternating tones. In fact, if the infant lost track of
which one of the pair of tones started the sequence, the two streams would be considered to
be exactly the same as they were with the original order of tones. Suppose, however, that the
infant does not segregate the high from the low tones. In this case the forward and the backward orders of tones are quite different from one another and remain so even if the infant
forgets which tone started the sequence.

    To summarize, the segregated streams are quite similar for the forward and backward
sequences whereas the unsegregated sequences are quite different. Using the
habituation/dishabituation method, Demany tried to determine whether the infants considered the forward and backward sequences the same or different. The results showed that
they were reacted to as being the same. This implied that stream segregation had occurred.
In addition, Demany showed that this result was not due to the fact that the infants were
incapable in general of distinguishing the order of tonal sequences. Pairs of sequences whose
segregated substreams did not sound similar to an adult were not reacted to as being the
same by infants. In general, the infant results paralleled those of adult perception and the
older and younger infants did not differ in their reactions.

    Undoubtedly more such research is required. After all, the infants were not newborns;
they had had some weeks of exposure to the world of sound. But after this pioneering study,
the burden of proof shifts to those who would argue that the basic patterns of auditory organization are learned. Unfortunately, working with very young infants is difficult and the
amount of data collected per experiment is small.

The unlearned constraints on organization can clearly not be the only ones. We know that a trained musician, for example, can hear the component sounds in a mixture that is impenetrable to the rest of us. I have also noticed that when researchers in my laboratory prepare studies on perceptual organization, they must listen to their own stimuli repeatedly. Gradually their intuitions about how easy it is to hear the stimulus in a particular way comes to be less and less like the performance of the untrained listeners who are to serve as the subjects of the experiment.

Undoubtedly there are learned rules that affect the perceptual organization of sound. I shall refer to the effects of these rules as "schema-based integration" (a schema is a mental representation of some regularity in our experience). Schema-based analysis probably involves the learned control of attention and is very powerful indeed. The learning is based on the encounter of individuals with certain lawful patterns of their environments, speech and music being but two examples. Since different environments contain different languages, musics, speakers, animals, and so on, the schema-based stream segregation skills of different individuals will come to have strong differences, although they may have certain things in common. In later chapters, I will give some examples of the effects of schema-governed scene analysis in the fields of music and language, and will discuss a theory of sequential integration of sound, proposed by Mari Reiss Jones, that is best understood as describing the influence of schemas on stream segregation.

7.8   VERIFICATION OF THE THEORY

The theory presented in this chapter proposes that there is an auditory stream-forming process that is responsible for a number of phenomena such as the streaming effect and the illusion of continuity, as well as for the everyday problems of grouping components correctly to hear that a car is approaching as we cross a street, or "hearing out" a voice or an instrument from a musical performance. This is not the type of theory that is likely to be accepted or rejected on the basis of one crucial experiment. Crucial experiments are rare in psychology in general. This is because the behavior that we observe in any psychological experiment is always the result of a large number of causal factors and is therefore interpretable in more than one way. When listeners participate in an experiment on stream segregation, they do not merely perceive; they must remember, choose, judge, and so on. Each experimental result is always affected by factors outside the theory, such as memory, attention, learning, and strategies for choosing one's answer. The theory must therefore be combined with extra assumptions to explain any particular outcome. Therefore it cannot easily be proven or falsified.

Theories of the type I am proposing do not perform their service by predicting the exact numerical values in experimental data. Rather they serve the role of guiding us among the infinite set of experiments that could be done and relationships between variables that could be studied. The notion of stream segregation serves to link a number of causes with a number of effects. Stream segregation is affected by the speed of the sequence, the frequency separation of sounds, the pitch separation of sounds, the spatial location of the sounds, and many other factors. In turn, the perceptual organization into separate streams influences a number of measurable effects, such as the ability to decide on the order of events, the tendency to hear rhythmic factors within each segregated stream, and the inability to judge the order of events that are in different streams. Without the simplifying idea of a stream-forming process, we would be left with a large number of empirical relations between individual causal influences and measurable behaviors.

A theory of this type is substantiated by converging operations. This means that the concepts of "perceptual stream" and "scene-analysis process" will gain in plausibility if a large number of different kinds of experimental tasks yield results that are consistent with these ideas.

SUMMARY

I started this chapter with a general introduction to a number of problems. I began with the claim that audition, no less than vision, must solve very complex problems in the interpretation of the incoming sensory stimulation. A central problem faced by audition was in dealing with mixtures of sounds. The sensory components that arise from distinct environmental events have to be segregated into separate perceptual representations. These representations (which I called streams) provide centers of description that connect sensory features so that the right combinations can serve as the basis for recognizing the environmental events. This was illustrated with three auditory phenomena, the streaming effect, the decomposition of complex tones (the ABC experiment), and perceptual closure through occluding sounds.

The explanation that I offered had two sides. It discussed both perceptual representations and the properties of the acoustic input that were used heuristically to do the segregation. I argued that one had to take the ecology of the world of sound into account in looking for the methods that the auditory system might be using, and claimed that this could serve as a powerful supplement to the Gestalt theorist's strategy of looking for formal similarities in the activity of different senses. Finally I proposed that there were two kinds of constraints on the formation of perceptual representations, unlearned primitive ones and more sophisticated ones that existed in learned packages called schemas.

NOTES

1. For example, those described by Deutsch (1975a).
2. From Guzman (1969).
3. Bregman and Rudnicky (1975).
4. Treisman and Schmidt (1982).
5. Julesz and Hirsh (1972).
6. Forms of this effect have been described by Vicario (1965, 1982) and Bregman and Achim (1973).
7. See discussion in van Noorden (1975). A more elaborate form of Körte's law in audition has been offered by Jones (1976).
8. Ogasawara (1936), Corbin (1942), and Attneave and Block (1973).
9. Bregman and Mills (1982).
10. See review in Warren (1982).
11. Bregman and Pinker (1978).
12. Cutting (1976).
13. Anstis and Saida (1985).
14. Shepard (1981).
15. Demany (1982).

REFERENCES

Anstis, S., and Saida, S. (1985). Adaptation to auditory streaming of frequency-modulated tones. *Journal of Experimental Psychology: Human Perception and Performance, 11,* 257–271.

Attneave, F., and Block, G. (1973). Apparent movement in tridimensional space. *Perception & Psychophysics, 13,* 301–307.

Bregman, A. S. (1981). Asking the "what for" question in auditory perception. In M. Kubovy and J. R. Pomerantz (Eds.), *Perceptual Organization.* Hillsdale, N.J.: Erlbaum.

Bregman, A. S., and Achim, A. (1973). Visual stream segregation. *Perception & Psychophysics, 13,* 451–454.

Bregman, A. S., and Campbell, J. (1971). Primary auditory stream segregation and perception of order in rapid sequences of tones. *Journal of Experimental Psychology, 89,* 244–249.

Bregman, A. S., and Mills, M. I. (1982). Perceived movement: The Flintstone constraint. *Perception, 11,* 201–206.

Bregman, A. S., and Pinker, S. (1978). Auditory streaming and the building of timbre. *Canadian Journal of Psychology, 32,* 19–31.

Bregman, A. S., and Rudnicky, A. (1975). Auditory segregation: Stream or streams? *Journal of Experimental Psychology: Human Perception and Performance, 1,* 263–267.

Corbin, H. H. (1942). The perception of grouping and apparent movement in visual depth. *Archives of Psychology,* no. 273.

Cutting, J. E. (1976). Auditory and linguistic processes in speech perception: Inferences from six fusions in dichotic listening. *Psychological Review, 83,* 114–140.

Dannenbring, G. L. (1976). Perceived auditory continuity with alternately rising and falling frequency transitions. *Canadian Journal of Psychology, 30,* 99–114.

Demany, L. (1982). Auditory stream segregation in infancy. *Infant Behavior and Development, 5,* 261–276.

Deutsch, D. (1975). Musical illusions. *Scientific American, 233,* 92–104.

Guzman, A. (1969). Decomposition of a visual scene into three-dimensional bodies. In A. Grasselli (Ed.), *Automatic Interpretation and Classification of Images.* New York: Academic Press.

Jones, M. R. (1976). Time, our lost dimensions: Toward a new theory of perception, attention, and memory. *Psychology Review, 83,* 323–355.

Julesz, B., and Hirsh, I. J. (1972). Visual and auditory perception — An essay of comparison. In E. E. David, Jr., and P. B. Denes (Eds.), *Human Communication: A Unified View.* New York: McGraw-Hill.

Ogasawara, J. (1936). Effect of apparent separation on apparent movement. *Japanese Journal of Psychology, 11,* 109–122.

CHAPTER EIGHT

PRINCIPLES OF CATEGORIZATION

ELEANOR ROSCH

The following is a taxonomy of the animal kingdom. It has been attributed to an ancient Chinese encyclopedia entitled the *Celestial Emporium of Benevolent Knowledge:*

> On those remote pages it is written that animals are divided into (a) those that belong to the Emperor, (b) embalmed ones, (c) those that are trained, (d) suckling pigs, (e) mermaids, (f) fabulous ones, (g) stray dogs, (h) those that are included in this classification, (i) those that tremble as if they were mad, (j) innumerable ones, (k) those drawn with a very fine camel's hair brush, (l) others, (m) those that have just broken a flower vase, (n) those that resemble flies from a distance. (Borges, 1966, p. 108)

Conceptually, the most interesting aspect of this classification system is that it does not exist. Certain types of categorizations may appear in the imagination of poets, but they are never found in the practical or linguistic classes of organisms or of man-made objects used by any of the cultures of the world. For some years, I have argued that human categorization should not be considered the arbitrary product of historical accident or of whimsy but rather the result of psychological principles of categorization, which are subject to investigation. This chapter is a summary and discussion of those principles.

The chapter is divided into five parts. The first part presents the two general principles that are proposed to underlie categorization systems. The second part shows the way in which these principles appear to result in a basic and primary level of categorization in the levels of abstraction in a taxonomy. It is essentially a summary of the research already reported on basic level objects (Rosch et al., 1976). Thus the second section may be omitted by the reader already sufficiently familiar with that material. The third part relates the principles of categorization to the formation of prototypes in those categories that are at the same level of abstraction in a taxonomy. In particular, this section

From Margolis, Eric and Laurence, Stephen, eds., *Concepts: Core Readings,* pp. 189–206, © 1978/1999 Massachusetts Institute of Technology, by permission of The MIT Press.

attempts to clarify the operational concept of prototypicality and to separate that concept from claims concerning the role of prototypes in cognitive processing, representation, and learning for which there is little evidence. The fourth part presents two issues that are problematical for the abstract principles of categorization stated in the first part: (1) the relation of context to basic level objects and prototypes; and (2) assumptions about the nature of the attributes of real-world objects that underlie the claim that there is structure in the world. The fifth part is a report of initial attempts to base an analysis of the attributes, functions, and contexts of objects on a consideration of objects as props in culturally defined events.

It should be noted that the issues in categorization with which we are primarily concerned have to do with explaining the categories found in a culture and coded by the language of that culture at a particular point in time. When we speak of the formation of categories, we mean their formation in the culture. This point is often misunderstood. The principles of categorization proposed are not as such intended to constitute a theory of the development of categories in children born into a culture nor to constitute a model of how categories are processed (how categorizations are made) in the minds of adult speakers of a language.

8.1   THE PRINCIPLES

Two general and basic principles are proposed for the formation of categories: The first has to do with the function of category systems and asserts that the task of category systems is to provide maximum information with the least cognitive effort; the second has to do with the structure of the information so provided and asserts that the perceived world comes as structured information rather than as arbitrary or unpredictable attributes. Thus maximum information with least cognitive effort is achieved if categories map the perceived world structure as closely as possible. This condition can be achieved either by the mapping of categories to given attribute structures or by the definition or redefinition of attributes to render a given set of categories appropriately structured. These principles are elaborated in the following.

8.1.1   Cognitive Economy

The first principle contains the almost common-sense notion that, as an organism, what one wishes to gain from one's categories is a great deal of information about the environment while conserving finite resources as much as possible. To categorize a stimulus means to consider it, for purposes of that categorization, not only equivalent to other stimuli in the same category but also different from stimuli not in that category. On the one hand, it would appear to the organism's advantage to have as many properties as possible predictable from knowing any one property, a principle that would lead to formation of large numbers of categories with as fine discriminations between categories as possible. On the other hand, one purpose of categorization is to reduce the infinite differences among stimuli to behaviorally and cognitively usable proportions. It is to the organism's advantage not to differentiate one stimulus from others when that differentiation is irrelevant to the purposes at hand.

8.1.2   Perceived World Structure

The second principle of categorization asserts that unlike the sets of stimuli used in traditional laboratory-concept attainment tasks, the perceived world is not an unstructured total set of equiprobable co-occurring attributes. Rather, the material objects of the world are perceived to possess (in Garner's, 1974, sense) high correlational structure. That is, given a knower who perceives the complex attributes of feathers, fur, and wings, it is an empirical fact provided by the perceived world that wings co-occur with feathers more than with fur. And given an actor with the motor programs for sitting, it is a fact of the perceived world that objects with the perceptual attributes of chairs are more likely to have functional sit-on-able-ness than objects with the appearance of cats. In short, combinations of what we perceive as the attributes of real objects do not occur uniformly. Some pairs, triples, etc., are quite probable, appearing in combination sometimes with one, sometimes another attribute; others are rare; others logically cannot or empirically do not occur.

It should be emphasized that we are talking about the perceived world and not a metaphysical world without a knower. What kinds of attributes *can* be perceived are, of course, species-specific. A dog's sense of smell is more highly differentiated than a human's, and the structure of the world for a dog must surely include attributes of smell that we, as a species, are incapable of perceiving. Furthermore, because a dog's body is constructed differently from a human's, its motor interactions with objects are necessarily differently structured. The "out there" of a bat, a frog, or a bee is surely more different still from that of a human. What attributes *will* be perceived given the ability to perceive them is undoubtedly determined by many factors having to do with the functional needs of the knower interacting with the physical and social environment. One influence on how attributes will be defined by humans is clearly the category system already existent in the culture at a given time. Thus, our segmentation of a bird's body such that there is an attribute called "wings" may be influenced not only by perceptual factors such as the gestalt laws of form that would lead us to consider the wings as a separate part (Palmer, 1977) but also by the fact that at present we already have a cultural and linguistic category called "birds." Viewing attributes as, at least in part, constructs of the perceiver does not negate the higher-order structural fact about attributes at issue, namely that the attributes of wings and that of feathers do co-occur in the perceived world.

These two basic principles of categorization, a drive toward cognitive economy combined with structure in the perceived world, have implications both for the level of abstraction of categories formed in a culture and for the internal structure of those categories once formed.

For purposes of explication, we may conceive of category systems as having both a vertical and horizontal dimension. The vertical dimension concerns the level of inclusiveness of the category — the dimension along which the terms collie, dog, mammal, animal, and living thing vary. The horizontal dimension concerns the segmentation of categories at the same level of inclusiveness — the dimension on which dog, cat, car, bus, chair, and sofa vary. The implication of the two principles of categorization for the vertical dimension is that not all possible levels of categorization are equally good or useful; rather, the most basic level of categorization will be the most inclusive (abstract) level at which the categories can mirror the structure of attributes perceived in the world. The implication of the principles of categorization for the horizontal dimension is that to increase the distinctiveness and flexibility of categories, categories tend to become defined in terms of prototypes or prototypical instances that contain the attributes most representative of items inside and least representative of items outside the category.

8.2   THE VERTICAL DIMENSION OF CATEGORIES: BASIC-LEVEL OBJECTS

In a programmatic series of experiments, we have attempted to argue that categories within taxonomies of concrete objects are structured such that there is generally one level of abstraction at which the most basic category cuts can be made (Rosch et al., 1976a). By *category* is meant a number of objects that are considered equivalent. Categories are generally designated by names (e.g., *dog, animal*). A *taxonomy* is a system by which categories are related to one another by means of class inclusion. The greater the inclusiveness of a category within a taxonomy, the higher the level of abstraction. Each category within a taxonomy is entirely included within one other category (unless it is the highest level category) but is not exhaustive of that more inclusive category (see Kay, 1971). Thus the term *level of abstraction* within a taxonomy refers to a particular level of inclusiveness. A familiar taxonomy is the Linnean system for the classification of animals.

Our claims concerning a basic level of abstraction can be formalized in terms of cue validity (Rosch et al., 1976a) or in terms of the set theoretic representation of similarity provided by Tversky (1977, and Tversky and Gati, 1978). Cue validity is a probabilistic concept; the validity of a given cue x as a predictor of a given category y (the conditional probability of y/x) increases as the frequency with which cue x is associated with categories other than y increases and decreases as the frequency with which cue x is associated with category y increases (Beach, 1964a, 1964b; Reed, 1972). The cue validity of an entire category may be defined as the summation of the cue validities for that category of each of the attributes of the category. A category with high cue validity is, by definition, more differentiated from other categories than one of lower cue validity. The elegant formulization that Tversky (1978) provides is in terms of the variable "category resemblance," which is defined as the weighted sum of the measures of all of the common features within a category minus the sum of the measures of all of the distinctive features. Distinctive features include those that belong to only some members of a given category as well as those belonging to contrasting categories. Thus Tversky's formalization does not weight the effect of contrast categories as much as does the cue validity formulation. Tversky suggests that two disjoint classes tend to be combined whenever the weight of the added common features exceeds the weight of the distinctive features.

A working assumption of the research on basic objects is that (1) in the perceived world, information-rich bundles of perceptual and functional attributes occur that form natural discontinuities, and that (2) basic cuts in categorization are made at these discontinuities. Suppose that basic objects (e.g., chair, car) are at the most inclusive level at which there are attributes common to all or most members of the category. Then both total cue validities and category resemblance are maximized at that level of abstraction at which basic objects are categorized. This is, categories one level more abstract will be superordinate categories (e.g., furniture, vehicle) whose members share only a few attributes among each other. Categories below the basic level will be bundles of common and, thus, predictable attributes and functions but contain many attributes that overlap with other categories (for example, kitchen chair shares most of its attributes with other kinds of chairs).

Superordinate categories have lower total cue validity and lower category resemblance than do basic-level categories, because they have fewer common attributes; in fact, the category resemblance measure of items within the superordinate can even be negative due to the high ratio of distinctive to common features. Subordinate categories have lower total cue validity than do basic categories, because they also share most attributes with contrasting subordinate categories; in Tversky's terms, they tend to be combined because the weight of the added common features tends to exceed the weight of the distinctive features. That basic objects are categories at the level of abstraction that maximizes cue validity and maximizes category resemblance is another way of asserting that basic objects are the categories that best mirror the correlational structure of the environment.

We chose to look at concrete objects because they appeared to be a domain that was at once an indisputable aspect of complex natural language classifications yet at the same time was amenable to methods of empirical analysis. In our investigations of basic categories, the correlational structure of concrete objects was considered to consist of a number of inseparable aspects of form and function, any one of which could serve as the starting point for analysis. Four investigations provided converging operational definitions of the basic level of abstraction: attributes in common, motor movements in common, objective similarity in shape, and identifiability of averaged shapes.

8.2.1   Common Attributes

Ethnobiologists had suggested on the basis of linguistic criteria and field observation that the folk genus was the level of classification at which organisms had bundles of attributes in common and maximum discontinuity between classes (see Berlin, 1978). The purpose of our research was to provide a systematic empirical study of the co-occurrence of attributes in the most common taxonomies of biological and man-made objects in our own culture.

The hypothesis that basic level objects are the most inclusive level of classification at which objects have numbers of attributes in common was tested for categories at three levels of abstraction for nine taxonomies: tree, bird, fish, fruit, musical instruments, tool, clothing, furniture, and vehicle. Examples of the three levels for one biological and one nonbiological taxonomy are shown in table 8.1. Criteria for choice of these specific items were that the taxonomies contain the most common (defined by word frequency) categories of concrete nouns in English, that the levels of abstraction bear simple class-inclusion relations to each other, and that those class-inclusion relations be generally known to our subjects (be agreed upon by a sample of native English speakers). The middle level of abstraction was the hypothesized basic level: For nonbiological taxonomies, this corresponded to the intuition of the experimenters (which also turned out to be consistent with Berlin's linguistic criteria); for biological categories, we assumed that the basic level would be the level of the folk generic.

Subjects received sets of words taken from these nine taxonomies; the subject's task was to list all of the attributes he could think of that were true of the items included in the class of things designated by each object name. Thus, for purposes of this study, attributes were defined operationally as whatever subjects agreed them to be with no implications for whether such analysis of an object could or could not be perceptually considered prior to

TABLE 8.1   Examples of Taxonomies Used in Basic Object Research

SUPERORDINATE	BASIC LEVEL	SUBORDINATE
Furniture	Chair	Kitchen chair
		Living-room chair
	Table	Kitchen table
		Dining-room table
	Lamp	Floor lamp
		Desk lamp
Tree	Oak	White oak
		Red oak
	Maple	Silver maple
		Sugar maple
	Birch	River birch
		White birch

knowledge of the object itself. Results of the study were as predicted: Very few attributes were listed for the superordinate categories, a significantly greater number listed for the supposed basic-level objects, and not significantly more attributes listed for subordinate-level objects than for basic-level. An additional study showed essentially the same attributes listed for visually present objects as for the object names. The single unpredicted result was that for the three biological taxonomies, the basic level, as defined by numbers of attributes in common, did not occur at the level of the folk generic but appeared at the level we had originally expected to be superordinate (e.g., *tree* rather than *oak*).

8.2.2   Motor Movements

Inseparable from the perceived attributes of objects are the ways in which humans habitually use or interact with those objects. For concrete objects, such interactions take the form of motor movements. For example, when performing the action of sitting down on a chair, a sequence of body and muscle movements are typically made that are inseparable from the nature of the attributes of chairs — legs, seat, back, etc. This aspect of objects is particularly important in light of the role that sensory-motor interaction with the world appears to play in the development of thought (Bruner, Olver, and Greenfield, 1966; Nelson, 1974; Piaget, 1952).

In our study of motor movements, each of the sets of words used in the previous experiment was administered to new subjects. A subject was asked to describe, in as much finely analyzed detail as possible, the sequences of motor movements he made when using or interacting with the object. Tallies of agreed upon listings of the same movements of the same body part in the same part of the movement sequence formed the unit of analysis. Results were identical to those of the attribute listings; basic objects were the most general classes to have motor sequences in common. For example, there are few motor programs we carry out to items of furniture in general and several specific motor programs carried out in regard to sitting down on chairs, but we sit on kitchen and living-room chairs using essentially the same motor programs.

8.2.3   Similarity in Shapes

Another aspect of the meaning of a class of objects is the appearance of the objects in the class. In order to be able to analyze correlational structures by different but converging methods, it was necessary to find a method of analyzing similarity in the visual aspects of the objects that was not dependent on subjects' descriptions, that was free from effects of the object's name (which would not have been the case for subjects' ratings of similarity), and that went beyond similarity of analyzable, listable attributes that had already been used in the first study described. For this purpose, outlines of the shape of two-dimensional representations of objects were used, an integral aspect of natural forms. Similarity in shape was measured by the amount of overlap of the two outlines when the outlines (normalized for size and orientation) were juxtaposed.

Results showed that the ratio of overlapped to nonoverlapped area when two objects from the same basic-level category (e.g., two cars) were superimposed was far greater than when two objects from the same superordinate category were superimposed (e.g., a car and a motorcycle). Although some gain in ratio of overlap to nonoverlap also occurred for subordinate category objects (e.g., two sports cars), the gain obtained by shifting from basic-level to subordinate objects was significantly less than the gain obtained by shifting from superordinate to basic-level objects.

8.2.4   Identifiability of Averaged Shapes

If the basic level is the most inclusive level at which shapes of objects of a class are similar, a possible result of such similarity may be that the basic level is also the most inclusive level at which an averaged shape of an object can be recognized. To test this hypothesis, the same normalized superimposed shapes used in the previous experiment were used to draw an averaged outline of the overlapped figures. Subjects were then asked to identify both the superordinate category and the specific object depicted. Results showed that basic objects were the most general and inclusive categories at which the objects depicted could be identified. Furthermore, overlaps of subordinate objects were no more identifiable than objects at the basic level.

In summary, our four converging operational definitions of basic objects all indicated the same level of abstraction to be basic in our taxonomies. Admittedly, the basic level for biological objects was not that predicted by the folk genus; however, this fact appeared to be simply accounted for by our subjects' lack of knowledge of the additional depth of real-world attribute structure available at the level of the folk generic (see Rosch et al., 1976a).

8.3   IMPLICATIONS FOR OTHER FIELDS

The foregoing theory of categorization and basic objects has implications for several traditional areas of study in psychology; some of these have been tested.

8.3.1   Imagery

The fact that basic-level objects were the most inclusive categories at which an averaged member of the category could be identified suggested that basic objects might be the most inclusive categories for which it was possible to form a mental image isomorphic to the appearance of members of the class as a whole. Experiments using a signal-detection paradigm and a priming paradigm, both of which have been previously argued to be measures of imagery (Peterson and Graham, 1974; Rosch, 1975c), verified that, in so far as it was meaningful to use the term *imagery,* basic objects appeared to be the most abstract categories for which an image could be reasonably representative of the class as a whole.

8.3.2   Perception

From all that has been said of the nature of basic classifications, it would hardly be reasonable to suppose that in perception of the world, objects were first categorized either at the most abstract or at the most concrete level possible. Two separate studies of picture verification (Rosch et al., 1976a; Smith, Balzano, and Walker, 1978) indicate that, in fact, objects may be first seen or recognized as members of their basic category, and that only with the aid of additional processing can they be identified as members of their superordinate or subordinate category.

8.3.3   Development

We have argued that classification into categories at the basic level is over-determined because perception, motor movements, functions, and iconic images would all lead to the same level of categorization. Thus basic objects should be the first categorizations of concrete objects made by children. In fact, for our nine taxonomies, the basic level was the first named. And even when naming was controlled, pictures of several basic-level objects were sorted into groups "because they were the same type of thing" long before such a technique of sorting has become general in children.

8.3.4   Language

From all that has been said, we would expect the most useful and, thus, most used name for an item to be the basic-level name. In fact, we found that adults almost invariably named pictures of the subordinate items of the nine taxonomies at the basic level, although they knew the correct superordinate and subordinate names for the objects. On a more speculative level, in the evolution of languages, one would expect names to evolve first for basic-level objects, spreading both upward and downward as taxonomies increased in depth. Of great relevance for this hypothesis are Berlin's (1972) claims for such a pattern for the evolution of plant names, and our own (Rosch et al., 1976a) and Newport and Bellugi's (1978) finding for American Sign Language of the Deaf, that it was the basic-level categories that were most often coded by single signs and super- and subordinate categories that were likely to be missing. Thus a wide range of converging operations verify as basic the same levels of abstraction.

8.4   THE HORIZONTAL DIMENSION: INTERNAL STRUCTURE OF CATEGORIES: PROTOTYPES

Most, if not all, categories do not have clear-cut boundaries. To argue that basic object categories follow clusters of perceived attributes is not to say that such attribute clusters are necessarily discontinuous.

In terms of the principles of categorization proposed earlier, cognitive economy dictates that categories tend to be viewed as being as separate from each other and as clear-cut as possible. One way to achieve this is by means of formal, necessary and sufficient criteria for category membership. The attempt to impose such criteria on categories marks virtually all definitions in the tradition of Western reason. The psychological treatment of categories in the standard concept-identification paradigm lies within this tradition. Another way to achieve separateness and clarity of actually continuous categories is by conceiving of each category in terms of its clear cases rather than its boundaries. As Wittgenstein (1953) has pointed out, categorical judgments become a problem only if one is concerned with boundaries — in the normal course of life, two neighbors know on whose property they are standing without exact demarcation of the boundary line. Categories can be viewed in terms of their clear cases if the perceiver places emphasis on the correlational structure of perceived attributes such that the categories are represented by their most structured portions.

By prototypes of categories we have generally meant the clearest cases of category membership defined operationally by people's judgments of goodness of membership in the category. A great deal of confusion in the discussion of prototypes has arisen from two sources. First, the notion of prototypes has tended to become reified as though it meant a specific category member or mental structure. Questions are then asked in an either-or fashion about whether something is or is not the prototype or part of the prototype in exactly the same way in which the question would previously have been asked about the category boundary. Such thinking precisely violates the Wittgensteinian insight that we can judge how clear a case something is and deal with categories on the basis of clear cases in the total absence of information about boundaries. Second, the empirical findings about prototypicality have been confused with theories of processing — that is, there has been a failure to distinguish the structure of categories from theories concerning the use of that structure in processing. Therefore, let us first attempt to look at prototypes in as purely structural a fashion as possible. We will focus on what may be said about prototypes based on operational definitions and empirical findings alone without the addition of processing assumptions.

Perception of typicality differences is, in the first place, an empirical fact of people's judgments about category membership. It is by now a well-documented finding that subjects overwhelmingly agree in their judgments of how good an example or clear a case members are of a category, even for categories about whose boundaries they disagree (Rosch, 1974, 1975b). Such judgments are reliable even under changes of instructions and items (Rips, Shoben, and Smith, 1973; Rosch, 1975b, 1975c; Rosch and Mervis, 1975). Were such agreement and reliability in judgment not to have been obtained, there would be no further point in discussion or investigation of the issue. However, given the empirical verification of degree of prototypicality, we can proceed to ask what principles determine which items will be judged the more prototypical and what other variables might be affected by prototypicality.

In terms of the basic principles of category formation, the formation of category prototypes should, like basic levels of abstraction, be determinate and be closely related to the initial formation of categories. For categories of concrete objects (which do not have a physiological basis, as categories such as colors and forms apparently do — Rosch, 1974), a reasonable hypothesis is that prototypes develop through the same principles such as maximization of cue validity and maximization of category resemblance[1] as those principles governing the formation of the categories themselves.

In support of such a hypothesis, Rosch and Mervis (1975) have shown that the more prototypical of a category a member is rated, the more attributes it has in common with other members of the category and the fewer attributes in common with members of the contrasting categories. This finding was demonstrated for natural language superordinate categories, for natural language basic-level categories, and for artificial categories in which the definition of attributes and the amount of experience with items was completely specified and controlled. The same basic principles can be represented in ways other than through attributes in common. Because the present theory is a structural theory, one aspect of it is that centrality shares the mathematical notions inherent in measures like the mean and mode. Prototypical category members have been found to represent the means of attributes that have a metric, such as size (Reed, 1972; Rosch, Simpson, and Miller, 1976).

In short, prototypes appear to be just those members of a category that most reflect the redundancy structure of the category as a whole. That is, if categories form to maximize the information-rich cluster of attributes in the environment and, thus, the cue validity or category resemblance of the attributes of categories, prototypes of categories appear to form in such a manner as to maximize such clusters and such cue validity still further within categories.

It is important to note that for natural language categories both at the superordinate and basic levels, the extent to which items have attributes common to the category was highly negatively correlated with the extent to which they have attributes belonging to members of contrast categories. This appears to be part of the structure of real-world categories. It may be that such structure is given by the correlated clusters of attributes of the real world. Or such structure, may be a result of the human tendency once a contrast exists to define attributes for contrasting categories so that the categories will be maximally distinctive. In either case, it is a fact that both representativeness within a category and distinctiveness from contrast categories are correlated with prototypicality in real categories. For artificial categories, either principle alone will produce prototype effects (Rosch et al., 1976b; Smith and Balzano, personal communication) depending on the structure of the stimulus set. Thus to perform experiments to try to distinguish which principle is the *one* that determines prototype formation and category processing appears to be an artificial exercise.

8.5   EFFECTS OF PROTOTYPICALITY ON PSYCHOLOGICAL DEPENDENT VARIABLES

The fact that prototypicality is reliably rated and is correlated with category structure does not have clear implications for particular processing models nor for a theory of cognitive representations of categories (see the introduction to Part III of Rosch and Lloyd, 1978 and

Palmer 1978). What is very clear from the extant research is that the prototypicality of items within a category can be shown to affect virtually all of the major dependent variables used as measures in psychological research.

8.5.1   Speed of Processing: Reaction Time

The speed with which subjects can judge statements about category membership is one of the most widely used measures of processing in semantic memory research within the human information-processing framework. Subjects typically are required to respond true or false to statements of the form: X item is a member of Y category, where the dependent variable of interest is reaction time. In such tasks, for natural language categories, responses of true are invariably faster for the items that have been rated more prototypical. Furthermore, Rosch et al. (1976b) had subjects learn artificial categories where prototypicality was defined structurally for some subjects in terms of distance of a gestalt configuration from a prototype, for others in terms of means of attributes, and for still others in terms of family resemblance between attributes. Factors other than the structure of the category, such as frequency, were controlled. After learning was completed, reaction time in a category membership verification task proved to be a function of structural prototypicality.

8.5.2   Speed of Learning of Artificial Categories (Errors) and Order of Development in Children

Rate of learning of new material and the naturally obtainable measure of learning (combined with maturation) reflected in developmental order are two of the most pervasive dependent variables in psychological research. In the artificial categories used by Rosch et al. (1976b), prototypicality for all three types of stimulus material predicted speed of learning of the categories. Developmentally, Anglin (1976) obtained evidence that young children learn category membership of good examples of categories before that of poor examples. Using a category-membership verification technique, Rosch (1973) found that the differences in reaction time to verify good and poor members were far more extreme for 10-year-old children than for adults, indicating that the children had learned the category membership of the prototypical members earlier than that of other members.

8.5.3   Order and Probability of Item Output

Item output is normally taken to reflect some aspect of storage, retrieval, or category search. Battig and Montague (1969) provided a normative study of the probability with which college students listed instances of superordinate semantic categories. The order is correlated with prototypicality ratings (Rosch, 1975b). Furthermore, using the artificial categories in which frequency of experience with all items was controlled, Rosch et al. (1976b) demonstrated that the most prototypical items were the first and most frequently produced items when subjects were asked to list the members of the category.

Effects of Advance Information on Performance: Set, Priming.   For colors (Rosch, 1975c), for natural superordinate semantic categories (Rosch, 1975b), and for artificial categories (Rosch et al., 1976b), it has been shown that degree of prototypicality determines whether advance information about the category name facilitates or inhibits responses in a matching task.

The Logic of Natural Language Use of Category Terms: Hedges, Substitutability into Sentences, Superordination in ASL.   Although logic may treat categories as though membership is all or none, natural languages themselves possess linguistic mechanisms for coding and coping with gradients of category membership.

1. *Hedges.*   In English there are qualifying terms such as "almost" and "virtually," which Lakoff (1972) calls "hedges." Even those who insist that statements such as "A robin is a bird" and "A penguin is a bird" are equally true, have to admit different hedges applicable to statements of category membership. Thus it is correct to say that a penguin is technically a bird but not that a robin is technically a bird, because a robin is more than just technically a bird; it is a real bird, a bird par excellence. Rosch (1975a) showed that when subjects were given sentence frames such as "*X* is virtually *Y*," they reliably placed the more prototypical member of a pair of items into the referent slot, a finding which is isomorphic to Tversky's work on asymmetry of similarity relations (Tversky & Gati, 1978).

2. *Substitutability into sentences.*   The meaning of words is intimately tied to their use in sentences. Rosch (1977) has shown that prototypicality ratings for members of superordinate categories predict the extent to which the member term is substitutable for the superordinate word in sentences. Thus, in the sentence "Twenty or so birds often perch on the telephone wires outside my window and twitter in the morning," the term "sparrow" may readily be substituted for "bird" but the result turns ludicrous by substitution of "turkey," an effect which is not simply a matter of frequency (Rosch, 1975d).

3. *Productive superordinates in ASL.*   Newport and Bellugi (1978) demonstrate that when superordinates in ASL are generated by means of a partial fixed list of category members, those members are the more prototypical items in the category.

In summary, evidence has been presented that prototypes of categories are related to the major dependent variables with which psychological processes are typically measured. What the work summarized does not tell us, however, is considerably more than it tells us. The pervasiveness of prototypes in real-world categories and of prototypicality as a variable indicates that prototypes must have some place in psychological theories of representation, processing, and learning. However, prototypes themselves do not constitute any particular model of processes, representations, or learning. This point is so often misunderstood that it requires discussion:

1. To speak of *a prototype* at all is simply a convenient grammatical fiction; what is really referred to are judgments of degree of prototypicality. Only in some artificial categories is there by definition a literal single prototype (for example, Posner,

Goldsmith, and Welton, 1967; Reed, 1972; Rosch et al., 1976b). For natural-language categories, to speak of a single entity that is the prototype is either a gross misunderstanding of the empirical data or a covert theory of mental representation.

2. Prototypes do not constitute any particular processing model for categories. For example, in pattern recognition, as Palmer (1978) points out, a prototype can be described as well by feature lists or structural descriptions as by templates. And many different types of matching operations can be conceived for matching to a prototype given any of these three modes of representation of the prototypes. Other cognitive processes performed on categories such as verifying the membership of an instance in a category, searching the exemplars of a category for the member with a particular attribute, or understanding the meaning of a paragraph containing the category name are not bound to any single process model by the fact that we may acknowledge prototypes. What the facts about prototypicality do contribute to processing notions is a constraint — process models should not be inconsistent with the known facts about prototypes. For example, a model should not be such as to predict equal verification times for good and bad examples of categories nor predict completely random search through a category.

3. Prototypes do not constitute a theory of representation of categories. Although we have suggested elsewhere that it would be reasonable in light of the basic principles of categorization, if categories were represented by prototypes that were most representative of the items in the category and least representative of items outside the category (Rosch and Mervis, 1975; Rosch, 1977), such a statement remains an unspecified formula until it is made concrete by inclusion in some specific theory of representation. For example, different theories of semantic memory can contain the notion of prototypes in different fashions (Smith, 1978). Prototypes can be represented either by propositional or image systems (see Kosslyn, 1978 and Palmer, 1978). As with processing models, the facts about prototypes can only constrain, but do not determine, models of representation. A representation of categories in terms of conjoined necessary and sufficient attributes alone would probably be incapable of handling all of the presently known facts, but there are many representations other than necessary and sufficient attributes that are possible.

4. Although prototypes must be learned, they do not constitute any particular theory of category learning. For example, learning of prototypicality in the types of categories examined in Rosch and Mervis (1975) could be represented in terms of counting attribute frequency (as in Neuman, 1974), in terms of storage of a set of exemplars to which one later matched the input (see Shepp, 1978 and the introduction to Part II of Rosch and Lloyd, 1978), or in terms of explicit teaching of the prototypes once prototypicality within a category is established in a culture (e.g., "Now that's a *real* coat.")

In short, prototypes only constrain but do not specify representation and process models. In addition, such models further constrain each other. For example, one could not argue for a frequency count of attributes in children's learning of prototypes of categories if one had reason to believe that children's representation of attributes did not allow for separability and selective attention to each attribute (see Garner, 1978 and the introduction to Part II of Rosch and Lloyd, 1978).

8.6   TWO PROBLEMATICAL ISSUES

8.6.1   The Nature of Perceived Attributes

The derivations of basic objects and of prototypes from the basic principles of categorization have depended on the notion of a structure in the perceived world — bundles of perceived world attributes that formed natural discontinuities. When the research on basic objects and their prototypes was initially conceived (Rosch et al., 1976a), I thought of such attributes as inherent in the real world. Thus, given an organism that had sensory equipment capable of perceiving attributes such as wings and feathers, it was a fact in the real world that wings and feathers co-occurred. The state of knowledge of a person might be ignorant of (or indifferent or inattentive to) the attributes or might know of the attributes but be ignorant concerning their correlation. Conversely, a person might know of the attributes and their correlational structure but exaggerate that structure, turning partial into complete correlations (as when attributes true only of many members of a category are thought of as true of all members). However, the environment was thought to constrain categorizations in that human knowledge could not provide correlational structure where there was none at all. For purposes of the basic object experiments, perceived attributes were operationally defined as those attributes listed by our subjects. Shape was defined as measured by our computer programs. We thus seemed to have our system grounded comfortably in the real world.

On contemplation of the nature of many of the attributes listed by our subjects, however, it appeared that three types of attributes presented a problem for such a realistic view: (1) some attributes, such as "seat" for the object "chair," appeared to have names that showed them not to be meaningful prior to knowledge of the object as chair; (2) some attributes such as "large" for the object "piano" seemed to have meaning only in relation to categorization of the object in terms of a superordinate category — piano is large for furniture but small for other kinds of objects such as buildings; (3) some attributes such as "you eat on it" for the object "table" were functional attributes that seemed to require knowledge about humans, their activities, and the real world in order to be understood (see Miller, 1978). That is, it appeared that the analysis of objects into attributes was a rather sophisticated activity that our subjects (and indeed a system of cultural knowledge) might well be considered to be able to impose only *after* the development of the category system.

In fact, the same laws of cognitive economy leading to the push toward basic-level categories and prototypes might also lead to the definition of attributes of categories such that the categories once given would appear maximally distinctive from one another and such that the more prototypical items would appear even more representative of their own and less representative of contrastive categories. Actually, in the evolution of the meaning of terms in languages, probably both the constraint of real-world factors and the construction and reconstruction of attributes are continually present. Thus, given a particular category system, attributes are defined such as to make the system appear as logical and economical as possible. However, if such a system becomes markedly out of phase with real-world constraints, it will probably tend to evolve to be more in line with those constraints — with redefinition of attributes ensuing if necessary. Unfortunately, to state the matter in such a way is to provide no clear place at which we can enter the system as analytical scientists. What is the unit with which to start our analysis? Partly in order to find a more basic real-world unit for analysis than attributes, we have turned our attention to the contexts in which objects occur — that is, to the culturally defined events in which objects serve as props.

8.6.2   The Role of Context in Basic-Level Objects and Prototypes

It is obvious, even in the absence of controlled experimentation, that a man about to buy a chair who is standing in a furniture store surrounded by different chairs among which he must choose will think and speak about chairs at other than the basic level of "chair." Similarly, in regard to prototypes, it is obvious that if asked for the most typical African animal, people of any age will not name the same animal as when asked for the most typical American pet animal. Because interest in context is only beginning, it is not yet clear just what experimentally defined contexts will affect what dependent variables for what categories. But it is predetermined that there will be context effects for both the level of abstraction at which an object is considered and for which items are named, learned, listed, or expected in a category. Does this mean that our findings in regard to basic levels and prototypes are relevant only to the artificial situation of the laboratory in which a context is not specified?

Actually, both basic levels and prototypes are, in a sense, theories about context itself. The basic level of abstraction is that level of abstraction that is appropriate for using, thinking about, or naming an object in most situations in which the object occurs (Rosch et al., 1976a). And when a context is not specified in an experiment, people must contribute their own context. Presumably, they do not do so randomly. Indeed, it seems likely that, in the absence of a specified context, subjects assume what they consider the normal context or situation for occurrence of that object. To make such claims about categories appears to demand an analysis of the actual events in daily life in which objects occur.

8.7   THE ROLE OF OBJECTS IN EVENTS

The attempt we have made to answer the issues of the origin of attributes and the role of context has been in terms of the use of objects in the events of daily human life. The study of events grew out of an interest in categorizations of the flow of experience. That is, our initial interest was in the question of whether any of the principles of categorization we had found useful for understanding concrete objects appeared to apply to the cutting up of the continuity of experience into the discrete bounded temporal units that we call *events*.

Previously, events have been studied primarily from two perspectives in psychology. Within ecological and social psychology, an observer records and attempts to segment the stream of another person's behavior into event sequences (for example, Barker and Wright, 1955; Newtson, 1976). And within the artificial intelligence tradition. Story Understanders are being constructed that can "comprehend," by means of event scripts, statements about simple, culturally predictable sequences such as going to a restaurant (Shank, 1975).

The unit of the event would appear to be a particularly important unit for analysis. Events stand at the interface between an analysis of social structure and culture and an analysis of individual psychology. It may be useful to think of scripts for events as the level of theory at which we can specify how culture and social structure enter the individual mind.

Could we use events as the basic unit from which to derive an understanding of objects? Could we view objects as props for the carrying out of events and have the functions, perceptual attributes, and levels of abstraction of objects fall out of their role in such events?

Our research to date has been a study rather than an experiment and more like a pilot study at that. Events were defined neither by observation of others nor by a priori units for scripts but introspectively in the following fashion. Students in a seminar on events were asked to choose a particular evening on which to list the events that they remembered of that day — e.g., to answer the question what did I do? (or what happened to me?) that day by means of a list of the names of the events. They were to begin in the morning. The students were aware of the nature of the inquiry and that the focus of interest was on the units that they would perceive as the appropriate units into which to chunk the days' happenings. After completing the list for that day, they were to do the same sort of lists for events remembered from the previous day, and thus to continue backwards to preceding days until they could remember no more day's events. They also listed events for units smaller and larger than a day: for example, the hour immediately preceding writing and the previous school quarter.

The results were somewhat encouraging concerning the tractability of such a means of study. There was considerable agreement on the kinds of units into which a day should be broken — units such as making coffee, taking a shower, and going to statistics class. No one used much smaller units: That is, units such as picking up the toothpaste tube, squeezing toothpaste onto the brush, etc., never occurred. Nor did people use larger units such as "got myself out of the house in the morning" or "went to all my afternoon classes." Furthermore, the units that were listed did not change in size or type with their recency or remoteness in time to the writing. Thus, for the time unit of the hour preceding writing, components of events were not listed. Nor were larger units of time given for a day a week past than for the day on which the list was composed. Indeed, it was dramatic how, as days further and further in the past appeared, fewer and fewer events were remembered although the type of unit for those that were remembered remained the same. That is, for a day a week past, a student would not say that he now only remembered getting himself out of the house in the morning (though such "summarizing" events could be inferred); rather he either did or did not remember feeding the cat that day (an occurrence that could also be inferred but for which inference and memory were introspectively clearly distinguishable). Indeed, it appeared that events such as "all the morning chores" as a whole do not have a memory representation separate from memory of doing the individual chores — perhaps in the way that superordinate categories, such as furniture, do not appear to be imageable per se apart from imaging individual items in the category. It should be noted that event boundaries appeared to be marked in a reasonable way by factors such as changes of the actors participating with ego, changes in the objects ego interacts with, changes in place, and changes in the type or rate of activity with an object, and by notable gaps in time between two reported events.

A good candidate for the basic level of abstraction for events is the type of unit into which the students broke their days. The events they listed were just those kinds of events for which Shank (1975) has provided scripts. Scripts of events analyze the event into individual units of action; these typically occur in a predictable order. For example, the script for going to a restaurant contains script elements such as entering, going to a table, ordering, eating, and paying. Some recent research has provided evidence for the psychological reality of scripts and their elements (Bower, 1976).

Our present concern is with the role of concrete objects in events. What categories of objects are required to serve as props for events at the level of abstraction of those listed by the students? In general, we found that the event name itself combined most readily with superordinate noun categories; thus, one gets dressed with clothes and needs various kitchen utensils to make breakfast. When such activities were analyzed into their script elements, the basic level appeared as the level of abstraction of objects necessary to script the events; e.g., in getting dressed, one puts on pants, sweater, and shoes, and in making breakfast, one cooks eggs in a frying pan.

With respect to prototypes, it appears to be those category members judged the more prototypical that have attributes that enable them to fit into the typical and agreed upon script elements. We are presently collecting normative data on the intersection of common events, the objects associated with those events and the other sets of events associated with those objects.[2] In addition, object names for eliciting events are varied in level of abstraction and in known prototypicality in given categories. Initial results show a similar pattern to that obtained in the earlier research in which it was found that the more typical members of superordinate categories could replace the superordinate in sentence frames generated by subjects told to "make up a sentence" that used the superordinate (Rosch, 1977). That is, the task of using a given concrete noun in a sentence appears to be an indirect method of eliciting a statement about the events in which objects play a part; that indirect method showed clearly that prototypical category members are those that can play the role in events expected of members of that category.

The use of deviant forms of object names in narratives accounts for several recently explored effects in the psychological literature. Substituting object names at other than the basic level within scripts results in obviously deviant descriptions. Substitution of superordinates produces just those types of narrative that Bransford and Johnson (1973) have claimed are not comprehended; for example, "The procedure is actually quite simple. First you arrange things into different groups. Of course, one pile may be sufficient [p. 400]." It should be noted in the present context that what Bransford and Johnson call context cues are actually names of basic-level events (e.g., washing clothes) and that one function of hearing the event name is to enable the reader to translate the superordinate terms into basic-level objects and actions. Such a translation appears to be a necessary aspect of our ability to match linguistic descriptions to world knowledge in a way that produces the "click of comprehension."

On the other hand, substitution of subordinate terms for basic-level object names in scripts gives the effect of satire or snobbery. For example, a review (Garis, 1975) of a pretentious novel accused of actually being about nothing more than brand-name snobbery concludes, "And so, after putting away my 10-year-old Royal 470 manual and lining up my Mongol number 3 pencils on my Goldsmith Brothers Formica imitation-wood desk, I slide into my oversize squirrel-skin L. L. Bean slippers and shuffle off to the kitchen. There, holding *Decades* in my trembling right hand, I drop it, *plunk,* into my new Sears 20-gallon, celadon-green Permanex trash can [p. 48]."

Analysis of events is still in its initial stages. It is hoped that further understanding of the functions and attributes of objects can be derived from such an analysis.

SUMMARY

The first part of this chapter showed how the same principles of categorization could account for the taxonomic structure of a category system organized around a basic level and also for the formation of the categories that occur within this basic level. Thus the principles described accounted for both the vertical and horizontal structure of category systems. Four converging operations were employed to establish the claim that the basic level provides the cornerstone of a taxonomy. The section on prototypes distinguished the empirical evidence for prototypes as structural facts about categories from the possible role of prototypes in cognitive processing, representation, and learning. Then we considered assumptions about the nature of the attributes of real-world objects and assumptions about context — insofar as attributes and contexts underlie the claim that there is structure in the world. Finally, a highly tentative pilot study of attributes and functions of objects as props in culturally defined events was presented.

NOTES

1. Tversky formalizes prototypicality as the member or members of the category with the highest summed similarity to all members of the category. This measure, although formally more tractable than that of cue validity, does not take account, as cue validity does, of an item's dissimilarity to contrast categories. This issue is discussed further later.

2. This work is being done by Elizabeth Kreusi.

REFERENCES

Anglin, J. (1976). Les premiers termes de référence de l'enfant. In S. Ehrlich and E. Tulving (Eds.), *La memoire sémantique.* Paris: Bulletin de Psychologie.

Barker, R., & Wright, H. (1955). *Midwest and its children.* Evanston, Ill.: Row-Peterson.

Battig, W. F., & Montague, W. E. (1969). Category norms for verbal items in 56 categories: A replication and extension of the Connecticut category norms. *Journal of Experimental Psychology Monograph, 80* (3, Pt. 2).

Beach, L. R. (1964). Cue probabilism and inference behavior. *Psychological Monographs. 78* (Whole No. 582). (a)

Beach, L. R. (1964). Recognition, assimilation, and identification of objects. *Psychological Monographs, 78* (Whole No. 583). (b)

Berlin, B. (1972). Speculations on the growth of ethnobotanical nomenclature. *Language in Society, 1,* 51–86.

Berlin, B. (1978). Ethnobiological classification. In E. Rosch and B. B. Lloyd (Eds.), *Cognition and categorization.* Hillsdale, NJ: Lawrence Erlbaum Associates, Inc.

Borges, J. L. (1966). *Other inquisitions 1937–1952.* New York: Washington Square Press.

Bower, G. (1976). *Comprehending and recalling stories.* Paper presented as Division 3 presidential address to the American Psychological Association, Washington, D.C., September.

Bransford, J. D., & Johnson, M. K. (1973). Considerations of some problems of comprehension. In W. Chase (Ed.), *Visual information processing.* New York: Academic Press.

Bruner, J. S., Olver, R. R., & Greenfield, P. M. (1966). *Studies in cognitive growth.* New York: Wiley.

Garis, L. (1975). The Margaret Mead of Madison Avenue. *Ms.,* March, pp. 47–48.

Garner, W. R. (1974). *The processing of information and structure.* New York: Wiley.

Garner, W. R. (1978). Aspects of a stimulus: Features, dimensions, and configurations. In E. Rosch and B. B. Lloyd (Eds.), *Cognition and categorization.* Hillsdale, NJ: Lawrence Erlbaum Associates, Inc.

Kay, P. (1971). Taxonomy and semantic contrast. *Language, 47,* 866–887.

Kosslyn, S. M. (1978). Imagery and internal representation. In E. Rosch and B. B. Lloyd (Eds.), *Cognition and Categorization.* Hillsdale, NJ: Lawrence Erlbaum Associates, Inc.

Lakoff, G. (1972). Hedges: A study in meaning criteria and the logic of fuzzy concepts. *Papers from the eighth regional meeting, Chicago Linguistics Society.* Chicago: University of Chicago Linguistics Department.

Miller, G. A. (1978). Practical and lexical knowledge. In E. Rosch and B. B. Lloyd (Eds.), *Cognition and categorization.* Hillsdale, NJ: Lawrence Erlbaum Associates, Inc.

Nelson, K. (1974). Concept, word and sentence: Interrelations in acquisition and development. *Psychological Review, 81,* 267–285.

Neuman, P. G. (1974). An attribute frequency model for the abstraction of prototypes. *Memory and Cognition, 2,* 241–248.

Newport, E. L., & Bellugi, U. (1978). Linguistic expression of category levels in a visual-gestural language: A flower is a flower is a flower. In E. Rosch and B. B. Lloyd (Eds.), *Cognition and categorization.* Hillsdale, NJ: Lawrence Erlbaum Associates, Inc.

Newtson, D. (1976). Foundations of attribution: The perception of ongoing behavior. In J. Harvey, W. Ickes, and R. Kidd (Eds.), *New directions in attribution research.* Hillsdale, N.J.: Lawrence Erlbaum Associates.

Palmer, S. (1977). Hierarchical structure in perceptual representation. *Cognitive Psychology, 9,* 441–474.

Palmer, S. E. (1978). Fundamental aspects of cognitive representation. In E. Rosch and B. B. Lloyd (Eds.), *Cognition and categorization.* Hillsdale, NJ: Lawrence Erlbaum Associates, Inc.

Peterson, M. J., & Graham, S. E. (1974). Visual detection and visual imagery. *Journal of Experimental Psychology, 103,* 509–514.

Piaget, J. (1952). *The origins of intelligence in children.* New York: International Universities Press.

Posner, M. I., Goldsmith, R., & Welton, K. E.(1967). Perceived distance and the classification of distorted patterns. *Journal of Experimental Psychology, 73,* 28–38.

Reed, S. K. (1972). Pattern recognition and categorization. *Cognitive Psychology, 3,* 382–407.

Rips, L. J., Shoben, E. J., & Smith, E. E. (1973). Semantic distance and the verification of semantic relations. *Journal of Verbal Learning and Verbal Behavior, 12,* 1–20.

Rosch, E. (1973). On the internal structure of perceptual and semantic categories. In T. E. Moore (Ed.), *Cognitive development and the acquisition of language.* New York: Academic Press.

Rosch, E. (1974). Linguistic relativity. In A. Silverstein (Ed.), *Human communication: Theoretical perspectives.* New York: Halsted Press.

Rosch, E. (1975). Cognitive reference points. *Cognitive Psychology, 7,* 532–547. (a)

Rosch, E. (1975). Cognitive representations of semantic categories. *Journal of Experimental Psychology: General, 104,* 192–233. (b)

Rosch, E. (1975). The nature of mental codes for color categories. *Journal of Experimental Psychology: Human Perception and Performance, 1,* 303–322. (c)

Rosch, E. (1975). Universals and cultural specifics in human categorization. In R. Brislin, S. Bochner, and W. Lonner (Eds.), *Cross-cultural perspectives on learning.* New York: Halsted Press. (d)

Rosch, E. (1977). Human categorization. In N. Warren (Ed.), *Advances in cross-cultural psychology* (Vol. 1). London: Academic Press.

Rosch, E., & Lloyd, B. B. (1978). *Cognition and categorization.* Hillsdale, NJ: Lawrence Erlbaum Associates, Inc.

Rosch, E., & Mervis, C. B. (1975). Family resemblances: Studies in the internal structure of categories. *Cognitive Psychology, 7,* 573–605.

Rosch, E., Mervis, C. B., Gray, W. D., Johnson, D. M., & Boyes-Braem, P. (1976). Basic objects in natural categories. *Cognitive Psychology, 8,* 382–439. (a)

Rosch, E., Simpson, C., & Miller, R. S. (1976). Structural bases of typicality effects. *Journal of Experimental Psychology: Human Perception and Performance. 2,* 491–502. (b)

Shank, R. C. (1975). The structure of episodes in memory. In D. G. Bobrow and A. Collins (Eds.), *Representation and understanding: Studies in cognitive science.* New York: Academic Press.

Shepp, B. E. (1978). From perceived similarity to dimensional structure: A new hypothesis about perspective development. In E. Rosch and B. B. Lloyd (Eds.), *Cognition and categorization.* Hillsdale, NJ: Lawrence Erlbaum Associates, Inc.

Smith, E. E., (1978). Theories of semantic memory. In W. K. Estes (Ed.), *Handbook of learning and cognitive processes* (Vol. 5). Hillsdale, N.J.: Lawrence Erlbaum Associates.

Smith, E. E., & Balzano, G. J. (1977). Personal communication, April.

Smith, E. E., Balzano, G. J., & Walker, J. H. (1978). Nominal, perceptual, and semantic codes in picture categorization. In J. Cotton and R. Klatzky (Eds.), *Semantic factors in cognition.* Hillsdale, N.J.: Lawrence Erlbaum Associates.

Tversky, A. (1977). Features of similarity. *Psychological Review, 84,* 327–352.

Tversky, A., & Gati, I. (1978). Studies of similarity. In E. Rosch and B. B. Lloyd (Eds.), *Cognition and categorization.* Hillsdale, NJ: Lawrence Erlbaum Associates, Inc.

Wittgenstein, L. (1953). *Philosophical investigations.* New York: Macmillan.

CHAPTER NINE

PHILOSOPHICAL INVESTIGATIONS, SECTIONS 65–78

LUDWIG WITTGENSTEIN

65. Here we come up against the great question that lies behind all these considerations. — For someone might object against me: "You take the easy way out! You talk about all sorts of language-games, but have nowhere said what the essence of a language-game, and hence of language, is: what is common to all these activities, and what makes them into language or parts of language. So you let yourself off the very part of the investigation that once gave you yourself most headache, the part about the *general form of propositions* and of language."

And this is true. — Instead of producing something common to all that we call language, I am saying that these phenomena have no one thing in common which makes us use the same word for all, — but that they are *related* to one another in many different ways. And it is because of this relationship, or these relationships, that we call them all "language." I will try to explain this.

66. Consider for example the proceedings that we call "games." I mean board-games, card-games, ball-games, Olympic games, and so on. What is common to them all? — Don't say: "There *must* be something common, or they would not be called 'games'" — but *look and see* whether there is anything common to all. — For if you look at them you will not see something that is common to *all,* but similarities, relationships, and a whole series of them at that. To repeat: don't think, but look! — Look for example at board-games, with their multifarious relationships. Now pass to card-games; here you find many correspondences with the first group, but many common features drop out, and others appear. When we pass next to ball-games, much that is common is retained, but much is lost. — Are they all 'amusing'? Compare chess with noughts and crosses. Or is there always winning and losing, or competition between players? Think of patience. In ball-games there is winning and losing; but when a child throws his ball at the wall and catches it again, this feature has disappeared.

Look at the parts played by skill and luck; and at the difference between skill in chess and skill in tennis. Think now of games like ring-a-ring-a-roses; here is the element of amusement, but how many other characteristic features have disappeared! And we can go through the many, many other groups of games in the same way; can see how similarities crop up and disappear.

And the result of this examination is: we see a complicated network of similarities overlapping and criss-crossing: sometimes overall similarities, sometimes similarities of detail.

67. I can think of no better expression to characterize these similarities than "family resemblances"; for the various resemblances between members of a family: build, features, colour of eyes, gait, temperament, etc. overlap and criss-cross in the same way. — And I shall say: 'games' form a family.

And for instance the kinds of number form a family in the same way. Why do we call something a "number"? Well, perhaps because it has a — direct — relationship with several things that have hitherto been called number; and this can be said to give it an indirect relationship to other things we call the same name. And we extend our concept of number as in spinning a thread we twist fibre on fibre. And the strength of the thread does not reside in the fact that some one fibre runs through its whole length, but in the overlapping of many fibres.

But if someone wished to say: "There is something common to all these constructions — namely the disjunction of all their common properties" — I should reply: Now you are only playing with words. One might as well say: "Something runs through the whole thread — namely the continuous overlapping of those fibres."

68. "All right: the concept of number is defined for you as the logical sum of these individual interrelated concepts: cardinal numbers, rational numbers, real numbers, etc.; and in the same way the concept of a game as the logical sum of a corresponding set of sub-concepts." — It need not be so. For I *can* give the concept 'number' rigid limits in this way, that is, use the word "number" for a rigidly limited concept, but I can also use it so that the extension of the concept is *not* closed by a frontier. And this is how we do use the word "game." For how is the concept of a game bounded? What still counts as a game and what no longer does? Can you give the boundary? No. You can *draw* one; for none has so far been drawn. (But that never troubled you before when you used the word "game.")

"But then the use of the word is unregulated, the 'game' we play with it is unregulated." — It is not everywhere circumscribed by rules; but no more are there any rules for how high one throws the ball in tennis, or how hard; yet tennis is a game for all that and has rules too.

69. How should we explain to someone what a game is? I imagine that we should describe *games* to him, and we might add: "This *and similar things* are called 'games.'" And do we know any more about it ourselves? Is it only other people whom we cannot tell exactly what a game is? — But this is not ignorance. We do not know the boundaries because none have been drawn. To repeat, we can draw a boundary — for a special purpose. Does it take that to make the concept usable? Not at all! (Except for that special purpose.) No more than it took the definition: 1 pace = 75 cm. to make the measure of length 'one pace' usable. And if you want to say "But still, before that it wasn't an exact

measure," then I reply: very well, it was an inexact one. — Though you still owe me a definition of exactness.

70. "But if the concept 'game' is uncircumscribed like that, you don't really know what you mean by a 'game.'" — When I give the description: "The ground was quite covered with plants" — do you want to say I don't know what I am talking about until I can give a definition of a plant?

My meaning would be explained by, say, a drawing and the words "The ground looked roughly like this." Perhaps I even say "it looked *exactly* like this." — Then were just *this* grass and *these* leaves there, arranged just like this? No, that is not what it means. And I should not accept any picture as exact in *this* sense.

Someone says to me: "Shew the children a game." I teach them gaming with dice, and the other says "I didn't mean that sort of game." Must the exclusion of the game with dice have come before his mind when he gave me the order?

71. One might say that the concept 'game' is a concept with blurred edges. — "But is a blurred concept a concept at all?" — Is an indistinct photograph a picture of a person at all? Is it even always an advantage to replace an indistinct picture by a sharp one? Isn't the indistinct one often exactly what we need?

Frege compares a concept to an area and says that an area with vague boundaries cannot be called an area at all. This presumably means that we cannot do anything with it. — But is it senseless to say: "Stand roughly there"? Suppose that I were standing with someone in a city square and said that. As I say it I do not draw any kind of boundary, but perhaps point with my hand — as if I were indicating a particular *spot*. And this is just how one might explain to someone what a game is. One gives examples and intends them to be taken in a particular way. — I do not, however, mean by this that he is supposed to see in those examples that common thing which I — for some reason — was unable to express; but that he is now to *employ* those examples in a particular way. Here giving examples is not an *indirect* means of explaining — in default of a better. For any general definition can be misunderstood too. The point is that *this* is how we play the game. (I mean the language-game with the word "game.")

72. *Seeing what is common.* Suppose I shew someone various multicoloured pictures, and say: "The colour you see in all these is called 'yellow ochre.'" — This is a definition, and the other will get to understand it by looking for and seeing what is common to the pictures. Then he can look *at,* can point *to,* the common thing.

Compare with this a case in which I shew him figures of different shapes all painted the same colour, and say: "What these have in common is called 'yellow ochre.'"

And compare this case: I shew him samples of different shades of blue and say: "The colour that is common to all these is what I call 'blue.'"

73. When someone defines the names of colours for me by pointing to samples and saying "This colour is called 'blue,' this 'green' . . . " this case can be compared in many respects to putting a table in my hands, with the words written under the colour-samples. — Though this comparison may mislead in many ways. — One is now inclined to extend the comparison: to have understood the definition means to have in one's mind an idea of the thing defined, and that is a sample or picture. So if I am shewn various different leaves and told "This is called a 'leaf,'" I get an idea of the shape of a leaf, a picture of it in my mind. — But what does the picture of a leaf look like when it does not shew us any particular shape,

but 'what is common to all shapes of leaf'? Which shade is the 'sample in my mind' of the colour green — the sample of what is common to all shades of green?

"But might there not be such 'general' samples? Say a schematic leaf, or a sample of *pure* green?" — Certainly there might. But for such a schema to be understood as a *schema,* and not as the shape of a particular leaf, and for a slip of pure green to be understood as a sample of all that is greenish and not as a sample of pure green — this in turn resides in the way the samples are used.

Ask yourself: what *shape* must the sample of the colour green be? Should it be rectangular? Or would it then be the sample of a green rectangle? — So should it be 'irregular' in shape? And what is to prevent us then from regarding it — that is, from using it — only as a sample of irregularity of shape?

74. Here also belongs the idea that if you see this leaf as a sample of 'leaf shape in general' you *see* it differently from someone who regards it as, say, a sample of this particular shape. Now this might well be so — though it is not so — for it would only be to say that, as a matter of experience, if you *see* the leaf in a particular way, you use it in such-and-such a way or according to such-and-such rules. Of course, there is such a thing as seeing in *this* way or *that;* and there are also cases where whoever sees a sample like *this* will in general use it in *this* way, and whoever sees it otherwise in another way. For example, if you see the schematic drawing of a cube as a plane figure consisting of a square and two rhombi you will, perhaps, carry out the order "Bring me something like this" differently from someone who sees the picture three-dimensionally.

75. What does it mean to know what a game is? What does it mean, to know it and not be able to say it? Is this knowledge somehow equivalent to an unformulated definition? So that if it were formulated I should be able to recognize it as the expression of my knowledge? Isn't my knowledge, my concept of a game, completely expressed in the explanations that I could give? That is, in my describing examples of various kinds of games; shewing how all sorts of other games can be constructed on the analogy of these; saying that I should scarcely include this or this among games; and so on.

76. If someone were to draw a sharp boundary I could not acknowledge it as the one that I too always wanted to draw, or had drawn in my mind. For I did not want to draw one at all. His concept can then be said to be not the same as mine, but akin to it. The kinship is that of two pictures, one of which consists of colour patches with vague contours, and the other of patches similarly shaped and distributed, but with clear contours. The kinship is just as undeniable as the difference.

77. And if we carry this comparison still further it is clear that the degree to which the sharp picture *can* resemble the blurred one depends on the latter's degree of vagueness. For imagine having to sketch a sharply defined picture 'corresponding' to a blurred one. In the latter there is a blurred red rectangle: for it you put down a sharply defined one. Of course — several such sharply defined rectangles can be drawn to correspond to the indefinite one. — But if the colours in the original merge without a hint of any outline won't it become a hopeless task to draw a sharp picture corresponding to the blurred one? Won't you then have to say: "Here I might just as well draw a circle or heart as a rectangle, for all the colours merge. Anything — and nothing — is right." — And this is the position you are in if you look for definitions corresponding to our concepts in aesthetics or ethics.

In such a difficulty always ask yourself: How did we *learn* the meaning of this word ("good" for instance)? From what sort of examples? in what language-games? Then it will be easier for you to see that the word must have a family of meanings.

78. Compare *knowing* and *saying:*

how many feet high Mont Blanc is —
how the word "game" is used —
how a clarinet sounds.

If you are surprised that one can know something and not be able to say it, you are perhaps thinking of a case like the first. Certainly not of one like the third.

CHAPTER TEN

REPRESENTATION AND KNOWLEDGE IN LONG-TERM MEMORY

Mind and Brain

EDWARD E. SMITH

STEPHEN M. KOSSLYN

You walk into a room. People are standing around a table covered with objects wrapped in a brightly colored covering. There is an object on a plate with small cylindrical projections coming out of it. Someone sets these sticks on fire. People exclaim things, but what do their words mean? Now the people begin to sing. They seem to be singing at or to you, and they seem to be happy and friendly. But it's hard to understand what they're singing, because while they all seem to know this song — it's quite short, melodically very simple — they are singing raggedly and not very well, although with enthusiasm.

Is this a dream? No. Through an exercise of the imagination, you just attended your own birthday party while being denied access to your knowledge in long-term memory — which meant you had no knowledge of your culture or tribal customs, no knowledge of the significance of the objects in front of you or the words called out or sung to you. This kind of knowledge normally comes to each of us easily, from the times of our earliest experiences in the world, and has an enormous influence on our lives. How is it stored, how is it used, how does it work?

10.1 ROLES OF KNOWLEDGE IN COGNITION

Knowledge is often thought of as constituting particular bodies of facts, techniques, and procedures that cultures develop, such as "knowledge of baseball statistics," "knowledge of the guitar," "knowledge of how to order a meal in a restaurant." Such knowledge in most cases comes consciously, after long and often difficult practice. But in its larger sense knowledge mostly exists and operates outside awareness: we are typically clueless about the constant and vast impact that knowledge has on us each moment. The formal sort of knowledge — the causes of the American Revolution or the designated-hitter rule in baseball — is a relatively small and uninfluential subset of the totality of what you know and of what affects your life. The bulk of your knowledge — and the knowledge that most influences your daily life — is relatively mundane knowledge about things such as clothing, driving, and love (well, perhaps not so mundane). Thus, **knowledge,** in its most iuclusive sense, and the sense in which the term is used in cognitive psychology, is information about the world that is stored in memory, ranging from the everyday to the formal. Knowledge is often further defined as information about the world that is likely to be true, that you have justification for believing, and that is coherent (for further discussion, see Carruthers, 1992; Lehrer, 1990).

Knowledge so defined makes ordinary life possible in a number of ways. It is essential for the competent functioning of most mental processes, not only in memory, language, and thought, but also in perception and attention. Without knowledge, *any* mental process would stumble into ineffectiveness. Just how would you experience your birthday party if knowledge simply switched off?

For one thing, you'd be unable to get beyond the surface of the objects and sensations that surround you in the world. Each one would be unique, without history or meaning. Specifically, you would be unable to *categorize* things. Categorization is the ability to establish that a perceived entity belongs to a particular group of things that share key characteristics. "Cakes," for example, form a category of entities that people perceive as related in their structure and use. Without knowledge, you can't categorize — so the cake on the table at your birthday party meant nothing to you. Consider a camera that registers on film an image of your birthday bash. Would the camera *know* that the scene contains a cake? No. A camera can show an image of the cake, but it is simply recording a particular arrangement of light on film, no different in quality or significance from any other arrangement of light; the camera lacks knowledge about meaningful entities and events in the world. And in the "thought experiment" of your birthday party, you have become something like a camera, able to register images but unable to grasp what they mean, what commonality they have with other entities present or not present in the scene. So categorization is one thing that would go if you lost your knowledge.

Once you assign a perceived entity to a category, further knowledge about the category becomes available for your use. If you know it is a cake, associations arise: Is this a celebration? Is this a special treat for dessert? Indeed, the whole point of categorization is to allow you to draw *inferences,* namely, to allow you to derive information not explicitly present in a single member of a category but available because of knowledge of the characteristics of the group or groups to which it belongs. Once you categorize a perceived entity, many useful inferences can follow. If you are able to assign an object wrapped in brightly colored paper to the category of "gifts," your knowledge of gifts would produce inferences about the wrapped object that go beyond what you-as-a-camera currently see — the object is a box, which might contain a thoughtful gift that a friend has bought you or a not-so-thoughtful gag. Though you cannot yet see inside the box, your inferential knowledge about gifts suggests these possibilities. Without being able to categorize, could you produce these inferences? Would a camera be able to infer that the wrapped box could contain a gift or a gag? Of course not, and neither would you if you had lost your knowledge.

Standing in the doorway, looking at this scene, you do not know it is your birthday party. You can't know this because you lack knowledge to draw inferences that go beyond what you see. What about *action?* Would you know what to do in this situation? Would you know to blow out the candles, respond to your friends' joshing, open your presents? There's no biological reflex that would help you here. So again, the answer is, no: no knowledge means no appropriate action. Think of the camera — on registering a box in its viewfinder, would it know that the box is a gift to be unwrapped? No, it wouldn't; and neither would you without knowledge about gifts.

Now someone is standing in front of the birthday table, obscuring from your view half your name on the uncut cake. Normally, you would readily infer the whole name. In your present no-knowledge state, however, would you? No; no more than would a camera. Without knowledge, you cannot complete the partial perception, but with knowledge you can. Ordinarily you constantly complete partial perceptions in this manner as you encounter occluded objects in the environment. What do you see in Figure 10.1? The letters l-e-a-r-t or the word *heart?* The nonword *leart* is actually closest to what is on the page, but your first categorization of the string of letters was probably *heart.* Why? Because — as we saw in Chapter 2 — knowledge of the word *heart* in memory led to the inference that the word was present but partially occluded by some sort of spill on the page; it's doubtful you have *leart* in memory. As we saw in Chapter 2, knowledge affects *perception.*

A party guest yells, "Look out the window! That looks like Madonna starting the truck in the driveway!" If you were in your normal, not your no-knowledge, state, when you look out the window, where would your *attention* go? You'd probably try to see inside the truck's cab, not scan its exterior. But nothing in the guest's exclamation directed your attention inside, so why would you look there? The obvious answer is that knowledge about what starting a vehicle entails guided your attention. Even if you don't drive yourself, you know generally where someone who is driving sits. But if you lacked knowledge — or, again, if you were a camera — you would have no idea where to focus your attention.

A few weeks before the party, you borrowed $50 from a friend, whom you've been avoiding because you haven't yet got the funds together to repay the loan. Now this friend

FIGURE 10.1   Knowledge leads to inferences during perception
Although the letters in the figure most closely approximate l-e-a-r-t, the likely assumption is the word *heart.* This inference comes from knowledge of familiar words and of how it is possible for spills to obscure them. Essentially, the brain reasons unconsciously that the word is more likely to be *heart* than *leart* and that a spill has partly obscured an "h."

is standing at the front of the crowd in your room, offering you one of the large boxes. Are you embarrassed? Nope. Without knowledge you'd be blissfully unaware that you should feel guilty about not having repaid your friend. Even if you remembered borrowing the money and when you borrowed it, you wouldn't be able to infer that you should have paid it back by now, and that because you haven't, you're a jerk. A specific memory without knowledge doesn't help you very much, because without knowledge you're not able to draw useful inferences from what you remember.

After the song, everyone at the party shouts at you in unison, "We love you!" Pretty nice — but you have no idea what they're saying. Why not? Because the ability to understand *language* requires knowledge. First, you need knowledge to recognize words and to know what they mean. If you didn't have knowledge about English, you would no more know that *love* is a word than that *loze* is not. Similarly, you would no more know that *love* means to hold people dear than to tattoo them. Second, you need knowledge to assemble the meanings of the words in a sentence. When your friends say, "We love you," how do you know they're saying that they love you, not that you love them? How do you know that "we" refers to the lovers and that "you" refers to the lovee? Why isn't it the other way around? Knowledge about the verb *to love* specifies that the lover comes before the verb in an active sentence, and that the lovee comes after it. In a passive sentence, such as "You are loved by us," your knowledge specifies that these roles are reversed. Instantly on hearing sentences like these, you are able, because of your knowledge, to make accurate interpretations of who is doing what to whom.

Now the party's in high gear, and the karaoke machine comes out. Two of your friends are singing, one of them a real belter. Another song, and now the belter is paired with someone who sings even louder. Now it's your turn, but you're a bit shy. The quieter singer from the first duet and the really loud one from the second both volunteer their services. You need the support of a really strong voice. Whom do you pick? The vocally fortified type from the second pair, of course. But wait — how did you unerringly pick her as the louder of the two volunteers — they haven't sung together, so how could you judge? Well, in a no-knowledge state, you couldn't. But you could with knowledge of the relationship described by the principle of transitivity, which you may or may not ever have heard of, but which nonetheless you have internalized through experience. If X is louder than Y, and Y is louder than Z, then X is louder than Z. So you can pick the singer who will make the duet with you a song to remember — but without knowledge you'd be up a creek, unable to draw the inference that successfully guided your choice. Transitivity is but one example of the many ways in which knowledge enables sophisticated *thought*. Knowledge underlies virtually every form that thought takes, including decision making, planning, problem solving, and reasoning in general.

Without knowledge in its various roles, in categorization and inference, action, perception and attention, memory, language, and thought, you'd be a zombie at the party. You'd simply be registering images of the scene passively like a camera, and that's about it. You'd be frustratingly inept at understanding anything about the situation, or acting suitably in it. Because knowledge is essential for the competent functioning of all mental processes, without it your brain couldn't provide any of the cognitive services it normally performs for you. To understand cognition, it is essential to understand knowledge and its ubiquitous presence in all aspects of mental activity.

10.2   REPRESENTATIONS AND THEIR FORMATS

A key aspect of knowledge is that it relies on representations. Representation is a complicated and controversial topic that cognitive scientists from many disciplines have argued about for a long, long time. No definition has been fully accepted, and most of those proposed are very technical. The definition we used here is relatively simplified, but it captures some of the core ideas in many accounts. (For diverse treatments of this important concept, see Dietrich & Markman, 2000; Dretske, 1995; Goodman, 1976; Haugeland, 1991; Palmet, 1978.) As noted in Chapter 1, a representation is a physical state (such as marks on a page, magnetic fields in a computer, or neural connections in a brain) that stands for an object, event, or concept. Representations also carry information about what they stand for. Consider a map of a subway system. The map is a representation because it stands for the various lines, stops, and connections, and it carries information about them, namely, the ordering of stops and the relative directions of the various lines. But representation involves more than this, as we explore in the following section.

10.2.1   Memories and Representations

Imagine that you're seeing a lava lamp for the first time at your birthday party. The lamp is not lit. Yon see a cone-shaped jar on a metal stand, the jar containing a mixture of colored liquids and solids. Now, to add to the festivities, the lamp is turned on. The contents of the jar brighten and globules of material inside begin undulating. A basic property of brains is that to some extent, but far from perfectly, they store perceived experiences — that is, they allow memories. When you store your first memory of a lava lamp, are you storing a representation? Well, does this memory meet the following criteria for a representation?

The intentionality criterion: A representation must be constructed intentionally to stand for something else. This may seem a little problematic. People usually don't try intentionally to set up their daily experiences for easy later recall. As you're watching the lava lamp for the first time, you probably aren't saying to yourself, "This is so cool, I have to remember it for the rest of my life." Nonetheless, you do remember its much research (and a good deal of anecdotal evidence) shows that your brain stores information automatically, even when you're not trying to fix it in your memory (e.g., Hasher & Zacks, 1979; Hyde & Jenkins, 1969). Indeed, trying consciously to preserve information for later recollection often leads to no improvement in memory relative to simply perceiving and processing the information well. This suggests that you have the unconscious goal of storing information about experience, independent of your conscious goals. It is as if the ability to store information is so important that evolution couldn't leave the job to people's conscious intentions (some of us can't even remember to take out the garbage). Instead, evolution entrusted part of the storage of information to unconscious automatic mechanisms in the brain.

So is the intentionality criterion met? Yes, because the brain at an unconscious level has the design feature of storing information about experiences of the world to stand for those experiences. If a camera is set by a photographer to take a picture every second whether the photographer is present or not, the intention to capture information is built into the system, whether or not the originator of the system, the photographer, is there to take each picture. Similarly, the intention to capture information is built into the brain system, whether or not you consciously direct each memory.

The information-carrying criterion: A representation must carry information about what it stands for. Does your first memory of a lava lamp meet this criterion? Imagine that on the next day, someone asks what's new, and you remember having seen a novel object, the lava lamp. Drawing on your memory of the lava lamp, you describe it. How are you able to do this? Because your memory of the lava lamp carries information about it — details of its shape, color, and function. Further evidence that your memory of the lamp carries information is that you are able to categorize from it. If you were to see another, not necessarily identical, lava lamp, you could say that it belongs to the same group of objects as the one in your memory. Because your memory of the first lava lamp carries information about what it looked like, you can use this information to recognize other things like it. Similarly, if the second lava lamp in your experience, the one you're looking at now, is unlit, you can consult your memory of the first one to conjecture that the second one can probably be turned on to make it brighten and cause its contents to undulate. Because your memory carries information about the first lava lamp, it can produce useful inferences about other ones you encounter.

In these ways, representations lay the groundwork for knowledge. Once the brain intentionally establishes memories that carry information about the world, all sorts of sophisticated cognitive abilities become possible.

10.2.2   Four Possible Formats for Representations

What more can we say about a mental representation? One aspect of a representation is its format. *Format* refers to the type of its code, as discussed in Chapter 1. We can now unpack this idea further. *Format* not only refers to the elements that make up a representation and how these elements are arranged, but also relies on characteristics of the processes that operate on them to extract information. As we will see, representations may be *modality specific,* that is, they may make use of perceptual or motor systems, or they may be *amodal,* residing outside the perceptual and motor modalities. Another aspect of a representation is its *content* — the information it conveys.

Modality-Specific Representations: Images.   In talking about the birthday party, the metaphor of a camera was useful. Images such as those that a camera captures are one possible representational format, which depicts information; perhaps the brain constructs a similar type of representation. Certainly we often talk as if it does, saying things like "I can't get that picture out of my mind" and "I see it clearly in my mind's eye." Let's look at what is involved in images, and see whether it is likely that the brain contains representations of this form.

Several wrapped boxes and a birthday cake are on a table. Part of the scene has been captured by a digital camera and registered by pixels, or "picture elements," the units of visual information in an image, and thus stored. Specifically, an image has three elements, which taken together determine its content: a *spatiotemporal window, storage units,* and *stored information.*

A photograph taken of the scene in front of the camera does not capture everything in that scene, but only that part of it within a spatiotemporal window (Figure 10.2a). Spatially, there are infinitely many pictures that a camera could take of the same scene, depending on its position relative to the scene — here the image has cut off the gifts and the table

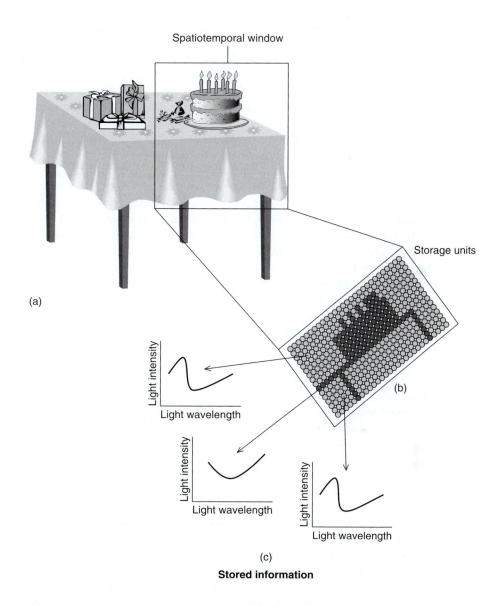

FIGURE 10.2   The components of an image: the birthday scene
(a) A spatiotemporal window of the information captured in the viewed scene. Within the spatiotemporal window, (b) an array of pixels captures the light information present. Each pixel stores (c) information about the intensity of light across the range of light wavelengths to which the pixel is sensitive. Together the stored information across pixels in the spatiotemporal window constitutes one possible image representation of the birthday scene.

legs. Temporally, the scene is not captured continuously over time, just in one time slice when the shutter is open. Thus, any image is defined to some extent by its spatiotemporal window.

Next consider the storage units (Figure 10.2b) of the image in the spatiotemporal window. An image contains an array of storage units — pixels if the camera is digital, or light-sensitive grains for a film camera — laid out in a grid. Each storage unit is sensitive to the light impinging on it. Like the complete array of storage units, each individual unit also has a spatiotemporal window. It captures only the information within a bounded spatial and temporal region nested within the larger window of the entire array.

Finally, consider the information in the storage units (Figure 10.2c). In the case of a photograph, this information is the intensity of light at visible wavelengths in each storage unit. Across storage units, the collective information specifies the content of the image.

Much additional — and important — information resides implicitly in the image. For example, a contiguous group of pixels might form a square. And distances between pixels correspond to distances in the world: if the horizontal distance between pixels A and B is shorter than the horizontal distance between pixels C and D, the points in the world that correspond to points A and B are closer horizontally than the points that correspond to points C and D. But extracting these additional types of information requires a processing system, and the camera does not possess such a system (or put another way, the camera's processing system is the brain of the human viewer using it). The essential question now is, do images constructed like the one of the birthday cake on the table in Figure 10.2 exist in the brain?

Many people (but not all) say that they experience mental images that they can "see with the mind's eye" or "hear with the mind's ear." Clearly self-reported experience is important, but scientific evidence is essential for drawing firm conclusions, especially given the illusions our minds are capable of producing. Much scientific evidence supports the presence of images in the human brain (for reviews, see Farah, 2000; Finke, 1989; Kosslyn, 1980, 1994; Kosslyn et al., 2006; Shepard & Cooper, 1982; Thompson & Kosslyn, 2000).

First, consider an example of evidence from brain anatomy research (Tootell et al., 1982). Figure 10.3a is the visual stimulus that a monkey viewed; Figure 10.3b shows activation in Area V1 of that monkey's occipital cortex, as measured by a neural tracer, while the monkey was looking at the stimulus. A striking correspondence is immediately apparent: the pattern of brain activation on the brain's surface roughly depicts the shape of the stimulus. The reason is that the corex of early visual processing areas is laid out somewhat like the pixels of a digital image and responds similarly. When neurons that are arranged in this manner fire, the pattern of activation forms a topographical map — their spatial layout in the brain is analogous to the layout of space in the environment. The presence of many such topographically organized anatomical structures in the brain suggests the presence of images.

Another example of neural evidence for images comes from the case of patient M.G.S. (Farah et al., 1992). Clinical diagnosis of M.G.S.'s seizures had localized their source in her right occipital lobe, the region that processes the left half of the visual field. To reduce her seizures, M.G.S. elected to have her right occipital lobe removed. In addition to reduction of seizures, another result was, as expected, blindness in her left visual field.

What would be the effect of this removal on M.G.S.'s ability to process visual images? Much research has shown that visual images are represented partly in the brain's occipital

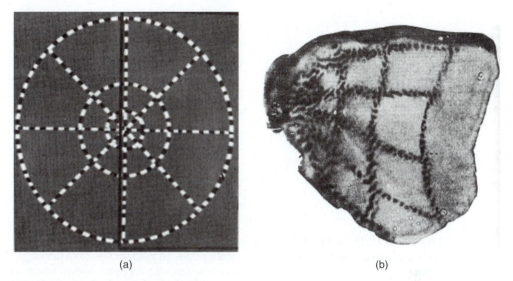

(a)   (b)

FIGURE 10.3   An image in the brain

(a) The "spokes of a wheel" stimulus shown to a monkey. (b) The activation that occurred on the surface of Area V1 of the monkey's brain in the left occipital lobe (which processed only the right half of the stimulus) as the monkey viewed the stimulus. The pattern of brain activation is similar to the visual pattern, suggesting that the brain is using some form of image-like representation in early visual processing.

(Tootell, R. B. H., Silverman, M. S., Switkes, E., & DeValois, R. L. [1982].)

lobes, and that the brain represents these images topographically, at least in some cases (e.g., Kosslyn et al., 1995, 2006). The investigators reasoned that if the occipital lobes do indeed represent visual images, then the loss of M.G.S.'s right occipital lobe should decrease the size of her visual images by one-half (a proportion analogous to her loss in vision). To test this hypothesis, the investigators measured the size of M.G.S.'s visual-imagery field before and after her surgery. As predicted, M.G.S.'s imagery field after the operation was approximately half its original size (Figure 10.4).

The two studies reviewed here, along with many others, have convinced most researchers that the brain uses images as one form of representation. Not only have mental images been found in the visual system, they have also been found in the motor system, as discussed in Chapter 11 (e.g., Grèzes & Decety, 2001; Jeannerod, 1995, 1997), and in the auditory system (e.g., Halpern, 2001).

In addition to all the neural evidence that has accumulated for mental images, much behavioral evidence has accumulated as well. Indeed many clever behavioral experiments provided the first evidence for imagery, preceding the neural evidence by two decades (for reviews, see Finke, 1989; Kosslyn, 1980; Shepard & Cooper, 1982). In these experiments, researchers asked research participants to construct mental images while performing a cognitive task. If the participants actually constructed mental images, then these images should have perceptual qualities, such as color, shape, size, and orientation. Experiment after experiment did indeed find that perceptual variables like these affected task performance,

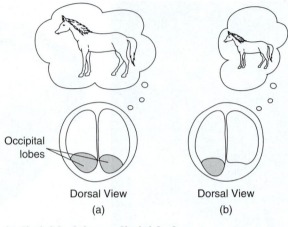

FIGURE 10.4   Brain diminished, image diminished
(a) Diagram of an intact, undamaged brain and a perceived visual image. (b) After surgery. Because visual images are represented in the occipital lobes, removing the right occipital lobe reduced image size by one-half (because the horizontal dimension was now restricted to one half of its previous extent).

(Fig. 66.2 from p. 96B of Farah, M. J. (2000). The neural bases of mental imagery. In M. S. Cazzaniga (ed.), *The Cognitive Neurosciences* (2nd ed., pp. 965–974). Cambridge, MA: The MIT Press. Reprinted with permission.)

suggesting that participants had constructed mental images having perceptual qualities. See the accompanying *A Closer Look* box for a detailed discussion of such a finding for the perceptual variable of size.

Although the camera has proved a useful metaphor in this discussion, brain images differ significantly from those taken by a camera. In particular, brain images are not as continuous and complete as photographs. For example, work on the phenomenon of change blindness, the failure to be aware of changing stimuli in the visual field (see Chapter 3), indicates that people's perceptual images do not have a uniform level of detail; some areas are not as well represented as others (e.g., Henderson & Hollingworth, 2003; Wolfe, 1999). Figure 10.5 illustrates this contrast. Figure 10.5a captures a relatively even and complete image of a scene, whereas an image in the brain, like the manipulated picture in Figure 10.5b, is much more uneven, with some areas better represented than others. Visual attention appears responsible for this unevenness: the well-represented patches of a scene are often regions where attention is focused (Hochberg, 1998). When attention does not focus on a region of a scene, the content of that region is not encoded as well into the image (e.g., Coltheart, 1999).

Another important qualification about mental images is that they are interpreted (e.g., Chambers & Reisberg, 1992). If you focus your attention on the left edge of the ambiguous object in Figure 6.5 on page 84, it appears to be a duck, but if you focus your attention on the right edge, it appears to be a rabbit. Depending on where you focus attention, your interpretation of the object varies. A photograph does not contain interpretations of the entities it contains. If you consider the image format in isolation, you can see that nothing in it offers the potential to aid in the interpretation of its contents. A photographic image is simply a record

(a)

(b)

FIGURE 10.5   Selective attention encodes some aspects of images better than others
(a) The birthday scene. (b) Rather than representing the scene at the top at equal resolutions across all points, attended parts of the image (in this case, the cake and gifts) are represented at a higher resolution than the unattended parts of the image (in this case, the table and everything in the background). As a result of the unequal distribution of attention, the image represents some parts of the scene better than others.

A CLOSER LOOK
BEHAVIORAL EVIDENCE FOR MENTAL IMAGERY

Although there has been considerable anecdotal evidence for mental imagery, scientific behavioral evidence was sought by Kosslyn; he reported his results in 1975 in "Information Representation in Visual Images," *Cognitive Psychology, 7,* 341–370.

INTRODUCTION

It is an obvious perceptual fact that when something is close up and large in the visual field, it is easy to recognize, but when it is far away and small, the task is not so easy. You have no trouble recognizing a friend standing just a few feet away, but recognizing your friend would be much harder if the two of you were at opposite ends of a football field. The investigator used this fact about perception to demonstrate that people have mental images.

METHOD

Participants were asked to visualize a target object (for example, a goose) next to one of two reference objects, a fly or an elephant. Each pair of objects was to fill the frame of a participant's mental image, and in each case the proportional size of the target object relative to that of the reference object was to be maintained. (Thus, the image of the goose would be larger when paired with the fly than when paired with the elephant.) While holding one of these two pairs of images in mind, such as goose-and-fly or goose-and-elephant, participants heard the name of a property (for example, "legs") and had to decide as quickly as possible whether or not the target animal has that property by referring to their image; the participants were told that if the animal has the property, they should be able to find it in the image.

RESULTS

Participants were an average of 211 milliseconds faster to verify properties when they imagined the target objects next to the fly than when next to the elephant. In a control condition, in which participants visualized enormous flies and tiny elephants next to the normal-sized animals, the results were reversed — the participants were faster when the queried animal was visualized next to a tiny elephant. So, it wasn't the fly or elephant per se that produced the results, but rather their size relative to that of the queried animal.

DISCUSSION

The finding parallels the motivating observation, namely, that recognizing a friend is easier up close than across a football field. When a given object was imaged as relatively large (next to a fly), it was easier to process visually than when it was imaged as relatively small (next to an elephant). As the property named became larger in the image, it was easier to identify. From this result, the investigator concluded that the participants used images to answer the questions asked of them and to verify the properties named.

The Mental Image Field

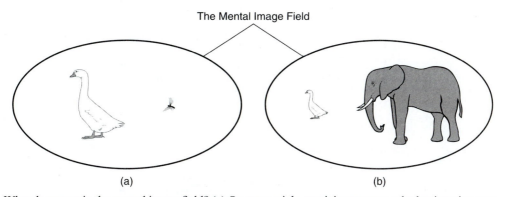

(a)   (b)

What do we see in the mental image field? (a) On some trials, participants were asked to imagine a target object, such as a goose, next to a fly. They were asked to fill the image field with the two objects, while maintaining their true relative sizes (that is, keeping the goose much larger than the fly). (b) On other trials, they were asked to imagine the same object next to an elephant, again while filling the image field and maintaining relative size. The size of the critical object (the goose, in this case) was larger in absolute terms when imaged next to the fly than when imaged next to the elephant. As a result, parts of the critical object (for example, the goose's legs) were larger next to the fly, and could be "seen" faster. This result provides behavioral evidence that we can use images to verify object properties.

of light energy that impinges on each pixel; it contains no categorizations of larger entities across pixels. But mental images are representations within a processing system that interprets them in specific ways; to understand imagery, we must consider both the representation and the accompanying processes. The importance of interpreting representations will become a central theme in this chapter.

Modality-Specific Representations: Feature Records.   From this point on, the representations we consider will be more sophisticated than those taken by image-capturing artifacts such as cameras. It will become clear that natural intelligence is superior to current technology when it comes to representation. Art will imitate nature: the future of sophisticated representational technology lies in implementing the natural representations we will be discussing.

At the heart of sophisticated representation lies the categorization of meaningful entities. A **meaningful entity** is an object or event that plays an important role in an organism's survival and pursuit of goals. In contrast, a pixel is a relatively meaningless entity. We don't just want to know whether light impinges on a particular point in space; we want to know what the patterns of pixels — or areas of neural activation — represent in the world. This doesn't mean that images are useless. Indeed, mote meaningful representations are derived from images.

The visual system of the frog presents a case of more sophisticated representation. If you were a frog, what would be meaningful to you? Bugs. What does a frog need in order to get bugs? Clearly it needs a motor system that can capture a bug flying by, but before it can do that it must be able to detect the bug. Here nature has applied meaningfulness and interpretation to the problem of representation, taking natural representational systems beyond images.

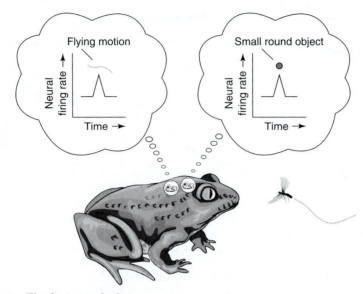

FIGURE 10.6   The frog sees the bug
In the frog's brain, one population of neurons is firing in response to the small round object; a second population is firing in response to the motion of this object. Together these two sets of neurons, along with others, allow the frog to detect the presence of a small, round, flying object.

Early and important work (Lettvin et al., 1959) showed that neurons in the frogs visual system respond differentially to small objects moving within the frog's visual field (Figure 10.6). These researchers inserted electrodes into individual neurons of a frog's brain and then varied the stimulus — sometimes a round stationary object, sometimes a moving object — to the frog's eyes. They found that some neurons fire in response to small round objects (largely independent of motion), whereas others fire in response to object movement (largely independent of the object). Different populations of neurons appeared to detect different types of information in the visual field.

The information that these neurons detect is information that is meaningful to frogs: "small, round" and "moving" are features of flying insects. We have discussed features in the two previous chapters, but will now look at them from a new point of view: A **feature** is a meaningful sensory aspect of a perceived stimulus. Unlike a pixel, which registers all light that falls on it in a general and undifferentiated accumulation of information, these frog neurons respond only when information meaningful to a frog is present. They could be tricked if a small, round, moving object in the frog's visual field isn't a bug — but in nature it probably *is* a bug, and that's the point. The function of these populations of neurons is to detect entities in the world meaningful to frogs. They don't constitute an image of the visual field, patchy or otherwise. Instead, they *interpret* regions of images as indicating the presence of a particular feature. When these feature-detecting neurons become active, they categorize a region of an image as containing a meaningful feature of an object or event. Feature detection is accomplished not by single neurons, but by populations of neurons. This allows for a graded, rather than an all-or-nothing, response and is therefore more reliable.

Furthermore, these neurons are often sensitive to more than a single feature, and the information to which they respond may change both with experience and with the organism's goals at a given time (e.g., Crist et al., 2001).

Do feature-detecting neurons meet the criteria for a representation? Yes. First, intentionality: they have been honed by evolution to stand for things in the world, to wit, bugs. Second, information: the neurons themselves, by their firing, carry information about the world. The evidence? If a frog blinks (closes its eyes), these neurons, once activated, *continue* to fire and carry information about the entity they collectively stand for — a bug.

As we saw in Chapter 2, the discovery the feature-detecting neurons in the brain revolutionized the field of perception. Since then, there have been hundreds if not thousands of follow-up studies, and much has been learned about such populations of neurons in the primate visual system. Examples of the processing stages to which such populations contribute are illustrated in Figure 10.7. As we saw in Chapter 2, as visual signals travel along pathways from the primary visual cortex in the occipital lobe to the temporal and parietal lobes, various types of features are extracted, such as the shape, orientation, color, and movement of objects. Farther along the processing stream, populations of conjunctive neurons, as their name suggests, integrate featural information extracted earlier into object representations. Conjunctive neurons, for example, might integrate information about size, shape, and movement to establish a featural representation of a flying bug, which can be of interest to humans as well as to frogs, especially in summer.

The collection of feature detectors active during the processing of a visual object constitutes a representation of that object. This representational format, unlike an image, is not

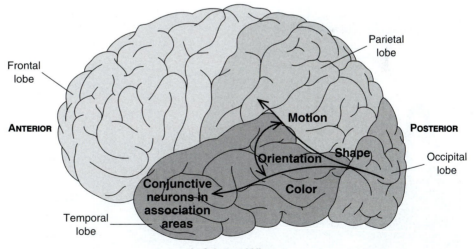

Left Lateral View

FIGURE 10.7   Visual processing systems in the human brain
From visual input, populations of neurons extract shape, color, orientation, and motion, along with other features, along pathways in the occipital, temporal, and parietal lobes. At later stages of processing, conjunctive neurons in various brain regions, such as the temporal lobes, combine these features to form integrated featural representations of perceived entities.

depictive; its elements do not correspond to spatial points of contrast, or to edges of the object. Instead, it draws on different meaningful features of the object, that is, aspects of meaningful entities found in an organism's environment. Such a representation built up of features complements an image of the same object that might reside in early topographically organized areas.

Researchers have found populations of feature-detecting neurons for all modalities, not just vision. Feature-detection systems also reside in audition, touch, taste, and smell (e.g., Bear et al., 2002).

Amodal Symbols.   Modality-specific representations reside in the perceptual and motor systems of the btain, and are thus perceptually related to the objects they represent. Is it possible that *amodal* representations exist that are built from arbitrary, abstract symbols? The dominant view is "yes," but the question is still open; see the accompanying *Debate* box.

How would amodal symbols work? Imagine the birthday scene, as in Figure 10.8a. An image of that scene resides early in the visual system. Farther along the ventral stream, feature detectors that represent aspects of meaningful entities have become active. Finally, amodal symbols — abstract and arbitrary — describe the properties of and relations among meaningful entities in the scene. Figures 10.8a–c present some examples of what these symbols might stand for.

Amodal symbols, lying outside the modalities and with no modality-specific characteristics, are usually assumed to reside in a knowledge system that constructs and manipulates descriptions of perceptual and motor states. Thus, the amodal representations in

FIGURE 10.8   Three amodal representations of elements in the birthday scene at left
(a) A frame, (b) a semantic network, and (c) a property list. Although words are used here for clarity, amodal representations are assumed to be constructed of nonlinguistic symbols.

DEBATE
DO AMODAL REPRESENTATIONS EXIST?

As useful as they are in building theory, a strong empirical case has never been established for amodal symbols in the brain (Barsalou, 1999). Nonetheless, the idea of amodal symbols has dominated theories of representation for decades. The intellectual reasons are attractive to many. First, amodal symbols provide powerful ways of expressing the meaningful content of images by representing objects (and their properties) and the relations between them. Second, the important functions of knowledge such as categorization, inference, memory, comprehension, and thought arise readily from the theory of amodal symbols (e.g.,). R. Anderson, 1976, 1983; Newell, 1990; Newell & Simon, 1972). Third, the idea of amodal symbols has allowed computers to implement knowledge; amodal descriptive representations can be easily implemented on computers.

There is in fact a theoretical gap as well as a deficiency of empirical support for amodal symbols. What are the mechanisms? What process links regions of visual images to the relevant amodal symbols? Conversely, when the amodal symbol for an object becomes active in memory, how does the symbol activate visual representations of the object's appearance? No one has yet figured out a compelling theory of how amodal symbols become linked to perceptual and motor states. Theorists are increasingly finding fault with the notion of amodal symbols (e.g., Barsalou, 1999; Glenberg, 1997; Lakoff, 1987; Newton, 1996). Some researchers are turning away from amodal symbols, arguing that other formats underlie knowledge representation in the brain.

Figure 10–8 describe the contents of a visual state but lie outside the visual system, and are part of a more general system that is used in language and other tasks that do not involve vision per se.

The content of the amodal representations in Figure 10.8 are symbols such as *ABOVE, LEFT-OF, candles.* So are amodal representations words? Certainly there's nothing in the line forms that constitute the word *candles* (or *velas* in Spanish, or *bougies* in French) that relates to a visually (or tactilely) perceived candle. So the answer is, close — but no cigar. Researchers exploring the idea of amodal symbols believe that amodal symbols and words *are two different things,* that words *stand for* the amodal symbols that underlie them. According to this view, underlying the word *candles,* for example, is an amodal symbol in the brain that stands for *candles.* To make this distinction clear, researchers could use a symbol like @ to stand for the things that are *candles.* They use the word *candles,* though, so that it is easier to see what the symbol stands for.

The amodal symbols named in Figure 10.8 build three types of amodal representations: *frames, semantic networks,* and *property lists.* A frame is a structure, rather like an algebraic expression, that specifies a set of relations that links objects in the environment. For example, the frame in Figure 10.8a specifies that the gifts are to the left of the cake, and that this LEFT-OF configuration is ABOVE the table. A **semantic network** (Figure 10.8b) represents essentially the same relations and objects in diagram form. A **property list** names the characteristics of the entities belonging to a category; for instance, the property list in Figure 10.8c names some of the properties of a cake, such as frosting and candles. Unlike frames and semantic networks, property lists omit the relations between properties. How do the properties in a property list differ from the features in modality-specific records? First, the symbols that represent properties in a property list are amodal, lying outside perceptual and motor systems, whereas the features in modality-specific records are modal, lying in a perceptual or motor system (for example, vision). Second, the properties in a property list capture relatively abstract aspects of an object, such as the presence of frosting, whereas the features in modality-specific records tend to capture fundamental perceptual details such as edges and colors.

Amodal symbols complement images in that they categorize the regions of an image meaningfully — they don't just record points of light or other sensory data. Amodal symbols continue the interpretive process begun when feature detectors categorize elementary properties of images, in the service of identifying meaningful entities. In the semantic network in Figure 10.8c, the amodal symbol for *cake* categorizes the respective region of the image as being a particular kind of thing. The same region could be categorized differently if different amodal symbols were assigned to it that categorize the same entity in different ways: *dessert, pastry, fattening food.* Furthermore, a symbol could categorize an entity inaccurately: you might dimly see the cake in the dark and categorize it as a hat — and meet with disaster when you put it on your head.

Statistical Patterns in Neural Nets.   Although amodal symbols work well in computers, it's not clear how well they would work in biological systems. Another possible means of representation is the neural net, a construct in which the cake in the birthday scene is represented by a statistical pattern such as 1100101000101 (Figure 10.9), which offers greater scope than the amodal system for two reasons (Smolensky, 1988).

1110101000101
1100011000111
1100101010101
1110001010111
1100111000101

FIGURE 10.9   Statistical patterns can represent the cake in the birthday scene
A 1 or 0 indicates whether a particular neuron in a population of neurons is firing (1) or not firing (0). Different statistical patterns can represent slightly different versions of the same thing (for example, a cake), although these patterns are usually highly similar to one another.

First, the elements of a statistical pattern can be viewed as neurons or as populations of neurons that are on or off — that fire or do not fire. Each 1 in the pattern represents a neuron (or neuron population) that fires, and each 0 represents one that does not. Thus the statistical approach has a natural neural interpretation that makes it a plausible candidate for biological representation. Second, whereas in an amodal system a single amodal symbol typically represents a category, in a neural net multiple statistical patterns can represent the same category, as in Figure 10.9. The flexibility offered by varying statistical patterns reflects the reality in the world: not all cakes are exactly the same. Because cakes differ, their representations should differ as well. And because even different cakes are more similar to one another than they are to tables, the representations of cakes should be more similar to one another than to the representations of tables. Although the representations that could stand for a cake differ to some extent, they should generally be highly similar. Statistical patterns capture these intuitions.

For these two reasons, statistical representations of knowledge have become increasingly interesting to researchers. Although amodal symbols are still used widely, models that rely on statistical approaches are increasingly plausible.

10.2.3   Multiple Representational Formats in Perception and Simulation

Some researchers have argued that an abstract descriptive representational format underlies all knowledge. But the brain is a complex system, and knowledge is used in many ways; representations play many roles in the myriad processes that constitute cognition. It is implausible that a single format would serve all these roles; it is much more likely that multiple formats — images, feature detectors, amodal symbols, and statistical patterns — are required.

Again imagine viewing your birthday party scene. On perceiving this scene, your brain constructs a somewhat patchy visual image of it, largely in the occipital cortex. As this image is developing, feature detection systems extract meaningful features from it in particular regions of the occipital, temporal, and parietal lobes. Finally, a statistical pattern in the temporal lobes becomes active to stand for the image and feature information extracted previously, and to associate all this information (Figure 10.10a). Because the neurons representing the statistical pattern are conjunctive neurons (that is, they have a linking function), the neurons active in the image, along with the neurons active in the feature analysis, all became associated with the neurons that represent the statistical pattern. Each element in the statistical pattern develops associations back to the image and feature units that activated it. Together, this sequence of processing phases establishes a multilevel representation of the scene as it is perceived.

It is possible, as it were, to "run the film backward." In a process known as **simulation,** a statistical pattern can reactivate image and feature information even after the original scene is no longer present (Figure 10.10b). For instance, say the following day, a friend reminds you how great the cake was. Your friend's words activate the statistical pattern that integrated information stored for the cake at the time you saw and tasted it. Now, in a top-down manner, this statistical pattern partially reactivates features extracted from the cake, along with aspects of the image that represented it. The associative structure linking all this information allows you to simulate the original experience. Whereas bottom-up processing through a perceptual system produces a statistical representation, top-down processing back

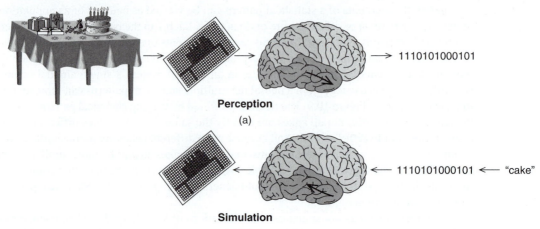

Perception

(a)

Simulation

(b)

FIGURE 10.10   Perception and simulation processes
(a) The levels of processing that occur during the perception of a scene; a patchy image in the occipital lobes; feature extraction in the occipital, temporal, and parietal lobes; and the integration of this information using a statistical pattern, perhaps in the temporal lobes. (b) An example of the simulation process, which is thought to be the process in part (a) run in reverse. Hearing someone say the word cake may activate the statistical pattern used previously to integrate information about the cake in the birthday scene that is now in the past. In turn, the statistical pattern would partially reactivate the features extracted for the cake, along with the accompanying image.

the other way reenacts, at least partially, the original visual processing. This top-down capability allows you to generate mental images and to remember past events. [. . .]

10.3   FROM REPRESENTATION TO CATEGORY KNOWLEDGE

The aim of an actor is to provide for the audience the "illusion of the first time" — the sense that what is happening now on stage has never happened before, neither in the real world nor in last night's performance. But the constant illusion of the first time in life would lead to chaos and confusion. When you arrived at your birthday party bereft of knowledge, the experience was bewildering. Representations are the means; the end is knowledge. The question before us now is how large assemblies of representations develop to provide knowledge about a category.

Category knowledge develops first from establishing representations of a category's individual members and second from integrating those representations. You have undoubtedly experienced members of the "cake" category many times. On each occasion, a multiformat representation became established in your brain. How might the representations of these different cakes have become integrated?

Consider the five different cakes in Figure 10.11a. Each cake produces a statistical pattern that integrates the results of its image and feature processing. Because the cakes are so similar, they produce similar statistical patterns, but because they differ to some

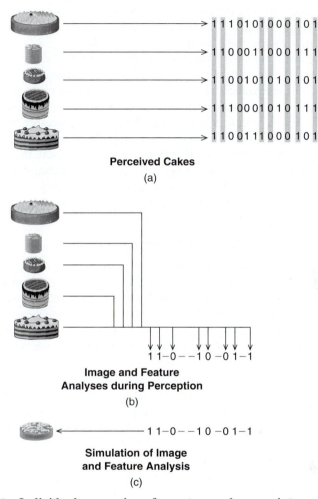

FIGURE 10.11   Individual memories of a category become integrated to establish category knowledge
(a) Five individual cakes perceived on different occasions are each represented with a unique statistical pattern; the conjunctive units common to all are highlighted. (b) The shared conjunctive units across statistical patterns establish a representation of the cake category. These shared units further integrate memories of the image and feature processing that occurred across cakes. (c) The shared statistical pattern becomes active in the absence of a particular cake, and produces a simulation of image and feature processing that is roughly the average of previously experienced cakes.

extent, the patterns are not identical. If you study the five individual patterns, you can see that 11–0 – – 10–01–1 is common to all five (where – indicates a unit that is not shared across cakes). The eight units corresponding to the 1s and 0s in this shared pattern offer a natural way of integrating the five memories. Because all five memories share these units, all the memories become associated to this common "hub" (Figure 10.11b). The result is the representation of a category. At one level, all category members become linked by virtue of the common statistical units they share. At another level, these shared units constitute a statistical representation of the category, not just of one member. (As we note later, though, natural concepts are less neat than this simple example — it's hard to think of a feature that's true of *all* possible cakes.)

Furthermore, the shared units offer a means of retrieving category members from memory. Because all category members become associated with a common hub, the hub serves as a mechanism for remembering category members at later times. When the associative structure is run in a top-down manner (Figure 10.11c), the hub reactivates the image and the feature processing associated with a category member, thereby simulating it. Notably, this process may often mix memories of multiple category members together during retrieval to produce a blending (e.g., Hintzman, 1986). As a result, the simulated category member may often be more like an average category member than like a specific one (as shown in Figure 10.11c). This process of simulating average category members provides one mechanism for generating prototypes, as will be described later.

10.3.1   The Inferential Power of Category Knowledge

Armed with the concept of category knowledge, we can begin to understand what makes organisms more intelligent than cameras. The power of category knowledge comes from capturing and integrating diverse pieces of information about a category. When you encounter a new category member, you activate the relevant knowledge of that general category, which provides a tremendous amount of useful information for dealing with this new entity. You aren't like a camera that operates exactly the same way whether its subject is making a first time appearance or has been photographed a hundred times before. Despite your parents' best efforts, how you dealt with your cake at your 3rd birthday party probably left something to be desired, but your 20th birthday cake presumably didn't end up in your hair. And when you encounter a new birthday cake at your next birthday party, your category knowledge about birthday cakes makes you an expert on it. You know how to act — blowing out the candles, cutting the cake, eating a piece of it. You can predict what will be inside, and pretty much how it will taste. You can explain generally how it was made and predict what will happen if it is left out for a few days. All these inferences are possible because you have integrated diverse pieces of information about birthday cakes into a body of category knowledge.

Even simply hearing the phrase "birthday cake" when there's nary a cake in sight activates your category knowledge of birthday cakes; you may not know whether it's chocolate or angel food, but you understand what's being talked about. In each case, as you encounter something associated with the category, other knowledge becomes active. Because your category knowledge contains diverse kinds of information that goes considerably beyond what's immediately before your eyes, you can draw many useful inferences and perform various intelligent functions (Bruner, 1957).

10.3.2   The Multimodal Nature of Category Knowledge

Cakes are not only seen, they are also tasted, smelled, touched, and acted on; perhaps the one modality by which cakes are not experienced much is sound. Guitars, on the other hand, are heard, seen, touched, and acted on, but neither tasted nor smelled. Depending on the category, a different profile of information across the six modalities of vision, audition, action, touch, taste, and smell is salient (Cree & McRae, 2003). Emotion and motivation offer further modes of experience that enter into a category's representation. Cakes are associated with positive emotion, poor grades with negative emotion; restaurants are associated with feeling hungry, pillows with feeling sleepy. The very name of a category opens the door to category knowledge: either through hearing the name, seeing its sign-language form, or, for the literate, seeing its orthographic (i.e., written) form or feeling its Braille configuration.

Integration is obviously the key: how does the brain do it, combining category name and all the relevant information across modalities? One proposal is the convergence zone theory (Damasio, 1989; for a more developed account, see Simmons & Barsalou, 2003). A **convergence zone** (also known as an **association area**) is a population of conjunctive neurons that associates feature information within a modality. These patterns integrate information from image and feature analyses within a given modality, such as vision. For cakes, image and feature information would similarly be integrated within the taste modality and also within the modalities for smell, touch, and action. Much neuroscience research indicates that association areas store modality-specific information (e.g., Tanaka, 1997).

Damasio (1989) further proposes that higher order convergence zones in the temporal, parietal, and frontal lobes integrate category knowledge *across* modalities, together with the category name. (Note that a convergence zone is *not* modality specific, suggesting the importance of amodal "symbols."). In general, these higher order convergence zones integrate the conjunctive neurons that reside in the earlier convergence zones for specific modalities. Thus, a convergence zone in the parietal lobe might integrate conjunctive neurons in visual and motor areas, which in turn integrate specific visual and motor features. Alternatively, convergence zones in the left anterior temporal lobe might integrate the names of categories with category knowledge. Throughout the brain, convergence zones integrate category knowledge in various ways, such that category knowledge captures the multimodal character of category members. As a result, all the relevant features across modalities for a category become integrated, so that they can all be retrieved together. When you think of cakes, higher order convergence zones activate how they look, taste, smell, and feel, and how you eat them.

If the convergence zone account of category knowledge is correct, two predictions follow. First, simulations in the brain's modality-specific areas should represent knowledge. To represent knowledge of how a cake looks, the relevant convergence zones should reactivate features that have previously been used to represent cakes in visual perception. Second, the simulations that represent a category should be distributed across the particular modalities that are relevant for processing it. The simulations that represent "cakes" should arise not only in the visual system but also in the taste and motor systems. Both behavioral and neural findings increasingly support these predictions (for reviews, see Barsalou, 2003b; Barsalou et al., 2003; Martin, 2001).

10.3.3   Multimodal Mechanisms and Category Knowledge: Behavioral Evidence

If simulations in perceptual systems underlie knowledge, then it should be possible to demonstrate the contribution of perceptual mechanisms in the representation of categories. To investigate this possibility, investigators focused on the perceptual mechanism of **modality switching,** a process in which attention is shifted from one modality to another, as, say, from vision to audition (Pecher et al., 2003). Researchers have shown that modality switching takes time. In one study, participants had to detect whether a stimulus — which might be a light, a tone, or a vibration — occurred on the left or right (Spence et al., 2000). Because the various stimuli were randomly mixed, participants had no way of predicting which particular type of signal would occur on a given trial. When the modality of the signal switched between two trials, participants took longer to detect the second signal than when the modality stayed the same. For example, the time to detect a tone was faster when the previous stimulus was a tone than when it was a light or a vibration. Switching modalities carries a cost.

Pecher and colleagues (2003) predicted that the perceptual mechanism of modality switching should be found not only in perception but also in category processing. They reasoned that if simulations represent category knowledge, then switching costs analogous to those incurred while processing perceptual information should be incurred while processing information about categories. Participants in this study verified the properties of objects. On a given trial, the word for a category (for example, "cakes") was followed by a word for a possible property, both words presented visually. Half the time the property was true of the category ("frosting") and half the time it was false ("crust"). As in the earlier perception experiment, sometimes the properties referred to the same modality on two consecutive trials: a participant might verify that "rustles" is a property of "leaves" and on the next trial verify that "loud" is a property of "blenders." Most of the time, however, the properties across two consecutive trials referred to different modalities.

Pecher and colleagues (2003) found that switching modalities in this property verification task produced a switching cost, just as in the perception experiment by Spence and colleagues (2000). When participants had to switch modalities to verify a property, they took longer than when they did not have to switch modalities. This finding is consistent with the idea that perceptual mechanisms are used in the representation of category knowledge: to represent the properties of categories, participants appeared to simulate them in the respective modalities.

Many other behavioral findings similarly demonstrate that perceptual mechanisms play a role in the representation of category knowledge. The visual mechanisms that process occlusion, size, shape, orientation, and similarity have all been shown to affect category processing (e.g., Solomon & Barsalou, 2001, 2004; Stanfield & Zwaan, 2001; Wu & Barsalou, 2004; Zwaan et al., 2002). Motor mechanisms have also been shown to play central roles (e.g., Barsalou et al., 2003; Glenberg & Kaschak, 2002; Spivey et al., 2000). Across modalities, behavioral findings increasingly implicate modality-based representations in the storage and use of category knowledge.

10.3.4 Multimodal Mechanisms and Category Knowledge: Neural Evidence

When talking about modality-specific mechanisms, conclusions drawn from behavioral evidence, no matter how suggestive, have their limits: behavioral experiments don't measure brain mechanisms directly. But neuroimaging does, and much supportive evidence for the perceptual underpinnings of category knowledge comes from neuroimaging research. In these studies, participants lie in a PET or fMRI scanner while performing various category-related tasks, such as naming visually presented objects (for example, a dog), listening to the names of categories (for example, "hammer"), producing the properties of a category (for example, "yellow" for a lemon), or verifying the properties of a category (for example, answering the question "Does a horse run?").

For example, in a study by Chao and Martin (2000), participants were asked to observe pictures of manipulable objects, buildings, animals, and faces while their brains were scanned using fMRI. The investigators found that when participants viewed manipulable objects such as hammers, a circuit in the brain that underlies the grasping of manipulable objects became active (Figure 10.12). This circuit did not become active when buildings, animals, or faces were observed. In much previous work, this grasping circuit has been found to become active while monkeys and humans perform actions with manipulable objects and while they watch others perform such actions (e.g., Rizzolatti et al., 2002). Even though Chao and Martin's participants were not allowed to move in the scanner, and even though they viewed no agents or actions, this grasping circuit nevertheless became active. From this result, the investigators concluded that activation of the grasping circuit constituted a motor inference about how to act on the perceived object. As participants viewed an object (for example, a hammer), they accessed category knowledge about it that included motor

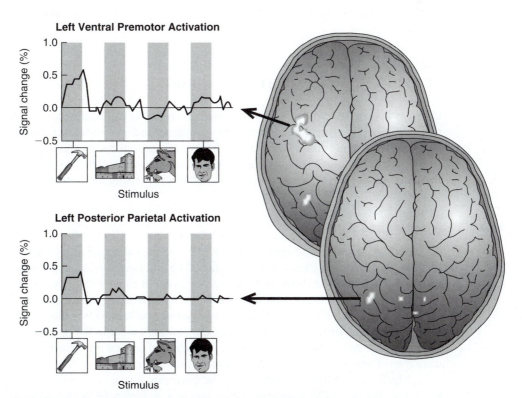

FIGURE 10.12   Neuroimaging support for category knowledge
The left-hemisphere grasping circuit (for night-handed participants) became active only while participants viewed pictures of tools, not while they viewed pictures of faces, animals, or buildings.

inferences (for example, "a hammer can be swung"). These inferences appear to be represented in the motor system, as we would expect if mental simulations are used to represent the objects and their categories.

Many further neuroimaging studies (reviewed by Martin, 2001; Martin & Chao, 2001; Martin et al., 2000) have shown that other modality-specific regions become active as other kinds of category knowledge are processed. In a striking correspondence, category knowledge about color, shape, and motion is processed near the respective brain areas that process this information in visual perception. When participants retrieve an object's shape properties, an area in the fusiform gyrus that overlaps visual shape processing areas becomes active during PET and fMRI scans. Similarly, when participants retrieve an object's color properties from category knowledge, an area in the occipital cortex that overlaps an area that processes color in perception (V4) becomes active. When participants think about performing actions on objects, motor areas become active. When participants retrieve an object's motion properties, regions in the posterior temporal gyrus that overlap motion processing areas in vision become active. When participants retrieve the sounds of objects, an auditory brain area becomes active (Kellenbach et al., 2001). And when they access knowledge of foods, gustatory areas in the brain become active that represent tastes (Simmons ct al., 2005). Together these findings demonstrate that an object category's representation is distributed across the brain's perceptual and motor systems.

10.4   STRUCTURES IN CATEGORY KNOWLEDGE

Category knowledge is not an undifferentiated mass of data; it contains many different structures, organized in many different ways. As we shall see in this section, exemplars, rules, prototypes, background knowledge, and schemata all play roles in creating the category knowledge that allows us to live lives cognizant of ourselves and the world around us. Furthermore, we possess powerful and dynamic abilities for using these structures.

10.4.1   Exemplars and Rules

The simplest structures that category knowledge contains are memories of individual category members; these are known as **exemplars.** The first time you see an unfamiliar type of dog and are told its breed, a memory of that dog is stored along with the name of the breed. As you see more of these dogs, a memory for each one similarly becomes associated with the breed name, and thereby with other memories of that breed. Over time, a collection of memories results for these category exemplars, all integrated in the appropriate memory store (as illustrated earlier in Figure 10.11a). This sort of content is relatively simple because each type of memory is stored independently of the others.

Much research has shown that exemplar memories are common in our category knowledge (e.g., Brooks, 1978; Lamberts, 1998; Medin & Schaffer, 1978; Nosofksy, 1984), and that they play a powerful role. For example, participants in a study by Allen and Brooks (1991) were told about two categories of imaginary animals; *builders* and *diggers.* Individual animals might have long or short legs, an angular or curved body, and spots or no spots.

A **rule** — that is, a precise definition of the criteria for a category — determined whether a particular animal was a *builder* or *digger:*

> An animal is a *builder* if it has *two* or *three* of the following properties: *long legs, angular body, spots;* otherwise it is a *digger.*

Some participants were told the two-out-of-three rule. These participants were then shown pictures of the imaginary animals sequentially and instructed to indicate which were *builders* and which were *diggers.* Presumably they used the rule to do this, counting the number of critical properties for each animal. If they made an error, the experimenter told them the correct category. Once the participants demonstrated that they could apply the rule for the categories effectively, they received a surprise test. On each trial they saw an animal that they hadn't seen earlier. Again they had to say whether the animal was a *builder* or *digger,* but this time the experimenter didn't say whether their categorizations were correct or incorrect.

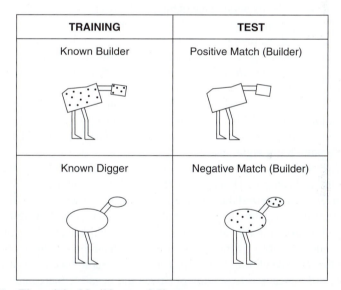

FIGURE 10.13   The original builders and diggers
Left column: A *builder* and a *digger* that participants studied while they learned the rule for *builders.* Right Column: Positive and negative test matches. A positive match was a *builder* that differed only by one property from a *builder* studied earlier; a negative match was a *builder* that differed only by one property from a *digger* studied earlier. If participants use only rules to categorize *builders,* the positive and negative matches should be equally easy to categorize, given that both have two of the three *builder properties.* Alternatively, if participants also use exemplars to categorize *builders,* the negative match should be harder to categorize because it is so similar to a member of the wrong category.

(Adapted from Allen, S. W., & Brooks, L. R. (1991). Specializing the operation of an explicit rule. *Journal of Experimental Psychology: General, 120,* pp. 3–19, Fig. 1, p. 4. Copyright © 1991 American Psychological Association. Adapted-with permission.)

Allen and Brooks (1991) suspected that even though participants knew a rule for the categories, they might nevertheless be storing exemplar memories and using them in categorization. From earlier research, the investigators believed that the human brain automatically stores and uses exemplar memories, even when doing so is not necessary. But how to determine this? Figure 10.13 illustrates the clever technique that the investigators used. In the test phase of the experiment, participants were shown some of the animals they had seen before and some new ones. Two of the new ones were *builders*. One of these differed from a builder seen during training in only one characteristic; this type of correspondence, between two entities of the same category, is referred to as a *positive match*. The other new builder, while fulfilling the rule, differed in only one characteristic from a *digger* seen previously; this kind of correspondence, between two entities of different categories, is a *negative match*.

Here's the key prediction. If participants do not store exemplar memories and use only the rule, the positive- and negative-match animals should be equally easy to categorize: both fulfill the rule for builders. If, however, participants stored exemplar memories — even though they did not have to in order to make the call — then the negative-match animal, which shared more characteristics with the *digger,* should be harder to categorize correctly than the positive-match one.

Why? Think about what happens when participants encounter the negative-match animal. If an exemplar memory of its counterpart from training exists, it is likely to become active. If it does, then because the two animals are so similar, sharing as they do two characteristics, the negative-match animal is a reminder of the counterpart seen earlier. *But the counterpart was in the other category!* So if the exemplar memory is active, the temptation to miscategorize is strong; rule and exemplar memory conflict.

What happens when participants encounter the positive-match animal and exemplar memory is active? Again, they will be reminded of the similar animal they saw in training, which in this case is in the correct category. This time both the exemplar memory and the rule point to the right answer.

Numbers told the story: the results demonstrated clearly not only that exemplar memories had been stored but also that they had a profound impact on categorization. Participants correctly categorized the positive-match exemplars 81 percent of the time, but correctly categorized the negative-match exemplars only 56 percent of the time. Even though participants knew a good rule for categorizing all the test animals, their memories of earlier exemplars intruded on categorization of negative-match animals, causing 25 percent more errors than in the other condition. If exemplar memories hadn't been stored, there shouldn't have been any difference in categorizing positive- and negative-march animals, given that both satisfied the rule equally well. Many similar findings in the literature demonstrate that exemplars are ubiquitous structures in category knowledge.

Does this finding suggest that we store only exemplars and not rules? Before we can answer, we need to look at another side of the coin. A second group of participants received the same training, learning by feedback from the experimenter whether their categorizations were correct. The difference? This second group was *not* told the rule for categorizing *builders* and *diggers*. These "no-rule" participants then were shown the same series of positive- and negative-match animals at test as the "rule" participants in the first group.

Two findings are of interest. Like the rule participants, the no-rule participants were more accurate on the positive-match animals (75 percent correct) than on the negative-match animals (15 percent correct). For these participants, similarity to exemplar memories played the central role in categorization. The effect of exemplar memories was significantly larger in the no-rule condition (incorrect negative-match categorization, 85 percent) than in the rule condition (incorrect negative-match categorization, 44 percent). Rule participants had stored a rule in their category knowledge that made them less vulnerable to exemplar memories than were no-rule participants. By applying the rule on some occasions, rule participants were more likely to categorize negative-match animals correctly. These and other results demonstrate that we can store rules for categories, not just exemplars (e.g., Ashby & Maddox, 1992; Blok et al., 2005; Nosofsky et al., 1994).

Thus the Allen and Brooks (1991) study established that, depending on the training conditions, we acquire exemplar memories, rules, *or both* for the categories we learn. To corroborate these behavioral findings with neural evidence, neuroimaging was conducted while two groups performed the task, either in the rule condition or the no-rule condition (Patalano et al., 2001; see also E. Smith et al., 1998). The investigators made the following predictions. First, in the no-rule condition, the brain areas used should be those that store exemplar memories (because the exemplars were experienced only visually, the primary sites of brain activation should be in the visual system). Second, in the rule condition, the primary brain areas used should be those that represent rules. (Because people rehearse a rule to themselves while they assess its fit to exemplars, motor areas that implement the implicit speech actions for rehearsal should become active.)

The results of the brain scans bear out the predictions. In the no-rule condition, most of the active sites were in occipital areas where vision is processed. As predicted, when participants did not know a rule, they primarily used visual memories of exemplars to categorize. In the rule condition, there were active sites in frontal motor areas. Again as predicted, when participants knew a rule, they rehearsed it silently to themselves, and the actions of internal rehearsal engaged the motor system.

The conclusion? Different brain systems become active to represent exemplars and to represent rules. Furthermore, the particular systems that become active support the notion that category knowledge is represented in modality-specific areas: visual areas represent the content of exemplars, motor areas implement the process of rehearsing rules. (For other work that also localizes various category representations in the brain, see Ashby & Ell, 2001.)

10.4.2   Prototypes and Typicality

Prototypes offer a different way to summarizing a category's members. Whereas an exemplar offers a reference for direct comparison, and a rule is a rigid requirement about the properties required for membership in a category, a **prototype** simply specifies what properties are *most likely* to be true of a category. A set of nine new *builders* is shown in Figure 10.14. These new builders have various combinations of horns, tails, ears, and a hump, as well as the familiar long legs, angular bodies, and spots.

What structures could represent these nine creatures, no two identical but all *builders?* Nine exemplar memories would do the job, but that doesn't seem very economical. A rule could summarize their shared properties. What rule? One possibility, borne out by inspection of this herd of nine, is that a creature possessing at least two of the following four properties — long legs, angular bodies, spots, horns — is a *builder.* This rule is good, but complicated to apply.

FIGURE 10.14   An augmented builder category
These *builders* can have the additional properties of horns, tail, ears, or hump, along with the usual properties of long legs, an angular body, or spots. The category prototype is a *builder* that has any property included in at least 60 percent of the population of nine *builders*.

Knowing the prototype — that is, knowing the combination of properties most likely to appear in a builder — seems the most efficient approach here. The prototype of the nine *builders* is the set of properties that occurs most often across builder-category members, excluding properties that occur rarely. Let's define a rare property as one that occurs less than 40 percent of the time, thus excluding tails, ears, and hump. All the remaining properties end up in the prototype, so the prototype of a *builder* is an animal with spots, angular body, long legs, and horns. Because the prototype summarizes statistical information about the category's most likely properties, the prototypical *builder* in Figure 10.14 results from combining the properties of spots (which appear in 78 percent of the population), angular body (in 67 percent,) long legs (in 67 percent), and horns (in 67 percent). Many theories assume that prototypes develop to represent categories. (For further discussion of prototype theories, see (Barsalou, 1990; Barsalou & Hale, 1993; E. Smith & Medin, 1981; J. Smith & Minda, 2002).

If a category has a prototype, category members similar to the prototype are viewed as typical category members, whereas category members different from the prototype are viewed as atypical. If the prototype for birds indicates that they tend to fly, nest in trees, and be small, then sparrows, which fit this prototype well, are typical; ostriches, on the other hand, which have none of these properties, do not fit the prototype and are therefore atypical. Typicality is not an on – off condition. Eagles fit the prototype moderately well, and so they are moderately typical. In general, the members of a category vary continuously in how similar they are to the prototype; thus, different birds vary continuously along this continuum of typicality, from highly typical to highly atypical. Such *typicality gradients* occur universally across categories (Barsalou, 1987; Rosch, 1973). Every category ever studied has one, even categories with precise rules (e.g., Armstrong et al., 1983).

Typicality gradients have substantial effects on how we process categories. When learning categories, we tend to learn typical members of a category before atypical ones (e.g., Mervis & Pani, 1980). When we categorize individuals, we categorize typical ones fastet than atypical ones (e.g., Rosch, 1975), and with greater accuracy (e.g., Posner & Keele, 1968). When we draw inferences from category members, we draw stronger ones from typical than from atypical category members (e.g., Osherson et al., 1990; Rips, 1975). In general, typical category members enjoy a privileged status in the kingdom of categories.

Such typicality effects have been widely viewed as implicating prototypes in the representation of categories (e.g., Hampton, 1979; Rosch & Mervis, 1975; E. Smith et al., 1974). Typicality effects can arise, however, even if no prototype is stored for a category and only exemplar memories represent the category (Medin & Schaffer, 1978). Much research has attempted to identify whether typicality gradients result from prototypes, exemplars, or other types of representations (e.g., Barsalou, 1985, 1987, 1990; Medin & Schaffer, 1978; J. Smith & Minda, 2002). Whatever way typicality gradients happen to originate, there is no doubt that categories have them, and that typicality is one of the most important factors in the acquisition and use of category knowledge.

10.4.3   Background Knowledge

An implicit assumption underlying exemplar memories, rules, and prototypes is that the properties constituting them are processed in a vacuum. To establish an exemplar memory of a chair, for example, the perceived object is simply added to a set of memorized exemplars of the object. To update a rule or prototype, newly perceived properties are simply integrated into its previously established property information. In either learning process, properties accumulate in relative isolation. Increasingly, however, researchers have come to appreciate that properties typically activate **background knowledge** in memory that specifies how properties originate, why they are important, and how they are related to one another (e.g., Ahn & Luhmann, 2005; Goodman, 1955; Murphy & Medin, 1985). Rather than being processed in a vacuum, properties are processed within a larger context of associated knowledge.

For instance, suppose that someone tells you that an object has wheels and a large sheet of canvas. In representing this object to yourself, do you assume that it has *only* these two properties and imagine a set of stationary wheels linked by a canvas axle? No. You could probably draw the additional inferences that the cloth is a sail, that the object uses wind power to roll along the ground, and that this "land sailboat" contains other parts, such as a metal axle, a mast, and a seat. Where did this interpretation come from? Background knowledge about wind, rolling, and transportation became active to explain and integrate the two stated properties. This example illustrates how readily background knowledge becomes active in interpretation and how it complements perceived properties. Rather than perceiving the properties of an entity in isolation, we almost always bring background knowledge to bear on interpreting them. (For a review of findings, see Murphy, 2000).

Here's another illustration (Barsalou, 1983). Participants were presented with the names of several objects — rock, chair, brick, potted plant — and asked to identify a category to which they all belong. (Not so easy — what's your guess?) But here's some background knowledge. The day is hot and windy. You want to keep your door open, but it keeps blowing shut. You decide to do something about it, maybe hold the door open with [. . .] right. With this information, people often instantly see that rock, chair, brick, and potted plant all belong to the category of things that will hold a door open on a windy day. The category did not become apparent until you activated the relevant background knowledge, another demonstration of the central role of background knowledge in processing categories.

A structure for representing background knowledge is the **schema,** a structured representation that captures the information that typically applies to a situation or event (for reviews, see Barsalou, 1992; Barsalou & Hale, 1993; Rumelhart & Norman, 1988). Schemata are described as "structured" because they are not lists of independent properties but instead establish coherent sets of relations that link properties. Thus the schema for a birthday party (like yours) might include guests, gifts, and cake; the structure is that the guests give gifts to the birthday celebrant, and that everyone eats cake. Schemata are similar to rules and prototypes in that they summarize the members of a category. They differ from rules and prototypes in that they contain much information that is not essential for categorizing entities but that is important for understanding the events surrounding them. The schema for a birthday party provides useful background knowledge about birthday cakes; seeing a birthday cake activates the schema for birthday parties, so useful inferences can be drawn about why the cake is there and how it will be used.

Much evidence for schemata can be found across all aspects of cognition. When processing visual scenes, we expect to see particular configurations of objects (e.g., Biederman, 1981; Palmer, 1975). In a given social situation, we expect to observe (and engage in) particular relations among the those present (e.g., Fiske & Taylor, 1991). In the realm of memory, schemata produce strong expectations about what is likely to have occurred in the past, expectations that can distort our memories (e.g., Bartlett, 1932; Brewer & Treyens, 1981; Schooler et al., 1997). Schemata play central roles in aspects of reasoning such as analogy, problem solving, and decision making (e.g., Gentner & Markman, 1997; Markman & Gentner, 2001; Markman & Medin, 1995; Ross, 1996).

10.4.4   Dynamic Representation

As we have seen, many different structures can underlie the knowledge of a given category: exemplars, rules, prototypes, and schemata. When we think of a particular category, do all the structures representing it become fully active? Or does the cognitive system vary the most active information about a category dynamically, highlighting the information most useful on the current occasions?

Much evidence indicates that not all possible information for a category is activated when the category is accessed, but rather information relevant in the current context is preferentially activated. **Dynamic representation** refers to the ability of the cognitive system to construct, and call on as necessary, many different representations of a category, each emphasizing the category knowledge currently most relevant.

One source of evidence for dynamic representation comes from cross-modality priming studies. Participants listen to a sentence over headphones. Immediately following the last spoken word, they see a string of letters. Their task is to indicate as quickly as possible whether the string forms a word (for example, *yellow*) or a non-word (for example, *yeelor*). This basic task can be used to demonstrate dynamic representation (e.g., Greenspan, 1986;

Tabossi, 1988). Here's how it works. Let's say that the last word of an auditorally presented sentence is *beachball* and that this word appears in one of two sentences:

> The swimmer saw the gently bobbing *beachball*.
> The air hissed out of the punctured *beachball*.

If *beachball* is represented dynamically in these two sentences, then the information active for it should vary, reflecting the most relevant property about beachballs in each situation. After presentation of the first sentence, the property "floats" should be more active than the property "is flat." But following the second sentence, "is flat" should be more active than "floats." If the representation of "beachball" is *not* dynamic, the activations of "floats" and "is flat" should not change across sentences. If all category knowledge is equally active for a category on every occasion, then the change of sentence should not affect the conceptual representation of "beachball."

Many experiments, using cross-modal priming and many other techniques, have consistently produced results that support dynamic representation (for reviews, see Barsalou, 1987, 1989; L. Smith & Samuelson, 1997; Yeh & Barsalou, 2004). The information that is most active varies from occasion to occasion. Furthermore, the most active information is typically relevant to the current context.

10.5   CATEGORY DOMAINS AND ORGANIZATION

For what domains in the world do we establish category knowledge? It seems we develop categories that reflect the kinds of things in the world — what philosophers concerned with ontology, the study of being or the essence of things, call **ontological types** (e.g., Sommers, 1963). Ontologists generally agree that important ontological types include living natural things ("kinds" in the language of ontology), nonliving natural kinds, artifacts, locations, events, mental states, times, and properties. Most ontologists believe that ontological categories are probably *universal;* that is, they are categories that every normal human knows regardless of culture. Psychologists believe that different domains of category knowledge develop for different ontological types (e.g., Keil, 1979).

Within each domain of category knowledge lie many more specific categories. "Living natural kinds" includes "mammals" and "trees." "Nonliving natural kinds" includes "water" and "gold." "Artifacts" includes "tools" and "clothes." "Locations" includes "oceans" and "parks." "Events" includes "meals" and "birthday parties." "Mental states" includes "emotions" and "ideas." "Times" includes "night" and "summer." "Properties" includes "green" and "expensive." Many of these more specific categories within domains also appear to be known universally across cultures (e.g., Malt, 1995). As categories become increasingly specific, though, they are less likely to be known in all cultures (for example, tank top, paper shredder, foods high in vitamin C).

10.5.1   Distinguishing Domains of Category Knowledge in the Brain

The various domains of category knowledge certainly seem different, at least intuitively: animals seem in their essence different from artifacts, objects seem different from thoughts. Are these intuitive differences realized in the brain's representational systems? Is knowledge of different categories stored in different regions of the brain? Or is all category knowledge stored in a single brain area? To address this question, researchers have assessed category knowledge in patients who have suffered brain lesions, seeking to learn which particular categories are lost and whether these losses can be associated with particular brain regions.

Typically when a brain-damaged patient loses category knowledge, only some knowledge is lost, while other knowledge is preserved. For example, Warrington and Shallice (1984) described four patients with brain damage who exhibited a deficit for animal categories (such as "dogs" and "robins"). But, although these patients had difficulty naming and defining various animals, they had little trouble naming and defining artifact categories (such as "hammers" and "chairs"). More rarely, patients show the opposite deficit (e.g., Warrington & McCarthy, 1983, 1987), exhibiting less knowledge of artifacts than of animals. This double dissociation of animals and artifacts suggests that different localized brain areas represent these two kinds of categories. Various deficits for other categories have been reported as well, such as deficits for number categories and abstract categories (e.g., Thioux et al., 1998; Tyler & Moss, 1997).

How can these selective deficits in category knowledge be explained? Modality-specific representations of categories may provide a clue. Both behavioral and neutal evidence suggest that the representation of a category is distributed across the modality-specific brain systems that process its properties. For example, in Western culture, at any rate, many people see animals (engaging the visual modality) far more often than they work with them (engaging the motor system). In contrast, knowledge of artifacts generally relies much more heavily on motor information than on visual information (try to describe a screwdriver while keeping your hands still). Given these different profiles of multimodal information, lesions to the visual system might produce larger deficits for living things than for artifacts, whereas lesions to the motor system might produce larger deficits for artifacts. Perhaps the multimodal profiles for different domains of categories interact with lesions in this way to produce different deficits in category knowledge when the corresponding brain area is damaged. Many theorists have reached this conclusion (e.g., Damasio & Damasio, 1994; Farah & McClelland, 1991; Gainotti et al., 1995; Humphreys & Forde, 2001; Pulvermüller, 1999). To the extent that this account is correct, it offers further evidence for the claim that category knowledge is distributed across the modality-specific systems that process it.

But the verdict is not in. Some researchers believe that this account is too crude to explain the subtle patterns of deficits that are often seen in patients with brain damage (Cree & McRae, 2003). Most typically, a patient does *not* lose just a single category but rather loses several. Foods can be lost along with living things, and so can musical instruments. Fruits and vegetables are typically lost together, and can be lost with either living things or non-living things. Figure 10.15 presents seven patterns of category deficits that Cree and McRae identified in their review of the literature; there is no way that loss of either visual or motor processing could explain all these different patterns.

Cree and McCrae (2003) believe that deficits result from specific losses to a much wider variety of properties, for which the processing is distributed across the brain. To assess this hypothesis, they asked people to produce the properties for the kinds of categories that patients lose following brain lesions, such as the properties of birds, fruit, and tools. Once they had established each category's properties, they assessed what *types* of properties the

Deficit Pattern	Shared Properties
1. Multiple categories that constitute living creatures	Visual motion, visual parts, color
2. Multiple categories that constitute nonliving things	Function, visual parts
3. Fruits and vegetables	Color, function, taste, smell
4. Fruits and vegetables with living creatures	Color
5. Fruits and vegetables with nonliving things	Function
6. Inanimate foods with living things (especially fruits and vegetables)	Function, taste, smell
7. Musical instruments with living things	Sound, color

FIGURE 10.15   Seven patterns of category deficits that result from brain lesions
These are sets of categories for which patients with brain damage simultaneously exhibit much poorer knowledge than normal. There is evidence that when a brain lesion compromises representations of particular properties, the categories that rely heavily on them are impaired.

various categories in each deficit pattern shared, along with the types that differed. Of central interest was whether the multiple categories in a particular deficit pattern had one or more property types in common — visual motion, say, or color? If so, lesions to areas that process a given property type could cause categories that share it to be lost together. For example, if color areas are damaged, then categories for which color is important, such as animals and foods, might be compromised simultaneously.

The results were illuminating (see Figure 10.15). Cree and McRae (2003) found, for example, that the categories in the first pattern of deficits, living creatures, typically share many properties: they generally move, have interesting and salient parts, and have relatively informative colors. The categories in the fifth pattern (fruits, vegetables, and nonliving things) share properties for functions, in that all these things have roles in our life — fruits and vegetables in our diet, nonliving artifacts in our manipulation of the world around us. Thus, a more complicated formulation of the original theory might explain the patterns of category-specific deficits found in the literature.

As provocative as these conclusions are, the issue of how the brain represents categories is far from settled. Cree and McRae (2003) show that factors besides shared properties are important, such as property uniqueness. Alternative accounts for category-specific deficits in terms of amodal symbols have also been offered (e.g., Capitani et al., 2003; Caramazza & Shelton, 1998; Tyler & Moss, 2001), and it is likely that a variety of mechanisms produce category-specific deficits, not just one (e.g., Coltheart et al., 1998; Simmons & Barsalou, 2003). Furthermore, studies of patients with brain damage suffer from a variety of methodological problems, including difficulties in measuring behavioral deficits, along with difficulties in measuring lesions and fully understanding their implications for brain operation (see Chapter 1). Nevertheless, a conclusion emerging from this research is that different types of categories are represented primarily in different brain areas. Consistent with the multimodal-simulation view, a category's representation appears, ar least in part, to be distributed across the modality-specific areas of the brain that process its members.

Further support for this conclusion comes from neuroimaging studies that have measured brain activity while participants process categories from different domains, particularly the domains of animals and artifacts. Different patterns of brain activity are observed for these domains. Consistent with findings from research with brain-damaged patients, for example, artifacts tend to activate premotor areas more than do animals (see Figure 10.12).

For the "animals" domain, studies of patients with brain damage and neuroimaging studies show an interesting difference (Martin, 2001). On the one hand, studies show that damage to the temporal lobes often produces a categorical deficit for animals; on the other hand, neuroimaging studies often show extensive activation for animals in the occipital lobes. Why do these different patterns occur? Martin suggests that the temporal lobes are *association areas* that work to integrate category knowledge. When there is damage to these areas, the statistical patterns stored there cannot trigger simulations in the occipital lobes that represent the properties of animal categories. When these association areas are intact, as they are for most participants in neuroimaging studies, the statistical patterns stored there can trigger simulations in the occipital lobes, which are then detected by neuroimaging. Thus, the differential pattern of results offers support for the idea that representations are distributed in the brain, as described earlier.

Neuroimaging studies also have found that using knowledge of object shape (for example, the shape of a cat) activates the fusiform gyrus, whereas using knowledge of object motion (for example, how a cat moves) activates the posterior temporal gyrus (Chao et al., 1999; Martin & Chao, 2001; Martin et al., 1996). Furthermore, these studies have found that accessing different kinds of categories activates somewhat different fusiform areas for shape, and somewhat different temporal areas for motion. Although the sites for shape are near each other, they differ. Whereas the shapes of animals, people, and faces tend to activate lateral fusiform areas, the shapes of tools tend to activate more medial ones. The same is true for motion sites. Whereas animals, people, and faces tend to activate superior temporal areas, tools tend to activate more inferior ones. These slightly different sites are a further indication that different domains of category knowledge rely on different brain systems. Increasingly, studies suggest that different domains of category knowledge are distributed differently across the brain's modality-specific areas. The intuitive differences that we experience for different domains indeed reflect important differences in the underlying neural implementations.

10.5.2   Taxonomies and the Search for a "Basic Level"

Within a domain of category knowledge, categories are not represented in isolation, but rather in various structures that link related categories. One important organizational form is the taxonomy, a set of nested categories that vary in abstraction, each nested category a subset of its higher order category (Figure 10.16). Thus, the category of objects includes living things and artifacts. "Artifacts" includes "tools," "vehicles," "clothing," [. . .] "Tools" includes "screwdrivers," "hammers," "saws," [. . .] "Screwdrivers" includes "slot," "Phillips," "ratchet" screwdrivers. [. . .] Taxonomies such as these examples sound like the result of formal education and, certainly, to some extent they are. But in fact taxonomies are found universally throughout cultures and are not dependent on formal training. After reviewing anthropological work on biological categories, Malt (1995) concluded

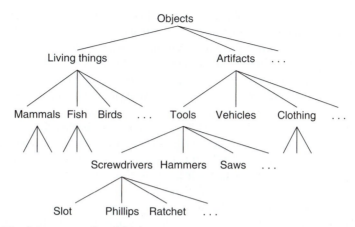

FIGURE 10.16   A taxonomy for objects
Increasingly specific categories are nested in more general ones.

that all cultures studied so far, including traditional, nonindustrial ones, have taxonomies for plants and animals.

A central question in this area has been the search for a *basic level* in taxonomies, a level that is more central than others in human cognition. In Figure 10.16, for example, which levels — the lower ones? the middle ones? the higher ones? — are likely to be the most important for cognition?

In classic anthropological work on biological categories, Berlin, Breedlove, and Raven (1973) argued that the middle levels are the most important. For one thing, more words for categories exist at middle levels than at those above and below — more words such as "dog," "horse," and "lion" exist than words such as "mammal" (above) or "collie," "poodle," and "terrier" (below). Although it is logically necessary that more categories become possible as you go *lower* in a taxonomy, the important finding here was that more single-word names exist for categories at middle levels than at lower ones. Another important finding was that names for categories at middle levels are shorter than names for categories above and below (for example, "dog" vs. "mammal" above and vs. "poodle" below). *Zipf's law* in linguistics states that the more frequently a word occurs in a language, the shorter it becomes as the language evolves over many generations of speakers. Names for categories at middle taxonomic levels are shortest, suggesting that these are the names used most often and therefore most important.

Cross-cultural conclusions from Malt (1995) further demonstrate the importance of middle-level categories in taxonomies. Across all cultures, traditional and developed, there is high agreement in middle-level categories: names for middle-level categories such as "deer," "eagle," and "alligator" tend to be found wherever these animals are part of the environment. Furthermore, these names refer to essentially the same groups of entities in the environment — "deer," for example, refers to pretty much the same creature across cultures. Finally, cultures typically have names for these categories even when they play no role in people's lives. Across cultures, many plants and animals that have no function still have names at the middle level. Middle-level categories in biological taxonomies are sufficiently salient perceptually that members of nearly all cultures perceive and develop names for them (for example, in our culture, many wild animals).

Much psychological research further shows that the middle levels in a taxonomy are most important. Investigators found that categories at mid-taxonomic levels are processed faster than are categories at other levels (Rosch et al., 1976). When participants have to match a pictured object to a category name (for example, "poodle," "dog," "animal"), they match middle-level names fastest (in this case, "dog"). These investigators also found that children learn names for middle-level categories earlier than they do the names for categories at other levels. Much other research has reported similar results (for a review, see Murphy & Lassaline, 1997). On the basis of results like these, Rosch and colleagues called middle-level categories the **basic level,** the level of a taxonomy used most often, learned most easily, and processed most efficiently.

Names for categories at higher and lower levels show much less agreement across cultures (e.g., Malt, 1995). For example, cultures that eat butterfly larvae have many categories for different kinds of larvae; cultures that don't, don't. When similar categories at higher and lower levels do exist in two cultures, they often do not refer to the same sets of things in the environment. One culture might have a category for "trees," another might have a category for "firewood" that includes only those trees that are burnable. Furthermore, both high- and low-level categories are more likely to deviate from scientific taxonomies than are middle-level categories.

So what is it about middle-level categories? *Why* do they show these advantages? Why are they the most common; why are their names shortest? Why are these the categories most agreed on across cultures and the closest to scientific taxonomies? Why do we learn and process them most easily?

Although this issue is far from settled, a dominant account has emerged (e.g., Malt, 1995; Tversky & Hemenway, 1985). Middle-level categories are important because their members (unlike members of categories at higher and lower levels) typically share a common configuration of physical parts, and this configuration differs from that of other categories at the same level. For example, deer have four legs, two ears, pointed hooves, a tail, and other physical properties in a particular arrangement; most butterflies have a specific arrangement of head, body, antennae, and large flat wings. For hundreds of years, biologists have used these morphological descriptions to define natural categories. Evolutionary and genetic theories have made it possible to link the genetic histories of species directly to these morphological structures.

At higher levels, there is no common morphological structure within a category — lots of mammals are built nothing like deer. At lower levels, such as varieties of butterflies, the morphology is shared across different categories, making different varieties confusable. To discriminate the difference between categories, it is necessary to learn subtle visual features that are much less salient than the motphological characteristics that distinguish the deer and butterflies categories at the middle level.

Why is the morphology of middle-level taxonomies so salient? One explanation is that our visual feature-detection systems have become tuned over evolutionary time to the features that distinguish different morphologies from one another. Laboratory evidence for this conclusion can be found in Tversky and Hemenway (1985), Jolicoeur et al. (1984), and Murphy and Brownell (1985); Biederman (1987) presents a related theory of object recognition.

Still, many researchers are reluctant to adopt the construct of a "basic level." One reason is that middle-level categories are not always the dominant ones. In Western culture, for example, the dominant level for categories of plants and birds is not at a mid-taxonomic level. Many Westerners know little about different types of plants and birds and cannot name the middle-level categories for them; besides, they often find higher level categories of plants and birds sufficiently informative for their purposes (e.g., Rosch et al., 1976). As Western culture has increasingly lost touch with the natural environment, the dominant taxonomic level for natural living kinds has shifted upward. Wolff and colleagues (1999) counted the taxonomic terms for trees in the *Oxford English Dictionary* from the sixteenth through the twentieth centuries, and discovered that the number of words for tree categories generally increased over this period, as knowledge about the natural world increased. In the twentieth century, however, names for tree categories decreased precipitately — especially for middle levels — indicating an upward taxonomic shift in knowledge about the natural environment.

So, one difficulty with middle-level categories as a basic level is that many people simply use higher level categories instead (see also Mandler & McDonough, 1998, 2000). A related problem, at the other end of the scale, is that when people become expert in a domain, they become able to process lower level taxonomic categories as effectively as middle-level ones (e.g., Gauthier et al., 1999; Johnson & Mervis, 1997; Tanaka & Curran, 2001; Tanaka & Gauthier, 1997).

Furthermore, the most useful taxonomic level can vary with the current goal (e.g., Cruse, 1977). You want your dog with you on a once-in-a-lifetime trip to London? In this situation, your travel agent does *not* use the basic level and simply tell you that all "dogs" coming into the United Kingdom are subject to a six-month quarantine. Because the law actually applies to all non-human *mammals,* your travel agent tells you that all non-human "mammals" coming into the United Kingdom are subject to quarantine. Even though the basic level is normally more salient than the next level up, your travel agent moves up a level so that you understand the full extent of the law. Under these conditions, a non-basic level is most important.

Thus, although there is an overall tendency for middle-level categories to dominate categories at other levels in many important ways, so many exceptions exist that many researchers believe that referring to middle-level categories as "basic" confers on them an objective reality not warranted by the data. The relative importance of a taxonomic level reflects a wide variety of mediating factors and fluctuates with need and circumstance.

REFERENCES

Ahn, W., & Luhmann, C. C. (2005). Demystifying theory-based categorization. In L. Gershkoff-Stowe & D. H. Rakison (Eds). *Building object categories in developmental time.* (pp. 277–300). Mahwah, NJ, US: Lawrence Erlbaum Associates, Publishers.

Allen, S. W., & Brooks, L. R. (1991). Specializing the operation of an explicit rule. *Journal of Experimental Psychology: General, 120,* 3–19.

Anderson, J. R. (1976). *Language, memory, and thought.* Hillsdale, NJ: Erlbaum.

Anderson, J. R. (1983). *The architecture of cognition.* Cambridge, MA: Harvard University Press.

Armstrong, S. L., Gleitman, L. R., & Gleitman, H. (1983). On what some concepts might not be. *Cognition, 13,* 263–308.

Ashby, F. G., & Ell, S. W. (2001). The neurobiology of human category learning. *Trends in Cognitive Sciences, 5,* 204–210.

Ashby, F. G., & Maddox, W. T. (1992). Complex decision rules in categorization: Contrasting novice and experienced performance. *Journal of Experimental Psychology: Human Perception and Performance, 18*, 50–71.

Barsalou, L. W. (1983). Ad hoc categories. *Memory & Cognition, 11*, 211–227.

Barsalou, L. W. (1985). Ideals, central tendency, and frequency of instantiation as determinants of graded structure in categories. *Journal of Experimental Psychology: Learning, Memory, and Cognition, 11*, 629–654.

Barsalou, L. W. (1987). The instability of graded structure: Implications for the nature of concepts. In U. Neisser (Ed.), *Concepts and conceptual development: Ecological and intellectual factors in categorization* (pp. 101–140). Cambridge, UK: Cambridge University Press.

Barsalou, L. W. (1989). Intraconcept similarity and its implications for interconcept similarity. In S. Vosniadou & A. Ortony (Eds.), *Similarity and analogical reasoning* (pp. 76–121). Cambridge, UK: Cambridge University Press.

Barsalou, L. W. (1990). On the indistinguishability of exemplar memory and abstraction in category representation. In T. K. Srull & R. S. Wyer (Eds.), *Advances in social cognition, Volume III: Content and process specificity in the effects of prior experiences* (pp. 61–88). Hillsdale, NJ: Lawrence Erlbaum Associates.

Barsalou, L. W. (1992). Frames, concepts, and conceptual fields. In E. Kittay & A. Lehrer (Eds.), *Frames, fields, and contrasts: New essays in semantic and lexical organization* (pp. 21–74). Hillsdale, NJ: Lawrence Erlbaum Associates.

Barsalou, L. W. (1999). Perceptual symbol systems. *Behavioral and Brain Sciences, 22*, 577–609.

Barsalou, L. W. (2003b). Situated simulation in the human conceptual system. *Language and Cognitive Processes, 18*, 513–562.

Barsalou, L. W., & Hale, C. R. (1993). Components of conceptual representation: From feature lists to recursive frames. In I. Van Mechelen, J. Hampton, R. Michalski, & P. Theuns (Eds.), *Categories and concepts: Theoretical views and inductive data analysis* (pp. 97–144). San Diego: Academic Press.

Barsalou, L. W., Niedenthal, P. M., Barbey, A., & Ruppert, J. (2003). Social embodiment. In B. Ross (Ed.), *The psychology of learning and motivation* (Vol. 43, pp. 43–92). San Diego: Academic Press.

Bartlett, F. C. (1932). *Remembering: A study in experimental and social psychology.* Cambridge, UK: Cambridge University Press.

Bear, M. F., Connors, B. W., & Paradiso, M. A. (2002). *Neuroscience: Exploring the brain* (2nd ed.). Baltimore: Lippincott Williams & Wilkins.

Berlin, B., Breedlove, D. E., & Raven, P. H. (1973). General principles of classification and nomenclature in folk biology. *American Anthropologist, 75*, 214–242.

Biederman, I. (1981). On the semantics of a glance at a scene. In M. Kubovy & J. R. Pomerantz (Eds.), *Perceptual Organization* (pp. 213–253). Hillsdale, NJ: Lawrence Erlbaum Associates.

Biederman, I. (1987). Recognition-by-components: A theory of human image understanding. *Psychological Review, 94*, 115–147.

Blok, S., Newman, G., & Rips, L. J. (2005). Individuals and their concepts. In W-K Ahn, R. L. Goldstone, B. C. Love, A. B. Markman, & P. Wolff (Eds). *Categorization inside and outside the laboratory: Essays in honor of Douglas L. Medin.* (pp. 127–149). Washington, DC, US: American Psychological Association.

Brewer, W. F., & Treyens, J. C. (1981). Role of schemata in memory for places. *Cognitive Psychology, 13*, 207–230.

Brooks, L. R. (1978). Nonanalytic concept formation and memory for instances. In E. Rosch & B. B. Lloyd (Eds.), *Cognition and categorization* (pp. 169–211). Hillsdale, NJ: Lawrence Erlbaum Associates.

Bruner, J. S. (1957). Going beyond the information given. In J. S. Bruner, E. Brunswik, L. Festinger, F. Heider, K. F. Muenzinger, C. E. Osgood, & D. Rapaport (Eds.), *Contemporary approaches to cognition* (pp. 41–69). Cambridge, MA: Harvard University Press.

Capitani, E., Laiacona, M., Mahon, B., & Caramazza, A. (2003). What are the facts of semantic category-specific deficits? A critical review of the clinical evidence. *Cognitive Neuropsychology, 20*, 213–261.

Caramazza, A., & Shelton, J. R. (1998). Domain-specific knowledge systems in the brain: The animate–inanimate distinction. *Journal of Cognitive Neuroscience, 10*, 1–34.

Carruthers, P. (1992). *Human knowledge and human nature.* Oxford: Oxford University Press.

Chambers, D., & Reisberg, D. (1992). What an image depicts depends on what an image means. *Cognitive Psychology, 24*, 145–174.

Chao, L. L., Haxby, J. V., & Martin, A. (1999). Attribute-based neural substrates in temporal cortex for perceiving and knowing about objects. *Nature Neuroscience, 2*, 913–919.

Chao, L. L., & Martin, A. (2000). Representation of manipulable man-made objects in the dorsal stream. *Neuroimage, 12*, 478–484.

Coltheart, M., Inglis, L., Cupples, L., Michie, P., Bates, A., & Budd, B. (1998). A semantic subsystem of visual attributes. *Neurocase, 4*, 353–370.

Coltheart, V. (Ed.). (1999). *Fleeting memories: Cognition of brief visual stimuli.* Cambridge, MA: The MIT Press.

Cree, G. S, & McRae, K. (2003). Analyzing the factors underlying the structure and computation of the meaning of chipmunk, cherry, chisel, cheese, and cello (and many other such concrete nouns). *Journal of Experimental Psychology: General, 132,* 163–201.

Crist, R. E., Li, W., & Gilbert, C. D. (2001). Learning to see: Experience and attention in primary visual cortex. *Nature Neuroscience, 4,* 519–525.

Cruse, D. A. (1977). The pragmatics of lexical specificity. *Journal of Linguistics, 13,* 153–164.

Damasio, A. R. (1989). Time-locked multiregional retroactivation: A systems-level proposal for the neural substrates of recall and recognition. *Cognition, 33,* 25–62.

Damasio, A. R., & Damasio, H. (1994). Cortical systems for retrieval of concrete knowledge: The convergence zone framework. In C. Koch & J. L. Davis (Eds.), *Large-scale neuronal theories of the brain: Computational neuroscience* (pp. 61–74). Cambridge, MA: The MIT Press.

Dietrich, E., & Markman, A. (Eds.) (2000). *Cognitive dynamics: Conceptual change in humans and machines.* Cambridge, MA: The MIT Press.

Dretske, F. (1995). *Naturalizing the mind.* Cambridge, MA: The MIT Press.

Farah, M. J. (2000). The neural bases of mental imagery. In M. S. Gazzaniga (Ed.), *The cognitive neurosciences* (2nd ed., pp. 965–974). Cambridge, MA: The MIT Press.

Farah, M. J., & McClelland, J. L. (1991). A computational model of semantic memory impairment: Modality specificity and emergent category specificity. *Journal of Experimental Psychology: General, 120,* 339–357.

Farah, M. J., Soso, M. J., & Dasheiff, R. M. (1992). Visual angle of the mind's eye before and after unilateral occipital lobectomy. *Journal of Experimental Psychology: Human Performance and Perception, 18,* 241–246.

Finke, R. A. (1989). *Principles of mental imagery.* Cambridge, MA: The MIT Press.

Fiske, S. T., & Taylor, S. E. (1991). *Social cognition* (2nd ed.). New York: McGraw-Hill.

Gainotti, G., Silveri, M. C., Daniele, A., & Giustolisi, L. (1995). Neuroanatomical correlates of category-specific semantic disorders: A critical survey. *Memory, 3,* 247–264.

Gauthier, I., Tarr, M. J., Anderson, A. W., Skudlarski, P., & Gore, J. C. (1999). Activation of the middle fusiform "face area" increases with expertise in recognizing novel objects. *Nature Neuroscience, 2,* 568–573.

Gentner, D., & Markman, A. B. (1997). Structure mapping in analogy and similarity. *American Psychologist, 52,* 45–56.

Glenberg, A. M. (1997). What memory is for. *Behavioral and Brain Sciences, 20,* 1–55.

Glenberg, A. M., & Kaschak, M. P. (2002). Grounding language in action. *Psychonomic Bulletin & Review, 9,* 558–569.

Goodman, N. (1955). *Fact, fiction, and forecast.* Cambridge, MA: Harvard University Press.

Goodman, N. (1976). *Languages of art.* Indianapolis, IN: Hackett.

Greenspan, S. L. (1986). Semantic flexibility and referential specificity of concrete nouns. *Journal of Memory and Language, 25,* 539–557.

Grèzes, J., & Decety, J. (2001). Functional anatomy of execution, mental simulation, observation, and verb generation of actions: A meta-analysis. *Human Brain Mapping, 12,* 1–19.

Halpern, A. R. (2001). Cerebral substrates of musical imagery. *Annals of the New York Academy of Sciences, 930,* 179–192.

Hampton, J. A. (1979). Polymorphous concepts in semantic memory. *Journal of Verbal Learning and Verbal Behavior, 18,* 441–461.

Hasher, L., & Zacks, R. T. (1979). Automatic and effortful processes in memory. *Journal of Experimental Psychology: General, 108,* 356–388.

Haugeland, J. (1991). Representational genera. In W. Ramsey, S. P. Stitch, & D. E. Rumelhart (Eds.), *Philosophy and connectionist theory* (pp. 61–89). Hillsdale, NJ: Lawrence Erlbaum Associates.

Henderson, J. M., & Hollingworth, A. (2003). Eye movements and visual memory: Detecting changes to saccade targets in scenes. *Perception and Psychophysics, 65,* 58–71.

Hintzman, D. L. (1986). "Schema abstraction" in a multiple-trace memory model. *Psychological Review, 93,* 411–428.

Hochberg, J. (1998). Gestalt theory and its legacy: Organization in eye and brain, in attention and mental representation. In J. Hochberg (Ed.), *Perception and cognition at century's end: Handbook of perception and cognition* (2nd ed., pp. 253–306). San Diego, CA: Academic Press.

Humphreys, G. W., & Forde, E. M. E. (2001). Hierarchies, similarity, and interactivity in object recognition: "Category-specific" neuropsychological deficits. *Behavioral & Brain Sciences, 24,* 453–509.

Hyde, T. S., & Jenkins, J. J. (1969). Differential effects of incidental tasks on the organization of recall of a list of highly associated words. *Journal of Experimental Psychology, 82,* 472–481.

Jeannerod, M. (1995). Mental imagery in the motor context. *Neuropsychologia, 33,* 1419–1432.

Jeannerod, M. (1997). *The cognitive neuroscience of action.* Cambridge, MA: Blackwell Press.

Johnson, K. E., & Mervis, C. B. (1997). Effects of varying levels of expertise on the basic level of categorization. *Journal of Experimental Psychology: General, 126,* 248–277.

Jolicoeur, P., Gluck, M., & Kosslyn, S. M. (1984). Pictures and names: Making the connection. *Cognitive Psychology, 16,* 243–275.

Keil, F. C. (1979). *Semantic and conceptual development: An ontological perspective.* Cambridge, MA: Harvard University Press.

Kellenbach, M. L., Brett, M., & Patterson, K. (2001). Large, colorful, and noisy? Attribute- and modality-specific activations during retrieval of perceptual attribute knowledge. *Cognitive, Affective, & Behavioral Neuroscience, 1,* 207–221.

Kosslyn, S. M. (1980). *Image and mind.* Cambridge, MA: Harvard University Press.

Kosslyn, S. M. (1994). *Image and brain: The resolution of the imagery debate.* Cambridge, MA: The MIT Press.

Kosslyn, S. M., Thompson, W. L., & Ganis, G. (2006). *The case for mental imagery.* New York: Oxford University Press.

Kosslyn, S. M., Thompson, W. L., Kim, I. J., & Alpert, N. M. (1995). Topographical representations of mental images in primary visual cortex. *Nature, 378,* 496–498.

Lakoff, G. (1987). *Women, fire, and dangerous things: What categories reveal about the mind.* Chicago: University of Chicago Press.

Lamberts, K. (1998). The time course of categorization. *Journal of Experimental Psychology: Learning, Memory, and Cognition, 24,* 695–711.

Lehrer, K. (1990). *Theory of knowledge.* Boulder, CO: Westview.

Lettvin, J. Y., Maturana, H. R., McCulloch, W. S., & Pitts, W. H. (1959). What the frog's eye tells the frog's brain. *Proceedings of the Institute of Radio Engineers, 47,* 1940–1951.

Malt, B. C. (1995). Category coherence in cross-cultural perspective. *Cognitive Psychology, 29,* 85–148.

Mandler, J. M., & McDonough, L. (1998). Studies in inductive inference in infancy. *Cognitive Psychology, 37,* 60–96.

Mandler, J. M., & McDonough, L. (2000). Advancing downward to the basic level. *Journal of Cognition and Development, 1,* 379–403.

Markman, A. B., & Gentner, D. (2001). Thinking. *Annual Review of Psychology, 52,* 223–247.

Markman, A. B., & Medin, D. L. (1995). Similarity and alignment in choice. *Organizational Behavior & Human Decision Processes, 63,* 117–130.

Martin, A. (2001). Functional neuroimaging of semantic memory. In R. Cabeza & A. Kingstone (Eds.), *Handbook of functional neuroimaging of cognition* (pp. 153–186). Cambridge, MA: The MIT Press.

Martin, A., & Chao, L. L. (2001). Semantic memory and the brain: Structure and process. *Current Opinion in Neurobiology, 11,* 194–201.

Martin, A., Ungerleider, L. G., & Haxby, J. V. (2000). Category-specificity and the brain: The sensory-motor model of semantic representations of objects. In M. S. Gazzaniga (Ed.), *The new cognitive neurosciences* (2nd ed., 1023–1036). Cambridge, MA: The MIT Press.

Martin, A., Wiggs, C. L., Ungerleider, L. G., & Haxby, J. V. (1996). Nerual correlates of category-specific knowledge. *Nature, 379,* 649–652.

Medin, D. L., & Schaffer, M. (1978). A context theory of classification learning. *Psychological Review, 85,* 207–238.

Mervis, C. B., & Pani, J. R. (1980). Acquisition of basic object categories. *Cognitive Psychology, 12,* 496–522.

Murphy, G. L. (2000). Explanatory concepts. In F. C. Keil & R. A. Wilson (Eds.), *Explanation and cognition* (pp. 361–392). Cambridge, MA: The MIT Press.

Murphy, G. L., & Brownell, H. H. (1985). Category differentiation in object recognition: Typicality constraints on the basic category advantage. *Journal of Experimental Psychology: Learning, Memory, and Cognition, 11,* 70–84.

Murphy, G. L., & Lassaline, M. E. (1997). Hierarchical structure in concepts and the basic level of categorization. In K. Lamberts & D. R. Shanks (Eds.), *Knowledge, concepts and categories.* (pp. 93–131). Cambridge, MA: The MIT Press.

Murphy, G. L., & Medin, D. L. (1985). The role of theories in conceptual coherence. *Psychological Review, 92,* 289–316.

Newton, N. (1996). *Foundations of understanding.* Philadelphia: John Benjamins.

Newell, A. (1990). *Unified theories of cognition.* Cambridge, MA: Harvard University Press.

Newell, A., & Simon, H. A. (1972). *Human problem solving.* Upper Saddle River, NJ: Prentice Hall.

Nosofsky, R. M. (1984). Choice, similarity, and the context theory of classification. *Journal of Experimental Psychology: Learning, Memory, and Cognition, 10,* 104–114.

Nosofsky, R. M., Palmeri, T. J., & McKinley, S. C. (1994). Rule-plus-exception model of classification learning. *Psychological Review, 101,* 53–79.

Osherson, D. N., Smith, E. E., Wilkie, O., Lopez, A., & Shafir, E. (1990). Category-based induction. *Psychological Review, 97,* 185–200.

Palmer, S. E. (1975). The effects of contextual scenes on the identification of objects. *Memory & Cognition, 3*, 519–526.

Palmer, S. E. (1978). Fundamental aspects of cognitive representation. In E. Rosch & B. B. Lloyd (Eds.), *Cognition and categorization* (pp. 259–303). Hillsdale, NJ: Lawrence Erlbaum Associates.

Patalano, A. L., Smith, E. E., Jonides, J., & Koeppe, R. A. (2001). PET evidence for multiple strategies of categorization. *Cognitive, Affective & Behavioral Neuroscience, 1*, 360–370.

Pecher, D., Zeelenberg, R., & Barsalou, L. W. (2003). Verifying properties from different modalities for concepts produces switching costs. *Psychological Science, 14*, 119–124.

Posner, M. I., & Keele, S. W. (1968). On the genesis of abstract ideas. *Journal of Experimental Psychology, 77*, 353–363.

Pulvermüller, F. (1999). Words in the brain's language. *Behavioral and Brain Sciences, 22*, 253–336.

Rips, L. J. (1975). Inductive judgments about natural categories. *Journal of Verbal Learning & Verbal Behavior, 14*, 665–681.

Rizzolatti, G., Fadiga, L., Fogassi, L., & Gallese, V. (2002). From mirror neurons to imitation: Facts and speculations. In A. N. Meltzoff & W. Prinz (Eds.), *The imitative mind: Development, evolution, and brain bases.* (pp. 247–266). New York: Cambridge University Press.

Rosch, E. (1973). On the internal structure of perceptual and semantic categories. In T. Moore (Ed.), *Cognitive development and the acquisition of language* (pp. 111–144). San Diego, CA: Academic Press.

Rosch, E. (1975). Cognitive representations of semantic categories. *Journal of Experimental Psychology: General, 104*, 192–233.

Rosch, E., & Mervis, C. B. (1975). Family resemblances: Studies in the internal structure of categories. *Cognitive Psychology, 7*, 573–605.

Rosch, E., Mervis, C. B., Gray, W. D., Johnson, D. M., & Boyes-Braem, P. (1976). Basic objects in natural categories. *Cognitive Psychology, 8*, 382–439.

Ross, B. H. (1996). Category learning as problem solving. In D. L. Medin (Ed.), *The psychology of learning and motivation: Advances in research and theory, 35*, 165–192.

Rumelhart, D. E., & Norman, D. A. (1988). Representation in memory. In R. C. Atkinson, R. J. Herrnstein, G. Lindzey, & R. D. Luce (Eds.), *Stevens' handbook of experimental psychology: Vol. 2. Learning and cognition* (pp. 511–587). New York: Wiley.

Schooler, J. W., Fiore, S. M., & Brandimonte, M. A. (1997). At a loss from words: Verbal overshadowing of perceptual memories. *The Psychology of Learning and Motivation, 37*, 291–340.

Shepard, R. N., & Cooper, L. A. (1982). *Mental images and their transformations.* New York: Cambridge University Press.

Simmons, W. K., & Barsalou, L. W. (2003). The similarity-in-topography principle: Reconciling theories of conceptual deficits. *Cognitive Neuropsychology, 20*, 451–486.

Simmons, W. K., Martin, A., & Barsalou, L. W. (2005). Pictures of appetizing foods activate gustatory cortices for taste and reward. *Cerebral Cortex, 15*, 1602–1608.

Smith, E. E., & Medin, D. L. (1981). *Categories and concepts.* Cambridge, MA: Harvard University Press.

Smith, E. E., Patalano, A. L., & Jonides, J. (1998). Alternative strategies for categorization. *Cognition, 65*, 167–196.

Smith, E. E., Shoben, E. J., & Rips, L. J. (1974). Structure and process in semantic memory: A featural model for semantic decisions. *Psychological Review, 81*, 214–241.

Smith, J. D., & Minda, J. P. (2002). Distinguishing prototype-based and exemplar-based processes in dot-pattern category learning. *Journal of Experimental Psychology: Learning, Memory, and Cognition, 28*, 800–811.

Smith, L. B., & Samuelson, L. K. (1997). Perceiving and remembering: Category stability, variability and development. In K. Lamberts & D. R. Shanks (Eds.), *Knowledge, concepts and categories.* (pp. 161–195). Cambridge, MA: The MIT Press.

Smolensky, P. (1988). On the proper treatment of connectionism. *The Behavioral and Brain Sciences, 11*, 1–74.

Solomon, K. O., & Barsalou, L. W. (2001). Representing properties locally. *Cognitive Psychology, 43*, 129–169.

Solomon, K. O., & Barsalou, L. W. (2004). Perceptual simulation in property verification. *Memory & Cognition, 32*, 244–259.

Sommers, F. (1963). Types and ontology. *Philosophical Review, 72*, 327–363.

Spence, C., Nicholls, M. E. R., & Driver, J. (2000). The cost of expecting events in the wrong sensory modality. *Perception & Psychophysics, 63*, 330–336.

Spivey, M., Tyler, M., Richardson, D., & Young, E. (2000). Eye movements during comprehension of spoken scene descriptions. *Proceedings of the 22nd Annual Conference of the Cognitive Science Society* (pp. 487–492). Mahwah, NJ: Lawrence Erlbaum Associates.

Stanfield, R. A., & Zwaan, R. A. (2001). The effect of implied orientation derived from verbal context on picture recognition. *Psychological Science, 12,* 153–156.

Tabossi, P. (1988). Effects of context on the immediate interpretation of unambiguous nouns. *Journal of Experimental Psychology: Learning, Memory, and Cognition, 14,* 153–162.

Tanaka, J. W., & Curran, T. (2001). A neural basis for expert object recognition. *Psychological Science, 12,* 43–47.

Tanaka, J. W., & Gauthier, I. (1997). Expertise in object and face recognition. In R. L. Goldstone, P. G. Schyns, & D. L. Medin (Eds.), *Psychology of learning and motivation series, special volume: Perceptual mechanisms of learning* (Vol. 36, pp. 83–125). San Diego, CA: Academic Press.

Tanaka, K. (1997). Inferotemporal cortex and object recognition. In J. W. Donahoe & V. P. Dorsel (Eds.), *Neural-network models of cognition: Biobehavioral foundations* (Vol. 121, pp. 160–188). Amsterdam: North-Holland/Elsevier Science Publishers.

Thioux, M., Pillon, A., Samson, D., de Partz, M. P., & Noël, M. P. (1998). The isolation of numerals at the semantic level. *Neurocase, 4,* 371–389.

Thompson, W. L., & Kosslyn, S. M. (2000). Neural systems activated during visual mental imagery: A review and meta-analysis. In A. W. Toga & J. C. Mazziotta (Eds.), *Brain mapping: The systems* (pp. 535–560). San Diego, CA: Academic Press.

Tootell, R. B. H., Silverman, M. S., Switkes, E., & DeValois, R. L. (1982). Deoxyglucose analysis of retinotopic organization in primates. *Science, 218,* 902–904.

Tversky, B., & Hemenway, K. (1985). Objects, parts, and categories. *Journal of Experimental Psychology: General, 113,* 169–193.

Tyler, L. K., & Moss, H. E. (1997). Imageability and category-specificity. *Cognitive Neuropsychology, 14,* 293–318.

Tyler, L. K., & Moss, H. E. (2001). Towards a distributed account of conceptual knowledge. *Trends in Cognitive Sciences, 5,* 244–252.

Warrington, E. K., & McCarthy, R. A. (1983). Category specific access dysphasia. *Brain, 106,* 859–878.

Warrington, E. K., & McCarthy, R. A. (1987). Categories of knowledge: Further fractionations and an attempted integration. *Brain, 110,* 1273–1296.

Warrington, E. K., & Shallice, T. (1984). Category specific semantic impairments. *Brain, 107,* 829–854.

Wolfe, J. M. (1999). Inattentional amnesia. In V. Coltheart (Ed.), *Fleeting memories: Cognition of brief visual stimuli* (pp. 71–94). Cambridge, MA: The MIT Press.

Wolff, P., Medin, D. L., & Pankratz, C. (1999). Evolution and devolution of folkbiological knowledge. *Cognition, 73,* 177–204.

Wu, L., & Barsalou, L. W. (2004). Perceptual simulation in property generation. Manuscript under review.

Yeh, W., & Barsalou, L. W. (2004). The situated character of concepts. Manuscript under review.

Zwaan, R. A., Stanfield, R. A., & Yaxley, R. H. (2002). Language comprehenders mentally represent the shapes of objects, *Psychological Science, 13,* 168–171.

CHAPTER ELEVEN

INTRODUCTION TO LEARNING

DOUGLAS H. HINTZMAN

Of all the animal species that inhabit this planet, we humans are truly exceptional. Our uniqueness finds expression in many ways: We use fire, build machines, domesticate animals and cultivate crops, communicate through spoken and written language, legislate our own social controls, visit such inaccessible places as the surface of the moon and the floor of the sea, and alter the face of the earth itself. Central to all these accomplishments is our great flexibility — our unparalleled capacity to change our behavior to suit the circumstances we are in.

Underlying the flexibility of our behavior are the processes we call learning and memory. *Learning* is a change in an organism, due to experience, which can affect the organism's behavior. *Memory* is the persistence of that change over time. The flexibility of human behavior rests on our ability to profit from experience — that is, on our unsurpassed ability to learn.

Very simple animals behave only in rigid, stereotyped ways. They are limited to genetically pre-programmed responses which can be changed by experience little, if at all. Moderately complex animals can learn, but for many of them learning requires direct experience. Being rewarded or punished will change an individual animal's behavior, but seeing a companion rewarded or punished will not. Still more complex organisms, particularly the higher primates, can learn "vicariously" from the successes and failures of others. They are, however, restricted in this learning to direct observation — that is, to the here and now. Human beings are free from even this limitation. Through the use of language, we can learn from the experiences of others. The experiences we learn about may concern events that were observed, inferred, or even imagined. Thus, we are freed in our learning not only from the here and now but also, to some extent, from reality.

The flexibility of human behavior has enabled us to adapt to an incredible variety of physical and social environments. Allowed free reign, human flexibility produces the great variability we see in the diversity of languages and social customs, and within cultures,

Printed with permission of Douglas H. Hintzman.

among social roles, occupations, and individual interests. Given direction, human flexibility can produce remarkable accomplishments such as the exploration of the solar system and the conquest of disease. It seems clear that an understanding of learning and memory — the processes that give human behavior its great flexibility — would be a major step toward understanding the nature of intelligence itself. While learning and memory are topics that have provoked much speculation by philosophers and experiments by scientists, the mysteries of their nature and function are still largely unsolved.

11.1   THE IMPORTANCE OF LEARNING AND MEMORY

To psychologists in particular, the problem of learning is a central one. Hardly an area of psychological investigation can ignore it. The differences among individuals that we call personality are believed to be strongly influenced by experience. Girls and boys adopt the sex roles modeled for them by adults. Whether a person is violent or peaceful, anxious or confident, gregarious or solitary, thoughtful or impulsive, deceitful or candid — all depend to some extent on learning. Early childhood experiences, such as weaning, toilet training, and interactions with parents and siblings, may exert a strong influence on emotional and cognitive development. It may even be — if one controversial hypothesis is to be believed — that a person's ultimate level of intellectual ability is determined by what happens to him during the first few years of life.

The aspects of social behavior we place under the heading of "culture" are primarily learned: language, sex roles, occupations, religious beliefs, and attitudes toward the family, neighborhood, community, and nation. Prejudices regarding race, social caste, and sex are acquired by experience; and it is through experience that they can be changed. The nature of modern society reflects, in large part, the speed with which humans adapt. We are absurdly easy to indoctrinate, which accounts for the variety and instability of political and religious views. And technological developments — which affect the ways we relate to work, to leisure, and to each other — produce a never-ending spiral in which learning-produced changes necessitate further learning, which brings about further change.

Clinical psychologists and psychiatrists have a strong interest in an understanding of learning. Many mental and behavioral problems are assumed to result, at least in part, from experience. Phobias, social anxiety, depression, psychosomatic symptoms, and habits such as smoking are examples. And most methods of psychotherapy are designed to provide an experience that will bring about a change in the patient — either in his mental state or in his behavior. Many therapists have looked directly to the psychology of learning for hints as to how therapeutic techniques might be improved.

Even perception — the way things look and sound to us — depends partly on learning. One might suppose the perception of stimuli to be entirely unaffected by past experience, but this is not the case. A person who is reading will perceive an "important" extraneous stimulus such as the mention of his own name, even though other words spoken by the same voice are easily ignored. A conversation that sounds like jabbering to someone unfamiliar with the language sounds quite different to one to whom the language is known; what looks like a series of random squiggles to a nonreader is immediately recognized as a coherent message to one who can read; and chess pieces on a board, arranged as in a position from a game, look quite different to a novice than they do to a chess master. A once-blind person whose vision is repaired sees things very differently than you or I. There is even some evidence, from experiments with cats, that normal development of cells in the visual areas of the brain depends on visual stimulation during infancy.

Physiological psychologists also have an interest in learning. The biological basis of learning and memory remains one of the great unsolved problems of science. Psychological investigations should play a crucial role in solving this problem. The search for a solution cannot be conducted exclusively at the level of neurochemistry, neurophysiology, and neuroanatomy, since it is only by observing an organism's behavior that we can determine that it has learned. In addition, the physiological psychologist is likely to find clues to the nature of the learning mechanism he is seeking in the results of behavioral experiments.

Areas outside psychology also are deeply concerned with learning and memory. The philosopher reflecting upon the nature of knowledge can hardly ignore what is known about the process by which knowledge is acquired. The physical anthropologist concerned with human evolution must take into consideration the remarkable capacity of humans to learn, and must ask not only what ecological pressures brought this ability about, but also how the developing ability may have exerted its own influence on evolution.

Many computer scientists, in the field called "artificial intelligence," are concerned with building machines that can duplicate or even exceed human abilities. How does one construct a computer that can translate languages, play games such as chess, think creatively, generate and follow its own elaborate plans, read handwriting, control skilled acts, and retrieve complex information quickly from a vast and efficient memory? Computer scientists attempting to answer such questions cannot, rationally, ignore the fact that a device that does all these things already exists, in the human mind, and that a general ability underlying all such special ones is the ability to learn.

Educators, of course, have always had a practical interest in learning and memory, and the application of learning principles to educational practice has always been regarded by learning psychologists as an ultimate goal of their work. How can instruction and training be made more effective and efficient? Can forgetting be slowed or prevented? How should teaching methods be matched to subject matter and to the abilities of students? What special methods should be used in training the retarded, the blind, or the deaf? How is knowledge acquired through reading? And how is this remarkable skill itself learned? Educators have looked to psychology, perhaps too trustingly, for answers to such questions; and psychologists have attempted, sometimes too readily, to comply. Applications of learning principles to education have not always been successful — but this should not be surprising. There is much about learning and memory we still do not understand.

Practical interest in learning and memory, of course, is not restricted to clinical psychology and education. Professional animal trainers and ordinary pet owners want to teach their animals good habits and eliminate bad ones; ranchers and farmers want to cure wild animals of their destructive behavior; and wildlife managers want to keep animals from endangering themselves. Parents want to influence the behavior and beliefs of their children. Corrections officers want to rehabilitate their prisoners. Athletes and musicians want to improve their respective skills; coaches, military officers, and factory managers want to improve the skills of those under them. Public speakers and entertainers want to improve their own memories; politicians, advertisers, and propagandists have messages they want people to remember and facts they want them to forget. Each of us, in his own way, curses his faulty memory when important names and faces, shopping lists, routine appointments, urgent deadlines, bizarre dreams, creative ideas, and even trivial facts are forgotten. In one way or another, learning and memory touch on nearly all human activities.

11.2   THE PRESENT STATUS OF THE FIELD

Given the potential impact of an accurate understanding of learning and memory both inside and outside psychology, the uncertain accomplishments of the field may be viewed with disappointment. An outsider who asks a physicist about falling bodies, electricity, or nuclear reactions will receive a definitive reply. Further, if he asks another physicist the same question, he can be confident the answer will be essentially the same. One who asks a psychologist how repetitive drill contributes to learning or what causes forgetting should expect either a discussion of several competing theories or a single, coherent analysis with which other psychologists will not fully agree. If he asks enough different psychologists, he will discover that not all of them agree even on how one should go about seeking the answers to such questions. Some explain effects of past experience on behavior in terms of mental, or conscious, events; others prefer theories based on the "machinery of the brain"; still others argue that the investigator should simply describe observable behavior and not attempt to explain it at all. Such theoretical and methodological disputes often strike the layman as unscientific. They are not what the "hard sciences" have led him to expect. Several things should be said about this attitude.

In the first place, it is a mistake to think of science as a body of agreed-upon knowledge. Science is, instead, a method by which knowledge is acquired. What distinguishes science from other modes of thought such as religion is not general agreement but the way the agreement is eventually reached. In the scientific method, ideas are subjected to skeptical analysis, and solid evidence is demanded in their support. In this respect, experimental psychology is no different from physics and chemistry — the frontiers of knowledge in those disciplines are, like psychology, often the scenes of vigorous disputes.

In the second place, experimental psychology is not without agreed-upon facts. Thousands of phenomena uncovered in psychology experiments have proven to be replicable; that is, similar investigations done in different laboratories reliably produce equivalent results. Replicable experimental results are a prerequisite for the existence of a scientific discipline, and although failures to replicate do occur in psychology (as in other areas), replicability of results is a prerequisite the field easily meets.

What the psychology of learning and memory is lacking is not the methodology and attitude of science, or reliable phenomena to be explained. What is lacking is theoretical interpretations of the phenomena with which all psychologists agree. Learning and memory have been the subject of numerous theories; but no theory of learning has attained the status of the theories of Newton, Einstein, or Darwin, in their respective disciplines. No single theory has provided the kind of elegant, coherent, and complete explanation of the phenomena of learning and memory that would lead to its acceptance by all those working within the field.

It is interesting to speculate about why no such generally accepted theory of learning and memory exists. Psychology as a science is young. Experimental psychology is just a little over a century old. Physics is much older: Galileo's experiments were done nearly four hundred years ago, and Newton's *Principia* appeared in 1687. Perhaps the field is still waiting for some genius to come along and put things in order. Many psychologists fantasize themselves as psychology's Newton, but so far even the most brilliant and concerted efforts have fallen short.

A more valid reason for the lack of a universal theory of psychology may be the complexity of psychology's subject matter. Each animal species has evolved to fit a particular ecological niche. And within a species, individuals differ from one another in a multitude of ways — a diversity assured by both genetics and past experience. The human brain is an incredibly complex device, and it is always undergoing change. It may never be in exactly the same state at two different times. The very flexibility the psychologist wants to study makes his job difficult. The subject in an experiment adapts to the artificial nature of the experimental situation, often finding ways of coping with the task that are more complex than the experimenter intended. The subject may try to discover the purpose of the experiment, to aid or hinder the investigation; he may even cheat. The "subjects" of physics experiments may be subtle and difficult to comprehend, but they are uniform in their structure and behavior, and they do not have an intelligence and a contrary will of their own.

Disagreements and controversies, then, are to be expected in a science so young dealing with a subject matter so complex, and they are certainly characteristic of the psychology of learning and memory. Many of them are fascinating; they are what make the area an exciting one in which to work. Some textbooks in the field, in an attempt to protect the student from confusion, try to hide controversy. They either ignore important issues altogether or present only one side as though it were an established fact. This seems a mistake. Only a person who knows something of the nature of these controversies and the attempts that have been made to resolve them can truly be said to understand the field.

Thus, this book is not only about phenomena we are sure we understand. It is also about theoretical issues — some old and some recent, some resolved and some recurring, some famous and some obscure, some active and some that have been abandoned due to an apparent lack of progress. Through the analysis of these issues, the reader should learn more than the facts of learning and memory; he or she should learn in addition that interpretations of facts in this area are subject to challenge and change. A theory in great favor yesterday may be rejected today, only to be resurrected tomorrow in slightly different form. An appreciation of the complexities of the issues faced by investigators in this field may help prevent the contagious fads occasionally spread by psychologists (and pseudopsychologists) suffering from attacks of premature enthusiasm about the far-reaching implications of their work. The sophisticated onlooker should be skeptical about such excesses. But one should also appreciate the real progress that is being made in understanding learning and memory and realize that the confusion, disagreement, and controversy of the field stem primarily from the subject matter itself. The human mind is the most difficult challenge science has ever faced.

11.3   BACKGROUND AND OVERVIEW

The psychology of learning and memory has roots in two different disciplines. It inherited from philosophy an interest in knowledge, and from biology an interest in adaptation. Philosophers (particularly those in the field of epistemology) are concerned with the structure of knowledge, the way it is acquired, and the way it is used. Biologists are concerned with adaptation, not only through genetic selection, but also through experience. Thus, the traditions of both parent disciplines are concerned with learning, but in different ways. One might expect the relationship of the two traditions within psychology to be complementary, but for the most part the relationship has been an antagonistic one.

The philosophical tradition is represented within psychology by a collection of attitudes sometimes called *cognitivism*. A psychologist of this persuasion is interested in cognitions, or mental events — ideas, thoughts, purposes, conscious awareness, images, feelings, and acts of will. Cognitivism views learning primarily as the acquisition of knowledge.

The biological tradition is represented in psychology by *behaviorism*. From the point of view of behaviorism, learning refers to a change in behavior. If a behaviorist is interested in anything beyond observable behavior itself, it is the principles of operation of the device producing the behavior. These principles may be understood by making use of mechanical analogies, but not by referring to mental events. As we shall see in the following chapters, behaviorists are strongly against mentalistic explanations of behavior, which they view as inherently unscientific.

The psychology of learning and memory is today split, not only into the somewhat opposed camps of cognitivism and behaviorism, but also into two broad interest areas. In one of these areas investigators do research on animal learning; in the other they do work on human memory. It should be no surprise that interest areas and theoretical persuasions are related: animal learning researchers tend to adopt a behaviorist view of learning, while most human memory investigators have a strong cognitive bias. The differences in theoretical orientation mean that communication between animal learning and human memory researchers is not as frequent or as sympathetic as it might be. Communication does occur, however, and there are signs that the split between the two interest areas is diminishing.

A theme of this book, superimposed on discussions of more specific issues, concerns the forces that brought about the split between cognitivism and behaviorism and that have maintained it for many years. The present state of the field cannot be presented accurately in cross-section; it can be understood only in historical context. Likewise, projections of the future of the field can only be made with some knowledge of what past states have been. For these reasons, the organization of this book is partly historical.

To give the reader a kind of road map of the area to be covered, a brief overview of the history of the psychology of learning and memory should be useful. Figure 11.1 represents the history of the field in terms of changes in the relative influence of the cognitivist and behaviorist traditions over time. The vertical axis represents time. There are two curves, one for cognitivism and one for behaviorism, and the horizontal axis — the distance of each curve from the center line — indicates in a rough way the degree of interest in that tradition at a particular time. There have been many outside influences on the psychological study of learning and memory. The ones that have had the most impact are represented in the figure by heavy arrows. The names of the most influential individuals and schools of thought within the cognitivist and behaviorist traditions are located at points on the time scale that correspond, very roughly, to their most important works.

From the beginning of the scientific study of learning in 1885 until around 1920, the field was dominated by interest in the roles in learning and memory of mental events (ideas, images, awareness, and so on) — the position we have called cognitivism. Most of the problems that were studied had already been discussed at great length by philosophers; experimental psychologists

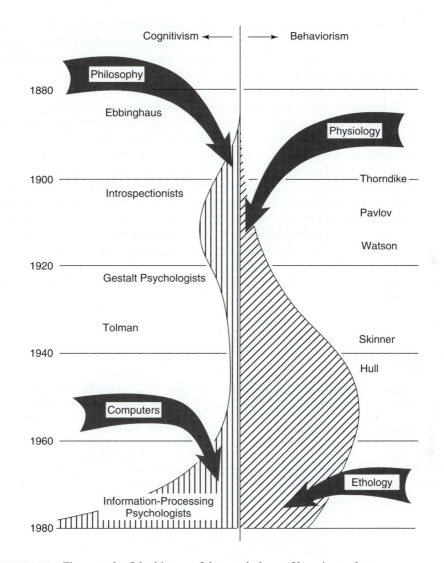

FIGURE 11.1   Time graph of the history of the psychology of learning and memory.

simply attacked the same problems using scientific methods. Most of the research during this period used human subjects. In the 1920s and 1930s, however, there was a shift of influence toward behaviorism. Most learning research — although certainly not all of it — was done on animals, and most theoretical explanations of animal or human behavior avoided reference to mental events.

The period from around 1960 to the present has seen a dramatic resurgence of interest in cognitivism and an attendant increase in human learning research. This resurgence, as Figure 11.1 suggests, has been strongly influenced by computers. The existence of "thinking machines" has greatly affected how psychologists theorize about mental processes, including those involved in learning and memory. The behaviorist tradition today has many adherents, but it has lost the iron grip it once had on the field. It is being pressured by the new-found popularity of cognitivism, on one side, and the concepts and findings of ethology, on the other. Ethology, the study of the behavior of animals in their natural surroundings, is forcing behaviorists to radically alter their views of learning.[. . .]

Influential individuals and groups of psychologists, listed alongside the undulating curves of Figure 11.1, include the following: (a) Ebbinghaus, who did the first formal experiments on human learning and memory (see Chapter 2); (b) the introspectionists, who tried to study mental events directly by "looking inward" on the mind (again, see Chapter 2); (c) Thorndike and Pavlov, who both conducted pioneering research on animal learning around the beginning of this century [. . .] (d) Watson, the founder of behaviorism [. . .] (e) the Gestalt psychologists, whose work on memory was not widely appreciated until the renaissance of cognitivism many years later [. . .] (f) Tolman, who championed a cognitivist theory of animal learning during a period when behaviorist sentiment prevailed [. . .] (g) Skinner and Hull, the most influential proponents of behaviorism [. . .] and (h) the information-processing psychologists, whose use of the computer analogy has revolutionized cognitive psychology in general and the area of human memory in particular [. . .].

[. . .]

REFERENCES

Ebbinghaus, H. (1911). *Grundzüge der Psychologie.* Vol. I 3rd Ed. Leipzig: Verlag von Veit and Company.

Hull, C. L. (1943). *Principles of Behavior: An Introduction to Behavior Theory.* New York: Appleton-Century-Crofts.

Pavlov, I. P. (1927). *Conditioned Reflexes.* Translated by G. V. Anrep. London: Oxford University Press.

Skinner, B. F. (1938). *The Behavior of Organisms.* New York: Appleton-Century-Crofts.

Thorndike, E. L. (1914). *The Psychology of Learning.* New York: Teachers College.

Tolman, E. C. (1932). *Purposive Behavior in Animals and Men.* New York: Appleton-Century-Crofts.

Watson, J. B. (1913). Psychology as the behaviorist views it. *Psychological Review, 20,* 158–177.

CHAPTER TWELVE

EXPERIMENTAL PROCEDURES IN ANIMAL LEARNING

DOUGLAS H. HINTZMAN

This chapter examines some of the basic types of animal learning experiments. Experiments, of course, differ from each other in many ways; but animal learning experiments are usually categorized into a few basic types. These types are referred to as experimental *paradigms*. The word paradigm, in general, means "pattern." Here it refers to the pattern around which an experiment is designed. This use of the term should be distinguished from Thomas Kuhn's concept of the scientific paradigm, referred to in the last chapter. Kuhn uses the word paradigm to refer to the conceptual framework through which a scientist views the research in his field. The two meanings of the term paradigm are quite different, although the "pattern" concept can be seen in both.

Four basic experimental paradigms will be described. They are (1) habituation and sensitization, (2) classical conditioning, (3) instrumental conditioning, and (4) operant conditioning. Most of the information in this chapter is relatively noncontroversial. The types of experimental manipulations defining each paradigm are described, along with typical results of those manipulations. Additional experimental results will be presented in later chapters, where they are relevant to theoretical issues under discussion. The material in the present chapter is intended to provide the background necessary for understanding those issues and the experiments bearing upon them.

12.1 HABITUATION AND SENSITIZATION

12.1.1 Habituation

In 1887, in an article entitled "Some Observations on the Mental Powers of Spiders," Peckham and Peckham described an experimental demonstration of a very simple type of learning. They repeatedly sounded a tuning fork near a spider in its web, recording each time the spider's response of dropping on its thread. With the first sounding of the stimulus, the response was pronounced. The response declined with repetitions of the tone on a given

Printed with permission of Douglas H. Hintzman.

day, recovering somewhat from one day to the next, and eventually ceased altogether. The decrease of an innate reaction to a stimulus due to repetition, as demonstrated by this experiment, is called *habituation*. To borrow terms from Pavlov, habituation can be considered a decrease in an unconditioned (or innate) reflex due to repetition of the UCS.

Habituation is considered by many investigators to be the simplest form of learning. While habituation undoubtedly has some limited adaptive value, the organism does not learn to do anything new, or to do something better, but only *not* to do something already in its unlearned behavioral repertoire. Habituation is also the most widespread form of adaptive change, common to all animals from the single-cell protozoa through humans (Razran, 1971). In vertebrates, habituation can apparently take place in the spinal cord, without involvement of the brain, for if the nerve fibers linking the brain and spinal cord are cut (producing what is called a "spinal" animal), reflexes mediated by the spinal cord, such as flexion of the hind limb in response to shock to the foot, will still habituate.

The number of stimulus exposures necessary to produce habituation varies widely, depending upon the organism being tested, the response being measured, and the strength of the stimulus used to elicit the response. Certain general characteristics of habituation, however, are remarkably independent of such factors. Thompson and Spencer (1966) have listed the common characteristics of habituation. The following discussion borrows from their account.

Typically, the magnitude of the UCR decreases with the number of stimulus presentations in the way illustrated in the first panel of Figure 12.1. A curve of that shape is described as a "negative exponential function." The magnitude of the response may or may not eventually reach zero. Whether it does or not depends partly on the strength of the stimulus (habituation is more effective with repetition of a weak stimulus than a strong one).

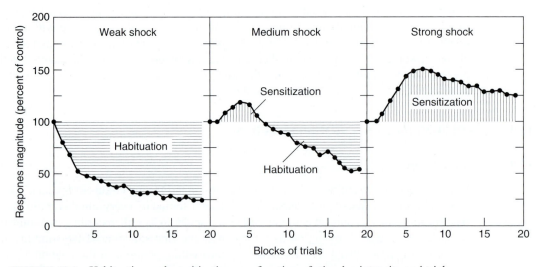

FIGURE 12.1   Habituation and sensitization as a function of stimulus intensity and trials. (Adapted from Groves and Thompson, 1970.)

Habituation shows stimulus generalization; that is, if a response is habituated by presenting a particular UCS repeatedly, tests with similar stimuli will tend to show habituation as well. The magnitude of the response increases as the test stimulus becomes less similar to the original UCS.

Habituated responses show *spontaneous recovery.* If the UCS is not presented for a time following habituation training, the tendency for the UCS to elicit the UCR will increase, eventually approaching its original level. If the response is then habituated again, allowed to recover again, rehabituated, and so on, habituation becomes more and more rapid each time it occurs.

How do we know that habituation is not simply a matter of fatigue? One bit of evidence is seen in stimulus generalization. If the response could not occur because of muscle fatigue, stimuli dissimilar to the original UCS would not be able to elicit it. The experimental evidence, however, is that they do. A second finding that is contrary to the fatigue explanation is a phenomenon called *dishabituation.* Suppose a UCS is repeatedly presented, resulting in habituation of the UCR. Then another, especially strong stimulus (such as a loud noise) occurs. If the UCS is presented immediately after the strong stimulus, it elicits the UCR at nearly its original strength. This is called dishabituation because it appears to eliminate the habituation that was produced by repetition of the UCS. An interesting finding regarding dishabituation is that it spontaneously disappears. In a matter of several seconds after presentation of the dishabituating stimulus, the habituation returns even without new repetitions of the UCS (Groves and Thompson, 1970). Dishabituation therefore appears to be a temporary increase in the strength of the response which leaves the underlying habituation intact.

By now it should be apparent that there are many parallels between the habituation of innate reflexes and the extinction of conditioned reflexes, as studied by Pavlov. Many of the manipulations are the same. In extinction, a *learned* response to a CS grows weaker because the CS is presented without the UCS. In habituation, an *innate* reflex to a UCS simply decreases with repeated presentation of the stimulus. Despite this difference, both phenomena show stimulus generalization and spontaneous recovery. And the phenomenon of dishabituation is remarkably similar to what Pavlov called disinhibition — a recovery of the response, due to presentation of a strong stimulus such as a loud noise. The similarities of habituation of the unconditioned reflex and extinction of the conditioned reflex have suggested to many investigators that the underlying mechanisms are essentially the same.

12.1.2   Sensitization

It is important to note that not all innate reflexes habituate. In fact, many reflexes that will habituate when the UCS is weak will not habituate when its is strong. Repetition of a strong stimulus can result in an effect opposite to that of habituation — namely, an increase in the magnitude of the response. Such an increase is called *sensitization.* An example of the effect of stimulus intensity on habituation and sensitization is shown in Figure 12.1. The data, taken from Groves and Thompson (1970), show how flexion of the hind limb in response to shock, in a spinal cat, changes with repetition of the shock stimulus. With a weak shock, the flexion response habituates; with a strong shock, sensitization occurs. An everyday example of the phenomenon shown in Figure 12.1 can be found in the effects of unwanted noise. If a neighbor's radio is playing softly, we may hear it at first but soon stop attending to it (habituation). However, if it is playing very loudly, it may become more and more distracting. With repeated exposure our annoyance increases (sensitization).

There is a rather interesting finding regarding the way habituation and sensitization are related to stimulus intensity, as illustrated in Figure 12.1. Ordinarily, the response to an intense stimulus will simply become sensitized with repetition. But the response can be habituated if the stimulus is first presented at a very weak intensity and then is gradually made more and more intense as training proceeds. Habituation training is much more effective following this gradual procedure than it is if the intense (final) stimulus is the only one presented. This outcome has been obtained with the startle response in rats (Davis and Wagner, 1969) and also with the hind limb flexion reflex in spinal cats (Groves and Thompson, 1970). This is one illustration of the effectiveness of gradual training procedures — a point to which we shall return later in this chapter.

The experimental operations for producing habituation and sensitization are the same. In both cases a UCS is presented repeatedly. If the strength of the UCR decreases, habituation has been obtained. If it increases, sensitization has been observed. As was just indicated, one factor determining which will occur in the intensity of the stimulus. Sensitization may be considered a higher form of learning than habituation. The simplest organisms in which it is found are planaria, or flatworms, and earthworms (Razran, 1971). Sensitization gives certain reflexes of these organisms a primitive ability to increase in strength with practice — an important characteristic of higher forms of learning.

12.1.3   Pseudoconditioning

Sensitization has not been studied thoroughly, so we can say little more about it. We do know, however, that sensitization generalizes to stimuli quite different from the original UCS. This fact has important consequences for the design of adequate conditioning experiments.

Suppose an investigator repeatedly elicits the hind limb reflex in a spinal cat, using shock to the leg as the UCS. He then pinches the animal's tail. Pinching the tail would not ordinarily elicit the hind limb flexion response. It may do so now, however, if the reflex has become highly sensitized and has generalized to stimuli quite different from the UCS. In other words, the tail pinch may be enough like leg shock to produce the flexion reflex, providing the reflex is highly sensitized. Ordinarily, it would not do so.

Now imagine the situation of an investigator who is attempting to condition the hind limb reflex by repeatedly pinching the tail (as a CS) and then shocking the leg (as the UCS). If after several trials the tail pinch alone elicits the reflex, he might very well conclude that he has obtained conditioning. In reality, however, the response to the pinch might have nothing to do with the *pairing* of the CS and UCS. It could result from sensitization, in the way just described; and sensitization does not involve the learning of new associations.

Since such a result could easily be mistaken for conditioning, it has been called *pseudoconditioning*. To make sure that the response to a CS reflects true conditioning, rather than pseudoconditioning, a careful investigator will compare the performance of a group of animals for which the CS and UCS are paired (the conditioning group) with that of another group of animals to which the CS and UCS are presented, but *not* paired (the pseudoconditioning control). Any sensitization resulting from repeated presentation of the UCS should be the same for both groups. Only if the CR is more pronounced in the conditioning group than in the control group is the investigator justified in concluding that conditioning has been obtained. (When this precaution is taken, many experiments on spinal animals fail to show evidence of conditioning. Others have produced positive evidence, however. Thus the possibility of true conditioning occurring in the spinal cord is still an open question.)

12.2   CLASSICAL CONDITIONING

In 1902, at about the time Pavlov's work on salivary conditioning was getting well under way, a graduate student named E. B. Twitmeyer submitted a PH.D. dissertation to the University of Pennsylvania, entitled "A Study of the Knee-Jerk." In it, he described a phenomenon he had discovered by accident. He had been conducting an experiment on the knee-jerk reflex. On each trial of the experiment a bell was sounded to warn the subject that a hammer was about to strike his knee. While testing one subject, Twitmeyer accidentally sounded the bell without tripping the hammer. The knee jerk occurred even though the natural stimulus for the reflex (the hammer blow) had not. Recognizing the importance of this discovery, Twitmeyer immediately redesigned his experiment in order to study it. Unfortunately, other psychologists showed little interest in the result, and Twitmeyer abandoned the project without even publishing his dissertation in a scientific journal. (Twitmeyer's experiments were finally published, in recognition of their historical importance, in the December, 1974, issue of the *Journal of Experimental Psychology.*)

The phenomenon Twitmeyer independently discovered is usually called *classical conditioning.* Other terms that are often applied are *respondent conditioning* and *Pavlovian conditioning.* If Twitmeyer had been a Nobel Prize winner instead of an unknown graduate student, or if he had possessed the determination and forceful personality of Pavlov, perhaps the procedure would be called Twitmeyerian conditioning today. If he had done nothing more than publish his dissertation, American psychology would have become familiar with the classical conditioning paradigm twenty years before Pavlov's work became widely known.

Recall that the classicial conditioning procedure involves the pairing of two stimuli: the CS, a neutral stimulus that does not elicit the response prior to conditioning, and the UCS, which elicits the response (UCR) before conditioning begins. Through pairing of the two stimuli, the CS alone comes to elicit the response (now called the CR). Thousands of experiments have been done using this procedure. Evidence of classical conditioning has been found in animals as simple as earthworms and as complex as humans. Baby chickens have been conditioned in the egg, and baby humans in the uterus. Responses that have been classically conditioned include salivation, changes in electrical rhythms of the brain (EEG), constriction of blood vessels, the knee jerk, vomiting, the eye-blink reflex, and changes in respiration (Kimble, 1961).

Several features of classical conditioning have already been mentioned in connection with Pavlov's work: Elimination of the UCS and presentation of the CS alone results in *extinction;* if time is allowed to pass following extinction and the CS is again presented alone, the CR shows partial *spontaneous recovery;* a strong unexpected stimulus results in *disinhibition,* the reappearance of the extinguished response. A CR that has been established using a particular CS will generalize to other stimuli according to their similarity to the CS; but generalization can be restricted by presenting during training both a CS+, which is followed by the UCS, and a CS− , which is not — a procedure called *differential conditioning.*

12.2.1 Temporal Arrangements of CS and UCS

An important variable in classical conditioning experiments has to do with the arrangement of the CS and UCS in time. In Figure 12.2 are presented several different types of conditioning arrangements. In the *simultaneous* procedures the CS and UCS are presented at exactly the same time. In the *delay* procedure, the CS goes on and remains on until the UCS is presented. The duration of the CS — that is, the delay from onset of the CS to onset of the UCS — can be varied. It is generally found that a delay of .5 to 1.0 second is most effective for conditioning, although there are striking exceptions to this rule. In the *trace* procedure, the CS comes on and then goes off some time before the UCS occurs. Conditioning presumably involves an internal trace of the CS, since the physical stimulus is no longer present when the UCS occurs. Conditioning is difficult to establish with traces longer than a few seconds, although it can be done. Long-trace conditioning is most easily established by first training with a delay or short-trace procedure, and then gradually lengthening the time from CS offset to UCS onset.

In the *backward* conditioning procedure, the UCS precedes the CS. Backward conditioning is difficult to achieve, and there is some controversy concerning whether it exists at

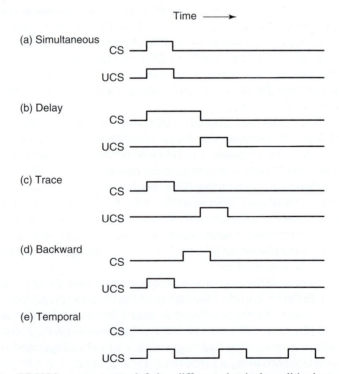

FIGURE 12.2 CS-UCS arrangements defining different classical conditioning paradigms.

all. One reason backward conditioning may be difficult to show has been discussed by Razran (1971). He points out that in the backward conditioning paradigm both the onset and the off-set of the UCS precede the CS. Because of this, the CS may become conditioned both to UCS-onset reactions and to UCS-offset reactions, and these reactions may be incompatible with each other. Consider the situation where the UCS is shock. The onset of shock produces a negative reaction which we might call "pain," while the offset produces a positive reaction which we might call "relief." Since the shock goes on and then off before the CS occurs, both reactions are available to become conditioned to the CS. The offset of the shock, however, is more nearly contiguous with the CS than is onset of the shock. Thus, according to the principle of contiguity, the "relief" reaction should be more strongly conditioned to the CS than the "pain" reaction. Since relief and pain are in a sense opposite responses, little if any evidence will be found that the negative "pain" response has been conditioned to the CS.

Finally, in the *temporal* conditioning procedure, there is no observable CS at all. The UCS is simply presented repeatedly, with the interval between presentations always the same. After prolonged training, the animal will come to make the response in anticipation of the UCS — that is, just before it occurs. The temporal conditioning procedure may be thought of as similar to the trace conditioning procedure; but in temporal conditioning it cannot be the "trace" of a CS that becomes conditioned to the response, since there is no CS as such. Instead, it may be the "trace" of the previous UCS (or possibly of the UCR). In one of Pavlov's experiments, temporal conditioning of the salivary reflex was achieved with an interval as long as 30 minutes (Pavlov, 1927).

12.2.2   CS Interactions

A number of important phenomena of classical conditioning, first discovered in Pavlov's laboratory, involve the pairing or combining of more than one CS. One such phenomenon is *higher-order conditioning.* A higher-order conditioned response is established in two stages. First, a CS such as a light is paired with a UCS such as food until it comes to elicit the response (salivation). Let us call the light CS_1. Next, another stimulus which we shall call CS_2 (say a buzzer) is paired repeatedly with CS_1, in the absence of the UCS. The CS_1, in this pairing, plays the role of the UCS in the simple conditioning paradigm. It does not elicit the response as an innate reflex, however, but as a previously conditioned one. Higher-order conditioning is established if the CS_2 comes to elicit the response through its pairing with the CS_1. Such conditioning can be obtained, but it is sometimes difficult. The UCS (food, in this case) is not presented during the second phase of the experiment, while the CS_1 and CS_2 are being paired. Thus, the response to the CS_1 tends to extinguish at the same time that we are trying to condition it to the CS_2. If extinction of the CS_1 — CR connection is too rapid or acquisition of the CS_2 — CR connection is too slow, higher-order conditioning will not occur.

A second phenomenon involving more than one CS is *compound stimulus conditioning.* Here, a compound stimulus, composed of CS_1 and CS_2, is paired with the UCS. The two CS's may be either from the same modality (for example, two lights) or from different modalities (for example, a light and a tone). They are presented together, followed by the UCS. Typically, once the CR has been conditioned to the compound stimulus, it can also be elicited by either CS_1 or CS_2 presented alone. After extensive training, however, it may be elicited only by the compound, and not by either component alone — showing that the animal is responding to the two-stimulus combination as a unit. This phenomenon is called "configuring."

A third result produced by CS interactions has attracted considerable recent interest. It is called *blocking*. Suppose that in a compound stimulus conditioning experiment, as just described, one of the component CS's we use has already been conditioned to the response. That is, our experiment has two stages: First, CS_1 is paired with the UCS, until it reliably elicits the response. Next, the compound stimulus CS_1 plus CS_2 is paired repeatedly with the UCS. Under these circumstances, CS_1, which was used in stage one of the experiment, maintains its power to elicit the CR, while CS_2, which is new, acquires little or no power to do so. Prior conditioning of one component of the compound stimulus apparently prevents, or blocks, the conditioning of the other component — hence the term "blocking." Just why this happens is not clear, but there is some indication that the animal fails, in the second stage, to pay attention to the CS_2 (Dickinson, Hall, and Mackintosh, 1976).

12.3   INSTRUMENTAL CONDITIONING

In 1898 a young American psychologist named Edward L. Thorndike published a mono-graph describing a number of experiments on the general topic of animal intelligence. The experiments, using cats, dogs, and baby chicks as subjects, were designed to provide objective experimental evidence regarding the reasoning abilities of animals. At the time, animals were thought by many authorities to be almost human in their ability to reason and solve problems. However, the evidence was unsystematic and fragmentary, and primarily based on anecdotes — a method that Thorndike considered untrustworthy. Not only were the situations in which the behavior occurred uncontrolled, but the anecdotal method itself was selective. It reported *only* remarkable occurrences and thereby made the unusual appear typical. As Thorndike put it:

> Dogs get lost hundreds of times and no one ever notices it or sends an account of it to a sci-entific magazine. But let one find his way from Brooklyn to Yonkers and the fact immediately becomes a circulating anecdote. Thousands of cats on thousands of occasions sit helplessly yowling, and no one takes thought of it or writes to his friend, the professor; but let one cat claw at the knob of a door supposedly as a signal to be let out, and straightaway this cat becomes representative of the cat-mind in all the books (Thorndike, 1898, p. 4).

Cats unlatching doors were supposed, by some, to understand the inner workings of the door latch. Thorndike's experiments suggested, however, that such behavior was learned in a blind trial-and-error fashion, and showed no reasoning ability whatever.

In the experiments for which Thorndike became best known, an "utterly hungry" cat was placed in a device called a *puzzle box*. Outside the box was placed some food. The puzzle box was constructed in such a way that the cat could escape by performing a response that released a latch holding the door. The response bringing freedom (and food) varied. Some boxes required pressing a lever; in others, pulling a string or sliding a bolt would open the door. Upon being confined in the box for the first time, the cat would thrash and jump about in a seemingly aimless fashion. Eventually, a response would be made that opened the door. Thorndike measured the animal's escape *latency* — that is, the amount of time it took for the correct response to occur. The cat was then returned to the box, and again it thrashed about until the response unlatching the door was made. This procedure was repeated over and over again; for each trial Thorndike recorded the latency of the correct response.

Escape latency varied considerably from trial to trial, but over a number of trials the latency tended to become shorter and shorter. The amount of thrashing gradually decreased until eventually the animal calmly performed the required response almost immediately after being placed in the box. The escape latency data of two of Thorndike's cats (one in Box A, which required pulling a wire loop hanging from the ceiling in front of the door, and one in Box C, which required rotating a wooden crosspiece) are presented in Figure 12.3 (Thorndike, 1898).

Thorndike's puzzle box experiments illustrate what is usually called *instrumental conditioning* or *instrumental learning*. This name derives from the fact that the behavior learned is instrumental in obtaining some desired outcome or reward. The neutral term *reinforcement* is often used in the psychological literature in place of the more common term *reward.* In the experiment by Thorndike just described, the reinforcer was food. (A second reinforcer was escape from the confines of the box, which the animals apparently found aversive.) The characteristic that differentiates instrumental from classical conditioning is that, in instrumental conditioning, the critical stimulus called the reinforcer is presented only if

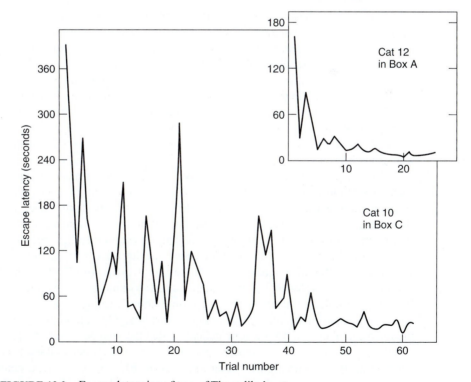

FIGURE 12.3   Escape latencies of two of Thorndike's cats.

(Adapted from Thorndike, 1898.)

the animal first makes an appropriate response. In classical conditioning, presentation of the reinforcer (the UCS) does not depend on whether or not the animal first responds.

12.3.1   Experimental Apparatus

The puzzle box has received little use since Thorndike's first experiments. Psychologists have devised a variety of types of apparatus for investigating instrumental conditioning. The apparatus used in a particular experiment depends upon a number of factors — primarily the organism being studied, the manipulations the experimenter wants to perform, and the type of response he wants to measure. A description of several kinds of apparatus will illustrate the variety of experimental situations used in the instrumental conditioning paradigm.

A device once popular in animal psychology but little used today is the *complex maze* (Figure 12.4a). Typically, a complex maze consists of a *start box,* where the animal is placed initially, a *goal box,* which contains the reward, and a pathway linking the start and goal boxes. The pathway may double back or branch off into many blind alleys. The experimenter places the animal in the start box, trial after trial, and on each trial measures either the *speed* with which the animal traverses the maze or the *number of errors* (that is, entrances into blind alleys). One finding regarding behavior in the complex maze is that the animal first learns to avoid entering blind alleys nearest the goal box. It appears that the ease of learning a choice between two paths depends in part on how quickly the choice is followed by reward.

Mastery of a complex maze obviously requires the learning of a complex sequence of behavior. To aid in the analysis of learning, psychologists have simplified the maze through a process of gradual evolution. A common apparatus used to study choice behavior is the *T-maze,* which as the name suggests is shaped like a T, having a start box at its base and a single choice point branching off toward two goal boxes (Figure 12.4b). The T-maze can be used to study preferences, by placing one reward (say sugar water) in one goal box and another (plain water) in the other goal box. It is also used to study *discrimination learning.* One arm of the T, for example, might be painted black and the other white. The black and white paths are switched back and forth randomly between the left and right sides from one trial to the next, and the animal must learn that the black path leads to reward, regardless of which side it is on.

More simple yet (and hardly deserving to be called a maze) is the *straight-alley maze* or straight runway, which consists of a start box and goal box with a runway in between (Figure 12.4c). Two measures of behavior are frequently used in the straight-alley maze: one is response *latency* — the amount of time from the opening of a door connecting the start box and the alley until the animal enters the alley; the other is response *speed* — the rate at which the animal traverses the alley once it has entered it. The straight-alley maze has found its greatest use in the investigation of effects on performance of reinforcement variables such as the amount of reward, kind of reward, and delay of reward. It is also possible, however, to study discrimination learning in a straight-alley. A tone might be sounded when the animal is in the start box, a high tone indicating that there is food in the goal box, and a low tone indicating that the goal box is empty. This type of task is called a *go — no go discrimination,* since the choice is between making the response and not making it. The situation is much like that of differential classical conditioning, in which the CS+ and CS− determine whether the animal responds or not. The two situations differ in one crucial respect, however. In the go — no go situation, the response is

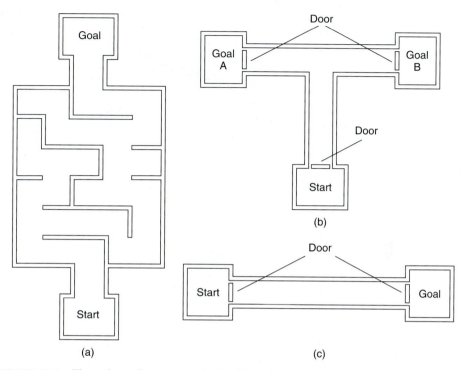

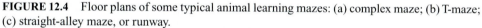

FIGURE 12.4   Floor plans of some typical animal learning mazes: (a) complex maze; (b) T-maze; (c) straight-alley maze, or runway.

an instrumental one that the animal must make in order to obtain the reinforcer, while in the classical conditioning situation the arrival of the reinforcer (the UCS) does not depend on whether the animal responds.

Another piece of apparatus, called the *shuttle box,* is often used to study the effects of aversive stimuli such as electric shock. The shuttle box consists of two compartments separated by a barrier over which the animal must jump. The floors of both compartments are electrified grids, which can be turned on independently. If the animal is in one compartment and shock is administered through the floor, it can escape the shock by jumping into the other compartment. The acquisition of a response that will terminate the aversive stimulus (for example, jumping the barrier) is called *escape learning* (see Figure 12.5a). A further complication can be introduced by preceding the onset of shock with a signal such as a tone or blinking light. By jumping the barrier shortly after the signal occurs, the animal can avoid the shock altogether. Learning to respond to a warning signal in a way that prevents any exposure to the aversive stimulus is called *avoidance learning* (Figure 12.5b). These two situations are easily confused, but the names given them point out the crucial difference. In escape learning, the animal receives no warning, but by responding quickly when the aversive stimulus first occurs, it can escape the pain. In avoidance learning, onset of the aversive stimulus is predictable — usually because it is heralded by a warning signal. By responding when the signal occurs, the animal can avoid any contact with the aversive stimulus.

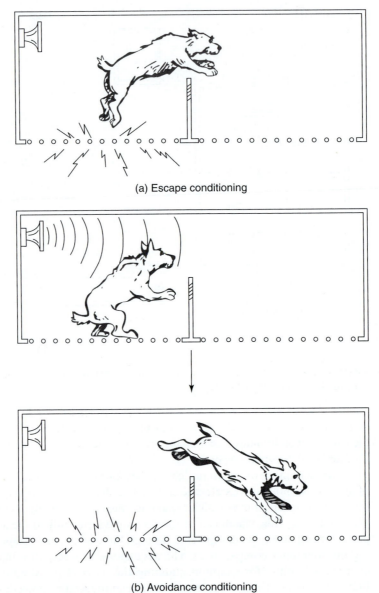

(a) Escape conditioning

(b) Avoidance conditioning

FIGURE 12.5   Two uses of the shuttle box: (a) escape conditioning and (b) avoidance conditioning.

12.3.2   Positive Versus Negative Reinforcement

In instrumental conditioning, the animal comes to make the response that leads to rein-forcement, and not to make responses that do not. Because reinforcement plays a central role in this process, investigators have been interested in just what reinforcement is and how it works. [...] Here we shall attempt to stay clear of controversy, while examining rein-forcement phenomena more closely.

Reinforcement is a manipulation that, if it follows a particular response, increases the tendency of that response to occur again. If the manipulation having this effect is the *presentation* of a stimulus, the stimulus is called a *positive reinforcer.* If the manipulation increasing the response tendency is the removal or *termination* of a stimulus, the stimulus is called a *negative reinforcer.* Thus negative reinforcement and escape learning (which was just described) are two ways of referring to the same manipulation.

Stimuli that are reinforcing because of the animal's genetic makeup, rather than because of the animal's experience, are called *primary reinforcers.* Primary positive reinforcers are usually stimuli that an appropriately deprived animal will approach, such as food, for a hungry animal, or water, for a thirsty one. Such stimuli are called *appetitive* stimuli (note the relation to the word *appetite*). Primary negative reinforcers are typically stimuli that an animal will learn to avoid (such as shock). Such stimuli are called *aversive* stimuli.

Negative reinforcement, then, is the termination of an aversive stimulus upon the performance of a response. Since the term suggests a negative consequence of the act, it has been used also to refer to *presentation* of an aversive stimulus following a response. The latter use of the term negative reinforcement, however, is no longer accepted, since reinforcement refers only to events that make the response more likely. Following a response with the presentation of an aversive stimulus is correctly referred to as *punishment.* Thus negative reinforcement and punishment are not synonyms. The two operations are quite different — and so are their effects on behavior.

12.3.3   Reinforcement Parameters

Fortunately, most of the laws governing the effects of reinforcement on behavior appear to be essentially the same for positive and negative reinforcers. Therefore, the following statements can be considered to apply to both types of reinforcement.

One frequently studied variable in instrumental conditioning is the *amount of reward.* "Amount" is a somewhat ambiguous term. It may refer to the size of a chunk of food, the number of food pellets, the concentration of a sugar solution, the amount of time a male is allowed to copulate with a female, or the degree of reduction of shock current. If animals are trained in a straight-alley runway, with different groups of animals receiving different amounts of reward in the goal box, the typical finding is that running speed increases with the magnitude of the reward. On the first trial, of course, running speeds are uniformly slow and do not depend on the amount of reward. As training progresses, speed increases for all the groups, but it levels off (reaches an *asymptote*) at a speed determined by the amount of reward. The larger the reward, the greater the speed. The same general relationship holds for the latency of the response of leaving the start box and entering the runway. (The larger the reward, the shorter the latency.)

Delay of reward is another variable that has strong effects on instrumental conditioning. By delay of reward we simply mean the time between performance of the response and administration of reinforcement. The effect of delay of reward depends to some extent on the species of animal being tested and on the nature of the task. With rats, even very short delays can have devastating effects on learning. This is well illustrated by an experiment done by Grice (1948). Grice required rats to make a black-white discrimination, taking a right-hand turn on some trials and a left-hand turn on others. Both the right and left pathways included a delay box, in which the animal's progress could be held up for a short time between the choice point and the goal box. One group of animals (the control group) was allowed to run straight through the delay box to the goal box. Other groups were delayed for different amounts of time before being allowed to continue to the goal box. The delays were 0.5, 1.2, 2.0, 5.0, and 10.0 seconds. Figure 12.6 shows how performance of the different groups of rats changed over trials. The shorter the delay, the more quickly the animals learned. Since there were two choices, the "chance" rate of success would be 50 percent. The animals with a 10-second delay of reward showed no evidence of improvement over the 50 percent rate even after several hundred trials.

If an animal has been trained to perform an instrumental response for reinforcement and the reinforcement is now withheld, the strength of the response gradually drops back to its original low level. As in the case of classical conditioning, the decrease in response tendency that results from withholding reinforcement is called *extinction*. Also similar to what is found in classical conditioning is the *spontaneous recovery* of an extinguished instrumental response with the passage of time. Extinction and spontaneous recovery are two of many properties that classical and instrumental conditioning have in common.

A manipulation with interesting effects on instrumental behavior is that of presenting reward on only some fraction of the training trials. Rewarding an animal on every trial is called 100 percent or *continuous reinforcement*. Rewarding the animal on some fraction of the trials is called *partial reinforcement*. If reinforcement is given randomly, with a certain probability of occurring on each trial, the manipulation is simply identified in terms of the

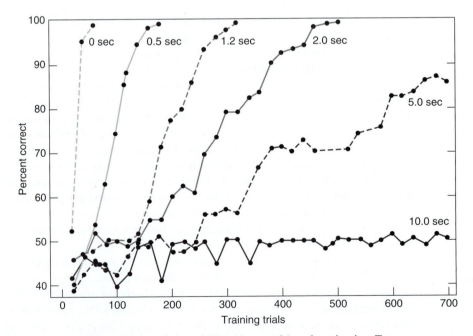

FIGURE 12.6   Effects of delay of reward (0 to 10 seconds) on learning in a T-maze.

(After Grice, 1948. Copyright 1948 by the American Psychological Association. Reprinted by permission.)

percentage of trials that are reinforced — say 25 percent or 50 percent. One of the most dramatic effects of partial reinforcement is seen in extinction. The responses of a group receiving partial reinforcement during training extinguish *more slowly* than those of a group receiving reinforcement on every trial. This counter-intuitive result is called the *partial-reinforcement effect* (sometimes abbreviated PRE). It has been the focus of a number of theoretical disputes.

A good example of the partial-reinforcement effect is found in an experiment by Bower (1960). Unlike most studies of the partial-reinforcement effect, this one used negative, rather than positive, reinforcement. The experimental apparatus was a straight-alley runway with an electrified grid as the floor. The grid in the start box and runway and the grid in the goal box could be turned on independently. At the start of a trial, a rat was placed in the start box and the shock turned on. On reinforced trials, the animal experienced termination of shock immediately upon entering the goal box. On nonreinforced trials, shock was present in the goal box, as well as in the alley (the animal was removed from the goal box after spending 20 seconds there). There were four groups of animals tested, receiving reinforcement on different proportions of trials: 100 percent, 75 percent, 50 percent, and 25 percent. Following training, extinction trials were administered to the 100 percent and 50 percent groups. During these trials, entering the goal box never produced termination of

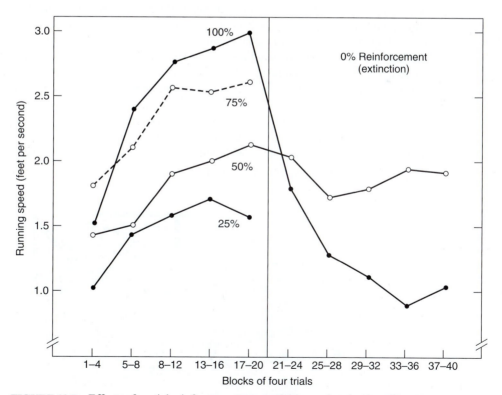

FIGURE 12.7   Effects of partial reinforcement on acquisition and extinction of an escape response. (After Bower, 1960. Copyright 1960 by the American Psychological Association. Reprinted by permission.)

shock (0 percent reinforcement). The acquisition and extinction data are presented in Figure 12.7. As the graph shows, the greater the probability of shock termination, the faster the animals ran during acquisition. However, the opposite was true during extinction. The running of group that had been rewarded with shock termination 100 percent of the time during acquisition extinguished much more rapidly than that of the group that had received 50 percent reinforcement. This is the partial-reinforcement effect.

12.4   OPERANT CONDITIONING

The apparatus most frequently used to study animal behavior is the *Skinner box*. Much of the popularity of this apparatus derives from the fact that experimental manipulations are easily automated, leaving the experimenter free from laboratory drudgery to construct theories, devise new experiments, and write. B. F. Skinner (1956) has given us a charming account of the evolution of the device that bears his name. The desire to avoid laboratory drudgery played an important role in development of the Skinner box. As a graduate student at Harvard University in the late 1920s, Skinner was studying the behavior of rats traversing an eight-food long runway for food. To save himself the trouble of having to move the rat from the goal box of the runway to the start box after every trial, he constructed a return path for the rat to take on his own. The result was a maze with a floor plan in the form of a rectangle, with a direct path from the start box to the goal (the original runway), and a roundabout path leading from the goal back to the start box. Next, Skinner invented a way to save himself the trouble of reinforcing the animal for each trip to the goal box. He constructed the ingenious apparatus shown in Figure 12.8. The entire rectangular-shaped runway was balanced in the center so that it tipped back and forth as the rat moved from one end to the other. Whenever the runway tipped back, the attached arm hooked a wheel and moved it one notch. This allowed a piece of food in one of the notches around the perimeter of the wheel to drop through a funnel into the food dish. Thus, the animal produced its own reward each time it shuttled back and forth in the maze. Finally, Skinner discovered that by winding a string around the central spindle of the wheel (which turned one notch each time the rat ran around the runway) and attaching the string to a pen held against a continuously moving drum, he

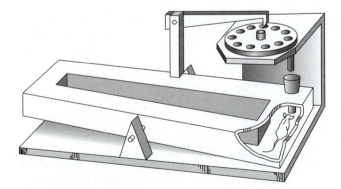

FIGURE 12.8   A precursor of the Skinner box.

(After Skinner, 1956. Copyright 1956 by the American Psychological Association. Reprinted by permission.)

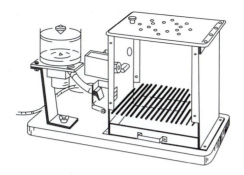

FIGURE 12.9   A Skinner box.

(Courtesy of Ralph Gerbrands Co., Arlington, Mass.)

could preserve a complete record of the behavior of the animal while the experimenter was out of the room. Each time the wheel turned, the string unwound slightly, displacing the string downward. The resulting curve was a stair-step tracing that was steep when the rat was active, and less steep when the animal made few trips around the maze.

12.4.1   The "Skinner Box"

The apparatus in Figure 12.8, of course, is nothing but a huge lever. From this realization, it was only a small step to the experimental chamber known as the "Skinner box." A diagram of a modern Skinner box is shown in Figure 12.9. The apparatus consists of a chamber, which may be sound-deadened to eliminate distracting noise, a floor which may or may not be an electrified grid designed for studying effects of shock, a food magazine for dispensing positive reinforcers, and a "manipulandum" — typically a lever for rats, or a pressure-sensitive key for pigeons. The manipulandum is connected to the food magazine (or shock apparatus) through an electronic circuit, allowing complex relations between responses and reinforcement to be programmed. In addition, secondary stimuli, called discriminative stimuli, may be presented in various ways to control the animal's behavior. The discriminative stimuli may be tones or lights. When a pigeon is tested, it is common practice to illuminate the response key from behind. In this way, various colors and patterns can be projected on the key as discriminative stimuli. The experimenter is assured that the bird will look at the stimulus, since it must peck the key in order to obtain a reward.

Behavior in a Skinner box is recorded by means of a *cumulative recorder*. In principle, the idea is the same as that behind Skinner's unwinding string. A sheet of paper is moved through the recorder at a slow, steady rate. A pen leaves a continuous line on the paper. If the animal makes no response, the pen does not move, and a straight horizontal line results. When the animal responds, the pen is displaced slightly upward, to a new position. The result is a *cumulative curve* that reflects the animal's *response rate*. If the animal responds at a fast rate, the curve is steep. If the response rate is slow, the slope of the curve is more gradual. Cumulative records showing acquisition, extinction, and spontaneous recovery of the lever-pressing response by a rat are shown in Figure 12.10. The data are taken from Skinner's *Behavior of Organisms* (1938).

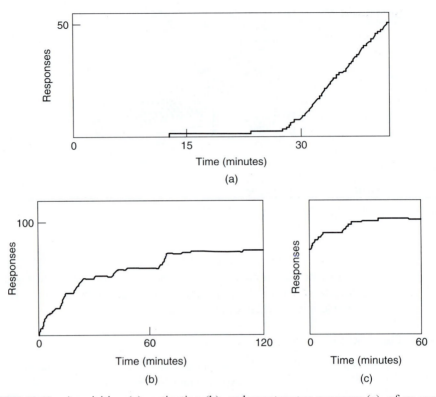

FIGURE 12.10   Acquisition (a), extinction (b), and spontaneous recovery (c), of an operant response.

(After B. F. Skinner, *The Behavior of Organisms: An Experimental Analysis,* © 1938 renewed 1966. Reprinted by permission of Prentice-Hall, Inc., Englewood Cliffs, N.J.)

A response (for example, pressing a lever) which the subject can repeat as often as desired is called a *free operant.* The term "operant" has essentially the same meaning as instrumental response. The response is called a free operant in this situation because there is no restriction on when the manipulandum is made available to the subject; the response can be made at any time. The learning of a free operant is often called *operant conditioning.* No important theoretical distinction is made between operant and instrumental conditioning; in fact, the terms are often used interchangeably. However, the term operant conditioning is used mostly in connection with a response that can be made at any time, while the term instrumental conditioning usually refers to the kinds of trial-by-trial learning situations described in the last section. While the instrumental situation gives the experimenter control over intervals between responses, which is an advantage for some purposes, the operant conditioning procedure allows one to measure response rate — a measure that is not possible in instrumental conditioning.

There are two areas of investigation in which the operant conditioning procedure has proved most useful. One is in the study of schedules of reinforcement, and the other is in the investigation of control of behavior by discriminative stimuli. We shall turn first to a discussion of schedules of reinforcement.

12.4.2   Schedules of Reinforcement

A *reinforcement schedule* is a rule relating the presentation of reward to the behavior of the animal. In *continuous reinforcement,* the animal receives a reward every time the correct response is made. Other schedules are called *intermittent,* because not all responses are reinforced. (The term intermittent, rather than partial, is customary in the operant conditioning literature.)

A simple intermittent schedule is the *fixed-ratio* schedule, in which every *n*th response is reinforced. Thus, if *n* is 5, the animal must make five responses for every reward. On a *variable-ratio* schedule, likewise, the animal must make a certain number of responses, *n,* to obtain the reward — but *n* varies from one reward to the next. Variable-ratio schedules are usually specified by the *average* number of responses necessary to produce the reward. Many games of chance can be viewed as variable-ratio schedules. Thus, in throwing a die for let us say a three, one wins on the average once every six throws. The schedule is a "variable ratio — 6." Ratio schedules are so named because there is a predetermined ratio of responses to reinforcements. The animal must make so many responses to obtain the reward; when he makes them does not matter.

In contrast to ratio schedules are *interval schedules.* In an interval schedule, regardless of the animal's behavior, a certain period of time must follow a reward before another reward can be obtained. On a *fixed-interval* schedule, responses can be rewarded no more often than once every *t* seconds. Thus on a fixed-interval 60-second schedule, the animal can receive at the most one reinforcer every 60 seconds. The first response occurring after 60 seconds have elapsed since the last reward will be reinforced; a response occurring sooner than 60 seconds after the last reward will not be reinforced. On a *variable-interval* schedule, likewise, a certain time interval must elapse after each reward before another reward can be obtained, but the length of the interval varies. A variable-interval schedule is usually identified by the *average* length of the interval during which reinforcement cannot occur.

Notice that with an interval schedule the number of reinforcements that can be obtained in a fixed period of time is strictly limited. This is not the case with a ratio schedule, in which the number of reinforcements is directly proportional to the rate of responding — the more responses per unit time, the more reinforcements are received.

Typical cumulative records for the simplest types of reinforcement schedules are shown in Figure 12.11. All four curves depict responding by hungry pigeons for food. A fixed-ratio schedule, once the animal is well trained, produces a faster rate of responding than does continuous reinforcement. However, there is usually a pause in responding just after each reward is consumed. At the end of the pause, responses are made at a steady, rapid rate until the next reinforcement occurs (curve *a* in Figure 12.11). A variable-ratio schedule produces a fairly steady, fast rate of responding, with shorter pauses following reward than those that characterize the fixed-ratio schedule. Generally, the higher the average ratio of a variable-ratio schedule (that is, the more responses per reward), the higher is the response rate (curve *b* in Figure 12.11). A fixed-interval schedule produces, with a well-practiced subject, what is called a *scallop.* Following each reward there is a pause and then a gradual increase in response rate, reaching a peak at just about the time reinforcement is due (curve *c* in Figure 12.11). It is the gradual, rather than abrupt, increase that differentiates the effect of a fixed-interval schedule from that of a fixed-ratio schedule. A variable-interval schedule produces a slow, steady rate of responding. The longer the average interval, the slower is the overall response rate (curve *d* in Figure 12.11).

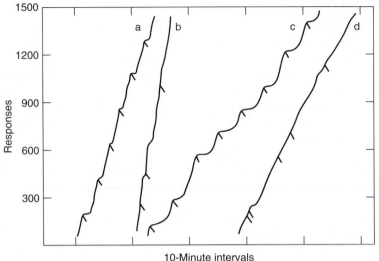

FIGURE 12.11   Cumulative records produced by four schedules of reinforcement: (a) fixed ratio, 200 responses per reinforcement; (b) variable ratio, 360 responses per reinforcement; (c) fixed interval, 4 minutes; (d) variable interval, 3 minutes.

(Adapted from Ferster and Skinner, 1957.)

In operant conditioning, as in instrumental conditioning, extinction is fastest following continuous reinforcement. It is slowest following variable-ratio and variable-interval schedules, and fixed-ratio and fixed-interval schedules fall in between.

There are many other types of schedules in addition to the ratio and interval varieties. For example, reinforcement can occur only when the animal responds at a slow rate (this is called the DRL schedule — for differential reinforcement of a low rate of responding). One can also train the animal to respond only with a certain degree of force. Deliberate manipulation of characteristics of the response, such as its force, is called *response differentiation*. An almost unlimited number of complex schedules can be created by combining simple schedules in various ways. Two schedules can alternate; they can be chained, so that the requirements of both must be satisfied in order to produce a reward; they can operate simultaneously, so that meeting the requirements of either will produce reinforcement; two operants (for example, two response keys), each with its own schedule, can be made available at the same time; and the nature of the schedule can be made to change, depending on the subject's performance. A whole area of research has grown up around complex reinforcement schedules.

12.4.3   Stimulus Control

If a special stimulus such as a tone or colored illumination of a key is present whenever responding leads to reinforcement and is absent when it does not, the animal learns to respond only when the stimulus is present. The behavior is then said to be under *stimulus control*, and the stimulus that signals availability of reward is called a *discriminative stimulus* (S^D). Following such training, the animal may be tested in the presence of other stimuli with varying degrees of similarity to the S^D. Response rates are higher the more the test stimulus resembles the S^D — thus, operant behavior displays *stimulus generalization.*

Suppose that nonavailability of reinforcement was signalled, not by the absence of the S^D as just described, but by presentation of another stimulus, similar to S^D. A stimulus associated with absence of reinforcement is denoted S^Δ. Both the S^D ("S-D") and the S^Δ ("S-Delta") are called discriminative stimuli; but the S^D indicates availability and the S^Δ non-availability of reward. The effect upon generalization of training with short periods of S^D interspersed with periods of S^Δ is compared, in Figure 12.12, with that of training without S^Δ. The data are taken from an experiment by Hanson (1959). The subjects in Hanson's experiments were pigeons, and the S^D was illumination of the key with light of 550-millimicron wavelength. In the control condition, where training did not include an S^Δ, the generalization test revealed a typical generalization gradient peaking at the wavelength of the S^D. However, when periods of S^D illumination were interspersed, during training, with periods of S^Δ illumination (570 millimicrons), signalling no reward, the form of the generalization gradient was different. Not only was the tendency to respond in the range of the S^Δ depressed (which simply indicates that a discrimination between the two stimuli developed), but there was a shift of the point of maximum responding, in the direction *away* from the S^Δ. Thus, the group of animals trained with both an S^D and S^Δ did not respond maximally to the S^D of 550; instead, a test stimulus of 540 produced the greatest response rate. This phenomenon, produced by the standard discrimination training procedure, is called the *peak shift,* because there is a shift in the peak of the generalization gradient.

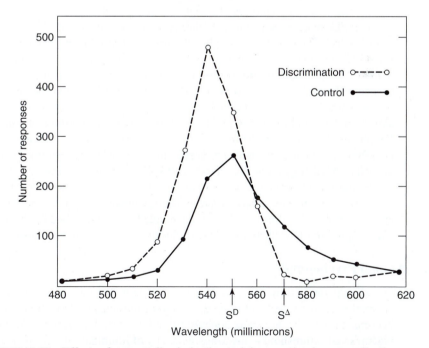

FIGURE 12.12   Effects of operant discrimination training on stimulus generalization.

(After Hanson, 1959. Copyright 1959 by the American Psychological Association. Reprinted by permission.)

12.4.4   Fading

A different procedure for training a discrimination between an S^D and S^Δ is called *fading*. This procedure has a number of interesting properties — among them the fact that it does not produce the peak shift. Consider one of a series of experiments on fading described by Terrace (1966). In the first stage of the experiment, pigeons were taught to peck a red response key (S^D). In the second stage, the key was first made to go dark very briefly every 30 seconds. The duration of the dark period was gradually increased to 30 seconds. During this phase of training, the pigeons pecked at the key when it was lighted, but never did so when it was dark. In the third stage, an S^Δ was introduced by illuminating the key with very dim green light during the darkened periods and gradually increasing the intensity of the green illumination. Thus, dark periods were gradually introduced in stage two, and then in stage three the darkened key was gradually changed into a green one. The pigeons learned to discriminate red from darkness, and then red from green, with virtually *no errors*. In a fourth stage of training, the birds were taught to discriminate between a horizontal and a vertical white bar — an even more difficult discrimination to establish using the standard procedure. First, the vertical line was superimposed on the red key (S^D), and the horizontal line was superimposed on the green key (S^Δ). Then the colors were gradually faded out. The result was that the difficult horizontal-vertical discrimination, like the simpler red — green one, was learned with no errors; the pigeons pecked the key only when it was illuminated with the vertical bar, and never when it was illuminated with the horizontal bar.

Terrace (1966) has noted a number of differences between the behavior of animals given errorless discrimination training, through the fading technique, and those learning a discrimination in the standard way, through alternated periods of S^D and S^Δ. First, fading produces errorless discrimination learning, while the standard procedure produces many errors. Second, when fading is used a test for generalization reveals no peak shift — the animal responds maximally to the S^D itself, not to a stimulus value displaced away from the S^Δ. Third, pigeons trained without errors calmly wait, in the presence of the S^Δ, for the S^D to appear, while those trained with errors demonstrate emotional behavior (wing flapping, jumping, and the like) similar to that produced in the presence of an aversive or punishing stimulus such as shock. Fourth, pigeons trained in the standard way often produce bursts of responses to the S^Δ, even after the discrimination has been completely mastered, while those trained without errors never do. It has been suggested that errorless discrimination learning and the standard error-producing procedure differ, not only in effectiveness, but in the underlying mechanism, as well. An S^Δ to which the subject has responded (without receiving reward) apparently acquires aversive properties, while one that has been faded in gradually and has never been responded to is simply part of the background from which the S^D — the signal to respond — is contrasted.

12.4.5   Animal Psychophysics

One of many uses to which operant conditioning techniques have been put is the study of "animal psychophysics" — the investigation of the sensory capabilities of animals. A pioneering study in this area was done by Blough (1958). The purpose was to investigate the pigeon's visual threshold — the lowest intensity of illumination the pigeon can see. Through a painstaking procedure, Blough taught a pigeon to peck two keys according to the appearance of a single visual stimulus above them. A peck on key A increased the intensity of the light very slightly. A peck on key B decreased it slightly. Pecks on key B also occasionally turned the stimulus off — an event heralding reinforcement. But of course the light could not go off unless it was on. Thus, when the illumination was too weak to be seen, the pigeon pecked key A, which eventually made it bright enough to be visible. But as soon as the stimulus could be seen, the bird pecked key B in an attempt to obtain reward. Since pecking key B produced reward only infrequently, and otherwise reduced the intensity of the stimulus, the stimulus-intensity value increased and decreased repeatedly, according to the animal's responses on the two keys. When light could be seen, the pigeon made it dimmer; and when it could not be seen, the bird made it brighter. The value around which the intensity fluctuated was taken to be the bird's visual threshold. The threshold was found to decrease with time in the dark (dark adaptation) and to vary with the wavelength or color of the stimulus in a regular way. Both types of data parallel similar findings from studies with humans. (Normal human adults, of course, do not have to be conditioned, since they can be instructed verbally how and when to respond.)

12.5   A COMPARISON OF PARADIGMS

Four basic experimental paradigms for studying animal learning have been described. In the first, a UCS — a stimulus reflexively eliciting an innate response — is presented repeatedly. Either of two opposite response tendencies may be produced by this manipulation: *habituation,* a decrease in the strength of the UCR; and *sensitization,* an increase in its strength. In the second paradigm, a neutral stimulus, the CS, is paired repeatedly with a UCS, and as a result comes to elicit the response when presented alone. This procedure is called Pavlovian, or *classical conditioning.* In the third paradigm, the animal makes a response and is rewarded, either through presentation of a positive reinforcer or through removal of an aversive stimulus or negative reinforcer. As a result, on the next trial, the reinforced response is more likely to occur. This procedure is called *instrumental conditioning.* In the fourth paradigm, as in the third, the animal makes a response which is then reinforced. Since the response is freely available (there are no discrete events called trials), the result is an increase in the rate or frequency with which the response is made. This is the *operant conditioning* paradigm.

12.5.1   Habituation and Sensitization Compared with Conditioning

It is interesting to note how much habituation and sensitization, both very primitive kinds of learning, have in common with the true conditioning procedures. Both, for example, display stimulus generalization, which is a prominent characteristic of classical, instrumental, and operant conditioning. Habituation is much like extinction of a conditioned response — not only in showing a decrease in response strength with repetition, but also in showing spontaneous recovery over time. Dishabituation, produced by an intense extraneous stimulus, is much like disinhibition of an extinguished conditioned reflex, as studied by Pavlov. It was once thought that disinhibition could not be obtained with instrumental or operant responses, but recent evidence shows that it can be (Brimer, 1970).

Another way in which habituation resembles conditioning is illustrated by the observation that a reaction to an intense stimulus can be habituated by first presenting the stimulus in weak form and then gradually increasing its intensity. A similar principle was used

FIGURE 12.13 Fading as a way of teaching reading.

by Mary Cover Jones (1924) to counter-condition fear in children. [...] The feared stimulus was introduced at a distance in a pleasant situation, and gradually brought closer. Likewise, Pavlov taught a difficult discrimination between white and light grey by first establishing an easy discrimination and then making the CS− more and more similar to the CS+. And in the operant conditioning situation, Terrace (1966) showed how a difficult discrimination between an S^D and S^Δ could be taught without errors through the use of fading. Perhaps the term *fading* could be used to refer to all these procedures. A simple principle seems common to all of them: A behavior that is difficult or even impossible to teach an organism by means of one technique may be produced readily if an easy version is trained first and then gradually made more and more like the difficult one.

The general principle of fading has proved useful in educational practice — particularly in training people who are physically and mentally handicapped. Indeed, the principle was applied in those fields more than a century before it was discovered in the learning laboratory. Lane (1976) recounts how Abbé Sicard, the eighteenth-century French educator of deaf-mutes, first taught his charges to read by inscribing a word inside a drawing of the corresponding object and then gradually fading out the outline and shape of the drawing, leaving the pupil to rely on the letters alone (see Figure 12.13). Related procedures were employed in the last century to teach skills to the deaf and the retarded, and in one celebrated case, to civilize the "wild boy of Aveyron" (Lane, 1976).

12.5.2   Classical Compared with Instrumental and Operant Conditioning

As we have seen, both instrumental and operant conditioning require the subject to make a particular response in order to obtain reward. But in instrumental conditioning the experimenter gives the animal individual opportunities (that is, discrete trials) to make the response, and measures the response's latency, amplitude, and probability; while in operant conditioning the response is always available, and the preferred measure is response rate. The two experimental procedures are so different that they have given rise to different ways of describing and thinking about learning research. Nevertheless, all theorists consider the mechanisms underlying learning in the two situations to be the same, and most writers, as a result, apply just one label (either instrumental or operant) to both. Since it is generally agreed that the underlying learning process is the same, we shall cease making the distinction for the remainder of this chapter. Whenever something is said about instrumental conditioning, it is meant to apply to operant conditioning as well.

A fundamental question theorists have debated is whether the mechanism underlying classical conditioning differs from that underlying instrumental conditioning. [...] For the present, we shall ignore this theoretical question; but it is important to understand the difference between the two forms of learning simply in terms of experimental procedure.

It is sometimes said that instrumental conditioning involves reinforcement, while classical conditioning does not. But this is misleading. The UCS plays a role in classical conditioning similar to that of the reward in instrumental conditioning — it is necessary in order for learning to occur, and when it is removed the behavior extinguishes. Indeed, many stimuli that can be used as the UCS in classical conditioning (for example, food and electric shock) also serve as reinforcers in instrumental conditioning.

The basic difference between the two conditioning procedures was pointed out by Skinner (1937). In both classical and instrumental conditioning there is a reinforcer or UCS; but in classical conditioning the reinforcer is presented just after the CS, while in instrumental conditioning it is presented just after the response. The difference, therefore, can be described in terms of *contingencies.* In classical conditioning, reinforcement is contingent on a stimulus (the CS), whereas in instrumental conditioning reinforcement is contingent on a response. Another way to describe the difference is to say that in classical conditioning reinforcement occurs regardless of whether the animal responds, while in instrumental conditioning the animal must respond in order to receive reinforcement.

An intriguing puzzle concerning the relationship between classical and instrumental conditioning has been pointed out by Razran (1971). Up to this point, we have treated the CS in the classical conditioning situation as a neutral stimulus that elicits no innate reaction. This is an oversimplification, however. A tone ordinarily causes a dog to prick up its ears and move its head; and a light will cause the animal to move its eyes and its head. This kind of reaction is called an *orienting response* (OR). In the classical conditioning situation, then, one really begins with two reflexes: the CS–OR orienting reflex, and the UCS–UCR reflex. Conditioning takes place when the CS–OR reflex is replaced by the CS–CR reflex (in which the CR is similar to the UCR).

Note, however, that the conditions for instrumental conditioning are seemingly satisfied by this arrangement. Suppose we present a tone (CS) and the animal pricks up its ears (OR). Then we present food (UCS) and the animal salivates (UCR). The response of pricking up the ears is followed by a positive reinforcer. Why doesn't instrumental conditioning occur? That is, why doesn't the probability of the OR increase? Instead, it decreases and is replaced by the CR of salivation. Razran (1971) has proposed that what determines whether classical or instrumental conditioning will occur is the *habituability* of the response that is followed by the reinforcer. Most OR's (such as pricking up the ears) habituate easily with repeated presentation of the CS; most responses that can be instrumentally learned are not easy to habituate. Razran's suggestion, then, is that instrumental conditioning will occur only if the response that is to be conditioned does not easily habituate. This hypothesis is beginning to receive some attention from other investigators (for example, Kimmel, 1973).

The above analysis shows that the classical conditioning situation includes the basic components of the instrumental conditioning paradigm — a response is followed by reward. It is also true that the basic elements of the classical conditioning paradigm are present during instrumental conditioning. In fact, classically conditioned behavior is often observed during instrumental learning. A dog performing an instrumental response for food will salivate; and a rat running in a straight alley for food may be seen to gnash its teeth and smack its lips — responses that would be elicited as UCR's by the food. Likewise, in avoidance learning, in which a signal warns that shock is about to occur, animals often respond to the signal by squealing, defecating, or crouching in a corner — behavior that would be reflexively elicited by the shock.

Theorists have had difficulty determining whether classical and instrumental conditioning involve different underlying mechanisms. One reason for this difficulty is that a "pure" case of instrumental conditioning — in which no classically conditioned behavior occurs — may be impossible to produce. In fact, the pecking of an illuminated key by a pigeon (the most commonly studied operant response) can be trained through a purely classical conditioning procedure. All one needs to do, apparently, is to repeatedly follow the lighting of the key (CS) by the delivery of food (UCS). The pecking response (the UCR to food) is transferred from the food to the key. Soon the pigeon is pecking the key, even though it need not do so in order to obtain the food (Brown and Jenkins, 1968). This phenomenon [. . .] has come to be known as *autoshaping* [. . .]

12.5.3   Secondary Reinforcement: A Mixed Paradigm

In the previous discussion of instrumental conditioning, the concept of primary reinforcement was introduced. Primary reinforcers, whose reinforcing power is genetically determined, are to be contrasted with secondary reinforcers, whose reinforcing power is acquired through learning. The paradigm demonstrating *secondary reinforcement* involves two stages: one of classical conditioning, and one of operant or instrumental conditioning. Consider a hungry rat fed in the presence of a previously neutral stimulus. We know that this situation fits the classical conditioning paradigm. The neutral stimulus is the CS; through its pairing with the UCS it can come to elicit the CR, part of the response the animal naturally makes to food. But the pairing of the CS and UCS has another effect on the animal's reaction to the CS, as well. It gives the CS the power to reinforce an instrumental response.

A good example of secondary reinforcement is provided by an experiment by Saltzman (1949). In the first stage of the experiment, hungry rats were fed in a distinctive goal box. For half the rats the goal box was white, and for the other half it was black. In the second stage the rats were given 15 trials of training in a maze which required a choice between two paths, one branching to the right and the other to the left. One of these paths led to the white goal box, and the other led to the black one; thus, for an individual rat, one goal box was the one in which food had been found during the first stage and the other was not. The animals were never fed in this maze; yet they learned to choose the path leading to the "correct" goal box — the one that had previously been associated with food — more often than the path leading to the "incorrect" one. Saltzman noted, however, that choices of the path leading to the previously rewarding goal box first increased, but then *declined* over the 15 trials. He suggested that in stage two the secondary reinforcing power of the goal box might have gradually extinguished because it was no longer paired with food. To test this hypothesis, he performed a second experiment. In this experiment the stage-one trials, in which food was paired with the goal box, were interspersed with the stage-two trials, which required a choice between the right and left paths of the maze. Under these conditions, the preference for the path leading to the "correct" goal box was maintained. The rats chose that path on 77 percent of the trials, as opposed to only 56 percent of the trials in the first experiment.

The experiments by Saltzman illustrate the crucial test of whether a CS has become a secondary reinforcer — it must have the power to reinforce *new learning*. In this case the animals learned to go left or right, even though this response was never directly reinforced with food. Stimuli of the goal box provided the only "reinforcement" for this behavior. The experiment also illustrates the fact that secondary reinforcers tend to lose their reinforcing power if they are not occasionally paired with the primary reinforcer (the UCS). Saltzman was able to forestall this loss in his second experiment by interspersing the choice tests with pairings of the goal box and food.

Secondary reinforcers, like primary reinforcers, can be either positive or negative. A *secondary positive reinforcer* is produced by pairing a neutral stimulus with a primary positive reinforcer, as in the Saltzman study. A *secondary negative reinforcer* is produced by pairing a neutral stimulus with a primary negative reinforcer, such as shock.

The test for secondary negative reinforcement, like that for secondary positive reinforcement, is whether or not the previously neutral stimulus will reinforce new learning. For example, suppose that in stage one a rat is placed in a white box (the CS), where it is repeatedly shocked (the UCS). In stage two the rat is again placed in a white box, but is never shocked. A lever is made available which, whenever it is pressed, opens a door permitting the rat to escape from the white box into another compartment. If the animal learns to make this response (and does so more quickly than a control rat that was never shocked in the white box), the white box has been shown to be a secondary negative reinforcer. Intuitively, an observer might assume that the rat had become "afraid" of the white box because it was shocked there. Thus, the paradigm for demonstrating secondary negative reinforcement is often referred to as a *fear conditioning* paradigm. Little Albert, in the experiment by Watson and Rayner (1920), performed an instrumental response (crawling away) to escape the white rat, which had become a secondary negative reinforcer by being paired with the loud noise.

A great deal of theoretical significance has been attached to secondary reinforcement as a link between animal learning studies and human behavior. While most complex human behavior appears to be instrumental or operant in the sense that it accomplishes a particular desired outcome, it is infrequent that the immediate outcome is a primary reinforcer. Students work for A's, laborers for wages, politicians for votes, celebrities for publicity, and amateur artists and hobbyists for whatever they produce plus occasional praise. Can the reinforcing power of such events be understood as examples of secondary reinforcement? That is, did these outcomes become reinforcing by being paired with primary (innate) reinforcers? There have been experimental attempts to make this connection. For example, a study by Wolfe (1936) found that chimpanzees that had learned to put a poker chip in a vending machine for a grape would work for poker chips even when the vending machine was not immediately available — a finding with an obvious parallel to the role of money in human behavior. The explanation of complex human behavior in terms of secondary reinforcement is not without its problems, however. It is not always evident that the "reinforcing" outcome has been paired with an appropriate primary reinforcer (with what UCS has the letter grade A been paired?), and there remains the fact that without such occasional pairings, most secondary reinforcers lose their reinforcing power. If A's, wages, votes, publicity, and praise are secondary reinforcers, they are remarkably resistant to extinction.

REFERENCES

Blough, D. S. (1958). A method for obtaining psychophysical thresholds from the pigeon. *Journal of the Experimental Analysis of Behavior, 1*, 31–43.

Bower, G. H. (1960). Partial and correlated reward in escape learning. *Journal of Experimental Psychology, 59*, 126–130.

Brimer, C. J. (1970). Disinhibition of an operant response. *Learning and Motivation, 1*, 346–371.

Brown, P. L., and Jenkins, H. M. (1968). Auto-shaping of the pigeon's keypeck. *Journal of the Experimental Analysis of Behavior, 11*, 1–8.

Davis, M., and Wagner, A. R. (1969). Habituation of startle response under incremental sequence of stimulus intensities. *Journal of Comparative and Physiological Psychology, 67*, 486–492.

Dickinson, A., Hall, G., and Mackintosh, N. J. (1976). Surprise and the attenuation of blocking. *Journal of Experimental Psychology: Animal Behavior Processes, 2*, 313–322.

Ferster, C. B., and Skinner, B. F. (1957). *Schedules of reinforcement*. New York: Appleton-Century.

Grice, G. R. (1948). The relation of secondary reinforcement to delayed reward in visual discrimination learning. *Journal of Experimental Psychology, 38*, 1–16.

Groves, P. M., and Thompson, R. F. (1970). Habituation: A dual-process theory. *Psychological Review, 77*, 419–450.

Hanson, H. M. (1959). Effects of discrimination training on stimulus generalization. *Journal of Experimental Psychology, 58*, 321–334.

Jones, M. C. (1924). The elimination of children's fears. *Journal of Experimental Psychology, 7*, 382–390.

Kimble, G. A. (1961). *Hilgard and Marquis' conditioning and learning*. New York: Appleton-Century-Crofts.

Kimmel, H. D. (1973). Reflex "habituability" as a basis for differentiating between classical and instrumental conditioning. *Conditional Reflex, 8*, 10–27.

Kuhn, T. S. (1962). *The structure of scientific revolutions*. Chicago: University of Chicago Press.

Lane, H. (1976). *The wild boy of Aveyron*. Cambridge, Mass.: Harvard University Press.

Pavlov, I. P. (1927). *Conditioned reflexes*. Translated by G. V. Anrep. London: Oxford University Press.

Peckham, G. W., and Peckham, E. G. (1887). Some observations on the mental powers of spiders. *Journal of Morphology, 1*, 383–419.

Razran, G. (1971). *Mind in evolution*. Boston: Houghton Mifflin.

Saltzman, I. J. (1949). Maze learning in the absence of primary reinforcement: A study of secondary reinforcement. *Journal of Comparative and Physiological Psychology, 42*, 161–173.

Skinner, B. F. (1937). Two types of conditioned reflex: A reply to Konorski and Miller. *Journal of General Psychology, 16*, 272–279.

Skinner, B. F. (1938). *The behavior of organisms*. New York: Appleton-Century-Crofts.

Skinner, B. F. (1956). A case history in scientific method. *American Psychologist, 11*, 221–233.

Terrace, H. S. (1966). Stimulus control. In W. H. Honig (Ed.), *Operant behavior: Areas of research and application*. New York: Appleton-Century-Crofts.

Thompson, R. F., and Spencer, W. A. (1966). Habituation: A model phenomenon for the study of neuronal substrates of behavior. *Psychological Review, 73*, 16–43.

Thorndike, E. L. (1898). Animal intelligence: An experimental study of the associative processes in animals. *Psychological Monographs, 2*, No. 8.

Twitmyer, E. B. (1974). A study of the knee jerk. *Journal of Experimental Psychology, 103*, 1047–1066.

Watson, J. B., and Rayner, R. (1920). Conditioned emotional reactions. *Journal of Experimental Psychology, 3*, 1–14.

Wolfe, J. B. (1936). Effectiveness of token-rewards for chimpanzees. *Comparative Psychology Monographs, 13*, No. 60.

CHAPTER THIRTEEN

MEMORY FOR MUSICAL ATTRIBUTES

DANIEL J. LEVITIN

13.1 INTRODUCTION

What is memory? As with many concepts in psychology, people have an intuition about what memory is until they are asked to define it. When we try to define memory, and break it up into its components, this becomes a complicated question. We talk about memorizing phone numbers, remembering a smell, remembering the best route to school. We talk about "knowing" that we're allergic to ragweed or that we had a haircut three weeks ago. Is this knowing a form of memory? A panty hose manufacturer boasts that its new fabric has memory. What do all these forms of memory and knowledge have in common? How do they differ? Psychology departments teach whole courses on memory. It is thus impossible to say much of importance about the topic in just a few introductory paragraphs, but what follows is a brief overview of some of the issues in memory research. Then we will discuss memory for musical events in more detail.

13.2 TYPES OF MEMORY

Psychologists tend to make conceptual distinctions among different types of memory. When we talk about different types of memory, an immediate question that comes to mind is whether these different types are conceptual conveniences, or whether they have an underlying neural basis. There is strong neurological evidence that particular memory systems are indeed localized in separate parts of the brain. The hippocampus and prefrontal cortex, for example, are known to play a role in the encoding and storage of particular forms of memory. However, the computational environment of the brain is massively parallel and widely distributed. It is likely that a number of processes related to memory are located throughout the brain. Further, some of the conceptual labels for memory systems, such as "procedural memory," actually encompass somewhat independent processes that are conveniently categorized together (for pedagogical reasons), but do not necessarily activate a single distinct brain structure. A more detailed discussion of the relation between brain and memory can be found in the book by Larry Squire (1987).

One kind of memory is the immediate sensory memory we experience as image persistence. For example, if you look outside the window on a bright day and then close your eyes, an afterimage stays on your retina for a few moments. This has been called *iconic memory* by Ulric Neisser (1967). We talk about the auditory equivalent of this as *echoic memory:* for a few moments after hearing a sound (such as a friend's voice) we are usually able to "hear" a trace of that sound in our mind's ear. Richard Atkinson and Richard Shiffrin (1968) referred to these immediate sensory memories as being held in a *sensory buffer.*

When you are holding a thought inside your head — such as what you are about to say next in a conversation, or as you're doing some mental arithmetic — it stands to reason that this requires some type of short-term, or immediate, memory. This kind of memory, the contents of your present consciousness and awareness, has been called "working memory" by Alan Baddelley (1990), and is similar to what Atkinson and Shiffrin called short-term memory.

Long-term memory is the kind of memory that most of us think of as memory — the ability to remember things that happened some time ago, or that we learned some time ago (usually more than a few minutes ago, and up to a life-time ago). For example, you might have stored in long-term memory images from your high school graduation, the sound of a locomotive, the capital of Colorado, or the definition of the word "protractor." (Actually, in the latter case, you might not be able to retrieve a definition of a protractor, but rather a visual image of what one looks like; this is also a form of long-term memory.) One of the important features of long-term memory is its durability. That is, we tend to think of long-term memories as staying with us for perhaps an indefinite period of time. We may not always be able to access them when we want (e.g., when you have somebody's name on the tip of your tongue but can't quite retrieve it), but we have the sense that the memories are "in there." This is in contrast to short-term memories, which decay rapidly without rehearsal, and are not durable unless they somehow are transferred to long-term memory. The sensory memory/short-term memory/long-term memory distinction appears to have validity at the neural level.

Psychologists also talk about different types of long-term memory, but it is not clear that these reflect different neural systems. Rather, they are different kinds of knowledge stored in long-term memory. It can be useful to make these distinctions for conceptual purposes. The psychologist Endel Tulving (1985) makes a distinction between episodic and semantic memory. There is something different between remembering your eighth birthday and remembering the capital of Colorado. Your eighth birthday is an episode that you can remember, one that occupied a specific time and place. There was also a time and place when you first learned the capitol of Colorado, but if you're like most people, you can't remember when you learned it, only the fact itself. Similarly, we remember what words mean, but usually not when and where the learning occurred. This is called *semantic memory.* Remembering how to ride a bicycle or tie your shoe is an example of another type of memory called *procedural memory.*

It is also important to make a distinction between *memory storage* (or encoding) and *memory retrieval.* One of the tricky parts about designing memory experiments is distinguishing between these operations. That is, if a subject cannot recall something, we need to distinguish between an encoding failure and a retrieval failure. Sometimes using different retrieval cues can bring up memories that seemed previously unreachable. Current memory researchers use a variety of different methods to study remembering, forgetting, storage, and retrieval processes.

13.3   WORKING MEMORY CAPACITY

George Miller (1956) pointed out that working memory has a limited capacity. The number of pieces of information we can juggle in short-term memory at any one time is between 5 and 9, or what he called "7 ± 2." As a demonstration, try to keep the following series of digits active in memory:

015514804707619

Most people can't keep this many (15) going at once. It is indeed a bit like juggling. But try again, by looking at the numbers when they are rearranged from right to left, as below:

916707408415510

If you're from California, you'll notice that these are the telephone area codes for the northern part of the state. If these are familiar to you, they become grouped — or "chunked," to use Miller's word — and voilà! — suddenly there are only five pieces of information to remember and it is possible to keep them active in working memory. As another example, consider the following string of fifteen letters:

FBICIAUSAATTIBM

If you are able to chunk this into the familiar three-letter abbreviations, the problem is reduced to keeping five chunks in memory, something most people can do easily.

What does chunking have to do with music? People who study ear-training and learn how to transcribe music are probably chunking information. For example, in a typical ear-training assignment, the instructor might play a recording of a four-piece combo: piano, bass, drums, and voice. The student's task is to write down, in real time, the chord changes, bass line, and melody. If you have never done this before, it seems impossible. But with chunking, the problem becomes more tractable. Although the chords on the piano each consist of three, four, five, or more notes, we tend to hear the chord as a chord, not as individual notes. Beyond this, musicians tend to hear not individual chords but chord progressions, or fragments of progressions, such as ii-V-I or I-vi-ii-V. This is analogous to seeing FBI as a chunk and not three individual letters. The chord changes can be parsed this way, and if the listener misses something, the part that is there provides constraints the listener can use to make an educated guess about the part that is missing. You can see the role of contextual constraints in reading. It is not hard to guess what the words below are, even though each is missing a letter:

basso_n cof_ee

13.4   REMEMBERING AND FORGETTING DETAILS

A common intuition is that the sole function of memory is to preserve the details of different experiences we've had. But there is a large body of research showing that our memory for details is actually pretty poor. Raymond Nickerson and Marilyn Adams (1979) showed people pictures of different pennies (figure 13.1). Americans see pennies every day, but people in the study could not reliably pick out the accurate picture. Similarly, people tend not to have a very good memory for the exact words of a conversation, but instead remember the "gist" of the conversation. What is the function of memory, then, if not to remember events accurately?

If you think about it, you can see that if we stored and retrieved every detail we encountered every day, we would soon become overloaded with millions of details. When children are first learning language, for example, it is important that they learn to generalize from

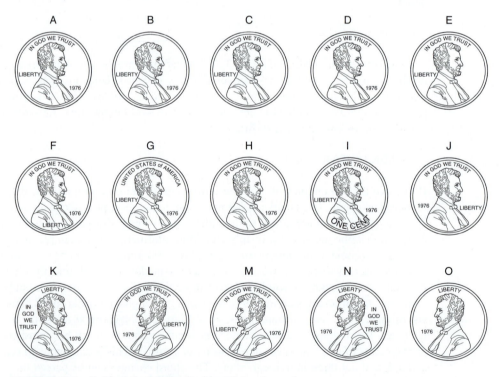

FIGURE 13.1   Subjects had difficulty identifying the real penny.

(Reprinted with permission from Nickerson and Adams, 1979.)

specific experiences. When a child learns the concept (and the word) "car" as his/her mother points to a car in the street, the child has to somehow disregard the differences among the different cars (the perceptual details) and extract what is common among them. A child who fails to do this, fails to learn the concept of car properly, or to use language properly. That is, the word "car" doesn't apply just to the 1981 Red Honda Accord the child first saw; it applies to objects that share certain properties. This doesn't necessarily mean the perceptual details are lost: the child may maintain a vivid image of the exact car; but the conceptual system of the brain, along with the memory system, by necessity must integrate details into generalizations. In fact, there is a great deal of evidence that memory does preserve both the details and the "gist" of experiences, and we are usually able to access information at the appropriate level.

13.5   MEMORY FOR MUSIC

Objects in the visual world have six perceptual attributes: size, color, location, orientation, luminance, and shape. What do we mean by "object"? This definition has been the subject of heated argument among theorists for many years. I propose that an object is something that maintains its identity across changes (or transformations) in these attributes. In other words, as we move an object through space, it is still the same object. If you were to change the color of your car, it will still be your car. Shape is a tricky attribute, because shape distortions can sometimes, but not always, alter an object's identity. For example, as was shown by William Labov (1973), a cup becomes a bowl if the ratio of its diameter to its height becomes too distorted.

A performance of music contains the following seven perceptual attributes: pitch, rhythm, tempo, contour, timbre, loudness, and spatial location (one might add reverberant environment as an eighth). Technically speaking, pitch and loudness are psychological constructs that relate to the physical properties of frequency and amplitude. The term *contour* refers to the shape of a melody when musical interval size is ignored, and only the pattern of "up" and "down" motion is considered. Each one of these eight attributes can be changed without changing the others. With the exception of contour, and sometimes rhythm, the recognizability of the melody is maintained when each of these attributes is changed. In fact, for many melodies, even the rhythm can be changed to some degree and the melody will still be recognizable (White, 1960).

To elaborate further, a melody is an auditory object that maintains its identity under certain transformations, just as a chair maintains its identity under certain transformations, such as being moved to the other side of the room or being turned upside down. A melody can generally retain its identity with transformations along the six dimensions of pitch, tempo, timbre, loudness, spatial location, and reverberant environment; sometimes with changes in rhythm; but rarely with changes in contour. So, for example, if you hear a song played louder than you're accustomed to, you can still identify it. If you hear it at a different tempo, played on a different instrument, or coming from a different location in space, it is still the same melody. Of course, extreme changes in any of these dimensions will render the song unrecognizable; a tempo of one beat per day, or a loudness of 200 dB SPL might stretch the limits of identification.

A specific case of transformation invariance for melodies concerns pitch. The identity of a melody is independent of the actual pitches of the tones played. A melody is defined by the pattern of tones, or the relation of pitches to each other. Thus, when we transpose a melody, it is still recognizable as the same melody. In fact, many melodies do not have a "correct" pitch, they just float freely in pitch space, starting anywhere one wants them to. "Happy Birthday" is an example of this. Now, you might object to all this and say that Beethoven's String Quartet in F Major ought to be played in F major, and that it loses something when it is transposed. The timbre of the stringed instruments changes with range, and if the piece is played in C major, the overall spectrum of the piece sounds different to the careful listener. But listeners will still recognize the melody because the identity of the melody is independent of pitch.

A number of controlled laboratory experiments have confirmed that people have little trouble recognizing melodies in transposition (Attneave and Olson, 1971; Dowling, 1978, 1982; Idson and Massaro, 1978). Also, at different times and different places, the tuning standard has changed; our present A440 system is arbitrary and was adopted only during the twentieth century. The absolute pitch of the melody's tones is not the most important feature. It is the pattern, or relation of pitches, that is important.

Note the parallel here with our earlier discussion of generalization and abstraction in memory. One of the reasons we are able to recognize melodies is that the memory system has formed an abstract representation of the melody that is pitch-invariant, loudness-invariant, and so on. We take for granted that our memory system is able to perform this important function. Recent evidence suggests that memory retains both the "gist" and the actual details of experience. But what about melodies? Do we retain pitch details, like the absolute pitch information, alongside the abstract representation? This is an interesting question that we will take up in section 13.9, after first reviewing research on memory for contour, lyrics, and failures of musical perception known as *amusias.*

13.6   CONTOUR

Recall that the term *contour* refers to the shape of a melody when musical interval size is ignored, and only the pattern of "up" and "down" motion is considered. At first, the idea of contour being an important attribute of melody seems counterintuitive. Contour is a relatively gross characterization of a song's identity. However, its utility has been shown in laboratory experiments. There is evidence that for melodies we do not know well (such as a melody we have only heard a few times), the contour is remembered better than the actual intervals (Massaro, Kallman, and Kelly, 1980). In contrast, the exact interval patterns of familiar melodies are well remembered, and adults can readily notice contour-preserving alterations of the intervallic pattern (Dowling, 1994). Infants respond to contour before they respond to melody; that is, infants cannot distinguish between a song and a melodic alteration of that song, so long as contour is preserved. Only as the child matures is he/she able to attend to the melodic information. Some animals show a similar inability to distinguish different alterations of a melody when contour is preserved (Hulse and Page, 1988). One explanation of why the contour of a melody might be more readily processed is that it is a more general description of the melody, and it subsumes the interval information. It is only with increasing familiarity, or increasing cognitive abilities, that the intervallic details become perceptually important.

13.7   LYRICS

The memory of ballad singers and tellers of epic poetry has been the focus of a great deal of recent research. On the surface, their memory capacity seems unbelievable for the amount of detail they can readily access. But Wanda Wallace and David Rubin of Duke University have shown that in fact these performers do not need to rely on remembering every detail, because the structures of songs and poems provide multiple constraints for the lyrics (Wallace and Rubin 1988a, 1988b). These constraints are based in part on rhyme, rhythm, alliteration, melodic emphasis, style, and story progression. As an example of lyric constraints, word phrases tend to have a unique stress pattern, such as weak-strong or strong-weak. Similarly, melodic phrases tend to be characterized by strong-weak or weak-strong patterns of accents. Thus, changing a word sequence could alter an entire line's rhythm.

Wallace and Rubin found that from one telling to another, minor alterations in the lyrics occur within these constraints. In a study of eleven singers performing the same ballad on two different occasions, they found that most of the lyric variations conformed to poetic and semantic constraints of the ballad. For example, many lyric changes are to synonyms or other words that do not affect the meaning, rhyme, or rhythm:

(a) "Can't you shovel in a little more coal" becomes
(a′) "Saying shovel in a little more coal"; or
(b) "She cried, 'Bold captain, tell me true' " becomes
(b′) "She cried, 'Brave captain, tell me true.' "

The lyrics and storyline together provide multiple redundant constraints to assist the recall of a passage. For example, even without music, given the first line of the following rock song, the last word of the second line is relatively easy to infer:

"Well, today a friend told me the sorry tale
As he stood there trembling and turning———
He said each day's harder to get on the scale."
(From A. Mann, "Jacob Marley's Chain," 1992)

The correct word to end the second line is "pale." Similarly, if one could recall the entire second line except for the word "pale," semantic constraints leave few alternatives. When one adds the contribution of melodic stress patterns, it becomes apparent that our recall of song lyrics is assisted by a number of constraints.

The experimental data corroborate our intuition that the memory representation for lyrics seems to be tied into the memory representation for melody (Serafine, Crowder, and Repp, 1984). Further evidence of this comes from a case report of a musician who suffered a stroke caused by blockage of the right cerebral artery. After the stroke, he was able to recognize songs played on the piano if they were associated with words (even though the words weren't being presented to him), but he was unable to recognize songs that were purely instrumentals (Steinke, Cuddy, and Jacobson, 1995).

13.8   AMUSIA

Amusia is the name given to a broad class of mental deficits, involving music perception, that usually appear after brain damage. The deficits include a sharp decrement in an individual's ability to grasp musical relationships in the perception of sounds, or in the ability to perform, read, or write music. Most amusiacs are capable of understanding spoken language, presumably because their neurological impairment spared the speech centers of the brain. However, in many cases amusia accompanies various auditory and speech disorders, such as the aphasias (the name given to various impairments in the production or perception of speech).

The degree to which music and speech rely on common neural mechanisms is not clear. A wealth of cases have shown clear dissociations between impairments in music and in speech, although there may also be individual differences in the way that music is handled by brains. Indeed, in many cases, amusia and aphasia co-occur. There are some separate brain structures, and some shared structures for processing music and speech. For example, Tallal, Miller, and Fitch (1993) found that some children who have trouble learning to speak are unable to process the correct temporal order of sounds. Presumably, if this is a low-level deficit (i.e., a deficit in a brain system shared by music and speech systems), it would also affect the ability to process the order of tones in a melody.

Our current knowledge of the brain's functional architecture is growing rapidly, in part due to advances in neuroimaging techniques. PET (positron-emission tomography), fMRI (functional magnetic resonance imaging), and ERP (event-related potentials) are three such techniques that are allowing neuroscientists to better localize specific brain functions (Posner and Levitin, 1997). For example, neuroscientists have demonstrated that there are specific brain anatomies for reading (Posner and Raichle, 1994), listening to music (Sergent, 1993), mentally practicing one's tennis serve (Roland, 1994), calculating numbers (Dehaene, 1998), and imagining a friend's face (Kosslyn, 1994). Lesions to certain parts of the brain render patients unable to recognize faces (known as prosopagnosia — Bruce, 1988; Young and Ellis, 1989), although their perception of other objects seems unimpaired. Other lesions cause an inability to read whole words (a type of alexia), although individual letters can still be made out.

Because music performance and perception involve a number of disparate and specialized skills, amusia includes a wide range of deficits. One patient developed an inability to read music note-by-note, but had an intact ability to read whole musical passages. In another case, a musician lost the ability to play the piano (his second instrument) although his ability to play the violin (his first instrument) remained intact. A pianist suffering from aphasia and alexia was unable to read written music or recognize previously familiar melodies; however, her music production abilities were spared, so that she could sing the melody and lyrics to many songs. Following brain damage, an aphasic composer could no longer understand speech but continued to compose without impairment (Luria, 1970).

A knowledge of some of the details of brain architecture makes clearer how some of these dissociations can occur. For example, reading music depends a great deal on the integration of spatial and form perception, because the identity of a musical note is determined both by its form and by its position on the musical staff. An established fact in neuroscience is that form perception and location perception follow different pathways in the visual system (Zeki, 1993). It is easy to see how musical alexia (an inability to read musical notes) could arise from damage to either of these two visual pathways, since reading music requires perception of both form and position. It is also easy to see that this damage would not necessarily interfere with other musical skills.

A relatively common dissociation is that found between lyric and melodic production. Oscar Marin (1982) reports the case of an aphasic patient who could sing with normal intonation and rhythm, so long as she wasn't required to sing lyrics. Her ability to join lyrics with melodies was totally impaired.

The neurological syndrome called auditory agnosia is a more general and severe perceptual deficit that usually arises from bilateral damage to the temporal lobes, in particular the auditory cortex (Heschl's area). Patients with auditory agnosia are unable to organize the sounds in the environment, so that speech, animal sounds, bells, and other noises are perceived as a jumbled, uninterpretable stream of noise. A few cases of purely musical agnosia have been described in which patients are unable to organize music into a coherent percept, although their ability to understand speech and nonmusical stimuli remains intact. The extent to which they can understand the "music" of normal speech (known as "prosody") has not been studied thoroughly. For example, are they able to distinguish a question from a statement if the only cue is a rising contour at the end of the sentence? These remain questions open for study.

13.9   MEMORY FOR MUSICAL PITCH AND TEMPO

To what extent do our memories of music retain perceptual details of the music, such as the timbre, pitch, and tempo of songs we have heard? Do we remember all the details of the piece, even details that are not theoretically important? Specifically, since melody is defined by the relation of pitches and rhythms, it would be easy to argue that people do not need to retain the actual pitch and tempo information in order to recognize the song. However, the music theorist Eugene Narmour (1977) argued that listening to music requires processing of both absolute information (schematic reduction) and relative information (irreducible idiostructural), so the question is whether both types of information reach long-term memory.

If people do encode the actual pitches of songs, this would be something like having "perfect pitch" or "absolute pitch" (AP). If you play a tone on the piano for most people and ask them which tone you played, they cannot tell you (unless they watched your hand). The person with AP can reliably tell you "that was a C#." Some APers can even do the reverse: if you name a tone, they can produce it without any external reference, either by singing or by adjusting a variable oscillator. Those with AP have memory for the actual pitches in songs, not just the relative pitches. In fact, most APers become agitated when they hear a song in transposition because it sounds wrong to them.

It has been estimated that AP is rare, occurring in only 1 out of 10,000 people. However, AP studies tend to test only musicians. There is an obvious reason for this — if you ask most non-musicians to sing an "E-flat," they will not understand. As a term project when I was a student in the Stanford CCRMA psychoacoustics class, I designed a test to determine whether non-musicians could demonstrate AP capabilities. The first test was to determine if non-musicians had an ability to remember pitches over a long period of time — even if they hadn't learned the fancy labels that musicians use. These subjects were given tuning forks, and they were asked to carry the forks around with them for a week, bang them every so often, and to try to memorize the pitch that the forks put out. After a week the tuning fork was taken away, and a week later the subjects were tested on their memory for the tone. Some of them were asked to sing it, and others had to pick it out from three notes played to them. The distribution of the subjects' productions is shown in figure 13.2. Notice that the modal response was perfect memory for the tone, and those who made errors were usually off by only a small amount.

Perhaps, then, absolute musical pitch is an attribute of sound that is encoded in long-term memory. In spite of all the interference — the daily bombardment by different sounds and noises — the subjects were able to keep the pitch of the tuning fork in their heads with great accuracy. A harder test would be to study non-musicians' memory for pitch when that pitch is embedded in a melody. Because melodies are transposition-invariant, the actual pitch information may be discarded once a melody is learned. On the other hand, if somebody hears a melody many times in the same key, we might expect that repeated playings would strengthen the memory trace for the specific pitches.

To test whether people can reproduce the absolute pitch of tones embedded in melodies, I asked subjects to come into the laboratory and sing their favorite rock 'n' roll song from memory (Levitin, 1994). The premise was that if they had memorized the actual pitches of the songs, they would reproduce them. It would then be easy to compare the tones they sang with the tones on the original compact disc (CD) version. Rock songs are especially suited to this task because people typically hear them in only one version, and they hear this over and over and over again. Contrast this with "Happy Birthday" or the national anthem, which have no objective key standard, and are likely to be sung in a variety of different keys.

The subjects were mostly introductory psychology students (and a few graduate students), they were not specially selected for musical ability or inability, and they didn't know ahead of time that they'd be participating in a music experiment. After they selected a song, they were asked to imagine that it was playing in their heads, and to sing or hum along with it when they were ready.

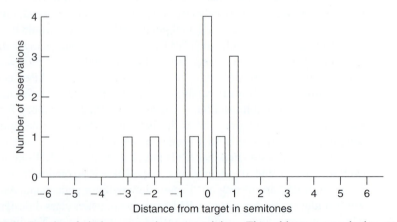

FIGURE 13.2   Results of pitch memory in non-musicians. The subjects were asked to retain the pitch of a tuning fork in memory for one week.

The subjects could sing as much or as little of the song as they wanted, and they could start wherever they wanted. The first five tones they sang were analyzed, then compared with the five corresponding tones on the CD. There was no difference in accuracy among the five tones or the average of the five tones. Octave errors were ignored (as is customary in absolute pitch research), and how many semitones they were away from the correct tone on the CD was recorded. Thus, the subjects could deviate from the correct pitch by six semitones in either direction.

Figure 13.3 is a plot of the distribution of the subjects' errors. If subjects were no good at this task, their errors would be uniformly distributed among the error categories. In fact, as the top portion of the figure shows, the modal response was to sing the correct pitch. Notice also that the errors cluster around the correct pitch in a mound-shaped distribution. In fact, 67 percent of the subjects came within two semitones of the correct pitch. The subjects sang a second song, and the findings were essentially the same (lower portion of the figure). Subjects were also consistent across trials, that is, if they were correct on the first song, they were likely to be correct on the second song. From these data, it appears that these nonmusical subjects have something much like absolute pitch. Instead of asking them to "sing a C# or a G," we can ask them to "sing 'Hotel California' or 'Papa Don't Preach,'" and they produce the correct tone. Whether or not they've learned the specialized vocabulary

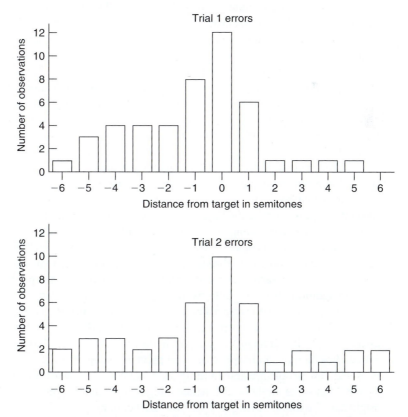

FIGURE 13.3   Results of pitch memory for the first tone of rock songs. (Upper) Trial 1; (Lower) Trial 2.

of the musician seems less important than the fact that they have learned to associate a consistent label with a specific tone. This finding has been replicated several times as of this writing (Ashley, 1997; Levitin, 1996; Wong, 1996).

A number of people have wondered if these results might be the product of something other than long-term memory for pitch. If people sing along with their favorite songs, the argument goes, they may have merely developed a "muscle sense" or "kinesthetic sense" from singing the song, and their knowledge of the proper vocal cord tension is driving the results. However, "muscle memory" is a form of long-term memory. All this argument does is specify the subsidiary mechanism in long-term memory that is at work. In addition, it turns out that muscle memory is not very good. W. Dixon Ward and Ed Burns (1978) asked vocalists to sing pitches from memory while being denied auditory feedback (loud white noise in headphones was used to mask the sound of their own voice). The singers were forced to rely solely on muscle memory to produce the requested tones. Their results showed errors as great as a major third, indicating that muscle memory alone cannot account for the precision of performance of the subjects in the sing-your-favorite-rock-song study.

These data support the idea that long-term memory encodes the absolute pitch of songs, even with a group of subjects in whom AP was not thought to exist. This finding also extends Narmour's theory about the two components required for musical perception, showing that both absolute and relative information are retained in long-term memory. A form of *latent* or *residue* absolute pitch is also implied by Fred Lerdahl and Ray Jackendoff's *strong reduction hypothesis* (1983).

Can a song's tempo be accurately encoded as well? The data collected for the pitch study were reanalyzed to test memory for tempo (Levitin and Cook, 1996). The subjects weren't explicitly instructed to reproduce tempo during the experimental session, so to the extent that they did, they did so on their own. Tempo would not necessarily have to be explicitly represented in memory, because a melody's identity does not depend on its being heard at exactly the same tempo every time. Because pitch and tempo are separable dimensions (Kubovy, 1981), it is possible that one would be preserved in memory and the other would not.

Some interesting properties of song memory are related to the idea of separable dimensions. When we imagine a song in our heads, most of us can easily imagine it in different keys without changing the speed of the song. This is not how a tape recorder works: if you speed up the tape to raise the key, you automatically speed up the tempo as well. Similarly, we can mentally scan a song at various rates without altering the pitch. If you are asked to determine as quickly as possible whether the word "at" appears in "The Star Spangled Banner," you will probably scan through the lyrics at a rate faster than you normally sing them. This does not necessarily raise your mental representation of the pitch.

In addition, different sections of songs seem to carry "flags" or "markers" that serve as starting points. If you were asked to sing the third verse of "The Twelve Days of Christmas," you might start right on the line: "On the third day of Christmas, my true love gave to me [. . .]" without having to start from the very beginning. Markers in songs are to some extent idiosyncratic, and depend on what parts of a song are salient, and how well you know the song. Few people are able to jump immediately to the word "at" in "The Star Spangled Banner," but some might be able to start singing it from the phrase "whose broad stripes and bright stars" without having to start from the beginning.

With respect to the other attributes of songs, most people can imagine a song being played loud or soft, being heard in their left ear or right ear or both, being performed inside or outside a large church, and the main melody being carried by various instruments. Most of these things can be imagined even if they have never been experienced before, just as we can imagine a polka-dot elephant, although it's unlikely we've ever seen one.

It is striking to listen to the tapes of non-musical subjects singing, superimposed on the corresponding passage from the CD. They are only singing along with their memory, but it appears that they hear the recording in their head. Enormous amounts of detail appear to be remembered — the subjects reproduce vocal affectations and stylistic nuances, so that it's hard to imagine they could perform any better if they were singing along with the CD.

It wasn't immediately obvious that people would encode tempo with great accuracy, but the data shown in figure 13.4 suggest that they do. As shown in that plot of subject-produced versus actual tempo, 72 percent of the subject's productions were within 8 percent of the correct tempo. How close is 8 percent? Carolyn Drake and Marie-Claire Botte (1993) found that the perceptual threshold for changes in tempo (the just-noticeable difference, or JND) was 6.2–8.8 percent. Thus it appears that people encode tempo information in memory with a high degree of precision.

We have seen that music has a number of different attributes, and that some of these attributes appear to be stored in memory in two forms: a relative encoding of relations and an absolute encoding of sensory features. The precision with which other attributes of musical performances, such as timbre and loudness, are encoded in memory, is the topic of experiments currently under way.

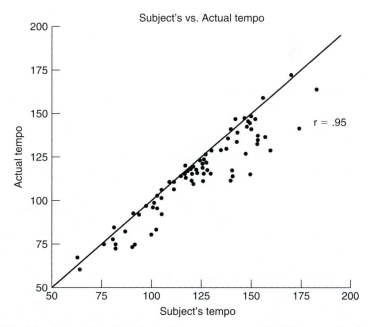

FIGURE 13.4 Bivariate scatter plot of actual tempo versus produced tempo of rock songs.

13.10 SUMMARY

The modern view is that memory is distributed throughout various parts of the brain, and that different types of memory engage separate neural structures. Memory for music, just like memory for prose or pictures, probably comprises different cognitive subsystems to encode the various aspects of music. There is a growing consensus that memory serves a dual function: it abstracts general rules from specific experiences, and it preserves to a great degree some of the details of those specific experiences.

ACKNOWLEDGMENTS

This chapter benefited greatly from comments by Michael C. Anderson, Gregg DiGirolamo, Gina Gerardi, Lewis R. Goldberg, and Douglas L. Hintzman. I received direct support from a graduate research fellowship from ONR (N-00014-89-J-3186), and indirect support both from CCRMA and from an ONR Grant to M. I. Posner (N-00014-89-3013).

REFERENCES

Ashley, C. (1997). "Does Pitch Memory Change with Age?" Paper presented at Illinois Junior Academy of Science meeting University of Illinois at Urbana.

Atkinson, R. C., and Shiffrin, R. M. (1968). "Human Memory: A Proposed System and Its Control Processes." In K. W. Spence and J. T. Spence, eds., *The Psychology of Learning and Motivation,* vol. 2, 89–105. New York: Academic Press.

Attneave, F., and Olson, R. K. (1971). "Pitch as a Medium: A New Approach to Psychophysical Scaling." *American Journal of Psychology,* 84, 147–166.

Baddeley, A. (1990). *Human Memory: Theory and Practice.* Boston: Allyn & Bacon.

Bruce, V. (1988). *Recognizing Faces.* Hillsdale, N.J.: Lawrence Erlbaum.

Dehaene, S. (1996). "The Organization of Brain Activations in Number Comparisons: Event Related Potentials and the Additive-Factors Method." *Journal of Cognitive Neuroscience,* 8 (1), 47–68.

Dowling, W. J. (1978). "Scale and Contour: Two Components of a Theory of Memory for Melodies." *Psychological Review,* 85 (4): 341–354.

———. (1982). "Melodic Information Processing and Its Development." In D. Deutsch, ed., *The Psychology of Music.* New York: Academic Press.

———. (1994). "Melodic Contour in Hearing and Remembering Melodies." In R. Aiello and J. A. Sloboda, eds., *Musical Perceptions,* 173–190. New York: Oxford University Press.

Drake, C., and Botte, M.-C. (1993). "Tempo Sensitivity in Auditory Sequences: Evidence for a Multiple-Look Model." *Perception & Psychophysics,* 54 (3): 277–286.

Hulse, S. H., and Page, S. C. (1988). "Toward a Comparative Psychology of Music Perception." *Music Perception,* 5 (4): 427–452.

Huxley, P. (1987). "Double Our Numbers." On the Columbia Records album *Sunny Nights.*

Idson, W. L., and Massaro, D. W. (1978). "A Bidimensional Model of Pitch in the Recognition of Melodies." *Perception and Psychophysics,* 246, 551–565.

Ivry, R. B., and Hazeltine, R. E. (1995). "The Perception and Production of Temporal Intervals Across a Range of Durations: Evidence for a Common Timing Mechanism." *Journal of Experimental Psychology: Human Perception and Performance,* 21 (1): 3–18.

Janata, P. (1995). "ERP Measures Assay the Degree of Expectancy Violation of Harmonic Contexts in Music." *Journal of Cognitive Neuroscience,* 7 (2): 153–164.

Kosslyn, S. (1994). *Image and Brain.* Cambridge, Mass.: MIT Press.

Kubovy, M. (1981). "Integral and Separable Dimensions and the Theory of Indispensable Attributes." In M. Kubovy and J. Pomerantz, eds., *Perceptual Organization.* Hillsdale, N.J.: Lawrence Erlbaum.

Lerdahl, F., and Jackendoff, R. (1983). *A Generative Theory of Tonal Music.* Cambridge, Mass.: MIT Press.

Levitin, D. J. (1994). "Absolute Memory for Musical Pitch: Evidence from the Production of Learned Melodies." *Perception & Psychophysics,* 56 (4): 414–423.

————. (1996). "Mechanisms of Memory for Musical Attributes." Doctoral dissertation, University of Oregon, Eugene, OR. Dissertation Abstracts International, 57(07B), 4755. (University Microfilms No. AAG9638097).

Levitin, D. J., and Cook, P. R. (1996). "Memory for Musical Tempo: Additional Evidence That Auditory Memory Is Absolute." *Perception & Psychophysics,* 58 (6): 927–935.

Loftus, E. (1979). *Eyewitness Testimony.* Cambridge, Mass.: Harvard University Press.

Luria, A. R., Tsvetkova, L. S., and Futer, D. S. (1965). "Aphasia in a Composer." *Journal of Neurological Science,* 2, 288–292.

Mann, A. (1992). "Jacob Marley's Chain," on the Imago Records album *Whatever.*

Marin, O. S. M. (1982). "Neurological Aspects of Music Perception and Performance." In D. Deutsch, ed., *The Psychology of Music.* New York: Academic Press.

Massaro, D. W., Kallman, H. J., and Kelly, J. L. (1980). "The Role of Tone Height, Melodic Contour, and Tone Chroma in Melody Recognition." *Journal of Experimental Psychology: Human Learning and Memory,* 6 (1): 77–90.

Miller, G. A. (1956). "The Magical Number Seven Plus or Minus Two: Some Limits on Our Capacity for Processing Information." *Psychological Review,* 63, 81–97.

Narmour, E. (1977). *Beyond Schenkerism: The Need for Alternatives in Music Analysis.* Chicago: University of Chicago Press.

Neisser, U. (1967). *Cognitive Psychology.* Englewood Cliffs, N.J.: Prentice-Hall.

Nickerson, R. S., and Adams, M. J. (1979). "Long-Term Memory for a Common Object." *Cognitive Psychology,* 11, 287–307.

Pavlov, I. P. (1927). *Conditioned Reflexes: An Investigation of the Physiological Activity of the Cerebral Cortex.* London: Oxford University Press.

Posner, M. I., and Levitin, D. J. (1997). "Imaging the Future." In R. L. Solso. ed., *Mind and Brain Sciences in the 21st Century,* 91–109. Cambridge, Mass.: MIT Press.

Posner, M. I., and Raichle, M. E. (1994). *Images of Mind.* New York: Scientific American Library.

Roland, P. (1994). *Brain Activation.* New York: Wiley-Liss.

Schacter, D. (1987). "Implicit Memory: History and Current Status." *Journal of Experimental Psychology: Learning, Memory, & Cognition,* 13 (3): 501–518.

Serafine, M. L., Crowder, R. G., and Repp, B. (1984). "Integration of Melody and Text in Memory for Songs." *Cognition,* 16, 285–303.

Sergent, J. (1993). "Mapping the Musician Brain." *Human Brain Mapping,* 1, 20–38.

Squire, L. R. (1987). *Memory and Brain.* New York: Oxford University Press.

Steinke, W. R., Cuddy, L. L., and Jacobson, L. S. (1995). "Evidence for Melodic Processing and Recognition Without Perception of Tonality in an Amusic Subject." Paper presented at Society for Music Perception and Cognition Conference, Berkeley, Calif.

Tallal, P., S. Miller, and Fitch, R. H. (1993). "Neurobiological Basis of Speech: A Case for the Preeminence of Temporal Processing." In P. Tallal, A. M. Galaburda, R. Llinas, and C. von Euler, eds., *Temporal Information Processing in the Nervous System: Special Reference to Dyslexia and Dysphasia,* 27–47. New York: New York Academy of Sciences.

Tulving, E. 1985. "How Many Memory Systems Are There?" *American Psychologist,* 40, 385–398.

Wallace, W. T., and Rubin, D. C. (1988a). "Memory of a Ballad Singer." In M. M. Gruneberg, P. E. Morris, and R. N. Sykes, eds., *Practical Aspects of Memory: Current Research and Issues,* vol. 1, *Memory in Everyday Life.* Chichester, U.K.: Wiley.

Wallace, W. T., and Rubin, D. C. (1988b). "'The Wreck of the Old 97': A Real Event Remembered in Song." In U. Neisser and E. Winograd, eds., *Remembering Reconsidered: Ecological and Traditional Approaches to the Study of Memory.* New York: Cambridge University Press.

Ward, W. D., and Burns, E. M. (1978). "Singing without Auditory Feedback." *Journal of Research in Singing and Applied Vocal Pedagogy,* 1, 24–44.

White, B. W. (1960). "Recognition of Distorted Melodies." *American Journal of Psychology, 73,* 100–107.

Wong, S. (1996). "Memory for Musical Pitch in Speakers of a Tonal Language." Undergraduate honors thesis, University of Oregon, Eugene.

Young, A. W., and Ellis, H. D. (1989). *Handbook of Research on Face Processing.* Amsterdam: North Holland.

Zeki, S. (1993). *A Vision of the Brain.* Oxford: Blackwell.

CHAPTER FOURTEEN

MEMORY

R. KIM GUENTHER

Donald Thompson, a noted expert on memory and a frequent expert witness in legal cases involving eyewitness memories, became a suspect in a case himself when he was found to match a rape victim's description of her rapist. Luckily, Thompson had an airtight alibi — he had been doing an interview on live television, where he was discussing how people can improve their memory for faces. He was cleared when it became apparent that the victim had been watching Thompson on television just prior to the rape and so had confused him with her memory of the actual rapist (this case is described in Schacter, 1996). Indeed, a number of cases have been reported in which eyewitnesses to crimes provided erroneous identifications of perpetrators after they encountered the accused outside the context of the crime (Read, Tollestrup, Hammersley, McFadzen, & Christensen, 1990; Ross, Ceci, Dunning, & Toglia, 1994). Why do people make such mistakes? What accounts for the fallibility of human memory?

In this chapter I will provide an overview of what cognitive psychologists have learned about memory, including how we learn new information, how we recollect previous experiences, and why we sometimes forget important information. I will focus on *explicit memory,* sometimes called *episodic memory,* which is our conscious recollection of personal experiences. In other chapters I will discuss the unconscious influence of past experiences on current thought and behavior and the physiological basis for memory and forgetting.

14.1 PERSPECTIVES ON MEMORY

14.1.1 Record-Keeping versus Constructionist Accounts of Memory

I will begin the discussion with the question: What is the principle function of human memory? One possible answer is that memory functions to preserve the past — that it is designed to retain records of previous experiences. Such a perspective has lead to an approach to memory I will label the *record-keeping* approach.

The essential idea of any record-keeping theory is that memory acts as a kind of storage bin in which records of experiences are placed, much as books might be placed in a library. The record keeping theory is really a family of theories that have in common the following principles: (1) Each experience adds a new record of the experience to the storage bin; consequently the number of records expands over time. Similarly, the number of books stored in a library increases over time. The records actually stored may be more accurately described as interpretations of experiences. (2) Remembering involves searching through a network of memory locations for some particular record, as one might search for a particular book in a library. Once found, the target memory record is "read" or in some sense reexperienced. The search need not be done haphazardly, since the memory records may be connected or organized in such a way as to improve the efficiency of the search. Libraries, for example, organize books by subject matter in order to make finding the books easier. (3) Forgetting is primarily due to search failure caused by the interfering effect of the presence of lots of memory records, just as in a library the huge number of books stored there makes finding any one book difficult. Some versions of the record-keeping theory claim that no memory record is ever really lost. All records of past experiences are potentially recoverable.

The metaphor of record keeping is compelling for several reasons. The word *memory* implies a preserving of the past; we sometimes have vivid and accurate recollections of the past, and nearly all of the artificial memory systems we know about, such as libraries, videotapes, and computers, are record-keeping systems designed to preserve information. Indeed, it is difficult to imagine any other basis for memory. Nevertheless, I will argue in this and other chapters that the record-keeping approach to human memory is a misleading one (Schacter, 1996). Human memory works according to a different set of principles.

An alternative to the record-keeping approach may be called a *constructionist* approach to memory. We know that knowledge from sources outside of the stimulus stream affects the perception of the stimulus. A similar notion plays a role in a constructionist account of memory.

The constructionist account begins with the important insight that human memory is not designed primarily to preserve the past, but to anticipate the future (Morris, 1988). Most constructionist theories are characterized by these principles: (1) Each new experience causes changes in the various cognitive systems that perceive, interpret, respond emotionally, and act on the environment, but no record-by-record account of the experiences that gave rise to those changes is stored anywhere. That is, memory reflects how the cognitive systems have adapted to the environment. Usually this adaptation takes the form of noting regularities in experiences and basing future responses on these regularities. The cognitive systems are also sensitive to unexpected exceptions to the regularities ordinarily observed. (2) Recollection of the past involves a reconstruction of past experiences based on information in the current environment and on the way cognitive processing is currently accomplished. Remembering is a process more akin to fantasizing or planning for the future than searching for and then "reading" memory records, or in any sense reexperiencing the past. The past does not force itself on a passive individual; instead, the individual actively creates some plausible account of her or his past. (3) Forgetting is not due to the presence of other memory records but to the continuous adaptive changes made to the various cognitive systems in response to events.

Let me distinguish between the record-keeping and constructionist approaches with a simple example. Suppose an individual — let's call him Jim — witnessed a robbery in a convenience store. Let's say that the burglar was wearing a black sweatshirt and black jeans, stole money from the cash register, and stole a radio that was lying on the counter. Suppose that after the burglar fled, Jim heard a customer claim that the burglar stole a camera. Later on, when questioned by the police and when testifying in a court of law, Jim must try to recollect as accurately as possible the details of the crime. For example, Jim might be asked: "What was the burglar wearing?" or "What did the burglar steal?"

Any record-keeping theory claims that witnessing the crime caused Jim to store a new record (or records) in his memory system. When later asked to recollect the crime, Jim must first search through his memory records until he finds the record representing the crime, and then try to "read" its contents. If Jim correctly answers questions about the crime, it is because he was able to locate the relevant memory record. If Jim forgets, it is because the presence of so many other memory records made it difficult for him to find the appropriate memory record or because he was unable to access all the details stored in the record.

According to constructionist theories, no record-by-record account of past events is maintained in a storage system. Instead, the cognitive systems for interpreting and acting on experiences change as a function of the event. For example, as a result of the crime experience, Jim might learn to avoid convenience stores and to distrust men who wear black clothes. Jim's cognitive systems function to anticipate possible future events. When Jim is asked questions about the crime, he has no memory records to "read." Instead, he uses the knowledge currently available in his cognitive systems to derive a plausible rendition of the past event. For example, he may use his newly acquired distrust of men in black clothes to deduce that the burglar must have worn black clothes. If Jim forgets, it is because his reconstruction of the past event was inaccurate. For example, he may remember something about a camera, and so reconstruct that he saw the burglar steal a camera when, in fact, the burglar stole a radio.

The main organizing theme of this chapter, then, is the contrast between record-keeping and constructionist accounts of memory. A number of cognitive scientists have noted that this contrast is fundamental to understanding approaches to memory (e.g., Neisser, 1967; Bransford, McCarrell, Franks, & Nitsch, 1977; Rosenfield, 1988; Howes, 1990). Still, probably no contemporary theory of memory entirely embodies the record-keeping theory. Even contemporary theories that may be characterized as predominantly record-keeping also make use of constructionist principles (see Bahrick, 1984; or Hall, 1990). For example, a theory based primarily on record-keeping may claim that people resort to reconstructing the past when they fail to find a relevant memory record. So the record-keeping theory discussed in this chapter serves mainly as a basis of contrast to help make clear how memory does not work. Examples of contemporary theories that primarily (but not exclusively) embody record-keeping principles can be found in Anderson (1983), Anderson and Milson (1989), Atkinson and Shiffrin (1968), Penfield (1969), and Raaijmakers and Shiffrin (1981). Approaches to memory that may be characterized as predominantly constructionist can be found in Bartlett (1932), Bransford et al. (1977), Loftus (1980, 1982), Neisser (1967, 1984), and Schacter (1996). Constructionist approaches to memory are also implicit in neural net (also known as connectionist or parallel distributed processing) models of memory (e.g., Rumelhart, Hinton & Williams, 1986; Grossberg & Stone, 1986; see Collins & Hay, 1994, for a summary). Raaijmakers and Shiffrin (1992) provide a technical description of various contemporary memory models, while Bolles (1988) provides a nontechnical overview of a constructionist approach to memory written by someone outside the field.

14.1.2   Historical Support for Record-Keeping Theories of Memory

Although I will champion the constructionist theory in this chapter, historically it has been record-keeping metaphors that have dominated thinking about memory (Roediger, 1980). The ancient Greek philosopher Plato, in the Theaetetus dialogue, likened memory to a wax tablet on which experiences leave an impression and likened the process of recollection to trying to capture birds in an aviary. We may not always be able to capture the one we seek. Saint Augustine (A.D. 354–430), an important Christian theologian, and John Locke (1631–1704), a British empiricist famous for his claim that there are no innate ideas, both characterized memory as a storehouse containing records of the past. More recently, cognitive psychologists have used libraries (e.g., Broad-bent, 1971), keysort cards (e.g., Brown & McNeill, 1966), tape recorders (e.g., Posner & Warren, 1972), stores (e.g., Atkinson & Shiffrin, 1968), and file systems (e.g., Anderson & Milson, 1989) as metaphors for memory.

The modern era of memory research is usually said to have begun with the publication of Hermann Ebbinghaus's *Uber das Gedachtnis* (*On Memory*) in 1885 (Ebbinghaus, 1885; Hoffman, Bringmann, Bamberg, & Klein, 1986). Ebbinghaus presented himself lists of arbitrarily ordered words or syllables (but not nonsense syllables, as is often claimed) and counted the number of recitations it took him to recall the list perfectly. In some experiments he later attempted to relearn those lists; the reduction in the number of trials to learn the list the second time constituted another, more indirect, measure of memory.

From years of doing these experiments, Ebbinghaus established several important principles of memory. One principle, sometimes known as the Ebbinghaus forgetting curve, is that most forgetting takes place within the first few hours and days of learning (see figure 14.1). After a few days, the rate at which information is lost from memory is very slow and gradual. He also showed that as the number of syllables on a list increased, the number of trials to learn the list increased exponentially. A list of 36 items took him 50 times the number of repetitions to learn as a list of 7 items. Ebbinghaus did not just study arbitrarily

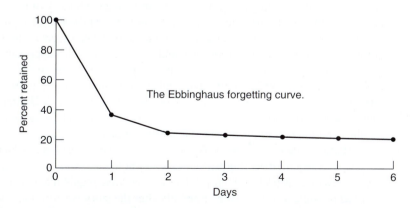

FIGURE 14.1   The Ebbinghaus forgetting curve.

ordered lists; he also tried to memorize more meaningful information, specifically various sections of the poem *Don Juan*. He found that he needed only one tenth as many recitations to memorize the poem as he needed to memorize the equivalent number of arbitrarily ordered syllables. Meaningful information is easier to memorize.

Ebbinghaus did not spend much time on developing theories about the nature of memory. His primary concern was to demonstrate that human memory is an orderly and measurable phenomenon that can be described with the same precision as biological phenomena. Still, Ebbinghaus's main legacy is his emphasis on memorization of lists of stimuli. Such an emphasis suggests that memory's most important function is to preserve detailed records of past events. Psychologists continue to use experimental methodologies that require subjects to memorize lists of stimuli, such as unrelated words or sentences. Sometimes psychologists make use of Ebbinghaus's relearning paradigm to test memory; more commonly, researchers use *free recall* tests (e.g., "Write down all the words on the lists"), *cued recall* tests (e.g., "What word was paired with *duck* on the list?"), or *recognition* tests (e.g., "Did the word *duck* appear on the list?").

Another development that encouraged the use of record-keeping theories of memory was the invention of the digital computer. Many memory theorists, especially those enamored of the information processing approach to human cognition, have perceived an analogy between how a computer stores information and human memory (e.g., Anderson, 1976, 1983; Winnograd, 1976). Computers store each piece of information by placing records of that information into separate locations, each of which has an address. The memory system in a computer is distinct from the central processing unit (CPU) that actually carries out the manipulation of information. Computers retrieve information either by scanning through the set of locations until the information is found or by going to the address of the memory location and accessing what is stored there. To some theorists, the computer's memory system seems a better metaphor for memory than do passive systems, like libraries. The programs that instruct computers can manipulate and transform stored information, just as we seem to do when we answer questions about and draw inferences from past experiences.

14.1.3   Historical Support for Constructionist Theories of Memory

Although record-keeping metaphors have dominated the history of memory research, there has been a constructionist countertradition. As Brewer (1984) noted, a constructionist conception of memory was the prevalent continental European view in the 1800s (Ebbinghaus notwithstanding). Sigmund Freud also held to a constructionist approach, writing frequently of how people falsify and remodel their past experiences in the course of trying to recollect them (Freud, 1900/1953; see Erdelyi, 1990). The constructionist approach to memory was introduced to Anglo-American psychology by Frederic Charles Bartlett in his 1932 book *Remembering*. Bartlett was also one of the first to establish a research program investigating the experimental implications of constructionism.

Bartlett's ideas about memory are illustrated in his most famous memory experiments, in which he presented his English subjects an English translation of a Native American folk story called "The War of the Ghosts." The subjects were required to recall the story in as much detail as possible at various time intervals after the story was originally presented to them. The story and one subject's recollection of it are presented in figure 14.2.

The War of the Ghosts

One night two young men from Egulac went down to the river to hunt seals, and while they were there it became foggy and calm. Then they heard warcries, and they thought: "Maybe this is a war party." They escaped to the shore, and hid behind a log. Now canoes came up, and they heard the noise of paddles, and saw one canoe coming up to them. There were five men in the canoe, and they said:

"What do you think? We wish to take you along. We are going up the river to make war on the people."

One of the young men said: "I have no arrows."

"Arrows are in the canoe," they said.

"I will not go along. I might be killed. My relatives do not know where I have gone. But you," he said, turning to the other, "may go with them."

So one of the young men went, but the other returned home.

And the warriors went on up the river to a town on the other side of Kalama. The people came down to the water, and they began to fight, and many were killed. But presently the young man heard one of the warriors say: "Quick, let us go home: that Indian has been hit." Now he thought: "Oh, they are ghosts." He did not feel sick, but they said he had been shot.

So the canoes went back to Egulac, and the young man went ashore to his house, and made a fire. And he told everybody and said: "Behold I accompanied the ghosts, and we went to fight. Many of our fellows were killed, and many of those who attacked us were killed. They said I was hit, and I did not feel sick."

He told it all, and then he became quiet. When the sun rose he fell down. Something black came out of his mouth. His face became contorted. The people jumped up and cried.

He was dead.

Subject's Reproduction

Two youths were standing by a river about to start seal-catching, when a boat appeared with five men in it. They were all armed for war.

The youths were at first frightened, but they were asked by the men to come and help them fight some enemies on the other bank. One youth said he could not come as his relations would be anxious about him; the other said he would go, and entered the boat.

In the evening he returned to his hut, and told his friends that he had been in a battle. A great many had been slain, and he had been wounded by an arrow; he had not felt any pain, he said. They told him that he must have been fighting in a battle of ghosts. Then he remembered that it had been queer and he became very excited.

In the morning, however, he became ill, and his friends gathered round; he fell down and his face became very pale. Then he writhed and shrieked and his friends were filled with terror. At last he became calm. Something hard and black came out of his mouth, and he lay contorted and dead.

FIGURE 14.2   The text of "The War of the Ghosts" and one subject's reproduction of it. From Bartlett, 1932.

"The War of the Ghosts" seems odd to people raised in Western cultures. It includes unfamiliar names, it seems to be missing some critical transitions, and it is based on a ghost cosmology not shared by educated Western people. Bartlett found that his subjects' recollections of the story were incomplete and often distorted. The subjects had trouble remembering the unusual proper names, they invented plausible transitions and, most important, they altered the facts about the ghosts. In fact, many subjects failed to remember anything at all about ghosts. Bartlett claimed that the subjects used their Western cultural knowledge of the nature of stories and other pertinent information to imaginatively reconstruct the story. When relevant cultural knowledge was missing or inappropriate to understanding a story from another culture, the Western subjects' memories were transformed to make their recollections more consistent with their own cultural knowledge. Bartlett's (1932) experiments on memory led him to conclude that remembering is a form of *reconstruction* in which various sources of knowledge are used to infer past experiences.

Another historically influential event in the development of the constructionist tradition was the publication of Ulric Neisser's *Cognitive Psychology* in 1967. In this book Neisser discussed his opposition to the idea that past experiences are somehow preserved and later reactivated when remembered. Instead, Neisser claimed that remembering is like problem solving, a matter of taking existing knowledge and memories of previous reconstructions to create a plausible rendition of some particular past event. Neisser used the analogy of reconstructing a complete dinosaur skeleton from a few bone fragments and knowledge of anatomy. He suggested that "executive routines" guide the process of gathering and interpreting evidence upon which a reconstruction of the past is based. Neisser thought that executive routines were strategies acquired through experience.

Another source of inspiration for a constructionist approach to memory comes from research on the neurophysiology of memory and cognition (see Squire, 1987; Carlson, 1994). Such research has revealed that there is no single place in the brain where past experiences are stored. That is, there does not seem to be anything that corresponds to a storage bin in the brain. Instead, memory reflects changes to neurons involved in perception, language, feeling, movement, and so on. Because each new experience results in altering the strengths of connections among neurons, the brain is constantly "tuning" itself in response to experiences. But it has no neural tissue dedicated only to storing a record of each experience.

14.2   RETAINING EXPERIENCES IN MEMORY

What is it that is retained in our cognitive system as a result of having experiences? The essential idea of a record-keeping theory is that a record of each experience is put into a kind of storage bin. Such records may take a variety of forms, including abstract descriptions or interpretations of events (see Anderson, 1983), lists of items and contextual information (see Raaijmakers & Shiffrin, 1981) or images of the perceptual qualities of events (see Paivio, 1971).

In contrast, the essential idea of a constructionist approach is that the various cognitive systems (e.g., the visual system, the language system) are changed by experiences, but no record-by-record accounts of the experiences are stored anywhere. Instead, the cognitive system is designed to extract the unchanging elements or patterns from experience and to note deviations from enduring patterns.

14.2.1   A Constructionist Account of Retention

To get a somewhat more precise sense of how a constructionist theory explains what is retained from experience, consider this simple example: remembering what you ate for dinner last Thursday night. Research on the effects of diet on health frequently relies on people's memory of what they have eaten. Is memory for food consumption reliable?

In general, research suggests that accurate recall of food items consumed declines to about 55% a week after the consumption (DeAngelis, 1988). The longer the retention interval, the poorer the memory for specific food items consumed (Smith, Jobe, & Mingay, 1991). Over time, people rely more on their generic knowledge of their own dieting behaviors than on a precise memory of any given meal (Smith et al., 1991). In some cases, knowledge of one's own dieting may distort memory. In one study, women on a low-fat diet remembered fewer of the snack items they had eaten the day before than did women on normal or high-fat diets (Fries, Green, & Bowen, 1995). People also tend to underestimate in their memories how much food they have eaten (Fries et al., 1995).

The constructionist account of memory for past meals would go something like the following (see figure 14.3). You have in your cognitive system concepts and ideas about food and food consumption. These include concepts such as iced tea, spaghetti, and entrees as well as ideas such as that snack foods are high in fat content and desserts are served at the end of a meal. The constructionist theory emphasizes that experiences change the strengths of the connections among these ideas and concepts.

To illustrate, suppose that on one night you have spaghetti for an entree and iced tea for a beverage, on the second night you have lamb chops and iced tea, and on the third night you have fried chicken and iced tea. On each night, then, the connections between the ideas of dinner and entree, between the ideas of dinner and beverage, and between the ideas

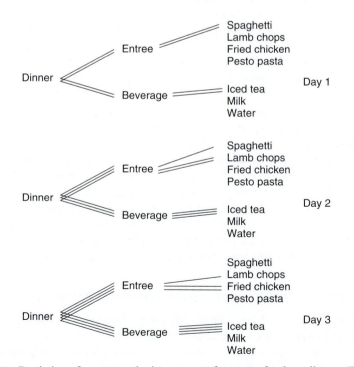

FIGURE 14.3   Depiction of a constructionist account of memory for three dinners. The more lines that connect one concept to another, the more likely the connections between those concepts will be remembered.

of beverage and iced tea will all be strengthened. These strong connections represent the enduring pattern in the dinner event. On the other hand, your cognitive system will not consistently strengthen the connection between the idea of an entree and the ideas that represent any particular entree (e.g., spaghetti), because the entrees change nightly. For instance, on the second night the connection between entree and lamb chops will be strengthened while the previously established connection between entree and spaghetti will weaken.

If you are later asked what you had for dinner on the first night, the strong connections between the dinner and entree ideas, between the dinner and beverage ideas, and between the beverage and iced tea ideas mean that you will reconstruct that you had some kind of an entree and iced tea. The connections between the idea of entree and any particular entree, such as spaghetti, will be relatively weak; consequently you will not be able to reconstruct as reliably which entree you had the first night. Instead, you may reconstruct only that you had an entree. Note that these reconstructions are accomplished without retrieving an actual record of each night's dinner. Other facts about food consumption may also influence your memory. If you are on a low-fat diet, for example, you may use your knowledge of fat content to deduce that you did not eat potato chips with your meal. In a later section of this chapter I will discuss in more detail how ideas and beliefs affect recollection. Although my example is greatly simplified, it at least illustrates how the cognitive system extracts the invariants of dinner experiences and uses them to form a plausible reconstruction of past dinner experiences.

Constructionist theory, then, predicts that people will not be able to remember very well the constantly changing details of events, such as the particular entree for any given dinner. Similarly, people might not be able to remember very well such things as what color shirt they wore on any given night out on the town or exactly where in the lot they parked their car on any given excursion to the beach. But it should be easy for people to remember the *invariants* or enduring patterns of events, such as always drinking a beverage with dinner, always wearing a casual shirt to the night club, or always parking in the cheaper lot at the beach.

Record-keeping theories, like constructionist theories, would also predict that accurate memory for any one event is likely to decline as more records are stored (see, for example, Anderson, 1976). But without embellishment, record-keeping theories have no ready way to explain why memory should be strong for the enduring patterns of experience. At the very least, a record-keeping theory would have to postulate the existence of another cognitive mechanism designed only to extract patterns from experiences. That is, it is not a natural consequence of keeping records that enduring patterns are extracted from those records. The advantage of constructionist theory is that it postulates that the creation of memories and the extraction of patterns from experience are accomplished by the same mechanism; namely, the altering of connection strengths among the concepts and ideas that constitute knowledge.

14.2.2   Evidence for the Constructionist Account of Retention

Empirical Evidence That Memory Preserves Patterns but Not Details of Experiences.   A nice example of the principle that memory preserves the enduring patterns and themes but not the changing elements in events comes from the testimony of John Dean, a key figure in the Watergate scandal of the early 1970s (Neisser, 1981). John Dean had been President Nixon's attorney and testified against him in a highly publicized Senate hearing on the Watergate break-in. Dean tried to recollect the details of meetings, including who participated, what was said, and when the meeting took place. Dean's memory seemed quite remarkable (and damaging to Nixon); he was able to supply many details that other members of Nixon's administration claimed to be unable to recall.

It was discovered later that all meetings in the Oval Office had been tape recorded, so that many of Dean's recollections could be compared with the actual transcripts of those meetings. It turns out that Dean was often inaccurate about details of the meetings but was accurate in his recollection of the general tenor of a number of the meetings; namely, that Nixon and other high-ranking members of his administration knew about the Watergate break-in and tried to cover it up. What distinguished Dean's testimony from that of the others was that Dean decided to tell the truth about the coverup. Dean's memory was not especially accurate about those elements that were always changing, like the details of conversations or which participants were at particular meetings, but his memory was quite accurate about the sorts of topics and issues that endured across many meetings.

Many memory experiments also make the point that our memories permit easier recall of enduring patterns than of details of specific experiences (e.g., Bartlett, 1932; Bransford & Franks, 1971; Thorndyke & Hayes-Roth, 1979). For example, participants in a weekly seminar on math were asked to recall the names of the other participants who had attended the last meeting of the seminar (Freeman, Romney, & Freeman, 1987). The subjects were not able to recall very accurately; about half of their responses were errors. The errors were revealing, however. Sometimes subjects mistakenly excluded someone who had attended the last meeting, but usually the excluded person had not regularly attended the seminar. And sometimes subjects mistakenly included someone who had missed the last meeting, but usually the included person had attended most of the other meetings. The errors suggest that the subjects had extracted the general pattern of attendance from their experiences in the seminar and had used that pattern, reasonably enough, to reconstruct who had attended the last meeting.

Memory for patterns is also reflected in the tendency for people to remember the gist but not the details of their experiences. Research has shown that subjects will forget the exact wording of any given sentence in a passage after reading only a few more sentences, but will usually be able to remember the meaning of the sentence (Sachs, 1967; for similar results with pictures, see Gernsbacher, 1985). Research has also shown that after studying a text or a set of pictures, people will tend to believe mistakenly that a sentence or picture was explicitly in the set of information they studied, when, in fact, it was only implied by the information (e.g., Bransford, Barclay, & Franks, 1972; Harris & Monaco, 1978; Maki, 1989; Sulin & Dooling, 1974; Thorndyke, 1976). For example, if a passage describes an event in which a long-haired customer sat in a barber's chair and later left the barbershop with short hair, a subject who had read that passage may mistakenly believe that the passage also contained a sentence describing the barber cutting the man's hair. The reason for the mistake is that the implicit information is likely to be consistent with the passage's essential themes, which would form the basis of the reconstruction of the details of the passage.

That memory is better for the patterns or invariants than for the ever-changing details of experiences is what enables memory to be adaptive, to anticipate the future. It is the invariants of experience that we are likely to encounter in future events, so a cognitive system that readily notices such patterns will be better prepared to respond to new experiences.

Good memory for the patterns or invariants of experience stands in contrast to our extremely poor memory for the details of the majority of experiences. Consider — can you describe in detail what you were doing around 3:00 P.M. on May 15th two years ago? Do you remember what the topic of conversation was when you first met your next-door neighbor? Or what your boss was wearing when you first met him or her? Or the first 10 sentences of this chapter? You see the point. What is especially remarkable about our memories is the almost complete lack of detail they provide about the majority of our past experiences! And it is easy to demonstrate experimentally that people do not remember very much about long-past experiences. For example, people have trouble remembering their infant-rearing practices, such as whether they fed their infants on demand (Robbins, 1963), their formerly held opinions on important political issues, such as whether they supported busing to equalize education (Goethals & Reckman, 1973); whether they voted in any given election (Parry & Crossley, 1950); and what they had to eat for dinner six weeks ago (Smith et al., 1991).

Accurate Memory.   A possible objection to the constructionist theory is the observation that people can sometimes remember past events accurately. A record-keeping theory of memory claims that accurate memory occurs when a person successfully locates a memory record. How can the constructionist theory account for accurate recollections? And, one might also object, what about people who have extraordinarily accurate memories, who seem to have a memory system that works like a videotape machine?

Constructionist theory implies that there are three circumstances in which memory is likely to be accurate. First, as I have already discussed, constructionist theory predicts that repetitious events, like always having iced tea with dinner, should be well remembered, because they promote the creation of strong connections among elements. A high probability, therefore, exists that at least some of the relevant connections created by the repetitive event will remain stable over time and so permit the accurate reconstruction of that event. Research shows that information that is repeated is more easily remembered than information that is presented only once (e.g., Jacoby, 1978; Greeno, 1964). To be fair, record-keeping theories also predict that repetition improves memory, because repetition would increase the number of records of that event, making any one record easier to find.

Second, constructionist theory predicts that recent events, such as what one ate for breakfast this morning, should be well remembered, because the strength of the connections among elements representing recent events would not yet be weakened by subsequent events. Researchers since Ebbinghaus have observed that recently experienced events are usually the easiest to remember (Ebbinghaus, 1885; Wickelgren, 1972).

Record-keeping theories need a modification to predict that recent events are better remembered. The modification is that recent events are stored in a more accessible manner or location. One way to visualize that is to imagine that events are stored in a push-down stack (Anderson & Bower, 1973). Recent events are first placed at the top of the stack but are gradually pushed further down into the stack by the continuous storage of even more recent events. The retrieval mechanism would begin its search at the top of the stack.

Third, constructionist theory predicts that unusual or distinctive events should be well remembered because they promote the creation of connections among elements that would not likely be reconfigured by future events. Consider an unusual event such as becoming nauseated after eating lamb chops. The connection between the feeling of nausea and the idea of lamb chops is not likely to be diminished by subsequent dinner experiences, because lamb chops would not ordinarily become associated with other ill feelings nor would nausea become associated with other entrees. Any subsequent activation of the lamb chops idea, then, is also likely to activate the feeling of nausea, permitting accurate memory for that experience of nausea.

Record-keeping theories could also predict that distinctive events are better remembered. One way to do so is to imagine that events are stored in locations that reflect the attributes of the event. Memories of happy experiences might be stored in one place, memories of car repair experiences might be stored in another place, and so on. A distinctive event has a collection of attributes that is different from other events and so would be stored in an uncluttered place in the memory system. It is easier to find a memory record in an uncluttered space than in a cluttered space, just as it would be easier to find *The Joy of Nausea* in a library that had only one book on the topic of nausea than in a library that carried hundreds of books on nausea.

That distinctive events are readily remembered has been well established by research (see Schmidt, 1991, for a review). In one experiment that required subjects to recall words from a list, the subjects were better able to remember that an animal name appeared on the list if the animal name was embedded in a list of names of countries than if the same animal name was embedded in a list of other animal names (Schmidt, 1985). This finding is an example of the *Von Restorff effect,* after the psychologist who first discovered it (Von Restorff, 1933). In another experiment, subjects were given photographs of human faces and were asked to judge the distinctiveness of each face. When later asked to recognize which faces they had previously studied, the subjects more accurately recognized the faces they rated as distinctive than the faces they rated as common (Cohen & Carr, 1975). At least some research shows that events associated with strong emotions, which are presumably distinctive, are better remembered than emotionally more neutral events (e.g., Waters & Leeper, 1936; Holmes, 1972).

Best-selling books on how to improve memory (e.g., Lorayne and Lucas, 1974) encourage the use of bizarre imagery to improve the memorability of verbal information, such as names of people. Bizarre images presumably make information more distinctive. But does the use of bizarre imagery really improve memory? The answer seems to be a qualified yes.

The standard experimental paradigm investigating the role of imagery in memory requires subjects to memorize word pairs (e.g., *chicken – cigar*) by making various kinds of images of the words. The results have shown that when people create bizarre images to connect the words (e.g., a chicken smoking a cigar), they will later recall more of the words than when they create common images (e.g., a chicken pecking a cigar) to connect the words (for a review, see Einstein, McDaniel, & Lackey, 1989). However, the advantage of bizarre over common images usually occurs only when the same person is required to make bizarre images for some of the words on the to-be-remembered list and ordinary images for the rest of the words on the list. When subjects are required to make bizarre images for all the words on the list, then the individual images are not as distinctive, and there is no longer an advantage of bizarre images over common images. Research also suggests that the superiority of the bizarre image technique is greater if the memory test is done days after studying the list (Webber & Marshall, 1978). When the delay between forming the images and recalling the words is only a few minutes, memory for the words is at least as good using the common image technique.

That distinctive events are memorable is also revealed in memory for real-life experiences. Erickson and Jemison (1991) had students record one event from their lives each day for 12 weeks, and 5 months later take several memory tests on the events.

They found that the more memorable events tended to be the distinctive ones — that is, the ones rated atypical, infrequent, or surprising. They also found that positive events were more memorable, possibly because positive events are likely to be thought about and discussed frequently.

When we have accurate memories of long-past events, these events are almost always remarkable — that is, distinctive — in some way. For example, I vividly remember a championship Little League baseball game in which I got five hits and scored the winning run (a newspaper account verifies that my memory is accurate). However, about all I remember from the many other Little League games in which I played is that I was good at throwing and catching but not so good at hitting.

Psychologists have studied memory of remarkable experiences by asking people what they were doing on the occasion of some historically significant event like the assassination of John F. Kennedy (Brown & Kulik, 1977; Pillemer, 1984). Usually people can describe what they were doing in great detail, although ordinarily the psychologist is unable to check the accuracy of the person's account. Memory for a remarkable event, sometimes called a *flashbulb memory,* is vivid (McCloskey, Wible, & Cohen, 1988) because the event is distinctive and because people talk about and think about the event much more frequently than about other, more mundane, experiences.

It should be noted, though, that memory for what one was doing at the time of a historically significant event is frequently wrong (McCloskey et al., 1988; Neisser & Harsch, 1991). For example, Neisser and Harsch (1991) asked students on the day after the Challenger disaster how they heard about the disaster and asked them again 3 years later. On the test conducted 3 years after the disaster, one third of the subjects gave inaccurate accounts, although they were confident that their accounts were accurate.

Brain Stimulation and Accurate Memory.   Sometimes memory researchers cite data that seem to indicate, as the record-keeping theory would have it, that human memory does contain records of nearly all past experiences, although it might ordinarily be hard to retrieve most of those records. Some of the most compelling data comes from the research of a brain surgeon named Wilder Penfield, who removed small portions of cortical tissue in order to prevent the spread of seizures in epileptic patients (Penfield & Jasper, 1954; Penfield & Perot, 1963). Ordinarily such patients are awake during the operation, because the cortex is impervious to pain. Penfield needed to electrically stimulate various portions of the cerebral cortex, in order to locate accurately the epileptic site. When he did so, some of the patients described vivid recollections of mostly trivial past experiences. Penfield reasoned that the cortex must therefore keep a record of all past experiences and that forgetting must be due to retrieval failure.

After Penfield began to publish his findings, some psychologists questioned his interpretations (Loftus & Loftus, 1980; Squire, 1987). First of all, only about 3% of Penfield's patients ever reported remembering past experiences in response to electrical stimulation. Furthermore, for those patients who did, the evidence suggested that they were not accurately recalling an actual experience but unintentionally fabricating one. One patient, for example, reported having a memory of playing at a lumberyard, but it turned out the patient had never been to the lumberyard. Another patient claimed to remember being born.

Recognition and Accurate Memory.   Another kind of data sometimes cited to support the claim that the brain stores records of virtually all experiences, any one of which is potentially retrievable, comes from research on recognition memory. In some recognition experiments, subjects are shown thousands of detailed pictures, such as magazine advertisements, and weeks to months later are given a recognition test in which they must discriminate the *old* pictures from *new* ones (e.g., Standing, 1973). In one of these experiments, subjects' recognition accuracy was 87% after one week (Shepard, 1967), while in another experiment recognition accuracy was 63% after a year (chance performance would be 50%) (Standing, Conezio, & Haber, 1970).

However, it also possible to design such experiments so that a person's recognition accuracy is not much better than chance, only minutes after viewing pictures (Goldstein & Chance, 1970). Critical to performance in recognition experiments is the similarity between the *old* stimuli and the *new* stimuli used as foils (Dale & Baddeley, 1962; Pezdek et al., 1988). When *old* and *new* pictures closely resemble one another, recognition accuracy is poor. But when the *old* and *new* pictures are dissimilar, subjects need not remember very much about a set of pictures to distinguish between *old* and *new* ones. Note that pictures of advertisements used in the high-accuracy memory experiments are relatively dissimilar from one another.

Still, the high percentage of correct responses in some recognition experiments does make the important point that we have much better memory for our experiences than we might ordinarily think. How good our memory seems to be for any given event depends critically on how we are tested. As I will discuss later, performance is usually better on recognition than on recall tests and is better the more cues there are in the environment to prompt memory. But it would be a mistake to assume that if a more sensitive test improves memory scores, then all experiences must be stored in, and therefore potentially retrievable from, memory.

Autobiographical Memory.   Another kind of finding sometimes used to support the notion that nearly all experiences are potentially retrievable comes from individuals who have for years kept records of details of important autobiographical experiences and later tried to recall some of those details (Linton, 1978; R. T. White, 1982, 1989). These individuals seem to remember something about nearly all the events they recorded.

Typical of this research is a study done by Willem Wagenaar (Wagenaar, 1986). Each day for six years Wagenaar selected an event or two and recorded what happened, who he was with when it happened, the date it happened, and where it happened. He tested his memory for an event by reading some details about the event (e.g., "I went to a church in Milano") and trying to recall other details (e.g., "I went to see Leonardo da Vinci's *Last Supper* on September 10, 1983"). He found that even years afterwards he was able to recall at least one detail of about 80% of the events he recorded.

Does his research contradict the constructionist theory that predicts forgetting of most events? I think not. First of all, Wagenaar deliberately selected salient, distinctive events to record; he avoided mundane events. The constructionist theory predicts good memory for distinctive events. It is interesting to note that after about one year, Wagenaar was able to recall accurately slightly less than 50% of the details of even these distinctive events. Furthermore, Wagenaar had no way to control for talking or thinking about the events later on;

consequently, many of these events were likely recycled many times through his cognitive systems. Also, he was often able to make plausible guesses about what happened. For example, given the cue "I went to a church in Milano" he may have been able to guess the approximate date by just remembering that his trip to Italy took place during the first two weeks of September in 1983. Finally, Wagenaar had no "foils" — events that could plausibly have happened to him but did not — to see if he could accurately discriminate between real events and foils. In fact, research demonstrates that people have a hard time distinguishing between actually experienced events and plausible foils in their recollections about important auto-biographical experiences (Barclay & Wellman, 1986).

In short, research on autobiographical memory does not prove that we have accurate and detailed memory for nearly all of our experiences. It suggests that we can remember, or at least infer, some of the details of our most distinctive experiences.

"Photographic" Memory?   But what about individuals who seem to have something akin to a photographic or videotape memory in which all experiences are accurately remembered? Wouldn't the existence of these people contradict the constructionist approach to memory? Incidentally, I do not intend for the notion of photographic memory to imply that the individual has only an especially good memory for visual information. Instead, "photographic" is meant to be a metaphor for extraordinary memory for all kinds of information.

A few extensive investigations of such rarely encountered individuals have been carried out. Probably the best-known memory expert was S. V. Shere-shevskii, usually referred to as *S. S* grew up around the turn of the century in Latvia and was a Moscow newspaper reporter when his editor noticed his exceptional memory. The editor recommended that *S* have his memory evaluated at the local university; there he met Aleksandr Luria, a great Russian psychologist.

Luria studied *S* over a period of about 30 years (Luria, 1968). Luria verified that *S*'s memory was quite extraordinary. For example, *S* was able to repeat back a series of 70 randomly selected numbers in order after hearing them only once. As another example, he was able to recall lists of arbitrary and randomly ordered words 15 years after Luria presented the words to him. *S* claimed that he formed vivid and detailed images of every stimulus he was asked to remember and often associated the images with images of familiar locations, like Gorky Street in Moscow. He would later retrieve the words from memory by taking a mental "walk," noticing the images associated with the landmarks. This *mnemonic technique* (i.e., a strategy for memorizing) is called the *method of loci,* and can be used effectively by anyone trying to memorize a list of stimuli (Groninger, 1971). Techniques like the method of loci improve memory for several reasons, one of which is that they help make information more distinctive.

S made use of other mnemonic techniques, as well. He seemed to have the exceedingly rare ability, known as *synesthesia,* to conjure up vivid images of light, color, taste, and touch in association with almost any sound. These images also helped him remember new information. For a time, *S* found work as a memory expert on stage. People would call out words or numbers for him to remember and he would try to recall them exactly. Interestingly, though, *S* sometimes needed to develop new mnemonic techniques to overcome occasional errors in memory and so improve his act. For example, he had difficulty remembering names and faces. If *S* had a photographic memory, he would have been able to memorize accurately any kind of information presented to him. His extraordinary memory, then, was not a result of possessing anything analogous to a photographic mind, but was rather a result of having an appropriate mnemonic strategy. Tragically, *S* ended his life in a Russian asylum for the mentally ill.

Some people, called *eidetic imagers,* seem to have an extraordinary ability to remember visual details of pictures. Eidetic imagers report that, after viewing a picture, they see an image of the picture localized in front of them and that the visual details disappear part by part. While they remember many more visual details of a picture than would the ordinary person, often the accuracy of their reports is far from perfect (Haber & Haber, 1988; see Searleman & Herrmann, 1994).

The all-time champion eidetic imager was an artist known as Elizabeth. Her most remarkable achievement had to do with superimposing two random-dot patterns to see a three-dimensional image. In one experiment (Stromeyer & Psotka, 1970), she was first presented with a 10,000-random-dot pattern to her right eye for 1 minute. The first pattern was then removed for 10 seconds and a second 10,000-random-dot pattern was presented to her left eye. She was instructed to superimpose her memory of the image of the first pattern onto the second. The patterns were designed so that when superimposed and examined through both eyes, a three-dimensional figure (e.g., a square floating in space) would appear. It was impossible to determine the three-dimensional image from either pattern alone, however. Elizabeth was able to superimpose a memory of the first pattern onto the second pattern and thus accurately identify the three-dimensional image. In fact, in one case, she was able to hold a 1,000,000-random-dot pattern in memory for 4 hours and then superimpose her memory of that pattern onto a second 1,000,000-random-dot pattern to identify successfully the three-dimensional image! It is possible to see the three-dimensional figure in the superimposed patterns even when one of the patterns is significantly blurred, although the blurring will also make the edges of the three-dimensional image more rounded. So Elizabeth need not have remembered the exact position of all of the dots to accomplish seeing the three-dimensional figure, although she claimed that the edges of her three-dimensional image were sharp and not rounded.

No one else has yet been found who can come close to Elizabeth's visual memory; indeed, some people are skeptical of her feats (see Searleman & Herrmann, 1994). As far as I know, Elizabeth was not tested for memory of anything other than visual information. It remains unclear, then, whether she had an outstanding all-purpose memory or an extraordinary memory for only visual information.

Another remarkable memorizer is Rajan Mahadevan, who has a phenomenal memory for numbers. He is able to recite the first 31,811 digits of pi from memory (I'm lucky if I can remember the first four digits!). In a series of experiments comparing his memory to that of college students, Rajan Mahadevan dramatically outperformed the students on any memory test involving numbers (Thompson, Cowan, Frieman, Mahadevan, & Vogel, 1991). For example, he recalled 43 randomly ordered digits presented to him once, while the college students recalled an average of only about 7 digits. Rajan Mahadevan claims that he does not use imagery to help him remember numbers but instead uses a rather vaguely described mnemonic system whereby numbers are associated with numerical locations in a series. It does not seem that he has anything analogous to a videotape or photographic memory, however. His recall for nonnumerical information, such as word lists or meaningful stories, was about equal to that of the average college student. For example, he recalled an average of about 41 ideas from several previously read Native American folk tales similar to "The War of the Ghosts," while the college students recalled about 47 ideas on average from the same stories.

A reasonable conclusion, then, is that individuals like *S* and Rajan Mahadevan make use of mnemonic devices that others could use to help make information more memorable (Ericsson & Polson, 1988; Hunt & Love, 1972). While the memorizing skill of these mnemonists can seem phenomenal, it is clear that their memories do not work like a videotape recorder; otherwise they would be able to remember the details of any and all of their experiences. Instead, their memory is good for classes of information in which they are experts (Elizabeth was a skilled artist) or for which they have learned mnemonic memorizing strategies. The Hollywood version of the person with a "photographic" mind probably does not exist.

14.2.3   The Assimilation Principle

Making information distinctive or associating information with distinctive images and ideas can promote better memory of that information. Such techniques may be called learning strategies. What other learning strategies help make information memorable? Another useful learning strategy is based on the principle that memory for an event will be improved to the extent that the event can be assimilated into something that already exists in memory (Stein & Bransford, 1979; Stein, Littlefield, Bransford, & Persampieri, 1984). This principle is called the *assimilation principle*.

Assimilation means that new information is incorporated into relevant pre-existing knowledge useful for interpreting the new information. For example, a passage describing the nature of electricity would be more memorable if the passage reminded readers of their knowledge of rivers. The passage would not be as memorable if it did not remind readers of relevant knowledge, nor would it be as memorable if it reminded readers of irrelevant knowledge, such as their knowledge of baseball. The constructionist theory explains the assimilation principle this way: When new information is assimilated into relevant pre-existing knowledge, there is widespread activation of the cognitive system for interpreting an event and an increase in the number and strength of the connections among elements of that cognitive system. Reconstruction of the event is improved to the extent that strong connections among elements in that cognitive system can be found.

Experimental Support for Assimilation.   A variety of research supports the assimilation principle. One kind of support comes from experiments that show that people remember more new information if that information is within their area of expertise than if the new information is outside their area of expertise (Bellezza & Buck, 1988; Chiesl, Spilich, & Voss, 1979; Morris, 1988). For instance, experienced bartenders remember better than do novices their customers' drink orders (Beach, 1988). Football experts can remember more about descriptions of fictitious football games than nonexperts (Bellezza and Buck, 1988). Chess experts will remember the positions of chess pieces on a chess-board better than chess novices, provided the pieces are arranged in a way consistent with the rules of chess. If the chess pieces are randomly arranged, however, the chess expert can remember their locations no better than the novice (Chase & Simon, 1973).

Sometimes when people must learn new material, like the material in this book, they have a hard time figuring out what general patterns or principles are implied by the material and so are unable to associate the material with the appropriate elements in their cognitive systems. Any aids that help people find such principles in the material will improve memory. If subjects are required to memorize a list of words, they will remember more of them if the words in the list are grouped according to categories, like animal names, than if the words are presented in a random order (Bower, Clark, Lesgold, & Winzenz, 1969; Mandler, 1979). Subjects given titles that clarify the meaning of otherwise obscure pictures or passages remember more than subjects not given titles (Bransford & Johnson, 1972). When subjects read technical or scientific passages, the subjects first given guides to help them associate the information with familiar ideas (e.g., electrical current is like a river) or help them see the relationships among key ideas in the text will later be able to recall more of the text than subjects not first given the guides (Dean & Kulhavy, 1981; Brooks & Dansereau, 1983; Lorch & Lorch, 1985). Most of the advantage for subjects receiving the guides is in remembering the conceptual information and not the technical detail (Mayer, 1980; Mayer & Bromage, 1980).

Levels of Processing and the Assimilation Principle.   Another manifestation of the assimilation principle is found in investigations of what is usually called *levels of processing* (Craik & Lockhart, 1972; Koriat & Melkman, 1987). This research establishes that when people think about the meaning of information, they remember more of it than when they think about the physical properties or when they merely try to rote memorize the information. Elaborating on the meaning is a more effective learning strategy than is rote memorizing.

In one example of research on levels of processing, subjects studied a list of words by making judgments about each word, and later recalled the words. Subjects recalled more words for which they had been asked to judge "How pleasant is the word?" than words for which they had been asked to judge "Does the word contain the letter *e?*" (Hyde & Jenkins, 1975; Parkin, 1984). Subjects who studied a list of words by elaborating each word into complete sentences (called elaborative rehearsal) later recalled more of the words than subjects who only rote memorized the words (called maintenance rehearsal) (Bjork, 1975; Bobrow & Bower, 1969).

The advantage of processing for meaning is not limited to verbal information. Subjects were better at recognizing pictures of faces if they previously thought about whether each face seemed friendly than if they previously thought about whether each face had a big nose (Smith & Winograd, 1978) and if they assessed faces for honesty rather than for the sex of the face (Sporer, 1991). In general, thinking about the meaning of a stimulus or elaborating on the stimulus is likely to permit the stimulus to be assimilated by a greater portion of a cognitive system, and so create more possibilities for reconstructing a memory of the stimulus later on. Elaboration may also help make information more distinctive (Craik & Lockhart, 1986; Winnograd, 1981).

Processing the meaning of a stimulus improves memory only when that processing connects the stimulus to relevant knowledge. For instance, asking a person whether a shirt is a type of clothing enhances memory for the word *shirt,* as opposed to the case where the person is asked whether the word *shirt* contains more vowels than consonants. However, asking a person whether a shirt is a type of insect does not promote very good memory for *shirt* (Craik & Tulving, 1975). In the latter case, answering the question does not encourage the person to connect *shirt* with knowledge of shirts (see Schacter, 1996).

Levels of processing research has been used to challenge the duplex model of short-term memory (see Klatzky, 1980). There is an important qualification to the general finding that thinking deeply about information promotes better memory than does thinking in a shallow manner about the information. The qualification is that it depends on how memory is tested. If the memory testing procedure matches the manner in which information is originally learned, then memory for that information is better than if there is a mismatch.

An example comes from a study by Morris, Bransford, and Franks (1977). Subjects were required to decide for each of a group of words whether the word could have a particular semantic property (e.g., "Does a train have a silver engine?") or whether the word rhymes with another word (e.g., "Does *train* rhyme with *rain?*"). The semantic task was the "deep" task and the rhyming task was the "shallow" task. Later, some subjects were given a standard recognition task in which they had to pick out the target word from a list of distractors. Subjects who had made the semantic judgment did better on the recognition task than did subjects who had made the rhyming judgment. But other subjects were given a very different test of memory in which they had to pick out from a list of words which word rhymed with one of the words previously studied. Now it was the subjects who had originally made the rhyming judgments who did better. This finding, usually called *transfer appropriate processing,* is discussed again later in this chapter.

14.2.4   Individual Differences in Memory

Why does one person have a better memory than another person? Record-keeping theories, especially those that liken human memory to the memories of computers or libraries, imply that there is an all-purpose memory system for storing every kind of experience. According to the record-keeping theory, the reason some people have better memories than others is that some people have more efficient mechanisms for storing or retrieving records. Even Plato talked about some people having a purer kind of wax tablet for storing experiences.

Constructionist theories, on the other hand, imply that there is no all-purpose memory system. Memory is instead a byproduct of changes to the various components of cognition that underlie perception, language, emotions, and so on. From the perspective of the constructionist approach, there are no storage and retrieval mechanisms whose efficiency varies from person to person. Instead, people vary with respect to how much they know about various domains of knowledge. According to constructionist theory, the main reason some people have better memories than others is that some people have more expertise in the domain of knowledge sampled by the test of memory. For example, a baseball expert can use the knowledge that runners on second base often score after a single to reconstruct that the home team scored a run in the previous inning. However, baseball knowledge would not help the baseball expert remember, say, a passage about climate in South America.

The constructionist theory claims, then, that the best predictor of how well a person remembers new information in some domain, such as baseball, is how much knowledge the person already possesses about that domain. General intellectual skills, especially skill at memorizing lists of information unrelated to the domain, should not predict individual differences in memory for information within some domain. If, instead, memory is an all-purpose system, it would follow that performance on tests of memory and on general intellectual skills would readily predict memory for new information.

The research supports the constructionist theory's explanation of individual differences in memory. Good memory for information within some domain is primarily a function of expertise in that domain and not a function of any general intellectual skill. Schneider, Korkel, and Weinert (1987) and Walker (1987) found that subjects who scored low on a test of general aptitude but happened to know a lot about baseball recalled more facts about a fictitious baseball game than did subjects who scored high on the general aptitude test but knew very little about baseball, and recalled as many facts as did high-aptitude subjects who knew a lot about baseball. Kuhara-Kojima and Hatano (1991) found that knowledge about music, but not performance on a test of memory for unrelated words, predicted how many new facts subjects recalled from a passage about music.

Merely possessing domain knowledge does not guarantee better memory for new information in that domain, however. DeMarie-Dreblow (1991) taught people about birds but found that the newly acquired bird knowledge did not help subjects recall a list of bird names any better than subjects not given the knowledge about birds. The knowledge has to be well-learned, and people need practice using the knowledge in the context of reconstructing a memory for the new information (Pressley & Van Meter, 1994).

For instance, Pressley and Brewster (1990) taught their Canadian subjects new facts about Canadian provinces. Some subjects were given prior knowledge in the form of pictures of some prominent setting in the province. By itself, this prior knowledge did not help subjects remember the new facts all that much better than the subjects not given the prior knowledge. Other subjects were given imagery instructions for which the subjects were to imagine the fact occurring in a setting unique to the province referred to by the new fact. Imagery instructions also did not help subjects all that much. However, subjects given both the prior knowledge and the imagery instructions did recall substantially more new facts than did subjects who did not have both the prior knowledge and the techniques (i.e., imagery) for using that knowledge to learn and remember new information.

The better predictor of memory for novel information, then, is a person's degree of expertise in that domain (provided the person knows how to use the knowledge for learning and remembering) and not the person's general intellectual level or memorizing ability for unrelated information. The main practical implication is that people develop good memory, not to the extent that they become better memorizers, but to the extent that they develop expertise in domains for which it is important to remember details accurately.

By way of summarizing this section, let me suggest how a student can make use of the material I have discussed. Suppose you must study this chapter on memory in preparation for an exam, and so are required to learn a lot of factual details. What can you do to make the chapter more memorable? Just repeatedly reading the facts will not in itself enhance your memory for this chapter very much. Instead, you must first look for the themes and patterns that serve to organize the material presented in the chapter. For example, the chapter presents two points of view about memory, the record-keeping theory and the constructionist theory, and argues that the constructionist theory is superior. You must then try to understand these themes by relating them to what you already know. You might note that the record-keeping theory is similar to how books are stored in and retrieved from a library. You should then attempt to figure out for each piece of information how it makes a distinctive contribution to the thesis. You might ask what unique insight each experiment makes concerning the predictions of the constructionist theory. Finally, and to anticipate the next section, you should practice studying the material in a way similar to the way you are going to be tested. If you know that the test will be an essay test, then write out answers to essay questions. Remember, human memory is designed to anticipate the future, not recapitulate the past.

14.3   RECOLLECTING THE PAST

So far I have focused on how cognitive systems change as a result of experiences. Now I wish to change the focus to the cognitive processes responsible for recollecting a past event. What is a good model of recollection?

14.3.1   Record-Keeping and Constructionist Models of Recollecting the Past

The record-keeping approach claims that recollecting the past means searching through a storehouse of records of past events until the target record is retrieved. Finding or "reading" the memory record is like reexperiencing the past event. The search process is thought to be guided by information in the current environment that acts as a sort of address for the location of the target record. The search through the records need not be haphazard, because the records may be organized, much the way books in a library are organized by content.

The constructionist approach to memory claims that recollecting the past is essentially a process of reconstructing the past from information in the current environment and from the connections serving the various cognitive systems. Recollection typically involves making plausible guesses about what probably happened. Recollection is an active process, akin to fantasizing or speculating about the future, whereby people recreate or infer their past rather than reexperience it. Another way to put it is that people learn reconstruction strategies that enable them to deduce past events. Loftus (1982) provides a discussion of some of the various types of reconstruction strategies.

To illustrate, suppose a person returns to the scene of a car accident and tries to recall the details of the accident, which occurred several days earlier. Returning to the intersection is likely to activate the same elements of the cognitive system involved in originally perceiving the accident; consequently some perceptual details necessary to reconstruct the accident will become available (e.g., cars move quickly through the intersection). Thoughts about a car accident may also activate knowledge of how cars work (e.g., brakes often squeak when a driver tries to stop a rapidly moving vehicle). Such knowledge may then become a basis for reconstructing the accident. Information that was provided to the person after the accident occurred may also be activated and inserted into the reconstruction of the accident (e.g., a friend at the scene of the accident later claimed to have seen a van cut in front of the car). The confluence of activated elements constitutes the memory of the accident (e.g., a van cut in front of a fast-moving car, which tried to stop, causing its brakes to squeal). The memory may appear to the person to be vivid and accurate, yet some details may be in error (e.g., perhaps the van never cut in front of the car).

14.3.2   Reconstructing the Past

An important implication of reconstruction is that when people try to recollect a past event, what they will remember about that event will depend on what they currently know or believe to be true about their lives. Errors in recollecting events will not be haphazard, but will instead reflect knowledge and beliefs. So researchers interested in demonstrating recon-struction often vary a person's current knowledge and show that the person's recollection of some past event will be distorted as a consequence (Dooling & Christiaansen, 1977; Hanawalt & Demarest, 1939; Snyder & Uranowitz, 1978; Spiro, 1977).

A nice demonstration of reconstruction is provided by Spiro (1977). In his experi-ment, subjects read a passage about a couple. Bob and Margie, who were engaged to be married. Bob was reluctant to tell Margie that he did not want to have children, but, by the end of the story, finally confronted Margie with his wishes. In one version of the story, Margie told Bob that she wanted children very badly. Afterwards, the subjects were told either that Bob and Margie are now happily married or that the engagement had been bro-ken off. Days to weeks later, subjects returned and tried to recall the details of the story. Subjects who were told that the engagement had been broken off tended to recall accurately that Bob and Margie disagreed sharply about having children. In some cases they even exag-gerated the disagreement. But the subjects told that Bob and Margie were now happily mar-ried tended to recall that the disagreement was much less severe than was actually depicted in the story. And the longer the time between reading the story and recalling it, the more likely these subjects distorted the story so as to resolve the inconsistency between the disagreement and the subsequent marriage. Furthermore, subjects who incorrectly recalled minimal dis-agreement between Bob and Margie were every bit as confident of their mistaken recollec-tions as they were of their accurate recollections about other aspects of the story.

These results make sense if we assume that subjects did not activate a memory record of the story, but instead used their belief that successful engagements require agreement about whether to have children, in order to reconstruct the story. If Bob and Margie are still married, then it would have seemed that any disagreement about children must not have been very serious.

An intriguing implication of a reconstructionist approach to memory is that it ought to be possible to create false memories — that is, memories of events that never happened. Some researchers have suggested that some memories of sexual abuse are actually false memories created by psychotherapeutic practices that encourage clients to interpret certain psychological symptoms as evidence of past abuse.

Eyewitness Memory and Reconstruction.   Reconstruction has been studied extensively in the context of eyewitness memory. A variety of research has shown that eyewitnesses tend to distort their memories of crimes and accidents based on information they receive after the crime or accident.

For example, eyewitness memory research demonstrates what is called *photo bias*. In one experiment on photo bias, subjects were first shown a film of a crime and were later presented photographs of suspects. Later still the subjects were required to pick the actual perpetrator out of a lineup. What happened was that subjects tend to be biased towards identifying as the perpetrator any suspect whose photograph they had recently seen, even when the person was innocent of the crime (Brown, Deffenbacher, & Sturgill, 1977). Apparently, when the subjects viewed the lineup, they recognized that they had seen one of the suspects before, and erroneously assumed that it must be because the suspect was the criminal.

Elizabeth Loftus, one of the most influential advocates of a reconstructionst approach to memory, has conducted a variety of experiments in which subjects are shown a film of an accident and are later asked questions about the film (Loftus, 1979; Loftus, Miller, & Burns, 1978; Loftus & Loftus, 1980; Loftus & Palmer, 1974). In one experiment, she asked one group of subjects leading questions like "Did another car pass the red Datsun while it was stopped at the stop sign?" when, in fact, the Datsun was stopped at a yield sign. (This particular experiment was conducted before Datsun changed its name to Nissan.) When questioned again about the film, these subjects were much more likely to claim they saw the Datsun stop at a stop sign than another group of subjects not initially asked the misleading question. In some cases, memory was tested by showing subjects two slides, a slide of a Datsun stopped at a stop sign and a slide of the Datsun stopped at a yield sign. Most of the misled subjects selected the slide displaying a stop sign, even when the misled subjects were offered a substantial reward ($25) for remembering accurately. Incidentally, this experimental paradigm usually contains a whole set of questions about various details of the accident or crime. I am illustrating the paradigm with only one of the questions that might be used. At any rate, the subjects were presumably using the information implied by the question to reconstruct the details of the accident. If the question falsely implied that the car stopped at a stop sign, then subjects reconstructed a stop sign in their recollections of the accident.

Exactly what would such a reconstruction be based on? One possibility is that mentioning a stop sign effectively erased or somehow undermined the connection between the accident and the yield sign and replaced it with a connection between the accident and the stop sign (Loftus & Loftus, 1980). There is another possibility, though. Maybe subjects do remember that the film contained, say, a yield sign and that the subsequent question mentioned a stop sign. But when given the choice between a yield and stop sign, the subjects figure that the experimenter wants them to say that they saw a stop sign in the film (otherwise, why would the experimenter ask the question?). In other words, maybe subjects' memories are just fine in this paradigm; maybe they are just responding to the demands characteristic of the experiment; maybe this research is not supportive of a construction approach to memory (McCloskey & Zaragoza, 1985).

To see if the question about the stop sign really erased the information about the yield sign (or, more generally, if misinformation erases previously acquired information), McCloskey and Zaragoza (1985) devised a somewhat different experimental paradigm (this paradigm, the Loftus paradigm, and a couple of other paradigms that I discuss below are all illustrated in figure 14.4). Subjects first saw a film that contained details like the yield sign, and then read a text that contained misinformation, such as a description of a stop sign, and then were asked to decide if the original film contained a yield sign or, say, a caution sign. Again, the actual paradigm includes several pieces of information, and not just information about traffic signs. If the misinformation really wiped out memory of the yield sign, subjects should be just as likely to choose the yield sign as to choose the caution sign. Instead, subjects overwhelmingly selected the correct alternative, the yield sign in this case.

So does this mean that the misinformation has no effect on eyewitness memory at all? No. In other research (see Lindsay, 1993), subjects were first shown a film (or slide show) of a crime or accident, then read a text that contained some misleading information, and then were asked of each piece of information whether the information was presented in the film, in the text, in both places, or in neither place. The memory test in this case (see figure 14.4) asks subjects the source of the information. The idea is to see whether source memory is worse for a detail in the film when there is misinformation in the text than when there is not misinformation in the text.

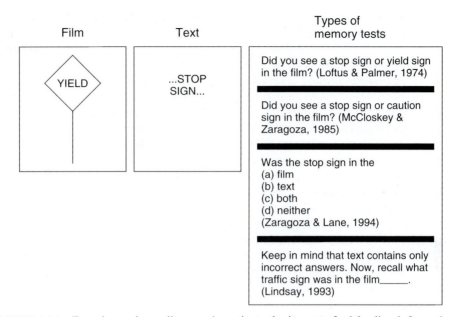

FIGURE 14.4   Experimental paradigms to investigate the impact of misleading information on eyewitness memory.

The main finding is that *source memory* tends to be good (i.e., subjects correctly remember that the stop sign was in the text and not in the film) when it is easy for subjects to discriminate between the experience of seeing the film and reading the text (e.g., Zaragoza & Lane, 1994; see Lindsay, 1993). One way to make the discrimination easy is to present the film on one day, wait until the next day to present the text, and then immediately follow the text with the memory test. Source memory tends to be poor (i.e., subjects think that the stop sign was in the film) when it is hard for subjects to discriminate between the experience of seeing the film and the experience of reading the text. For example, a way to make the discrimination hard is to present the text right after the film, ask subjects to visualize the text, and present the memory test the next day. Source memory also tends to be poor if the misleading suggestions contained in the text are repeated several times rather than presented in the text only once (Zaragoza & Mitchell, 1996).

One other paradigm (see figure 14.4) that suggests that memory really is affected by subsequently presented misinformation comes from Lindsay (1990; also Weingardt, Loftus, & Lindsay, 1995; see Lindsay, 1993). Again, say that subjects see a yield sign in the film and later read a text about a stop sign. The description of a stop sign is misinformation. Now subjects are correctly informed that the text did not contain any correct answers to a subsequent memory test. In the memory test, subjects are asked to report details about the traffic sign, and subjects know that the correct answer comes from the film and not from the text. When it is hard to discriminate between the film and text experiences, subjects are likely to recall incorrectly details from the text, such as that the traffic sign was a stop sign. Such incorrect recall occurs less often when subjects are asked to recall details from the film about which no misinformation was given in the text. Here the demand characteristics of the experiment unambiguously push subjects to recall only the information in the film, yet they frequently recall inaccurately the information in the text.

I went through these experimental paradigms in some detail because I want you to see exactly how researchers refine their paradigms in response to alternative interpretations of findings. In this case, we can say that misinformation is likely to affect recollection when it is relatively difficult for people to discriminate between the misinformation event and the to-be-remembered event (Lindsay, 1993). So, for example, our hypothetical Jim — mentioned at the beginning of this chapter — might be prone to remember incorrectly that the thief stole a camera (when, in fact, he saw the thief steal a radio) because he heard someone at the crime scene tell the police that the thief stole a camera. But Jim would be far less likely to remember incorrectly that the thief stole a camera if he heard someone talking about a missing camera the day after the theft and in a different physical setting than where the theft took place.

Loftus (1986) estimates that thousands of people in the United States are wrongfully convicted each year, and that many of these wrongful convictions are due to inaccurate eye-witness testimony. Juries deliberating the fate of people accused of crimes need to be made aware of the fallibility of human memory and the ease with which details of the past can be inaccurately recollected.

Hypnosis and Memory. Sometimes it is supposed that hypnosis can help people better recollect crimes and accidents. As it turns out, psychologists debate whether hypnosis is a distinctive state of waking consciousness that is different from ordinary wakefulness or is merely an occasion in which some people are unusually motivated to carry out the requests of the hypnotist (see Farthing, 1992). Whatever the exact nature of hypnosis, certainly it is commonly believed that hypnosis promotes such accurate recall of the past that nearly all events must be stored in memory. The reality, though, is that when hypnosis is used to help eyewitnesses recollect a crime, accident, or any past event, hypnotized people do not remember details any more accurately than do nonhypnotized people. Hypnotized people, though, may be more confident about their recollections than nonhypnotized people (Buckhout, Eugenio, Licitia, Oliver, & Kramer, 1981; Krass, Kinoshita, & McConkey, 1989). Furthermore, hypnotized eyewitnesses are influenced by misleading questions even more than are non-hypnotized people.

Putnam (1979) presented subjects a videotape of a car accident and later hypnotized some subjects. When asked a misleading question like "Did you see the license plate number on the car?" some hypnotized subjects claimed to remember the numbers on the license plate when, in fact, the license plate was not visible in the film. Note that by using the phrase "the license plate," the question implies that the license plate was visible. Some of the hypnotized subjects presumably used the misleading implication in the question to reconstruct a number for the license plate. The subjects who were not hypnotized were less likely to fall for the misleading questions.

Hypnosis has also been used to attempt age regression, in which hypnotized adults may claim that they are really reliving some experience from childhood. But investigations reveal that the recollected details are often inaccurate (Nash, 1987). In one case, an adult who was hypnotically age-regressed remembered inaccurately a first-grade teacher's name. In another case, an adult who was hypnotically regressed to age 6 was asked to draw a picture. While the picture the adult produced looked childlike, it did not resemble the subject's own drawings made at age 6. Instead, the drawing reflected an adult's conception of a childish drawing, but not real children's drawings.

In brief, hypnosis, which is supposed to help people relive past experiences, does not really work. The research on hypnosis and memory is consistent with the idea that records of past experiences are not routinely maintained in memory, but must be reconstructed.

The Influence of Beliefs on Memory.   The idea that recollecting is reconstructing suggests that we reconstruct a memory of our past from our current beliefs and what we believe to be true about human personality in general (Ross, 1989). One idea that people have about personality is that beliefs remain rather stable over time. As a result, people tend to remember that their past beliefs were similar to their currently held beliefs, even when their beliefs have, in fact, changed over time. Let me provide a few experimental demonstrations.

In one study (Goethals & Reckman, 1973; see also Markus, 1986), high school students filled out a survey asking them for their opinion on various topics, including forced busing. About two weeks later, students met with a respected high school senior who presented a carefully crafted and well-rehearsed argument to the students about busing that was the opposite of the students' own opinion. For example, students who were opposed to forced busing heard a counterargument in favor of forced busing. Following the counterargument, students were again asked their opinion on busing, and were also asked to try to recall how they had filled out the survey two weeks earlier. The instructions emphasized the importance of accurate recall.

The counterarguments were effective; students tended to reverse their opinion about busing after hearing the counterargument. The result, consistent with reconstruction, was that the students tended to remember that they originally filled out the survey question about busing in a way consistent with their newly formed opinion and inconsistent with the way they actually had originally answered the busing question. For example, the students who were originally opposed to forced busing but heard a persuasive argument in favor of forced busing tended to remember that they had been in favor of forced busing all along. It was as if the students examined their current belief about busing, assumed that attitudes remain stable over the short period of two weeks, and so reconstructed that they must have held their current attitude two weeks earlier.

Galotti (1995) studied the criteria students use when selecting a college. Galotti asked students to recall the criteria that they had listed in a previously filled-out questionnaire assessing the basis on which they decided where to go to college. Galotti also asked the students to describe the ideal criteria that they thought, in retrospect, they ought to have used. The questionnaires had been filled out 8 to 20 months earlier. Subjects recalled about half of the criteria they had used when originally making the decision about where to go to college. But the overlap between what they recalled and the ideal criteria was substantially greater than the overlap between what they recalled and the criteria they had actually used. It was as if subjects used their current sense of the ideal decision criteria to reconstruct a memory of the criteria they used when originally making the college decision.

Many people, at least in our culture, believe that a woman's mood is likely to become more negative just before and during menstruation. It turns out, though, that this belief may be false. Based on diary studies, there seems to be no reliable correlation between a woman's mood and her menstrual cycle, at least when large numbers of women are studied (see Ross,

1989). The idea of reconstruction suggests that women may use this belief about mood and menstruation to remember inaccurately that their mood had been worse during a previous menstruation phase than during an intermenstrual phase of the cycle.

Evidence consistent with the reconstruction hypothesis is provided by Ross (1989). He reports a study in which a group of women was asked to keep detailed diaries in which they recorded various life events and daily moods. The women were not told that the study focused on the menstrual cycle. At one point in the experiment, the women were asked to recall their mood from a day two weeks earlier. The women were supplied the date and day of the week and a small portion of their diary entries, including an entry that indicated whether they were menstruating. For one group, the to-be-recalled day was during the menstruation phase of their cycle, while for the other group the to-be-recalled day was during the intermenstrual phase. The actual diary entries for the to-be-recalled days indicated that the women's mood was no worse on average during the menstrual phase than during the intermenstrual phase. Yet the women tended to recall that their mood was worse on the menstrual day. Moreover, the more the women believed in a correlation between menstruation and mood (as assessed by an attitude survey), the more likely they were to exaggerate how negative their mood was on the day when they were menstruating.

14.3.3   Confidence and Accuracy

As I suggested earlier, record-keeping theories of human memory may concede that recollection of the past often involves reconstruction. The record-keeping theory could claim that a person resorts to reconstruction when the retrieval process fails to locate the necessary record. The constructionist theory claims instead that people use a reconstruction strategy every time they reflect on the past.

The record-keeping theory implies that people should be able to tell the difference between when they are able to read a record that accurately preserves the details of the past event, and when they are unable to locate the record and so must resort to making guesses about the past. People would presumably have more confidence in their memory for a past event if they are reading the record than if they are only reconstructing it. Therefore, according to the record-keeping theory, people's confidence in the accuracy of their memory for a past event should be reliably greater when the event is remembered accurately than when an event is remembered inaccurately.

The constructionist theory, on the other hand, claims that all recollection is reconstruction. Constructionist theory suggests that confidence and accuracy may sometimes be related, particularly when people have developed learning and reconstruction strategies for which they have been provided feedback as to how well those strategies work. In such cases, people may use their knowledge about how well a strategy has worked in the past to predict accurately how well it will work in the future. However, constructionist theory predicts that confidence will not be strongly related to accuracy when people have had no opportunity to develop adequate learning and reconstructive strategies, or when there is misleading information that fools people into thinking that they have accurately reconstructed an event. In these latter two situations, people may be as confident in the accuracy of an incorrectly reconstructed event as they are of a correctly reconstructed event.

Consistent with the predictions of constructionist theory, a variety of experiments have demonstrated that the correlation between confidence and accuracy is typically quite low, especially in situations where eyewitnesses to crimes and accidents must recollect details of those crimes and accidents (Wells & Murray, 1984; Donders, Schooler, & Loftus, 1987; Smith, Kassin, & Ellsworth, 1989). Presumably most people have not had much practice developing learning and reconstruction strategies for eyewitness information, and therefore have not learned when such strategies produce accurate recollections (see Perfect, Watson, & Wagstaff, 1993).

On the other hand, the correlation between confidence and accuracy is reliably higher in situations where people have had such practice. For example, the correlation between confidence and accuracy is moderately high when subjects are asked to answer general knowledge questions, such as "Who wrote *The Mill on the Floss?*" (e.g., Hart, 1967; Perfect et al., 1993; see Nelson, 1988, for a review). Presumably most people have learned how good they are at answering general knowledge questions (Perfect et al., 1993). The correlation between confidence and accuracy is also moderately high when subjects are asked to answer questions about short texts they have recently read (e.g., Stephenson, 1984; Stephenson, Clark, & Wade, 1986). In this case, experience in academic settings has presumably taught most people how good they are at answering questions about texts.

Record-keeping theories of memory would predict that any variable that decreases memory accuracy should also decrease confidence in the accuracy of the memory. Contrary to the record-keeping prediction, Chandler (1994) reported a series of studies in which accuracy was decreased but confidence increased. Chandler had subjects study nature pictures, such as pictures of lakes. Later, subjects were required to determine which of two related pictures (e.g., two different lakes) had been previously displayed and to indicate their confidence in their recognition judgment. When the subjects had also studied a third related picture (e.g., a third lake), their recognition performance declined but their confidence in their selection increased (compared to the case when there was no third picture). The constructionist explanation is that subjects become more familiar with the general theme (e.g., scenic lakes) of the pictures as they study more of the related pictures. Both alternatives on the recognition test fit the theme, making discrimination between them difficult, so recognition memory performance declines. But because the selected picture fits the theme, confidence in the selection is high.

Also consistent with constructionist theory is the finding that people become confident of inaccurate recollections when those recollections are reconstructed from misleading information supplied to them by an experimenter (e.g., Davis & Schiffman, 1985; Spiro, 1977). Consider a study by Ryan and Geiselman (1991). They presented subjects a film of a robbery and a week later had them read a summary description of the film. For some of the subjects the summary included a misleading detail, such as "The police car is at a brown house" (in fact, the house in the film was white). The subjects then answered questions about the film (e.g., "What was the color of the house?"). The interesting finding was that subjects who were biased by the incorrect detail, and therefore gave the wrong answer (e.g., "The house was brown"), were more confident of their wrong answer than were the subjects who were not given the misleading detail and so usually gave the correct answer (e.g., "The house was white").

People may become confident of their inaccurate memories when some inaccurately remembered piece of information is nevertheless consistent with the gist of some previously presented information. For instance, Roediger and McDermott (1995; see also Deese, 1959) presented subjects list of words (e.g., *bed, rest, awake*) for which every word on a list was related to a target word (e.g., *sleep*) not presented on the list. Later, on tests of recall and recognition, subjects remembered that the target words (e.g., *sleep*) were on the list about as often and with about the same confidence as they remembered the words that were actually presented on the lists. Moreover, the greater the number of related words presented on the list, the more likely subjects were to recall or recognize the target word not presented on the list (Robinson & Roediger, 1997). Presumably, the tendency to think of the target word when studying the list created a false memory for that target word that seemed as real to subjects as their memories of actually presented words.

14.3.4   The Overlap Principle

The fact that memory makes use of reconstruction strategies, such as relying on one's current beliefs to deduce past beliefs, means that remembering is often inaccurate. But recollections of the past are not inevitably inaccurate. The study of memory has established that memory of an event is more accurate when the environment at the time of recollection resembles the environment of the originally experienced event (Begg & White, 1985; Guthrie, 1959; Tulving, 1983; Tulving & Thomson, 1973). This principle may be called the *overlap principle* — people's memory for a past event improves to the extent that the elements of the recollection environment overlap with the elements of the past event. By environment, I mean a person's cognitive and emotional state, as well as the person's physical environment. The overlap principle also goes by the name of *encoding specificity,* to emphasize that how an event is processed or "encoded" will determine what kinds of cues will later be effective at promoting memory for the event (Tulving & Thomson, 1973).

Experimental Evidence for the Overlap Principle.   A good experimental demonstration of the overlap principle comes from research designed to help eyewitnesses more accurately remember crimes and accidents. Courts of law place strong emphasis on eyewitness accounts when assessing responsibility and punishment. Yet people often have a hard time remembering important details of crimes and accidents they have witnessed, a point I used earlier to illustrate the concept of reconstruction in memory. A variety of research suggests that eyewitness memory improves if the context surrounding the event is reinstated (see Geiselman, 1988).

Cutler and Penrod (1988; see also Geiselman, Fisher, MacKinnon, & Holland, 1985) had subjects view a videotape of a robbery and a few days later pick out the robber from a lineup. Some subjects were given photographs (not containing the robber) taken from the scene of the crime, or were asked to think back through the events from beginning to end while imagining the robbery. These subjects tended to identify the robber more accurately than subjects not given any context-reinstating cues.

Other experiments have demonstrated that memory for an event is more accurate if retrieval takes place in the same physical environment as the one where the event originally occurred (e.g., Canas & Nelson, 1986; see Smith, 1988 for a review). In one of my favorite studies, subjects who learned a list of words while scuba diving later recalled more of the words if the recall test took place while the subjects were again scuba diving than if the recall test took place on land (Godden & Baddeley, 1975).

It should be noted, though, that the overlap of physical environments is probably an important determinant of memory when the to-be-learned information can be associated with the physical environment (Baddeley, 1982; Fernandez & Glenberg, 1985). An eyewitness may be more likely to remember the events of an accident, such as a car crashing into a tree, if the eyewitness recollects at the scene of the accident, than if the eyewitness recollects in the police station. The tree at the crash site is associated with the accident, so that seeing the tree is likely to activate information that may be used to reconstruct the accident. On the other hand, it is probably not as important that a student take an exam in the same room where he or she studied for the exam (Saufley, Otaka, & Bavaresco, 1985) since academic information would not ordinarily be associated with the physical elements of a room. Much more important is that the student understand the academic material, organize the material, and make the details contained within the material distinctive.

One demonstration that the overlap principle depends more on the similarity of cognitive processing than on similarity of physical stimuli comes from research on mood. The usual finding is that subjects induced to feel elated or depressed will more likely and quickly recall past events experienced in the same mood, than those experienced in a different mood (Snyder & White, 1982; Teasdale & Fogarty, 1979; see Blaney, 1986, for a review). In experiments conducted by Eich (1995), subjects were placed in a setting (e.g., a laboratory) and then responded to a list of 16 words designed to prompt memories of past experiences. The subjects' mood was also measured. Later, subjects were placed in either the same physical setting or a different setting, and were induced to feel either happy or sad. Mood was induced by having subjects listen to either joyful musical pieces while entertaining elating thoughts or melancholy musical pieces while entertaining depressing thoughts. The subjects then had to recall the 16 prompt words and the events the prompts elicited. Recall was better when the mood at the time of recall matched the mood experienced when the prompt words were first presented. Overlap in physical setting, on the other hand, did not matter to recall.

Problem Solving and the Overlap Principle.   Another interesting demonstration that the overlap principle is based on similarity in the way events are processed, and not on the mere presence of overlapping stimulus cues, comes from research on problem solving. A seemingly perplexing finding of this research is that people often fail to remember facts that would help them solve a problem (Perfetto, Bransford, & Franks, 1983; Weisberg, Dicamillo, & Phillips, 1978). To illustrate with a hypothetical example, suppose a student in a psychology class learned the fact that, paradoxically, ignoring a young child who is whining and crying promotes the development of a dependent personality. On an examination, the student remembers this information and so correctly answers questions based on it. Yet when the student becomes a parent and encounters the whining of the child, the parent chooses to ignore the child, in the mistaken belief that the child will thereby become more independent.

Why does the parent fail to remember and make use of the relevant information previously learned in school? The answer is that trying to solve problems is unlikely to engage the portion of the cognitive system used to memorize facts, so the memorized facts play no role in the attempt to arrive at a solution. Perhaps if the parent had practiced solving child-rearing problems in school, rather than only memorizing facts about child rearing, the parent would have been more likely to transfer the information to real problems.

My hypothetical example about child rearing was inspired by experiments conducted by Adams et al. (1988); Perfetto et al. (1983); Lockhart, Lamon, and Glick (1988), and Needham and Begg (1991), among others. In one of these experiments (Perfetto et al., 1983), one group of subjects read a list of sentences that included sentences like "A minister marries several people a week" while a control group of subjects did not read the sentences. Both groups of subjects were then asked to solve brain teasers like "How can it be that a man can marry several women a week, never get divorced, yet break no law?" Note that the sentences the first group read were designed to help them solve the problems presented later on. Surprisingly, the subjects who first read the helpful sentences were no more likely to solve the brain teasers than the control subjects.

What would it take to get the subjects to make use of previously studied information to solve a new problem? Adams et al. (1988) and Lockhart et al. (1988) presented groups of subjects with sentences like this: "The man married ten people each week" and, 5 seconds after each sentence, gave the subjects a clue to help solve the puzzle suggested by the sentence — for example "a minister." Note that the subjects were not memorizing the sentences but instead approaching each sentence as a kind of miniature problem for which they were quickly given the solution. Subjects asked to approach the sentences as a set of problems were later on better at solving the brain teasers than either the subjects who first only memorized the sentences or the control subjects who never read any sentences. When the experiment ensured that the information processing activity required by the brain teaser matched the information processing activity required by the original presentation of the sentences, the subjects were able to make use of the sentences to help them solve the brain teasers.

These findings are examples of transfer appropriate processing (discussed earlier in the chapter), and are a manifestation of the overlap principle. If the kind of cognitive processing taking place in the testing environment resembles that taking place in the original learning environment, then what is learned will likely transfer to the test. Other experiments demonstrating transfer appropriate processing can be found in Blaxton (1989); in Glass, Krejci, and Goldman (1989); and in the Morris, Bransford, and Franks (1977) study I discussed in the "levels of processing" section earlier in this chapter. The obvious educational implication of transfer appropriate processing is that if schools want to increase the odds that what students learn in school will help them solve problems later in life, then schools should engage students in solving problems that resemble those encountered outside of school. Students who demonstrate on examinations that they remember the material are not necessarily going to be able to use the material to solve problems they encounter later on.

Recognition versus Recall.   Another demonstration of the overlap principle is the finding that, under most circumstances, people can recognize more accurately than they can recall a past event (McDougall, 1904). A recognition test usually supplies more information about the original event than does a recall test, because the correct answer to any memory question is contained in the recognition test. For example, subjects asked to recall as many names as they could remember from their high school class that graduated 47 years earlier recalled on average only about 20 names (about 30% of the class), but accurately recognized about 45 names (about 65% of the class) (Bahrick, Bahrick, & Wittlinger, 1975).

It is possible, however, to devise situations for which people can recall what they are unable to recognize (Watkins & Tulving, 1975; see Klatzky, 1980, for a review). Such situations are characterized by a recall testing environment that more closely resembles the original learning environment than does the recognition testing environment.

In one experiment demonstrating recall without recognition (Nilsson, Law, & Tulving, 1988), subjects were presented a list of famous names (e.g., George Washington) in the context of descriptive phrases (e.g., "He was the first in a long line but the only one on horseback — George Washington"). Seven days later the subjects were given a recognition test in which a set of famous names was presented. This set contained the previously studied names as well as foils (e.g., Charles Darwin). Subjects had to indicate which names they had studied a week earlier. Then subjects were given the descriptive phrases and had to recall the famous names (e.g., "He was the first in a long line but the only one on horseback — ?"). Subjects were often able to recall famous names that they did not recognize.

14.4   FORGETTING

Forgetting past experiences, if not in their entirety, at least in most of their detail, seems the rule. Why do we so easily forget most of our past? Certainly, if we fail to pay attention to certain information contained in an event then we are unlikely to remember that information later on. Or if we are not motivated to try to remember an event, or are not given enough information to enable us to be sure what it is we are supposed to remember, then we are not likely to remember the event.

14.4.1   Interference

Another important reason for forgetting, besides those mentioned above, is that one's memory for any given event from one's past is undermined by the occurrence of other events. When memory for an event is undermined by events that precede it, the result is called *proactive interference.* When memory for an event is undermined by events that follow it, the result is called *retroactive interference.*

A variety of experimental paradigms have been used to demonstrate interference (see Klatzky, 1980, or Watkins, 1979, for a review). The classic demonstration of retroactive interference comes from Jenkins and Dallenbach (1924). In their experiment, subjects were first presented a list of nonsense syllables, then spent the following 8 hours either asleep or awake, and then tried to recall the nonsense syllables. The subjects who remained awake, and so experienced more interfering events, recalled fewer syllables than did the subjects who went to sleep. This experiment is not the ideal demonstration of retroactive interference, though, because the subjects who experienced less interference also experienced a night of sleep. Maybe people are more motivated or less fatigued after sleeping, and so perform better on memory tests.

An example of a better controlled experiment demonstrating interference is provided by Kalbaugh and Walls (1973; also see Barnes & Underwood, 1959; McGeoch, 1942; Melton & Irwin, 1940). They required their eighth-grade subjects to study a critical passage describing the essential biographical details of a fictional character. Some subjects read no other passages while other subjects read either two or four other biographical passages. The additional passages were presented either before the critical passage or after the critical passage. As summarized in figure 14.5, the experiment demonstrated both retroactive and proactive interference. The subjects who read additional passages, whether presented

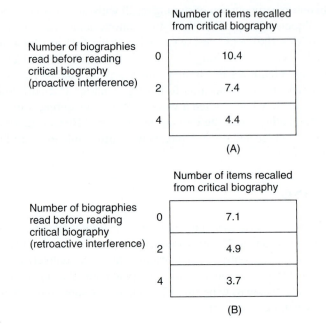

FIGURE 14.5   Proactive and retroactive interference. Based on Kalbaugh and Walls, 1973.

before or after the critical passage, recalled less about the critical passage than subjects who read only the critical passage. The more additional passages the subjects read, the poorer was their recall of the critical passage.

Another way in which interference is demonstrated is in experiments that measure how fast people can decide whether a fact about a concept was on a previously memorized list of facts. Interference in this paradigm takes the form of an increased response latency to facts whose concepts are found in lots of other facts on the list. In one such experiment, subjects memorized sentences that described a professional in some location (e.g., "The lawyer was in the park"). The number of facts about any one professional or about any one location varied. Subjects might memorize two facts about a lawyer (e.g., "The lawyer was in the park," "The lawyer was at the beach") and one fact about a doctor (e.g., "The doctor was in the park") and might memorize two facts that involved parks and one fact that involved beaches. The typical result (illustrated in figure 14.6 for "true" responses) is that the more facts associated with a character or with a location, the longer it takes to decide if the fact is true or false (Anderson, 1974, 1976). Sometimes this finding is known as the *fan effect.* The more facts that "fan off" a concept, the longer it takes to verify whether any given fact about the concept was previously memorized.

14.4.2   Explaining Interference

The record-keeping theory has an easy explanation for interference. People search memory records by first finding in memory a target element, such as a character's profession. People then scan through the set of facts associated with the target element until the desired fact

Number of facts about a location

1	2	3
1.169	1.196	1.248

Reaction time, in seconds, to respond "true"

Number of facts about a profession

1	2	3
1.144	1.202	1.267

Reaction time, in seconds, to respond "true"

FIGURE 14.6   The more facts about a professional or location, the longer the response time to verify the fact. Based on Anderson, 1974.

is found, or until the search is exhausted. The more associations to be searched, or the longer or more effort it takes to find the desired fact, the more likely the fact will not be found. It is as if all of the associations, facts, and lists of facts stored in memory compete with the target information for the attention of the search process (Anderson, 1976, 1983; McGeoch, 1942; Postman, Stark, & Fraser, 1968).

The ease with which a record-keeping theory explains interference in memory experiments is one of the most compelling sources of evidence for it. But the explanation leads to a paradox (Smith, Adams, & Schoor, 1978). As we go through life, the number of associations with elements in our memory should continually increase. It follows, then, that over time we should become increasingly inefficient at finding information stored in our memory. Becoming an expert would be especially difficult, because the expert learns many facts about a set of concepts. Experts, then, would be expected to have an ever-increasing difficulty in remembering information in their area of expertise. Obviously this does not happen. The record-keeping theory's explanation for interference observed in many memorization experiments cannot easily explain the obvious facts that an adult's memory skill remains stable over time and that experts get better, and not worse, at remembering information in their area of expertise.

The difficulty that the record-keeping theory of memory has with explaining everyday observations about memory reminds us that explanations must have *ecological validity*. That is, theories of memory should explain how memory works in the actual environment in which we use our memory. Some memory theorists, notably Ulric Neisser (Neisser, 1978), have argued that a lot of memory research does not look at memory in realistic settings and so may not be ecologically valid. Neisser has urged the cognitive psychological community to make more use of experimental paradigms that resemble real-life situations. I have tried to include a fair number of such experiments in this chapter. Some memory theorists, however, have complained that experiments that have resembled real-life situations have not really uncovered any new principle of memory (Banaji & Crowder, 1989; see articles in the January 1991 issue of the *American Psychologist*).

Perhaps, though, the contrast between the results of list memorization experiments and the everyday observations that memory is stable over time and that experts have good memory constitutes a compelling example of the importance of conducting ecologically valid research.

The constructionist theory is able to explain both the decline in memory performance exhibited in the memorization experiments and the lack of decline in memory observed in ordinary day-to-day situations or in experts. Memorization of related lists of words should generally present difficulties because the same elements would be used repeatedly to understand each new list. A subject who must memorize two lists of state-city associations, for example, would find that the connections among the cognitive elements used to understand and recollect the first list would be reconfigured when the second list was studied, thereby undermining memory for the details of the first list. Memorization, therefore, should be poorer or slower if a person has to memorize several related lists than if a person has to memorize unrelated lists. Furthermore, the repeated use of similar lists would make accurate and detailed reconstruction of any one list difficult.

The stability in an adult's memory skill occurs because the elements used to understand experiences do not expand in number as a result of having many experiences. Only the connections among elements change with experience. Experts become good at remembering information in their area of expertise because the portions of their cognitive system that support the expertise will have many enduring patterns of connections to represent and reconstruct that information. For example, an expert on climate may be able to remember that Seattle has a milder winter than Denver by activating the general principle that oceans moderate climate. Much of what is involved in becoming an expert is understanding the general principles that a body of information entails.

One of the important predictions of the constructionist account of interference is that interference is not inevitable. Interference is expected when there is no effective learning strategy for extracting the patterns that integrate increasingly larger bodies of information. If such patterns can be extracted and used to reconstruct the information, then increasing the amount of information should not produce interference. Research confirms this prediction.

In one experiment, Jones and Anderson (1987) required subjects to memorize varying numbers of facts about hypothetical characters. In some cases, the facts were all related by a common theme. For example, subjects might learn that John has a rifle, John is a hunter, and John is in the forest. In other cases the facts were unrelated — for example: Jerry has a rifle, Jerry is a researcher, and Jerry is at the beach. As in other experiments investigating the fan effect, the subjects were then asked to verify whether particular facts were true (e.g., "John has a rifle") or false (e.g., "John is a researcher"). When the facts were unrelated, the usual fan effect was observed. Subjects took longer to verify facts about a character when there were six unrelated facts about that character to memorize than when there was only one fact to memorize. But when the facts were related by a common theme, the fan effect was greatly reduced. When the facts were related by a theme, subjects took about as long to verify facts about a character when there were six related facts to memorize about that character as when there was only one fact to memorize. Similar results have been obtained by Radvansky and Zacks (1991) and by Smith, Adams, and Schorr (1978). The constructionist explanation is that when the facts are related by a theme, that theme can be used to reconstruct whether a fact fits the theme and so must be true, or does not fit the theme, and so must be false.

The constructionist theory of memory also implies that interference depends on what kind of information subjects are asked to remember. If subjects in list-memorizing experiments were asked to remember the general pattern of information in the lists, rather than the unique details of each list, then presenting subjects with several lists should promote better memory of the general pattern, even while undermining memory for the unique details of each list.

Evidence consistent with the constructionist prediction is provided by Reder and Ross (1983). They required subjects to memorize a varying number of facts about hypothetical characters. Later, some subjects were required to indicate whether a particular fact was explicitly on the memorized list, while other subjects were asked to indicate whether a particular fact was similar to (implied by) other facts on the list. For example, subjects might learn three facts about Marvin: Marvin skied down the slope, Marvin waited in the lift line, and Marvin waxed his skis. The usual fan effect was observed if the memory test required subjects to judge whether a particular fact was explicitly on the list (e.g., Marvin waited in the lift line). The greater the number of memorized facts about a character, the longer to verify whether any given fact about the character was on the list. The opposite of the usual fan effect was observed if the test required that subjects decide whether a fact was implied by other facts on the list (e.g., Marvin adjusted his skis). The greater the number of facts about a character, the faster subjects could verify whether a fact was similar to one of the memorized facts. The constructionist explanation is that the similarity judgment allowed subjects to compare a fact to the pattern or theme extracted from the memorized facts. The more facts there were to memorize, the more likely that such patterns would be extracted.

Another demonstration that increasing the amount of information can improve memory for patterns but undermine memory for details comes from an experiment by Bower (1974). Bower required his subjects to learn a critical passage describing the biography of a hypothetical character. The basic form of the biography described the time and place of birth, the occupation of the character's father, the way the father died, and so on. Subjects then studied some additional passages. For some subjects, the additional passages were biographies similar in form but different in detail from the critical passage. For other subjects, the additional passages were unrelated to the critical passage in form and in detail. Later, all subjects had to recall the same critical passage. Bower found that subjects who studied the related passages recalled fewer details of the critical passage (e.g., the father was a servant) but more of the general pattern of the passage (e.g., the passage described the father's occupation) than did subjects who studied unrelated passages.

Students often feel overwhelmed by the amount of material they must learn for an exam. Perhaps it would hearten them to learn that interference for newly acquired information is not inevitable. If students can relate each piece of information to a common theme, then interference is not likely to occur. The student should be able to remember large sets of information as well as small sets. Similarly, if the examination tests for general principles rather than specific details, then again interference is not inevitable. The more information one must learn, the more likely the general principles can be extracted from the information.

SUMMARY AND CONCLUSIONS

In the first section of this chapter, I introduced two competing types of theories of memory. One is the record-keeping theory, which argues that memory is a system for storing records of past events, that recollection is searching through and reading the records, and that forgetting is caused primarily by the distracting presence of many memory records. The second is the constructionist theory, which argues that memory reflects changes to the cognitive systems used to interpret events, that recollection is reconstructing the past, and that forgetting is caused primarily by the continuous changes each new experience makes to the cognitive systems that interpret and act on stimuli. Few contemporary theories of memory embody all the features of record-keeping theories, although some contemporary theories, especially those that use computers as metaphors for memory, seem closer in spirit to the record-keeping than to the constructionist theory. Certainly the record-keeping theory has dominated the history of memory research and seems to reflect the ordinary person's view of memory (Loftus & Loftus, 1980).

I have argued that the evidence overall supports the constructionist theory over the record-keeping theory. In the second section, I discussed how experiences are retained in memory. Evidence consistent with constructionist theory is that memory is good for invariants or patterns that endure across many experiences, but is poor for the details of specific experiences. Usually people remember the details of a particular experience because those details are unusual or distinctive in some way. Even people with very remarkable memory for details, such as Luria's *S,* make use of mnemonic devices and learning strategies that help them make information more distinctive.

The constructionist approach claims that memory reflects the strength of connections among elements of the cognitive systems used to perceive, think about, and act on events. Such connections undergo continuous reconfiguration in response to experiences. In a sense, memory is only a byproduct of connections among the components of various cognitive systems. There is no separate memory system in which information is "stored." Consistent with the idea of memory as a byproduct is the assimilation principle: How well people remember new information about a topic depends on how much they already know about that topic. Also consistent is the observation that individual differences in memory are largely attributable to expertise in the relevant domain of knowledge. General intellectual skill, or skill at memorizing, does not seem to predict memory for new information from some domain of knowledge as well as does expertise in that domain.

Especially telling for the constructionist theory is that conscious recollection of the past depends on current knowledge and on recollection strategies. As I discussed in the third section, a person's recollections of the past are often distorted by misleading questions or general knowledge. For example, eye-witnesses to crimes and accidents sometimes mistakenly remember details, like a car going through a stop sign, that they never observed. Usually such mistakes are made when someone or some process implies that the details were a part of the crime or accident. Especially difficult for the record-keeping theory is the finding that people are often as confident of inaccurate as of accurate reconstructions of past events.

Although forgetting is common, people certainly are able to reconstruct accurately some of their past experiences. Memory is more accurate when there is considerable similarity between the retrieval and original learning environment, a phenomenon called the overlap (also called the encoding specificity) principle. The constructionist theory explains the overlap principle by claiming that memory is improved when the retrieval environment activates the same portions of the cognitive system used to interpret the original environment. For instance, people are more likely to use information previously learned in one environment to solve a new problem if the original environment also required them to use that information to solve problems.

The most important principle of forgetting, called interference, is that the more information a person must memorize, the more likely the person will be unable to remember or will be slower at remembering any given piece of information. As I discussed in the fourth section, the record-keeping theory suggests that interference is primarily due to the distracting effects of other memory records, which increase in number as the amount of information to be remembered increases. But the record-keeping theory implies a paradox: Adults should show a gradual decline in their memory as they learn more about various topics. Experts should have especially poor memory in their domains of expertise. Yet neither of these propositions is true.

The constructionist theory predicts interference when no distinctive patterns enable the person to reconstruct information, as is likely to happen in list memorization experiments. Because the constructionist theory claims that no memory records are kept, an adult's memory remains stable over time. Because experts learn to find patterns in and to develop reconstruction strategies for their domain of expertise, experts have a good memory for that domain. The constructionist theory correctly predicts that interference usually observed in list learning experiments is eliminated if the memorized facts can be integrated by a common theme, or if the memory test requires people to remember the patterns rather than the details contained within the memorized material.

Although constructionist accounts of memory are currently influential (see Schacter, 1996), some cognitive psychologists continue to support record-keeping theories (see Hall, 1990). One might argue that, with suitable modifications, the record-keeping theory can explain the data I claimed support the constructionist theory. For example, a record-keeping theory could include a pattern recognition system that either stores descriptions of patterns or examines memory records to find patterns in events. Consequently, patterns of experiences would be readily remembered. A record-keeping theory could posit that reconstruction strategies are used when a sought-after memory record is not located.

It is true that such modifications would make the record-keeping theory work more like real human memory. Note, though, that the proposed modifications have the effect of making the record-keeping theory more like the constructionist theory. Furthermore, the modifications are not intrinsic to, or a natural consequence of, the central idea that memory is a matter of storing records of experiences. There is nothing about putting a record of an experience someplace in a storage bin that inevitably leads to extracting a pattern. There is nothing about reading memory records that leads to making plausible guesses about what happened in the past. These modifications are just tacked on, because without them the system does not resemble human memory. To put it another way, the record-keeping theory so modified lacks theoretical elegance.

In contrast, consider that the central idea of the constructionist theory, that the cognitive systems change the strength of their connections in response to events, does lead naturally to how human memory actually works. Remembering patterns, but not details, is a natural consequence of such a system, because the invariants in experiences strengthen already existing connections. No pattern recognition system has to be added on. Reconstruction happens because no records of past experiences are ever "read" or "reexperienced"; rather, past events must be inferred from the current state of connections. And a constructionist theory of memory more closely reflects what is known about the neurophysiology of learning and remembering.

[...]

REFERENCES

Adams, J. L., Kasserman, J. E., Yearwood, A. A., Perfetto, G. A., Bransford, J. D., & Franks, J. J. (1988). Memory access: The effects of fact-oriented versus problem-oriented acquisition. *Memory and Cognition, 16,* 167–175.

Anderson, J. R. (1974). Retrieval of prepositional information from long-term memory. *Cognitive Psychology, 5,* 451–474.

Anderson, J. R. (1976). *Language, memory, and thought.* Hillsdale, NJ: Erlbaum.

Anderson, J. R. (1983). *The architecture of cognition.* Cambridge, MA: Harvard University Press.

Anderson, J. R., & Bower, G. H. (1973). *Human associative memory.* Washington, D.C.: Winston.

Anderson, J. R., & Milson, R. (1989). Human memory: An adaptive perspective. *Psychological Review, 96,* 703–719.

Atkinson, R. C., & Shiffrin, R. M. (1968). Human memory: A proposed system and its control processes. In K. W. Spence & J. T. Spence (Eds.), *The psychology of learning and motivation: Advances in research and theory* (Vol. 2). New York: Academic Press.

Baddeley, A. D. (1982). Domains of recollection. *Psychological Review, 22,* 88–104.

Bahrick, H. P., Bahrick, P. C., & Wittlinger, R. P. (1975). Fifty years of memories for names and faces: A cross-sectional approach. *Journal of Experimental Psychology, 104,* 54–75.

Banaji, M. R., & Crowder, R. G. (1989). The bankruptcy of everyday memory. *American Psychologist, 44,* 1185–1193.

Barclay, C. R., & Wellman, H. M. (1986). Accuracies and inaccuracies in autobiographical memories. *Journal of Memory and Language, 25,* 93–106.

Barnes, J. M., & Underwood, B. J. (1959). "Fate: of first-list associations in transfer theory. *Journal of Experimental Psychology, 58,* 97–105.

Bartlett, F. C. (1932). *Remembering: A study in experimental and social psychology.* Cambridge, England: Cambridge University Press.

Beach, K. D. (1988). The role of external mnemonic symbols in acquiring an occupation. In M. M. Gruensberg, P. E. Morris, & R. N. Sykes (Eds.), *Practical aspects of memory: Current research and issues* (Vol. 1, pp. 342–346). Chichester, England: Wiley.

Begg, I., & White, P. (1985). Encoding, specificity in interpersonal communication. *Canadian Journal of Psychology, 39,* 70–87.

Bellezza, F. S., & Buck, D. K. (1988). Expert knowledge as mneumonic cues. *Applied Cognitive Psychology, 2,* 147–162.

Bjork, R. A. (1975). Short-term storage: The ordered output of a central processor. In F. Restle, R. M. Shiffrin, N. J. Castellan, H. R. Lindeman, & D. B. Pisoni (Eds.), *Cognitive Theory* (Vol. 1). Hillsdale, NJ: Erlbaum.

Blaney, P. H. (1986). Affect and memory: A review. *Child Development, 53,* 799–810.

Blaxton, T. A. (1989). Investigating dissociations among memory measures: Support for a transfer-appropriate processing framework. *Journal of Experimental Psychology: Learning, Memory, and Cognition, 15,* 657–668.

Bobrow, S., & Bower, G. H. (1969). Comprehension and recall of sentences. *Journal of Experimental Psychology, 80,* 455–461.

Bower, G. H. (1974). Selective facilitation and interference in retention of prose. *Journal of Educational Psychology, 66,* 1–8.

Bower, G. H., Clark, M. C., Lesgold, A. M., & Winzenz, D. (1969). Hierarchical retrieval schemes in recall of categorical word lists. *Journal of Verbal Learning and Verbal Behavior, 8,* 303–343.

Bransford, J. D., & Franks, J. J. (1971). The abstraction of linguistic ideas. *Cognitive Psychology, 2,* 331–350.

Bransford, J. D., & Johnson, M. K. (1972). Contextual prerequisite for understanding: Some investigations of comprehension and recall. *Journal of Verbal Learning and Verbal Behavior, 11,* 717–726.

Bransford, J. D., Barclay, J. R., & Franks, J. J. (1972). Sentence memory: A constructive versus interpretive approach. *Cognitive Psychology, 3,* 193–209.

Bransford, J. D., McCarrell, N. S., Franks, J. J., & Nitsch, K. E. (1977). Toward unexplaining memory. In R. S. Shaw & J. D. Bransford (Eds.), *Perceiving, Acting and Knowing: Toward an Ecological Psychology.* Hillsdale, NJ: Erlbaum.

Brewer, W. F. (1984). The nature and function of schema. In J. Strachey & T. K. Srult (Eds.), *Hand-book of Social Cognition* (Vol. 1, pp. 119–160). Hillsdale, NJ: Erlbaum.

Brooks, L. W., & Dansereau, D. F. (1983). Effects of structural schema training and text organization on expository prose processing. *Journal of Educational Psychology, 75,* 811–820.

Brown, R., & Kulik, J. (1977). Flashbulb memories. *Cognition, 5,* 73–99.

Brown, R., & McNeill, D. (1966). The "tip of the tongue" phenomemon. *Journal of Verbal Learning and Verbal Behavior, 5,* 325–337.

Brown, E., Deffenbacher, K., & Sturgill, W. (1977). Memory for faces and the circumstances of encounter. *Journal of Applied Psychology, 62,* 311–318.

Buckhout, R., Eugenio, P., Licitia, T., Oliver, L., & Kramer, T. H. (1981). Memory, hypnosis, and evidence: Research or eyewitnesses. *Social Action and the Law, 7,* 67–72.

Canas, J. J., & Nelson, D. C. (1986). Recognition and environmental context: The effects of testing by phone. *Bulletin of the Psychonomic Society, 24,* 407–109.

Carlson, N. R. (1994). *Physiology of behavior.* Boston: Allyn & Bacon.

Chandler, C. C. (1994). Studying related pictures can reduce accuracy, but increase confidence, in a modified recognition test. *Memory and Cognition, 22,* 273–280.

Chase, W. G., & Simon, H. A. (1973). Perception in chess. *Cognitive Psychology, 4,* 55–81.

Chiesi, H., Spilich, G., & Voss, J. F. (1979). Acquisition of domain related information in relation to high and low domain knowledge. *Journal of Verbal Learning and Verbal Behavior, 18,* 257–273.

Cohen, M. E., & Carr, W. J. (1975). Facial recognition and the VonRestorff effect. *Bulletin of the Psychonomic Society, 6,* 383–384.

Collins, A. F., & Hay, D. C. (1994). Connectionism and memory. In P. E. Morrise & M. Gruneberg (Eds.), *Theoretical aspects of memory* (pp. 196–237). New York: Routledge.

Craik, F. I. M., & Lockhart, R. S. (1972). Levels of processing: A framework for memory research. *Journal of Verbal Learning and Verbal Behavior, 11,* 671–684.

Craik, F. I. M., & Tulving, E. (1975). Depth of processing and the retention of words in episodic memory. *Journal of Experimental Psychology: General, 104,* 268–294.

Dale, H. C. A., & Baddeley, A. D. (1962). On the nature of alternatives used in testing recognition of memory. *Nature, 196,* 93–94.

Davis, J., & Schiffman, H. R. (1985). The influence of the wording of interrogatives on the accuracy of eyewitness recollection. *Bulletin of the Psychonomic Society, 23,* 394–396.

Dean, R. S., & Kulhavy, R. W. (1981). Influence of spatial organization in prose learning. *Journal of Educational Psychology, 73,* 64–97.

DeAngelis, T. (1988). Dietary recall is poor: Recall study suggests. *APA Monitor, 19,* 14.

Deese, J. (1959). On the prediction of occurrence of particular verbal intrusions in immediate recall. *Journal of Experimental Psychology, 58,* 17–22.

DeMarie-Dreblow, D. (1991). Relation between knowledge and memory: A reminder that correlation does not imply causation. *Child Development, 62,* 484–498.

Donders, K., Schooler, J. W., & Loftus, E. F. (1987, November). *Troubles with memory.* Paper presented at the annual meeting of the Psychonomic Society, Seattle, WA.

Dooling, D. J., & Christiaansen, R. E. (1977). Episodic and semantic aspects of memory for prose. *Journal of Experimental Psychology: Human Learning and Memory, 3,* 428–436.

Ebbinghaus, H. (1885). *Uber das Gedachtnis.* Leipzig: Dunker and Humbolt.

Ericssson, K. A., & Polson, P. G. (1988). An experimental analysis of the mechanisms of a memory skill. *Journal of Experimental Psychology: Learning, Memory, and Cognition, 14,* 305–316.

Erickson, J. R., & Jemison, C. R. (1991). Relations among measures of autobiographical memory. *Bulletin of the Psychonomic Society, 29,* 233–236.

Farthing, G. W. (1992). *The psychology of consciousness.* Upper Saddle River, NJ: Prentice-Hall.

Fernandez, A., & Glenberg, A. M. (1985). Changing environmental context does not reliably affect memory. *Memory and Cognition, 13,* 333–336.

Freeman, L. C., Romney, A. K., & Freeman, S. C. (1987). Cognitive structure and informant accuracy. *American Anthropologist, 89,* 310–325.

Fries, E., Green, P., & Bowen, D. J. (1995). What did I eat yesterday? Determinants of accuracy in 24-hour food memories. *Applied Cognitive Psychology, 9,* 143–155.

Galiotti, K. M. (1995). Memories of a "decision-map": Recall of real-life decision. *Applied Cognitive Psychology, 9,* 307–319.

Geiselman, R. E. (1988). Improving eyewitness memory through mental reinstatement of context. In G. M. Davies & D. M. Thompson (Eds.), *Memory in context: Context in memory* (pp. 231–244). Chichester, England: Wiley.

Geiselman, R. E., Fisher, R. P., MacKinnon, D. P., & Holland, H. L. (1985). Eyewitness memory enhancement in the police interview: Cognitive retrieval mneumonics versus hypnonsis. *Journal of Applied Psychology, 70,* 401–412.

Gernsbacher, M. A. (1985). Surface information loss in comprehension. *Cognitive Psychology, 17,* 324–363.

Glass, A. L., Krejci, J., & Goldman, J. (1989). The necessary and sufficient conditions for motor learning, recognition, and recall. *Journal of Memory and Language, 28,* 189–199.

Godden, N. N., & Baddeley, A. D. (1975). Context-dependent memory in two natural environments: On land and underwater. *British Journal of Psychology, 66,* 325–332.

Goethals, G. R., & Reckman, R. F. (1973). The perception of consistency in attitudes. *Journal of Experimental Psychology, 9,* 491–501.

Goldstein, A. G., & Chance, J. (1970). Visual recognition memory for complex configurations. *Perception and Psychophysics, 9,* 237–241.

Greeno, J. G. (1964). Paired-associate learning with massed and distributed repetition of items. *Journal of Experimental Psychology, 67,* 286–295.

Groninger, L. D. (1971). Mnemonic imagery and forgetting. *Psychonomic Science, 23,* 161–163.

Grossberg, S., & Stone, G. (1986). Neural dynamics of word recognition and recall: Attentional priming, learning, and resonance. *Psychological Review, 93,* 46–74.

Guthrie, E. R. (1959). Association of contiguity. In S. Koch (Ed.), *Psychology: A study of science* (Vol. 2). New York: McGraw-Hill.

Haber, R. N., & Haber, L. R. (1988). The characteristic of eidetic imagery. In L. K. Obler & D. Fein (Eds.), *The exceptional brain: Neuropsychology of talent and special abilities* (pp. 218–241). New York: Guilford Press.

Hall, J. F. (1990). Reconstructive and reproductive models of memory. *Bulletins of the Psychonomic Society, 28,* 191–194.

Hanawalt, N. G., & Demarest, I. H. (1939). The effect of verbal suggestion in the recall period upon the production of visually perceived forms. *Journal of Experimental Psychology, 251,* 151–174.

Harris, R. O., & Monaco, G. E. (1978). Psychology of pragmatic implication: Information processing between the lines. *Journal of Experimental Psychology: General, 107,* 1–22.

Hart, J. T. (1967). Memory and the memory-monitoring process. *Journal of Verbal Learning and Verbal Behavior, 76,* 685–691.

Hoffman, R. R., Bringmann, W., Bamberg, M., & Klein, R. (1986). Some historical observations on Ebbinghaus. In D. Gorgein & R. Hoffman (Eds.), *Memory and learning: The Ebbinghaus centennial conference.* Hillsdale, NJ: Erlbaum.

Holmes, D. S. (1972). Repression or interference: A further investigation. *Journal of Personality and Social Psychology, 221,* 163–170.

Howes, M. B. (1990). *The psychology of human cognition: Mainstream and Genevan tradtionsI.* New York: Pergamon Press.

Hunt, E., & Love, T. (1972). How good can memory be? In A. W. Melton & E. Martin (Eds.), *Coding processes in human memory.* Washington, DC: Winston.

Hyde, J. S., & Jenkins, J. J. (1975). Recall for words as a function of semantic, graphic, and syntactic orienting tasks. *Journal of Verbal Learning and Verbal Behavior, 12,* 471–480.

Jacoby, L. L. (1978). On interpreting the effects of repetition: Solving a problem versus remembering a solution. *Journal of Verbal Learning and Verbal Behavior, 17,* 649–667.

Jenkins, J. G., & Dallenbach, K. M. (1924). Oblivescence during sleep and working. *American Journal of Psychology, 35,* 605–612.

Jones, W. P., & Anderson, J. R. (1987). Short- and long-term memory retrieval: A comparison of the effects of information load and relatedness. *Journal of Experimental Psychology: General, 116,* 137–153.

Kalbaugh, G. L., & Walls, R. T. (1973). Retroactive and proactive interference in prose learning of biographical and science materials. *Journal of Educational Psychology, 65,* 244–251.

Klatzky, R. L. (1980). *Human memory: Structure and processes.* San Francisco: Freeman.

Koriat, A., & Melkman, R. (1987). Depth of processing and memory organization. *Psychological Records, 49,* 183–187.

Krass, J., Kinoshita, S., & McConkey, K. M. (1989). Hypnotic memory and confidence reporting. *Applied Cognitive Psychology, 3,* 35–51.

Kuhara-Kojima, K., & Hatano, G. (1991). Contribution of content knowledge and learning ability to the learning of facts. *Jornal of Educational Psychology, 83,* 253–263.

Lindsay, D. S. (1990). Misleading questions can impair eyewitnesses' ability to remember details. *Journal of Experimental Psychology: Learning, Memory, and Cognition, 16,* 1077–1083.

Lindsay, D. S. (1993). Eyewitness suggestibility. *Current Directions in Psychological Science, 3,* 86–89.

Linton, M. (1978). Real world memory after six years: An in vivo study of very long term memory. In M. M. Gruneberg, P. E. Morris, & R. N. Sykes (Eds.), *Practical aspects of memory.* Orlando, FL/London: Academic Press.

Lockhart, R. S., Lamon, M., & Glick, M. L. (1988). Conceptual transfer in simple insight-problems. *Memory and Cognition, 16,* 36–44.

Loftus, E. F. (1979). *Eyewitness testimony.* Cambridge, MA: Harvard University Press.

Loftus, E. F. (1980). *Memory.* Menlo Park, CA: Addison-Wesley.

Loftus, E. F. (1982). Remembering recent experiences. In L. S. Cermak (Ed.), *Human memory and amnesia.* Hillsdale, NJ: Erlbaum.

Loftus, E. F. (1993). The reality of repressed memories. *American Psychologist, 48,* 518–537.

Loftus, G. R., & Loftus, E. F. (1980). The influence of one memory retrieval on a subsequent memory retrieval. *Memory and Cognition, 2,* 467–471.

Loftus, E. F., & Palmer, J. C. (1974). Reconstruction of automobile destruction: An example of the interaction between language and memory. *Journal of Verbal Learning and Verbal Memory, 13,* 585–589.

Loftus, E. F., Miller, D. G., & Burns, H. J. (1978). Semantic integration of verbal information into visual memory. *Journal of Experimental Psychology: Human Learning and Memory, 4,* 19–31.

Lorayne, H., & Lucas, J. (1974). *The memory book.* New York: Ballantine.

Lorch, R. F., & Lorch, E. P. (1985). Topic structure representation and text recall. *Journal of Educational Psychology, 77,* 137–148.

Luria, A. R. (1968). *The mind of mnemonist.* New York: Basic Books.

Maki, R. (1989). Recognition of added and deleted details in scripts. *Memory and Cognition, 17,* 274–282.

Mandler, J. M. (1978). A code in the node: The use of a story schema in retrieval. *Discourse Processes, 1,* 14–35.

Markus, G. B. (1986). Stability and change in political attitudes: Observe, recall, and "explain." *Political Behavior, 8,* 21–44.

Mayer, R. E. (1980). Elaboration techniques that increase the meaningfulness of technical text: An experimental test of the learning strategy hypothesis. *Journal of Educational Psychology, 72,* 770–784.

Mayer, R. E., & Bromage, B. D. (1980). Different recall protocols for technical tests due to advance organizers. *Journal of Educational Psychology, 72,* 209–225.

McCloskey, M., & Zaragoza, M. (1985). Misleading post-event information and memory for events: Arguments and evidence against memory impairment hypotheses. *Journal of Experimental Psychology: General, 114,* 1–16.

McCloskey, M., Wible, C. G., & Cohen, N. J. (1988). Is there a special flash-bulb memory mechanism? *Journal of Experimental Psychology: General, 117,* 171–181.

McDougall, R. (1904). Recognition and recall. *Journal of Philosophical and Scientific Methods, 1,* 229–233.

McGeoch, J. A. (1942). *The psychology of human learning.* New York: Longmans, Green.

Melton, A. W., & Irwin, J. M. (1940). The influence of degrees of interpolated learning on retroactive inhibitions and the overt transfer of specific responses. *Journal of Experimental Psychology, 53,* 173–203.

Morris, P. (1998). Memory research: Past mistakes and future prospects. In G. Claxton (Ed.), *Growth points in cognition.* London: Routledge.

Morris, C. D., Bransford, J. D., & Franks, J. J. (1977). Levels of processing versus transfer appropriate processing. *Journal of Verbal Learning and Verbal Behavior, 16,* 519–534.

Nash, M. (1987). What, if anything, is regressed about hypnotic age regression? A review of the literature. *Psychological Bulletin, 102,* 42–52.

Needham, D. R., & Begg, I. M. (1991). Problem-oriented training promotes spontaneous analogical transfer: Memory-oriented training promotes memory for training. *Memory and Cognition, 19,* 543–557.

Neisser, U. (1967). *Cognitive psychology.* New York: Appleton-Century-Crofts.

Neisser, U. (1978). Memory: What are the important questions? In M. M. Gruneberg, P. E. Morris, & R. N. Sykes (Eds.), *Practical aspects of memory* (pp. 3–24). London: Academic Press.

Neisser, U. (1981). John Dean's memory: A case study. *Cognition, 9,* 1–22.

Neisser, U., & Harsch, N. (1991). Phantom flashbulbs: False recognition of hearing the news about the *Challenger.* In E. Winnograd & U. Neisser (Eds.), *Flashbulb memories: Recalling the Challenger explosion and other disasters.* New York: Cambridge University Press.

Nelson, T. O. (1988). Predictive accuracy of feeling of knowing across different criterion tasks and across different subject populations and individuals. In M. M. Gruneberg, P. E. Morris, & R. N. Sykes (Eds.), *Practical aspects of memory: Current research and issues* (Vol. 1, pp. 190–196). Chichester, England: Wiley.

Paivio, A. (1971). *Imagery and verbal processes.* New York: Holt, Rinehart and Winston.

Parkin, A. J. (1984). Levels of processing, context, and facilitation of pronunciation. *Acta pscyhologica, 55,* 19–29.

Parry, H., & Crossley, H. (1950). Validity of responses to survey questions. *Public Opinion Quarterly, 14,* 61–80.

Penfield, W. W. (1969). Consciousness, memory, and man's conditioned reflexes. In K. Pribram (Ed.), *On the biology of learning.* New York: Harcourt, Brace and World.

Penfield, W. W., & Jasper, H. (1954). *Epilepsy and the functional anatomy of the human brain.* Boston: Little, Brown.

Penfield, W. W., & Perot, P. (1963). The brain's record of auditory and visual experience. *Brain, 86,* 595–696.

Perfect, T. J., Watson, E. L., & Wagstaff, G. F. (1993). Accuracy of confidence ratings associated with general knowledge and eyewitness memory. *Journal of Applied Psychology, 78,* 144–147.

Perfetto, G. A., Bransford, J. D., & Franks, J. J. (1983). Constraints on access in a problem-solving context. *Memory and Cognition, 11,* 24–31.

Pezdek, K., Maki, R., Valencea-Lover, D., Whetstone, T., Stoeckert, J., & Dougherty, T. (1988). Picture memory: Recognizing added and deleted details. *Journal of Experimental Psychology: Learning, Memory and Cognition, 14,* 468–476.

Pillemer, D. B. (1984). Flashbulb memories of the assassination attempt on President Reagan. *Cognition, 16,* 63–80.

Posner, M. I., & Warren, R. E. (1972). Traces, concepts, and conscious constructions. In A. W. Melton & T. E. Martin (Eds.), *Coding processes in human memory.* Washington, DC: Winston.

Postman, L., Stark, K., & Fraser, J. (1968). Temporal changes in interference. *Journal of Verbal Learning and Verbal Behavior, 7,* 672–694.

Pressley, M., & Brewster, M. E. (1990). Cognitive elaboration of illustrations to facilitate acquisition of facts: Memories Prince Edward School. *Applied Cognitive Psychology, 4,* 359–369.

Pressley, M., & Van Meter, P. (1994). What is memory development the development of? In P. E. Morris & M. Cruneberg (Eds.), *Theoretical aspects of memory* (pp. 79–129). London: Routledge.

Putnam, B. (1979). Hypnosis and distortions in eyewitness memory. *International Journal of Clinical and Experimental Hypnosis, 27,* 437–448.

Raaijmakers, J. G. W., & Shiffrin, R. M. (1981). Search of associative memory. *Psychological Review, 88,* 93–134.

Raaijmakers, J. G. W., & Shiffrin, R. M. (1992). Models for recall and recognition. *Annual Review of Psychology, 43,* 205–234.

Radavansky, G. A., & Zacks, R. T. (1991). Mental models and the fan effect. *Journal of Experimental Psychology: Learning, Memory, and Cognition, 17,* 940–953.

Reder, L. M., & Ross, B. H. (1983). Integrated knowledge in different tasks: The role of retrieval strategy on fan effects. *Journal of Experimental Psychology: Learning, Memory, and Cognition, 9,* 55–72.

Robbins, L. C. (1963). The accuracy of parental recall of aspects of child development and of child rearing practices. *Journal of Abnormal and Social Psychology, 66,* 261–270.

Robinson, K. J., & Roediger, H. L. (1997). Associative processes in false recall and false recognition. *Psychological Science, 8,* 231–237.

Roediger, H. L. (1980). Memory metaphors in cognitive psychology. *Memory and Cognition, 8,* 231–246.

Roediger, H. L., & McDermott, K. B. (1995). Creating false memories: Remembering words not presented in lists. *Journal of Experimental Psychology: Learning, Memory, and Cognition, 21,* 803–814.

Rosenfeld, I. (1988). *The invention of memory.* New York: Basic Books.

Ross, M. (1989). Relation of implicit theories to the construction of personal histories. *Psychological Review, 96,* 341–357.

Ross, D. F., Ceci, S. J., Dunning, D., & Toglia, M. P. (1994). Unconscious transference and mistaken identity: When a witness misidentifies a familiar but innocent person. *Journal of Applied Psychology, 79,* 990–892.

Rumelhart, D. E., Hinton, G. E., & Williams, R. J. (1986). Learning internal representation by error propagation. In D. E. Rumelhart & J. L. McClelland (Eds.), *Parallel distributed processing: Explorations in the microstructure of cognition* (Vol. 1, pp. 216–271). Cambridge, MA: MTT Press.

Ryan, R. H., & Geiselman, R. E. (1991). Effects of biased information on the relationship between eyewitness confidence and accuracy. *Bulletin of the Psychonomic Society, 29,* 7–9.

Sachs, J. D. S. (1967). Recognition memory for syntactic and semantic aspects of connected discourse. *Perception and Psychophysics, 2,* 437–442.

Saufley, W. H., Otaka, S. R., & Bavaresco, J. L. (1985). Context effects: Classroom tests and context independence. *Memory and Cognition, 13,* 522–528.

Schacter, D. L. (1996). *Searching for memory.* New York: Basic Books.

Schmidt, S. R. (1985). Encoding and retrieval processes in the memory for conceptually distinctive events. *Journal of Experimental Psychology: Learning, Memory, and Cognition, 11,* 565–578.

Schmidt, S. R. (1991). Can we have a distinctive theory of memory? *Memory and Cognition, 19,* 523–542.

Schneider, W., Korkel, J., & Weinert, F. E. (1987). *The knowledge base and memory performance: A comparison of academically successful and unsuccessful learners.* Paper presented at the meeting of the American Educational Research Association, Washington, DC.

Searleman, A., & Hermann, D. (1994). *Memory from a broader perspective.* New York: McGraw-Hill.

Shephard, R. N. (1967). Recognition memory for words, sentences, and pictures. *Journal of Verbal Learning and Verbal Behavior, 6,* 156–163.

Smith, E. E. (1988). Concepts and thought. In R. J. S. Sternberg & E. E. Smith (Eds.), *The psychology of human thought.* Cambridge, England: Cambridge University Press.

Smith, A. D., & Winograd, E. (1978). Adult age differences in remembering faces. *Developmental Psychology, 14,* 443–444.

Smith, E. E., Adams, N., & Schorr, D. (1978). Fact retrieval and the paradox of interference. *Cognitive Psychology, 10,* 438–464.

Smith, V. L., Kassin, S. M., & Ellsworth, P. C. (1989). Eyewitness accuracy and confidence: Within versus between-subjects correlations. *Journal of Applied Psychology, 74,* 356–359.

Smith, A. F., Jobe, J. B., & Mingay, D. J. (1991). Retrieval from memory of dietary information. *Applied Cognitive Psychology, 5,* 269–296.

Snyder, M., & Uranowitz, S. W. (1978). Reconstructing the past: Some cognitive consequences of person perception. *Journal of Personality and Social Psychology, 36,* 941–950.

Snyder, M., & White, P. (1982). Moods and memories: Elation, depression, and the remembering of the events of one's life. *Journal of Personality, 50,* 142–167.

Spiro, R. J. (1977). Remembering information from text: The state of the schema approach. In R. C. Anderson, R. J. Spiro, & W. E. Monague (Eds.), *Schooling and the acquisition of knowledge.* Hillsdale, NJ: Erlbaum.

Sporer, S. L. (1991). Deep-deeper-deepest? Encoding strategies and the recognition of human faces. *Journal of Experimental Psychology: Learning, Memory, and Cognition, 17,* 323–333.

Squire, L. R. (1987). *Memory and brain.* New York: Oxford University Press.

Standing, L. (1973). Learning 10,000 pictures. *Quarterly Journal of Experimental Psychology, 25,* 207–222.

Standing, L., Conezio, J., & Haber, R. N. (1970). Perception and memory for pictures: Single trial learning of 2560 visual stimuli. *Psychonomic Science, 19,* 73–74.

Stein, B. S., & Bransford, J. D. (1979). Constraints on effective elaboration: Effects of precision and subject generation. *Journal of Verbal Learning and Verbal Behavior, 18,* 769–777.

Stein, B. S., Littlefield, J., Bransford, J. D., & Persampieri, M. (1984). Elaboration and knowledge acquisition. *Memory and Cognition, 12,* 522–529.

Stephenson, G. M. (1984). Accuracy and confidence in testimony: A critical review and some fresh evidence. In D. J. Muller, D. E. Blackman, & A. J. Chapman (Eds.), *Psychology and law: Topics from an international conference* (pp. 229–249). Chichester, England: Wiley.

Stephenson, G. M., Clark, N. K., & Wade, G. S. (1986). Meetings make evidence: An experimental study of collaborative and individual recall of a simulated police interrogation. *Journal of Personality and Social Psychology, 50,* 1113–1122.

Stromeyer, C. F. Ill, & Psotka, J. (1970). The detailed textures of eidetic images. *Nature, 225,* 346–349.

Sulin, R. A., & Dooling, D. J. (1974). Intrusion of a thematic idea in retention of prose. *Journal of Experimental Psychology, 103,* 255–262.

Teasdale, J. D., & Fogarty, S. J. (1979). Differential effects of induced mood on retrieval of pleasant and unpleasant events from episodic memory. *Journal of Abnormal Psychology, 188,* 248–257.

Thompson, C. P., Cowan, T., Frieman, J., Mahadevan, R. S., & Vogel, R. J. (1991). Rahan: A study of a memorist. *Journal of Memory and Language, 30,* 702–724.

Thorndyke, P. W. (1976). The role of inferences in discourse comprehension. *Journal of Verbal Learning and Verbal Behavior, 15,* 437–446.

Thorndyke, P., & Hayes-Roth, B. (1979) The use of schemata in the acquisition and transfer of knowledge. *Cognitive Psychology, 11,* 82–106.

Tulving, E. (1983). *Elements of episodic memory.* New York: Oxford University Press.

Tulving, E., & Thompson, D. M. (1973). Encoding specificity and retrieval processes in episodic memory. *Psychological Review, 80,* 352–373.

Von Restorff, H. (1933). Uber die Wirkung von Bereichsbildungen in Spurenfeld. *Psychologisch Forschung, 18,* 299–342.

Walker, C. H. (1987). Relative importance of domain knowledge and overall aptitude on acquisition of domain-related information. *Cognition and Instruction, 4,* 24–42.

Waters, R., & Leeper, R. (1936). The relation of affective tone to the retention of experience in everyday life. *Journal of Experimental Psychology, 19,* 203–215.

Watkins, M. J. (1979). Engrams as cuegrams and forgetting as cue overload: A cueing approach to the structure of memory. In C. R. Puff (Ed.), *Memory organization and structure.* New York: Academic Press.

Watkins, M. J., & Tulving, E. (1975). When recognition fails. *Journal of Experimental Psychology: General, 104,* 5–29.

Webber, E. U., & Marshall, P. H. (1978). Priming in a distributed memory system. Implications for models of implicit memory. In S. Lewandowsky, J. C. Dunn, & K. Kirsner (Eds.), *Implicit memory: Theoretical Issues* (pp. 87–98). Hillsdale, NJ: Erlbaum.

Weingardt, K. R., Loftus, E. F., & Lindsay, D. S. (1995). Misinformation revisited: New evidence on the suggestibility of memory. *Memory and Cognition, 23,* 72–82.

Weisberg, R., Dicamillo, M., & Phillips, D. (1978). Transferring old associations to new problems: A nonautomatic process. *Journal of Verbal Learning and Verbal Behavior, 17,* 219–228.

Wells, G. L., & Murray, D. M. (1984). Eyewitness confidence. In G. L. Wells & E. F. Loftus (Eds.), *Eyewitness testimony: Psychological Perspectives* (pp. 155–170). New York: Cambridge University Press.

White, R. T. (1982). Memory for personal events. *Human Learning, 1,* 171–183.

White, R. T. (1989). Recall of autobiographical events. *Applied Cognitive Psychology, 3,* 127–135.

Wickelgren, W. A. (1972). Trace resistance and the decay of long-term memory. *Journal of Mathematical Psychology, 9,* 418–455.

Winnograd, T. (1976). Computer memories: A metaphor for memory organization. In C. N. Cofer (Ed.), *The structure of human memory.* San Francisco: Freeman.

Zaragoza, M. S., & Lane, S. M. (1994). Source misattributions and the suggestibility of eyewitness memory. *Journal of Experimental Psychology: Learning, Memory, and Cognition, 20,* 934–945.

Zaragoza, M. S., & Mitchell, K. J. (1996). Repeated exposure to suggestion and the creation of false memories. *Psychological Science, 7,* 294–300.

CHAPTER FIFTEEN

ATTENTION

MARK H. ASHCRAFT AND RAYMOND KLEIN

Everyone knows what attention is. It is the taking possession by the mind, in clear and vivid form, of one out of what seem several simultaneously possible objects or trains of thought. Focalization, concentration, of consciousness are of its essence. It implies withdrawal from some things in order to deal effectively with others.

(James, 1890, pp. 381–382)

As he did every morning after waking, Bill went into the bathroom to begin his morning ritual. After squeezing toothpaste onto his toothbrush, he looked into the mirror and began to brush his teeth. Although he brushed the teeth on the right side of his mouth quite vigorously, for the most part he ignored those on the left side. [. . .] He shaved all the stubble from the right side of his face impeccably but did a spotty job on the left side. [. . .] [After eating at a diner,] when Bill asked for the check, the waitress placed it on the left side of the table. After a few minutes, he waved the waitress over and complained, saying "I asked for my tab 5 minutes ago. What is taking so long?"

(Banich, 1997, p. 235)

Attention, one of cognitive psychology's most important topics and one of our oldest puzzles in the study of the mind, in Ulric Neisser's (1976) description is "psychology's most elusive target." What does it mean to pay attention to something? To direct your attention to something? To be unable to pay attention because of boredom, lack of interest, or fatigue? What sorts of things, whether external stimuli or internal thoughts, grab or capture our attention? How much control do we have over our attention? Is it always a matter of concentration and determination when you pay attention to something? Or are some things easy to attend to, and if so why? (Cognitive science says "attend to," meaning "pay attention," even though the dictionary claims that to be an archaic usage.) The authors of this book have to work at paying attention to some things (most topics in a faculty meeting, for example). But for other topics, it seems effortless: A good spy novel can rivet our attention, just as a great cognition lecture rivets yours (!).

15.1   MULTIPLE MEANINGS OF ATTENTION

Attention is one of the most pervasive topics in cognitive psychology and one of the thorniest, possibly because we mean so many different things by the term. We apply the term *attention* to a huge range of phenomena, from the basic notion of arousal and alertness all the way up to consciousness and awareness. Some attentional processes are extremely rapid, so that we are aware only of their outcomes, and others are slow enough that we seem to be aware of them — and able to control them — throughout. In some cases, attention is very much like a reflex. Even when we are deliberately concentrating on something, that concentration can be disrupted and redirected by an unexpected, attention-grabbing event, such as a sudden loud noise in an otherwise quiet library. In other cases, we are frustrated that our deliberate attempts to focus attention on some task are so easily disrupted by another train of thought; you try very hard to pay attention to a lecture, only to find yourself daydreaming about last weekend's party.

Table 15.1 presents a list of four different connotations of the term *attention* — different processes, phenomena, or ideas that in one way or another are involved in a study of attention. For organizational purposes, this chapter is structured around that list to impose some coherence on an otherwise confusing field, to help you see the forest and prevent your getting lost in the trees. Although other organizational schemes are possible, this approach should at least help you develop an understanding of the topic of attention and see how certain topics flow into others. The list will also help us avoid some of the confusion that arises when the general term *attention* is used for processes or mechanisms more precisely described by another term, such as *arousal*.

We'll rely on everyday examples and your intuitive understanding, but only so far as they help us understand the empirical concept of attention. And, at every turn, we confront four interrelated ideas:

1. We are constantly confronted with much more information than we can pay attention to.
2. There are serious limitations in how much we can attend to at any one time.
3. We can respond to some information and perform some tasks with little if any attention.
4. With sufficient practice and knowledge, some tasks become less and less demanding of our attentional processes.

TABLE 15.1   Four Meanings of Attention

Alertness and arousal

Orienting and searching

Filtering and selecting

Mental resources and conscious processing

15.2   BASICS OF ATTENTION

Let's start by giving two rather general definitions for the concept of attention, both of which apply throughout the list in Table 15.1.

15.2.1   Attention as a Mental Process

Attention can be thought of as the mental process of concentrating effort on a stimulus or a mental event. By this definition we mean that attention is an activity that occurs within the cognitive system, a process. This process focuses a mental commodity — effort — on either an external stimulus or an internal event. So when you examine a picture like that in Figure 15.1, you focus your mental energies on an external stimulus, the splotches and patches of black and white in a puzzling photograph. If you have never seen the photograph before, you struggle to identify it, to recognize the pattern in it; you are reduced to very heavy reliance on data-driven processing. As you puzzle and wonder, searching for clues, you focus this mental effort in an attempt to identify the pattern; the effort you focused was attention. Attention is the mental process that focused your eyes on the figure and encoded the photograph into your visual system. Sustained attention then led, possibly after a long while, to identifying the Dalmatian in the photo.

In principle, this focusing of your attention on a visual stimulus is no different than when you focus purely mental attention on a word, idea, or concept. For example, your professor says something unexpected (e.g., describing an idea as "green"), and you puzzle over the remark, trying to find a way of interpreting the remark that makes sense (can an idea that promotes conservation and ecology be described as "green"? [. . .]. It is this concentration of attention we are illustrating here, attention focused on and driving the mental event of remembering, searching for information stored in your long-term memory, attempting to comprehend.

FIGURE 15.1   First identification of the pattern relies almost exclusively on data-driven processing, whereas later identification relies heavily on conceptually driven processing.

15.2.2   Attention as a Limited Mental Resource

Now consider attention as a mental resource, a kind of mental fuel. In this sense, attention is *the limited mental energy or resource that powers the mental system*. It is a mental commodity, the stuff that gets focused when we pay attention. According to this definition, attention is the all-important mental resource necessary to run the cognitive system, to make it operate.

A fundamentally important idea here is the notion of limitations: Attention is limited, finite. We usually state this idea by talking about the limited capacity of the attentional system. Countless experiments, to say nothing of everyday experiences, show that there is a limitation in our attentional capacity, the capacity to attend to stimuli, to remember events that just happened, to remember things we are supposed to do. In short, there is a limit to how many different things we can attend to and do all at once.

It does not take very long to think of everyday situations that reveal these attentional limitations. I can easily drive down an uncrowded highway in daylight while I carry on a conversation with someone, maybe on a cellphone. I can easily listen to the news on the radio under normal driving conditions. In the middle of a heavy rainstorm, however, I can't talk to the person sitting in the passenger seat; in rush hour traffic, I can't (or shouldn't try to) do business on the cellphone. Under such demanding circumstances, the radio is an annoyance or an irritating distraction, and I have to turn down the volume.

Try a demonstration right now. First, count backward by threes out loud, starting from some arbitrary number such as 741. Get good at it, to the point that you can keep up a steady, challenging rhythm. Now, try counting backward by threes while you read a paragraph from this book. Neither of these tasks is too difficult by itself, another way of saying that neither task exceeds your attentional capacity. Doing them simultaneously, however, overtaxes the attentional system; you probably slowed down in your backward counting or your reading, or made some counting errors. Although you have sufficient attentional capacity to do either task alone, there is not enough to do them both together.

15.3   ALERTNESS AND AROUSAL

It almost seems axiomatic to say that part of what we mean by attention involves the basic capacity to respond to the environment. This most basic sense refers to alertness and arousal as a necessary state of the nervous system: The nervous system must be awake, responsive, and able to interact with the environment. At the physiological level, arousal is at least partly a function of the reticular activating system (RAS), a lower brain stem system in charge of, among other things, basic arousal and consciousness (Kolb & Whishaw, 1996). It seems clear, intuitively, that the nervous system must be aroused in order to pay attention. You cannot attend to stimuli while you are unconscious, of course, although certain stimuli can impinge on us and rouse us to a conscious state (e.g., alarm clocks, smoke detectors, or other loud noises).

States of alertness and arousal may last for relatively long periods of time and change rather gradually. Such changes are referred to as *tonic*. The sleep-wakefulness cycle is perhaps the best-known example of tonic changes in alertness and arousal. Entrained by the light-dark cycle, a biological clock (Rusak, 1989) controls many physiological parameters (such as your body temperature), and causes us to become tired and fall asleep (usually in the evening) and to wake up from sleep (usually in the morning). Of course, through our own behaviours (such as drinking coffee or making a dedicated effort to meet a deadline) we may stay awake beyond when our internal clock signals that it is time for bed. And rather than waking up when our internal clock provides the arousal signal, we may rely on our alarm clock. Another example of a tonic change in arousal is the fatigue or loss of vigilance we encounter when performing a task (like driving) for long periods of time.

In contrast to tonic changes, alertness and arousal may also be controlled *phasically.* A typical example of phasic arousal might occur when a sudden, unexpected change in the environment is detected. Perhaps due to a drop in vigilance after a long trip, you may become drowsy while stopped at a red light. The loud horn blast from the impatient driver behind you will cause an abrupt, phasic increase in your state of arousal — among other changes, your heart rate will increase. Phasic changes in alertness or arousal can also be produced voluntarily, as when you use a warning signal to prepare to encode and respond to an upcoming target stimulus (Posner & Boies, 1971).

Although it is generally accepted that a state of arousal and alertness is necessary for most cognitive processing, this view emphasizes a kind of mental processing known as explicit processing. [. . .] Explicit processes are those *involving conscious processing, conscious awareness that a task is being performed, and usually conscious awareness of the outcome of that performance.* The opposite is known as implicit processing, *processing with no necessary involvement of conscious awareness* (Schacter, 1989, 1996). As you will see later in the book, the distinction between implicit and explicit is often in terms of memory performance, especially long-term memory. When I ask you to learn a list of words and then name them back, that's an explicit memory task: You are consciously aware of being tested and aware that you are remembering words you just studied on the list. By contrast, you can also demonstrate memory for information without being aware of remembering it, a demonstration of implicit memory. For example, you can reread a passage of text more rapidly than you read it the first time, even if you have no recollection of ever reading the passage before (Masson, 1984).

Much evidence shows that some important mental processing can be accomplished with only minimal attentional involvement. Much of this is discussed later in the book, especially in sections on long-term memory. For now, consider just one study on alertness and arousal, conducted by Bonebakker et al. (1996). These investigators presented tape-recorded lists of words to surgery patients, one list just before and another during surgery, and then tested their memory for the words up to 24 hours later. Despite the fact that all the patients were given general anaesthesia and were therefore unconscious during the surgery itself, they nonetheless demonstrated memory for words they heard during the surgery.

The powerful part of the demonstration was that performance was based on an implicit memory task, the *word stem completion task.* Patients were given word stems and told to complete them with the first word they thought of. To ensure that the task was measuring only implicit memory, patients were further asked to leave out or exclude any words they explicitly remembered hearing, such as the words they remembered hearing before receiving anaesthesia. For example, say that they heard *BOARD* before surgery and *LIGHT* during surgery. When tested 24 hours after surgery, the patients completed the word stems (e.g., *LI___*) with words they had heard during surgery (*LIGHT*) significantly more frequently than they did with presurgery words (*BO___*) or with control words that had never been presented on the tapes. In other words, they remembered hearing *BOARD* and excluded it on the word stem task. Because they did not explicitly remember *LIGHT,* they finished *LI___* with *GHT,* presumably because their memory of *LIGHT* was implicit. The results demonstrated clearly that the patients had implicit memory of the word lists they had heard while they were under the anaesthesia, a state very close to no alertness or arousal at all.

So that you will understand this procedure better, and because we will encounter it several times in later chapters, here is a more focused, written version of the task. Imagine that you saw a list of words including *SCHOOL* and *SHELF.* Relying on explicit memory, you would probably complete the stem *SCH___* with *SCHOOL.* But if I asked you to exclude words you explicitly remembered, you would find another way of completing that stem, say *SCHEME;* likewise, you might exclude *SHELF* and write *SHELL.* By chance alone, you might complete the stem *CRA___* with *CRADLE* or *CRAYON,* neither of which you saw on the list. Here is the implicit part of the demonstration — if it works. Try it yourself. Complete the following word stems with the first word that comes to your mind: *PAP___;* *GRE___.* *PAPER* is a pretty common completion for the first one, but probably only because paper is a fairly common word (it has not appeared in this chapter yet). But if you completed the second one as *GREEN* without explicitly remembering that you read about "green ideas" earlier, then that probably was an implicit memory effect.

15.4   ORIENTING AND SEARCHING

Orienting refers to the alignment of information pickup mechanisms with a source of information. As we will see, orienting may be controlled *reflexively* in response to sudden changes in the environment or *voluntarily* in response to our own intentions. This distinction between reflexive and voluntary control is sometimes referred to as control by *bottom-up* and *top-down processing.* Whether under voluntary or reflexive control, orienting may involve overt responses such as eye [. . .] and head movements or, in the absence of an observable behavioural response, orienting may involve an internal mental change that is called covert orienting of attention. The modes of orienting that follow from this pair of distinctions (first described by Michael Posner in 1980) are illustrated in Figure 15.2 and described in the next two sections of this chapter. The interested reader is referred to *Orienting of Attention,* a recent book by Canadian scientists Richard Wright (Simon Fraser University) and Lawrence Ward (University of British Columbia) that provides comprehensive coverage of the topic (Wright & Ward, 2008).

15.5   REFLEXIVE ORIENTING

In a quiet room, an unexpected noise immediately grabs your attention away from what you were doing and often involves a reflexive turning of your head toward the source of the sound. In vision, of course, you turn your eyes and head toward the unexpected stimulus, the flash of light, or sudden movement detected in your peripheral vision. This is the orienting reflex or orienting response, *the reflexive redirection of attention that orients you toward the unexpected stimulus.* This response is found at all levels of the animal kingdom and is present very early in life. The orienting reflex, then, is initiated by external stimulation and

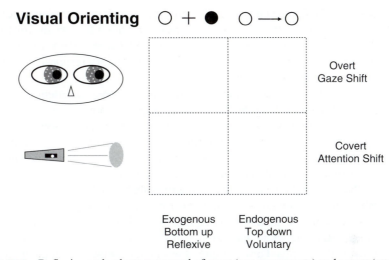

FIGURE 15.2   Reflexive and voluntary control of overt (eye movements) and covert (attention) orienting yield four modes of orienting that were distinguished by Posner (1980).

Redrawn from Klein (2005).

often involves the redirection of sensory receptors toward the source of this stimulation. In vision this might be accomplished by eye and head movements. When such an orienting reflex can be observed in the behaviour of the organism, it is referred to as *overt reflexive orienting* (Posner, 1980). Importantly — particularly in a chapter about attention — when one's eyes and head remain stationary, unexpected events can elicit reflexive redirection of attention in the form of internal (mental) adjustments of information processing. This kind of orienting of attention without the assistance of an overt response is referred to as *covert reflexive orienting.*

Whether the orienting reflex is overt or covert, current thinking suggests that it is a location-finding response of the nervous system. That is, an unexpected stimulus, a noise or a flash of light, triggers the reflex so that you can locate the stimulus, find where it is in space, and respond to it appropriately. The orienting reflex enables you to protect yourself against danger, in the reflexive, survival sense; after all, what if the unexpected movement you detect is a rock thrown at you or some other kind of threat (e.g., Ohman, Flykt, & Esteves, 2001)? Given that the response helps you locate the stimulus, it is not surprising that some of the neural pathways involved in this response correspond to the "where" pathway (a companion to the "what" pathway involved in object recognition). Briefly, the "where" pathway projects from the visual cortex to upper (superior) rearward (dorsal) regions of the parietal lobe in the brain; in fact, the "where" pathway is also called the dorsal pathway (and the "what" pathway is also called the ventral pathway).

Cowan (1995) noted that the kinds of stimuli that trigger the orienting reflex boil down to two basic categories: stimuli that are significant for the organism (the rock thrown toward your head) and stimuli that are novel. We orient toward a novel stimulus in an otherwise constant, unchanging, even monotonous background. We orient when something *different* occurs: the unexpected sound in the quiet library, sudden and unexpected movement (Abrams

& Christ, 2003), the change in pitch in a professor's voice during a lecture, maybe the word *different* in italics in a textbook paragraph. Orienting focuses the organism so it can devote deliberate attention to the stimulus if warranted; Cowan (1995) called these voluntary attentive processes. In this sense, orienting is a preparatory response, one that prepares the system for further voluntary processing.

On the other hand, if the stimulus that triggered the orienting reflex then occurs over and over again, it is no longer novel or different; now it has become part of the normal, unchanging background. At this point the process of habituation begins to take over, *a gradual reduction of the orienting response back to baseline.* For example, if the unexpected noise in the quiet library is the ventilation fan coming on, you first notice it but then grow accustomed to it as it continues. You have oriented to the stimulus, and then that response has habituated, to the point that you will probably orient again when the fan *stops* running. When the constant noise stops, that is a change that triggers the orienting response.

Cowan (1995), among others, believes that a thorough understanding of this orienting reflex, along with habituation, can go a long way toward helping us understand attention in all its forms. For one thing, it is a kind of bridge, from the built-in reflexive process of attention to the voluntary, deliberate attentional system that we turn to next. Second, as you will soon see, there are some important parallels between orienting and habituation on the one hand and selective attention on the other. And third, there is even evidence that top-down processes and expectations can affect the orienting response (Hommel, Pratt, Colzato, & Godijn, 2001; Sussman, Winkler, & Schroger, 2003).

15.6   VOLUNTARY ORIENTING

Fortunately, our attention is not completely under the control of immediate external stimulation. In many situations we choose the objects or locations in space that we want to analyze or pay attention to. Voluntary control over orienting can and often does involve overt changes, as when we shift our gaze so that the sensitive fovea will be directed to objects in and regions of space containing the information we are seeking. But just as reflexive orienting can control attention covertly without an overt shift of gaze, so too can voluntary orienting. [. . .] The results from Yarbus's experiment [. . .] illustrate how voluntary or top-down control of overt orienting coordinates with the bottom-up scene that is before us. In this case the eye movements made to inspect the same painting are very different depending on the instructions that the participant is given (i.e., what the participant is looking for). We will return to this coordination in our discussion of visual search, but at this point we will focus on voluntary covert orienting: voluntary shifts of attention made without overt shifts in gaze.

15.7   A SPATIAL CUEING TASK FOR EXPLORING
THE SPOTLIGHT OF ATTENTION

Michael Posner and his colleagues (Posner, 1980; Posner, Snyder & Davidson, 1980; Posner & Cohen, 1984) developed a model task for exploring covert orienting of attention in the visual modality. There are two versions of this task, one for exploring voluntary control and one for exploring reflexive control.

In a typical study, the initial display consists of three boxes arranged horizontally as illustrated at the top of the top two panels of Figure 15.3, Subjects in this cued detection

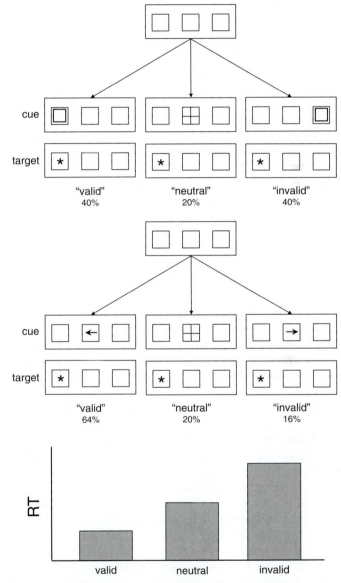

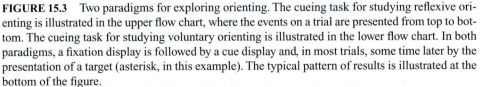

FIGURE 15.3   Two paradigms for exploring orienting. The cueing task for studying reflexive orienting is illustrated in the upper flow chart, where the events on a trial are presented from top to bottom. The cueing task for studying voluntary orienting is illustrated in the lower flow chart. In both paradigms, a fixation display is followed by a cue display and, in most trials, some time later by the presentation of a target (asterisk, in this example). The typical pattern of results is illustrated at the bottom of the figure.

task are asked to fixate on the centre box throughout the trial. A directional cue is then presented, and finally, on most trials, a simple target (e.g., an asterisk) is presented in one of the peripheral boxes. The subject's' task is simply to press a button when they detect the target (and to refrain from responding on the small percentage of "catch" trials when no target is presented.

The version used to explore reflexive control is illustrated in the top part of Figure 15.3. In this case a peripheral event (the brief brightening of one of the peripheral boxes) is used to attract attention reflexively. When purely reflexive orienting is studied with this task, the peripheral cue is entirely uninformative (i.e., regardless of which peripheral box is cued, the target, when one is presented, is equally likely to be presented in either peripheral box). Because the reflexive capture of attention by the peripheral event is both rapid and brief, the target must be presented relatively quickly after the cue if we want to measure performance when attention is at the cued location (e.g. the interval between the appearance of the cue and the appearance of the target should be 100 ms or less).

The version used to explore voluntary control is illustrated in the middle part of Figure 15.3. As used by Posner, Snyder, & Davidson (1980), arrow cues that point left or right are presented in the central box to inform the participant which location is likely to contain the target. For 80% of the trials with arrow cues, the arrow points toward the box where the target will actually appear 1 s later. On the remaining 20% of the trials with arrow cues, however, the cue is invalid: It points to the wrong side for the upcoming target. Neutral trials (a plus sign instead of an arrow) provide an uninformative cue, indicating that the target will appear equally often on the left or right.

The typical results, at the bottom of Figure 15.3, reveal that reaction time (RT) to detect the target is faster on valid trials than on invalid trials. In many cases, RT on neutral trials falls between valid and invalid RT. The advantage on valid relative to neutral trials is known as a benefit. The disadvantage on invalid relative to neutral trials is known as a cost. Posner would later describe the difference in performance: disengaging attention from its current focus, moving the attention to the target's true location, then engaging attention at that new location.

Posner et al. (1980) concluded from this and related experiments that the attentional focus the subjects were switching was a thoroughly cognitive phenomenon: It was not tied to eye movements or other overt behaviour, but to an internal focusing mechanism. They also suggested that "attention can be likened to a spotlight that enhances the efficiency of detection of events within its beam" (p. 172). So spotlight attention is *the covert focusing of attention that prepares you to encode stimulus information.*

As Cave and Bichot (1999) pointed out, countless studies of visual attention, many of them inspired by Posner's work, have adopted the spotlight metaphor in investigating visual attention. Much of that work has explored the characteristics and limits of visual attention, attempting to evaluate how useful the metaphor is. For instance, when a real spotlight shifts its beam from one location to another, it illuminates the locations between those two locations as it moves; the time it takes to change locations also depends on how far away the new location is. The evidence of visual attention, however, suggests that the mental spotlight does not sweep, enhancing the intermediate locations along the way, but instead that it jumps (much as the saccade does). On the other hand, there is also supportive evidence for the similarity between a real spotlight and spotlight attention. For example, there is evidence that the size of the spotlight beam can be altered, depending on circumstances, that a zoomlike process is part of the attentional spotlight, and that stimuli toward the centre of the beam are facilitated more than stimuli on the fringes (see Cave & Bichot, 1999, for their extensive review of the literature).

Among scholars who study covert visual orienting, it is generally assumed that there is one mental spotlight of attention that is controlled by *bottom-up* (reflexive) and by *top-down* (voluntary) *processes.* Many of the differences between reflexive and voluntary covert visual orienting seem simply to reflect the properties of the different controllers: reflexive orienting is faster, less influenced by target probabilities, and less affected by giving the subject a secondary memory task (Jonides, 1981). A variety of findings, however (e.g., Briand & Klein, 1987), are consistent with the idea that the two control systems may be controlling different beams. If this view is correct (see Klein, 2004a, for a review), then how — and how well — the spotlight metaphor characterizes covert shifts of attention may depend on whether these shifts are controlled reflexively or voluntarily.

One such difference between these two modes of controlling orienting can be seen after attention has been removed from the cued location. Posner and Cohen (1984) combined the cueing task illustrated at the bottom of Figure 15.3 with two methods for encouraging participants to return their attention to the centre box immediately after it had been captured by the peripheral cue. As illustrated in Figure 15.4, in this experiment they also varied the interval between the cue and target. When the interval was short, RT for targets at the cued location was faster than to targets at the uncued location. This difference reflects the capture of attention by the uninformative cue which, as described above, generates benefits for the processing of validly cued targets and costs for the processing of invalidly cued targets. However, after about 200 to 300 ms there is a crossover in the functions, and RT to validly cued

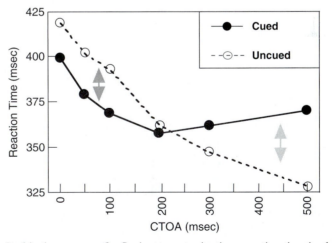

FIGURE 15.4   In this timecourse of reflexive covert orienting, reaction time is plotted for targets presented at the cued (valid) and uncued (invalid) locations in a spatial cueing task with uninformative peripheral cues. Results are plotted as a function of the interval between the onset of the cue and the onset of the target (also called the cue-target onset asynchrony, or CTOA). The dark-blue arrow illustrates facilitation due to capture of attention by the cue; the light-blue arrow illustrates the inhibitory aftereffect that has been called inhibition of return.

Redrawn from Posner & Cohen (1984).

targets becomes slower than to invalidly cued targets. Posner and Cohen speculated that this phenomenon, which was later called "inhibition of return," might serve as a novelty-seeking mechanism. According to this view, once attention is removed from a recently attended location it is inhibited from returning there. (Inhibition is *a mental process that restrains behaviour or impedes another mental process.*) *Importantly,* this "been there, done that" inhibitory aftermath of orienting is not observed following a voluntary shift of attention in response to a central cue (Posner & Cohen, 1984; Rafal, Calabresi, Brennan, & Sciolto, 1989). In the next section we learn a bit more about inhibition of return, including evidence suggesting that inhibition of return may operate to help make visual search more efficient.

15.8   VISUAL SEARCH

The joint operation of bottom-up and top-down control of attention is nicely illustrated in visual search, such as when you are looking for something particular on your desk (e.g., a pen) or on your virtual desktop (a particular icon). The actual scene you are looking at offers, in a bottom-up sense, salient objects and contours for you to inspect while your intention to find the target must collaborate with your representation of the scene to control the search sequence. In the laboratory, cognitive psychologists interested in attention and pattern recognition have simplified this real-world situation. Look at Figure 15.5. In the first panel, search for either a letter *T* or a boldfaced letter; in the other two panels, search for a boldfaced *T*.

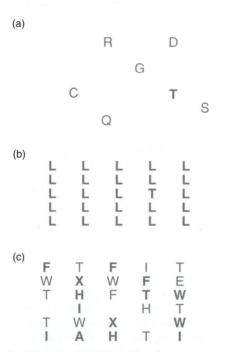

FIGURE 15.5   In the top panel, search either for a capital *T* or a boldfaced letter. In the other two panels, search for a boldfaced capital *T*.

As you performed these searches, you surely noticed that searching for *T* in the first panel was stunningly simple; it hardly seemed like a search, did it? Instead, didn't the *T* just "pop out" at you from the page? In contrast, searching for *T* in the middle panel probably was a slow process, and finding it in the last panel probably took even longer.

A distinguished series of studies by Anne Treisman and her associates (Treisman, 1982, 1988, 1991; Treisman & Gelade, 1980) examined spotlight attention in terms of visual search and pattern recognition. Typically, participants in the experiments were told to search the visual display for either of two simple features (e.g., letter S or a blue letter) or a conjunction of two features (e.g., a green *T*). The search for a simple feature was called the *disjunction condition*: Participants responded "yes" when they detected the presence of either of the specified features, either a letter *S* or a blue letter. In the conjunction condition, they had to search for the combination of two features, *T* and the colour green. In the searches you conducted, the first panel search was a disjunction search, and the last panel illustrated a conjunction search (the target had to be both boldfaced and a *T*).

In the typical result (Treisman & Gelade, 1980, Experiment 1), subjects could search rapidly for either colour or shape, and it made little or no difference whether they searched through a small or a large display; for instance, subjects were able to search through as few as 5 patterns or as many as 30 in about the same amount of time, approximately 500 ms. Because there was no increase in RT across the display sizes in the disjunction search condition, Treisman and Gelade concluded that visual search for a dimension such as shape or colour occurs in parallel across the entire region of visual attention. Such a search, they suggested, must be largely automatic and must represent very early visual processing. In the results, shown in Figure 15.6, this is the flat, low function of the graph.

But when subjects had to search for a conjunction of features, such as a green *T*, they took much more time, up to 2400 ms, as more and more distractor items filled the display (distractors for both conditions were brown *T*s and green *X*s). Such conjunction search, Treisman and Gelade reasoned, must be occurring in a more serial, one-by-one fashion and seemed to be a far more conscious, deliberate act. This is the steeply increasing function in Figure 15.6.

There is some debate about these interpretations, along with many follow-up studies. For example, Duncan and Humphreys (1989) showed that visual search rates depend critically on the kinds of distractor patterns through which subjects are searching and the similarity of those patterns to the targets (see also Duncan & Humphreys, 1992; Treisman, 1992). This is surely the case because finding the boldfaced *T* in the middle panel was difficult, in part because all the letters were angular and boldfaced. And it was even harder in the last panel because of the many near misses, the large number of *T*s and boldfaced letters, all of which matched on one but not both of the target letter's features.

Aside from differences of opinion in interpreting the results from this area, one clear-cut conclusion deserves special mention here. Treisman's two conditions provided clear evidence of both a very quick, automatic attentional process — essentially the capture of attention due to "pop-out" — and a much slower, serial, and more deliberate attention, the type needed for the conjunction search. Although it may seem reasonable to view these two modes of search as corresponding to reflexive and voluntary orienting discussed in the preceding section, it is probably more accurate to consider each search mode as having both reflexive and voluntary components, with the balance favouring reflexive control in "pop-out" search and favouring voluntary control in serial search.

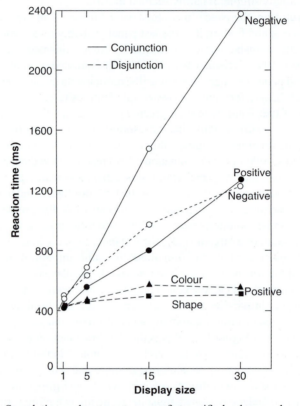

FIGURE 15.6   Search times when targets were of a specified colour or shape. The dashed lines are for the disjunction search conditions (e.g., search for either a capital T or a boldfaced letter). The solid lines show search times for the conjunction condition (e.g., search for a boldfaced T). The important result is that disjunctive search times did not increase as the display size grew larger, but the conjunction search times did.

The linearly increasing functions relating RT to display size and the roughly 2:1 ratio in target absent to target present slopes (rates of increase in RT with display size) have been used to infer a serial self-terminating search. In such a search, the spotlight of attention inspects each item (or perhaps small groups of items) one at a time until the target is found (yielding a "yes" response) or until the entire array has been inspected with no target found (yielding a "no" response). Unless the items are very small or the target is camouflaged — in which case foveation of the individual items will be required — these functions are more or less the same whether subjects are allowed to move their eyes or are precluded from moving their eyes in their search for the target (Klein & Farrell, 1989). (Foveation refers to *an eye movement that places the region of a scene that requires fine, detailed processing onto the sensitive fovea.*) It is findings like this that lead us to believe that search functions like those shown in Figure 15.6 are generated by primarily mental or covert shifts of attention.

Two questions arise about the guidance system for serial search: (1) How does the system decide the order in which objects or regions of the display will be inspected? (2) Once a sequence of inspections has begun, how does the system keep track of which objects and regions have already been inspected? Search would be relatively inefficient without a mechanism to prevent re-inspections. It is generally believed that bottom-up and top-down signals contribute to something called an *activation map* that controls orienting (Wolfe, Cave, & Franzel, 1989). In a "winner-take-all" strategy, the most activated region in this map will guide attention toward inspecting the object(s) in the selected region. A problem with this strategy is that after this region is inspected, without some reduction in its activation level, (1) it will remain the most activated region, (2) the inspection process will perseverate (keep returning to the most salient region), and (3) search will fail (unless this region contains the target). In an article entitled: "Inhibitory Tagging System Facilitates Search," Klein (1988) suggested that the novelty-seeking mechanism we discussed at the end of the last section — inhibition of return — might perform this function. For evidence supporting this proposal, see the Research in Action box.

15.9   FILTERING: VOLUNTARY CONTROL OF SELECTIVE ATTENTION

We turn now to several senses of the term *attention* that point to the controlled, voluntary nature of attentional processes. We have already discussed voluntary control of the spotlight of attention, but for the most part (e.g. in Posner's cueing paradigm) this kind of control was in advance of the target and without the requirement to filter out irrelevant signals. Controlled attention, in contrast, refers to forms of processing in which there is *a deliberate, voluntary allocation of mental effort* or concentration. A critical feature of situations requiring controlled attention is the competition between inputs for the control of actions. *You* decide to pay attention to this stimulus and ignore others, to perform this task and not that one. It is this act of paying attention that may be effortful. The study of this later, controlled kind of attention begins with classic research done in the 1950s and 1960s on the process of selective attention.

Cognitive psychology has always been intrigued by the observation that at any moment, scores of different sensory messages are impinging on our senses. We can neither attend to all of them (we would be overwhelmed instantly), nor afford for our attention to be captured by one, then another, then another of the multiple sensory inputs (we would lose all coherence, all continuity). Therefore, it has always made sense to ask questions about selective attention, *the ability to attend to one source of information while ignoring or excluding other ongoing messages around us.* How do our mental processes enable us to do this? How do you screen out the surrounding noises so you can hear just one? How can you listen covertly to the person on your right, who is gossiping about someone you know, while overtly pretending to listen to a conversational partner on your left? (And how did you notice in the first place that the person on your right was gossiping?) Somewhat the converse of selective attention is the topic of divided attention: How do we divide or share our attentional capacity across more than one source of information at a time, and how much information are we picking up from the several attended sources? Can we really talk on a

■ ■ ■ ■ ■

RESEARCH IN ACTION
INHIBITION OF RETURN: FACILITATES SEARCH BY DISCOURAGING RE-INSPECTIONS

Extending Posner and Cohen's (1984) suggestion that inhibition of return (IOR) was a novelty-seeking mechanism, Raymond Klein (1988) proposed that IOR facilitates serial search by discouraging attention from revisiting previously inspected objects or regions of the search display.

In experiments conducted at Dalhousie University, he tested this proposal using a dual task in which, immediately following the primary search task, a probe dot was displayed on the screen. The participants' secondary task was simply to press a button whenever they detected this probe. The experiments made use of the two kinds of search identified by Treisman as requiring (serial search) or not requiring (pop-out search) the inspection, by attention, of each item in the array.

According to Klein's proposal (see figure below), IOR should be present at the locations of items following serial search when the target was absent (because attention would have visited the location of each of these items). Following a search for a target that pops out, IOR should not be present because attention is not needed to find the target in this kind of search. To the extent IOR was present, response times to the probes should be delayed. The figure below shows what was found (as replicated by Klein, R.M., & MacInnes, W.J. (1999). Inhibition of return is a foraging facilitator in visual search. Psychological Science, 10, 346–352. Müller, H., & von Mühlenen, A. (2000). Probing distractor inhibition in visual search. Journal of Experimental Psychology: Human Perception & Performance. 26, 1591–1605. Takeda, Y., & Yagi, A. (2000). Inhibitory tagging in visual search can be found if search stimuli remain visible. Perception & Psychophysics, 62, 927–934.

For IOR to facilitate search, it must have the following properties:

1. In the real world we typically move our eyes when we are searching for something, and the scene we are inspecting is often dynamic in the sense that the items we inspect may move during search (as when looking for your friend in a busy train station). Confirming this property, it has also been demonstrated that IOR is not retinotopic (i.e., relative to the current fixation point) but rather is coded environmentally when an eye movement intervenes between a cue and target (Maylor & Hockey, 1985) and is coded in object coordinates when the item that was cued moves before the target is presented (Tipper, Driver, & Weaver, 1991).
2. IOR should be graded, such that the inhibited regions are neither too small nor too large to be useful. Several laboratories have demonstrated that there is a gradient of inhibition around a previously attended location (e.g., Bennett & Pratt, 2001; Maylor & Hockey, 1985).
3. IOR would be relatively useless as a search facilitator if only one object or location could be inhibited. Although such a limit was suggested by Pratt and Abrams (1995) using a two-location cueing task, Snyder and Kingstone (2000) found that up to five locations could be simultaneously inhibited when they used an eight-item array.
4. The duration of IOR must be long enough to be effective over the duration of a typical visual search. Samuel and Kat (2003) demonstrated that IOR lasts for at least 3 seconds.
5. IOR must begin very quickly after attention has inspected an item in a search array.

(Continued)

The relatively slow appearance of IOR in the cueing paradigm (see Figure 15-4) might lead the reader to think that IOR begins too slowly to be useful during a search task. When participants in a cueing paradigm had an incentive to remove attention from the cued location to a different one, Dahziger and Kingstone (1999) found IOR at the cued location within 50 ms of the cue's onset. Neuroscientific data (for a review, see Klein, 2004b) suggests that IOR is present from the onset of the cue; its impact on performance may not be strong enough to overcome the early facilitation from reflexive attention until attention has been removed from the cued location.

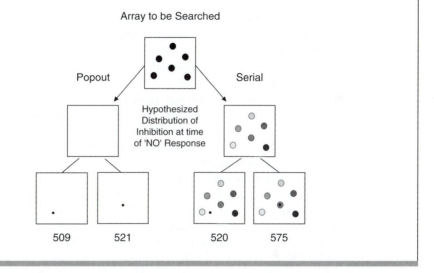

cellphone and drive at the same time without one or the other activity suffering? Apparently dividing our attention between two demanding tasks is difficult and driving performance does suffer when we devote some of our mental capacity to a cellphone conversation (Spence & Read, 2003; Strayer & Johnston, 2001). When do we start reaching the limits of our attentional capacity?

15.9.1   Selective Attention and the Cocktail Party Effect

When you try to ignore the many stimuli or events around you so you can focus on just one, the ones you are trying to ignore are distractions that must be eliminated or excluded. *The mental process of eliminating those distractions, eliminating unwanted messages,* is called filtering or selecting. Some aspect of the attention mechanism seems to filter out the unwanted, extraneous sources of information so we can select the one message we want to pay attention to.

Selective attention and the process of filtering seems to be straightforward in vision: You move your eyes, thereby selecting what you will pay attention to. As you just saw, however, attention is separate from eye movements: You can shift your mental attention even without eye movements. But in human hearing (in some animals the ears orient toward the source of an auditory event), attention has no outward, behavioural component that is analogous to eye movements, so psychologists have always realized that the selective attention process in hearing was thoroughly cognitive. This accounts for cognitive psychology's heavy investment in filter theories of auditory perception. If we cannot avoid hearing something, we then must select among the stimuli by some mental process, filtering out the unimportant and attending to the important. We turn now to investigations of selective attention in audition; in the process we bump into the need for more global theories of attention, memory, and cognition.

Dual Task Procedures. A general characteristic of many attention experiments, whether on vision or audition, involves the procedure of overload. In brief, we can overload the sensory system by presenting more information than it can handle at once and then test accuracy for some part of the information. That was the strategy in Sperling's partial report studies [. . .], which led to the concept of iconic memory. In studies of auditory perception, this has usually involved a dual task procedure. *Two tasks or messages are presented such that one task or message consumes the person's attentional resources as completely as possible.* Because the attentional capacity is used up by this primary task, there are few if any resources left over for conscious attention to the other information being presented. By varying the auditory characteristics or content of the messages, we can make the listener's job easier or harder. For instance, paying attention to a message spoken in one ear while trying to ignore the other ear's message is especially difficult when both messages are spoken by the same person. We can conclude from this that the initial encoding of the messages in auditory sensory memory included purely auditory features such as pitch and intonation.

Going one step further, when we examine performance to the attended task, we can ask about the accuracy with which the message is perceived and about the degree of interference caused by the second message. We can also look at the subject's accuracy for information that was not in the primary message, the unattended message in the other ear. If the subject shows any evidence of remembering the unattended message, or even some of its auditory features, we can discuss how unattended information is processed and registered in memory.

The Shadowing Experiments. Some of the earliest cognitive research on auditory pattern recognition and selective attention was performed by E. Colin Cherry (1953; Cherry & Taylor, 1954). Cherry was interested in the basic phenomena of speech recognition and attention. He characterized his research procedures, as well as the question he was asking, as the cocktail party problem: How do we pay attention to and recognize what one person is saying when we are surrounded by other spoken messages? To simulate this real-world situation in the laboratory, Cherry (see also Broadbent, 1952) devised the workhorse task of auditory perception research, the shadowing task. In this task, Cherry recorded spoken messages of different sorts on tape, then played the tape to a subject who was wearing headphones. The subject's task was to "shadow" the message coming into the right ear, that is, *to repeat the message out loud as soon as it was heard.* In most of the experiments, subjects were also told to ignore the other message, the one coming to the left ear. (It makes no difference which ear is shadowed and which is ignored, of course. For simplicity, assume that the right ear always receives the to-be-shadowed attended message and the left ear receives the unattended message.)

Although this procedure sounds simple, it takes a surprising amount of attention and concentration to shadow a message accurately. On one hand, subjects were quite accurate in producing "shadows" and reported that the task was easy. Nonetheless, Cherry found that subjects' spoken shadows usually were produced in a monotone voice, with little intonational stress, and generally lagged behind the taped message by a second or so. Interestingly, subjects seem unaware of the strangeness of their spoken shadows and usually cannot remember much of the content of the shadowed message once the task is over.

Assured that the task consumed enough attention to leave little, if any, for other purposes, Cherry then began to vary the unattended message. In a typical session, the tape began with a continuous coherent message presented to the right (attended) ear and another coherent message to the left (unattended ear). Once the subject began to shadow, the message in the left ear was changed. At the end of some amount of time, subjects were interrupted and asked what, if anything, they could report about the unattended message.

Generally, subjects could report accurately on a variety of physical characteristics of the unattended message. For instance, they noticed if it changed from human speech to a tone. They usually detected a change from a male voice to a female voice. On the other hand, when the unattended message was changed to reversed speech, only a few subjects noticed "something queer about it." Changes from English to a different language generally went unnoticed, and, overall, the subjects were unable to identify words or phrases that had been on the unattended message. In a dramatic confirmation of this last result, Neville Moray (1959) found that even a word presented 35 times in the unattended message was never recalled by the subjects (see also Wood & Cowan, 1995b).

15.9.2   Selection Models

It appears that almost any physical difference between the messages permits the subject to distinguish between them and eases the job of selectively attending to the target message (Johnston & Heinz, 1978). Eysenck (1982) called this Stage 1 selection; other investigators routinely call it early selection. Regardless of the name, this refers to some of the earliest phases of perception, an acoustic analysis based on physical features of the message. The evidence is that people can select a message based on Stage 1 sensory information — based on loudness, location of the sound source, pitch, and so on (Egan, Carterette, & Thwing, 1954; Spieth, Curtis, & Webster, 1954; Wood & Cowan, 1995a).

Broadbent's Filter Theory.   This evidence, indicating that subjects could somehow tune their auditory mechanisms to one message and ignore the other, prompted Donald Broadbent (1958) to propose a filter theory of auditory perception (actually, Broadbent's theory also covered memory, learning, and other more complex topics). In Broadbent's view, the auditory mechanism acts as a selective filter, as shown in Figure 15.7. Regardless of how many competing channels or messages are coming in, the filter can be tuned, or switched, to any one of the messages, based on characteristics such as loudness or pitch. Note that only one message can be passed through the filter at a time in Broadbent's theory. In other words, despite the many incoming signals, only one message can be sent along through the filter into the "limited-capacity decision channel," essentially the same as short-term memory. Only the information on the attended, "passed-along" message can affect performance, in Broadbent's view, because only it gets past the filtering mechanism.

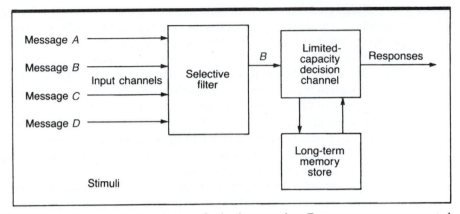

FIGURE 15.7 Broadbent's filter theory of selective attention. Four messages are presented, yet only one is selected and passed to the limited-capacity decision mechanism.

Adapted from Broadbent (1958).

It was realized very quickly that Broadbent's filter approach had some serious short-comings. For one, intuition tells us that we often notice information from a message we are not attending, as when you hear your name spoken in a crowded, noisy place. Moray (1959) found an exact laboratory parallel to this intuitive example: Although people did not recall a word presented 35 times to the unattended ear, fully a third of his sample heard their name spoken on the unattended channel (see Wood & Cowan, 1995b, for a modern replication of this effect). If Broadbent's theory were correct, then only the attended and passed-along information should be available for further cognitive processing, where attention is directed by physical cues. Yet clear evidence was available that unattended information could some-how slip past the filter (but see Lachter, Forster, & Ruthruff, 2004, who argue that some small amount of attention had been devoted to the "unattended" stimuli).

Treisman's Attenuation Theory. Anne Treisman (1960, 1964) performed an important series of investigations to explore this slippage more closely. Treisman used the standard shadowing task, but varied the nature of the unattended message across a much more subtle range of differences. She first replicated Cherry's findings that selective attention was easy when various physical differences existed between the messages. Then she turned to the situation in which physical differences were absent; both the attended and unattended messages were tape-recorded by the same speaker. Because the same pitch, intonation, stress, and so on were on both messages, Stage 1 selection should not be possible. Yet she found that subjects could shadow quite accurately; they could attend selectively to one message while ignoring the other. The basis for the selection, however, was not any physical characteristic of the messages. Instead, subjects now performed their selection on the basis of *message content*, what the message was about rather than what it sounded like. Eysenck (1982) called this *Stage 2* selection, in which the grammatical and semantic features are the basis for selection (*semantic* refers to meaning). A more conventional term for selection at this point is *middle selection*, certainly later in the stream of processing than early selection based on sensory features, yet earlier than selection just at the moment of having to respond out loud with the shadowed speech.

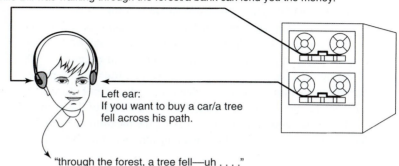

Right ear:
While Bill was walking through the forest/a bank can lend you the money.

Left ear:
If you want to buy a car/a tree
fell across his path.

"through the forest, a tree fell—uh . . . ."

FIGURE 15.8 The shadowing task. Two messages are played simultaneously into different ears; then, at the slash, the ear-of-arrival is switched for the two messages.

From Lindsay, *Human Information Processing,* 2nd edition. (c) 1977 Wadsworth, a part of Cengage Learning, Inc. Reproduced by permission. www.cengage.com/permissions

To show the power of selection based on the content of the message, Treisman conducted a study that is now considered a classic (1960); the setup for the experiment is depicted in Figure 15.8. Treisman arranged the tape recording so that the coherent message being shadowed by the subject was unexpectedly shifted to the unattended channel. Quite literally, the sentence the subject was saying switched from the right to the left ear. Despite a high degree of practice in shadowing the right ear and the high level of concentration needed, subjects routinely switched to the left ear message, the one that completed the meaning of the sentence they were shadowing. Although they did not continue to shadow the "wrong" ear for very long, when the meaningful sentence switched to the other ear, they also switched. Clearly, there must be some consideration of the unattended message, unlike the prediction from Broadbent's theory. Semantic elements of the unattended channel must be receiving some analysis, Treisman reasoned, or there would be no basis for preferring it when the sentences switched ears.

Based on such results, Treisman rejected the "early selection" notion embodied in Broadbent's theory, Eysenck's Stage 1 selection. Instead, she claimed that all incoming messages receive some amount of low-level analysis, including an analysis of the physical characteristics of the message. When the unattended messages yield no useful or important information, those messages are attenuated, in Treisman's terms; they are reduced not in their volume or physical characteristics but in their informational importance to ongoing processing. In the process of shadowing, we arrive at an identification of the words and phrases on the attended message.

Treisman (1965) felt that it was during this process of semantic analysis that we make our selection among messages — at Stage 2, selection at a "middle" stage. This scheme places selective attention well within the cognitive apparatus, of course, and permits attention to be affected by the semantic aspects of the message — that is, a top-down effect. The more extreme view, proposed by Deutsch and Deutsch (1963), claimed that selection takes place only after *all* messages have received full acoustic and semantic analysis (i.e., just before the response stage). This was a late selection theory, at Stage 3 in Eysenck's (1982) terminology, where the outcomes of all earlier analyses become conscious (for modern results against late selection, see Wood & Cowan, 1995a).

So the evidence is that much more information is getting into the cognitive system than strict selection or filtering would permit: the meaning of the words on the unattended channel, for example, in Treisman's study (1960; see also Lewis, 1970; Carr, McCauley, Sperber, & Parmelee, 1982, found comparable results for visually presented stimuli). Intrusion of the word *tree* into the subject's shadow, as shown in Figure 15.8, makes sense only if *tree* has been recognized as related to the forest theme of the shadowed message, an effect that implies some rapid process of accessing the meanings of words. How are such spoken patterns processed to the level of meaningfulness in the absence of explicit attention?

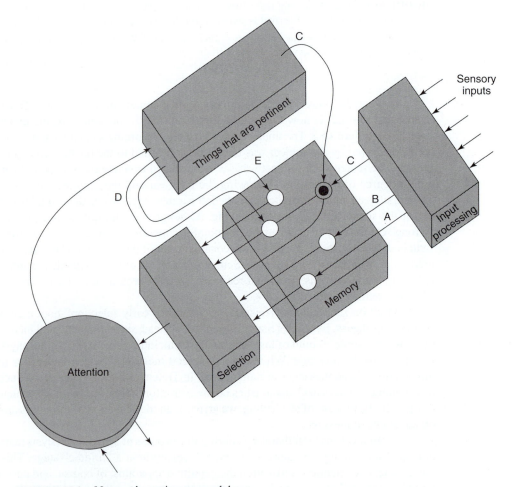

FIGURE 15.9   Norman's pertinence model.

Adapted from "*Toward a Theory of Memory and Attention*" by D. A. Norman, Psychological Review, 75, (1968), pp. 522–536. Copyright (c) 1968 by American Psychological Association. Used with permission.

Norman's Pertinence Model.   Donald Norman (1968) proposed a useful modification to the Treisman scheme; his model, which specifically included a mechanism for top-down processing, is depicted in Figure 15.9. Despite the more complex illustration, the model is rather straightforward and very appealing. It claims that at any instant in time, attention to some piece of information, some message, is determined by two factors: sensory activation and pertinence.

Consider sensory activation first. If the message is loud, in a distinct voice, or otherwise salient from a sensory standpoint, its sensory activation will be high; that is the message you will pay attention to. In simple terms, if the stereo at the party is much louder than anything else, you will be unable to attend to anything but the music. The figure shows that messages A, B, and C have some degree of sensory activation — maybe the music and the two nearest conversations.

Now add pertinence to the mixture. At any moment in time, certain things — ideas, words, and so forth — are highly pertinent to you, and others are low in pertinence. Pertinence can be temporary, as in Treisman's results on message content; if you're listening to a message about a forest, words such as *tree* are high in pertinence. But pertinence can also be relatively permanent; your name probably stays at a high level of pertinence on a permanent basis, for instance. In either case, the higher an item is in pertinence, the closer that item is to its criterion or threshold for awareness. In the figure, items C, D, and E are highly pertinent. So pertinence is *the momentary importance of information, whether caused by permanent or transitory factors.*

Now all we have to do is add the pertinence and sensory activations together. In Norman's model, the items in memory that have the highest combination of sensory and pertinence scores are the ones that are selected for attention. Thus, selective attention in Norman's theory is a continuous process. On a moment-by-moment basis, the item with the highest combination score is selected for conscious, deliberate attention. In the figure, this is represented by the darkened item C; it is pertinent and has high sensory activation (maybe it's your name in one of those nearby conversations). To continue the shadowing example, hearing *forest* makes concepts such as *tree* temporarily pertinent. That pertinence combines with the sensory input from the unattended channel ("a tree fell across his path"), so *tree* is selected and thus enters the attention component of the model.

Multimode Model of Attention.   Where does this leave us, you ask? It leaves us with knowledge about two aspects of selective attention: when, in the information processing sequence, attention can operate, and what kinds of factors influence its operation. Selective attention can occur very early in the processing sequence, based on very low-level, physical characteristics, as Broadbent proposed. It can also occur later, based on meaning or message content, as Treisman demonstrated. It can be influenced by both permanent and temporary factors. Permanent factors include highly important information, such as your name and highly overlearned and personally important factors. Like you, we always hear our names, even when it is just a coincidence that a passerby happens to say one of our names. But we also always hear the word *psychology,* even when it's spoken on an unattended message. So names are not the only possible items that can be permanently boosted in their pertinence. Temporary pertinence factors include message content as well as momentary fluctuations in interests. In short, attention is flexible.

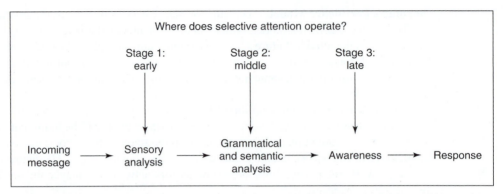

FIGURE 15.10   The sequence of processes in the shadowing task, with early, middle, and late operation of the selective attention mechanism.

Adapted from Johnston & Heinz (1978).

An important article, by Johnston and Heinz (1978), said just that — that attention is a highly flexible process that can operate in multiple modes. By modes, these authors meant the sort of factors described here as Stage 1, 2, or 3 models — operating in a physical mode, a meaning-based mode, and the like. This is illustrated in Figure 15.10. Johnston and Heinz's answer to the question "Where does selective attention operate?" is: "Anywhere. Selective attention can operate in multiple modes: early, middle, or late."

There is an important limitation to this flexibility, however, which involves capacity. Johnston and Heinz pointed out that although selective attention can vary from quite early to quite late, the downside of this flexibility is that later selection uses more of our limited attentional capacity. Therefore, later selection tends to be slower or less accurate when it comes to remembering the information that was attended to.

Their data illustrated this tradeoff quite clearly. In their experiments, the subjects listened to multiple messages, some differing physically, some differing in terms of meaning, and some differing in both meaning and physical characteristics. The subjects always had to remember information from one message, the target, and try to ignore any other messages that were also presented. While listening to the messages, they also had to monitor a light in front of them and press a button as soon as it came on. To make this challenging, the light came on at random, unpredictable intervals. The reasoning here was that detecting the light would be slower when participants listened to multiple messages because listening would use more attentional capacity. If selective attention is more difficult in some conditions because of similarities in the competing messages, this should slow down detection of the light.

This is exactly what happened, as illustrated in Figure 15.11. The figure shows the costs in performance — in other words, how much slower the responses to the light were compared with baseline (higher costs on the graph mean worse performance than in the baseline condition). Having to listen to one message slowed down light detection by about 60 ms; this is the first point on the graph. It shows that burdening the attentional system with the extra task, listening to the target message, used some of the available attentional capacity, thus slowing down light detection.

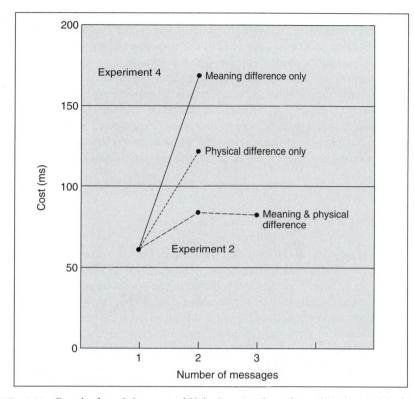

FIGURE 15.11   Results from Johnston and Heinz's research on the multimode model of attention. Data from Johnston and Heinz (1978).

Johnston and Heinz then went on to show how much more attentional capacity was drained when two or more messages were presented simultaneously, as in the shadowing research described earlier. In a second experiment, the target message was presented along with either one or two extra messages, the distractor messages (for a total number of messages of either two or three). But because the distractors differed both physically and in meaning from the target, this added only another 20 ms to the participants' time to detect the light; this is shown in the bottom curve in Figure 15.11. In other words, it took very little extra attention when given two types of cues, physical and meaning, to help them ignore the distractors. (It is not that difficult to ignore one or two nearby conversations if they are about different topics.)

But their fourth experiment examined the more taxing conditions for selective attention that you read about before (i.e., when the extra message differs only physically from the target or when it differs only in meaning). As the middle curve in the figure shows, the "physical difference only" task added 120 ms to participants' responses, showing a large drain on attentional capacity because of the difficulty of the listening task. This is rather like saying that Stage 1 selection, based on physical differences, costs the attentional system an extra 120 ms. And when it was only meaning that differentiated the messages, the cost to light detection speed was a whopping 170 ms.

This is the crux of Johnston and Heinz's multimode model. Selective attention can operate early in the sequence of processing, or it can operate late. But as it operates later and later, extra capacity is consumed by the attentional mechanism. This slows down (and makes less accurate) any other ongoing process because it subtracts from the total pool of mental resources that are available for performance (see also Wood & Cowan, 1995a, 1995b).

In short, it boils down to the issue of capacity. We started with the notion of limited capacity, then worked through the models of selective attention. And now we run into the capacity issue again. Selective attention is flexible but consumes some of the limited capacity of the human processing system. The harder it is to attend selectively to just one of several competing messages, the more capacity the selective attention process uses.

15.10   ATTENTION AS A MENTAL RESOURCE

An important and far-reaching meaning of the term *attention* — this one may be closer to our everyday meaning – treats attention as mental effort, as a mental resource that fuels cognitive activity. If we selectively attend to one particular message, we are deliberately focusing some mental effort on that message, concentrating on it to the exclusion of other messages (clearly what James had in mind in the quotation at the beginning of the chapter). This sense usually involves the notion that attention is a limited resource, that there is only so much of the critical mental fuel to be devoted here or there at any one time (Kahneman, 1973, also suggested that capacity might be somewhat elastic in that increasing the task load might also increase the subject's arousal, thus making additional resources available; see Eysenck, 1982, for a discussion of this point). Approaches that emphasize this meaning of the term are called resource theories.

A corollary to this idea of limited capacity is that attention, loosely speaking, is the same thing as consciousness or awareness. After all, if you can be consciously aware of only one thing at a time, doesn't that illustrate the limited capacity of attention? Even on a much smaller scale, when we process very simple stimuli, there is evidence of this attentional limit. If you are required to process a target stimulus and then immediately process a second target stimulus, processing of the second target may suffer because some of the resources needed to process it may still be operating on the first stimulus. When the first and second targets each require a speeded response, the RT to the second target will be delayed. This phenomenon was discovered in the 1950s, when it was called the psychological refractory period (for a review see Pashler, 1994). Even when neither target requires a speeded response, Jane Raymond, Kimron Shapiro, and Karen Arnell (1992) discovered, in studies conducted at the University of Calgary, that a similar processing bottleneck can impede performance. When they presented a rapid stream of items containing the two targets, accuracy in identifying the second target declined sharply as soon as the two were presented close together in time. They called this the "attentional blink." Under some conditions (Visser, Bischoff, & Di Lollo, 1999), when the two targets are adjacent to one another in the stream, the second one can be spared from the deleterious effects of the attentional blink — as if the second target was processed along with the first one before the "blink" took place. Although first demonstrated in the visual modality, the limitation seen in the attentional blink — like that seen in the psychological refractory period — has been observed in audition and cross-modally (Arnell & Jolicoeur, 1999), suggesting it is a basic limitation of attention and not of vision. Pierre Jolicoeur (1999) has suggested that these two phenomena (the psychological refractory period when speeded responses are measured and the attentional blink when accuracy is measured) may reflect the same process: Allocating attention to the first stimulus momentarily deprives you of the attention needed for the second stimulus, for example. (Jolicoeur was at the University of Waterloo when this paper was published, but is currently at the Université de Montréal.)

A related idea, which you encountered in the previous section, is that this kind of attention is deliberate, willful, intended — *controlled attention.* You decide to pay attention to a signal, a stimulus coming into the mental system, or you decide not to pay attention to the signal. *You* decide to pay attention to the lecture instead of your memory of last night's date, and when you realize your attention has wandered, you willfully redirect it to the lecture, determined not to daydream about last night until class is over.

The James quotation at the beginning of this chapter is also interesting because of another insight he had about attention: the idea that probably only one process of conception can occur at a time, but that we may seem to do more than one thing at a time if the other processes are habitual. When processes are less automatic, however, attention must oscillate among them if they are done simultaneously, with no consequent gain of time. The key point, of course, involves the idea of automatic processes, that some mental events can happen automatically without draining the pool of mental resources we call attention. Putting it simply, the germ of James's idea, automaticity, has become central to cognitive psychology's views on attention, pattern recognition, and a host of other topics. And cognitive science has devoted a huge amount of effort to recasting James's ideas about automaticity and attention into more formal, quantifiable concepts.

15.10.1   Automatic and Conscious Processing Theories

In place of the former approach, the limited-capacity attentional mechanism and the need for filtering in selective attention, the current view is that a variety of perceptual and cognitive processes can be executed in an automatic fashion, *with little or no necessary involvement of a conscious, limited-attention mechanism.* Two such explicit theories of automaticity have been proposed, one by Posner and Snyder (1975) and one by Shiffrin and Schneider, 1977; (Schneider & Shiffrin, 1977). These theories differ in some of their details but are similar in their overall message (see also Logan & Etherton, 1994; for discussions that oppose the idea of mental resources, see Navon, 1984, and Pashler, 1994).

Automatic Processing.   Posner and Snyder described three characteristics that are necessary for the "diagnosis" of an automatic process, listed for convenience in Table 15.2:

1. An automatic process occurs without intention; in other words, an automatic process occurs whether you consciously want it to or not. A standard and compelling example of this is the result obtained in a Stroop task (named after the task described in Stroop, 1935). Words such as *RED GREEN BLUE YELLOW* were presented visually to subjects, written in mismatching colours of ink (e.g., *RED* printed in green ink). When subjects have to name the ink colour, they must try to ignore the printed words themselves. This leads to tremendous interference, a dramatic slowing of the ink colour

TABLE 15.2 Diagnostic Criteria for Automatic and Conscious Processing

AUTOMATIC	CONSCIOUS
The process occurs without intention, without a conscious decision.	The process occurs only with intention, with a deliberate decision.
The mental process is not open to conscious awareness or introspection.	The process is open to awareness and introspection.
The process consumes few if any conscious resources; that is, it consumes little if any conscious attention.	The process uses conscious resources; that is, it drains the pool of conscious attentional capacity.
(Informal) The process operates very rapidly, usually within 1 s.	(Informal) The process is slow, taking more than a second or two for completion.

naming, caused by the mismatching colours and the contradictory impulses to name the word and the ink colour (this is an extremely easy demonstration to perform, by the way).

In Posner and Snyder's terms, accessing the meaning of the written symbol RED is automatic: It requires no intention; it happens whether you want it to or not. In the research that demonstrates automatic access to word meaning, the term we use is priming. A word automatically activates or primes its meaning in memory and, as a consequence, primes or activates meanings closely associated with it. This priming then makes related meanings easier to access: Because of priming, they are boosted up, or given an extra advantage or head start (just as wellwater is pumped more easily when you prime the pump; see Dunbar & MacLeod, 1984, and MacLeod, 1991, for an explanation of Stroop interference based on priming). This is obviously the mechanism underneath Treisman's "tree — forest" result in the shadowing task, as well as the Lewis (1970) and Carr et al. (1982) results.

2. An automatic process does not reveal itself to conscious awareness. You cannot describe the mental processes of looking up the word *RED* in memory. The look-up processes are automatic and are not available to conscious awareness. You are not aware of the operation of automatic processes, such as the perceptual mechanisms of looking at the visual pattern *T* and recognizing what it is. [. . .]

3. The third criterion of automaticity, according to Posner and Snyder, is that a fully automatic process consumes few if any conscious resources. Such a process should not interfere with other tasks, certainly not those that rely on conscious resources.[1] As an obvious example, walking is so automatic for adults that it simply does not interfere with other processes; you can walk and talk at the same time.

A fourth criterion is informal but nonetheless useful and is commonly noted as a characteristic of automaticity. Automatic processes tend to be very fast; as a rule, a response taking no more than 1 s is heavily automatic. (For evidence of very slow automatic processing, in a person with brain damage, see Wingfield, Goodglass, & Lindfield, 1997.)

Conscious Processing. Let's contrast these diagnostic criteria for automaticity with those for conscious or controlled processing (see Table 15.2). First, conscious processes occur only with intention. They are optional and can be deliberately performed or not performed

PROVE IT
THE STROOP TASK

An almost fall-safe demonstration of automaticity, in particular the automatic nature of access-ing word meaning, involves the Stroop task.

With several different colours of marker pens, write a dozen or so colour names on a sheet of paper, making sure to use a different colour of ink than the word signifies (e.g., write red in green ink); alternatively, create a deck of 3- × 5-inch cards, with one word per card. Make a control list of noncolour words (e.g., *hammer, card, wall*), again in coloured inks. (And try it yourself right now — name the colour of the ink for the words in Figure 4 inside the front cover of the book.)

Explain to your subject that the task is to name the *ink colour* as rapidly as possible. Time the subject (the second hand/display on your watch is more than sufficient; or keep track of naming errors, another way to measure the Stroop interference) on each kind of list. The standard result is that the colour word list will require substantially longer for ink colour nam-ing than the control list. Other useful control lists are simple bletches of colour, to check on the speed of naming the colours, and pseudowords ("manty," "zoople," and the like) written in dif-ferent ink colours.

According to several recent studies (e.g., Besner & Stolz, 1999; Marnwell, Roberts, & Besner, 2004; Vecera, Behrmann, and McGoldrick, 2000), you should be able to eliminate the Streep effect by getting your subjects to focus on just part of the word or to say the first letter position (this might be easier if you used the 3- × 5-inch card method) or by, printing only one letter in colour. This work suggests that reading the whole word is a kind of "default" set-ting for visual attention, which might be changed depending on the task and instructions and that our selective attention mechanism can select either whole objects (words) or their parts (let-ters) as the focus.

by the subject. Second, conscious processes are open to awareness; we know they are going on, and within limits we know what they consist of. Finally, and of greatest importance to the research, conscious processes use *attention*. They consume some of the limited attentional resources we have in the cognitive system.

A demanding conscious process should leave very few resources still available for use by a second task that also uses conscious processing. Driving during a hard rainstorm consumes too many resources for you to listen simultaneously to the news on the radio. Of course, if the second task can be processed fairly automatically, then both tasks may be able to proceed without interference; for example, you can walk while carrying on a serious conversation.

Integration with Conceptually Driven Processes.   We can go one step further now, integrating this explanation into the notion of conceptually driven processing. Attending to one of two incoming messages and shadowing that message out loud demands conscious, deliberate attention. Such a process is under the subject's direct control, the subject is aware of performing the process, and the process consumes most of the available mental resources that can be allocated. Presumably, no other conscious process can be performed simultaneously with the shadowing task without affecting performance in one or the other task (or both). When the messages are acoustically similar, the subject must rely on differences of content or meaning to keep them separate. But by tracking the meaning of a passage, the person's conceptually driven processes come into play in an obvious way. Just as subjects "restored" the missing sound in "the *eel was on the axle" (Warren & Warren, 1970), the shadowing subject "supplies" information about the message from long-term memory. Once you have begun to understand the content of the shadowed message, then your conceptually driven processes assist you by narrowing down the possible alternatives, by suggesting what might come next.

Saying that conceptually driven processes suggest what might come next is an informal way of referring to the important process of priming. You shadow "While Bill was walking through the forest." Your semantic analysis primes related information and thereby suggests the likely content of the next clause in the sentence; it is likely to be about trees, and it is unlikely to be about banks and cars. At this instant in time, your "forest" knowledge has been primed or activated in memory. It is ready (indeed, almost *eager*) to be perceived because it is so likely to be contained in the rest of the sentence. Then *tree* occurs on the unattended channel. Because we seem to access the meanings of words in an automatic fashion, the extra boost given to *tree* by the priming process pushes it over into the conscious attention mechanism. Suddenly, you're saying "a tree fell across" rather than sticking with the right-ear message. Automatic priming of long-term memory has exerted a top-down influence on the earliest of your cognitive processes, auditory pattern recognition and attention.

The Role of Practice and Memory.   If accessing word meaning is automatic, then you might be wondering about some of the shadowing research described earlier in which subjects were insensitive to the unshadowed message, failing to detect the word presented 35 times, the reversed speech, and so on. If word access is automatic, why didn't these subjects recognize the words on the unattended channel? A very plausible explanation, in view of recent research, is practice. It now seems very likely that subjects' inability to detect or to be influenced by the unattended message was caused by their relative lack of practice on the shadowing task. As several studies have shown, with greater degrees of practice even a seemingly complex and attention-consuming task becomes easy, or less demanding of attention's full resources. In fact, Logan and Klapp, 1991; (see also Zbrodoff & Logan, 1986) suggested that the effect of practice is to store the relevant information in memory; that is, that the necessary precondition for automatic processing is memory. Interestingly, once a process or procedure has become quite automatic, devoting explicit attention to it can even lead to worse performance (e.g., Beilock & Carr, 2001).

One of the most compelling strengths of the Shiffrin and Schneider (1977) theory of automatic and conscious processing (actually, they use the term *controlled* instead of *conscious* processing) is the role they award to old-fashioned, repetitive practice. Their experiments asked subjects to detect one or more target stimuli in successively presented displays (e.g., hold targets 2 and 7 in memory, then search for either of them in successively presented displays of stimuli). For some subjects, the targets were consistent across hundreds of trials — always digits, for instance. This was called Consistent Mapping. For subjects in the Varied Mapping groups, the targets were varied across trials (e.g., 2 and 7 might be targets on one trial, 3 and B on another, M and Z on yet another).

The essential ingredient here is practice on the stimuli and task. Unlike the Varied Mapping groups, subjects who received Consistent Mapping had enormous amounts of practice in scanning for the same targets. Across many experiments, subjects in the Consistent Mapping conditions developed quick automatic detection processes for their unchanging targets, to the point that they could search for any of four targets in about 450 ms, even in the largest display size (four characters shown at once). Subjects in the Varied Mapping conditions, on the other hand, needed greater search times for larger displays. At the large display size, their four-target search time was 1300 ms (Experiment 2, Schneider & Shiffrin, 1977). In the authors' interpretation, these subjects had not developed automatic detection processes because the stimuli they had to detect kept changing from trial to trial. In short, their search used conscious or controlled processing.

Rounding out their evidence on the effect of prolonged practice, Shiffrin and Schneider administered 2,100 detection trials to another group of subjects, consistently using one set of letters for the targets and a different set for the distractors. In the authors' words, "The subjects all reported extensive, attention-demanding rehearsal [. . .] during the first 600 trials of Experiment 1, but they gradually became unaware of rehearsal or other attention-demanding controlled processing after this point. [. . .] [They] gradually shifted to automatic detection" (1977, p. 133). After this lengthy procedure, Shiffrin and Schneider reversed the target and distractor sets, forcing subjects to search for targets that were previously distractors and to ignore distractors that were previously targets. Shiffrin and Schneider suspected that "automatic detection would prove impossible and that the subject would be forced to revert to controlled search" (p. 133). This is exactly what happened. As shown in Figure 15.12, panel A, RTs after the reversal took 2,400 trials before they were as rapid as the search times became in the initial testing condition. And as panel B shows, accuracy quickly climbed above 80% in the initial testing condition, but it took 1,800 trials after the reversal of targets and distractors before accuracy reached near 80% again.

15.10.2   A Synthesis for Attention and Automaticity

Attention, in its usual, everyday sense, is essentially equivalent to conscious mental capacity or conscious mental resources. We can devote these attentional resources to only one demanding task at a time or to two somewhat less demanding tasks simultaneously, as long as the two together do not exceed the total capacity available. This devotion of resources means that few, if any, additional resources are available for other demanding tasks. Alternatively, if a second task is performed largely at the automatic level, then it can occur simultaneously with the first because it does not draw from the conscious resource pool (or, to change the metaphor, the automatic process has achieved a high level of skill; see Hirst & Kalmar, 1987). The more automatically a task can be performed, the more mental resources are available for other processes.

The route to automaticity, it appears, is practice and memory. With repetition and overlearning comes the ability to perform in an automatic fashion what formerly needed conscious processing. A particularly dramatic illustration of the power of practice is the Spelke, Hirst, and Neisser (1976) demonstration. With extensive practice, two subjects eventually were able to read stories at normal rates and with high comprehension, while they simultaneously copied words at dictation or even categorized the dictated words according

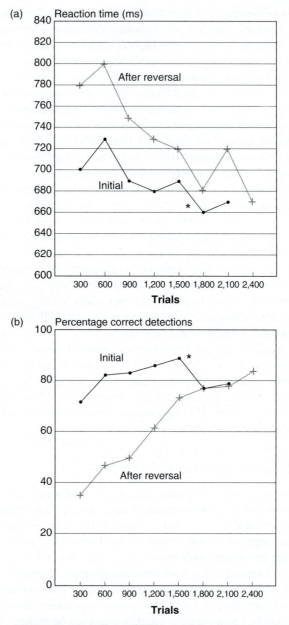

FIGURE 15.12   **(a)** Reaction times from Shiffrin and Schneider's detection task for the initial 2,100 trials of detection and for the 2,400 trials after the target and distractor sets were reversed. **(b)** Percentage of correct detections of targets for the same initial and after-reversal conditions. In both, the asterisk denotes the point during the initial condition when the time for stimulus presentation was reduced from 200 ms to 120 ms.

to meaning. The Shiffrin and Schneider results tracked the changes in performance across practice, showing a steady shift or migration from conscious to automatic. Significantly, once practice has yielded automatic performance, it seems especially difficult to undo the practice, to overcome what has now become an automatic and, in a sense, autonomous process (Zbrodoff & Logan, 1986).

Different degrees of practice, and therefore different degrees of automaticity, probably account for the varied results from the shadowing studies as well. As subjects gain more experience with the shadowing task, their shadowing presumably uses less and less conscious attention. This would release some of their conscious resources for other purposes. Among those other purposes is the conscious detection of related information, as Treisman found, or even detection of unattended channel information while shadowing (Moray himself, with presumably much practice at shadowing, outperformed less practiced subjects in reporting unattended channel information).

15.10.3 Disadvantages of Automaticity

We have been talking as if automaticity is a completely positive, desirable characteristic for mental processes, as if anything that reduces the drain on the limited available mental capacity is a good thing. This is not entirely true, however. There are several situations in which achieving automaticity can lead to difficulties (Reason, 1990).

You have encountered one of these already, in a sense. Schneider and Shiffrin's (1977) participants learned automatic detection processes in the Consistent Mapping condition: It took them no more time to search for four targets than for one after 2,100 trials. But when the target letters were switched, it took more than 2,100 additional trials for them to overcome the automaticity they achieved. It is hard to undo what has become automatic, in other words.

But does this have any practical application? Of course. We are often confronted with change, with situations that differ enough from what we have become accustomed to that some relearning has to take place. Your new car has some of its controls in a different location from where they were on the older one, so you have to overcome the habit of reaching to the left dashboard to turn on the lights (this is why some controls, e.g., accelerator and brake pedals, do not change position). If you switch to a new word processor after becoming fluent with a different system, it takes some relearning to overcome your accumulated practice with the old system.

More critically, sometimes we *should* be consciously aware of information or processes that have become too routine and automatic. Barshi and Healy (1993) provided an excellent example, using a proofreading procedure that mimics how we use checklists. All participants in their study scanned pages of simple multiplication problems. Five mistakes such as "$7 \times 8 = 63$" were embedded in the pages of problems. All participants saw the same sets of 10 problems over and over. But in the *fixed order* condition, the problems were in the same order each time; in the *varied order* condition, the problems were in a different order each time. Those tested in the fixed order condition missed significantly more of the embedded mistakes than those in the varied order condition; an average of 23% missed in fixed order, but only 9% missed with varied orders. Figure 15.13 shows this result across the five

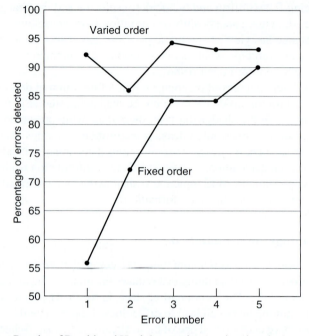

FIGURE 15.13   Results of Barshi and Healy's experiment, showing the percentage of participants detecting the five embedded errors in proofreading multiplication problems. Problems were presented in fixed or varied order.

Data from Barshi & Healy (1993).

embedded errors. Performance did improve in the fixed order condition as more and more of the mistakes were encountered. But the first multiplication error was detected only 55% of the time, compared with the 90% detection rate for the varied order group.

The fixed order of problems encouraged automatic proofreading, which disrupted accuracy at detecting errors. In fact, it took either an earlier error that was detected or a specific alerting signal (Experiment 3) to overcome the effects of routine, automatic proofreading.

The implications of this kind of result should be clear, as Barshi and Healy pointed out. Pilots are required to go through checklist procedures, say for landing an airplane, to ensure safety. Yet because the items on the checklist are in a fixed order, repeated use of the list probably leads to a degree of automaticity and probably a tendency to miss errors. This is exactly what happened in March 1983: A plane landed in Casper, Wyoming, without its landing gear down, even though the flight crew had gone through its standard checklist procedure and had "verified" that the wheels were down. In Barshi and Healy's words, this incident "reminded the crew and the rest of the aviation community that the countless repetition of the same procedure can lead to a dangerous automatization" (1993, p. 496). It's interesting to wonder which is worse, too much automatization of procedures, as exemplified by the Barshi and Healy study, or too much attention paid to the procedures, as in the Haines (1991) study you read about in Chapter 3 (hint: experienced pilots in flight simulators).

15.11   A DISORDER OF ATTENTION: HEMINEGLECT

We turn now to the cognitive neuroscience of attention, an increasingly important adjunct to cognitive studies of attentional mechanisms. The approach we will explore in this section uses a particular disorder of attention to help us understand how attention might operate in the normal brain. [. . .] Some actively researched disorders of attention, including complex syndromes such as attention deficit hyperactivity disorder (ADHD) are beyond the scope of this book. But one in particular deserves consideration here because it has a bearing on normal attention in several direct ways.

Go back to the beginning of the chapter and reread the quotation from Banich (1997) about Bill. Bill suffers from hemineglect, a syndrome that leads to such behaviour as brushing only the teeth on his right, washing only his right arm, and shaving only the right side of his face. To most people, this phenomenon is almost too bizarre to believe, maybe because the processes of mental attention have always been so closely tied to perception and voluntary movement and so automatic that we think they are indivisible parts of the same process. Look at yourself in a mirror, then look at the left side of your face — no problem, you merely move your eyes, shift your direction of gaze, and look at it. If I ask you to stare straight ahead and then attend to something in your left field of vision, say the letter *X* on a computer screen, your normal response is to shift your eyes toward the left and focus on the target. You simply look at the *X* and pay attention to it. And as you read earlier, you can shift your mental attention to the left even without moving your eyes.

The syndrome known as hemineglect, or hemi-inattention, is a disruption in the ability to do just that, to refocus your attention to one side of your face or the other, to the *X* on the left of the computer screen. It is a *disruption or decreased ability to look at something in the* (often) *left field of vision and pay attention to it. Hemi* means "half," and *neglect* and *inattention* mean "to ignore" or "to fail to perceive." Thus hemineglect is a disorder of attention in which one half of the perceptual world is neglected to some degree and cannot be attended to as completely or accurately as normal. Very often, the neglect is of the left visual field, for stimuli to the left of the current fixation, the current focus of attention. And because of the principle of contralaterality, it is not surprising that the brain damage leading to hemineglect is often in the right hemisphere — in particular, certain regions of the right parietal lobe (see Intriligator & Cavanagh, 2001, for evidence that localizes selective attention in the parietal lobe).

Here are the facts (see Banich, 1997, or Rafal, 1997, for complete treatments). A patient with hemineglect cannot voluntarily direct attention to half of the perceptual world, whether the to-be-perceived stimulus is visual, auditory, or any other type of sensation. In some cases, the neglect is nearly total, as if half of the perceptual world has simply vanished, is simply not there in any normal sense of the word. In other cases, the neglect is not total, so for such people it is more accurate to say that they are *less* able to redirect their controlled attention than are normal people. In either case, there is a disruption in the ability to control attention. Note that this is not a case of sensory damage like blindness or deafness. The patient with hemineglect receives input from both sides of the body and can make voluntary muscle movements on both sides. And in careful testing situations, such patients can also respond to stimuli in the neglected field. But somehow, the deliberate devotion of controlled attention to one side is deficient.

Bisiach and Luzatti (1978) presented a compelling description of patients with hemineglect. The afflicted individuals were from Milan, Italy, so before their brain damage they were quite familiar with the city, and in particular the main piazza in town, a broad open square with buildings and shops along the sides and a large cathedral at one end. These patients were asked to imagine themselves standing at one end of the piazza, facing toward the cathedral, and were asked to describe what they could see. They uniformly described only the buildings and shops on the right side of the piazza. When asked to imagine themselves standing on the steps of the cathedral, facing back the opposite way, they once again described what was on their right side. From this second view, of course, what they described on their right was exactly what they had omitted from their earlier descriptions. Likewise, what they now omitted was what they had described earlier, the buildings and shops that now would be in their left visual field.

Critically important here is the observation that these reports, based on memory, were exactly the kind of reports patients with hemineglect give when actually viewing a scene; if these patients had been taken to the piazza, they probably would have seen and described it the same way in person as they did from memory. (For a similar account, see "Eyes Right!" in Sacks, 1970; the patient there eats the right half of everything on her dinner plate, then complains about not getting enough food.) [. . .] The illustrations in Figure 15.14 show a similarly revealing result. Here, the patient was asked to look at the top drawing in that panel and then draw the black part. Then the patient was asked to look at and draw the white part of the figure. In both cases, the patient was able to focus on whichever part was called for but could pay attention only to the right half of that part. Because the right half of the white part does not have a jagged edge, neither did the patient's drawing, and because the right half of the black part does have a jagged edge, the patient's drawing did as well.

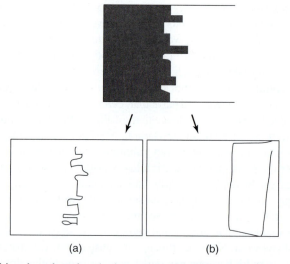

(a)   (b)

FIGURE 15.14   Object-based neglect is demonstrated by the copying performance of a patient with left hemispatial neglect. **(a)** When asked to copy the black object, the patient did well because the jagged contour is on the right side of the black object. **(b)** When asked to copy the white object, the patient was unable to copy the jagged contour because it is on the left side of the object being attended.

From Marshall & Halligan (1994).

A careful analysis of the range of disruptions seen in patients with hemineglect has recently been provided by Duncan et al. (1999) in the context of an umbrella theory called the Theory of Visual Attention (Bundesen, 1990). Duncan et al. noted that several important advances in our understanding of hemineglect have been made recently, especially when the patients are tested with some standardized cognitive tasks such as Posner's spatial cueing task, which you read about earlier. For example, it turns out that patients with hemineglect often can attend to stimuli in the neglected field but only if nothing else is displayed visually that might attract their attention. That is, they can detect a simple stimulus in the left visual field (or, more properly, the field contralateral to their brain damage), even if that is the field they normally neglect. But this ability to detect the same stimulus is dramatically reduced if a stimulus in the right visual field (a stimulus in the ipsilateral or same-side field) is presented at the same time (see Danziger, Kingstone, & Rafal, 1998, for evidence of an orienting response in the neglected field).

This tendency to ignore the contralateral field when a competing stimulus is presented in the ipsilateral field is called extinction. It is apparently caused by something like attentional capture. When a right-side (ipsilateral) stimulus is presented, it captures the person's attention and prevents attention from being devoted to the left (contralateral). In a sense then, hemineglect patients may neglect one side only because there is usually something on the other side that captures their attention. In a very real sense, Bill might have been able to focus on shaving the left side of his face if he had not been able to see his right side.

In a curious way, hemineglect seems to disrupt both the reflexive and the voluntary control of attention. First, attention seems to be captured by stimuli in the "good" or preserved field, the ipsilateral field (the term *ipsilesional* is also used, meaning "same side as the brain lesion"). Second, in terms that Posner used to describe mental activity in the spatial cueing task, it appears that hemineglect patients have difficulty disengaging attention from that ipsilateral stimulus. Because attention was captured and then held by stimuli on the right side, patients have difficulty shifting their attention voluntarily to the left. Thus, bottom-up capture of attention on one side has disrupted a shift of top-down, voluntary attention toward the other side.

In their analysis, Duncan et al. (1999) noted that their patients with hemineglect showed standard deficits in attention to the contralateral side but also some rather strong bilateral deficits related to attentional capacity; in other words, there were accuracy deficits on the neglected side but capacity difficulties on both sides. Interestingly, there was little evidence that the conceptually driven aspects of their attention were affected. It may be some time before such results and their implications for the normal processes of attention are fully digested. Moreover, the deficits experienced by patients with hemineglect are not restricted to spatial attention (e.g., Danckert & Ferber, 2006). But even now, it is clear that such fractionation of performance — some abilities preserved, some disrupted — will be important in our further understanding of attention (for a neural net modelling approach to hemineglect, see Monaghan & Shillcock, 2004).

NOTES

1. Interference in the Stroop task occurs in part because the two automatic processes, reading the word and detecting the ink colour, eventually compete with one another when it is time to make a response. That is, both processes are trying to output their results to the same speech mechanism, but the responses are incompatible ("red," "green"). When we say that an automatic process generally does not interfere with other processes, it is assumed that we are speaking of situations in which the two processes are not compering for the same response mechanism.

REFERENCES

Abrams, R. A., & Christ, S. E. (2003). Motion onset captures attention. *Psychological Science, 14,* 427–432.

Arnell, K. M., & Jolicoeur, P. (1999). The attentional blink across stimulus modalities: Evidence for central processing limitations. *Journal of Experimental Psychology: Human Perception & Psychophysics, 25,* 630–648.

Banich, M. T. (1997). *Neuropsychology: The neural bases of mental function.* Boston: Houghton Mifflin.

Barshi, I., & Healy, A. F. (1993). Checklist procedures and the cost of automaticity. *Memory & Cognition, 21,* 496–505.

Beilock, S. L., & Carr, T. H. (2001). On the fragility of skilled performance: What governs choking under pressure? *Journal of Experimental Psychology, 130,* 701–725.

Bennett, P. J., & Pratt, J. (2001). The spatial distribution of inhibition of return. *Psychological Science, 12,* 76–80.

Besner, D., & Stolz, J. A. (1999). What kind of attention modulates the Stroop effect? *Psychonomic Bulletin & Review, 6,* 99–104.

Bisiach, E., & Luzzatti, C. (1978). Unilateral neglect of representational space. *Cortex, 14,* 129–133.

Bonebakker, A. E., Bonke, B., Klein, J., Wolters, G., Stijnen, T., Passchier, J., & Merikle, P. M. (1996). Information processing during general anesthesia: Evidence for unconscious memory. *Memory & Cognition, 24,* 766–776.

Briand, K., & Klein, R. M. (1987). Is Posner's beam the same as Treisman's glue? On the relationship between visual orienting and feature integration theory. *Journal of Experimental Psychology: Human Perception & Performance, 13*(2), 228–247.

Broadbent, D. E. (1952). Speaking and listening simultaneously. *Journal of Experimental Psychology, 43,* 267–273.

Broadbent, D. E. (1958). *Perception and communication.* London: Pergamon.

Bundesen, C. (1990). A theory of visual attention. *Psychological Review, 97,* 523–547.

Carr, T. H., McCauley, C., Sperber, R. D., & Parmalee, C. M. (1982). Words, pictures, and priming: On semantic activation, conscious identification, and the automaticity of information processing. *Journal of Experimental Psychology: Human Perception and Performance, 8,* 757–777.

Cave, K. R., & Bichot, N. P. (1999). Visuospatial attention: Beyond a spotlight model. *Psychonomic Bulletin & Review, 6,* 204–223.

Cherry, E. C. (1953). Some experiments on the recognition of speech, with one and with two ears. *Journal of the Acoustical Society of America, 25,* 975–979.

Cherry, E. C., & Taylor, W. K. (1954). Some further experiments on the recognition of speech with one and two ears. *Journal of the Acoustical Society of America, 26,* 554–559.

Cowan, N. (1995). *Attention and memory: An integrated framework.* New York: Oxford University Press.

Danckert, J., & Ferber, S. (2006). Revisiting unilateral neglect. *Neuropsychologia, 44,* 987–1006.

Danziger, S., Kingstone, A., & Rafal, R. D. (1998). Orienting to extinguished signals in hemispatial neglect. *Psychological Science, 9,* 119–123.

Danziger, S., & Kingstone, A. (1999). Unmasking the inhibition of return phenomenon. *Perception & Psychophysics, 61,* 1024–1037.

Deutsch, J. A., & Deutsch, D. (1963). Attention: Some theoretical considerations. *Psychological Review, 70,* 80–90.

Dunbar, K., & MacLeod, C. M. (1984). A horse race of a different color: Stroop interference patterns with transformed words. *Journal of Experimental Psychology: Human Perception and Performance, 10,* 622–639.

Duncan, J., & Humphreys, G. W. (1989). Visual search and stimulus similarity. *Psychological Review, 96,* 433–458.

Duncan, J., & Humphreys, G. W. (1992). Beyond the search surface: Visual search and attentional engagement. *Journal of Experimental Psychology: Human Perception and Performance, 18,* 578–588.

Duncan, J., Bundesen, C., Olson, A., Humphreys, G., Chavda, S., & Shibuya, H. (1999). Systematic analysis of deficits in visual attention. *Journal of Experimental Psychology: General, 128,* 450–478.

Egan, P., Carterette, E. C., & Thwing, E. J. (1954). Some factors affecting multichannel listening. *Journal of the Acoustic Society of America, 26*, 774–782.

Eysenck, M. W. (1982). *Attention and arousal: Cognition and performance.* Heidelberg: Springer-Verlag.

Haines, R. F. (1991). A breakdown in simultaneous information processing. In G. Obrecht & L. W. Stark (Eds.), *Presbyopia research* (pp. 171–175). New York: Plenum Press.

Hirst, W., & Kalmar, D. (1987). Characterizing attentional resources. *Journal of Experimental Psychology: General, 116*, 68–81.

Hommel, B., Pratt, J., Colzato, L., & Godijn, R. (2001). Symbolic control of visual attention. *Psychological Science, 12*, 360–365.

Intriligator, J., & Cavanagh, P. (2001). The spatial resolution of visual attention. *Cognitive Psychology, 43*, 171–216.

James, W. (1890). *The principles of psychology.* New York: Dover.

Johnston, W. A., & Heinz, S. P. (1978). Flexibility and capacity demands of attention. *Journal of Experimental Psychology: General, 107*, 420–435.

Jolicoeur P. (1999). Concurrent response-selection demands modulate the attentional blink. *Journal of Experimental Psychology: Human Perception & Performance, 25*, 1097–1113.

Jonides, J. (1981). Voluntary versus automatic control over the mind's eye's movement. In J. [B.] Long & A. [D.] Baddeley (Eds.), *Attention and performance IX* (pp. 187–203). Hillsdale, NJ: Erlbaum.

Kahneman, D. (1973). *Attention and effort.* Englewood Cliffs, NJ: Prentice Hall.

Klein, R. M. (1988). Inhibitory tagging system facilitates visual search. *Nature, 334*, 430–431.

Klein, R. M. (2004a). On the control of orienting. In M. I. Posner (Ed.), *Cognitive neuroscience of attention* (pp. 29–44). New York: Guilford Press.

Klein, R. M. (2004b). Orienting and inhibition of return. In M. S. Gazzaniga (Ed.), *The cognitive neurosciences*, 3rd ed. (pp. 545–560). Cambridge, MA: MIT Press.

Klein, R. M. (2005). On the role of endogenous orienting in the inhibitory aftermath of exogenous orienting. In U. Mayr, E. Awh, & S. Keele, *Developing individuality in the human brain: A feschrift for Michael Posner* (pp. 45–64). Washington, DC: APA Books.

Klein, R. M., & Farrell, M. (1989). Search performance without eye movements. *Perception & Psychophysics, 46*(5), 476–482.

Klein, R. M., & MacInnes, W. J. (1999). Inhibition of return is a foraging facilitator in visual search. *Psychological Science, 10*, 346–352

Kolb, B., & Whishaw, I. Q. (1996). *Fundamentals of human neuropsychology* (4th ed.). New York: Freeman.

Lachter, J., Forster, K. I., & Ruthruff, E. (2004). Forty-five years after Broadbent (1958): Still no identification without attention. *Psychological Review, 111*, 880–913.

Lewis, J. L. (1970). Semantic processing of unattended messages using dichotic listening. *Journal of Experimental Psychology, 85*, 225–228.

Lindsay, P. H., & Norman, D. A. (1977). *Human information processing: An introduction to psychology.* New York: Academic Press.

Logan, G. D., & Etherton, J. L. (1994). What is learned during automatization? The role of attention in constructing an instance. *Journal of Experimental Psychology: Learning, Memory, and Cognition, 20*, 1022–1050.

Logan, G. D., & Klapp, S. T. (1991). Automatizing alphabet arithmetic: 1. Is extended practice necessary to produce automaticity? *Journal of Experimental Psychology: Learning, Memory, and Cognition, 17*, 179–195.

MacLeod, C. M. (1991). Half a century of research on the Stroop effect: An integrative review. *Psychological Bulletin, 109*, 163–203.

Manwell, L. A., Roberts, M. A., & Besner, D. (2004). Single letter coloring and spatial cuing eliminates a semantic contribution to the Stroop effect. *Psychonomic Bulletin & Review, 11*, 458–462.

Marshall, J. C., & Halligan, P. W. (1994). The yin and yang of visuospatial neglect: A case-study. *Neuropsychologia, 32*, 137–157.

Masson, M. E. J. (1984). Memory for the surface structure of sentences: Remembering with and without awareness. *Journal of Verbal Learning and Verbal Behavior, 23*, 579–592.

Maylor, E. A., & Hockey, R. (1985). Inhibitory component of externally controlled covert orienting in visual space. *Journal of Experimental Psychology: Human Perception and Performance, 11*, 777–787.

Monaghan, P., & Shillcock, R. (2004). Hemispheric asymmetries in cognitive modeling: connectionist modeling of unilateral visual neglect. *Psychological Review, 111*, 283–308.

Moray, N. (1959). Attention in dichotic listening: Affective cues and the influence of instructions. *Quarterly Journal of Experimental Psychology, 11*, 56–60.

Müller, H., & von Mühlenen, A. (2000). Probing distractor inhibition in visual search. *Journal of Experimental Psychology: Human Perception & Performance. 26*, 1591–1605.

Navon, D. (1984). Resources: A theoretical soup stone? *Psychological Review, 91*, 216–234.

Neisser, U. (1976) *Cognition and reality.* San Francisco: Freeman.

Norman, D. A. (1968). Toward a theory of memory and attention. *Psychological Review, 75*, 522–536.

Ohman, A., Flykt, A., & Esteves, F. (2001). Emotion drives attention: Detecting the snake in the grass. *Journal of Experimental Psychology: General, 130,* 466–478.

Pashler, H. (1994) Dual-task interference in simple tasks: Data and theory. Psychological Bulletin, 116, 220–244.d

Posner, M. I. (1980). Orienting of attention. *Quarterly Journal of Experimental Psychology, 32,* 3–25.

Posner, M. I., & Boies, S. J. (1971) Components of attention. *Psychological Review, 78,* 391–408.

Posner, M. I., & Cohen, Y. (1984). Components of visual orienting. In H. Bouma & D. G. Bouwhuis (Eds.), *Attention and performance X* (pp. 531–556). Hillsdale, NJ: Erlbaum.

Posner, M. I., & Snyder, C. R. R. (1975). Facilitation and inhibition in the processing of signals. In P. M. A. Rabbitt & S. Dornic (Eds.), *Attention and performance V* (pp. 669–682). New York: Academic Press.

Posner, M. I., Snyder, C. R. R., & Davidson, B. J. (1980). Attention and the detection of signals. *Journal of Experimental Psychology: General, 109,* 160–174.

Pratt, J., & Abrams, R. A. (1995). Inhibition of return to successively cued spatial locations. *Journal of Experimental Psychology: Human Perception & Performance, 21,* 1343–1353.

Rafal, R. D. (1997). Hemispatial neglect: Cognitive neuropsychological aspects. In T. E. Feinberg & M. J. Farah (Eds.), *Behavioral neurology and neuropsychology* (pp. 319–336). New York: McGraw-Hill.

Rafal, R. D., Calabresi, P. A., Brennan, C. W., & Sciolto, T. K. (1989). Saccade preparation inhibits reorienting to recently attended locations. *Journal of Experimental Psychology: Human Perception and Performance, 15,* 673–685.

Raymond, J. E., Shapiro, K. L., & Arnell, K. M. (1992). Temporary suppression of visual processing in an RSVP task: An attentional blink. *Journal of Experimental Psychology: Human Perception & Performance, 18,* 849–860.

Reason, J. (1990). *Human error.* New York: Cambridge University Press.

Rusak, B. (1989). The mammalian circadian system: Models and physiology. *Journal of Biological Rhythms, 4,* 121–134.

Sacks, O. (1970). *The man who mistook his wife for a hat.* New York: Harper & Row.

Samuel, A. G., & Kat, D. (2003). Inhibition of return: A graphical meta-analysis of its time course and an empirical test of its temporal and spatial properties. *Psychonomic Bulletin & Review, 10,* 897–906.

Schacter, D. L. (1989). Memory. In M. I. Posner (Ed.), *Foundations of cognitive science* (pp. 683–725). Cambridge, MA: MIT Press.

Schacter, D. L. (1996). *Searching for memory.* New York: Basic Books.

Schneider, W., & Shiffrin, R. M. (1977). Controlled and automatic human information processing: I. Detection, search, and attention. *Psychological Review, 84,* 1–66.

Shiffrin, R. M., & Schneider, W. (1977). Controlled and automatic human information processing: II. Perceptual learning, automatic attending, and a general theory. *Psychological Review, 84,* 127–190.

Snyder, J. J. & Kingstone, A. (2000). Inhibition of return and visual search: How many separate loci are inhibited. *Perception and Psychophysics, 62,* 452–458.

Spelke, E., Hirst, W., & Neisser, U. (1976). Skills of divided attention. *Cognition, 4,* 215–230.

Spence, C., & Read, L. (2003). Speech shadowing while driving: On the difficulty of splitting attention between eye and ear. *Psychological Science, 14,* 251–256.

Spieth, W., Curtis, J. F., & Webster, J. C. (1954). Responding to one of two simultaneous messages. *Journal of the Acoustical Society of America, 26,* 391–396.

Strayer, D. L., & Johnson, W. A. (2001). Driven to distraction: Dual-task studies of stimulated driving and conversing on a cellular phone. *Psychological Science, 12,* 462–466.

Stroop, J. R. (1935). Studies of interference in serial verbal reactions. *Journal of Experimental Psychology, 18,* 643–662.

Sussman, E., Winkler, I., & Schroger, E. (2003). Top-down control over involuntary attention switching in the auditory modality. *Psychonomic Bulletin & Review, 10,* 630–637.

Takeda, Y., & Yagi, A. (2000). Inhibitory tagging in visual search can be found if search stimuli remain visible. *Perception & Psychophysics, 62,* 927–934.

Tipper, S. P., Driver, J., & Weaver, B. (1991). Object-centred inhibition of return of visual attention. *Quarterly Journal of Experimental Psychology [A], 43,* 289–298.

Treisman, A. (1982). Perceptual grouping and attention in visual search for features and for objects. *Journal of Experimental Psychology: Human Perception and Performance, 8,* 194–214.

Treisman, A. (1988). Features and objects: The Fourteenth Bartlett Memorial Lecture. *Quarterly Journal of Experimental Psychology, 40A,* 201–237.

Treisman, A. (1991). Search, similarity, and integration of features between and within dimensions. *Journal of Experimental Psychology: Human Perception and Performance, 17*, 652–676.

Treisman, A. (1992). Spreading suppression or feature integration? A reply to Duncan and Humphreys (1992). *Journal of Experimental Psychology: Human Perception and Performance, 18*, 589–593.

Treisman, A. M. (1960). Contextual cues in selective listening. *Quarterly Journal of Experimental Psychology, 12*, 242–248.

Treisman, A. M. (1964). Monitoring and storage of irrelevant messages in selective attention. *Journal of Verbal Learning and Verbal Behavior, 3*, 449–459.

Treisman, A. M. (1965). The effects of redundancy and familiarity on translating and repeating back a foreign and a native language. *British Journal of Psychology, 56*, 369–379.

Treisman, A., & Gelade, G. (1980). A feature integration theory of attention. *Cognitive Psychology, 12*, 97–136.

Vecera, S. P., Behrmann, M., & McGoldrick, J. (2000). Selective attention to the parts of an object. *Psychonomic Bulletin & Review, 7*, 301–308.

Visser, T. A. W., Bischof, W. F., & Di Lollo, V. (1999). Attentional switching in spatial and nonspatial domains: Evidence from the attentional blink. *Psychological Bulletin, 125*, 458–469.

Warren, R. M., & Warren, R. P. (1970). Auditory illusions and confusions. *Scientific American, 223*, 30–36.

Wingfield, A., Goodglass, H., & Lindfield, K. C. (1997). Separating speed from automaticity in a patient with focal brain atrophy. *Psychological Science, 8*, 247–249.

Wolfe, J. M., Cave, K. R., & Franzel, S. L. (1989). Guided search: An alternative to the feature integration model for visual search. *Journal of Experimental Psychology: Human Perception & Performance, 15*, 419–433.

Wood, N. L., & Cowan, N. (1995a). The cocktail party phenomenon revisited: Attention and memory in the classic selective listening procedure of Cherry (1953). *Journal of Experimental Psychology: General, 124*, 243–262.

Wood, N., & Cowan, N. (1995b). The cocktail party phenomenon revisited: How frequent are attention shifts to one's name in an irrelevant auditory channel? *Journal of Experimental Psychology: Learning, Memory, and Cognition, 21*, 255–260.

Wright, R. D., & Ward, L. M. (2008). *Orienting of attention.* Oxford University Press: New York.

Zbrodoff, N. J., & Logan, G. D. (1986). On the autonomy of mental processes: A case study of arithmetic. *Journal of Experimental Psychology: General, 115*, 118–130.

CHAPTER SIXTEEN

FEATURES AND OBJECTS
IN VISUAL PROCESSING

ANNE TREISMAN

If you were magically deposited in an unknown city, your first impression would be of recognizable objects organized coherently in a meaningful framework. You would see buildings, people, cars, and trees. You would not be aware of detecting colors, edges, movements, and distances, and of assembling them into multidimensional wholes for which you could retrieve identities and labels from memory. In short, meaningful wholes seem to precede parts and properties, as the Gestalt psychologists emphasized many years ago.

This apparently effortless achievement, which you repeat innumerable times throughout your waking hours, is proving very difficult to understand or to simulate on a computer — much more difficult, in fact, than the understanding and simulation of tasks that most people find quite challenging, such as playing chess or solving problems in logic. The perception of meaningful wholes in the visual world apparently depends on complex operations to which a person has no conscious access, operations that can be inferred only on the basis of indirect evidence.

Nevertheless, some simple generalizations about visual information processing are beginning to emerge. One of them is a distinction between two levels of processing. Certain aspects of visual processing seem to be accomplished simultaneously (that is, for the entire visual field at once) and automatically (that is, without attention being focused on any one part of the visual field). Other aspects of visual processing seem to depend on focused attention and are done serially, or one at a time, as if a mental spotlight were being moved from one location to another.

In 1967, Ulric Neisser, then at the University of Pennsylvania, suggested that a "preattentive" level of visual processing segregates regions of a scene into figures and ground so that a subsequent, attentive level can identify particular objects. More recently,

From *Scientific American* 255, no. 5 (1986): 114–125. Reprinted with permission.

David C. Marr, investigating computer simulation of vision at the Massachusetts Institute of Technology, found it necessary to establish a "primal sketch": a first stage of processing, in which the pattern of light reaching an array of receptors is converted into a coded description of lines, spots, or edges and their locations, orientations, and colors. The representation of surfaces and volumes and finally the identification of objects could begin only after this initial coding.

In brief, a model with two or more stages is gaining acceptance among psychologists, physiologists, and computer scientists working in artificial intelligence. Its first stage might be described as the extraction of features from patterns of light; later stages are concerned with the identification of objects and their settings. The phrase "features and objects" is therefore a three-word characterization of the emerging hypothesis about the early stages of vision.

I think there are many reasons to agree that vision indeed applies specialized analyzers to decompose stimuli into parts and properties, and that extra operations are needed to specify their recombination into the correct wholes. In part the evidence is physiological and anatomical. In particular, the effort to trace what happens to sensory data suggests that the data are processed in different areas of considerable specialization. One area concerns itself mainly with the orientation of lines and edges, another with color, still another with directions of movement. Only after processing in these areas do data reach areas that appear to discriminate between complex natural objects.

Some further evidence is behavioral. For example, it seems that visual adaptation (the visual system's tendency to become unresponsive to a sustained stimulus) occurs separately for different properties of a scene. If you stare at a waterfall for a few minutes and then look at the bank of the river, the bank will appear to flow in the opposite direction. It is as if the visual detectors had selectively adapted to a particular direction of motion independent of *what* is moving. The bank looks very different from the water, but it nonetheless shows the aftereffects of the adaptation process.

How can the preattentive aspect of visual processing be further subjected to laboratory examination? One strategy is suggested by the obvious fact that in the real world parts that belong to the same object tend to share properties: they have the same color and texture, their boundaries show a continuity of lines or curves, they move together, they are at roughly the same distance from the eye. Accordingly the investigator can ask subjects to locate the boundaries between regions in various visual displays and thus can learn what properties make a boundary immediately salient — make it "pop out" of a scene. These properties are likely to be the ones the visual system normally employs in its initial task of segregating figure from ground.

It turns out that boundaries are salient between elements that differ in simple properties such as color, brightness, and line orientation but not between elements that differ in how their properties are combined or arranged (figure 16.1). For example, a region of *T*s segregates well from a region of tilted *T*s but not from a region of *L*s made of the same components as the *T*s (a horizontal line and a vertical line). By the same token, a mixture of blue *V*s and red *O*s does not segregate from a mixture of red *V*s and blue *O*s. It seems that the early "parsing" of the visual field is mediated by separate properties, not by particular combinations of properties. That is, analysis of properties and parts precedes their synthesis. And if parts or properties are identified before they are conjoined with objects, they must have some independent psychological existence.

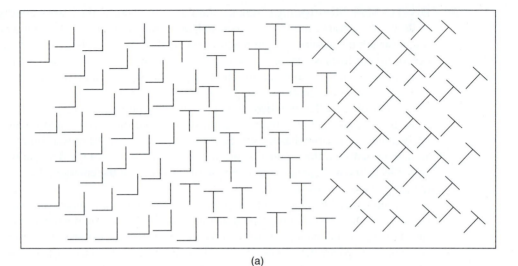

(a)

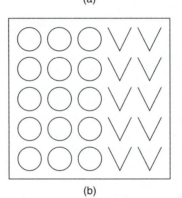

(b)

FIGURE 16.1   Boundaries that "pop out" of a scene are likely to reveal the simple properties, or features, of the visual world that are seized on by the initial stage of visual processing. For example, a boundary between *Ts* and tilted *Ts* pops out, whereas a boundary between *Ts* and *Ls* does not (a). The implication is that line orientations are important features in early visual processing but that particular arrangements of conjunctions of lines are not. A boundary between *Os* and *Vs* pops out (b). The implication is that simple shape properties (such as line curvature) are important.

    This leads to a strong prediction, which is that errors of synthesis should sometimes take place. In other words, subjects should sometimes see illusory conjunctions of parts or properties drawn from different areas of the visual field. In certain conditions such illusions take place frequently. In one experiment my colleagues and I flashed three colored letters, say a blue *X*, a green *T*, and a red *O*, for a brief period (200 milliseconds, or a fifth of a second) and diverted our subjects' attention by asking them to report first a digit shown at each side of the display and only then the colored letters. In about one trial in three, the subjects reported the wrong combinations — perhaps a red *X*, a green *O*, or a blue *T*.

    The subjects made these conjunction errors much more often than they reported a color or shape that was not present in the display, which suggests that the errors reflect genuine exchanges of properties rather than simply misperceptions of a single object. Many of these errors appear to be real illusions, so convincing that subjects demand to see the display again to convince themselves that the errors were indeed mistakes.

We have looked for constraints on the occurrence of such illusory conjunctions. For example, we have asked whether objects must be similar for their properties to be exchanged. It seems they do not: Subjects exchanged colors between a small, red outline of a triangle and a large, solid blue circle just as readily as they exchanged colors between two small outline triangles. It is as if the red color of the triangle were represented by an abstract code for red rather than being incorporated into a kind of analogue of the triangle that also encodes the object's size and shape.

We also asked if it would be harder to create illusory conjunctions by detaching a part from a simple unitary shape, such as a triangle, than by moving a loose line. The answer again was no. Our subjects saw illusory dollar signs in a display of Ss and lines. They also saw the illusory signs in a display of Ss and triangles in which each triangle incorporated the line the illusion required (figure 16.2). In conscious experience the triangle looks like a cohesive whole. Nevertheless, at the preattentive level, its component lines seem to be detected independently.

To be sure, the triangle may have an additional feature, namely the fact that its constituent lines enclose an area, and this property of closure might be detected preattentively. If so, the perception of a triangle might require the detection of its three component lines in the correct orientations and also the detection of closure. We should then find that subjects do not see illusory triangles when they are given only the triangles' separate lines in the proper orientations (figure 16.3). They may need a further stimulus, a different closed shape (perhaps a circle), in order to assemble illusory triangles. That is indeed what we found.

Another way to make the early, preattentive level of visual processing the subject of laboratory investigation is to assign visual-search tasks. That is, we ask subjects to find a target item in the midst of other, "distractor" items. The assumption is that if the preattentive

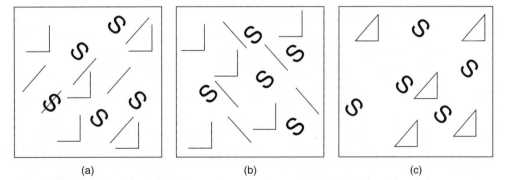

(a)   (b)   (c)

FIGURE 16.2   Illusory dollar signs are an instance of false conjunctions of features. Subjects were asked to look for dollar signs in the midst of Ss and line segments (a). They often reported seeing the signs when the displays to which they were briefly exposed contained none (b). They had the same experience about as often when the line segment needed to complete a sign was embedded in a triangle (c). The experiment suggests that early visual processing can detect the presence of features independent of location.

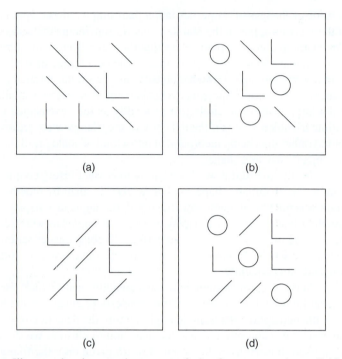

FIGURE 16.3   Illusory triangles constitute a test of what features must be available to support the perception of triangles. Subjects seldom reported seeing a triangle when they were briefly exposed to displays consisting of the line segments that make up a triangle (a). They saw triangles far more often when the displays also included closed stimuli, that is, shapes that enclose a space, in this case *Os* (b). Evidently, closure is a feature analyzed in early visual processing. This conclusion was supported by showing displays that lack the diagonal line to make a triangle (c, d). Subjects seldom saw triangles in such displays.

processing occurs automatically and across the visual field, a target that is distinct from its neighbors in its preattentive representation in the brain should "pop out" of the display. The proverbial needle in a haystack is hard to find because it shares properties of length, thickness and orientation with the hay in which it is hidden. A red poppy in a haystack is a much easier target; its unique color and shape are detected automatically.

We find that if a target differs from the distractors in some simple property, such as orientation or color or curvature, the target is detected about equally fast in an array of 30 items and in an array of three items. Such targets pop out of the display, so that the time it takes to find them is independent of the number of distractors. This independence holds true even when subjects are not told what the unique property of the target will be. The subjects take slightly longer overall, but the number of distractors still has little or no effect.

On the other hand, we find that if a target is characterized only by a conjunction of properties (for example, a red *O* among red *N*s and green *O*s), or if it is defined only by its particular combination of components (for example, an *R* among *P*s and *Q*s that together incorporate all the parts of the *R*), the time taken to find the target or to decide that the target is not present increases linearly with the number of distractors. It is as if the subjects who are placed in these circumstances are forced to focus attention in turn on each item in the display in order to determine how the item's properties or parts are conjoined. In a positive trial (a trial in which a target is present) the search ends when the target is found; on the average, therefore, it ends after half of the distractors have been examined. In a negative trial (in which no target is present) all the distractors have to be checked. As distractors are added to the displays, the search time in positive trials therefore increases at half the rate of the search time in negative trials.

The difference between a search for simple features and a search for conjunctions of features could have implications in industrial settings. Quality-control inspectors might, for example, take more time to check manufactured items if the possible errors in manufacture are characterized by faulty combinations of properties than they do if the errors always result in a salient change in a single property. Similarly, each of the symbols representing, say, the destinations for baggage handled at airline terminals should be characterized by a unique combination of properties.

In a further series of experiments on visual-search tasks, we explored the effect of exchanging the target and the distractors. That is, we required subjects to find a target distinguished by the fact that it *lacks* a feature present in all the distractors. For example, we employed displays consisting of *O*s and *Q*s, so that the difference between the target and the distractors is that one is simply a circle whereas the other is a circle intersected by a line segment (figure 16.4). We found a remarkable difference in the search time depending on whether the target was the *Q* and had the line or was the *O* and lacked the line. When the target had the line, the search time was independent of the number of distractors. Evidently, the target popped out of the display. When the target lacked the line, the search time increased linearly with the number of distractors. Evidently, the items in the display were being subjected to a serial search.

The result goes against one's intuitions. After all, each case involves the same discrimination between the same two stimuli: *O*s and *Q*s. The result is consistent, however, with the idea that a pooled neural signal early in visual processing conveys the presence but not the absence of a distinctive feature. In other words, early vision extracts simple properties, and each type of property triggers activity in populations of specialized detectors. A target with a unique property is detected in the midst of distractor items simply by a check on whether the relevant detectors are active. Conversely, a target lacking a property that is present in the distractors arouses only slightly less activity than a display consisting exclusively of distractors. We propose, therefore, that early vision sets up a number of what might be called *feature maps*. They are not necessarily to be equated with the specialized visual areas that are mapped by physiologists, although the correspondence is suggestive.

We have exploited visual-search tasks to test a wide range of candidate features we thought might pop out of displays and so reveal themselves as primitives: basic elements in the language of early vision. The candidates fell into a number of categories: quantitative properties such as length or number; properties of single lines such as orientation or curvature; properties of line arrangements; topological and relational properties such as the connectedness of lines, the presence of the free ends of lines or the ratio of the height to the width of a shape.

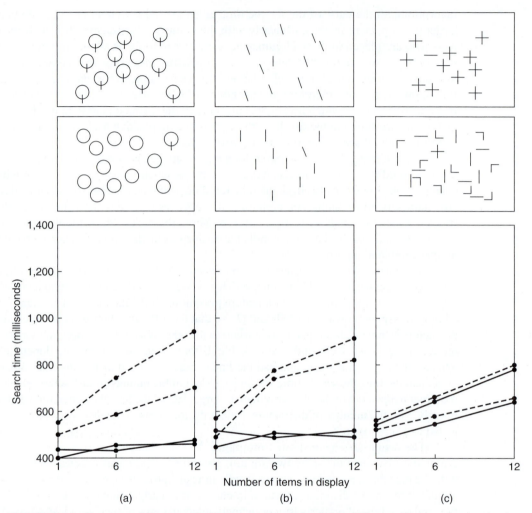

FIGURE 16.4   Presence of absence of a feature can have remarkably different effects on the time it takes to find a target in the midst of distractors. In one experiment (a) the target was a circle intersected by a vertical line segment or a circle without that feature. The search time for the intersected circle (solid) proved to be largely independent of the number of items in the display, suggesting that the feature popped out. The search time for the plain circle (dashed) increased steeply as distractors were added, suggesting that a serial search of the display was being made. A second experiment (b) required subjects to search for a vertical line (dashed) or a tilted line (solid). The tilted line could be found much faster; evidently only the tilted line popped out of the displays. A third experiment (c) tested an isolated line segment (dashed) or intersecting lines in the form of a plus sign (solid). Evidently neither popped out.

Among the quantitative candidates, my colleagues and I found that some targets popped out when their discriminability was great. In particular, the more extreme targets — the longer lines, the darker grays, the pairs of lines (when the distractors were single lines) — were easier to detect. This suggests that the visual system responds positively to "more" in these quantitative properties and that "less" is coded by default. For example, the neural activity signaling

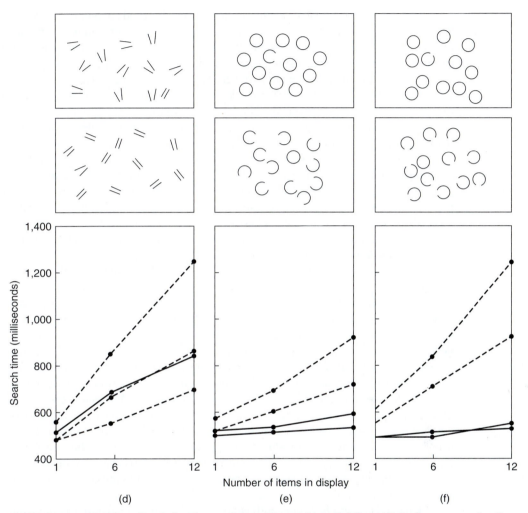

FIGURE 16.4 (Continued) A fourth experiment (d) tested parallel lines (dashed) or converging lines (solid). Again neither popped out. A fifth experiment (e) tested closure with complete circles (dashed) or circles with a gap of a fourth of their circumference (solid). A sixth experiment (f), again testing closure, had complete circles (dashed) or circles with smaller gaps (solid). The size of the gap seemed to make no difference: The incomplete circle popped out. On the other hand, a complete circle became harder to find as the size of the gaps in distractors was reduced. Open dots represent data from trials in which the display included only distractors.

line length might increase with increasing length (up to some maximum), so that a longer target is detected against the lower level of background activity produced by short distractors. In contrast, a shorter target, with its concomitant lower rate of firing, is likely to be swamped by the greater activity produced by the longer distractors. Psychophysicists have known for more than a century that the ability to distinguish differences in intensity grows more acute with decreasing background intensity. We suggest that the same phenomenon, which is known as Weber's law, could account for our findings concerning the quantitative features.

Our tests of two simple properties of lines, orientation and curvature, yielded some surprises. In both cases we found pop-out for one target, a tilted line among vertical distractors and a curved line among straight lines, but not for the converse target, a vertical line among tilted distractors and a straight line among curves. These findings suggest that early vision encodes tilt and curvature but not verticality or straightness. That is, the vertical targets and the straight targets appear to lack a feature the distractors possess, as if they represent null values on their respective dimensions. If our interpretation is correct, it implies that in early vision, tilt and curvature are represented relationally, as deviations from a standard or norm that itself is not positively signaled.

A similar conclusion emerged for the property of closure. We asked subjects to search for complete circles in the midst of circles with gaps and for circles with gaps among complete circles. Again we found a striking asymmetry, this time suggesting that the gap is preattentively detectable but that closure is not — or rather that it becomes preattentively detectable only when the distractors have very large gaps (that is, when they are quite open shapes like semicircles). In other words, closure is preattentively detectable, but only when the distractors do not share it to any significant degree. On the other hand, gaps (or the line ends that gaps create) are found equally easily whatever their size (unless they are too small for a subject, employing peripheral vision, to see).

Finally, we found no evidence that any property of line arrangements is preattentively detectable. We tested intersections, junctions, convergent lines and parallel lines. In every case we found that search time increases with an increasing number of distractors. The targets become salient and obvious only when the subject's attention is directed to them; they do not emerge automatically when that attention is disseminated throughout the display.

In sum, it seems that only a small number of features are extracted early in visual processing. They include color, size, contrast, tilt, curvature, and line ends. Research by other investigators shows that movement and differences in stereoscopic depth are also extracted automatically in early vision. In general the building blocks of vision appear to be simple properties that characterize local elements, such as points or lines, but not the relations among them. Closure appears to be the most complex property that pops out preattentively. Finally, our findings suggest that several preattentive properties are coded as values of deviation from a null, or reference, value.

Up to this point I have concentrated on the initial, preattentive stages of vision. I turn now to the later stages. In particular I turn to the evidence that focused attention is required for conjoining the features at a given location in a scene and for establishing structured representations of objects and their relations.

One line of evidence suggesting that conjunctions require attention emerges from experiments in which we asked subjects to identify a target in a display and say where it was positioned. In one type of display only a simple feature distinguished the target from the distractors. For example, the target was a red *H* in the midst of red *O*s and blue *X*s or an orange *X* among red *O*s and blue *X*s. In other displays, the target differed only in the way its features were conjoined. For example, it was a blue *O* or a red *X* among red *O*s and blue *X*s.

We were particularly interested in the cases in which a subject identified the target correctly but gave it the wrong location. As we expected, the subjects could sometimes identify a simple target, say a target distinguished merely by its color, but get its location wrong. Conjunction targets were different: The correct identification was completely dependent on the correct localization. It does indeed seem that attention must be focused on a location in order to combine the features it contains.

In a natural scene, of course, many conjunctions of features are ruled out by prior knowledge. You seldom come across blue bananas or furry eggs. Preattentive visual processing might be called "bottom up," in that it happens automatically, without any recourse to such knowledge. Specifically, it happens without recourse to "top down" constraints. One might hypothesize that conjunction illusions in everyday life are prevented when they conflict with top-down expectations. There are many demonstrations that we do use our knowledge of the world to speed up perception and to make it more accurate. For example, Irving Biederman of the State University of New York at Buffalo asked subjects to find a target object such as a bicycle in a photograph of a natural scene or in a jumbled image in which different areas had been randomly interchanged. The subjects did better when the bicycle could be found in a natural context [. . .].

In order to explore the role of prior knowledge in the conjoining of properties. Deborah Butler and I did a further study of illusory conjunctions. We showed subjects a set of three colored objects flanked on each side by a digit. Then, some 200 milliseconds later, we showed them a pointer, which was accompanied by a random checkerboard in order to wipe out any visual persistence from the initial display. We asked the subjects to attend to the two digits and report them, and then to say which object the pointer had designated. The sequence was too brief to allow the subjects to focus their attention on all three objects.

The crucial aspect of the experiment lay in the labels we gave the objects. We told one group of subjects that the display would consist of "an orange carrot, a blue lake, and a black tire." Occasional objects (one in four) were shown in the wrong color to ensure that the subjects could not just name the color they would know in advance ought to be associated with a given shape. For another group of subjects the same display was described as "an orange triangle, a blue ellipse, and a black ring."

The results were significant. The group given arbitrary pairings of colors and shapes reported many illusory conjunctions: 29 percent of their responses represented illusory recombinations of colors and shapes from the display, whereas 13 percent were reports of colors or shapes not present in the display. In contrast, the group expecting familiar objects saw rather few illusory conjunctions: They wrongly recombined colors and shapes only 5 percent more often than they reported colors and shapes not present in the display.

We occasionally gave a third group of subjects the wrong combinations when they were expecting most objects to be in their natural colors. To our surprise we found no evidence that subjects generated illusory conjunctions to fit their expectations. For example, they were no more likely to see the triangle (the "carrot") as orange when another object in the display was orange than they were when no orange was present. There seem to be two implications: Prior knowledge and expectations do indeed help one to use attention efficiently in conjoining features, but prior knowledge and expectations seem not to induce illusory exchanges of features to make abnormal objects normal again. Thus illusory conjunctions seem to arise at a stage of visual processing that precedes semantic access to knowledge of familiar objects. The conjunctions seem to be generated preattentively from the sensory data, bottom-up, and not to be influenced by top-down constraints.

How are objects perceived once attention has been focused on them and the correct set of properties has been selected from those present in the scene? In particular, how does one generate and maintain an object's perceptual unity even when objects move and change? Imagine a bird perched on a branch, seen from a particular angle and in a particular illumination. Now watch its shape, its size, and its color all change as it preens itself, opens its wings, and flies away. In spite of these major transformations in virtually all its properties, the bird retains its perceptual integrity: It remains the same single object.

Daniel Kahneman of the University of California at Berkeley and I have suggested that object perception is mediated not only by recognition, or matching to a stored label or description, but also by the construction of a temporary representation that is specific to the object's current appearance and is constantly updated as the object changes. We have drawn an analogy to a file in which all the perceptual information about a particular object is entered, just as the police might open a file on a particular crime, in which they collect all the information about the crime as the information accrues. The perceptual continuity of an object would then depend on its current manifestation being allocated to the same file as its earlier appearances. Such allocation is possible if the object remains stationary or if it changes location within constraints that allow the perceptual system to keep track of which file it should belong to.

In order to test this idea we joined with Brian Gibbs in devising a letter-naming task (figure 16.5). Two letters were briefly flashed in the centers of two frames. The empty frames then moved to new locations. Next, another letter appeared in one of the two frames. We devised the display so that the temporal and spatial separations between the priming letter and the final letter were always the same; the only thing that differed was the motion of the frames. The subjects' task was to name the final letter as quickly as possible.

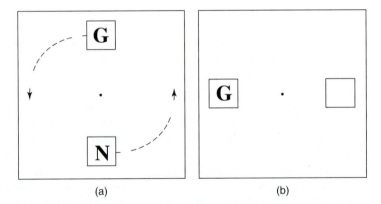

(a)   (b)

FIGURE 16.5   Integration of sensory information into what amounts to a file on each perceptual object was tested by the motion of frames. In each trial, two frames appeared, then two letters were briefly flashed in the frames (a). The frames moved to new locations, and a letter appeared in one of the two (b). The subject's task was to name the final letter as quickly as possible. If the final letter matched the initial letter and appeared in the same frame, the naming was faster than if the letter had appeared in the other frame or differed from the initial letter. The implication is that it takes more time to create or update a file on an object than it does simply to perceive the same object a second time.

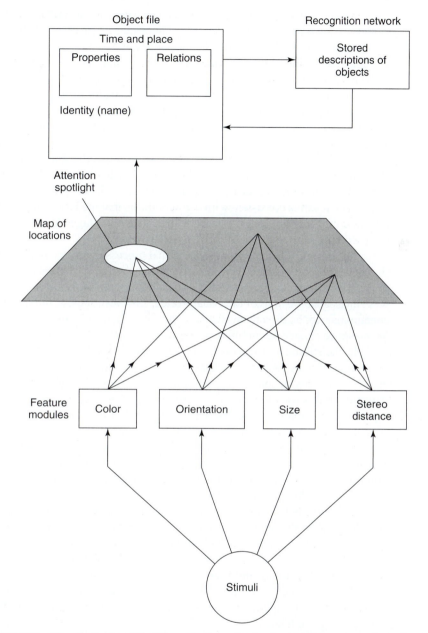

FIGURE 16.6 Hypothetical model of the early stages in visual perception emerges from the author's experiments. The model proposes that early vision encodes some simple and useful properties of a scene in a number of feature maps, which may preserve the spatial relations of the visual world but do not themselves make spatial information available to subsequent processing stages. Instead, focused attention (employing a master map of locations) selects and integrates the features present at particular locations. At later stages, the integrated information serves to create and update files on perceptual objects. In turn, the file contents are compared with descriptions stored in a recognition network. The network incorporates the attributes, behavior, names, and significance of familiar objects.

We knew that the prior exposure to a given letter should normally lessen the time it takes to identify the same letter on a subsequent appearance; the effect is known as *priming*. The question that interested us was whether priming would occur only in particular circumstances. We argued that if the final letter is the same as the priming letter and appears in the same frame as the priming letter, the two should be seen as belonging to the same object; in this case, we could think of the perceptual task as simply re-viewing the original object in its shifted position. If, on the other hand, a new letter appears in the same frame, the object file should have to be updated, perhaps increasing the time it takes for subjects to become aware of the letter and name it.

Actually the priming was found to be object-specific: Subjects named the final letter some 30 milliseconds faster if the same letter had appeared previously in the same frame. They showed no such benefit if the same letter had appeared previously in the other frame. The result is consistent with the hypothesis that the later stages of visual perception integrate information from the early, feature-sensitive stages in temporary object-specific representations.

The overall scheme I propose for visual processing can be put in the form of a model (figure 16.6). The visual system begins by coding a certain number of simple and useful properties in what can be considered a stack of maps. In the brain such maps ordinarily preserve the spatial relations of the visual world itself. Nevertheless, the spatial information they contain may not be directly available to the subsequent stages of visual processing. Instead the presence of each feature may be signaled without a specification of *where* it is.

In the subsequent stages, focused attention acts. In particular, focused attention is taken to operate by means of a master map of locations, in which the presence of discontinuities in intensity or color is registered without specification of what the discontinuities are. Attention makes use of this master map, simultaneously selecting, by means of links to the separate feature maps, all the features that currently are present in a selected location. These are entered into a temporary object representation, or file.

Finally, the model posits that the integrated information about the properties and structural relations in each object file is compared with stored descriptions in a "recognition network." The network specifies the critical attributes of cats, trees, bacon and eggs, one's grandmothers, and all other familiar perceptual objects, allowing access to their names, their likely behavior, and their current significance. I assume that conscious awareness depends on the object files and on the information they contain. It depends, in other words, on representations that collect information about particular objects, both from the analyses of sensory features and from the recognition network, and continually update the information. If a significant discontinuity in space or time occurs, the original file on an object may be canceled: it ceases to be a source of perceptual experience. As for the object, it disappears and is replaced by a new object with its own new temporary file, ready to begin a new perceptual history.

CHAPTER SEVENTEEN

THE DEVELOPMENT OF MUSIC PERCEPTION AND COGNITION

W. JAY DOWLING

I. INTRODUCTION

An adult listening attentively to a piece of music and understanding it performs an enormous amount of information processing very rapidly. Most of this processing is carried out automatically below the level of conscious analysis, because there is no time for reflective thought on each detail as the piece steadily progresses. This process is closely parallel to what happens when a native speaker of a language listens to and understands a sentence. The elements of the sentence are processed very rapidly — so rapidly that the listener cannot attend individually to each detail, but simply hears and understands the overall meaning. The rapidity of automatic speech processing depends on extensive perceptual learning with the language in question. Similarly, the music listener's facility in grasping a piece of music depends on perceptual learning gained through experience with the music of a particular culture. Further, we can see in the development of language from its earliest stages the predisposition of the child to speak, and the ways in which basic elements of language, already present in infancy, are molded through perceptual learning and acculturation into adult structures (Brown, 1973). Similarly, we can find elements of adult cognitive structures for music in young infants, and can watch them develop in complexity under the influence of culture and individual experience. In both speech and music, then, there are specific patterns of behavior that emerge in infancy that bear the unmistakable stamp of "speech" or "music" behavior. We can trace the elaboration of those incipient speech and music patterns in the course of development.

A point to be emphasized is the ease and rapidity with which adults perform complex cognitive tasks in domains of speech and music familiar to them, and the degree to which that facility depends on prior experience. For example, when the processing of a melody is complicated by the temporal interleaving of distractor notes among the notes of the melody,

From chapter 15 in *The Psychology of Music,* 2d ed., ed. D. Deutsch (San Diego: Academic Press, 1999), 603–625. Reprinted with permission of Elsevier, Ltd..

listeners are more accurate in judging pitches that match familiar, culturally determined norms than those that do not (Dowling, 1992, 1993a). Furthermore, the ability to discern a target melody in the midst of temporally interleaved distractors grows gradually through childhood, and the importance of the culturally defined tonal scheme to the performance of that task grows as well (Andrews & Dowling, 1991). Perceptual learning with the music of a culture provides the listener with a fund of implicit knowledge of the structural patterns of that music, and this implicit knowledge serves to facilitate the cognitive processing of music conforming to those patterns.

Calling the knowledge amassed through perceptual learning "implicit" indicates that it is not always available to conscious thought. Neither the knowledge base itself nor the cognitive processes through which it is applied are entirely accessible to consciousness (Dowling, 1993a, 1993b). Listeners typically engage in far more elaborate processing than they are aware of. For example, there is evidence that listeners with a moderate amount of musical training encode the diatonic scale-step ("*do, re, mi*") values of the notes of melodies they hear (Dowling, 1986). Yet those listeners are not aware that they are even capable of categorizing melodic pitches according to their scale-step values, much less that they do it routinely when hearing a new melody. Implicit knowledge of Western musical scale structure has accrued over years of experience, and that knowledge is applied automatically and unconsciously whenever the adult listens to music.

This sensorimotor learning undoubtedly has consequences for brain development, as illustrated by Elbert, Pantev, Wienbruch, Rockstroh, and Taub's (1995) demonstration of the enhanced allocation of cortical representation to fingers of the left hand in string players, especially for those who begin study of the instrument before the age of 12. Recent results by Pantev, Oostenveld, Engelien, Ross, Roberts, and Hoke (1998) concerning cortical allocation in processing musical tones tend to confirm this supposition.

In looking at the development of music perception and cognition, one of our goals is to distinguish between cognitive components that are already present at the earliest ages and components that develop in response to experience. We can look at the content of the adult's implicit knowledge base in contrast to the child's. We can also look at the developmental sequence by which the individual goes from the infant's rudimentary grasp of musical structure to the experienced adult's sophisticated knowledge and repertoire of cognitive strategies for applying it.

II. DEVELOPMENT

A. Infancy

Over the past 20 years, much has been learned about the infant's auditory world. Researchers have isolated several kinds of changes that infants can notice in melodies and rhythmic patterns, and those results give us a picture consistent with the notion that infant auditory perception uses components that will remain important into adulthood. In broad outline it is clear that infants are much like adults in their sensitivity to the pitch and rhythmic grouping of sounds. This is seen in infants' tendency to treat melodies with the same melodic contour (pattern of ups and downs in pitch) as the same and to respond to the similarity of rhythmic patterns even across changes of tempo. Similarly, we find that in children's spontaneous singing, rhythmic grouping and melodic contour are important determinants of structure and that when children begin singing, their singing is readily distinguishable from speech in terms of its patterns of pitch and rhythm. In both perception and production, we find that the child's cognition of musical patterns contains the seeds of the adult's cognition.

1. Prenatal Experience.   Even before birth, the infant appears to be sensitive to music, or at least to patterns of auditory stimulation. Research has shown that prenatal auditory stimulation has effects on the infant's behavior after birth. Shetler (1989) has reviewed studies showing that the fetus is responsive to sounds at least as early as the second trimester. Very young infants recognize their mother's voice (DeCasper & Fifer, 1980; Mehler, Bertoncini, Barrière, & Jassik-Gerschenfeld, 1978), and this may derive from neonatal experience with the mother's characteristic patterns of pitch and stress accents. Such an interpretation is plausible in light of the demonstration by DeCasper and Spence (1986) that patterns of a speech passage read repeatedly by their mothers during the third trimester of pregnancy were later preferred by babies. DeCasper and Spence had newborns suck on a blind nipple in order to hear one or another children's story. Children who had been read a story in the womb sucked more to hear that story, while babies who had not been read stories in the womb had no preference between the two stories. Spence and DeCasper (1987) also demonstrated that babies who had been read stories in the womb liked speech that was low-pass filtered (resembling speech heard before birth) as much as normal unfiltered speech, whereas babies who had not been read to did not.

2. Perceptual Grouping.   Infants' grouping of sounds in the pitch and time domain appears to follow much the same overall rules of thumb as it does for adults. Just as adults segregate a sequence of notes alternating rapidly between two pitch ranges into two perceptual streams (Bregman & Campbell, 1971; Dowling, 1973; McAdams & Bregman, 1979), so do infants (Demany, 1982). A converging result of Thorpe and Trehub (1989) illustrates this. Thorpe and Trehub played infants repeating six-note sequences such as AAAEEE (where A and E have frequencies of 440 and 660 Hz, a musical fifth apart). They trained the infants to turn their heads to see a toy whenever they heard a change in the stimuli being presented. A background pattern (AAAEEE) would be played over and over. Once in a while a changed pattern would appear. The changes consisted of temporal gaps introduced within perceptual groups (AAAE EE) or between groups (AAA EEE). The infants noticed the changes when they occurred within groups, but not between groups. An additional gap separating patterns that were already perceptually separate was simply lost in processing (as it tends to be by adults).

3. Pitch.   Infant pitch perception is quite accurate and also displays some of the sophistication of adult pitch processing. Adults display "octave equivalence" in being able to distinguish easily between a pair of tones an octave apart and a pair of tones not quite an octave apart (Ward, 1954), and so do infants (Demany & Armand, 1984). Adults also have "pitch constancy" in the sense that complex tones with differing harmonic structure (such as different vowel sounds with different frequency spectra) have the same pitch as long as their fundamental frequencies are the same. That is, we can sing "ah" and "ooh" on the same pitch, the listener will hear them that way, and the pitch can be varied independently of vowel timbre by changing our vocal chord vibration rate (and hence the fundamental frequency of the vowel).

Even eliminating the fundamental frequency entirely from a complex tone will not change the pitch as long as several harmonics remain intact (Schouten, Ritsma, & Cardozo, 1962). Clarkson and Clifton (1985) used conditioned head turning to demonstrate that the same is true for infants 7 or 8 months old. Also, Clarkson and Rogers (1995) showed that, just like adults, infants have difficulty discerning the pitch when the harmonics that are present are high in frequency and remote from the frequency of the missing fundamental.

Regarding pitch discrimination, Thorpe (1986, as cited in Trehub, 1987) demonstrated that infants 7–10 months old can discriminate direction of pitch change for intervals as small as 1 semitone. Infants 6–9 months old can also be induced to match the pitches of vowels that are sung to them (Kessen, Levine, & Wendrich, 1979; Révész, 1954; Shuter-Dyson & Gabriel, 1981).

4. Melodic Pitch Patterns.   Since early demonstrations by Melson and McCall (1970) and Kinney and Kagan (1976) that infants notice changes in melodies, a substantial body of research by Trehub (1985, 1987, 1990; Trehub & Trainor, 1990) and her colleagues has explored the importance for infants of a variety of dimensions of melodies. Figure 17.1 illustrates kinds of changes we can make in the pitch pattern of a melody, in this case "Twinkle, Twinkle, Little Star." We can shift the whole melody to a new pitch level, creating a transposition that leaves the pitch pattern in terms of exact intervals from note to note intact (figure 17.1b). We can shift the melody in pitch while preserving its contour (pattern of ups and downs) but changing its exact interval pattern (figures 17.1c and 17.1d), creating a same-contour imitation. The altered pitches of the same-contour imitation in figure 17.1c remain within a diatonic major scale, while those in figure 17.1d depart from it. Finally, we can change the contour (figure 17.1e), producing a completely different melody. Changes of contour are easily noticed by adults, whereas patterns with diatonic changes of intervals (figure 17.1c) are often hard to discriminate from transpositions (figure 17.1b; Dowling, 1978; Dowling & Fujitani, 1971).

Chang and Trehub (1977a) used heart-rate deceleration to indicate when a 5-month-old notices something new. Babies adapted to a continuously repeating six-note melody. Then Chang and Trehub substituted an altered melody to see if the baby would notice. When the stimulus was simply transposed 3 semitones (leaving it in much the same pitch range as before) the babies did not notice, but when the melody was shifted 3 semitones in pitch and its contour was altered, the babies showed a heart-rate deceleration "startle" response. For infants as for adults, the transposition sounds like the same old melody again, whereas the different-contour melody sounds new.

This result was refined in a study of 8- to 10-month-olds by Trehub, Bull, and Thorpe (1984). As in Thorpe and Trehub's (1989) study just described, Trehub et al. used conditioned head turning as an index of the infant's noticing changes in the melody. A background melody was played over and over. When a comparison melody replaced the background melody on a trial, the infants were able to notice all the changes Trehub et al. used: transpositions, same-contour-different-interval imitations, different-contour patterns, and patterns in which individual notes were displaced by an octave in a way that either violated, or did not violate, the contour. In this last transformation, the changes preserved *pitch class* by substituting a note an octave away that changed the contour. Pitch class depends on octave equivalence; all the members of a pitch class lie at octave multiples

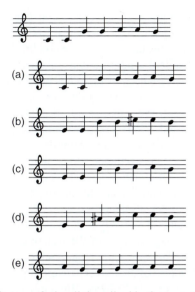

FIGURE 17.1   Examples of types of stimuli described in the text. At the top is the first phrase of the familiar melody, "Twinkle, Twinkle, Little Star," with the intervals between successive notes in semitones of [0, +7, 0, +2, 0, −2]. Following it are (a) an exact repetition of [0, +7, 0, +2, 0, −2]; (b) a transposition to another key [0, +7, 0, +2, 0, −2]; (c) a tonal imitation in the key of the original [0, +7, 0, +1, 0, −1]; (d) an imitation not in any major key [0, +6, 0, +2, 0, −1]; and (e) a melody with a different contour ("Mary Had a Little Lamb") [−2, −2, +2, +2, 0, 0].

from each other. Contour changes were most noticeable. In a second experiment, Trehub et al. used the same task but made it more difficult by interposing three extra tones before the presentation of the comparison melody. In that case, infants did not notice the shift to transpositions and contour-preserving imitations, but they did notice changes in contour. This result was replicated with stimuli having even subtler contour changes by Trehub, Thorpe, and Morrongiello (1985).

The foregoing studies show that infants, like adults, easily notice differences in melodic contour. But, as Trehub, Thorpe, and Morrongiello (1987) point out, the studies do not demonstrate that infants in fact treat contour as a feature of melodies to be remembered. To show that, we would need to show that infants were abstracting a common property, an invariant, from a family of similar melodies that share only contour, and contrasting that property with that of melodies from another family with a different contour. To accomplish this, Trehub et al. (1987) used the conditioned-head-turning paradigm but with a series of background patterns that varied. In one condition, the background melodies varied in key and were all transpositions of one another. In a second condition, the background melodies were all contour-preserving imitations of one another, but not exact transpositions. In fact, infants were able to notice changes among the background melodies, which were changes involving pitches (in the transposition set) and both intervals and pitches (in the imitation set). But they noticed changes of contour even more, supporting the notion that infants, like adults, encode and remember the contours of melodies they hear.

The results reviewed so far suggest considerable qualitative similarity between infants and adults in their memory for melodies. Both are able to notice changes in intervals and pitch levels of melodies under favorable conditions, but both find changes of melodic contour much more salient. The principal differences between infants and adults in the processing of pitch information in melodies arise from the acculturation of the adults in the tonal scale system of a particular culture. Virtually every culture in the world has at least one systematic pattern for the organization of pitch classes that repeats from octave to octave (Dowling & Harwood, 1986). The most common pattern in Western European music is that of the major ("*do, re, mi*") scale. Melodies that conform to that pattern are easier for Western European adults to encode and remember than melodies that do not (Cuddy, Cohen, & Mewhort, 1981; Dowling, 1991). However, as can be inferred from their cross-cultural variation, such scale patterns are not innate. There is no reason a priori for infants to find one pitch pattern easier than another.

This last point will probably strike psychologists as noncontroversial, but there is a very strong tradition among theorists of Western music going back to Pythagoras that attributes the structure of the Western scale system not only to innate cognitive tendencies, but, even further, to the structure of the universe itself in terms of simple whole-number ratios (Bernstein, 1976; Helmholtz, 1877/1954; Hindemith, 1961). The most sensible answer to these questions appears to be that there are certain constraints of human cognition that apply to musical scale structures but that within those constraints a very wide range of cultural variation occurs (Dowling & Harwood, 1986). The main constraints are octave equivalence (involving a 2/1 frequency ratio), a weaker tendency to give importance to the perfect fifth (a 3/2 ratio), coupled with a limit of seven or so pitch classes within the octave, in agreement with George Miller's (1956) argument concerning the number of categories along a perceptual dimension that humans can handle.

In a study bearing on the inherent importance of the perfect fifth, Trehub, Cohen, Thorpe, and Morrongiello (1986) used conditioned head turning to assess the performance of 9- to 11-month-olds in detecting changes of single pitches in a simple diatonic melody (C-E-G-E-C) and in a corresponding non-diatonic melody with an augmented fifth (C-E-G♯-E-C). They found no difference between the two background melodies, suggesting the lack of a strong inherent preference for the size of the fifth. Children between 4 and 6 years of age, however, did show a difference favoring the diatonic melody. Thus acculturation in the tonal scale system is already well begun by that age.

There is some evidence, however, in favor of the primacy of the perfect fifth. Cohen, Thorpe, and Trehub (1987) complicated the task used by Trehub et al. (1986) by transposing the background melody to a new pitch level with each repetition. In that case, the task could not be solved simply by noticing changes of single pitches, but would require the abstraction of the invariant interval pattern of the background melody. Under those conditions, 7- to 11-month-olds found changes easier to detect in the diatonic pattern (C-E-G-E-C) than in the nondiatonic pattern (C-E-G♯-E-C). Seven to 11 months is a rather wide age range in the life of a rapidly changing infant. Lynch and Eilers (1992) differentiated the ends of that range by running 6-month-olds and 12-month-olds in parallel tasks. They found that although the 12-month-olds performed like the 7- to 11-month-olds in the Cohen, Thorpe, and Trehub (1987) study, the 6-month-olds performed equally well with the diatonic and nondiatonic patterns. That is, the younger infants were not yet acculturated to the standard Western diatonic scale as distinct from other arrangements of semitone intervals, whereas the older infants were.

In addition to the diatonic and nondiatonic patterns using Western "tonal material" (Dowling, 1978) consisting of intervals constructed of semitones, Lynch and Eilers (1992) also included a non-Western pattern: a Javanese *pélog* scale pattern that did not contain a perfect fifth and in which some of the pitches approximated quarter steps lying in between the semitones on the piano. The performance of the 6-month-olds, which was better than chance (and equally good) for diatonic and nondiatonic Western patterns, decreased to chance levels for the Javanese pattern (as did the performance of the 12-month-olds). Thus the 6-month-olds were either acculturated at the level of Western tonal material, or there is something about scale structures constructed with a logarithmic modulus such as the semitone (shared by the diatonic and nondiatonic patterns) that makes patterns constructed in them naturally easier to process. I favor the former explanation in terms of acculturation, because if conformity to "natural" pitch intervals were important, the most obvious candidate for a natural interval conducive to "good" pattern construction (in the Gestalt sense) is the perfect fifth (C-G, the 3/2 ratio) contained in the diatonic but not the other two patterns. This possibility is suggested by Trainor (1993), Trehub, Thorpe, and Trainor (1990), and Schellenberg and Trehub (1994) in their discussions of the diatonic/nondiatonic distinction made by the older infants. The perfect fifth is a fundamental building block in the traditional scale systems of India, China, and the American Indians, as well as of Europe (Dowling & Harwood, 1986), and is represented in the harmonic structure of complex tones such as vowel sounds, and also is prevalent in music (as at the start of "Twinkle, Twinkle," Figure 17.1). Thus if the perfect fifth, as a natural interval, were an important determinant of infant responses to scale patterns, the 6-month-olds would have performed better with the diatonic patterns than with the other two patterns. They did not, so it seems unlikely to me that the semitone, rarely explicitly present in the patterns and a far more remote candidate for natural interval, would play such a role.

If the younger infants are acculturated in terms of semitones, it remains nevertheless true that they are not sensitive to subtler aspects of the diatonic scheme. This is seen in their indifference both to the diatonic/nondiatonic distinction and to diatonic key membership of target tones, as shown by Trainor and Trehub (1992). Trainor and Trehub tested 8-month-olds using a strongly diatonic background melody. Comparison melodies had an altered pitch that either remained within the key of the background melody or went outside it. Infants detected the change equally well whether it remained within the key or not. Their performance was unaffected by tonal scale structure. Adults, in contrast, found out-of-key alterations much easier to detect. (In fact, out-of-key alterations sound quite startling to adults unless they are "anchored" to a new key as the result of modulation — Bartlett, 1993; Bartlett & Dowling, 1988; Bharucha, 1984, 1996.) In fact, infants' performance with within-key alterations was superior to that of adults! Adults found the within-key alterations difficult to detect because the tonal framework they had acquired through lifelong perceptual learning made the within-key notes sound like natural continuations of the melody, even though they were the wrong notes. (Trainor & Trehub, 1993, extended these results to show that infants were more sensitive to changes in both patterns when they were transposed to a closely related key vs. a distant key — see the discussion of key-distance effects later.)

In summary, we can say that infants, like adults, find melodic contour a very salient feature of melodies. However, the process of acculturation in pitch-scale patterns is a long, slow process. By 6 months the infant is beginning that process at the level of the tonal material. By 1 year the infant responds differently to diatonic and nondiatonic patterns. But, as described below, listeners require more years of acculturation before they hear pitches automatically in terms of a tonal frame of reference.

5. Rhythm.   As noted in the earlier discussion of perceptual grouping, infants' temporal grouping of tone sequences is much like that of adults. Infants have been shown to discriminate between different rhythmic patterns (Chang & Trehub, 1977b; Demany, McKenzie, & Vurpillot, 1977). However, those tasks could have been solved on the basis of absolute rather than relative temporal relationships. Just as a melody retains its identity across transposition, so that relative and not absolute pitches are important, so a rhythmic pattern retains its identity across changes in tempo, where relative rather than absolute timing of the notes is important (Monahan & Carterette, 1985). And just as infants are sensitive to changes in patterns of relative pitch, they are sensitive to changes in the relative temporal patterns of rhythms. Trehub and Thorpe (1989), again using conditioned head turning, showed that infants 7–9 months old could notice changes in rhythmic patterns (such as XX XX vs. XXX X) even across variations in tempo. Just as for adults, a rhythmic pattern retained its identity when presented faster or slower.

Infants' broader rhythmic organization of musical phrases is like adults' in a surprising way. Krumhansl and Jusczyk (1990) presented 4- and 5-month-olds with Mozart minuets that had pauses inserted between phrases or within phrases. The infants preferred to listen to versions with pauses between phrases, suggesting that the infants were sensitive to cues to adult phrase structure of musical pieces. It remains to be seen exactly what cues the infants were responding to. Jusczyk and Krumhansl (1993) extended those results to show that the infants were really responding to phrase structure (and not just Mozart's beginning and ending patterns in the minuets) and that the pitch contour and note duration are important determinants of the infants' response to structural pauses. Furthermore, infants tended not to notice pauses inserted at phrase boundaries in naturally segmented minuets.

B. Childhood

During their second year, children begin to recognize certain melodies as stable entities in their environment and can identify them even after a considerable delay. My older daughter at 18 months would run to the TV set when she heard the "Sesame Street" theme come on, but not for other tunes. At 20 months, after a week or so of going around the house singing "uh-oh" rather loudly to a descending minor third, she responded with the spoken label "uh-oh" when I played that pattern on the piano.

1. Singing.   Children begin to sing spontaneously somewhere around the age of 9 months or a year. At first this can take the form of vocal play that includes wild excursions over the child's entire pitch range, but it also includes patterns of vowel sounds sung on locally stable pitches. This last is a feature that distinguishes singing from the child's incipient speech at this age.

Especially after 18 months, the child begins to generate recognizable, repeatable songs (Ostwald, 1973). The songs of a child around the age of 2 years often consist of brief phrases repeated over and over. Their contours are replicable, but the pitch wanders. The same melodic and rhythmic contour is repeated at different pitch levels, usually with different intervals between the notes. The rhythm of these phrases is coherent, with rhythms often those of speech patterns. Accents within phrases and the timing of the phrases themselves is determined by a regular beat pattern. This two-level organization of beat and within-phrase rhythm is another feature that distinguishes singing from speech and is characteristic of adult musical organization (Dowling, 1988; Dowling & Harwood, 1986).

An example of a spontaneous song from my daughter at 24 months consisted of an ascending and descending phrase with the words "Come a duck on my house" repeated 10 or 12 times at different pitch levels with small pitch intervals within phrases. This song recurred for 2 weeks and then disappeared. Such spontaneous songs have a systematic form and display two essential features of adult singing: they use discrete pitch levels, and they use the repetition of rhythmic and melodic contours as a formal device. They are unlike adult songs, however, because they lack a stable pitch framework (a scale) and use a very limited set of phrase contours in one song — usually just one or two (Dowling, 1984). A more sophisticated construction by the same child at 32 months can be seen in figure 17.2. The pitch still wanders but is locally stable within phrases. Here three identifiable phrases are built into a coherent song.

The preceding observations are in general agreement with those of Davidson, McKernon, and Gardner (1981; Davidson, 1985; McKernon, 1979) on spontaneous singing by 2-year-olds. Davidson et al. extended naturalistic observation by teaching a simple song to children across the preschool age range. Two- and 3-year-olds generally succeeded in reproducing the contours of isolated phrases. Older children were able to concatenate more phrases *in* closer approximations to the model. It was only very gradually across age that the interval relationships of the major scale began to stabilize. Four-year-olds could stick to a stable scale pattern within a phrase but would often slip to a new key for the next phrase, just as the 3-year-old in figure 17.2. It was not until after age 5 that the children could hold onto a stable tonality throughout the song. Further, with a little practice, 5-year-olds were able to produce easily recognizable versions of the model. My own observations suggest that the typical 5-year-old has a fairly large repertoire of nursery songs of his or her culture. This emerges when children are asked to sing a song and can respond with a great variety of instances. It is also apparent from their better performance on memory tasks using familiar materials (vs. novel melodies; Andrews & Dowling, 1991). Through the preschool years, the use of more or less stable tonalities for songs comes to be established.

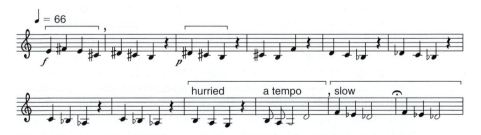

FIGURE 17.2   A child's spontaneous song at 32 months. Each note was vocalized to the syllable "Yeah." Brackets indicate regions of relatively accurate intonation. Elsewhere intonation wandered.

2. Absolute Pitch.   Absolute pitch is the ability to identify pitches by their note names even in the absence of musical context. Absolute pitch is not an essential ability for the understanding of most music, although it can aid in the tracking of key relationships in extended passages of tonal music (as in Mozart and Wagner) and in singing 12-tone music on sight. There are times when it can be a hindrance to music cognition by discouraging some of its possessors from developing sophisticated strategies for identifying pitch relationships in tonal contexts (Miyazaki, 1993). Absolute pitch has typically been quite rare even among musicians, occurring in only about 4–8%. However, in cultures where early music training is encouraged, such as in present-day Japan, the incidence of absolute pitch among the musically trained is much higher, possibly near 50% (Miyazaki, 1988). Ogawa and Miyazaki (1994) suggest on the basis of studies of 4- to 10-year-old children in a keyboard training program that most children have the underlying ability to acquire absolute pitch. In their review of the literature, Takeuchi and Hulse (1993) argue in favor of an "early-learning" hypothesis — that absolute pitch can be acquired by anyone, but only during a critical period ending in the fifth or sixth year.

Although relatively few adults can identify pitches, adults typically are able to approximate the pitch levels of familiar songs, a capacity that Takeuchi and Hulse (1993) call "residual absolute pitch." For example, Halpern (1989) found that adults would typically begin the same song on close to the same pitch after an extended delay. Levitin (1994), using the album cover as a retrieval cue, found that young adults sang popular songs they had heard only in one recorded version at approximately the correct pitch level. (Two thirds of the subjects were within 2 semitones of the correct pitch.)

The studies on pitch encoding cited earlier (Dowling, 1986, 1992) suggest that with a moderate amount of training people develop a "temporary and local" sense of absolute pitch that leads them to encode what they hear (and produce) in terms of the tonal framework provided by the current context.

3. Melodic Contour and Tonality.   In perception and in singing, melodic contour remains an important basis for melodic organization throughout childhood. Morrongiello, Trehub, Thorpe, and Capodilupo (1985) found 4- to 6-year-olds very capable in discriminating melodies on the basis of contour. Pick, Palmer, Hennessy, Unze, Jones, and Richardson (1988) replicated that result and found that 4- to 6-year-olds could also use contour to recognize same-contour imitations of familiar melodies. In another task emphasizing the recognition of similarity among same-contour imitations of familiar tunes, Andrews and Dowling (1991) found 5- and 6-year-olds performed equally well at recognizing familiar versions and both tonal and atonal imitations. It was not until ages 7 and 8 that tonality began to be a factor in that experiment and only by ages 9 or 10 that a difference appeared between familiar versions and same-contour imitations (the adult pattern of performance).

Studies of perception and memory provide converging evidence with that from singing concerning the 5- or 6-year-old's acquisition of a stable scale structure. With highly familiar tunes such as "Happy Birthday" and "Twinkle, Twinkle," even 4-year-olds can notice "funny" sounding versions with out-of-key pitches (Trehub, Morrongiello, & Thorpe, 1985). And Bartlett and Dowling (1980, Experiment 4) found that 5-year-olds can use musical key differences to discriminate between melodies. On each trial of the experiment, a familiar melody was presented, followed by either a transposition or a same-contour imitation. The comparison was either in the same key as the standard or a nearly related key, or it was in a distant key. (Near keys share many overlapping pitches in their scales; distant keys share few.) Adults in this task are highly accurate in saying "Same" to transpositions (>90%) and not saying "Same" to imitations (<10%). The pattern for 5-year-olds was very different: they tend to say "Same" to near-key comparisons (both transpositions and imitations) and "different" to far-key comparisons. Five-year-olds have one component of the adult behavior pattern — the ability to distinguish near from far keys — but not the other component — the ability to detect changes of interval sizes in the tonal imitations. They accept same-contour imitations as versions of the tune. As the child grows older, the pattern of response moves in the adult direction, so that an 8-year-old accepts near-key imitations less often than far-key transpositions. Eight-year-olds can use both key distance and interval changes to reject a same-contour imitation, whereas 5-year-olds rely principally on key distance.

The 5- to 6-year-old's grasp of stable tonal centers fits other results in the literature. For example, in a series of studies Riley and McKee (1963; Riley, McKee, Bell, & Schwartz, 1967; Riley, McKee & Hadley, 1964) found that first graders have an overwhelming tendency to respond by choosing a pitch match rather than an interval match. This tendency to respond to the pitch tasks in terms of a stable frame of reference contrasted with the same children's ability to respond to loudness-comparison tasks in terms of relative (not absolute) loudness.

The emergence of tonal scale relationships among the child's cognitive structures has implications for the conduct of research. Using atonal materials with infants has little impact on the results, because babies do not respond to tonal scale structures as such (Trainor & Trehub, 1992). But Wohlwill's (1971) use of atonal (and to the adult ear rather strange sounding) melodies probably led to his result that first graders could distinguish targets from different-contour lures at a level barely better than chance. At any rate, Wohlwill's conclusion that "the establishment of pitch as a directional dimension is a relatively late phenomenon" could not be true in the light of Thorpe's result with infants (1986, cited in Trehub, 1987). What is true is that first graders have trouble using words to describe pitch direction (Hair, 1977; Zimmerman & Sechrest, 1970).

During later childhood, the child continues to develop sophistication in the use of the tonal scale framework determined by the culture. This progress is illustrated by Zenatti (1969), who studied memory for sequences of three, four, and six notes with subjects from age 5 years up. On each trial, a standard melody was followed by a comparison melody in which one note of the standard had been changed by 1 or 2 semitones. The subject had to say which of the notes had been changed — a very difficult task. Zenatti found that for the three-note sequences, 5-year-olds performed at about chance with both tonal and atonal stimuli. From ages 6 through 10, the results for tonal and atonal sequences diverged, with better performance on tonal sequences. Then, at around age 12, processing of the atonal sequences caught up. For four- and six-note sequences, the same pattern appeared, but the tonal-atonal difference remained until adulthood. Experience with the tonal scale system leads people to improve on recognition of tonal melodies but not atonal melodies. With simple stimuli such as the three-note melodies, atonal performance catches up relatively soon, but longer sequences continue to benefit from the tonal framework throughout childhood.

(This result converges with that of Morrongiello & Roes, 1990.) Superiority of recognition with tonal materials has been often observed with adults (Dowling, 1978; Francès, 1958/1988); Zenatti's study shows that the effect can be used as an index of the child's acquisition of the scale structures of the culture.

Trainor and Trehub (1994) took the development of the role of tonality in the ability to detect melodic pitch changes one step further. In addition to alterations that either remained within key or departed from the key, Trainor and Trehub introduced changes that remained in the key but departed from the particular harmony implied by the melody. For example, the first four notes of "Twinkle, Twinkle" (Figure la: C-C-G-G) imply harmonization with the tonic triad (C-E-G). A change of the third note from G to E would remain within both the key and the implied harmony. A change to F would remain within the key, but violate the harmony. Trainor and Trehub found that 7-year-olds, like adults, could detect the out-of-key and out-of-harmony changes much more easily than the within-harmony changes, whereas 5-year-olds reliably detected only the out-of-key changes. As Trainor and Trehub (1994, p. 131) conclude, "5-year-olds have implicit knowledge of key membership but not of implied harmony, whereas 7-year-olds, like adults, have implicit knowledge of both aspects of musical structure." In a result that converges with these studies, Imberty (1969, chapter 4) found that 7-year-olds could tell when a melody had been switched in midstream from one key to another or from the major mode to the minor.

Krumhansl and Keil (1982) provide a good picture of the child's progress in grasping the tonal framework. They had children judge the goodness of melodic patterns beginning with an outline of the tonic triad (C-E-G) and ending on an arbitrarily chosen pitch. Krumhansl (1990) had found that adults in that task, especially musically experienced adults, produce a profile in which important notes in the tonal hierarchy (such as those of the tonic triad) receive high ratings and less important notes receive progressively lower ratings in accordance with their importance in the key. Krumhansl and Keil found that 6-and 7-year-olds distinguished simply between within-key notes and outside-of-key notes. The structure of the tonal hierarchy became more differentiated with age, so that by the age of 8 or 9 children were distinguishing between the pitches of the tonic triad and the other pitches within the key.

Two similar studies illustrate the importance of seemingly minor methodological details in research on the development of the tonal hierarchy. Cuddy and Badertscher (1987) simplified the task by using patterns with five notes instead of six. In that case, even 6- and 7-year-olds displayed the principal features of the adult hierarchy. And Speer and Meeks (1985) used an unstable context of the first seven notes of a C-major scale, ending on B or D (in contrast to the stable triad context in Krumhansl & Keil, 1982), to find that 8- and 11-year-olds perform very much like adults.

Lamont and Cross (1994) criticize the use of triads and scales as contexts in the foregoing three studies on two grounds. First, they suggest that these prototypical contexts, always the same throughout a condition of the experiment, are not very representative of the varied character of real tonal music. Second, they note that if children are exposed to any music class activities, the children will probably already have encountered scales and arpeggios. As Lamont and Cross (1994, p. 31) say, "Presented with an overlearned pattern,[. . .] the listener [could be expected] to give an overlearned response appropriate to that pattern." To produce more representative contexts, Lamont and Cross borrowed a method from West and Fryer (1990) of using a different random permutation of the notes of the major scale on each trial, and they also used chord progressions establishing the key. The study included five groups of children between 6 and 11 years old. Like Speer and Meeks (1985) and Cuddy and Badertscher (1987), Lamont and Cross found the children relatively sophisticated in their differentiation of the tonal hierarchy, but they also found, in agreement with Krumhansl and Keil (1982), that the children's representations of musical pitch gained in sophistication through the elementary school years. Lamont and Cross supplemented this study with converging evidence from a series of more open-ended tasks, such as arranging chime bars in order according to pitch and arranging them to create a tune.

In summary, the development of melody-processing skills can be seen as a progression from the use of gross, obvious features to the use of more and more subtle features. Babies can distinguish pitch contours and produce single pitches. Around the age of 5, the child can organize songs around stable tonal centers (keys) but does not yet have a stable tonal scale system that can be used to transpose melodies accurately to new keys. The scale system develops during the elementary school years and confers on tonal materials an advantage in memory that remains into adulthood.

4. Rhythm.   There are two aspects of musical rhythm that I wish to discuss in terms of development in childhood. First is the development of the ability to control attention in relation to the temporal sequence of events, using regularities in the rhythm of occurrence of critical features in a piece to aim attention at important elements. Second is the development of the ability to remember and reproduce rhythmic patterns.

Adults in listening to speech and music are able to use their experience with similar patterns to focus their attention on critical moments in the ongoing stream of stimuli to pick up important information (Jones, 1981). This ability requires perceptual learning to develop. Andrews and Dowling (1991) studied the course of this development using a "hidden melodies" task in which the notes of a target melody such as "Twinkle, Twinkle" are temporally interleaved with random distractor notes in the same pitch range, the whole pattern being presented at 6 or 8 notes/sec. After about an hour of practice, adults can discern the hidden melody when they are told which target melody to listen for (Dowling, 1973; Dowling, Lung, & Herrbold, 1987). Andrews and Dowling (1991) included an easier condition in which the interleaved distractor notes were presented in a separate pitch range from the notes of the target. They reasoned that as listeners learned to aim attention in pitch, the listeners would find it easier to discern the targets in a separate pitch range. Five- and 6-year-olds perform barely better than chance on this task and find targets equally difficult to discern whether in a separate range from the distractors or not. It is not until the age of 9 or 10 that the separation of pitch ranges confers an advantage, suggesting that by that age listeners are able to aim their attention at a particular pitch range. Ability to aim attention in time improves steadily from age 6 on, and by age 9, discerning hidden targets with distractors in the same pitch range has reached 70% (with chance at 50%). Musically untrained adults achieve about 80% on this task, while musically experienced adults find the hidden targets equally easy to discern (about 90%) with distractors inside as well as outside the target pitch range.

There is evidence for the importance of a hierarchical organization of rhythm in 5-year-olds' reproductions of rhythmic patterns. Drake (1993) found 5-year-olds able to reproduce rhythms with two levels of organization: a steady beat and varying binary subdivisions of the beat. Although children that age find it easy to tap isochronous (steady, nonvarying) sequences in either binary or ternary rhythm, they find binary sequences with varying patterns within the beat easier than ternary. Drake reports that by the age of 7, children improve in reproducing models that include a variety of different durations in the same sequence, having gained facility with greater rhythmic complexity.

Accents in music can occur on various levels of structure. In particular, accents can be produced in terms of the two levels of beat and rhythmic organization. The beat or meter provides accents at regular time intervals. Rhythmic accents are generally conferred on the first and last members of rhythmic groups. A third level of accents can arise from discontinuities in the melodic contour, such as leaps and reversals of direction. Drake, Dowling, and Palmer (1991) constructed songs in which accents on those levels either coincided or did not. Desynchronization of accent structure lowered children's performance in singing the songs, but there was little change in singing accuracy for children who are between 5 and 11 years old.

These results suggest that by the age of 5 children are responding to more than one level of rhythmic organization and that the songs they learn are processed as integrated wholes in the sense that events at one level affect performance at another; for example, complication of accent structure produces decrements in pitch accuracy in singing. An additional example is provided by Gérard and Auxiette (1988), who obtained rhythm reproductions from 5-year-olds. Gérard and Auxiette either provided the children with a plain rhythmic model to reproduce or provided additional context for the rhythm by providing either words to be chanted to it, or a melody to be sung to it, or both. They found that children with musical training performed best in tapping the rhythm when there was a melody, and children without musical training performed best when there were words. Having words or melody aided in the processing of the rhythm. Gérard and Auxiette (1992) also found that 6-year-old musicians were better able than nonmusicians to synchronize their tapping and their verbalizations in such a task.

The picture that emerges of the development of rhythmic organization is that a multilevel structure appears early and that by the age of 5, the child is quite sophisticated. There is some development in the school-age years, but Drake (1993), for example, found little difference between 7-year-olds and adult non-musicians. Already the spontaneous songs of a 2-year-old show two levels of rhythmic organization, the beat and rhythmic subdivisions (often speech rhythms) overlaid on that, and the 5-year-old follows the same hierarchical organization in tapped reproductions. Finally, rhythmic organization is not easily separable from other aspects of structural organization in a song, so that in perception and production other aspects of melody are intertwined with rhythmic structure.

5. Emotion.   Ample evidence has accumulated that children during the pre-school years learn to identify the emotional states represented in music, and this ability improves during the school years. For example, both Cunningham and Sterling (1988) and Dolgin and Adelson (1990) showed that by the age of 4, children perform well above chance in assigning one of four affective labels (essentially "happy," "sad," "angry," and "afraid") to musical excerpts in agreement with adults' choices. (With the exception of Cunningham and Sterling, all the studies reviewed here had subjects choose schematic faces expressing the emotions in making their responses.) Both of these studies also showed that performance improves over the school years. Performance was less than perfect at the earlier ages, and in particular, Cunningham and Sterling found that 4-year-olds were not consistently above chance with "sad" and "angry," nor 5-year-olds with "afraid," whereas Dolgin and Adelson found 4-year-olds at about chance with "afraid." In a similar study, Terwogt and Van Grinsven (1991) found that 5-year-olds performed very much like adults, but that all ages tended to confuse "afraid" and "angry." These studies were able in a general way to attribute the children's responses to features of the music, but there are other studies that have focused on specific musical features such as the contrast between major and minor.

The issue of whether the major mode in Western music is a cue to happy emotions, and the minor mode a cue to sad ones, has been a perennial issue for both musicologists and psychologists. A particular developmental issue arises here, because we can ask whether responses to the affective connotations of major and minor appear earlier than the specific cognitive recognition of the difference, which, according to the foregoing review, appears around the age of 5. In exploring these issues, Gerardi and Gerken (1995) restricted responses to the choice of two faces, "happy" or "sad," and used adaptations of musical passages that differed in mode (major vs. minor) and predominant melodic contour (up vs. down). They found that 8-year-olds and adults, but not 5-year-olds, applied "happy" and "sad" consistently to excerpts in the major and minor, respectively. Only adults consistently chose "happy" for ascending contours and "sad" for descending, although that variable was probably not manipulated very strongly. (For example, "Che faro" from Gluck's *Orfeo ed Euridice* fails to ascend or descend unambiguously.)

In contrast to Gerardi and Gerken, Kastner and Crowder (1990) allowed subjects a choice of four faces — "happy," "neutral," "sad," and "angry" — and used versions of three different tunes presented in the major and minor, and with or without accompaniment. They found that when relatively positive responses (happy or neutral) were contrasted with negative responses (sad or angry), even 3-year-olds consistently assigned positive faces to major and negative faces to minor. This tendency became stronger between 3 and 12 years of age. Therefore, we can say that there is some indication that preschoolers are able to grasp the emotional connotations of the two modes at an earlier age than they can differentiate their responses in a more cognitively oriented task.

C. Adulthood

Rather than include here a comprehensive review of adults' implicit knowledge of musical structure, I shall concentrate on some issues concerned with tonality and the tonal scale framework. Adults in Western European cultures vary greatly in musical ability. Sometimes these individual differences are reflected in performance on perception and memory tasks. Untrained subjects usually do not find contour recognition more difficult than trained subjects (Dowling, 1978) but do find interval recognition (Bartlett & Dowling, 1980; Cuddy & Cohen, 1976) and the hearing out of partials in a complex tone (Fine & Moore, 1993) more difficult. Even where nonmusicians perform worse overall on tasks involving memory for melodies, they are often just as influenced as musicians by variables such as tonality, performing worse with atonal than with tonal melodies (Dowling, 1991). Also, nonmusicians are just as error prone as musicians when dealing with nonstandard quarter steps that fall in cracks in the musical scale (Dowling, 1992). Such qualitative results show that nonmusicians have acquired at least a basic tonal scale framework from their experience in the culture and that that framework has a psychological reality independent of its use as a pedagogical tool.

During the past few years, evidence has been accumulating that listeners routinely encode the music they hear in absolute, and not relative, terms. For example, when presented with novel melodies and then tested after filled delays of up to 1.5 min, listeners find it easier to discriminate between targets (like figure 17.1b, only novel) and same-contour lures (like figure 17.1c), than between targets and different-contour lures (like figure 17.1e; Dowling, Kwak, & Andrews, 1995). (With familiar melodies such as those shown in figure 17.1, those abilities are about equal after 2 min.) That is, after a delay, listeners find it easier to discriminate very fine differences between the test melody and the melody they heard than to discriminate gross differences (DeWitt & Crowder, 1986; Dowling & Bartlett, 1981). Their memory represents very precisely what they have heard. This evidence converges with the demonstration by Levitin (1994), reviewed earlier, that nonmusicians come very close to the correct absolute pitch when singing familiar popular songs and with the similar demonstration by Levitin and Cook (1996) that their approximations of the tempos of such songs are quite accurate. This makes it seem likely that memory for music typically operates in terms of more precise representations of particular stimuli than has been generally thought (e.g., by Dowling, 1978).

Among adults, striking differences in performance based on different levels of musical experience sometimes appear, illustrating different ways in which knowledge of scale structure can be used. Dowling (1986) demonstrated differences among three levels of sophistication in a study of memory for novel seven-note melodies. Dowling presented the melodies in a context of chords that defined each melody as built around the tonic (the first degree of the scale, *do*) or the dominant (the fifth degree, *sol*). Listeners had to say whether notes had been altered when the melody was presented again. The test melodies were also presented with a chordal context, and that context was either the same as before or different. The test melodies were either exact transpositions or altered same-contour imitations of the original melodies. Musically untrained listeners performed equally well with same or different chord context at test. Listeners with moderate amounts of training in music (around 5 years of lessons when they were young) performed much worse with changed context. That suggests that those listeners were initially encoding the melodies in terms of the tonal scale values provided by the context, so that when the context was shifted, the melody was very difficult to retrieve. In contrast, nonmusicians simply remembered the melody independent of its relation to the context. Professional musicians performed very well with both changed and unchanged contexts. Their sophistication gave them the flexibility to ignore the context where it was not useful.

III. SUMMARY

Adults bring a large store of implicit knowledge to bear in listening to music. This knowledge includes implicit representations of the tonal framework of the culture in terms of which expected events are processed efficiently and in terms of which pitches are interpreted in their musical context. This store of knowledge includes knowledge of the timing patterns of music in the culture, so that the listener is able to focus attention on moments in time at which critical information is likely to occur. Although musical experience leads, as we have seen, to greater sophistication in the store of implicit knowledge, nevertheless non-musicians have typically acquired the fundamentals of this knowledge from their experience listening to music throughout their lives. Thus nonmusicians are sensitive to shifts in tonal-ity and to the multilevel structure of rhythmic organization.

The implicit knowledge of adults is built on elements present even in infancy: the importance of melodic and rhythmic contours, the use of discrete, steady pitch levels, the organization of rhythmic patterns into a steady beat and an overlay of more complicated rhythms, and octave equivalence, to name a few. These elements provide the groundwork for perceptual learning and acculturation throughout life to build upon.

ACKNOWLEDGMENT

I thank Melinda Andrews for her thoughtful contributions to the development of this chapter.

REFERENCES

Andrews, M. W., & Dowling, W. J. (1991). The development of perception of interleaved melodies and control of auditory attention. *Music Perception, 8,* 349–368.

Bartlett, J. C. (1993). Tonal structure of melodies. In T. J. Tighe & W. J. Dowling (Eds.), *Psychology and music: The understanding of melody and rhythm* (pp. 39–61). Hillsdale, NJ: Erlbaum.

Bartlett, J. C., & Dowling, W. J. (1980). The recognition of transposed melodies: A key-distance effect in developmental perspective. *Journal of Experimental Psychology: Human Perception & Performance, 6,* 501–515.

Bartlett, J. C., & Dowling, W. J. (1988). Scale structure and similarity of melodies. *Music Perception, 5,* 285–314.

Bernstein, L. (1976). *The unanswered question.* Cambridge, MA: Harvard University Press.

Bharucha, J. J. (1984). Anchoring effects in music: The resolution of dissonance. *Cognitive Psychology, 16,* 485–518.

Bharucha, J. J. (1996). Melodic anchoring. *Music Perception, 13,* 383–400.

Bregman, A., & Campbell, J. (1971). Primary auditory stream segregation and perception of order in rapid sequences of tones. *Journal of Experimental Psychology, 89,* 244–249.

Brown, R. (1973). *A first language: The early stages.* London: George Allen & Unwin.

Chang, H. W., & Trehub, S. E. (1977a). Auditory processing of relational information by young infants.

Journal of Experimental Child Psychology, 24, 324–331.

Chang, H. W., & Trehub, S. E. (1977b). Infant's perception of temporal grouping in auditory patterns. *Child Development, 48,* 1666–1670.

Clarkson, M. G., & Clifton, R. K. (1985). Infant pitch perception: Evidence for responding to pitch categories and the missing fundamental. *Journal of the Acoustical Society of America, 77,* 1521–1528.

Clarkson, M. G., & Rogers, E. C. (1995). Infants require low-frequency energy to hear the pitch of the missing fundamental. *Journal of the Acoustical Society of America, 98,* 148–154.

Cohen, A. J., Thorpe, L. A., & Trehub, S. E. (1987). Infants' perception of musical relations in short transposed tone sequences. *Canadian Journal of Psychology, 41,* 33–47.

Cuddy, L. L., & Badertscher, B. (1987). Recovery of the tonal hierarchy: Some comparisons across age and levels of musical experience. *Perception & Psychophysics, 41,* 609–620.

Cuddy, L. L., & Cohen, A. J. (1976). Recognition of transposed melodic sequences. *Quarterly of Experimental Psychology, 28,* 255–270.

Cuddy, L. L., Cohen, A. J., & Mewhort, D. J. K. (1981). Perception of structure in short melodic sequences. *Journal of Experimental Psychology: Human Perception & Performance, 7,* 869–883.

Cunningham, J. G., & Sterling, R. S. (1988). Developmental change in the understanding of affective meaning of music. *Motivation & Emotion, 12,* 399–413.

Davidson, L. (1985). Tonal structures in children's early songs. *Music Perception, 2,* 361–374.

Davidson, L., McKernon, P., & Gardner, H. (1981). The acquisition of song: A developmental approach. In *Documentary report of the Ann Arbor Symposium* (pp. 301–315). Reston, VA: Music Educators National Conference.

DeCasper, A. J., & Fifer, W. P. (1980). Of human bonding: Newborns prefer their mothers' voices. *Science, 208,* 1174–1176.

DeCasper, A. J., & Spence, M. J. (1986). Prematernal speech influences newborns' perception of speech sounds. *Infant Behavior & Development, 9,* 133–150.

Demany, L. (1982). Auditory stream segregation in infancy. *Infant Behavior & Development, 5,* 261–276.

Demany, L., & Armand, F. (1984). The perceptual reality of tone chroma in early infancy. *Journal of the Acoustical Society of America, 76,* 57–66.

Demany, L., McKenzie, B., & Vurpillot, E. (1977). Rhythm perception in early infancy. *Nature, 266,* 718–719.

DeWitt, L. A., & Crowder, R. G. (1986). Recognition of novel melodies after brief delays. *Music Perception, 3,* 259–274.

Dolgin, K. G., & Adelson, E. H. (1990). Age changes in the ability to interpret affect in sung and instrumentally-presented melodies. *Psychology of Music, 18,* 87–98.

Dowling, W. J. (1973). The perception of interleaved melodies. *Cognitive Psychology, 5,* 322–337.

Dowling, W. J. (1978). Scale and contour: Two components of a theory of memory for melodies. *Psychological Review, 85,* 341–354.

Dowling, W. J. (1984). Development of musical schemata in children's spontaneous singing. In W. R. Crozier & A. J. Chapman (Eds.), *Cognitive processes in the perception of art* (pp. 145–163). Amsterdam: North-Holland.

Dowling, W. J. (1986). Context effects on melody recognition: Scale-step versus interval representations. *Music Perception, 3,* 281–296.

Dowling, W. J. (1988). Tonal structure and children's early learning of music. In J. Sloboda (Ed.), *Generative processes in music* (pp. 113–128). Oxford: Oxford University Press.

Dowling, W. J. (1991). Tonal strength and melody recognition after long and short delays. *Perception & Psychophysics, 50,* 305–313.

Dowling, W. J. (1992). Perceptual grouping, attention and expectancy in listening to music. In J. Sundberg (Ed.), *Gluing tones: Grouping in music composition, performance and listening* (pp. 77–98).

Stockholm: Publications of the Royal Swedish Academy of Music, no. 72.

Dowling, W. J. (1993a). Procedural and declarative knowledge in music cognition and education. In T. J. Tighe & W. J. Dowling (Eds.), *Psychology and music: The understanding of melody and rhythm* (pp. 5–18). Hillsdale, NJ: Erlbaum.

Dowling, W. J. (1993b). La structuration melodique: Perception et chant. In A. Zenatti (Ed.), *Psychologie de la musique* (pp. 145–176). Paris: Presses Universitaires de France.

Dowling, W. J., & Bartlett, J. C. (1981). The importance of interval information in long-term memory for melodies. *Psychomusicology, 1*(1), 30–49.

Dowling, W. J., & Fujitani, D. S. (1971). Contour, interval, and pitch recognition in memory for melodies. *Journal of the Acoustical Society of America, 49,* 524–531.

Dowling, W. J., & Harwood, D. L. (1986). *Music cognition.* New York: Academic Press.

Dowling, W. J., Kwak, S.-Y., & Andrews, M. W. (1995). The time course of recognition of novel melodies. *Perception & Psychophysics, 57,* 136–149.

Dowling, W. J., Lung, K. M.-T., & Herrbold, S. (1987). Aiming attention in pitch and time in the perception of interleaved melodies. *Perception & Psychophysics, 41,* 642–656.

Drake, C. (1993). Reproduction of musical rhythms by children, adult musicians, and adult non-musicians. *Perception & Psychophysics, 53,* 25–33.

Drake, C., Dowling, W. J., & Palmer, C. (1991). Accent structures in the reproduction of simple tunes by children and adult pianists. *Music Perception, 8,* 315–334.

Elbert, T., Pantev, C., Wienbruch, C., Rockstroh, B., & Taub, E. (1995). Increased cortical representation of the fingers of the left hand in string players. *Science, 270,* 305–307.

Fine, P. A., & Moore, B. J. C. (1993). Frequency analysis and musical ability. *Music Perception, 11,* 39–54.

Francès, R. (1988). *The perception of music* (W. J. Dowling, Trans.). Hillsdale, NJ: Erlbaum. (Original publication 1958).

Gérard, C., & Auxiette, C. (1988). The role of melodic and verbal organization in the reproduction of rhythmic groups by children. *Music Perception, 6,* 173–192.

Gérard, C., & Auxiette, C. (1992). The processing of musical prosody by musical and nonmusical children. *Music Perception, 10,* 93–126.

Gerardi, G. M., & Gerken, L. (1995). The development of affective responses to modality and melodic contour. *Music Perception, 12,* 279–290.

Hair, H. I. (1977). Discrimination of tonal direction on verbal and nonverbal tasks by first-grade children.

Journal of Research on Music Education, 25, 197–210.

Halpern, A. R. (1989). Memory for the absolute pitch of familiar songs. *Memory & Cognition, 17,* 572–581.

Helmholtz, H. von. (1954). *On the sensations of tone.* (A. J. Ellis, Trans.). New York: Dover. (Original work published 1877.)

Hindemith, P. A. (1961). *Composer's world.* New York: Doubleday.

Imberty, M. (1969). *L'acquisition des structures tonales chez l'enfant.* Paris: Klincksieck.

Jones, M. R. (1981). Only time can tell: On the topology of mental space and time. *Critical Inquiry, 7,* 557–576.

Jusczyk, P. W., & Krumhansl, C. L. (1993). Pitch and rhythmic patterns affecting infants' sensitivity to musical phrase structure. *Journal of Experimental Psychology: Human Perception & Performance, 19,* 627–640.

Kastner, M. P., & Crowder, R. G. (1990). Perception of major/minor: IV. Emotional connotations in young children. *Music Perception, 8,* 189–202.

Kessen, W., Levine, J., & Wendrich, K. A. (1979). The imitation of pitch in infants. *Infant Behavior & Development, 2,* 93–99.

Kinney, D. K., & Kagan, J. (1976). Infant attention to auditory discrepancy. *Child Development, 47,* 155–164.

Krumhansl, C. L. (1990). *Cognitive foundations of musical pitch.* New York: Oxford University Press.

Krumhansl, C. L., & Jusczyk, P. W. (1990). Infants' perception of phrase structure in music. *Psychological Science, 1,* 70–73.

Krumhansl, C. L., & Keil, F. C. (1982). Acquisition of the hierarchy of tonal functions in music. *Memory & Cognition, 10,* 243–251.

Lamont, A., & Cross, I. (1994). Children's cognitive representations of musical pitch. *Music Perception, 12,* 27–55.

Levitin, D. J. (1994). Absolute memory for musical pitch: Evidence from the production of learned melodies. *Perception & Psychophysics, 56,* 414–423.

Levitin, D. J., & Cook, P. R. (1996). Memory for musical tempo: Additional evidence that auditory memory is absolute. *Perception & Psychophysics, 58,* 927–935.

Lynch, M. P., & Eilers, R. E. (1992). A study of perceptual development for musical tuning. *Perception & Psychophysics, 52,* 599–608.

McAdams, S., & Bregman, A. (1979). Hearing musical streams. *Computer Music Journal, 3*(4), 26–43, 60.

McKernon, P. E. (1979). The development of first songs in young children. *New Directions for Child Development, 3,* 43–58.

Mehler, J., Bertoncini, J., Barrière, M., & Jassik-Gerschenfeld, D. (1978). Infant recognition of mother's voice. *Perception, 7,* 491–497.

Melson, W. H., & McCall, R. B. (1970). Attentional responses of five-month girls to discrepant auditory stimuli. *Child Development, 41,* 1159–1171.

Miller, G. A. (1956). The magical number seven, plus or minus two: Some limits on our capacity for processing information. *Psychological Review, 63,* 81–97.

Miyazaki, K. (1988). Musical pitch identification by absolute pitch possessors. *Perception & Psychophysics, 44,* 501–512.

Miyazaki, K. (1993). Absolute pitch as an inability: Identification of musical intervals in a tonal context. *Music Perception, 11,* 55–72.

Monahan, C. B., & Carterette, E. C. (1985). Pitch and duration as determinants of musical space. *Music Perception, 3,* 1–32.

Morrongiello, B. A., & Roes, C. L. (1990). Developmental changes in children's perception of musical sequences: Effects of musical training. *Developmental Psychology, 26,* 814–820.

Morrongiello, B. A., Trehub, S. E., Thorpe, L. A., & Capodilupo, S. (1985). Children's perception of melodies: The role of contour, frequency, and rate of presentation. *Journal of Experimental Child Psychology, 40,* 279–292.

Ogawa, Y., & Miyazaki, K. (1994, July). *The process of acquisition of absolute pitch by children in Yamaha music school.* Paper presented at the Third International Conference for Music Perception and Cognition, Liège, Belgium.

Ostwald, P. F. (1973). Musical behavior in early childhood. *Developmental Medicine & Child Neurology, 15,* 367–375.

Pantev, C., Oostenveld, R., Engelien, A., Ross, B., Roberts, L. E., & Hoke, M. (1998). Increased auditory cortical representation in musicians. *Nature, 392,* 811.

Pick, A. D., Palmer, C. F., Hennessy, B. L., Unze, M. G., Jones, R. K., & Richardson, R. M. (1988). Children's perception of certain musical properties: Scale and contour. *Journal of Experimental Child Psychology, 45,* 28–51.

Révész, G. (1954). *Introduction to the psychology of music.* Norman: University of Oklahoma Press.

Riley, D. A., & McKee, J. P. (1963). Pitch and loudness transposition in children and adults. *Child Development, 34,* 471–483.

Riley, D. A., McKee, J. P., Bell, D. D., & Schwartz, C. R. (1967). Auditory discrimination in children: The effect of relative and absolute instructions on retention and transfer. *Journal of Experimental Psychology, 73,* 581–588.

Riley, D. A., McKee, J. P., & Hadley, R. W. (1964). Prediction of auditory discrimination learning and transposition from children's auditory ordering ability. *Journal of Experimental Psychology, 67,* 324–329.

Schellenberg, E. G., & Trehub, S. E. (1994). Frequency ratios and the perception of tone patterns. *Psychonomic Bulletin & Review, 2,* 191–201.

Schouten, J. F., Ritsma, B. J., & Cardozo, B. L. (1962). Pitch of the residue. *Journal of the Acoustical Society of America, 34,* 1418–1424.

Shetler, D. J. (1989). The inquiry into prenatal musical experience: A report of the Eastman Project, 1980–1987. *Pre- and Peri-Natal Psychology, 3,* 171–189.

Shuter-Dyson, R., & Gabriel, C. (1981). *The psychology of musical ability.* London: Methuen.

Speer, J. R., & Meeks, P. U. (1985). School children's perception of pitch in music. *Psychomusicology, 5,* 49–56.

Spence, M. J., & DeCasper, A. J. (1987). Prenatal experience with low-frequency maternal-voice sounds influence neonatal perception of maternal voice samples. *Infant Behavior & Development, 10,* 133–142.

Takeuchi, A. H., & Hulse, S. H. (1993). Absolute pitch. *Psychological Bulletin, 113,* 345–361.

Terwogt, M. M., & Van Grinsven, F. (1991). Musical expression of moodstates. *Psychology of Music, 19,* 99–109.

Thorpe, L. A., & Trehub, S. E. (1989). Duration illusion and auditory grouping in infancy. *Developmental Psychology, 25,* 122–127.

Trainor, L. J. (1993, March). *What makes a melody intrinsically easy to process: Comparing infant and adult listeners.* Paper presented to the Society of Research in Child Development, New Orleans.

Trainor, L. J., & Trehub, S. E. (1992). A comparison of infants' and adults' sensitivity to Western tonal structure. *Journal of Experimental Psychology: Human Perception & Performance, 18,* 394–402.

Trainor, L. J., & Trehub, S. E. (1993). Musical context effects in infants and adults: Key distance. *Journal of Experimental Psychology: Human Perception & Performance, 19,* 615–626.

Trainor, L. J., & Trehub, S. E. (1994). Key membership and implied harmony in Western tonal music: Developmental perspectives. *Perception & Psychophysics, 56,* 125–132.

Trehub, S. E. (1985). Auditory pattern perception in infancy. In S. E. Trehub & B. A. Schneider (Eds.), Auditory development in infancy (pp. 183–195). New York: Plenum.

Trehub, S. E. (1987). Infants' perception of musical patterns. *Perception & Psychophysics, 41,* 635–641.

Trehub, S. E. (1990). Human infants' perception of auditory patterns. *International Journal of Comparative Psychology, 4,* 91–110.

Trehub, S. E., Bull, D., & Thorpe, L. A. (1984). Infants' perception of melodies: The role of melodic contour. *Child Development, 55,* 821–830.

Trehub, S. E., Cohen, A. J., Thorpe, L. A., & Morrongiello, B. A. (1986). Development of the perception of musical relations: Semitone and diatonic structure. *Journal of Experimental Psychology: Human Perception & Performance, 12,* 295–301.

Trehub, S. E., Morrongiello, B. A., & Thorpe, L. A. (1985). Children's perception of familiar melodies: The role of intervals. *Psychomusicology, 5,* 39–48.

Trehub, S. E., & Thorpe, L. A. (1989). Infants' perception of rhythm: Categorization of auditory sequences by temporal structure. *Canadian Journal of Psychology, 43,* 217–229.

Trehub, S. E., Thorpe, L. A., & Morrongiello, B. A. (1985). Infants' perception of melodies: Changes in a single tone. *Infant Behavior & Development, 8,* 213–223.

Trehub, S. E., Thorpe, L. A., & Morrongiello, B. A. (1987). Organizational processes in infants' perception of auditory patterns. *Child Development, 58,* 741–749.

Trehub, S. E., Thorpe, L. A., & Trainor, L. J. (1990). Infants' perception of good and bad melodies. *Psychomusicology, 9,* 5–19.

Trehub, S. E., & Trainor, L. J. (1990). Rules for listening in infancy. In J. Enns (Ed.), *The development of attention: Research and theory* (pp. 87–119). Amsterdam: Elsevier.

Ward, W. D. (1954). Subjective musical pitch. *Journal of the Acoustical Society of America, 26,* 369–380.

West, R. J., & Fryer, R. (1990). Ratings of suitability of probe tones as tonics after random ordering of notes of the diatonic scale. *Music Perception, 7,* 253–258.

Wohlwill, J. F. (1971). Effect of correlated visual and tactual feedback on auditory pattern learning at different age levels. *Journal of Experimental Child Psychology, 11,* 213–228.

Zenatti, A. (1969). Le développement génétique de la perception musicale. *Monographies Françaises de Psychologie, No. 17.*

Zimmerman, M. P., & Sechrest, L. (1970). Brief focused instruction and musical concepts. *Journal of Research on Music Education, 18,* 25–36.

CHAPTER EIGHTEEN

PROSPECTS AND LIMITS OF THE EMPIRICAL STUDY OF EXPERTISE: AN INTRODUCTION

K. ANDERS ERICSSON AND JACQUI SMITH

Research on expertise may be one of the most rapidly expanding areas within cognitive psychology and cognitive science. Typically, when a topic becomes popular in psychology, the research approach and the methodology associated with it are also accepted, and the pressure to demonstrate the utility and feasibility of the approach diminishes. Efforts are directed instead toward the theoretical integration of research findings. Furthermore, popularity of a new approach nearly always means that many investigators will adopt it. An even larger number of investigators, however, will adopt only the terminology and will attempt to modify other research approaches to encompass the new concepts. That, in turn, leads to diffusion of the defining characteristics of the "new" approach, making straightforward attempts to integrate published research findings difficult. Because of this process of diffusion, often the new approach will no longer be readily distinguishable from previous alternative research approaches.

In this chapter we attempt to provide a conceptual framework for distinguishing important characteristics of the *original expertise approach*. Our chapter consists of three sections. The first section attempts to characterize the study of expertise in the most general and domain-independent manner so that we can compare the expertise approach with a number of alternative approaches that had similar objectives. The focus of this section is on briefly reviewing some of the outcomes and failures of the earlier approaches. Our goal is to show that the expertise approach can account for these failures at the expense of greater empirical and theoretical complexity. In the second section we specify the nature of the original

From K. Anders Ericsson, Jacqui Smith, *Toward a General Theory of Expertise,* "Prospects and limits of the empirical study of expertise: an introduction," pp. 1–30.

expertise approach and methodology. Here the pioneering work on chess expertise by de Groot (1978) and Chase and Simon (1973) is used to exemplify the sequence of research steps that characterized the original expertise approach. In the final section we elaborate criteria for these steps and use these criteria to discuss and review the prospects for, and limits of, more recent research on expertise.

18.1   DEFINITION OF OUTSTANDING PERFORMANCE AND EXPERTISE: A COMPARISON

On the most general level, the study of expertise seeks to understand and account for what distinguishes outstanding individuals in a domain from less outstanding individuals in that domain, as well as from people in general. We deliberately use the vague term "outstanding" because by not specifying more detailed criteria we are able to point to a number of distinctly different scientific approaches that have addressed the same problem.

In nearly all human endeavors there always appear to be some people who perform at a higher level than others, people who for some reason stand out from the majority. Depending on the historical period and the particular activity involved, such individuals have been labeled exceptional, superior, gifted, talented, specialist, expert, or even lucky. The label used to characterize them reflects an attribution of the major factor responsible for their outstanding behavior, whether it is intended to or not. Scientific efforts to understand the sources of such outstanding behavior have been guided by similar conceptions and attributions.

We limit our discussion to those cases in which the outstanding behavior can be attributed to relatively stable characteristics of the relevant individuals. We believe that stability of the individual characteristics is a necessary condition for any empirical approach seeking to account for the behavior with reference to characteristics of the individual. This constraint does not distinguish whether the characteristics are inherited or acquired. It does, however, eliminate a large number of achievements due to unique immediate environmental circumstances.

The most obvious achievements to be excluded by the stability constraint are those that involve events of fair games of chance, such as winning a large amount of money in a single lottery. More interestingly, the same criterion rules out achievements that occur only once in a lifetime, such as a single scientific discovery, a major artistic creation, a historically significant decision or prediction, or a single victory in a sport. This, of course, does not mean that we reject the possibility of defining criteria for outstanding performances in the arts, sciences, and sports arenas. It does mean, however, that a single achievement in a unique situation does not allow us to infer that the achievement was solely due to the particular individual's characteristics.

In order to support an attribution to the stable characteristics of a person, ideally one would require a series of outstanding achievements under different circumstances. Furthermore, one would like to have a larger group of other individuals (a "control" group of sorts) who have experienced similar opportunities to make contributions or to achieve. In the case in which many other individuals would be equally likely to achieve in similar situations, there is no need to attribute the achievement to special personal characteristics. Almost by definition the numbers of individuals given opportunities in some life realms to achieve and to stand out from the majority are small (e.g., heads of state, army generals, people with vast economic resources). In such cases, even a stable series of achievements cannot unambiguously be linked to stable personal characteristics, because of the confounding influence of a unique stable situation.

Examination of our simple stable-characteristic constraint indicates that many achievements popularly acknowledged as evidence for expertise must be questioned and carefully scrutinized. Another important consequence of this constraint is more indirect and concerns the validity of social evaluation and perception of outstanding performance or ability. One would expect social evaluation to be greatly influenced by observations of previous performances (not all by the same individual) occurring under unique circumstances. A social judgment, then, might not be the most precise evaluation of an individual's current ability to perform. Ideally, one needs to determine the unique situation of the individual and to observe performances in standardized situations that allow interindividual comparisons (e.g., laboratory tasks or tests). Once it is possible to measure superior performance under standardized conditions, there is no need to rely on social indicators. Attuned to some of the difficulties of definition and assessment, let us now proceed to discuss some scientific approaches that have been directed toward accounting for outstanding or superior performance.

18.2   SCIENTIFIC APPROACHES TO ACCOUNTING FOR OUTSTANDING PERFORMANCE

Several different scientific approaches have been used to investigate outstanding performance. The constructs that have been investigated have primarily reflected popular attributions regarding the source of the outstanding behavior. These conceptualizations, in turn, have directly influenced what empirical evidence has been considered and collected. Table 18.1 summarizes the different types of stable personal characteristics that have been hypothesized to underlie outstanding performance and links those attributions to associated theoretical constructs and research methods. The attributed personal characteristics noted in table 18.1 reflect a basic belief that behavior either is predominantly influenced by inherited qualities or is a function of learning and acquisition. Further, outstanding performance is attributed either to some general characteristic of the individual or to a specific aspect. The associated theoretical constructs and methodologies reflect these dimensions: *inherited* versus *acquired, general* versus *specific.* So, for example, the researcher will focus either on the effects of general traits (e.g., intelligence, personality), specific abilities (e.g., musical ability, spatial ability), and general life and educational experience (e.g., language, study strategies) or on domain-specific training and practice.

One's conception of the likely origins of outstanding performances will greatly influence the group of people selected for study, as well as the type of information sought concerning these individuals. For example, investigators pursuing an account in terms of general inherited capacities would be likely to consider individuals regardless of their domains and would be particularly interested in information allowing assessment of the genetic contribution. A longitudinal study of individuals identified as having exceptionally

TABLE 18.1   Different Approaches to Accounting for Outstanding Performance

ATTRIBUTION	CONSTRUCT	RESEARCH APPROACH
Primarily inherited		
General abilities	Intelligence, personality	Correlation with personality profile, general intelligence
Specific abilities	E.g., music ability, artistic ability, body build	Correlation with measures of specific ability
Primarily acquired		
General learning and experience	General knowledge and cognitive strategies	Investigation of common processing strategies
Domain-specific training and practice	Domain- or task-specific knowledge	Analysis of task performance, i.e., the expertise approach

high intelligence, by Terman and his associates (Oden, 1968; Stanley, George, & Solano, 1977; Terman & Oden, 1947), illustrates this approach. A focus on domain-specific acquired characteristics would lead investigators to constrain themselves to one domain or task and to try to assess what was acquired (e.g., specific memory strategies), as well as the process of acquisition.

On a priori grounds one can argue that the most parsimonious theoretical account of outstanding performance is in terms of general, predominantly inherited characteristics. Indeed, in the history of scientific research on superior performance, that approach was initially preferred. It was primarily because of inability to explain certain empirical observations that accounts based on more specific abilities and acquired characteristics came to be seriously considered. We shall briefly consider some of those failures before turning to a consideration of the expertise approach that exemplifies the belief that specific acquired characteristics underlie outstanding performance.

18.2.1   Accounts in Terms of General and Specific Inherited Characteristics

If one wants to attribute outstanding performance to general inherited characteristics, it is reasonable to rely on readily available criteria to identify instances of outstanding behavior and of individuals who exhibit that behavior, criteria such as social evaluation and recognition by one's peers. In the first major study in that area, Galton (1869) used social recognition to identify eminent individuals in a wide range of fields and then studied their familial and genetic origins. Galton argued that individuals gained eminence in the eyes of others because of a long-term history of achievement. Such achievement, he suggested, was the product of a blend of intellectual (natural) ability and personal motivation. He reported strong evidence for eminence's being limited to a relatively small number of families stemming from common ancestors, and he inferred that eminence was genetically determined.

Contemporary work in Galton's time and subsequent studies were directed at uncovering the loci of individual differences in general ability. The genetic nature of those general capacities led investigators to search for differences in basic characteristics of processes, such as the speed of mental processes as reflected by reaction time. In subsequent studies, however, individual differences in performance of simple tasks showed disappointingly low correlations, both among tasks and between performance and indices of ability, such as grade in school (Guilford, 1967).

More recent effort to uncover general basic cognitive processes that could account for individual differences have been inconclusive (Baron, 1978; Carroll, 1978; Cooper & Regan, 1982; Hunt, 1980). For example, research on individual differences in general memory ability has found low correlations of memory performance across different types of material and methods of testing, leading investigators to reject the idea of a general memory ability (Kelley, 1964). More direct evidence against stable basic memory processes comes from repeated demonstrations that memory performance for specific types of material can be drastically improved even after short periods of practice (Ericsson, 1985; Kliegl, Smith, & Baltes, 1989). Moreover, as Cooper and Regan noted (1982, p. 163), inadequacies in the definition and design of both cognitive tasks and intelligence measures create serious problems for interpreting correlations between measures of basic cognitive processes and ability.

Tests measuring general intelligence have been extremely useful for prediction and diagnosis in a wide range of situations, although there is considerable controversy about what they actually measure (Resnick, 1976; Sternberg, 1982). IQ tests, however, have been remarkably unsuccessful in accounting for individual differences in levels of performance in the arts and sciences and advanced professions, as measured by social indicators (e.g., money earned, status) and judgments (e.g., prizes, awards) (Tyler, 1965).

There were other lines of research that examined subjects with reliably superior performances and compared them with control groups. Much of that research was similarly motivated by the belief that exceptionally high levels of performance would reflect some basic exceptional ability involving attention (power or concentration), memory, general speed of reaction, or command of logic. Some investigators, however, focused on other stable individual characteristics, such as features of personality, motivation, and perceptual style (e.g., Cattell, 1963; Roe, 1953).

In the 1920s, three Russian professors examined the performance of eight grand masters (world-class chess players) on a wide range of laboratory tests for basic cognitive and perceptual abilities (de Groot, 1946/1978). Surprisingly, the grand masters did not differ from control subjects in those basic abilities, but they were clearly superior in memory tests involving chess positions.

In the case of exceptional chess performance, superior spatial ability often is assumed to be essential (Chase & Simon, 1973; Holding, 1985). Doll and Mayr (1987) compared the performances of about thirty of the best chess players in what was then West Germany with those of almost ninety normal subjects of similar ages, using an IQ test with seven subscales. Only three of the subscales showed reliable differences, and somewhat surprisingly the largest difference between the two groups concerned higher scores for numeric calculation for the chess masters. Doll and Mayr (1987) found no evidence that chess players were selectively better on spatial tasks. In accounting for the unexpected superiority of the chess players on two of the subscales, Doll and Mayr (1987) argued that one reason could be that elite chess players had prior experience in coping with time pressure because of their past chess competitions. When the analysis was restricted to the group of elite chess players, none of the subscales of the IQ test was found to have a reliable correlation with chess-playing performance.

Of the research that has focused not on intelligence but on other relatively stable characteristics of individuals, that by Cattell (1963; Cattell & Drevdahl, 1955) is probably the best example. Cattell sought to determine whether the personality profiles for eminent researchers in physics, biology, and psychology could be distinguished from those of teachers and administrators in the same fields and from those of the general population. Compared with all other groups, top researchers were found to exhibit a consistent profile, being more self-sufficient, dominant, emotionally unstable, introverted, and reflective. Such a profile supports Galton's earlier opinion that eminence and outstanding achievement in a field are products not only of ability but also of aspects of personal motivation. Motivation and striving for excellence often are focused on a small number of domains or even a single domain, suggesting that aspects of motivation may well be acquired.

Despite these hints at possible personality patterns, the research approach of accounting for outstanding and superior performance in terms of general inherited characteristics has been largely unsuccessful in identifying strong and replicable relations. The search for links to specific inherited abilities has been similarly inconclusive. Indeed, as the specific characteristics proposed to account for the superior performance become integral to that performance, it becomes difficult to rule out the possibility that such characteristics have not been acquired as a result of many years of extensive training and practice. Investigators have therefore focused their attention on characteristics that appear in children and that reflect basic capacities for which a genetic origin is plausible. We shall briefly consider two examples of such basic capabilities, namely, absolute pitch among musicians and physiological differences among elite athletes.

A recent review of the research on absolute pitch shows that most of the empirical evidence favors an account in terms of acquired skill (Ericsson & Faivre, 1988). The ability to recognize musical pitch is not an all-or-none skill, and many musicians have it to various degrees. They display the best performance on their own instruments, and their performance decreases as artificial tones from a tone generator are presented (Bachem, 1937). The ability to name pitches correctly is closely related to the amount of one's formal musical training (Oakes, 1955). Furthermore, pitch recognition can be dramatically improved with training, and one musician has documented how he acquired absolute pitch through long-term training (Brady, 1970).

Similarly, a recent review shows that many anatomical characteristics of elite athletes, such as larger hearts, more capillaries for muscles, and the proportions of different types of muscle fibers, are acquired during years of practice (Ericsson, 1990). Such findings showing the far-reaching effects of training do not, however, rule out possible genetic constraints. An individual's height and overall physique are determined by genetic factors (Wilson, 1986). Height and physique, for example, impose important constraints in many physical and sports domains, such as basketball, high jumping, gymnastics, ballet, and professional riding. It is also conceivable that genetic factors might influence the rate of improvement due to training. Nevertheless, training and preparation appear to be necessary prerequisites and important determinants of outstanding performance. We turn to a brief discussion of accounts of outstanding and superior performance based on acquired characteristics.

18.2.2 Accounts in Terms of Specific Acquired Characteristics: The Expertise Approach

In this brief review we have seen that the more parsimonious theoretical approaches relying on stable inherited characteristics seem inadequate to account for outstanding and superior performance. It is therefore necessary to consider accounts based on acquired characteristics. Here we need to identify not only what the acquired characteristics are but also the process by which they are acquired.

How long is the acquisition period, and over what time frame do we need to observe and monitor changes in performance? Simon and Chase (1973) were the first to observe that 10 years or more of full-time preparation are required to attain an international level of performance in chess. Studies by Hayes (1981) and Bloom (1985) revealed that a decade of intensive preparation is necessary to become an international performer in sports or in the arts or sciences. In a recent review, Ericsson and Crutcher (1990) found consistent support for the requirement of 10 years of intensive preparation in a wide range of studies of international levels of performance. Furthermore, Ericsson and Crutcher (1990) found for many domains that most international-level performers had been seriously involved in their domains before the age of 6 years. The period of preparation for superior performance appears to cover a major proportion of these individuals' development during adolescence and early adulthood.

A detailed analysis of acquisition processes extending over decades under widely different environmental circumstances is extraordinarily difficult to conduct. Without a theoretical framework to outline the relevant aspects, the number of possible factors that could be critical to attain superior performance is vast. One can, of course, gain some idea of the range of factors by reading biographies and analyses of unusual events or circumstances in the lives of outstanding scientists and artists (Albert, 1983; McCurdy, 1983). It is unlikely, though, that descriptive studies seeking correlations between ultimate performance of individuals and information about their developmental histories will ever be able to yield conclusive results. A much more promising approach is offered by a careful analysis of the attained performance. This is the crux of the expertise approach.

The expertise approach differs from the approaches discussed earlier in some important respects. The other approaches were attempts to measure independently the constructs hypothesized to be the sources and bases of outstanding performance. In contrast, the expertise approach is an attempt to describe the critical performance under standardized conditions, to analyze it, and to identify the components of the performance that make it superior.

Two features distinguish the expertise approach from other approaches: first, the insistence that it is necessary to identify or design a collection of representative tasks to capture the relevant aspects of superior performance in a domain and to elicit superior performance under laboratory conditions; second, the proposal that systematic empirical analysis of the processes leading to the superior performance will allow assessment of critical mediating mechanisms. Moreover, it is possible to analyze the types of learning or adaptation processes by which these mechanisms can be acquired and to study their acquisition in real life or under laboratory conditions.

The expertise approach is more limited in its application than the other approaches reviewed earlier. Whereas the other approaches can use social indicators as criterion variables of outstanding performance, the expertise approach requires the design of a set of standardized tasks wherein the superior performance can be demonstrated and reliability reproduced. With this important limitation in mind, we now turn to a closer examination of the original expertise approach.

18.2.3   The Original Expertise Approach: The Pioneering Work on Chess

There is no consensus on how the expertise approach should be characterized. If one takes the original work on chess expertise by de Groot (1978) and Chase and Simon (1973), however, it is possible to extract three general characteristics. First, the focus is on producing and observing outstanding performance in the laboratory under relatively standardized conditions. Second, there is a theoretical concern to analyze and describe the cognitive processes critical to the production of an outstanding performance on such tasks. Finally, the critical cognitive processes are examined, and explicit learning mechanisms are proposed to account for their acquisition.

If one is interested in reproducing superior performance under standardized conditions, one should give preference to domains in which there are accepted measures of performance. Chess provides such a domain. It is possible to measure an individual's chess-playing ability from the results of matches against different opponents in different tournaments (Elo, 1978). It is easy to select groups of chess players who differ sufficiently in chess ability that the probability of one of the weaker players beating one of the stronger players in a particular game is remote.

A critical issue in the expertise approach is *how to identify standardized tasks* that will allow the real-life outstanding performance to be reproduced in the laboratory. Because of the interactive nature of chess games and the vast number of possible sequences of moves, the same sequences of chess moves are hardly ever observed in two different chess games. Better chess players will consistently win over weaker chess players employing a wide variety of chess-playing styles. One could therefore argue that the better chess players consistently select moves as good as, or better than, the moves selected by weaker players. De Groot (1978) argued that it is possible to develop a collection of well-defined tasks capturing chess expertise by having chess players select the "best next move" for a number of different chess positions. Measurement of performance in this task requires that it be possible to evaluate qualitatively, on a priori grounds, the dependent variable, that is, the next chess move selected for a given chess position. It is not currently possible to evaluate the quality of chess moves for an arbitrary chess position. In fact, one international chess master claims to have spent a great part of his life unsuccessfully seeking to determine the best move for one particular chess position (Saariluoma, 1984).

De Groot (1978) collected think-aloud protocols from chess players of widely differing levels of expertise while they selected their best next moves for several chess positions. After extended analysis of these classic positions, however, he found that only *one* of them differentiated between grand masters and other chess experts who differed greatly in chess ability: All of the very best chess players selected better moves than did any of the comparatively weak players (nonoverlapping). Hence, he inferred that the task of selecting moves for that chess position must elicit cognitive processes that differentiate chess players at different levels of expertise.

Another pioneering aspect of de Groot's study was his use of verbal protocols. He was able to localize differences in cognitive processes between the grand masters and the other class experts by analyzing think-aloud protocols from his best-next-move task. He found that both masters and experts spent about 10 minutes before deciding on a move. In the beginning, the players familiarized themselves with the chess position, evaluated the position for strengths and weaknesses, and identified a range of promising moves. Later they explored in greater depth the consequences of a few of those moves. On average, both masters and experts considered more than thirty move possibilities involving both Black and White and considered three or four distinctly different first moves.

De Groot (1978) first examined the possibility that, compared with chess experts, the grand masters were able to explore longer move combinations and thereby uncover the best move. He found, however, that the maximum depth of the search (i.e., the length of move combinations) was virtually the same for the two groups. When de Groot then focused his analysis on how the players came to consider different moves for the position, he did find differences. Few of the chess experts initially mentioned the best move, whereas most of the grand masters had noticed the best move during the familiarization with the position. More generally, de Groot argued, on the basis of his analysis of the protocols, that the grand masters perceived and recognized the characteristics of a chess position and evaluated possible moves by relying on their extensive experience rather than by uncovering those characteristics by calculation and evaluation of move possibilities. In some cases the discovery of promising chess moves was linked to the verbal report of a localized weakness in the opponent's chess position. Other grand masters discovered the same move without any verbal report of a mediating step (de Groot, 1978, p. 298). The superior chess-playing ability of more experienced chess players, according to de Groot, is attributable to their extensive experience, allowing retrieval of direct associations in memory between characteristics of chess positions and appropriate methods and moves. De Groot (1978, p. 316) argued that mastery in "the field of shoemaking, painting, building, [or] confectionary" is due to a similar accumulation of experiential linkings.

To examine the critical perceptual processing occurring at the initial presentation of a chess position, de Groot (1978) briefly showed subjects a middle-game chess position (2–10 seconds). Shortly after the end of the presentation the chess players gave retrospective reports on their thoughts and perceptions during the brief presentation and also recalled the presented chess position as best they could. From the verbal reports, de Groot found that the position was perceived in large complexes (e.g., a pawn structure, a castled position) and that unusual characteristics of the position (such as an exposed piece or a far-advanced pawn) were noticed. Within this brief time, the chess masters were found to integrate all the characteristics of the position into a single whole, whereas the less experienced players were not able to do so. The chess masters also often perceived the best move within that short exposure time. The analysis of the amount recalled from the various chess positions was consistent with the evidence derived from the verbal reports. Chess masters were able to recall the positions of all the 20–30 chess pieces virtually perfectly, whereas the positions recalled by the less experienced chess experts ranged from 50 to 70 percent.

The classic study of Chase and Simon (1973) followed up on this superior memory performance by chess masters for briefly presented chess positions. They designed a standardized memory task in which subjects were presented with a chess position for 5 seconds with the sole task of the subjects being to recall the locations of as many chess pieces as possible. We shall later review more carefully to what extent this new task can be viewed as capturing the cognitive processes underlying superior chess-playing performance.

With that memory task, Chase and Simon (1973) were able to corroborate de Groot's earlier finding that chess players with higher levels of expertise recalled the correct locations of many more pieces for representative chess positions. They also went a significant step farther and experimentally varied the characteristics of the presented configurations of the chess pieces. For chessboards with randomly placed pieces, the memory performances of the chess masters were no better than those of novice chess players, showing that the superior memory performance of the master depends on the presence of meaningful relations between the chess pieces, the kinds of relations seen in actual chess games.

Chase and Simon (1973) found that a player's ability to reproduce from memory the previously presented chess position proceeded in bursts in which chess pieces were rapidly placed, with pauses of a couple of seconds between bursts. The pieces belonging to a burst were shown to reflect meaningfully related configurations of pieces (i.e., chunks) that corresponded well to the complexes discovered by de Groot (1978). The chess masters were found to differ from other chess players primarily in the number of pieces belonging to a chunk, that is, the size of the chunk. In support of the hypothesis that memory and perception of chess positions rely on the same encoding processes, Chase and Simon (1973) demonstrated that the recall process had a structure similar to that of the process of reproducing perceptually available chess positions. Rather than discuss the large number of additional empirical studies by Chase and Simon (1973), we shall change the focus and consider their theoretical effort to specify the detailed processes underlying superior memory performance and the relation of these processes to general constraints on human information processing.

One of the most severe constraints on an account that is based on acquired knowledge and skill involves explicating what has been acquired and showing that the acquired characteristics are sufficient to account for the superior performance without violating the limitations of the general capacities of human information processing (Newell & Simon, 1972). The superior recall of 15–30 chess pieces by chess masters would at first glance seem to be inconsistent with the limited capacity of short-term memory in humans, which allows storage of around 7 chunks (Miller, 1956). Chase and Simon (1973) found that the number of chunks recalled by chess players at all skill levels was well within the limit of around 7 ± 2. They attributed the difference in memory performance between strong and weak players to the fact that the more expert chess players were able to recognize more complex chunks, that is, chunks with a larger number of chess pieces per chunk.

On the basis of computer simulations of the encoding and recall of middle-game chess positions, Simon and Gilmartin (1973) were able to show that 1,000 chunks were sufficient to reproduce the memory performance of a chess expert. They estimated that simulation of the performance of a chess master would require between 10,000 and 100,000 chunks. Assuming that the superior performance of the expert depends on the recognition of familiar patterns that index previously stored relevant knowledge of successful methods (actions), the time-consuming process of becoming an expert would consist in acquiring those patterns and the associated knowledge. Simon and Chase (1973) estimated that around 3,000 hours are required to become an expert, and around 30,000 hours to become a chess master. They also commented that "the organization of the Master's elaborate repertoire of information takes thousands of hours to build up, and the same is true of any skilled task (e.g., football, music). That is why *practice* is the major independent variable in the acquisition of skill" (p. 279). Whether or not one agrees with the Chase and Simon theory of expertise, it would be unwise to confound the methodology of their research with the theoretical assumptions of their specific theory. Indeed, Chase and Simon (1973) were rather cautious when they proposed their theory, describing it as simply a rough first approximation.

18.3   THE THREE STEPS OF THE ORIGINAL EXPERTISE APPROACH

From our review of the pioneering research on chess expertise we have extracted three steps. The first step involves capturing the essence of superior performance under standardized laboratory conditions by identifying representative tasks. In the following sections we try to distinguish between collections of tasks that capture the superior performance and collections of tasks that measure a related function or ability. In our review of the initial work on chess, we argued that only the task that required that subjects consistently select the "best moves" meets the criterion of capturing the nature of superior performance. Two other tasks, one involving perception and the other measuring memory for briefly presented chess positions, assess related functions but do not directly represent chess-playing skill.

The second step involves a detailed analysis of the superior performance. The pioneering research on chess nicely illustrates the use of refined analyses of sequences of verbal reports and placement of chess pieces to infer the underlying cognitive processes mediating the superior performance, as well as the use of experimental manipulation of stimulus materials.

The third and final step involves efforts to account for the acquisition of the characteristics and cognitive structures and processes that have been found to mediate the superior performances of experts. A persistent failure to identify conditions under which the critical characteristics could be acquired or improved would provide strong evidence that those characteristics are unmodifiable and hence basic and most likely inherited.

Our explication of the original expertise approach imposes clear limits for its successful application. Unless the essence of the superior performance of the expert can be captured in the laboratory (satisfying the criterion for the first step), there will not be a performance to be further analyzed in terms of its mediating processes. Similarly, failure to identify mediating processes that can account for the superior performance during the second step will leave the investigator with only the original differences in overall performance and will make the third step essentially superfluous.

At the same time, our explication of the expertise approach is applicable to any phenomenon involving reliably superior performance that can be captured in the laboratory. We believe that an attempt to encompass phenomena normally labeled as perceptual (e.g., chicken sexing), motoric (e.g., typing), or knowledge-based (e.g., physics) within the same overall approach will allow us to identify common methodological and theoretical issues and to consider a common and more differentiated set of learning mechanisms in accounting for achievement of superior performance in any one of these different domains. Such an approach will have the additional advantage of allowing us to consider the many different perceptual, memory, motoric, and knowledge-based aspects of superior performance in domains like chess (Charness, 1991), physics (Anzai, 1991), medicine (Patel & Groen, 1991), performing arts and sports (Allard & Starkes, 1991), and music (Sloboda, 1991).

18.3.1   Capturing Superior Performance: The First Step

The first step in the expertise approach involves finding or designing a collection of tasks to capture the superior performance in the appropriate domain. If one is able to identify such a collection of tasks, the following important advantages will accrue: First, the performance of the designed tasks will reflect the stable characteristics of the superior real-life performance. More important, the availability of such a collection of tasks will allow us to study the performance of the experts extensively in order to accumulate sufficient information on the mediating processes to make a detailed assessment and analysis. During these extensive observations of performance, we should not expect significant changes due to learning and practice, as we shall be monitoring stable processes that have been adapted and perfected over a long period of time. The period during which performance will be observed will be negligible in comparison.

Finally, these collections of tasks will provide us with an excellent testing ground for studying how rapidly the various identified characteristics can be acquired through practice. In fact, one could argue that with an adequate collection of tasks, the rates of acquisition should be comparable for practice with the collection of tasks and in real life. If, on the other hand, the collection of designed tasks does not elicit the mechanisms that mediate superior real-life performance, or does so only partially, then we are likely to see substantial learning and changes in the processes as a result of further practice. Collections of tasks that lead to rapid rises in levels of performance by experts with further practice are unlikely to yield an adequate representation of superior performance. Even more devastating evidence against the claim that such a collection can capture superior performance comes from situations in which novices have matched or surpassed the performance levels of experts after only a few weeks or months of practice.

For some types of expertise it is easy to identify such a collection of tasks, but in most cases it is the most difficult step. We shall first describe some simple cases and then turn to the difficult issues involved in designing a collection of tasks to characterize real-life expertise. We shall also consider the advantages and problems of designing a collection of memory tasks to study superior memory performance by experts, as opposed to studying directly the superior performance of experts.

Tasks Capturing Real-Life Expertise.   There are few instances of real-life expertise in which superior performance can be demonstrated under relatively standardized conditions. Mental calculators and memory experts provide such instances. They often exhibit their performance under conditions similar to those used in traditional experiments. In both of these cases it is easy to define a large pool of different stimuli (e.g., 10 billion possible multiplications of two 5-digit numbers, or 100 trillion digit sequences of 14 digits). Drawing on this pool of items, the experimenter can observe the performance in a large number of different trials and accumulate information on the cognitive processes underlying the expertise. Similarly, some types of psychomotor performance, such as typing, and some sporting events can easily be imported into the laboratory.

Apart from the preceding cases, the design of standardized tasks to capture real-life expert performance is difficult. The problem is somewhat similar to that of isolating phenomena in the natural and biological sciences. By careful analysis of the expert performance in real life, we try to identify recurrent activities that can be reproduced under controlled conditions. In those domains in which expertise can be measured, it is important to restrict the focus to those activities that are involved in producing the relevant performance or resulting product. One should search for goal-directed activities that result in overt behavior that can be reproduced by presentation of the appropriate stimuli.

A nice illustration of this procedure comes from the previously described research on chess, in which de Groot (1978) designed the task of selecting the best next move for a given middle-game position. It should be possible to collect a large number of such positions with which even top-level chess players would be unfamiliar. In extracting out a single chess position from a chess game, one is faced with a problem that is common in research on expertise, namely, the determination of the correct response, or the reliable evaluation of selected moves. Given that currently there was no method available that could have provided that information objectively, de Groot (1978) spent an extended period carefully analyzing the selected chess position to evaluate the relative merits of different moves. A different method of dealing with this problem was offered in a recent study by Saariluoma (1984), who selected chess positions that had clearly discernible best next moves. Both of these methods are oriented toward finding or designing a small set of tasks, and they cannot easily be extended into specifying a large population of tasks that could be claimed to capture the chess expertise.

In most other complex task domains, such as physics and medical diagnosis, investigators tend to select a small number of tasks without specifying the population from which those tasks were chosen to be a representative sample. One reason for this is that a detailed task analysis of even a single complex problem is difficult and extraordinarily time-consuming. More important, our knowledge of complex domains of expertise is incomplete, and it would not at this time be possible to specify a population of tasks to capture such expertise. Many scientists, however, are working on building expert systems in which the tasks and prerequisite knowledge must be specified, and other researchers are working on describing the formal characteristics of various task environments. (see Charness, 1991).

In many domains, experts produce complex products such as texts on a given topic or performances of a given piece of music. Although judges can reliably assess the superior quality of the product, it is difficult to analyze such products in order to identify the measurable aspects capturing the superior quality of the product. Hence, in their analysis of expertise in writing, Scardamalia and Bereiter (1991) focus on systematic characteristics of the cognitive processes involved in designing and writing a text in an effort to differentiate expert from novice writers.

It is, of course, possible to give up the hope of designing a collection of tasks that could capture the full extent of the superior performance and focus instead on one or more well-defined activities involved in the expertise or measuring knowledge about the task domain. In adopting such an approach, one no longer can be certain that one is examining cognitive structures and processes essential to the superior performance. Occasionally, expected differences between the performance of novices and that of experts in component activities are not found. For example, Lewis (1981) found no reliable differences in performance on algebra problems between expert mathematicians and the top third of a group of college students. The most frequently studied activity related to expert performance is memory for meaningful stimuli from the task domain.

Tasks Focusing on Domain-Specific Memory Performance.   In the context of the difficulties of identifying a collection of tasks that can capture the expertise, it is easy to see the attractiveness of studying memory performance. It is possible to evaluate memory performance for presented information by means of recognition and reproduction of literal details (e.g., correct placement of chess pieces), which does not involve any in-depth analysis of tasks or prior knowledge in the given domain. Large samples of different meaningful stimuli can relatively easily be extracted from a given domain even though no formal description of the corresponding population of stimuli is given. Similarly, it is relatively easy to assemble unrepresentative or even meaningless stimuli by recombining stimulus elements in an arbitrary or random manner.

In a wide range of different domains, experts have been shown to display superior memory performance for representative stimuli from their domains of expertise when adaptations of Chase and Simon's (1973) original procedure have been used: chess (for a review, see Charness, 1991); bridge (Charness, 1979; Engle & Bukstel, 1978); go (Reitman, 1976); music notation (Sloboda, 1976); electronic circuit diagrams (Egan & Schwartz, 1979); computer programming (McKeithen, Reitman, Rueter, & Hirtle, 1981); dance, basketball, and field hockey (Allard & Starkes, 1991). Other studies have shown superior retention of domain-related information as a function of the subject's amount of knowledge of the domain, such as baseball (Chiesi, Spilich, & Voss, 1979; Spilich, Vesonder, Chiesi, & Voss, 1979; Voss, Vesonder, & Spilich, 1980) or soccer (Morris, Gruneberg, Sykes, & Merrick, 1981; Morris, Tweedy, & Gruneberg, 1985). Hence, many studies have found evidence supporting a monotonic relation between recall performance for a domain and expertise in that domain. There are, however, several lines of research that have questioned the generality of that relation. Sloboda (1991) points out the striking similarity in accuracy and structure of recall of presented melodies between musicians and non-musicians, which he attributes to shared extensive experience with music. Allard and Starkes (1991) show that superior recall of briefly presented game situations by elite players, as compared with intramural players, is not always found in sports with speed stress, such as volleyball. Finally, Patel and Groen (1991) demonstrate that levels of medical expertise have nonmonotonic relations to the amounts of information recalled from presented medical cases, which they attribute in part to the ability of experts to efficiently identify the information relevant to the medical diagnosis. These findings show that superior memory performance is not an inevitable consequence of attaining expertise.

It is thus questionable that a collection of tasks to measure the superior memory of experts can be claimed to really capture the expertise in question. With the exception of experts on memory tasks, superior performance by experts in many domains does not include explicit tests of memory performance. Moreover, there is no reason to believe that experts explicitly train with the goal of increasing their memory performance. It is therefore unlikely that their memory performance would have reached a stable maximum. We shall later discuss in more detail the cognitive processes relating memory performance and expertise.

An issue shared by studies of superior memory performance and studies of superior performance in other realms is the problem of determining the stimulus characteristics necessary to evoke performance in the laboratory analogous to real-life expertise.

Finding the Appropriate Stimuli to Evoke Superior Performance.   In capturing expert-level performance, one attempts to create a situation that is maximally simple and yet sufficiently similar to the real-life situation to allow the reproduction of the expertise under laboratory conditions. The mere demonstration that an expert-level performance can be reproduced under controlled laboratory conditions reveals something important about the mechanisms underlying the corresponding expertise. It reduces the number of possible stimulus variables that are critical to performance, and it can also eliminate a number of systematic covariations that would make the real-life performance much easier than it would initially appear. Despite the critical importance of the process of finding appropriate stimuli to evoke superior performance, that process has rarely been documented. Ericsson and Polson (1988a, 1988b) investigated the ability of expert waiters and waitresses to match meal orders to customers. They reproduced under laboratory conditions the superior memory performance related to dinner orders by simulating actual customers with photos of faces. Similarly, Bennett (1983) reproduced the superior memory performance related to drink orders by cocktail waitresses in a simulated situation with dolls representing customers. Hence, highly schematic stimuli are sufficient to elicit the perceptual and representational mechanisms that mediate superior memory performance. Similarly, Chase and Simon (1973) found that the memory performance of two chess experts did not differ for chessboards with real pieces and schematic diagrams of chess positions, whereas a beginner at chess showed poorer recall with schematic diagrams because of lack of familiarity with the diagram notation. When they exposed a chess expert to an unfamiliar type of letter diagram representing the chess positions, his memory performance was only half as good as his performance with a real board. But after only 16 trials, his performance with the unfamiliar diagrams had improved to the level of his performance with the real board. Charness (1991) provides a review of the current research using different visual representations of chess positions.

There is some evidence that there are limits to the extent to which stimuli can be abstracted. Gilhooly, Wood, Kinnear, and Green (1988) demonstrated that the lack of superior memory performance by expert map users, as compared with the novices studied by Thorndyke and Stasz (1980), could be attributed to their use of schematic maps (mainly used by tourists) as stimuli. By studying recall of both schematic maps and more advanced contour maps by expert and novice map users, Gilhooly et al. (1988) found, as expected, superior memory of contour maps by the experts, but no differences between experts and novices for the commonly available schematic maps. The fact that superior performances can be reproduced in the laboratory with schematic stimuli is important not only for practical purposes but also for theoretical analyses of the mediating mechanisms.

The issues of how to design representative laboratory tasks are discussed in many chapters in this volume. For example, Patel and Groen (1991) consider the differences between medical diagnoses based on written texts presenting medical cases and diagnoses based on interviews with real patients. Dörner and Schölkopf (chapter 9, this volume) report on the management of simulations of very complex systems.

Summary.   The essential first step of the study of expert performance involves identifying a collection of standardized tasks that can capture the superior performance under controlled conditions. It is a necessary condition for further analysis that superior performance by experts be reliably shown for the designed tasks. In complex domains it is often especially difficult to identify a population of tasks to capture the expertise; it may be possible to identify instead a small number of representative tasks to elicit superior performance. Nonetheless, it may be useful to think of expertise in terms of a corresponding population of tasks. Various experts may, however, require different populations of tasks. [. . .] Similar specialization is to be expected in most complex domains. To capture specialized expertise adequately, it is necessary to design special populations of tasks appropriate for a small group of experts or even individual experts (case studies). Superior memory performance by an expert is a legitimate subject for study as long as we keep in mind that the processes underlying the superior memory performance may only partially overlap with those that generally underlie the superior performance of experts.

The fact that it is possible to reproduce expert performance in a laboratory task has important theoretical implications. It reduces the significance of large numbers of factors that influence complex real-life situations. Furthermore, it indicates a fair degree of generalizability, especially concerning the detailed stimulus representation. Let us now turn to further analysis of the processes that mediate superior performance.

18.3.2   Analysis of Expert Performance: The Second Step

After identifying collection of tasks that can capture the superior performance of experts, one can apply the full range of methods of analysis in cognitive psychology to examine the phenomena associated with a particular type of expertise. In the following sections we present a brief outline of the wide range of observations that can be made to infer information about the processes mediating superior performance. We then discuss different research paradigms, such as comparisons of performance by experts and novices in a small number of tasks, and extended analysis of individual experts. Finally, we report on analyses of particular types of superior performance, such as superior memory performance.

Performance Analysis: Methods of Inferring Mediating Processes.   It is clear that one cannot directly observe mediating cognitive processes, but what can be observed concurrently with cognitive processes can be related to the underlying cognitive processes within the information-processing theory of cognition. Figure 18.1 shows a number of different types of observations that can be collected on any cognitive process. At the top of figure 18.1, cognitive processing is represented schematically as a series of internal processing steps, as proposed by the information-processing theory of human cognition. These internal processing steps cannot, of course, be observed directly, but it is possible to specify hypotheses about the relations between the internal processing steps and

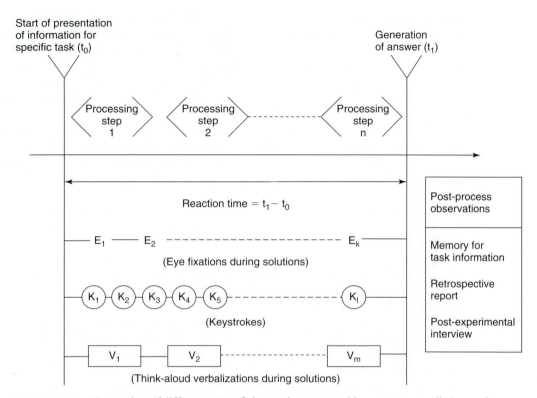

FIGURE 18.1   An overview of different types of observations on cognitive processes mediating performance on a task, adapted from a figure in Ericsson and Oliver (1988).

observable behavior. For example, when a subject fixes his or her gaze on a specific item in a visually presented table of information, we can infer that the corresponding internal steps involve processing that information. On the basis of veridical recall of the presented information after the task has been completed and the presented information is no longer available to the subject, one can infer that that information was processed during the completion of the task. In research on transcription typing, it is possible to determine what part of the text the typist is looking at and what part of the text is simultaneously being typed. The general finding is that the higher the skill level of the typist, the farther ahead in the text the typist looks during typing. Being able to look ahead in the text appears to be critical to the superior typing speeds of expert typists, because when their freedom to look ahead is experimentally restricted, their typing speeds are reduced to levels approaching those for novice typists [. . .].

It is possible to extend our analysis beyond the processing of presented information and consider one's access of preexisting knowledge and procedures. In that case, a *task analysis* of the particular task should be performed before the data collection. A task analysis involves specifying a number of different sequences of processing steps that could generate the correct answer for a specific task given the subjects' preexisting knowledge. In well-defined task domains, such as mental multiplication or problem solving in logic, it is relatively easy to specify nearly exhaustively the different sequences of processing steps leading to a correct answer in an efficient manner. In more complex domains, the a priori task analysis makes explicit the pool of hypothesized processing sequences that is being considered. On the basis of the think-aloud verbalizations of subjects, one can determine only that the verbalized information was accessed. A task analysis is critical for relating the verbalized information to the underlying cognitive processes leading to its access or generation (Ericsson & Simon, 1984).

Analysis of think-aloud verbalizations is time-consuming, and therefore researchers in expertise using these types of data tend to collect data on many subjects for a small number of tasks (expert-novice comparisons) or to collect data on individual subjects for a large number of tasks (case studies).

Expert—Novice Comparisons.   Comparison of think-aloud verbalizations by experts and novices is the best-known method of assessing differences in the mediating processes as functions of the subjects' levels of expertise: Subjects at different levels of expertise are asked to think aloud while carrying out a small number of representative tasks. The number of tasks usually is not sufficient for assessing stable characteristics of individual subjects; the focus is on comparing the groups of subjects to identify salient differences in regard to mediating knowledge and processes.

The types of differences found in a wide range of domains of expertise are remarkably consistent with those originally noted by de Groot (1978) in the domain of chess. Expert performers tend to retrieve a solution method (e.g., next moves for a chess position) as part of the immediate comprehension of the task, whereas less experienced subjects have to construct a representation of the task deliberately and generate a step-by-step solution, as shown by research on physics problems (Anzai, 1991; Chi, Glaser, & Rees, 1982; Larkin, McDermott, Simon, & Simon, 1980; Simon & Simon, 1978) and algebra-word problems (Hinsley, Hayes, & Simon, 1977). Medical experts generate their diagnoses by studying the symptoms (forward reasoning), whereas less experienced medical students tend to check the correctness of a diagnosis by inspecting relevant symptoms (backward reasoning) (Patel & Groen, 1991).

On the same theme, expert performers have a body of knowledge that not only is more extensive than that for nonexperts but also is more accessible (Feltovich, Johnson, Moller, & Swanson, 1984; Johnson et al., 1981; Voss, Greene, Post, & Penner, 1983). Whenever knowledge is relevant, experts appear to access it efficiently (Jeffries, Turner, Polson, & Atwood, 1981). The experts are therefore able to notice inconsistencies rapidly, and thus inconsistent hypotheses are rejected rapidly in favor of the correct diagnosis (Feltovich et al., 1984; Johnson et al., 1981). On presentation, information in the problem is integrated with the relevant domain knowledge (Patel & Groen, 1986, 1991).

Similar characteristics of expert performance are found across different domains of expertise. The studies cited earlier suggest several important characteristics that can be more effectively studied in relation to tasks particularly designed to elicit them in a more controlled manner. We shall consider such research shortly.

Extensive Case Studies of Single Subjects.   In contrast to the group studies discussed earlier, in which small numbers of tasks were used to elicit the cognitive processes of experts, we shall briefly consider two examples of research efforts that have used detailed case studies in order to describe the cognitive processes underlying superior performance.

The first example draws on several case studies of calendar calculations. Calendar calculation is the rather astounding ability to name the day of the week on which a given date falls. For example, when asked on what day of the week August 5, 1934, fell, such a subject would be able to say, correctly, that it was a Sunday. A major interest in this curious ability derives from the fact that several individuals with this skill have been severely mentally retarded, and little is known about how the ability emerged or was acquired. Analysis of this performance is further complicated by the low intelligence of the subjects. On the basis of a task analysis, where no knowledge about calculation can be assumed for these mentally retarded subjects, one is led to assume that the subjects must have memorized the information for all dates.

Investigators have examined a fairly large number of individuals for whom the ability of calendar calculation has been substantiated (for reviews, see Ericsson & Faivre, 1988, and Howe & Smith, 1988). Most calendar calculators can demonstrate that ability for only a limited range of years. All such subjects examined have been unable to explain how they know the correct answers. Some investigators, however, have been able to assess mediating steps by analyzing these subjects' mumblings prior to reporting an answer. Other investigators have been able to obtain informative retrospective reports on mediating steps. The most reasonable conclusion seems to be that the detailed structures of these subjects' processes differ from subject to subject and rely on a combination of memory for specific dates and some limited specialized calculation (Howe & Smith, 1988). The rare calendar calculators whose abilities extend from A.D. 0 to A.D. 999,999 appear to use a version of known algorithms that can be mastered by a graduate student within a couple of weeks to reach a comparable level of performance (Addis & Parson, described in Ericsson & Faivre, 1988).

A second example of single-subject research to analyze expert performance draws on the many case studies of memory experts. Studies of expert memory performances are particularly suited for the laboratory and can capitalize on the long tradition of experimental research on memory. The same research tradition has primarily used stimuli that have been selected to be meaningless, or at least has minimized the role of knowledge in order to capture basic memory processes. It has, however, been difficult to account for vastly superior memory performance within this tradition, and occasionally investigators have suggested that such exceptional individuals are endowed with structurally different memory systems (Luria, 1968; Wechsler, 1952). Analysis of expert memory performance is difficult even in the information-processing tradition, because it is virtually impossible to conduct an a priori task analysis specifying the mediating processing steps and the relevant knowledge used to store information efficiently in memory.

One of the methods available is to use think-aloud and retrospective verbal reports to identify the knowledge used by an individual memory expert and experimentally evaluate hypotheses about the mediating role of that knowledge. For each individual expert it is possible to hypothesize which stimuli could and could not be successfully encoded using the uncovered mediating knowledge. By comparing memory performances for compatible and incompatible stimuli, it is possible to validate hypotheses about the mediating knowledge using the general method developed by Chase and Simon (1979). In a study of a long-distance runner who acquired an exceptional digit span through extended training, Chase and Ericsson (1981) found that the runner encoded sequences of three digits (513) as familiar running times (5 minutes and 13 seconds in a mile race) whenever possible. When the runner was presented with experimentally prepared sequences of triplets of digits that could not be encoded as running times (483 would be 4 minutes and 83 seconds), his digit-span performance was dramatically reduced, and for prepared sequences of triplets all of which could be encoded as running times, his performance was reliably improved over his performance with random digit sequences. Similarly, Sloboda (1991) shows that superior memory performance for classical music by idiots savants is mediated by knowledge of that type of music and cannot be generalized to modern atonal music.

Case studies of memory experts have revealed that the knowledge used to encode the presented information varies greatly from expert to expert. Similarly, the details of the acquired cognitive structures (retrieval structures) to store information in retrieval form in long-term memory also differ. Chase and Ericsson (1982; Ericsson, 1985), however, found three principles of skilled memory that described the general characteristics of essentially all memory experts who have been systematically studied.

Studies of Particular Aspects of Expert Performance.   Up to this point we have discussed studies of expert performance using tasks selected to capture the essence of that performance. It was pointed out that in many cases particular cognitive activities associated with expertise could be identified that could be more effectively examined in tasks designed to focus on those particular cognitive activities. For example, in their study of experts in physics, Chi et al. (1981) focused on the initial encoding of physics problems to account for these experts' immediate availability of plans for complete solutions to those problems. They asked experts and novices to sort a large number of physics problems into categories of similar problems. Consistent with the hypothesis that experts' encodings would incorporate information about solution methods, the experts' categories of problems reflected the physical principles underlying the solutions, whereas the novices' categories were based on the situations and objects mentioned in the problem text. In this case, the knowledge uncovered stands in close correspondence to the knowledge evoked during the solution of the physics problems. Several other investigators have used similar sorting methods to assess the immediate encodings of mathematical problems (Berger & Wilde, 1987, 1981), as well as encodings of pictures of situations in team sports (Allard & Starkes, 1991). It is, of course, possible to examine the knowledge of experts more generally. In their study of representation of expert knowledge, Olson and Biolsi (1991) discuss a wide range of methods. Attempts to measure knowledge about chess directly with psychometric tests have been quite successful, and scores on these tests show a clear correlation with rated chess performance (Charness, 1991).

During a study of the selection of the best move for an unfamiliar chess position, de Groot (1978) also found that the critical differences in cognitive processes relating to chess expertise occurred within the initial perception of the chess position. After a brief exposure to an unfamiliar chess position, the chess masters could give very informative verbal reports about the perceived characteristics of the presented chess position, along with virtually perfect recall of the locations of all chess pieces. In subsequent research, superior memory performance and superior perceptual performance of experts have been studied in specially designed tasks.

As reported earlier, Chase and Simon (1973) accounted for the superior memory performance of chess masters in terms of their storage of chess positions in short-term memory using complex independent chunks of chess pieces. The assumptions of storage in short-term memory and of independence of chunks have been seriously questioned by more recent investigators. Carefully designed studies of superior memory performance for chess positions, as reviewed by Charness (chapter 2, 1991), showed that chess experts store information about chess positions in long-term memory, not solely in short-term memory as Chase and Simon (1973) originally proposed.

Subsequent researchers have questioned Chase and Simon's (1973) assumption that chunks of chess pieces were distinct and that a given chess piece could therefore belong to only a single chunk. Chi (1978) showed that occasionally a chess piece can belong to more than one chunk, a finding that suggests relations between the chunks from a given chess position. On the basis of retrospective verbal reports of grand masters and masters after brief exposures to chess positions, de Groot (1978) found clear evidence of perception of chess pieces in chunks, or complexes, as well as of encodings relating chunks to one another to form a global encoding of the position. It appears necessary to assume that global and integrating encodings account for the ability of chess experts to recall accurately more than one briefly presented chess position at a single trial (Frey & Adesman, 1976).

In analyses of superior memory performance in domains other than chess, evidence of global integration of the presented information has also been found (Egan & Schwartz, 1979; Reitman, 1976). Studies in other domains, however, have also revealed differences from the findings regarding chess experts. In domains with complex stimuli, such as medicine (Patel & Groen, 1991) and computer programming (Adelson, 1984), it is clear that part of the integration of the presented information involves identification of the relevant and critical information, and any analysis of subsequent recall must distinguish between relevant and irrelevant information. For different domains of expertise, the processes of encoding presented information will be quite different, depending on the demands of the particular type of expertise (Allard & Starkes, 1991). Expert dancers display superior memory for presented dance sequences, whereas skilled volleyball players can detect the location of the volleyball with superior speed. Superior perceptual processing has also been demonstrated as a function of chess expertise for tasks involving simple perceptual judgments about critical aspects of presented chess positions (Charness, 1991).

General Comments on the Analysis of Expert Performance. Once the expert performance can be elicited by a collection of tasks in the laboratory, the full range of methods in cognitive science can be applied to assess the mediating cognitive structures and processes. The mediating mechanism for an expert performance should be stable and not much influenced by the additional experience in the laboratory, as the laboratory experience will constitute only a minor fraction of the experts' total experience of tasks in their domains. In fact, an absence of further improvement during extended laboratory testing should provide a nice index for evaluating our ability to capture the mechanisms underlying the real-life expertise.

On the basis of this argument, one immediately realizes some potential dangers of studying aspects of "real" expert performance with tasks not encountered in the normal environments of the experts. If we provide an expert with unfamiliar tasks, we need to consider the possibility that the expert may resort to nonoptimal and unstable strategies that can be rapidly improved even during just a couple of sessions. With respect to memory for briefly presented chess positions, Ericsson and Oliver (Ericsson & Staszewski, 1989) found substantial improvement in the memory performance of a candidate chess master during a few months of testing. They found no evidence of changes in the mediating processes, however, only a marked speedup of the processes.

We have been unable to find much evidence concerning the effects of extended testing of experts. Ericsson (1985) reported several instances of marked improvements in the performance of memory experts when they were observed on several test occasions. In several cases the tests were separated by several years, and one cannot distinguish between the effects of testing and the improvement due to accumulated experience outside the laboratory. Ericsson and Polson (1988b) found continual improvements in their expert waiter's performance of their standard task during about two years of weekly testing. It is likely that part of the observed speedup resulted from the particular constraints of the dinner orders studied. A more important determinant of the speedup, however, was the fact that the real-life task of memorizing dinner orders was not constrained by speed, because the customers required more time to decide on their dinner selections than the waiter needed to memorize them. Only in the laboratory situation with preselected dinner orders did the time required for memorization become critical.

In sum, differences between real-life situations and analogous laboratory tasks with respect to demands for maximum speed and the presented perceptual information are likely to lead to practice effects, even for experts, during extended testing. But as long as the practice effects for the experts remain comparatively small and the performance of the experts remains reliably superior to those for novices even after extended practice, we would claim that such a collection of tasks can successfully capture the superior expert performance.

The effects of extended practice for novices will provide a major source of empirical evidence as we now turn to a review of theoretical accounts of how the superior performance of experts can be acquired through extensive training.

18.3.3   Accounting for Superior Performance by Experts: The Third Step

In all the studies discussed earlier, the assessed mechanisms mediating superior performance implicated cognitive structures that were specific to the relevant task domains. The nature of the mediating cognitions allows us to infer that they reflect acquired knowledge and previous experiences in the domain. In order to account for those aspects of superior performance that are acquired, it is critical to understand the role of knowledge acquisition and the important effects of practice and training for their acquisition.

When we restrict ourselves to those task domains in which superior performance has been adequately captured, the empirical findings can be summarized relatively easily. The superior performance consists of faster response times for the tasks in the domain, such as the superior speed of expert typists, pianists, and Morse code operators. In addition, chess experts exhibit superior ability to plan ahead while selecting a move (Charness, 1981). In a wide range of task domains, experts have been found to exhibit superior memory performance.

What is acquired by experts? Superior performance in different domains reflects processes and knowledge specific to the particular domain. The challenge is to account for the widest range of empirical phenomena with the smallest of learning mechanisms and processes responsible for changes as a function of long-term practice. Because it is not possible to observe subjects during a decade of intensive practice, most of the empirical evidence is based on extrapolation of changes in performance found as a result of practice at laboratory tasks over much shorter terms. Another important constraint is that the proposed descriptions cannot posit performance capacities that would violate the known limits of human information processing.

In this section we shall consider various accounts concerning the processes and knowledge that experts have acquired. We shall first briefly describe the Chase and Simon theory of expertise. Then we shall briefly review some of the empirical evidence concerning speedup of performance, superior memory performance, and superior ability to plan, with the intent of pointing to issues requiring further attention and elaboration.

The Chase and Simon Theory.   Chase and Simon (1973) argued that the main differences among masters, experts, and novices in a wide range of domains were related to their immediate access to relevant knowledge. Chase and Simon's (1973) elegant theoretical account of chess expertise provided an account of how the masters rapidly retrieved the best move possibilities from long-term memory. The recognized configurations of chess pieces (chunks) served as cues to elicit the best move possibilities, which had been stored in memory at an earlier time. The chess masters' richer vocabulary of chunks thus played a critical role in the storage and retrieval of superior chess moves.

Within the same theoretical framework, the speedup in selecting moves can be accounted for in terms of recognition of chess configurations and direct retrieval of knowledge about appropriate move selections. Similarly, Chase and Simon (1973) proposed that the superior memory performance for the briefly presented chess positions was due to recognition of familiar configurations of chess pieces by the masters. The near-perfect recall by the chess masters, involving more than twenty chess pieces, was assumed to be mediated by approximately seven chunks or configurations — within the postulated limits of short-term memory.

Finally, with respect to planning, Chase and Simon (1973) outlined a mechanism whereby the experts' chess knowledge could be accessed in response to internally planned moves in the mind's eye. Given that no evidence was available to show that the depth of planning increased with a rise in the level of expertise (Charness, 1981), they did not consider the acquisition of such a mechanism.

Accounts Focusing on Practice and Learning.   Across a wide range of tasks, an improvement in performance is a direct function of the amount of practice, and this relation can be remarkably accurately described by a power function (Newell & Rosenbloom, 1981). This consistent relation between performance and practice has been given a theoretical account by Newell and Rosenbloom (1981) using a uniform mechanism of learning chunks, which they explicitly relate to Chase and Simon's (1973) analysis of chess expertise.

It is possible to describe skill acquisition in a broader range of tasks and domains in which the subject at the outset does not have the prerequisite knowledge to produce error-free performance. In systematizing a large body of data on the acquisition of skills, Fitts (1964) proposed three different acquisition stages: The "cognitive stage" is characterized by an effort to understand the task and its demands and to learn to what information one must attend. The "associative stage" involves making the cognitive processes efficient to allow rapid retrieval and perception of required information. During the "autonomous stage," performance is automatic, and conscious cognition is minimal. More recently, Anderson (1982) provided a theoretical model with three different learning mechanisms, each corresponding to a stage of the Fitts model. Anderson was able to derive a power law for relating performance to the amount of practice.

It is clear that the learning mechanisms that mediate increasing improvements from repeated practice trials must play important roles in the acquisition of expertise. It may even be useful to consider such mechanisms with an eye to identifying some limits to their applicability.

First, it is important to distinguish between practice and mere exposure or experience. It is well known that learning requires feedback in order to be effective. Hence, in environments with poor or even delayed feedback, learning may be slow or even nonexistent. Making predictions and forecasts for complex environments that are dynamically changing can present difficult information-extraction problems, which may, at least in part, account for the poor performance of expert consultants and decision-makers (Camerer & Johnson, 1991). In addition, merely performing a task does not ensure that subsequent performance will be improved. From everyday experience, anyone can cite countless examples of individuals whose performance never appears to improve in spite of more than 10 years of daily activity at a task. These observations deserve to be considered in more detail, but we shall limit ourselves to one issue relevant to research on expertise: On the basis of the foregoing considerations, one should be particularly careful about accepting one's number of years of experience as an accurate measure of one's level of expertise.

Second, the learning mechanisms discussed can account only for making the initial cognitive processes more efficient and ultimately automatic. In real-life perceptual motor skills, there exist a wide range of motor movements that can allow realization of a given goal. There is good evidence from sports that the beginner's spontaneously adopted baseline strokes in tennis or basic strokes in swimming are nonoptimal and that it is impossible to improve their efficiency by iterative refinement. Hence, the first thing a coach will do when beginners start training is to have them relearn their basic strokes to achieve correct form. Only then can the basic motor patterns be perfected through further training. It is thus possible that the final performance levels may reflect differences in the initial representations used by different subjects.

Third, once we are willing to consider the effects that result from weeks, months, and years of daily practice, it is likely that we cannot limit the consideration to purely cognitive effects on the central nervous system. Research on sports performance shows that extensive and intensive training is associated with a full range of changes related to the blood supply and the efficiency of muscles (Ericsson, 1990). Such changes will influence the speed of performance. It is possible that the correlations concerning speed of movements, as measured by maximum rate of tapping and speed of typewriting (Keele & Hawkins, 1982; Salthouse, 1984), should be considered not only as reflections of inherited characteristics but also as adaptations of the motor system during years of practice.

Finally, and most important, these types of learning mechanisms focus only on how performance can be made faster and more efficient; they do not take into account the acquisition of new cognitive structures, processes that are prerequisites for the unique ability of experts to plan and reason about problem situations.

Accounts Focusing on Memory Functioning.   The Chase-Simon hypothesis that the superior memory of the expert reflects storage of more complex independent chunks in short-term memory has been seriously questioned, and most of the empirical evidence also suggests storage of interrelated information in long-term memory, as mentioned earlier. Even without the constraints of independence of chunks and storage in a limited-capacity short-term memory, human information-processing theory suggests a number of limits and processing constraints that must be taken into consideration in any acceptable account. But let us first review some of the empirical characteristics of the superior memory of experts.

Over a broad range of domains, experts have superior memory restricted to information in their domains of expertise. Furthermore, de Groot (1978) and Chase and Simon (1973) found that chess skill among a small number of subjects was monotonically related to their memory performance, which would suggest a high correlation between skill level and memory performance. Subsequent studies with representative samples involving large numbers of subjects found reliable correlations, but the strength of the association was lower than would have been expected from the Chase-Simon theory (Charness, 1991; Holding, 1985).

Although experts with decades of experience nearly always exhibit memory performance superior to that of subjects lacking expertise, there is at least one intriguing counterexample: Even though experts in mental calculation show far better memory performance for numbers than do normal subjects, their performance is far inferior to that of subjects who have practiced memorizing digits over extended periods (Chase & Ericsson, 1982; Ericsson, 1985). Whereas the mental-calculation experts rely predominantly on their vast mathematical knowledge of numbers, the trained subjects draw on a variety of knowledge essentially unrelated to mathematics. The most important difference between mental calculators and memory experts is that mental calculators require years and decades of practice to achieve memory performance comparable to what can be achieved by normal subjects after 50–100 hours of practice in a memory task. Hence, it is possible that the superior memory performance of experts has only a weak association with their expert knowledge.

Similarly, superior memory for briefly presented chess positions can be trained. Ericsson and Harris (1989) found that after 50 hours of practice, a subject without chess-playing experience was able to recall chess positions at a level of accuracy approaching that of some chess masters. In similarity to the digit-span experts, a close examination of the mediating processes revealed that the subject's performance was mediated by perceptually salient configurations of chess pieces, without implications for playing chess. Hence, it appears that by means of practice directed toward improving memory of performance, subjects without expertise can, after a couple of months of daily practice, match or surpass the superior memory performance of experts.

To account for the results concerning memory experts and long-term training studies, Chase and Ericsson (1981, 1982; Ericsson, 1985, 1988; Ericsson & Staszewski, 1989) proposed a skilled-memory theory to account for how memory performance can be improved within the known limits of human information processing. Chase and Ericsson proposed that experts can develop skilled memory to rapidly store and retrieve information using long-term memory for information in their domains of expertise. Building on the distinction between a limited short-term memory and a vast long-term memory, this theory sees the key problem to be selective access to information stored in long-term memory. Skilled-memory theory postulates that at the time of encoding, experts acquire a set of retrieval cues that are associated in a meaningful way with the information to be stored. At a later time, the desired information can be retrieved from long-term memory by using the appropriate retrieval cue. After extensive practice using a stable set of retrieval cues with meaningful information in the domain, one's speed of encoding and retrieval is assumed to approach that for short-term memory. The best empirical evidence regarding the structure and operation of skilled memory comes from studies of subjects who achieved exceptional levels of performance on the digit-span task (Chase & Ericsson, 1981, 1982; Staszewski, 1987). The retrieval cues used for rapid storage of meaningful encodings of three- and four-digit groups (up to a total of more than a hundred digits) can be used to access digits in presented matrices in a manner earlier believed to require a raw visual image (Ericsson & Chase, 1982). Studies of other types of expertise have given clear evidence for retrieval cues indexing content (e.g., specific intermediate products in mental calculation) (Ericsson & Staszewski, 1989; Staszewski, 1988).

The most direct evidence suggesting the use of retrieval structures in chess comes from a series of studies with a candidate chess master by Ericsson and Oliver (Ericsson & Staszewski, 1989). They found that the chess master could read the description of the sequence of chess moves in a game and mentally generate the sequence of intermediate chess positions almost as fast as he could play out similar chess games by actually moving the pieces on a chessboard. During the process of mentally playing out the chess games, sometimes they would interrupt him and test his ability to name the piece on a given square for the current chess position, which he could do within a few seconds. In other experiments, his speed of access to different types of information for a briefly presented middle-game chess position was examined. The chess master could name the piece located on a given square within a second, and within seconds he could report the number of his opponent's pieces that were attacking a given square, which suggests remarkable availability of many different types of information about the presented chess position. Ericsson and Oliver (Ericsson & Staszewski, 1989) found evidence for rapid and flexible retrieval using a retrieval structure. This research raises the possibility that acquisition of expert-level chess skill involves the development of skilled memory for chess positions.

Once it is accepted that mediating mechanisms are acquired, that raises a number of challenging issues. One can no longer assume that superior performance is automatically achieved merely as a function of practice. The history of expert memory performance provides a number of cases in which individuals who have had extensive practice and experience have settled for suboptimal methods. Crutcher and Ericsson (Ericsson & Polson, 1988b) found that several waiters and waitresses who on a daily basis memorized dinner orders relied on less effective encoding methods than did the expert waiter JC, who exhibited vastly superior performance. Chase and Eriesson (1981, 1982) documented extended problem-solving efforts by digit-span experts to identify strategies and encoding methods to increase their digit-span performance, as well as similar efforts by other subjects, whose performance never improved or did not improve beyond a certain level. When that evidence is considered together with studies of other memory experts (Ericsson, 1985, 1988) past and present, it appears that all memory experts rely on the same limited set of mechanisms (Chase & Ericsson, 1982). Given that most memory experts have not been instructed but have themselves discovered the structures necessary for their memory skills over extended periods, the importance of problem solving for their ultimate performance can hardly be overestimated. Similarly, studies of the development of a number of perceptual motor skills suggest the importance of discovered methods and strategies for performing tasks such as juggling (Norman, 1976). There appears to exist a wealth of phenomena such that successful performance in the future cannot be predicted on the basis of current performance. Similarly, there is no reason to believe that such problem solving is limited to the early stages in the development of expert performance.

Accounts Focusing on the Ability to Plan and Reason.   Analyses in several different domains of expertise have revealed that experts engage in a number of complex mental activities involving reasoning that relies on mental models and internal representations. The most frequently studied activity has been the planning of chess moves. Charness (1981) found that the depth to which a possible move sequence for a chess position was explored was closely related to the level of chess skill, at least for chess players at or below the level of chess experts. Mental planning and evaluation of possible move sequences place greater demands on memory as the depth increases, and such a cognitive activity will be particularly tractable using acquired skilled memory to represent chess positions.

As noted earlier, de Groot (1978) found no reliable differences in regard to depth of search among advanced chess players with differing levels of chess ability. Holding (1985) suggested that the differences were too small to be detected, because of the small number of subjects. Charness (1989), however, presented a case study suggesting that the depth of search may increase with chess skill only up to some level of chess skill and then level off. One should also keep in mind that the task of searching for a move for a middle-game chess position is not designed to measure the capacity to make deep searches and hence may well reflect pragmatic criteria for sufficient depth of exploration to evaluate a prospective move.

In support of the findings of remarkable capacities to explore chess positions mentally, it is well known that chess players at the master level can play while blindfolded with only a minor reduction in chess capability without any prior specialized practice (Holding, 1985). In the absence of a strict time constraint, there appears to be no clear limit to the depth to which a chess master can explore a position. Ericsson and Oliver (Ericsson & Staszewski, 1989) found that a candidate chess master was able to access all the information about a mentally generated chess position rapidly and accurately, and they showed that the memory representation of the chess position was consistent with the characteristics of skilled-memory theory (Chase & Ericsson, 1982; Ericsson & Staszewski, 1989).

The need to represent and integrate large amounts of presented information internally is common to a wide range of different types of expertise. Charness (1989) showed that expertise at the game of bridge was closely linked with the capacity to generate success-ful plans for playing the cards in the optimum order. In medical diagnosis, the medical expert has to integrate many different pieces of information that are not simultaneously available perceptually. The internal representation of the presented medical information must be sufficiently precise to allow extensive reasoning and evaluation of consistency, but also must be sufficiently flexible to allow reinterpretation as new information becomes available (Lesgold et al., 1985; Patel & Groen, 1991). Anzai (1991) reviews the critical role of effective representations in solving physics problems and how methods of generat-ing such representations can be developed through practice. In order to account for exper-tise, it is essential to describe emerging skills for managing extended memory demands, as well as their efficient processing and manipulation.

Comments on the Problem of Accounting for Expert Performance. Chase and Simon (1973) may have been correct in their claim that access to aggregated past experience is the single most important factor accounting for the development of expertise. More recent research, however, shows that to describe the structure of expertise accurately, several other factors must be considered, ranging from acquired skill allowing for an extended working memory to increased physiological efficiency of the motor system due to adaptation to intensive practice. We believe that the research on superior expert performance is benefited more by the development of a taxonomy of different types of mechanisms acquired through different types of learning and adaptation processes than by restricting the definition of expertise to a specific type of acquisition through learning.

SUMMARY

In this chapter we initially contrasted the study of expertise with a number of other approaches studying outstanding and superior performance, and we found that one distinguishing feature was the claim that the superior performance was predominantly acquired. Drawing on the pioneering work on chess, we identified three important steps in the study of expertise: first, identification of a collection of representative tasks by means of which the superior performance of experts can be reproduced; second, analysis of the cognitive processes mediating that performance, followed by design of experimental tasks to elicit the critical aspects of such performance in a purer form; third, theoretical and empirical accounts of how the identified mechanisms can be acquired through training and practice.

The most effective approach to organizing the results across different domains of expertise is to propose a small number of learning mechanisms that can account for the development of similar performance characteristics in different domains within the limits of human information capabilities. There is now overwhelming empirical support for the theory of acquisition of skill with mechanisms skin to those originally proposed by Chase and Simon (1973). They proposed their account as "simply a rough first approximation" (p. 252), and it would therefore make sense to seek a fuller account, both looking for the conditions limiting those principles and supplying other principles that can account for the complete range of performance capacities. Next we looked at some of those additional mechanisms. It would seem that one of the strengths of a generalized study of superior performances lies in a careful consideration of learning mechanisms and associated acquired characteristics uncovered across different domains.

We believe that both the excellent prospects and the clear-cut limitations of the expertise approach lie in its exacting methodological criteria, particularly the criterion that superior performance should be demonstrated as well as captured by a collection of laboratory tasks. To the extent that we are studying mechanisms and phenomena that have emerged as a result of intensive preparation during years or decades, we can be certain that tens or hundreds of hours of laboratory testing are not likely to alter their structure seriously. This affords excellent opportunities to examine and to describe carefully the mechanisms mediating the observed superior performance. In this regard, the superior expert performance is a phenomenon that is particularly well suited for laboratory study and experimental analysis.

A major limitation of the approach is the fact that many types of expertise have not yet been adequately captured. In some cases, the lack of success in capturing the essence of an expertise is so well documented that there may not be a legitimate phenomenon to study. Perhaps the most important limitation concerns the difficulty of studying the development of superior performance in real-life expertise. To understand the many factors underlying why some individuals attain the highest levels of performance whereas others do not, we need to broaden our approach. Indeed, in many cases we may well be forced to rely on correlational methods. As our ability to describe the structures of different types of expert performance improves, we shall be able to focus on the essential aspects, which can be monitored in longitudinal studies.

On the most general level, the study of expert performance provides us with a range of capacities and associated characteristics that can be acquired. A careful systematization of those should allow us to map out the potential for human performance that can be acquired through experience.

ACKNOWLEDGMENTS

The thoughtful suggestions and comments on earlier drafts of this chapter by Ralf Krampe, Natalie Sachs-Ericsson, Herbert Simon, and Clemens Tesch-Römer are gratefully acknowledged.

REFERENCES

Adelson, B. (1984). When novices surpass experts: The difficulty of the task may increase with expertise. *Journal of Experimental Psychology: Learning, Memory, and Cognition, 10,* 483–495.

Albert, R. S. (1983). Family positions and the attainment of eminence. In R. S. Albert (Ed.), *Genius and eminence* (pp. 141–154). Oxford: Pergamon Press. (Original work published 1980.)

Allard, F., & Burnett, N. (1985). Skill in sport. *Canadian Journal of Psychology, 39,* 294–312.

Allard, F., & Starkes, J. L. (1991). Motor-skill experts in sports, dance, and other domains. In K. A. Ericsson & J. Smith (Eds.), *Toward a General Theory of Expertise* (pp. 126–152). New York: Cambridge University Press.

Anderson, J. R. (1982). Acquisition of cognitive skill. *Psychological Review, 89,* 369–406.

Anzai, Y. (1991). Learning and use of representations for physics expertise. In K. A. Ericsson & J. Smith (Eds.), *Toward a General Theory of Expertise* (pp. 64–92). New York: Cambridge University Press.

Bachem, A. (1937). Various types of absolute pitch. *Journal of the Acoustical Society of America, 9,* 146–151.

Baron, J. (1978). Intelligence and general strategies. In G. Underwood (Ed.), *Strategies in information processing* (pp. 403–450). London: Academic Press.

Bennett, H. L. (1983). Remembering drink orders: The memory skill of cocktail waitresses. *Human Learning, 2,* 157–169.

Berger, D. E., & Wilde, J. M. (1987). A task analysis of algebra word problems. In D. E. Berger, K. Pezdek, & W. P. Banks (Eds.), *Application of cognitive psychology: Problem solving, education and computing* (pp. 123–137). Hillsdale, NJ: Erlbaum.

Bloom, B. S. (Ed.). (1985). *Developing talent in young people.* New York: Ballantine Books.

Brady, P. T. (1970). The genesis of absolute pitch. *Journal of the Acoustical Society of America, 48,* 883–887.

Camerer, C. F., & Johnson, E. J. (1991). In K. A. Ericsson & J. Smith (Eds.), *Toward a General Theory of Expertise* (pp. 195–217). New York: Cambridge University Press.

Carroll, J. B. (1978). How shall we study individual differences in cognitive abilities? Methodological and theoretical perspectives. *Intelligence, 2,* 87–115.

Cattell, R. B. (1963). The personality and motivation of the researcher from measurements of contemporaries and from bibliography. In C. W. Taylor & F. Barron (Eds.), *Scientific creativity: Its recognition and development* (pp. 119–131). New York: Wiley.

Cattell, R. B., & Drevdahl, J. E. (1955). A comparison of the personality profile (16 PF) of eminent researchers with that of eminent teachers and administrators, and of the general population. *British Journal of Psychology, 46,* 248–261.

Charness, N. (1976). Memory for chess positions: Resistance to interference. *Journal of Experimental Psychology: Human Learning and Memory, 2,* 641–653.

Charness, N. (1979). Components of skill in bridge. *Canadian Journal of Psychology, 33,* 1–6.

Charness, N. (1981). Search in chess: Age and skill differences. *Journal of Experimental Psychology: Human Perception and Performance, 7,* 467–476.

Charness, N. (1989). Expertise in chess and bridge. In D. Klahr & K. Kotovsky (Eds.), *Complex information processing: The impact of Herbert A. Simon* (pp. 183–208). Hillsdale, NJ: Erlbaum.

Charness, N. (1991). Expertise in chess: the balance between knowledge and search. In K. A. Ericsson & J. Smith (Eds.), *Toward a General Theory of Expertise* (pp. 39–63). New York: Cambridge University Press.

Chase, W. G., & Ericsson, K. A. (1981). Skilled memory. In J. R. Anderson (Ed.), *Cognitive skills and their acquisition* (pp. 141–189). Hillsdale, NJ: Erlbaum.

Chase, W. G., & Ericsson, K. A. (1982). Skill and working memory. In G. H. Bower (Ed.), *The psychology of learning and motivation* (Vol. 16, pp. 1–58). New York: Academic Press.

Chase, W. G., & Simon, H. A. (1973). The mind's eye in chess. In W. G. Chase (Ed.), *Visual information processing* (pp. 215–281). New York: Academic Press.

Chi, M. T. H. (1978). Knowledge structures and memory development. In R. S. Siegler (Ed.), *Children's thinking: What develops?* (pp. 73–96). Hillsdale, NJ: Erlbaum.

Chi, M. T. H., Feltovich, P. J., & Glaser, R. (1981). Categorization and representation of physics problems by experts and novices. *Cognitive Science, 5,* 121–152.

Chi, M. T. H., Glaser, R., & Rees, E. (1982). Expertise in problem solving. In R. S. Sternberg (Ed.), *Advances in the psychology of human intelligence* (Vol. 1, pp. 1–75). Hillsdale, NJ: Erlbaum.

Chiesi, H. L., Spilich, G. J., & Voss, J. F. (1979). Acquisition of domain-related information in relation to high and low domain knowledge. *Journal of Verbal Learning and Verbal Behavior, 18,* 257–273.

Cooper, L. A., & Regan, D. T. (1982). Attention, perception and intelligence. In R. J. Sternberg (Ed.), *Handbook of human intelligence* (pp. 123–169). Cambridge: Cambridge University Press.

de Groot, A. (1978). *Thought and choice in chess.* The Hague: Mouton. (Original work published 1946.)

Doll, J., & Mayr, U. (1987). Intelligenz und Schachleistung — eine Untersuchung an Schachexperten. [Intelligence and achievement in chess — A study of chess masters]. *Psychologische Beiträge, 29,* 270–289.

Dörner, D., & Schölkopf, J. (1991). Controlling complex systems; or, Expertise as "grandmother's know-how." In K. A. Ericsson & J. Smith (Eds.), *Toward a General Theory of Expertise* (pp. 218–239). New York: Cambridge University Press.

Egan, D. E., & Schwartz, B. J. (1979). Chunking in recall of symbolic drawings. *Memory and Cognition, 7,* 149–158.

Elo, A. E. (1978). *The rating of chessplayers, past and present.* London: Batsford.

Engle, R. W., & Bukstel, L. H. (1978). Memory processes among bridge players of differing expertise. *American Journal of Psychology, 91,* 673–689.

Ericsson, K. A. (1985). Memory skill. *Canadian Journal of Psychology, 39,* 188–231.

Ericsson, K. A. (1988). Analysis of memory performance in terms of memory skill. In R. J. Sternberg (Ed.), *Advances in the psychology of human intelligence* (Vol. 5, pp. 137–179). Hillsdale, NJ: Erlbaum.

Ericsson, K. A. (1990). Peak performance and age: An examination of peak performance in sports. In P. B. Baltes & M. M. Baltes (Eds.), *Successful aging: Perspectives from the behavioral sciences* (pp. 164–195). Cambridge: Cambridge University Press.

Ericsson, K. A., & Chase, W. G. (1982). Exceptional memory. *American Scientist, 70,* 607–615.

Ericsson, K. A., Chase, W. G., & Faloon, S. (1980). Acquisition of a memory skill. *Science, 208,* 1181–1182.

Ericsson, K. A., & Crutcher, R. J. (1990). The nature of exceptional performance. In P. B. Baltes, D. L. Featherman, & R. M. Lerner (Eds.), *Life-span development and behavior* (Vol. 10, pp. 187–217). Hillsdale, NJ: Erlbaum.

Ericsson, K. A., & Faivre, I. (1988). What's exceptional about exceptional abilities? In L. K. Obler & D. Fein (Eds.), *The exceptional brain: Neuropsychology of talent and special abilities* (pp. 436–473). New York: Guilford.

Ericsson, K. A., & Harris, M. (1989). *Acquiring expert memory performance without expert knowledge: A case study in the domain of chess.* Unpublished manuscript.

Ericsson, K. A., & Oliver, W. (1988). Methodology for laboratory research on thinking: Task selection, collection of observation and data analysis. In R. J. Sternberg & E. E. Smith (Eds.), *The psychology of human thought* (pp. 392–428). New York: Cambridge University Press.

Ericsson, K. A., & Polson, P. G. (1988a). An experimental analysis of a memory skill for dinner-orders. *Journal of Experimental Psychology: Learning, Memory, and Cognition, 14,* 305–316.

Ericsson, K. A., & Polson, P. G. (1988b). Memory for restaurant orders. In M. Chi, R. Glaser, & M. Farr (Eds.), *The nature of expertise* (pp. 23–70). Hillsdale, NJ: Erlbaum.

Ericsson, K. A., & Simon, H. A. (1984). *Protocol analysis: Verbal reports as data.* Cambridge, MA: Bradford Books/MIT Press.

Ericsson, K. A., & Staszewski, J. (1989). Skilled memory and expertise: Mechanisms of exceptional performance. In D. Klahr & K. Kotovsky (Eds.), *Complex information processing: The impact of Herbert A. Simon* (pp. 235–267). Hillsdale, NJ: Erlbaum.

Feltovich, P. J., Johnson, P. E., Moller, J. H., & Swanson, D. B. (1984). LCS: The role and development of medical knowledge in diagnostic expertise. In W. J. Clancey & E. H. Shortliffe (Eds.), *Readings in medical artificial intelligence* (pp. 275–319). Reading, MA: Addison-Wesley.

Fitts, P. M. (1964). Perceptual-motor skill learning. In A. W. Melton (Ed.), *Categories of human learning* (pp. 243–285). New York: Academic Press.

Frey, P. W., & Adesman, P. (1976). Recall memory for visually presented chess positions. *Memory and Cognition, 4,* 541–547.

Galton, F. (1869). *Hereditary genius.* New York: Macmillan.

Gilhooly, K. J., Wood, M., Kinnear, P. R., & Green, C. (1988). Skill in map reading and memory for maps. *Quarterly Journal of Experimental Psychology, 40A,* 87–107.

Guilford, J. P. (1967). *The nature of human intelligence.* New York: McGraw-Hill.

Hayes, J. R. (1981). *The complete problem solver.* Philadelphia: Franklin Institute Press.

Hinsley, D. A., Hayes, J. R., & Simon, H. A. (1977). From words to equations: Meaning and representation in algebra word problem. In M. A. Just & P. A. Carpenter (Eds.), *Cognitive processes in comprehension* (pp. 89–108). Hillsdale, NJ: Erlbaum.

Holding, D. H. (1985). *The psychology of chess skill.* Hillsdale, NJ: Erlbaum.

Howe, M. J. A., & Smith, J. (1988). Calendar calculating in "idiot savants": How do they do it? *British Journal of Psychology, 79,* 371–386.

Hunt, E. (1980). Intelligence as an information processing concept. *Journal of British Psychology, 71,* 449–474.

Jeffries, R., Turner, A. A., Polson, P. G., & Atwood, M. E. (1981). The processes involved in designing software.

In J. R. Anderson (Ed.), *Cognitive skills and their acquisition* (pp. 255–283). Hills-dale, NJ: Erlbaum.

Johnson, P. E., Duran, A. A., Hassebrock, F., Moller, J., Prietula, M., Feltovich, P. J., & Swanson, D. B. (1981). Expertise and error in diagnostic reasoning. *Cognitive Science, 5,* 235–283.

Keele, S. W., & Hawkins, H. L. (1982). Explorations of individual differences relevant to high level skill. *Journal of Motor Behavior, 14,* 3–23.

Kelley, H. P. (1964). Memory abilities: A factor analysis. *Psychometric Society Monographs, 11,* 1–53.

Kliegl, R., Smith, J., & Baltes, P. B. (1989). Testing-the-limits and the study of adult age differences in cognitive plasticity of a mnemonic skill. *Developmental Psychology, 25,* 247–256.

Larkin, J., McDermott, J., Simon, D. P., & Simon, H. A. (1980). Expert and novice performance in solving physics problems. *Science, 208,* 1335–1342.

Lesgold, A., Rubinson, H., Feltovich, P., Glaser, R., Klopfer, D., & Wang, Y. (1985). *Expertise in a complex skill: Diagnosing X-ray pictures.* LRDC, University of Pittsburgh Technical Report.

Lewis, C. (1981). Skill in algebra. In J. R. Anderson (Ed.), *Cognitive skills and their acquisition* (pp. 85–110). Hillsdale, NJ: Erlbaum.

Luria, A. R. (1968). *The mind of a mnemonist.* New York: Avon.

McCurdy, H. G. (1983). The childhood pattern of genius. In R. S. Albert (Ed.), *Genius and eminence* (pp. 155–169). Oxford: Pergamon Press. (Original work published 1957.)

McKeithen, K. B., Reitman, J. S., Rueter, H. H., & Hirtle, S. C. (1981). Knowledge organization and skill differences in computer programmers. *Cognitive Psychology, 13,* 307–325.

Miller, G. A. (1956). The magical number seven, plus or minus two. *Psychological Review, 63,* 81–97.

Morris, P. E., Gruneberg, M. M., Sykes, R. N., & Merrick, A. (1981). Football knowledge and the acquisition of new results. *British Journal of Psychology, 72,* 479–483.

Morris, P. E., Tweedy, M., & Gruneberg, M. M. (1985). Interest, knowledge and the memorization of soccer scores. *British Journal of Psychology, 76,* 415–425.

Newell, A., & Rosenbloom, P. S. (1981). Mechanisms of skill acquisition and the law of practice. In J. R. Anderson (Ed.), *Cognitive skills and their acquisition* (pp. 1–55). Hillsdale, NJ: Erlbaum.

Newell, A., & Simon, H. A. (1972). *Human problem solving.* Englewood Cliffs, NJ: Prentice-Hall.

Norman, D. A. (1976). *Memory and attention* (2nd ed.). New York: Wiley.

Oakes, W. F. (1955). An experimental study of pitch naming and pitch discrimination reaction. *Journal of Genetic Psychology, 86,* 237–259.

Oden, M. H. (1968). The fulfillment of promise: Forty-year follow-up of the Terman gifted group. *Genetic Psychology Monographs, 77,* 3–93.

Olson, J. R., & Biolosi, K. J. (1991). Techniques for representing expert knowledge. In K. A. Ericsson & J. Smith (Eds.), *Toward a General Theory of Expertise* (pp. 240–285). New York: Cambridge University Press.

Patel, V. L., & Groen, G. L. (1986). Knowledge based solution strategies in medical reasoning. *Cognitive Science, 10,* 91–116.

Patel, V. L., & Groen, G. J. (1991). The general and specific nature of medical expertise: a critical look. In K. A. Ericsson & J. Smith (Eds.), *Toward a General Theory of Expertise* (pp. 93–125). New York: Cambridge University Press.

Reitman, J. (1976). Skilled perception in go: Deducing memory structures from interresponse times. *Cognitive Psychology, 8,* 336–356.

Resnick, L. B. (Ed.). (1976). *The nature of intelligence.* Hillsdale, NJ: Erlbaum.

Roe, A. (1953). A psychological study of eminent psychologists and anthropologists, and a comparison with biological and physical scientists. *Psychological Monographs, 67,* 1–55.

Saariluoma, P. (1984). *Coding problem spaces in chess: A psychological study.* Helsinki: Societas Scientiarum Fennica.

Salthouse, T. A. (1984). Effects of age and skill in typing. *Journal of Experimental Psychology: General, 113,* 345–371.

Scardamalia, M., & Bereiter, C. (1991). Literate expertise. In K. A. Ericsson & J. Smith (Eds.), *Toward a General Theory of Expertise* (pp. 172–194). New York: Cambridge University Press.

Silver, E. A. (1981). Recall of mathematical information: Solving related problems. *Journal for Research and Mathematical Education, 12,* 54–64.

Simon, D. P., & Simon, H. A. (1978). Individual differences in solving physics problems. In R. S. Siegler (Ed.), *Children's thinking: What develops?* (pp. 325–348). Hillsdale, NJ: Erlbaum.

Simon, H. A., & Chase, W. G. (1973). Skill in chess. *American Scientist, 61,* 394–403.

Simon, H. A., & Gilmartin, K. (1973). A simulation of memory for chess positions. *Cognitive Psychology, 8,* 165–190.

Sloboda, J. (1976). Visual perception of musical notation: Registering pitch symbols in memory. *Quarterly Journal of Experimental Psychology, 28,* 1–16.

Sloboda, J. (1991) Musical expertise. In K. A. Ericsson & J. Smith (Eds.), *Toward a General Theory of Expertise* (pp. 153–171). New York: Cambridge University Press.

Spilich, G. J., Vesonder, G. T., Chiesi, H. L., & Voss, J. F. (1979). Text processing of domain-related information for individuals with high and low domain knowledge. *Journal of Verbal Learning and Verbal Behavior, 18,* 275–290.

Stanley, J. C., George, W. C., & Solano, C. H. (1977). *The gifted and creative: A fifty-year perspective.* Baltimore: Johns Hopkins University Press.

Staszewski, J. J. (1987). *The psychological reality of retrieval structures: An investigation of expert knowledge.* Unpublished doctoral dissertation, Cornell University, Ithaca, NY.

Staszewski, J. J. (1988). Skilled memory and expert mental calculation. In M. T. H. Chi, R. Glaser, & M. J. Farr (Eds.), *The nature of expertise* (pp. 71–128). Hillsdale, NJ: Erlbaum.

Sternberg, R. J. (Ed.). (1982). *Handbook of human intelligence.* Cambridge University Press.

Terman, L. M., & Oden, M. H. (1947). *Genetic studies of genius. Vol. 4: The gifted child grows up.* Stanford, CA: Stanford University Press.

Thorndyke, P. W., & Stasz, C. (1980). Individual differences in procedures for knowledge acquisition from maps. *Cognitive Psychology, 12,* 137–175.

Tyler, L. E. (1965). *The psychology of human differences.* New York: Appleton-Century-Crofts.

van Dijk, T. A., & Kintsch, W. (1983). *Strategies of discourse comprehension.* New York: Academic Press.

Varon, E. J. (1935). The development of Alfred Binet's psychology. *Psychological Monographs, 46* (Whole No. 207).

Voss, J. F., Greene, T. R., Post, T. A., & Penner, B. C. (1983). Problem-solving skill in the social sciences. *Psychology of Learning and Motivation, 17,* 165–213.

Voss, J. F., Vesonder, G. T., & Spilich, G. J. (1980). Text generation and recall by high-knowledge and low-knowledge individuals. *Journal of Verbal Leaning and Verbal Behavior, 19,* 651–667.

Wechsler, D. (1952). *The range of human capacities.* Baltimore: Williams & Wilkins.

Wilson, R. S. (1986). Twins: Genetic influence on growth. In R. M. Malina & C. Bouchard (Eds.), *Sports and human genetics* (pp. 1–21). Champaign, IL: Human Kinetics Publishing.

CHAPTER NINETEEN

THREE PROBLEMS IN TEACHING GENERAL SKILLS

JOHN R. HAYES

We need educational practices that will help people to adapt to a rapidly changing environment. We want students to acquire general skills — skills likely to transfer to the new situations that will face them. I was asked to consider whether there are any general skills to be taught. I believe that there are, and I also believe that it will not be as easy as we would like to teach them.

In this chapter, I discuss three problems that anyone who wants to teach general skills must face. The first is that proficiency in some general skills may require vast bodies of knowledge — knowledge that could take years to acquire. A second problem is that the task of teaching learning and thinking skills may be complicated by their number. If there were just three or five candidate strategies, it would be a relatively straightforward matter to set about evaluating them and teaching the useful ones. However, I argue that there are actually several hundred plausible strategies we might teach. Finally, the third problem with teaching general skills is that even after we identify a useful strategy and teach it successfully in one application, students may and frequently do fail to transfer that strategy to other applications.

19.1   THE REQUIREMENTS FOR KNOWLEDGE

The work of DeGroot (1965), Simon and Chase (1973), and Simon and Gilmartin (1973) has demonstrated clearly that skillful chess players employ an enormous amount of knowledge of chess patterns. To acquire this knowledge, the chess player must spend thousands of hours of preparation — playing chess, reading chess magazines, and studying chess positions. Simon and Chase (1973) note that it is very rare for a person to reach the grandmaster level of skill with less than 10 years of intensive study.

From chapter 17 in *Thinking and Learning,* Vol. 2, ed. J. Segal, S. Chipman, and R. Glaser (Hillsdale, NJ: Erlbaum, 1985), 391–405. Reprinted with permission.

I do not want to argue that chess is an important general skill. It may well be that chess knowledge equips people to do little beyond playing chess. However, I do want to argue that there are valuable skills — specifically musical composition, painting, and perhaps other skills — that like chess depend on acquiring large bodies of knowledge. To explore this question in the area of music, I examined the lives of famous composers.

I started my investigation with the incredibly precocious Mozart because he is the composer who seems least likely to have required a long period of preparation. He began to study music at four and wrote his first symphony at the age of eight.

I have graphed the number of works that Mozart produced in each year of his career in figure 19.1. The figure shows that Mozart's productivity increased steadily for the first 10 or 12 years of his career, as reported by Groves (1954) and Koechel (1965). It also shows that Mozart did produce works in the very early part of his career when he had had only a year or two of preparation. If these are works of very high quality, then we could conclude, for Mozart at least, that long preparation is not a necessary condition for the production of outstanding musical works. However, these early works may not be of very high quality. Perhaps they have been preserved for their historical rather than for their musical value.

To obtain some measure of the quality of Mozart's work, I turned to Schwann's *Record and Tape Guide.* I reasoned that an excellent work is likely to be recorded more often than a poor one. The decision to record a work presumably reflects both musical judgment and popular taste — that is, it reflects the musical judgment by a conductor that the work is worthwhile and the belief of the record companies that the record will sell.

Figure 19.2 shows the number of recordings listed in Schwann's guide (August, 1979) of works written in each year of Mozart's career. Although about 12% of Mozart's works were written in the first 10 years of his career, only 4.8% of the recordings came from this early period. Further, many of the recordings of early works are included in collections with labels such as, "The Complete Symphonies of Mozart." Perhaps the early works were included for reasons of completeness rather than excellence. When recordings included in complete collections are omitted from the calculations, the percentage of recordings in this early period drops to 2.4. These observations suggest that Mozart's early works are not of the same high quality as his later ones. The music critic, Harold Schonberg (1970), is of the same opinion. He says:

> It is strange to say of a composer who started writing at six, and lived only thirty-six years, that he developed late, but that is the truth. Few of Mozart's early works, elegant as they are, have the personality, concentration, and richness that entered his music after 1781. (pp. 82–84)

In 1782, Mozart was in the 21st year of his career.

Some works are recorded two or three times in different complete collections. Therefore, to weed out works recorded for reasons other than musical quality, I defined a masterwork (for the purposes of this study) as one for which five different recordings are currently listed in Schwann's guide. By this definition, Mozart's first masterwork was written in the 12th year of his career.

To explore the question about creativity and preparation more generally, I searched for biographical material about all the composers discussed in Schonberg's *The Lives of the Great Composers* (1970). For 76 of these composers, I was able to determine when they

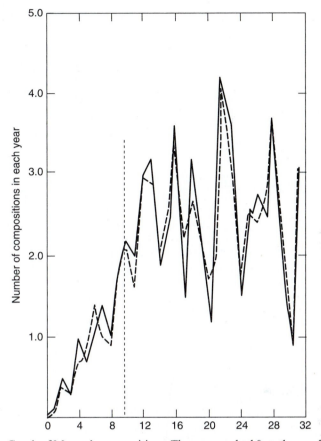

FIGURE 19.1   Graph of Mozart's compositions. The year marked 0 on the graph is 1760, the year when Mozart was 4 and began intensive musical training. The solid line in the figure is based on information from *Grove's Dictionary of Music* (1954). The dashed line is based on Koechel's listings (1965) as revised by modern musicologists. These two sources are in reasonable agreement about what works were produced when.

started intensive study of music. Incidentally, all these composers had at least one work listed in Schwann's guide, and 64 had one or more works available on five different records.

In figure 19.3 all of the careers of the composers are shown on the same scale, that is, the 10th year of Handel's career is graphed in the same place as the 10th year of Brahms' career. The figure shows that very few composers produced masterworks with less than 10 years of preparation. There are just three exceptions: Satie's "Trois Gynopédies," written in year 8; Shostakovich's Symphony #1, and Paganini's Caprices, both written in year 9. Between year 10 and year 25, there is a rapid and essentially linear increase in productivity from almost zero to slightly more than half a work per composer per year.

I have not continued figure 19.3 beyond year 25 because to do so would have given a misleading impression of changes in productivity with age. All the composers in our sample had careers of 25 years or more. However, some composers died quite young. Schubert,

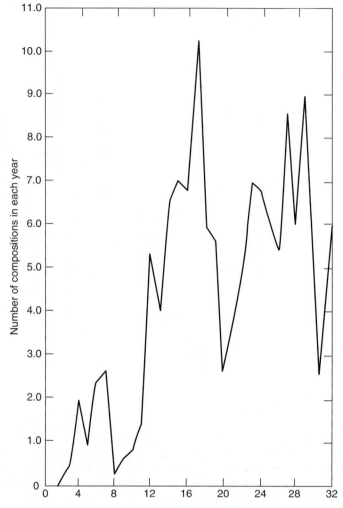

FIGURE 19.2   Number of recordings listed in *Schwann's Guide* (August, 1979) of works written in each year of Mozart's career.

for example, died in the 25th year of his career and Mozart died in the 31st year of his. Famous composers who die young tend to be unusually productive. This observation does not imply that especially creative musicians compose themselves to death. Rather, we believe that it is a statistical artifact captured by Hayes' maxim, "Late bloomers who want to be famous shouldn't die young."

If Handel and Verdi had died as young as Schubert, they would probably not be considered major composers. All their major works were written after they had been in music for 25 years. Averaging together short and long careers would make it appear that composers get less productive after 25 or 30. Actually, this is not so. This distortion is avoided in figure 19.4 by including only composers who have had careers of 40 years or more, and in figure 19.5 by including only composers who had careers of 55 and 60 years or more.

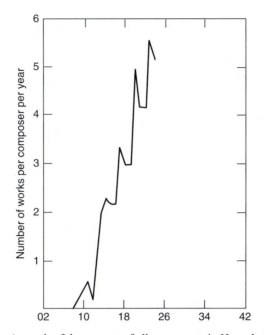

FIGURE 19.3   A graph of the careers of all composers in Hayes' study.

Figure 19.4 shows that composers maintain their productivity at least through the 40th year of their careers. Figure 19.5 indicates that a decline in productivity begins at about 50 years into the composers' careers. These figures, of course, do not take the composer's health into account. If we were to consider only composers in good physical and mental health, the decline in productivity might be much less marked. Clearly, productivity can continue far beyond the 50th year of the composer's musical career. For example, Albeniz's first masterwork was written in the 72nd year of his career!

It is reasonable to ask whether the important factor in the composers' productivity is really preparation or if perhaps the important factor is simply age. It is conceivable, for example, that composers have to be, say, 16 or 22, before they can write good music. Perhaps it is experience in life rather than experience in music that is critical. To test this possibility, I divided the composers into three groups. The first consisted of 14 composers who had begun their careers between the ages of 3 and 5. The second consisted of 30 composers who began their careers between 6 and 9 years of age. The third group consisted of 20 composers who began their careers at 10 or later.

I reasoned that if age were the critical factor, those who started their careers early would have to wait longer to produce good work than those composers who started late. In fact, this was not the case. The median number of years to first notable composition was 16.5 for the first group, 22 for the second group, and 21.5 for the third group.

It appears then that what composers need to write good music is not maturing but rather musical preparation. The results make it dramatically clear that no one composes outstanding music without first having about 10 years of intensive musical preparation.

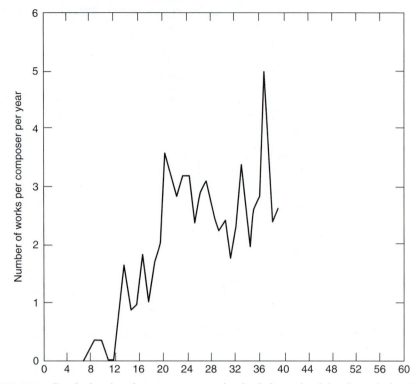

FIGURE 19.4   Graph showing that composers maintain their productivity through the 40th year of their career.

These results *do not* mean that there is no such thing as genius. They *do not* mean that just anyone with 10 to 25 years of experience can write great music. They *do* mean that even a person endowed with the genius of Mozart or Beethoven will still need 10 years or more of intense preparation to realize his or her potential.

Do painters also require years of intense preparation to be productive? Sandra Bond, Carol Janik, Felicia Pratto, and I have conducted a parallel study of painters designed to answer this question. For the purpose of the study, we defined an outstanding painting as one reproduced in any of 11 standard histories of art. We defined the beginning of the artist's career as the point at which he or she began intensive study of art. For many, this point was marked by the beginning of an apprenticeship or by entry into an art academy.

Figure 19.6 shows how productivity (the number of outstanding works produced per year per painter) varies with the painters' years of experience in the profession. The 16-year curve presents data for 132 painters who had careers of at least 16 years. The 40-year curve presents data for 102 painters who had careers of at least 40 years.

The results for painters are generally similar to those for composers. The productivity curve for painters has an initial period of very low productivity followed by a period

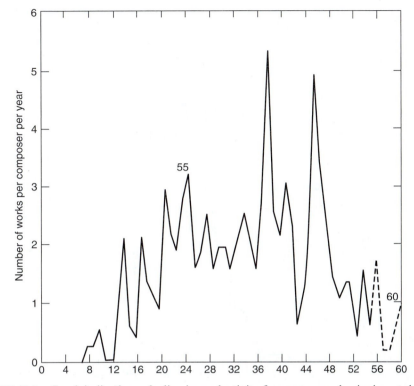

FIGURE 19.5   Graph indicating a decline in productivity for composers, beginning at about the 50th year of their careers.

in which productivity increases very rapidly. Then there is a long period of stable productivity followed by a gradual decline. The period of rapid increase in productivity occurs between 6 and 12 years for painters rather than between years 10 and 24 as was observed for composers. This difference may reflect differences in the nature of the skills involved in the fields or differences in our criteria for identifying outstanding works in the two fields. In part, we believe it reflects a difference in the sensitivity of our biographical measures to experience in music and art. We believe that parents are more likely to notice and record musical activity, perhaps because it makes a noise, than drawing. For many of the painters, there was evidence of early but undated drawing activity. Because it was unquantifiable, this early experience could not be included in our study as part of the painter's preparation.

If skill in chess, musical composition, and painting depend on large amounts of knowledge, it is easy to believe that there are other skills that do so as well, for example, skills in writing poetry, fiction, or expository prose, and skill in science, history, and athletics as well as many others. Strategies may help in acquiring or executing such skills. However, it is unlikely that the use of strategies can circumvent the need to spend large amounts of time acquiring a knowledge base for such skills.

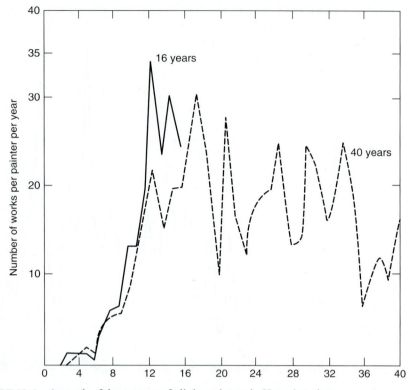

FIGURE 19.6   A graph of the careers of all the painters in Hayes' study.

19.2   THE LARGE NUMBER OF REASONABLE STRATEGIES

People differ in their proficiency in learning, in reasoning, and in problem solving, and in the strategies they employ to do these things. It seems reasonable to teach the strategies used by good learners and thinkers to those who are less proficient. I teach a course at Carnegie Mellon University intended to do just this. It is a freshman course that assumes little sophistication on the part of the student. Its structure is reflected in my text, *The Complete Problem Solver* (1981). In the course, I teach basic strategies in problem finding, representation, solution search, decision making, memory, and learning. In examining the course materials, I was surprised to find that I present at least 50 different strategies during the semester. The strategies, listed in table 19.1, include such diverse procedures as searching for counterexamples, working backward, perspective drawing, brainstorming, fractionation, satisficing, the keyword method, and time management skills.

When I say that the strategies are diverse, I mean that they are quite distinct. They are not simple variants of a few general strategies. They have different purposes and different contexts and must be taught separately. I am not suggesting that the strategies taught in my course are exactly the right ones. Of course, each of them seems plausible to me, but most of them have not been evaluated. I am suggesting, though, that the number of plausible strategies is large.

Another person teaching a course with the same orientation as mine might choose to teach many of the same strategies. However, there are many different ways to orient a basic strategies course. For example, a course could be focused on human relations problems or on math, on writing or on spoken communication, on learning through reading or on the analysis of arguments. Further, courses could be aimed at college students, or high school or grammar school students. Each focus and each age level would require a very different selection of strategies. Polya's *How To Solve It* (1973), which focuses on mathematics, includes some 60 strategies. Relatively few of these, perhaps 15, overlap with those in table 19.1. Taken together, these courses might easily include several hundred different plausible strategies — perhaps as many as a thousand.

The large number of plausible strategies poses a problem for us. Evaluating hundreds of strategies is a major research task — one that will not soon be completed. Fortunately, some excellent strategy evaluation work is already under way. However, until much more is done, choosing which strategies to teach will involve guesses and potentially faulty judgment.

Being mistaken about strategies can have serious consequences. For example, a student in my course had written an essay that had omitted an important qualification of its major point. The student's teaching assistant pointed out this flaw and precipitated the following dialogue:

Student:	"I know, but I already have three paragraphs."
TA:	"What?"
Student:	"I've already proposed three ideas, so I've used up my three paragraphs."
TA:	"What?"
Student:	"An essay has just three paragraphs."
TA:	"What?"
Student:	"Beginning, middle, and end. So you see, I just couldn't add an extra idea."

Clearly, this student has learned some rather odd strategies for writing that put serious constraints on what he was able to do with language.

College English teachers report that they frequently observe equally bizarre strategies. One teacher, for example, reported that a student had asked her, "Aren't you going to give me extra credit because I didn't use any pronouns in my paper?"

19.3   FAILURE TO GENERALIZE STRATEGIES

Sometimes a strategy that ought to generalize does not. Herb Simon and I have worked a good deal with problem isomorphs (1976) — that is, with sets of problems that have the same underlying structure, but different cover stories. For example, we have developed and studied a set of problems, all of which are identical in form to the famous Tower of Hanoi

TABLE 19.1   Strategies Taught in Problem-Solving Course

Problem Finding

Bug lists for identifying needed innovations

Search for counter-examples

Search for alternative interpretations

Representation

When in difficulty, examine problem statement to see if information has been properly extracted

When in difficulty, search for a new problem representation

  Change point of view

  Choose new sensory code, e.g., imagery

  Work backwards

  Try hypothetical reasoning

  Try proof by contradiction

Be active in defining ill-defined problems by

  Making gap filling decisons

  Trying to solve the problem as a method for understanding it

Use external representations where possible

  Use perspective drawing

  Use matrices for keeping track of information

  Use drawing to find implicit relations in the problem

Search

Brainstorm

Use heuristic search where possible

  Planning

  Means-End analysis

  Auxiliary problems

  Fractionation

  Analogies

Decision Making

Explicit decision methods help

  Satisficing

  Dominance

  Additive weighting

  Expected value

  Signal detection model

  Bayes' Theorem

  Minimax

  Minimize maximum regret

TABLE 19.1
(CONTINUED)

Cost benefit analysis

  Bargaining strategies

  Schelling's task

Memory and Learning

Use external memory aids

Mnemonics

  Method of loci

  Keyword method

Learning strategies

  Elaborative rehearsal

  Notice hierarchical structure

  Use overlearning

  Monitor own learning

  Generate examples

  Use information in word roots

Evaluation

Check results

Get external criticism

General

Consolidate

Examine own process

Time management skills

puzzle. Four of these problems, which involve the actions of an imaginary set of "monsters," are shown in table 19.2. In the first puzzle, the monsters pass globes of various sizes back and forth; in the second, they move themselves from globe to globe; in the third, they change the sizes of the globe; and in the fourth, they change their own sizes.

Ideally, because these problems are formally identical, people who have solved one of them should behave as if they had solved them all. In fact, this is not the case. There is a lot of transfer between problems that involve moving either monsters or globes, and there is a lot of transfer between problems that involve changing the sizes of either monsters or globes. But there is relatively little transfer between move and change problems.

Failure of transfer is a frustrating reality in our classrooms. A statistics teacher at CMU who had taught the Poisson distribution to this class through a distance example was surprised that the next day his students could not apply the distribution to an example involving time.

TABLE 19.2   Four Monster Problems

1. *Monster Problem (Transfer Form 1).*   Three five-handed extraterrestrial monsters were holding three crystal globes. Because of the quantum-mechanical peculiarities of their neighborhood, both monsters and globes come in exactly three sizes with no others permitted: small, medium, and large. The medium-sized monster was holding the small globe; the small monster was holding the large globe; and the large monster was holding the medium-sized globe. Because this situation offended their keenly developed sense of symmetry, they proceeded to transfer globes from one monster to another so that each monster would have a globe proportionate to its own size.

    Monster etiquette complicated the solution of the problem because it requires that:

    1. only one globe may be transferred at a time;
    2. if a monster is holding two globes, only the larger of the two may be transferred;
    3. a globe may not be transferred to a monster who is holding a larger globe.

    By what sequence of transfers could the monsters have solved this problem?

2. *Monster Problem (Transfer Form 2).*   Three five-handed extraterrestrial monsters were standing on three crystal globes. Because of the quantum-mechanical peculiarities of their neighborhood, both monsters and globes come in exactly three sizes with no others permitted: small, medium, and large. The medium-sized monster was standing on the small globe; the small monster was standing on the large globe; and the large monster was standing on the medium-sized globe. Because this situation offended their keenly developed sense of symmetry, they proceeded to transfer themselves from one globe to another so that each monster would have a globe proportionate to its own size.

    Monster etiquette complicated the solution of the problem because it requires that:

    1. only one monster may be transferred at a time;
    2. if two monsters are standing on the same globe, only the larger of the two may be transferred;
    3. a monster may not be transferred to a globe on which a larger monster is standing.

    By what sequence of transfers could the monsters have solved this problem?

3. *Monster Problem (Change Form 1).*   Three five-handed extraterrestrial monsters were holding three crystal globes. Because of the quantum-mechanical peculiarities of their neighborhood, both monsters and globes come in exactly three sizes with no others permitted: small, medium, and large. The medium-sized monster was holding the small globe; the small monster was holding the large globe; and the large monster was holding the medium-sized globe. Because this situation offended their keenly developed sense of symmetry, they proceeded to shrink and expand globes so that each monster would have a globe proportionate to its own size.

    Monster etiquette complicated the solution of the problem because it requires that:

    1. only one globe may be changed at a time;
    2. if two globes have the same size, only the globe held by the larger monster may be changed;
    3. a globe may not be changed to the same size as the globe of a larger monster.

    By what sequence of changes could the monsters have solved this problem?

TABLE 19.2
(CONTINUED)

4. *Monster Problem (Change Form 2).*   Three five-handed extraterrestrial monsters were holding three crystal globes. Because of the quantum-mechanical peculiarities of their neighborhood, both monsters and globes come in exactly three sizes with no others permitted:
small, medium, and large. The medium-sized monster was holding the small globe; the small
monster was holding the large globe; and the large monster was holding the medium-sized
globe. Because this situation offended their keenly developed sense of symmetry, they proceeded to shrink and expand themselves so that each monster would have a globe proportion
to its own size.

Monster etiquette complicated the solution of the problem because it requires that:

1. only one monster may be changed at a time;
2. if two monster have the same size, only the monster holding the large globe may be changed;
3. a monster may not be changed to the same size as a monster holding a larger globe.

By what sequence of changes could the monsters have solved this problem?

Note: From Hayes, J. R., & Simon, H. A. (1976). Psychological differences among problem isomorphs. In
N. Castellan, Jr., D. Pisoni, & G. Potts (Eds.), *Cognitive theory* (Vol. II, pp. 23–24). Potomac, MD: Lawrence
Erlbaum Associates.

19.4   POSSIBLE RESPONSES TO THESE PROBLEMS

The possibility that mastery of a field may take many years is an important item of metacognitive knowledge that we ought to teach to our students. Some students may be inappropri-
ately discouraged by early setbacks because they believe that failure indicates lack of talent
rather than lack of knowledge. Others, perhaps too well endowed with self-confidence, may
believe that they are destined to perform great acts of creativity with little or no effort on
their part. Some may even defend themselves against knowledge on the grounds that it may
spoil the purity of their individual spark. Students of either type could profit by learning
that large quantities of knowledge may be essential for skilled performance in their fields.

The possibility that there are several hundred plausible learning and thinking strategies may be an important piece of metacognitive knowledge for teachers and educational
researchers. As teachers, this knowledge should lead us to question whether we can expect
very much general benefit from teaching any single strategy and to consider instead designing courses that allow students to choose among large numbers of strategies. As educational
researchers, the knowledge may lead us to try to simplify the evaluation task by searching
for categories of strategies that may be evaluated together.

What can we do to reduce the difficulty that people experience in transferring skills?
I offer the following speculation based distantly on observations made by Simon and me:
People employ certain fundamental categories when they construct representations. I sug-
gest that the most fundamental ones are object, event, action, location, time, and attribute.

When the elements of one problem isomorph fall in the same categories as the corresponding elements of another isomorph, then transfer between the two will be easy. For example, it should be easy to transfer from a problem isomorph in which people are moved among apartments to one in which checkers are moved among board positions, because people and checkers are both objects and apartments and board positions are both locations. However, transfer should be difficult to a third isomorph in which events are shuffled in time, because the categories of the elements of the first two problems are different from those in the third problem.

If this speculation is correct, it would suggest that we should not expect students to transfer knowledge across category boundaries without help. Rather, when full understanding of a principle requires students to generalize across category boundaries, we should be prepared to provide the student with examples that illustrate the application of the principle in each major category.

REFERENCES

DeGroot, A. D. (1965). *Thought and choice in chess.* The Hague: Mouton.

Grove's dictionary of music and musicians. (1954). J. A. F. Maitland (Ed.). Philadelphia: T. Presser.

Hayes, J. R. (1981). *The complete problem solver.* Philadelphia: The Franklin Institute Press.

Hayes, J. R., & Simon, H. A. (1976). Psychological differences among problem isomorphs. In N. Castellan, Jr., D. Pisoni, & G. Potts (Eds.), *Cognitive theory* (Vol. II). Potomac, MD: Lawrence Erlbaum Associates.

Koechel ABC. (1965). H. Von Hase (Ed.). New York: C. F. Peters Corporation.

Polya, G. (1973). *How to solve it.* (2nd ed.). Princeton, NJ: Princeton University Press.

Schonberg, H. C. (1970). *The lives of the great composers.* New York: Norton.

Schwann-1 Record & Tape Guide. (1979, August). Boston: ABC Schwann.

Simon, H. A., & Chase, W. G. (1973). Skill in chess. *American Scientist, 61,* 394–403.

Simon, H. A., & Gilmartin, K. (1975). A simulation of memory for chess positions. *Cognitive Psychology, 5,* 29–46.

Simon, H. A., & Hayes, J. R. (1976). The understanding process: Problem isomorphs. *Cognitive Psychology, 8,* 165–190.

CHAPTER TWENTY

MUSICAL EXPERTISE

JOHN A. SLOBODA

This chapter treats six connected issues having to do with musical expertise. Section 20.1 examines the difficulties associated with characterizing expertise in a way that offers a genuine foothold for cognitive psychology, and I suggest that expertise may not, in fact, be "special" in any cognitively interesting sense. Section 20.2 goes on to review some experimental studies of music, which suggest that most members of a culture possess tacit musical expertise, expressed in their ability to use high-level structural information in carrying out a variety of perceptual tasks. This expertise seems to be acquired through casual exposure to the musical forms and activities of the culture. Section 20.3 provides two detailed examples of exceptional musical expertise (a musical savant and a jazz musician) that apparently developed in the absence of formal instruction, suggesting that normal and "exceptional" expertise may be parts of a single continuum. The evidence presented in Section 20.4 suggests that a major difference between musical expertise and many other forms of expertise is that musical expertise requires an apprehension of a structure-emotion mapping. Without this, the ability to perform with "expression" cannot be acquired. Section 20.5 outlines some evidence to suggest that these structure-emotion links become firmly established during middle childhood, under certain conditions, and that these conditions are predictive of future development of musical expertise. Finally, Section 20.6 reviews some research efforts that are attempts to clarify the precise nature of the structure-emotion link and are showing that definite types of structures seem to mediate distinct emotions.

20.1   WHAT IS EXPERTISE?

In beginning to think about how a psychologist who deals with music could contribute in a specific way to a volume on expertise, it became clear to me that most of the recently published work on musical competence has made little attempt to define or characterize

From K. Anders Ericsson, Jacqui Smith, *Toward a General Theory of Expertise,* "Musical expertise," by John Sloboda (pp. 153–171).

musical expertise. What we have, instead, is a varied collection of empirical studies on single aspects of what some musicians do. The topics of such studies range from pitch memory (Ward & Burns, 1982), through synchronization in performance (Rasch, 1988), to planning a composition (Davidson & Welsh, 1988), and it is not immediately clear that such accomplishments have anything in common other than the fact that they are different aspects of handling the organized sounds our various societies label as music.

That observation led back to a logically prior question: Is there anything that all examples of expertise *in general* should or might have in common? More precisely, is there anything about the *internal* psychological structures of certain accomplishments that marks them out as examples of expertise? It is important to remember that when someone is declared an expert, that is a social act that may or may not correspond to an intrinsic characteristic of the person so designated.

One possible definition of an expert is "someone who performs a task significantly better (by some specified criterion) than the majority of people." According to this definition, Chase and Ericsson's (1981) digit memorizer SF is an expert. If, however, digit-span recall became a popular hobby, then he might well be overtaken by sufficient numbers of people so that he would cease to be considered an expert. Such a relativistic attribution of expertise clearly would preclude the possibility of any *cognitive* account of expertise, because the cognitive apparatus that earned SF expert status would remain precisely the same after SF was no longer labeled an expert. It does, however, seem to me that exactly such a relativistic conception underlies much common talk of expertise, and to a certain extent determines the agendas of "expertise" research.

For cognitive psychology to have an authentic foothold, we have to find a characterization of expertise that will allow any number of people (up to and including all) to be expert in a particular area. For instance, many would, I think, agree that the vast majority of people are expert speakers of their native languages. I shall later suggest that the majority of our population possess particular types of musical expertise. A possible definition with this outcome might relate to the reliable attainment of specific goals within a specific domain. So, for instance, one is an expert diner if one can get a wide variety of foodstuffs from plate to mouth without spilling anything.

An apparent problem with this definition, however, is that there is no lower limit to the simplicity or specificity of the task to which one can apply it. For instance, this definition would allow each of us to be expert at pronouncing his or her own name or at folding his or her arms. It may seem that we need more than goal attainment to attribute expertise. For instance, one may want to say that an expert is someone who can make an appropriate response to a situation that contains a degree of unpredictability. So the expert bridge player is one who can work out the play most likely to win with a hand that the player has never seen before; the expert doctor is one who can provide an appropriate diagnosis when faced with a configuration of symptoms never before encountered. In this way we might be able to carve out precisely the set of activities in which various experts have been interested.

On further examination, however, it is not as easy to apply this distinction as it might first appear. Pronouncing one's own name can also be seen as an act requiring the handling of unpredictability. It is an act that is occasioned by cues (external or internal) that can vary. One must be able to retrieve and execute the required motor program regardless of the immediate mental context. The complexity of these apparently simple acts is soon revealed when one attempts to construct machines that can do the same tasks, as the discipline of artificial intelligence has amply documented (e.g., visual recognition, Marr, 1982).

It is difficult for me to escape the conclusion that we should abandon the idea that expertise is something special and rare (from a cognitive or biological point of view) and move toward the view that the human organism is in its essence expert. The neonatal brain is already an expert system. "Becoming expert" in socially defined ways is the process of connecting "intrinsic" expertise to the outside world so that it becomes manifest in particular types of behaviors in particular types of situations. I believe that Fodor (1975), from another point of view, was articulating a similar proposal: To broadly paraphrase Fodor, "You can't learn anything you don't already know."

To look at expertise in this way may require reversal of some of our perspectives on familiar situations. For instance, when considering Chase and Ericsson's (1981) study of SF, it is easy to allow one's focus of attention to fall on the two hundred hours of practice that moved him from average to the world's best, implicitly equating the acquisition of the expertise with the work that went on in the practice period under observation. The perspective to which I am increasingly drawn suggests that we focus our attention instead on what SF brought to the experimental situation. SF's intimate knowledge of running times was, from this perspective, the principal manifestation of expertise that "bootstrapped" the digit-span task, and it seems to me that the most interesting psychological considerations are how and why that knowledge came to be applied to the task in hand when it did. What determined that it would be applied after about fifteen hours of practice rather than instantaneously or not at all? A plausible answer to that question may well be "chance" (e.g., a particular sequence of numbers that strongly reminded SF of a well-known running time).

In other words, the broad answer to the question of how SF became expert at the digit-span task is that he was able to increment his expertise by approximately 0.01 percent in a situation in which he was already expert at a number of things, including running times, that supplied the other 99.99 percent of what was needed. And each of those preceding areas of expertise was likewise resting on other forms of expertise in the same relationship in a constant, unbroken sequence back to birth and beyond. What made SF "exceptional" in conventional terms was no more than a unique set of life experiences. In the sections that follow, I pursue some implications of this way of looking at expertise as applied to music.

20.2   ACQUIRING MUSICAL SKILL

One of the principal reasons for studying expertise is practical. Given that it would be socially desirable for certain manifestations of expertise to be more widespread than they are, we want to know what we can do to assist people to acquire them. The issue becomes acute in relation to formal education, where the general perception is that we set up environments that are supposed to encourage expertise, but that many individuals still do not achieve levels that we know to be possible (whether it be learning a foreign language, a musical instrument, or physics skill). We want to be able to tell teachers that there are principled things that they can do to increase the frequency of those 0.01 percent increments in learning.

Music is no exception to this, and music teachers are continually inquiring of psychologists how psychological insights can inform their work. It is their perception that musical expertise is taught and acquired with great difficulty. They speak of "tone-deaf" children (usually children unable to sing in tune); they speak of the difficulty of teaching sight reading, of teaching rhythm, of teaching good intonation on a string instrument, and so on.

My early research on the skill of sight reading has been summarized elsewhere (Sloboda, 1984). That research was carried out under the influence of the previously published work of Chase and Simon (1973) on chess perception. Their research showed that, like playing chess, reading of music depended on an ability to pick up various sorts of patterns in the stimulus. For instance, good sight readers were found to be much more prone than poor sight readers to a sort of "proofreader's error" (Sloboda, 1976a) whereby notational mistakes out of character with the genre were automatically corrected back to what the genre would have predicted. Their ability to use music structure to "chunk" notes could account for their superior short-term memory for notation (Halpern & Bower, 1982; Sloboda, 1976b).

Encouraging as it was to find results for music that so clearly paralleled Chase's findings, I became progressively more disheartened as I talked about those results to groups of teachers. The question they all asked was of what prescriptions I would draw from my results for the teaching of sight reading, and after some hand waving I really had to admit that there were no prescriptions that I could draw at that time. I did not know how one could teach children to "see" structures.

Since then I have come to realize that in order to "see" musically significant structures, one first must be able to "hear" those structures, and I have learned from reading some excellent recent research that the process of coming to "hear" musical structure is a process that occurs quite naturally for the majority of children as a function of normal enculturation. For instance, Zenatti (1969) showed that children at age 7 show a distinct memory advantage for sequences conforming to rules of normal tonal progression, as compared with atonal sequences. This advantage is not shared by children of age 5. Similar results were obtained from studying children's songs (Dowling, 1982, 1988; Gardner, Davidson, & McKernon, 1981). There is a definite age progression from tonal inconsistency and instability toward conformity to the norms of the tonal culture.

An experiment I conducted earlier (Sloboda, 1985a) showed that the progressing of the ability to discriminate between "legal" and "illegal" sequences did not seem to depend on children's receiving any sort of formal music instruction. Almost no children at age 5 made meaningful discriminations, whereas almost all 11-year-olds made discriminations in accordance with those of adults (and music harmony textbooks). The children who were receiving formal music lessons did not fare better than other children.

Although many experiments with adults have shown cognitive differences between musicians and nonmusicians, some studies have shown little difference. For instance, Deliege and El Ahmahdi (1990) showed that musicians and nonmusicians were remarkably similar in the segmentations they suggested for an atonal piece. That may have been partly attributable to the relative unfamiliarity of the genre to both groups. More strikingly, Bigand (1990) showed that nonmusicians had an ability similar to that of musicians to classify superficially different conventional tonal melodies into groups containing underlying structural similarities. Studies of memory recall for melodies (Sloboda & Parker, 1985) have shown that musicians and nonmusicians have similar abilities to preserve higher-order structure at the expense of note-to-note detail.

The research literature, therefore, leads to the conclusion that human beings pick up quite high-level implicit (or tacit) knowledge about some major structural features of the music of their culture. They gradually improve their ability to do this over the first ten or more years of life and preserve this ability into adulthood. We may presume that this is achieved through informal engagement in the everyday musical activities that abound in almost all human cultures (e.g., nursery rhymes, hymns, dances, popular songs, playground games). In our own culture these forms are, of course, massively reinforced through the broadcast media.

In this way, almost every member of a culture is a musical expert, but the expertise is usually hidden and tacit. It may not exhibit itself in abilities to sing or play. It is, however, manifested in a variety of perceptual and memory tasks. Nearly all of us can identify some kinds of "wrong notes" when we hear them, even though we cannot always say why the notes are "wrong."

Tacit expertise depends, in part, on being in a culture in which one is exposed to products in the specified domain without the necessity for active engagement. This allows the dissociation between receptive expertise and productive expertise. Such a dissociation would not normally occur in chess, or bridge, or physics, because the only way one normally gets exposure to the relevant structures is by *doing* the activity.

It is not the purpose of this essay to give an account of the various developments in understanding what it is that people know when they know about music structure. Suffice it to say that it seems necessary to postulate mechanisms for representing music that are multidimensional and hierarchical. This means that music can be characterized by points of greater or lesser prominence or distance from one another and that various dimensions may be in synchrony or in opposition. This gives rise to complex patterns of tension and resolution at different hierarchical levels. Some of the most influential characterizations of musical representation have been offered by Lerdahl and Jack-endoff (1983), Krumhansl (1990), and Meyer (1973).

More pertinent for our current purposes is the observation that at least some of these structures seem capable of being represented in a connectionist network (Bharucha, 1987). A connectionist model of the brain shows one way in which it might be possible for knowledge of complex structures to be built up simply as a result of frequent exposure to relevant examples. Such an activity seems to be an essential requirement of any mechanism that acquires expertise from environments that are not engineered to be instructional (i.e., most environments).

20.3   ACQUISITION OF MUSICAL EXPERTISE IN NONINSTRUCTIONAL SETTINGS

Musical expertise, in the foregoing sense, is possessed by the majority of untutored members of any culture. This is not, however, what most people mean when they refer to musical expertise; they mean overt skills of performance or composition. Surely these cannot be acquired other than through formal instruction. It is certain that such skills are acquired mainly through instruction, at least in our culture, but there is some evidence that such instruction is not necessary. Several cases of overt expertise have apparently arisen without any formal tuition or intervention by other experts. An examination of these cases is particularly important if we are to isolate the general conditions for the acquisition of expertise.

20.3.1   Musical Prodigies and Savants

There have been several documented cases of children who showed exceptional precocity at various musical skills. Some of them, such as Mozart, went on to become exceptional adults. Others did not sustain their exceptionality into adult life (see Bamberger, 1986, for a cognitive account of adolescent "burnout" among musical prodigies). One of the fullest accounts of a child musical prodigy was given by Revesz (1925), who made an intensive study of the young Hungarian prodigy Erwin Nyherigazy (EN). Although EN had a great deal of formal tuition and support from professional musicians from an early age, he soon surpassed his teachers in his ability to commit tonal piano music to memory on one or two exposures.

There is another group of prodigies who, by and large, do not receive formal instruction: the so-called idiots savants (see Treffert, 1988, for a review). The savant is a person of generally low IQ, usually male, and often autistic, who has developed a skill in one defined area to a level quite exceptional compared with the general population. Although such cases have been reported in the literature for many years, the reports have mostly been only anecdotal and impressionistic contributions to the psychiatric literature. Only in the past decade have systematic investigations of musical savants been reported in the cognitive literature (e.g., Miller, 1987).

One of these studies concerned the autistic savant NP (Sloboda, Hermelin, & O'Connor, 1985). At the time of detailed study, NP was in his early twenties, and we were able to document his ability to recall a tonal piano movement almost perfectly twelve minutes after first hearing it. Two features of the study were particularly noteworthy: (1) His ability did not extend to a simple atonal piece, and (2) the few errors in his recall of the tonal piece were largely in conformity with the rules of the genre. We concluded that NP's recall ability was predicated on his ability to code and store tonal music in terms of its structural features. In that respect, NP's ability was every bit as "intelligent" as the memory performance of chess masters. Other studies of musical savants (Hermelin, O'Connor, & Lee, 1987; Miller, 1987; Treffert, 1988) have confirmed the importance of structural knowledge in supporting their skills.

Because NP was still relatively young when studied, it was possible to talk to people who knew him at different points in his life and observed his ability develop. It seems that NP's early life was one of considerable cultural deprivation. As far as we know, he had few, if any, opportunities to interact with musical instruments and was not encouraged to sing or to engage with music. His precocity was first noticed at about the age of 6 years, when he spontaneously reproduced at the piano a song that a staff member at his day-care center had just played. From the point on, he was given many opportunities and encouragements to interact with music and musical instruments, although nothing approaching "instruction" was ever possible with this profoundly nonverbal individual. Even now his "lessons" consist of a pianist playing pieces that NP then reproduces. A tape recording of his accomplishments at the age of 8 years shows memory and performance skills that were impressive for an autistic child, though by no means as polished and outstanding as his current performances.

How did NP's skill compare with "normal" skill at the various stages of his life? At age 6 or 7, it was not clear that his memorization abilities were abnormally good. Most untutored children of that age are capable of memorizing short songs, and many can succeed in picking them out on a piano by a process of trial and error. What distinguished NP at that age was his ability to map his internal knowledge of songs directly and without error onto the piano keyboard and to choose appropriate fingering patterns. His performances of tonal music have always been characterized by an absence of hesitation or experimentation, no doubt assisted by his possession of absolute pitch. We have no information that would help us to explain how NP acquired his knowledge without having had any known opportunity to practice before the age of 6.

For the period of his early twenties, the comparison with normals showed a somewhat different pattern. His technical accomplishments were then not unusual. Many reasonably proficient pianists can choose appropriate fingerings for musical passages immediately and automatically. What made NP quite unusual was the *length* of the musical material he could commit to accurate memory after a single hearing. This is a skill shared by few adults at any level of musical expertise, although there are adult musicians of my acquaintance who claim that they could do what NP does when they were age 12 or 13. They no longer can do it, because it has not seemed interesting or worthwhile for them to practice and maintain that particular skill.

We may ask what conditions seem to be associated with the acquisition of the expertise of NP and other savants. The first common factor seems to be a high degree of intrinsic motivation for engagement with a single activity sustained over many years. Such motivation usually has a strong obsessional component, in that given freedom, the savant will spend all available time on the activity, without ever tiring of it.

The second factor is an environment that provides frequent opportunities for the practice of the skill in question. In the case of a musical savant, this may include the provision of regular access to instruments, broadcast media, and musical events. It is possible to suppose that whatever level of cultural deprivation NP suffered during his earliest years, he at least would have been exposed to music through the broadcast media.

The third factor is, of course, the exceptional amount of time spent in cognitive engagement with the materials and activities relevant to the skill in question (practice). It is difficult to estimate the amount of time NP spent thinking about music when not playing or listening to it, but obvious external involvement probably amounted to four to five hours per day.

The fourth factor, therefore, is the availability of the time and opportunity to "indulge" the obsession. It may be because fewer societal demands are made on people with low IQs that they are "allowed," even encouraged, to devote their attentions in this way.

The fifth factor is the complete absence of negative external reinforcement related to attainment or lack of it. There is, therefore, little possibility of a savant's developing self-doubt, fear of failure, or any of the other blocks that inhibit and sometimes prevent normal or exceptional accomplishment.

20.3.2   Jazz Musicians

It is probable that many of the world's musical cultures, particularly the informal, nonliterate "folk" cultures, have been breeding grounds for expertise. Some anthropological work (e.g., Blacking, 1976) suggests that this is true of indigenous Third World cultures. The jazz culture of New Orleans in the early part of this century may not have been greatly different from those other cultures in many respects. Its advantage for us is that jazz rapidly spread from New Orleans to become part of mass culture and contributed an entirely new facet to the face of Western culture. Its leaders became cult heroes, and jazz itself became a subject for intensive academic scrutiny. For these reasons, we have far more detailed biographical information about jazz musicians than about the musicians from all of the world's other nonliterate cultures put together.

It appears that most of the early jazz players were self-taught. Among the self-taught players who became international names were Bix Beiderbecke, Roy Eldridge, and Louis Armstrong. Collier's (1983) study of Armstrong is particularly detailed, and it allows us to look at Armstrong's musical development in some detail as a "prototype" of untutored expertise.

Armstrong spent most of his early years in a neighborhood known as "Black Storeyville," an area designated for black prostitution. One of the features of that neighborhood was the continual live music, performed by dance bands and "tonk" bands, which often would play on the street to attract customers. Having little knowledge of the world outside, Armstrong had little more than pimps and musicians as male role models. His father had abandoned his mother before he was born. His childhood was one of extreme poverty and deprivation, and from the age of 7 years he had to work, steal, and hustle to make money for his mother and himself. At the age of 8 or 9 years he formed a vocal quartet with some other boys in order to pick up pennies on street corners. The group lasted two or three years and probably practiced and performed in public two or three times per week. That provided several hundred hours of improvised part singing, which as Collier observed, "would have constituted a substantial course in ear training — far more than most conservatory instrumentalists get today."

At the age of 13 or 14 years, Armstrong was involved in an incident with a gun and was, as a result, sent to the Colored Waif's Home (known as the Jones Home). There the boys were taught reading, writing, and arithmetic, with gardening as a sideline. The home had a band that played once a week around the city. After six months in the home, Armstrong was allowed to join the band, first playing tambourine, then drums, then alto horn. It is clear from contemporary accounts that many of the bands playing in the streets of New Orleans were fairly informal groups with an "anything goes" attitude. It was quite easy for a novice to join in the general noise, just playing the notes he knew, and his mistakes and split notes would pass without comment. Armstrong quickly learned how to get sounds out of the horn, and his vocal experience made it easy for him to work out appropriate parts to the songs the band played. His talent was noticed, and he was promoted to bugle player. He gradually improved to become the band's leader, but he left the home and the band after two years, at age 16. Nothing he experienced in the home would merit the term "formal teaching."

Armstrong found casual work driving a coal cart, which occupied his days, but during the evenings he began playing jazz in the blues bands of the tonks. He did not at that stage own a cornet, and so it was impossible for him to practice. He simply went around to the various bands asking cornetists to let him sit in for a few numbers. Blues music provided a good vehicle for gaining jazz expertise. Blues songs featured slow tempos in two or three of the easiest keys. The set melodies were of the simplest sort; in many cases there was no set melody at all, and the cornetist would string phrases together from a small repertoire of stock figures.

At age 17, Armstrong acquired his first cornet and began to practice and work regularly at one of the tonks. The work paid little, and so he kept his coal job during the day. At some point in that period Armstrong met Joe Oliver, acknowledged as the best cornetist in

New Orleans. Armstrong began hanging around the places where Oliver played, running errands, carrying his case, and eventually sitting in for him. Oliver became Armstrong's sponsor and to some extent his teacher. According to Collier, however, Oliver did not influence Armstrong's style and probably did little more than show Armstrong some new tunes and possibly a few alternative fingerings.

By age 19, Armstrong was finding employment on local riverboat excursions. Then, for three summers running, he made long trips, playing every day. For the first time in his life music had become his predominant activity. The band played seven nights per week, doing fourteen numbers and encores each night. They rehearsed two afternoons per week, and the repertoire changed every two weeks. It was only after joining the riverboats that Armstrong learned how to read music and had to acquire the discipline of playing what was written rather than what he felt like playing. When he left the riverboats at age 23, he was an established professional musician.

If Armstrong's early life was a prototype for untutored acquisition of expertise, which of its features might we highlight for future corroboration? One obvious feature was the casual immersion in a rich musical environment with many opportunities to listen and observe. A second feature was the early systematic exploration of a performance medium (in his case, voice). Third, as far as we can judge, his early experiences allowed a great deal of freedom to explore and experiment without negative consequences. A fourth feature was a lack of distinction between "practice" and "performance." The learning took place on the job. A fifth feature was an enduring motivation to engage in music — in Armstrong's case, a complex mix of internal and external motivations, but arguably with internal motivations dominating. A sixth feature was a graded series of opportunities and challenges available or sought out as the expertise developed.

In many ways, this list of features fits the case of a savant such as NP. The principal differences in the two examples cited here relate to motivation and challenge. NP's motivation did not have a significant external component, and partly for that reason it is not clear that his challenges either arose or were grasped with the same frequency as those of Armstrong. It is easy to imagine NP remaining on a performance plateau. Armstrong went on growing and changing throughout his life.

What these case studies show is that high levels of expertise are achievable without instruction. This does not, of course, mean that instruction is useless. By providing a structured progression of information and challenges for a learner, geared precisely to the learner's capacities at a given time, a teacher may be able to accelerate a learner's progress. Not every person has the opportunity to extract the relevant experiences from the "natural" environment that Armstrong had. A formal instructional environment can engineer the conditions for such extraction. The danger of all such environments is that goals and standards are imposed on the learner, rather than being chosen. The consequence can be to inhibit intrinsic motivation and originality (Amabile, 1983). If external constraints are extreme, it may even be that the ability to enjoy music will be destroyed.

In this connection, one other difference between NP and Armstrong has not been brought out thus far. One of the most striking aspects of NP's musical life was its lack of affect. All pieces in his repertoire were played in a "wooden," unexpressive manner. Although his immediate reproduction showed some of the expressive features of the model, within twenty-four hours all expressive variation was "washed out," leaving a rigid metronomical husk. It was as if NP had no means of understanding (and thus relating to the structure of) the small variations in timing, loudness, and timbre that are the lifeblood of musical performances. From the earliest recording we have of Armstrong's music, in contrast, we find a richly expressive, flexible performance that bends tone and time in ways that have a strong impact on many listeners. Armstrong is not hailed as the king of jazz for his technique, impressive as it was. There are others who match or surpass him in technique. He is revered for the life he could breathe into the simplest material.

NP was one of a rather small number of people who appear to gain complete satisfaction from relating to music as pure structure or syntax. What brings the vast majority of us to music, and keeps us with it, is something additional: its power to mediate a vast range of emotionally toned states, ranging from the subtle to the overwhelming. Because modern systematic studies of music have approached it with the tools of cognitive science and linguistics, the emotional aspect of music has been virtually overlooked, and naive readers of modern research studies might be forgiven for thinking that music is simply another kind of complex structure to be apprehended, like chess or physics.

I know that those who are expert in chess or physics say that there is beauty and emotion in those activities too, but there is a sense in which such things are not central to the skill. One can write a perfectly effective computer program for chess that will not need any information about how particular chess positions or games will affect the emotions of certain human players. I think there is a strong case for saying that a computer could never adequately simulate Louis Armstrong without some implementation of a theory of the emotions.

20.4   EXPRESSION AND EMOTION AS FOUNDATIONAL ASPECTS OF MUSICAL EXPERTISE

Those approaching music with the prejudices and preoccupations of experimental psychology have been wary of examining the emotional aspect, for methodological and conceptual reasons. Rather than examine these reasons in detail, I should like to point to some investigations that seem to have "opened doors" into this area.

The advent of the microcomputer and microtechnology has, for the first time, made possible easy and accurate transfer of detailed performance information into computers for sophisticated analysis. The 1980s saw a number of studies (Clarke, 1985; Gabrielsson, 1983; Shaffer, 1981; Sloboda, 1983; Sundberg, 1988; Todd, 1985) that measured minute expressive variations in performance loudness and timing. These studies showed several things: (1) A given player can consistently repeat given variations on successive performances; (2) these perturbations are not random but, rather, are intentional, and performers can alter them to a greater or lesser extent at will; (3) many of these perturbations are rule-governed and relate to the formal structure of the music in systematic ways.

My own studies (Sloboda, 1983, 1985b), for instance, have shown that timing deformations are organized around the strong metrical beats of tonal melodies in a way that makes the metrical structure clearer for listeners than it is when such deformations are not present. Although we do not yet have the evidence, this line of research suggests that all effective expression may be systematic and rule-governed in this way, helping to highlight musical structures in a way that makes their emotion-bearing content more manifest to listeners.

The other line of contemporary thinking that converges with the experimental work on expression is the music-theory work of such writers as Leonard Meyer (Meyer, 1956, 1973) and Fred Lerdahl (1988a, 1988b; Lerdahl & Jack-endoff, 1983). Meyer has convincingly argued that emotion in music arises out of the complex, often subliminal web of expectations and violations of expectations that musical structures unfold over time (Narmour, 1977). Lerdahl (1988b) takes this a step farther by suggesting that only structures that have certain formal properties (such as discreteness and hierarchical organization) can be directly detected by listeners (Balzano, 1980; Shepard, 1982). Only such structures will be effective in creating the types of tensions and resolutions that can support the emotional activities and responses peculiar to music. Lerdahl has particularly enraged certain sections of the avant-garde music community by claiming that traditional tonal music satisfies his criteria, whereas such forms as serial music do not. This could be used as an explanation of why tonality has been able to resist all attempts to oust it from center stage in music and why many avant-garde genres have but limited appeal. The general thrust of all this thinking about music gets independent support from cognitive theorists (e.g., Ortony, Clore, & Collins, 1988) who characterize the cognitive substrate of all emotion in terms of the violations of various classes of expectations.

These strands of work lead toward the following set of working hypotheses about the vast central bulk of the world's music:

1. One major function of music is to suggest or mediate a range of emotional responses.
2. Common musical structures have particular perceptible properties that support the patterns of expectation underlying such emotions.
3. Expression in musical performance has the effect of making these structural features more prominent, and thus of heightening the emotional response.

20.5   THE ROOTS OF MUSICAL EXPERTISE

At the beginning of this chapter, I asked whether all aspects of musical expertise have anything in common. By a rather circuitous route I now come to a proposed answer, which is that they involve apprehension and use of the structure–emotion link. At whatever level, and for whatever activity, what makes the behavior *musically,* as opposed to technically or perceptually, expert is its manifestation of this link. I take it as axiomatic that emotions do not have to be learned (although they may be refined and differentiated through experience). They are part of the "expert system" with which we are born. So what must be learned is how to apprehend those features of musical structures that can be mapped onto and therefore evoke our existing emotions.

Hevner's (1936) pioneering work showed that adult members of a culture generally agree on the emotional characterization of a passage of music, in that they tend to select similar adjectives to describe it (e.g., majestic, gloomy, playful). Gardner (1973) has shown that this ability develops through childhood, with younger children able to use only rather crude descriptions (such as "loud" or "jumpy"). It is, of course, possible that particular kinds of music have come to acquire conventional meanings by routes that do not involve the listener's own emotions. Laboratory studies of people's abilities to *describe* music do not show how these abilities were acquired.

Direct observational studies of children's emotional responses to music have been rare. Moog's (1976) studies showed that preverbal infants could demonstrate quite strong expressions of delight or fear on hearing music. The available evidence suggests that tone quality is the aspect of music that elicits the strongest early reactions. Smooth, treble-register sounds seem to elicit the strongest reactions of attention and pleasure. Most children below the age of 5 years seem not to be particularly interested in unpitched rhythms and seem not to differentiate emotionally between music played in conventional harmony and that played dissonantly.

As children grow older, it is less easy to record emotional responses by direct observation. Socialization leads to significant suppression of direct emotional expression. An alternative approach that I have been pursuing (Sloboda, 1989) is to ask adults to recall musical experiences from the first ten years of life. The literature on autobiographical memory (Brown & Kulik, 1977; Rubin & Kozin, 1984) suggests that experiences connected with significant emotion may be particularly retrievable. The method also has the advantage of tapping musical experience in a range of naturalistic contexts, rather than in restricted experimental contexts. In addition to asking these adults for information about childhood events and their contexts, I also ask them if those experiences had any particular significance for them. Information about the involvement of music in their lives, including formal music tuition, is also collected.

The findings from these studies indicate that most subjects seem to be capable of producing at least one memory. Some people readily recalled as many as ten different events. No event was recalled from an age earlier than 3 years, but from 4 to 10 years the age spread was fairly even. Analysis of the words used by adults to describe the character of their experiences (both of the music itself and of their reaction to it) showed an interesting age progression. Memories from around age 5 tended to characterize music in rather neutral descriptive terms (e.g., "fast," "loud," "simple"), and the responses to it in terms of general positive enjoyment (e.g., "love," "like," "enjoy," "excited," "happy"). Looking back to age 8, subjects characterized music in terms of its affective or sensual characteristics (e.g., "beautiful," "liquid," "funny"), and the responses to it were recalled in terms of wonder or surprise (e.g., "enthralled," "incredulous," "astounded," "overwhelmed," "awe-struck"). Finally, harking back to around age 9, some memories contained strong feelings of sadness (e.g., "melancholy," "sad," "apprehensive").

It is of particular significance that the ability to respond to music in terms of wonder arises at about the age when children can be shown to distinguish reliably between tonal and atonal music. This strongly suggests that the particular violations of expectations that mediate some of the more "advanced" emotional responses to music require the ability to represent music in terms of the structural categories of tonal music. It is also significant that the progression of responsivity seems to owe nothing to explicit formal instruction. The majority of the experiences reported *preceded* the onset of formal musical training, and in several cases such an experience spurred the child to seek instruction. Learning the structure–emotion link seems to proceed in the absence of formal instruction.

Some of the memories reported clearly had the status of what some people call "peak experiences" — unusual and deeply rewarding experiences of a complex emotional/ intellectual character. The research showed that people who have had such peak experiences were more likely than others to pursue involvement with music for the rest of their life. The experiences provided a strong source of internal motivation to engage with music in a systematic way (arguably in part to increase the likelihood of replicating the experiences). Educators wishing to raise the general level of musical skill might well be advised to consider how they can help increase the frequency of such experiences in the population, because it is clear that not every child has them.

The memory research provided some interesting clues on this latter point as well. It was discovered that almost none of those peak experiences had occurred in situations of external constraint or anxiety. The most likely environment for a peak experience was at home, on one's own or with friends and family, and while listening to music. The least promising environment was at school, with teachers, while performing. The individual stories graphically revealed the kinds of anxieties and humiliations many children were made to suffer in relation to music by insensitive adults or through insensitive educational practices. These acted as strong disincentives to further engagement with music and seemed to block the possibility of making links between emotions and the intrinsic characteristics of music.

A similar lesson emerges from a recent study of leading American concert pianists by Sosniak (1989). None of those in her sample showed exceptional promise as a child, but in every case their early lessons were associated with fun and exploration, rather than with practical achievement. It seems that, at least for the crucial early stages of musical development, there is no special strategy we should recommend to educators, other than to stop worrying about particular apparent skill deficiencies and concentrate on not getting in the way of children's enjoyment and exploration of music. In such contexts, children become natural experts who spontaneously seek what they require to bring their expertise to bear on particular practical accomplishments.

20.6   MUSICAL STRUCTURE AND EMOTION

The final question I wish to raise in this chapter concerns the precise nature of the structure–emotion link: What structures elicit what emotions, and why? Although musicologists have long debated this point (e.g., Cooke, 1959; Meyer, 1956), there have been remarkably few attempts to collect empirical data on it. A few physiological studies (e.g., Goldstein, 1980; Nakamura, 1984) have shown that reliable changes in such indices as heart rate and skin conductance can be shown as people listen to specific pieces of music. But such studies generally have not involved subjecting the music itself to detailed structural analysis. A particular characteristic of emotional responses to music is that they often change in nature and intensity over the duration of a piece and are linked to specific events (rather than being a general "wash" of a particular mood). In this respect, they are similar in nature to emotional responses to drama or fiction. To my knowledge, no published studies provide data on the specific points in musical compositions at which intense or peak emotional experiences take place. One problem is that it is difficult to get intersubjective agreement on how to characterize these experiences. Some of my own research entails an attempt to circumvent this problem by asking people to report (retrospectively, at this stage) on the locations in musical compositions at which they reliably experience direct physical manifestations of emotion (e.g., tears, shivers). A significant minority of subjects have been willing and able to do this and have provided a corpus of some 165 "moments" of reliable emotional response. Full details of this study are reported in Sloboda (1991). An analysis of the subset comprising classical instrumental excerpts has revealed three clusters of structural features associated with three different types of responses. These are summarized in table 20.1. This pattern requires confirmation with other types of music and also by direct observation in experimental situations. If confirmed, it will show that many of the emotional responses to music require that the listener, at some level, represent high-level structure. For instance, one cannot define "melodic appoggiatura" apart from a description of music in terms of strong and weak beats within a metrical structure and of discord and resolution within a tonal framework. This is one reason we find it difficult to respond emotionally to the music of other cultures as do the members of those cultures. We have not yet assimilated the means of representing their musical structures that would allow the appropriate structure–emotion links to be activated.

We have many interesting and important questions to explore, such as why these particular structures mediate these particular emotions in the way that they do. Research, however, has begun to clarify a major strand in musical expertise that distinguishes it starkly from the other forms of expertise represented in this volume. It suggests that the central conditions for acquisition of musical expertise are as follows:

1. Existence in a musical culture of forms that have perceptible structures of certain kinds (as specified by Lerdahl and others)
2. Frequent informal exposure to examples of these forms over a lifetime
3. Existence of a normal range of human emotional responses
4. Opportunity to experience these emotions mediated through perceived musical structures, which in itself requires
5. Opportunity to experience music in contexts free of externally imposed constraints or negative reinforcements

TABLE 20.1   Emotion and Musical Structure

EMOTIONAL RESPONSE	ASSOCIATED STRUCTURAL FEATURES
Tears or lump in throat	Descending circle of 5ths in harmony
	Melodic appoggiatura
	Melodic or harmonic sequence
	Harmonic or melodic acceleration to cadence
Shivers down spine or goose pimples	Enharmonic change
	Delay of final cadence
	New or unprepared harmony
	Sudden dynamic or textural change
Racing heart and "pit of stomach" sensations	Harmonic or melodic acceleration
	Sudden dynamic or textural change
	Repeated syncopation
	Prominent event arriving earlier than expected

If we can ensure these conditions, then the problems associated with bringing individuals to levels of achievement we would currently regard as exceptional may turn out to be trivial.

REFERENCES

Amabile, T. M. (1983). *The social psychology of creativity.* New York: Springer-Verlag.

Balzano, G. J. (1980). The group-theoretic description of twelvefold and microtonal pitch systems. *Computer Music Journal, 4,* 66–84.

Bamberger, J. (1986). Cognitive issues in the development of musically gifted children. In R. J. Sternberg & J. E. Davidson (Eds.), *Conceptions of giftedness* (pp. 388–416). Cambridge: Cambridge University Press.

Bharucha, J. J. (1987). Music cognition and perceptual facilitation: A connectionist framework. *Music Perception, 5,* 1–30.

Bigand, E. (1990). Abstraction of two forms of underlying structure in a tonal melody. *Psychology of Music, 19,* 45–59.

Blacking, J. (1976). *How musical is man?* London: Faber.

Brown, R., & Kulik, J. (1977). Flashbulb memories. *Cognition, 5,* 73–99.

Chase, W. G., & Ericsson, K. A. (1981). Skilled memory. In J. R. Anderson (Ed.), *Cognitive skills and their acquisition* (pp. 141–189). Hillsdale, NJ: Erlbaum.

Chase, W. G., & Simon, H. A. (1973). The mind's eye in chess. In W. G. Chase (Ed.), *Visual information processing* (pp. 215–281). New York: Academic Press.

Clarke, E. F. (1985). Structure and expression in rhythmic performance. In P. Howell, I. Cross, & R. West (Eds.), *Musical structure and cognition* (pp. 209–236). London: Academic Press.

Collier, J. L. (1983). *Louis Armstrong: An American genius.* New York: Oxford University Press.

Cooke, D. (1959). *The language of music.* London: Oxford University Press.

Davidson, L., & Welsh, P. (1988). From collections to structure: The developmental path of tonal thinking. In J. A. Sloboda (Ed.), *Generative processes in music: The psychology of performance, improvisation and composition* (pp. 260–285). London: Oxford University Press.

Deliege, I., & El Ahmahdi, A. (1990). Mechanisms of cue extraction in musical groupings: A study of perception, on *Sequenza VI* for viola solo by Luciano Berio. *Psychology of Music, 19,* 18–44.

Dowling, W. J. (1982). Melodic information processing and its development. In D. Deutsch (Ed.), *The psychology of music* (pp. 413–430). New York: Academic Press.

Dowling, W. J. (1988). Tonal structure and children's early learning of music. In J. A. Sloboda (Ed.), *Generative processes in music: The psychology of performance, improvisation and composition* (pp. 113–128). London: Oxford University Press.

Foder, J. A. (1975). *The language of thought.* Hassocks, Sussex: Harvester Press.

Gabrielsson, A. (1988). Timing in music performance and its relation to music experience. In J. A. Sloboda (Ed.), *Generative processes in music: The psychology of performance, improvisation and composition* (pp. 27–51). London: Oxford University Press.

Gardner, H. (1973). Children's sensitivity to musical styles. *Merrill-Palmer Quarterly of Behavioral Development, 19,* 67–77.

Gardner, H., Davidson, L., & McKernon, P. (1981). The acquisition of song: A developmental approach. In *Documentary report of the Ann Arbor Symposium.* Music Educators' National Conference, Reston, VA.

Goldstein, A. (1980). Thrills in response to music and other stimuli. *Physiological Psychology, 8,* 126–129.

Halpern, A. R., & Bower, G. H. (1982). Musical expertise and melodic structure in memory for musical notation. *American Journal of Psychology, 95,* 31–50.

Hermelin, B., O'Connor, N., & Lee, S. (1987). Musical inventiveness of five idiots-savants. *Psychological Medicine, 17,* 79–90.

Hevner, K. (1936). Experimental studies of the elements of expression in music. *American Journal of Psychology, 48,* 246–268.

Krumhansl, C. (1990). *Tonal structures and music cognition.* New York: Oxford University Press.

Lerdahl, F. (1988a). Tonal pitch space. *Music Perception, 5,* 315–350.

Lerdahl, F. (1988b). Cognitive constraints on compositional systems. In J. A. Sloboda (Ed.), *Generative processes in music: The psychology of performance, improvisation and composition* (pp. 231–259). London: Oxford University Press.

Lerdahl, F., & Jackendoff, R. (1983). *A generative theory of tonal music.* Cambridge, MA: MIT Press.

Marr, D. A. (1982). *Vision.* San Francisco: Freeman.

Meyer, L. B. (1956). *Emotion and meaning in music.* Chicago: University of Chicago Press.

Meyer, L. B. (1973). *Explaining music.* Berkeley: University of California Press.

Miller, L. K. (1987). Sensitivity to tonal structure in a developmentally disabled musical savant. *Psychology of Music, 15,* 76–89.

Moog, H. (1976). *The musical experience of the preschool child* (C. Clarke, Trans.). London: Schott.

Nakamura, H. (1984). Effects of musical emotionality upon GSR and respiration rate: The relationship between verbal reports and physiological responses. *Japanese Journal of Psychology, 55,* 47–50.

Narmour, E. (1977). *Beyond Schenkerism: The need for alternatives in music analysis.* Chicago: University of Chicago Press.

Ortony, A., Clore, G. L., & Collins, A. (1988). *The cognitive structure of the emotions.* Cambridge: Cambridge University Press.

Rasch, R. A. (1988). Timing and synchronization in ensemble performance. In J. A. Sloboda (Ed.), *Generative processes in music: The psychology of performance, improvisation and composition* (pp. 70–90). London: Oxford University Press.

Revesz, G. (1925). *The psychology of a musical prodigy.* London: Kegan Paul, Trench, & Trubner.

Rubin, D. C., & Kozin, M. (1984). Vivid memories. *Cognition, 16,* 81–95.

Shaffer, L. H. (1981). Performance of Chopin, Bach, and Bartok: Studies in motor programming. *Cognitive Psychology, 13,* 326–376.

Shepard, R. N. (1982). Structural representations of musical pitch. In D. Deutsch (Ed.), *The psychology of music* (pp. 344–390). New York: Academic Press.

Sloboda, J. A. (1976a). The effect of item position on the likelihood of identification by inference in prose reading and music reading. *Canadian Journal of Psychology, 30,* 228–236.

Sloboda, J. A. (1976b). Phrase units as determinants of visual processing in music reading. *British Journal of Psychology, 68,* 117–124.

Sloboda, J. A. (1983). The communication of musical metre in piano performance. *Quarterly Journal of Experimental Psychology, A35,* 377–396.

Sloboda, J. A. (1984). Experimental studies of music reading: A review. *Music Perception, 2,* 222–236.

Sloboda, J. A. (1985a). *The musical mind: The cognitive psychology of music.* London: Oxford University Press.

Sloboda, J. A. (1985b). Expressive skill in two pianists: Style and effectiveness in music performance. *Canadian Journal of Psychology, 39,* 273–293.

Sloboda, J. A. (1989). Music as a language. In F. Wilson & F. Roehmann (Eds.), *Music and child development: Proceedings of the 1987 Biology of Music Making Conference* (pp. 28–43). St. Louis: MMB Music.

Sloboda, J. A. (1991). Music structure and emotional response: Some empirical findings. *Psychology of Music, 19* (2), 110–120.

Sloboda, J. A., Hermelin, B., & O'Connor, N. (1985). An exceptional musical memory. *Music Perception, 3,* 155–170.

Sloboda, J. A., & Parker, D. H. H. (1985). Immediate recall of melodies. In P. Howell, I. Cross, & R. West (Eds.), *Musical structure and cognition* (pp. 143–167). London: Academic Press.

Sosniak, L. (1989). From tyro to virtuoso: A long-term commitment to learning. In F. Wilson & F. Roehmann (Eds.), *Music and child development: Proceedings of the 1987 Biology of Music Making Conference* (pp. 274–290). St. Louis: MMB Music.

Sundberg, J. (1988). Computer synthesis of musical performance. In J. A. Sloboda (Ed.), *Generative processes in music: The psychology of performance, improvisation and composition* (pp. 52–59). London: Oxford University Press.

Todd, N. (1985). A model of expressive timing in tonal music. *Music Perception, 3,* 33–58.

Treffert, D. A. (1988). The idiot savant: A review of the syndrome. *American Journal of Psychiatry, 145,* 563–572.

Ward, W. D., & Burns, E. M. (1982). Absolute pitch. In D. Deutsch (Ed.), *The psychology of music* (pp. 431–452). New York: Academic Press.

Zenatti, A. (1969). *Le développement génétique de la perception musicale.* Monographies Français Psychologique No. 17.

CHAPTER TWENTY-ONE

JUDGMENT UNDER UNCERTAINTY: HEURISTICS AND BIASES

AMOS TVERSKY AND DANIEL KAHNEMAN

Many decisions are based on beliefs concerning the likelihood of uncertain events such as the outcome of an election, the guilt of a defendant, or the future value of the dollar. These beliefs are usually expressed in statements such as "I think that [. . .]," "chances are [. . .]," "it is unlikely that [. . .]," and so forth. Occasionally, beliefs concerning uncertain events are expressed in numerical form as odds or subjective probabilities. What determines such beliefs? How do people assess the probability of an uncertain event or the value of an uncertain quantity? This article shows that people rely on a limited number of heuristic principles which reduce the complex tasks of assessing probabilities and predicting values to simpler judgmental operations. In general, these heuristics are quite useful, but sometimes they lead to severe and systematic errors.

The subjective assessment of probability resembles the subjective assessment of physical quantities such as distance or size. These judgments are all based on data of limited validity, which are processed according to heuristic rules. For example, the apparent distance of an object is determined in part by its clarity. The more sharply the object is seen, the closer it appears to be. This rule has some validity, because in any given scene the more distant objects are seen less sharply than nearer objects. However, the reliance on this rule leads to systematic errors in the estimation of distance. Specifically, distances are often overestimated when visibility is poor because the contours of objects are blurred. On the other hand, distances are often underestimated when visibility is good because the objects are seen sharply. Thus, the reliance on clarity as an indication of distance leads to common biases. Such biases are also found in the intuitive judgment of probability. This article describes three heuristics that are employed to assess probabilities and to predict values. Biases to which these heuristics lead are enumerated, and the applied and theoretical implications of these observations are discussed.

From *Science* 185, no. 415 (1974): 1124–1131. Reprinted with permission from AAAS.

21.1   REPRESENTATIVENESS

Many of the probabilistic questions with which people are concerned belong to one of the following types: What is the probability that object A belongs to class B? What is the probability that event A originates from process B? What is the probability that process B will generate event A? In answering such questions, people typically rely on the representativeness heuristic, in which probabilities are evaluated by the degree to which A is representative of B, that is, by the degree to which A resembles B. For example, when A is highly representative of B, the probability that A originates from B is judged to be high. On the other hand, if A is not similar to B, the probability that A originates from B is judged to be low.

For an illustration of judgment by representativeness, consider an individual who has been described by a former neighbor as follows: "Steve is very shy and withdrawn, invariably helpful, but with little interest in people, or in the world of reality. A meek and tidy soul, he has a need for order and structure, and a passion for detail." How do people assess the probability that Steve is engaged in a particular occupation from a list of possibilities (for example, farmer, salesman, airline pilot, librarian, or physician)? How do people order these occupations from most to least likely? In the representativeness heuristic, the probability that Steve is a librarian, for example, is assessed by the degree to which he is representative of, or similar to, the stereotype of a librarian. Indeed, research with problems of this type has shown that people order the occupations by probability and by similarity in exactly the same way (Kahneman & Tversky, 1973, 4). This approach to the judgment of probability leads to serious errors, because similarity, or representativeness, is not influenced by several factors that should affect judgments of probability.

21.1.1   Insensitivity to Prior Probability of Outcomes

One of the factors that have no effect on representativeness but should have a major effect on probability is the prior probability, or base-rate frequency, of the outcomes. In the case of Steve, for example, the fact that there are many more farmers than librarians in the population should enter into any reasonable estimate of the probability that Steve is a librarian rather than a farmer. Considerations of base-rate frequency, however, do not affect the similarity of Steve to the stereotypes of librarians and farmers. If people evaluate probability by representativeness, therefore, prior probabilities will be neglected. This hypothesis was tested in an experiment where prior probabilities were manipulated (Kahneman & Tversky, 1973, 4). Subjects were shown brief personality descriptions of several individuals, allegedly sampled at random from a group of 100 professionals — engineers and lawyers. The subjects were asked to assess, for each description, the probability that it belonged to an engineer rather than to a lawyer. In one experimental condition, subjects were told that the group from which the descriptions had been drawn consisted of 70 engineers and 30 lawyers. In another condition, subjects were told that the group consisted of 30 engineers and 70 lawyers. The odds that any particular description belongs to an engineer rather than to a lawyer should be higher in the first condition, where there is a majority of engineers, than in the second condition, where there is a majority of lawyers. Specifically, it can be shown by applying Bayes' rule that the ratio of these odds should be $(.7/.3)^2$, or 5.44, for each description. In a sharp violation of Bayes' rule, the subjects in the two conditions produced essentially the same probability judgments. Apparently, subjects evaluated the likelihood that a particular description belonged to an engineer rather than to a lawyer by the degree to which this description was representative of the two stereotypes, with little or no regard for the prior probabilities of the categories.

The subjects used prior probabilities correctly when they had no other information. In the absence of a personality sketch, they judged the probability that an unknown individual is an engineer to be .7 and .3, respectively, in the two base-rate conditions. However, prior probabilities were effectively ignored when a description was introduced, even when this description was totally uninformative. The responses to the following description illustrate this phenomenon:

> Dick is a 30 year old man. He is married with no children. A man of high ability and high motivation, he promises to be quite successful in his field. He is well liked by his colleagues.

This description was intended to convey no information relevant to the question of whether Dick is an engineer or a lawyer. Consequently, the probability that Dick is an engineer should equal the proportion of engineers in the group, as if no description had been given. The subjects, however, judged the probability of Dick being an engineer to be .5 regardless of whether the stated proportion of engineers in the group was .7 or .3. Evidently, people respond differently when given no evidence and when given worthless evidence. When no specific evidence is given, prior probabilities are properly utilized; when worthless evidence is given, prior probabilities are ignored (Kahneman & Tversky, 1973, 4).

21.1.2   Insensitivity to Sample Size

To evaluate the probability of obtaining a particular result in a sample drawn from a specified population, people typically apply the representativeness heuristic. That is, they assess the likelihood of a sample result, for example, that the average height in a random sample of ten men will be 6 feet (180 centimeters), by the similarity of this result to the corresponding parameter (that is, to the average height in the population of men). The similarity of a sample statistic to a population parameter does not depend on the size of the sample. Consequently, if probabilities are assessed by representativeness, then the judged probability of a sample statistic will be essentially independent of sample size. Indeed, when subjects assessed the distributions of average height for samples of various sizes, they produced identical distributions. For example, the probability of obtaining an average height greater than 6 feet was assigned the same value for samples of 1000, 100, and 10 men (Kahneman & Tversky, 1972, 3). Moreover, subjects failed to appreciate the role of sample size even when it was emphasized in the formulation of the problem. Consider the following question:

> A certain town is served by two hospitals. In the larger hospital about 45 babies are born each day, and in the smaller hospital about 15 babies are born each day. As you know, about 50 percent of all babies are boys. However, the exact percentage varies from day to day. Sometimes it may be higher than 50 percent, sometimes lower.
>
> For a period of 1 year, each hospital recorded the days on which more than 60 percent of the babies born were boys. Which hospital do you think recorded more such days?
> The larger hospital (21)
> The smaller hospital (21)
> About the same (that is, within 5 percent of each other) (53)

The values in parentheses are the number of undergraduate students who chose each answer.

Most subjects judged the probability of obtaining more than 60 percent boys to be the same in the small and in the large hospital, presumably because these events are described by the same statistic and are therefore equally representative of the general population. In contrast, sampling theory entails that the expected number of days on which more than 60 percent of the babies are boys is much greater in the small hospital than in the large one, because a large sample is less likely to stray from 50 percent. This fundamental notion of statistics is evidently not part of people's repertoire of intuitions.

A similar insensitivity to sample size has been reported in judgments of posterior probability, that is, of the probability that a sample has been drawn from one population rather than from another. Consider the following example:

> Imagine an urn filled with balls, of which $\frac{2}{3}$ are of one color and $\frac{1}{3}$ of another. One individual has drawn 5 balls from the urn, and found that 4 were red and 1 was white. Another individual has drawn 20 balls and found that 12 were red and 8 were white. Which of the two individuals should feel more confident that the urn contains $\frac{2}{3}$ red balls and $\frac{1}{3}$ white balls, rather than the opposite? What odds should each individual give?

In this problem, the correct posterior odds are 8 to 1 for the 4:1 sample and 16 to 1 for the 12:8 sample, assuming equal prior probabilities. However, most people feel that the first sample provides much stronger evidence for the hypothesis that the urn is predominantly red, because the proportion of red balls is larger in the first than in the second sample. Here again, intuitive judgments are dominated by the sample proportion and are essentially unaffected by the size of the sample, which plays a crucial role in the determination of the actual posterior odds (Kahneman & Tversky, 1972). In addition, intuitive estimates of posterior odds are far less extreme than the correct values. The underestimation of the impact of evidence has been observed repeatedly in problems of this type (W. Edwards, 1968, 25; Slovic & Lichtenstein, 1971). It has been labeled "conservatism."

21.1.3   Misconceptions of Chance

People expect that a sequence of events generated by a random process will represent the essential characteristics of that process even when the sequence is short. In considering tosses of a coin for heads or tails, for example, people regard the sequence H-T-H-T-T-H to be more likely than the sequence H-H-H-T-T-T, which does not appear random, and also more likely than the sequence H-H-H-H-T-H, which does not represent the fairness of the coin (Kahneman & Tversky, 1972b, 3). Thus, people expect that the essential characteristics of the process will be represented, not only globally in the entire sequence, but also locally in each of its parts. A locally representative sequence, however, deviates systematically from chance expectation: it contains too many alternations and too few runs. Another consequence of the belief in local representativeness is the well-known gambler's fallacy. After observing a long run of red on the roulette wheel, for example, most people erroneously believe that black is now due, presumably because the occurence of black will result in a more representative sequence than the occurrence of an additional red. Chance is commonly viewed as a self-correcting process in which a deviation in one direction induces a deviation in the opposite direction to restore the equilibrium. In fact, deviations are not "corrected" as a chance process unfolds, they are merely diluted.

Misconceptions of chance are not limited to naive subjects. A study of the statistical intuitions of experienced research psychologists (Tversky & Kahneman, 1971, 2) revealed a lingering belief in what may be called the "law of small numbers," according to which even small samples are highly representative of the populations from which they are drawn. The responses of these investigators reflected the expectation that a valid hypothesis about a population will be represented by a statistically significant result in a sample — with little regard for its size. As a consequence, the researchers put too much faith in the results of small samples and grossly overestimated the replicability of such results. In the actual conduct of research, this bias leads to the selection of samples of inadequate size and to overinterpretation of findings.

21.1.4   Insensitivity to Predictability

People are sometimes called upon to make such numerical predictions as the future value of a stock, the demand for a commodity, or the outcome of a football game. Such predictions are often made by representativeness. For example, suppose one is given a description of a company and is asked to predict its future profit. If the description of the company is very favorable, a very high profit will appear most representative of that description; if the description is mediocre, a mediocre performance will appear most representative. The degree to which the description is favorable is unaffected by the reliability of that description or by the degree to which it permits accurate prediction. Hence, if people predict solely in terms of the favorableness of the description, their predictions will be insensitive to the reliability of the evidence and to the expected accuracy of the prediction.

This mode of judgment violates the normative statistical theory in which the extremeness and the range of predictions are controlled by considerations of predictability. When predictability is nil, the same prediction should be made in all cases. For example, if the descriptions of companies provide no information relevant to profit, then the same value (such as average profit) should be predicted for all companies. If predictability is perfect, of course, the values predicted will match the actual values and the range of predictions will equal the range of outcomes. In general, the higher the predictability, the wider the range of predicted values.

Several studies of numerical prediction have demonstrated that intuitive predictions violate this rule, and that subjects show little or no regard for considerations of predictability (Kahneman & Tversky, 1973, 4). In one of these studies, subjects were presented with several paragraphs, each describing the performance of a student teacher during a particular practice lesson. Some subjects were asked to *evaluate* the quality of the lesson described in the paragraph in percentile scores, relative to a specified population. Other subjects were asked to *predict,* also in percentile scores, the standing of each student teacher 5 years after the practice lesson. The judgments made under the two conditions were identical. That is, the prediction of a remote criterion (success of a teacher after 5 years) was identical to the evaluation of the information on which the prediction was based (the quality of the practice lesson). The students who made these predictions were undoubtedly aware of the limited predictability of teaching competence on the basis of a single trial lesson 5 years earlier; nevertheless, their predictions were as extreme as their evaluations.

21.1.5   The Illusion of Validity

As we have seen, people often predict by selecting the outcome (for example, an occupation) that is most representative of the input (for example, the description of a person). The confidence they have in their prediction depends primarily on the degree of representativeness (that is, on the quality of the match between the selected outcome and the input) with little or no regard for the factors that limit predictive accuracy. Thus, people express great confidence in the prediction that a person is a librarian when given a description of his personality which matches the stereotype of librarians, even if the description is scanty, unreliable, or outdated. The unwarranted confidence which is produced by a good fit between the predicted outcome and the input information may be called the illusion of validity. This illusion persists even when the judge is aware of the factors that limit the accuracy of his predictions. It is a common observation that psychologists who conduct selection interviews often experience considerable confidence in their predictions, even when they know of the vast literature that shows selection interviews to be highly fallible. The continued reliance on the clinical interview for selection, despite repeated demonstrations of its inadequacy, amply attests to the strength of this effect.

The internal consistency of a pattern of inputs is a major determinant of one's confidence in predictions based on these inputs. For example, people express more confidence in predicting the final grade-point average of a student whose first-year record consists entirely of B's than in predicting the grade-point average of a student whose first-year record includes many A's and C's. Highly consistent patterns are most often observed when the input variables are highly redundant or correlated. Hence, people tend to have great confidence in predictions based on redundant input variables. However, an elementary result in the statistics of correlation asserts that, given input variables of stated validity, a prediction based on several such inputs can achieve higher accuracy when they are independent of each other than when they are redundant or correlated. Thus, redundancy among inputs decreases accuracy even as it increases confidence, and people are often-confident in predictions that are quite likely to be off the mark (Kahneman & Tversky, 1973, 4).

21.1.6   Misconceptions of Regression

Suppose a large group of children has been examined on two equivalent versions of an aptitude test. If one selects ten children from among those who did best on one of the two versions, he will usually find their performance on the second version to be somewhat disappointing. Conversely, if one selects ten children from among those who did worst on one version, they will be found, on the average, to do somewhat better on the other version. More generally, consider two variables X and Y which have the same distribution. If one selects individuals whose average X score deviates from the mean of X by k units, then the average of their Y scores will usually deviate from the mean of Y by less than k units. These observations illustrate a general phenomenon known as regression toward the mean, which was first documented by Galton more than 100 years ago.

In the normal course of life, one encounters many instances of regression toward the mean, in the comparison of the height of fathers and sons, of the intelligence of husbands and wives, or of the performance of individuals on consecutive examinations. Nevertheless, people do not develop correct intuitions about this phenomenon. First, they do not expect regression in many contexts where it is bound to occur. Second, when they recognize the occurrence of regression, they often invent spurious causal explanations for it (Kahneman & Tversky, 1973, 4). We suggest that the phenomenon of regression remains elusive because it is incompatible with the belief that the predicted outcome should be maximally representative of the input, and, hence, that the value of the outcome variable should be as extreme as the value of the input variable.

The failure to recognize the import of regression can have pernicious consequences, as illustrated by the following observation (Kahneman & Tversky, 1973, 4). In a discussion of flight training, experienced instructors noted that praise for an exceptionally smooth landing is typically followed by a poorer landing on the next try, while harsh criticism after a rough landing is usually followed by an improvement on the next try. The instructors concluded that verbal rewards are detrimental to learning, while verbal punishments are beneficial, contrary to accepted psychological doctrine. This conclusion is unwarranted because of the presence of regression toward the mean. As in other cases of repeated examination, an improvement will usually follow a poor performance and a deterioration will usually follow an outstanding performance, even if the instructor does not respond to the trainee's achievement on the first attempt. Because the instructors had praised their trainees after good landings and admonished them after poor ones, they reached the erroneous and potentially harmful conclusion that punishment is more effective than reward.

Thus, the failure to understand the effect of regression leads one to over-estimate the effectiveness of punishment and to underestimate the effectiveness of reward. In social interaction, as well as in training, rewards are typically administered when performance is good, and punishments are typically administered when performance is poor. By regression alone, therefore, behavior is most likely to improve after punishment and most likely to deteriorate after reward. Consequently, the human condition is such that, by chance alone, one is most often rewarded for punishing others and most often punished for rewarding them. People are generally not aware of this contingency. In fact, the elusive role of regression in determining the apparent consequences of reward and punishment seems to have escaped the notice of students of this area.

21.2   AVAILABILITY

There are situations in which people assess the frequency of a class or the probability of an event by the ease with which instances or occurrences can be brought to mind. For example, one may assess the risk of heart attack among middle-aged people by recalling such occurrences among one's acquaintances. Similarly, one may evaluate the probability that a given business venture will fail by imagining various difficulties it could encounter. This judgmental heuristic is called availability. Availability is a useful clue for assessing frequency or probability, because instances of large classes are usually reached better and faster than instances of less frequent classes. However, availability is affected by factors other than frequency and probability. Consequently, the reliance on availability leads to predictable biases, some of which are illustrated below.

21.2.1   Biases Due to the Retrievability of Instances

When the size of a class is judged by the availability of its instances, a class whose instances are easily retrieved will appear more numerous than a class of equal frequency whose instances are less retrievable. In an elementary demonstration of this effect, subjects heard a list of well-known personalities of both sexes and were subsequently asked to judge whether the list contained more names of men than of women. Different lists were presented to different groups of subjects. In some of the lists the men were relatively more famous than the women, and in others the women were relatively more famous than the men. In each of the lists, the subjects erroneously judged that the class (sex) that had the more famous personalities was the more numerous (Tversky & Kahneman, 1973, 11).

In addition to familiarity, there are other factors, such as salience, which affect the retrievability of instances. For example, the impact of seeing a house burning on the subjective probability of such accidents is probably greater than the impact of reading about a fire in the local paper. Furthermore, recent occurrences are likely to be relatively more available than earlier occurrences. It is a common experience that the subjective probability of traffic accidents rises temporarily when one sees a car overturned by the side of the road.

21.2.2   Biases Due to the Effectiveness of a Search Set

Suppose one samples a word (of three letters or more) at random from an English text. Is it more likely that the word starts with r or that r is the third letter? People approach this problem by recalling words that begin with r (road) and words that have r in the third position (car) and assess the relative frequency by the ease with which words of the two types come to mind. Because it is much easier to search for words by their first letter than by their third letter, most people judge words that begin with a given consonant to be more numerous than words in which the same consonant appears in the third position. They do so even for consonants, such as r or k, that are more frequent in the third position than in the first (Tversky & Kahneman, 1973, 11).

Different tasks elicit different search sets. For example, suppose you are asked to rate the frequency with which abstract words (*thought, love*) and concrete words (*door, water*) appear in written English. A natural way to answer this question is to search for contexts in which the word could appear. It seems easier to think of contexts in which an abstract concept is mentioned (*love* in love stories) than to think of contexts in which a concrete word (such as *door*) is mentioned. If the frequency of words is judged by the availability of the contexts in which they appear, abstract words will be judged as relatively more numerous than concrete words. This bias has been observed in a study (Galbraith & Underwood, 1973) which showed that the judged frequency of occurrence of abstract words was much higher than that of concrete words, equated in objective frequency. Abstract words were also judged to appear in a much greater variety of contexts than concrete words.

21.2.3   Biases of Imaginability

Sometimes one has to assess the frequency of a class whose instances are not stored in memory but can be generated according to a given rule. In such situations, one typically generates several instances and evaluates frequency or probability by the ease with which the relevant instances can be constructed. However, the ease of constructing instances does not always reflect their actual frequency, and this mode of evaluation is prone to biases. To illustrate, consider a group of 10 people who form committees of k members, $2 \leq k \leq 8$. How many different committees of k members can be formed? The correct answer to this problem is given by the binomial coefficient $\binom{10}{K}$ which reaches a maximum of 252 for $k = 5$. Clearly, the number of committees of k members equals the number of committees of $(10 - k)$ members, because any committee of k members defines a unique group of $(10 - k)$ nonmembers.

One way to answer this question without computation is to mentally construct committees of k members and to evaluate their number by the ease with which they come to mind. Committees of few members, say 2, are more available than committees of many members, say 8. The simplest scheme for the construction of committees is a partition of the group into disjoint sets. One readily sees that it is easy to construct five disjoint committees of 2 members, while it is impossible to generate even two disjoint committees of 8 members. Consequently, if frequency is assessed by imaginability, or by availability for construction, the small committees will appear more numerous than larger committees, in contrast to the correct bell-shaped function. Indeed, when naive subjects were asked to estimate the number of distinct committees of various sizes, their estimates were a decreasing monotonic function of committee size (Tversky & Kahneman, 1973, 11). For example, the median estimate of the number of committees of 2 members was 70, while the estimate for committees of 8 members was 20 (the correct answer is 45 in both cases).

Imaginability plays an important role in the evaluation of probabilities in real-life situations. The risk involved in an adventurous expedition, for example, is evaluated by imagining contingencies with which the expedition is not equipped to cope. If many such difficulties are vividly portrayed, the expedition can be made to appear exceedingly dangerous, although the ease with which disasters are imagined need not reflect their actual likelihood. Conversely, the risk involved in an undertaking may be grossly underestimated if some possible dangers are either difficult to conceive of, or simply do not come to mind.

21.2.4   Illusory Correlation

Chapman and Chapman (1969) have described an interesting bias in the judgment of the frequency with which two events co-occur. They presented naive judges with information concerning several hypothetical mental patients. The data for each patient consisted of a clinical diagnosis and a drawing of a person made by the patient. Later the judges estimated the frequency with which each diagnosis (such as paranoia or suspiciousness) had been accompanied by various features of the drawing (such as peculiar eyes). The subjects markedly overestimated the frequency of co-occurrence of natural associates, such as suspiciousness and peculiar eyes. This effect was labeled illusory correlation. In their erroneous judgments of the data to which they had been exposed, naive subjects "rediscovered" much of the common, but unfounded, clinical lore concerning the interpretation of the draw-a-person test. The illusory correlation effect was extremely resistant to contradictory data. It persisted even when the correlation between symptom and diagnosis was actually negative, and it prevented the judges from detecting relationships that were in fact present.

Availability provides a natural account for the illusory-correlation effect. The judgment of how frequently two events co-occur could be based on the strength of the associative bond between them. When the association is strong, one is likely to conclude that the events have been frequently paired. Consequently, strong associates will be judged to have occurred together frequently. According to this view, the illusory correlation between suspiciousness and peculiar drawing of the eyes, for example, is due to the fact that suspiciousness is more readily associated with the eyes than with any other part of the body.

Lifelong experience has taught us that, in general, instances of large classes are recalled better and faster than instances of less frequent classes; that likely occurrences are easier to imagine than unlikely ones; and that the associative connections between events are strengthened when the events frequently co-occur. As a result, man has at his disposal a procedure (the availability heuristic) for estimating the numerosity of a class, the likelihood of an event, or the frequency of co-occurrences, by the ease with which the relevant mental operations of retrieval, construction, or association can be performed. However, as the preceding examples have demonstrated, this valuable estimation procedure results in systematic errors.

21.3   ADJUSTMENT AND ANCHORING

In many situations, people make estimates by starting from an initial value that is adjusted to yield the final answer. The initial value, or starting point, may be suggested by the formulation of the problem, or it may be the result of a partial computation. In either case, adjustments are typically insufficient (Slovic & Lichtenstein, 1971). That is, different starting points yield different estimates, which are biased toward the initial values. We call this phenomenon anchoring.

21.3.1   Insufficient Adjustment

In a demonstration of the anchoring effect, subjects were asked to estimate various quantities, stated in percentages (for example, the percentage of African countries in the United Nations). For each quantity, a number between 0 and 100 was determined by spinning a wheel of fortune in the subjects' presence. The subjects were instructed to indicate first whether that number was higher or lower than the value of the quantity, and then to estimate the value of the quantity by moving upward or downward from the given number. Different groups were given different numbers for each quantity, and these arbitrary numbers had a marked effect on estimates. For example, the median estimates of the percentage of African countries in the United Nations were 25 and 45 for groups that received 10 and 65, respectively, as starting points. Payoffs for accuracy did not reduce the anchoring effect.

Anchoring occurs not only when the starting point is given to the subject, but also when the subject bases his estimate on the result of some incomplete computation. A study of intuitive numerical estimation illustrates this effect. Two groups of high school students estimated, within 5 seconds, a numerical expression that was written on the blackboard. One group estimated the product

$$8 \times 7 \times 6 \times 5 \times 4 \times 3 \times 2 \times 1$$

while another group estimated the product

$$1 \times 2 \times 3 \times 4 \times 5 \times 6 \times 7 \times 8$$

To rapidly answer such questions, people may perform a few steps of computation and estimate the product by extrapolation or adjustment. Because adjustments are typically insufficient, this procedure should lead to underestimation. Furthermore, because the result of the first few steps of multiplication (performed from left to right) is higher in the descending sequence than in the ascending sequence, the former expression should be judged larger than the latter. Both predictions were confirmed. The median estimate for the ascending sequence was 512, while the median estimate for the descending sequence was 2,250. The correct answer is 40,320.

21.4.1   Biases in the Evaluation of Conjunctive and Disjunctive Events

In a recent study by Bar-Hillel (1973) subjects were given the opportunity to bet on one of two events. Three types of events were used: (i) simple events, such as drawing a red marble from a bag containing 50 percent red marbles and 50 percent white marbles; (ii) conjunctive events, such as drawing a red marble seven times in succession, with replacement, from a bag containing 90 percent red marbles and 10 percent white marbles; and (iii) disjunctive events, such as drawing a red marble at least once in seven successive tries, with replacement, from a bag containing 10 percent red marbles and 90 percent white marbles. In this problem, a significant majority of subjects preferred to bet on the conjunctive event (the probability of which is .48) rather than on the simple event (the probability of which is .50). Subjects also preferred to bet on the simple event rather than on the disjunctive event, which has a probability of .52. Thus, most subjects bet on the less likely event in both comparisons. This pattern of choices illustrates a general finding. Studies of choice among gambles and of judgments of probability indicate that people tend to overestimate the probability of conjunctive events (Cohen, Chesnick, & Haran, 1972, 24) and to underestimate the probability of disjunctive events. These biases are readily explained as effects of anchoring. The stated probability of the elementary event (success at any one stage) provides a natural starting point for the estimation of the probabilities of both conjunctive and disjunctive events. Since adjustment from the starting point is typically insufficient, the final estimates remain too close to the probabilities of the elementary events in both cases. Note that the overall probability of a conjunctive event is lower than the probability of each elementary event, whereas the overall probability of a disjunctive event is higher than the probability of each elementary event. As a consequence of anchoring, the overall probability will be overestimated in conjunctive problems and under-estimated in disjunctive problems.

Biases in the evaluation of compound events are particularly significant in the context of planning. The successful completion of an undertaking, such as the development of a new product, typically has a conjunctive character: for the undertaking to succeed, each of a series of events must occur. Even when each of these events is very likely, the overall probability of success can be quite low if the number of events is large. The general tendency to overestimate the probability of conjunctive events leads to unwarranted optimism in the evaluation of the likelihood that a plan will succeed or that a project will be completed on time. Conversely, disjunctive structures are typically encountered in the evaluation of risks. A complex system, such as a nuclear reactor or a human body, will malfunction if any of its essential components fails. Even when the likelihood of failure in each component is slight, the probability of an overall failure can be high if many components are involved. Because of anchoring, people will tend to underestimate the probabilities of failure in complex systems.

Thus, the direction of the anchoring bias can sometimes be inferred from the structure of the event. The chain-like structure of conjunctions leads to overestimation, the funnel-like structure of disjunctions leads to underestimation.

21.4.2   Anchoring in the Assessment of Subjective Probability Distributions

In decision analysis, experts are often required to express their beliefs about a quantity, such as the value of the Dow-Jones average on a particular day, in the form of a probability distribution. Such a distribution is usually constructed by asking the person to select values of the quantity that correspond to specified percentiles of his subjective probability distribution. For example, the judge may be asked to select a number, X_{90}, such that his subjective probability that this number will be higher than the value of the Dow-Jones average is .90. That is, he should select the value X_{90} so that he is just willing to accept 9 to 1 odds that the Dow-Jones average will not exceed it. A subjective probability distribution for the value of the Dow-Jones average can be constructed from several such judgments corresponding to different percentiles.

By collecting subjective probability distributions for many different quantities, it is possible to test the judge for proper calibration. A judge is properly (or externally) calibrated in a set of problems if exactly Π percent of the true values of the assessed quantities fall below his stated values of X_{Π}. For example, the true values should fall below X_{01} for 1 percent of the quantities and above X_{99} for 1 percent of the quantities. Thus, the true values should fall in the confidence interval between X_{01} and X_{99} on 98 percent of the problems.

Several investigators (Alpert & Raiffa, 1969, 21; Staël von Holstein, 1971; Winkler, 1967) have obtained probability disruptions for many quantities from a large number of judges. These distributions indicated large and systematic departures from proper calibration. In most studies, the actual values of the assessed quantities are either smaller than X_{01} or greater than X_{99} for about 30 percent of the problems. That is, the subjects state overly narrow confidence intervals which reflect more certainty than is justified by their knowledge about the assessed quantities. This bias is common to naive and to sophisticated subjects, and it is not eliminated by introducing proper scoring rules, which provide incentives for external calibration. This effect is attributable, in part at least, to anchoring.

To select X_{90} for the value of the Dow-Jones average, for example, it is natural to begin by thinking about one's best estimate of the Dow-Jones and to adjust this value upward. If this adjustment — like most others — is insufficient, then X_{90} will not be sufficiently extreme. A similar anchoring effect will occur in the selection of X_{10}, which is presumably obtained by adjusting one's best estimate downward. Consequently, the confidence interval between X_{10} and X_{90} will be too narrow, and the assessed probability distribution will be too tight. In support of this interpretation it can be shown that subjective probabilities are systematically altered by a procedure in which one's best estimate does not serve as an anchor.

Subjective probability distributions for a given quantity (the Dow-Jones average) can be obtained in two different ways: (i) by asking the subject to select values of the Dow-Jones that correspond to specified percentiles of his probability distribution and (ii) by asking the subject to assess the probabilities that the true value of the Dow-Jones will exceed some specified values. The two procedures are formally equivalent and should yield identical distributions. However, they suggest different modes of adjustment from different anchors. In procedure (i), the natural starting point is one's best estimate of the quality. In procedure (ii), on the other hand, the subject may be anchored on the value stated in the question. Alternatively, he may be anchored on even odds, or 50–50 chances, which is a natural starting point in the estimation of likelihood. In either case, procedure (ii) should yield less extreme odds than procedure (i).

To contrast the two procedures, a set of 24 quantities (such as the air distance from New Delhi to Peking) was presented to a group of subjects who assessed either X_{10} or X_{90} for each problem. Another group of subjects received the median judgment of the first group for each of the 24 quantities. They were asked to assess the odds that each of the given values exceeded the true value of the relevant quantity. In the absence of any bias, the second group should retrieve the odds specified to the first group, that is, 9:1. However, if even odds or the stated value serve as anchors, the odds of the second group should be less extreme, that is, closer to 1:1. Indeed, the median odds stated by this group, across all problems, were 3:1. When the judgments of the two groups were tested for external calibration, it was found that subjects in the first group were too extreme, in accord with earlier studies. The events that they defined as having a probability of .10 actually obtained in 24 percent of the cases. In contrast, subjects in the second group were too conservative. Events to which they assigned an average probability of .34 actually obtained in 26 percent of the cases. These results illustrate the manner in which the degree of calibration depends on the procedure of elicitation.

21.5   DISCUSSION

This article has been concerned with cognitive biases that stem from the reliance on judgmental heuristics. These biases are not attributable to motivational effects such as wishful thinking or the distortion of judgments by payoffs and penalties. Indeed, several of the severe errors of judgment reported earlier occurred despite the fact that subjects were encouraged to be accurate and were rewarded for the correct answers (Kahneman & Tversky, 1972, 3; Tversky & Kahneman, 1973, 11).

The reliance on heuristics and the prevalence of biases are not restricted to laymen. Experienced researchers are also prone to the same biases — when they think intuitively. For example, the tendency to predict the outcome that best represents the data, with insufficient regard for prior probability, has been observed in the intuitive judgments of individuals who have had extensive training in statistics (Kahneman & Tversky, 1973, 4; Tversky & Kahneman, 1971, 2). Although the statistically sophisticated avoid elementary errors, such as the gambler's fallacy, their intuitive judgments are liable to similar fallacies in more intricate and less transparent problems.

It is not surprising that useful heuristics such as representativeness and availability are retained, even though they occasionally lead to errors in prediction or estimation. What is perhaps surprising is the failure of people to infer from lifelong experience such fundamental statistical rules as regression toward the mean, or the effect of sample size on sampling variability. Although everyone is exposed, in the normal course of life, to numerous examples from which these rules could have been induced, very few people discover the principles of sampling and regression on their own. Statistical principles are not learned from everyday experience because the relevant instances are not coded appropriately. For example, people do not discover that successive lines in a text differ more in average word length than do successive pages, because they simply do not attend to the average word length of individual lines or pages. Thus, people do not learn the relation between sample size and sampling variability, although the data for such learning are abundant.

The lack of an appropriate code also explains why people usually do not detect the biases in their judgments of probability. A person could conceivably learn whether his judgments are externally calibrated by keeping a tally of the proportion of events that actually occur among those to which he assigns the same probability. However, it is not natural to group events by their judged probability. In the absence of such grouping it is impossible for an individual to discover, for example, that only 50 percent of the predictions to which he has assigned a probability of .9 or higher actually come true.

The empirical analysis of cognitive biases has implications for the theoretical and applied role of judged probabilities. Modern decision theory (de Finetti, 1968; Savage, 1954) regards subjective probability as the quantified opinion of an idealized person. Specifically, the subjective probability of a given event is defined by the set of bets about this event that such a person is willing to accept. An internally consistent, or coherent, subjective probability measure can be derived for an individual if his choices among bets satisfy certain principles, that is, the axioms of the theory. The derived probability is subjective in the sense that different individuals are allowed to have different probabilities for the same event. The major contribution of this approach is that it provides a rigorous subjective interpretation of probability that is applicable to unique events and is embedded in a general theory of rational decision.

It should perhaps be noted that, while subjective probabilities can sometimes be inferred from preferences among bets, they are normally not formed in this fashion. A person bets on team A rather than on team B because he believes that team A is more likely to win; he does not infer this belief from his betting preferences. Thus, in reality, subjective probabilities determine preferences among bets and are not derived from them, as in the axiomatic theory of rational decision (Savage, 1954).

The inherently subjective nature of probability has led many students to the belief that coherence, or internal consistency, is the only valid criterion by which judged probabilities should be evaluated. From the standpoint of the formal theory of subjective probability, any set of internally consistent probability judgments is as good as any other. This criterion is not entirely satisfactory, because an internally consistent set of subjective probabilities can be incompatible with other beliefs held by the individual. Consider a person whose subjective probabilities for all possible outcomes of a coin-tossing game reflect the gambler's fallacy. That is, his estimate of the probability of tails on a particular toss increases with the number of consecutive heads that preceded that toss. The judgments of such a person could be internally consistent and therefore acceptable as adequate subjective probabilities according to the criterion of the formal theory. These probabilities, however, are incompatible with the generally held belief that a coin has no memory and is therefore incapable of generating sequential dependencies. For judged probabilities to be considered adequate, or rational, internal consistency is not enough. The judgments must be compatible with the entire web of beliefs held by the individual. Unfortunately, there can be no simple formal procedure for assessing the compatibility of a set of probability judgments with the judge's total system of beliefs. The rational judge will nevertheless strive for compatibility, even though internal consistency is more easily achieved and assessed. In particular, he will attempt to make his probability judgments compatible with his knowledge about the subject matter, the laws of probability, and his own judgmental heuristics and biases.

SUMMARY

This chapter described three heuristics that are employed in making judgments under uncertainty: (i) representativeness, which is usually employed when people are asked to judge the probability that an object or event A belongs to class or process B; (ii) availability of instances or scenarios, which is often employed when people are asked to assess the frequency of a class or the plausibility of a particular development; and (iii) adjustment from an anchor, which is usually employed in numerical prediction when a relevant value is available. These heuristics are highly economical and usually effective, but they lead to systematic and predictable errors. A better understanding of these heuristics and of the biases to which they lead could improve judgments and decisions in situations of uncertainty.

ACKNOWLEDGMENTS

This research was supported by the Advanced Research Projects Agency of the Department of Defense and was monitored by the Office of Naval Research under contract N00014-73-C-0438 to the Oregon Research Institute, Eugene. Additional Support for this research was provided by the Research and Development Authority of the Hebrew University, Jerusalem, Israel.

REFERENCES

Alpert, M., & Raiffa, H. "Unpublished manuscript."

Bar-Hillel, M. (1973). On the subjective probability of compound events. *Organizational Behavior and Human Decision Processing 9*(3): 396–406.

Chapman, L. J., & Chapman, J. P. (1969). Illusory correlation as an obstacle to the use of valid psychodiagnostic signs. *Journal of Abnormal Psychology 74*(3): 271–280.

Cohen, J., Chesnick, E. I. & Haran, D. (1972). A confirmation of the intertial-PSI effect in sequential choice and decision. *British Journal of Psychology 63*(1): 41–46.

De Finetti, B. (1968). *International Encyclopedia of the Social Sciences.* D. E. Sills. New York, MacMillan. 12: 496–504.

Edwards, W. (1968). In B. Kleinmuntz (Ed.), *Formal Representation of Human Judgment.* New York, Wiley.

Galbraith, R. C., & Underwood, B. J. (1973). Perceived frequency of concrete and abstract words. *Memory Cognition 1*(1): 56–60.

Kahneman, D., & Tversky, A. (1972). Subjective probability: a judgment of representativeness. *Cognitive Psychology 3*(3): 430–454.

Kahneman, D., & Tversky, A. (1973). On the psychology of prediction. *Psychological Review 80*(4): 237–251.

Savage, L. J. (1954). *The Foundations of Statistics.* New York, Wiley.

Slovic, P., & Lichenstein, S. (1971). Comparison of Bayesian and regression analysis approaches to the study of information processing in judgment. *Organizational Behavior and Human Decision Processing 6*(6): 649–744.

Staël von Holstein, C. A. (1971). Two techniques for assessment of subjective probability judgments: An experimental study. *Acta Psychologica 35*(6): 478–494.

Tversky, A., & Kahneman, D. (1971). Belief in law of small numbers. *Psychological Bulletin 76*(2): 105–110.

Tversky, A., & Kahneman, D. (1973). Availability: A heuristic for judging frequency and probability. *Cognitive Psychology 5*(2): 207–232.

Winkler, R. L. (1967). The quantification of judgment: Some methodological suggestions. *Journal of the American Statistical Association 62*(320): 1105–1120.

CHAPTER TWENTY-TWO

DECISION MAKING

ARTHUR B. MARKMAN AND DOUGLAS L. MEDIN

University of Texas, Austin, TX

Northwestern University, Evanston, IL

Abstract

For much of the 20th century, decision making research was strongly influenced by theories in economics. Economic models predict that people strive to make optimal decisions. True optimality is impossible to achieve given limitations in processing ability, and so much research examined the heuristics that people use to make good decisions in most natural situations. We begin by reviewing this work. However, there has been growing interest in the relationship between decision making and other aspects of psychological processing. The core areas of this emerging research are discussed in the second half of this chapter. First, we present research relating goals, motivation, and emotion to decision making. Then, we consider the role of expertise, analogical comparison and problem solving strategies in choice. Finally, we explore the types of choices people make and how those choices are influenced by culture. In this way, we examine the ways that decision making research has gone beyond its roots in economic models of choice.

22.1 WHAT IS DECISION MAKING?

Psychological research is often organized around particular tasks, such as problem solving and categorization. Research on decision making has also historically taken this approach. Decision situations are generally defined as those in which the decision maker has some unsatisfied goal and a set of options that might satisfy the goal. The decision maker must then evaluate the options in some way and select one. For example, a business executive may fly to Chicago and have to get from the airport to a downtown hotel. There are many ways to get there, including limousine, taxi, shuttle, and train. These options differ in their comfort, convenience, and price. Typically these attributes trade off, so that higher-priced options provide greater comfort and convenience. The executive might be on an expense account, in which case comfort and convenience may be factored into the decision more heavily than is price. The executive may choose to ride downtown by taxi and then implement this decision by standing on line and taking a taxi to the hotel.

To bring these sorts of decision situations into the laboratory, researchers commonly focused on the goal of obtaining money, which they assume is shared across people. In the prototypical task, subjects are given choice options that differ in probability and amount. The use of gambles enabled researchers to explore decision making under risk. Often, a number of different choices are made in a single experimental session, and the pattern of choices across sets is analyzed. For example, people might be asked whether they prefer a 45% chance to win $200 or a 50% chance to win $150. Later in the same session, they might be asked whether they prefer a 90% chance to win $200 or a 100% chance to win $150. At issue in studies like these is the consistency of people's choices. The analyses would involve an examination of whether the people who preferred the 45% chance to win $200 also preferred the 90% chance to win $200.

These sorts of betting situations can be powerful diagnostic tools. For example, standard economic models (e.g., subjective expected utility models) are constrained to predict that people's choices are consistent across transformations of choices. Thus, if people opt for the 45% chance for $200 instead of the 50% chance to win $150, then they should also prefer the 90% chance for $200 over the 100% chance to win $150. In point of fact, however, people often prefer the 45% chance for $200 but the 100% chance for $150, in violation of this prediction. It is not surprising, therefore, that some have referred to choices varying in amount and probability as the fruit flies of decision research.

If this review of decision-making research were written in the 1970s or 1980s, it would tell a simple and coherent story with a clear moral. The drama would be organized around the question of whether human choice behavior is rational and optimal, with economists arguing that it is (at least as a first approximation) and psychologists arguing that it is not. The upshot of this tale would be that the psychologists won the debate. Human decision-making behavior violates the fundamental axioms of economic models of choice in predictable ways. These violations reflect people's reliance on heuristics, biases and strategies that perform reasonably well in most cases but can lead to systematic errors (e.g., Dawes, 1988; Kahneman, Slovic, & Tversky, 1982). Things got a bit more complicated in the later 1980s and 1990s, but not enough to overturn the essential message that people are far from optimal decision makers.

In short, writing the review would have been relatively easy; we would take the definition of choice behavior in the first paragraph as a starting point, and then describe economic approaches to choice that define the normative practice of decision making. Next, we would present research that examined the degree to which human decision makers approach this normative ideal. This would largely consist of a catalog of heuristics and biases, along with a discussion of why they might be adaptive much of the time (e.g., Hogarth, 1990) and of what is known about overcoming these biases (e.g., Fischhoff, 1988; Fischhoff, Lichtenstein, Slovic, Derby, & Keeney, 1981). We would likely have ended with a description of mechanisms that people use to make choices in this prototypical context, and with some discussion about the effectiveness of these strategies in normal situations.

Starting in the 1990s, however, the sharp focus on the target (or foil) of rationality/ optimality gave way to series of new developments that are still unfolding.[1] First of all, decision research began to question the adequacy of the simple definition of the standard decision situation. A brief examination of these sorts of bets suggests that many elements involved in choice are missing. For example, the set of available options is often not specified in advance. In addition, many choices (such as deciding whether to have children or even what flavor of ice cream to buy) do not involve money but rather have a strong emotional component. In principle, models of choice should work as well here; one simply has to determine what value or utility the child or ice cream has and combine this with some measure of (psychological) probability to determine the expected utility or value. The key question is how well this straightforward approach works, or even whether it can be applied to these new situations at all.

A related issue concerns how goals might influence choice. If John goes to Las Vegas and loses all of his money and needs $80 to rent a room for the night, he may prefer a 50% chance to gain $80 to a 100% chance of gaining $60 (Lopes, 1983, 1987). This situation does not seem too complicated. But what about situations in which multiple goals might be active? Suppose Joan is trying to quit smoking, and her friends (who smoke) invite her to a bar for a drink. How does she reach a decision when she is confronted with balancing her goal of maintaining friendships with the potential costs of resuming smoking? Joan's assessment of the attractiveness of these options will change dynamically with the strength of goals and desires (as anyone who has tried to quit smoking will readily attest).

Furthermore, in many cases where a decision is possible, a person does not appear to actually make a choice. When traveling to Chicago, for example, an executive may simply take a taxi without considering any other alternative methods for getting from the airport to a hotel. Thus, it is not clear what circumstances require the evaluation of multiple options. Does taking the cab count as a decision? Certainly people may experience regret when they find themselves stuck in traffic and realize that they could have saved an hour by taking the train into the city. See Svenson (1999) for an analysis of types and levels of decisions.

These and related developments have placed decision research in a state of flux. In this chapter, we want to provide an overview of the ways that researchers have begun to explore decision making. To place the new research in perspective, we begin with a brief summary of the standard approach to decision making in the 1970s and 1980s. Then, we explore the underlying assumptions of this approach and discuss what is missing. Next, we summarize some of these new areas of research and show how they bear on the earlier framework. It is not feasible to provide a comprehensive presentation of current research in decision making (see Schneider & Shanteau, for a book-length effort to do so); instead, we focus on a cross section of research in order to give a sense of the scope of current research trends. We conclude by noting how these trends have transformed the focus of decision research from the structure of options to the dynamic structure of decision makers themselves.

22.1.1   The Standard Story

In order to place the discussion of decision making in context, we provide a brief description of economic models of choice and of the psychological research that was motivated by them. At the end of each of the following sections, we provide some suggested readings for those who want a more detailed treatment of these issues.

Economic Approaches to Choice.   In the standard decision setting a person selects one of a set of options in order to satisfy some goal. Much research on the psychology of choice was motivated by economic theories that suggest how choices ought to be made. These economic theories assume that people are rational and that they want to make the optimal choice in a given setting. In this case, optimal is defined as the choice that best reflects a person's preferences. It might not actually be the choice that is best for that person in the kind of objective third-party sense that parents use when suggesting to their children that they should do what is "best" for themselves.

Rationality requires that people make consistent choices across settings. To capture this desirable property, economic models typically assume that options are evaluated relative to some global preference scale. In modern economic theory, this global preference is called utility (e.g., Edwards, 1954; Luce & Raiffa, 1957; Savage, 1954; von Neumann & Morgenstern, 1944). The notion of utility implicitly assumes that a person's goals are important for determining their preferences. For example, what is the psychological value of $10? That depends in part on what the $10 can be used for. For people with very little money, $10 might allow them to eat a healthy meal or buy a new shirt. For wealthy people, there may be few things that this additional $10 will allow them to accomplish. Thus, the utility of $10 will be greater for the poor person than for the wealthy one. In our earlier example in which John needed $80 to get a room, the utility of $80 might be more than twice the utility of $60. Of course, there are some constraints on subjective utility; for example, it is assumed that the utility of money is monotonically increasing. Thus, more money is always better than less.

In order to calculate the overall utility of an option, most models assume that the attributes (or features) of an option can be treated independently. Thus, each attribute has a utility that indicates the degree to which that property helps to achieve the decision maker's goals. Each attribute also has an importance, or weight. Attributes are weighted by multiplying the utility of the attribute by its importance weight. The overall utility of an option is then the sum of the weighted utilities of the attributes. Once the utility of each option has been determined, making a choice is just a straightforward process of selecting the item with the highest utility. In the case of probabilistic outcomes, subjective utility theory assumes that the utility of an outcome is multiplied by the probability that it will occur.

Utility models have a number of nice properties. First, they take into account all available information about the choice options. Each attribute is weighted by its importance, and thus there are no attributes of options that are ignored. Second, because preference is translated onto a single utility scale, any pair of options can be compared. Third, once the utility of each option is selected, a consistent preference structure is established (i.e., options are ordered by their utility). In short, subjective utility provides a clear bottom line. Thus, by using the overall utility of options, decision makers are guaranteed that if they prefer option A to option B in one setting, then they will prefer option A to option B in another setting as well (except, of course, if new attribute information that changes the evaluation of the options becomes available).

Economic models make a number of predictions about people's choice behavior. One prediction involves the effect of equivalent transformations. If option A is preferred to option B, then if the same information is added to both options, preference for the options should not change. A second important prediction is consistency across measures of preference. There are many ways to assess people's preference. For example, people can be given a set of options and asked to choose one, or they can be given a set of options and asked how much they would be willing to pay for each one. Consistency suggests that if a person selects option A over option B, that person should also be willing to pay more for option A than for option B. Related to consistency is independence. Utility models assume that options are evaluated independently, so adding a new option to a choice set should not change the relative preferences of the other options (Luce, 1959).

In the next section, we present some tests of these predictions. This description of economic models has been brief and cursory. Readers interested in more detail about economic models are encouraged to consult Edwards (1992). Birnbaum and Chavez (1997), Quiggin (1993), and Luce and Marley (2000).

Testing Economic Models.   Economic models of choice behavior inspired considerable psychological research. This work was based on the general assumption that human behavior is rational. Thus, if economic models define the rational standard for choice behavior, people's choices should conform to the predictions of rational models (within limitations of human processing ability; Simon, 1956). Although a complete catalog of tests of the predictions of economic models is beyond the scope of this chapter, we discuss evidence that bears on the four predictions described in the previous section.

One prediction we described earlier was the influence of equivalent transformations. An early observation in the study of decision making was that choice behavior violated this prediction. One demonstration of this violation is the Allais paradox (Allais, 1953), which involves pairs of decision problems such as the one that follows. If people are asked to select either option A or option B, many people prefer option A to option B:

> Option A: $1,000 with probability 1.00
> Option B: $1,000 with probability .89
> $5,000 with probability .10
> $0 with probability .01

If they are asked to select from options C and D, however, they often select option D:

> Option C: $1,000 with probability .11
> $0 with probability .89
> Option D: $5,000 with probability .10
> $0 with probability .90

The second pair of options in this set are generated by removing a .89 probability of winning $1,000 from each option. Thus, the same amount has been taken away from each option; and, like weights on a balance scale, if A has more utility than B, then C must have more utility than D. In short, normative economic models must predict that these two pairs of options will be treated equivalently so that people who prefer option A should also prefer option C, and those who prefer option B should also prefer option D. In this case, however, people tend to exhibit a certainty bias in which they prefer option A over option B because there is a small possibility of winning nothing in B (perhaps they imagine how much regret they might feel if they pick B and receive nothing; see Loomes and Sugden, 1982) whereas A is a certain gain. In contrast, in the choice between C and D, both options have a high probability of winning nothing, so the disparity in payoffs is salient. These results suggest that people are risk averse when there is a possible gain. That is, they would prefer not to take a risk to win a larger amount of money in the presence of an option that involves a certain gain.

Another violation of the equivalence across transformations has been found in research on framing effects (e.g., Tversky & Kahneman, 1974, 1981; see Levin, Schneider, & Gaeth, 1998, for a recent review). In the classic disease problem, people are told to imagine the impending outbreak of a rare disease. People given a gain frame are told that the disease is expected to kill 600 people. They are asked to choose between one prevention program that will save 200 people, and a second program that will save all 600 people with a one-third probability and save no people with a two-thirds probability. People given these options often choose to save 200 people. A second group is given the same scenario, but the options are described differently. They are told that if the first prevention program is adopted, 400 people will die, but if the second is adopted, then there is a one-third probability that no people will die and a two-thirds probability that 600 people will die. People given these options often choose the program with the small chance to save all 600 people.

The two pairs of options are equivalent in the number of people who will be saved and who will die. What differs is whether the framing of the options focuses on lives saved or lives lost. As discussed earlier, people tend to be risk averse for gains. Thus, when the options are framed in terms of lives saved, people tend to select the least risky option. In contrast, people tend to be risk seeking for losses. That is, they prefer a chance to lose nothing (or a small amount) over a certain large loss. When the options are framed in terms of lives lost, people tend to select the risky option. This framing effect violates the prediction that equivalent transformations will not influence relative preference. Simply changing how the options are described changes people's preferences for them.

Other research has demonstrated violations of the prediction that preferences will be stable across different measures of preference. As one example, a number of preference reversals have been demonstrated in which two different measures of preference lead to a preference for different options (Slovic, 1995; Tversky, Sattath, & Slovic, 1988; see Hsee, 2001, and Hsee, Loewenstein, Blount, & Bazerman, 1999, for recent reviews). In a classic study, Slovic and Lichtenstein (1983) gave people a pair of gambles such as the following:

Bet E: 11/12 chance to win 12 gambling chips
      1/12 chance to lose 24 chips
Bet F: 2/12 chance to win 79 chips
      10/12 chance to lose 5 chips

People were asked both to choose which bet they would prefer to play and to say how much they would be willing to sell each gamble for. If different measures of preference yield consistent results, then the gamble chosen by the most people should also be the one they would want the most money to sell. In contrast to this prediction, participants selected bets E and F equally often, but they set a higher selling price for F than for E 88% of the time.

This result has often been explained as a type of compatibility effect. When asked to choose between gambles, people give weight both to the probability of winning and to the magnitude of the payoffs. In contrast, when setting a selling price, people focus on the monetary outcomes. Because the potential gain in Bet F is much higher than the gain in Bet E, people set a higher selling price for F than for E.

Compatibility effects have also been observed for acceptance and rejection of options. Shafir (1993, 1995) asked participants to consider a pair of vacations. One of the vacations was rather bland (e.g., average weather and average nightlife). The other vacation had both very good features (e.g., lots of sunshine) and very bad features (e.g., no nightlife). One group in this study was asked to select one of the vacations. The other group was told that they had reserved both vacations and that they should cancel the one they did not want. Shafir suggested that the selection task should focus people on positive features of the vacations. In contrast, the cancellation task should focus people on negative features of the vacations. Because one of the options had both many good features and many bad features, Shafir predicted that this option would often be selected by one group and canceled by the other group. If canceling is just the converse of selection, then percent cancellations plus selections should sum to 100%. However, the results showed that cancellations plus rejections of the choice with good and bad features summed to reliably more than 100 percent, as Shafir predicted. In short, this framing produced a reliable preference reversal, suggesting that people's preferences may change as a function of the task used to measure preference.

The third prediction of economic models that we discuss is that options should be evaluated independently so that the addition of a new option to a set should not affect the relative preference of the other options. Two interesting violations of this prediction are found in the attraction effect and the compromise effect (Huber, Payne, & Puto, 1982; Huber & Puto, 1983; Simonson, 1989).

In the attraction effect, options are presented as shown in the left panel of Figure 22.1 (Huber et al., 1982; Simonson, 1989). For each of these two dimensions, higher values are preferred to lower values. In this graph, option A is better than option B along dimension 1, but worse than option B along dimension 2. Assume that the particular values possessed by A and B along these dimensions have been selected so that the two options are equally preferable. What should happen if a new option is added to this set? According to economic models, options are evaluated independently. Thus, a new option (in this case, option C) should steal some choices from A and some from B. The only outcome that cannot occur (according to these models) is that the addition of option C should not *increase* the proportion of choices of option A or B (the original options).

In the left panel of Figure 1, option C is included in the choice set. This option is asymmetrically dominated. That is, C is worse than A along both dimensions. There is still a trade-off between C and B, however, as option C is better along dimension 1 and worse along dimension 2 than is option B. When participants are given a choice set like this one that has an asymmetrically dominated alternative, they are typically *more* likely to select option A than they were when just choosing between A and B. This outcome is called the attraction effect, because the new option attracts choices to the dominating alternative.

A similar context effect can occur when options like those in the right panel of Figure 22.1 are presented (Simonson, 1989). Imagine that options D and E are created so that they are equally preferable. What happens if option F is added to this set? Option F is much better than the other options along one dimension, but much worse along the other. In this choice set, option D is selected more often than it was when options D and E were presented alone, in violation of economic models. In this case, option D becomes

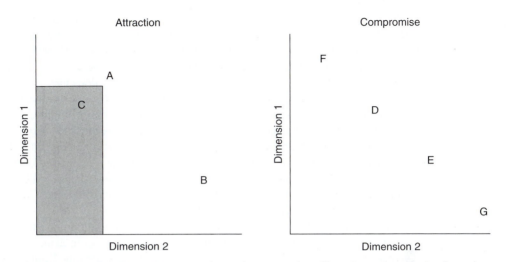

FIGURE 22.1   Examples of the attraction and compromise effects. In each example, the options are described along two dimensions. Goodness of each attribute increases with distance from the origin. In the attraction effect, options A and B are selected so that people are indifferent between them. Options placed in the shaded region will be eliminated by Option A. Option C is then added. In the compromise effect, options D and E are selected so that people are indifferent between them. Option F or G is then added.

a compromise option between E and F. Compared to each of these options, it has reasonable values along both dimensions. If instead of option F some option G is added that makes E the compromise choice, then choices of E increase.

The examples in this section are demonstrations of violations of three basic predictions of economic models of choice. Starting in the 1950s, psychologists cataloged many such violations. These findings are typically quite robust. Furthermore, it can prove difficult to "de-bias" people and make them obey the dictates of rational economic models. This presentation of violations of the predictions of economic models has been brief. More complete discussions of these violations and their theoretical implications can be found in Bazerman (1998); Luce (2000); Tversky and Fox (1995); and the book edited by Kahneman and Tversky (2000).

Heuristics and Biases.   Demonstrations that people's choices do not follow the predictions of normative models of choice led to research on the processes that people do use to make choices. Much of this research, particularly that carried out from the late 1960s through the 1990s, came to be known as the heuristics and biases approach (Kahneman, Knetsch, & Thaler, 1991; Kahneman et al., 1982; Kahneman & Tversky, 1984; Tversky & Kahneman, 1974, 1986). A heuristic is a (fairly simple) rule that can be used to perform some cognitive task. In general, heuristics are efficient and lead to accurate choices (see Polya, 1945, for an extensive discussion of heuristics). In this section, we discuss a few of the heuristics that have been explored.

First, however, it is important to discuss some of the philosophical underpinnings of the heuristics and biases approach. Economic models of choice are computationally expensive to carry out. They require that the decision maker consider all available information and weight it appropriately. In many decision situations, it may not be possible to find out every relevant piece of information. Even if it were possible, most options have so many possible features that it would take too long to consider every relevant piece of information.

The use of heuristics falls within Simon's (1957) notion of bounded rationality. In this view people seek to evaluate information as completely as possible subject to the limitations of human cognitive processing (e.g., limitations on working memory and attentional processes). In many situations, according to Simon, people may stop their information search when they find an option that will meet their goals. That is, they *satisfice*. The idea was that the heuristics used by the cognitive system are accurate enough, often enough, to be useful, even though they may sometimes lead to sub-optimal decisions.

Simon's notion of satisficing creates a fuzzy border between rationality and optimality on the one hand, and biases and heuristics on the other. In order to demonstrate that people were using a particular heuristic, researchers typically have identified situations in which using that rule would lead to a violation of the predictions of normative models. Thus, studies of decision making tended to focus on cases in which people made suboptimal decisions. Rarely was there corresponding work that would allow researchers to see how effective or ineffective a strategy might be across a representative sample of situations in which the strategy might be applied. More recent work has actually explored some of the most popular heuristics and has demonstrated that they are indeed quite accurate in many real-world situations (Gigerenzer & Goldstein, 1996). From one perspective the debate might be whether the glass is one-quarter empty or three-quarters full. At the same time, however, we think that there is compelling evidence that human decision making is not limited solely by computational resources (Kahneman & Tversky, 1996) and that it can be improved (e.g., Larrick, Nisbett, & Morgan 1993; Nisbett, Fong, Lehman, & Cheng, 1987).

We begin our discussion of heuristics with a presentation of some choice heuristics. These are methods for carrying out choices that are often accurate but do not take into account all of the available information about a set of options. Then, we discuss some evaluation heuristics. These heuristics focus on sources of information that can be used to evaluate particular choice options.

Choice Heuristics   Decision-making researchers have studied a variety of processes that people use to make decisions. These heuristics all have in common that they are methods for making reasonably good choices without having to evaluate all of the available information about an option. As we noted earlier, one of the earliest choice heuristics is satisficing, whereby the decision maker searches for the first option that will satisfy the goal of the decision and then selects that option. For example, if you are trying to hire someone to mow your lawn, you might interview a succession of candidates until a satisfactory one is found. It is very unlikely that you would interview *everyone* who might have some interest in the job and only then decide whom to hire. Selecting the first option that satisfies the goal may be appropriate because the degree of accuracy (i.e., how close the decision is to optimal) does not justify additional expenditure of effort (Payne, Bettman, & Johnson, 1988, 1993).

More elaborate decision heuristics have also been described. For example, Tversky (1972) presented elimination by aspects. According to this heuristic, people take the set of choice options and start by considering the most important attribute. Then, they eliminate all options that have unsatisfactory values of this attribute. Next, they consider the second most important attribute and eliminate the options that have unsatisfactory values of this attribute. This process continues, considering attributes in order of their importance. The process ends when there is only a single option left. For example, when buying a car, safety might be the most important attribute, so all models that are not sufficiently safe might be rejected. Then, the next most important attribute (e.g., engine power) might be considered.

This strategy uses more information about options than does simple satisficing, though it need not take into account all of the information about a set of options. Despite its efficiency, elimination by aspects is often quite accurate. Gigerenzer and Goldstein (1996) examined the elimination by aspects heuristic in the context of making judgments. They applied elimination by aspects to a variety of naturalistic judgment problems (e.g., judging the relative populations of cities) and found that it often gave results that were as good as an optimal model for that domain, suggesting that this heuristic is well worth using in many natural situations.

To summarize, both satisficing and elimination by aspects provide ways of making reasonably good decisions without expending significant effort. Elimination by aspects uses more information than does satisficing, and it tends to provide somewhat more accurate choices. Thus, a decision maker can select from among decision strategies in order to use one that provides an acceptable level of choice accuracy and also a reasonable degree of choice effort. For a more detailed discussion of choice heuristics and the trade-off between effort and accuracy, see Payne et al. (1993). They make the point that the theoretically optimal decision rule may be far from optimal if the time to decide is limited, and they also show that people are capable of adjusting their decision procedure as the decision deadline varies.

Evaluation Heuristics   According to economic models, evaluating options involves weighting each attribute value by its importance and then adding up these weighted evaluations. This view suggests that there must be some way of evaluating the relative goodness of attributes as well as the importance (or probability) associated with these attributes. Some research on heuristics has focused on strategies that can be used to evaluate the goodness and importance of options and their attributes (Tversky & Kahneman, 1974). In this section, we discuss two prominent heuristics: availability and representativeness.

The availability heuristic is used to assess the likelihood of an occurrence. This heuristic assumes that the ease with which an option comes to mind is related to the frequency with which it has been encountered in the past, and presumably the likelihood that it will be encountered again in the future. For example, it is easier for us to think of times that we or someone we know has had a cold than to think of times when we or someone we know has had shingles. Thus, we might judge (correctly) that colds are more common than shingles.

As with all heuristics, of course, there are cases in which this heuristic fails to give an accurate assessment of relative likelihood. For the availability heuristic, these cases tend to be of two kinds. First, retrieving something from memory is a function of both the presence of that item in memory and the match between the cue and the item in memory. Thus, more specific cues may make information in memory more accessible, thereby skewing judgments of likelihood (Tversky & Kahneman, 1974). It is readily demonstrated that people estimate that there are more words in English that end in ing than n (where the penultimate letter is an *n*). Of course, the set of words ending in ing is a proper subset of the words whose penultimate letter is *n*. However, -ing is a more specific retrieval cue than -n- (and it is also a meaningful unit in English). Thus, it forms a better retrieval cue. Because people are using availability to assess likelihood, they are mistaken in their estimates of word frequency.

A second heuristic that people use when making evaluations is representativeness, which refers to the degree to which an item is similar to an ideal. When evaluating some new item, if it is very similar to the ideal object for satisfying some goal, then it is also probably going to be useful for satisfying the goal. The operation of this heuristic can be seen in elections when candidates are evaluated for the degree to which they appear to be "presidential." Although having a commanding presence need not be a sign that a person will be a good leader, the fact that many prior presidents have had this quality seems to play a role in our evaluations.

Availability and representativeness are just two evaluation heuristics that have been described in the judgment literature. A number of good papers and books have summarized the evaluation heuristics that people use (Bazerman, 1998; Dawes, 1988; Kahneman & Tversky, 1984). In general, the research strategy for presenting these heuristics has been to describe the type of information used by subjects and then to demonstrate how the heuristic can sometimes lead to suboptimal evaluations. To reiterate the point raised earlier, however, the observation that these heuristics sometimes lead to suboptimal judgments should not be taken as a sign that they are not usually a good basis for people's judgments. Kahneman and Tversky have suggested that some heuristics and biases are analogous to perceptual illusions and are resistant to change. Of course, the fact that we are susceptible to perceptual illusions does not mean that our perceptual system does not function quite well much of the time. To extend the analogy, perception researchers have identified situations, such as airplane takeoffs and landings, in which limitations of human perception can have literally disastrous consequences and in which it is necessary to take steps to compensate for these limitations. The same likely holds for decision making.

Prospect Theory.   One way that decision-making researchers responded to findings like those that emerged from the heuristics and biases research was to develop new models that could account for these findings. The models often had the same general structure as normative economic models, but they differed in the way that options were evaluated (Kahneman & Tversky, 1979; Shafir, Osherson, & Smith, 1993b). Although there were a large number of demonstrations of the limitations of human decision making, the publication of *Prospect Theory* (Kahneman & Tversky, 1979) marks an inflection point for the increasing interest and influence of psychological models of decision making.

In prospect theory, as in the economic models described earlier, the evaluation of an option is the sum of the goodness of each of its attributes weighted by the importance of that attribute. Where Prospect Theory differs from economic models is that it uses psychologically motivated functions for evaluating the goodness and importance of attributes and for the weighting of probabilities.

In economic models, the goodness of an attribute is measured on an absolute rather than a relative scale. That is why people should treat saving 200/600 lives in the same way as losing 400/600 lives in the well-known Asian disease scenario. In Prospect Theory, attributes are evaluated relative to a reference point. Furthermore, consistent with observations about differences between gains and losses, the evaluation function changes more steeply

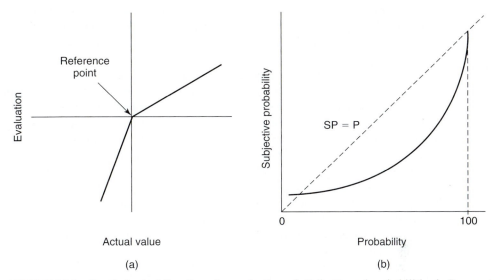

FIGURE 22.2   Psychological functions for evaluation of attributes and probabilities in Prospect Theory. Left panel: A hypothetical function for evaluating attribute values relative to a reference point. The function for losses is steeper than the function for gains. Right panel: A hypothetical function for the psychological perception of probability. According to this curve, people are relatively insensitive to changes in small probabilities and relatively sensitive to small changes in large probabilities.

for losses (relative to the reference point) than for gains. A sample function of this type is shown in the left panel of Figure 22.2. In this figure, the reference point is the x-axis. The reference point is typically the status quo in a problem. For example, in the disease problem, the status quo in the lives-saved frame is 0 lives saved (and thus each life saved is a gain), but the status quo in the lives-lost frame is 0 lives lost (and thus each life lost is a loss relative to the reference point). Finally, as shown, a positive change of a particular magnitude has a lower evaluation than does a negative evaluation of the same magnitude. (Often the curve is actually negatively accelerated rather than a line to capture the fact that the perceived magnitude of a constant change is smaller as the distance from the reference point gets larger. We drew this figure with straight lines to highlight the difference in value between gains and losses.)

Prospect Theory also places importance on probability weights on a psychological scale. In many of the examples considered earlier, the choices involved monetary gambles. In these items, the importance weights are subjective probabilities. The right panel of Figure 22.2 shows a typical psychological scaling for probabilities. There are two key aspects of this curve. First, the area of the curve near 0 is relatively flat. That is, people are relatively insensitive to changes in small probabilities, but the change from a zero to a nonzero probability is a qualitative shift. Furthermore, the weighting of small probabilities is above the diagonal (shown as a dashed line), suggesting that people are giving small probabilities a higher weight than they would get if people treated probabilities veridically. Conversely, there is a sharp qualitative change as one goes from certainty to probabilities less than one, reflecting that people give a high weight to certain outcomes.

In general, for high probabilities people are hypersensitive to changes, and any probability less than certainty is subjectively much smaller than certainty. This weighting reflects the certainty bias that is evident in the Allais paradox and in the risk-seeking behavior for losses in the examples above.

Clearly, both the subjective evaluation of gains and losses and the subjective probability evaluation in Prospect Theory are based on previous experimental findings. Thus, it should not be surprising that Prospect Theory can be used to account for patterns of data that violate the assumptions of normative models. The power of Prospect Theory is that it is formulated in terms that are similar to those used in normative economic models (see Kahneman & Tversky, 1992, for recent developments in Prospect Theory and Camerer, 2000, for a summary of relevant applications and observations). Thus, it is a psychological model that was accessible to economists. As such, it led many economists to begin thinking about the psychology of choice behavior. Indeed, behavioral economics has become a thriving area of research that explores the way people make decisions (see Hertwig & Ortmann, for a discussion of the relative merits of methods in behavioral economics and psychology for the study of decision making).

22.1.2   Summary

So far, we have given a brief version of the state of research on decision making up to about 1990. Normative economic models provided an initial set of hypotheses about human behavior that could be tested. Because these assumptions were likely too strong (because people do not have the unlimited processing capacity necessary to make optimal decisions in all situations), there was good reason to expect violations of the predictions of normative models. Psychologists were not disappointed, as the central predictions of rational models often were violated at least in some circumstances.

The news was not all bad, of course. The strategies that people use to make decisions are often quite good. They give reasonably accurate results using very little effort (Gigerenzer & Todd, 2000; Tversky and Kahneman, 1974, 1981). Thus, although the heuristics that people use can be shown to lead to suboptimal choices under some conditions, people's decisions based on heuristics are pretty good, pretty often.

The initial response to data like those reviewed so far was to generate new models that resemble the economic models in many respects but that incorporate more psychologically realistic assumptions about the way attributes and probability (or importance) are evaluated. As we will see, however, there has been a second and more radical reaction to the research program outlined so far.

Researchers in psychology and related, more-applied disciplines such as management and consumer behavior have begun to examine what is missing from the standard story about decision making. Economic models start with a particular definition of a choice: There is a set of options, and the chooser must decide from among them. However, there are many decision situations that do not resemble this archetypal case at all. For example, studies of naturalistic decision making suggest that experts often consider only a single option under time pressure, and yet they typically make good decisions (Klein, 2000). Consumers at the store often purchase the same products in every trip, suggesting that they are making these choices automatically without considering many options (Guidagni & Little, 1983). As a final example, there has been a growing recognition that the set of choice options may not be known at the start of a decision situation, but rather must be constructed (Kardes, Kalyanaram, Chandrashekaran, & Dornoff, 1993; Shapiro, Macinnis, & Heckler, 1997).

Perhaps more important, there is a growing recognition that topics central to cognitive and social psychology, such as problem solving, goals and motivations, emotions, expertise, categorization, and memory, must be incorporated into decision-making research. If decision making is an important psychological process, then process models of decision making are needed (e.g., Busemeyer, Hastie, & Medin, 1995). The rest of this chapter will explore the emerging research that ties decision making to more basic psychological processes. As with many emerging fields, there is no consensus on the right way to conduct research. Nonetheless, we feel that it is important to impose some structure on current research in order to avoid a simple laundry list of studies. Thus, in the next section we suggest three general themes that have guided current research. Our review of the literature is selective; nonetheless, we feel that this presentation provides a balanced view of research on choice.

22.2   RECASTING DECISION MAKING

In order to go beyond the research program that is framed by the goal of undermining economic models of choice, it is important to understand the biases that the rationality/optimality approach introduces into decision-making research. Once these biases have been identified and called into question, it is possible to extend work in new directions that were not explored previously. In this section we begin by discussing four biases of the economic approach to choice. Then, we discuss some important extensions that need to be made to choice research. The remainder of the paper then summarizes more recent research that has begun to address these issues.

22.2.1   Biases of the Economic Approach

It is common in psychology for explanatory models to influence the kinds of data that are collected. In particular, the studies that test a particular model must yield data that are compatible with the explanatory constructs and knowledge representations assumed by the model [. . .]. As a result, a subtle confirmation bias may be introduced into research because experiments may be designed to collect data in the image of the model being tested.

In decision research based on economic models of choice, three important aspects have strongly influenced paradigms and procedures. First, these models assume that options are evaluated relative to some common scale, such as utility. Second, the models assume that there is a fixed set of options that are being evaluated relative to this common scale. Third, the evaluation of options assumes that people assess the goodness of each attribute and weight it by the attribute's importance. These assumptions have led to the use of options like gambles for which the goodness and importance of the attributes can be defined objectively. Finally, using economic models as the standard of evaluation for psychological models leads to a focus on the importance of rational or optimal behavior, which may overestimate the importance of optimality in human performance.

The idea that preference can be measured along a common scale is important for normative models because it enables the models to ensure that preferences will be consistent.

If one cannot achieve a common scale, it is not easy to see how a coherent decision can even be made or how priorities can be weighed (Baron and Spranca, 1997; Weber, Baron, and Loomes, 2001). The assumption of a common currency often leads researchers to use measures that assess outcomes on a common scale; indeed, it's hard to see any alternative to this practice.

Nonetheless, people's judgments may not show a corresponding coherence. For example, Chapman (1996) explored people's preferences for health and money. She points out that these two types of outcomes are very different but that utility approaches allow them to be placed on a single scale. However, in order to make these domains comparable, the monetary questions in her study involved amounts of money to be won, whereas the health questions involved assessing the value of a medical procedure by asking for the number of years of full health it would have to produce.

Thus, because a utility model was assumed as the basis of this research, the dependent measures obtained focused on numerical outcomes. Furthermore, this same theoretical framework implies that people should discount the future at the same rate for health as they do for money, or else their judgments will be incoherent and subject to Dutch-book ploys.[2] Nonetheless, Chapman finds that people do not discount health and money at the same rates.

Another influence of the common-currency approach to choice is that it tends to focus research on choice outcomes rather than on choice processes. That is, if all options can be evaluated against some common metric, then focusing on the consistency of people's selections is a good research strategy. The specific psychological processes that people use to make choices can be inferred from the pattern of selections because normative models and economically inspired evaluation models (e.g., prospect theory) all assume that options are evaluated relative to a common metric.

This focus on outcomes parallels the development of research on similarity (Medin, Goldstone, & Markman, 1995). In early studies of similarity, researchers tended to focus on similarity ratings (and other assessments of the similarity of pairs of items) under the assumption that there was some common similarity scale against which pairs could be judged (e.g., Shepard, 1962; Tversky, 1977). Later work assumed that the feeling of similarity is a reflection of the way concepts are compared and that variability in similarity ratings suggested that the malleability of similarity masked stability in performance at the level of underlying processes (Gentner & Markman, 1997; Medin, Goldstone, & Gentner, 1993). Thus, more recent research in similarity has focused on the processes underlying similarity comparisons rather than on people's similarity judgments. As we will see later, moving beyond the economic framework in choice research has also led to greater attention to the processes underlying decision making.

The second bias introduced by economic models is that people decide from among a set of options. Two aspects of this bias creep into research. First, these models assume that there is some set of options that people consider. Thus, studies often present people with a fixed set of options and ask them to pick one. Many of the examples presented in the previous section involved selections of one of a set of items. Some research explores variations of this theme. For example, some studies have explored how people make choices when options are presented sequentially rather than simultaneously (e.g., Read, Antonides, van den Ouden, & Trienekens, 2001), or from memory rather than with the options present (Hastie & Park, 1986). In addition, some researchers have allowed decision makers the option to defer a choice until some later time rather than selecting one of the available options (e.g., Tversky & Shafir, 1992a). All of this research is done against a background assumption that a choice is based on a set of options.

There are two aspects of this assumption that are potentially problematic. First, a substantial part of the choice process may involve developing the consideration set, which is the set of options that is actually being considered (Kardes et al., 1993; Nedungadi, 1990; Shapiro et al., 1997). Second, there may be many cases in which a decision maker only considers a single option. In these cases, experts may be retrieving potential options sequentially and accepting or rejecting them immediately rather than explicitly comparing a set of options. This process of generation and evaluation may differ substantially from comparative choice processes (Klein, 2000). We discuss these issues in more detail later.

The third assumption of economic models is that options are evaluated by assessing the goodness and importance of the attributes of options. In order to carry out this research, it is useful to have options that have obvious attributes whose goodness and importance can be assessed in some way. In this way, good experimental control can be established in studies of choice. In many naturalistic settings, the attributes of the options are not obvious. For example, if a person goes to a pet store to buy a dog, it is not clear what attributes of dogs will be relevant to the choice. That does not mean that attributes are not used to make choices, only that it is difficult for decision makers to know which attributes are being used.

Thus, it is not surprising that decision researchers have often turned to monetary gambles as stimuli. Gambles have nice properties for assessing normative models of choice. They have an explicit set of outcomes, each of which can be treated as an attribute of the gamble. These outcomes have a monetary value. The monetary value can be varied as a way of changing the goodness of the attributes. Finally, each outcome has a probability, which can serve as a stand-in for the importance of that outcome. Thus, the structure of gambles maps closely to the structure of normative models. (Indeed, an early economic model, the expected value model, assessed the value of gambles by simply multiplying the monetary value of the outcome by its probability of occurrence.)

Goldstein and Weber (1995) argued that decision-making research must go beyond the use of gambles as materials. They drew an analogy between the use of gambles in decision-making studies and the use of nonsense syllables in memory research. In memory research, nonsense syllables were meant to provide a way to assess the underlying principles of memory without having to worry about the effects of the content of what is being remembered. For example, if people are given a list of words like "dog, cat, cup," they might imagine dogs and cats sitting in cups to help them recall the list. In contrast, if they are given the list "fep, dax, vod," they cannot use the meanings of these syllables to help them recall the list later. Presumably, more elementary memory processes would be involved in remembering this list. As many theorists have pointed out, however, the purpose of memory is to remember the content of previous situations, so excising the content from the experimental materials leads people to use strategies that do not reflect what occurs in more naturalistic situations (e.g., Bransford & Johnson, 1973; Glenberg, 1997).

Similarly, people's decisions involving gambles may lead them to use strategies that do not reflect more general processes in choice. In particular, gambles focus people selectively on the evaluation of attributes and the importance of those attributes. Research that focuses selectively on gambles will systematically underestimate the contribution of other processes that go beyond evaluation and importance. It will also miss influences of the emerging decision on the evaluation of attributes (Holyoak & Simon, 1999).

Finally, economic models suggest that process models of choice behavior should be rooted in optimal behavior. Thus, the normative economic models had two influences on theories of decision-making behavior. First, they tended to dampen interest in psychological processes. Second, to the extent that these theories were considered process models, they provided an oversimplified and misleading view of what people are doing. Consider the following example from Frisch and Clemen (1994):

> Imagine that a person has a $1,000 balance on his or her VISA card and pays 17% annual interest. Imagine that this person also has $2,000 in a savings account earning 4% interest. From the perspective of utility theory one would conclude that the utility to this person from having money in a savings account (e.g., feeling of security) outweighed the cost of paying the high interest on the VISA bill.

As Frisch and Clemen point out, however, whether this choice reflects the results of an explicit assessment of value or utility should be an empirical question, not a given. They suggest that it may reflect a habit of keeping the money in savings, and it is easy to think of other possibilities (as Medin & Bazerman, 1999, note). For example, (a) the person may not have remembered that they had money in a savings account during times when they paid their bill; (b) the savings may have been a gift from a relative and may be linked to a moral prohibition from using it to pay current expense bills (Zelizer, 1994); or (c) the credit card bill may have been produced by impulsive purchases and the person in question may be protecting themselves from future impulse buying by leaving a balance near his or her credit limit (Shefrin & Thaler, 1992). The point is that when treated as a process model, utility theory prejudges the basis for decisions and forecloses on the exploration of other motivations. As we shall see, researchers have recently begun to explore the possibilities that people may have multiple selves that must negotiate before decisions are reached (Bazerman, Tenbrunsel, & Wade-Benzonl, 1998) or that cognition and emotion may play differing roles in determining decisions without necessarily even being integrated into an overall evaluation (Loewenstein, 1996).

In summary, the use of economic models of choice and the focus on human rationality has led to systematic biases in the way research is carried out. Studies of choice tend to focus on measures that allow options to be evaluated against some common metric. These studies also focus on choice outcomes rather than on choice processes and on the underlying goals and motivations that underlie choice. This work typically presents participants with a fixed set of options to be evaluated. The use of gambles (and other choices that fall outside the range of participants' general experience) may have led to a focus on specialized procedures for evaluating gambles that may not be applicable to more naturalistic situations. Finally, the use of economic models has led to an assumption that choice behavior should be evaluated with respect to a normative ideal.

22.2.2   Moving Forward

Because decision research has focused historically on comparisons of human performance to normative models, this area of research has not been closely connected to other research in cognitive and social psychology. Although articles on decision making do appear in general psychology journals such as the branches of the *Journal of Experimental Psychology* as well as the *Journal of Personality and Social Psychology,* there are many specialized journals that focus on decision making research, such as *Organizational Behavior and Human Decision Processes* and the *Journal of Behavioral Decision Making.* There is also a professional society, the Society for Judgment and Decision Making, which promotes research on decision making and holds an annual conference.

As decision-making researchers have gone beyond economic models as a theoretical basis for research, there has been a growing recognition that decisions involve a variety of cognitive and motivational processes that are also important in other areas of psychological research (see also Goldstein & Weber, 1995). This work has focused on broadening the constraints that economic models have placed on research. To set the stage for our discussion of other areas of research, we begin by examining how more recent research has gone beyond the boundaries established by economic models of choice.

In recognition of the limitations of the common currency assumption in economic models, research has begun to focus on factors that influence the evaluation of choices. Some of this research has explored the influence of motivational processes on choice. Other work has examined how goals and goal activation influence choice. Related to this research is the study of emotion and its effect on evaluation. The distinction between "hot" emotional processing and "cool" reason-based choices has been a target of current work. Finally, a stream of research has explored how the evaluation of options is affected by the ease of comparison of options in a choice set and the ease of evaluation of individual attributes.

Research attempting to elucidate decision processes has looked at the influence of a variety of component choice processes. For example, one important line of research has examined parallels between problem solving and choice. Other work has looked at the role of causal reasoning processes on decision making. Research has also been directed at the assumption that decisions are made by choosing from among a fixed set of options. One line of research has focused on the way that the consideration set (i.e., the set of options being evaluated) is determined. A stream of research has explored situations in which only a single option is considered. This work often looks at expert decision making, particularly in cases where the choices must be made under time pressure. One theme that emerges from this research is that no single process will suffice to explain all kinds of decisions. Instead, people bring a variety of strategies to bear on choices. Some are used when choices are being made in novel situations. Others are specific to particular conditions.

Finally, decision-making research has broadened out from its traditional focus on gambles. The domain of consumer choice has looked at the way people make decisions about consumer goods ranging from items purchased at supermarkets to more significant purchases such as buying a house.[3] Other research has explored the moral content of decision making, looking at how issues of fairness and values influence choice. In addition, a variety of different kinds of expert decision making have been explored, such as military decisions and medical diagnostic choices. Finally, as with many other areas of psychology, there has been a growing recognition of the importance of culture on the way people make choices. This research has demonstrated important variations in choice behavior across cultures.

In the following sections, we briefly take up each of these research topics. While reading the descriptions of this research, it is worth considering how this work goes beyond the assumptions associated with economic models. Because there are many types of decisions as well as cultural and expertise differences in decision processing, there may be no single framework for studying choice. Instead, the main lesson of this work is that decision making integrates across topics that have traditionally been studied by cognitive and social psychology.

22.3   CHOICE EVALUATION: GOALS, MOTIVATION, AND EMOTION

Moving beyond economic models of choice opens up a number of avenues for exploring the way choice options are evaluated. Economic models focused on evaluations in which attribute goodness was weighted by importance. Evaluation of information in the environment has been a topic of study in a number of areas of psychology. In this section, we first discuss the role of goals in evaluation and present some research that bears on the activation and use of goals. Then, we turn to the more general issue of motivational systems. Motivation and emotion are tightly intertwined, and there is growing evidence that emotional states are important for generating evaluations. This work involves both behavioral and neurophysiological evidence.

22.3.1   Goals and Choice

Theories of behavior often assume that agents control their behavior by pursuing some desired state of the world using some kind of feedback loop to compare the state of the world to the desired state (e.g., Miller, Galanter, & Pribram, 1960). These desired states of the world are called goals. When the end state of the goal is something desirable, then the goal is called an approach goal. For example, if an agent wants to eat, then food is the end state of an approach goal. When the end state is something undesirable, then the goal is called an avoidance goal. When an organism is trying to protect itself from predators, then being eaten is the end state of an avoidance goal. Intelligent systems are typically designed to decrease their psychological distance to the end states of approach goals and to increase their psychological distance to the end state of avoidance goals. Approach and avoidance goals must work in concert. There are many ways to avoid something (e.g., there are many directions one may run away from a dangerous object). Having approach goals in addition to avoidance goals will direct people away from one state and toward another (e.g., Carver & Scheier, 1990, 1998).

The cognitive system decides between goals by allowing them to wax and wane in their strength or activation (e.g., Lewin, 1935). While the details of goal activation are still being studied, a few general principles can be stated. First, goal activation drives behavior. Thus, agents attend to goal-relevant stimuli in the environment, and they prefer items that will enable them to satisfy goals to those that will not. Second, some goals have a physiological basis. These goals (e.g., hunger or thirst) are often called drives or needs, but like more cognitive goals (e.g., buying a toaster), they guide behavior. Third, active goals that have not yet been satisfied tend to remain active and will draw attention to information in the environment that will enable the goals to be satisfied (Patalano & Seifert, 1997; Zelgarnik, 1927). Finally, all else being equal, the strength of avoidance goals increases faster than the strength of approach goals as the end state of the avoidance goal draws nearer (Miller, 1959; see Busemeyer & Townsend, 1993, for a more recent treatment). This aspect of goals enables agents to explore potentially noxious options without doing something too dangerous.

To the extent that an intelligent agent uses goals to guide action, goals become a standard against which options can be evaluated. Using goals as a basis for action permits cognitive agents to solve a key problem that common-currency models of choice were developed to avoid. In particular, if all options are evaluated on a single scale (e.g., utility), then when the evaluation of all options is complete, one option will have the highest value on the scale, and it can be chosen. Thus, the common-currency models of choice guarantee that a selection will be made.

One danger in moving away from common-currency models is that the evaluations of different options will be incommensurable. Such an outcome would lead to indecision. For example, a person deciding whether to buy a smoke alarm or a toaster might determine that a particular smoke alarm is good because it has long battery life and a loud buzzer. The toaster might be deemed good because it has ten heat settings and an optional broiler attachment. How should the decision maker determine which of these options should be selected? These evaluations still require more global trade-offs.

Because agents have goals to guide actions, using goals as the basis of evaluations in decision situations means that options are being evaluated in service of action. One way to conceptualize this change is that normative economic models posited a global common currency against which all options could be compared. An approach based on goals assumes that options are evaluated against the agent's current goals. For example, if a person needs to be able to make breakfast each morning, then the toaster in the example above may be selected rather than the smoke alarm because it satisfies the person's active goals.

Thus, the dynamics of goal activation typically ensure that an agent will continue pursuing actions instead of getting lost in decision processes. Certain goals (like the physiological needs just described) will continue to increase in activation if not satisfied and thus will eventually exceed the activation of other goals and drive behavior. In many other situations, the activation of one goal tends to inhibit competing goals. However, in some cases there are conflicts among goals that do not go away just through the mechanisms of goal activation. This situation typically occurs for cognitive goals of great importance. For example, in the classic approach-approach conflict, two options may seem important (though perhaps for different reasons). Focusing on one option makes it seem like the best, but switching focus to the other makes it also seem attractive (Houston, Sherman, & Baker, 1989).

People often develop strategies for carrying out difficult choices that involve goal conflicts. One such strategy is the omission bias (Spranca, Minsk, & Baron, 1991). People generally judge decision makers to be more culpable when they carry out an act than when they fail to carry out an act that leads to the same consequence. For example, if a doctor vaccinates a child and the child subsequently dies, that doctor is considered to be more of a "cause" of the child's death than is a doctor who fails to vaccinate a child who later dies. This omission bias is observed in choice situations as well. For example, younger people (e.g., college students) tend to avoid performing actions that they feel they will regret later. Interestingly, older people tend to regret actions that they did not take more than they regret their sins of commission (Gilovich & Medvec, 1995). While the regret associated with omissions is often just a general wistfulness, there are times when it is a more powerful despair (Gilovich, Medvec, & Kahneman, 1998). These policies are used in those situations in which simple goal activation is not sufficient to allow a choice to be made.

Goals allow actions to be carried out through their interaction with motivational systems. The activation of a goal engages motivations to approach or avoid situations. Thus, in order to understand the influence of the dynamics of goal activation on behavior, it is also important to have some understanding of motivational systems. Furthermore, goal satisfaction (or failure) will also lead to emotions (see, e.g., Carver & Scheier, 1998). We discuss the connections between goals, motivations, and emotions after discussing research related to goals and evaluation.

To start things off, we explore research that bears on two important predictions of this view of goals. First, because the activation of goals changes over time, factors that influence the activation of a goal will also influence the evaluation of objects relevant to the goal. Thus, if some factor increases the activation of a goal, then evaluations of goal-related items should get more positive to the degree that they facilitate goal satisfaction. Second, to the extent that evaluation depends on goal activation in a context, people should be quite poor at predicting their future preferences. This difficulty should arise because the effects of future goal activation cannot be simulated in the present.

Goal Activation and Evaluation.   In general, goals are assumed to increase in activation as they become more important. There are many factors that govern goal activation (see Gollwitzer & Moskowitz, 1996, for a discussion of goal activation). Physiological needs increase in their activation as a function of both underlying physical states and social factors. For example, a smoker's need to smoke will increase both because of nicotine withdrawal and because of environmental cues associated with smoking. For goals with a physiological basis activation of the goal decreases almost immediately upon satisfaction (e.g., smoking a cigarette).

Goals that are more cognitively based (i.e., those without a clear physiological basis) are strongly influenced by both environmental factors and internal cognitive states. Cues from the environment may increase activation of a goal and may provide opportunities for goal fulfillment (Gollwitzer, 1999; Heckhausen & Beckmann, 1990). For example, an advertisement for a stereo might activate the goal to purchase a new CD player. Passing by a stereo store may serve as a cue that the goal can be satisfied by entering the store. In addition, cognitive structures can support goal activation. For example, thinking about home improvements might lead to setting a goal to purchase a new CD player.

Gollwitzer (1999) discusses the importance of the environment in satisfaction of these cognitive goals. He points out that many intentions to satisfy a goal are thwarted but that people are much more likely to satisfy a goal when they also envision specific circumstances in which they will fulfill that goal. Gollwitzer suggests that people will be reminded of these specific circumstances at times when goal satisfaction is possible.

The idea that goal activation waxes and wanes over time suggests that people's momentary evaluations of options should be influenced by the activation of goals relevant to those options. There is certainly a lot of anecdotal evidence consistent with this claim. For example, food seems to taste better when we are hungry than when we are not. Nisbett and Kanouse (1969) confirmed the intuition that people tend to purchase more at the supermarket when they are hungry than when they are not (though interestingly this effect does not occur for obese people, whose food consumption tends to be driven by external factors such as time of day). Presumably, hungry people purchase more at the store than do sated people because the food at the store is more attractive for them.

Markman and Brendl (2000) describe another study that suggests that current goal activation influences evaluation. In this study, German college students who were habitual smokers were approached after a large lecture class finished. They were offered the opportunity to purchase raffle tickets (for about a quarter apiece) for one of two lotteries, one with a cash prize and one with a cigarette prize. Participants were offered only one of the two lotteries and were not aware of the other lottery. The raffle would be held two weeks from the date of the study, so the prize could not be used to satisfy any current goal. Half of the smokers were approached before smoking a postclass cigarette (and hence they had a strong goal to smoke a cigarette). The other half were approached just after smoking their postclass cigarette (and hence the strength of the goal to smoke a cigarette was diminished). Consistent with the idea that active goals influence value, those who had not smoked yet purchased more raffle tickets to win cigarettes than did those who had already smoked. In contrast, those who had not smoked yet purchased fewer raffle tickets for the cash prize than did those who had already smoked.

One implication of the view that evaluations are based on active goals is that people should have difficulty predicting their preferences in those cases in which goals that are not currently active will become active. A number of researchers have provided evidence for this claim. For example, Kahneman and Snell (1992); see also Loewenstein & Adler (1995) found that people's judgments about which flavor of ice cream they would prefer in the future were only moderately correlated with their actual choices.

Loewenstein and his colleagues have explored varieties of what they call an empathy gap (Loewenstein, 1996; Van Boven, Dunning, & Loewenstein, 2000). Essentially, people have difficulty understanding the emotional (or what Loewenstein calls visceral) influences on evaluation. Thus, people exhibit an egocentric bias, assuming that other people will feel as they do now and that they will feel in the future the way they do now. The hypothesized empathy gaps (between self and others and between self at different times) can explain a number of preference anomalies. For example, people's inability to predict their own future preferences (as in the Kahneman and Snell finding) falls out naturally from this view.

Another finding that arises from an empathy gap is that people systematically mispredict other people's preferences. For example, there is a well-known choice anomaly called the endowment effect (Kahneman et al., 1991). In a typical experimental demonstration of the endowment effect, half of the people in a room are given an object such as a mug. After receiving the mug, they are asked how much they would be willing to sell it for. The rest of the people in the room (who were not given mugs) are asked how much they would be willing to pay for the mug. In general, the selling prices set by people with mugs are significantly higher than the buying prices set by people without mugs. This phenomenon is called the endowment effect because it has been suggested that the people given the mugs endow them with additional value because they own the mugs. As a control condition, a group of people are asked to set a selling price but are not given a mug. This group sets a price similar to that given by the buyers. Thus, the difference between the buyers and sellers is not due simply to a schema in which buyers and sellers are both trying to get a good deal (i.e., buy low, sell high).

Van Boven et al. (2000) suggested that this effect occurs because buyers are unable to simulate the endowment effect. That is, they cannot simulate the increase in value that comes from not owning an object. Similarly, the sellers are unable to recognize that they are adding value to the mug simply because they own it. Thus, they cannot factor in the added value that they place on the mug when setting a selling price.

Taken together, the research described in this section suggests that people use their active goals to evaluate objects. Using active goals allows people to make evaluations in service of carrying out actions. A potential danger with using active goals as a source of activation is that the strengths of goals wax and wane. Thus, people's evaluations are labile. This variability can be a particular problem when people must make determinations about future preferences. In this case, if people's current goals differ from their future goals, they will systematically misestimate their future preferences.

Mental Accounting.   Active goals can also influence how people perceive the relationship among events in a choice situation. We start with an example. Kahneman and Tversky (1984) described a situation in which people went to a store and selected a calculator that cost $25 and a jacket that cost $120. Some people were told that if they drove across town to a new store they could save $15 on the calculator. Others were told that they could save $15 on the jacket. People who could save money on the calculator were more likely to say that they would go across town than were people who could save money on the jacket. This finding suggests that people are segregating the costs associated with the calculator and the jacket.

What factors govern whether people will integrate the costs of two events or segregate them? One suggestion is that people create mental accounts that are analogous to the sorts of accounts used by businesses to segregate expenses (Heath, 1995; Heath & Fennema, 1996; Thaler, 1985, 1999). On this view, people do not treat all monetary gains and losses as the same, despite the fact that money is fungible and thus could be treated in a single account. Instead, people have a set of topical accounts that enable them to combine those gains and losses that come from particular events. Often, these mental accounts are organized around the satisfaction of a particular goal.

For example, Kahneman and Tversky (1984) presented a scenario in which people went to a theater to see a play. When they arrived at the theater, half of the people were told that they discovered they had lost the ticket they purchased earlier. The other half were told that they had not yet purchased a ticket, but that they discovered they had lost an amount of money equal to the purchase price of the ticket. People who were told that they had lost cash were much more likely than were people who were told that they lost a ticket to purchase another ticket to see the show. This finding suggests that people who had lost a ticket were combining the price of the initial ticket with the potential purchase price of a second ticket. In contrast, the people who were told they had lost cash were treating this lost cash as if it came from a separate account. In this case, the account was organized around the goal of seeing a show.

A final example of mental accounting is the house-money effect (Thaler & Johnson, 1990). When people gamble, if they win money early in the gambling session, they often pursue riskier gambles later compared to situations in which they lose money early. This observation suggests that people are treating the early gambling winnings as if they are playing with someone else's money (in this case, the gambling establishment's money). The only case in which Thaler and Johnson found that people tended to be risk seeking was when they were losing money toward the end of a gambling session. At this point, they would risk money in order to make a bet that would eliminate their losses for the day. This finding suggests that people do not like to close a mental account that has a negative balance (see Thaler, 1999, for more discussion of this issue).

Examples like these make mental accounting seem as though it is primarily a source of poor decisions. However, mental accounting can play an important self-regulatory role. In particular, mental accounts can protect long-term goals from competing (and potentially attractive) short-term goals (Shefrin & Thaler, 1992). For example, it is often important for people to save money for the future in order to be able to make large purchases such as buying a house or sending a child to college. It may be difficult to save money because a long-term goal whose outcome is many years off may seem remote compared to an attractive option that can be obtained in the near future.

One way people handle this situation is by creating different types of money. For example, people treat money in retirement accounts separately from the rest of their money, and people are quite reluctant to spend it. Money in long-term investments such as stocks, bonds, and home equity are treated as wealth, and people are reluctant to spend it as well (though less reluctant than they are to spend retirement income). In contrast, many people are quite willing to spend money in savings accounts. Thus, by physically segregating money into different types of accounts, people are able to protect long-term goals (see Zelizer, 1994, for an extensive sociological discussion of this issue). Thus, mental accounts can serve as a source of policies for resolving goal competition.

To summarize, in the previous section we discussed the role of goals in evaluating specific options. The research on mental accounting extends the role of goals to multiple outcomes. A set of outcomes is treated as part of the same event when it is related to a common goal (e.g., entertainment or retirement). Outcomes are treated as part of different events when they are related to different goals. The creation of mental accounts can lead to suboptimal choices in situations in which it would be advantageous to integrate outcomes that are placed in different accounts. In general, however, mental accounts permit people to protect long-term goals from potentially enticing short-term goals.

22.3.2 Motivation and Emotion

Goals enable actions to be taken by engaging motivational systems, which enable people to approach desired situations and avoid noxious ones. Satisfaction (or failure to satisfy) goals can lead to the experience of emotions. These emotions serve both as a holistic evaluation of options and choice settings and also as a force that may influence choice processing. In this section, we begin by discussing the role that approach (or promotion) and avoidance (or prevention) motivation play in motivation and choice. Then, we discuss the relationship between emotion and risk. Finally, we discuss some research on the role that emotion plays in choice processing.

Motivation and Self-Regulation.   There are many proposals for mechanisms that allow people to achieve their goals (e.g., Ajzen, 1991; Anderson, 1983; Carver & Scheier, 1998; Gollwitzer, 1999; Vallacher & Wegner, 1985). In this section, we briefly discuss regulatory-focus theory (Higgins, 1987, 1997). This theory explores the relationship between motivation and cognition and also the relationship between motivation and emotion. Finally, the theory has been extended to choice and evaluation. Thus, it provides a nice example of the way motivational issues can be explored in decision making.

According to regulatory-focus theory, active goals engage motivational systems. Following the distinction between approach goals and avoidance goals, there are two motivational systems: the promotion system and the prevention system. The promotion system is engaged to achieve desired states of the world (i.e., gains). The prevention system is engaged to protect against undesired states of the world (i.e., losses). This distinction between motivational systems is also compatible with research from neuroscience suggesting that avoidance-related motivation (e.g., fear conditioning) involves brain regions that differ from those involved in approach-related motivations (e.g., appetitive conditioning; Fanselow, 1995; see also Cacioppo & Gardener, 1999, for a corresponding analysis of the human emotional system).

Regulatory-focus theory can also be applied to emotions. Basic theories of emotion distinguish between positively and negatively valenced emotions (Mellers, 2000). On this view, goal satisfaction leads to positive emotions (e.g., joy), and goal failure leads to negative emotions (e.g., sadness). Regulatory-focus theory posits distinct emotions associated with each motivational system. Satisfaction of an approach goal (e.g., winning a game) leads to joy. In contrast, satisfaction of an avoidance goal (e.g., finding out that you passed a difficult exam) leads to relief. Failure to satisfy an approach goal (e.g., losing a game) leads to dejection. In contrast, failure to satisfy an avoidance goal (e.g., failing a difficult exam) leads to anxiety. Thus, the particular emotions experienced in a situation depend on the kind of motivational system that was engaged.

The motivational system engaged also influences how tasks are performed. In promotion situations, people attempt to achieve correct performance. In prevention situations, people attempt to avoid making mistakes. For tasks that involve solving multiple problems (e.g., anagrams), people will often stay on task longer in promotion than in prevention situations, because that will enable them to maximize the number of correct trials (Crowe & Higgins, 1997).

The motivational system engaged during choice may also influence the way decisions are processed. Luce, Bettman, and Payne (1997) examined the way people process information when making choices with negative emotional content. These decisions were ones that would engage prevention motivation (e.g., selecting a child to receive financial support, where the negative emotion arose from the knowledge that the children not chosen would be unlikely to receive support). Relative to a control group (e.g., where the children not chosen would also be likely to receive support), people in the negative emotion condition tended to spend more time on the decisions, but they engaged in less complex processing. Less complex processing in this case meant more attribute-based comparisons and less holistic processing of individual options relative to the control group. If people are trying to avoid errors, then we would expect them to examine a lot of information. It is not clear exactly why the prevention situation led to increased use of comparison-based processing, but it is possible that the attributes were difficult to evaluate in isolation and that comparison-based strategies provided the best method for evaluating options (Hsee, 1996).

Regulatory-focus theory has been extended to explore aspects of decision making (Idson, Liberman, & Higgins, 2000; Shah & Higgins, 1997). In one study, college students were put in a promotion focus (by framing a decision in terms of the likelihood of getting into an honors society) or in a prevention focus (by framing a decision in terms of the likelihood of being rejected by an honors society). Students were then asked whether they would take a particular difficult course in their major. Consistent with regulatory-focus theory, students were much more likely to say that they would take the class in the promotion case than in the prevention case.

The benefits of using the promotion system for goal attainment suggest that people may adopt strategies that allow them to frame new situations in terms of approach goals (Schneider, 2001). Most real-world situations are inherently ambiguous, and thus they can be framed in terms of either approach or avoidance goals. For example, a student applying to college can either view the experience as an attempt to get into the best possible academic school (an approach goal) or to avoid being rejected by colleges (an avoidance goal). By framing this decision in terms of approach goals, promotion motivation will be engaged, which will lead to risk taking (such as applying to reach schools that carry a high probability of rejection combined with an opportunity for admission to a high-caliber school). Often, in order to keep this promotion focus, people must view the world optimistically, which requires interpreting potentially ambiguous information (e.g., mediocre SAT scores) in the best possible light.

In summary, regulatory-focus theory assumes that approach goals engage promotion motivation and that avoidance goals engage prevention motivation. Promotion motivation (which is associated with emotions of joy and dejection) leads people to focus on achieving positive or correct outcomes. Prevention motivation (which is associated with emotions of relief and anxiety) leads people to focus on avoiding negative or incorrect outcomes. This distinction has been shown to influence cognitive strategies as well as the way people form preferences.

Emotions and Decision Making.   A large body of empirical and theoretical work suggests that emotions interfere with rational decision making by affecting both the cognitive and motivational forces that shape decisions. First, emotions are said to produce impulsive choices at the expense of options that provide larger long-term gains (e.g., DeSousa, 1987; Metcalfe & Mischel, 1999). Second, emotions adversely affect decision-making by interfering systematically with proper belief-formation (Lazar, 1999). The consensus has been that emotions stand in the way of rationality (DeSousa, 1987).

Recently, however, a number of philosophers and psychologists have suggested that emotions play a positive role in decision making (e.g., Frank, 1988; Wollheim, 1999). Specifically, it has been suggested that anticipatory feelings such as guilt (Baumeister & Heatherton, 1996) or regret (Loomes & Sugden, 1982) may guide decisions. For example, people given a lottery ticket are often reluctant to exchange that ticket with a friend's ticket for the same lottery even though each has an equal chance to win. One explanation for this phenomenon is that they are unwilling to trade because they would regret giving up the ticket if the ticket they gave away were the winner.

Other theories posit a more central role for emotions, arguing that emotional reactions provide information about aspects of decisions that are not accessible to consciousness and deliberation (e.g., Wilson & Schooler, 1991). In this vein, Damasio (1994) conjectured that anticipatory somatic feedback (skin conductance response) from the emotional system is necessary for proper decision making.

Damasio and his associates have reported a series of striking observations about the effects of damage to the ventro-medial prefrontal cortex. This type of damage is correlated with impairments in emotional regulation and decision making (Damasio, 1994; Bechara, Damasio, Tranel, & Damasio, 1997). Importantly, poor decision making and emotional regulation characterize patients who have both normal working memory and normal IQ (Bechara, Damasio, Tranel, & Damasio, 1997). These deficits are well-known in the personal lives of patients with prefrontal damage, but Bechara et al. (1994) have succeeded in showing these deficits in laboratory tasks. First, patients with prefrontal damage show deficits in emotional conditioning: Unlike normal control patients, they never develop anticipatory skin conductance responses when evaluating risky choices (Bechara, Damasio, Damasio, & Lee, 1999; Bechara, Damasio, Tranel, & Damasio, 1997).

The performance of prefrontal patients on some gambling tasks is even more striking. Damasio and his associates (Bechara et al., 1994) constructed a risky decision task that they thought would capture many important properties of real-world decision making. Patients were allowed to choose cards from any of four decks: A, B, C, or D. Decks A and B offered a sure gain of 100 points (patients were given play money, and points translated directly into money), whereas decks C and D offered a sure gain of 50 points. However, all decks were associated with occasional, unpredictable punishments or losses. These losses were larger for decks A and B than for decks C and D such that overall, the expected value for decks C and D was greater than the expected value for decks A and B. Decks A and B differed only in that one had larger but more infrequent punishments than the other, balanced such that their expected value was equal. Decks C and D had an analogous difference in probability and amount of punishments and did not differ from each other in expected value. Normal patients tended to be attracted to the larger gains offered by decks A and B initially, but after experiencing the larger punishments learned to rely on decks C and D, which offer better long-term prospects. In contrast, patients with prefrontal damage did not learn to choose the better decks within the 100 trial limit of the study. In fact, they tended to choose from decks A and B more than from decks C and D.

These results could be explained by the hypothesis that patients with prefrontal damage are either hypersensitive to rewards or insensitive to punishments. To evaluate this possibility, Bechara, Tranel, and Damasio (2000) ran a version of the four-deck task in which the pattern of rewards was reversed. That is, two decks had high immediate punishment but much higher occasional rewards, and the other decks had small, consistent punishments but much lower occasional rewards, such that the former two decks had the better long-term consequences. Patients with prefrontal damage tended to choose the disadvantageous decks and failed to learn to choose the decks offering the better payoffs over the long run. Bechara et al. argued that their findings are consistent with the generalization that prefrontal patients are relatively insensitive to future consequences but instead are guided by immediate consequences. Damasio and his associates concluded that anticipatory emotional responses in the form of somatic arousal are necessary intermediaries for performance on risky decision-making tasks. They call this view the somatic-marker hypothesis.

The fact that patients with normal IQ but prefrontal damage show deficits on the laboratory gambling task is striking from a number of perspectives. If normal IQ implies that the patients have sufficient computational resources to calculate expected values, why are these deficits seen? Bechara et al. did report anecdotal evidence that prefrontal patients may know which decks are "better" but still fail to choose them. Although Damasio, Bechara, and their associates described the deficits in terms of immediate versus delayed outcomes, it would be more precise to say that the contrast is between certain and probabilistic outcomes. Thus, one could conclude that the prefrontal patients approach higher certain gains and avoid higher certain losses, giving much less weight to uncertain events.

This research puts a new spin on the role of emotion in decision making. While emotions may sometimes stand in the way of rational choice, emotions are also important for the proper evaluation of options. Future research must establish more precisely the deficits in decision making that follow prefrontal damage and must explore the positive role of emotion in choice.

Emotions and Risk.   Emotions also influence choices that involve risk. One of the earliest influences is the loss aversion. As discussed previously, Prospect Theory assumes that the negative (emotional) impact of losses is larger than the positive (emotional) impact of equivalent gains. Of course, Prospect Theory still shares the utility assumption with earlier normative models of choice. More recent work has explored Prospect Theory's assumption that the impact of a given probability is a function of the magnitude of the probability without regard to the outcome to which it is attached. In contrast to this supposition, Loewenstein, Weber, Hsee, and Welch (2001) proposed a framework on the role of emotions in decision making that questions this independence. Specifically, emotionally vivid options involving fear or hope may yield a subjective probability function different from that associated with less emotionally salient events (see also Finucane, Peters, & Slovic, 2000).

In the first experiment by Rottenstreich and Hsee (2001) provided a nice demonstration of the interaction between affect and subjective probability. The general idea is that the probability weighting function used by Prospect Theory (shown in the right panel of Figure 22.2) will be more extreme for emotionally vivid events than for blander options. For positive events, the implication is that going from a zero probability to a nonzero probability triggers hope, whereas going from certainty to less than certainty triggers fear. The greater the vividness, the greater the jump in subjective probability as one moves from a zero probability, and the greater the drop as one moves from certainty to uncertainty.

In the first experiment by Rottenstreich and Hsee, participants were told that they could receive either $50 in cash or "the opportunity to meet and kiss your favorite movie star." Half the participants chose between those two options, and half chose between lotteries offering a 1% chance for these options. In the certainty condition, 70% of the participants chose the cash over the kiss, but in the lottery condition 65% preferred the chance for a kiss to the chance for the money. This finding is consistent with the prediction based on the idea that vivid outcomes (e.g., a kiss) show less sensitivity to differences at the low end of the probability scale. In a follow-up study, participants valued a 1% chance for a $500 coupon for a trip to Europe (a vivid event) four times as much as a 1% chance for a $500 coupon for tuition reduction (a less vivid event). When the probabilities were shifted to 99%, the valuations reversed, again as predicted. In other studies Rottenstreich and Hsee showed that this same pattern held for aversive events (electric shock, a vivid event, versus loss of money, a less vivid event).

These results support the idea that the probability weighting function is not independent of the outcome under consideration. Specifically, the probability weighting function (shown in the right panel of Figure 22.2) appears to be flatter for emotionally rich outcomes than for less engaging outcomes. Rottenstreich and Hsee concluded that probability-outcome independence may hold for different monetary outcomes but not for different affective values.

22.3.3   Summary

In this section we have explored the role of goals, motivation, and emotions in evaluation. The normative economic models described at the beginning of this chapter are "cool" reasoning models in that they assume that each attribute can be evaluated and weighted without considering the role of emotion and motivation directly. Indeed, emotions are typically assumed to be factors that decrease the rationality of decisions.

We suggested that options are evaluated relative to a decision maker's active goals. The more strongly a goal is activated, the more an option is valued. Furthermore, the two kinds of goals — approach and avoidance goals — are associated with different kinds of motivational systems that support goal satisfaction. The promotion system is concerned with satisfying approach goals. The prevention system is associated with satisfying avoidance goals.

Finally, goal satisfaction and failure are associated with emotions. These emotions not only are a result of goal satisfaction but are also used as a source of evaluative information about the goodness of options and the degree of risk. Current evidence suggests that patients with damage to emotional processing systems are actually worse at making decisions than are people who experience emotions normally.

22.4   CHOICE PROCESSES: CATEGORIZATION, MEMORY, AND PROBLEM SOLVING

One result of the move away from economic models of choice behavior is a growing recognition that decision making involves a variety of cognitive (and social-cognitive) processes that are shared with other common tasks such as problem solving, causal reasoning, analogical reasoning, and similarity comparison. In this section, we review some of the work that has explored parallels between decision making and cognitive processing more generally.

22.4.1   Knowledge, Explanation, and Problem Solving

One important theme in current decision-making research is that choice involves constructive processes that make extensive use of a decision maker's background knowledge (Goldstein & Weber, 1995). In this section, we review two types of constructive processes. First, decision makers may use analogies to previous scenarios to generate a consideration set and to evaluate options. Second, they may develop causal stories that connect available information in order to evaluate options. Both analogy and causal reasoning are more general cognitive processes used for many tasks in addition to decision making.

The prototypical decision-making experiment presents the subject with a set of options and asks them to choose one (or to provide some other measure of preference). This situation is similar to what happens when people shop in settings where a range of options is available in a single store. In many naturalistic decision contexts, however, the set of options must be generated. In these more ill-defined cases, people often rely on their previous experience to determine the consideration set.

Analogy can play a prominent role in consideration-set formation (Gregan-Paxton & Roedder, 1997; Markman & Moreau, 2001). A decision maker may see a new situation as analogous to a prior episode, which may suggest potential options. The role of analogy in generating options has been explored extensively in the domain of political decision making (Holyoak & Thagard, 1995; Khong, 1992; May, 1973; Shimko, 1994). In particular, historians have examined the analogies that have influenced important political decisions.

For example, prior to the Vietnam War, politicians in the United States were trying to decide whether and how to intervene in the growing tension in Vietnam (Khong, 1992; May, 1973). Three interesting points emerge from an analysis of the analogies used. First, many of the analogies tended to come from similar situations. When generating military options for Vietnam, decision makers used other similar political situations (such as the experience of the United States in the Korean conflict in the 1950s) instead of drawing parallels from far-flung domains such as domestic disputes (see also Dunbar, 1997). Similar domains were used so that specific aspects of prior situations could be carried over from prior conflicts rather than just abstract principles. That is, by drawing analogies from Vietnam to previous conflicts such as World War II and Korea, specific diplomatic and military options could be drawn from these base domains. If Vietnam had been compared to a marital dispute, then only general principles (such as strategies for negotiating with an adversary) could be drawn (assuming that military action is not a key aspect of most marital disputes).

Second, the analogy that was selected placed strong constraints on the options that were considered. In the end, the dominant analogy used in the Vietnam conflict drew a parallel between Vietnam and the Korean conflict. One of the major difficulties faced by U.S. military forces during Korea was that the Chinese entered the conflict on the side of North Korea. Because Vietnam was being compared to the Korean conflict, military leaders spent considerable time developing options that would avoid having the Chinese commit military forces. There is some speculation that this constraint imposed by the analogy kept the United States from using sufficient force early in the conflict and thus contributed to the protracted hostilities.

The third interesting aspect of this use of analogy is that political leaders tended to consider only a small number of analogies (often only one or two; May, 1973). One important reason why a small number of analogies were used is that analogies tend to provide a causal structure for thinking about a domain (Gentner, 1983). Once an analogy has been used to suggest how the events in a political situation are related, new analogies no longer seem apt. Thus, people are strongly influenced by the first analogy they consider.

The importance of the first analogy presented has also been demonstrated in consumer choice (Moreau, Markman, & Lehman, 2001). In this work, people were shown advertisements about digital cameras that compared them either to scanners or to film-based cameras. In general, people who were unfamiliar with digital cameras got a better impression of them when they were compared to film-based cameras than when they were compared to scanners. Of interest, if people were shown both the scanner and film-based camera ads sequentially, their impression of the camera was based primarily on the first ad. This finding suggests that once the new product is conceptualized in one way (on the basis of the first analogy), subsequent potential analogies no longer provide a good base domain for reasoning about the new product.

The importance of structuring a domain in order to make decisions about it also emerges from research on explanation-based choice (Pennington & Hastie, 1988, 1992). This research suggests that in some cases people make choices on the basis of which option provides the most coherent account of the available information. For example, when people serve on a jury, their verdicts may depend on whether assuming the guilt or innocence of the defendant provides the story that most coherently fits the evidence. Furthermore, given the standards of evidence in the United States, if the prosecution in a case is unable to provide a coherent story that connects the evidence, then a juror is likely to decide that the defendant is not guilty, even if the defense has not provided a coherent story for the defendant's innocence.

These results suggest that the ease of creating an explanation may influence people's evaluation of an option. Other research extends this view by suggesting that people may select a particular option because of the reason they can give for their choice (Shafir, Simonson, & Tversky, 1993a). As one example, Tversky and Shafir (1992b) told students to imagine that they had just taken a difficult final exam and that they did not yet know whether they passed. They were told about a vacation trip to Hawaii that was available at a travel agency for a reduced price. They could elect to purchase the trip, decline the trip, or pay $5 to reserve a seat and make a final decision the following day (at which point they would know the outcome of the exam). Given this scenario, 61% of people elected to pay the $5 to reserve a seat and thus to defer the final choice. Interestingly, two other groups of participants were run, one of which was told that they had taken a difficult exam and passed, and the other of which was told that they had failed. In both of these groups, over 50% of the participants elected to go on the trip. This finding suggests that at least some of the participants in the first group paid $5 to obtain a piece of information that would not influence their choice (as they would elect to go on the trip whether they passed or failed).

One explanation for why people might have been willing to pay for this "irrelevant" information is that it may have provided a reason for going on the trip. If the student passed the exam, then the trip was a celebration. If the student failed the exam, then the trip was consolation. Without knowing the outcome of the exam, the reason for making the decision was not known, and thus the decision could not be made.

In other cases, a choice may be made because it is easy to justify (Simonson, 1989). People may believe that their choices will be evaluated by others, and hence they select an option in order to facilitate the process of justifying the choice. For example, Simonson (1989) explored the attraction effect described earlier (see also Aaker, 1991). Recall that in the attraction effect people are more likely to select one of a pair of options in the presence of a third option that it dominates (see the left panel of Figure 22.1). Simonson found that the attraction effect was stronger when people were told that their decisions would be scrutinized by others than when they were told that their decisions would be kept confidential.

With choice settings such as the attraction effect, it is not clear how to interpret the way choice is influenced by the necessity of giving a reason. After all, self-presentation goals are important, so it would make sense that options that a person feels would make them appear more positive would get good evaluations. Nonetheless, there is evidence that having to give reasons may cause a person to make worse decisions in some cases (Wilson et al., 1993; Wilson & Schooler, 1991). In one study, Wilson and Schooler (1991) found that people who had to consider reasons for their preferences for brands of jam were less well correlated with the preferences of experts than were people who did not consider reasons. Wilson and Schooler speculated that thinking about reasons may lead people to consider easily accessible verbal information, while some preferences (e.g., taste preferences) may involve attributes that are not easy to state. Furthermore, Wilson et al. (1993) found that choices made immediately after considering reasons led to lower satisfaction with the choice a few weeks later than did choices made without considering reasons. These results suggest that thinking about reasons led to a focus on information about the domain that was not important to people in the long run.

The importance of analogy, causal explanation, and reasons in choices suggests that choice processing bears many similarities to problem solving. In particular, when solving problems, people must find some kind of causal structure that connects the elements in a problem domain in order to overcome the obstacles that prevent the satisfaction of some goal. Similarly, in many ill-defined decision situations, the options that permit a goal to be satisfied must be generated and evaluated.

22.4.2   Similarity, Comparison, and Choice

Often, when faced with a consideration set, people compare options to each other in order to make a choice (though see the discussion of expert decision making later). The process of comparison has also been the focus of study in research on similarity. Thus, it might make sense to search for parallel phenomena in similarity and choice (Medin et al., 1995). As discussed earlier, research on similarity first focused on the output of similarity judgments. Later work focused more on the processes underlying similarity comparisons. To illustrate why this shift was made, we discuss a finding suggesting that similarity judgments and preference judgments differ. Then, we present other research focused on processing that suggests that both similarity comparisons and choices involve common processes.

Earlier, we examined research on the compromise effect illustrated in the right panel of Figure 22.1 (Simonson, 1989; Simonson & Tversky, 1992). In compromise, people tend to select an option that provides a moderate value along the dimensions on which a choice is described rather than an option that is extremely good along one dimension and poor along another. This finding is actually the opposite of what is found in many similarity situations. Tversky and Gati (1982) provided evidence for a coincidence (pronounced *coincide-ence*) effect. They collected similarity judgments for a variety of pairs of objects that could be described by two feature dimensions (analogous to the items pictured in the right panel of Figure 22.1). They found that pairs that had an exact match along one dimension and a dissimilar value along a second dimension were generally perceived as more similar than were pairs that had moderate dissimilarities along both dimensions. Thus, coincidence and compromise appear to be distinct phenomena involving a similar task structure. Indeed, Kaplan and Medin (1997) used the same stimulus sets in studies of similarity comparison and preference construction and found a tendency toward coincidence in similarity judgments and a tendency toward compromise in preference.

This finding would seem to suggest that similarity and choice are distinct. However, it is also possible that these two tasks involve some common processes (e.g., comparison) and some unique processes (e.g., weighting of common and distinctive properties). Much research now suggests that similarity and decision making involve the same process of comparison.

Research on similarity suggests that mental representations contain information about objects and the features of those objects as well as structural information about relations among features and objects [. . .]. Comparisons of these structured representations (using a process called structural alignment) permit people to see the commonalities and differences of the items (Gentner & Markman, 1997; Medin et al., 1993). In particular, because there are relationships among items, some differences between items are connected to commonalities. For example, cars and motorcycles both have wheels. That is a commonality of this pair. Cars have four wheels, but motorcycles have two. This difference can only be found because of the commonality that both have wheels. Thus, this difference is called an alignable difference (Gentner & Markman, 1997; Markman & Gentner, 1993). In contrast, some properties of one item have no correspondence at all in the other. For example, cars have seatbelts, and motorcycles do not. These differences, which are not related to the commonalities, are called nonalignable differences. Considerable research on similarity suggests that alignable differences are a more focal output of comparisons than are nonalignable differences (Gentner & Markman, 1997).

There is mounting evidence that alignable differences of options are also more important to decisions than are nonalignable differences. In an early study of judgment, Slovic and MacPhillamy (1974) asked people to make judgments about the first-year grade point averages of two students, each of whom was described by two test scores. One score was from a test taken by both students (i.e., it was an alignable difference). The other score was from a test taken by one student but not the other (i.e., it was a nonalignable difference). Participants in this study tended to focus primarily on the score from the shared test rather than the score from the unique test, suggesting that alignable differences were important for these judgments. Other studies also demonstrated that dimensions with missing information tended to be discounted during choice (e.g., Levin, Johnson, & Faraone, 1984).

Other studies have manipulated the presence of alignable and nonalignable differences more directly. In a study by Markman and Medin (1995), people decided which of a pair of video games would sell best and had to justify their decisions. The descriptions were set up to have some alignable differences and some nonalignable differences. The justifications mentioned significantly more alignable differences than nonalignable differences. Finally, Zhang and Markman (1998) demonstrated that when people are learning about new options, they tend to focus on alignable differences first, and those alignable differences influence their preferences for the new items.

People are also quite good at finding a level of abstraction that enables them to compare sets of items along alignable attributes. Johnson (1984, 1988) found that when people are given sets of options that are easily comparable (e.g., a pair of toasters), they focus on specific properties of the items (e.g., the number of slots or the number of heat settings). In contrast, when they are given sets of options that are hard to compare (e.g., a toaster and a smoke alarm) they focus on more abstract properties such as the degree to which they need a toaster or a smoke alarm. Thus, the evaluation of options takes place at a level of abstraction that permits the representations of the options to be aligned.

There are two reasons why alignable differences play a central role in judgments. First, studies of similarity suggest that alignable differences often signal information that is likely to be important. Thus, attending to alignable differences permits the cognitive system to focus on information about a new situation that is likely to be useful. Second, alignable differences are easier to evaluate than are nonalignable differences (Hsee, 1996). In order to evaluate an alignable difference, it is only necessary to know which value is better. In contrast, in order to evaluate a nonalignable difference, it is necessary to know the value of an attribute on an absolute scale. Both of these factors are likely to contribute to the observed advantage of alignable differences over nonalignable differences in choice.

22.4.3   Summary

The studies summarized in this section are examples of research suggesting that decision making involves general cognitive processes that are also involved in many other tasks. Thus, general processes of evaluation and causal explanation that occur across higher cognitive processes such as problem solving are also important in decision making. Furthermore, analogical reasoning and comparison processes more generally, which have been shown to be part of a variety of fundamental cognitive processes such as categorization, are also central to the ways that people make choices.

With the growing recognition that cognitive processing involves many of the same mechanisms involved in other tasks comes the sense that decision-making research can be used to illuminate these other cognitive processes. For example, Hutchinson and Alba (1991) used a context in which people were exposed to consumer products as a way to explore the role of analytic and holistic processing in category acquisition. As the links between decision making and other areas of cognition become clearer, research of this type will become more commonplace.

22.5   TYPES OF DECISIONS I: FAIRNESS, VALUES, AND TRADE-OFFS

In the next two sections we concentrate on how choice processing varies in different settings. This section focuses on how decision making may change as a function of context. In some contexts, people may take the fairness of a decision into account when evaluating options, while in other contexts fairness is not an issue. As another example, what people do when they make choices about consumer products differs from what they do when they make choices about moral situations. Furthermore, people must have strategies for dealing with conflicts in values that they hold. For example, there are often trade-offs between the speed of a car and its goodness for the environment. After we discuss the influence of context on choice processing, we examine how person variables such as personality, expertise, and culture influence choice processing.

22.5.1   Commensurability, Trade-Offs, and Protected Values

Values, meaning, and morality may all affect the ways that people make choices. Departures from normative or prescriptive descriptions of choice behavior go well beyond cognitive heuristics and biases. In this section we review research on the moral side of decision making. Not only do people depart from rational choice, but also there are circumstances in which people's performance is "better than rational." Research on values and meaning also shows limited commensurabillty and a reluctance to make certain types of trade-offs (often to the consternation of policy makers).

Fairness.   Consider the following ultimatum game (Guth, Schmittberger, and Schwarze, 1982; Roth, 1991). Participants are paired off, and one person (A) is allowed to propose an allocation of some resource, and the other (B) must either accept or reject it. If the offer is accepted, both players receive their allocation; however, if B rejects the offer, neither player receives anything. For example, the resource may be $10, and A may propose to take $9 and give B $1. From one point of view B's decision is quite simple: B should accept any nonnegative outcome because it is better than nothing.

To the contrary, Bs typically reject such an unequal distribution on grounds that it is not fair. Furthermore, the modal offer by As is a 50-50 split, even when the participants do not know each other and are unlikely to interact again in the future. These basic ultimatum results have been replicated time after time (Bazerman et al., 1998). At least for modest amounts of money, Bs are quite willing to punish greedy As. Thaler (1985) suggested that transactions involve two kinds of utility: acquisition utility and transaction utility. The former depends on the value of the good in itself, and the latter refers to the perceived merits of the deal. For the above example, the acquisition utility is positive, but the transaction utility may be negative. Kahneman et al. (1991) provided numerous other examples in which judgments of fairness fail to correspond to standard economic models. Interestingly, notions of fairness, trust, and reciprocity, which have no role in rational analyses of social dilemmas, appear to allow groups to achieve levels of outcomes that are better than rational in that they exceed what is predicted by rational-choice analysis (see Ostrum, 1998, for a review and Axelrod, 1997, for a set of formal models for cooperation). These standards of fairness are another policy that people use to help them out of a situation in which goals might potentially conflict.

Attributional Aspects of Decision Making.   Judgments of fairness convey one attributional aspect of decision making. The point is that people make attributions about the behaviors of others and that decisions may constitute particularly meaningful behaviors. That is, decisions often convey information both to the decision maker and to others. This attributional, or meaning, component of decisions gives rise to complexities that undermine attempts to use monetary value or straightforward notions of a homogeneous currency (e.g., subjective utility) as a close proxy or descriptive framework for judgments.

Sometimes people make decisions with the explicit goal of conveying information. For example, a person completely unhappy with his or her dining experience in a restaurant may choose to leave a one-cent tip rather than no tip at all. The goal of leaving a one-cent tip is to ensure that the message of dissatisfaction is conveyed, because the waiter could possibly attribute leaving no tip to the customer's forgetfulness or stinginess. To verify this intuition, Medin, Schwartz, Biok, and Bimbaum (1999) asked undergraduates to imagine that they had a job waiting on tables in a restaurant and then queried them as to whether they would rather receive no tip or a one-cent tip. The overwhelming majority indicated that they would prefer no tip. Their comments indicated that a one-cent tip would be perceived as an unkind act. Note that these judgments imply a nonmonotone relation between monetary value and utility, in which no tip and a large tip are preferred to a very small tip.

Meaning may depend on inferences about goals even within a narrow domain. For example, Medin et al. (1999) found that within the sphere of donations, attributions are not some straightforward function of monetary values. They asked undergraduates to rate their liking for a person who donated $500 to Princeton University. The person was described as being either a billionaire CEO or a shoe salesman. The shoe salesman received positive ratings 92% of the time compared with only 20% for the CEO (the CEO was also described by participants in very negative terms in an open-ended, descriptive-adjective task). Of course, these judgments could reveal a general dislike for CEOs. However, when the CEO was described as donating a first edition of poems valued at $500 to Princeton instead of cash, positive ratings for the CEO increased from 20% to 75%.

In a follow-up study, the multibillionaire scenario was described in two stories in which the final use of the donation was the same. Undergraduates rated the multibillionaire after reading one of two scenarios. In the first vignette the donation was $500 to the Princeton University Library to be used to purchase books. In the second story the multibillionaire found the first edition of poems in an antique desk he purchased at an auction, was told that it was worth $500, and then donated it to the Princeton University Library. The story continued that the library already had several first editions, and the head librarian sold the gift for $400 and used the proceeds to purchase books. Note that the latter scenario undermines the idea that the book had strong sentimental value for the multibillionaire or that the gift met a special need for the library. Note also that the final value for the library was less in the second vignette than the first. Nonetheless, the multibillionaire was rated reliably more favorably after the second story than after the first. Apparently, the book donation suggests a different kind of intention than does the money donation, and the latter evokes the multibillionaire's wealth as the context for evaluating the gift. In brief, it is the perceived intention that serves to determine attributions, not the value of the gift by itself.

22.5.2   Kinds of Decisions

Decisions may be divisible into kinds based on the values, meaning, or evaluation procedure associated with them (e.g., Beattie & Baron, 1995; Chapman, 1996, 1998; Goldstein and Weber, 1995; Irwin & Baron, -b). Furthermore, there are both across-and within-kind obstacles to notions of common currency or simple exchangeability.

A focus on meaning is also consistent with the idea that different kinds of decisions may be associated with different principles and strategies. These sorts of influences are most readily seen in studies in which the same context (more or less) is involved but cues are present that bias the interpretation of the context in one way or another. For example, Larrick and Blount (1997) presented participants with a game that could be seen either as a social dilemma or as involving fairness (an ultimatum game). They varied whether the situation was described in terms of "claiming" versus "accepting or rejecting" offers. Larrick and Blount reasoned that the accept or reject framing is more compatible with an ultimatum game than with a social dilemma. They found that the description affected both the offers made and their likelihood of being accepted; when the situation was framed in terms of accepting versus rejecting, participants were less willing to accept small shares than they were when the situation was framed in terms of claiming.

Tenbrunsel and Messick (1999) presented research participants with resource dilemmas in which individual self-interest conflicted with a cooperative solution that would protect the resource. In one study participants played the role of managers of manufacturing plants that were faced with the problem of toxic gas emissions. Their plants had smokestacks equipped with scrubbers that could eliminate the toxicity. Operating the scrubbers cost money, and participants had to decide what percentage of the time their scrubbers would run. As in the usual dilemma, accepting the expense of running scrubbers would produce clean air only if managers cooperated. In one condition mild sanctions for failure to run scrubbers were introduced, and in the other there were no penalties. Tenbrunsel and Messick found that mild sanctions for noncooperation actually increased noncooperation compared with no sanctions. Other measures suggested that without sanctions, people viewed the dilemma as involving a personal or ethical decision; with mild sanctions, people tended to see the dilemma as a business decision (see also Bazerman et al., 1998, for related evidence). Thus, when the dilemma was viewed as an ethical choice, participants playing the role of managers were more likely to operate the scrubbers than when the choice was viewed solely as a business decision.

Social-Relation Theory.   One specific theory about kinds of decisions is the Fiske and Tetlock (1997) social-relation theory. Their analysis includes four types of social relationships: communal sharing, authority ranking, equality matching, and market pricing. Communal sharing is categorical in character. Members do not keep track of favors, nor is direct reciprocity involved. For example, a father who helps his daughter move into a new apartment would not expect to be compensated (monetarily or otherwise). Friendships typically correspond to equality matching in which there is something of a loose reciprocity, and problems may arise if exchanges get too far out of balance. In contrast, business exchanges embody a market-pricing relationship in which exchanges are precisely monitored and money is the prototypical medium. The fourth type of relation, authority ranking, involves dominance as in, for example, the relationship between a queen and her subjects. In dominance relations, exchange may be asymmetrical (e.g., subordinates pay tribute). In short, according to Fiske and Tetlock, there is a semantics of exchange that varies as a function of the type of relation.

Although some forms of exchange may involve culture-specific conventions, the general rules of exchange for a given type of relation are held to be universal. Fiske and Tetlock's main argument is that exchanges between entities in different domains are often painful, condemned as unethical, or just plain taboo. Parents selling their children into slavery is an extreme example of the forbidden mixture between community sharing and market pricing. Other cross-domain trade-offs are less offensive and may only be perceived as tactless. For example, offering money to a neighbor who helped you with a spare tire is not immoral, but it may be seen as a display of bad taste. Money is an appropriate exchange only for the right relationships and only for certain kinds of exchanges (see Medin et al., 1999, for empirical evidence supporting the Fiske and Tetlock theory). Conversely, nonmonetary goods and services are inappropriate in contexts in which only money will do.

Commensurability, Trade-Offs, and Protected Values.   Decision making involves judgments about values. Some values may be easy to compare and thus may lend themselves to a common measure. For example, if two business projects are considered, then the one that generates more cash flow may be accepted as more valuable and more worth investing in. However, not all values can be converted to a common currency. For the same two projects, if the one that generates more cash flow does so using manufacturing techniques that endanger the lives of workers, then one might reject it as an investment. It is commonly said that one cannot put a price on a human life, suggesting that people are unwilling to make trade-offs between money and lives (at least when they are asked to do so explicitly). Many people think of such values (e.g., protecting the natural environment, human life, sacred objects, etc.) as absolute, not to be traded off for anything else, particularly economic values. Such values are known as protected values (Baron & Ritov, 1994; Baron & Spranca, 1997; Fiske & Tetlock, 1997; Ritov & Baron, 1999).

An interesting phenomenon associated with protected values is that people who indicate some value as protected appear to show a larger than average omission bias. Ritov and Baron (1999) used examples like: An epidemic will cause 1,000 children to die, and a vaccine is available that would prevent these deaths but would also cause 100 children to die. Would you use the vaccine? They report that many subjects oppose such a vaccine both for their own child and as a matter of policy (Ritov and Baron 1990, 1999). When asked for a threshold amount of harm from action, a few participants said zero. That is, they would not vaccinate a group of children if the vaccine had caused a single death. Of course, many more participants give some number between 0 and 1,000. Importantly people who were found to hold protected values (by an independent measure) showed a larger omission bias than people who did not indicate a protected value. Thus, even though a vaccine is also likely to save children, these participants prefer to avoid taking an action that might harm some children.

In brief, researchers (Baron & Spranca, 1997; Ritov & Baron, 1999) have found that protected values are associated with a particularly large bias against harmful acts that undermine the value in question, as opposed to harmful omissions. Apparently, it is much worse to cause something bad to happen by one's actions than to allow something bad to happen through one's inaction. That is, protected values represent prohibitions against actions (Baron & Spranca, 1997).

In most of the studies concerning omission bias, a decision is made between two alternatives: omission (status quo) and active commission that may incur loss as well as gain. The losses or gains are about human or animal lives, the natural environment, or other potentially protected values. Even though the act of commission involves trade-offs that might generate a net gain, many participants do not readily accept them.

One explanation for omission bias is that the status quo is taken as a reference point and that alternatives are evaluated relative to it. Furthermore, losses loom larger than gains (Baron & Ritov, 1994). In the vaccine example, a loss of 80 children caused by a vaccine may be weighted more heavily than the gain of 100 lives that would have been saved from the disease. This observation suggests that the size of the omission bias may vary with how readily the gain and loss alternatives can be integrated. When the gain and loss items involved in the trade-off (human lives, for example) are from the same samples, omission bias appears to be significantly smaller. For the vaccine example, Ritov and Baron (1990) found that omission bias was reduced when people were told that the vaccine did not actually cause deaths but rather that the deaths occurred when the vaccine was ineffective against the disease. Perhaps more relevant, omission bias was also reduced when subjects were told that the children who would die from the vaccine were the same ones who would have died anyway from the disease (Ritov and Baron, 1995). This is consistent with the idea that gains and losses are more easily integrated or made commensurable when the deaths from vaccination are a proper subset of the potential deaths from the disease.

The most straightforward account of why people with protected values show a larger omission bias is the idea suggested by Baron and Spranca (1997) that protected values represented prohibitions against actions that are harmful. In this sense, they may simply represent an exaggerated form of normal behavior that results in omission bias. As Baron and Spranca point out, the defining characteristic of a protected value is an unwillingness to consider trade-offs. Recall from our previous discussion that one reason why people may be unwilling to consider trade-offs is that trade-offs ease choices in situations in which there are competing goals.

One potential problem with this view of protected values is that it risks circularity. People indicate protected values by their attitude toward trade-offs, so it is perhaps not surprising that they are often unwilling to make trade-offs in the scenarios. Thus, what are being called protected values might just be prominent examples of situations in which people show an omission bias. They are notable because they occur in emotionally charged contexts.

Contingent Valuation.   In general it has proven difficult to get people to place monetary value on certain sorts of goods. For example, policy makers have been interested in the importance or value that people place on things such as national parks or clean air in order to determine priorities in expenditures or penalties to be imposed on polluters. Two common measures employed are people's willingness to pay (WTP) to ensure some good or outcome and people's willingness to accept (WTA) money to give up some good or outcome. These attempts have been met consistently with frustration. Not only do the WTA and WTP measures disagree, but also people's judgments show insensitivity to quantity. For example, Kahneman and Knetsch (1992) found that the WTP to clean up all lakes in Ontario was barely higher that the WTP to clean up the lakes in specific regions of Ontario (see also Baron & Greene, 1996). Kahneman and Knetsch suggested that, if anything, WTP might correspond to the "purchase of moral satisfaction," in other words, a symbolic act to mark the fact that the person has the appropriate values. In general, respondents seem to treat such goods as things that cannot be traded off for money (see also Baron, 2001; Beattie and Barlas, 2001; Ritov and Kahneman, 1997). Indeed, in a series of studies Irwin and Baron (2001) find that alternatives to pricing responses (e.g., a rating of a person's willingness to purchase some item) are more sensitive to moral values than are pricing responses.

22.5.3   Summary

The straightforward framework in which values are assigned to entities and the resulting values provide the basis for a common currency to mediate exchanges is severely limited when morality and meaning are at stake. A further important qualification is that value and exchange are relation-dependent. This means that findings from the prototypical market-pricing context may not generalize beyond that context. Instead, it appears that a lack of commensurability is the norm when moral values are engaged. Yet to be systematically explored are the interrelationships between values and emotions, though Baron and Spranca (1997) note that the mere offer of an exchange involving protected values may trigger moral outrage. We now turn to the role of expertise and cultural differences in choice.

22.6   TYPES OF DECISIONS II: EXPERTISE AND CULTURAL DIFFERENCES

So far, we have discussed decision making as if all people make choices in approximately the same way, even if their choices of strategy may be influenced by the domain in which the choices are made. Recently, researchers have shown significant interest in the way people may differ in their choice strategies, even within a given domain. In this section we review research that explores how expert decision making may differ from novice decision making. In addition, we examine other kinds of individual differences, particularly those that result from cultural differences. This work illustrates current thinking about how people vary in the way they approach choice situations.

22.6.1   Individual Differences

An important theme in decision research is concern with ecological validity. Do people respond to real bets the same way they do to hypothetical ones? In general, results from laboratory studies have held up surprisingly well when tested, for example, on the floor of a casino or at the race track (see Camerer, 2000, for a review). Of course, generality is multifaceted and can include task variable, context, and participant characteristics. In keeping with our theme of a shift between a focus on the structure of decisions to a concern with the structure of the decision maker, in this section we consider individual difference variables and their role in decision making.

One place where people differ is in their degree of risk aversion. The Prospect-Theory weighting function (shown in Figure 22.2) is aimed at describing aggregate data, and how well individuals conform to it is an open question. Lopes (1987, 1995; Lopes & Oden, 1999) argued that an important individual difference variable is the degree to which individuals are risk seeking versus risk averse (corresponding more or less to promotion versus prevention motivation). She suggested that people who are risk averse pay more attention to the worst outcomes associated with an option, whereas risk-seeking individuals attend more to the best outcomes.

Another variable in her theory is a person's aspiration level. The idea is that a person sets some criterion or goal and gives extra weight to options that meet or exceed this aspiration level. For example, if a person's goal is to break even at the race track and he or she is behind by $30 going into the last race, then the person might prefer to bet on a horse with long odds and a small chance to win over a favorite with very short odds. According to her SP/A theory (SP stands for security bias versus potential bias, A for aspiration level), choices are a function of the security-potential weighting functions and the aspiration level. Although the SP/A theory shares some characteristics with cumulative Prospect Theory (Tversky and Kahneman, 1992), there are some differences that center around the contrast between reference points and aspiration levels (see Lopes & Oden, 1999, for details).

Another approach to individual differences is to wonder if results from undergraduates and business students hold for other populations. For example, Nisbett and his colleagues (Lehman & Nisbett, 1993; Lehman, Nisbett, & Lempert, 1993) found that social science graduate students and majors are less susceptible to some cognitive biases than are humanities or natural science majors. They attribute this difference not to self-selection but rather to specific learning experiences involving, for example, probabilistic reasoning. Nisbett, Fong, Lehman, and Cheng (1987) provided clear evidence that training students on probabilistic reasoning (e.g., concepts such as regression to the mean) has enduring effects outside the classroom (see also Larrick, Morgan, & Nisbett, 1990). Larrick et al. (1993) reported that the use of cost-benefit decision rules among University of Michigan faculty (avoiding sunk costs, attending to opportunity costs, etc.) correlated significantly with economics training and salary.

Tentori, Osherson, Hasher, and May (in press) observed that older adults were far less susceptible to biases such as framing effects than were younger adults (see Wang, 1996, for another age-related difference in risk-sensitive choices involving family members). All of the above results suggest that there are clear individual differences in decision making. Furthermore, they may be tied to learning and experience. We now look more directly at expertise effects.

22.6.2   Expertise

An important way that people differ from each other is in the knowledge they acquire. Acquisition of expertise can have a number of important effects on decision making (Alba & Hutchinson, 1987). First, expertise may influence the way decision makers perceive a domain. Second, experts can bring domain knowledge to bear on choice and thus may be able to retrieve a possible solution without having to compare a set of options. Third, expertise may allow decision makers to go beyond the information given. Finally, there may be situations in which expertise may hinder decision processing. Often, these negative effects of expertise arise when a new option (such as an innovative product) is developed that goes beyond the expert's knowledge. In this section we present examples of each of these phenomena.

Expertise influences the way people encode information about options. Increasing expertise can actually change people's perception of visual stimuli. For example, Lesgold and his colleagues (1988) found that expert radiologists (doctors with many years of experience) making diagnostic decisions focused on much smaller aspects of X-ray films than did residents who had much less experience interpreting X-ray films. Thus, the basic input to diagnostic decisions changes based on expertise.

The perceptual changes are not just a matter of some kind of hardwiring of the perceptual system that changes with experience. Conceptual information may interact with available perceptual information in the environment to determine what is seen in a stimulus. For example, physicians use conceptual information to influence their perception during diagnosis. Brooks, LeBlanc, and Norman (2000) showed doctors different case histories along with textbook pictures of dermatological disorders. When the case history was consistent with the disorder, the doctors saw the proper symptoms in the pictures nearly all the time. In contrast, when the case did not suggest a particular disorder, doctors were much less likely to perceive the same features in the pictures. Thus, the perceptual information that an expert seeks will depend in part on conceptual information that is active during decision making.

The role of conceptual information in diagnostic decision making suggests that doctors are constructing choices rather than selecting from among a set of possible options. This view of choice is consistent with Klein's (2000) observations of expert decision makers in practical situations. His work with firefighters and military decision makers suggests that it is rare for experts to consider and compare multiple options. Instead, decision makers appear to use their background knowledge to remind them of prior situations in which particular solution strategies were carried out. For example, an expert firefighter who approaches the scene of a fire will be able to decide how to configure the trucks and deploy firefighters by carrying out variations of plans used while fighting previous fires.

Nearly all of the potential decisions studied by Klein and his colleagues involved this kind of constructive processing rather than choices among options. Indeed, most of the cases in which people compared a set of options occurred when a novice was forced to make a decision or when an expert decision maker had to act in a situation that went beyond his or her domain of expertise.

Even when experts did not have a specific case in memory to handle a new situation, they tended to consider one option at a time. The experts would generate a potential course of action and mentally simulate the outcome in an attempt to find flaws in their plan. If the mental simulation revealed a fatal flaw in the plan, then another option was generated. Thus, even when multiple options were considered, they were examined serially. Klein (2000) refers to this type of decision making as recognition-primed decision making and suggests that it characterizes most of expert behavior.

Why then do most studies of decision making suggest that people are making comparisons among options? One reason is that decision researchers (and indeed most decision theorists) assume that decision making involves explicit choices from among a set of options. Thus, most studies are designed to force people to choose from among a set of options. Second, although Klein found recognition-primed decision making among the experts in his studies, he observed that novices tended to compare a set of options to each other (as did the experts working outside of their domain of expertise). Many psychological studies of expertise tend to use weak manipulations of expertise, having graduate students or people with self-professed familiarity serve as experts (see Shanteau, 1988, for an insightful discussion of this issue). For this reason, changes in decision processing that occur with "real" experts may go unnoticed.

Another benefit of expertise is that experts can bring their knowledge structures to bear in cases in which insufficient information has been presented. Earlier, we discussed that people tend to discount dimensions with missing information, leading to greater use of alignable differences than nonalignable differences. In many cases, a nonalignable difference is a property that people know about for one option and they simply do not know the corresponding attribute for the other option. Although it might be advantageous to find out the missing value, people often ignore that dimension instead. However, experts are able to recognize when important information is missing and to use their background knowledge to make plausible guesses about the values of the missing properties. For example, Sanbonmatsu, Kardes, and Herr (1992) found that bicycle experts were more likely than novices to recognize that the weight of some models of bicycles in a consideration set were missing and to make reasonable guesses about the weight of those bicycles on the basis of the other values provided. One reason why experts may be better at processing information about missing information is also that they have a better sense of the criteria against which a set of options should be evaluated than do novices (Bettman & Sujan, 1987).

Finally, expertise can have negative consequences when people must learn about new products. When people become experts, part of what they do is to acquire information about relationships among properties of objects. For example, camera experts know how the parts of cameras are connected. They also know the conceptual relationships among parts, so they can predict the influence of changing the film speed, the shutter speed, or the size of the aperture. Novices may know about some of these parts, but they do not know as many relations among them.

Sloman, Love, and Ahn (1998) suggest that people have more difficulty incorporating a property change into their knowledge when that property has many relational connections than when it has few. Thus, a camera expert will have more difficulty learning about products that change critical features of cameras than will novices. Support for this conjecture comes from research demonstrating that camera experts have more difficulty processing information about digital cameras than do novices (Moreau, Lehman, & Markman, 2001). This research suggests that camera experts find more potential risks of a new product because they have many goals that can be satisfied by film-based cameras, and they do not know how those goals will be satisfied by the new product. This processing difficulty actually makes camera experts feel less inclined than novices to purchase a digital camera.

22.6.3   Culture

No one doubts that there are cultural differences in decision making. For example, one might expect cultural differences as well as individual differences in prevention versus promotion goals (e.g., Lee, Aaker, & Gardner, 2000). Although cultural differences may have practical implications for international commerce, a critical question is whether cultural and individual differences can be captured in terms of variations in the parameters of a single model or whether a different type of theory is needed to describe decision makers in different cultures. It is premature to try to answer this question, if only because the field of decision making is so broad and because there is no single unifying theory that covers all or even most of the major facets. Current progress takes the form of addressing two less ambitious questions: (a) how well the generalizations developed so far concerning judgment and decision making carry over into other cultures and (b) whether one can use cultural differences in values, goals, and orientations to develop and test predictions of current theories. We will briefly consider examples of each of these questions.

Generality.   Nisbett, Peng, Choi, and Norenzayan (2001) argued that holistic versus analytic processing styles characterize a critical differences between East Asian and Western thought. East Asians are said to be more dialectical and focused on relations, whereas Westerners are more comfortable with formal logic and are focused on individuals. Nisbett et al. documented a series of cultural differences in judgment that they argue follow from these differences. For example, East Asians are less likely to make the fundamental attribution error (Ross, 1977) but more likely to show hindsight bias. Nisbett et al. argued that East Asians also may tend to seek the middle way in reconciling conflicts or contradictions. In a more or less literal test of this idea, Briley, Morris, and Simonson (2000) examined the compromise effect in East Asians and European Americans and found that asking for justifications for choices increased compromise choices for East Asians but decreased them for European Americans.

These examples suggest that cultural differences do influence patterns of judgment and choice and that what we have considered to be cognitive universals in decision making may sometimes be more specific to particular cultures. The cut between Eastern and Western cultures made in this section is quite broad, and there are likely to be important differences within these categories. For example, Yates, Lee, Shinotsuka, Patalano, and Sieck (1998; see also Yates, Lee, & Shinotsuka, 1996) found that Chinese students showed a much larger overconfidence effect than American students and that Japanese students showed the least overconfidence. Much additional research is required to elucidate these issues.

Comparisons as Theory Tests.   An exciting application of cultural differences is to use cross-cultural comparisons as a way of testing broader theories of choice. One important distinction among cultures that has been the basis of current research is the difference between individualist and collectivist cultures. An individualist culture (such as in the United States) tends to place emphasis on the individual and on independence. A collectivist culture (such as in many Asian cultures) tends to value relationships among people. See Hofstede (1980, 1983) and Triandis (1989) for a general review of individualist versus collectivist cultures and their cognitive implications.

Gelfand and Christakopolou (1999) suggested that members of a collectivist culture (Greece in their study) should differ from members of an individualistic culture (the United States) in negotiation processes. Specifically, they predicted that participants from the individualistic cultures would have more difficulty than members of a collectivist culture in negotiating a mutually advantageous settlement. Instead, members of the individualistic culture tended to treat negotiations as a zero-sum game in which gains by one side should be matched by losses on the other.

A more typical pattern of cross-cultural research starts with a puzzle (e.g., why do the cultures differ?) and then is followed by some detective work to pin down the basis for differences. A nice example of this approach is provided by the work of Weber and Hsee (1999). The initial observation was that although American and Chinese students did not differ in their attitude toward risk, Chinese students saw financial risk situations as significantly less risky than did Americans (incidentally, this is the opposite of the intuitions of both groups about cultural differences; Hsee and Weber).

Why did this difference in risk perception occur? Based on some ethnographic observations, Hsee and Weber (1999) suggested what they call the cushion hypothesis. The basic idea is that in a collectivist culture, in which the extended family is important, people are more likely to receive financial help if they need it than in a more individualistic culture (like that of the United States), in which the nuclear family tends to be more important than the extended family. An analysis of American and Chinese proverbs (Weber, Hsee, & Sokolowska, 1998) indicated that American proverbs are less applicable to the social domain than are Chinese proverbs. Furthermore, Chinese students perceived proverbs to advocate more risk seeking than American students, but only for financial risks and not for social risks.

If this analysis is correct, then Chinese students may be more risk seeking only in the financial domain. In support of this hypothesis, Hsee and Weber (1999) looked at risk preferences in the domains of finance, academics, and medicine. They replicated the cultural difference for financial decisions but found no difference in the academic or health domains. In a review of this and related research on cultural differences in risk perception, Weber and Hsee (1999) argued that, where possible, cross-cultural research should be guided by and relevant to a theory or model (as opposed to a simple catalog of cultural differences).

As another example of cross-cultural research focused on model testing, Aaker and Lee (in press) predicted that people with a highly accessible independent self-concept would tend to have a promotion focus when evaluating consumer products, whereas people with a highly accessible interdependent self-concept would tend to have a prevention focus. To explore this issue, one study examined American and Chinese participants. As members of an individualistic culture, the American participants were expected to have a relatively independent self-concept. In contrast, as members of a collectivist culture, Chinese participants were expected to have a relatively interdependent self-concept. Consistent with their hypothesis, American participants showed relatively better recall of information related to promotion than of information related to prevention, and Chinese participants showed better recall of information related to prevention than of information related to promotion. It is important to note, however, that a manipulation of regulatory focus (which focused people on winning or not losing a prize) had a larger effect on people's recall than did their dominant culture. Thus, although cultural differences can provide a chronic source of motivational focus, situational effects are likely to be stronger.

Cultural differences in choice behavior may also be used as a way of assessing underlying mental models of the choice domain. As an example, Atran et al. (1999) began with the observation that three cultural groups living in the lowland rainforest of Guatemala had distinct differences in the sustainability of their agroforestry practices. The indigenous group, the Itza' Maya, appears to operate sustainably. Two other groups that immigrated to the area — Ladinos and Q'eqchi' Maya — are more destructive than the Itza', and the Q'eqchi' are much more destructive than the Ladinos.

In order to explore why the Ladinos and Q'eqchi' choose to be more environmentally destructive than the Itza', Atran et al. collected observations on social and expert networks, on folk-ecological models of the forest (i.e., how plants and animals affect each other), and on human impact (both self-report and direct measurements on farmers' lands). They found dramatic differences in mental models. Only the Itza' Maya see animals as helping plants. Itza' and Ladinos have a common model for how plants affect animals, and this model is much richer than the Q'eqchi' model. Furthermore, there is evidence that the Ladinos are learning from the Itza': Ladino network distance from the most expert Itza' correlates reliably with the number of plant-animal relations known by the Ladino participants. Regression analyses on human impact indicate that the cash value predicts what Ladinos say they protect, whereas total uses and ecological centrality predict Itza' impact.[4] Interestingly, Q'eqchi' see themselves as having less impact, though they do report (correctly) that they tend to destroy rather than protect species. These observations are correlational, and it is possible that the folk-ecological models are consequences rather than causes of sustainable agroforestry practice, as Atran et al. note. What is unequivocal is that surface differences in environmental decision can be accompanied by striking differences in cognitive models of resources.

The studies described in this section used cultural differences as a lever for studying cognitive processing. Research has begun to use the distinction between individualist and collectivist cultures as a way to explore hypotheses about risk aversion and motivational focus. This work also permits an examination of the differences between chronic motivational focus (imbued by culture) and situational motivational focus (determined by the current context). Finally, cultural differences permit the exploration of more complex topics such as the influence of mental models on choice behavior. This work is particularly interesting because there is not enough time in laboratory settings to provide participants with the kinds of detailed mental models that are necessary to influence decisions.

22.6.4   Summary

Research on individual differences, and especially on cultural differences, is in its infancy (see Chen, 1995; Hui, Triandis, & Yee, 1991; Leung, Bond, & Schwartz, 1995; and the edited volume by Earley & Minam, 1997, for a review of culture and decision making). The safest prediction of our review is that this topic will receive dramatically greater attention in the

21st century. The globalization of economies, as well as the recognition of multiculturalism within nations, demands consideration, if only to demonstrate the generality of current theories. We believe that comparative studies will provide a rich source of observations that will lead the field toward better theories.

22.7   CONCLUSIONS

It is difficult to provide a single summary of a chapter as long as this one is. We have covered a lot of ground. In particular, we have suggested that research on decision making is organized differently than it was in the 1970s and 1980s. The field has moved from one dominated by normative models borrowed from economics to one based on psychological models that inform (and in turn are informed by) the study of choice.

One key change is the shift in focus from an analysis of performance with particular sets of options to an exploration of psychological processes within decision makers. Research motivated by normative economic models created sets of decision situations designed to highlight anomalies in choice. There was concern for the way decision makers would process these decisions, but the interest was clearly centered on the particular choice settings. One way to see this focus is to note that many of the key decision settings were given names such as the "jacket scenario" (i.e., the mental-accounting demonstration involving the jacket and the calculator), the "disease problem" (i.e., the problem illustrating framing effects), and the "theater ticket scenario" (i.e., the example of mental accounting involving a lost ticket).

Current research is focused less on these particular choice scenarios and more on the characteristics of decision makers. Researchers are now more interested in the psychological processes underlying choice behavior than in cataloging violations of normative models of choice.

Unlike many areas of psychology, the study of decision making cuts across traditional areas. The study of goals and motivations often appears in social psychology journals. The exploration of reasoning, problem solving, and similarity is generally presented in cognitive psychology. Explorations of fairness and values appear in management and public policy journals. The study of emotion and its links to decision making appears in law, philosophy, and psychology journals. To understand decision-making behavior, however, all of these relevant areas must be integrated. Thus, decision making has moved from a peripheral to a central area of psychology.

END NOTES

1. This is not to say that all decision-making research before 1990 focused on gambles and rationality. Indeed, many of the papers cited here that go beyond gambles were published before 1990. It is just that there was more consensus about the main issues in decision-making research before 1990 than after.

2. A Dutch book is a set of gambles in which each successive pair is close in probability and value. When people choose among these similar gambles, they typically focus on the differences in the amount to be won and select the gamble with the higher potential winnings. If they are then given the first and last gamble in the series (which differ in both probability and payoff), they often switch their choice to the item with the higher probability of winning. A judiciously selected set of gambles like this can lead to the case in which people consistently favor gambles

that favor the house. Thus, a Dutch book can become a money pump.

3. There is even a burgeoning field of behavioral accounting that focuses on how financial statements are interpreted and used to make decisions (e.g., Hunton, 1998).

4. An interesting follow-up observation is that the Itza' believe that the forest spirits, or *arux,* not only value forest plants in accordance with their ecological

centrality but also play an active role in protecting the forest. For example, Itza' attributed a man's falling out of a tree to the *arux*'s punishing him for cutting down a tree that should have been preserved. Note that this shift in a resource from passive to responsive changes the very conception of the resource dilemma. Although both of the other groups vouch for the presence of the *arux,* in neither group do the *arux* play any such role.

REFERENCE

Aaker, J. (1991). The negative attraction effect? A study of the attraction effect under judgment and choice. *Advances in Consumer Research,* **18,** 462–469.

Aaker, J. L., & Lee, A. Y. (1991). "I" seek pleasures and "we" avoid pains: The role of self-regulatory goals in information processing and persuasion. *Journal of Consumer Research.*

Ajzen, I. (1991). The theory of planned behavior. *Organizational Behavior and Human Decision Processes,* **50,** 179–211.

Alba, J. W., & Hutchinson, J. W. (1987). Dimensions of consumer expertise. *Journal of Consumer Research,* **13,** 411–454.

Allais, M. (1953). Le comportement de I' homme rationnel devant le risque, critique des postulats et axiomes de I'école Américaine. *Econometrica,* **21,** 503–546.

Anderson, J. R. (1983). *The architecture of cognition.* Cambridge: Harvard University Press.

Atran, S., Medin, D. L., Ross, N., Lynch, E., Coley, J., Ucan Ek, E., & Vapnarsky, V. (1999). Folkecology and commons management in the Maya lowlands. *Proceedings of the National Academy of Sciences, USA,* **96,** 7598–7603.

Axelrod, R. (1997). *The complexity of cooperation: Agent-based models of competition and collaboration.* Princeton: Princeton University Press.

Baumeister, R. F., & Heatherton, T. F. (1996). Self-regulation failure: An overview. *Psychological Inquiry,* **7,** 1–15.

Baron, J. (2001). Measuring value trade-offs: Problems and some solutions. In E. U. Weber, J. Baron, & G. Loomes (Eds.), *Conflict and trade-offs in decision making* (pp. 231–258). New York: Cambridge University Press.

Baron, J., & Greene, J. (1996). Determinants of insensitivity to quantity in valuation of public goods: contribution, warm glow, budget constraints, availability and prominence. *Journal of Applied Experimental Psychology,* **2,** 107–125.

Baron, J., & Ritov, I. (1994). Reference points and omission bias. *Organizational Behavior and Human Decision Processes,* **59,** 475–498.

Baron, J., & Spranca, M. (1997). Protected values. *Organizational Behavior and Human Decision Processes,* **70,** 1–16.

Bazerman, M. H. (1998). *Judgment in managerial decision making* (4th ed.). New York: Wiley.

Bazerman, M. H., Tenbrunsel, A. E., & Wade-Benzoni, K. A. (1998). Negotiating with yourself and losing: Understanding and managing conflicting internal preferences. *Academy of Management Review,* **23,** 225–241.

Beattie, J., & Barlas, S. (2001). Predicting perceived differences in trade-off difficulty. In E. U. Weber, J. Baron, & G. Loomes (Eds.), *Conflict and Trade-Offs in Decision Making* (pp. 25–64). New York: Cambridge University Press.

Beattie, J., & Baron, J. (1995). In-kind vs. out-of kind penalties: Preference and valuation. *Journal of Experimental Psychology: Applied,* **1,** 136–151.

Bechara, A., Damasio, H., Damasio, A., & Anderson, S. (1994). Insensitivity to future consequences following damage to human prefrontal cortex. *Cognition,* **50,** 7–15.

Bechara, A., Damasio, H., Damasio, A. R., & Lee, G. P. (1999). Different contributions of the human amygdala and ventromedial prefrontal cortex to decision making. *Journal of Neuroscience,* **19,** 5473–5481.

Bechara, A., Damasio, H., Tranel, D. & Damasio, A. R. (1997). Deciding advantageously before knowing the advantageous strategy. *Science,* **275,** 1293–1295.

Bechara, A., Tranel, D., & Damasio, H. (2000). Characterization of the decision-making deficit of patients with ventromedial prefrontal cortex lesions. *Brain,* **123**(11), 2189–2202.

Bettman, J. R., & Sujan, M. (1987). Effects of framing on evaluation of comparable and noncomparable alternatives by expert and novice consumers. *Journal of Consumer Research,* **14,** 141–154.

Birnbaum, M. H., & Chavez, A. (1997). Test of theories of decision-making: Violations of branch independence and distribution independence. *Organizational Behavior and Human Decision Processes,* **72,** 161–194.

Bransford, J. D., & Johnson, M. K. (1973). Considerations of some problems of comprehension. In W. G. Chase (Ed.), *Visual information processing* (pp. 383–438). New York: Academic Press.

Briley, D. A., Morris, M., & Simonson, I. (2000). Reasons as carriers of culture: Dynamics vs. dispositional models of cultural influence on decision-making. *Journal of Consumer Research,* **27,** 157–178.

Brooks, L. R., LeBlanc, V. R., & Norman, G. R. (2000). On the difficulty of noticing obvious features in patient appearance. *Psychonomic Bulletin and Review,* **11**(2), 112–117.

Busemeyer, J. R., Hastie, R., & Medin, D. L. (1995). Preface. In J. R. Busemeyer, R. Hastie, & D. L. Medin (Eds.), *The psychology of learning and motivation* (Vol. **32,** pp. XI–XV). San Diego: Academic Press.

Busemeyer, J. R., & Townsend, J. T. (1993). Decision field theory: A dynamic-cognitive approach to decision making in an uncertain environment. *Psychological Review,* **100,** 432–459.

Cacioppo, J. T., & Gardener, W. L. (1999). Emotion. *Annual Review of Psychology,* **50,** 191–214.

Camerer, C. F. (2000). Prospect theory in the wild: Evidence form the field. In D. Kahneman & A. Tversky (Eds.), *Choices, values and frames.* New York: Cambridge University Press.

Carver, C. S., & Scheier, M. F. (1990). Principles of self-regulation: Action and emotion. In E. T. Higgins & R. M. Sorrentino (Eds.), *Handbook of motivation and cognition* (Vol. **2,** pp. 3–52). New York: Guilford Press.

Carver, C. S., & Scheier, M. F. (1998). *On the self-regulation of behavior.* New York: Cambridge University Press.

Chapman, G. (1996). Temporal discounting and utility for health and money. *Journal of Experimental Psychology: Learning, Memory, and Cognition,* **22**(3), 771–791.

Chapman, G. (1998). Sooner or later: The Psychology of intertemporal choice. In D. L. Medin (Ed.), *The psychology of learning and motivation: Advances in research and theory* (pp. 83–113). San Diego: Academic Press.

Chen, C. C. (1995). New trends in rewards allocation preferences: A Sino-U.S. comparison. *Academy of Management Journal,* **38,** 408–428.

Crowe, E., & Higgins, E. T. (1997). Regulatory focus and strategic inclinations: Promotion and prevention in decision-making. *Organizational Behavior and Human Decision Processes,* **69**(2), 117–132.

Damasio, A. R. (1994). *Descartes' error: Emotion, reason and the human brain.* New York: Putnam.

Dawes, R. M. (1988). *Rational choice In an uncertain world.* Orlando, FL: Harcourt Brace Jovanovich.

DeSousa, R. (1987). *The rationality of emotion.* Cambridge: MIT Press.

Dunbar, K. (1997). How scientists think: On-line creativity and conceptual change in science. In T. B. Ward, S. M. Smith, & J. Vaid (Eds.), *Creative thought: An investigation of conceptual structures and processes* (pp. 461–493). Washington, DC: American Psychological Association.

Earley, P. C., & Miriam, E. (Eds.). (1997). *New perspectives on international and industrial-organizational psychology.* San Francisco: New Lexington Press.

Edwards, W. (1954). The theory of decision making. *Psychological Bulletin,* **51,** 380–417.

Edwards, W. (Ed.). (1992). *Utility theories: Measurements and applications.* Boston: Kluwer.

Fanselow, M. S. (1995). Neural organization of the defensive behavior system responsible for fear. *Psychonomic Bulletin and Review,* **1**(4), 429–438.

Finucane, M., Peters, E., & Slovic, P. (2000). Judgment and decision making: The dance of affect and reason. In Schneider, S. L., & Shanteau, J. (Eds.), *Emerging Perspectives on Judgment and Decision Research.* Cambridge University Press.

Fischhoff, B. (1988). Judgment and decision-making. In R. J. Sternberg & E. E. Smith (Eds.), *The psychology of human thought.* Cambridge: Cambridge University Press.

Fischhoff, B., Lichtenstein, S., Slovic, P., Derby, S., & Keeney, R. L. (1981). *Acceptable risk.* New York: Cambridge University Press.

Fiske, A. P., & Tetlock, P. E. (1997). Taboo trade-offs: Reactions to transactions that transgress the spheres of justice. *Political Psychology,* **18,** 255–297.

Frisch, D., & Clemen, R. T. (1994). Beyond expected utility: Rethinking behavioral decision research. *Psychological Bulletin,* **116,** 46–54.

Frank, R. H. (1988). *Passions within reason: The strategic role of the emotions.* New York: Morton.

Gelfand, M. J., & Christakopolou, S. (1999). Culture and negotiator cognition: Judgment accuracy and negotiation processes in individualistic and collectivist cultures. *Organizational Behavior and Human Decision Processes,* **79**(3), 248–269.

Gentner, D. (1983). Structure-mapping: A theoretical framework for analogy. *Cognitive Science,* **7,** 155–170.

Gentner, D. D., & Markman, A. B. (1997). Structural alignment in analogy and similarity. *American Psychologist,* **52**(1), 45–56.

Gigerenzer, G., & Goldstein, D. G. (1996). Reasoning the fast and frugal way: Models of bounded rationality. *Psychological Review,* **103**(4), 650–669.

Gigerenzer, G., & Todd, P. M. (2000). *Simple heuristics that make us smart.* New York: Oxford University Press.

Gilovich, T., & Medvec, V. H. (1995). The experience of regret: What, when, and why. *Psychological Review,* **102**(2), 379–395.

Gilovich, T., Medvec, V. H., & Kahneman, D. (1998). Varieties of regret: A debate and a partial resolution. *Psychological Review,* **105**(3), 602–605.

Glenberg, A. M. (1997). What memory is for. *Behavioral and Brain Sciences,* **20**(1), 1–55.

Goldstein, W. M., & Weber, E. U. (1995). Content and discontent: Indications and implications of domain specificity in preferential decision making. In J. Busemeyer, R. Hastie, & D. L. Medin (Eds.), *Decision making from a cognitive perspective* (Vol. **32**, pp. 83–136). San Diego: Academic Press.

Gollwitzer, P. (1999). Implementation intentions: Strong effects of simple plans. *American Psychologist,* **54,** 493–503.

Gollwitzer, P. M., & Moskowitz, G. B. (1996). Goal effects on action and cognition. In E. T. Higgins & A. W. Kruglanski (Eds.), *Social psychology: Handbook of basic principles* (pp. 361–399). New York: Guilford Press.

Gregan-Paxton, J., & Roedder, J. D. (1997). Consumer learning by analogy: A model of internal knowledge transfer. *Journal of Consumer Research,* **24,** 266–284.

Guidagni, P. M., & Little, J. D. C. (1983). A logit model of brand choice calibrated on scanner data. *Marketing Science,* **2,** 203–238.

Guth, W., Schmittberger, R., & Schwarze, B. (1982). An experimental analysis of ultimatum bargaining. *Journal of Economic Behavior and Organization,* **3,** 367–388.

Hastie, R., & Park, B. (1986). The relationship between memory and judgment depends on whether the judgment task is memory-based or on-line. *Psychological Review,* **93**(3), 258–268.

Heath, C. (1995). Escalation and de-escalation of commitment in response to sunk costs: The role of budgeting in mental accounting. *Organizational Behavior and Human Decision Processes,* **62**(1), 38–54.

Heath, C., & Fennema, M. G. (1996). Mental depreciation and marginal decision making. *Organizational Behavior and Human Decision Processes,* **68**(2), 95–108.

Heckhausen, H., & Beckmann, J. (1990). Intentional action and action slips. *Psychological Review,* **97**(1), 36–48.

Hertwig, R., & Ortmann, A. (in press). Experimental practices in economics: A methodological challenge for psychologists? *Behavioral and Brain Sciences.*

Higgins, E. T. (1987). Self-discrepancy: A theory relating self and affect. *Psychological Review,* **94**(3), 319–340.

Higgins, E. T. (1997). Beyond pleasure and pain. *American Journal of Psychology,* **52**(12), 1280–1300.

Hofstede, G. (1980). *Cultures consequences: International differences in work related values.* Beverly Hills: Sage.

Hofstede, G. (1983). Dimensions of national cultures in fifty countries and three regions. In J. B. Deregowski, S. Dziurawiec, & R. C. Annis (Eds.), *Expectations in cross-cultural psychology.* Lisse, Netherlands: Swets and Zeitlinger.

Hogarth, R. M. (Ed.), (1990). *Insights in decision making: A tribute to Hillel J. Einhorn.* Chicago: University of Chicago Press.

Holyoak, K. J., & Simon, D. (1999). Bidirectional reasoning in decision making. *Journal of Experimental Psychology: General,* **128**(1), 3–31.

Holyoak, K. J., & Thagard, P. (1995). *Mental leaps: Analogy in creative thought.* Cambridge: MIT Press.

Houston, D. A., Sherman, S. J., & Baker, S. M. (1989). The influence of unique features and direction of comparison on preferences. *Journal of Experimental Social Psychology,* **25,** 121–141.

Hsee, C. K. (1996). The evaluability hypothesis: An explanation for preference reversals between joint and separate evaluations of alternatives. *Organizational Behavior and Human Decision Processes,* **67**(3), 247–257.

Hsee, C. K. (2001). Attribute evaluability: Its implications for joint-separate evaluation reversals and beyond. In D. Kahneman & A. Tversky (Eds.), *Choices, values and frames* (pp. 543–563). New York: Cambridge University Press.

Hsee, C. K., Loewenstein, G. F., Blount, S., & Bazerman, M. H. (1999). Preference reversals between joint and separate evaluations of options: A review and theoretical analysis. *Psychological Bulletin,* **125,** 576–590.

Hsee, C., & Weber, E. U. (1999). Cross-national differences in risk preference and lay predictions. *Journal of Behavioral Decision Making,* **12,** 165–179.

Huber, J., Payne, J. W., & Puto, C. (1982). Adding asymmetrically dominated alternatives: Violations of regularity and the similarity hypothesis. *Journal of Consumer Research,* **9,** 90–98.

Huber, J., & Puto, C. (1983). Market boundaries and product choice: Illustrating attraction and substitution effects. *Journal of Consumer Research,* **10,** 31–44.

Hui, C. H., Triandis, H. C., & Yee, C. (1991). Cultural differences in reward allocation: Is collectivism the explanation? *British Journal of Social Psychology,* **30,** 145–157.

Hunton, J. E. (Ed.). (1998). *Advances in accounting behavioral research* (Vol. 1). Stamford, CT: Jai Press.

Hutchinson, J. W., & Alba, J. W. (1991). Ignoring irrelevant information: Situational determinants of consumer learning. *Journal of Consumer Research,* **18,** 325–345.

Idson, L. C., Liberman, N., & Higgins, T. (2000). Distinguishing gains from nonlosses and losses from nongains: A regulatory focus perspective on hedonic intensity. *Journal of Experimental and Social Psychology,* **36,** 252–274.

Irwin, J. R., & Baron, J. (2001). Response mode effects and moral values. *Organizational Behavior and Human Decision Processes,* **84**(2), 177–197.

Irwin, J. R., & Baron, J. (in press). Values and decisions. In H. Kunreuther & S. Hoch (Eds.), *Wharton on decision making.* New York: Wiley.

Johnson, M. D. (1984). Consumer choice strategies for comparing noncomparable alternatives. *Journal of Consumer Research,* **11,** 741–753.

Johnson, M. D. (1988). Comparability and hierarchical processing in multialternative choice. *Journal of Consumer Research,* **15,** 303–314.

Kahneman, D., & Knetsch, J. L. (1992). Valuing public goods: The purchase of moral satisfaction. *Journal of Environmental Economics and Management,* **22,** 57–70.

Kahneman, D., Knetsch, J. L., & Thaler, R. H. (1991). Anomalies: The endowment effect, loss aversion and status quo bias. *Journal of Economic Perspectives,* **5**(1), 193–206.

Kahneman, D., Slovic, P., & Tversky, A. (1982). *Judgment under uncertainty: Heuristics and biases.* New York: Cambridge University Press.

Kahneman, D., & Snell, J. S. (1992). Predicting a changing taste: Do people know what they will like? *Journal of Behavioral Decision Making,* **5**(3), 187–200.

Kahneman, D., & Tversky, A. (1979). Prospect theory: An analysis of decision under risk. *Econometrica,* **47,** 263–291.

Kahneman, D., & Tversky, A. (1984). Choices, values, and frames. *American Psychologist,* **39**(4), 341–350.

Kahneman, D., & Tversky, A. (1992). Advances in prospect theory: Cumulative representation of uncertainty. *Journal of Risk and Uncertainty,* **5,** 297–324.

Kahneman, D., & Tversky, A. (1996). On the reality of cognitive illusions. *Psychological Review,* **105,** 582–596.

Kahneman, D., & Tversky, A. (Eds.). (2000). *Choices, values, and frames.* New York: Cambridge University Press.

Kaplan, A. S., & Medin, D. L. (1997). The coincidence effect in similarity and choice. *Memory & Cognition,* **25**(4), 570–576.

Kardes, F. R., Kalyanaram, G., Chandrashekaran, M., & Dornoff, R. J. (1993). Brand retrieval, consideration set, composition, consumer choice, and the pioneering advantage. *Journal of Consumer Research,* **20,** 62–75.

Khong, Y. F. (1992). *Analogies at war.* Princeton: Princeton University Press.

Klein, G. (2000). *Sources of power.* Cambridge: MIT Press.

Larrick, R. P., & Blount, S. (1997). The claiming effect: Why players are more generous in social dilemmas than in ultimatum games. *Journal of Personality and Social Psychology,* **723,** 810–825.

Larrick, R. P., Morgan, J. N., & Nisbett, R. E. (1990). Teaching the use of cost benefit reasoning in everyday life. *Psychological Science,* **1**(6), 362–371.

Larrick, R. P., Nisbett, R. E., & Morgan, J. N. (1993). Who uses the cost benefit rules of choice? Implications for the normative status of microeconomic theory. *Organizational Behavior and Human Decision Processes,* **56,** 331–347.

Lazar, A. (1999). Deceiving oneself or self-deceived? On the formation of beliefs "under the influence." *Mind,* **108,** 265–290.

Lee, A. Y., Aaker, J. L., & Gardner, W. (2000). The pleasures and pains of distinct self-construals: The role of interdependence in regulatory focus. *Journal of Personality and Social Psychology,* **78,** 122–134.

Lehman, D. R., & Nisbett, R. E. (1993). A longitudinal study of the effects of undergraduate training on reasoning. In R. E. Nisbett (Ed.), *Rules for reasoning* (pp. 340–357). Hillsdale, NJ: Erlbaum.

Lehman, D. R., Nisbett, R. E., & Lempert, R. O. (1993). The effects of graduate training on reasoning: Formal discipline and thinking about everyday life events. In R. E. Nisbett (Ed.), *Rules for reasoning* (pp. 315–339). Hillsdale, NJ: Erlbaum.

Lesgold, A., Rubinson, H., Feltovich, P., Glaser, R., Klopfer, D., & Wang, Y. (1988). Expertise in a complex skill: Diagnosing X-ray pictures. In M. T. H. Chi, R. Glaser, & M. J. Farr (Eds.), *The nature of expertise* (pp. 311–342). Hillsdale, NJ: Erlbaum.

Leung, K., Bond, M. H., & Schwartz, S. H. (1995). How to explain cross cultural differences: Values, valences and expectancies? *Asian Journal of Psychology,* **1,** 70–75.

Levin, I. P., Johnson, R. D., & Faraone, S. V. (1984). Information integration in price-quality trade-offs: The effect of missing information. *Memory & Cognition,* **12,** 96–102.

Levin, I. P., Schneider, S. L., & Gaeth, G. J. (1998). All frames are not created equal: A typology and critical analysis of framing effects. *Organizational Behavior and Human Decision Processes,* **76**(2), 149–188.

Lewin, K. (1935). *A dynamic theory of personality.* New York: McGraw-Hill.

Loewenstein, G. (1996). Out of control: Visceral influences on behavior. *Organizational Behavior and Human Decision Processes, 65,* 272–292.

Loewenstein, G., & Adler, D. (1995). A bias in the prediction of tastes. *Economic Journal, 105,* 929–937.

Loewenstein, G., Weber, E. U., Hsee, C. K., & Welch, E. S. (2001). Risk as feelings. *Psychological Bulletin, 127*(2), 267–286.5.

Loomes, G., & Sugden, R. (1982). Regret theory: An alterative theory of rational choice under uncertainty. *The Economic Journal, 92,* 805–824.

Lopes, L. L. (1983). Some thoughts on the psychological concepts of risk. *Journal of Experimental Psychology: Human Perception and Performance, 9*(1), 137–144.

Lopes, L. L. (1987). Between hope and fear: The psychology of risk. *Advances in Experimental Social Psychology, 20,* 255–295.

Lopes, L. L. (1995). Algebra and processes in the modeling of risky choice. *The Psychology of Learning and Motivation, 32,* 177–220.

Lopes, L. L., & Oden, G. C. (1999). The role of aspiration level in risky choice: A comparison of cumulative prospect theory and SP/A theory. *Journal of Mathematical Psychology, 43,* 286–313.

Luce, M. F., Bettman, J. R., & Payne, J. W. (1997). Choice processing in emotionally difficult decisions. *Journal of Experimental Psychology: Learning, Memory, and Cognition, 23*(2), 384–405.

Luce, R. D. (1959). *Individual choice behavior.* New York: Wiley.

Luce, R. D. (2003). Rationality in choice under certainty and uncertainty. In Schneider, S. L., & J. Shanteau (Eds.), *Emerging Perpectives on Judgment and Decision Research.* Cambridge University Press, pp. 64–83.

Luce, R. D., & Marley, A. A. J. (2000). Separable and additive representations of binary gambles of gains? *Mathematical Social Sciences, 40,* 237–356.

Luce, R. D., & Raiffa, H. (1957). *Games and decisions.* New York: Wiley.

Markman, A. B., & Brendl, C. M. (2000). The influence of goals on value and choice. In D. L. Medin (Ed.), *The psychology of learning and motivation* (Vol. 39), pp. 97–129). San Diego: Academic Press.

Markman, A. B., & Gentner, D. (1993). Splitting the differences: A structural alignment view of similarity. *Journal of Memory and Language, 32*(4), 517–535.

Markman, A. B., & Medin, D. L. (1995). Similarity and alignment in choice. *Organizational Behavior and Human Decision Processes, 63*(2), 117–130.

Markman, A. B., & Moreau, C. P. (2001). Analogy and analogical comparison in choice. In D. Gentner, K. J. Holyoak, & B. Kokinov (Eds.), *The analogical mind: Perspectives from cognitive science* (pp. 363–400). Cambridge: MIT Press.

May, E. R. (1973). *'Lessons' of the past.* New York: Oxford University Press.

Medin, D. L., & Bazerman, M. H. (1999). Broadening behavioral decision research: Multiple levels of cognitive processing. *Psychonomic Bulletin and Review, 6*(4), 533–547.

Medin, D. L., Goldstone, R. L., & Gentner, D. (1993). Respects for similarity. *Psychological Review, 100*(2), 254–278.

Medin, D. L., Goldstone, R. L., & Markman, A. B. (1995). Comparison and choice: Relations between similarity processing and decision processing. *Psychonomic Bulletin and Review, 2*(1), 1–19.

Mcdin, D. L., Schwartz, II. C., Blok, S., & Bimbaum, L. (1999). The semantic side of decision making. *Psychonomic Bulletin and Review, 6*(4), 562–569.

Mellers, B. A. (2000). Choice and the relative pleasure of consequences. *Psychological Bulletin, 126*(6), 910–924.

Metcalfe, J., & Mischel, W. (1999). A hot/cool system analysis of delay of gratification: Dynamics of willpower. *Psychological Review, 106,* 3–19.

Miller, G. A., Galanter, E., & Pribram, K. H. (1960). *Plans and the structure of behavior.* New York: Holt, Reinhart and Winston.

Miller, N. E. (1959). Liberalization of basic S-R concepts: Extensions to conflict behavior, motivation, and social learning. In S. Koch (Ed.), *Psychology: A study of a science. General and systematic formulations, learning, and special processes* (Vol. 2, pp. 196–292). New York: McGraw Hill.

Moreau, C. P., Lehman, D. R., & Markman, A. B. (2001). Entrenched category structures and resistance to "really" new products. *Journal of Marketing Research, 38*(1), 14–29.

Moreau, C. P., Markman, A. B., & Lehman, D. R. (2001). 'What is it?' Categorization flexibility and consumers' responses to really new products. *Journal of Consumer Research, 27,* 489–498.

Nedungadi, P. (1990). Recall and consumer consideration sets: Influencing choice without altering brand evaluations. *Journal of Consumer Research, 17,* 263–276.

Nisbett, R. E., Fong, G. T., Lehman, D. R., & Cheng, P. W. (1987). Teaching reasoning. *Science, 238,* 625–631.

Nisbett, R. E., & Kanouse, D. E. (1969). Obesity, food deprivation, and supermarket shopping behavior. *Journal of Personality and Social Psychology, 12*(4), 289–294.

Nisbett, R. E., Peng, K., Choi, I., & Norenzayan, A. (2001). Culture and systems of thought: Holistic vs. analytic cognition. *Psychological Review,* **108**(2), 291–310.

Ostrum, E. (1998). A behavioral approach to the rational choice theory of collective action. *American Political Science Review,* **92,** 1–22.

Patalano, A. L., & Seifert, C. M. (1997). Opportunistic planning: Being reminded of pending goals. *Cognitive Psychology,* **34,** 1–36.

Payne, J. W., Bettman, J. R., & Johnson, E. J. (1988). Adaptive strategy selection in decision making. *Journal of Experimental Psychology: Learning, Memory, and Cognition,* **14**(3), 534–552.

Payne, J. W., Bettman, J. R., & Johnson, E. J. (1993). *The adaptive decision maker.* New York: Cambridge University Press.

Pennington, N., & Hastie, R. (1988). Explanation-based decision making: Effects of memory structure on judgment. *Journal of Experimental Psychology: Learning, Memory, and Cognition,* **14**(3), 521–533.

Pennington, N., & Hastie, R. (1992). Explaining the evidence: Tests of the story model for juror decision making. *Journal of Personality and Social Psychology,* **62**(2), 189–206.

Polya, G. (1945). *How to solve it.* Princeton: Princeton University Press.

Quiggin, J. (1993). *Generalized expected utility theory: The rank-dependent model.* Boston: Kluwer.

Read, D., Antonides, G., van den Ouden, L., & Trienekens, H. (2001). Which is better: Simultaneous or sequential choice? *Organizational Behavior and Human Decision Processes,* **84**(1), 54–70.

Ritov, I., & Baron, J. (1990). Reluctance to vaccinate: Omission bias and ambiguity. *Journal of Behavioral Decision Making,* **3,** 263–277.

Ritov, I., & Baron, J. (1995). Outcome knowledge, regret and omission bias. *Organizational Behavior and Human Decision Processes,* **64,** 119–127.

Ritov, I., & Baron, J. (1999). Protected values and mission bias. *Organizational Behavior and Human Decision Processes,* **79,** 79–94.

Ritov, I., & Kahneman, D. (1997). How people value the environment: Attitudes versus economic values. In M. H. Bazerman, D. M. Messick, A. E. Tenbrusel, & K. A. Wed-Benzoni (Eds.), *Environment, ethics and behavior* (pp. 33–51). San Francisco: New Lexington Press.

Ross, L. (1977). The intuitive psychologist and his shortcomings: Distortions in the attribution process. In L. Berkowitz (Ed.), *Advances in experimental social psychology* (Vol. **10,** pp. 173–220). San Diego: Academic Press.

Roth, A. E. (1991). An economic approach to the study of bargaining. In M. H. Bazerman, R. J. Lewicki, & B. H. Sheppard (Eds.), *Handbook of negotiation research: Research in negotiation in organizations* (Vol. **III**). Greenwich, CT: JAI Press.

Rottenstreich, Y., & Hsee, C. K. (2001). Money, kisses and electric shocks: On the affective psychology of risk. *Psychological Science,* **12,** 185–190.

Sanbonmatsu, D. M., Kardes, F. R., & Herr, P. M. (1992). The role of prior knowledge and missing information in multiattribute evaluation. *Organizational Behavior and Human Decision Processes,* **51,** 76–91.

Savage, L. J. (1954). *The foundations of statistics.* New York: Wiley.

Schneider, S. L. (2001). In search of realistic optimism: Meaning, knowledge, and warm fuzziness. *American Journal of Psychology,* **56**(3), 250–263.

Schneider, S. L., & Shanteau, J. (Eds.) (in press). *Emerging Perspectives on Judgment and Decision Research.* Cambridge University Press.

Shafir, E. (1993). Choosing versus rejecting: Why some options are both better and worse than others. *Memory & Cognition,* **21**(4), 546–556.

Shafir, E. (1995). Compatibility in cognition and decision. In J. Busemeyer, R. Hastie, & D. L. Medin (Eds.), *Cognitive approaches to decision making* (Vol. **32,** pp. 247–274). San Diego: Academic Press.

Shafir, E., Simonson, I., & Tversky, A. (1993a). Reason-based choice. *Cognition,* **49,** 11–36.

Shafir, E. B., Osherson, D. N., & Smith, E. E. (1993b). The advantage model: A comparative theory of evaluation and choice under risk. *Organizational Behavior and Human Decision Processes,* **55,** 325–378.

Shah, J., & Higgins, E. T. (1997). Expectancy * value effects: Regulatory focus as determinant of magnitude and direction. *Journal of Personality and Social Psychology,* **73**(3), 447–458.

Shanteau, J. (1988). Psychological characteristics and strategies of expert decision makers. *Acta Psychologica,* **68,** 203–215.

Shapiro, S., Macinnis, D. J., & Heckler, S. E. (1997). The effects of incidental ad exposure on the formation of consideration sets. *Journal of Consumer Research,* **24,** 94–104.

Shefrin, H. M., & Thaler, R. H. (1992). Mental accounting, saving, and self-control. In G. Loewenstein & J. Elster (Eds.), *Choice over time* (pp. 287–330). New York: Sage.

Shepard, R. N. (1962). The analysis of proximities: Multidimensional scaling with an unknown distance function, I. *Psychometrika,* **27**(2), 125–140.

Shimko, K. L. (1994). Metaphors and foreign policy decision making. *Political Psychology,* **15**(4), 665–671.

Simon, H. (1957). *Models of man.* New York: Wiley.

Simon, H. A. (1956). Rationale choice and the structure of the environment. *Psychological Review,* **63,** 129–138.

Simonson, I. (1989). Choice based on reasons: The case of attraction and compromise effects. *Journal of Consumer Research,* **16,** 158–174.

Simonson, I., & Tversky, A. (1992). Choice in context: Trade-off contrast and extremeness aversion. *Journal of Marketing Research,* **29,** 281–295.

Sloman, S. A., Love, B. C., & Ahn, W. K. (1998). Feature centrality and conceptual coherence. *Cognitive Science,* **22**(2), 189–228.

Slovic, P. (1995). The construction of preference. *American Psychologist,* **50**(5), 364–371.

Slovic, P., & Lichtenstein, S. (1983). Preference reversals: A broader perspective. *American Economic Review,* **73,** 596–605.

Slovic, P., & MacPhillamy, D. (1974). Dimensional commensurability and cue utilization in comparative judgment. *Organizational Behavior and Human Performance,* **11,** 172–194.

Spranca, M., Minsk, E., & Baron, J. (1991). Omission and commission in judgment and choice. *Journal of Experimental Social Psychology,* **27,** 76–105.

Svenson, O. (1999). Differentiation and consolidation theory: Decision making processes before and after a choice. In Juslin, P., & H. Montgomery (Eds.), *Judgment and Decision Making: Neo Brunswikian and Process-Tracing Approaches.* Hillsdale, NJ: Erlbaum.

Svenson, O. (in press). Values, affect and processes in human decision making: A differentiation and consolidation theory perspective. In S. L. Schneider & J. Shanteau (Eds.), *Emerging perspectives on judgment and decision research* New York: Cambridge University Press.

Tenbrunsel, A., & Messick, D. (1999). Sanctioning systems, decision frames and cooperation. *Administrative Science Quarterly,* **44,** 684–707.

Tentori, K., Osherson, D., Hasher, L., & May, C. (in press). Irrational preferences in college students but not older adults. *Cognition.*

Thaler, R. H. (1985). Mental accounting and consumer choice. *Marketing Science,* **4,** 199–214.

Thaler, R. H. (1999). Mental accounting matters. *Journal of Behavioral Decision Making,* **12**(3), 183–206.

Thaler, R. H., & Johnson, E. J. (1990). Gambling with the house money and trying to break even: The effects of prior outcomes on risky choice. *Management Science,* **36**(6), 643–660.

Triandis, H. C. (1989). The self and social behavior in differing cultural context. *Psychological Review,* **96,** 506–520.

Tversky, A. (1972). Elimination by aspects: A theory of choice. *Psychological Review,* **79**(4), 281–299.

Tversky, A. (1977). Features of similarity. *Psychological Review,* **84**(4), 327–352.

Tversky, A., & Fox, C. R. (1995). Weighing risk and uncertainty. *Psychological Review,* **102**(2), 269–283.

Tversky, A., & Gati, I. (1982). Similarity, separability and the triangle inequality. *Psychological Review,* **89**(2), 123–154.

Tversky, A., & Kahneman, D. (1974). Judgment under uncertainty: Heuristics and biases. *Science,* **185,** 1124–1131.

Tversky, A., & Kahneman, D. (1981). The framing of decisions and the psychology of choice. *Science,* **185,** 1124–1131.

Tversky, A., & Kahneman, D. (1986). Rational choice and the framing of decisions. *Journal of Business,* **59**(4), S251–S278.

Tversky, A., & Kahneman, D. (1992). Advances in Prospect Theory: Cumulative representation of uncertainty. *Journal of Risk and Uncertainty,* **5,** 297–323.

Tversky, A., Sattath, S., & Slovic, P. (1988). Contingent weighting in judgment and choice. *Psychological Review,* **95**(3), 371–384.

Tversky, A., & Shafir, E. (1992a). Choice under conflict: The dynamics of deferred decision. *Psychological Science,* **3**(6), 358–361.

Tversky, A., & Shafir, E. (1992b). The disjunction effect in choice under uncertainty. *Psychological Science,* **3**(5), 305–309.

Vallacher, R. R., & Wegner, D. M. (1985). *A theory of action identification.* Hillsdale, NJ: Erlbaum.

Van Boven, L., Dunning, D., & Loewenstein, G. (2000). Egocentric empathy gaps between owners and buyers: Misperceptions of the endowment effect. *Journal of Personality and Social Psychology,* **79**(1), 66–76.

von Neumann, J., & Morgenstern, O. (1944). *Theory of games and economic behavior.* Princeton: Princeton University Press.

Wang, X. T. (1996). Evolutionary hypotheses of risk-sensitive choice: Age differences and perspective change. *Ethology and Sociobiology,* **17,** 1–15.

Weber, E. U., Baron, J., & Loomes (2001). *Conflict and tradeoffs in decision making.* Cambridge, UK: Cambridge University Press.

Weber, E. U., Hsee, C., & Sokolowska, J. (1998). What folklore tells us about risk and risk taking: Cross-cultural comparisons of American, German and Chinese proverbs. *Organizational Behavior and Human Decision Processes,* **75**(2), 170–186.

Weber, E. U., & Hsee, C. (1998). Cross-cultural differences in risk perception, but cross-cultural similarities in attitudes towards perceived risk. *Management Science,* **44**(9), 1205–1217.

Weber, E. U., & Hsee, C. (1999). Models and mosaics: Investigating cross-cultural differences in risk perception and risk preference. *Psychonomic Bulletin and Review, 6*(4), 611–617.

Wilson, T. D., Lisle, D. J., Schooler, J. W., Hodges, S. D., Klaaren, K. J., & LaFleur, S. J. (1993). Introspecting about reasons can reduce post-choice satisfaction. *Personality and Social Psychology Bulletin, 19*(3), 331–339.

Wilson, T. D., & Schooler, J. W. (1991). Thinking too much: Introspection can reduce the quality of preferences and decisions. *Journal of Personality and Social Psychology, 60*(2), 181–192.

Wollheim, R. (1999). *On the emotions.* New Haven and London: Yale University Press.

Yates, J. F., Lee, J. W., & Shinotsuka, H. (1996). Beliefs about overconfidence, including its cross-national variation. *Organizational Behavior and Human Decision Processes, 65,* 138–147.

Yates, J. F., Lee, J. W., Shinotsuka, H., Patalano, A. L., & Sieck, W. R. (1998). Cross-cultural variations in probability judgment accuracy: Beyond general knowledge overconfidence. *Organizational Behavior and Human Decision Processes, 74*(2), 89–117.

Zeigarnik, B. (1927). Das Behalten eriedigter unt unerledigter Handlungen [The retention of completed and uncompleted actions]. *Psychologische Forschung, 9,* 1–85.

Zelizer, V. A. (1994). *The social meaning of money.* New York: Basic Books.

Zhang, S., & Markman, A. B. (1998). Overcoming the early entrant advantage: The role of alignable and non-alignable differences. *Journal of Marketing Research, 35,* 413–426.

ABBREVIATIONS

SP/A: SP stands for security bias versus potential bias, A for aspiration level

WTA: willingness to accept
WTP: willingness to pay

CHAPTER TWENTY-THREE

ADAPTATIONS, EXAPTATIONS, AND SPANDRELS

DAVID M. BUSS, MARTIE G. HASELTON,
TODD K. SHACKELFORD, APRIL L. BLESKE,
AND JEROME C. WAKEFIELD

Over the past decade, evolutionary psychology has emerged as a prominent new theoretical perspective within the field of psychology. Evolutionary psychology seeks to synthesize the guiding principles of modern evolutionary theory with current formulations of psychological phenomena (Buss, 1995; Daly & Wilson, 1988; Pinker, 1997b; Symons, 1987; Tooby & Cosmides, 1992). The concepts of adaptation and natural selection are central to evolutionary approaches and, therefore, have figured prominently in this emerging perspective. At the same time, criticisms have been leveled at the concept of adaptation and the importance of natural selection, especially as they are applied to human behavior. In particular, Gould (1991), in an influential and widely cited analysis, suggested that "exaptation," a feature not arising as an adaptation for its current function but rather co-opted for new purposes, may be a more important concept for the emerging paradigm of evolutionary psychology.

Psychologists in cognitive, developmental, social, personality, and clinical psychology are increasingly incorporating the evolutionary concepts of adaptation and exaptation in their theoretical frameworks and empirical research (e.g., Buss, 1994; Cosmides, 1989; Cosmides & Tooby, 1994; Daly & Wilson, 1988; Kenrick & Keefe, 1992; Lilienfeld & Marino, 1995; MacNeilage, 1997; Piattelli-Palmarini, 1989; Pinker & Bloom, 1992; Richters & Cicchetti, 1993; Sedikedes & Skowronski, 1997; Wakefield, 1992, 1999). Much confusion exists, however, about what these central concepts mean, how they should be distinguished, and how they are to be applied to psychological phenomena.

The confusion can be traced to several factors. First, psychologists typically receive no formal training in evolutionary biology and, therefore, cannot be expected to wade through what has become a highly technical field. Second, although evolutionary theorizing about

From *American Psychologist,* Vol. 53(5), May 1998, 533–548.

humans has a long history (e.g., Baldwin, 1894; Darwin, 1859/1958; James, 1890/1962; Jennings, 1930; Morgan, 1896; Romanes, 1889), the empirical examination within psychology of evolutionary hypotheses regarding human psychological mechanisms is much more recent, and confusion often inheres in newly emerging approaches as practitioners struggle, often with many false starts, to use an incipient set of theoretical tools.[1] Third, psychologists dating back to Darwin's time have had a history of wariness about evolutionary approaches and, therefore, often have avoided a serious consideration of their potential utility. Fourth, there are genuine differences in scientific opinion about which concepts should be used, what the concepts actually mean, and how they should be applied. This article seeks to provide psychologists with a guide to the basic concepts involved in the current dispute over evolutionary explanations and to clarify the role that each of these concepts plays in an evolutionary approach to human psychology.

23.1   THE EVOLUTIONARY PROCESS

The process of evolution — changes over time in organic structure — was hypothesized to occur long before Charles Darwin (1859/1958) formulated his theory of evolution. What the field of biology lacked, however, was a causal mechanism to account for these changes. Darwin supplied this causal mechanism in the form of natural selection.

Darwin's task was more difficult than it might appear at first. He wanted not only to explain why life-forms have the characteristics they do and why these characteristics change over time but also to account for the particular ways in which they change. He wanted to explain how new species emerge (hence the title of his book, *On the Origin of Species by Means of Natural Selection;* Darwin, 1859/1958) as well as how others vanish. Darwin wanted to explain why the component parts of animals — the long necks of giraffes, the wings of birds, the trunks of elephants, and the proportionately large brains of humans — exist in the particular forms they do. In addition, he wanted to explain the apparent purposive quality of these complex organic forms, or why they seem to function to help organisms to accomplish specific tasks.

Darwin's (1859/1958) answer to all these puzzles of life was the theory of natural selection. Darwin's theory of natural selection had three essential ingredients: variation, inheritance, and selection. Animals within a species vary in all sorts of ways, such as wing length, trunk strength, bone mass, cell structure, fighting ability, defensive maneuverability, and social cunning. This variation is essential for the process of evolution to operate. It provides the raw materials for evolution.

Only some of these variations, however, are reliably passed down from parents to offspring through successive generations. Other variations, such as a wing deformity caused by a chance environmental accident, are not inherited by offspring. Only those variations that are inherited play a role in the evolutionary process.

The third critical ingredient of Darwin's (1859/1958) theory was selection. Organisms with particular heritable attributes produce more offspring, on average, than those lacking these attributes because these attributes help to solve specific problems and thereby contribute to reproduction in a particular environment. For example, in an environment in which the primary food source is nut-bearing trees or bushes, some finches with a particular shape of beak might be better able to crack nuts and get at their meat than finches with alternative beak shapes. More finches that have the beaks better shaped for nut-cracking survive than those with beaks poorly shaped for nut-cracking. Hence, those finches with more suitably shaped beaks are more likely, on average, to live long enough to pass on their genes to the next generation.

Organisms can survive for many years, however, and still fail to contribute inherited qualities to future generations. To pass on their qualities, they must reproduce. Differential reproductive success, by virtue of the possession of heritable variants, is the causal engine of evolution by natural selection. Because survival is usually necessary for reproduction, survival took on a critical role in Darwin's (1859/1958) theory of natural selection.

Darwin (1859/1958) envisioned two classes of evolved variants — one playing a role in survival and one playing a role in reproductive competition. For example, among humans, sweat glands help to maintain a constant body temperature and thus presumably help humans to survive. Humans' tastes for sugar and fat presumably helped to guide their ancestors to eat certain foods and to avoid others and thus helped them to survive. Other inherited attributes aid more directly in reproductive competition and are said to be sexually selected (Darwin, 1871/1981). The elaborate songs and brilliant plumage of various bird species, for example, help to attract mates, and hence to reproduce, but may do nothing to enhance the individual's survival. In fact, these characteristics may be detrimental to survival by carrying large metabolic costs or by alerting predators.

In summary, although differential reproductive success of inherited variants was the crux of Darwin's (1859/1958) theory of natural selection, he conceived of two classes of variants that might evolve — those that help organisms survive (and thus indirectly help them to reproduce) and those that more directly help organisms in reproductive competition. The theory of natural selection unified all living creatures, from single-celled amoebas to multicellular mammals, into one grand tree of descent. It also provided for the first time a scientific theory to account for the exquisite design and functional nature of the component parts of each of these species.

In its modern formulation, the evolutionary process of natural selection has been refined in the form of inclusive fitness theory (Hamilton, 1964). Hamilton reasoned that classical fitness — a measure of an individual's direct reproductive success in passing on genes through the production of offspring — was too narrow to describe the process of evolution by selection. He proposed that a characteristic will be naturally selected if it causes an organism's genes to be passed on, regardless of whether the organism directly produces offspring. If a person helps a brother, a sister, or a niece to reproduce and nurture offspring, for example, by sharing resources, offering protection, or helping in times of need, then that person contributes to the reproductive success of his or her own genes because kin tend to share genes and, moreover, contributes to the reproductive success of genes specifically for brotherly, sisterly, or niecely assistance (assuming that such helping is partly heritable and, therefore, such genes are likely to be shared by kin). The implication of this analysis is that parental care — investing in one's own children — is merely a special case of caring for kin who carry copies of one's genes in their bodies. Thus, the notion of classical fitness was expanded to inclusive fitness.

Technically, inclusive fitness is not a property of an individual organism but rather a property of its actions or effects (Hamilton, 1964; see also Dawkins, 1982). Inclusive fitness can be calculated from an individual's own reproductive success (classical fitness) plus the effects the individual's actions have on the reproductive success of his or her genetic relatives, weighted by the appropriate degree of genetic relatedness.

It is critical to keep in mind that evolution by natural selection is not forward looking or intentional. A giraffe does not notice juicy leaves stirring high in a tree and "evolve" a longer neck. Rather, those giraffes that happen to have slightly longer necks than other giraffes have a slight advantage in getting to those leaves. Hence, they survive better and are more likely to live to pass on genes for slightly longer necks to offspring. Natural selection acts only on those variants that happen to exist. Evolution is not intentional and cannot look into the future to foresee distant needs.

23.2   PRODUCTS OF THE EVOLUTIONARY PROCESS: ADAPTATIONS, BY-PRODUCTS, AND RANDOM EFFECTS

In each generation, the process of selection acts like a sieve (Dawkins, 1996). Variants that interfere with successful solutions to adaptive problems are filtered out. Variants that contribute to the successful solution of an adaptive problem pass through the selective sieve. Iterated over thousands of generations, this filtering process tends to produce and maintain characteristics that interact with the physical, social, or internal environment in ways that promote the reproduction of individuals who possess the characteristics or the reproduction of the individuals' genetic relatives (Dawkins, 1982; Hamilton, 1964; Tooby & Cosmides, 1990a; Williams, 1966). These characteristics are called adaptations.

There has been much debate about the precise meaning of adaptation, but we offer a provisional working definition. An *adaptation* may be defined as an inherited and reliably developing characteristic that came into existence as a feature of a species through natural selection because it helped to directly or indirectly facilitate reproduction during the period of its evolution (after Tooby & Cosmides, 1992). Solving an adaptive problem — that is, the manner in which a feature contributes to reproduction — is the function of the adaptation. There must be genes for an adaptation because such genes are required for the passage of the adaptation from parents to offspring. Adaptations, therefore, are by definition inherited, although environmental events may play a critical role in their ontogenetic development.

Ontogenetic events play a profound role in several ways. First, interactions with features of the environment during ontogeny (e.g., certain placental nutrients, aspects of parental care) are critical for the reliable development and emergence of most adaptations. Second, input during development may be required to activate existing mechanisms. There is some evidence, for example, that experience in committed sexual relationships activates sex-linked jealousy adaptations (Buss, Larsen, Westen, & Semmelroth, 1992). Third, developmental events may channel individuals into one of several alternative adaptive paths specified by evolved decision rules. Lack of an investing father during the first several years of life, for example, may incline individuals toward a short-term mating strategy, whereas the presence of an investing father may shift individuals toward a long-term mating strategy (e.g., Belsky, Steinberg, & Draper, 1991; for alternative theories, see Buss & Schmitt, 1993; Gangestad & Simpson, 1990). Fourth, environmental events may disrupt the emergence of an adaptation in a particular individual, and thus the genes for the adaptation do not invariantly result in its intact phenotypic manifestation. Fifth, the environment during development may affect where in the selected range someone falls, such as which language a person speaks or how anxious a person tends to be. Developmental context, in short, plays a critical role in the emergence and activation of adaptations (see DeKay & Buss, 1992, for a more extended discussion of the role of context).

To qualify as an adaptation, however, the characteristic must reliably emerge in reasonably intact form at the appropriate time during an organism's life. Furthermore, adaptations tend to be typical of most or all members of a species, with some important exceptions, such as characteristics that are sex-linked, that exist only in a subset because of frequency-dependent selection, or that exist because of temporally or spatially varying selection pressures.

Adaptations need not be present at birth. Many adaptations develop long after birth. Bipedal locomotion is a reliably developing characteristic of humans, but most humans do not begin to walk until a year after birth. The breasts of women and a variety of other secondary sex characteristics reliably develop, but they do not start to develop until puberty.

The characteristics that make it through the filtering process in each generation generally do so because they contribute to the successful solution of adaptive problems — solutions that either are necessary for reproduction or enhance relative reproductive success. Solutions to adaptive problems can be direct, such as a fear of dangerous snakes that solves a survival problem or a desire to mate with particular members of one's species that helps to solve a reproductive problem. They can be indirect, as in a desire to ascend a social hierarchy, which many years later might give an individual better access to mates. Or they can be even more indirect, such as when a person helps a brother or a sister, which eventually helps that sibling to reproduce or nurture offspring. Adaptive solutions need not invariably solve adaptive problems in order to evolve. The human propensity to fear snakes, for example, does not inevitably prevent snakebites, as evidenced by the hundreds of people who die every year from snakebites (Than-Than et al., 1988). Rather, adaptive designs must provide reproductive benefits on average, relative to their costs and relative to alternative designs available to selection, during the period of their evolution.

Each adaptation has its own period of evolution. Initially, a mutation occurs in a single individual. Most mutations disrupt the existing design of the organism and hence hinder reproduction. If the mutation is helpful to reproduction, however, it will be passed down to the next generation in greater numbers. In the next generation, therefore, more individuals will possess the characteristic. Over many generations, if it continues to be successful, the characteristic will spread among the population. In sum, natural selection is the central explanatory concept of evolutionary theory, and adaptation refers to any functional characteristic whose origin or maintenance must be explained by the process of natural selection.[2]

Most adaptations, of course, are not caused by single genes. The human eye, for example, takes thousands of genes to construct. An adaptation's environment of evolutionary adaptedness (EEA) refers to the cumulative selection processes that constructed it piece by piece until it came to characterize the species. Thus, there is no single EEA that can be localized at a particular point in time and space. The EEA will differ for each adaptation and is best described as a statistical aggregate of selection pressures over a particular period of time that are responsible for the emergence of an adaptation (Tooby & Cosmides, 1992).

The hallmarks of adaptation are features that define *special design* — complexity, economy, efficiency, reliability, precision, and functionality (Williams, 1966). These qualities are conceptual criteria subject to empirical testing and potential falsification for any particular hypothesis about an adaptation. Because, in principle, many alternative hypotheses can account for any particular constellation of findings, a specific hypothesis that a feature is an adaptation is, in effect, a probability statement that it is highly unlikely that the complex, reliable, and functional aspects of special design characterizing the feature could have arisen as an incidental by-product of another characteristic or by chance alone (Tooby & Cosmides, 1992). As more and more functional features suggesting special design are documented for a hypothesized adaptation, each pointing to a successful solution to a specific adaptive problem, the alternative hypotheses of chance and incidental by-product become increasingly improbable.

Although adaptations are the primary products of the evolutionary process, they are not the only products. The evolutionary process also produces by-products of adaptations as well as a residue of noise. By-products are characteristics that do not solve adaptive problems and do not have to have functional design. They are carried along with characteristics that do have functional design because they happen to be coupled with those adaptations. The whiteness of bones, for example, is an incidental by-product of the fact that they contain large amounts of calcium, which was presumably selected because of properties such as strength rather than because of whiteness (see Symons, 1992).

An example from the domain of humanly designed artifacts illustrates the concept of a by-product. Consider a particular lightbulb designed for a reading lamp; this lightbulb is designed to produce light. Light production is its function. The design features of a lightbulb — the conducting filament, the vacuum surrounding the filament, and the glass encasement — all contribute to the production of light and are part of its functional design. Lightbulbs also produce heat, however. Heat is a by-product of light production. It is carried along not because the bulb was designed to produce heat but rather because heat tends to be a common incidental consequence of light production.

A naturally occurring example of a by-product of adaptation is the human belly button. There is no evidence that the belly button, per se, helped human ancestors to survive or reproduce. A belly button is not good for catching food, detecting predators, avoiding snakes, locating good habitats, or choosing mates. It does not seem to be involved directly or indirectly in the solution to an adaptive problem. Rather, the belly button is a by-product of something that is an adaptation, namely, the umbilical cord that formerly provided the food supply to the growing fetus. As this example illustrates, establishing the hypothesis that something is a by-product of an adaptation generally requires the identification of the adaptation of which it is a by-product and the reason it is coupled with that adaptation (Tooby & Cosmides, 1992). In other words, the hypothesis that something is a by-product, just like the hypothesis that something is an adaptation, must be subjected to rigorous standards of scientific confirmation and potential falsification. As we discuss below, incidental by-products may come to have their own functions or may continue to have no evolved function at all, and they may be ignored or valued and exploited by people in various cultures.

The third and final product of the evolutionary process is noise, or random effects. Noise can be produced by mutations that neither contribute to nor detract from the functional design of the organism. The glass encasement of a lightbulb, for example, often contains perturbations from smoothness due to imperfections in the materials and the process of manufacturing that do not affect the functioning of the bulb; a bulb can function equally well with or without such perturbations. In self-reproducing systems, these neutral effects can be carried along and passed down to succeeding generations, as long as they do not impair the functioning of the mechanisms that are adaptations. Noise is distinguished from incidental by-products in that it is not linked to the adaptive aspects of design features but rather is independent of such features.

In summary, the evolutionary process produces three products: naturally selected features (adaptations), by-products of naturally selected features, and a residue of noise. In principle, the component parts of a species can be analyzed, and empirical studies can be conducted to determine which of these parts are adaptations, which are by-products, and which represent noise. Evolutionary scientists differ in their estimates of the relative sizes of these three categories of products. Some argue that many obviously important human qualities, such as language, are merely incidental by-products of large brains (e.g., Gould, 1991). Others argue that qualities such as language show evidence of special design that render it highly improbable that it is anything other than a well-designed adaptation for communication and conspecific manipulation (Pinker, 1994). Despite these differences among competing scientific views about the importance and prevalence of adaptations and by-products, all evolutionary scientists agree that there are many constraints on optimal design.

23.3   CONSTRAINTS ON OPTIMAL DESIGN

Adaptationists are sometimes accused of being *panglossian,* a term named after Voltaire's (1759/1939) Pangloss, who proposed that everything was for the best (Gould & Lewontin, 1979). According to this criticism, adaptationists are presumed to believe that selection creates optimal design, and practitioners are presumed to liberally spin adaptationist stories. Humans have noses designed to hold up eyeglasses and laps designed to hold computers, and they grow bald so that they can be more easily spotted when lost! This sort of fanciful storytelling, lacking rigorous standards for hypothesis formulation and evidentiary evaluation, would be poor science indeed. Although some no doubt succumb to this sort of cocktail banter, evolutionists going back to Darwin have long recognized important forces that prevent selection from creating optimally designed adaptations (see Dawkins, 1982, for an extensive summary of these constraints).

First, evolution by selection is a slow process, so there will often be a lag in time between a new adaptive problem and the evolution of a mechanism designed to solve it. The hedgehog's antipredator strategy of rolling into a ball is inadequate to deal with the novel impediment to survival created by automobiles. The moth's mechanism for flying toward light is inadequate for dealing with the novel challenge to survival of candle flames. The existence in humans of a preparedness mechanism for developing a fear of snakes may be a relic not well designed to deal with urban living, which currently contains hostile forces far more dangerous to human survival (e.g., cars, electrical outlets) but for which humans lack evolved mechanisms of fear preparedness (Mineka, 1992). Because of these evolutionary time lags, humans can be said to live in a modern world, but they are burdened with a Stone Age brain designed to deal with ancient adaptive problems, some of which are long forgotten (Allman, 1994).

A second constraint on adaptation occurs because of local optima. A better design may be available, in principle, atop a "neighboring mountain," but selection cannot reach it if it has to go through a deep fitness valley to get there. Selection requires that each step and each intermediate form in the construction of an adaptation be superior to its predecessor form in the currency of fitness. An evolutionary step toward a better solution would be stopped in its tracks if that step caused too steep a decrement in fitness. Selection is not like an engineer who can start from scratch and build toward a goal. Selection works only with the available materials and has no foresight. Local optima can prevent the evolution of better adaptive solutions that might, in principle, exist in potential design space (Dennett, 1995; Williams, 1992).

Lack of available genetic variation imposes a third constraint on optimal design. In the context of artificial selection, for example, it would be tremendously advantageous for dairy breeders to bias the sex ratio of offspring toward milk-producing females rather than non-lactating males. But all selective-breeding attempts to do this have failed, presumably because cattle lack the requisite genetic variation to bias the sex ratio (Dawkins, 1982). Similarly, it might, in principle, be advantageous for humans to evolve X-ray vision to see what is on the other side of obstacles or telescopic vision to spot danger from miles away. But the lack of available genetic variation, along with other constraints, has apparently precluded such adaptations.

A fourth constraint centers on the costs involved in the construction of adaptations. At puberty, male adolescents experience a sharply elevated production of circulating plasma testosterone. Elevated testosterone is linked to onset of puberty, an increase in body size, the production of masculine facial features, and the commencement of sexual interest and activity. But elevated testosterone also has an unfortunate cost — it compromises the immune system, rendering men more susceptible than women to a variety of diseases (Folstad & Karter, 1992; Wedekind, 1992). Presumably, averaged over all men through many generations, the benefits of elevated testosterone outweighed its costs in the currency of fitness. It evolved despite these costs. The key point is that all adaptations carry costs — sometimes minimal metabolic costs and at other times large survival costs — and these costs impose constraints on the optimal design of adaptations.

A fifth class of constraints involves the necessity of coordination with other mechanisms. Adaptations do not exist in a vacuum, isolated from other evolved mechanisms. Selection favors mechanisms that coordinate well with, and facilitate the functioning of, other evolved mechanisms. This process of coordination, however, often entails compromises in the evolution of an adaptation that render it less efficient than might be optimal in the absence of these constraints. Women, for example, have been selected both for bipedal locomotion and for the capacity for childbirth. The widened hips and birth canal that facilitate childbirth, however, compromise the ability to locomote with great speed. Without the need to coordinate design for running with design for childbirth, selection may have favored slimmer hips like those found on men, which facilitate running speed. The departure from optimal design for running speed in women, therefore, presumably occurs because of compromises required by the need to coordinate adaptive mechanisms with each other.[3] Thus, constraints imposed by the coordination of evolved mechanisms with each other produce design that is less than might be optimal if the mechanisms were not required to coexist.

Time lags, local optima, lack of available genetic variation, costs, and limits imposed by adaptive coordination with other mechanisms all constitute some of the major constraints on the design of adaptations, but there are others (Dawkins, 1982; Williams, 1992). Adaptations are not optimally designed mechanisms. They are better described as jerry-rigged, meliorative solutions to adaptive problems constructed out of the available materials at hand, constrained in their quality and design by a variety of historical and current forces.

23.4   EXAPTATIONS AND SPANDRELS

Recently, Stephen J. Gould (1991, 1997b; see also Gould & Lewontin, 1979; Gould & Vrba, 1982) proposed that the concept of exaptation is a crucial tool for evolutionary psychology, providing a critical supplement to the concept of adaptation. According to this argument, some evolutionary biologists and psychologists have conflated the historical origins of a mechanism or structure with its current utility. For example, the feathers of birds may have originated as evolved mechanisms for thermal regulation. Over evolutionary time, however, the feathers appear to have been co-opted for a different function — flight. According to this distinction, the term *adaptation* would be properly applied to the original thermal regulation structure and function, but the term *exaptation* would be more appropriate for describing the current flight-producing structure and function.

Gould (1991) provided two related definitions of exaptations. First, an exaptation is "a feature, now useful to an organism, that did not arise as an adaptation for its present role, but was subsequently co-opted for its current function" (p. 43). Second, exaptations are "features that now enhance fitness, but were not built by natural selection for their current role" (p. 47). On the basis of these related definitions, a mechanism must have a function and must enhance the fitness of its bearer to qualify as an exaptation.

It should be noted that Gould was inconsistent in his usage of the concept of exaptation, even within a single article (e.g., Gould, 1991). Although the definitions of exaptation quoted verbatim here appear to reflect his most common usage (indeed, the quoted 1991 definition was first introduced by Gould and Vrba in 1982), at other times, he seemed to use the term to cover novel but functionless uses or consequences of existing characteristics. For conceptual clarity, it is critical to distinguish between exaptation, as Gould (1991) defined it in the quoted passages, and by-products that are unrelated to function in the biological sense. In the next section, we examine Gould's various usages of the term *exaptation*. However, in this article, we use *exaptation*, consistent with the above quoted definitions, to refer only to mechanisms that have new biological functions that are not the ones that caused the original selection of the mechanisms. Biologically functionless uses are referred to as "effects," "consequences," or "by-products." These two easily confused strands of Gould's discussion of exaptation are thus disentangled here and treated separately.

According to Gould (1991), exaptations come in two types. In the first type, features that evolved by selection for one function are co-opted for another function. We use the term *co-opted adaptation* to describe this first category. The feathers of birds first having evolved for thermal regulation but then later co-opted for flight is an example of a co-opted adaptation. In the second type, "presently useful characteristics did not arise as adaptations [. . .] but owe their origin to side consequences of other features" (Gould, 1991, p. 53). Gould called such side effects of the organism's architecture "spandrels." The term *spandrels* is an architectural term that refers to the spaces left over between structural features of a building. The spaces between the pillars of a bridge, for example, can subsequently be used by homeless persons for sleeping, even though such spaces were not designed for providing such shelter.

In sum, Gould (1991) proposed two types of functional exaptations — adaptations that initially arose through natural selection and were subsequently co-opted for another function (co-opted adaptations) and features that did not arise as adaptations through natural selection but rather as side effects of adaptive processes and that have been co-opted for a biological function (co-opted spandrels). In both cases, according to Gould's primary definition, a mechanism must possess a biological function that contributes to fitness to qualify as an exaptation.

As an example of an exaptation, Gould (1991) used the large size of the human brain and its function of enabling humans to produce speech. The large brain size, according to his argument, originally arose as an adaptation for some (unspecified) functions in humans' ancestral past (Gould, 1991). But the complexity of the human brain produces many by-products that are not properly considered to be functions of the brain: "The human brain, as nature's most complex and flexible organ, throws up spandrels by the thousands for each conceivable adaptation in its initial evolutionary restructuring" (Gould, 1991, p. 58). Among the spandrels he cited as being by-products of large brains are religion, reading, writing, fine arts, the norms of commerce, and the practices of war. These seem to be intended as func-tionless uses or by-products rather than true fitness-enhancing, co-opted spandrels. Gould (1991) concluded that among features of interest to psychologists, such by-products are "a mountain to the adaptive molehill" (p. 59).

From these arguments, Gould (1991) concluded that the concepts of exaptations and spandrels provide a "one-line refutation of [...] an ultra-Darwinian theory based on adaptation" (p. 58). The two standard pillars of evolutionary biology — natural selection and adaptation — cannot, in principle, account for human behavior "without fatal revisions in its basic intent" (p. 58). Note that Gould was not challenging the importance of evolu-tionary biology for understanding human behavior. Indeed, as we show later in this article, understanding the nature of the adaptation responsible for producing spandrels (in this case, the nature of the large human brain) is critical to the analysis. Rather, he argued that there has been an overreliance on explanation in terms of adaptation, and to this important explanatory concept must be added the concept of exaptation, which is "a crucial tool for evolutionary psychology" (Gould, 1991, p. 43).

23.5   TERMINOLOGICAL AND CONCEPTUAL CONFUSIONS IN THE INVOCATION OF EXAPTATION AND ADAPTATION

To apply evolutionary concepts to psychology and to properly evaluate and contrast the concepts of exaptation and adaptation as potentially critical tools for evolutionary psychology, several dis-tinctions need to be made, and some common terminological confusions should be clarified.

23.5.1   Confusion 1: Adaptation versus Intuitions about Psychological Adjustment

Psychologists often use the term *adaptive* or *maladaptive* in a colloquial nonevolutionary sense. Often, these usages refer to notions such as personal happiness, social appropriate-ness, the ability to adjust to changing conditions, or other intuitive notions of well-being. It is important to distinguish these colloquial uses from the technical evolutionary uses, although evolved mechanisms may eventually turn out to be important in explaining personal happiness, well-being, or the ability to adjust to changing conditions (see, e.g., Nesse, 1990).

23.5.2   Confusion 2: Current Utility versus Explanation in Terms of Past Functionality

Taken literally, Gould's (1991) cited definition of exaptation requires that a feature be co-opted for its current function and that it now enhances fitness. It may seem from these phrases that exaptations concern only functions operating at the present moment, whether or not they operated in the past. However, evolutionary psychologists and biologists are generally interested in explaining existing features of organisms. Obviously, a characteristic cannot be explained by current fitness-enhancing properties that came about after the characteristic already existed. When evolutionists attempt to explain the existence of a feature, they must do so by reference to its evolutionary history. All evolutionary explanations of the existence of species-wide mechanisms are to this extent explanations in terms of the past fitness effects of that kind of mechanism that led to the current existence of the mechanism in the species. The fact that a mechanism currently enhances fitness, by itself, cannot explain why the mechanism exists or how it is structured (Tooby & Cosmides, 1990b).

There are good reasons to think that it is not scientifically illuminating to demonstrate a feature's current correlation with fitness (Symons, 1992; Tooby & Cosmides, 1990b), unless such correlations reveal longer term, past selective pressures. It is not clear that such correlations shed any light on the mechanism's design or status as an adaptation. Such correlations may reveal the current direction of selection, although even this assumes that such correlations will continue to be obtained in future generations — a questionable assumption given the rapidly changing biotic and abiotic environments. Evolutionary explanation focuses on explaining why a feature exists, not what incidental interactions the feature may be having with the current environment.

23.5.3   Confusion 3: Current Functions versus Past Functions That Are No Longer Active

Another confusion lurking in Gould's (1991) language is that it seems to imply that the past functions that explain the existence of a mechanism must still be operating now and literally be a current function to be an adaptation or exaptation. The concepts of adaptation and exaptation are intended as explanatory concepts, and they may be explanatorily useful even when the cited functions are no longer operative. Selected features often cease having the fitness-enhancing effects that got them selected in the first place; for example, it is possible that a selected taste for fatty foods to ensure adequate caloric intake is no longer fitness-enhancing in industrial societies where excessive fat is harmfully common and available for consumption. When evolutionists attempt to explain why humans have a taste for fatty foods, however, they generally say that this taste likely is (or was) an adaptation to ensure adequate caloric intake. Current fitness enhancement is not at issue; at issue is the past function explaining the existence of the mechanisms behind the taste for fatty foods.

A similar point holds for an exaptation. For example, if birds that fly subsequently were to become nonflying, so their feathers would no longer have the exapted function of supporting flight, the existence of feathers at that future time would still need to be explained in terms of (a) an original adaptation for heat insulation and (b) a later exaptation for flying, followed by (c) a functionless period too short for feathers to be selected out. So, the use of exaptation as an evolutionary explanatory concept does not require that there be a current function, any more than the use of adaptation requires such a current function. However, the use of exaptation requires, as Gould (1991) was trying to convey, that there be an original function and a distinct later function (he appeared to use "current" to conveniently distinguish the later function from the original function). What is required for exaptational explanation is not that there be an active current function but that there was an active function at the time that the feature is claimed to have served as an exaptation.

23.5.4   Confusion 4: Function versus Functionless By-Product

The most central confusion in applying Gould's (1991) ideas pertains to distinguishing between exaptations, as Gould defined them, and the novel use of existing features that are currently unrelated to function and fitness. Although Gould (1991) defined an exaptation as a feature "coopted for its current function" (p. 43) and features that "now enhance fitness, but were not built by natural selection for their current role" (p. 46), he sometimes argued that "function" does not describe the utility of exaptations; instead, he suggested that the utility of an exaptation is better described as "effect" (p. 48). Even more confusing, he referred to "culturally useful features" (p. 58) of the brain as exaptations. Gould's stated definitions seem to require that these effects and culturally useful features must contribute to fitness and have specifiable biological functions to qualify as exaptations, but it seems implausible that Gould intended to claim that such cultural practices as reading and writing are explainable by biological functions. Accordingly, exaptations must be distinguished from novel uses of existing mechanisms, where the novel uses are not explained by a biological function.

Consider the human hand as an adaptation. Clearly, the human hand is now used for many activities that were not part of its original set of functions — playing handball or disc golf, manipulating a joystick on a Super Nintendo game, or writing a computer program by pecking on a keyboard. But it seems unlikely that Gould (1991) meant to claim that these activities serve any functions in the formal sense, as solutions to adaptive problems that contribute to reproduction, although they certainly serve *functions* in the colloquial meaning of the term — helping to achieve some goal (e.g., staying in shape, engaging in a stimulating and distracting activity). The same problem arises for many of the activities enumerated by Gould as hypothesized exaptations of the large human brain. Indeed, many of the features Gould claimed to be exaptations or spandrels in human behavior do not seem to fall under his own definitions of exaptation or spandrel and seem instead to be functionless by-products. The key point is that novel uses of existing mechanisms that are not explained by biological function or fitness (i.e., functionless by-products) must be distinguished from true functional exaptations, such as the feathers of birds co-opted for flight.

23.5.5   Confusion 5: What Causal Process or Mechanism Is Doing the Co-opting?

Intimately related to the confusion between exaptations and functionless by-products is a confusion pertaining to the causal process responsible for co-opting an existing structure (see Pinker, 1997a). In the example of birds' feathers, which were originally evolved for thermal regulation but subsequently co-opted for flight, it is clearly natural selection that is responsible for transforming an existing structure into a new, modified structure with a different function. In other cases, however, Gould (1991) appeared to imply that human psychological capacities, such as cognitive capacities, human instrumental actions, or motivational mechanisms, are responsible for the co-opting.

The distinction that evolutionary psychologists make between underlying mechanisms and manifest behavior is helpful in clarifying this confusion. Both adaptations and exaptations, as underlying mechanisms, may be subsequently used for novel behaviors that may have no functional relevance whatsoever. When people use their hands to grip a tennis racquet, for example, this evolutionarily recent manifest behavior is clearly not the function for which the hands evolved. A full understanding of this novel behavior, however, requires an understanding of the underlying mechanism that is used (the hand) and is aided by insight into the functions for which it was designed (e.g., the power grip). The activity (e.g., tennis) may be partially understood by invoking evolved motivational mechanisms (e.g., social networking, hierarchy negotiation, enhancement of appearance) that are responsible for humans co-opting or exploiting existing mechanisms to pursue this novel activity.

In this example, human motivational mechanisms conjoined with current cognitive and physical capacities, not natural selection, are responsible for co-opting the existing mechanism of the hand. The same logic applies to many of Gould's (1991) other examples of exaptations, such as reading and writing — these are evolutionarily novel activities that are presumably too recent to have been co-opted by natural selection and so apparently must have been invented and co-opted by existing human psychological mechanisms. Such human co-optation must be distinguished from biological exaptations that natural selection has transformed from one function to another.

In summary, evolutionary functional analysis is useful regardless of whether natural selection or some other causal process, such as an existing human motivation, is responsible for the co-opting. Even in cases where a feature has no biological function and is proposed to be a functionless by-product, an understanding of novel behaviors must involve (a) an understanding of the evolved mechanisms that make humans capable of performing the behavior and (b) an understanding of the evolved cognitive and motivational mechanisms that led humans to exploit such capabilities. It is not sufficient from a scientific point of view to merely present a long speculative list of purported exaptations, however interesting or intuitively compelling they might be.

The hypothesis that something is an exaptation or even a functionless effect should be subjected to reasonable standards of hypothesis formulation and empirical verification, just as hypotheses about adaptation must meet these standards. The hypothesis that religion, to use one of Gould's (1991) examples, is an exaptation would seem to require a specification of (a) the original adaptations or by-products that were co-opted to produce religion; (b) the causal mechanism responsible for the co-opting (e.g., natural selection or an existing motivational mechanism); and (c) the exapted biological function of religion, if any; that is, the manner in which it contributes to the solution to an adaptive problem of survival or reproduction. These predictions can then be subjected to evidentiary standards of empirical testing and potential falsification.

Hypotheses about functionless by-products must meet rigorous scientific standards that include a functional analysis of the original adaptations responsible for producing the functionless by-products and the existing human cognitive and motivational mechanisms responsible for the co-opting. Without this specification, the mere assertion that this or that characteristic is an exaptation encounters the same problem that Gould (1991) leveled against adaptationists — the telling of "just-so stories."

23.5.6   Confusion 6: Are Exaptations Merely Adaptations?

A final conceptual issue pertains to whether the concept of exaptation is usefully distinct from the concept of adaptation. Dennett (1995) argued that it is not:

> According to orthodox Darwinism, every adaptation is one sort of exaptation or the other — this is trivial, since no function is eternal; if you go back far enough, you will find that every adaptation has developed out of predecessor structures each of which either had some other use or no use at all. (p. 281)

If all adaptations are exaptations, and all exaptations are adaptations, then having two terms to describe one thing would certainly be superfluous.

Although Dennett's (1995) argument has some merit in pointing to the limits of the distinction between adaptation and exaptation, we think he is wrong in suggesting that there is no difference, and we believe that there is utility in differentiating between the two concepts. Granted, the distinction may end up being more a matter of degree than an absolute distinction because exaptations themselves often involve further adaptations; nonetheless, understanding the degree to which a new function is superimposed on a predecessor structure that already existed as an adaptation or as a by-product may indeed shed light on its nature. The notion that a bird's feathers originally were designed for thermal regulation rather than for flying, for example, may help to explain some of its current features that do not seem to contribute to flight (e.g., insulating, heat-retention features).

In sum, Gould's (1991) concept of exaptation can be meaningfully distinguished from adaptation. Both concepts invoke function; therefore, both must meet the conceptual and evidentiary standards for invoking function. The concepts differ, however, in that adaptations are characteristics that spread through the population because they were selected for some functional effect, whereas exaptations are structures that already exist in the population and continue to exist, albeit sometimes in modified form, for functional reasons different from the ones for which they were originally selected.

23.6   THE ROLE OF NATURAL SELECTION IN ADAPTATIONS AND EXAPTATIONS

Some readers of Gould (1997a) come away believing that the role of natural selection is somehow diminished to the degree that exaptations are important. This is a mistake, as Gould himself took pains to point out: "I accept natural selection as the only known cause of 'eminently workable design' and [. . .] 'adaptive design must be the product of natural selection'" (p. 57). Natural selection plays a key role in both adaptations and exaptations.

When exaptations are co-opted adaptations, where the mechanism being co-opted for a new function was an adaptation, selection is required to explain the original adaptation being co-opted. Fishes' fins designed for swimming may have been co-opted to produce mammalian legs for walking. Birds' feathers, perhaps originally designed for thermal regulation, may have been co-opted for flying. In all these cases, however, natural selection is required to explain the origins and nature of the adaptations that provided the existing structures capable of being co-opted.

When exaptations are co-opted spandrels, where the mechanism being co-opted for a new function was not an adaptation but rather an incidental by-product of an adaptation, then selection is required to explain the adaptation that produced the incidental by-product. Recall that the hypothesis that a mechanism with a function is a spandrel implies that the mechanism was a by-product, and supporting a by-product hypothesis generally requires specifying the adaptation responsible for producing the by-product (Tooby & Cosmides, 1992). Natural selection is required to explain the origin and design of the adaptation — it is the only known causal process capable of producing adaptation. Without specifying the origin of the adaptation that produced the by-product that was co-opted to become a spandrel, the hypothesis that something is a spandrel generally cannot be tested.

Selection is necessary not only to explain the adaptations and by-products that are available for co-optation but also to explain the process of exaptation itself. Selection is required to explain the structural changes in an existing mechanism that enable it to perform the new exapted function: "Exaptations almost always involve structural changes that enable the preexisting mechanism, designed for another function, to perform the new function; these changes require explanation by natural selection" (Wakefield, 1999). When feathers for thermal regulation become wings capable of flight, it is highly unlikely that the new function can occur without any modification of the original mechanism. Selection would have to act on the existing feathers, favoring those individuals that possess more aerodynamic features over those possessing less aerodynamic features. Furthermore, these changes would have to be coordinated with other changes, such as a musculature capable of generating sufficient flapping, alterations in the visual system to accommodate the new demands of aerial mobility, and perhaps modifications of the feet to facilitate landing without damage (e.g., a redesigned shape of the feet). All these changes require the invocation of natural selection to explain the transformation of the original adaptation to an exaptation (e.g., an adaptation with a new function). Similar explanations would generally be necessary for explaining how functionless by-products are transformed into co-opted spandrels that perform specific functions.

Selection is also required to explain the maintenance of an exaptation over evolutionary time, even if no changes in structure occur: "Even in rare cases where exaptations involve no structural changes whatsoever, selective pressures must be invoked to fully explain why the mechanism is maintained in the population" (Wakefield, 1999). The forces of selection, of course, are never static. The fact that more than 99% of all species that have ever existed are now extinct is harsh testimony to the changes in selection over time (Thiessen, 1996). If the selection pressure responsible for the original adaptation becomes neutral or reversed, then the adaptation will eventually degrade over time because of forces such as the cumulative influx of new mutations and competing metabolic demands of other mechanisms. Selection is not only the force responsible for their maintenance. Thus, even in the odd event that an existing mechanism is co-opted for a new function with no change whatsoever, selection is required to explain why this mechanism and its new function are maintained in the population over time.

In summary, adding exaptation to the conceptual toolbox of evolutionary psychology does not diminish the importance of natural selection as the primary process responsible for creating complex organic design — a point apparently endorsed by all sides involved in these conceptual debates. Selection is responsible for producing the original adaptations that are then available for co-optation. It is responsible for producing the adaptations, of which spandrels are incidental by-products. It is responsible for producing structural changes in exaptations in order to fulfill their new functions. And it is responsible for maintaining exaptations in the population over evolutionary time, even in the rare cases where no structural changes occurred. The distinctions between exaptation and adaptation are important, and Gould (1991) deserves credit for highlighting them. However, the distinctions should not be taken to mean that natural selection is not the basic explanatory principle in biology and evolutionary psychology.

23.7 TESTING HYPOTHESES ABOUT ADAPTATIONS, EXAPTATIONS, AND SPANDRELS

Evolutionary psychological hypotheses about adaptations are sometimes derided as mere storytelling, but the same accusation can be leveled at hypotheses about exaptations and spandrels, and even at more standard social science notions such as socialization, learning, and culture as causal explanations (Tooby & Cosmides, 1992). In all these approaches, as in the case of evolutionary hypotheses about adaptation, it is easy to concoct hypotheses about how a feature might be explained. The key issue is not whether a hypothesis is a story or not — at some level, all scientific hypotheses can be viewed as stories. Rather, the key questions are (a) Is the evolutionary psychological hypothesis formulated in a precise and internally consistent manner? (b) Does the hypothesis coordinate with known causal processes in evolutionary biology, much as hypotheses in cosmology must coordinate with known laws of physics? (Tooby and Cosmides [1992] called this "conceptual integration") (c) Can new specific empirical predictions about behavior or psychology be derived from the hypothesis for which data are currently lacking? (d) Can the hypothesis more parsimoniously account for known empirical findings, and overall, is it more evidentially compelling than competing hypotheses? and (e) Is the proposed psychological mechanism computationally capable of solving the hypothesized problem (Cosmides & Tooby, 1994; Marr, 1982)? These are scientific criteria that can be applied whether the hypothesis is or is not explicitly evolutionary and whether the hypothesis invokes an adaptation, exaptation, spandrel, or functionless by-product.

There is nothing about the fact that a hypothesis is explicitly evolutionary that makes it virtuous or more likely to be correct. Many evolutionarily inspired hypotheses turn out to be wrong, however reasonable they may seem. The hypothesis that the female orgasm functions to facilitate sperm transport, for example, is eminently reasonable on evolutionary grounds and leads to specific testable predictions. At present, however, the evidence for this hypothesis is weak (Baker & Bellis, 1995). In contrast, the hypothesis that male sexual jealousy has evolved to serve the function of combating paternity uncertainty has accrued a reasonable volume of empirical support across diverse methods, samples, and cultures (Baker & Bellis, 1995; Buss, 1988; Buss et al., 1992; Buss & Shackelford, 1997;

Buunk, Angleitner, Oubaid, & Buss, 1996; Daly & Wilson, 1988; Daly, Wilson, & Weghorst, 1982; Shackelford & Buss, 1996; Symons, 1979; Wiederman & Allgeier, 1993; Wilson & Daly, 1992).

When a particular hypothesis about an evolved mechanism fails to be supported empirically, then a number of options are available to researchers. First, the hypothesis may be right but may have been tested incorrectly. Second, the hypothesis may be wrong, but an alternative functional hypothesis could be formulated and tested. Third, the phenomenon under examination might not represent an adaptation or exaptation at all but might instead be an incidental by-product of some other evolved mechanism, and this hypothesis could be tested.

Researchers then can empirically test these alternatives. Suppose, for example, that the sperm transport hypothesis of the female orgasm turned out to be wrong, with the results showing that women who had orgasms were no more likely to conceive than were women who did not have orgasms. The researchers could first scrutinize the methodology to see whether some flaw in the research design may have gone undetected (e.g., had the researchers controlled for the ages of the women in the two groups, because inadvertent age differences may have concealed the effect?). Second, the researchers could formulate an alternative hypothesis — perhaps the female orgasm functions as a mate selection device, providing a cue to the woman about the quality of the man or his investment in her (see Rancour-Laferriere, 1985, for a discussion of this and other hypotheses about the female orgasm) — and this alternative could be tested. Third, the researchers could hypothesize that the female orgasm is not an adaptation at all but rather an incidental by-product of some other mechanism, such as a common design shared with men, who do possess the capacity for orgasm for functional reasons (see Symons, 1979, for the original proposal of this functionless by-product hypothesis, and Gould's, 1987, subsequent endorsement of this hypothesis). In this case, researchers could try to disconfirm all existing functional explanations and could try to identify how the known mechanisms for development of naturally selected male orgasmic capacities led to the female orgasmic capacities as a side effect. Different researchers undoubtedly will have different proclivities about which of these options they pursue. The key point is that all evolutionary hypotheses — whether about adaptations, exaptations, spandrels, or functionless by-products — should be formulated in a precise enough manner to produce empirical predictions that can then be subjected to testing and potential falsification.

It should be noted that evolutionary hypotheses range on a gradient from well-formulated, precise deductions from known evolutionary principles on the one hand to evolutionarily inspired hunches on the other (see, e.g., Symons, 1992). Evolutionary psychology often provides a heuristic, guiding scientific inquiry to important domains that have a priori importance, such as events surrounding reproduction (e.g., sexuality, mate selection). Just as with a precise evolutionary hypothesis, an evolutionary hunch may turn out to be right or wrong. It would seem reasonable to hypothesize, for example, that men would have evolved mechanisms designed to detect when women ovulate, because such a mechanism would help to solve the adaptive problems of identifying fecund women and channeling mating effort more efficiently. But there is little solid empirical evidence that such a mechanism exists (see Symons, 1995). Such hunches, however, can often be useful in guiding investigations. Thus, evolutionary psychology, at its best, has both heuristic and predictive value for psychological science.

23.8   DISCUSSION

In principle, we agree with Gould's (1991, 1997b) suggestion to be pluralistic about the conceptual tools of evolutionary psychology, although it is clear that many evolutionary psychologists already embody the pluralism advocated (e.g., Tooby & Cosmides, 1990a, 1992). Researchers may differ about which of these tools they believe are most scientifically valuable for particular purposes. One reasonable standard for judging the value of such conceptual tools is the heuristic and predictive empirical harvest they yield. Table 23.1 shows 30 recent examples of the empirical findings about humans whose discovery was guided by hypotheses anchored in adaptation and natural selection.

From this empirical evidence, hypotheses about adaptations appear to have considerable value. In some cases, adaptation-minded researchers have generated and tested specific empirical predictions not generated from nonadaptationist theories, such as sex-linked causes of divorce (Betzig, 1989), causes of the intensity of mate retention effort (Buss & Shackelford, 1997), predictable conditions under which spousal homicide occurs (Daly & Wilson, 1988), sex differences in the nature of sexual fantasy (Ellis & Symons, 1990), and shifts in mate preferences across the life span (Kenrick & Keefe, 1992). In other cases, adaptation-mindedness has proved heuristic, guiding researchers to important domains not previously examined or discovered, such as the role of symmetry in mate attraction (Thornhill & Gangestad, 1993), the role of deception in mate attraction (Tooke & Camire, 1991), and the specific conflicts of interest that occur in stepfamilies (Wilson & Daly, 1987). Using the same criterion, we could not find a single example of an empirical discovery made about humans as a result of using the concepts of exaptations or spandrels (but see MacNeilage, 1997, for a testable exaptation hypothesis about the origins of human speech production). Of course, this relative lack of fruitfulness at this time does not imply that over time, the concepts of exaptation and spandrels cannot be useful in generating scientific hypotheses and producing empirical discoveries.

In this article, we have attempted to elucidate the defining criteria of adaptations, exaptations, spandrels, and functionless by-products. Tables 23.2 and 23.3 summarize several important conceptual and evidentiary standards applicable to each of these concepts.

Adaptations and exaptations — in the form of either co-opted adaptations or co-opted spandrels — share several common features. All invoke selection at some point in the causal sequence. All invoke function. All must meet conceptual criteria for the proposed function — the hallmarks of special design, including specialization of function for solving a particular adaptive problem. And all must meet evidentiary standards, such as generating specific testable empirical predictions and parsimoniously accounting for known empirical findings.

These concepts differ, however, in the role of selective origins and fitness in explaining a feature. Although all three invoke selection, adaptations that arose de novo from mutations invoke selection in the original construction of the mechanism as a species-wide feature. Co-opted adaptations invoke selection in the original construction of the mechanism that is co-opted as well as in any reconstruction necessary for reshaping the mechanism for its new function and in maintaining the mechanism in the population because of its new function. And co-opted spandrels invoke selection in explaining the adaptations of which they are by-products, in explaining the reshaping of the by-product for its new function, and in

TABLE 23.1   Thirty Recent Examples of Empirical Discoveries about Humans Generated by Thinking about Adaptation and Selection

EXAMPLE	SOURCE
Evolved landscape preferences	Orions & Heerwagen (1992)
Sexually dimorphic mating strategies	Thiessen (1993); Thiessen, Young, & Burroughs (1993)
Waist-to-hip ratio as a determinant of attractiveness judgments	Singh (1993)
Standards of beauty involving symmetry	Grammer & Thornhill (1994)
Women's desire for mates with resources found in 37 cultures	Buss (1989)
Men's preference for younger mates documented in 37 cultures	Buss (1989)
Cheater detection procedure in social exchange	Cosmides (1989)
Stepchild abuse at 40 times the rate of nonstepchild abuse	Wilson & Daly (1987)
Relationship-specific sensitivity to betrayal	Shackelford & Buss (1996)
Sex-linked shifts in mate preference across the life span	Kenrick & Keefe (1992)
Predictable patterns of spousal and same-sex homicide	Daly & Wilson (1988)
Pregnancy sickness as an adaptation to teratogens	Profet (1992)
Mother-fetus conflict	Haig (1993)
Predictably patterned occurrence of allergies	Profet (1991)
Different human sperm morphs	Baker & Bellis (1995)
Superior female spatial location memory	Silverman & Eals (1992)
Design of male sexual jealousy	Buss et al. (1992); Daly et al. (1982)
Sex differences in sexual fantasy	Ellis & Symons (1990)
Deception in mating tactics	Tooke & Camire (1991)
Profiles of sexual harassers and their victims	Studd & Gattiker (1991)
Sex differences in desire for sexual variety	Clark & Hatfield (1989)
Facial asymmetry as an indicator of poor psychological and physical health	Shackelford & Larsen (1997)
Frequentist reasoning in human cognition	Cosmides & Tooby (1996); Gigerenzer & Hoffrage (1995)
Predictable causes of conjugal dissolution in 89 cultures	Betzig (1989)
Socialization practices across cultures differing by sex and mating system	Low (1989)
Patterns of risk taking in intrasexual competition for mates	Wilson & Daly (1985)
Shifts in grandparental investment according to sex of grandparent and sex of parent	DeKay (1995); Euler & Weitzel (1996)
Perceptual adaptations for entraining, tracking, and predicting animate motion	Heptulla-Chatterjee, Freyd, & Shiffrar (1996)
Universal perceptual adaptations to terrestrial living	Shepard (1984, 1992)
Mate guarding as a function of female reproductive value	Buss & Shackelford (1997); Dickemann (1981)

TABLE 23.2   Conceptual and Evidentiary Criteria for Evaluating the Core Concepts of Adaptations, Exaptations, Spandrels, and Functionless By-Products

DIFFERENTIATION CRITERIA	ADAPTATION	EXAPTATION: CO-OPTED ADAPTATION	CO-OPTED SPANDREL	FUNCTIONLESS BY-PRODUCT
Origin and maintenance	History of selection	Selection operating on previous adaptation	Selection operating on previous by-product	History of selection for mechanism that produced by-product
Role of fitness	Correlated with fitness in past during period of its evolution	Currently correlated with fitness	Currently correlated with fitness	Not directly related to fitness
Critical features	Solved adaptive problem in past	Has new function	Has new function	No previous or current function

Note: Exaptations and *spandrels* are used here according to Gould's (1991) primary meanings, that is, as features co-opted for new current functions; *functionless by-product* is the term used for Gould's other and less common usages of exaptations and spandrels, that is, as incidental, nonfunctional consequences of other characteristics. In the evolutionary literature, these are usually called "by-products." In Gould's usage, "currently enhances fitness" presumably refers to the period of evolutionary time during which selection transformed a previous adaptation or by-product into a new function. Note also that Gould sometimes used the term *exaptation* to cover both co-opted adaptations and co-opted spandrels; we treat these separately.

explaining the maintenance of the by-product in the population because of its new function. Consequently, relative to initial adaptations, exaptations carry the additional evidentiary burden of showing that a current function is distinct from an earlier function or from a functional original structure.

The most important differences, however, center on the temporal aspect of function and fitness. Adaptations exist in the present because their form was shaped in the past by selection for a particular function (Darwin, 1859/1958; Symons, 1979; Tooby & Cosmides, 1990b; Williams, 1966). Exaptations, in contrast, exist in the present because they were co-opted from previous structures that evolved for reasons different from those of the later exapted function (Gould, 1991). Although all three concepts require documentation of special design for a hypothesized function, co-opted exaptations and spandrels carry the additional evidentiary burdens of documenting both later co-opted functionality and a distinct original adaptational functionality. To our knowledge, none of the items on Gould's (1991) list

TABLE 23.3   Standards Common to Adaptations, Exaptations (Co-Opted Adaptations), and Co-Opted Spandrels

STANDARDS	CRITERIA
Conceptual	Hallmarks of special design for proposed function: complexity, efficiency, reliability, specificity, capability of solving adaptive problem, and evolvability
Empirical	Capable of generating specific and falsifiable empirical predictions; must account for known data better than alternative hypotheses

of proposed spandrels and exaptations — language, religion, principles of commerce, warfare, reading, writing, and fine arts — have met these standards of evidence. Moreover, even if they did meet such standards, this would in no way diminish the need to place such items within an overall evolutionary framework in order to adequately understand and explain them — a point agreed on by all sides of these debates.

Evolutionary psychology is emerging as a promising theoretical perspective within psychology. As with many emerging theoretical perspectives, there is often controversy about the meaning and scientific utility of the new explanatory concepts. Although most psychologists cannot be expected to become steeped in all of the formal complexities of the highly technical discipline of evolutionary theory, we hope that this article will serve as a guide to some of the most theoretically useful core concepts and some of the most interesting controversies within this emerging perspective in psychological science.

ACKNOWLEDGMENTS

William Bevan served as action editor for this article.

We thank Rick Arnold, George Bittner, Leda Cosmides, Helena Cronin, Todd DeKay, Randy Diehl, Rob Kurzban, Don Symons, Del Thiessen, and John Tooby for discussions and commentary on the ideas contained in this article.

NOTES

1. The empirical application of evolutionary ideas to the study of nonhuman animal behavior, of course, has a long and rich history of success (see Alcock, 1993). Indeed, theory and research emerging from the study of animal behavior have been of great benefit to evolutionary psychology, and comparative psychology continues to inform research about humans (Tooby & Cosmides, 1992). Furthermore, over the past 40 years, ethologists have applied evolutionary functional analysis to manifest human behavior, such as in the study of fixed action patterns (e.g., Lorenz, 1952; Tinbergen, 1951) and universals of facial expression (Ekman, 1973). It was not until the late 1980s, however, that underlying psychological mechanisms, such as those postulated by cognitive psychologists subsequent to the cognitive revolution in psychology, were explored empirically from an evolutionary perspective (e.g., Buss, 1989; Cosmides, 1989).

2. Obviously, the inheritance of selected characteristics and their spread throughout a population are much more complex topics than we can do justice to here; for more extended treatments, see Dawkins (1982), Tooby and Cosmides (1992), and Williams (1966).

3. These and other examples throughout this article are used to illustrate the conceptual points being made and should be regarded at this early stage in the development of evolutionary psychology as hypotheses to be subjected to empirical verification.

REFERENCES

Alcock, J. (1993). *Animal behavior: An evolutionary approach* (5th ed.). Sunderland, MA: Sinauer.

Allman, W. F. (1994). *The Stone Age present.* New York: Simon & Schuster.

Baker, R. R., & Bellis, M. A. (1995). *Human sperm competition.* London: Chapman & Hall.

Baldwin, J. M. (1894). *Mental development in the child and the race.* New York: Kelly.

Belsky, J., Steinberg, L., & Draper, P. (1991). Childhood experience, interpersonal development, and reproductive strategy: An evolutionary theory of socialization. *Child Development, 62,* 647–670.

Betzig, L. (1989). Causes of conjugal dissolution: A cross-cultural study. *Current Anthropology, 30,* 654–676.

Buss, D. M. (1988). From vigilance to violence: Tactics of mate retention among American undergraduates. *Ethology and Sociobiology, 9,* 291–317.

Buss, D. M. (1989). Sex differences in human mate preferences: Evolutionary hypotheses tested in 37 cultures. *Behavioral and Brain Sciences, 12,* 1–49.

Buss, D. M. (1994). *The evolution of desire: Strategies of human mating.* New York: Basic Books.

Buss, D. M. (1995). Evolutionary psychology: A new paradigm for psychological science. *Psychological Inquiry, 6,* 1–30.

Buss, D. M., Larsen, R. J., Westen, D., & Semmelroth, J. (1992). Sex differences in jealousy: Evolution, physiology, and psychology. *Psychological Science, 3,* 251–255.

Buss, D. M., & Schmitt, D. P. (1993). Sexual strategies theory: An evolutionary perspective on human mating. *Psychological Review, 100,* 204–232.

Buss, D. M., & Shackelford, T. K. (1997). From vigilance to violence: Tactics of mate retention in married couples. *Journal of Personality and Social Psychology, 72,* 346–361.

Buunk, A. B., Angleitner, A., Oubaid, V., & Buss, D. M. (1996). Sex differences in jealousy in evolutionary and cultural perspective: Tests from The Netherlands, Germany, and the United States. *Psychological Science, 7,* 359–363.

Clark, R. D., & Hatfield, E. (1989). Gender differences in receptivity to sexual offers. *Journal of Psychology and Human Sexuality, 2,* 39–55.

Cosmides, L. (1989). The logic of social exchange: Has natural selection shaped how humans reason? *Cognition, 31,* 187–276.

Cosmides, L., & Tooby, J. (1994). Beyond intuition and instinct blindness: Toward an evolutionarily rigorous cognitive science. *Cognition, 50,* 41–77.

Cosmides, L., & Tooby, J. (1996). Are humans good intuitive statisticians after all? Rethinking some conclusions from the literature on judgment under uncertainty. *Cognition, 58,* 1–73.

Daly, M., & Wilson, M. (1988). *Homicide.* Hawthorne, NY: Aldine de Gruyter.

Daly, M., Wilson, M., & Weghorst, S. J. (1982). Male sexual jealousy. *Ethology and Sociobiology, 3,* 11–27.

Darwin, C. (1958). *On the origin of species by means of natural selection.* New York: New American Library. (Original work published 1859)

Darwin, C. (1981). *The descent of man and selection in relation to sex.* Princeton, NJ: Princeton University Press. (Original work published 1871)

Dawkins, R. (1982). *The extended phenotype.* San Francisco: Freeman.

Dawkins, R. (1996). *Climbing Mount Improbable.* New York: Norton.

DeKay, W. T. (1995, June). *Grandparental investment and the uncertainty of kinship.* Paper presented at the Seventh Annual Meeting of the Human Behavior and Evolution Society, Santa Barbara, CA.

DeKay, W. T., & Buss, D. M. (1992). Human nature, individual differences, and the importance of context: Perspectives from evolutionary psychology. *Current Directions in Psychological Science, 1,* 184–189.

Dennett, D. C. (1995). *Darwin's dangerous idea.* New York: Simon & Schuster.

Dickemann, M. (1981). Paternal confidence and dowry competition: A biocultural analysis of purdah. In R. D. Alexander & D. W. Tinkle (Eds.), *Natural selection and social behavior* (pp. 417–438). New York: Chiron.

Ekman, P. (1973). Cross-cultural studies of facial expression. In P. Ekman (Ed.), *Darwin and facial expression* (pp. 169–222). New York: Academic Press.

Ellis, B. J., & Symons, D. (1990). Sex differences in sexual fantasy: An evolutionary psychological approach. *Journal of Sex Research, 27,* 527–556.

Euler, H. A., & Weitzel, B. (1996). Discriminative grandparental solicitude as reproductive strategy. *Human Nature, 7,* 39–59.

Folstad, I., & Karter, A. J. (1992). Parasites, bright males, and the immunocompetence handicap. *American Naturalist, 139,* 603–622.

Gangestad, S. W., & Simpson, J. A. (1990). Toward an evolutionary history of female sociosexual variation. *Journal of Personality, 58,* 69–96.

Gigerenzer, G., & Hoffrage, U. (1995). How to improve Bayesian reasoning without instruction: Frequency formats. *Psychological Review, 102,* 684–704.

Gould, S. J. (1987). Freudian slip. *Natural History, 96*(1), 14–21.

Gould, S. J. (1991). Exaptation: A crucial tool for evolutionary psychology. *Journal of Social Issues, 47,* 43–65.

Gould, S. J. (1997a, October 9). Evolutionary psychology: An exchange. *New York Review of Books, XLIV,* 53–58.

Gould, S. J. (1997b). The exaptive excellence of spandrels as a term and prototype. *Proceedings of the National Academy of Sciences, 94,* 10750–10755.

Gould, S. J., & Lewontin, R. C. (1979). The spandrels of San Marco and the Panglossian paradigm: A critique of the adaptationist programme. *Proceedings of the Royal Society of London B, 205,* 581–598.

Gould, S. J., & Vrba, E. S. (1982). Exaptation: A missing term in the science of form. *Paleobiology, 8,* 4–15.

Grammer, K., & Thornhill, R. (1994). Human facial attractiveness and sexual selection: The role of symmetry and averageness. *Journal of Comparative Psychology, 108,* 233–242.

Haig, D. (1993). Maternal-fetal conflict in human pregnancy. *Quarterly Review of Biology, 68,* 495–532.

Hamilton, W. D. (1964). The genetical evolution of social behavior. *Journal of Theoretical Biology, 7,* 1–52.

Heptulla-Chatterjee, S., Freyd, J. J., & Shiffrar, M. (1996). Configural processing in the perception of apparent biological motion. *Journal of Experimental Psychology: Human Perception and Performance, 22,* 916–929.

James, W. (1962). *Principles of psychology.* New York: Dover. (Original work published 1890)

Jennings, H. S. (1930). *The biological basis of human nature.* New York: Norton.

Kenrick, D. T., & Keefe, R. C. (1992). Age preferences in mates reflect sex differences in human reproductive strategies. *Behavioral and Brain Sciences, 15,* 75–133.

Lilienfeld, S. O., & Marino, L. (1995). Mental disorder as a Roschian concept: A critique of Wakefield's "harmful dysfunction" analysis. *Journal of Abnormal Psychology, 104,* 411–420.

Lorenz, K. Z. (1952). *King Solomon's ring.* New York: Cromwell.

Low, B. S. (1989). Cross-cultural patterns in the training of children: An evolutionary perspective. *Journal of Comparative Psychology, 103,* 313–319.

MacNeilage, P. (1997). What ever happened to articulate speech? In M. C. Corballis & S. Lea (Eds.), *Evolution of the hominid mind.* New York: Oxford University Press.

Marr, D. (1982). *Vision.* San Francisco: Freeman.

Mineka, S. (1992). Evolutionary memories, emotional processing, and the emotional disorders. In D. Medin (Ed.), *The psychology of learning and motivation* (Vol. 28). New York: Academic Press.

Morgan, C. L. (1896). *Habit and instinct.* London: Arnold.

Nesse, R. M. (1990). Evolutionary explanations of emotions. *Human Nature, 1,* 261–289.

Orions, G. H., & Heerwagen, J. H. (1992). Evolved response to landscapes. In J. H. Barkow, L. Cosmides, & J. Tooby (Eds.), *The adapted mind* (pp. 555–580). New York: Oxford University Press.

Piattelli-Palmarini, M. (1989). Evolution, selection, and cognition: From "learning" to parameter setting in biology and the study of language. *Cognition, 31,* 1–44.

Pinker, S. (1994). *The language instinct.* New York: Morrow.

Pinker, S. (1997a, October 9). Evolutionary psychology: An exchange. *New York Review of Books, XLIV,* 55–56.

Pinker, S. (1997b). *How the mind works.* New York: Norton.

Pinker, S., & Bloom, P. (1992). Natural language and natural selection. In J. H. Barkow, L. Cosmides, & J. Tooby (Eds.), *The adapted mind* (pp. 451–493). New York: Oxford University Press.

Profet, M. (1991). The function of allergy: Immunological defense against toxins. *Quarterly Review of Biology, 66,* 23–62.

Profet, M. (1992). Pregnancy sickness as adaptation: A deterrent to maternal ingestion of teratogens. In J. H. Barkow, L. Cosmides, & J. Tooby (Eds.), *The adapted mind* (pp. 327–365). New York: Oxford University Press.

Rancour-Laferriere, D. (1985). *Signs of the flesh: An essay on the evolution of hominid sexuality.* New York: Mouton de Gruyter.

Richters, J. E., & Cicchetti, D. (1993). Mark Twain meets *DSM-III-R:* Conduct disorder, development, and the concept of harmful dysfunction. *Development & Psychopathology, 5,* 5–29.

Romanes, G. (1889). *Mental evolution in man: Origin of human faculty.* New York: Appleton.

Sedikedes, C., & Skowronski, J. J. (1997). The symbolic self in evolutionary context. *Personality and Social Psychology Review, 1,* 80–102.

Shackelford, T. K., & Buss, D. M. (1996). Betrayal in mateships, friendships, and coalitions. *Personality and Social Psychology Bulletin, 22,* 1151–1164.

Shackelford, T. K., & Larsen, R. J. (1997). Facial asymmetry as an indicator of psychological, emotional, and physiological distress. *Journal of Personality and Social Psychology, 72,* 456–466.

Shepard, R. N. (1984). Ecological constraints on internal representation: Resonant kinematics of perceiving, imagining, thinking, and dreaming. *Psychological Review, 91,* 417–447.

Shepard, R. N. (1992). The perceptual organization of colors: An adaptation to regularities of the terrestrial world? In J. H. Barkow, L. Cosmides, & J. Tobby (Eds.), *The adapted mind* (pp. 495–532). New York: Oxford University Press.

Silverman, I., & Eals, M. (1992). Sex differences in spatial abilities: Evolutionary theory and data. In J. H. Barkow, L. Cosmides, & J. Tooby (Eds.), *The adapted mind* (pp. 533–549). New York: Oxford University Press.

Singh, D. (1993). Adaptive significance of female physical attractiveness: Role of waist-to-hip ratio. *Journal of Personality and Social Psychology, 65,* 293–307.

Studd, M. V., & Gattiker, U. E. (1991). The evolutionary psychology of sexual harassment in organizations. *Ethology and Sociobiology, 12,* 249–290.

Symons, D. (1979). *The evolution of human sexuality.* New York: Oxford University Press.

Symons, D. (1987). If we're all Darwinians, what's the fuss about? In C. Crawford, D. Krebs, & M. Smith

(Eds.), *Sociobiology and psychology* (pp. 121–146). Hillsdale, NJ: Erlbaum.

Symons, D. (1992). On the use and misuse of Darwinism in the study of human behavior. In J. H. Barkow, L. Cosmides, & J. Tooby (Eds.), *The adapted mind* (pp. 137–159). New York: Oxford University Press.

Symons, D. (1995). Beauty is in the adaptations of the beholder: The evolutionary psychology of human female sexual attractiveness. In P. R. Abramson & S. D. Pinkerton (Eds.), *Sexual nature, sexual culture* (pp. 80–118). Chicago: University of Chicago Press.

Than-Than, Hutton, R. A., Myint-Lwin, Khin-EiHan, Soe-Soe, Tin-Nu-Swe, Phillips, R. E., & Warrell, D. A. (1988). Haemostatic disturbances in patients bitten by Russell's viper *(Vipera russelli siamensis)* in Burma. *British Journal of Haematology, 69,* 513–520.

Thiessen, D. (1993). Environmental tracking by females: Sexual lability. *Human Nature, 5,* 167–202.

Thiessen, D. (1996). *Bittersweet destiny.* New Brunswick, NJ: Transaction.

Thiessen, D., Young, R. K., & Burroughs, R. (1993). Lonely hearts advertisements reflect sexually dimorphic mating strategies. *Ethology and Sociobiology, 14,* 209–229.

Thornhill, R., & Gangestad, S. W. (1993). Human facial beauty: Averageness, symmetry, and parasite resistance. *Human Nature, 4,* 237–270.

Tinbergen, N. (1951). *The study of instinct.* London: Oxford University Press.

Tooby, J., & Cosmides, L. (1990a). On the universality of human nature and the uniqueness of the individual: The role of genetics and adaptation. *Journal of Personality, 58,* 17–68.

Tooby, J., & Cosmides, L. (1990b). The past explains the present: Emotional adaptations and the structure of ancestral environments. *Ethology and Sociobiology, 11,* 375–424.

Tooby, J., & Cosmides, L. (1992). Psychological foundations of culture. In J. H. Barkow, L. Cosmides, & J. Tooby (Eds.), *The adapted mind* (pp. 19–136). New York: Oxford University Press.

Tooke, J., & Camire, L. (1991). Patterns of deception in intersexual and intrasexual mating strategies. *Ethology and Sociobiology, 10,* 241–253.

Voltaire, F. M. A. (1939). *Candide.* London: Nonesuch Press. (Original work published 1759)

Wakefield, J. C. (1992). The concept of mental disorder: On the boundary between biological facts and social values. *American Psychologist, 47,* 373–388.

Wakefield, J. C. (1999). Evolutionary versus prototype analyses of the concept of disorder. *Journal of Abnormal Psychology, 108,* 374–399.

Wedekind, C. (1992). Detailed information about parasites revealed by sexual ornamentation. *Proceedings of the Royal Society of London B, 247,* 169–174.

Wiederman, M. W., & Allgeier, E. R. (1993). Gender differences in sexual jealousy: Adaptationist or social learning explanation? *Ethology and Sociobiology, 14,* 115–140.

Williams, G. C. (1966). *Adaptation and natural selection.* Princeton, NJ: Princeton University Press.

Williams, G. C. (1992). *Natural selection.* New York: Oxford University Press.

Wilson, M., & Daly, M. (1985). Competitiveness, risk-taking, and violence: The young male syndrome. *Ethology and Sociobiology, 6,* 59–73.

Wilson, M., & Daly, M. (1987). Risk of maltreatment of children living with stepparents. In R. J. Gelles & J. B. Lancaster (Eds.), *Child abuse and neglect* (pp. 215–232). Hawthorne, NY: Aldine de Gruyter.

Wilson, M., & Daly, M. (1992). The man who mistook his wife for a chattel. In J. H. Barkow, L. Cosmides, & J. Tooby (Eds.), *The adapted mind* (pp. 289–322). New York: Oxford University Press.

CHAPTER TWENTY-FOUR

TOWARD MAPPING THE EVOLVED FUNCTIONAL ORGANIZATION OF MIND AND BRAIN

JOHN TOOBY AND LEDA COSMIDES

Nothing in biology makes sense except in the light of evolution.

— T. Dobzhansky

It is the theory which decides what we can observe.

— A. Einstein

24.1   SEEING WITH NEW EYES: TOWARD AN EVOLUTIONARILY INFORMED COGNITIVE NEUROSCIENCE

The task of cognitive neuroscience is to map the information-processing structure of the human mind and to discover how this computational organization is implemented in the physical organization of the brain. The central impediment to progress is obvious: The human brain is, by many orders of magnitude, the most complex system that humans have yet investigated. Purely as a physical system, the vast intricacy of chemical and electrical interactions among hundreds of billions of neurons and glial cells defeats any straightforward attempt to build a comprehensive model, as one might attempt to do with particle collisions, geological processes, protein folding, or host-parasite interactions. Combinatorial explosion makes the task of elucidating the brain's computational structure even more overwhelming: There is an indefinitely large number of specifiable inputs, measurable outputs, and possible

From Gazzaniga, Michael, ed., *The New Cognitive Neurosciences,* second edition, pp. 1167–1178, © 1999 Massachusetts Institute of Technology, by permission of The MIT Press.

relationships between them. Even worse, no one yet knows with certainty how computations are physically realized. They depend on individuated events within the detailed structure of neural microcircuitry largely beyond the capacity of current technologies to observe or resolve. Finally, the underlying logic of the system has been obscured by the torrent of recently generated data.

Historically, however, well-established theories from one discipline have functioned as organs of perception for others (e.g., statistical mechanics for thermodynamics). They allow new relationships to be observed and make visible elegant systems of organization that had previously eluded detection. It seems worth exploring whether evolutionary biology could provide a rigorous metatheoretical framework for the brain sciences, as they have recently begun to do for psychology (Shepard, 1984, 1987a, 1987b; Gallistel, 1990; Cosmides and Tooby, 1987; Pinker, 1994, 1997; Marr, 1982; Tooby and Cosmides, 1992).

Cognitive neuroscience began with the recognition that the brain is an organ designed to process information and that studying it as such would offer important new insights. Cognitive neuroscientists also recognize that the brain is an evolved system, but few realize that anything follows from this second fact. Yet these two views of the brain are intimately related and, when considered jointly, can be very illuminating.

24.2   WHY BRAINS EXIST

The brain is an organ of computation that was built by the evolutionary process. To say that the brain is an organ of computation means that (1) its physical structure embodies a set of programs that process information, and (2) that physical structure is there *because* it embodies these programs. To say that the brain was built by the evolutionary process means that its functional components — its programs — are there *because* they solved a particular problem-type in the past. In systems designed by natural selection, function determines structure.

Among living things, there are whole kingdoms filled with organisms that lack brains (plants, Monera, fungi). The sole reason that evolution introduced brains into the designs of some organisms — the reason brains exist at all — is because brains performed computations that regulated these organisms' internal processes and external activities in ways that promoted their fitness. For a randomly generated modification in design to be selected — that is, for a mutation to be incorporated by means of a nonrandom process into a species-typical brain design — it had to improve the ability of organisms to solve adaptive problems. That is, the modification had to have a certain kind of effect: It had to improve the organisms' performance of some activity that systematically enhanced the propagation of that modification, summed across the species' range and across many generations. This means that the design of the circuits, components, systems, or modules that make up our neural architecture must reflect, to an unknown but high degree, (1) the computational task demands inherent in the performance of those ancestral activities and (2) the evolutionarily long-enduring structure of those task environments (Marr, 1982; Shepard, 1987a; Tooby and Cosmides, 1992).

Activities that promoted fitness in hominid ancestral environments differ in many ways from activities that capture our attention in the modern world, and they were certainly performed under radically different circumstances. (Consider: hunting vs. grocery shopping; walking everywhere vs. driving and flying; cooperating within a social world of ~200 relatives and friends vs. 50,000 strangers in a medium-sized city). The design features of the brain were built to specifications inherent in ancestral adaptive problems and selection pressures, often resulting in talents or deficits that seem out of place or irrational in our world. A baby cries — alerting her parents — when she is left to sleep alone in the dark, not because hyenas roam her suburban household, but because her brain is designed to keep her from being eaten under the circumstances in which our species evolved.

There is no single algorithm or computational procedure that can solve every adaptive problem (Cosmides and Tooby, 1987; Tooby and Cosmides, 1990a, 1992). The human mind (it will turn out) is composed of many different programs for the same reason that a carpenter's toolbox contains many different tools: Different problems require different solutions. To reverse-engineer the brain, one needs to discover functional units that are native to its organization. To do this, it is useful to know, as specifically as possible, what the brain is for — which specific families of computations it was built to accomplish and what counted as a biologically successful outcome for each problem-type. The answers to this question must be phrased in computational terms because that is the only language that can capture or express the functions that neural properties were naturally selected to embody. They must also refer to the ancestral activities, problems, selection pressures, and environments of the species in question because jointly these define the computational problems each component was configured to solve (Cosmides and Tooby, 1987; Tooby and Cosmides, 1990a, 1992).

For these reasons, evolutionary biology, biological anthropology, and cognitive psychology (when integrated, called *evolutionary psychology*) have the potential to supply to cognitive neuroscientists what might prove to be a key missing element in their research program: a partial list of the native information-processing functions that the human brain was built to execute, as well as clues and principles about how to discover or evaluate adaptive problems that might be proposed in the future.

Just as the fields of electrical and mechanical engineering summarize our knowledge of principles that govern the design of human-built machines, the field of evolutionary biology summarizes our knowledge of the engineering principles that govern the design of organisms, which can be thought of as machines built by the evolutionary process (for overviews, see Daly and Wilson, 1984; Dawkins, 1976, 1982, 1986; Krebs and Davies, 1997). Modern evolutionary biology constitutes, in effect, a foundational "organism design theory" whose principles can be used to fit together research findings into coherent models of specific cognitive and neural mechanisms (Tooby and Cosmides, 1992). To apply these theories to a particular species, one integrates analyses of selection pressures with models of the natural history and ancestral environments of the species. For humans, the latter are provided by hunter-gatherer studies, biological anthropology, paleoanthropology, and primatology (Lee and DeVore, 1968).

24.3   FIRST PRINCIPLES: REPRODUCTION, FEEDBACK, AND THE ANTIENTROPIC CONSTRUCTION OF ORGANIC DESIGN

Within an evolutionary framework, an organism can be described as a self-reproducing machine. From this perspective, the defining property of life is the presence in a system of "devices" (organized components) that cause the system to construct new and similarly reproducing systems. From this defining property — self-reproduction — the entire deductive structure of modern Darwinism logically follows (Dawkins, 1976; Williams, 1985; Tooby and Cosmides, 1990a). Because the replication of the design of the parental machine is not always error free, randomly modified designs (i.e., mutants) are introduced into populations of reproducers. Because such machines are highly organized so that they cause the otherwise improbable outcome of constructing offspring machines, most random modifications interfere with the complex sequence of actions necessary for self-reproduction. Consequently, such modified designs will tend to remove themselves from the population — a case of negative feedback.

However, a small residual subset of design modifications will, by chance, happen to constitute improvements in the design's machinery for causing its own reproduction. Such improved designs (by definition) cause their own increasing frequency in the population — a case of positive feedback. This increase continues until (usually) such modified designs outreproduce and thereby replace all alternative designs in the population, leading to a new species-standard design. After such an event, the population of reproducing machines is different from the ancestral population: The population- or species-standard design has taken a step "uphill" toward a greater degree of functional organization for reproduction than it had previously. This spontaneous feedback process — natural selection — causes functional organization to emerge *naturally*, that is, without the intervention of an intelligent "designer" or supernatural forces.

Over the long run, down chains of descent, this feedback cycle pushes designs through state-space toward increasingly well-organized — and otherwise improbable — functional arrangements (Dawkins, 1986; Williams, 1966, 1985). These arrangements are functional in a specific sense: the elements are improbably well organized to cause their own reproduction in the environment in which the species evolved. Because the reproductive fates of the inherited traits that coexist in the same organism are linked together, traits will be selected to enhance each other's functionality (however, see Cosmides and Tooby, 1981, and Tooby and Cosmides, 1990a, for the relevant genetic analysis and qualifications). As design features accumulate, they will tend to sequentially fit themselves together into increasingly functionally elaborated machines for reproduction, composed of constituent mechanisms — called *adaptations* — that solve problems that either are necessary for reproduction or increase its likelihood (Darwin, 1859; Dawkins, 1986; Thornhill, 1991; Tooby and Cosmides, 1990a; Williams, 1966, 1985). Significantly, in species like humans, genetic processes ensure that complex adaptations virtually always are species-typical (unlike nonfunctional aspects of the system). This means that *functional* aspects of the architecture will tend to be universal at the genetic level, even though their expression may often be sex or age limited, or environmentally contingent (Tooby and Cosmides, 1990b).[1]

Because design features are embodied in individual organisms, they can, generally speaking, propagate themselves in only two ways: by solving problems that increase the probability that offspring will be produced either by the organism they are situated in or by that organism's kin (Hamilton, 1964; Williams and Williams, 1957; however, see Cosmides and Tooby, 1981, and Haig, 1993, for intragenomic methods). An individual's relatives, by virtue of having descended from a recent common ancestor, have an increased likelihood of having the same design feature as compared to other conspecifics. This means that a design modification in an individual that causes an increase in the reproductive rate of that individual's kin will, by so doing, tend to increase its own frequency in the population. Accordingly, design features that promote both direct reproduction and kin reproduction, and that make efficient trade-offs between the two, will replace those that do not. To put this in standard biological terminology, design features are selected to the extent that they promote their inclusive fitness (Hamilton, 1964).

In addition to selection, mutations can become incorporated into species-typical designs by means of chance processes. For example, the sheer impact of many random accidents may cumulatively propel a useless mutation upward in frequency until it crowds out all alternative design features from the population. Clearly, the presence of such a trait in the architecture is not explained by the (nonexistent) functional consequences that it had over many generations on the design's reproduction; as a result, chance-injected traits will not tend to be coordinated with the rest of the organism's architecture in a functional way.

Although such chance events play a restricted role in evolution and explain the existence and distribution of many simple and trivial properties, organisms are not primarily chance agglomerations of stray properties. Reproduction is a highly improbable outcome in the absence of functional machinery designed to bring it about, and only designs that retain all the necessary machinery avoid being selected out. To be invisible to selection and, therefore, not organized by it a modification must be so minor that its effects on reproduction are negligible. As a result, chance properties do indeed drift through the standard designs of species in a random way, but they are unable to account for the complex organized design in organisms and are, correspondingly, usually peripheralized into those aspects that do not make a significant impact on the functional operation of the system (Tooby and Cosmides, 1990a, 1990b, 1992). Random walks do not systematically build intricate and improbably functional arrangements such as the visual system, the language faculty, face recognition programs, emotion recognition modules, food aversion circuits, cheater detection devices, or motor control systems, for the same reason that wind in a junkyard does not assemble airplanes and radar.

24.4 BRAINS ARE COMPOSED PRIMARILY OF ADAPTIVE PROBLEM-SOLVING DEVICES

In fact, natural selection is the only known cause of and explanation for complex functional design in organic systems. Hence, all naturally occurring functional organization in organisms should be ascribed to its operation, and hypotheses about function are likely to be correct only if they are the kinds of functionality that natural selection produces.

This leads to the most important point for cognitive neuroscientists to abstract from modern evolutionary biology: Although not everything in the designs of organisms is the product of selection, all complex functional organization is. Indeed, selection can only account for functionality of a very narrow kind: approximately, design features organized to promote the reproduction of an individual and his or her relatives in ancestral environments (Williams, 1966; Dawkins, 1986). Fortunately for the modern theory of evolution, the only naturally occurring complex functionality that ever has been documented in undomesticated plants, animals, or other organisms is functionality of just this kind, along with its derivatives and by-products.

This has several important implications for cognitive neuroscientists:

1. *Technical Definition of Function.*   In explaining or exploring the reliably developing organization of a cognitive device, the *function* of a design refers solely to how it systematically caused its own propagation in ancestral environments. It does not validly refer to any intuitive or folk definitions of function such as "contributing to personal goals," "contributing to one's well-being," or "contributing to society." These other kinds of usefulness may or may not exist as side effects of a given evolved design, but they can play no role in explaining how such designs came into existence or why they have the organization that they do.

It is important to bear in mind that the evolutionary standard of functionality is entirely independent of any ordinary human standard of desirability, social value, morality, or health (Cosmides and Tooby, 1999).

2. *Adapted to the Past.*   The human brain, to the extent that it is organized to do anything functional at all, is organized to construct information, make decisions, and generate behavior that would have tended to promote inclusive fitness in the ancestral environments and behavioral contexts of Pleistocene hunter-gatherers and before. (The preagricultural world of hunter-gatherers is the appropriate ancestral context because natural selection operates far too slowly to have built complex information-processing adaptations to the post-hunter-gatherer world of the last few thousand years.)

3. *No Evolved "Reading Modules."*   The problems that our cognitive devices are designed to solve do not reflect the problems that our modern life experiences lead us to see as normal, such as reading, driving cars, working for large organizations, reading insurance forms, learning the oboe, or playing Go. Instead, they are the odd and seemingly esoteric problems that our hunter-gatherer ancestors encountered generation after generation over hominid evolution. These include such problems as foraging, kin recognition, "mind reading" (i.e., inferring beliefs, desires, and intentions from behavior), engaging in social exchange, avoiding incest, choosing mates, interpreting threats, recognizing emotions, caring for children, regulating immune function, and so on, as well as the already well-known problems involved in perception, language acquisition, and motor control.

4. *Side Effects are Personally Important but Scientifically Misleading.*   Although our architectures may be capable of performing tasks that are "functional" in the (nonbiological) sense that we may value them (e.g., weaving, playing piano), these are incidental side effects of selection for our Pleistocene competencies — just as a machine built to be a hairdryer can, incidentally, dehydrate fruit or electrocute. But it will be difficult to make sense of our cognitive mechanisms if one attempts to interpret them as devices designed to perform functions that were not selectively important for our hunter-gatherer ancestors, or if one fails to consider the adaptive functions these abilities are side effects of.

5. *Adaptationism Provides New Techniques and Principles.*   Whenever one finds better-than-chance functional organization built into our cognitive or neural architecture, one is looking at adaptations — devices that acquired their distinctive organization from natural selection acting on our hunter-gatherer or more distant primate ancestors. Reciprocally, when one is searching for intelligible functional organization underlying a set of cognitive or neural phenomena, one is far more likely to discover it by using an adaptationist framework for organizing observations because adaptive organization is the only kind of functional organization that is there to be found.

Because the reliably developing mechanisms (i.e., circuits, modules, functionally isolable units, mental organs, or computational devices) that cognitive neuroscientists study are evolved adaptations, all the biological principles that apply to adaptations apply to cognitive devices. This connects cognitive neuroscience and evolutionary biology in the most direct possible way. This conclusion should be a welcome one because it is the logical doorway through which a very extensive body of new expertise and principles can be made to apply to cognitive neuroscience, stringently constraining the range of valid hypotheses about the functions and structures of cognitive mechanisms. Because cognitive neuroscientists are usually studying adaptations and their effects, they can supplement their present research methods with carefully derived adaptationist analytic tools.

6. *Ruling Out and Ruling In.* Evolutionary biology gives specific and rigorous content to the concept of function, imposing strict rules on its use (Williams, 1966; Dawkins, 1982, 1986). This allows one to rule out certain hypotheses about the proposed function of a given cognitive mechanism. But the problem is not just that cognitive neuroscientists sometimes impute functions that they ought not to. An even larger problem is that many fail to impute functions that they ought to. For example, an otherwise excellent recent talk by a prominent cognitive neuroscientist began with the claim that one would not expect jealousy to be a "primary" emotion — that is, a universal, reliably developing part of the human neural architecture (in contrast to others, such as disgust or fear). Yet there is a large body of theory in evolutionary biology — sexual selection theory — that predicts that sexual jealousy will be widespread in species with substantial parental investment in offspring (particularly in males); behavioral ecologists have documented mate-guarding behavior (behavior designed to keep sexual competitors away from one's mate) in a wide variety of species, including various birds, fish, insects, and mammals (Krebs and Davies, 1997; Wilson and Daly, 1992); male sexual jealousy exists in every documented human culture (Daly et al., 1982; Wilson and Daly, 1992); it is the major cause of spousal homicides (Daly and Wilson, 1988), and in experimental settings, the design features of sexual jealousy have been shown to differ between the sexes in ways that reflect the different adaptive problems faced by ancestral men and women (Buss, 1994). From the standpoint of evolutionary biology and behavioral ecology, the hypothesis that sexual jealousy is a primary emotion — more specifically, the hypothesis that the human brain includes neurocognitive mechanisms whose function is to regulate the conditions under which sexual jealousy is expressed and what its cognitive and behavioral manifestations will be like — is virtually inescapable (for an evolutionary/cognitive approach to emotions, see Tooby and Cosmides, 1990a, 1990b). But if cognitive neuroscientists are not aware of this body of theory and evidence, they will not design experiments capable of revealing such mechanisms.

7. *Biological Parsimony, Not Physics Parsimony.* The standard of parsimony imported from physics, the traditional philosophy of science, or from habits of economical programming is inappropriate and misleading in biology, and hence, in neuroscience and cognitive science, which study biological systems. The evolutionary process never starts with a clean work board, has no foresight, and incorporates new features solely on the basis of whether they lead to systematically enhanced propagation. Indeed, when one examines the brain, one sees an amazingly heterogeneous physical structure. A correct theory of evolved cognitive functions should be no less complex and heterogeneous than the evolved physical structure itself and should map on to the heterogeneous set of recurring adaptive tasks faced by hominid foragers over evolutionary time. Theories of engineered machinery involve theories of the subcomponents. One would not expect that a general, unified theory of robot or automotive mechanism could be accurate.

8. *Many Cognitive Adaptations.* Indeed, analyses of the adaptive problems humans and other animals must have regularly solved over evolutionary time suggest that the mind contains a far greater number of functional specializations than is traditionally supposed, even by cognitive scientists sympathetic to "modular" approaches. From an evolutionary perspective, the human cognitive architecture is far more likely to resemble a confederation of hundreds or thousands of functionally dedicated computers, designed to solve problems endemic to the Pleistocene, than it is to resemble a single general purpose computer equipped with a small number of domain-general procedures, such as association formation, categorization, or production rule formation (for discussion, see Cosmides and Tooby, 1987, 1994; Gallistel, 1990; Pinker, 1997; Sperber, 1994; Symons, 1987; Tooby and Cosmides, 1992).

9. *Cognitive Descriptions are Necessary.* Understanding the neural organization of the brain depends on understanding the functional organization of its computational relationships or cognitive devices. The brain originally came into existence and accumulated its particular set of design features only because these features functionally contributed to the organism's propagation. This contribution — that is, the evolutionary function of the brain — is obviously the adaptive regulation of behavior and physiology *on the basis of information* derived from the body and from the environment. The brain performs no significant mechanical, metabolic, or chemical service for the organism — its function is purely informational, computational, and regulatory in nature. Because the function of the brain is informational in nature, its precise functional organization can only be accurately described in a language that is capable of expressing its informational functions — that is, in cognitive terms, rather than in cellular, anatomical, or chemical terms. Cognitive investigations are not some soft, optional activity that goes on only until the "real" neural analysis can be performed. Instead, the mapping of the computational adaptations of the brain is an unavoidable and indispensable step in the neuroscience research enterprise. It must proceed in tandem with neural investigations and provides one of the primary frameworks necessary for organizing the body of neuroscience results.

The reason is straightforward. Natural selection retained neural structures on the basis of their ability to create adaptively organized relationships between information and behavior (e.g., the sight of a predator activates inference procedures that cause the organism to hide or flee) or between information and physiology (e.g., the sight of a predator increases the organism's heart rate, in preparation for flight). Thus, it is the information-processing structure of the human psychological architecture that has been functionally organized by natural selection, and the neural structures and processes have been organized insofar as they physically realize this cognitive organization. Brains exist and have the structure that they do because of the computational requirements imposed by selection on our ancestors. The adaptive structure of our computational devices provides a skeleton around which a modern understanding of our neural architecture should be constructed.

24.5   BRAIN ARCHITECTURES CONSIST OF ADAPTATIONS, BY-PRODUCTS, AND RANDOM EFFECTS

To understand the human (or any living species') computational or neural architecture is a problem in reverse engineering: We have working exemplars of the design in front of us, but we need to organize our observations of these exemplars into a systematic functional and causal description of the design. One can describe and decompose brains into properties according to any of an infinite set of alternative systems, and hence there are an indefinitely large number of cognitive and neural phenomena that could be defined and measured. However, describing and investigating the architecture in terms of its adaptations is a useful place to begin, because (1) the adaptations are the cause of the system's organization (the reason for the system's existence), (2) organisms, properly described, consist largely of collections of adaptations (evolved problem-solvers), (3) an adaptationist frame of reference allows cognitive neuroscientists to apply to their research problems the formidable array of knowledge that evolutionary biologists have accumulated about adaptations, (4) all of the complex functionally organized subsystems in the architecture are adaptations, and (5) such a frame of reference permits the construction of economical and principled models of the important features of the system, in which the wealth of varied phenomena fall into intelligible, functional, and predictable patterns. As Ernst Mayr put it, summarizing the historical record, "the adaptationist question, 'What is the function of a given structure or organ?' has been for centuries the basis for every advance in physiology" (Mayr, 1983, p. 32). It should prove no less productive for cognitive neuroscientists. Indeed, all of the inherited design features of organisms can be partitioned into three categories: (1) adaptations (often, although not always, complex); (2) the by-products or concomitants of adaptations; and (3) random effects. Chance and selection, the two components of the evolutionary process, explain different types of design properties in organisms, and all aspects of design must be attributed to one of these two forces. The conspicuously distinctive cumulative impacts of chance and selection allow the development of rigorous standards of evidence for recognizing and establishing the existence of adaptations and distinguishing them from the nonadaptive aspects of organisms caused by the nonselectionist mechanisms of evolutionary change (Williams, 1966, 1985; Pinker and Bloom, 1992; Symons, 1992; Thornhill, 1991; Tooby and Cosmides, 1990a, 1990b, 1992; Dawkins, 1986).

24.5.1   Design Evidence

Adaptations are systems of properties ("mechanisms") crafted by natural selection to solve the specific problems posed by the regularities of the physical, chemical, developmental, ecological, demographic, social, and informational environments encountered by ancestral populations during the course of a species' or population's evolution (table 24.1). Adaptations are recognizable by "evidence of special design" (Williams, 1966) — that is, by recognizing certain features of the evolved species-typical design of an organism "as

TABLE 24.1   The Formal Properties of an Adaptation

An adaptation is:

1. A cross-generationally recurring set of characteristics of the phenotype

2. that is reliably manufactured over the developmental life history of the organism,

3. according to instructions contained in its genetic specification,

4. in interaction with stable and recurring features of the environment (i.e., it reliably develops normally when exposed to normal ontogenetic environments),

5. whose genetic basis became established and organized in the species (or population) over evolutionary time, because

6. the set of characteristics systematically interacted with stable and recurring features of the ancestral environment (the "adaptive problem"),

7. in a way that systematically promoted the propagation of the genetic basis of the set of characteristics better than the alternative designs existing in the population during the period of selection. This promotion virtually always takes place through enhancing the reproduction of the individual bearing the set of characteristics, or the reproduction of the relatives of that individual.

Adaptations. The most fundamental analytic tool for organizing observations about a species' functional architecture is the definition of an adaptation. To function, adaptations must evolve such that their causal properties rely on and exploit these stable and enduring statistical structural regularities in the world, and in other parts of the organism. Things worth noticing include the fact that an adaptation (such as teeth or breasts) can develop at any time during the life cycle, and need not be present at birth; an adaptation can express itself differently in different environments (e.g., speaks English, speaks Tagalog); an adaptation is not just any individually beneficial trait, but one built over evolutionary time and expressed in many individuals; an adaptation may not be producing functional outcomes currently (e.g., agoraphobia), but only needed to function well in ancestral environments; finally, an adaptation (like every other aspect of the phenotype) is the product of gene–environment interaction. Unlike many other phenotypic properties, however, it is the result of the interaction of the species-standard set of genes with those aspects of the environment that were present and relevant during the species' evolution. For a more extensive definition of the concept of adaptation, see Tooby and Cosmides, 1990b, 1992.

---

components of some special problem-solving machinery" (Williams, 1985, p. 1). Moreover, they are so well organized and such good engineering solutions to adaptive problems that a chance coordination between problem and solution is effectively ruled out as a counterhypothesis. Standards for recognizing special design include whether the problem solved by the structure is an evolutionarily long-standing adaptive problem, and such factors as economy, efficiency, complexity, precision, specialization, and reliability, which, like a key fitting a lock, render the design too good a solution to a defined adaptive problem to be coincidence (Williams, 1966). Like most other methods of empirical hypothesis testing, the demonstration that something is an adaptation is always, at core, a probability assessment concerning how likely a set of events is to have arisen by chance alone. Such assessments are made by investigating whether there is a highly nonrandom coordination between the recurring properties of the phenotype and the structured properties of the adaptive problem, in a way that meshed to promote fitness (genetic propagation) in ancestral environments

(Tooby and Cosmides, 1990b, 1992). For example, the lens, pupil, iris, retina, visual cortex, and other parts of the eye are too well coordinated, both with each other and with features of the world, such as the properties of light, optics, geometry, and the reflectant properties of surfaces, to have co-occurred by chance. In short, like the functional aspects of any other engineered system, they are recognizable as adaptations for analyzing scenes from reflected light by their organized and functional relationships to the rest of the design and to the structure of the world.

In contrast, concomitants or by-products of adaptations are those properties of the phenotype that do not contribute to functional design per se, but that happen to be coupled to properties that are. Consequently, they were dragged along into the species-typical architecture because of selection for the functional design features to which they are linked. For example, bones are adaptations, but the fact that they are white is an incidental by-product. Bones were selected to include calcium because it conferred hardness and rigidity to the structure (and was dietarily available), and it simply happens that alkaline earth metals appear white in many compounds, including the insoluble calcium salts that are a constituent of bone. From the point of view of functional design, by-products are the result of "chance," in the sense that the process that led to their incorporation into the design was blind to their consequences (assuming that they were not negative). Accordingly, such by-products are distinguishable from adaptations by the fact that they are not complexly arranged to have improbably functional consequences (e.g., the whiteness of bone does nothing for the vertebrae).

In general, by-products will be far less informative as a focus of study than adaptations because they are consequences and not causes of the organization of the system (and hence are functionally arbitrary, unregulated, and may, for example, vary capriciously between individuals). Unfortunately, unless researchers actively seek to study organisms in terms of their adaptations, they usually end up measuring and investigating arbitrary and random admixtures of functional and functionless aspects of organisms, a situation that hampers the discovery of the underlying organization of the biological system. We do not yet, for example, even know which exact aspects of the neuron are relevant to its function and which are by-products, so many computational neuroscientists may be using a model of the neuron that is wildly inaccurate.

Finally, entropic effects of many types are always acting to introduce disorder into the design of organisms. Traits introduced by accident or by evolutionary random walks are recognizable by the lack of coordination that they produce within the architecture or between the architecture and the environment, as well as by the fact that they frequently cause uncalibrated variation between individuals. Examples of such entropic processes include genetic mutation, recent change in ancestrally stable environmental features, and developmentally anomalous circumstances.

24.6   HOW WELL-ENGINEERED ARE ADAPTATIONS?

The design of our cognitive and neural mechanisms should only reflect the structure of the adaptive problems that our ancestors faced to the extent that natural selection is an effective process. Is it one? How well or poorly engineered are adaptations? Some researchers have argued that evolution primarily produces inept designs, because selection does not produce perfect optimality (Gould and Lewontin, 1979). In fact, evolutionary biologists since Darwin have been well aware that selection does not produce perfect designs (Darwin, 1859; Williams, 1966; Dawkins, 1976, 1982, 1986; for a recent convert from the position that organisms are optimally designed to the more traditional adaptationist position, see Lewontin, 1967, 1979; see Dawkins, 1982, for an extensive discussion of the many processes that prevent selection from reaching perfect optimality). Still, because natural selection is a hill-climbing process that tends to choose the best of the variant designs that actually appear, and because of the immense numbers of alternatives that appear o er the vast expanse of evolutionary time, natural selection tends to cause the accumulation of very well-engineered functional designs.

Empirical confirmation can be gained by comparing how well evolved devices and human engineered devices perform on evolutionarily recurrent adaptive problems (as opposed to arbitrary, artificial modern tasks, such as chess). For example, the claim that language competence is a simple and poorly engineered adaptation cannot be taken seriously, given the total amount of time, engineering, and genius that has gone into the still unsuccessful effort to produce artificial systems that can remotely approach — let alone equal — human speech perception, comprehension, acquisition, and production (Pinker and Bloom, 1992).

Even more strikingly, the visual system is composed of collections of cognitive adaptations that are well-engineered products of the evolutionary process, and although they may not be "perfect" or "optimal" — however these somewhat vague concepts may be interpreted — they are far better at vision than any human-engineered system yet developed.

Wherever the standard of biological functionality can be clearly defined — semantic induction, object recognition, color constancy, echolocation, relevant problem-solving generalization, chemical recognition (olfaction), mimicry, scene analysis, chemical synthesis — evolved adaptations are at least as good as and usually strikingly better than human engineered systems, in those rare situations in which humans can build systems that can accomplish them at all. It seems reasonable to insist that before a system is criticized as being poorly designed, the critic ought to be able to construct a better alternative — a requirement, it need hardly be pointed out, that has never been met by anyone who has argued that adaptations are poorly designed. Thus, although adaptations are certainly suboptimal in some ultimate sense, it is an empirically demonstrable fact that the short-run constraints on selective optimization do not prevent the emergence of superlatively organized computational adaptations in brains. Indeed, aside from the exotic nature of the problems that the brain was designed to solve, it is exactly this sheer functional intricacy that makes our architecture so difficult to reverse-engineer and to understand.

24.7   COGNITIVE ADAPTATIONS REFLECT THE STRUCTURE OF THE ADAPTIVE PROBLEM AND THE ANCESTRAL WORLD

Four lessons emerge from the study of natural competences, such as vision and language: (1) most adaptive information-processing problems are complex; (2) the evolved solution to these problems is usually machinery that is well engineered for the task; (3) this machinery is usually specialized to fit the particular nature of the problem; and (4) its evolved design often embodies substantial and contentful "innate knowledge" about problem-relevant aspects of the world.

Well-studied adaptations overwhelmingly achieve their functional outcomes because they display an intricately engineered coordination between their specialized design features and the detailed structure of the task and task environment. Like a code that has been torn in two and given to separate couriers, the two halves (the structure of the mechanism and the structure of the task) must be put together to be understood. To function, adaptations evolve such that their causal properties rely on and exploit these stable and enduring statistical and structural regularities in the world. Thus, to map the structures of our cognitive devices, we need to understand the structures of the problems that they solve and the problem-relevant parts of the hunter-gatherer world. If studying face recognition mechanisms, one must study the recurrent structure of faces. If studying social cognition, one must study the recurrent structure of hunter-gatherer social life. For vision, the problems are not so very different for a modern scientist and a Pleistocene hunter-gatherer, so the folk notions of function that perception researchers use are not a problem. But the more one strays from low-level perception, the more one needs to know about human behavioral ecology and the structure of the ancestral world.

24.8   EXPERIMENTING WITH ANCESTRALLY VALID TASKS AND STIMULI

Although bringing cognitive neuroscience current with modern evolutionary biology offers many new research tools (Preuss, 1995), we have out of necessity limited discussion to only one: an evolutionary functionalist research strategy (see Tooby and Cosmides, 1992, for a description; for examples, see chapters in Barkow et al., 1992; Daly and Wilson, 1995; Gaulin, 1995). The adoption of such an approach will modify research practice in many ways. Perhaps most significantly, researchers will no longer have to operate purely by intuition or guesswork to know which kinds of tasks and stimuli to expose subjects to. Using knowledge from evolutionary biology, behavioral ecology, animal behavior, and hunter-gatherer studies, they can construct ancestrally or adaptively valid stimuli and tasks. These are stimuli that would have had adaptive significance in ancestral environments, and tasks that resemble (at least in some ways) the adaptive problems that our ancestors would have been selected to be able to solve.

The present widespread practice of using arbitrary stimuli of no adaptive significance (e.g., lists of random words, colored geometric shapes) or abstract experimental tasks of unknown relevance to Pleistocene life has sharply limited what researchers have observed and can observe about our evolved computational devices. This is because the adaptive specializations that are expected to constitute the majority of our neural architecture are designed to remain dormant until triggered by cues of the adaptively significant situations that they were designed to handle. The Wundtian and British Empiricist methodological assumption that complex stimuli, behaviors, representations, and competences are compounded out of simple ones has been empirically falsified in scores of cases (see, e.g., Gallistel, 1990), and so, restricting experimentation to such stimuli and tasks simply restricts what researchers can find to a highly impoverished and unrepresentative set of phenomena. In contrast, experimenters who use more biologically meaningful stimuli have had far better luck, as the collapse of behaviorism and its replacement by modern behavioral ecology have shown in the study of animal behavior. To take one example of its applicability to humans, effective mechanisms for Bayesian inference — undetected by 20 years of previous research using "modern" tasks and data formats — were activated by exposing subjects to information formatted in a way that hunter-gatherers would have encountered it (Brase et al., 1998; Cosmides and Tooby, 1996; Gigerenzer and Hoffrage, 1995). Equally, when subjects were given ancestrally valid social inference tasks (cheater detection, threat interpretation), previously unobserved adaptive reasoning specializations were activated, guiding subjects to act in accordance with evolutionarily predicted but otherwise odd patterns (Cosmides, 1989; Cosmides and Tooby, 1992).

Everyone accepts that one cannot study human language specializations by exposing subjects to meaningless sounds: the acoustic stimuli must contain the subtle, precise, high level relationships that make sound language. Similarly, to move on to the study of other complex cognitive devices, subjects should be exposed to stimuli that contain the subtle, ancestrally valid relationships relevant to the diverse functions of these devices. In such an expanded research program, experimental stimuli and tasks would involve constituents such as faces, smiles, disgust expressions, foods, the depiction of socially significant situations, sexual attractiveness, habitat quality cues, animals, navigational problems, cues of kinship, rage displays, cues of contagion, motivational cues, distressed children, species-typical "body language," rigid object mechanics, plants, predators, and other functional elements that would have been part of ancestral hunter-gatherer life. Investigations would look for functional sub-systems that not only deal with such low-level and broadly functional competences as perception, attention, memory, and motor control, but also with higher-level ancestrally valid competences as well — mechanisms such as eye direction detectors (Baron-Cohen, 1994), face recognizers (e.g., Johnson and Morton, 1991), food memory subsystems (e.g., Hart et al., 1985; Caramazza and Shelton, 1998), person-specific memory, child care motivators (Daly and Wilson, 1995), and sexual jealousy modules.

Although these proposals to look for scores of content-sensitive circuits and domain-specific specializations will strike many as bizarre and even preposterous, they are well grounded in modern biology. We believe that in a decade or so they will look tame. If cognitive neuroscience is anything like investigations in domain-specific cognitive psychology (Hirschfeld and Gelman, 1994) and in modern animal behavior, researchers will be rewarded with the materialization of a rich array of functionally patterned phenomena that have not been observed so far because the mechanisms were never activated in the laboratory by exposure to ecologically appropriate stimuli. Although presently, the functions of most brain structures are largely unknown, pursuing such research directions may begin to populate the empty regions of our maps of the brain with circuit diagrams of discrete, functionally intelligible computational devices.

In short, because theories and principled systems of knowledge can function as organs of perception, the incorporation of a modern evolutionary framework into cognitive neuroscience may allow the community to detect ordered relationships in phenomena that otherwise seem too complex to be understood.

CONCLUSION

The aforementioned points indicate why cognitive neuroscience is pivotal to the progress of the brain sciences. There are an astronomical number of physical interactions and relationships in the brain, and blind empiricism rapidly drowns itself among the deluge of manic and enigmatic measurements. Through blind empiricism, one can equally drown at the cognitive level in a sea of irrelevant things that our computational devices can generate, from writing theology or dancing the mazurka to calling for the restoration of the Plantagenets to the throne of France. However, evolutionary biology, behavioral ecology, and hunter-gatherer studies can be used to identify and supply descriptions of the recurrent adaptive problems humans faced during their evolution. Supplemented with this knowledge, cognitive research techniques can abstract out of the welter of human cognitive performance a series of maps of the functional information-processing relationships that constitute our computational devices and that evolved to solve this particular set of problems: our cognitive architecture. These computational maps can then help us abstract out of the ocean of physical relationships in the brain that exact and minute subset that implements those information-processing relationships because it is only these relationships that explain the existence and functional organization of the system. The immense number of other physical relationships in the brain are incidental by-products of those narrow aspects that implement the functional computational architecture. Consequently, an adaptationist inventory and functional mapping of our cognitive devices can provide the essential theoretical guidance for neuroscientists that will allow them to home in on these narrow but meaningful aspects of neural organization and to distinguish them from the sea of irrelevant neural phenomena.

ACKNOWLEDGMENTS

The authors gratefully acknowledge the financial support of the James S. McDonnell Foundation, the National Science Foundation (NSF grant BNS9157-449 to John Tooby), and a Research Across Disciplines grant (Evolution and the Social Mind) from the UCSB Office of Research.

NOTE

1. The genes underlying complex adaptations cannot vary substantially between individuals because if they did, the obligatory genetic shuffling that takes place during sexual reproduction would break apart the complex adaptations that had existed in the parents when these are recombined in the offspring generation. All the genetic subcomponents necessary to build the complex adaptation rarely would reappear together in the same individual if they were not being supplied reliably by both parents in all matings (for a discussion of the genetics of sexual recombination, species-typical adaptive design, and individual differences, see Tooby, 1982; Tooby and Cosmides, 1990b).

REFERENCES

Barkow, J., L. Cosmides, & Tooby, J. eds. (1992). *The Adapted Mind: Evolutionary Psychology and the Generation of Culture.* New York: Oxford University Press.

Baron-Cohen, S. (1994). The eye-direction detector: A case for evolutionary psychology. In *Joint-Attention: Its Origins and Role in Development,* C. Moore and P. Dunham, eds. Hillsdale, N.J.: Erlbaum.

Brase, G., L. Cosmides, & Tooby, J. (1998). Individuation, counting, and statistical inference: The role of frequency and whole-object representations in judgment under uncertainty. *J. Exp. Psychol. Gen.* 127:3–21.

Buss, D. (1994). *The Evolution of Desire.* New York: Basic Books.

Caramazza, A., & Shelton, J. (1998). Domain-specific knowledge systems in the brain: The animate-inanimate distinction. *J. Cogn. Neurosci.* 10:1–34.

Cosmides, L. (1989). The logic of social exchange: Has natural selection shaped how humans reason? Studies with the Wason selection task. *Cognition* 31:187–276.

Cosmides, L., & Tooby, J. (1981). Cytoplasmic inheritance and intragenomic conflict. *J. Theor. Biol.* 89:83–129.

Cosmides, L., & Tooby, J. (1987). From evolution to behavior: Evolutionary psychology as the missing link. In *The Latest on the Best: Essays on Evolution and Optimality,* J. Dupre, ed. Cambridge, Mass.: MIT Press, pp. 277–306.

Cosmides, L., & Tooby, J. (1992). Cognitive adaptations for social exchange. In *The Adapted Mind: Evolutionary Psychology and the Generation of Culture,* J. Barkow, L. Cosmides, and J. Tooby, eds. New York: Oxford University Press, pp. 163–228.

Cosmides, L., & Tooby, J. (1994). Beyond intuition and instinct blindness: The case for an evolutionarily rigorous cognitive science. *Cognition* 50:41–77.

Cosmides, L., & Tooby, J. (1996). Are humans good intuitive statisticians after all? Rethinking some conclusions from the literature on judgment under uncertainty. *Cognition* 58:1–73.

Cosmides, L., & Tooby, J. (1999). Toward an evolutionary taxanomy of treatable conditions. *J. Abnorm. Psychol.* 108:435–464.

Daly, M., & Wilson, M. (1984). *Sex, Evolution and Behavior,* Second Edition. Boston: Willard Grant.

Daly, M., & Wilson, M. (1988). *Homicide.* New York: Aldine.

Daly, M., & Wilson, M. (1995). Discriminative parental solicitude and the relevance of evolutionary models to the analysis of motivational systems. In *The Cognitive Neurosciences,* M. S. Gazzaniga, ed. Cambridge, Mass.: MIT Press, pp. 1269–1286.

Daly, M., Wilson, M. & Weghorst, S. J. (1982). Male sexual jealousy. *Ethol. Sociobiol.* 3:11–27.

Darwin, C. (1859). *On the Origin of Species.* London: Murray. New edition: Cambridge, Mass.: Harvard University Press.

Dawkins, R. (1976). *The Selfish Gene.* New York: Oxford University Press.

Dawkins, R. (1982). *The Estended Phenotype.* San Francisco: W. H. Freeman.

Dawkins, R. (1986). *The Blind Watchmaker.* New York: Norton.

Gallistel, C. R. (1990). *The Organization of Learning.* Cambridge, Mass.: MIT Press.

Gaulin, S. (1995). Does evolutionary theory predict sex differences in the brain? In *The Cognitive Neurosciences,* M. S. Gazzaniga, ed. Cambridge, Mass.: MIT Press, pp. 1211–1225.

Gigerenzer, G., & Hoffrage, U. (1995). How to improve Bayesian reasoning without instruction: Frequency formats. *Psychol. Rev.* 102:684–704.

Gould, S. J., & Lewontin, R. C. (1979). The spandrels of San Marco and the Panglossian program: A critique of the adaptationist programme. *Proc. R. Soc. Lond.* 205:281–288.

Haig, D. (1993). Genetic conflicts in human pregnancy. *Q. Rev. Biol.* 68:495–532.

Hamilton, W. D. (1964). The genetical evolution of social behavior. *J. Theor. Biol.* 7:1–52.

Hart, J. Jr, R. S. Berndt, & Caramazza, A. (1985). Category-specific naming deficit following cerebral infarction. *Nature* 316:439–440.

Hirschfeld, L., & Gelman, S. eds. (1994). *Mapping the Mind: Domain Specificity in Cognition and Culture.* New York: Cambridge University Press.

Johnson, M., & Morton, J. (1991). *Biology and Cognitive Development: The Case of Face Recognition.* Oxford: Blackwell.

Krebs, J. R., & Davies, N. B. (1997). *Behavioural Ecology: An Evolutionary Approach,* 4th edition. London: Blackwell Science.

Lee, R. B., & DeVore, I. (1968). *Man the Hunter.* Chicago: Aldine.

Lewontin, R. (1967). Spoken remark in *Mathematical Challenges to the Neo-Darwinian Interpretation of*

Evolution, P. Moorhead and M. Kaplan, eds. *Wistar Institute Symposium Monograph* 5:79.

Lewontin, R. (1979). Sociobiology as an adaptationist program. *Behav. Sci.* 24:5–14.

Marr, D. (1982). *Vision: A Computational Investigation into the Human Representation and Processing of Visual Information.* San Francisco: Freeman.

Mayr, E. (1983). How to carry out the adaptationist program. *Am. Naturalist* 121:324–334.

Pinker, S. (1994). *The Language Instinct.* New York: Morrow.

Pinker, S. (1997). *How the Mind Works.* New York: Norton.

Pinker, S., & Bloom, P. (1992). Natural language and natural selection. Reprinted in *The Adapted Mind: Evolutionary Psychology and the Generation of Culture,* J. Barkow, L. Cosmides, and J. Tooby, eds. New York: Oxford University Press, pp. 451–493.

Preuss, T. (1995). The argument from animals to humans in cognitive neuroscience. In *The Cognitive Neurosciences,* M. S. Gazzaniga, ed. Cambridge, Mass.: MIT Press, pp. 1227–1241.

Shepard, R. N. (1984). Ecological constraints on internal representation: Resonant kinematics of perceiving, imagining, thinking, and dreaming. *Psychol. Rev.* 91:417–447.

Shepard, R. N. (1987a). Evolution of a mesh between principles of the mind and regularities of the world. In *The Latest on the Best: Essays on Evolution and Optimality,* J. Dupre, ed. Cambridge, Mass.: MIT Press, pp. 251–275.

Shepard, R. N. (1987b). Towards a universal law of generalization for psychological science. *Science* 237:1317–1323.

Sperber, D. (1994). The modularity of thought and the epidemiology of representations. *In Mapping the Mind: Domain Specificity in Cognition and Culture,* L. Hirschfeld and S. Gelman, eds. New York: Cambridge University Press, pp. 39–67.

Symons, D. (1987). If we're all Darwinians, what's the fuss about? In *Sociobiology and Psychology,* C. B. Crawford, M. F. Smith, and D. L. Krebs, eds. Hillsdale, N.J.: Erlbaum, pp. 121–146.

Symons, D. (1992). On the use and misuse of Darwinism in the study of human behavior. In *The Adapted Mind: Evolutionary Psychology and the Generation of Culture,* J. Barkow, L. Cosmides, and J. Tooby, eds. New York: Oxford University Press, pp. 137–159.

Thornhill, R. (1991). The study of adaptation. In *Interpretation and Explanation in the Study of Behavior,* M. Bekoff and D. Jamieson, eds. Boulder, Colo.: Westview Press.

Tooby, J. (1982). Pathogens, polymorphism, and the evolution of sex. *J. Theor. Biol.* 97:557–576.

Tooby, J., & Cosmides, L. (1990a). The past explains the present: Emotional adaptations and the structure of ancestral environments. *Ethol. Sociobiol.* 11:375–424.

Tooby, J., & Cosmides, L. (1990b). On the universality of human nature and the uniqueness of the individual: The role of genetics and adaptation. *J. Pers.* 58:17–67.

Tooby, J., & Cosmides, L. (1992). The psychological foundations of culture. In *The Adapted Mind: Evolutionary Psychology and the Generation of Culture,* J. Barkow, L. Cosmides, and J. Tooby, eds. New York: Oxford University Press, pp. 19–136.

Williams, G. C. (1966). *Adaptation and Natural Selection: A Critique of Some Current Evolutionary Thought.* Princeton, N.J.: Princeton University Press.

Williams, G. C. (1985). A defense of reductionism in evolutionary biology. *Oxford Surv. Biol.* 2:1–27.

Williams, G. C., &. Williams, D. C (1957). Natural selection of individually harmful social adaptations among sibs with special reference to social insects. *Evolution* 17:249–253.

Wilson, M., & Daly, M. (1992). The man who mistook his wife for a chattel. In *The Adapted Mind: Evolutionary Psychology and the Generation of Culture,* J. Barkow, L. Cosmides, and J. Tooby, eds. New York: Oxford University Press, pp. 289–322.

CHAPTER TWENTY-FIVE

THE INVENTION OF LANGUAGE BY CHILDREN: ENVIRONMENTAL AND BIOLOGICAL INFLUENCES ON THE ACQUISITION OF LANGUAGE

LILA R. GLEITMAN AND ELISSA L. NEWPORT

Human children grow up in cultural settings of enormous diversity. This differentiation sometimes leads us to overlook those aspects of development that are highly similar, even universal to our species. For example, under widely varying environmental circumstances, while learning different languages within different cultures and under different conditions of child rearing, with different motivations and talents, all normal children acquire their native tongue to a high level of proficiency within a narrow developmental time frame. Evidence from the study of the language learning process suggests that this constancy of outcome, despite variation in environment, has its explanation in biology. Language is universal in the species just because the capacity to learn it is innately given. In Descartes's (1662/1911) words: "It is a very remarkable fact that there are none ... without even excepting idiots, that they cannot arrange different words together, forming of them a statement by which they make known their thoughts; while on the other hand, there is no other animal, however perfect and fortunately circumstanced it may be, which can do the same."

  In other words, some part of the capacity to learn languages must be "innate." At the same time, it is equally clear that language is "learned." There are about five thousand different languages now in use on the earth, and the speakers of one cannot understand the speakers of the next. Moreover, specific exposure conditions strikingly influence how each of these is acquired: there is a massive correlation between being born in England and

From Gleitman, Lila, Mark Liberman, and Daniel N. Osherson, eds., *An Invitation to Cognitive Science,* second edition, Volume 1: Language, pp. 1–24, © 1995 Massachusetts Institute of Technology, by permission of The MIT Press.

coming to speak English and being born in France and speaking French. This immediately shows that the language function is heavily affected by specific environmental stimulation.

How can both of these claims (language is innate, and it is learned from the environment) be true? Like many developmental processes that have been studied in animals, *language acquisition in humans seems to involve a type of learning that is heavily constrained, or predisposed to follow certain limited courses, by our biology.* Clearly, no specific language is innate; the particular languages we come to speak must be learned. Yet, the commonalities among human languages are, upon careful study, far more striking than the differences among them. Every human language is organized in terms of a hierarchy of structures, composed of speech sounds that lawfully combine into morphemes and words, which in turn combine into phrases and sentences. Every human language has the wherewithal to express approximately the same meanings (that is, they are intertranslatable). Apparently, human children are in some sense prepared by nature to learn only languages that have just these formal and substantive properties, and to learn such languages relatively effortlessly during the natural course of maturation.

This chapter reviews two kinds of evidence for the claim that there is an important biological endowment in humans that supports and shapes language acquisition: (1) language learning proceeds uniformly within and across linguistic communities despite extensive variability of the input provided to individuals; (2) the child acquires many linguistic generalizations that experience could not have made available.

25.1   UNIFORMITY OF LEARNING

25.1.1   Milestones of Normal Development

Language learning follows the same course in all of the many languages that have been investigated. Isolated words appear at about one year of age. These are mainly nouns that describe simple objects and a few social words such as "bye-bye." Sometime during the second year of life, there is a sudden spurt of vocabulary growth accompanied by the appearance of rudimentary sentences. At first these are limited to two or three words; for example, "Throw ball," "Kiss teddy," and the like. These early sentences display considerable structure despite their brevity. Roughly speaking, there is a place for the noun and a place for the verb; moreover, the subject and object noun are positioned differently within the sentence. Thus, though the young learner never says long sentences like "Mommy should promptly throw that ball," the distinction between subject and object will show up in such foreshortened attempts as "Mommy throw" (the subject precedes the verb) versus "Throw ball" (the direct object follows the verb). As soon as children begin to combine words at all, they reserve structurally determined positions for subjects and direct objects. This ability to hone in on such a crucial and fundamentally linguistic distinction forms a kind of skeletal base of language learning; this shows up early and in much the same way in two-year-olds all over the world.

Language use by the child in normal learning settings undergoes considerable elaboration between the ages of 2 and 5. Complex (multiclausal) sentences appear, and the function morphemes (prepositions, articles, bound morphemes like *-ed,* and so forth) make their appearance. By age 5 or before, youngsters sound essentially adult.

Lenneberg (1967) argued that these uniformities in the course of learning for children exposed to different languages are indicators that language learning has a significant biological basis. Like the regularities of physical and motor development (the appearance of teeth, or of walking), they suggest that language learning is controlled, at least in part, by some underlying maturational timetable. He provided some normative evidence that the achievement of basic milestones in language learning can be predicted from the child's age and seem, in fact, to be intercalated tightly with the aspects of physical development that are known to be maturationally dependent. For instance, youngsters utter first words just when they stand, two-word sentences just when they walk, and elaborate sentence structures just when they jump.

These findings alone, however, cannot prove the position that Lenneberg proposed, for they are consistent as well with other quite different conjectures about the processes that underlie language learning. Possibly, children move from talking childishly to speaking with great sophistication because of the maturation of their brains; but, on the other hand, they may go through these regular stages because such stages are the only logical way to learn, through time and exposure, all the detailed facts about the language that they are hearing from adults around them. (After all, foreign adults first arriving in a new linguistic community will also say things like "Throw ball" and later speak in longer and more complex sentences; but this is surely not because they are biologically changing from a primitive to a more advanced maturational state.)

A stronger way to test this view is somehow to disentangle the environmental exposure from the maturation of the learner. We will therefore next consider these two aspects separately, looking first at how language learning proceeds when the learning environment is changed, and second at how language learning proceeds when the maturational status of the learners themselves is changed. As we will show, while languages are in some sense certainly learned from the environment, alterations in the environment over a very large range do not change the fundamental character of acquisition. In contrast, changing the learner's maturational status has substantial effects on the nature and success of acquisition.

25.1.2   Altering the Learning Environment

There are several ways in which one might examine alterations in the linguistic environment to observe the consequences for acquisition. We will consider three: first, the modest natural variations in the degree to which mothers adjust the complexity of their speech to children; second, a much more radical change, in the presence versus absence of any conventional linguistic input; and third, a similarly radical change, in the presence versus absence of the visual non-linguistic world during language learning. In each case, we will argue, young children proceed on a remarkably stable course of early acquisition.

Variation in Motherese.   It is obvious that mothers talk differently to their young children than they do to other adults. This natural simplification is clearly an adaptation both to the fact that children are cognitively immature and to the fact that their understanding of the language is primitive. But it has sometimes been asserted that this simple kind of speech does more than serve the immediate communicative needs of caretakers and infants. Simplified speech (often fondly called *Motherese;* Newport, Gleitman, and Gleitman, 1977) may play a causal role in the language-learning process itself. The idea would be that the caretaker first teaches the child some easy structures and contents, and then moves on to more advanced lessons — essentially, provides smallest sentences to littlest ears. For instance, perhaps the fact that the child learns nouns before verbs and declarative sentences before interrogative sentences is a straightforward consequence of caretakers' natural behavior toward infants.

This hypothesis, though plausible, turns out to be false. By and large, mothers speak in whole sentences even to youngest learners. Nouns, verbs, prepositions, and so forth occur in speech even to the youngest learners, and yet the children all select the nouns as the first items to utter. Worse, contrary to intuition, maternal speech is not characterized by simple declarative sentences of the kind that children utter first, such as "Mommy throw ball." In fact, these apparently simplest declarative formats occur in speech to youngest learners only about 25 percent of the time. Instead, the mother's speech is replete with questions ("Where is your nose?") and commands ("Get your foot out of the laundry!"), while the child's own first sentences are mostly declaratives.

Most interestingly, variations in maternal speech forms have been investigated to see if they are predictive of the child's learning: perhaps some mothers know just how to talk to help their children learn; other mothers may not be inclined to speak in ways that facilitate the learning process, in which case their children should progress more slowly in language knowledge. One method for studying this (Newport et al., 1977) is to select a group of young children who are at the same stage of language knowledge (for example, 15-month-olds who speak only in single isolated words) and to collect samples of their caretakers' speech. If learning is a function of the caretaker's speech style, then variation among the mothers at this time should predict the further progress of these children. To study this, the children's speech was sampled again six months later. Analyzing the children's speech at these two times (ages 15 months, then 21 months), one can compute growth scores for each child on various linguistic dimensions (the length and structure of the sentences, the size of the vocabulary, and so forth). The question is whether properties of the mother's speech (in the first measurement, at age 15 months) predict the child's rate of growth on each measured dimension and explain the child's language status at the second measurement six months later.

The outcome of these studies was that, while the details of mothers' use of a few particular constructions of English predicted the children's rate of acquiring these same few constructions, the mothers' overall simplicity did not predict the rate at which their children progressed through the stages of acquisition. In this sense, then, the children's learning rate was largely unaffected by differences in their mothers' speech. Each child seemed to develop according to a maturational schedule that was essentially indifferent to maternal variation.

While such studies preclude certain strong versions of the view that language is learned just because it is taught, they also unfortunately leave almost all details unresolved. This is because the absence of measurable environmental effects may be attributable to threshold effects of various sorts. After all, though the mothers differed in their speech styles to some degree, presumably they all uttered speech that fell into some "normal range" for talking to children. This complaint is quite fair. To find out how the environment causes (or does not cause) a child to learn its native tongue, we would need to look at cases in which the environment is much more radically altered. The most straight-forward technique would be to maroon some infants on a desert island, rearing them totally apart from adult language users. If they could and would invent a human language on their own hook, and if this invented language developed just as it developed in infants acquiring English or Urdu, this would constitute a stronger argument for a biological basis for language learning.

Classical cognoscenti will recall that, according to Herodotus (ca. 410 B.C./ 1942), this ultimate language-learning, experiment has been performed. A certain Egyptian king, Psammetichus, placed two infants ("of the ordinary sort") in an isolated cabin. Herdsmen were assigned to feed them but were not to speak to them, on pain of death. Psammetichus's experimental intent was to resolve the question of which (Egyptian or Phrygian!) was the first of all languages on earth. Appropriately enough for a king, he appears to have been a radical innatist, for he never considered the possibility that untutored children would fail to speak at all. Herodotus tells us that two years later ("after the indistinct babblings of infancy were over") these children began to speak Phrygian, whereupon "the Egyptians yielded their claims, and admitted the greater antiquity of the Phrygians."

In effect, if Herodotus is to be believed, these children reinvented Phrygian rather than merely learning it: though the children were isolated from input, Phrygian emerged as the pure reflection of the language of the soul, the original innate language.

Of course, modern scientists have reason to doubt the reliability of these particular findings, but the concept of Psammetichus's experiment (modified by our increased concern for the possibility that the children might require more kindly environments) is still highly pertinent to the questions of languages and language acquisition. While we would no longer conduct this experiment on purpose, it has been possible, surprisingly enough, to observe natural circumstances that reproduce some of the essentials of Psammetichus's experiment in modern times. In the sections below, we will discuss several examples of language learning in environmentally deprived circumstances. As we will see, the outcome is not Phrygian. All the same, we will apply the same reasoning to the findings as did Psammetichus: those aspects of language that appear in children without environmental stimulation or support must reflect preprogrammed tendencies of the human brain.

Language Invention by the Isolated Deaf Child.   Extensive study over the past thirty years has shown that the sign languages used among the deaf differ but little from the spoken languages of the world (Klima, Bellugi et al., 1982; Supalla and Newport, 1978). Their vocabularies are the same, and their organizational principles are the same; that is, they are composed of a small set of primitive gestural parts (analogous to speech sounds), organized into morphemes and words, which in turn are organized into meaningful phrases and sentences. Moreover, deaf or hearing children who acquire a sign language from their deaf parents follow the learning course typical of spoken-language learning (Newport and Meier, 1985).

Most deaf infants, though, are born into hearing families in which the parents know no sign language. In many cases the parents make the decision not to allow the children access to sign language at all. They believe that the children can come to know a spoken language by formal "oralist" training in which the children are taught to lip-read and utter English. (This method has at best mixed results; few totally deaf children ever come to control spoken English adequately.) Because the children are not exposed to a sign language and, at the same time, are not able to hear a spoken language, they are effectively deprived of linguistic stimulation during their early years. They cannot learn the language around them (spoken English) just because they cannot hear it. And they cannot learn an alternative — one of the sign languages of the deaf — because they have not been exposed to it. The question is whether, like the Psammetichus children, these youngsters will invent a language in circumstances that provide no opportunity to learn one.

Goldin-Meadow and her colleagues (Feldman, Goldin-Meadow, and Gleitman, 1978; Goldin-Meadow and Mylander 1984) have studied the development of language in ten of these language-isolated, congenitally deaf children, from the ages 1–4 years (the period during which they would ordinarily be acquiring an environmental language). The findings were quite startling. As mentioned earlier, normally circumstanced learners acquiring English or Urdu from their caretakers produce isolated words starting around their first birthday. The deaf isolates in this same time period began to produce single manual gestures, much like the single words of the youngsters next door who were learning English "from" their caretakers. These gestures were understandable because of their iconicity; for example, the deaf children would flutter their fingers for "snow," and they would cup their hands behind their ears to render "Mickey Mouse." The hearing parents much more rarely produced such gestures; instead, they more frequently simply pointed at objects or pantomimed an action using a nearby object, hoping that their oral speech would itself thereby be comprehensible enough. Nevertheless, the size and content of the children's gestural vocabulary approximated that of their hearing peers even though they had to invent their own "words."

At about age 2, again in common with their hearing peers, the deaf children began to sequence their gestures in rudimentary two- and three-sign sentences, with occasional examples of yet further complexity. For example, a child would point to a chicken on the table and then extend his open palm ("give"), or point at himself ("me") and then produce a gesture at his mouth ("eat"). Most surprising of all, when these signed sentences were analyzed like sentences of hearing children, it was discovered that they were structurally organized, with distinct structural positions assigned to the verb and nouns in each utterance. For instance, just like the youngest English speakers, the deaf children had structurally distinctive ways of expressing "Chicken eat" and "Eat chicken." This syntactic structuring of signed sentences was not observed in their hearing caretakers.

Evidently, where the environment provides no language samples, children have the internal wherewithal to invent their own forms to render the same meanings. What is more, the timing of language development — at least at the early stages investigated here — is approximately the same whether one is exposed to a fully elaborated natural language or not: first words at age 1, rudimentary sentences at age 2, and elaborations beginning to appear at age $2\frac{1}{2}$ to 3. The appearance of the skeletal base of a language is thus part of the biology of normally developing children; it appears on the maturationally appropriate timetable even when a normal linguistic environment is absent.

At the same time, it is important to point out that the development of this homemade system does not appear to advance to anywhere near the level of full natural languages, whether signed or spoken. In particular, the function morphemes, such as articles, verbal auxiliaries, and bound morphemes marking tense and case, are virtually nonexistent in these children's signing. As we stressed at the beginning, languages are not fully innate, but instead are acquired as a product of both linguistic input and biology. Many complex aspects of linguistic structure do not therefore appear in full without linguistic input; in a later section (see "Pidgins and Creoles") we will discuss more about the circumstances of input and maturation in which these more complex elements appear. The important point to notice for now is the rather remarkable achievement of the early parts of language development, which the isolated learners can produce without an environmental language at all.

Language Development in the Blind Child.   The case just considered involved children who were cut off from opportunities to observe a language. Evidently, they could invent something like a skeletal human language all the same, demonstrating that there is something within the human child that makes it "natural" to develop a language of a certain type — one that has words, phrases, and so forth. But a little reflection reveals that, in some ways, language invention seems an easier task than ordinary language learning. After all, the inventors of a new language are free to choose their own instantiations of each item that is dictated by the internal predispositions for language. Those who want a word for Mickey Mouse can just make one up, say, by mimicking Mickey's big ears through an iconic gesture. The learners of English or Greek have no such freedom. They must learn just which sound (such as the sound "snow") is used to express the concept *snow* in the linguistic community around them.

How is this done? Clearly, learners observe the real world contexts in which words are uttered; thus, presumably, they will notice that "cup" is uttered in the presence of cups, "jump" is uttered in the presence of jumping, and so forth. But if this is the whole story of vocabulary learning, then we should expect delays and perhaps distortions in the language learning of the blind. After all, some words refer to things that are too large, distant, or gossamer for the blind child to apprehend through tactile means — such as mountains, birds, and clouds. Overall, the restrictions on blind children's access to contextual information ought to pose acquisitional problems. Yet study of their progress demonstrates that there is neither delay nor distortion in their language growth (Landau and Gleitman, 1985). They acquire approximately the same words at the same maturational moments as do sighted children, and their syntactic development is unexceptional, with phrases and sentences occurring at the ordinary time.

A particularly surprising aspect of blind children's learning has to do with their acquisition of terms that (seem to) describe the visual experience in particular — words like *look* and *see* (Landau and Gleitman, 1985). Because blind children cannot experience visual looking and seeing, one would think that these terms would be absent from their early spoken vocabularies. Yet, in fact, these are among the very first verbs to appear in blind (as well as sighted) children's spontaneous speech. And these words are meaningful to their blind users. For instance, sighted 3-year-olds (even if blindfolded) will tilt their faces upward in response to the command "Look up!" presumably because they understand that *look* has to do with visual-perceptual inspection. Blind children raise their hands instead, keeping the head immobile, as though they too realize that *look* has to do with perceptual inspection — but in the absence of a working visual system, this perceptual inspection must necessarily be by hand. This interpretation is reinforced by the finding that blind youngsters distinguish between the perceptual term *look* and the contact term *touch*. Thus, if told "You can touch that table but don't look at it!" the blind 3-year-old responds by gingerly tapping the table. And then if told "Now you can look at it," the child systematically explores all the surfaces of the table with her hands. Despite radical differences in the observational opportunities offered to blind and sighted babies, both populations come up with interpretations of quite abstract words in a way that is fitting to their own perceptual lives.

Let us now try to organize these facts. Clearly, learning a language is a matter of discovering the relations between the sounds (or gestures) and the meanings that language can express. Thus, the novice English speaker must learn that there is a relation between the sound "see" and the meaning *inspect by eye* (or *by hand,* if the learner is blind), while the

Spanish novice must discover that the sound "see" means *yes*. The deaf isolates were deprived of the sound side of this equation. They neither heard sounds nor saw formal gestures; as a result, they could not learn any of the languages of the community around them. All the same, they were capable of inventing the rudiments of such a system, assigning distinct, spontaneously invented gestures to particular objects and events that they could observe in the world around them. In contrast, the blind children had access to all the sounds and structures of English, for they could hear. Their deprivation had to do with simultaneous observation of some of the things in the world to which their parents' speech referred, and which could provide the clues to the meanings of the various words. For instance, when the blind child's mother asks her to "look at the pumpkin," the child decidedly cannot look, in the visual sense of this term. All the same, blind learners come up with a perceptual interpretation of the word — a haptic-perceptual interpretation, to be sure — that is relevant to their perceptual functioning. In content as well as in form, properties of mind appear to legislate the development and character of human language.

To summarize the effects of altering the learning environment: While language may not be quite as innate as Psammetichus reported (none of the subjects of these studies spoke Phrygian), there is a remarkable range of environments in which the normal milestones of language structure and content appear. Apparently, then, significant aspects of language development are dictated by our biology. In the next section we will examine the opposite manipulation, in which normal environments are presented to learners who vary in their maturational status (that is, who vary in their biology). If what we have said thus far is correct, it should be the case that changes in the biology of learners have far more dramatic effects on the process of learning a language.

25.1.3   Changing the Learner's Mental Endowment

Deprivation of First Language Exposure until Late in Life.   Thus far, we have argued that language learning is the natural product of the developing human mind and brain, that linguistic-learning events in the child's life are the natural consequences of maturation rather than rote outcomes of what children hear and see in the world around them. After all, various children hear different sentences in different contexts, but they all learn the language of their communities in just the same way. But if maturation is a serious limiting factor in acquisition, learning should look different if it takes place later in life than in the usual case: Presentation of a full and complete environment for language learning, but at a time after the usual maturational sequence should have been completed, would on this view not result in normal acquisition. Where can one find cases in which learners are exposed to normal linguistic input only late in life?

One such case is the (fortunately) occasional situation in which children have been reared, like Romulus and Remus, by wolves or bears, and then attempts are made to rehabilitate them into human society. Unfortunately such "pure" cases of isolation defy interpretation, owing to the collateral physical, nutritional, and other deprivations that accompany such individuals' language deprivations (Brown, 1958).

More interpretable cases involve children raised by humans under conditions that are almost unimaginably inhumane. "Isabelle" (a code name) was hidden away in an attic by a deranged mother, apparently never spoken to at all, and provided with only the minimal attention necessary to sustain her life. She was discovered at age 6. Unsurprisingly, she had learned no language, and her cognitive development was below that of a normal 2-year-old. But within a year Isabelle learned to speak at the level of her 7-year-old peers. Her tested intelligence was normal, and she took her place in an ordinary school (Davis, 1947).

The first lesson from this case is that a 7-year-old child, with one year of language practice, can speak about as well as her second-grade peers, all of whom had seven years of practice. Relatedly, bilingual children (who presumably hear only half as much of each language they are learning as do monolingual children, unless they sleep less) acquire both languages in about the same time that it takes the monolingual child to learn one language. That is, bilinguals speak at the level appropriate to their age, not the level appropriate to their exposure time. Such findings argue that maturational level, not extent of opportunities for practice, is the chief limiting factor in language growth. But the second inference from Isabelle's case seems to be that learning can begin late in maturational time and yet have the normal outcome: native-level fluency.

However, any such conclusion would be premature. Rehabilitation from isolation does seem to depend on maturational state. A child, "Genie," discovered in California about twenty years ago, was 13 years old when she was removed from the hideous circumstances of her early life. From the age of about 20 months, she had lived tied to a chair in a darkened room, was frequently beaten, and never was spoken to — in fact, she was barked at because her deranged father said she was no more than a dog. But despite intensive long-term rehabilitation attempts by a team of sophisticated psychologists and linguists, Genie's language learning never approached normality (Curtiss, 1977; Fromkin et al., 1974). She did rapidly pass through the stages we have discussed thus far and identified as the skeletal base of the language-learning capacity: she acquired vocabulary items and put them together in meaningful propositions much as 2-year-olds do — for example, "Another house have dog," "No more take wax." But she never progressed beyond this stage to complex sentences or acquisition of the function words that characterize normal 3- and 4-year-olds' speech.

Another case of late language learning, but without the extreme abuse suffered by Genie, has been reported in a study of a woman called "Chelsea" (Curtiss, 1989). Born deaf, Chelsea was mistakenly diagnosed by a series of doctors as retarded or emotionally disturbed. Her family did not believe that she was retarded, but, because of these diagnoses, she was raised at home and never exposed to either sign language or speech training. She was, however, otherwise healthy and emotionally and neurologically normal. At age 31 she was referred to a neurologist, who recognized that she was merely deaf. When she was provided with hearing aids, her hearing tested at near-normal levels. Intensive rehabilitation, along with several years of this radically improved hearing, has led to her acquisition of a sizable vocabulary, as well the production of multiword utterances. However, her sentences do not have even the rudimentary aspects of grammatical structure found in Genie's. For example, Chelsea says such things as "Breakfast eating girl" and "Banana the eat."

Why did Genie and Chelsea not progress to full language knowledge while Isabelle did? The best guess is that the crucial factor is the age at which exposure to linguistic stimulation began. Age 6 (as in Isabelle's case) is late, but evidently not too late. Age 13 or 31 is too late by far. There appears to be a critical or sensitive period for language acquisition, a consequence of maturational changes in the developing human brain.

The notion of a critical period for learning has been studied primarily in animals. Acquisition of a number of important animal behavior patterns seems to be governed by the timing of environmental stimulation. One example is the attachment of the young of various species to their mothers, which generally can be formed only in early childhood (Hess, 1973; Suomi and Harlow, 1971). Another is bird song. Male birds of many species have a song that is characteristic of their own kind. In some species this song is entirely innate, but in other species the song is partially acquired or modified through exposure. They learn this song by listening to adult males of their own species. However, this exposure will be effective only if it occurs at a certain period in the fledgling's life. This has been documented for the white-crowned sparrow (Marler, 1970). To learn the white-crowned sparrow song in all its glory (complete with special trills and grace notes), the baby birds must hear an adult song sometime between the seventh and sixtieth days of life. The next forty days are a marginal period. If the fledgling is exposed to an adult male's song during that period but not before, he will acquire only some skeletal basics of the sparrow song, without the full elaborations heard in normal adults. If the exposure comes still later, it has no effect at all: the bird will never sing normally.

It is tempting to extend such findings to the cases of Isabelle, Genie, and Chelsea. Though Isabelle's exposure to language was relatively late, it might have fallen full square within the critical period. Genie's later exposure might have been at the "marginal" time, allowing her to achieve only the skeletal base of a human language. Chelsea's even later exposure might have been entirely too late. But in order to draw any such grand conclusions, it is necessary to look beyond such complex and tragic individual cases at a more organized body of evidence to examine the effects of brain state on the capacity to learn a language.

Second Language Learning.   Much of the literature on this topic has traditionally come from studies of second-language learning, for the obvious reason that it is hard to find adults who have not been exposed to a first language early in life. But individuals acquire second — and third, and fifth — languages throughout their life spans. Do they acquire these differently as a consequence of differences in their degree of brain maturation?

The facts are these. In the first stages of learning a second language, adults appear to be more efficient than children (Snow and Hoefnagel-Hohle, 1978). The adult second-language learners produce primitive sentences almost immediately, whereas the young child displaced into a new language community is often shocked into total silence and emotional distress. But the long-range outcome is just the reverse. After a few years very young children speak the new language fluently and sound just like natives. This is highly uncommon in adults.

This point has been made by investigators who studied the long-run outcome of second-language learning as a function of the age at first exposure to it (Johnson and Newport, 1989; Oyama, 1978; Patkowski, 1980). In the study by Johnson and Newport, the subjects were native Chinese and Korean speakers who came to the United States and were immersed in English at varying ages. The East Asian languages were chosen because they are maximally dissimilar to English. The subjects were tested for English-language knowledge after they had been in the United States for at least five years; therefore, they had ample exposure and practice time. Finally, all of them were students and faculty members at a large midwestern university, so they shared some social background and presumably were about equally motivated to learn the new language so as to succeed in their jobs and social roles.

These subjects listened to English sentences, half of which were clearly ungrammatical ("The farmer bought two pig at the market, The little boy is speak to a policeman"); the other half were the grammatical counterparts of the ungrammatical sentences. The task was to identify the grammatical and ungrammatical sentences. The results were clear-cut. Those learners who (like Isabelle) had been exposed to English before age 7 performed just like native speakers. Thereafter, there was an increasing decrement in performance as a function of age at first exposure. The later they were exposed to English, the worse they performed.

Late Exposure to a First Language.   Immediate objections can be raised to the outcomes just described as bearing on the critical period hypothesis. The first is anecdotal. All of us know, or know of, individuals (such as Joseph Conrad or Vladimir Nabokov) who learned English late in life and controlled it extraordinarily well. But the point of the studies just mentioned has to do with population characteristics, not extraordinary individuals. Every child of normal mentality exposed to a (first or second) language before age 6 or 7 learns it at native level. It is a rarity, the subject of considerable admiration and awe, if anyone does as well when exposure begins in adulthood.

The second objection is more substantive. Perhaps the difficulties of the learners just discussed had to do specifically with second-language learning. Maybe older individuals are not worse at learning language but rather are troubled by their sophisticated knowledge of the first language. One body of language knowledge may interfere with the other.

For this reason, it is of interest to look at acquisition of a first language late in life. The best available line of evidence comes from work on the acquisition of sign language. As we saw earlier (see the section "Language Invention by the Isolated Deaf Child"), most deaf children are born into hearing families and are therefore not exposed to a gestural language from birth. These individuals invent a skeletal communication system that compares quite well with language in the normally circumstanced 2-year-old (Feldman et al., 1978; Goldin-Meadow and Mylander, 1984). Yet they do not advance to an elaborate language system containing function morphemes and other very complex linguistic devices. In some ways their spontaneous development seems akin to Genie's; early in life these isolates control no elaborate linguistic system. At varying points in life, as accidents of personal history, most of these individuals do come in contact with a formal language of the deaf, such as American Sign Language (ASL), which they then learn and use for all their everyday communicative needs. Sometimes contact with a formal sign language comes relatively early in life but sometimes as late as 15 or 20 years of age. These individuals are essentially learning a first language at an unusually late point in maturational time.

Does this late start matter? Newport (1990) studied the production and comprehension of ASL in three groups of congenitally deaf people. All of them had been using ASL as their primary means of communication for at least thirty years, a virtual guarantee that they were as expert in this language as they would ever be. The only difference among them was the age at which they had first been exposed to ASL. The first group consisted of deaf children of deaf parents who had been exposed to ASL from birth. The second consisted of early learners, those who had been exposed to ASL between ages 4 and 6. The third group had come into contact with ASL after the age of 12. All subjects were at least 50 years of age when tested. The findings were dramatic. After thirty years or more of exposure and constant use, only those who had been exposed to ASL before age 6 showed native-level fluency. There were subtle defects in the middle group, and those whose exposure occurred after the age of 12 evinced significant deficits. Their particular problems (as usual) were with the ASL equivalents of the function morphemes and with complex sentences.

Pidgins and Creoles.   A fascinating line of research concerns the process of language formation among linguistically heterogeneous adults who are thrown together for limited times or purposes (Bickerton, 1975, 1981; Sankoff and LaBerge, 1973). They may be occasional trading partners of different language backgrounds who have to communicate about the costs of fish and vegetables, or foreign coworkers who come to a new country to earn money and then return to their native land, or citizens of a region in which there are too many languages for everyone to learn them all. In order to communicate across language barriers, these individuals often develop a rough-and-ready contact language, a lingua franca, or *pidgin*. Not surprisingly from what we have discussed so far, these pidgin languages are rudimentary in form, perhaps because all their speakers are late learners. Thus, there are interesting overlaps between the pidgins and the first attempts of young children learning an elaborated natural language (Slobin, 1977). For example, at the first stages of both, the sentences are one clause long and have a rigid simple structure and few if any function words.

Very often, a pidgin will develop into a full language. An example is Tok Pisin ("Talk Pidgin"), a language of Papua, New Guinea, with pidgin origins. When the speakers of different language groups began to marry, they used this pidgin as the only means of linguistic communication. Most important, they had babies whose only language input was the pidgin itself. Once a pidgin language has native speakers (and thus by definition is called a *creole*), it undergoes rapid change and expansion of just the sort one might expect based on the learning data we have presented so far: Multiclausal sentences and a variety of function morphemes appeared in the users who heard the pidgin from birth rather than acquiring it during adulthood. Sankoff and LaBerge (1973) (see also Bickerton, 1975, 1981) showed that this elaboration of structure was carried out primarily by the child learners who, between the ages of about 4 and 7 years, refined and expanded upon the formal resources available in the pidgin.

Singleton and Newport (1994) have shown a related effect for the children of late learners of ASL. Recall that the late learners, even after thirty years of exposure and practice, have substantial problems with the complex parts of ASL: While they may have good control over the basic vocabulary and simple clauses of ASL, they use more complex structures of ASL inconsistently, and they often omit multiclausal sentences and function morphemes altogether. In this sense, then, their late-learned language is somewhat like a pidgin (see Schumann, 1978 for a similar analogy between late-acquired second languages and pidgins). When two late learners marry, their children (learning ASL in the family home from their parents) are therefore like creole speakers. Singleton and Newport observed such a child, "Simon," from the time he was about 2 years old until he was 9, and recorded both his parents' and his own use of ASL. Simon's parents provided his only input to ASL; as is common for deaf children, no one at Simon's school knew ASL at all. His parents showed the characteristic restrictions of late learners of ASL described above. In contrast, however, Simon's own ASL surpassed his parents'. At the appropriate maturational time (ages 4 to 7), he refined, expanded, and grammaticized the resources of his input, creating an elaborated language complete with complex sentences and function elements.

In a nutshell, both for the spoken creole of Sankoff and LaBerge and the gestural creole of Singleton and Newport, the first language-learning situation, carried out at the correct maturational moment, creates new resources that are not properties of the input pidgin, are highly abstract, and are the very hallmarks of full natural languages.

25.2   EVERY LEARNER IS AN ISOLATE

Most of our discussion so far has focused on language learning in unusual and apparently especially difficult conditions — when the learner was blocked from getting information of various kinds by accidents of nature or circumstance, or even when there was no full language out there in the world for the learner to observe. Rising above these inadequacies in the data provided, children learned language even so. These findings point to a human "linguistic nature" that rescues learners from inadequacies in relevant nurture.

In one sense, these populations provide the most solid and dramatic evidence for our understanding of language learning because they extensively remove or reduce the contributions from one of the components of the nature/nurture equation and thereby reveal the effects of the other. But in an important sense, it was not really necessary to look at special populations to conclude that language learning must be largely "from the inside out" rather than being "outside in." The special cases serve only to dramatize what are actually the ordinary conditions for language acquisition. For every learner of a human language, no matter how fortunately circumstanced, is really in the same boat as, say, the blind child or the learner exposed to a rudimentary contact language: isolated from much of the information required to learn a language from mere exposure. At best, the child's environment offers some fragmentary and inconclusive clues, with human nature left to fill in the rest. In short, children are able to acquire English or German or Tlingit just because in some sense they know, from their biological predispositions, the essence of language.

We can document this point with a few examples. Consider the information children are given for learning that the sound "dog" means *dog.* No one tells the child the meaning of the word (perhaps, *cute, furry, tame, four-legged, midsized mammal of the canine variety*). Instead, the child will see a few dogs — say, a chihuahua and a Great Dane — and in their presence the caretaker will utter, "That's a dog," "Be careful; that dog bites!" "I'm glad we don't have a dirty dog like that at home," or something of the sort. From such adventitious encounters with dogs along with sentences about dogs, rather than from any direct encounters with the meaning of *dog,* novices must deduce that there is a category *dog,* labeled "dog" in English, that can be applied to certain kinds of creatures in the world. Though their observations may include only the chihuahua and the Great Dane, they must be able to apply the word to future terriers and poodles as well, but not to cats or elephants. That is, the use of even the homeliest words is creative. Once learned, they are applicable to instances never previously observed, so long as they fit the category. But just what the appropriate extensions are, from the particular examples they have seen to new things in the world, is left to the children to figure out on their own.

Such are the real conditions for vocabulary acquisition. The category (or *concept*) is never directly encountered, for there are no categories indicated directly in the world; there are only individual things, complex events, and so forth. Learners are thrown upon their own internal resources to discover the category itself. Yet the most ordinary child by age 6 has acquired about ten thousand words, hardly any of them ever directly defined by the adult community.

To see the real dimensions of this vocabulary acquisition task, consider now the acquisition of *know,* a vocabulary item within the range of every self-respecting 4-year-old. In certain conversational contexts the novice will hear, "Do you know where your blocks are?" "I don't know what you're crying about," "You know Aunt Mary, don't you? You met her at Bobby's house last week." In consequence of such contacts with the world and the word, children come to understand the meaning of *know*. How do they manage to do this? What is the meaning of *know*, such that it refers truly and relevantly to the (infinitely many) new knowing situations but not to the infinitely many other new situations that involve no knowing? Just what are the situations that license uttering "know"?

All in all, it seems that the word learner is "isolated" from direct information about word meanings, even under optimal environmental conditions. The instances offered by experience are insufficient to warrant discovery of these meanings, but the child does so anyway, and for a formidably large set of words.

Lay observers are often impressed with the fact that very young children may sometimes overextend some term — for example, calling the dog in the street "Fido" if that is the name of the child's own dog, or calling the man in the street "Daddy." But these errors are quite rare, even in the toddler (perhaps that is why they are so treasured), and have largely disappeared by age 2. More important, the rare errors in applying a word are highly constrained: no child uses the word *dog* for an onion or jumping or redness. Even when toddlers are slightly off the mark in using first words, they are admirably close to correct, despite the fact that the information presented in the environment is ludicrously impoverished. It must be that the categories in which language traffics are lavishly prefigured in the human mind.

Similar arguments for the poverty of the stimulus information (and thus the need to look to nature to understand the emergence of language in children) can be made by looking at almost any property of syntactic structure. No mother explains English grammar to her child. One reason is that no one knows the grammar in any conscious way and so could not explain it if they tried. Another is that the babies would not understand the explanations. Just as in the case of vocabulary, acquisition of syntactic structure proceeds on the basis of examples rather than explanations. One can thus ask, for syntax as well as vocabulary, whether the example utterances that children hear are really sufficient to account for what they come to know about the structure of their language. The structures we will use for illustration come from a discussion by Chomsky (1975).

In simple English declarative sentences, the verb occurs after the subject noun phrase: for example, *The man is a fool*. To form the interrogative, the *is* "moves" into initial position preceding the subject (*Is the man a fool?*). But can any *is* in a declarative sentence be moved to form an interrogative? It is impossible to judge from one-clause sentences alone. The issue is resolved by looking at more complex sentences, which can contain more than one instance of *is*, for example:

1. The man who is a fool is amusing.
2. The man is a fool who is amusing.

Which of the two *is*'s in each of these sentences can move to initial position to form an interrogative? Suppose we say that it is the first of the two *is*'s that can move. This will yield:

1'. Is the man who a fool is amusing?
2'. Is the man a fool who is amusing?

Sentence (2') is fine, but (1') is clearly ungrammatical. No one talks that way. Therefore, the "rule" for forming an interrogative cannot be anything like "move the first *is*." But a new trouble results if we try to move the second *is* instead. This would yield:

1″. Is the man who is a fool amusing?
2″. Is the man is a fool who amusing?

Now sentence (2″) has come out wrong. Thus *no* rule that alludes to the serial order of the two *is*'s will correctly account for what is and what is not a grammatical interrogative. The only generalization that will work is that the *is* in the *main clause* (rather than the subordinate clause, the one introduced by *who*) moves. The problem with (1′) and with (2″) is that we tried to move the *is* in the subordinate clause, a violation of English syntactic structure.

English speakers by age 4 are capable of uttering complex interrogatives like those we have just looked at. No one has ever observed a youngster to err along the way, producing sentences like (1′) or (2″). But how could they have learned the appropriate generalization? No one whispers in a child's ear. "It's the *is* in the main clause that moves." And even such a whispered hint would be insufficient, for the task would still be to identify these clauses. Sentences uttered to children are not marked off into clauses such as:

3. The man [who is a fool] is amusing.

nor are clauses marked "main" and "subordinate" anywhere in the speech stream. No one hears sentences like:

4. beginning-of-main clause: "The man," subordinate clause: "who is a fool," end-of-main clause: "is amusing."

In short, the analysis of utterances required for forming the correct generalization is not offered in the language input that the child receives. Even so, every child forms this generalization, which operates in terms of structures (such as "the main clause") rather than according to the serial order of items (such as "the first *is*").

The distinction between main and subordinate clauses — or, in modern linguistic parlance, "higher" and "lower" clauses — is no arcane byway of English grammar. Consider as one more instance the interpretation of pronouns. Very often, pronouns follow their antecedent, as in:

5. When John arrived home, he ate dinner.

But we cannot account for the antecedent/pronoun relation simply by alluding to their serial order in the sentence (just as we could not account for the movement of *is* by alluding to its serial position in a sentence). This is because a pronoun can sometimes precede its antecedent noun as in:

6. When he arrived home, John ate dinner.

But this is not always possible, as shown by:

7. He arrived home when John ate dinner.

Sentence (7) is perfectly grammatical, but its *he* cannot be John, while the *he* in sentence (6) can be John.

What is the generalization that accounts for the distinction in the interpretation of (6) and (7)? It is (very roughly) that the pronoun in the main (higher) clause cannot corefer with a noun in the subordinate (lower) clause. Again, it is necessary to invoke structures within sentences, rather than the serial order of words (here, nouns and pronouns), to understand how to interpret the sentences.

How could a child learn that the principles of English syntax are — always, as it turns out — *structure-dependent* rather than serial-order-dependent? Why are errors not made on the way to this generalization? The problem is that sentences spoken and heard by children in no way transparently provide the structural information. The "stimulus information" (the utterances) is too impoverished — just a bunch of words strung in a row — to sustain the correct generalizations. And yet these generalizations are formed anyway.

The solution seems to be that learners are innately biased to assume that generalizations in natural languages will always be structure-dependent rather than serial-order-dependent. Indeed, extensive linguistic investigation shows this to be true of all languages, not just English. With this principle in hand, children have a crucial leg up in acquiring any natural language to which they are exposed.

To summarize this discussion, every real learner is isolated from many of the kinds of elaborate information that would be necessary for discovering the word meanings and grammatical forms of a human language. Children use neither dictionaries nor grammar texts to redress this paucity of the information base. It follows that innate principles must be guiding their linguistic development. Children can learn language because they are disposed by nature to represent and manipulate linguistic data in highly circumscribed ways.

25.3   CONCLUSIONS

In the preceding sections we have presented some of the complex facts about language and language learning. We have suggested that these facts support the notion that there are biologically given dispositions toward certain types of language structure and toward a particular maturationally based sequence in which these structures appear. We have given evidence that, to a surprising degree, language is the product of the young human brain, such that virtually any exposure conditions short of total isolation and vicious mistreatment will suffice to bring it forth in every child. In retrospect, this is scarcely surprising. It would be just as foolish for evolution to have created human bodies without human "programs" to run these bodies as to have created giraffe bodies without giraffe programs or white-crowned-sparrow bodies without white-crowned-sparrow programs. It is owing to such biological programming that language is universal in our species and utterly closed to other species — including even college-educated chimpanzees.

The universality of language is, moreover, no quirk or back corner of human mentality but rather one of the central cognitive properties whose possession makes us truly human. If we humans ever get to another planet and find organisms who speak like us, it is likely that we will feel some strong impetus to get to know them and understand them — rather than trying to herd them or milk them — even if they look like cows.

While we have emphasized the biological underpinnings of language acquisition, we must also repeat that part of the normal acquisition process clearly involves learning from the environment as well: English children learn English, not Greek or Urdu. The surface manifestations of human languages are marvelously variable, and children learn whichever of these manifestations they are presented with (as long as what they hear is organized in accord with the general principles of human language, and as long as it is presented at the proper maturational moment). Language acquisition is therefore a complex interaction between the child's innate capacities and the social, cognitive, and linguistic supports provided in the environment. What we have tried to emphasize, however, is that acknowledgment of significant environmentally caused variation should not blind us to the pervasive commonalities among all languages and among all their learners. Specific languages are apparently acquired within the constraints of a specialized and highly evolved biological endowment, which learns languages only in particular ways and only at particular moments of life.

Perhaps it would repay serious inquiry to investigate other complex human functions in ways similar to those that have been exploited in the study of language learning. There are vast differences in human artifacts and social functions in different times and places, with some humans riding on camels while others rocket to the moon. All the same, it may well be that — as is the case for language — human individuals and cultures do not differ from one another without limit. There may be more human universals than are visible to the naked eye. Beneath the kaleidoscopic variation in human behavior that we easily observe, there may be many universal organizing principles that constrain us and contribute to the definition of what it is to be a human.

ACKNOWLEDGMENTS

The writing of this paper and some of the research reported herein were supported in part by NIH grant DC00167 to E. Newport and T. Supalla, and by a NSF Science & Technology grant to the University of Pennsylvania. We are grateful to Steve Pinker for helpful suggestions on an earlier draft of this chapter.

REFERENCES

Berlin, B., & Kay, P. (1969). *Basic color terms: Their universality and evolution.* Berkeley: University of California Press.

Bickerton, D. (1975). *Dynamics of a creole system.* Cambridge: Cambridge University Press.

Bickerton, D. (1981). *Roots of language.* Ann Arbor: Karoma Press.

Borer, H., & Wexler, K. (1982). Bi-unique relations and the maturation of grammatical principles. *Natural Language and Linguistic Theory* 10, 147–189.

Brown, R. (1958). *Words and things.* New York: Free Press, Macmillan.

Brown, R., & Lenneberg, E. (1954). A study in language and cognition. *Journal of Abnormal and Social Psychology* 49, 454–462.

Chomsky, N. (1959). A review of B. F. Skinner's *Verbal Behavior. Language* 35, 26–58.

Chomsky, N. (1975). *Reflections on language.* New York: Pantheon.

Curtiss, S. (1977). *Genie: A psycholinguistic study of a modern day "wild child."* New York: Academic Press.

Curtiss, S. (1989). The case of Chelsea: A new test case of the critical period for language acquisition. Manuscript, University of California, Los Angeles.

Davis, K. (1947). Final note on a case of extreme social isolation. *American Journal of Sociology* 52, 432–437.

Descartes, R. (1662). *Discours de la méthode,* part 5. In *Philosophical works,* translated by F. Haldane and

G. Ross, 1911. Cambridge, England: Cambridge University Press.

Feldman, H., Goldin-Meadow, S. & Gleitman, L. R. (1978). Beyond Herodotus: The creation of language by linguistically deprived deaf children. In A. Lock, ed., *Action, symbol, and gesture.* New York: Academic Press.

Fowler, E. E., Gelman, R. & Gleitman, L. R. (1994). The course of language learning in children with Down Syndrome. In H. Tager-Flusberg, ed., *Constraints on language acquisition: Studies of atypical children.* Hillsdale, NJ: Erlbaum.

Fromkin, V., Krashen, S. Curtiss, S. Rigler, D. & Rigler, M. (1974). The development of language in Genie: A case of language acquisition beyond the critical period. *Brain and Language* 1, 81–107.

Goldin-Meadow, S., & Mylander, C. (1984). Gestural communication in deaf children: The non-effects of parental input on early language development. *Monographs of the Society for Research in Child Development* 49 (3–4), serial no. 207.

Heider, E. R., & Oliver, D. C. (1972). The structure of the color space in naming and memory for two languages. *Cognitive Psychology* 3, 337–354.

Herodotus (ca. 410 B.C.). *The Persian wars,* book 2, chapter 2. New York: Rawlinson, 1942.

Hess, E. H. (1973). *Imprinting.* New York: Van Nostrand.

Johnson, J. S., & Newport, E. L. (1989). Critical period effects in second-language learning: The influence of maturational state on the acquisition of English as a second language. *Cognitive Psychology* 21, 60–90.

Johnston, J. (1988). Specific language disorders in the child. In N. Lass, L. McReynolds, J. Northern, and D. Yoder, eds., *Handbook of speech-language pathology and audiology.* Philadelphia: Decker.

Klima, E. S., Bellugi, U. et al. (1979). *The signs of language.* Cambridge, MA: Harvard University Press.

Landau, B., & Gleitman, L. R. (1985). *Language and experience: Evidence from the blind child.* Cambridge, MA: Harvard University Press.

Landau, B., & Jackendoff, R. (1993). "What" and "where" in spatial language and spatial cognition. *Behavioral and Brain Sciences* 16, 217–266.

Lenneberg, E. (1967). *Biological foundations of language.* New York: Wiley.

Marler, P. (1970). A comparative approach to vocal learning: Song development in white crowned sparrows. *Journal of Comparative and Physiological Psychology,* monograph 7, 1–25.

Nadel, L. (1988). *The psychobiology of Down Syndrome.* Cambridge, MA: MIT Press.

Newport, E. L. (1990). Maturational constraints on language learning. *Cognitive Science* 14, 11–28.

Newport, E. L., Gleitman, H. & Gleitman, L. R. (1977). Mother, I'd rather do it myself: Some effects and noneffects of maternal speech style. In C. Snow and C. Ferguson, eds., *Talking to children: Language input and acquisition.* Cambridge: Cambridge University Press.

Newport, E. L., & Meier, R. (1985). The acquisition of American Sign Language. In D. I. Slobin (ed.), *The crosslinguistic study of language acquisition.* Hillsdale, NJ: Erlbaum.

Oyama, S. (1978). The sensitive period and comprehension of speech. *Working Papers on Bilingualism* 16, 1–17.

Patkowski, M. (1980). The sensitive period for the acquisition of syntax in a second language. *Language Learning* 30, 449–472.

Sankoff, G., & LaBerge, S. (1973). On the acquisition of native speakers by a language. *Kivung 6,* 32–47.

Schumann, J. H. (1978). *The pidginization process: A model for second language acquisition.* Rowley, MA: Newbury House.

Singleton, J., & Newport, E. L. (1994). When learners surpass their models: The acquisition of American Sign Language from impoverished input. Manuscript, University of Rochester.

Slobin, D. I. (1977). Language change in childhood and in history. In J. Macnamara, ed., *Language learning and thought.* New York: Academic Press.

Snow, C., & Hoefnagel-Hohle, M. (1978). The critical period for language acquisition: Evidence from second language learning. *Child Development* 49, 1114–1128.

Starkey, P., Spelke, E. S. & Gelman, R. (1990). Numerical abstraction by human infants. *Cognition* 36, 97–127.

Suomi, S., & Harlow, H. (1971). Abnormal social behavior in young monkeys. In J. Helmuth, ed., *Exceptional infant: Studies in abnormalities.* Vol. 2. New York: Brunner/Mazel.

Supalla, T., & Newport, E. L. (1978). How many seats in a chair? The derivation of nouns and verbs in American Sign Language. In P. Siple, ed., *Understanding language through sign language research.* New York: Academic Press.

Whorf, B. L. (1956). *Language, thought, and reality.* Cambridge, MA: MIT Press.

CHAPTER TWENTY-SIX

STATISTICAL LANGUAGE LEARNING: MECHANISMS AND CONSTRAINTS

JENNY R. SAFFRAN[1]

Abstract

What types of mechanisms underlie the acquisition of human language? Recent evidence suggests that learners, including infants, can use statistical properties of linguistic input to discover structure, including sound patterns, words, and the beginnings of grammar. These abilities appear to be both powerful and constrained, such that some statistical patterns are more readily detected and used than others. Implications for the structure of human languages are discussed.

Imagine that you are faced with the following challenge: You must discover the underlying structure of an immense system that contains tens of thousands of pieces, all generated by combining a small set of elements in various ways. These pieces, in turn, can be combined in an infinite number of ways, although only a subset of those combinations is actually correct. However, the subset that is correct is itself infinite. Somehow you must rapidly figure out the structure of this system so that you can use it appropriately early in your childhood.

This system, of course, is human language. The elements are the sounds of language, and the larger pieces are the words, which in turn combine to form sentences. Given the richness and complexity of language, it seems improbable that children could ever discern its structure. The process of acquiring such a system is likely to be nearly as complex as the system itself, so it is not surprising that the mechanisms underlying language acquisition are a matter of long-standing debate. One of the central focuses of this debate concerns the innate and environmental contributions to the language-acquisition process, and the degree to which these components draw on information and abilities that are also relevant to other domains of learning.

In particular, there is a fundamental tension between theories of language acquisition in which learning plays a central role and theories in which learning is relegated to the sidelines. A strength of learning-oriented theories is that they exploit the growing wealth of evidence suggesting that young humans possess powerful learning mechanisms. For example, infants can rapidly capitalize on the statistical properties of their language environments, including the distributions of sounds in words and the orders of word types in sentences, to discover important components of language structure. Infants can track such statistics, for example, to discover speech categories (e.g., native-language consonants; see, e.g., Maye, Werker, & Gerken, 2002), word boundaries (e.g., Saffran, Aslin, & Newport, 1996), and rudimentary syntax (e.g., Gomez & Gerken, 1999; Saffran & Wilson, 2003).

However, theories of language acquisition in which learning plays a central role are vulnerable to a number of criticisms. One of the most important arguments against learning-oriented theories is that such accounts seem at odds with one of the central observations about human languages. The linguistic systems of the world, despite surface differences, share deep similarities, and vary in nonarbitrary ways. Theories of language acquisition that focus primarily on pre-existing knowledge of language do provide an elegant explanation for cross-linguistic similarities. Such theories, which are exemplified by the seminal work of Noam Chomsky, suggest that linguistic universals are prespecified in the child's linguistic endowment, and do not require learning. Such accounts generate predictions about the types of patterns that should be observed cross-linguistically, and lead to important claims regarding the evolution of a language capacity that includes innate knowledge of this kind (e.g., Pinker & Bloom, 1990).

Can learning-oriented theories also account for the existence of language universals? The answer to this question is the object of current research. The *constrained statistical learning framework* suggests that learning is central to language acquisition, and that the specific nature of language learning explains similarities across languages. The crucial point is that learning is constrained: learners are not open-minded, and calculate some statistics more readily than others. Of particular interest are those constraints on learning that correspond to cross-linguistic similarities (e.g., Newport & Aslin, 2000). According to this framework, the similarities across languages are indeed nonaccidental, as suggested by the Chomskian framework — but they are not the result of innate linguistic knowledge. Instead, human languages have been shaped by human learning mechanisms (along with constraints on human perception, processing, and speech production), and aspects of language that enhance learnability are more likely to persist in linguistic structure than those that do not. Thus, according to this view, the similarities across languages are not due to innate knowledge, as is traditionally claimed, but rather are the result of constraints on learning. Further, if human languages were (and continue to be) shaped by constraints on human learning mechanisms, it seems likely that these mechanisms and their constraints were not tailored solely for language acquisition. Instead, learning in nonlinguistic domains should be similarly constrained, as seems to be the case.

A better understanding of these constraints may lead to new connections between theories focused on nature and theories focused on nurture. Constrained learning mechanisms require both particular experiences to drive learning and preexisting structures to capture and manipulate those experiences.

26.1   LEARNING THE SOUNDS OF WORDS

In order to investigate the nature of infants learning mechanisms, my colleagues and I began by studying an aspect of language that we knew must certainly be learned: word segmentation, or the boundaries between words in fluent speech. This is a challenging problem for infants acquiring their first language, for speakers do not mark word boundaries with pauses, as shown in Figure 26.1. Instead, infants must determine where one word ends and the next begins without access to obvious acoustic cues. This process requires learning because children cannot innately know that, for example, *pretty* and *baby* are words, whereas *tyba* (spanning the boundary between *pretty* and *baby*) is not.

One source of information that may contribute to the discovery of word boundaries is the statistical structure of the language in the infant's environment. In English, the syllable *pre* precedes a small set of syllables, including *ty, tend,* and *cedes:* in the stream of speech, the probability that *pre* is followed by *ty* is thus quite high (roughly 80% in speech to young infants). However, because the syllable *ty* occurs word finally, it can be followed by any syllable that can begin an English word. Thus, the probability that *ty* is followed by *ba,* as in *pretty baby,* is extremely low (roughly 0.03% in speech to young infants). This difference in sequential probabilities is a clue that *pretty* is a word, and *tyba* is not. More generally, given the statistical properties of the input language, the ability to track sequential probabilities would be an extremely useful tool for infant learners.

To explore whether humans can use statistical learning to segment words, we exposed adults, first graders, and 8-month-olds to spoken nonsense languages in which the only cues to word boundaries were the statistical properties of the syllable sequences (e.g., Saffran et al., 1996). Listeners briefly heard a continuous sequence of syllables containing multisyllabic words from one of the languages (e.g., *golabupabikututibubabupugolabubabupu* [. . .]). We then tested our participants to determine whether they could discriminate the words from the

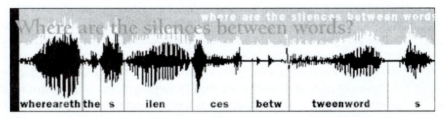

FIGURE 26.1   A speech waveform of the sentence "Where are the silences between words?" The height of the bars indicates loudness, and the *x*-axis is time. This example illustrates the lack of consistent silences between word boundaries in fluent speech. The vertical gray lines represent quiet points in the speech stream, some of which do not correspond to word boundaries. Some sounds are represented twice in the transcription below the waveform because of their continued persistence over time.

language from sequences spanning word boundaries. For example, we compared performance on words like *golabu* and *pabiku* with performance on sequences like *bupabi,* which spanned the boundary between words. To succeed at this task, listeners would have had to track the statistical properties of the input. Our results confirmed that human learners, including infants, can indeed use statistics to find word boundaries. Moreover, this ability is not confined to humans: Cotton-top tamarins, a New World monkey species, can also track statistics to discover word boundaries (Hauser, Newport, & Aslin, 2001).

One question immediately raised by these results is the degree to which statistical learning is limited to language-like stimuli. A growing body of results suggests that sequential statistical learning is quite general. For example, infants can track sequences of tones, discovering "tone-word boundaries" via statistical cues (e.g., Saffran, Johnson, Aslin, & Newport, 1999), and can learn statistically defined visual patterns (e.g., Fiser & Aslin, 2002; Kirkham, Slemmer, & Johnson, 2002); work in progress is extending these results to the domain of events in human action sequences.

Given that the ability to discover units via their statistical coherence is not confined to language (or to humans), one might wonder whether the statistical learning results actually pertain to language at all. That is, do infants actually use statistical learning mechanisms in real-world language acquisition? One way to address this question is to ask what infants are actually learning in our segmentation task. Are they learning statistics? Or are they using statistics to learn language? Our results suggest that when infants being raised in English-speaking environments have segmented the sound strings, they treat these nonsensical patterns as English words (Saffran, 2001b). Statistical language learning in the laboratory thus appears to be integrated with other aspects of language acquisition. Related results suggest that 12-month-olds can first segment novel words and then discover syntactic regularities relating the new words — all within the same set of input. This would not be possible if the infants formed mental representations only of the sequential probabilities relating individual syllables, and no word-level representations (Saffran & Wilson, 2003). These findings point to a constraint on statistical language learning: The mental representations produced by this process are not just sets of syllables linked by statistics, but new units that are available to serve as the input to subsequent learning processes.

Similarly, it is possible to examine constraints on learning that might affect the acquisition of the sound structure of human languages. The types of sound patterns that infants learn most readily may be more prevalent in languages than are sound patterns that are not learnable by infants. We tested this hypothesis by asking whether infants find some phonotactic regularities (restrictions on where particular sounds can occur; e.g., /fs/ can occur at the end, but not the beginning, of syllables in English) easier to acquire than others (Saffran & Thiessen, 2003). The results suggest that infants readily acquire novel regularities that are consistent with the types of patterns found in the world's languages, but fail to learn regularities that are inconsistent with natural language structure. For example, infants rapidly learn new phonotactic regularities involving generalizations across sounds that share a phonetic feature, while failing to learn regularities that disregard such features. Thus, it is easier for infants to learn a set of patterns that group together /p/, /t/, and /k/, which are all voiceless, and that group together /b/, /d/, and /g/, which are all voiced, than to learn a pattern that groups together /d/, /p/, and /k/, but does not apply to /t/.[2] Studies of this sort may provide explanations for why languages show the types of sound patterning that they do; sound structures that are hard for infants to learn may be unlikely to recur across the languages of the world.

26.2   STATISTICAL LEARNING AND SYNTAX

Issues about learning versus innate knowledge are most prominent in the area of syntax. How could learning-oriented theories account for the acquisition of abstract structure (e.g., phrase boundaries) not obviously mirrored in the surface statistics of the input? Unlike accounts centered on innate linguistic knowledge, most learning-oriented theories do not provide a transparent explanation for the ubiquity of particular structures cross-linguistically. One approach to these issues is to ask whether some nearly universal structural aspects of human languages may result from constraints on human learning (e.g., Morgan, Meier, & Newport, 1987). To test this hypothesis, we asked whether one such aspect of syntax, phrase structure (groupings of types of words together into subunits, such as noun phrases and verb phrases), results from a constraint on learning: Do humans learn sequential structures better when they are organized into subunits such as phrases than when they are not? We identified a statistical cue to phrasal units, predictive dependencies (e.g., the presence of a word like *the* or *a* predicts a noun somewhere downstream; the presence of a preposition predicts a noun phrase somewhere downstream), and determined that learners can use this kind of cue to locate phrase boundaries (Saffran, 2001a).

In a direct test of the theory that predictive dependencies enhance learn-ability, we compared the acquisition of two nonsense languages, one with predictive dependencies as a cue to phrase structure, and one lacking predictive dependencies (e.g., words like *the* could occur either with or without a noun, and a noun could occur either with or without words like *the:* neither type of word predicted the presence of the other). We found better language learning in listeners exposed to languages containing predictive dependencies than in listeners exposed to languages lacking predictive dependencies (Saffran, 2002). Interestingly, the same constraint on learning emerged in tasks using nonlinguistic materials (e.g., computer alert sounds and simultaneously presented shape arrays). These results support the claim that learning mechanisms not specifically designed for language learning may have shaped the structure of human languages.

26.3   DIRECTIONS FOR FUTURE RESEARCH

Results to date demonstrate that human language learners possess powerful statistical learning capacities. These mechanisms are constrained at multiple levels: there are limits on what information serves as input, which computations are performed over that input, and the structure of the representations that emerge as output. To more fully understand the contribution of statistical learning to language acquisition, it is necessary to assess the degree to which statistical learning provides explanatory power given the complexities of the acquisition process.

For example, how does statistical learning interact with other aspects of language acquisition? One way we are addressing this question is by investigating how infants weight statistical cues relative to other cues to word segmentation early in life. The results of such studies provide an important window into the ways in which statistical learning may help infant learners to determine the relevance of the many cues inherent in language input. Similarly, we are studying how statistics meet up with meaning in the world (e.g., are statistically defined "words" easier to learn as labels for novel objects than sound sequences spanning word boundaries?) and how infants in bilingual environments cope with multiple sets of statistics. Studying the intersection between statistical learning and the rest of language learning may provide new insights into how various nonstatistical aspects of language are acquired. Moreover, a clearer picture of the learning mechanisms used successfully by typical language learners may increase researchers understanding of the types of processes that go awry when children do not acquire language as readily as their peers.

It is also critical to determine which statistics are available to young learners and whether those statistics are actually relevant to natural language structure. Researchers do not agree on the role that statistical learning should play in acquisition theories. For example, they disagree about when learning is best described as statistically based as opposed to rule based (i.e., utilizing mechanisms that operate over algebraic variables to discover abstract knowledge), and about whether learning can still be considered statistical when the input to learning is abstract. Debates regarding the proper place for statistical learning in theories of language acquisition cannot be resolved in advance of the data. For example, although one can distinguish between statistical versus rule-based learning mechanisms, and statistical versus rule-based knowledge, the data are not yet available to determine whether statistical learning itself renders rule-based knowledge structures, and whether abstract knowledge can be probabilistic. Significant empirical advances will be required to disentangle these and other competing theoretical distinctions.

Finally, cross-species investigations may be particularly informative with respect to the relationship between statistical learning and human language. Current research is identifying species differences in the deployment of statistical learning mechanisms (e.g., Newport & Aslin, 2000). To the extent that nonhumans and humans track different statistics, or track statistics over different perceptual units, learning mechanisms that do not initially appear to be human-specific may actually render human-specific outcomes. Alternatively, the overlap between the learning mechanisms available across species may suggest that differences in statistical learning cannot account for cross-species differences in language-learning capacities.

CONCLUSION

It is clear that human language is a system of mind-boggling complexity. At the same time, the use of statistical cues may help learners to discover some of the patterns lurking in language input. To what extent might the kinds of statistical patterns accessible to human learners help in disentangling the complexities of this system? Although the answer to this question remains unknown, it is possible that a combination of inherent constraints on the types of patterns acquired by learners, and the use of output from one level of learning as input to the next, may help to explain why something so complex is mastered readily by the human mind. Human learning mechanisms may themselves have played a prominent role in shaping the structure of human languages.

ACKNOWLEDGMENTS

The preparation of this manuscript was supported by grants from the National Institutes of Health (HD37466) and National Science Foundation (BCS-9983630). I thank Martha Alibali, Erin McMullen, Seth Pollak, Erik Thiessen, and Kim Zinski for comments on a previous version of this manuscript.

NOTES

1. Address correspondence to Jenny R. Saffran, Department of Psychology, University of Wisconsin-Madison, Madison, WJ 53706; e-mail: jsaffran@wisc.edu.
2. Voicing refers to the timing of vibration of the vocal cords. Compared with voiceless consonants, voiced consonants have a shorter lag time between the initial noise burst of the consonant and the subsequent vocal cord vibrations.

REFERENCES

Fiser, J., & Aslin, R. N. (2002). Statistical learning of new visual feature combinations by infants. *Proceedings of the National Academy of Sciences,* USA, *99,* 15822–15826.

Gomez, R. L., & Gerken, L. (1999). Artificial grammar learning by 1-year-olds leads to specific and abstract knowledge. *Cognition, 70,* 109–135.

Hauser, M., Newport, E. L., & Aslin, R. N. (2001). Segmentation of the speech stream in a nonhuman primate: Statistical learning in cotton-top tamarins. *Cognition, 78,* B41–B52.

Kirkham, N. Z., Slemmer, J. A., & Johnson. S. P. (2002). Visual statistical learning in infancy. Evidence of a domain general learning mechanism. *Cognition, 83,* B35–B42.

Maye, J., Werker, J. F., & Gerken. L. (2002). Infant sensitivity to distributional information can affect phonetic discrimination. *Cognition, 82,* B101–B111.

Morgan, J. L., Meier, R. P., & Newport, E. L. (1987). Structural packaging in the input to language learning: Contributions of intonational and morphological marking of phrases to the acquisition of language. *Cognitive Psychology, 19,* 498–550.

Newport, E. L., & Aslin. R. N. (2000). Innately constrained learning: Blending old and new approaches to language acquisition. In S.C. Howell, S.A. Fish, & T. Keith-Lucas (Eds.), *Proceedings of the 24th Boston University Conference on Language Development* (pp. 1–21). Somerville, MA: Cascadilla Press.

Pinker, S., & Bloom, P. (1990). Natural language and natural selection. *Behavioral and Brain Sciences, 13,* 707–784.

Saffran, J. R. (2001a). The use of predictive dependencies in language learning. *Journal of Memory and Language, 44,* 493–515.

Saffran, J. R. (2001b). Words in a sea of sounds: The output of statistical learning. *Cognition, 81,* 149–169.

Saffran, J. R. (2002). Constraints on statistical language learning. *Journal of Memory and Language, 47,* 172–196.

Saffran, J. R., Aslin, R. N., & Newport, E. L. (1996). Statistical learning by 8-month-old infants. *Science, 274,* 1926–1928.

Saffran, J. R., Johnson, E. K., Aslin, R. N., & Newport, E. L. (1999). Statistical learning of tone sequences by human infants and adults. *Cognition, 70,* 27–52.

Saffran, J. R., & Thiessen, E. D. (2003). Pattern induction by infant language learners. *Developmental Psychology, 39,* 484–494.

Saffran, J. R., & Wilson, D. P. (2003). From syllables to syntax: Multi-level statistical learning by 12month-old infants *Infancy, 4,* 273–284.

CHAPTER TWENTY-SEVEN

LOGIC AND CONVERSATION

H. P. GRICE

It is a commonplace of philosophical logic that there are, or appear to be, divergences in meaning between, on the one hand, at least some of what I shall call the formal devices—$\sim$, $\wedge$, $\vee$, $\supset$, $(\forall x)$, $(\exists x)$, (ιx) (when these are given a standard two-valued interpretation) — and, on the other, what are taken to be their analogues or counterparts in natural language — such expressions as *not, and, or, if, all, some* (or *at least one*), *the*. Some logicians may at some time have wanted to claim that there are in fact no such divergences; but such claims, if made at all, have been somewhat rashly made, and those suspected of making them have been subjected to some pretty rough handling.

Those who concede that such divergences exist adhere, in the main, to one or the other of two rival groups, which I shall call the formalist and the informalist groups. An outline of a not uncharacteristic formalist position may be given as follows: Insofar as logicians are concerned with the formulation of very general patterns of valid inference, the formal devices possess a decisive advantage over their natural counterparts. For it will be possible to construct in terms of the formal devices a system of very general formulas, a considerable number of which can be regarded as, or are closely related to, patterns of inferences the expression of which involves some or all of the devices: Such a system may consist of a certain set of simple formulas that must be acceptable if the devices have the meaning that has been assigned to them, and an indefinite number of further formulas, many of which are less obviously acceptable and each of which can be shown to be acceptable if the members of the original set are acceptable. We have, thus, a way of handling dubiously acceptable patterns of inference, and if, as is sometimes possible, we can apply a decision procedure, we have an even better way. Furthermore, from a philosophical point of view, the possession by the natural counterparts of those elements in their meaning, which they do not share with the corresponding formal devices, is to be regarded as an imperfection of natural languages; the elements in question are undesirable excrescences. For the presence of these elements has the result both that the concepts within which they appear cannot be precisely or clearly defined,

From chapter 2 in *Syntax and Semantics 3: Speech Acts,* ed. P. Cole and J. Morgan (New York: Academic Press, 1975), 26–40. Reprinted with permission.

and that at least some statements involving them cannot, in some circumstances, be assigned a definite truth value; and the indefiniteness of these concepts not only is objectionable in itself but also leaves open the way to metaphysics — we cannot be certain that none of these natural language expressions is metaphysically "loaded." For these reasons, the expressions, as used in natural speech, cannot be regarded as finally acceptable, and may turn out to be, finally, not fully intelligible. The proper course is to conceive and begin to construct an ideal language, incorporating the formal devices, the sentences of which will be clear, determinate in truth value, and certifiably free from metaphysical implications; the foundations of science will now be philosophically secure, since the statements of the scientist will be expressible (though not necessarily actually expressed) within this ideal language. (I do not wish to suggest that all formalists would accept the whole of this outline, but I think that all would accept at least some part of it.)

To this, an informalist might reply in the following vein. The philosophical demand for an ideal language rests on certain assumptions that should not be conceded; these are, that the primary yardstick by which to judge the adequacy of a language is its ability to serve the needs of science, that an expression cannot be guaranteed as fully intelligible unless an explication or analysis of its meaning has been provided, and that every explication or analysis must take the form of a precise definition that is the expression or assertion of a logical equivalence. Language serves many important purposes besides those of scientific inquiry; we can know perfectly well what an expression means (and so a fortiori that it is intelligible) without knowing its analysis, and the provision of an analysis may (and usually does) consist in the specification, as generalized as possible, of the conditions that count for or against the applicability of the expression being analyzed. Moreover, while it is no doubt true that the formal devices are especially amenable to systematic treatment by the logician, it remains the case that there are very many inferences and arguments, expressed in natural language and not in terms of these devices, which are nevertheless recognizably valid. So there must be a place for an unsimplified, and so more or less unsystematic, logic of the natural counterparts of these devices; this logic may be aided and guided by the simplified logic of the formal devices but cannot be supplanted by it. Indeed, not only do the two logics differ, but sometimes they come into conflict; rules that hold for a formal device may not hold for its natural counterpart.

On the general question of the place in philosophy of the reformation of natural language, I shall, in this essay, have nothing to say. I shall confine myself to the dispute in its relation to the alleged divergences. I have, moreover, no intention of entering the fray on behalf of either contestant. I wish, rather, to maintain that the common assumption of the contestants that the divergences do in fact exist is (broadly speaking) a common mistake, and that the mistake arises from inadequate attention to the nature and importance of the conditions governing conversation. I shall, therefore, inquire into the general conditions that, in one way or another, apply to conversation as such, irrespective of its subject matter. I begin with a characterization of the notion of "implicature."

27.1   IMPLICATURE

Suppose that A and B are talking about a mutual friend, C, who is now working in a bank. A asks B how C is getting on in his job, and B replies, *Oh quite well, I think; he likes his colleagues, and he hasn't been to prison yet.* At this point, A might well inquire what B was implying, what he was suggesting, or even what he meant by saying that C had not yet been to prison. The answer might be any one of such things as that C is the sort of person likely to yield to the temptation provided by his occupation, that C's colleagues are really very unpleasant and treacherous people, and so forth. It might, of course, be quite unnecessary for A to make such an inquiry of B, the answer to it being, in the context, clear in advance. It is clear that whatever B implied, suggested, meant in this example, is distinct from what B said, which was simply that C had not been to prison yet. I wish to introduce, as terms of art, the verb *implicate* and the related nouns *implicature* (cf. *implying*) and *implicatum* (cf. *what is implied*). The point of this maneuver is to avoid having, on each occasion, to choose between this or that member of the family of verbs for which *implicate* is to do general duty. I shall, for the time being at least, have to assume to a considerable extent an intuitive understanding of the meaning of *say* in such contexts, and an ability to recognize particular verbs as members of the family with which *implicate* is associated. I can, however, make one or two remarks that may help to clarify the more problematic of these assumptions, namely, that connected with the meaning of the word *say*.

In the sense in which I am using the word *say,* I intend what someone has said to be closely related to the conventional meaning of the words (the sentence) he has uttered. Suppose someone to have uttered the sentence *He is in the grip of a vice.* Given a knowledge of the English language, but no knowledge of the circumstances of the utterance, one would know something about what the speaker had said on the assumption that he was speaking standard English, and speaking literally. One would know that he had said, about some particular male person or animal *x,* that at the time of the utterance (whatever that was), either (1) *x* was unable to rid himself of a certain kind of bad character trait or (2) some part of *x*'s person was caught in a certain kind of tool or instrument (approximate account, of course). But for a full identification of what the speaker had said, one would need to know (a) the identity of *x,* (b) the time of utterance, and (c) the meaning, on the particular occasion of utterance, of the phrase *in the grip of a vice* [a decision between (1) and (2)]. This brief indication of my use of *say* leaves it open whether a man who says (today) *Harold Wilson is a great man* and another who says (also today) *The British Prime Minister is a great man* would, if each knew that the two singular terms had the same reference, have said the same thing. But whatever decision is made about this question, the apparatus that I am about to provide will be capable of accounting for any implicatures that might depend on the presence of one rather than another of these singular terms in the sentence uttered. Such implicatures would merely be related to different maxims.

In some cases the conventional meaning of the words used will determine what is implicated, besides helping to determine what is said. If I say (smugly), *He is an Englishman; he is, therefore, brave,* I have certainly committed myself, by virtue of the meaning of my words, to its being the case that his being brave is a consequence of (follows from) his being an Englishman. But while I have said that he is an Englishman, and said that he is brave, I do not want to say that I have *said* (in the favored sense) that it follows from his being an Englishman that he is brave, though I have certainly indicated, and so implicated, that this is so. I do not want to say that my utterance of this sentence would be, *strictly speaking,* false should the consequence in question fail to hold. So *some* implicatures are conventional, unlike the one with which I introduced this discussion of implicature.

I wish to represent a certain subclass of nonconventional implicatures, which I shall call *conversational* implicatures, as being essentially connected with certain general features of discourse; so my next step is to try to say what these features are. The following may provide a first approximation to a general principle. Our talk exchanges do not normally consist of a succession of disconnected remarks, and would not be rational if they did. They are characteristically, to some degree at least, cooperative efforts; and each participant recognizes in them, to some extent, a common purpose or set of purposes, or at least a mutually accepted direction. This purpose or direction may be fixed from the start (e.g., by an initial proposal of a question for discussion), or it may evolve during the exchange; it may be fairly definite, or it may be so indefinite as to leave very considerable latitude to the participants (as in a casual conversation). But at each stage, *some* possible conversational moves would be excluded as conversationally unsuitable. We might then formulate a rough general principle which participants will be expected (ceteris paribus) to observe, namely: Make your conversational contribution such as is required, at the stage at which it occurs, by the accepted purpose or direction of the talk exchange in which you are engaged. One might label this the Cooperative Principle.

On the assumption that some such general principle as this is acceptable, one may perhaps distinguish four categories under one or another of which will fall certain more specific maxims and submaxims, the following of which will, in general, yield results in accordance with the Cooperative Principle. Echoing Kant, I call these categories Quantity, Quality, Relation, and Manner. The category of Quantity relates to the quantity of information to be provided, and under it fall the following maxims:

1. Make your contribution as informative as is required (for the current purposes of the exchange).
2. Do not make your contribution more informative than is required.

(The second maxim is disputable; it might be said that to be overinformative is not a transgression of the Cooperative Principle but merely a waste of time. However, it might be answered that such overinformativeness may be confusing in that it is liable to raise side issues; and there may also be an indirect effect, in that the hearers may be misled as a result of thinking that there is some particular *point* in the provision of the excess of information. However this may be, there is perhaps a different reason for doubt about the admission of this second maxim, namely, that its effect will be secured by a later maxim, which concerns relevance.)

Under the category of Quality falls a supermaxim — "Try to make your contribution one that is true" — and two more specific maxims:

1. Do not say what you believe to be false.
2. Do not say that for which you lack adequate evidence.

Under the category of Relation I place a single maxim, namely, "Be relevant." Though the maxim itself is terse, its formulation conceals a number of problems that exercise me a good deal: questions about what different kinds and focuses of relevance there may be, how these shift in the course of a talk exchange, how to allow for the fact that subjects of conversation are legitimately changed, and so on. I find the treatment of such questions exceedingly difficult, and I hope to revert to them in later work.

Finally, under the category of Manner, which I understand as relating not (like the previous categories) to what is said but, rather, to *how* what is said is to be said, I include the supermaxim — "Be perspicuous" — and various maxims such as:

1. Avoid obscurity of expression.
2. Avoid ambiguity.
3. Be brief (avoid unnecessary prolixity).
4. Be orderly.

And one might need others.

It is obvious that the observance of some of these maxims is a matter of less urgency than is the observance of others; a man who has expressed himself with undue prolixity would, in general, be open to milder comment than would a man who has said something he believes to be false. Indeed, it might be felt that the importance of at least the first maxim of Quality is such that it should not be included in a scheme of the kind I am constructing; other maxims come into operation only on the assumption that this maxim of Quality is satisfied. While this may be correct, so far as the generation of implicatures is concerned it seems to play a role not totally different from the other maxims, and it will be convenient, for the present at least, to treat it as a member of the list of maxims.

There are, of course, all sorts of other maxims (aesthetic, social, or moral in character), such as "Be polite," that are also normally observed by participants in talk exchanges, and these may also generate nonconventional implicatures. The conversational maxims, however, and the conversational implicatures connected with them, are specially connected (I hope) with the particular purposes that talk (and so, talk exchange) is adapted to serve and is primarily employed to serve. I have stated my maxims as if this purpose were a maximally effective exchange of information; this specification is, of course, too narrow, and the scheme needs to be generalized to allow for such general purposes as influencing or directing the actions of others.

As one of my avowed aims is to see talking as a special case or variety of purposive, indeed rational, behavior, it may be worth noting that the specific expectations or presumptions connected with at least some of the foregoing maxims have their analogues in the sphere of transactions that are not talk exchanges. I list briefly one such analogue for each conversational category.

1. *Quantity.*   If you are assisting me to mend a car, I expect your contribution to be neither more nor less than is required. If, for example, at a particular stage I need four screws, I expect you to hand me four, rather than two or six.
2. *Quality.*   I expect your contributions to be genuine and not spurious. If I need sugar as an ingredient in the cake you are assisting me to make, I do not expect you to hand me salt; if I need a spoon, I do not expect a trick spoon made of rubber.
3. *Relation.*   I expect a partner's contribution to be appropriate to the immediate needs at each stage of the transaction. If I am mixing ingredients for a cake, I do not expect to be handed a good book, or even an oven cloth (though this might be an appropriate contribution at a later stage).
4. *Manner.*   I expect a partner to make it clear what contribution he is making and to execute his performance with reasonable dispatch.

These analogies are relevant to what I regard as a fundamental question about the Cooperative Principle and its attendant maxims, namely, what the basis is for the assumption which we seem to make, and on which (I hope) it will appear that a great range of implicatures depends, that talkers will in general (ceteris paribus and in the absence of indications to the contrary) proceed in the manner that these principles prescribe. A dull but, no doubt at a certain level, adequate answer is that it is just a well-recognized empirical fact that people do behave in these ways; they learned to do so in childhood and have not lost the habit of doing so; and, indeed, it would involve a good deal of effort to make a radical departure from the habit. It is much easier, for example, to tell the truth than to invent lies.

I am, however, enough of a rationalist to want to find a basis that underlies these facts, undeniable though they may be; I would like to be able to think of the standard type of conversational practice not merely as something that all or most do *in fact* follow but as something that it is *reasonable* for us to follow, that we *should not* abandon. For a time, I was attracted by the idea that observance of the Cooperative Principle and the maxims, in a talk exchange, could be thought of as a quasi-contractual matter, with parallels outside the realm of discourse. If you pass by when I am struggling with my stranded car, I no doubt have some degree of expectation that you will offer help, but once you join me in tinkering under the hood, my expectations become stronger and take more specific forms (in the absence of indications that you are merely an incompetent meddler); and talk exchanges seemed to me to exhibit, characteristically, certain features that jointly distinguish cooperative transactions:

1. The participants have some common immediate aim, like getting a car mended; their ultimate aims may, of course, be independent and even in conflict — each may want to get the car mended in order to drive off, leaving the other stranded. In characteristic talk exchanges, there is a common aim even if, as in an over-the-wall chat, it is a second-order one, namely, that each party should, for the time being, identify himself with the transitory conversational interests of the other.
2. The contributions of the participants should be dovetailed, mutually dependent.
3. There is some sort of understanding (which may be explicit but which is often tacit) that, other things being equal, the transaction should continue in appropriate style unless both parties are agreeable that it should terminate. You do not just shove off or start doing something else.

But while some such quasi-contractual basis as this may apply to some cases, there are too many types of exchange, like quarreling and letter writing, that it fails to fit comfortably. In any case, one feels that the talker who is irrelevant or obscure has primarily let down not his audience but himself. So I would like to be able to show that observance of the Cooperative Principle and maxims is reasonable (rational) along the following lines: that anyone who cares about the goals that are central to conversation/communication (such as giving and receiving information, influencing and being influenced by others) must be expected to have an interest, given suitable circumstances, in participation in talk exchanges that will be profitable only on the assumption that they are conducted in general accordance with the Cooperative Principle and the maxims. Whether any such conclusion can be reached, I am uncertain; in any case, I am fairly sure that I cannot reach it until I am a good deal clearer about the nature of relevance and of the circumstances in which it is required.

It is now time to show the connection between the Cooperative Principle and maxims, on the one hand, and conversational implicature on the other.

A participant in a talk exchange may fail to fulfill a maxim in various ways, which include the following:

1. He may quietly and unostentatiously *violate* a maxim; if so, in some cases he will be liable to mislead.
2. He may *opt out* from the operation both of the maxim and of the Cooperative Principle; he may say, indicate, or allow it to become plain that he is unwilling to cooperate in the way the maxim requires. He may say, for example, *I cannot say more; my lips are sealed.*
3. He may be faced by a *clash:* He may be unable, for example, to fulfill the first maxim of Quantity (Be as informative as is required) without violating the second maxim of Quality (Have adequate evidence for what you say).
4. He may *flout* a maxim; that is, he may blatantly fail to fulfill it. On the assumption that the speaker is able to fulfill the maxim and to do so without violating another maxim (because of a clash), is not opting out, and is not, in view of the blatancy of his performance, trying to mislead, the hearer is faced with a minor problem: How can his saying what he did say be reconciled with the supposition that he is observing the overall Cooperative Principle? This situation is one that characteristically gives rise to a conversational implicature; and when a conversational implicature is generated in this way, I shall say that a maxim is being *exploited.*

I am now in a position to characterize the notion of conversational implicature. A man who, by (in, when) saying (or making as if to say) that *p* has implicated that *q,* may be said to have conversationally implicated that *q,* provided that (1) he is to be presumed to be observing the conversational maxims, or at least the Cooperative Principle; (2) the supposition that he is aware that, or thinks that, *q* is required in order to make his saying or making as if to say *p* (or doing so in *those* terms) consistent with this presumption; and (3) the speaker thinks (and would expect the hearer to think that the speaker thinks) that it is within the competence of the hearer to work out, or grasp intuitively, that the supposition mentioned in (2) is required. Apply this to my initial example, to B's remark that C has not yet been to prison. In a suitable setting A might reason as follows: "(1) B has apparently violated the maxim 'Be relevant' and so may be regarded as having flouted one of the maxims conjoining perspicuity, yet I have no reason to suppose that he is opting out from the operation of the Cooperative Principle; (2) given the circumstances, I can regard his irrelevance as only apparent if, and only if, I suppose him to think that C is potentially dishonest; (3) B knows that I am capable of working out step (2). So B implicates that C is potentially dishonest."

The presence of a conversational implicature must be capable of being worked out; for even if it can in fact be intuitively grasped, unless the intuition is replaceable by an argument, the implicature (if present at all) will not count as a conversational implicature; it will be a conventional implicature. To work out that a particular conversational implicature is present, the hearer will rely on the following data: (1) the conventional meaning of the words used, together with the identity of any references that may be involved; (2) the Cooperative Principle and its maxims; (3) the context, linguistic or otherwise, of the utterance; (4) other items of background knowledge; and (5) the fact (or supposed fact) that all relevant items falling under the previous headings are available to both participants and both participants know or assume this to be the case. A general pattern for the working out of a conversational implicature might be given as follows: "He has said that p; there is no reason to suppose that he is not observing the maxims, or at least the Cooperative Principle; he could not be doing this unless he thought that q; he knows (and knows that I know that he knows) that I can see that the supposition that he thinks that q is required; he has done nothing to stop me thinking that q; he intends me to think, or is at least willing to allow me to think, that q; and so he has implicated that q."

27.2 EXAMPLES OF CONVERSATIONAL IMPLICATURE

I shall now offer a number of examples, which I shall divide into three groups.

Group A: *Examples in which no maxim is violated, or at least in which it is not clear that any maxim is violated*

A is standing by an obviously immobilized car and is approached by B; the following exchange takes place:

    1. A: *I am out of petrol.*
         B: *There is a garage round the corner.*

(Gloss: B would be infringing the maxim "Be relevant" unless he thinks, or thinks it possible, that the garage is open, and has petrol to sell; so he implicates that the garage is, or at least may be open, etc.)

In this example, unlike the case of the remark *He hasn't been to prison yet,* the unstated connection between B's remark and A's remark is so obvious that, even if one interprets the supermaxim of Manner, "Be perspicuous," as applying not only to the expression of what is said but also to the connection of what is said with adjacent remarks, there seems to be no case for regarding that supermaxim as infringed in this example. The next example is perhaps a little less clear in this respect:

    2. A: *Smith doesn't seem to have a girlfriend these days.*
         B: *He has been paying a lot of visits to New York lately.*

B implicates that Smith has, or may have, a girlfriend in New York. (A gloss is unnecessary in view of that given for the previous example.)

In both examples, the speaker implicates that which he must be assumed to believe in order to preserve the assumption that he is observing the maxim of Relation.

Group B: *Examples in which a maxim is violated, but its violation is to be explained by the supposition of a clash with another maxim*

A is planning with B an itinerary for a holiday in France. Both know that A wants to see his friend C, if to do so would not involve too great a prolongation of his journey:

    3. A: *Where does C live?*
         B: *Somewhere in the South of France.*

(Gloss: There is no reason to suppose that B is opting out; his answer is, as he well knows, less informative than is required to meet A's needs. This infringement of the first maxim of Quantity can be explained only by the supposition that B is aware that to be more informative would be to say something that infringed the second maxim of Quality. "Don't say what you lack adequate evidence for," so B implicates that he does not know in which town C lives.)

Group C: *Examples that involve exploitation, that is, a procedure by which a maxim is flouted for the purpose of getting in a conversational implicature by means of something of the nature of a figure of speech*

In these examples, though some maxim is violated at the level of what is said, the hearer is entitled to assume that that maxim, or at least the overall Cooperative Principle, is observed at the level of what is implicated.

(1a) *A flouting of the first maxim of Quantity*

A is writing a testimonial about a pupil who is a candidate for a philosophy job, and his letter reads as follows: "Dear Sir, Mr. X's command of English is excellent, and his attendance at tutorials has been regular. Yours, etc." (Gloss: A cannot be opting out, since if he wished to be uncooperative, why write at all? He cannot be unable, through ignorance, to say more, since the man is his pupil; moreover, he knows that more information than this is wanted. He must, therefore, be wishing to impart information that he is reluctant to write down. This supposition is tenable only if he thinks Mr. X is no good at philosophy. This, then, is what he is implicating.)

Extreme examples of a flouting of the first maxim of Quantity are provided by utterances of patent tautologies like *Women are women* and *War is war.* I would wish to maintain that at the level of what is said, in my favored sense, such remarks are totally noninformative and so, at that level, cannot but infringe the first maxim of Quantity in any conversational context. They are, of course, informative at the level of what is implicated, and the hearer's identification of their informative content at this level is dependent on his ability to explain the speaker's selection of this particular patent tautology.

(1b) *An infringement of the second maxim of Quantity, "Do not give more information than is required," on the assumption that the existence of such a maxim should be admitted*

A wants to know whether *p,* and B volunteers not only the information that *p,* but information to the effect that it is certain that *p,* and that the evidence for its being the case that *p* is so-and-so and such-and-such.

B's volubility may be undesigned, and if it is so regarded by A it may raise in A's mind a doubt as to whether B is as certain as he says he is ("Methinks the lady doth protest too much"). But if it is thought of as designed, it would be an oblique way of conveying that it is to some degree controversial whether or not *p.* It is, however, arguable that such an implicature could be explained by reference to the maxim of Relation without invoking an alleged second maxim of Quantity.

(2a) *Examples in which the first maxim of Quality is flouted*

Irony. X, with whom A has been on close terms until now, has betrayed a secret of A's to a business rival. A and his audience both know this. A says *X is a fine friend.* (Gloss: It is perfectly obvious to A and his audience that what A has said or has made as if to say is something he does not believe, and the audience knows that A knows that this is obvious to the audience. So, unless A's utterance is entirely pointless, A must be trying to get across some other proposition than the one he purports to be putting forward. This must be some obviously related proposition; the most obviously related proposition is the contradictory of the one he purports to be putting forward.)

Metaphor. Examples like *You are the cream in my coffee* characteristically involve categorial falsity, so the contradictory of what the speaker has made as if to say will, strictly speaking, be a truism; so it cannot be *that* that such a speaker is trying to get across. The most likely supposition is that the speaker is attributing to his audience some feature or features in respect of which the audience resembles (more or less fancifully) the mentioned substance.

It is possible to combine metaphor and irony by imposing on the hearer two stages of interpretation. I say *You are the cream in my coffee,* intending the hearer to reach first the metaphor interpretant "You are my pride and joy" and then the irony interpretant "You are my bane."

Meiosis. Of a man known to have broken up all the furniture, one says *He was a little intoxicated.*

Hyperbole. Every nice girl loves a sailor.

(2b) Examples in which the second maxim of Quality, "Do not say that for which you lack adequate evidence," is flouted are perhaps not easy to find, but the following seems to be a specimen. I say of X's wife, *She is probably deceiving him this evening.* In a suitable context, or with a suitable gesture or tone of voice, it may be clear that I have no adequate reason for supposing this to be the case. My partner, to preserve the assumption that the conversational game is still being played, assumes that I am getting at some related proposition for the acceptance of which I do have a reasonable basis. The related proposition might well be that she is given to deceiving her husband, or possibly that she is the sort of person who would not stop short of such conduct.

(3) *Examples in which an implicature is achieved by real, as distinct from apparent, violation of the maxim of Relation* are perhaps rare but the following seems to be a good candidate. At a genteel tea party, A says *Mrs. X is an old bag.* There is a moment of appalled silence, and then B says *The weather has been quite delightful this summer, hasn't it?* B has blatantly refused to make what he says relevant to A's preceding remark. He thereby implicates that A's remark should not be discussed and, perhaps more specifically, that A has committed a social gaffe.

(4) *Examples in which various maxims falling under the supermaxim "Be perspicuous" are flouted*

Ambiguity. We must remember that we are concerned only with ambiguity that is deliberate, and that the speaker intends or expects to be recognized by his hearer. The problem the hearer has to solve is why a speaker should, when still playing the conversational game, go out of his way to choose an ambiguous utterance. There are two types of cases:

(a) Examples in which there is no difference, or no striking difference, between two interpretations of an utterance with respect to straightforwardness; neither interpretation is notably more sophisticated, less standard, more recondite or more far-fetched than the other. We might consider Blake's lines: "Never seek to tell thy love, Love that never told can be." To avoid the complications introduced by the presence of the imperative mood, I shall consider the related sentence, *I sought to tell my love, love that never told can be.* There may be a double ambiguity here. *My love* may refer to either a state of emotion or an object of emotion, and *love that never told can be* may mean either "Love that cannot be told" or "love that if told cannot continue to exist." Partly because of the sophistication of the poet and partly because of internal evidence (that the ambiguity is kept up), there seems to be no alternative to supposing that the ambiguities are deliberate and that the poet is conveying both what he would be saying if one interpretation were intended rather than the other, and vice versa; though no doubt the poet is not explicitly saying any one of these things but only conveying or suggesting them (cf. "Since she [nature] pricked thee out for women's pleasure, mine be thy love, and thy love's use their treasure").

(b) Examples in which one interpretation is notably less straightforward than another. Take the complex example of the British General who captured the province of Sind and sent back the message *Peccavi*. The ambiguity involved ("I have Sind"/"I have sinned") is phonemic, not morphemic; and the expression actually used is unambiguous, but since it is in a language foreign to speaker and hearer, translation is called for, and the ambiguity resides in the standard translation into native English.

Whether or not the straightforward interpretant ("I have sinned") is being conveyed, it seems that the nonstraightforward interpretant must be. There might be stylistic reasons for conveying by a sentence merely its nonstraightforward interpretant, but it would be pointless, and perhaps also stylistically objectionable, to go to the trouble of finding an expression that nonstraight-forwardly conveys that *p,* thus imposing on an audience the effort involved in finding this interpretant, if this interpretant were otiose so far as communication was concerned. Whether the straightforward interpretant is also being conveyed seems to depend on whether such a supposition would conflict with other conversational requirements, for example, would it be relevant, would it be something the speaker could be supposed to accept, and so on. If such requirements are not satisfied, then the straightforward interpretant is not being conveyed. If they are, it is. If the author of *Peccavi* could naturally be supposed to think that he had committed some kind of transgression, for example, had disobeyed his orders in capturing Sind, and if reference to such a transgression would be relevant to the presumed interests of the audience, then he would have been conveying both interpretants: otherwise he would be conveying only the nonstraightforward one.

Obscurity. How do I exploit, for the purposes of communication, a deliberate and overt violation of the requirement that I should avoid obscurity? Obviously, if the Cooperative Principle is to operate, I must intend my partner to understand what I am saying despite the obscurity I import into my utterance. Suppose that A and B are having a conversation in the presence of a third party, for example, a child, then A might be deliberately obscure, though not too obscure, in the hope that B would understand and the third party not. Furthermore, if A expects B to see that A is being deliberately obscure, it seems reasonable to suppose that, in making his conversational contribution in this way, A is implicating that the contents of his communication should not be imparted to the third party.

Failure to be brief or succinct. Compare the remarks:

(a) *Miss X sang "Home Sweet Home."*
(b) *Miss X produced a series of sounds that corresponded closely with the score of "Home Sweet Home."*

Suppose that a reviewer has chosen to utter (b) rather than (a). (Gloss: Why has he selected that rigmarole in place of the concise and nearly synonymous *sang?* Presumably, to indicate some striking difference between Miss X's performance and those to which the word *singing* is usually applied. The most obvious supposition is that Miss X's performance suffered from some hideous defect. The reviewer knows that this supposition is what is likely to spring to mind, so that is what he is implicating.)

27.3   GENERALIZED CONVERSATIONAL IMPLICATURE

I have so far considered only cases of what I might call "particularized conversational implicature" — that is to say, cases in which an implicature is carried by saying that *p* on a particular occasion in virtue of special features of the context, cases in which there is no room for the the idea that an implicature of this sort is normally carried by saying that *p*. But there are cases of generalized conversational implicature. Sometimes one can say that the use of a certain form of words in an utterance would normally (in the absence of special circumstances) carry such-and-such an implicature or type of implicature. Noncontroversial examples are perhaps hard to find, since it is all too easy to treat a generalized conversational implicature as if it were a conventional implicature. I offer an example that I hope may be fairly noncontroversial.

Anyone who uses a sentence of the form *X is meeting a woman this evening* would normally implicate that the person to be met was someone other than X's wife, mother, sister, or perhaps even close platonic friend. Similarly, if I were to say *X went into a house yesterday and found a tortoise inside the front door,* my hearer would normally be surprised if some time later I revealed that the house was X's own. I could produce similar linguistic phenomena involving the expressions *a garden, a car, a college,* and so on. Sometimes, however, there would normally be no such implicature ("I have been sitting in a car all morning"), and sometimes a reverse implicature ("I broke a finger yesterday"). I am inclined to think that one would not lend a sympathetic ear to a philosopher who suggested that there are three senses of the form of expression *an X:* one in which it means roughly "something that satisfies the conditions defining the word X," another in which it means approximately "an X (in the first sense) that is only remotely related in a certain way to some person indicated by the context," and yet another in which it means "an X (in the first sense) that is closely related in a certain way to some person indicated by the context." Would we not much prefer an account on the following lines (which, of course, may be incorrect in detail): When someone, by using the form of expression *an X,* implicates that the X does not belong to or is not otherwise closely connected with some identifiable person, the implicature is present because the speaker has failed to be specific in a way in which he might have been expected to be specific, with the consequence that it is likely to be assumed that he is not in a position to be specific. This is a familiar implicature situation and is classifiable as a failure, for one reason or another, to fulfill the first maxim of Quantity. The only difficult question is why it should, in certain cases, be presumed, independently of information about particular contexts of utterance, that specification of the closeness or remoteness of the connection between a particular person or object and a further person who is mentioned or indicated by the utterance should be likely to be of interest. The answer must lie in the following region: Transactions between a person and other persons or things closely connected with him are liable to be very different as regards their concomitants and results from the same sort of transactions involving only remotely connected persons or things; the concomitants and results, for instance, of my finding a hole in my roof are likely to be very different from the concomitants and results of my finding a hole in someone else's roof. Information, like money, is often given without the giver's knowing to just what use the recipient will want to put it. If someone to whom a transaction is mentioned gives it further consideration, he is likely to find himself wanting the answers to further questions that the speaker may not be able to identify in advance; if the appropriate specification will be likely to enable the hearer to answer a considerable variety of such questions for himself, then there is a presumption that the speaker should include it in his remark; if not, then there is no such presumption.

Finally, we can now show that, conversational implicature being what it is, it must possess certain features:

1. Since, to assume the presence of a conversational implicature, we have to assume that at least the Cooperative Principle is being observed, and since it is possible to opt out of the observation of this principle, it follows that a generalized conversational implicature can be canceled in a particular case. It may be explicitly canceled, by the addition of a clause that states or implies that the speaker has opted out, or it may be contextually canceled, if the form of utterance that usually carries it is used in a context that makes it clear that the speaker is opting out.

2. Insofar as the calculation that a particular conversational implicature is present requires, besides contextual and background information, only a knowledge of what has been said (or of the conventional commitment of the utterance), and insofar as the manner of expression plays no role in the calculation, it will not be possible to find another way of saying the same thing, which simply lacks the implicature in question, except where some special feature of the substituted version is itself relevant to the determination of an implicature (in virtue of one of the maxims of Manner). If we call this feature nondetachability, one may expect a generalized conversational implicature that is carried by a familiar, nonspecial locution to have a high degree of nondetachability.

3. To speak approximately, since the calculation of the presence of a conversational implicature presupposes an initial knowledge of the conventional force of the expression the utterance of which carries the implicature, a conversational implicatum will be a condition that is not included in the original specification of the expression's conventional force. Though it may not be impossible for what starts life, so to speak, as a conversational implicature to become conventionalized, to suppose that this is so in a given case would require special justification. So, initially at least, conversational implicata are not part of the meaning of the expressions to the employment of which they attach.

4. Since the truth of a conversational implicatum is not required by the truth of what is said (what is said may be true — what is implicated may be false), the implicature is not carried by what is said, but only by the saying of what is said, or by "putting it that way."

5. Since, to calculate a conversational implicature is to calculate what has to be supposed in order to preserve the supposition that the Cooperative Principle is being observed, and since there may be various possible specific explanations, a list of which may be open, the conversational implicatum in such cases will be disjunction of such specific explanations; and if the list of these is open, the implicatum will have just the kind of indeterminacy that many actual implicata do in fact seem to possess.

CHAPTER TWENTY-EIGHT

THE THEORY OF MULTIPLE INTELLIGENCES: IN A NUTSHELL

HOWARD E. GARDNER

Allow me to transport all of us to the Paris of 1900 — La Belle Epoque — when the city fathers of Paris approached a psychologist named Alfred Binet with an unusual request: Could he devise some kind of a measure that would predict which youngsters would succeed and which would fail in the primary grades of Paris schools? As everybody knows, Binet succeeded. In short order, his discovery came to be called the "intelligence test"; his measure, the "IQ." Like other Parisian fashions, the IQ soon made its way to the United States, where it enjoyed a modest success until World War I. Then, it was used to test over one million American recruits, and it had truly arrived. From that day on, the IQ test has looked like psychology's biggest success — a genuinely useful scientific tool.

What is the vision that led to the excitement about IQ? At least in the West, people had always relied on intuitive assessments of how smart other people were. Now intelligence seemed to be quantifiable. You could measure someone's actual or potential height, and now, it seemed, you could also measure someone's actual or potential intelligence. We had one dimension of mental ability along which we could array everyone.

The search for the perfect measure of intelligence has proceeded apace. Here, for example, are some quotations from an ad for a widely used test:

> Need an individual test which quickly provides a stable and reliable estimate of intelligence in four or five minutes per form? Has three forms? Does not depend on verbal production or subjective scoring? Can be used with the severely physically handicapped (even paralyzed) if they can signal yes or no? Handles two-year-olds and superior adults with the same short series of items and the same format? Only $16.00 complete.

Now, that's quite a claim. The American psychologist Arthur Jensen suggests that we could look at reaction time to assess intelligence: a set of lights go on; how quickly can the subject react? The British psychologist Hans Eysenck suggests that investigators of intelligence should look directly at brain waves.

There are also, of course, more sophisticated versions of the IQ test. One of them is called the Scholastic Aptitude Test (SAT). It purports to be a similar kind of measure, and if you add up a person's verbal and math scores, as is often done, you can rate him or her along a single intellectual dimension. Programs for the gifted, for example, often use that kind of measure; if your IQ is in excess of 130, you're admitted to the program.

I want to suggest that along with this one-dimensional view of how to assess people's minds comes a corresponding view of school, which I will call the "uniform view." In the uniform school, there is a core curriculum, a set of facts that everybody should know, and very few electives. The better students, perhaps those with higher IQs, are allowed to take courses that call upon critical reading, calculation, and thinking skills. In the "uniform school," there are regular assessments, using paper and pencil instruments, of the IQ or SAT variety. They yield reliable rankings of people; the best and the brightest get into the better colleges, and perhaps — but only perhaps — they will also get better rankings in life. There is no question but that this approach works well for certain people — schools such as Harvard are eloquent testimony to that. Since this measurement and selection system is clearly meritocratic in certain respects, it has something to recommend it.

But there is an alternative vision that I would like to present — one based on a radically different view of the mind, and one that yields a very different view of school. It is a pluralistic view of mind, recognizing many different and discrete facets of cognition, acknowledging that people have different cognitive strengths and contrasting cognitive styles. I would also like to introduce the concept of an individual-centered school that takes this multifaceted view of intelligence seriously. This model for a school is based in part on findings from sciences that did not even exist in Binet's time: cognitive science (the study of the mind), and neuroscience (the study of the brain). One such approach I have called my "theory of multiple intelligences." Let me tell you something about its sources, its claims, and its educational implications for a possible school of the future.

Dissatisfaction with the concept of IQ and with unitary views of intelligence is fairly widespread — one thinks, for instance, of the work of L. L. Thurstone, J. P. Guilford, and other critics. From my point of view, however, these criticisms do not suffice. The whole concept has to be challenged; in fact, it has to be replaced.

I believe that we should get away altogether from tests and correlations among tests, and look instead at more naturalistic sources of information about how peoples around the world develop skills important to their way of life. Think, for example, of sailors in the South Seas, who find their way around hundreds, or even thousands, of islands by looking at the constellations of stars in the sky, feeling the way a boat passes over the water, and noticing a few scattered landmarks. A word for intelligence in a society of these sailors would probably refer to that kind of navigational ability. Think of surgeons and engineers, hunters and fishermen, dancers and choreographers, athletes and athletic coaches, tribal chiefs and sorcerers. All of these different roles need to be taken into account if we accept the way I define intelligence — that is, as the ability to solve problems, or to fashion products, that are valued in one or more cultural or community settings. For the moment I am saying nothing about whether there is one dimension, or more than one dimension, of intelligence; nothing about whether intelligence is inborn or developed. Instead I emphasize the ability to solve problems and to fashion products. In my work I seek the building blocks of the intelligences used by the aforementioned sailors and surgeons and sorcerers.

The science in this enterprise, to the extent that it exists, involves trying to discover the *right* description of the intelligences. What is an intelligence? To try to answer this question, I have, with my colleagues, surveyed a wide set of sources which, to my knowledge, have never been considered together before. One source is what we already know concerning the development of different kinds of skills in normal children. Another source, and a very important one, is information on the ways that these abilities break down under conditions of brain damage. When one suffers a stroke or some other kind of brain damage, various abilities can be destroyed, or spared, in isolation from other abilities. This research with brain-damaged patients yields a very powerful kind of evidence, because it seems to reflect the way the nervous system has evolved over the millennia to yield certain discrete kinds of intelligence.

My research group looks at other special populations as well: prodigies, idiot savants, autistic children, children with learning disabilities, all of whom exhibit very jagged cognitive profiles — profiles that are extremely difficult to explain in terms of a unitary view of intelligence. We examine cognition in diverse animal species and in dramatically different cultures. Finally, we consider two kinds of psychological evidence: correlations among psychological tests of the sort yielded by a careful statistical analysis of a test battery; and the results of efforts of skill training. When you train a person in skill A, for example, does that training transfer to skill B? So, for example, does training in mathematics enhance one's musical abilities, or vice versa?

Obviously, through looking at all these sources — information on development, on breakdowns, on special populations, and the like — we end up with a cornucopia of information. Optimally, we would perform a statistical factor analysis, feeding all the data into a computer and noting the kinds of factors or intelligences that are extracted. Alas, the kind of material with which I was working didn't exist in a form that is susceptible to computation, and so we had to perform a more subjective factor analysis. In truth, we simply studied the results as best we could, and tried to organize them in a way that made sense to us, and hopefully, to critical readers as well. My resulting list of seven intelligences is a preliminary attempt to organize this mass of information.

I want now to mention briefly the seven intelligences we have located, and to cite one or two examples of each intelligence. Linguistic intelligence is the kind of ability exhibited in its fullest form, perhaps, by poets. Logical-mathematical intelligence, as the name implies, is logical and mathematical ability, as well as scientific ability. Jean Piaget, the great developmental psychologist, thought he was studying *all* intelligence, but I believe he was studying the development of logical-mathematical intelligence. Although I name the linguistic and logical-mathematical intelligences first, it is not because I think they are the most important — in fact, I am convinced that all seven of the intelligences have equal claim to priority. In our society, however, we have put linguistic and logical-mathematical intelligences, figuratively speaking, on a pedestal. Much of our testing is based on this high valuation of verbal and mathematical skills. If you do well in language and logic, you should do well in IQ tests and SATs, and you may well get into a prestigious college, but whether you do well once you leave is probably going to depend as much on the extent to which you possess and use the other intelligences, and it is to those that I want to give equal attention.

Spatial intelligence is the ability to form a mental model of a spatial world and to be able to maneuver and operate using that model. Sailors, engineers, surgeons, sculptors, and painters, to name just a few examples, all have highly developed spatial intelligence. Musical intelligence is the fourth category of ability we have identified: Leonard Bernstein had lots of it; Mozart, presumably, had even more. Bodily-kinesthetic intelligence is the ability to solve problems or to fashion products using one's whole body, or parts of the body. Dancers, athletes, surgeons, and craftspeople all exhibit highly developed bodily-kinesthetic intelligence.

Finally, I propose two forms of personal intelligence — not well understood, elusive to study, but immensely important. Interpersonal intelligence is the ability to understand other people: what motivates them, how they work, how to work cooperatively with them. Successful salespeople, politicians, teachers, clinicians, and religious leaders are all likely to be individuals with high degrees of interpersonal intelligence. Intrapersonal intelligence, a seventh kind of intelligence, is a correlative ability, turned inward. It is a capacity to form an accurate, veridical model of oneself and to be able to use that model to operate effectively in life.

These, then, are the seven intelligences that we have uncovered and described in our research. This is a preliminary list, as I have said; obviously, each form of intelligence can be subdivided, or the list can be rearranged. The real point here is to make the case for the plurality of intellect. Also, we believe that individuals may differ in the particular intelligence profiles with which they are born, and that certainly they differ in the profiles they end up with. I think of the intelligences as raw, biological potentials, which can be seen in pure form only in individuals who are, in the technical sense, freaks. In almost everybody else the intelligences work together to solve problems, to yield various kinds of cultural endstates — vocations, avocations, and the like.

This is my theory of multiple intelligence in capsule form. In my view, the purpose of school should be to develop intelligences and to help people reach vocational and avocational goals that are appropriate to their particular spectrum of intelligences. People who are helped to do so, I believe, feel more engaged and competent, and therefore more inclined to serve the society in a constructive way.

These thoughts, and the critique of a universalistic view of mind with which I began, lead to the notion of an individual-centered school, one geared to optimal understanding and development of each student's cognitive profile. This vision stands in direct contrast to that of the uniform school that I described earlier.

The design of my ideal school of the future is based upon two assumptions. The first is that not all people have the same interests and abilities; not all of us learn in the same way. (And we now have the tools to begin to address these individual differences in school.) The second assumption is one that hurts: it is the assumption that nowadays no one person can learn everything there is to learn. We would all like, as Renaissance men and women, to know everything, or at least to believe in the potential of knowing everything, but that ideal clearly is not possible anymore. Choice is therefore inevitable, and one of the things that I want to argue is that the choices that we make for ourselves, and for the people who are under our charge, might as well be informed choices. An individual-centered school would be rich in assessment of individual abilities and proclivities. It would seek to match individuals not only to curricular areas, but also to particular ways of teaching those subjects. And after the first few grades, the school would also seek to match individuals with the various kinds of life and work options that are available in their culture.

I want to propose a new set of roles for educators that might make this vision a reality. First of all, we might have what I will call "assessment specialists." The job of these people would be to try to understand as sensitively and comprehensively as possible the abilities and interests of the students in a school. It would be very important, however, that the assessment specialists use "intelligence-fair" instruments. We want to be able to look specifically and directly at spatial abilities, at personal abilities, and the like, and not through the usual lenses of the linguistic and logical-mathematical intelligences. Up until now nearly all assessment has depended indirectly on measurement of those abilities; if students are not strong in those two areas, their abilities in other areas may be obscured. Once we begin to try to assess other kinds of intelligences directly, I am confident that particular students will reveal strengths in quite different areas, and the notion of general brightness will disappear or become greatly attenuated.

In addition to the assessment specialist, the school of the future might have the "student-curriculum broker." It would be his or her job to help match students' profiles, goals, and interests to particular curricula and to particular styles of learning. Incidentally, I think that the new interactive technologies offer considerable promise in this area: it will probably be much easier in the future for "brokers" to match individual students to ways of learning that prove comfortable for them.

There should also be, I think, a "school-community broker," who would match students to learning opportunities in the wider community. It would be this person's job to find situations in the community, particularly options not available in the school, for children who exhibit unusual cognitive profiles. I have in mind apprenticeships, mentorships, internships in organizations, "big brothers," "big sisters" — individuals and organizations with whom these students might work to secure a feeling for different kinds of vocational and avocational roles in the society. I am not worried about those occasional youngsters who are good in everything. They're going to do just fine. I'm concerned about those who don't shine in the standardized tests, and who, therefore, tend to be written off as not having gifts of any kind. It seems to me that the school-community broker could spot these youngsters and find placements in the community that provide chances for them to shine.

There is ample room in this vision for teachers, as well, and also for master teachers. In my view, teachers would be freed to do what they are supposed to do, which is to teach their subject matter, in their preferred style of teaching. The job of master teacher would be very demanding. It would involve, first of all, supervising the novice teachers and guiding them; but the master teacher would also seek to ensure that the complex student-assessment-curriculum-community equation is balanced appropriately. If the equation is seriously imbalanced, master teachers would intervene and suggest ways to make things better.

Clearly, what I am describing is a tall order; it might even be called utopian. And there is a major risk to this program, of which I am well aware. That is the risk of premature billeting — of saying, "Well, Johnny is four, he seems to be musical, so we are going to send him to Juilliard and drop everything else." There is, however, nothing inherent in the approach that I have described that demands this early overdetermination — quite the contrary. It seems to me that early identification of strengths can be very helpful in indicating what kinds of experiences children might profit from; but early identification of weaknesses can be equally important. If a weakness is identified early, there is a chance to attend to it before it is too late, and to come up with alternative ways of teaching or of covering an important skill area.

We now have the technological and the human resources to implement such an individual-centered school. Achieving it is a question of will, including the will to withstand the current enormous pressures toward uniformity and unidimensional assessments. There are strong pressures now, which you read about every day in the newspapers, to compare students, to compare teachers, states, even entire countries, using one dimension or criterion, a kind of a crypto-IQ assessment. Clearly, everything I have described today stands in direct opposition to that particular view of the world. Indeed that is my intent — to provide a ringing indictment of such one-track thinking.

I believe that in our society we suffer from three biases, which I have nick-named "Westist," "Testist," and "Bestist." "Westist" involves putting certain Western cultural values, which date back to Socrates, on a pedestal. Logical thinking, for example, is important; rationality is important; but they are not the only virtues. "Testist" suggests a bias towards focusing upon those human abilities or approaches that are readily testable. If it can't be tested, it sometimes seems, it is not worth paying attention to. My feeling is that assessment can be much broader, much more humane than it is now, and that psychologists should spend less time ranking people and more time trying to help them.

"Bestist" is a not very veiled reference to a book by David Halberstam called *The best and the brightest.* Halberstam referred ironically to figures such as Harvard faculty members who were brought to Washington to help President John F. Kennedy and in the process launched the Vietnam War. I think that any belief that all the answers to a given problem lie in one certain approach, such as logical-mathematical thinking, can be very dangerous. Current views of intellect need to be leavened with other more comprehensive points of view.

It is of the utmost importance that we recognize and nurture all of the varied human intelligences, and all of the combinations of intelligences. We are all so different largely because we all have different combinations of intelligences. If we recognize this, I think we will have at least a better chance of dealing appropriately with the many problems that we face in the world. If we can mobilize the spectrum of human abilities, not only will people feel better about themselves and more competent; it is even possible that they will also feel more engaged and better able to join the rest of the world community in working for the broader good. Perhaps if we can mobilize the full range of human intelligences and ally them to an ethical sense, we can help to increase the likelihood of our survival on this planet, and perhaps even contribute to our thriving.

ACKNOWLEDGMENTS

This chapter is based on an informal talk given at the 350th anniversary of Harvard University on 5 September 1986. The work reported in this article was supported by the Rockefeller Foundation, the Spencer Foundation, and the Bernard Van Leer Foundation.

CHAPTER TWENTY-NINE

INDIVIDUAL DIFFERENCES
IN COGNITION

R. KIM GUENTHER

People differ with respect to their intellectual capabilities. Historically, the attempt to measure differences in intellectual ability has been the most conspicuous and influential branch of cognitive psychology.

Perspectives on Individual Differences in Intelligence: Hereditarian, Unitary Models versus Multifaceted, Domain-Specific Models of Intelligence
The assumptions historically made by researchers in the intelligence testing movement constitute a theory of intelligence that Steven Jay Gould calls the *hereditarian theory* (Gould, 1981; also Mackintosh, 1986). The hereditarian theory of intelligence makes two separate claims. First, it claims that intelligence is *unitary* — it is a reflection of an all-purpose system or process that permeates all intellectual activity. Another way of making this claim is to say that intelligence is *generic.* An implication of the generic notion is that intelligence is measurable using tests that are meaningfully converted into numbers that reflect the amount of intelligence a person possesses. The second claim, from which the hereditarian theory derives its name, is that the primary basis of intellectual differences among people is to be found in the genes they inherit; that is, intelligence is primarily *genetically determined.* Although these claims are logically distinct (intelligence could be unitary but differences among people could still be due primarily to environmental differences), historically they have been associated.

The main theme of this chapter will be a comparison between the unitary or generic view of individual cognitive differences, on the one hand, and a *domain-specific* or *multifaceted* view of individual cognitive differences, on the other (Gardner, 1983). The multifaceted view claims that people may display superior talent or skill in one intellectual domain without necessarily being superior in other domains. As I did in chapter 8: Problem Solving, I will champion here the domain-specific approach to individual intellectual differences. I will also discuss the evidence for a genetic basis for intellectual differences and try to make clear what are and are not reasonable implications of this evidence. Included in the section on the genetic basis of intelligence is a discussion of sex differences in cognitive skills.

29.1   HISTORICAL BACKGROUND AND THE RISE OF THE HEREDTARIAN THEORY OF INTELLIGENCE

A confluence of several developments taking place in the 1800s led to an interest in the measurement of individual differences in cognition, culminating in the creation of *intelligence quotient (IQ)* tests around the turn of the 20th century. One development was the theory of evolution, which focuses on individual differences. For traits like abstract reasoning or language to evolve in a species, members of predecessor species must differ from one another on that trait. Only then can natural selection produce an increase in the number of individuals possessing the more adaptive trait. A second development was the growing acceptance of materialism — the view that what we label mental activity reflects only brain processes. In this view, any intellectual differences between people must also be reflected in differences in their brains. A third development was the rise of psychological experimentation and measurement. Sophisticated techniques for investigating and quantifying human behavior were being developed in the experimental laboratories of Europe and North America. Finally, the industrialized nations had become committed to universal education. But not everyone seemed to profit very much by formal education. Consequently, educators became interested in identifying students who might need special educational intervention.

29.1.1   The Rise of the Intelligence Testing Movement

Francis Galton.   Francis Galton, Darwin's cousin and one of the founders of the intelligence testing movement, was a bright, independently wealthy man who had a passion for measuring things. He was the first to suggest that fingerprints be used for personal identification. He measured the degree of boredom at scientific lectures, and tried to find out which country had the most beautiful women.

Galton, along with his friend Karl Pearson (1867–1936), devised the concept and formula for *correlation* (see Boring, 1950; Gould, 1981; Hergenhahn, 1986). As it turns out, the concept of correlation is extremely important to the research on intelligence. Correlation is a measure of the degree to which two measurements are linearly related. Correlations range between +1 and −1. A positive correlation indicates that when scores on one measure increase, scores on the other measure tend to increase as well. A negative correlation indicates that when scores on one measure increase, scores on the other measure tend to decrease. A lack of correlation between two measures means that when scores on one measure increase, scores on the other measure tend neither to increase nor decrease. Height and weight are positively correlated — people who are tall also tend to be people who weigh more. Smoking and longevity are negatively correlated — people who smoke more tend to live fewer years. The last digit of one's social security number and one's annual income in dollars are not correlated — people with higher last digits are not likely to earn more money or less money.

It is important to note that just because two measures are correlated does not mean that there is a causal relationship between them. However, if there is a causal relationship, it is certain that the two measures will be correlated. There is a positive correlation between the speed with which a sprinter runs and the number of wins in a track meet. Here the faster speed is the cause of the winning. But there is also a positive correlation between the number of ice cream cones consumed in New York City on any given day and the number of deaths in Bombay, India on the same given day. Obviously, though, the eating of ice cream cones in New York does not cause people in Bombay to die; rather, both measures probably reflect global climate. When it is hot in the Northern Hemisphere, people in New York eat ice cream cones and people in Bombay endure heat and disease. Many correlations are simply coincidental. The gross national product of the United States in any given year is positively correlated to the distance between the North American continent and the European continent — both are increasing over time.

Based on his correlational and measuring techniques, Galton (1883) decided that intelligence is primarily a reflection of energy and the perceptual acuteness of the senses. Intelligent people, thought Galton, were especially good at perceptually discriminating between similar stimuli, such as between two similar colors differing only slightly in frequency. In 1884 he set up an anthropometric laboratory at the International Exposition where visitors, by paying a threepence, could have their skulls measured and have various tests taken of their perceptual functions. Some of the tests included judging the relative weight of a series of identical-looking objects, trying to detect very high frequency sounds, and reacting as quickly as possible to an auditory stimulus by punching a bag. This laboratory, later transferred to South Kensington Museum in London, constituted the first large-scale testing of individual differences.

Galton claimed that mentally retarded people did not discriminate heat, cold, and pain as well as "normal" people, and used this finding to bolster his argument that sensory discriminatory capacity underlies intelligence (Galton, 1883). Other research seemed to show that children classified by their teachers as "bright" tended to have faster reaction times than children classified as below average (Gilbert, 1894). Galton's procedures for measuring intelligence were adopted by James Cattell (1860–1944), who administered them to college students in the United States (Cattell, 1890).

Later research discredited some of Galton's ideas, when it was shown that an individual's performance on sensory and reaction time tests showed little relationship from test to test, and was unrelated to grades in school or to a teacher's estimates of intelligence (e.g., Wissler, 1901). More recent research (discussed below) suggests that there might be a modest relationship between performance on sensory or reaction-time tests and other measures of intellectual prowess.

Galton's interest in evolution led him to study the possibility that intelligence runs in families. Based on a study of families of people who were highly acclaimed scientists, artists, writers, and politicians, Galton found that children of illustrious people were more likely to be illustrious than children of ordinary folks (Galton, 1884). Galton concluded that the basis of high intelligence was favorable genes that the illustrious passed on to their offspring. Galton advocated a form of eugenics, in which the government would pay highly intelligent people to marry and bear children.

Alfred Binet.   Alfred Binet (1857–1911), one of the founders of experimental psychology in France, conducted research on hypnotism, cognitive development, memory, and creativity.

Some of his work with children was similar to that later conducted by Jean Piaget (see Boring, 1950; Gould, 1981; Hergenhahn, 1986).

In 1903 Binet and Theodore Simon (1878–1961) were commissioned by the French government to develop a test that could identify learning disabled or mentally retarded children, so that they could be given special education. At the time, tests based on Galton's theories were used, but, as discussed before, some research seemed to discredit Galton's ideas about the basis of individual differences. Besides, as Binet noted, children with vision and hearing impairments would be erroneously classified as retarded. Binet proposed instead that more complex tests of reasoning, motor performance, spatial thinking, and memory be used to assess a child's cognitive abilities. Binet and Simon's tests included reasoning problems, reflecting Binet's belief that the intelligent person was one who showed reasoned judgments when confronted with problems (Binet, 1911; Binet & Simon, 1916). Typical items on the test required children to define common words, name objects in pictures, tell how two objects are alike, draw designs from memory, repeat back a string of spoken digits, and answer abstract questions such as "When a person has offended you and comes to offer his apologies, what should you do?"

Binet ordered his hodgepodge of tests from simple ones, which most two-year-old children could answer, to difficult ones, which children could not answer but most adults could answer. The age associated with the most difficult tasks that the child could perform was designated the child's mental age, which was then compared with the child's chronological age. In 1911 William Stern (1871–1938) proposed that mental age be divided by chronological age and then multiplied by 100 to produce the familiar IQ score. Using this formula, if a 10-year-old child is able to answer most of the items that a typical 12-year-old could answer, then the 10-year-old child's IQ score would be $(12/10) \times 100 = 120$. More recently, IQ has been measured by looking at the average for the age group and determining how far above or below the average the test taker's score lies. Average is set as equal to 100; standard deviation (a measure of dispersion) is usually set as equal to 15. Using this formula, a person who scores two standard deviations above the average would be assigned an IQ score of 130.

Binet did not believe that an IQ score was a measure of intelligence, which he regarded as too complex to capture with a single number. He made it clear that IQ was not like weight or height, in that IQ does not represent a quality possessed by a person. Again, Binet believed that his test was good only as a guide to help identify children who needed special help. Furthermore, Binet did not believe that scores on IQ tests necessarily represented a genetically based intellectual potential. Rather, he was optimistic that, with special education, many children who scored low on the IQ test could greatly improve their reasoning, memory, and verbal skills. Binet recommended that special education be tailored to the individual's needs and aptitudes, that classrooms for special education be kept small, and that the initial focus be kept on motivation and work discipline.

29.1.2   Correlates of IQ

Since the early 1900s, a large number of intelligence tests have been developed. These include the Stanford-Binet (a modification of Binet's original test), the Wechsler scales for children (WISC) and adults (WAIS), each of which computes a verbal IQ score and a performance IQ score; the Raven's Matrices, a nonverbal test of intelligence; and college entrance tests like the SAT.

Research on IQ tests demonstrates that various IQ test scores are positively correlated with one another; for example, the Wechsler IQ score correlates about .8 with the Stanford-Binet. IQ tests are also moderately correlated with grades in school (the correlation is usually about .5), number of years of formal education, occupational status, and, to a lesser extent, with success in an occupation (Kline, 1991; Neisser, Boodoo, et al., 1996). The correlation between success in an occupation (measured, for example, by supervisor ratings) and IQ scores is typically about .3. So people who get good grades, go to school for a long time, have professional jobs such as doctors and lawyers, and get higher ratings from supervisors evaluating their work tend to score higher on IQ tests than do people who get poor grades, drop out early, have jobs such as factory workers, and get lower evaluations from their supervisors.

Keep in mind that these correlations do not tell us much about the causes of the relationship between IQ scores and other measures, such as grades in school. It could be, for example, that the superior intellect some people possess causes them to score higher on IQ tests, do better in school, and get better jobs. But there are other possibilities. Perhaps motivation to succeed is the cause (or at least one of the causes) of the correlations — a generally motivated person will try harder to do well on IQ tests, stay in school longer, and work harder on the job. Or maybe health is a cause of the correlations — a generally healthy person is more likely than an unhealthy person to be alert in school, acquire the knowledge necessary to do well on IQ tests, and perform well on the job. It could also be that the economic advantage some people enjoy is what enables them to do better on IQ tests, do better in school, and get better jobs (McClelland, 1973).

It should be pointed out, however, that the relationship between IQ performance and educational and occupational success cannot be attributed entirely to socioeconomic factors (Barrett & Depinet, 1991). Parental background variables like parental income and education do not predict occupational achievement as well as do IQ test scores (Gottfredson & Brown, 1981). Grades in school are more strongly correlated with SAT scores than with parental income (Baird, 1984).

29.2   IS INTELLIGENCE UNITARY?

As I suggested at the beginning of this chapter, much of the recent work on the nature of intellectual differences has taken the form of a reaction to the historically entrenched hereditarian theory of intelligence and the IQ enterprise it established. In this section I will discuss the evidence that intelligence is unitary, that it reflects a generic intellectual system. In the next major section I will develop the argument for a multifaceted model of intellectual differences.

29.2.1   Evidence for the Unitary View

Charles E. Spearman (1863–1945) was one of the first psychologists to demonstrate that people who do well on any one subtest of the IQ inventory tend to do well on any other subtest. That is, the various subtests that make up the IQ inventory are positively correlated (Kline,

1991). Spearman thought that the prevalence of positive correlations reflected a physical property of the brain, namely, a kind of mental energy that some brains happened to possess more of than other brains (Spearman, 1927). He labeled this idea "g," to stand for the *general factor* that underlies all intellectual activity. More recent but similar interpretations of g are that g reflects the capacity to pay attention to information (Hunt, 1980; Jensen, 1979), reflects nerve conduction velocity and rate of neural decay (Jensen, 1993), or reflects the ability of neurons to change connections (Larson & Saccuzzo, 1989).

Spearman, and many others since, have noted that subtests of the IQ inventory that are similar to one another are even more positively correlated than are dissimilar subtests. For example, two different subtests that measure spacial reasoning will be more highly correlated than a subtest that measures spacial reasoning and a subtest that measures vocabulary. This pattern of correlations, analyzed by a statistical technique called factor analysis, is sometimes interpreted as indicating that intelligence has a general (also known as *fluid*) component that reflects some genetically determined biological aspect of the cognitive system, and a series of specialized (also called *crystallized)* components that reflect various learned skills (Kline, 1991).

There is other evidence for the unitary nature of intelligence. Correlations among IQ tests are significant even when one IQ test is verbal and the other IQ test is nonverbal. For example, the correlations between the Raven's Matrices (a nonverbal IQ test) and conventional IQ tests range from about $+.40$ to $+.75$ (Anastasi, 1988). That IQ scores predict performance in very different situations, such as school settings and job settings, also suggests that there is a unitary aspect to intelligence.

29.2.2   What Underlies Unitary Intelligence? Contributions of Information Processing

Elsewhere I have criticized information processing models that postulate that all problems are solved by the same, generic information processing system. A similar sort of information processing perspective has been used as an account for why intelligence seemingly has a unitary character.

A generic information processing approach to intellectual differences has all intellectual tasks performed by a single information processing system. Individual differences in intellectual performance reflect differences in the speed and efficiency with which the various components of the system are executed. I do wish to note that information processing cognitive psychologists need not postulate a generic information processing model of individual differences. Perhaps human cognition is composed of many different, relatively autonomous information processing systems. However, the idea of a generic information processing system is implicit in most information processing approaches to cognition (Lachman, Lachman, & Butterfield, 1979), and so it is the generic form of it that I will critique here.

The information processing approach rose to prominence in the 1950s, 1960s, and 1970s. An important claim of information processing is that any given cognitive process can be broken down into a set of fundamental components, such as perceiving information, transforming information, storing information in memory, and retrieving symbols from memory. Most information processing accounts claim that there is a limited-capacity working memory — a place that holds the currently activated information and the program for manipulating it. More discussion of information processing can be found in the introductory chapter.

The contribution of information processing to the study of intelligence is its claim that any or all of these components of cognition could be the basic and essential source of individual differences in intellectual activity (e.g., Carroll, 1983; Jensen, 1982; Vernon, 1983; Sternberg, 1985; Hunt, 1983; Pellegrino & Glaser, 1979). Some people might be more intelligent than others because they can more quickly and efficiently process stimulus input, retrieve information from memory, or transform information from one form into another.

An Example of Research Based on Information Processing: Inspection Time.   The information processing perspective has produced a variety of experimental paradigms for measuring the speed and efficiency with which people can carry out any component of cognitive processing. In the typical information processing experiment, researchers use established experimental paradigms to obtain from each subject an estimate of how quickly or efficiently the subject can execute one of the components, and then measure the correlation between that estimate and the subject's score on an IQ test.

One task that has been studied extensively is called the *inspection time task* (Deary & Stough, 1996). In a typical version of this task, subjects are given two parallel vertical lines joined at the top by a horizontal line. One of the vertical lines is longer than the other. An example of a stimulus used in the inspection time task is provided in figure 29.1. Over a series of trials the longer line is presented on the left side about as often as it is presented on the right. Subjects must identify which is the longer line and can take as long as they want to make the decision. The task is made difficult by limiting the amount of time the stimulus is exposed to the subjects; that is, the inspection time is kept brief. The range of exposure

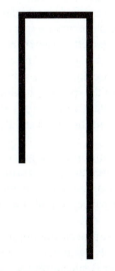

FIGURE 29.1   A typical stimulus used in the inspection time task. From a very brief exposure to such a stimulus, subjects must decide whether the left or the right vertical line is longer. (See Deary and Stough, 1996.)

durations is usually between 100 milliseconds to less than around 10 milliseconds. Any given subject's inspection time is usually expressed as the stimulus duration necessary for the subject to reach a given accuracy level, such as 75%. Be clear that inspection time does not refer to how long it takes a subject to make this simple discrimination; rather, it refers to how long the stimulus was exposed in order that the subject might reach an acceptable level of performance.

The main finding of interest is that inspection times correlate with performance on standard tests of intelligence (e.g., Nettelbeck & 1976; Deary, 1993; see Deary & Stough, 1996). People whose inspection times are short tend to score higher on the intelligence tests. Across a variety of studies the correlation is usually around .5, a moderately strong correlation (Deary & Stough, 1996). One interpretation of the correlation is that inspection time measures a basic information processing component — namely, the speed with which information is taken in or initially perceived.

Other information processing measures have also been correlated to IQ. These include estimates of the span of working or short-term memory (Hunt, 1978; Schofield & Ashman, 1986; Daneman & Carpenter, 1980; Dark & Benbow, 1991; see Dempster, 1981), the speed with which subjects supposedly scan short term memory (Keating & Bobbit, 1978; Vernon, 1983), the speed with which people mentally rotate a visual stimulus (Mumaw Pellegrino, Kail, & Carter, 1984), the speed with which people access the name of a letter (Hunt, 1978, 1983; Hunt, Lunneborg & Lewis, 1975), and the speed with which subjects access the meaning of a word in memory (Goldberg, Schwartz, & Stewart, 1977; Vernon, 1983). Measures of the speed of information processing tasks correlate with scores on IQ tests even when the IQ test itself is not timed (Vernon & Kantor, 1986).

Problems with the Information Processing Perspective on Intellectual Differences.   There are, however, problems with the information processing account of individual differences in cognition. One problem is that not every researcher finds a correlation between measures of the speed or efficiency of a component and IQ performance (e.g., Keating, 1982; Ruchalla, Scholt & Vogel, 1985; see Long-streth, 1984; Barrett, Eysenck, & Luching, 1989). Further, when a correlation is found, that correlation is often achieved by comparing college students to mentally retarded people. When the studies are done using subjects who are not mentally retarded, the correlation between any estimate of the speed with which a cognitive component is executed and IQ scores is usually quite modest, in the .3 to .4 range (see Kline, 1991; Mackintosh, 1986). The correlation between inspection time and IQ scores seems a bit more robust, however (Deary & Sough, 1996).

A more fundamental problem is that the information processing approach relies too much on establishing correlations between measures of information processing and IQ scores. What is generally lacking from this line of inquiry are demonstrations that measures of information processing can predict performance on real life tasks better than conventional IQ tests (Richardson, 1991).

Another difficulty with the information processing approach to individual differences is that of establishing cause and effect. Is the efficiency with which information is initially processed the cause of intelligence, or is speed of processing the effect of intelligence, whose cause is undetermined? Even if it is conceded that perception speed, as measured in tasks like the inspection time task, is a causal determinant of intelligence, what then causes there to be differences in perception speed (see Richardson, 1991)? What would be the biological basis for mental speed, or for any other component of cognition measured by information processing tasks?

Research on the Physiological Basis of Intelligence.   Another way to get at the underlying nature of intelligence is to examine neurophysiological correlates of individual differences in cognition. Typically, research and theory studying the neurophysiological basis for intelligence has assumed, at least implicitly, that intelligence is a unitary phenomenon. For instance, researchers have speculated that the brain of a highly intelligent person has more synapses among neurons (Birren, Woods, & Williams, 1979), more efficiently metabolizes energy (Smith, 1984), or more efficiently reconfigures connections among neurons (Larson & Saccuzzo, 1989). Unfortunately, it is difficult to obtain clear-cut evidence for or against any of these conjectures, because the research on the physiological underpinnings of individual differences in cognition is meager and inconclusive. One of the main difficulties lies in measuring the critical physiological processes, which are likely to be dynamic phenomena reflected in the way neurons communicate with one another.

Are Smart Brains Metabolically Efficient?   Recently, brain imaging technology, such as positron emission tomography scanning (PET scans), has allowed researchers to study metabolic activity in various sections of the brain of an alive and awake person. Some studies suggest that people who do better on intelligence tests tend to display lower neural metabolic activity. Haier, Siegel, Nuechterlein, et al. (1988) found that performance on the Raven's Matrices was negatively correlated with overall cortical metabolic rate. Subjects who scored higher on the Raven's Matrices test (a nonverbal intelligence test) tended to have lower overall cortical metabolic rates than subjects who scored lower on the test. The authors speculated that people who are good at reasoning tasks have more efficient neural circuits which therefore use less energy than the neural circuits of people who have more trouble with the reasoning tasks.

Haier, Siegel, MacLachlan, et al. (1992) measured cortical metabolic activity during the initial stages of learning the complex computer game TETRIS, and again several weeks later after subjects practiced the game. They found that subjects who improved the most on the computer game displayed the largest drop in cortical metabolic activity while playing the game. Similar results have been found by Parks, et al. (1988).

In apparent contradiction to these studies, though, is research that has uncovered a positive correlation between metabolic rate and performance on IQ tests. This research, however, has usually used elderly subjects, some of whom have Alzheimer's disease and other forms of dementia (e.g., Butler, Dickinson, Katholi, & Halsey, 1983; Chase et al., 1984). Aging and disease may alter the normal functioning of the brain.

Even if the negative correlation between performance on intelligence tests and cortical metabolic activity proves reliable, interpretation problems remain. It is not clear what makes neural circuits more efficient. Is it the density of the neurons, the ease with which neurons affect the activity of other neurons, the number of glial cells that support the neurons, or any of a number of other possibilities? Furthermore, there may be other reasons for the slower cortical metabolic rate in people who score higher on the intelligence tests. Perhaps people who are able to remain calm while taking intelligence tests have lower cortical metabolic rates as a result, and thus do better on the tests. Both intelligence test performance and metabolic rate may be affected by control over anxiety. Haier et al. (1988)

dismiss this possibility because their subjects did not appear to be anxious, and because other research suggests that anxiety increases metabolic rates primarily in the frontal lobes. The authors found that metabolic rate changes related to learning occurred primarily in the posterior regions. However, it is possible that anxiety responses interacting with the responses necessary to do cognitive tasks may produce a different pattern of cortical metabolic rate than observed in other situations.

Neural Conduction Rate and Smart Brains.   Some recent research suggests that the rate at which neurons conduct electrical activity may be faster for people who score higher on intelligence tests. Reed and Jensen (1992) presented subjects with visual stimuli and measured the latency with which an evoked potential was detected in primary visual cortex. Shorter latencies imply faster neural conduction. They found a .37 correlation between scores on the Raven's Matrices test and conduction rates. Similar findings have been reported by Vernon and Mori (1992).

Again, though, the conduction latency results are not easy to interpret. What is different about the neural structure between people whose neurons conduct impulses faster and people whose neurons conduct impulses more slowly? Does the variation in conduction latency reflect intellectual efficiency, motivation, consistency of performance, or what?

Let me make one final comment on the studies of the physiological basis of individual intellectual differences. It is possible that certain physiological features on which people differ and which determine intelligence permeate much of the brain. There may be something about the development of neurons such that virtually all of them are more efficient in some people. In such a case, intelligence would have a unitary character, as much of the research on the neurophysiology of intelligence implicitly assumes. On the other hand, it is also possible that the relative efficiency of neurons varies across neural domains within any given brain. Such variability in efficiency within a single brain could be due to environmental experiences, genetic "programming," or some interaction between the two. At any rate, neural domain variability would give rise to a multifaceted form of intelligence. And it is to a multifaceted view of intelligence that I will now direct my discussion.

29.3   BUILDING THE CASE FOR A MULTIFACETED APPROACH TO INTELLIGENCE

29.3.1   Interpreting the Evidence for Unitary Models of Intelligence

There have been a number of reactions to the unitary intelligence interpretation of the positive correlations observed among various measures of intelligence and information processing. One reaction is that the g factor has many possible interpretations besides the interpretation that it reflects the intrinsic efficiency of the cognitive system (Gould, 1981; Richardson, 1991). One possibility is that g reflects the encouragement people receive as they grow up. Children who are encouraged to learn and perform well, or are made to feel secure, may try harder and/or be less anxious when taking the various subtests of the IQ test. Such children would be expected to do well on the subtests of the IQ inventory and well in academic situations. Certainly it has been established that measures of a person's attitude and motivation tend to correlate with that person's performance on IQ tests (see Anastasi, 1988).

For example, people who have positive attitudes toward learning and have a desire to succeed tend to do better in school and score higher on tests of intelligence (Anastasi, 1985; Dreger, 1968).

The connection between performance in information processing paradigms and performance on IQ tests may also be interpreted as a matter of attitude and motivation, and not necessarily a matter of the intrinsic efficiency of the cognitive system. Consider that from the perspective of the subject, tasks like the inspection time task are tedious. Subjects who try hard, especially by concentrating on every trial, will tend to have short inspection times. Subjects who occasionally let their attention wander, on the other hand, will get the occasional long inspection time that will increase their overall average (Mackintosh, 1986). If the subjects who try hard on the information processing tasks are also the ones who try hard on the IQ test, then there will be correlations between measures of the information processing task and IQ performance, as is observed.

29.3.2 Expanding the Concept of Intelligence: Creativity, Sociability, Practicality

To some extent, the issue of whether a given test of the intellect correlates with other tests depends on what sorts of tests one wishes to consider as revealing of intelligence. When people are given tests that are dissimilar in content to those found in conventional IQ inventories, researchers often find that performance on such tests (e.g., writing plots from descriptions of short stories) does not correlate with performance on the conventional tests (Guilford, 1964, 1967; Thurstone, 1938).

Creativity. One way to expand the concept of intelligence is to consider creativity as an aspect of intelligence. Recall that I first discussed creativity in chapter 8: Problem Solving. Most IQ tests have no measures of creativity, an admittedly difficult concept to define and measure objectively. Creativity usually refers to ideas or works that are novel and valuable to others. Einstein was creative when he declared that "$E = mc^2$," because the equation was novel and valuable, at least to physicists. Had he declared "$E = mc^3$" his equation would still have been novel, but not valuable.

A variety of research suggests that creativity, as measured by peer assessments, number of publications, and so on, bears little relationship to scores on IQ tests (Baird, 1982; Barron, 1969; MacKinnon, 1962; Wallach, 1976; see Perkins, 1988). For example, Yong (1994) studied Malaysian secondary students and found that a test of figural creativity was unrelated to scores on the Cattell Culture Fair test of intelligence.

Some disciplines requiring creativity tend to be populated by people who score high on IQ tests. For example, if one were to examine the general population, one would find a positive correlation between creative achievement in architecture and IQ performance. That is because nearly all of the creative efforts are accomplished by professional architects who, as a group, do well on IQ tests. But if one examines only professional architects, one does not find a strong relationship between degree of creative achievement (measured by peer ratings of creativity) and IQ performance (MacKinnon, 1962). Similarly, among psychology graduate students, Graduate Record Exam scores did not correlate significantly with faculty advisor ratings of the students' creative abilities (Sternberg and Williams, 1997). These results suggest that people who score very low on IQ tests tend to show less evidence of creative talent than people who score higher on IQ tests. But among people whose IQ performance is in the average-to-above-average range, IQ is at best only weakly related to performance on tests of creativity. Creativity, then, is a different aspect of the intellect or involves a different kind of motivation than the skills and motivations that enable people to do well on IQ tests (McDermid, 1965; Richards, Kinney, Benet, & Merzel, 1988).

Social Skill.   One might also consider social skill as an aspect of intelligence, although IQ tests do not usually measure it. Again, social skill is a concept that is difficult to measure objectively. Research on social skill suggests that if social skill is measured using the same sorts of items that appear on IQ tests, then measures of social intelligence do correlate with IQ performance. An example of this is that memory for face-name associations and the tendency to correctly answer multiple choice questions about what to do in social situations are correlated with performance on IQ tests, especially IQ tests that measure verbal skills (Thorndike, 1936; Woodrow, 1939).

When social skill is assessed by directly observing people in social situations, however, there seems to be almost no relationship between it and IQ performance. Wong, Day, Maxwell, and Meara (1995) showed that people's performance on tests designed to measure cognitive aspects of social intelligence was only weakly related to their performance on tests of behavioral aspects of social intelligence. Frederiksen, Carlson, and Ward (1984) observed the interviewing skills of medical students who had to interact with "simulated" patients in several types of situations, including one in which the medical students had to inform the patient that she had breast cancer. Various aspects of the students' interviewing performance were rated by independent judges, in order to obtain a social skill score for each medical student. These scores were unrelated to the medical students' IQ scores and unrelated to their knowledge of science, as assessed by another test. Similarly, Rothstein, Paunonen, Rush, and King (1994) found that social-personality variables, especially self-confidence and a willingness to be the center of attention, predicted classroom performance (presenting convincing solutions, communicating clearly, and contributing to others' learning) in graduate school better than did standard measures of intellectual aptitude.

Practical Intelligence.   Most people recognize a distinction between academic intelligence (book smarts) and practical intelligence (street smarts) (Sternberg, Wagner, Williams, & Horvath, 1995). Academic intelligence as measured by standard IQ tests is disembedded from an individual's ordinary experience. Practical intelligence, however, has to do with the actual attainment of goals that are valued. Sternberg and his colleagues (see Sternberg et al., 1995) have developed tests that supposedly measure *practical intelligence* (also known as *tacit knowledge*). Their tests typically present subjects with a set of work-related problems (e.g., how to achieve rapid promotion within a company) along with choices of strategies for solving the problem (e.g., write an article on productivity for the company newsletter, find ways to make sure that your supervisors are aware of your accomplishments). The subjects rank-order the strategies according to which is likely to achieve the goal. Their responses are then compared to those of acknowledged experts or to established rules of thumb used by experts. The greater the response overlap between subject and expert, the higher the subject's score on the test of practical intelligence.

A variety of studies suggest that scores on tests of practical intelligence correlate moderately with success on the job (see Sternberg et al., 1995). For instance, in one study, the correlation between practical intelligence test scores and performance ratings for the category "generating new business for the bank" was .56 (Wagner & Sternberg, 1985). However, scores on tests of practical intelligence are essentially unrelated to performance on standard IQ tests (Wagner & Sternberg, 1990). For instance, among Air Force recruits, the median correlation between scores on a test of practical intelligence and scores on various batteries of a standard IQ-type test was −.07 (Eddy, 1988, in Sternberg et al., 1995).

Similarly, Ceci and Liker (1986) found that, among avid racetrack patrons, the complexity of reasoning about handicapping horse races and success at predicting a horse's speed was unrelated to their IQ performance. Dorner and Kreuzig (1983) found that the sophistication of strategies used to solve city management problems was unrelated to a person's IQ. Yekovich, Walker, Ogle, and Thompson (1990) found that expertise in football, and not IQ, predicts who identifies the important facts in a passage about football, and who derives appropriate inferences about a football game. Lave (1988) showed that subjects who were easily able to perform algebraic calculations in the context of selecting which product is the best buy in a supermarket were unable to perform essentially the same calculations when the calculations were presented as math problems on a paper-and-pencil test.

The main point of the studies on creativity, social skill, and practicality is that if we expand our sense of the intellect, we find that people are not equally skilled in all areas. These observations suggest that the prevalence of g (the tendency for performance on the subtests of the IQ inventory to correlate) is largely an artifact of the restricted range of skills that the IQ inventory samples. It is probably true that the range of skills prized in academia tends to be limited to mathematical, reasoning, and verbal skills. Creativity, social skill, and practical skill, among other examples, are not usually emphasized in school.

29.3.3   Gardner's Frames of Mind

Howard Gardner, a cognitive scientist from Harvard University, proposed an influential theory on intelligence in a book entitled *Frames of Mind* (Gardner, 1983). In contrast to unitary theorists, Gardner postulated six distinct, relatively autonomous categories of intelligence. These categories are *verbal intelligence,* exemplified by the poet; *logical intelligence,* exemplified by the mathematician; *musical intelligence,* exemplified by the composer; *spatial intelligence,* exemplified by the painter; *bodily-kinesthetic intelligence,* exemplified by the athlete or the dancer; and *social-emotional intelligence,* exemplified by the political leader or gifted parent. Gardner claimed that intellectual skill in one category is unrelated to intellectual skill in any other category. Similar claims have been made by Guilford (1964, 1967) and Thurstone (1938).

There are several remarkable features of Gardner's theory. First, he acknowledges the wide range of intellectual competencies that may be regarded as aspects of intelligence. Very few IQ tests examine the social-emotional realm, probably because, as I noted before, it is difficult to develop objective tests to see how well a person can motivate another person or understand his or her own feelings. Yet these sorts of skills are among the most prized in virtually all cultures. Very few IQ tests examine the musical or bodily-kinesthetic realm, because in our culture the intellect has historically been equated with verbal and logical intelligence. We have a hard time regarding a talented musician or dancer or athlete as unusually intelligent. Yet in many other cultures, these sorts of competencies are so regarded.

Evidence for Gardner's Frames.   Gardner's theory is also remarkable for the kinds of evidence used to support it. Gardner has broken with the IQ tradition of examining patterns of correlations among subtests of the IQ inventory. Instead, he uses brain damage evidence, isolated talents, anthropological evidence, and the nature of mental operations to support his theory.

The brain damage evidence suggests that damage can interfere with one intellectual competency but leave the others intact. Damage to the left frontal and temporal regions of the brain can interfere with the use of language, but leave other skills, like logical or musical skill, intact. Damage to posterior portions of the right cerebral hemisphere can produce amusia — a difficulty in expressing and appreciating music. Yet spoken language, which also uses the auditory system, is unaffected. Similarly, damage to the anterior portions of the frontal lobes can interfere with certain aspects of emotional expression, yet language and all the other intellectual skills may remain intact.

The phenomenon of isolated talents also provides evidence for Gardner's theory. There are cases of people who are unusually talented in one realm, such as music or art, but are unremarkable and sometimes even retarded in other realms, such as logical reasoning. Similar support for Gardner's theory comes from the previously discussed findings that among people who score average or above on IQ tests, musical and social skill are unrelated to IQ performance, which tends to reflect language and reasoning skills (Shuter-Dyson, 1982; Frederiksen et al., 1984). Some research also suggests that logical reasoning skills are minimally correlated with language proficiency skills, especially when the logical reasoning task uses simple vocabulary (Boyle, 1987). Research also suggests that when memory span is measured using digits, it does not correlate with language proficiency, but when memory span is measured by words in a sentence, it does correlate with language proficiency (Daneman & Carpenter, 1980; King & Just, 1991; Perfetti & Lesgold, 1977). In my own research (Guenther, 1991), I found that the rate at which people could scan their memory of sentences that varied in word length (e.g., "Lions run quickly," "Lions jog") for a target word (e.g., "lions") was unrelated to the rate at which the same people could scan their memory of pictures of objects containing a variable number of properties (a house containing a door, window, and roof, a house containing a door and window) for some target property (e.g., a picture of a particular door).

Gardner notes that people in all cultures develop and appreciate his six proposed categories of intelligence. In all cultures virtually everyone learns something about music, movement skills such as those used in sports, spatial skills such as those used in drawing or navigating, social skills such as those used in soothing a troubled child, reasoning skills such as those underlying the exchange of goods and services, and language skills necessary to communicate. Although the IQ industry and academia implicitly claim that reasoning and language skills are of overwhelming importance, in most other cultures, including segments of our own culture outside of academia, skills such as musical and social skill are also prized.

Finally, Gardner notes that the mental operations are quite different in each category of intelligence. Language, for example, uses rules of grammar for combining symbols that bear an arbitrary relationship to ideas. Music uses rhythm and pitch to create aesthetically pleasing sounds. Logical reasoning entails comparing patterns or sequences and deriving implications, often from symbols that are quite abstract. Social intelligence involves understanding emotions and motivation. The dissimilarity among these mental operations suggests qualitative differences among categories of intellectual skill.

Criticisms of Gardner's Frames.   Gardner's theory is not without its critics (see Sternberg, 1990; Richardson, 1991). One complaint is that it and any multifaceted theory of individual differences fail to explain the positive correlations among subtests of IQ inventories. For example, people who do well at explaining a proverb also tend to do well on spatial, nonverbal tests. A reasonable response to this complaint is the one already discussed, namely, that conventional IQ tests sample from a limited range of possibilities. There are few, if any, objective tests of musical, social, or kinesthetic skill, few measures of creativity, few tests measuring how well people learn new information, and few tests that confront people with problems like those actually encountered in real life.

Another complaint about Gardner's theory is that it seems to divide up the human intellect in a somewhat arbitrary way. Why, for example, is there no separate category for mechanical intelligence, which Gardner subsumes under bodily-kinesthetic? Is it not possible that a person could be a skilled mechanic but not a skilled dancer or athlete? Even Gardner admits, and others have found, that within a category like spatial intelligence, people who are good at one aspect of the skill are not necessarily good at other aspects of the skill. Kosslyn, Brunn, Cave, and Wallach (1984) found that people who are good at producing accurate visual images from verbal descriptions are not necessarily the same people who are able to make rapid rotational transformations of visual images. As another example, brain damage can interfere with the grammatical aspect of language but leave the semantic aspect more or less intact.

Gardner also seems to exclude categories that might be considered types of intelligence. Why is there not a category for religious intelligence? Have not virtually all cultures developed religion? Or for culinary intelligence? Is not food preparation essential to survival and is it not related to the brain mechanisms underlying olfactory and taste perceptions? Why not a category for practical intelligence? Are not measures of practical intelligence related to performance on the job (Sternberg, Wagner, Williams, & Horvath, 1995)?

It seems, then, that there may be an inherent arbitrariness to picking categories of intelligence. The concept of intelligence seems to reflect the values and ideology of a culture, or of an institution within a culture. Different value systems imply different notions of intelligence and different ways to measure intelligence. Advocates of this intelligence-as-ideology position include Garcia (1981), Berry (1974), Heath (1983), Helms (1992), and Keating (1982). From their perspective, the notion that one possesses a single kind of intelligence may be regarded as absurd. People possess skills of varying kinds that may be measured in many ways. Actually describing a skill and inventing a way to measure it reflects the values and goals of institutions, and not some essence of intelligence residing in a person. IQ tests tend to reflect the value the academic culture places on verbal and abstract reasoning skills, and on the objective measurement of people.

I think, then, that the unitary or generic view of intelligence is misleading. Instead, intelligence is multifaceted; it reflects performance on particularized, relatively autonomous skills. As I mentioned before, the multifaceted model of intelligence is reminiscent of the domain-specific nature of problem solving (discussed in the previous chapter). Just as there is no generic problem-solving system that kicks into action whenever a problem is encountered, there is no single unitary trait that permeates all of human cognition and gives rise to individual differences in intellectual performance.

29.4   IS INTELLIGENCE DETERMINED PRIMARILY BY GENES?

Explicit in the hereditarian theory of intelligence is the idea that intelligence is a genetically determined intellectual potential. IQ is supposed to be an approximation of the amount of this potential. In this view, then, intellectual differences among people are largely attributable to their genetic differences. Most advocates of the genetic basis for intelligence concede that the environment can either nurture or thwart the acquisition of intellectual competency. But they contend that genes are the primary determinant of one's intellectual potential, and that in most cases IQ performance provides a rough index of this potential.

The hereditarian claim is often taken to imply that: (a) environmental intervention is not likely to help people who are "intellectually at risk" and that (b) ethnic or racial differences in IQ performance are caused primarily by genetic differences, and not by social or cultural factors. It is important to see that advocates of the hereditarian theory need not draw these implications, as I will discuss later. Indeed, my main purpose in this section is to demonstrate that the evidence for a genetic component to intellectual differences does not support these two claims.

29.4.1   Evidence for a Genetic Basis for Intelligence

Familial IQ Correlations.   Advocates of the hereditarian theory base the genetic hypothesis on the finding that intelligence (at least as measured by IQ tests) runs in families. For example, the correlation between parents' and children's performance on IQ tests is about .4 (see Bouchard & McCue, 1981, or Kline, 1991, for references on familial correlations in IQ scores). Especially compelling is the finding that the correlation between the IQ scores of children adopted at birth and the IQ scores of their biological parents is higher (about .32) than is the correlation between the children's IQ scores and the IQ scores of their adopted parents (about .15) (Horn, Loehlin, & Willerman, 1975). Figure 29.2 provides a table of familial correlations in IQ performance.

Evidence relevant to the genetic hypothesis comes from research on identical twins reared apart (e.g., Bouchard & McCue, 1981; Shields, 1962). In this situation, the individuals have virtually the same genes, but grow up in different environments. The usual finding is that the correlation between the IQ scores of twins reared apart is about .7, a high correlation. So despite a dissimilarity in environments, identical twins reared apart score about the same on IQ tests. This correlation is almost as high as the correlation in IQ between identical twins reared together (about .8) and much higher than the correlation between biologically unrelated siblings reared together (about .3). Biologically unrelated siblings reared together share family environments but not genes. So the inescapable conclusion seems to be that genes are a primary determinant of intelligence, at least as measured by IQ tests.

Problems with the Evidence Supporting a Genetic Basis for Intelligence.   The interpretation that the familial IQ correlations support an overpowering influence of genes on intelligence is problematic, however. The pattern of familial correlations does not rule out a substantial influence of the environment on intellectual differences. After all, people learn child-rearing practices and other skills relevant to the cognitive development of the child from their parents. For example, children may acquire an interest in reading from their parents and

Relationship	Correlation
Identical twins reared together	.86
Identical twins reared apart	.72
Fraternal twins reared together	.60
Siblings reared together	.47
Siblings reared apart	.24
Biological parent and child, living together	.42
Biological parent and child, separated by adoption	.22
Unrelated children living together	.32
Adoptive parent and adopted child	.19

FIGURE 29.2   Familial correlations in IQ performance. The source of these correlations is Bouchard and McCue (1981).

pass this interest on to their own children. Children who become interested in reading are likely to read more, get better at reading, and so do well on IQ tests that are typically saturated with test items that depend on language skills.

The importance of the environment in accounting for familial IQ correlations is suggested by the fact that children and their parents are likely to grow up in similar cultural and economic circumstances. Even adopted children are likely to be placed in homes similar in educational and economic background to the homes of the biological parents. Furthermore, children adopted as infants may be more likely to have suffered from prenatal problems, which may undermine their intellectual development and reduce the correlation between their IQ scores and the IQ scores of the adopted parents.

Some of the familial correlations demonstrate an important effect of environment on intellectual differences. The IQ correlation between unrelated children living together is about .3, which is certainly much greater than zero. So there is at least some tendency for people who have dissimilar genes but similar family backgrounds to have similar IQ scores. Also, the correlation between IQ scores for ordinary biologically related siblings is about .4, which is much lower than the correlation for fraternal twins reared together (about .6), even though the genes of fraternal twins are no more similar than the genes of ordinary siblings. Presumably, though, the family environments of fraternal twins are more similar than the family environments of ordinary siblings, because twins share the same period of family history.

Turning to the twins-reared-apart paradigm, it is worth noting that the environments of twins reared apart are not necessarily all that different from those of siblings reared together. As I mentioned before, adoption agencies usually try to place adoptees in homes similar to the home of the biological parents. Furthermore, when twins are raised separately, one twin is often reared by another family member; twins are not usually separated until later childhood; and the twins often remain in contact with one another. In other words, there is a kind of environmental "contamination" that may make the environmental influences on the twins reared apart more similar than is commonly appreciated. Finally, twins are more susceptible to prenatal trauma, which can result in mental retardation, reflected in lowered IQ scores for both twins, even if reared apart. This inflates the IQ correlation between twins (see Anastasi, 1988).

Another kind of problem with the twins-reared-apart paradigm is that it does not identify which shared genes are the underlying cause of the similarity in IQ scores. One possibility is that the genes that produce the high correlations influence biological functions that are directly involved in many cognitive processes. But there are other possibilities.

Consider the following hypothetical scenario. Identical twins share facial and bodily features, the characteristics of which are established primarily by genes. How people are treated depends to some extent on their physical appearance. Consequently, people's social skills, confidence, and so on depend to some extent on their physical appearance. Social skills and confidence, in turn, may influence how one performs on IQ tests. The result would be that identical twins, even when reared apart, will tend to perform similarly on IQ tests, yet the similarity in performance has nothing to do with their intellectual potential. Instead, it has to do with their physical appearance. It could be that one twin, should she or he grow up in an environment that downplays physical appearance, might obtain a very different IQ score than the other twin.

There are other hypothetical examples I could work out. Maybe, for example, the similarity in IQ between twins reared apart is due to similarity of their metabolic rates, or to their resistance to diseases, or to any of a number of other factors that may be genetically inherited and indirectly affect performance on IQ tests. The point of these hypothetical examples is to show that establishing that twins reared apart perform similarly on IQ tests does not necessarily prove that there is a direct genetic basis for intellectual performance. Incidentally, the same argument can be made with respect to the higher IQ correlation between the biological parents and their children whom they do not raise than between the adoptive parents and those same children. Some of the genes the adopted children inherit from their biological parents influence their scores on IQ tests, but it remains unclear what aspect of biology those inherited genes control.

29.4.2 The Role of Environmental Factors in Intellectual Differences

One of the unfortunate implications sometimes drawn from the hereditarian theory of intelligence is that environmental factors are likely to have a rather meager effect on intelligence. Consequently, it is not worth spending money and effort trying to improve substantially the intelligence of people who might seem "intellectually at risk." Now, strictly speaking, one need not draw this implication from hereditary theory, because hereditarians concede that the environment can have an impact on intellectual development. But the problem is that an emphasis on the genetic basis of intellectual differences can blind one to the possibility that environmental factors may have a rather potent effect on intelligence. Genetically based differences lead to the idea of inevitable differences (Gould, 1981). Yet a variety of studies have demonstrated that environmental intervention can substantially improve intellectual capabilities.

Family and School Environments.   Some studies have looked at the behaviors of parents to see which are correlated with their children's intellectual competence. For example, the parents' use of language correlates with their children's performance on IQ tests (Hart & Risley, 1992). Child-rearing practices also correlate with the child's intellect. White (1978), for example, found that parents who reared intellectually competent children tended to do three things: first, they provided a structured, safe, and interesting physical environment for their children. Second, they spent a lot of time helping their children solve problems. Third, they established and enforced clear-cut rules, but in a loving and respectful manner.

Such studies suggest the importance of parenting styles in the acquisition of intellectual competence. The hereditarian could, however, still argue that is the favorable genes of the parents that lead them to use reasonable parenting techniques, and that the intellectual competence of their children is mainly a consequence of inheriting these favorable genes. A better way to show that parenting styles and other environmental variables have a causal effect on the acquisition of intelligence would be to rear one group of children under one set of environmental conditions and a comparable group under a different set of conditions. Ideally, the children should be randomly assigned to the two conditions, but random assignment is obviously socially and ethically impossible.

Still, some research comes close to performing the ideal experiment. Observations of children growing up in orphanages reveals that children who receive loving affection from the caretakers will tend to average higher on IQ tests than children who do not get the affection (Skeels, 1966). Other research has provided training to a group of low-income preschool children on the intellectual skills necessary to do well in school, and has shown that such children improve their IQ performance by an average of 10 to 15 points. Unfortunately, these sorts of studies typically reveal that the gains are temporary. By the fourth grade, the average IQ performance of the group that got the training declines to the level of comparable children who did not receive the training (Bronfenbrenner, 1974; Klaus & Gray, 1968; Ramey, Campbell, & Finkelstein, 1984). However, if the intervention program is extended into the school years, evidence suggests that the intervention has a beneficial effect on IQ performance that extends beyond the first few years of school (Lazar, Darlington, Murray, Royce, & Snipper, 1982; Miller & Bizzell, 1984).

A fairly dramatic environmental effect on IQ performance was accomplished by Garber (1988), who placed a group of children who were previously labeled to be at risk for mental retardation in an extensive home enrichment program. Garber found that, by age 6, the group scored 30 points higher on an IQ test than did a control group, and even by age 14 still scored about 10 points higher than the control group. Another dramatic case is the Carolina Abecedarian Project (Campbell & Ramey, 1994). In this project, infants from low-income families were placed into intellectually enriched environments until they began school. Compared with controls, the enriched children scored higher on tests of intelligence, even 7 years after the end of the intervention.

Generational Environmental Changes: IQ Scores Are Rising.   One intriguing piece of evidence for an environmental influence on IQ performance is the finding that in this century there has been a steady worldwide rise in IQ scores (Flynn, 1984, 1987; see Neisser et al., 1996). The average gain has been about 3 IQ points per decade. The result is that most intelligence tests have to be periodically restandardized in order to keep the mean equal to a score of 100. So people who score 100 on an IQ test today (in 1997) would have averaged about 115 in 1947.

No one knows why IQ scores are rising. Among the proposed reasons (see Neisser et al., 1996) is the idea that the world's cultures are becoming informationally more complex, because of television, urbanization, prolonged schooling, and so on. Such complexity then produces improvements in the development of intellectual skill. Another idea is that the IQ increases are due to nutritional improvements, perhaps the same improvements that have also led to nutritionally based increases in height. Whatever the reason, it must be something in the environment that is producing the rising IQ scores. Certainly the gene pool of the humans species cannot be changing as rapidly as IQ scores are rising. Indeed, there is no evidence that people who score higher on IQ tests are reproducing at greater rates. If anything, the evidence suggests that people who score high on intelligence tests have lower fertility rates, at least within the last century (Van Court & Bean, 1985).

In general, then, the research is consistent with the notion that environmental factors can have a large effect on the development of intellectual competency, even as measured by conventional IQ tests. The fact that people inherit genes that somehow influence intelligence, however measured, does not mean that intelligence is immutable.

29.4.3   Ethnic Differences in IQ Performance

Another unfortunate implication sometimes drawn from the hereditarian theory of intelligence is based on the finding that people from minority groups, such as Native Americans and African Americans, tend to score lower on IQ tests than people from majority groups such as European Americans (Herrnstein & Murray, 1994; Neisser et al., 1996). Yet IQ tests predict academic performance among minority people, suggesting that the tests are not unreasonable measures of intelligence in minority populations (Scarr-Salapatek, 1971; Oakland, 1983). The unfortunate implication sometimes drawn from these findings is that European people possess a genetically determined intellectual potential that exceeds that possessed by peoples from other parts of the world (Jensen, 1969). Some hereditarians claim that Asian people possess the most favorable genes for intellectual potential (Rushton, 1988, 1991). Such claims have historically been used to justify racial segregation and racist social and economic policies. They have also been used to discourage the spending of economic resources on the education of people from minority cultures.

Again, the implication that ethnic differences in performance on IQ tests are genetic need not be drawn from a hereditarian theory of intelligence. It is perfectly consistent with the hereditarian view that individual differences in intelligence are primarily due to genes but ethnic differences in measured intelligence are primarily due to environmental factors. I think that the consensus position is that ethnic differences in IQ performance reflect differences in cultural environments. Specifically, the cultural environment of the typical European (and in some cases, Asian) is more conducive to learning the skills that enable a person to do well on IQ tests than is the cultural environment of the typical African American or Hispanic American or Native American.

Evidence against a Genetic Basis for Ethnic IQ Differences.   Several lines of evidence support the claim that ethnic differences in IQ performance are a consequence of environmental and cultural factors and not a matter of genetic differences.

First of all, when children from a minority group that typically scores lower on IQ tests are raised in the same environment as children from the majority culture, the IQ scores of those minority children are similar to the IQ scores of the majority children. Scarr and Weinberg (1976, 1983) examined the IQ scores of African-American children born of mostly lower income parents but adopted by European-American families from mostly the middle and upper middle economic brackets. The IQ scores of the adopted African Americans averaged about 20 points higher than the IQ scores of other African Americans living in lower income circumstances. Clearly, the family environment had a huge effect on the development of skills underlying the performance on IQ tests. Further-more, these and other adoption studies indicate that when African-American children are adopted into European-American families, their average IQ performance typically comes to be nearly equal to that of the European Americans (Flynn, 1980; Eyferth, 1961; Tizard, Cooperman, Joseph, & Tizard, 1972; Scarr & Weinberg, 1976, 1983). Yet the IQ correlation between the African-American adopted children and their biological parents is greater than the correlation between the African-American children and their adopted parents. Again, that seemingly paradoxical result is because correlation reflects rank order. The IQ scores of the adopted African-American children may have been improved by their environment, but the environment did not affect their rank order on the IQ test. The rank order of the IQ scores of the adopted children continued to reflect the rank order of the IQ scores of their biological parents.

Other research that examines children in similar environments but with different racial backgrounds has also contradicted the hereditarian claim of a racial difference in intelligence. Loehlin, Lindzey, and Spuhler (1975) examined the IQ scores of children born to German mothers and American fathers stationed in Germany after World War II. One group of children was fathered by African Americans, while the other group was fathered by European Americans. Both groups were raised by German mothers in roughly similar economic circumstances. The averages of the IQ scores of the two groups of children were equal, even though one group received half of its genes from people of African descent. Furthermore, there is no correlation between degree of African ancestry of African Americans and their performance on IQ tests (Scarr, Pakstis, Katz, & Barker, 1977).

It is true that some Asian-American people, such as Japanese Americans, score higher on average on IQ tests than do European Americans. But cross-cultural studies that take into account cultural factors, such as the proportions of rural and urban dwellers, suggest no difference between Asians and Europeans in IQ test performance (Stevenson et al., 1985). Furthermore, some Asian groups that have immigrated to the West and subsequently endured poverty in the West score lower on IQ tests than do Europeans (see Mackintosh, 1986).

Sometimes people use the high correlations in IQ performance between twins reared apart as evidence that ethnic differences in IQ performance must be due to genetic differences. In fact, though, even if one overlooks the interpretation problems associated with this paradigm, the twin findings are perfectly consistent with an environmental explanation for group differences in IQ performance.

To see why, consider the following hypothetical situation. Suppose we have three sets of twins (Jerry and Gerry, Robin and Robyn, and Sara and Seri) who are reared apart. On

IQ tests, Jerry and Gerry both obtain 100, Robin and Robyn both obtain 110, and Sara and Seri both obtain 120. So the correlation between the IQ scores of the twins is 1.0. Now suppose the second member of each pair (Gerry, Robyn, and Seri) is each given extensive training so that each improves his or her IQ performance by 20 points. So now the IQ scores will be 100 and 120 for Jerry and Gerry respectively, 110 and 130 for Robin and Robyn respectively, and 120 and 140 for Sara and Seri respectively. Yet the correlation between the IQ scores of the twins will still be 1.0, because correlations reflect rank order, which remains the same. This hypothetical example makes clear that even when the correlation between twins reared apart is as high as it can be (1.0), the environment can still dramatically affect group differences in IQ performance.

Why Are There Ethnic Differences in IQ Performance? If differences in IQ performance among ethnic groups are not due to genetics, what are they due to? Nobody knows for sure (Neisser et al., 1996). A clue comes from the finding that many politically and economically disadvantaged groups from all over the world tend to do less well in school and to score lower on IQ-type tests than do the more advantaged groups (Ogbu, 1978, 1994). The kinds of minority groups that score lower on IQ tests are those that became a minority group involuntarily or those that are regarded by the culture as caste-like (Ogbu, 1978, 1994). Immigrants who come to a country voluntarily may be optimistic that they can control and improve their conditions. These groups typically do well on IQ tests. Groups that are involuntarily displaced, such as Native Americans, African Americans, and the Maori in New Zealand, or are excluded, like the "untouchables" of India or non-European Jews of Israel, may lack the conviction that hard schoolwork and serious commitment to the educational enterprise will be rewarded. It is these groups that tend to do poorly on IQ tests.

Furthermore, IQ tests take place in settings in which motivation and attitudes can affect performance (see Helms, 1992; Miller-Jones, 1989). Children from a minority culture that emphasizes the interpersonal nature of learning may be more likely to regard a lack of feedback from the tester as evidence that they are doing well on the test (Miller-Jones, 1989). These children may refrain from varying their strategies in the course of taking the test and consequently obtain a lower score. In some cultures, it is unusual for an adult who already knows the answer to a question to ask that question of a child, or for children to explain what they know (Heath, 1989; Rogoff & Morelli, 1989).

It is frequently observed that people from other cultures often misunderstand the instructions and fail to take seriously the test's requirements. Sinha (1983), for example, has provided an analysis of some of the cultural reasons why Asiatic Indians who have not been enculturated by the West have trouble with IQ tests. Asiatic Indians typically do not know that responses like "I don't know" or "I can't decide" will cause one to get lower scores on IQ tests. Also, Asiatic Indians are typically inhibited in responding, especially when the task seems pointless to them. In some cultures, such as the culture in which many African Americans are raised, a premium is placed on the creativity of responses. Sometimes African-American children are surprised to learn that they are expected to provide obvious answers on IQ tests (Heath, 1989; Helms, 1992). The creative answers they often do provide get them lower scores. Boykin (1994) argues that many African Americans are alienated from education and the accompanying psychometric enterprise because these institutions implicitly conflict with a heritage that emphasizes spirituality, harmony, expressive individualism, communalism, and orality, and not talent sorting and talent assessment. A consequence of that alienation may be a poorer average performance on IQ tests.

29.4.4   Cultural Differences in Prized Intellectual Competencies

In general, then, research shows that when the cultural and economic environments of ethnic groups are roughly equated, performance on IQ tests is roughly equated as well. But impoverished minority groups involuntarily displaced or shunned by the culture as a whole tend to do poorly on IQ tests. It would be a mistake, though, to conclude from the research that the poverty and cultural alienation endured by many minorities invariably suppresses intellectual development. Rather, people from different cultures place emphasis on different kinds of intellectual development (Garcia, 1981; Heath, 1983, 1989; Helms, 1992; Miller-Jones, 1989).

IQ tests were developed by middle- and upper-middle-class Europeans and people of European descent, so it is unsurprising that the intellectual skills relevant to IQ testing are emphasized more in their culture than in most other cultures. But the skills developed in other cultures in response to their environments, including impoverished environments, may be "invisible" to IQ tests. If care is taken to develop tests that reflect the intellectual competencies prized by a minority culture, but not necessarily by the majority culture, then the minority culture will do as well, and sometimes even better, on such tests.

Heath (1983) studied children from low-income African-American families, low-income European-American families, and middle-income European-American families. She noted that, on average, there were differences in the kinds of intellectual competencies with which these children began school. The African-American children from low-income families tended to be very skilled at responding to novel situations, defending themselves against a verbal insult, and telling creative stories. The European-American children from middle-income families were typically good at responding to requests, responding quickly when timed by a psychologist administering a test, and answering "why" questions. In general, then, this study makes the point that poverty or lack of formal education does not necessarily depress intellectual development; rather, it can lead to the development of intellectual skills different from those at which well-educated Europeans tend to excel and to measure with IQ tests.

Similar conclusions may be drawn from cross-cultural studies. Berry (1974) found that people from hunting cultures tend to do better on tests of perceptual discrimination and spacial processing than people from cultures in which hunting is less important. Rice farmers from Liberia are better than Americans at estimating quantities (Gay & Cole, 1967).

Children from Botswana, accustomed to storytelling, are better than American children at remembering stories (Dube, 1982). In one of my favorite examples, Cole, Gay, Glick, and Sharp (1971) asked adult Kpelle tribespeople to sort 20 familiar objects, such as knives, oranges, and so on, into groups of things that belong together. The Kpelle separated the objects into functional groups (e.g., knife with orange) and not taxonomic groups (e.g., knife with fork). Western adults, on the other hand, sort on the basis of taxonomy, as do children who receive higher IQ scores. But when the Kpelle adults were asked to sort the objects the way a "stupid" person would do it, the Kpelle sorted like the Western adults and high IQ children — that is, on the basis of taxonomy. At least with respect to those objects, the typical Kpelle adult regarded the functional grouping as more useful than the taxonomic grouping.

29.4.5   Sex Differences in Intellectual Competencies

Perhaps because people are fascinated by male–female differences, there have been many studies of sex differences in cognition. Many of these studies report that males tend to do better in tests of mathematical and spatial ability, and females tend to do better in tests of verbal ability (reviewed in Maccoby and Jacklin, 1974; Bjorklund, 1995; Kimura, 1992; Halpern, 1992). Examples of tasks that favor males and tasks that favor females are provided in figure 29.3. Men and women do not differ in IQ scores, vocabulary tests, or reasoning tasks.

The nature of the sex differences depends on how cognitive skills are measured. To illustrate, males do slightly better than females on spatial tests that measure the ability to orient oneself in relationship to objects or to mentally transform spatial information. But females do slightly better than males on spatial tests measuring ability to learn and remember spatial relationships (Silverman & Eals, 1992). Although males do better on most objective tests of mathematical ability, females get better grades in math courses than do males (Kimball, 1989).

TASKS FAVORING WOMEN	TASKS FAVORING MEN
Perceptual Speed Find the house that exactly matches the one on the left.	**Spatial Relations** A hole has been punched in the folded sheet. How will the sheet appear when unfolded?

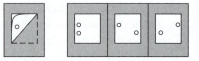

Verbal Fluency
Indicate another word that begins with the same letter, not included in the list.

Mathematical Reasoning
In the space at the left, write the answer to the following problem.

Limp, Livery, Love, Laser, Liquid, Low, Like, Lag, Live, Lug, Light, Lift, Liver, Lime, Leg, Load, Lap, Lucid

If only 60% of seedlings will survive, how many must be planted to obtain 660 trees?

Answers:
The house at the far right; Life or any other word beginning with L.

Answers:
The middle sheet; 1,100 seedlings.

FIGURE 29.3   Problem-solving tasks favoring women and problem-solving tasks favoring men.

From *Psychology* by Fernald, Dodge, © 1994. Reprinted with permission of Prentice-Hall, Inc., Upper Saddle River, NJ.

It should be noted that there is considerable controversy surrounding sex differences in cognition. Some researchers claim that the average differences between males and females are usually small and often statistically insignificant (Hyde, 1981) whereas others claim that the differences are substantial (Eagly, 1995). Some researchers claim that the differences may have been declining in recent years (Feingold, 1988; Voyer, Voyer, & Bryden, 1995) but others claim that the differences have remained stable (Halpern, 1992). And, of course, the biggest controversy has to do with whether cognitive differences between the sexes are due to the different genes that the sexes inherit or to the different environments and cultures in which they grow up.

Genetic Basis of Sex Differences in Cognition.   What is the cause of the sex differences in cognition? Obviously, boys and girls are treated differently and encouraged in different ways (Halpern, 1992). Boys are more likely to be encouraged to pursue careers in science, engineering, and mechanics, where mathematical and spatial skills are important. Girls are more likely to be encouraged to pursue careers in teaching and in child rearing, where communication skills are important.

Still, many researchers have proposed genetically based biological explanations for male–female differences in cognition (e.g., Kimura, 1992). Usually the ultimate cause of sex differences is attributed to the supposedly different selective pressures on males and females as humans evolved. Supposedly, males did the hunting, and so evolved better spatial skills for orienting to and transforming spatial information; and females did the gathering and child rearing, and so evolved better spatial memory and verbal skills.

What biological mechanism might be controlled by the genes that underlie sex differences in cognition? One example of a biological mechanism that may plausibly be coded for in the genes and that may give rise to sex differences in cognition is the production of sex hormones. Sex hormones, such as testosterone, are known to influence the organization of the mammalian brain during critical periods in prenatal development (Geschwind & Galabura, 1987; Halpern & Cass, 1994). A variety of research supports a correlation between sex hormones and performance on sex-differentiating cognitive tasks.

Women who were exposed to abnormally high levels of the male hormone androgen *in utero* score higher than do controls on tests of spatial ability (Resnick, Berenbaum, Gottesman, & Bouchard, 1986). Older males given testosterone improve on visual-spatial tasks (Janowsky, Oviatt, & Orwoll, 1994). Women do better on cognitive tasks that favor women over men, like verbal skills, and worse on cognitive tasks that favor men, like spatial rotation, when they are in the midluteal phase of the menstrual cycle than when they are in the late menstrual phase. Levels of estrogen and progesterone are higher during the midluteal phase (Hampson & Kimura, 1988; Hampson, 1990a, 1990b; see Kimura & Hampson, 1994). Men do better on tasks that favor men over women during the spring, when their testosterone levels are relatively low, than in the autumn, when their testosterone levels are relatively high (Kimura & Toussaint, 1991; see Kimura & Hampson, 1994). And it isn't just that men do better in the spring, when a young man's fancy supposedly turns to love–men's performance on tasks that do not favor men over women, such as reasoning, is the same in spring as in autumn. Apparently, average to below-average levels of testosterone are associated with optimal performance on visual-spatial tasks in men (Gouchie & Kimura, 1991).

What is it that sex hormones do to the brain that gives rise to differences in cognition? One possibility is that hormones affect how the cerebral hemispheres distribute their function. Recall that in most people the left hemisphere is more involved than the right in the control of language whereas the right hemisphere is more involved than the left in the control of spatial processing. Perhaps the female advantage for some verbal skills reflects the involvement of more right-hemisphere neural tissue in language–neural tissue that at the same time encroaches on the neural tissue that would have been used for spatial processing. At least some evidence suggests that there is less tendency among women for their left hemisphere to control language more than their right hemisphere (e.g., Shaywitz et al., 1995), although not all studies find a sex difference in hemispheric specialization (Newcombe & Bandura, 1983; Waber, Mann, Merola, & Moylan, 1985).

Another possible neurological model of sex hormone differences in brain organization has been developed by Kimura (1992). Kimura suggests that the organization of functions within the left hemisphere differs between the sexes. For language functions, women may make more use of the anterior portions of the left hemisphere whereas men make more use of the posterior left hemisphere. Such a difference may give rise to the tendency for women to do better on tests of verbal fluency, because the grammatical aspect of language may be more anatomically connected to the planning and strategic components of information processing. The more intimate connection in males between language centers and the centers involved in visual perception may give rise to the male advantages on spatial reasoning tasks. One line of evidence consistent with this view is that aphasia (language disturbance) occurs more often in women when the damage is near the front of the left hemisphere, but more often in men when the damage is in the posterior area of the left hemisphere (Kimura, 1992).

It is important to point out that the supposed differences in the brains of men and women may not necessarily reflect the effects of sex hormones; those differences may be mediated by some other biological mechanism. Furthermore, the sex differences in relevant biological mechanisms need not be entirely or even at all due to genes. It may be that experiences, like playing with toys or studying mathematics, affect the production of hormones (and any other relevant biological mechanism) and thereby produce sex differences in certain cognitive skills.

Environmental Explanations of Sex Differences in Cognition.   My own belief is that it remains a viable possibility that sex differences in cognition are due mostly to environmental factors (how is that for a hedge!). One line of evidence for an environmental explanation of sex differences is that parental attitudes and expectations are correlated with performance on math (Raymond & Benbow, 1986) and verbal tests (Roe, Drivas, Karagellis, & Roe, 1985). An especially compelling line of evidence is research that shows that, with practice and feedback, women improve as much as men do on spatial tasks (e.g., Law, Pellegrino, & Hunt, 1993; see Halpern, 1992 for a review). Some cross-cultural work shows that among Canadian Eskimos, a culture in which both males and females travel far from home and hunt, there are no differences in spatial abilities between males and females (Berry, 1966).

Indeed, at present in our culture, it is at least debatable whether there are any reliable male–female differences in verbal and math skills. Hyde and Linn (1986, 1988) reviewed 165 studies of verbal ability representing over 1.4 million people and found no average difference between males and females. Moreover, Hyde, Fennema, and Lamon (1990) reviewed 100 studies of mathematical performance and found that sex differences were quite small, but tended to favor females in large samples that are taken from the general population. It is only in the population of mathematically gifted individuals that males outperform females, on the average.

Carol Tavris, in her splendid book *The Mismeasure of Woman* (Tavris, 1992), reviews evidence that suggests that male and female brains learn, reason, and process information in similar ways. Tavris also discusses the bias against publishing research that finds no sex differences in cognition, and the unfortunate consequences this bias has for women. For example, a belief that males have superior mathematical skills, sustained by a bias against publishing studies that show no sex differences in mathematical skill, provides a rationale for excluding women from the sciences and for denigrating the few women who do manage to become scientists.

29.4.6   Conclusions about the Genetic Basis of Intelligence

There seems to be no easy way to summarize the evidence relevant to the genetic basis for intelligence. Because we are unable to conduct controlled experiments that vary genes and environments, we remain ignorant of how to interpret correlations in the IQ scores of individuals who share genes. Individuals who share genes almost always share environments. With regard to sex differences in cognition, it is difficult to disentangle the influence of sex-linked genes and sex-linked environments. It is true that the twins-reared-apart studies, as well as other research on adoption, suggest that something that is genetically inherited causes differences in scores on IQ tests. However, it is not clear what genetically controlled biological mechanism is responsible for the similarity in IQ scores. Indeed, at this point we do not really know what biological mechanisms are the underlying basis for individual differences in any of the potentially limitless kinds of skills a person can acquire. All we can say with certainty is that the biological mechanisms underlying intellectual development are, especially in our species, designed to enable us to learn from the environment. Consequently, any act of the intellect will invariably reflect both biological and environmental factors. Genetic models of intellectual differences to date lack any clear explanation of what biological mechanisms underlie individual differences. Sex hormones may be a basis for male–female differences in cognition; however, it is possible that sex hormone production may be the effect of different environments and not necessarily the direct cause of cognitive differences.

Any useful model needs to explain how a genetically determined biological mechanism interacts with various aspects of the environment to produce intellectual development. It seems pointless to argue about whether intellectual development is primarily determined by the genes or by the environment, because either can dominate depending on the circumstances. If people are given no exposure to music, for example, they will not develop musical skill. If people are born deaf as a result of a genetic defect, they will not develop any musical skill.

And, of course, the role of genes and the biological mechanisms controlling intellectual differences is invariably complicated by the difficulty in defining and measuring intelligence. As I suggested in earlier sections of this chapter, a good case can be made that there are a potentially vast number of relatively autonomous skills that a person can acquire, any one of which could be assessed in many different ways. The effects of genetically controlled biological mechanisms and environmental variables could be quite different depending on what aspect of intelligence one cares to study.

My own sense is that the influence of genes and environmental variables is so complex and intertwined, the research limitations on the effects of genes so intractable, and the notion of intelligence so potentially multifaceted, that it is not possible to know exactly how genes and environmental variables interact to produce individual differences in cognition. This need not be a distressing state of affairs, however. Our goal as psychologists and educators should be to try to create the best possible environments for fostering the acquisition of intellectual competence in our children, regardless of their genetic makeup.

SUMMARY AND CONCLUSIONS

The integrating theme for this chapter was a contrast between a hereditarian approach to individual differences in intelligence and a multi-faceted approach. The hereditarian approach make two essential claims: intelligence is unitary and is determined primarily by the genes one inherits. The multi-faceted approach claims that there are many different and relatively autonomous domains of intelligence. Intellectual skill in one domain is typically unrelated to intellectual skill in other domains.

In the first section, I discussed the rise of the hereditarian approach to intelligence and the intelligence testing movement. Probably the most historically significant event in the history of intelligence testing was the development of IQ tests. IQ tests are known to be moderately correlated with grades in school, occupational status, and success in an occupation.

In section 29.2, I discussed the main evidence for a unitary view of intelligence, which is that performance on the subtests that make up the IQ inventory and between IQ scores and academic achievement are positively correlated. A generic information processing perspective proposes that intellectual tasks are performed by a common information processing system. Differences in intellectual capability are due to the speed and efficiency with which various stages of the system are executed. One line of evidence in support of the information processing perspective comes from research that shows that the shorter the stimulus exposure time at which people can accurately discriminate between the length of two lines, the higher the person's IQ score. In a sense, the rise of the information processing analysis of individual differences represents a re-emergence of the ideas of Francis Galton, who espoused them about 100 years ago.

Recent physiological research has suggested correlations between performance on intelligence tests and physiological measures such as cortical metabolic rate or neural conduction speed. Usually, these neurophysiologically based models implicitly suppose that intelligence is unitary — that some aspect of neurophysiology that permeates all intellectual tasks is the factor that gives rise to individual differences in cognition. While intriguing, such research has not yet elucidated the underlying biological mechanisms or the causes of such correlations.

At any rate, correlations among IQ subtests or between IQ tests and academic success can be explained without supposing that all intellectual differences represent differences in a single underlying substrate of the various cognitive systems. In section 29.3 I discuss how the correlations could reflect motivation or the limited range of skills measured by IQ tests and taught in schools. Indeed, if one examines creativity, social skills, or practical skills used in everyday life, the correlations between such skills and IQ tests are essentially nonexistent.

One alternative to the unitary model is the claim that there are several distinct, relatively autonomous categories of intelligence. Howard Gardner (1983), for example, claims that there are six different categories of intelligence, and cites physiological and anthropological evidence to bolster his claim. Another alternative claims that there are potentially an unlimited number of categories of intelligence, any one of which may be measured in a potentially unlimited number of ways. The ways a culture defines and measures intelligence reflect the values and goals of the culture, and not something intrinsic to the biology of people.

In section 29.4 I discuss the hereditarian claim that intelligence is largely genetically determined. The claim is supported by familial correlations in IQ performance, and by the high correlation between the IQ scores of identical twins reared apart. However, the familial pattern of correlations is also consistent with a substantial impact of environmental factors on intelligence. The twins-reared-apart findings only show that some genetically determined biological mechanism underlies IQ performance. That mechanism might control intellectual processes, but it might also control physical appearance, metabolic rate, resistance to disease and/or any of a number of other traits.

One unfortunate implication sometimes drawn from a theory that emphasizes the genetic basis of intelligence is that environmental factors are likely to have minimal influence on intellectual development. In fact, though, a variety of studies demonstrate that appropriate environmental intervention can improve the intellectual performance of individuals who might otherwise be at "intellectual risk." Furthermore, performance on IQ tests is rising about 3 IQ points a decade all around the world.

Another unfortunate implication historically drawn by hereditarians is that ethnic differences in IQ performance reflect genetic differences among racial and other ethnic groups. However, adoption studies and other research convincingly makes the case that differences among the average IQ scores of ethnic groups reflect environmental and cultural differences among groups. If members from two different ethnic groups are raised in similar circumstances, their average IQ performances will be similar as well. Furthermore, some research suggests that different ethnic groups, in response to their respective environments, are likely to develop different skills, not all of which are measured by IQ tests.

Sex differences in cognition have been explored as well. Some hereditarian approaches have claimed that the superior performance of the average male on spacial and mathematical tests, and the superior performance of the average female on verbal tests, reflect sex-linked genetic differences between the sexes. Fluctuations in sex hormones are correlated with performance on just those tasks on which the sexes are different. However, once again, the sex differences may be largely attributable to environmental factors. I am personally impressed with the research that shows that, with practice and feedback, women improve as much as men do on spatial tasks. There is some admittedly controversial evidence that sex differences in cognition are shrinking over time, possibly because of cultural changes made in recent years whereby more women are encouraged to attend college and pursue careers in which mathematical and spatial skills are important.

Certainly both the biological mechanisms put into place by the genes and the environment invariably contribute to intellectual growth and individual differences. How could it be otherwise? A useful model of biology's role in intelligence must specify precisely how any given biological mechanism responds to the various aspects of the environment in the course of intellectual development. Given that controlled experiments are ethically and biologically impossible, we may never completely understand the precise contributions that genes and environmental factors make to individual intellectual differences.

REFERENCES

Anastasi, A. (1985). Reciprocal relations between cognitive and affective development: With implications for sex differences. In T. B. Sonderegger (Ed.), *Psychology and gender* (Nebraska Symposium on Motivation, Vol. 32, pp. 1–35). Lincoln: University of Nebraska Press.

Anastasi, A. (1988). *Psychological testing.* New York: Macmillan.

Baird, L. L. (1982). *The role of academic ability in high-level accomplishment and general success* (College Board Repl No. 82–6). New York: College Entrance Examination Board.

Baird, L. L. (1984). Relationships between ability, college attendance, and family income. *Research in Higher Education, 21,* 373–395.

Barrett, G. V., & Depinet, R. L. (1991). A reconsideration of testing for competence rather than for intelligence. *American Psychologist, 46,* 1012–1024.

Barrett, P., Eysenck, H. J., & Luching, S. (1989). Reaction time and intelligence: A replicated study. *Intelligence, 10,* 9–40.

Berry, J. W. (1996). Temne and Eskimo perceptual skill. *International Journal of Psychology, 1,* 207–229.

Berry, J. W. (1974). Radical cultural relativism and the concept of intelligence. In J. W. Berry & P. R. Dasen (Eds.), *Culture and cognition: Readings in cross-cultural psychology* (pp. 225–229). London: Methuen.

Binet, A. (1911). *Les indees modernes sur les enfants.* Paris: Flamarion.

Binet, A., & Simon, T. (1916). *The intelligence of the feeble-minded.* Baltimore: Williams and Wilkins.

Birren, J. E., Woods, A. M., & Williams, M. V. (1979). Speed of behavior as an indicator of age changes and the integrity of the nervous system. In F. Hoffmeister & C. Muller (Eds.), *Brain function in old age.* New York: Springer-Verlag.

Bjorklund, D. F. (1995). *Children's thinking: Developmental function and individual differences.* Pacific Grove, CA: Brooks/Cole.

Boring, E. G. (1950). *A history of experimental psychology.* New York: Appleton-Century-Crofts.

Bouchard, T. J., & McCue, M. (1981). Familial studies of intelligence: A review. *Science, 212,* 1055–1059.

Boykin, A. W. (1994). Harvesting talent and culture: African-American children and educational reform. In R. Rossi (Ed.), *Schools and students at risk,* (pp. 116–138). New York: Teachers College Press.

Boyle, J. P. (1987). Intelligence, reasoning, and language proficiency. *The Modern Language Journal, 71,* 277–288.

Bronfenbrenner, U. (1974). *Is early intervention effective? A report on longitudinal evaluations of preschool programs* (Vol. 2). Washington, DC: Department of Health, Education, and Welfare, Office of Child Development.

Butler, M. S., Dickinson, W. A., Katholi, C., & Halsey, J. H. (1983). The comparative effects of organic brain disease on cerebral blood flow and measured intelligence. *Annals of Neurology, 13,* 155–159.

Campbell, F. A., & Ramey, C. T. (1994). Effects of early intervention on intellectual and academic achievement: A follow-up study on children from low-income families. *Child Development, 65,* 684–698.

Carroll, J. B. (1983). Individual differences in cognitive abilities. In S. H. Irvine & J. W. Berry (Eds.), *Human assessment and cultural factors.* New York: Plenum.

Ceci, S. J., & Liker, J. K. (1986). A day at the races: A study of IQ, expertise, and cognitive complexity. *Journal of Experimental Psychology: General, 115,* 255–266.

Chase, T. N., Fedio, P., Foster, N. L., Brooks, R., DiChiro, G., & Mansi, L. (1984). Wechsler Adult Intelligence Scale Performance. Cortical location by flurodeoxyglucose F 18-positron emission tomography. *Archives of Neurology, 41,* 1244–1247.

Cole, M., Gay, J., Glick, J., & Sharp, D. W. (1971). *The cultural context of learning and thinking.* New York: Basic Books.

Daneman, M., & Carpenter, P. A. (1980). Individual differences in working memory and reading. *Journal of Verbal Learning and Verbal Behavior, 9,* 450–466.

Dark, V. J., & Benbow, C. P. (1991). Differential enhancement of working memory with mathematical versus versus verbal precocity. *Journal of Educational Psychology, 83,* 48–60.

Deary, I. J. (1993). Inspection time and WAIS-R IQ subtypes: A confirmatory factor analysis study. *Intelligence, 17,* 223–236.

Deary, I. J., & Stough, C. (1996). Intelligence and inspection time: Achievements, prospects, problems. *American Psychologist, 51,* 599–608.

Dempster, F. N. (1981). Memory span: Sources of individual and developmental differences. *Psychological Bulletin, 89,* 63–100.

Dorner, D., & Kreuzig, H. (1983). Problemosefahigkeit and intelligenz. *Psychologische Rundhaus, 34,* 185–192.

Dreger, R. M. (1968). General temperament and personality factors related to intellectual performances. *Journal of Genetic Psychology, 113,* 275–293.

Dube, E. F. (1982). Literacy, cultural familiarity, and "intelligence" as determinants of story recall. In U. Neisser (Ed.), *Memory observed: Remembering in natural contexts* (pp. 274–292). New York: Freeman.

Eagly, A. H. (1995). The science and politics of comparing women and men. *American Psychologist, 50,* 145–158.

Eddy, D. M. (1988). Probabilistic reasoning in clinical medicine: Problems and opportunities. In D. Kahneman, P. Slovic, & A. Tversky (Eds.), *Judgment under uncertainty: Heuristics and biases* (pp. 249–267). Cambridge, England: Cambridge University Press.

Eyferth, K. (1961). Leistungen verschiedener Gruppen con Besatzungskindern in Hamburg-Weschler Intelligenztest fur Kinder (HAWIK). *Archiv fur die gesamte Psychologie, 113,* 223–241.

Feingold, A. (1988). Cognitive gender differences are disappearing. *American Psychologist, 42,* 95–103.

Flynn, J. R. (1980). *Race, IQ and Jensen.* London: Routledge & Kegan Paul.

Flynn, J. R. (1984). The mean IQ of Americans: Massive gains 1932–1978. *Psychological Bulletin, 95,* 29–51.

Flynn, J. R. (1987). Massive IQ gains in 14 nations: What IQ tests really measure. *Psychological Bulletin, 95,* 29–51.

Frederiksen, N., Carlson, S., & Ward, W. C. (1984). The place of social intelligence in a taxonomy of cognitive abilities. *Intelligence, 8,* 315–337.

Galton, F. (1883). *Inquiries into human faculty and its development.* London: Macmillan.

Galton, F. (1884). *Hereditary genius.* New York: D. Appleton.

Garber, H. L. (1988). *The Milwaukee Project: Preventing mental retardation in children at risk.* Washington, DC: American Association of Mental Retardation.

Garcia, J. (1981). The logic and limits of mental aptitude testing. *American Psychologist, 36,* 1172–1180.

Gardner, H. (1983). *Frames of mind.* New York: Basic Books.

Gay, J., & Cole, M. (1967). *The new mathematics and old culture: A study of learning among the Kpelle of Liberia.* New York: Holt, Rinehart & Winston.

Geschwind, N., & Galabura, A. M. (1987). *Cerebral lateralization: Biological mechanisms, associations, and pathology.* Cambridge, MA: MIT Press.

Gilbert, J. A. (1894). Researches on the mental and physical development of school children. *Studies from the Yale Psychological Laboratory, 2,* 40–100.

Goldberg, R. A., Schwartz, S., & Stewart, M. (1977). Individual differences in cognitive processes. *Journal of Educational Psychology, 66,* 325–332.

Gottfredson, L. S., & Brown, V. C. (1981). Occupational differences among white men in the first decade after high school. *Journal of Vocational Behavior, 19,* 251–289.

Gouchie, C., & Kimura, D. (1991). The relationship between testosterone levels and cognitive ability patterns. *Psychoneuroendocrinology, 16,* 323–344.

Gould, S. J. (1981). *The mismeasure of man.* New York: Norton.

Guenther, R. K. (1991). Generic versus specialized information processing. *American Journal of Psychology, 104,* 193–209.

Guilford, J. P. (1964). Zero correlations among tests of intellectual abilities. *Psychological Bulletin, 61,* 401–404.

Guilford, J. P. (1967). *The nature of human intelligence.* New York: McGraw-Hill.

Haier, R. J., Siegel, B. V., Nuechterlein, K. H., Hazlett, E., Wu, J. C., Paek, J., Browning, H. L., & Buchsbaum, M. S. (1988). Cortical glucose metabolic rate correlates of abstract reasoning and attention studies with positron emission tomography. *Intelligence, 12,* 199–217.

Haier, R. J., Siegel, B. V., MacLachlan, A., Soderling, E., Lottenberg, S., & Buchsbaum, M. S. (1992). Regional glucose metabolic changes after learning a complex, visio-spatial-motor task: A positron emission tomography study. *Brain Research, 570,* 134–143.

Halpern, D. F. (1992). *Sex differences in cognitive abilities* (2d ed.). Hillsdale, NJ: Erlbaum.

Halpern, D. F. & Cass, M. (1994). Laterality, sexual orientation, and immune system functioning: Is there a relationship? *International Journal of Neuroscience, 77,* 167–180.

Hampson, E. (1990). Variations in sex-related cognitive abilities across the menstrual cycle. *Brain and Cognition, 14,* 26–43.

Hampson, E. (1990). Estrogen-related variations in human spatial and articulatory motor skills. *Psychoneuroendocrinology, 15,* 97–111.

Hampson, E., & Kimura, D. (1988). Reciprocal effects of hormonal fluctuations on human motor and perceptual-spatial skills. *Behavioral Neuro-science, 102,* 456–459.

Hart, B., & Risley, T. R. (1992). American parenting of lan-guage-learning children: Persisting differences in family-child interaction observed in natural home environments. *Developmental Psychology, 28,* 1096–1105.

Heath, S. B. (1983). *Ways with words.* Cambridge, Eng-land: Cambridge University Press.

Heath, S. B. (1989). Oral and literate traditions among Black Americans living in poverty. *American Psy-chologist, 44,* 367–373.

Helms, J. E. (1992). Why is there no study of cultural equivalence in standardized cognitive ability test-ing? *American Psychologist, 47,* 1083–1101.

Hergenhahn, B. R. (1986). *An introduction to the history of psychology.* Belmont, CA: Wadsworth.

Hernstein, R., & Murray, C. (1994). *The bell curve.* New York: Free Press.

Horn, J. L., Loehlin, J., & Willerman, L. (1975). Prelimi-nary report of Texas adoption project. In Munsinger, H., The adopted child's IQ: A critical review. *Psychological Bulletin, 82,* 623–659.

Hunt, E. (1978). Mechanisms of verbal ability. *Psycho-logical Review, 85,* 199–230.

Hunt, E. (1980). Intelligence as an information-processing concept. *British Journal of Psychology, 71,* 449–474.

Hunt, E. (1983). On the nature of intelligence. *Science, 219,* 141–146.

Hunt, E., Lunneborg, C., & Lewis, J. (1975). What does it mean to be high verbal? *Cognitive Psychology, 7,* 194–227.

Hyde, J. S. (1981). How large are cognitive gender differ-ences? A meta-analysis using w2 and d. *American Psychologist, 36,* 892–901.

Hyde, J. S., & Linn, M. C. (1988). Gender differences in verbal ability: A meta-analysis. *Psychological Bul-letin, 104,* 53–69.

Hyde, J. S., & Linn, M. C. (Eds.) (1986). *The psychology of gender advances through meta-analysis.* Balti-more: Johns Hopkins University Press.

Hyde, J. S., Fennema, E., & Lamon, S. J. (1990). Gender differences in mathematics performance: A meta-analysis. *Psychological Bulletin, 107,* 139–155.

Jensen, A. R. (1969). How much can we boost IQ and scholastic achievement? *Harvard Educational Review,* 39, 1–123.

Jensen, A. R. (1979). G: Outmoded theory or uncon-quered frontier? *Creative Science Technology, 2,* 16–29.

Jensen, A. R. (1982). Reaction time and psychometric g. In H. J. Eysenck (Eds.), *A model for intelligence* (pp. 93–123). Berlin: Springer-Verlag.

Jensen, A. R. (1993). Why is reaction time correlated with psychometric g? *Current Directions in Psycholog-ical Science, 2,* 53–56.

Keating, D. P. (1982). The emperor's new clothes: The "new look" in intelligence research. In R. Sternberg (Ed.), *Advances in the psychology of human intelligence* (Vol. 2, pp. 1–45).

Keating, D. P., & Bobbit, B. L. (1978). Individual and developmental differences in cognitive-processing components of mental ability. *Child Development, 49,* 155–167.

Kimball, M. M. (1989). A new perspective on women's math achievement. *Psychological Bulletin, 105,* 198–214.

Kimura, D. (1992). Sex differences in the brain. *Scientific American, 267,* 118–125.

Kimura, D., & Hampson, E. (1994). Cognitive pattern in men and women is influenced by fluctuation in sex hormones. *Current Directions in Psychological Sci-ence, 3,* 57–61.

King, J., & Just, M. A. (1991). Individual differences in syntactic processing: The role of working memory. *Journal of Memory and Languages, 30,* 580–602.

Klaus, R. A., & Gray, S. (1968). The early training project for disadvantaged children: A report after five years. *Monographs of the Society for Research in Child Development, 33* (Serial No. 120).

Kline, P. (1991). *Intelligence: The psychometric view.* New York: Routledge.

Kosslyn, S. M., Brunn, J., Cave, K. R., & Wallach, R. W. (1984). Individual differences in mental imagery ability: A computational analysis. *Cognition, 18,* 195–243.

Lachman, R., Lachman, J. L., & Butterfield, E. C. (1979). *Cognitive psychology and information processing: An introduction.* Hillsdale, NJ: Erlbaum.

Larson, G. E., & Saccuzzo, D. P. (1989). Cogntive corre-lates of general intelligence: Toward a process the-ory of g. *Intelligence, 13,* 5–31.

Lave, J. (1988). *Cognition in practice.* Cambridge, Eng-land: Cambridge University Press.

Law, D. J., Pellegrino, J. W., & Hunt, E. B. (1993). Com-paring the tortoise and the hare. Gender differences and experience in dynamic spatial reasoning tasks. *Psychological Science, 41,* 35–40.

Lazar, I., Darlington, R., Murray, H., Royce, J., & Snipper, A. (1982). Lasting effects of early education: A report from the Consortium for Longitudinal Studies. *Monographs of the Society for Research in Child Development, 47* (Serial No. 195).

Loehlin, J. C., Lindzey, G., & Spuhler, J. N. (1975). *Race differences in intelligence.* San Francisco: Freeman.

Longstreth, L. (1984). Jensen's reaction-time investigations of intelligence: A critique. *Intelligence, 8,* 139–160.

Maccoby, E. E., & Jacklin, C. N. (1974). *The psychology of sex differences.* Stanford, CA: Stanford University Press.

MacKinnon, D. W. (1962). The nature and nurture of creative talent. *American Psychologist, 17,* 484–495.

Mackintosh, J. J. (1986). The biology of intelligence? *British Journal of Psychology, 77,* 1–18.

McClelland, D. C. (1973). Testing for competence rather than for "intelligence." *American Psychologist, 28,* 1–14.

McDermid, C. D. (1965). Some correlates of creativity in engineering personnel. *Journal of Applied Psychology, 49,* 14–19.

Miller-Jones, D. (1989). Culture and testing. *American Psychologist, 44,* 360–366.

Miller, L. B., & Bizzell, R. P. (1984). Long-term effects of four preschool programs: Ninth and tenth-grade results. *Child Development, 55,* 1570–1587.

Mumaw, R. J., Pellegrino, J. W., Kail, R. V., & Carter, P. (1984). Different slopes for different folks: Process analysis of spatial aptitude. *Memory and Cognition, 12,* 515–521.

Neisser, U., Boodoo, G., Bouchard, T. J., Boyken, A. W., Brody, N., Ceci, S. J., Halpern, D. F., Loehlin, J. C., Perloff, R., Sternberg, R. J., & Urbiva, S. (1996). Intelligence: Knowns and unknowns. *American Psychologist, 51,* 77–101.

Nettlebeck, T., & Lally, M. (1976). Inspection time and measured intelligence. *British Journal of Psychology, 67,* 17–22.

Newcombe, N., & Bandura, M. M. (1983). Effects of age at puberty on spatial ability in girls: A question of mechanism. *Developmental Psychology, 19,* 215–244.

Oakland, T. (1983). Joint use of adaptive behavior and IQ to predict achievement. *Journal of Consulting and Clinical Psychology, 51,* 298–301.

Ogbu, J. U. (1978). *Minority education and caste: The American system in cross-cultural perspective.* New York: Academic Press.

Ogbu, J. U. (1994). From cultural differences to differences in cultural frames of reference. In P. M. Greenfield & R. R. Cocking (Eds.), *Cross-cultural roots of minority child development* (pp. 365–391). Hillsdale, NJ: Erlbaum.

Parks, R. W., Loewenstein, D. A., Dodril, K. L., Barker, W. W., Yoshi, F., Chang, J. Y., Emran, A., Apicella, A., Shermata, W. A., & Duara, R. (1988). Cerebral metabolic effects of a verbal fluency test: A PET scan study. *Journal of Clinical and Experimental Neuropsychology, 10,* 565–575.

Pellegrino, J. W., & Glaser, R. (1979). Cognitive correlates and components in the analysis of individual differences. *Intelligence, 3,* 187–214.

Perfetto, G. A., & Lesgold, A. M. (1977). Discourse comprehension and sources of individual differences. In M. A. Just & P. A. Carpenter (Eds.), *Cognitive processes in comprehension* (pp. 141–183). Hillsdale, NJ: Erlbaum.

Perkins, D. N. (1988). Creativity and the quest for mechanism. In R. J. Sternberg & E. E. Smith (Eds.), *The psychology of human thought.* Cambridge, England: Cambridge University Press.

Ramey, C. T., Campbell, F. A., & Finkelstein, N. W. (1984). Course and structure of intellectual development in children at risk for developmental retardation. In P. H. Brooks, R. Sperber, & C. McCauley (Eds.), *Learning and cognition in the mentally retarded.* Hillsdale, NJ: Erlbaum.

Raymond, C. L., & Benbow, C. P. (1986). Gender differences in mathematics: A function of parental support and student sex typing? *Developmental Psychology, 22,* 808–819.

Reed, T. E., & Jensen, A. R. (1992). Conduction velocity in a brain nerve pathway of normal adults correlates with intelligence level. *Intelligence, 16,* 259–272.

Resnick, S. M., Berenbaum, S. A., Gottesman, I. F., & Bouchard, T. J., Jr. (1986). Early hormonal influence on cognitive functioning in congential adrenal hyperplasia. *Developmental Psychology, 22,* 191–198.

Richards, R., Kinney, D. K., Benet, M., & Merzel, A. P. C. (1988). Assessing everyday creativity characteristics of the lifetime creativity scales and validation with three large samples. *Journal of Personality and Social Psychology, 54,* 476–485.

Richardson, K. (1991). *Understanding intelligence.* Philadelphia: Open University Press.

Roe, K. V., Drivas, A., Karagellis, A., & Roe, A. (1985). Sex differences in vocal interaction with mother and stranger in Greek infants: Some cognitive implications. *Developmental Psychology, 21,* 372–377.

Rogoff, B., & Morelli, G. (1989). Perspectives on children's development from cultural psychology. *American Psychologist, 44,* 343–348.

Rothstein, M. G., Paunonen, S. V., Rush, J. C., & King, G. A. (1994). Personality and cognitive ability indicators of performance in graduate business school. *Journal of Educational Psychology, 86,* 516–530.

Ruchalla, E., Scholt, E., & Vogel, F. (1985). Relations between mental performance and reaction time: New aspects of an old problem. *Intelligence, 9,* 189–205.

Rushton, J. P. (1988). Race differences in behaviour: A review and evolutionary analysis. *Personality and Individual Differences, 9,* 1009–1024.

Rushton, J. P. (1991). Do r-K strategies underlie human race differences? *Canadian Psychology, 32,* 29–42.

Scarr, S., Pakstis, A. J., Katz, S. H., & Barker, B. (1977). Absence of a relationship between degree of white ancestry and intellectual skills within a Black population. *Human Genetics, 39,* 69–86.

Scarr, S., & Weinberg, R. A. (1976). IQ test performance of black children adopted by white families. *American Psychologist, 31,* 726–739.

Scarr, S., & Weinberg, R. A. (1983). The Minnesota adoption studies: Genetic differences and malleability. *Child Development, 54,* 260–267.

Scarr-Salapatek, S. (1971). Race, social class, and IQ. *Science, 174,* 1285–1295.

Schofield, N. J., & Ashman, A. F. (1986). The relationship between digit span and cognitive processing across ability groups. *Intelligence, 10,* 59–73.

Shaywitz, B. A., Shaywitz, S. E., Pugh, K. R., Constable, R. T., Skudlarski, P., Fulbright, R. K., Bronen, R. A., Fletcher, J. M., Shankweller, D. P., Katz, L., & Gore, J. C. (1995). Sex differences in the functional organization of the brain for language. *Nature, 373,* 607–609.

Shields, J. (1962). *Monozygotic twins brought up apart and brought together.* London: Oxford University Press.

Shuter-Dyson, R. (1982). Musical ability. In D. Deutsch (Ed.), *The psychology of music.* New York: Academic Press.

Silverman, I., & Eals, M. (1992). Sex differences in spatial abilities: Evolutionary theory and data. In J. Barkow, L. Cosmides, & J. Tooby (Eds.), *The adapted mind: Evolutionary psychology and the generation of culture* (pp. 539–549). New York: Oxford University Press.

Smith, C. B. (1984). Aging and changes in cerebral energy metabolism. *Trends in Neurosciences, 7,* 203–208.

Spearman, C. (1927). *The abilities of man.* New York: Macmillan.

Sternberg, R. J. (1985). *Beyond IQ: A triarchic theory of human intelligence.* Cambridge, MA: Cambridge University Press.

Sternberg, R. J. (1990). *Metaphors of mind: Conceptions of the nature of intelligence.* Cambridge, England: Cambridge University Press.

Sternberg, R. J., Wagner, R. K., Williams, W. M., & Horvath, J. A. (1995). Testing common sense. *American Psychologist, 50,* 912–927.

Stevenson, H. W., Stigler, J. W., Lee, S., Lucker, G. W., Kitamura, S., & Hsu, C. (1985). Cognitive performance and academic achievement of Japanese, Chinese, and American children. *Child Development, 56,* 718–734.

Tavris, C. (1992). *The mismeasure of woman: Why women are not the better sex, the inferior sex, or the opposite sex.* New York: Simon & Schuster.

Thorndike, E. L. (1936). Factor analysis of social and abstract intelligence. *Journal of Educational Psychology, 27,* 231–233.

Thurstone, L. L. (1938). *Primary mental abilities.* Chicago: University of Chicago Press, Psychometric Monographs, No. 1.

Tizard, B., Cooperman, O., Joseph, A., & Tizard, J. (1972). Environmental effects of language development: A study of young children in long-stay residential nurseries. *Child Development, 43,* 337–358.

Van Court, M., & Bean, F. D. (1985). Intelligence and fertility in the United States: 1912–1982. *Intelligence, 9,* 23–32.

Vernon, P. A. (1983). Speed of information processing and general intelligence. *Intelligence, 7,* 53–70.

Vernon, P. A., & Kantor, L. (1986). Reaction time correlates with intelligence test scores obtained under either timed and untimed conditions. *Intelligence, 10,* 315–330.

Vernon, P. A., & Mori, M. (1992). Intelligence, reaction times, and peripheral nerve conductor velocity. *Intelligence, 16,* 273–288.

Voyer, D., Voyer, S., & Bryden, M. F. (1995). Magnitude of sex difference in spatial abilities: A meta-analysis and consideration of critical variables. *Psychological Bulletin, 117,* 250–270.

Waber, D. P., Mann, M. B., Merola, J., & Moylan, P. (1985). Physical maturation rate and cognitive performance in early adolescence: A longitudinal examination. *Developmental Psychology, 21,* 666–681.

Wagner, R. K., & Sternberg, R. J. (1985). Practical intelligence in real-world pursuits: The role of tacit knowledge. *Journal of Personality and Social Psychology, 49,* 436–458.

Wagner, R. K., & Sternberg, R. J. (1990). Streetsmarts. In K. E. Clark & M. B. Clark (Eds.), *Measures of leadership* (pp. 493–504). West Orange, NJ: Leadership Library of American.

Wallach, M. A. (1976). Tests tell us little about talent. *American Scientist, 64,* 57–63.

White, B. L. (1978). *Experience and environment: Major influences on the development of the young child* (Vol. 2). Englewood Cliffs, NJ: Prentice Hall.

Wissler, C. (1901). The correlation of mental and physical tests. *Psychological Review Monograph Supplements, 3(6),* Whole No. 16.

Wong, G. M. T., Day, J. D., Maxwell, S. E., & Meara, N. M. (1995). A multitrait-multimethod study of academic and social intelligence in college students. *Journal of Educational Psychology, 87,* 117–133.

Woodrow, H. (1939). The common factos in fifty-two mental tests. *Psychometrika, 4,* 99–108.

Yekovich, F. R., Walker, C. H., Ogle, L. T., & Thompson, M. A. (1990). The influence of domain knowledge on inferencing in low-aptitude individuals. *The Psychology of Learning and Motivation, 25,* 259–278.

Yong, L. M. S. (1994). Relations between creativity and intelligence among Malaysian pupils. *Perceptual and Motor Skills, 79,* 739–742.

CHAPTER THIRTY

LOCALIZATION OF COGNITIVE OPERATIONS IN THE HUMAN BRAIN

MICHAEL I. POSNER, STEVEN E. PETERSEN, PETER T. FOX, AND MARCUS E. RAICHLE

Introduction

The question of localization of cognition in the human brain is an old and difficult one (Churchland, 1986). However, current analyses of the operations involved in cognition (Anderson, 1980) and new techniques for the imaging of brain function during cognitive tasks (Raichle, 1983) have combined to provide support for a new hypothesis. The hypothesis is that elementary operations forming the basis of cognitive analyses of human tasks are strictly localized. Many such local operations are involved in any cognitive task. A set of distributed brain areas must be orchestrated in the performance of even simple cognitive tasks. The task itself is not performed by any single area of the brain, but the operations that underlie the performance are strictly localized. This idea fits generally with many network theories in neuroscience and cognition. However, most neuroscience network theories of higher processes (Mesolam, 1981; Goldman-Rakic, 1988) provide little information on the specific computations performed at the nodes of the network, and most cognitive network models provide little or no information on the anatomy involved (McClelland & Rumelhart, 1986). Our approach relates specific mental operations as developed from cognitive models to neural anatomical areas.

The study of reading and listening has been one of the most active areas in cognitive science for the study of internal codes involved in information processing (Posner, 1986). In this chapter we review results of studies on cognitive tasks that suggest several separate codes for processing individual words. These codes can be accessed from input or from attention. We also review studies of alert monkeys and brain-lesioned patients that provide

From *Science* 240 (1988): 1627–1631. Reprinted with permission from AAAS.

evidence on the localization of an attention system for visual spatial information. This system is apparently unnecessary for processing single, foveally centered words. Next, we introduce data from positron emission tomography (PET) concerning the neural systems underlying the coding of individual visual (printed) words. These studies support the findings in cognition and also give new evidence for an anterior attention system involved in language processing. Finally, we survey other areas of cognition for which recent findings support the localization of component mental operations.

30.1   INTERNAL CODES

The most advanced efforts to develop cognitive models of information processing have been in the area of the coding of individual words through reading and listening (Posner, 1986; Marshall & Newcombe, 1973; LaBerge & Samuels, 1974; Carr & Pollatsek, 1985; Coltheart, 1985). These efforts have distinguished between a number of internal codes related to the visual, phonological, articulatory, and semantic analysis of a word. Operations at all these levels appear to be involved in understanding a word.

This view began with efforts to develop detailed measurements of the time it takes to execute operations on codes thought to be involved in reading. Figure 30.1 shows the amount

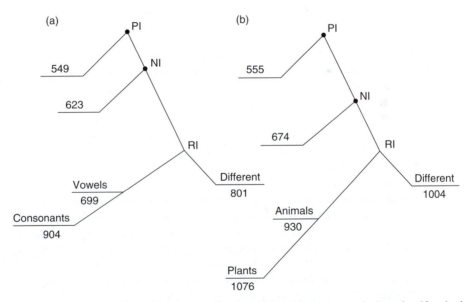

FIGURE 30.1   Results of reaction time studies in which subjects were asked to classify whether pairs of letters were both vowels or both consonants (a) or whether pairs of words were both animal or both plants (b) Reaction times are in milliseconds. Each study involved 10 to 12 normal subjects. Standard deviations are typically 20% of the mean value. Data argue in favor of these matches being made on different internal codes.

(Posner, 1986; Marshall & Newcombe, 1973; LaBerge & Samuels, 1974; Carr & Pollatsek, 1985; Coltheart, 1985). Abbreviations: PI, physical identity; NI, name identity; and RI, rule identity. [Reprinted from Posner, Lewis, & Conrad (1972) with permission of MIT Press.]

of time needed to determine if two simultaneously shown visual letters or words belong to the same category (Posner, Lewis, & Conrad, 1972). The reaction time to match pairs of items that are physically identical (for example, AA) is faster than reaction time for matches of the same letters or words in the opposite case (Aa), which are in turn faster than matches that have only a common category (Ae). These studies have been interpreted as involving a mental operation of matching based on different codes. In the case of visual identity the code is thought to be the visual form, whereas in cross-case matching it is thought to be the letter or word name. The idea that a word consists of separable physical, phonological, and semantic codes and that operations may be performed on them separately has been basic to many theories of reading and listening (Marshall & Newcombe, 1973; LaBerge & Samuels, 1974; Carr & Pollatsek, 1985; Coltheart, 1985). Thus the operation of rotating a letter to the upright position is thought to be performed on the visual code (Cooper, 1976), whereas matching to determine if two words rhyme is said to be performed on a phonological representation of the words (Kleiman, 1975). These theories suggest that mental operations take place on the basis of codes related to separate neural systems.

It is not easy to determine if any operation is elementary or whether it is based on only a single code. Even a simple task such as matching identical items can involve parallel operations on both physical and name codes. Indeed, there has been controversy over the theoretical implications of these matching experiments (Boles & Everland, 1981). Some results have suggested that both within- and cross-case matches are performed on physical (visual) codes, whereas others have suggested that they are both performed on name codes (Boles & Everland, 1981). A basic question is to determine whether operations performed on different codes involve different brain areas. This question cannot be resolved by performance studies, since they provide only indirect evidence about localization of the operations performed on different codes.

It has been widely accepted that there can be multiple routes by which codes interact. For example, a visual word may be sounded out to produce a phonological code and then the phonology is used to develop a meaning (Posner, 1986; Marshall & Newcombe, 1973; LaBerge & Samuels, 1974; Carr & Pollatsek, 1985; Coltheart, 1985). Alternately, the visual code may have direct access to a semantic interpretation without any need for developing a phonological code (Posner, 1986; Marshall & Newcombe, 1973; LaBerge & Samuels, 1974; Carr & Pollatsek, 1985; Coltheart, 1985). These routes are thought to be somewhat separate because patients with one form of reading difficulty have great trouble in sounding out nonsense material (for example, the nonword "caik"), indicating they may have a poor ability to use phonics; but they have no problems with familiar words even when the words have irregular pronunciation (for example, pint). Other patients have no trouble with reading nonwords but have difficulty with highly familiar irregular words. Although there is also reason to doubt that these routes are entirely separate, it is often thought that the visual to semantic route is dominant in skilled readers (Marshall & Newcombe, 1973; LaBerge & Samuels, 1974; Carr & Pollatsek, 1985; Coltheart, 1985).

30.2   VISUAL SPATIAL ATTENTION

Another distinction in cognitive psychology is between automatic activation of these codes and controlled processing by means of attention (Posner, 1986; Marshall & Newcombe, 1973; LaBerge & Samuels, 1974; Carr & Pollatsek, 1985; Coltheart, 1985). Evidence indicates that a word may activate its internal visual, phonological, and even semantic codes without the person having to pay attention to the word. The evidence for activation of the internally stored visual code of a word is particularly good. Normal subjects show evidence that the stimulus duration necessary for perceiving individual letters within words is shorter than for perceiving the same letter when it is presented in isolation (Reicher, 1969; McClelland & Rumelhart, 1981).

What is known about the localization of attention? Cognitive, brain lesion, and animal studies have identified a posterior neural system involved in visual spatial attention. Patients with lesions of many areas of the brain show neglect of stimuli from the side of space opposite the lesion (DeRenzi, 1982). These findings have led to network views of the neural system underlying visual spatial attention (Mesulam, 1984). However, studies performed with single-cell recording from alert monkeys have been more specific in showing three brain areas in which individual cells show selective enhancement due to the requirement that the monkey attend to a visual location (Mountcastle, 1978; Wurtz, Goldberg, & Robinson, 1980; Petersen & Robinson, 1985). These areas are the posterior parietal lobe of the cerebral cortex, a portion of the thalamus (part of the pulvinar), and areas of the midbrain related to eye movements — all areas in which clinical studies of lesioned patients find neglect of the environment opposite the lesion.

Recent studies of normal (control) and patient populations have used cues to direct attention covertly to areas of the visual field without eye movements (Posner, Walker, Friedrich, & Rafal, 1984). Attention is measured by changes in the efficiency of processing targets at the cued location in comparison with other uncued locations in the visual field. These studies have found systematic deficits in shifting of covert visual attention in patients with injury of the same three brain areas suggested by the monkey studies. When the efficiency of processing is measured precisely by a reaction time test, the nature of the deficits in the three areas differs. Patients with lesions in the parietal lobe show very long reaction times to targets on the side opposite the lesion only when their attention has first been drawn to a different location in the direction of the lesion (Posner, Walker, Friedrich, & Rafal, 1984). This increase in reaction time for uncued but not cued contralesional targets is consistent with a specific deficit in the patient's ability to disengage attention from a cued location when the target is in the contralesional direction. In contrast, damage to the midbrain not only greatly lengthens overall reaction time but increases the time needed to establish an advantage in reaction time at the cued location in comparison to the uncued location (Posner, Cohen, & Rafal, 1982). This finding is consistent with the idea that the lesion causes a slowing of attention movements. Damage to the thalamus (Rafal & Posner, 1987) produces a pattern of slowed reaction to both cued and uncued targets on the side opposite the lesion. This pattern suggests difficulty in being able to use attention to speed processing of targets irrespective of the time allowed to do so (engage deficit). A similar deficit has been found in monkeys performing this task when chemical injections disrupt the performance of the lateral pulvinar (Petersen, Robinson, & Reys, 1985). Thus the simple act of shifting attention to the cued location appears to involve a number of distinct computations (figure 30.2) that must be orchestrated to allow the cognitive performance to occur. We now have an idea of the anatomy of several of these computations.

Damage to the visual spatial attention system also produces deficits in recognition of visual stimuli. Patients with lesions of the right parietal lobe frequently neglect (fail to report) the first few letters of a nonword. However, when shown an actual word

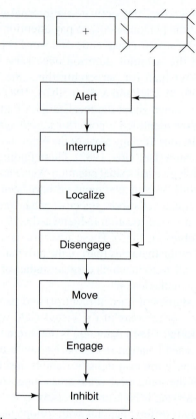

FIGURE 30.2   Top of figure illustrates an experimental situation in which attention is summoned from fixation (center) to righthand box by brightening of the box. This is followed by a target at the cued location or on the opposite side. The boxes below indicate mental operations thought to begin by presentation of the cue. The last four operations involve the posterior visual–spatial attention system; specific deficits have been found in patients with lesions in the parietal (disengage), midbrain (move), and thalmic (engage) areas.

(Posner, Walker, Friedrich, & Rafal, 1984; Posner, Cohen, & Rafal, 1982; Rafar and Posner, 1987). [Reprinted from Posner, Inhoff, Friedrich, & Cohen (1987) with permission of the Psychonomics Society.]

that occupied the same visual angle, they report it correctly (Sieroff, Palatsek, & Posner, 1988). Cognitive studies have often shown a superiority of words over nonwords (Reicher, 1969; McClelland & Rumelhart, 1984). Our results fit with the idea that words do not require scanning by a covert visual spatial attention system.

30.3   ATTENTION FOR ACTION

In cognitive studies it is often suggested that attention to stimuli occurs only after they have been processed to a very high degree (Allport, 1980; Duncan, 1980). In this view, attention is designed mainly to limit the conflicting actions taken toward stimuli. This form of attention is often called "attention for action." Our studies of patients with parietal lesions suggest that the posterior visual spatial attention system is connected to a more general attention system that is also involved in the processing of language stimuli (Posner, Inhoff, Friedrich, & Cohen, 1987). When normal subjects and patients had to pay close attention to auditory, or spoken, words, the ability of a visual cue to draw their visual spatial attention was retarded. Cognitive studies have been unclear on whether access to meaning requires attention. Although semantic information may be activated without attention being drawn to the specific lexical unit (Marcel, 1983), attention strongly interacts with semantic activation (Henik, Friedrich, & Kellogg, 1983; Hoffman & Macmillan, 1985). Considerable evidence shows that attention to semantic information limits the range of concepts activated. When a person attends to one meaning of a word, activation of alternative meanings of the same item tends to be suppressed (Neely, 1977).

30.4   PET IMAGING OF WORDS

How do the operations suggested by cognitive theories of lexical access relate to brain systems? Recently, in a study with normal persons, we used PET to observe brain processes that are active during single word reading (Petersen, Fox, Posner, Mintun, & Raichle, 1988). This method allows examination of averaged changes in cerebral blood flow in localized brain areas during 40 seconds of cognitive activity (Fox, Mintun, Reiman, & Raichle, 1988). During this period we presented words at a rate of one per second. Previous PET studies have suggested that a difference of a few millimeters in the location of activations will be sufficient to separate them (Fox et al., 1986).

To isolate component mental operations we used a set of conditions shown in table 30.1. By subtracting the control state from the stimulus state, we attempted to isolate areas of activation related to those mental operations present in the stimulus state but not in the control state. For example, subtraction of looking at the fixation point, without any stimuli, from the presentation of passive visual words allowed us to examine the brain areas automatically activated by the word stimuli.[1]

30.4.1   Visual Word Forms

We examined changes in cerebral blood flow during passive looking at foveally presented nouns. This task produced five areas of significantly greater activation than found in the fixation condition. They all lie within the occipital lobe: two along the calcarine fissure in left

TABLE 30.1   Conditions for PET Subtractive Studies of Words

CONTROL STATE	STIMULUS STATE	COMPUTATIONS
Fixation	Passive words	Passive word processing
Repeat words	Generate word use	Semantic association, attention
Passive words	Monitor category	Semantic association, attention (many targets)[a]

[a]The extent of attentional activation increases with the number of targets.

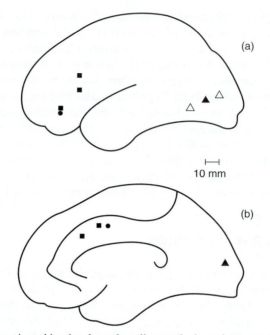

FIGURE 30.3   Areas activated in visual word reading on the lateral aspect of the cortex (a) and on the medial aspect (b). Triangles refer to the passive visual task minus fixation (black triangle, left hemisphere; white triangle, right hemisphere). Only occipital areas are active. Squares refer to generate minus repeat task. Circles refer to monitor minus passive words task. Solid circles and squares in (a) denote left hemisphere activation; however, in (b), on the midline it is not possible to determine if activation is left or right. The lateral area is thought to involve a semantic network while the midline areas appear to involve attention.

(Petersen, Fox, Posner, Mintun, & Raichle, 1988).

and right primary visual cortex and three in left and right lateral regions (figure 30.3). As one moves to more complex naming and semantic activation tasks, no new posterior areas are active. Thus the entire visually specific coding takes place within the occipital lobe. Activated areas are found as far anterior as the occipital temporal boundary. Are these activations specific to visual words? The presentation of auditory words does not produce any activation in this area. Visual stimuli known to activate striate cortex (for example, checkerboards or dot patterns) do not activate the prestriate areas used in word reading (Fox et al., 1986; Fox, Miezin, Allman, Van Essen, & Raichle, 1987). All other cortical areas active during word reading are anterior. Thus it seems reasonable to conclude that visual word forms are developed in the occipital lobe.

It might seem that occipital areas are too early in the system to support the development of visual word forms. However, the early development of the visual word form is supported by our evidence that patients with right parietal lesions do not neglect the left side of foveally centered words even though they do neglect the initial letters of nonword strings (Sieroff, Pollatsek, & Posner, 1988). The presence of pure alexia from lesions of the occipital temporal boundary (Damasio & Damasio, 1983) also supports the development of the visual word form in the occipital area.

Precise computational models of how visual word forms are developed (McClelland & Rumelhart, 1986; Reicher, 1969; McClelland & Rumelhart, 1981) involve parallel computations from feature, letter, and word levels and precise feedback among these levels. The prestriate visual system would provide an attractive anatomy for models relying on such abundant feedback. However, presently we can only tentatively identify the general occipital areas that underlie the visual processing of words.

30.4.2   Semantic Operations

We used two tasks to study semantic operations. One task required the subject to generate and say aloud a use for each of 40 concrete nouns (for example, a subject may say "pound" when presented with the noun "hammer"). We subtracted the activations from repeating the nouns to eliminate strictly sensory and motor activations. Only two general areas of the cortex were found to be active (figure 30.3, square symbols). A second semantic task required subjects to note the presence of dangerous animals in a list of 40 visually presented words. We subtracted passive presentation of the word list to eliminate sensory processing. No motor output was required and subjects were asked to estimate only the frequency of targets after the list was presented. The same two areas of cortex were activated (figure 30.3, circles).

One of the areas activated in both semantic tasks was in the anterior left frontal lobe. Figure 30.4 shows an illustration of this area from averaged scans in auditory and visual generate (minus repeat) and in visual monitoring (minus passive words). This area is strictly left lateralized and appears to be specific to semantic language tasks. Moreover, lesions of this area produce deficits in word fluency tests (Benton, 1968). Thus we have concluded that this general area is related to the semantic network supporting the type of word associations involved in the generate and monitoring tasks.

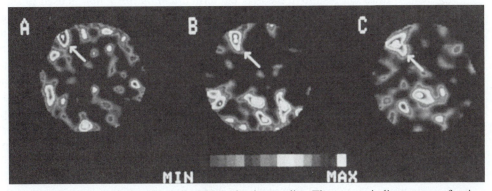

FIGURE 30.4   Sample data from the PET activation studies. The arrows indicate areas of activation in the left inferior prefrontal cortex found active in all three semantic processing conditions. (Left) Monitoring visual words for dangerous animals (minus passive visual words). (Middle) Generating uses (minus repeat) for visual stimuli. (Right) Generating uses (minus repeat) for auditory stimuli. In each condition an area of cortical activation was found in the anterior cingulate gyrus on a higher slice (figure 30.3). The color scale indicates the relative strength of activation (black indicates the minimum and white, the maximum, for that condition).
(Petersen, Fox, Posner, Mintun, & Raichle, 1988).

30.4.3   Phonological Coding

When words are presented in auditory form, the primary auditory cortex and an area of the left temporoparietal cortex that has been related to language tasks are activated (Geschwind, 1965). This temporoparietal left-lateralized area seemed to be a good candidate for phonological processing. It was surprising from some perspectives that no visual word reading task activated this area. However, all of our visual tasks involved single common nouns read by highly skilled readers. According to cognitive theories of reading (Marshall & Newcombe, 1973; LaBerge & Samuels, 1974; Carr & Pollatsek, 1985; Coltheart, 1985), these tasks should involve the visual to semantic route. One way of requiring a phonological activation would be to force subjects to tell whether two simultaneous words (for example, pint-lint or row-though) rhymed. This method has been used in cognitive studies to activate phonological codes (Kleiman, 1975). Recent data from our laboratory (Petersen, Fox, Posner, & Raichle, unpub.) show that this task does produce activation near the supramarginal gyrus. We also assume that word reading that involves difficult words or requires storage in short-term memory or is performed by unskilled readers would also activate phonological operations.

30.4.4   Anterior Attention

There is no evidence of activation of any parts of the posterior visual spatial attention system (for example, parietal lobe) in any of our PET language studies. However, it is possible to show that simple tasks that require close monitoring of visual input or that use visual imagery (Petersen, Fox, Miezin, & Raichle, 1988) do activate this parietal system. We conclude, in agreement with the results of our lesion work (Sieroff, Pollatsek, & Posner, 1988), that visual word reading is automatic in that it does not require activation of the visual spatial attention system.

In recent cognitive theories the term *attention for action* is used to summarize the idea that attention seems to be involved in selecting those operations that will gain control of output systems (Allport, 1980). This kind of attention system does not appear to be related to any particular sensory or cognitive content and is distinct from the more strictly visual functions assigned to the visual-spatial attention system. Although attention for action seems to imply motor acts, internal selections involved in detecting or noting an event may be sufficient to involve attention in this sense (Duncan, 1980). Whenever subjects are active in this way, we see an increase in blood flow in areas of the medial frontal lobe (figure 30.3B, square symbols). When motor output is involved (for example, naming words), these areas tend to be more superior and posterior (supplementary motor area); but when motor activity is subtracted away or when none is required, they appear to be more anterior and inferior (anterior cingulate gyrus). The anterior cingulate has long been thought to be related to attention (Mesulam, 1988) in the sense of generating actions, since lesions of this area produce akinetic mutism (Damasio & Van Hoesen, 1983).

We tested the identification of the anterior cingulate with attention and the left lateral frontal area with a word association network. This was done by applying a cognitive theory that attention would not be much involved in the semantic decision of whether a word belonged to a category (for example, dangerous animal) but would be involved in noting the targets even though no specific action was required. The special involvement of attention with target detection has been widely argued by cognitive studies (Duncan, 1980). These studies have suggested that monitoring produces relatively little evidence of heavy attentional involvement, but when a target is actually detected there is evidence of strong interference so that the likelihood of detecting a simultaneous target is reduced. Thus we varied the number of dangerous animals in our list from one (few targets) to 25 (many targets). We found that blood flow in the anterior cingulate showed much greater change with many targets than with few targets. The left frontal area showed little change in blood flow between these conditions. Additional work with other low-target vigilance tasks not involving semantics also failed to activate the anterior cingulate area.[2] Thus the identification of the anterior cingulate with some part of an anterior attention system that selects for action receives some support from these results.

CONCLUSIONS

The PET data provide strong support for localization of operations performed on visual, phonological, and semantic codes. The ability to localize these operations in studies of average blood flow suggests considerable homogeneity in the neural systems involved, at least among the right-handed subjects with good reading skills who were used in our study.

The PET data on lexical access complement the lesion data cited here in showing that mental operations of the type that form the basis of cognitive analysis are localized in the human brain. This form of localization of function differs from the idea that cognitive tasks are performed by a particular brain area. Visual imagery, word reading, and even shifting visual attention from one location to another are not performed by any single brain area. Each of them involves a large number of component computations that must be orchestrated to perform the cognitive task.

Our data suggest that operations involved both in activation of internal codes and in selective attention obey the general rule of localization of component operations. However, selective attention appears to use neural systems separate from those involved in passively collecting information about a stimulus. In the posterior part of the brain, the ventral occipital lobe appears to develop the visual word form. If active selection or visual search is required, this is done by a spatial system that is deficient in patients with lesions of the parietal lobe (Friedrich, Walker, & Posner, 1985; Riddoch & Humphreys, 1987). Similarly, in the anterior brain the lateral left frontal lobe is involved in the semantic network for coding word associations. Local areas within the anterior cingulate become increasingly involved when the output of the computations within the semantic network is to be selected as a relevant target. Thus the anterior cingulate is involved in the computations in selecting language or other forms of information for action. This separation of anterior and posterior attention systems helps clarify how attention can be involved both in early visual processing and in the selection of information for ontput.

Several other research areas also support our general hypothesis. In the study of visual imagery, models distinguish between a set of operations involved in the generation of an image and those involved in scanning the image once it is generated (Kosslyn, 1980). Mechanisms involved in image scanning share components with those in visual spatial attention. Patients with lesions of the right parietal lobe have deficits both in scanning the left side of an image and in responding to visual input to their left (Bisiach & Luzzatti, 1978). Although the right hemisphere plays an important role in visual scanning, it apparently is deficient in operations needed to generate an image. Studies of patients whose cerebral hemispheres have been split during surgery show that the isolated left hemisphere can generate complex visual images whereas the isolated right hemisphere cannot (Kosslyn, Holtzman, Farah, & Gazzaniga, 1985).

Patients with lesions of the lateral cerebellum have a deficit in timing motor output and in their threshold for recognition of small temporal differences in sensory input (Ivry, Keele, & Diener, 1988). These results indicate that this area of the cerebellum performs a critical computation for timing both motor and sensory tasks. Similarly, studies of memory have indicated that the hippocampus performs a computation needed for storage in a manner that will allow conscious retrieval of the item once it has left current attention. The same item can be used as part of a skill even though damage to the hippocampus makes it unavailable to conscious recollection (Squire, 1986).

The joint anatomical and cognitive approach discussed in this article should open the way to a more detailed understanding of the deficits found in the many disorders involving cognitive or attentional operations in which the anatomy is poorly understood. For example, we have attempted to apply the new knowledge of the anatomy of selective attention to study deficits in patients with schizophrenia (Early, Posner, & Reiman, Posner, Early, Reiman, Pardo, et al., 1988).

NOTES

This work was supported by the Office of Naval Research contract N00014-86-K-0289 and by the McDonnell Center for Higher Brain Studies. The imaging studies were performed at the Malinckrodt Institute of Radiology of Washington University with the support of NIH grants NS 06833, HL 13851, NS 14834, and AG 03991. We thank M. K. Rothbart and G. L. Shulman for helpful comments.

1. Subtraction was used to infer mental processes by F. C. Donders in 1868 for reaction time data. The method has been disputed because it is possible that subjects use different strategies as the task is made more complex. By using PET, we can study this issue. For example, when subtracting the fixation control from the generate condition, one should obtain only those active areas found in passive (minus fixation) plus repeat (minus passive) plus generate (minus repeat). Our preliminary analyses of these conditions generally support the method.

2. The studies of the visual monitoring task were conducted by S. E. Petersen, P. T. Fox, M. I. Posner, and M. E. Raichle. Unpublished studies on vigilance were conducted by J. Pardo, P. T. Fox, M. I. Posner, and M. E. Raichle, using somatosensory and visual tasks.

REFERENCES

Allport, D. A. (1980). In G. Claxton (Ed.), *Cognitive psychology: New directions* (pp. 112–153). Boston: Routledge & Kegan Paul.

Anderson, J. R. (1980). *Cognitive psychology and its implications.* San Francisco: Freeman.

Benton, A. L. (1968). *Neuropsychologia 18,* 53.

Bisiach, E., & Luzzatti, C. (1978). *Cortex 14,* 129.

Boles, D. B., & Eveland, D. C. (1983). *J. Exp. Psychol. Hum Percept. Perform. 9,* 657; Proctor, R. W. (1981). *Psychol. Rev. 88,* 291.

Churchland, P. S. (1986). *Neurophilosophy.* Cambridge, MA: MIT Press.

Cooper, L. A. (1976). *Percept. Psychophys. 7,* 20.

Damasio, A. R., & Damasio, H. (1983). *Neurology 33,* 1573.

Damasio, A. R., & Van Hoesen, G. W. (1983). In K. M. Heilman and P. Satz (Eds.), *Neuropsychology of Human Emotion* (pp. 85–110). New York: Guilford.

DeRenzi, E. (1982). *Disorders of space exploration and cognition.* New York: Wiley.

Duncan, J. (1980). *Psychol. Rev. 87,* 272.

Fox, P. T. et al. (1986). *Nature 323,* 806.

Fox, P. T., Miezin, F. M., Allman, J. M., Van Essen, D. C., & Raichle, M. E. (1987). *J. Neurosci. 7,* 913.

Fox, P. T., Mintun, M. A., Reiman, E. M., Raichle, M. E. (1988). Enhanced detection of focal brain responses using intersubject averaging and change-distribution analysis of subtracted PET images. *J. Cereb. Blood Flow Metab. 8(5),* 642–653.

Friedrich, F. J., Walker, J. A., & Posner, M. I. (1985). *Cog. Neuropsychol. 2,* 250; Riddoch, J. M., & Humphreys, G. W. (1980). In M. Jeannerod (Ed.), *Neurophysiological and neuropsychological aspects of spatial neglect* (pp. 151–181). New York: Elsevier.

Geschwind, N. (1965). *Brain 88,* 227.

Henik, A., Friedrich, F. J., & Kellogg, W. A. (1983). *Mem. Cognit. 11,* 363; Hoffman, J. E., & Macmillan, F. W. In M. I. Posner and O. S. M. Marin (Eds.), *Attention and performance XI* (pp. 585–599). Hillsdale, NJ: Erlbaum.

Ivry, R. I., Keele, S. W., & Diener, H. C. (1988). *Exp. Brain Res. 73,* 167–180.

Kleiman, G. M. (1975). *J. Verb. Learn. Verb. Behav. 24,* 323.

Kosslyn, S. W. (1980). *Image and mind.* Cambridge, MA: Harvard Univ. Press.

Kosslyn, S. W., Holtzman, J. D., Farah, M. J., & Gazzaniga, M. S. (1985). *J. Exp. Psychol. Gen. 114,* 311.

Marcel, A. (1983). *Cog. Psychol. 15,* 197.

Marshall, J. C., & Newcombe, F. J. (1973). *J. Psychol. Res. 2,* 175; LaBerge, D., & Samuels, J. (1974). *Cog. Psychol. 10,* 293; Carr, T. H., & Pollatsek, A. (1985). In D. Besner, D. Waller, & G. E. Mackinnon (Eds.), *Reading research,* vol. 5. New York: Academic Press, pp. 1–82; Coltheart, M. (1985). In M. I. Posner & O. S. M. Marin (Eds.), *Attention and performance XI,* Hillsdale, NJ: Erlbaum, pp. 3–37.

McClelland, J. L., & Rumelhart, D. E. (1986). *Parallel distributed processing,* vol. 2. Cambridge, MA: MIT Press, pp. 170–215.

Mesulam, M. M. (1981). *Ann. Neurol. 10,* 309; Goldman-Rakic, P. S. (1988). *Annu. Rev. Neurosci. 11,* 156.

Mountcastle, V. B. (1978). *J. R. Soc. Med. 71,* 14; Wurtz, R. H., Goldberg, M. E., & Robinson, D. L. (1980). *Prog. Psychobiol. Physiol. Psychol. 9,* 43; Petersen, S. E., Robinson, D. L., & Keys, W. (1985). *J. Neurophysiol. 54,* 367.

Neely, J. (1977). *J. Exp. Psychol. Gen. 3,* 226.

Petersen, S. E., Fox, P. T., Miezin, F. M., & Raichle, M. E. (1988). *Invest. Ophthalmol. Vis. Sci. 29,* 22 (abstr.).

Petersen, S. E., Fox, P. T., Posner, M. I., Mintun, M., & Raichle, M. E. (1988). *Nature 331,* 585.

Petersen, S. E., Fox, P. T., Posner, M. I., & Raichle, M. E., unpublished data.

Petersen, S. E., Robinson, D. L., & Keys, W. J. (1985). *Neurophysiology 54,* 207.

Posner, M. I. (1986). *Chronometric explorations of mind.* Oxford: Oxford Univ. Press.

Posner, M. I., Cohen, Y., & Rafal, R. D. (1982). *Proc. R. Soc. London Ser. B 298,* 187; Posner, M. L., Choate, L., Rafal, R. D., & Vaughan, J. (1985). *Cog. Neuropsychol. 2,* 250.

Posner, M. I., Early, T. S. Reiman, E., Pardo, P., et al. (1988). Asymetries in hemispheric control of attention in schizophrenia. *Archives of General Psychiatry, 4S(9),* 814–821.

Posner, M. I., Inhoff, W. R., Friedrich, F. J., & Cohen, A. (1987). *Psychobiology 15,* 107.

Posner, M. I., Lewis, J., & Conrad, C. (1972). In J. F. Kavanaugh & I. G. Mattingly (Eds.), *Language by ear and by eye.* Cambridge, MA: MIT Press, pp. 159–192.

Posner, M. I., Walker, J., Friedrich, F. J., & Rafal, R. D. (1984). *J. Neurosci. 4,* 1863.

Rafal, R. D., & Posner, M. I. (1987). *Proc. Natl. Acad. Sci. U.S.A. 84,* 7349.

Raichle, M. E. (1983). *Annu. Rev. Neurosci. 6,* 243.

Reicher, G. M. (1969). *J. Exp. Psychol. 81,* 274; McClelland, J. L., & Rumelhart, D. E. (1981). *Psychol. Rev. 88,* 375.

Sieroff, E., Pollastek, A., and Posner, M. (1988) Recognition of visual letter strings following injury to the posterior visual spatial attention system. *Cog. Neuropsychol. 5(4),* 451–472.

Squire, L. R. (1986). *Science 232,* 1612.

CHAPTER THIRTY-ONE

HOW THE BRAIN GIVES RISE TO THE MIND

EDWARD E. SMITH AND STEPHEN M. KOSSLYN

31.1 WHY THE BRAIN?

At its inception, cognitive psychology was concerned only with function, only with characterizing mental activity (Neisser, 1967). More recently, cognitive psychology has come to rely on facts about the brain. This development has occurred for two main reasons, which concern the concepts of identifiability and adequacy. *Identifiability* refers to the ability to specify the correct combination of representations and processes used to accomplish a task. The problem is that, in principle, different sorts of information processing can produce the same result; thus, additional sorts of evidence — such as knowledge of specific brain activity — are necessary to discover how mental processing in fact takes place. The goal of any theory in science is to discover the facts of the matter, to understand the principles and causes that underlie phenomena. Just as you can correctly or incorrectly describe the way a particular computer program operates, you can correctly or incorrectly describe mental representations, processes, and the ways they are used during a specific mental activity. You can get it right or get it wrong.

It is difficult to disagree with the idea that some theories (or aspects of theories) are correct and some are incorrect, but identifiability is much easier said than achieved. One reason this black-and-white approach has proven difficult to realize is that theories in cognitive psychology can be undermined by *structure–process trade-offs*. This is a key idea, so let's pause to consider an example.

Saul Sternberg (1969b) developed a method to examine how information is accessed in memory. He gave people sets of digits, each set containing one to six items. He then presented single items and asked the participants to decide as quickly as they could whether those

---

items had been in the set. For example, the participants first would memorize "1, 8, 3, 4" and would later be asked to decide whether "3" was in the set, whether "5" was in the set, and so on. A key result was that the time to respond increased linearly for increasingly large memorized sets; that is, an equal increment of time was added for each additional item included in the set. This led Sternberg to hypothesize that people hold *lists* of items in memory and *serially scan* these lists (when asked whether "3" was in the set, they go through and check each item in the list of numbers they are holding in their memory). The theory thus specified a representation (a list) and an accompanying process (serial scanning). However, it wasn't long before others (e.g., Monsell, 1978; Townsend, 1990; Townsend & Ashby, 1983) formulated alternative theories that varied the representation and compensated for this change by varying the accompanying process. For example, instead of a list, the items could be stored as an *unordered collection,* like pool balls sitting in a bowl. Instead of searching them one at a time, they could be searched *in parallel,* all at the same time (Figure 31.1). But how would this theory explain the increase in time for larger sets? The essential idea is that — as in everything else in nature — there is variation in the time to examine each item, whether it's examining them one at a time in a list or in parallel as a group. Think about the amount of time people spend in a job interview: some interviews finish up very quickly (for better or worse!), some end up dragging on at length. Just as in interviews, some comparisons of remembered information are faster than others. And here's the trick that makes this alternative theory work: the larger the number of items to be considered, the more likely it is that one of the comparisons will be particularly slow, just as it is more likely that there will be a particularly long interview as the number of people interviewed increases. Thus, if all items must be checked before a decision is made, then the more items, the more time in general will be required until all comparisons are complete.

In short, the two theories, list-with-serial-scan and collection-with-parallel comparison, can mimic each other. The point: we can change the theory of the representation,

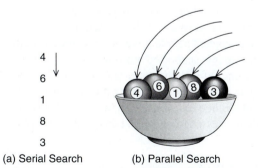

(a) Serial Search   (b) Parallel Search

FIGURE 31.1   Two theories of memory scanning
(a) A set of digits can be ordered into a list and scanned serially, one digit at a time. (b) Alternatively, the representation can be changed, creating an unordered collection, and the process can then be changed to compensate for the change in representation–with all digits examined in parallel. This structure–process trade-off can produce models that can mimic each other, both predicting increased times when larger sets of digits must be searched.

and compensate for that change by altering the theory of the process. The representation and process trade off against each other, with change in one compensating for change in the other.

Anderson (1978) proved mathematically that information-processing theorists can always use this sort of structure–process trade-off to create a theory that mimics another theory. The problem is that all the characteristics of both the representations and the processes are up for grabs; a theorist can change one aspect and then can adjust the other aspects of the theory arbitrarily — nothing is nailed down in advance. Anderson also pointed out, however, that the brain can serve to limit this arbitrariness. A theorist *cannot* make up properties of the brain willy-nilly to account for data. Cognitive theories are limited by facts about the brain; the facts don't dictate the theories, but they limit the range of what can be proposed. Facts about the brain anchor theories so that theorists cannot always use structure-process trade-offs to invent alternative accounts for sets of data; the accompanying *Debate* box illustrates an example of the way such facts can help us understand mental activity.

Turning to the brain helps us to grapple with the challenge of identifiability. But this is not all that can be gained by considering the brain when formulating theories of mental activity. Facts about the brain can help us test the *adequacy* of a theory, which lets us know whether a theory is — to that point — valid.

How do we know when a theory, taken on its own terms (and not compared to another, competing theory), is worth its salt? At first glance, this seems obvious: a theory should be taken seriously if it explains all relevant phenomena and makes correct predictions. That standard holds to evaluate a final, complete theory — but it is not clear that such theories ever really exist! What about theories that are just being worked out now, as is true in almost all of cognitive psychology? How do we know whether we are on the right track? Clearly, the theory must be testable, and it must be capable of being disproved; if a theory can explain any result *and* its opposite, it explains nothing at all.

In addition, in psychology we can use facts about the structure and function of the brain to help us evaluate theories; such facts can provide strong justification and support for a theory (what Chomsky, 1967, called *explanatory adequacy*). For example, a cognitive theory might claim that nouns and verbs are stored separately, and this theory might perhaps be based on differences in how easily the two categories can be learned. If researchers can then show that the brain "respects" this distinction, perhaps by showing that different parts of the brain are active when people produce or comprehend the two types of words, the theory is supported. And it is supported more strongly than it would be if you simply collected more data on learning, of the sort that were used to formulate the theory in the first place. In this book, we use facts about the brain in this way, as a separate source of justification and support for cognitive theories. If a theory incorporates two distinct processes, this theory gains support when researchers show that different parts of the brain carry out each process.

31.2   THE COGNITIVE BRAIN

Volumes and volumes have been written about the brain, but fortunately we need not concern ourselves here with most of this avalanche of information. Rather, we need focus only on those aspects that can be brought to bear on theories of mental activity. This section is a brief overview, which will be supplemented in later chapters as the need arises. Although we

■ ■ ■ ■ ■ ■

DEBATE
WHAT IS THE NATURE OF VISUAL MENTAL IMAGERY?

Perception occurs after our sense organs (e.g., our eyes and ears) register a stimulus that is physically present and our brain allows us to organize the sensory input; mental imagery occurs when you have a similar experience of perception, but is based on information you previously stored in memory. For example, can you recall how many windows there are in your bedroom? To answer, most people visualize their room, which is an example of using mental imagery. Although mental imagery may seem similar to perception, it clearly is not the same thing; we can change our images at will (for instance, by adding or deleting windows), and the images fade very quickly.

The "imagery debate" concerns the nature of the representations used during mental imagery, and has focused on visual mental imagery (although the issues apply equally well to other forms of imagery, such as the auditory images you have when you "hear" a song in your mind). This debate began when Zenon Pylyshyn (1973) claimed that mental imagery relies entirely on the same sorts of descriptive representations that are used in language. Kosslyn and Pomerantz (1977) marshaled both theoretical arguments and empirical results in an attempt to counter Pylyshyn's assertion and to support the idea that imagery relies in part on depictive representations. In depictive representations, each point in the representation corresponds to a point on the object being depicted such that the distances between points in the representation correspond to the distances between the corresponding points on the object. Pictures are an example of a depictive representation. Many exchanges followed, without conclusion. Every finding produced by the depictive camp was quickly undermined by the descriptive camp. Structure–process trade-offs ran rampant (Anderson, 1978; Kosslyn, Thompson & Canis, 2006).

Today, the debate finally appears to be going somewhere, thanks to new knowledge of key facts about the brain mechanisms used in vision. In the monkey brain, some areas involved in visual processing are *topographically organized,* and new methods have shown that the human brain also has such visual areas (e.g., Sereno et al., 1995). These brain areas (such as areas 17 and 18, as the regions are known) literally use space on the surface of the brain to represent space in the world. When you see an object, the pattern of activity on your retinas is projected back into the brain, where it is reproduced (although with some distortions) on the surface of the brain. There literally is a "picture in your head"; brain areas support genuinely depictive representations. And at least two of these topographically organized areas (the largest ones) are also activated when participants close their eyes and visualize objects clearly enough that they could "see" fine details (Kosslyn & Thompson, 2003). Moreover, the size and orientation of the image affects activation in these areas in very much the same way as when people actually see objects at different sizes or orientations (Klein et al., 2003; Kosslyn et al., 1995). In fact, temporarily disrupting neural functioning in these areas temporarily disrupts both visual perception and visual mental imagery — and does so to the same extent (Kosslyn et al., 1999).

However, some patients with brain damage in these areas apparently still retain at least some forms of imagery (e.g., Behrmann, 2000; Goldenberg et al., 1995), and thus the precise role of these brain areas in imagery has yet to be established. If future research conclusively shows that at least some forms of imagery rely on depictive representations in topographically organized brain areas, the debate will either end or be forced to change direction.

note the major functions of different brain structures, we must emphasize from the outset that virtually all cognitive functions are *not* carried out by a single brain area; rather, as we will see in later chapters, systems of brain areas working together allow us to perform specific tasks. Nevertheless, each brain area plays a role in some functions and not others — and knowing these roles will help in understanding later discussions.

31.2.1   Neurons: The Building Blocks of the Brain

What do neurons have to do with mental processes? That's a bit like wondering what the properties of bricks, boards, and steel have to do with architecture. It is true that architecture cannot be reduced to these components, but they nevertheless influence architecture. For example, London, England, is relatively flat and spread out because most of it was built before steel was readily available — and you cannot build skyscrapers with just brick because the weight of upper stories becomes so great that the walls at street level cannot support them. Although the building materials do not *dictate* the way they are used, they place limitations — *constraints* — on the types of possible architectures. So too with the components of nervous systems. As we will see in this book, the nature of our neurons and the ways they interact feed into theories of how large groups of neurons can function in mental activity.

Brain activity arises primarily from the activities of neurons. *Sensory neurons* are activated by input from sensory organs such as the eyes and ears; *motor neurons* stimulate muscles, causing movements. *Interneurons,* the vast majority of the neurons in the brain, stand between sensory and motor neurons or between other interneurons; often interneurons are connected to other interneurons, forming vast networks. In addition to 100 billion neurons or so, the brain also contains *glial cells.* Glial cells initially were thought to be involved solely in the care and feeding of neurons, but now are recognized to play a critical role in the way connections among neurons are set up (Ullian et al., 2001). They also modulate chemical interactions among neurons (Newman & Zahs, 1998). There are about 10 times as many glial cells as neurons in the brain.

The crucial parts of a neuron (Figure 31.2) are its dendrites, axon, and cell body. The *dendrites* receive input from other neurons, as does the *cell body,* and the *axon* transmits output to other neurons. The axon is usually covered with myelin, a fatty insulator that improves transmission. Typical neurons have thousands of dendrites, and the axon branches at the end so that each neuron can in turn affect thousands of other neurons. The connection between neurons is called a *synapse,* and the gap in the synapse is called the *synaptic cleft.* Most neurons affect others by releasing specific *neurotransmitters* at the tip of the axon via small structures known as *terminal buttons.* Neurotransmitters cross the synaptic cleft, moving from the axon of one neuron to the dendrites (or, sometimes, directly on the cell membrane, the outer covering of the cell body itself) of another.

The effects of a neurotransmitter depend on the *receptors* present on the receiving end. The standard analogy is to a lock and key: the chemical corresponds to a key, and the receptor to a lock. When the appropriate "messenger molecule," the neurotransmitter, binds to a receptor, it can excite the neuron (making it more active) or inhibit it (damping down its activity). The same neurotransmitter can have different effects depending on the nature of the receptor. If the excitatory input reaching a neuron is sufficiently greater than the inhibitory input, the neuron will produce an *action potential;* that is, it will "fire." Neurons obey an all-or-none law: either they fire or they don't.

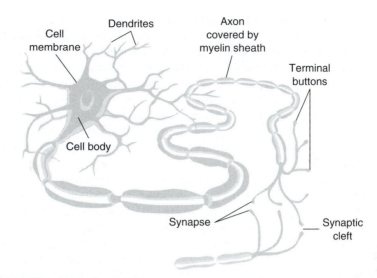

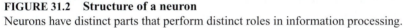

FIGURE 31.2   Structure of a neuron
Neurons have distinct parts that perform distinct roles in information processing.

31.2.2   Structure of the Nervous System

The nervous system is traditionally considered to have two major parts, the *central nervous system* (CNS) and the *peripheral nervous system* (PNS). The CNS consists of the brain and spinal cord; the PNS consists of the skeletal nervous system and the *autonomic nervous system* (ANS). We start with the more basic, and (in evolutionary terms) older, PNS and then turn to the brain itself.

The Peripheral Nervous System.   The skeletal system governs *striated* (that is, very finely "striped") muscles, which are under voluntary control. The skeletal system plays a major role in motor cognition and mental simulation [. . .]. In contrast, most of the functions of the ANS are carried out by smooth muscles, but the ANS also controls some glands. Smooth muscles, found in the heart, blood vessels, stomach lining, and intestines, are usually not under voluntary control. The ANS plays a key role in emotion and it also affects how memory works.

The ANS is traditionally divided into two major parts, the sympathetic and parasympathetic nervous systems. The *sympathetic nervous system* prepares an animal to respond more vigorously and accurately during an emergency. Among other things, it:

- increases the heart rate (so more oxygen and nutrients are delivered to organs),
- increases the breathing rate (thus providing more oxygen),
- dilates the pupils (resulting in greater sensitivity to light),
- causes the palms of the hands to become moist (thus providing better grip),
- reduces digestive functions, including salivation (putting them "on hold"), and
- relaxes the bladder (suspending another function that isn't crucial in an emergency).

These changes prepare an organism for successful challenge or successful escape, and are often called the *fight-or-flight response*. Why should we care about this response in a book on cognition? For one thing, the events surrounding this response can actually improve memory [. . .], while at the same time they can disrupt reasoning [. . .].

We modern human beings have the same sympathetic nervous system that served our ancestors well, but now its responses can be activated by stimuli very different from those encountered in previous eras. If during a job interview you are asked to explain some weak spot on your résumé, you may not find the features of the fight-or-flight responses so adaptive — it is not easy making your explanation when your heart is pounding and you have a dry mouth!

The *parasympathetic nervous system* in many ways counters the sympathetic nervous system. Whereas the sympathetic system tends to rev things up, the parasympathetic system dampens them down. Moreover, whereas the sympathetic system causes a whole constellation of effects (producing arousal in general), the parasympathetic system targets single organs or small sets of organs. In a job interview, you are grateful when the interviewer moves onto another part of your résumé where you are on rock-solid ground — and the parasympathetic system then dampens down the fight-or-flight response you were struggling to contain.

The Cerebral Cortex.   Now let's consider the central nervous system, specifically the brain — the seat of mental activity. Imagine that you are in a neuroanatomy lab, dissecting a human brain. The first thing you see, covering the surface of the brain, is the topmost of three membranes, called the *meninges.* Putting on surgical gloves (an absolute necessity to guard yourself against viruses), you peel back the meninges to uncover a rich network of blood vessels clinging to the surface of the brain, like ivy clinging to a wall. The surface of the brain contains most of the cell bodies of neurons, which are a gray color, hence the term "gray matter." These cells are in a layer about 2 millimeters deep, which is called the *cerebral cortex.* The cortex of the brain is noticeably wrinkled; the wrinkles allow more cortex to be crammed into the skull. Each up-bulging fold is called a *gyrus,* and each crease a *sulcus.* The various gyri and sulci have individual names, and as we shall see throughout this book, many have been identified as playing a role in particular mental activities.

In your neuroanatomy lab you are equipped with a scalpel as well as surgical gloves. Now slice into the brain and examine its interior. The interior is packed with white fibers (the color giving rise to the term "white matter"), which connect the neurons. Keep exploring deeper to find the *subcortical structures* (so called because they lie beneath the cortex), which contain gray matter, and — at the very center of the brain — a series of connected cavities, the *ventricles.* The ventricles are filled with the same fluid that runs inside the spinal cord.

The brain is best considered not as a single entity but rather as a collection of components that work together, in the same way that the hand is a collection of separate bones, tendons, and muscles, all of which depend on one another to carry out the functions of the hand. One of the first things you have noticed in the neuroanatomy lab is that the brain is divided into two halves, the left and right *cerebral hemispheres.* Although the same physical structures are duplicated in the two cerebral hemispheres, they can differ both in their size and their functions (as will be discussed later in the book). The hemispheres are connected in the interior of the brain by a massive collection of nerve fibers (some 250 to 300 million of them), called the *corpus callosum,* as well as several smaller, less important connections.

Modern neuroanatomy divides each hemisphere into four major parts, or *lobes:* the *occipital,* at the posterior (rear) of the brain; the *temporal,* directly under the temples; the *parietal,* at the superior (upper) posterior part of the brain; and the *frontal,* at the anterior (front) part of the brain, right behind the forehead (Figure 31.3). The lobes are named after the bones of the skull that cover them, and hence this organization of the brain is somewhat arbitrary — so you won't be surprised to find that mental activities are not neatly assigned to one or another lobe. Nevertheless, at least some mental representations and processes occur mainly in a specific lobe, and we can make some generalizations about the different functions of the various lobes. But always keep in mind that the lobes work together, like the bones, tendons, and muscles of the hand.

The occipital lobes process only visual input, both from the eyes and from memory (at least in some cases, in mental imagery). If you were to slip while roller skating and fall on the back of your head, you would probably "see stars." This visual effect (which is not worth the pain of inducing it) occurs because the impact causes compression of the neurons in the occipital lobes. Curiously, if you stare straight ahead, the left occipital lobe receives inputs from the right side of space, and the right occipital lobe receives inputs from the left side of space. Why? The back of the eye, the retina, is actually part of the brain that's been

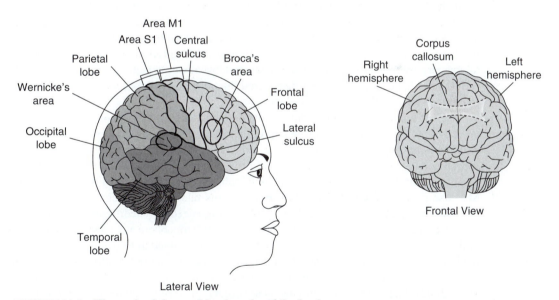

FIGURE 31.3   The major lobes and landmarks of the brain
The anatomical landmarks of the brain only imperfectly correspond to distinct functions, but these landmarks nevertheless are useful ways to describe brain location. Specific terms are used to describe locations in the brain: *Medial* means closer to the midline; thus, the medial views show the inside of the brain. *Lateral* means toward the side, farther away from the midline; thus the lateral views show the outside surface of the cerebral cortex. The terms *dorsal* (the "back" side) and *ventral* (the "stomach" side) are also used. Because we stand fully upright, these terms have no literal meaning with reference to the human brain, but by convention *dorsal,* like *superior,* describes "above," and *ventral,* like *inferior,* describes "below."

pushed forward during development (Dowling, 1992); hence the left side of each eye (not just the left eye) is connected to the left part of the brain, and the right side of each eye (not just the right eye) is connected to the right side of the brain. When you stare straight ahead, light from your left strikes the right sides of each eye, and light from your right strikes the left sides of each eye. Vision, like all cognitive functions, is itself carried out by a set of distinct representations and processes. In fact, the occipital lobes contain numerous different areas, each of which plays a key role in a different aspect of vision: for example, some areas primarily process motion, others color, and others shape. If the occipital lobes are damaged, partial or complete blindness results.

The temporal lobes are involved in many different sorts of functions. One of them is the retention of visual memories. In addition, they receive input from the occipital lobes and match visual input to visual memories. When you've already stored an image of what you currently are seeing, this matching process makes the stimulus seem familiar. The temporal lobes also process input from the ears, and the posterior portion of the left temporal lobe contains *Wernicke's area,* which is crucial for comprehending language. At the anterior (i.e., front) portion of the temporal lobes are a number of areas that are critical for storing new information in memory, and areas involved in deriving meaning and in emotion.

The parietal lobes are crucially involved in representing space and your relationship to it. The most anterior gyrus of the parietal lobes, the *somatosensory cortex* (area S1), represents sensations on different parts of the body; S1 is organized so that the different parts of the body are registered by different portions of cortex. In addition, the left-hemisphere S1 registers sensations on the right side of the body, and vice versa for the right hemisphere. The parietal lobes also are important for consciousness and attention. Moreover, they are also involved in mathematical thinking. Albert Einstein (1945) reported that he relied on mental imagery when reasoning, and often imagined "what would happen if. . . . " This is interesting: after his death researchers discovered that his parietal lobes were about 15 percent larger than normal (Witelson et al., 1999).

The frontal lobes are generally involved in managing sequences of behaviors or mental activities. They play a major role in producing speech; *Broca's area* is usually identified with the third frontal gyrus in the left hemisphere, and this area is crucial for programming speech sounds. Several other areas in the frontal lobes are involved in controlling movements. The most posterior gyrus in the frontal lobes is called the *primary motor cortex* (area M1; also called the *motor strip*); this area controls fine motor movements, such as those necessary to type up your résumé. Like S1, M1 is organized so that different parts of the cortex correspond to different parts of the body. The left-hemisphere M1 controls the right part of the body, and vice versa. The frontal lobes are also involved in looking up specific information stored in memory, in planning and reasoning, in storing information briefly in memory so that it can be used in reasoning, in some emotions, and even in personality (Davidson, 1998, 2002). The frontal lobes obviously are crucial in helping you decide what sort of job to pursue, and will play crucial roles in allowing you to do well in your chosen career.

Although many functions are duplicated in the corresponding lobes in the two hemispheres (just as they are in our two lungs and two kidneys), in some cases the lobes function differently on the left and right sides. For example, the left-hemisphere parietal lobe produces representations that describe spatial relations (such as, "one object is *above* another"), whereas the right produces representations of continuous distances (Laeng et al., 2002). However, even when the hemispheres are specialized differently, in most

cases the difference is a matter of degree, not of kind. Other than for some language functions, both hemispheres generally can carry out most functions, but perhaps not equally
well (Hellige, 1993).

Subcortical Areas.   The subcortical areas of the human brain (Figure 31.4) often appear
very similar to those of other animals, and research suggests that these areas perform similar
functions in various species. This is not to say that these areas perform simple functions: they
typically carry out complex functions that either are essential for life or fundamental to the
survival of the organism.

The *thalamus* is usually regarded as a kind of switching station. The sensory organs,
such as the eye and the ear, as well as parts of the brain involved in controlling voluntary
movements, send fibers to the thalamus, and the thalamus in turn sends fibers widely throughout the brain. The thalamus is ideally situated to regulate the flow of information in the
brain, and it does: *attention* is the selective aspect of information processing, and parts of
the thalamus play a crucial role in attention. The *pulvinar nucleus* (a nucleus, in neuroanatomy, is a cluster of cells) is involved in focusing attention. The thalamus is also important in regulating sleep.

Directly under the thalamus lies the *hypothalamus,* which controls many bodily
functions, including maintaining a constant body temperature and blood pressure, eating
and drinking, keeping the heart rate within appropriate limits, and regulating sexual

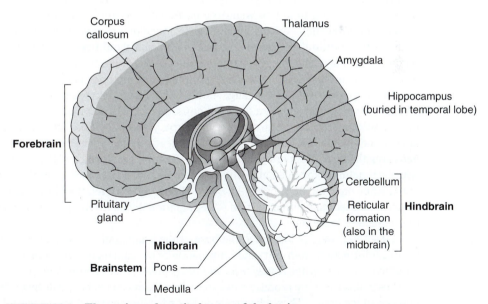

FIGURE 31.4   The major subcortical areas of the brain
The mammalian brain is divided into the *forebrain, midbrain,* and *hindbrain.* In nonhuman mammals, these are essentially in front-to-back order. In humans, *hindbrain* seems a misnomer, both
because of human posture and the evolutionary expansion of the forebrain over the midbrain and
the hindbrain.

behavior. Some of these functions are accomplished by various hormones (which are chemicals that affect various organs, and can even modulate the activity of neurons) regulated by the hypothalamus.

The *hippocampus* is located at the anterior of the temporal lobes, tucked inside. Its internal structure and connections to other areas allow it to play a central role in entering new information into memory. The hippocampus itself is not the repository of new memories; rather, it governs processes that allow memories to be stored elsewhere in the brain (such as in other regions of the temporal lobe).

The *amygdala* (named, based on its shape, for the Greek word for "almond") nestles next to the hippocampus, and for good reason. The amygdala is central both in the appreciation of emotion in others and in the production of behaviors that express our own emotions, especially fear. The amygdala can modulate the functioning of the hippocampus, a relationship that helps you store vivid memories of highly emotional information. The amygdala and hypothalamus serve to connect the CNS to the PNS. Both structures are central to triggering fight-or-flight responses.

The amygdala and hippocampus, along with several other subcortical structures, are part of the *limbic system*. At one time researchers believed that the limbic system regulated emotion, but this turned out to be incorrect. Not only are some parts of the limbic system used in other ways (such as in encoding new memories), but also other structures (such as the frontal lobes) are involved in emotion (Davidson, 2002; LeDoux, 1996).

The *basal ganglia* are absolutely critical for day-to-day life, allowing us to plan movements and to develop habits. Can you imagine what life would be like if you had to think through everything you do every time you do it? Think about the difference between the second time you went to a particular classroom in a basement of an unfamiliar building (which you now remember from the previous visit) and the tenth time you sauntered in: without the basal ganglia, every visit would be like that effortful, alert, second time. The basal ganglia lie at the outer sides of the thalami. The *nucleus accumbens,* a structure that is near the basal ganglia and sometimes considered to be part of it, plays an important role in learning. As the behaviorists emphasized, animals will learn a behavior when it produces a pleasant consequence. (If you make eye contact with the interviewer and receive a warm smile in return, you are likely to make eye contact again later in the interview.) This happy consequence is called a *reward.* The nucleus accumbens signals other brain areas when reward occurs (Tzschentke & Schmidt, 2000), both when it is actually received and when an animal only anticipates receiving it (Hall et al., 2001; Knutson et al., 2001; Pagnoni et al., 2002). By studying the brain, then, researchers have discovered that a mental state — anticipation — can affect the brain in a way that in turn enhances learning.

The *brainstem* is located at the base of the brain, and contains many structures that receive information from and send information to the spinal cord. A set of small structures, collectively known as the *reticular formation,* is involved in sleep and alertness. Some of the neurons in this structure produce *neuromodulators,* which are chemicals that affect far-flung portions of the brain. (These chemicals do just what their name suggests: they alter, or modulate, the functions of neurons.) The *pons* ("bridge" in Latin) connects the brainstem to the cerebellum, and contributes to functions that both structures perform, such as controlling sleep and forming facial expressions.

Finally, the *cerebellum* is concerned with physical coordination. It is also involved in some aspects of attention and in the estimation of time. The surface area of the cerebellum is about the same as the surface area of the cerebral cortex, which implies that this structure is engaged in many complex processes; researchers have only begun to comprehend its functions.

31.3   STUDYING COGNITION

Cognition is investigated in several fields, each of which uses a different approach. When first conceived, *cognitive psychology* focused exclusively on the level of information processing (e.g., Lindsay & Norman, 1977; Neisser, 1967). *Artificial intelligence* (AI), concentrating at the same level of analysis, is the field in which researchers attempt to program computers to perform cognitive tasks. Many AI researchers believe that cognition is so complicated that figuring out how to build a processing system that performs comparably to humans will lend insight into human cognition (Minsky, 1986). Neither early cognitive psychology nor AI pays much attention to the way such information processing takes place in the brain. But even computer buffs have noted that it isn't quite right to assume that information processing is independent of the machine itself: some programs rely on specific features of the hardware, such as the presence of a certain amount of RAM or a particular graphics or sound card. Studying the hardware can lead to insights about what the machine does and how it functions.

In fact, taking this view further, other researchers argue that understanding the hardware in sufficient detail allows you to understand its function. *Neuroscience* aims to understand the "wetware," the brain itself, which also must be understood at different levels of analysis. At one extreme, we must understand the nature of the genetic and molecular events that regulate cells in order to know how individual neurons work; at the other extreme, we must understand the functions of lobes and interactions among the different brain regions in order to know how the brain as a whole operates. Theories of such large-scale interactions among brain areas meld into theories of information processing (cf. Dowling, 1992).

Cognitive neuroscience stands at the intersection of neuroscience and cognitive psychology. The guiding idea is "the mind is what the brain does." Cognition is information processing, but information processing carried out by a brain with specific characteristics. Thus, cognitive neuroscience uses knowledge of the brain, such as the existence of brain areas that are specialized for different processes, in theories of processing systems. However, as indicated by the name of the approach, in which *neuroscience* is the noun that's modified by *cognitive,* cognitive neuroscience is focused on understanding the brain itself — what different parts of it do and how they interact.

In this book we focus on the subject matter of cognitive psychology — the study of mental activity — and draw on related fields to further the investigation. Our goal is twofold: to integrate what has been learned about cognition from the various approaches and to integrate the brain into the traditional laboratory approaches of cognitive psychology. As we conceive it, the goal of the new cognitive psychology is to understand mental activity so well that you could program a computer to mimic the way the brain functions when we perform tasks.

31.3.1   Converging Evidence for Dissociations and Associations

The first thing you will notice as we continue is that there are a lot of different methods. No one method is ideal; they all have limitations and potential problems. But — and this is a critical point — they have *different* limitations and potential problems. Using several different methods has two desirable outcomes. First, a more complete picture can be painted. For example, some sorts of neuroimaging (also called brain scanning) require a relatively long time to obtain an image, but can detect changes in relatively small parts of the brain, and the opposite is true of other neuroimaging methods. By using both types of methods, researchers can learn about different aspects of the same phenomenon. Second, the results from any one study are rarely conclusive; findings from any method are typically open to more than one interpretation. But if the results from different methodologies all point in the same direction, the weaknesses of any one method are compensated by the strengths of another. Thus, converging evidence, different types of results that imply the same conclusion, lies at the heart of successful investigations in cognitive psychology.

Many of the methods in cognitive psychology are used to accomplish two general types of goals. The first is to establish a dissociation, that is, to establish that an activity or a variable affects the performance of one task (or aspect of one task) but not of another. A dissociation, therefore, is evidence for the existence of a specific process. For example, Alan Baddley (1986) has argued that people can use at least two distinct types of "working memory" structures, one that briefly holds visual-spatial information and one that briefly holds articulatory-verbal information. If you look up a phone number and keep it in mind as you cross the room to the telephone, you are holding that information in the articulatory-verbal working memory. In contrast, if you are given a map of how to find the office where a job interview will take place, you might hold that map in visual-spatial working memory after you enter the building and begin to walk down the halls. The primary evidence for the existence of these two types of memory structures is a dissociation between the two kinds of memories in the effects of different sorts of interference. Having to count backward disrupts the ability to retain articulatory-verbal information, but not visual-spatial information; in contrast, having to trace a route through a maze has the opposite effect. In this example, we have a double dissociation: in this case, an activity or variable affects one process but not another and a second activity or variable has the reverse properties (e.g., Sternberg, 2003). Double dissociations are powerful evidence for the existence of two distinct processes, and they can be obtained with virtually any of the methods used in cognitive psychology.

In addition to dissociations, cognitive psychologists try to document associations. An association, in this sense, occurs when the effects of an activity or variable on one task are accompanied by effects on another task. Such shared effects indicate that common representations or processes are being affected. For example, if someone suffered brain damage that led to the inability to recognize faces (which actually does happen, and is discussed in Chapter 2), you might want to test whether that patient also had difficulty forming mental images of faces. In fact, if patients have one problem, they often have the other. This association suggests that a common representation or process is shared by perception and mental imagery.

So much for goals and general approaches. How do we actually get on with it? How do we actually collect observations — data — and formulate theories? Researchers in cognitive psychology ask a wide variety of questions about information processing, and many different methods can be used to answer them. In this book you will see how different methods complement one another, and how researchers have used methods in clever ways to discover some of the secrets of one of Nature's most intricate and intriguing creations — the human mind. So to get oriented, let's open the toolbox and see what's inside.

31.3.2   Behavioral Methods

A behavioral method measures directly observable behavior, such as the time to respond or the accuracy of a response. Researchers attempt to draw inferences about internal representation and processing from such directly observable responses. Table 31.1 summarizes the main behavioral measures and methods used in cognitive psychology and their primary advantages and disadvantages. We pause briefly here to consider some observations about the most important behavioral methods.

First, the accuracy with which participants perform a task is used to address a wide variety of types of processing, ranging from those that require making a discrimination (either perceptually or from memory) to those that require recall. With all accuracy measures, however, researchers must be on guard against two possible hazards:

1. If the task is too easy, participants may exhibit *ceiling effects,* where no differences are seen in the responses because the participants all score the highest possible score. For

TABLE 31.1   Major Behavioral Measures and Methods Used in Cognitive Psychology

MEASURE OR METHOD	EXAMPLE	ADVANTAGES	LIMITATIONS
Accuracy (percent correct or percent error)	Memory recall, such as trying to remember the main job requirements during an interview	Objective measure of processing effectiveness	Ceiling effects (no differences because the task is too easy); floor effects (no differences because the task is too hard); speed — accuracy trade-off ("jumping the gun")
Response time	Time to answer a specific question, such as whether you know the requirements of a certain job	Objective and subtle measure of processing, including unconscious processing	Sensitive to experimental expectancy effects and to effects of task demands: speed-accuracy trade-off
Judgments	Rating on a seven-point scale how successful you felt an interview was	Can assess subjective reactions; easy and inexpensive to collect	Participant may not know how to use the scale; may not have conscious access to the information; may not be honest
Protocol collection (speaking aloud one's thoughts about a problem)	Talking through the pros and cons of various job possibilities	Can reveal a sequence of processing steps	Cannot be used for most cognitive processes, which occur unconsciously and in a fraction of a second

example, if you want to know whether emotion boosts memory and you test only two highly emotional items and two neutral ones, the participants will recall all the items so well that no difference will emerge. But that result does not mean that no difference exists, merely that your test was too easy to demonstrate it. Similarly, if the task is too difficult, participants may exhibit *floor effects,* where no differences are seen among responses because the participants are doing terribly on all the conditions.

2. Participants can make errors because they are jumping the gun, that is, responding before they are ready. This pattern of responses produces a *speed — accuracy trade-off* in which errors go up as response times go down. Such a trade-off can be detected only if response times are assessed at the same time as accuracy. Therefore, as a rule, the two measures should be taken together. Incidentally, this problem is not limited to the laboratory: such speed — accuracy trade-offs can occur in real life, which is why you should be sure to reflect on your decisions: there's truth in "haste makes waste."

Second, a large amount of research in cognitive psychology rests on measures of the amount of time participants take to respond when making a judgment. In general, participants should require more time to respond when a task requires more cognitive processing.

Finally, some researchers also collect judgments of various sorts (such as ratings of confidence that a participant recalls information correctly) and others collect protocols (such as records of what participants say they are doing as they work through a problem).

In general, purely behavioral methods are prone to a number of problems:

1. Participants sometimes change their speed of responding after figuring out what the investigator expects, trying, perhaps unconsciously, to cooperate. The influence of the investigator on the participant's responses is known as *experimental expectancy effects.*

2. Participants may respond to *task demands,* aspects of the task itself that participants believe require them to respond in a particular way. For example, results of mental imagery scanning experiments might reflect such task demands (Pylyshyn, 1981, 2002, 2003). In these experiments, participants are asked to scan an object in their visual mental image, with their eyes closed, until they have focused on a specific target (at which point they press a button). Response times typically increase with the distance scanned (for a review, Denis & Kosslyn, 1999). This result could be explained if participants *interpret the task* as requiring them to mimic what would happen in the corresponding perceptual situation, and thus take more time when they think they should be scanning longer distances. Task demands can be ruled out, but this requires clever experimentation. For example, the scanning results have been obtained even when no instructions to scan, or even to use imagery, are employed (Finke & Pinker, 1982, 1983).

3. Behavioral methods are necessarily incomplete. They cannot give us a rich picture of underlying processing, in part because of structure–process trade-offs. These methods are probably most useful when employed to test a specific theory that makes specific predictions about the specific measures being collected.

31.3.3   Correlational Neural Methods: The Importance of Localization

Cognitive psychology has become extraordinarily exciting during the past decade because researchers have developed relatively inexpensive, high-quality methods for assessing how the human brain functions. These methods are *correlational:* although they reveal the pattern of brain activity that accompanies information processing, they do not show that activation in specific brain areas actually results in the task's being carried out. Correlation does not necessarily imply causation. Some of the activated brain areas could be just along for the ride — activated because they are connected to other areas that do play a functional role in processing. One of the main virtues of these methods is that they allow researchers to begin to *localize* mental activity, to show that particular parts of the brain either give rise to specific representations or carry out specific processes.

Such data can establish both dissociations and associations, thereby giving insight into the nature of representations and processes used during mental activity. On the one hand, if two tasks activate different brain areas (a dissociation), this is evidence that they are accomplished at least in part by separate representations or processes. For example, the parts of the brain used when one holds verbal information in working memory (sometimes refered to as "short-term memory") are different from those used when one recalls previously stored information (Nyberg et al., 1996; Smith, 2000), showing that working memory is not just an activated portion of the information previously stored in memory. On the other hand, if the same brain area is activated in two tasks (an association), this is evidence that at least some of the same representations or processes may be used in the two tasks. For example, once part of the parietal lobe was shown to be involved in representing space, Dehaene and colleagues (1999) could interpret activation in this region when participants compare relative magnitudes of numbers. They argued that people use a "mental number line" in this task. Their interpretation was then supported with a variety of additional forms of evidence. However, this sort of inference must be made with great caution: what appears to be activation of the same area in two different tasks may in fact be activation in two different, nearby areas, but the technique is too insensitive to register the difference. As usual, we must be very careful in affirming the null hypothesis; that is, in claiming that a failure to *find* a difference means that there is in fact no difference.

We can evaluate the various correlational neural methods on four dimensions: (1) *spatial resolution,* how precisely they localize the brain area that produces a signal; (2) *temporal resolution,* how precisely they track changes in brain activity over time; (3) *invasiveness,* the degree to which they require introduction of foreign substances into the brain; and (4) *cost,* both for the equipment (and any special facilities) and for its use in each participant test. The three most important neuroimaging methods for cognitive psychology currently are event-related potentials (ERP), positron emission tomography (PET), and functional magnetic resonance imaging (fMRI), and so it is worth considering them briefly in more detail. Table 31.2 summarizes these methods.

The oldest correlational methods record brain activity from the scalp. *Electroencephalography* (EEG) uses electrodes placed on the scalp to record fluctuations in electrical activity over time (Figure 31.5). These "brain waves" are analyzed to reveal how much activity is present in different "bands," which are sets of frequencies. For example, the "alpha rhythm" is 8 to 12 Hz (that is, 8 to 12 cycles per second), and the amplitude of waves in this range increases when a participant becomes relaxed. Recording *event-related potentials*

TABLE 31.2 Correlational Neuroimaging Methods

METHOD	EXAMPLE	SPATIAL RESOLUTION	TEMPORAL RESOLUTION	INVASIVE-NESS	COST (INITIAL; USE)
Electrical (electroen-cephalography, EEG; event-related potentials, ERP)	Track stages of sleep (EEG), brain response to novelty (ERP)	Poor (perhaps 1 inch)	Excellent (milliseconds)	Low	Low purchase cost; low use cost
Magnetoen-cephalography (MEG)	Detect activity in auditory cortex to tones of different pitches	Good (under 1 centimeter), but only in sulci, not in gyri (because of the way dendrites line up)	Excellent (milliseconds)	Low	High purchase cost (and needs a special magnetically shielded room); medium use cost (needs servicing so superconductors remain extremely cold)
Positron emission tomography (PET)	Detect activity in language areas as participants speak	Good (about 1 centimeter, but in theory higher)	Poor (an image every 40 seconds)	High (must introduce radiation)	High purchase cost (needs a cyclotron plus the PET cam-era); high use cost (about $2,000 per participant)
Magnetic resonance imaging (MRI) and functional magnetic resonance imaging (fMRI)	Show structure of the brain (for MRI), show activity in brain areas, same as PET (for fMRI)	Superb (millimeter range); fMRI often about 0.5 centimeter	Depends on level of resolution; typically several seconds	Low	High purchase cost (needs a specially shielded room); medium use cost (needs servicing)
Optical imaging	Show activity in brain areas, same as PET	Poor at present (about 2 centimeters)	Depends on level of resolution; typically several minutes	Medium/ low (light is shined through the skull)	Low purchase cost; low use cost

(a)

FIGURE 31.5A   Recording the brain
(a) An EEG machine, which records electrical activity.

(Photograph by Deep Light Production. Courtesy of Photo Researchers, Inc.)

also relies on scalp electrodes, but here they are used to observe fluctuations in activity in response to a specific stimulus. Investigators note changes in electrical activity, positive or negative, that occur specific amounts of time after a stimulus has been presented. For example, the "P-300" is a positive fluctuation that occurs about 300 milliseconds after a stimulus; this fluctuation is thought to reflect detection of novelty. These methods have several drawbacks:

1. Both EEG and ERP are disrupted by slight movements because muscles produce electric activity when they twitch.
2. Both techniques have relatively poor spatial resolution, in part because electrical waves travel over the surface of the brain and the scalp, and in part because the electrical activity at any point on the scalp is a composite of activity that has originated from various places in the brain. It is as if you were measuring the amount of water falling into paper cups during a rainstorm, and trying to figure out how much water the cloud immediately overhead held; the water you collect came from multiple parts of the cloud (the wind affects where raindrops land) as well as from multiple altitudes. Researchers are working on techniques to use recordings at multiple electrodes to try

to zero in on the source of electric activity, but these techniques are still being developed. At present, the spatial resolution of electric techniques is probably about 1 inch, but this is a rough estimate. In spite of their poor spatial resolution, these techniques have several virtues: they have excellent temporal resolution, they are not invasive, and both purchase and use of the equipment are relatively inexpensive.

A relatively recent variant of ERP, *magnetoencephalography* (MEG), records magnetic rather than electric fields (Figure 31.5b). Unlike electrical fields, magnetic fields are not distorted as they pass through bone and they do not travel over the surface of the brain or the scalp. MEG has relatively good spatial resolution (probably under a centimeter), but because of the way dendrites are arranged in cortex it primarily detects activity in sulci, not on gyri. It has superb temporal resolution (detecting fluctuations of a few milliseconds) and is not invasive. However, MEG is expensive; the machine must be housed in a special magnetically shielded room, and the detectors must be serviced regularly. (They need to be extremely cold, so that superconductors can detect the faint magnetic fields in the brain.)

PET provides a different type of information than what we can learn from ERP and thus is very useful as a complementary technique (Figure 31.6). The most common use of PET in cognitive psychology relies on a radioactive isotope of oxygen, ^{15}O. Water in which some of the oxygen is in the form of this isotope is injected into a participant who is performing a task. When a part of the brain becomes active, it draws more blood to it (rather like the way a washing machine draws more water from the main when the machine is turned on). As more blood flows to an area, more of the radioactively tagged water goes along with it. Detectors surrounding the head record the amount of radioactivity, and computers later reconstruct a three-dimensional image from this information. This technique can detect activity in structures smaller than 1 centimeter across (in theory as small as 2 millimeters, but in practice perhaps three times larger than that). Among the drawbacks are the following:

1. Although the levels of radiation are very low (10 scans deliver about the same amount of radiation as what an airline pilot typically receives in a year and a half), the technique is still invasive.
2. The temporal resolution is relatively poor; it takes at least 40 seconds to obtain an image.
3. PET is expensive, requiring radioactive material that is manufactured immediately before use (because the radiation decays quickly) and special machines to perform the scans.

Another technique has recently come to replace most of the research that used to be done with PET. This technique grew out of magnetic resonance imaging (MRI). So, let's first look at MRI, and then consider the newer functional magnetic resonance imaging methods that assess brain activity. The American Paul C. Lauterbur and the Englishman Peter Mansfield won the 2003 Nobel Prize in Physiology or Medicine for their roles in developing MRI. Their discoveries not only changed the face of medicine for all time but also dramatically improved our ability to understand the brain. The original use of MRI was to assess brain structure, not function. For example, this technique has revealed that musicians who play string instruments (such as violins) have a larger area M1 in their right

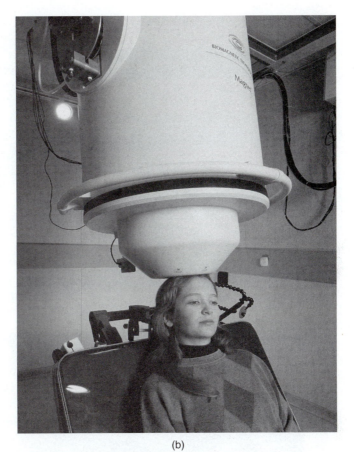

(b)

FIGURE 31.5B   (b) A MEG machine, which records magnetic activity, in use.

hemispheres (controlling their left hands) than is present for other members of an orchestra (Münte et al., 2002). MRI uses magnetic fields to alter the orientations of specific atoms in a substance. A strong reference magnet is turned on, causing all the atoms to line up with it (atoms have a north and south pole, and line up accordingly with a large magnet). A quick pulse of radio waves is then used to disorient the atoms, which give off detectable signals when they return to normal. (This pulse is created by magnets that are so strong that they flex when they are turned on, and they displace air, which creates a sound, just as a loudspeaker pushes air to create sound. But in the case of MRI, the sound is a loud knocking noise.) The MRI records a signal as the atoms return to their original alignment; the recorded current is then amplified and used to create an image. Gray matter and white matter can be identified by the way their component atoms resonate to different frequencies of radio waves. MRI has extraordinarily good spatial resolution (less than 1 millimeter, in principle), good temporal resolution (an image can be created in a few seconds), and it is noninvasive. But the machines are very expensive and require special facilities (Figure 31.6).

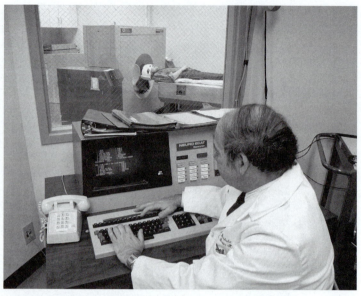

(a)

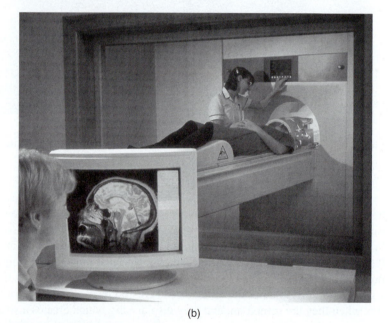

(b)

FIGURE 31.6   Neuroimaging methods.
PET and fMRI are probably the most common neuroimaging methods used today. (a) A PET scan in progress. (b) An MRI machine.

(Photograph by Spencer Grant. Courtesy of PhotoEdit Inc.) (Photograph by Geoff Tompkinson. Courtesy of Photo Researchers. Inc.)

Functional magnetic resonance imaging is based on the same principles as structural MRI. However, instead of charting the structure of the brain, fMRI tracks activity in different parts of the brain. The most common fMRI technique is called BOLD, for *blood oxygenation level dependent.* Red blood cells contain iron (in the hemoglobin), which can have oxygen bound to it or can have oxygen stripped off when it is used up in metabolism. When a brain area begins to function, it draws more oxygenated red blood cells than it actually needs, and thus oxygenated red blood cells pile up. The iron-with-oxygen and the iron-without-oxygen affect the nearby hydrogen atoms in water (the major constituent of blood) differently. And that's the key: the magnetic pulse sequence is designed to reveal where oxygenated red blood cells have piled up, which is an indirect measure of activity in that brain area. fMRI has about the same spatial resolution as structural MRI (at least 1 millimeter) and is noninvasive. Nevertheless, this technique does have drawbacks, including these:

1. fMRI can detect changes that occur over the course of about 6 seconds, which is much less precise than ERP or MEG.
2. The machines (and the necessary specially shielded rooms) are expensive.
3. The machines are very noisy (which can make participants uncomfortable and therefore make certain studies hard to do).
4. The tube in which participants lie is very narrow, which some people find disturbing.

Finally, it is worth mentioning a very new member of the neuroimaging toolbox, which holds promise of becoming increasingly popular in the near future. *Optical imaging* takes advantage of two facts about light: first, the skull is transparent to near-infrared light; second, some frequencies of such light are absorbed more by oxygenated hemoglobin than by hemoglobin stripped of its oxygen (Obrig & Villringer, 2003). The *diffuse optical tomography* (DOT) method positions a collection of very weak lasers at different locations on the skull and shines light onto the cortex; the reflected light is measured by detectors placed on the scalp. Each laser flickers at a distinct rate, and thus it is possible to calculate where the reflected light originated. This technique allows researchers to track blood flow in the cortex. It is relatively inexpensive to build the machines and costs almost nothing to use them. Although the technique is in a sense invasive, it is very safe; the level of light reaching the cortex is less than what an uncovered bald head receives outdoors on a sunny day (the technique has been approved for use with very young infants). The major drawbacks are as follows:

1. Light penetrates only 2 or 3 centimeters before it becomes too diffuse to be recorded accurately, and thus no subcorrical areas can be assessed and only about 80 percent of the cortex can be reached.
2. This technique has about the same temporal resolution as BOLD fMRI, and the spatial resolution depends on the number and placement of the lasers and detectors.

In general, neuroimaging techniques suffer from a number of weaknesses, which should make you cautious when interpreting their results:

■ First, we cannot tell the difference between results caused by excitatory or inhibitory activity.

- Second, more activation does not necessarily mean more processing. A champion runner can run a mile faster than a couch potato and use less energy in the process; similarly, if you are an expert at specific processes, you may be able to accomplish them with less brain processing.
- Third, the same functional area can lie in slightly different anatomical regions in different brains, which makes averaging over participants difficult.
- Fourth, the brain is always "on," even during sleep. Thus, researchers always must compare two conditions and observe how activation changes from one to the other. The problem is that we do not know exactly what processing takes place during either a "test" or "baseline" comparison condition, and so the difference between the two conditions can be difficult to interpret.
- Fifth, if no difference in activation between two tasks is found in a brain area, this can mean that the process was active in both tasks, not active in either task, or the difference was too subtle to detect. This last possibility is particularly worrisome because blood vessels can expand only so much, and therefore increases in blood flow with neural activity cannot be linear — they cannot increase by the same increment for each additional increment of processing. If an area is relatively active in two conditions, the difference in blood flow between them may not reflect the difference in processing.
- Finally, processes need not be implemented in distinct neural tissue. For example, area 17 contains neurons that process color, and these neurons are interspersed among those that process shape (Livingstone & Hubel, 1984). If we average over a centimeter or so (the resolution used in most PET and fMRI studies), we cannot distinguish these two classes of neurons. In short, "converging evidence" must be our watchword!

31.3.4   Causal Neural Methods

Researchers have depended on other types of studies to establish causal connections between brain activation and performance. Such methods, summarized in Table 31.3, show that activity in a particular brain area actually gives rise to specific representations or carries out specific processes.

If a part of the brain plays a key role in performing a specific task, then a patient should have difficulty performing that task if that part of the brain has been damaged. Following this logic, researchers have tried to use deficits in performance of particular tasks (such as reading, writing, or arithmetic) following brain damage to infer the causal role of specific parts of the brain. People suffer brain damage primarily for one or the other of five reasons:

- They have a stroke, an event that occurs when blood flow — with its life-sustaining oxygen and nutrients — to the brain is disrupted. When this happens, neurons in part of the brain may die.
- Surgery to remove a tumor may also have removed specific parts of the brain.
- They have suffered various sorts of head injuries that can damage the brain. (In a car, use the seat belt! On a bike, wear a helmet!)

TABLE 31.3   Causal Neural Methods Used in Cognitive Psychology

METHOD	EXAMPLE	ADVANTAGES	LIMITATIONS
Neuropsychological studies (of patients with localized or diffuse brain damage)	Examine deficit in understanding nouns but not verbs	Tests theories of causal role of specific brain areas; tests theories of shared and distinct processing used in different tasks; relatively easy and inexpensive to collect	Damage is often not limited to one area; patients may have many deficits
Transcranial magnetic stimulation (TMS)	Temporarily disrupt occipital lobe and show that this has the same effects on visual perception and on visual mental imagery	Same as for neuropsychological studies, but the transient "lesion" is more restricted, and the participant can be tested before and after TMS	Can be used only for brain areas near the surface (TMS affects only tissue about 1 inch down)
Drugs that affect specific brain systems	Disrupt the action of nor-adrenaline, which is crucial for the operation of the hip-pocampus	Can alter the processing of specific brain systems; typically is reversible; can be tested in advance with animals	Many drugs affect many different brain systems; the temporal resolution may be very poor

- They have a brain-damaging disease. Alzheimer's disease, for example, initially selectively impairs parts of the brain involved in memory.
- They have ingested brain-damaging toxins. Drinking too much alcohol for too long, for example, can lead to bad dietary habits, which in turn damage specific parts of the brain involved in memory. (The problem is not the alcohol per se, but rather how drinking too much affects nutrition.)

Researchers have studied patients with brain damage in order to discover which cognitive abilities are disrupted and which are left intact. Their goal is to document dissociations and associations (Caramazza, 1984, 1986; Shallice, 1988). In these studies, a dissociation is said to occur when one ability is impaired while another is spared, and an association is said to occur when two tasks are always disrupted together (suggesting that the two tasks rely on at least one common underlying representation or process). However, associations can also occur because nearby brain areas are damaged together (or neurons that have different functions are present in the same area).

In general, it can be difficult to relate changes in performance after brain damage to the normal function of damaged areas. Why?

1. Brain damage typically affects a large area of neural tissue, and also affects connections among brain areas.
2. Such damage does not leave the rest of the brain as it was before the injury; rather, the brain compensates in various ways. Gregory (1961) offers a useful metaphor: if you

remove a resistor from a radio and it begins to howl, this does not mean that the resistor was a howl suppressor. Removing the part changes the way the entire system works.

Nevertheless, if one has a theory of what a specific brain area does, then damage to that area provides a strong test of the role of that area: if an area does play a causal role in a particular type of performance, then damage to that part of the brain should disrupt such tasks (Fellows et al., 2005).

A new technique sidesteps many of the difficulties encountered when studying people with brain damage. *Transcranial magnetic stimulation* (TMS) temporarily disrupts normal brain activity in a relatively small area, perhaps 1 cubic centimeter (Walsh & Pascual-Leone, 2003). TMS involves placing a coil on the participant's skull and briefly running a large current through the coil (Figure 31.7). The current produces a magnetic field, which in turn temporarily disrupts neural activity of brain areas beneath the coil. There are two main variants of this technique. In the single-pulse version, a pulse is delivered a specific amount of time after a stimulus is presented. This method can be used to discover the duration of particular processes, as well as their causal roles in a specific task. In the other version, known as repetitive TMS (rTMS), a series of magnetic pulses is delivered to a brain area before a task is performed. If enough pulses are delivered, the neurons eventually become less responsive and continue to be sluggish for a period thereafter. Thus, researchers can deliver rTMS to a particular part of the cortex and then observe performance in specific tasks. This technique in some ways induces a temporary lesion,

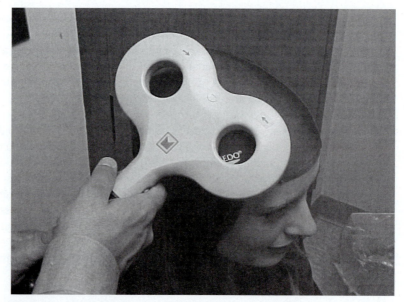

FIGURE 31.7   Investigation by transcranial magnetic stimulation
A TMS test, as shown here, can be administered easily in a laboratory; it can temporarily impair very specific cognitive processing.

(Courtesy of Julian Paul Keenan, PhD.)

but does not disrupt connections. For example, if TMS is delivered to Broca's area, the result is difficulty in producing speech immediately afterward. It is not always clear, however, exactly which areas are affected by the pulses, nor is it clear whether affecting one area also affects another to which it is connected. The method has drawbacks:

1. The effects of stimulating one area can be transmitted to other areas, which can make it difficult to infer which area is in fact responsible for observed effects.
2. If not used according to safety guidelines, rTMS can produce seizures.
3. The technique affects only the cortex, and only the portions of it that lie directly beneath the skull.
4. Muscles at the sides of the forehead twitch when TMS is applied to that area, which can be uncomfortable.

Finally, another method involves administering drugs that affect the workings of specific brain systems. This technique provides another way to demonstrate that particular brain systems play a causal role in particular types of performance. For example, Cahill and colleagues (1994) showed participants pictures that either illustrated neutral events (such as walking past a junk yard) or aversive events (such as being in a horrible accident). One hour after seeing the pictures, they gave the participants one of two pills: half the participants took a drug that interferes with noradrenaline, a neurotransmitter that is crucial for the operation of the hippocampus; this drug thus impaired the operation of that brain structure, which is crucial for entering new information into memory. The other half of the participants received a placebo, a medically inert substance. (The participants did not know whether they received the active drug or a placebo.) A week later, the participants were tested — without being warned in advance that such a test was in the works — on their memory for the pictures. The group that received the placebo recalled more pictures of emotional events than pictures of neural events. Why? The answer may be that the group that received the drug that blocks noradrenaline did not show the typical memory advantage for emotional events, which is evidence that the hippocampus (along with the amygdala) plays a role in our enhanced memory for emotional material. However, this method also has drawbacks:

1. Drugs often affect many different brain systems.
2. Drugs may take a relatively long time to operate and their effects may linger for a relatively long time.

In general, the causal methods are most effective when used in combination with neuroimaging techniques, which can establish that certain areas are active during a task; those areas then can be specifically examined (in patients with brain damage or by TMS or specific drugs). Advances in localizing activation in individual participants are allowing researchers to use TMS with increasing precision, and this technique is likely to play an increasingly large role in research.

REFERENCES

Anderson, J. R. (1978). Arguments concerning representations for mental imagery. *Psychological Review, 85*, 249–277.

Baddeley, A. (1986). *Working memory*. New York: Clarendon Press/Oxford University Press.

Behrmann, M. (2000). The mind's eye mapped onto the brain's matter. *Current Directions in Psychological Science, 9*, 50–54.

Cahill, L., Prins, B., Weber, M., & McGaugh, J. L. (1994). β-Adrenergic activation and memory for emotional events. *Nature, 371*, 702–704.

Caramazza, A. (1984). The logic of neuropsychological research and the problem of patient classification in aphasia. *Brain and Language, 21*, 9–20.

Caramazza, A. (1986). On drawing inferences about the structure of normal cognitive systems from the analysis of patterns of impaired performance: The case for single-patient studies. *Brain and Cognition, 5*, 41–66.

Chomsky N. (1967). *Current issues in linguistic theory*. The Hague: Mouton.

Davidson, R. J. (1998). Affective style and affective disorders: Perspectives from affective neuroscience. *Cognition and Emotion, 12*, 307–330.

Davidson, R. J. (2002). Anxiety and affective style: Role of prefrontal cortex and amygdala. *Biological Psychiatry, 51*, 68–80.

Dehaene, S., Spelke, E., Pinel, P., Stanescu, R., & Tsivkin, S. (1999). Sources of mathematical thinking: Behavioral and brain-imaging evidence. *Science, 284*, 970–974.

Denis, M., & Kosslyn, S. M. (1999). Scanning visual images: A window on the mind. *Cahiers de Psychologie Cognitive/Current Psychology of Cognition, 18*, 409–465.

Dowling, J. E. (1992). *Neurons and networks: An introduction to neuroscience*. Cambridge, MA: The Belknap Press of Harvard University Press.

Einstein, A. (1945). A testimonial from Professor Einstein (Appendix II). In J. Hadamard (Ed.), *An essay on the psychology of invention in the mathematical field* (pp. 142–143). Princeton, NJ: Princeton University Press.

Fellows, L. K., Heberlein, A. S., Morales, D. A., Shivde, G., Waller, S., & Wu, D. H. (2005). Method matters: An empirical study of impact in cognitive neuroscience. *Journal of Cognitive Neuroscience, 17*, 850–858.

Finke, R. A., & Pinker, S. (1982). Spontaneous mental image scanning in mental extrapolation. *Journal of Experimental Psychology: Learning, Memory, and Cognition, 8*, 142–147.

Finke, R. A., & Pinker, S. (1983). Directional scanning of remembered visual patterns. *Journal of Experimental Psychology: Learning, Memory, and Cognition, 9*, 398–410.

Goldenberg, G., Mullbacher, W., & Nowak, A. (1995). Imagery without perception—a case study of anosognosia for cortical blindness. *Neuropsychologia, 33*, 1373–1382.

Gregory, R. L. (1961). The brain as an engineering problem. In W. H. Thorpe & O. L. Zangwill (Eds.), *Current problems in animal behaviour* (pp. 547–565). Cambridge, UK: Cambridge University Press.

Hall, J., Parkinson, J. A., Connor, T. M., Dickinson, A., & Everitt, B. J. (2001). Involvement of the central nucleus of the amygdala and nucleus accumbens core in mediating Pavlovian influences on instrumental behaviour. *European Journal of Neuroscience, 13*, 1984–1992.

Hellige, J. B. (1993). *Hemispheric asymmetry: What's right and what's left*. Cambridge, MA: Harvard University Press.

Klein, I., Dubois, J., Mangin, J., Kherif, F., Flandin, G., Poline, J., Denis, M., Kosslyn, S. M., & Le Bihan, D. (2004). Retinotopic organization of visual mental images as revealed by functional magnetic resonance imaging. *Cognitive Brain Research, 22*, 26–31.

Knutson, B., Adams, C. M., Fong, G. W., & Hommer, D. (2001). Anticipation of increasing monetary reward selectively recruits nucleus accumbens. *Journal of Neuroscience, 21*, RC159.

Kosslyn, S. M., Pascual-Leone, A., Felician, O., Camposano, S., Keenan, J. P., Thompson, W. L., et al. (1999). The role of area 17 in visual imagery: Convergent evidence from PET and rTMS. *Science, 284*, 167–170.

Kosslyn, S. M., & Pomerantz, J. R. (1977). Imagery, propositions, and the form of internal representations. *Cognitive Psychology, 9*, 52–76.

Kosslyn, S. M., & Thompson, W. L. (2003). When does visual mental imagery activate early visual cortex? *Psychological Bulletin, 129*, 723–746.

Kosslyn, S. M., Thompson, W. L., & Ganis, G. (2006). *The case for mental imagery*. New York: Oxford University Press.

Kosslyn, S. M., Thompson, W. L., Kim, I. J., & Alpert, N. M. (1995). Topographical representations of mental images in primary visual cortex. *Nature, 378*, 496–498.

Laeng, B., Chabris, C. F., & Kosslyn, S. M. (2002). Asymmetries in encoding spatial relations. In

R. J. Davidson & K. Hugdahl (Eds.), *Brain asymmetry* (2nd edition). Cambridge, MA: The MIT Press.

Lindsay, P. H., & Norman, D. A. (1977). *Human information processing: An introduction to psychology* (2nd ed.). New York: Academic Press.

Livingstone, M. S., & Hubel, D. H. (1984). Anatomy and physiology of a color system in the primate visual cortex. *Journal of Neuroscience, 4*, 309–356.

Minsky, M. (1986). *The society of mind*. New York: Simon and Schuster.

Monsell, S. (1978). Recency, immediate recognition memory, and reaction time. *Cognitive Psychology, 10*, 465–501.

Montague, P. R., & Berns, G. S. (2002). Neural economics and biological substrates of valuation. *Neuron, 36*, 265–284.

Münte, T. F., Altenmüller, E., & Jäncke, L. (2002). The musician's brain as a model of neuroplasticity. *Nature Reviews Neuroscience, 3*, 473–478.

Neisser, U. (1967). *Cognitive psychology*. New York: Appleton-Century-Crofts.

Newman, E. A., & Zahs, K. R. (1998). Modulation of neuronal activity by glial cells in the retina. *Journal of Neuroscience, 18*, 4022–4028.

Nyberg, L., Habib, R., & McIntosh, A. R. (2000). Reactivation of encoding-related brain activity during memory retrieval. *Proceedings of the National Academy of Sciences USA, 97*, 11120–11124.

Obrig, H., & Villringer, A. (2003). Beyond the visible — imaging the human brain with light. *Journal of Cerebral Blood Flow and Metabolism, 23*, 1–18.

Pagnoni, G., Zink, C. F., Montague, P. R., & Berns, G. S. (2002). Activity in human ventral striatum locked to errors of reward prediction. *Nature Neuroscience, 5*, 97–98.

Pylyshyn, Z. W. (1973). What the mind's eye tells the mind's brain: A critique of mental imagery. *Psychological Bulletin, 80*, 1–24.

Pylyshyn, Z. W. (1981). The imagery debate: Analogue media versus tacit knowledge. *Psychological Review, 87*, 16–45.

Pylyshyn, Z. W. (2002). Mental imagery: In search of a theory. *Behavioral & Brain Sciences, 25*, 157–238.

Pylyshyn, Z. (2003). Return of the mental image: Are there pictures in the brain? *Trends in Cognitive Sciences, 7*, 113–118.

Sereno, M. I., Dale, A. M., Reppas, J. B., & Kwong, K. K. (1995). Borders of multiple visual areas in humans revealed by functional magnetic resonance imaging. *Science, 268*, 889–893.

Shallice, T. (1988). *From neuropsychology to mental structure* (2nd ed.). Cambridge, UK: Cambridge University Press.

Smith, E. E. (2000). Neural bases of human working memory. *Current Directions in Psychological Science, 9*, 45–49.

Sternberg, S. (1969b). Memory-scanning: Mental processes revealed by reaction-time experiments. *American Scientist, 57*, 421–457.

Sternberg, S. (2003). Process decomposition from double dissociation of subprocesses. *Cortex, 39*, 180–182.

Townsend, J. T. (1990). Serial vs parallel processing: Sometimes they look like tweedledum and tweedledee but they can (and should) be distinguished. *Psychological Science, 1*, 46–54.

Townsend, J. T., & Ashby, F. G. (1983). *The stochastic modeling of elementary psychological processes*. Cambridge, UK: Cambridge University Press.

Tzschentke, T. M., & Schmidt, W. J. (2000). Functional relationship among medial prefrontal cortex, nucleus accumbens, and ventral tegmental area in locomotion and reward. *Critical Reviews in Neurobiology, 14*, 131–142.

Ullian, E. M., Sapperstein, S. K., Christopherson, K. S., & Barres, B. A. (2001). Control of synapse number by glia. *Science, 291*, 657–661.

Walsh, V., & Pascual-Leone, A. (2003). *Transcranial magnetic stimulation: A neurochronometrics of mind*. Cambridge, MA: The MIT Press.

Witelson, S. F., Kigar, D. L., & Harvey, T. (1999). The exceptional brain of Albert Einstein. *Lancet, 353*, 2149–2153.

CHAPTER THIRTY-TWO

SOME PROPOSITIONS ABOUT THE RELATIONS BETWEEN CULTURE AND HUMAN COGNITION

ROY D'ANDRADE

Cognitive anthropology has been an ongoing enterprise for more than 25 years. In this period much has been learned about the relationship between culture and cognition. This chapter summarizes some of that work. I have tried to organize what has been learned as a series of interrelated propositions with supporting material. These propositions represent not proven facts but rather my assessment of what is most probably the case.

Before the propositions are presented, something should be said about the terms *culture* and *cognition.* With respect to human cognition, this essay assumes an information-processing approach based on the model developed at UCSD by Mandler, Norman, Rumelhart, and associates. This model treats the mind as a complex of structures composed of parallel-distributed processing networks. Through these structures events are interpreted, remembered, and acted upon (Mandler, 1984; Rumelhart & McClelland, 1986).

It is assumed here that culture consists of learned and shared systems of meaning and understanding, communicated primarily by means of natural language. These meanings and understandings are not just representations about what is in the world; they are also directive, evocative, and reality constructing in character. Through these systems of meanings and understandings individuals adapt to their physical environment, structure interpersonal relationships, and adjust psychologically to problems and conflicts (D'Andrade, 1985). These systems of meanings and understandings are only one set of variables that influence human behavior; social and environmental conditions, the distribution of power, economic opportunity, personality characteristics, genetic constitution, and other classes of variables also influence what people do and think.

This paper has benefited from critiques by James Boster, Paul Kay, Willet Kempton, and Naomi Quinn. From chapter 2 in *Cultural Psychology: Essays on Comparative Human Development,* ed. J. W. Sitgler, R. A. Shweder, and G. Herdt (New York: Cambridge University Press, 1990), 65–129. Reprinted with permission.

The abstract definition of culture first given fails to indicate the pervasiveness and importance of culture in normal human life. If we try to enumerate the actions that a normal person carries out in an average day, we quickly discover that a great deal of what people do is culturally shaped — culturally shaped in the sense that both the goal and the means to the goal are part of a learned and shared system of understandings about the appropriate thing to do (Swartz & Jordan, 1976). For example, an average American adult, on waking, does things like shaving, showering, dressing, eating breakfast, and reading the morning newspaper. These conventional actions, evaluated by conventional standards, are replicated daily by millions of other Americans, but not performed at all by millions of non-Americans.

It is sometimes said that social scientists are unsuccessful at predicting behavior. Whether this statement is true for other fields, it is clearly untrue with reference to the study of culture. Since culture tends to be stable over time, a description of yesterday's conventions will serve as predictions of tomorrow's actions. A simple English dictionary, for example, can be viewed as a huge compilation of predictions about tomorrow's discourse. Similarly, a standard ethnography can also be considered a predictive account of what people will do. For example, LeVine (1984) writes:

> From 1955 to 1957, I conducted fieldwork in a Gusii community. I had read the publications of Philip Mayer, who carried out fieldwork among the Gusii from 1946 to 1949 in an area about ten miles away. Guided by his descriptions of Gusii culture, I was nevertheless constantly searching for points in which my community might deviate from what he had written. I found that his account of Gusii beliefs concerning witches (Mayer, 1954) forecast my informants' descriptions down to the smallest details, not only as beliefs attributed to the community in general but also in narratives concerning personal experience. In other words, the Gusii I worked with for eighteen months told me stories of their own current encounters with witches for which Mayer's account provided the basic script, though his statements were based on interviews with other informants in a community some distance away. I discovered that Gusii accounts of personal experience with witches were in fact highly predictable in the social situations of their occurrence, the images of witches and victims, the narrative sequences of action, the emotional reactions attributed to self and other, and the outcomes of attempts to combat witchcraft. These were the most intense emotional experiences reported by my friends and neighbors about themselves and members of their immediate families, yet the form and contents of their reports were standardized, apparently following a conventional script with a single set of symbols and meanings. (p. 71)

If anthropologists are so good at predicting behavior, is there anything left for psychologists and other social scientists to do? First, it should be noted that although large chunks of behavior come culturally "packaged," there is always selection at the individual level among alternative packages. In greeting a friend, one can say "hello," or "how's it going," or "good morning," and it is reasonable to expect that extracultural variables — psychological and social — will account for who selects which alternatives. Second, culture changes, and a theory is needed that can account for the way the chunks get repackaged. Third, there is much behavior that is not already conventionalized — some idiosyncratic, some aberrant, some produced in laboratories — which cannot be accounted for by referring to culture and convention. Finally, there is more to doing science than making successful predictions. Success at prediction is not a good measure of how well a science is progressing.

If the only theory in anthropology were that people continue to do the conventional actions they did before, anthropology would make many successful predictions but would not be a good science (see D'Andrade, 1986, for further discussion of this point).

One issue taken up in this chapter has to do with the ways in which culture "structures" or "packages" or "conventionalizes" human cognition. Given that so much of human behavior is culturally shaped, it would be surprising indeed if culture did not also shape human cognition. Can culture affect the way people perceive, reason, and feel? If so, to what degree? And, conversely, is culture shaped by the way human cognitive processes work? If so, to what degree? Any attempt to understand the human condition must pay close attention to these issues.

32.1   SYMBOLIC REPRESENTATION

What then, have anthropologists, psychologists, and others discovered about relationships between culture and cognition? To start off, a basic area of continuing interest is the general process of *categorization,* especially the type of categorization found in natural language. The emphasis on natural language leads immediately to questions about the nature of symbolic representation. What does it mean to say that something is a *symbol?* A considerable amount of work has been done on defining a symbol, but most of it seems to involve synonym mongering. It does not help to say that "a symbol is a physical sign that stands for something else," without saying what "stands for" means. One can, however, get at what representation by symbols really is by discovering something about what an animal has to learn before one can say that the animal is really using symbols.

To my knowledge, the most effective experimental paradigm for the investigation of symbolic representation by animals is that developed by Savage-Rumbaugh and her associates (1980), who taught chimpanzees to label objects and classes of objects using plastic tokens (lexigrams). First, the animals were taught to sort real objects (bread, orange, key, stick) into two different bins — one for the "foods," and one for the "tools." Next, the animals were taught to sort these objects into the proper bin and then select the proper lexigram representing either food or tool. The bins were then removed, and subjects taught to label each object as a food or tool. Once the animals reached a high level of expertise in performing this task, a test was made by introducing new tools and foods, testing whether or not the animals could make the appropriate generalization and label correctly the new items. It turned out that two of the three chimpanzees could do this, and one — Lana — could not. Lana had been trained just to label specific objects, and had not used lexigrams to communicate with other animals. It is interesting that Lana could, when shown new tools, correctly place them in the original bins. Thus she understood the distinction between food and tool, but had not learned that the lexigrams stood for this distinction.

In further work, the two successful animals were also taught to label photographs of the original training items with the food and tool lexigrams, and then were tested to see if they could label correctly photographs of new items. Again, both animals were successful. Finally, the animals were taught to select the appropriate food or tool lexigram when presented with previously learned lexigrams for the specific training items. The test for this phase was to present the animals with lexigrams for new items that they had not learned to label with the food or tool lexigram, and to see if they could correctly label these new lexigrams. In fact, both animals were quite successful at this final test of labeling labels.

It seems clear that symbolic representation is involved in these animals' ability to generalize a sign from a small class of specific objects to a larger abstract class of tools or foods, and further to generalize a sign from a small class of signs to a larger class of signs. What appears to have been learned is not just a link between a specific object and a physical sign (something any mammal can learn), but rather a complex linkage between physical signs, physical objects, *and abstract concepts*.

However, the success of some chimpanzees in learning symbolic representations should not obscure the great difference between humans and other animals with respect to the degree to which humans are genetically ready and eager to learn a language (Lenneberg, 1967). For example, research by Goldin-Meadow and Feldman (1977) with deaf children who have never been exposed to a sign language indicates that even without tuition of any direct kind children will spontaneously invent a structured sign system that not only uses symbolic representation, but also combines signs into semantically meaningful phrases. In sum,

1. Humans and some other animals are capable of using true symbolic representations, but humans differ from other animals in being much more interested in and successful at acquiring and using language.

32.2   COGNITIVE EFFECTS OF CATEGORIZATION

Given the capacity and importance of language for humans, the question of the relationship between culture and cognition has been investigated primarily in terms of the relationship between language and cognition. One historically important formulation of this relationship is the *Sapir-Whorf hypothesis*. This hypothesis has been stated in a number of ways, but one reasonable form, derived from Kay and Kempton (1984), is

2. Language differences in the way objects are categorized and distinguished are paralleled by cognitive differences in the perception of similarity between such objects, and in the degree to which these objects are accurately remembered.

As Kay and Kempton point out, for the Sapir-Whorf hypothesis to be of any interest there must be at least moderate differences between languages, or between domains in categorization within languages. They quote Whorf: "In our language ... plurality and cardinal numbers are applied in two ways: to real plurals and imaginary plurals. Or more exactly if less tersely: perceptible spatial aggregates and metaphorical aggregates: We say 'ten men' and 'ten days'" (Whorf, 1956:139).

Kay and Kempton (1984) go on to say:

> The claim here is that some things really are plural (or really are experienced directly as plural) while other things have the conceptual structure of plurality imposed on them by a metaphor that in another language could be and often is avoided. Everybody, Whorf seems to be saying, has to experience ten men as an aggregate, but we English speakers extend this aggregate schema to days, while the Hopi do not. A few lines later Whorf again suggests that he conceives of experience having two tiers: one, a kind of rock bottom, inescapable seeing-things-as-they-are (or at least as human beings cannot help but see them), and a second, in which the metaphors implicit in the grammatical and lexical structures of language cause us to classify things in ways that could be otherwise. (p. 76)

Thus there is a factor that potentially limits any effects of the Sapir-Whorf hypothesis, namely, the amount of human experience that rests on the bottom tier of inescapable seeing-things-as-they-are in contrast to the amount of human experience that could be seen differently.

Much of the research on the Sapir-Whorf hypothesis has been carried out in the domain of color. Color is a practical domain for this type of research because there are between-language and within-language differences in the way in which various parts of the color space are categorized, and because it is difficult to discriminate among the many fine gradations of color. Consequently, at least some color perception must rest on Whorf's second rather than first tier of human experience. Munsell color chips have been used to elicit ethnographic color terms in response to standardized stimuli, and to make a controlled comparison between the ranges of color terms in languages as different as English and Zuni (Lenneberg & Roberts, 1956). In their landmark study, Brown and Lenneberg (1954), using an array varying by hue and brightness at the highest level of saturation, found that Munsell color chips with short agreed-upon names were more accurately remembered than chips without short agreed-upon names. However, using a different array, in which chips vary by hue but are at the same level of saturation and brightness, Lenneberg (1961) found that chips *without* short agreed-upon names were more accurately remembered than chips with short names. It should be noted that the chips in this second array, the Farnsworth Munsell array, do not include the focal colors, since focal colors are defined at high levels of saturation, and the Farnsworth Munsell array chips are all at *relatively low* levels of saturation. One hypothesis about why Lenneberg got these results is simply that basic color terms are poor descriptors of the chips in the Farnsworth Munsell array.

Research by Lantz and Stefflre (1964) reestablished the potential of the Sapir–Whorf hypothesis by using a different linguistic measure. Rather than using the short agreed-upon names as a measure of how language categorizes a domain, Stefflre developed a measure of communication accuracy, which measures the degree to which a speaker of a language can describe a chip within an array so that other speakers of the same language can correctly select that chip from the array. Using the Farnsworth Munsell array, Lantz and Stefflre found this measure of communication accuracy correlated strongly with accuracy of recognition. Stefflre, Castillo Vales, and Moreley (1966) extended the study of communication accuracy to Spanish and Yucatec Mayan speakers, and found the same strong correlation between communication accuracy and recognition accuracy for each language, although, in general, the speakers of these languages differed with respect to which chips were most easily remembered and described. These researchers also found that mistakes in memory are *systematically distorted,* for when subjects misremembered which chip they had seen, they tended to select a chip in the direction of the median chip selected as typical of that chip's description. For example, a chip that is called *rose* may not be as good an example of the color rose as some other chip. When trying to select from memory this "rose-but-not-the-best-rose" chip, subjects will tend to err in the direction of the "best-rose" chip.

In the late 1960s the emphasis in research shifted from how language influences perception and memory to how the bedrock of human experience of color is so inescapably what it is that languages naturally conform to this experience. In *Basic Color Terms,* Berlin and Kay (1969), using Munsell's 320-chip array of varying hue and brightness at maximal saturation, found that speakers of different languages agreed closely on the best exemplars for basic color terms, and that although languages had varying numbers of basic color terms, these terms form a Guttman scale-like order. Rosch (Heider 1972), using a 160 Munsell array, found that the chips universally selected as best exemplars of basic color terms (focals) were more accurately remembered, regardless of naming. However, Lucy and Shweder (1979) observed that the focal color chips were easier to find (they gave a subject a chip and timed how long it took the subject to find the same chip in a randomized array), and that in an array in which the discriminability of chips was controlled, that focality did not correlate with accuracy of recognition, but that communication accuracy did. Later work by Garro (1986) and Lucy and Shweder (1988) revealed that under certain conditions both focality and communication accuracy correlate with recognition.

Up to this point, the discussion of the Sapir–Whorf hypothesis has been solely concerned with memory effects. Recently Kay and Kempton (1984) tested the Sapir–Whorf hypothesis by comparing American-English speakers to Tarahumara speakers using specific color chips in the blue-green area. Tarahumara differs from English in having only one basic-level term for the blue and green region. Kempton and Kay used three chips differing only in hue, where the middle and one end chip fall on the same side of the English blue-green boundary, but the middle and the other end chip are actually closer together with respect to hue. They found that American English speakers, compared with Tarahumara speakers, tended to select as the most different the chip that has a different English color name, whereas Tarahumara speakers more often selected on the basis of actual similarity in hue.

In a second, ingenious experiment, Kay and Kempton devised an apparatus in which three chips were arranged in a container with a sliding top so that the subject could see either of two pairs of the three chips, but not all three at once. The chips selected for this experiment were the same as those selected for the first experiment in which two chips fell on one side of the boundary and one fell on the other. The subject was then asked "tell me which is bigger: the difference in greenness between the two chips on the left or the difference in blueness between the two chips on the right." The central chip, which is intermediate in hue between the other two, is in view at all times.

Although formally the same judgment was being asked in this experiment as in the first experiment, where subjects could see all three chips at once, the use of the apparatus apparently blocked the application of different names as a factor in the perception of difference. What happened here was that American subjects reversed the judgment about which two chips were furthest apart, and more accurately saw a greater difference between the two chips on the same side of the blue-green boundary. The effect is like a perceptual illusion — as soon as the sliding cover is taken off and all three chips are seen, the difference between the two chips of the same color suddenly appears to be the smaller difference. Kay and Kempton (1984) concluded:

> There do appear to be incursions of linguistic categorization into apparently nonlinguistic processes of thinking, even incursions that result in judgments that differ from those made on a purely perceptual basis. Thus . . . the English speaker judges chip B to be more similar to A than to C because the blue-green boundary passes between B and C, even though B is perceptually closer to C than to A. The name strategy seems to demand two facilitating conditions:
>   (1) it must not be blocked by context, as in experiment 2; (2) the original judgment must be in some sense hard to make. (p. 77)

It would be interesting to determine the age at which American children begin to show this linguistic effect on color perception. One might guess the effect would not show up until some period after the age at which the child can use color terms correctly, since rehearsal time should be needed to establish what Whorf called *habitual* thought.

Another example of the effect of categorization on memory can be found in the various studies of the *systematic distortion effect* in memory-based personality assessment procedures (D'Andrade, 1965, 1974b, 1985; Shweder, 1972, 1977a, 1977b, 1977c; Shweder and D'Andrade, 1979, 1980). These studies show that the correlational structure of memory-based assessment ratings, such as the Norman five factors or the MMPI Alpha factor, can be replicated using only informants' judgments about the similarity of the rating items, and that in many cases the correlational structure of directly observed behavior does not correspond to the correlational structure of memory-based ratings. These findings are just part of a wide range of studies that show that recall data are influenced by preexisting ideas about the world — that memory is constructive and schema-driven (Mandler, 1984).

The cross-cultural study of emotion is like the cross-cultural study of color in that it also involves problems concerning potential universals of experience and the cognitive effects of different lexically coded systems of categorization (see Lutz & White's 1986 review of studies of emotion in anthropology). Although there is evidence that the facial patterns that are postulated to express the basic emotions are universally lexically differentiated (Ekman, 1971), exactly what is meant when a speaker of a non-Western language uses a particular term to refer to a particular facial expression remains controversial. Anthropologists (e.g., Gerber 1975, 1985; Levy, 1973, 1985; Lutz, 1982, 1985; Poole, 1985) who have studied discourse about emotion ethnographically have found that emotion terms often are defined with reference to complex culturally stereotyped scenarios. Since these complex scenarios are often culturally idiosyncratic, emotion terms are difficult to translate exactly from one language to another, although partial synonyms can usually be found. Wierzbicka (1986), for example, discusses the Polish term *tesknota,* a frequently used emotion term that has no exact English translation. Wierzbicka defines this feeling as follows:

> X feels "tesknota" to Y *means*
> X is far away from Y
> X thinks of Y
> X feels good feelings towards Y
> X wants to be together with Y
> X knows he (she) can't be together with Y
> X feels something bad because of that.

Wierzbicka discusses the ways in which *tesknota* differs from such partial English synonyms as *pine* (for which the object can be places and things as well as people, and which carries the connotation that the person becomes sickly as well), *miss* (which is not necessarily a strong feeling, and also can take as its object places and things as well as people), and *homesick* (which is for a place where certain people are, not an individual person). The problem is not just with Polish, however, although the evidence is not as systematic as one would like. Wierzbicka suggests that the distinctions between the English terms *disgust, revulsion,* and *dislike,* and the distinctions between *shame, embarrassment,* and *fear* are quite different from the distinctions found in many other languages around the world. The issue here is not whether there are universal basic affects, but whether the distinctions found in English make the best prototype for basic affects.

Gerber, in her investigation of Samoan emotion terms (1985), sums up the problem of the relation between *basic affects* and cultural influence as follows:

> The subjective experience of all but a few emotions is shaped both by basic affect patterns and by complex cultural influences. Some emotions, however, have relatively specific cultural scenarios to which they are considered relevant. . . . Because of this specificity, terms that express such feelings cover relatively narrow ranges of meaning. Other terms are more global, and therefore available to be used to express something closer to a basic affect pattern. "Nostalgia-for-the-lilacs-of-yesteryear" is an example of the former sort of emotion, while "sadness," . . . is an example of the latter. . . . Both of these concepts are given force by the same basic affect; to the extent that nostalgia is capable of moving us, it is because we are innately programmed to respond to loss. Equally, every experience of loss, whether described by a specific or more global term, is culturally defined and conditioned. We are taught which experiences appropriately trigger the loss program, what behavioral reactions to it are expectable, and what the appropriate subjective tone of the experience ought to be. (pp. 129–130)

An important question here is to what extent do the different cultural organizations of emotion terms affect perception and memory? In languages that do not distinguish between "fear" and "shame," what do people feel when something "frightening" happens to them? And do they have the same feeling when something "shameful" happens to them? Feelings appear to be difficult to tell apart, which makes them good material for "incursions of linguistic categorization into apparently nonlinguistic processes of thinking."

Cultural understandings about emotions do more than segment the domain of basic affects. Because culturally defined eliciting situations and behavior responses are included as part of the definition of emotions, emotion terms can convey covert cultural ideologies. Gerber (1985) has analyzed some of the cultural ideology carried by Samoan emotion terms. For example, the term *alofa,* best translated by the English term *love,* has the following basic culturally conventional scenario: An old person, hot, tired, and perhaps ill, is seen walking down the road carrying a heavy load. This makes one feel *alofa,* which prompts one to provide help, perhaps by taking the burden or by offering a cool drink and a place to rest. The emphasis in *alofa* is on caring, giving, and obligation, not intimacy, physical affection, and the appreciation of individual uniqueness, as expressed by the English term *love. Alofa* is the normal feeling toward kin, and the behaviors that are thought to express and are prompted by this feeling are generally morally correct and socially obligatory. Thus a good child works for his or her parents and thereby expresses *alofa.* The emotions thought to be similar to *alofa* are feelings of peacefulness, absence of angry thoughts, forgiveness, humility, generosity, and agreeableness. *Alofa* is thought to be the way good people feel. The cultural ideology here, an ideology that strengthens obligations to elders and kin and mutes resentment and rebellion, is readily apparent to most Americans, since they have not been raised within this particular reality-defining system. The ideology invoked by English emotion terms is probably less apparent to most Americans (see Lutz, 1986, for an analysis of this ideology).

3. Category systems that bring together definitional attributes from a number of domains, such as emotion terms, have the capacity to reinforce certain values. Typically, these systems bring together representations of situations, actions, and the self along with a strong evaluational component.

There is an interesting relation between emotion terms and colors. A series of studies of the association between emotion terms and Munsell color chips in four cultures (D'Andrade & Egan, 1974; Kieffer, 1974; Johnson, Johnson, & Baksh, 1986) demonstrates that informants tend to select similar chips out of various arrays as the best examples of translations of the English emotion terms *happy, sad, angry,* and *frightened* in all four cultures. There is also considerable agreement among all four cultures on which color chips are *good, bad, strong,* and *weak.* This is not to say there are no cultural differences. However, the cultural differences seem to be small compared to the general similarity in emotional response to colors.

32.3   THE PROBLEM OF DEFINITION

There is a great deal of controversy about how the meaning of words is formulated. Linguists, psychologists, and anthropologists have proposed a number of models to explain this process. Miller and Johnson-Laird (1976) carried out an early pioneering effort to relate word meaning to explicit cognitive processes. Recent empirical work by researchers such as Chafe, Fillmore, Kay, Kempton, Labov, Lakoff, Langacker, Rosch, Sweetser, and Talmy has brought to light a wide range of phenomena that are badly in need of critical examination. Unfortunately, only a brief summary of some of this work can be presented here.

At present there is some agreement that the so-called classical view of meaning as an if-and-only-if relation between the item to be defined and a conjunctively connected class of features or attributes is insufficient to describe the semantics of natural language. Perhaps the most detailed metalanguage for semantics is that developed by Langacker (1986, 1987). For Langacker, the unit to be defined, whether a grammatical particle, word, phrase, or sentence, has two basic parts, a *base* and a *profile.* The base is the background object, relation, or event that is differentiated by the profile. For example, the term *hypotenuse* has as its base a right angle triangle and as its profile the line segment opposite to the right angle; the term *finger* has as its base some kind of hand and as its profile an elongated terminal segment of the hand; and the term *mother* has as its base a woman and as its profile the fact that this woman has given birth to a child. Langacker does not give a set theoretical formulation for the terms *base* and *profile;* rather he conceives of these terms as having a psychological relationship of a gestaltlike *figure/ground* type. (Interestingly, Langacker's base/profile relationship is closer to the true classical analysis of meaning — that is, Aristotle's notion that definition is constituted by the specification or differentiation of a "genus," the type example being *man* is a *rational animal,* where *animal* is the base and *rational* is what is profiled — than it is to the classical checklist model.)

The assumption of a psychological foundation for meaning is quite explicit in Langacker's work. For Langacker, the base that is profiled by a term is really a knowledge base, composed of cognitive schemas. The right-triangle base of the term *hypotenuse,* for example, involves the coordination of the cognitive schemas of *line segment* and *angle,* which in turn are complex conceptualizations built of even simpler schemas involving conceptually basic representations of space, markings, straightness, and so on. An exhaustive definition of the meaning of a term would require a complete description of all the hierarchical levels of schemas presupposed by the term, but such an endeavor generally is not feasible.

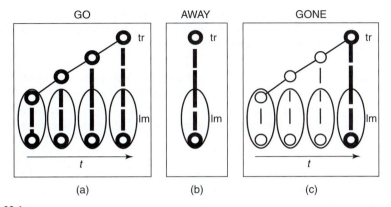

FIGURE 32.1

Langacker has developed a set of concepts and a method of using diagrams to describe the way predications are built up. This approach permits one to identify relatively subtle aspects of meaning. Consider the meanings of *go, away,* and *gone,* as in

    a. You have been here long enough — please *go* now.
    b. California is very far *away.*
    c. By the time I arrived, she was already *gone.*

The time process designated by *go* is diagrammed in Figure 32.1(a). This example is taken directly from Langacker (1986). Time, which is one salient domain for this verb, is indicated by an arrow. The diagram for *go* displays only four states out of a continuous series. There are two main participants, represented by circles. Langacker calls one of these the *trajector* and the other the *landmark*. The dotted lines signify "correspondence"; they connect the trajector from state to state, and the landmark from state to state. The heavy dashed lines connecting the trajector and the landmark within each state represent the profiled interconnection marking the distance of the trajector relative to the region to the landmark. In the initial state the trajector is in the neighborhood of the landmark, as given by the ellipse. The trajector's position changes from state to state over time, and in the final state it lies outside the neighborhood of the landmark. For *away,* time is not an active domain. Figure 32.1(b) shows a single configuration that is identical to the final state of *go.* Thus the process designated by *go* results in the locative state of being *away.*

The analysis for *gone* is more complex. As diagrammed in Figure 32.1(c) *gone* matches *away* in profiling (the dark lines) a single locative arrangement in which the trajector is outside the neighborhood of the landmark. However, these two terms differ in their base; for *away,* the base is just a spatial region, whereas for *gone* the base is the entire process diagrammed for *go.* That is, something is *gone* because it is the result of the process of *going.*

This brief excursus gives some indication of the complex relations to be found in the construction of meaning. *Profile* and *base, trajector* and *landmark* are complex relational terms needed to analyze the information carried by a term like *gone.* These relationships are basically psychological; they involve cognitive processes that have not been well studied in the laboratory. However, if Langacker is right about the necessity of postulating such relationships in semantic analysis, then these must be frequently used and highly practiced cognitive processes, and one would expect to find them in other areas of intellective functioning outside natural language.

4. Semantic analysis of natural language terms requires an understanding of complex cognitive processes such as the profiling of a base and the establishment of the relationship of a trajector to a landmark. Meaning is not reducible to a conjunctive association of features, or some similar logically based formulation.

The way in which the word *gone* builds on the structure of *go*, which is built on the structure of increasing "awayness" across time, illustrates a major characteristic of human semantics: the "chunking" of structures into cognitive "units" that serve as the parts of more complex structures. An early finding in the field of cognitive psychology was that humans are limited in their capacity to process information (Miller, 1956). Anthony Wallace extended Miller's finding to cultural terminological systems (Wallace, 1961). In a survey of kin-term systems and other lexical sets in which every item is in direct contrast with every other item — such as an alphabet, a phonemic system, pieces of a game, and verb systems — he found that the number of items in such systems range from 14 to 50 and seem to be constrained to a number smaller than the number of items that can be discriminated by 2^6 binary bits of information.

The limitations of short-term memory also appear to affect both the depth and width of folk taxonomic systems. Rarely do folk taxonomies exceed more than five hierarchical levels (since each level down adds an independent predication to the level above, and so the most specific level involves at least five different chunks). Also, rarely do the terms that fall directly under any one node (and so form a direct contrast set) exceed the 50-item limit, as would be expected from the size constraints just discussed (Berlin, Breedlove, & Raven, 1966, 1973).

Since human short-term memory is limited with regard to the number of items it can independently discriminate, natural language symbol systems have developed elaborate uses of chunking to get around this constraint. That is, by treating a complex structure such as the structure of awayness, as a single item, a number of such structures can be cognitively processed simultaneously, as in the term *go*. This more complex structure can then be packaged into a single chunk and made part of even more complex structures, such as *gone* (or *deserted*).

5. Limits on short-term memory restrict the number of items that can be independently discriminated, and thereby constrain the size of directly contrasting lexical sets to 64 or so items and constrain the size of folk taxonomic systems to five or so levels. However, the complexity of structure found within a single term may exceed what might be expected from short-term memory constraints alone because of the cognitive operation of chunking, which makes it possible to package together previously formed structures and treat them as if they were single objects.

The way in which meanings are constructed cannot be fully explained without taking into account *polysemy,* or the multiple senses of a single term. Take the term *ring.* It has a number of senses. These senses are diagrammed in Figure 32.2 (taken from Langacker,

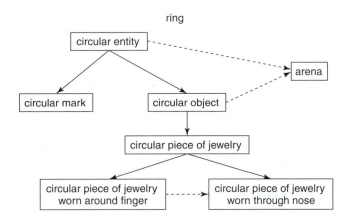

FIGURE 32.2

1986). The solid arrows in the diagram indicate that the sense under the arrow is a more elaborated or more highly specified conceptualization of the sense above the arrow. The dotted arrows indicate an *extension* of the sense; that is, some features of the original sense have been retained, but contrasing features have also been added. Thus a *boxing ring* is an enclosed area, but, unlike the other senses of *ring*, does not refer to a circular form.

Anthropological studies provide numerous discussions of polysemy in connection with kinship terms. In many cultures the basic kin terms *(mother, father, son, daughter)* have at least two senses. One sense is genealogical — genealogically, a *father* is related to someone else by being that person's genitor. Another sense is *role designating* — behaviorally, a *father* is someone who provides basic support and guidance for ego (Schneider & Roberts, 1953). The two senses contrast in the following sentences:

> Sam never even met his father.
> Jim wasn't the father he wanted to be.

According to one view of polysemy, the meaning of any term can be reduced to a single sense and its other senses derive from the basic sense from context, or are metaphorical extensions that need not be treated as lexical meanings. This may be done by taking the most *abstract* sense as the basic or primary meaning. For the term *father,* one might posit an upper-level sense defined as "the male generally responsible for the reproduction of offspring," and then treat the genealogical and role-designating senses as contextually defined specifications of being "generally responsible for reproduction." A different tactic is to arrange the terms in some kind of logical, temporal, or physical order of *priority* and take the most prior sense as the basic or primary sense. For the term *father,* one might argue that the genealogical sense is prior because the role-designating sense is based on an understanding of what it is that genealogical fathers *do,* and hence the genealogical sense is the basic or primary sense, whereas the role-designating sense is given by context.

Each of these tactics depends on being able to trace out kinds of relations among the senses of terms, and then arguing that analysis of these relations allows the analyst to fix one meaning as primary or basic. Their major drawback is that there is no principled reason to accept any one of these ways of deciding which sense is primary as the right method (D'Andrade, 1976, 1986; Fillmore, 1977; Lakoff, 1987; Langacker, 1987). However, the analyses of the relations between senses point to an important empirical generalization:

6. The different senses of a term tend to be related to each other in complex ways; by abstraction, or by logical, spatial, or temporal priority, or by empirical or culturally based associations, and so are motivated rather than arbitrary.

This argument is made with an extensive range of cultural materials by Lakoff (1987).

An aspect of meaning that is often overlooked in linguistic and anthropological treatments of semantics is its *intersubjective* character. To communicate what one means to someone requires not just that the speaker have a set of meanings for the sounds produced, but also that the hearer have the *same* set of meanings. Further, the speaker must assume that the hearer has the same set of meanings for the words produced, for otherwise there would be no communication and no point in speaking. Still further, the speaker must assume that the hearer assumes that the speaker has the same set of meanings for what is said; otherwise the hearer could not assume that the speaker had intended to communicate whatever was said. Interestingly, the assumption of inter-subjectivity has the secondary effect of producing a psychological sense of intersubjectivity, in that talking to someone who talks back appropriately appears to establish that it must be true that both parties are in contact with the same realities. However, the often-cited example of people who do not know they are *not* talking to a therapist when using the Eliza program shows that people can be fooled about this relatively easily.

7. Symbolic communication requires the establishment of intersubjectivity, although it may be the case that much actual language use in which intersubjectivity is assumed in fact rests only on a limited commonality.

32.4 SEMANTIC NETWORKS

The simplest kinds of networks among terms are those created by the very attributes of the terms. One of these is the *contrast set*. A contrast set is composed of terms that all possess at least one salient attribute in common but that differ from each other with respect to other attributes. In some special domains the attributes on which terms differ are orthogonal or cross-cutting, which result in *paradigmatic sets* such as the often-used example of kinship terms. Thus, within the domain of genealogical relationships the paradigmatic relations of *mother, father, aunt, uncle, daughter, son, niece,* and *nephew* can be displayed as shown in Figure 32.3. These terms all share the attribute of being nonaffinal kin, but differ on the attributes of gender *(male* vs. *female),* descent *(direct* vs. *collateral),* and generational polarity *(ascending* vs. *descending).* (For a detailed analysis of American kin terms, see Romney & D'Andrade, 1964.)

There are few fully paradigmatically organized sets of terms in the lexicon. They occur mainly in domains containing dyadic relationships between a small class of objects, such as kin terms, pronouns, and verb inflections. In some cases alternative analyses can

	direct		*collateral*	
	male	*female*	*male*	*female*
ascending	father	mother	uncle	aunt
descending	son	daughter	nephew	niece

FIGURE 32.3

be made using different selections of attributes. In these cases it is possible to use information judgments of various kinds to determine which analysis corresponds best to the psychological distinctions made by native speakers (Romney & D'Andrade, 1964; Wexler & Romney, 1972).

An interesting empirical finding about paradigmatic sets based on the space defined by the attributes is that the great majority of terms are conjunctively or relationally composed, and are *not* disjunctively composed. To illustrate, consider the attributes by which sibling terms can be distinguished (Nerlove & Romney, 1967). One such attribute is gender; in English, for example, *brother* refers to a male sibling and *sister* refers to a female sibling. Another attribute is the *relative age* of the sibling; some languages contain just two sibling terms, one for *older* sibling, one for *younger* sibling. A third attribute is the *cross/parallel* relation between the sex of the speaker and the sex of the sibling; some languages have just two sibling terms, one for sibling of the *same sex* as the speaker, one for sibling of the *opposite sex* of the speaker. These three binary attributes define a space of eight kin types. Working from ethnographic and linguistic sources, Nerlove and Romney collected the sibling kin-term systems for 245 distinct cultural groups and found that only 4 of these systems contained any disjunctive categories.

8. Although natural language categories are often polysemous, containing motivated extensions that make definition by a simple conjunctive or relational composition of attributes impossible, it is nonetheless rare for natural language categories to be arbitrarily disjunctive.

32.5 PSYCHOLOGICAL PROCESSES AND CONTRASTIVE FEATURES

Several examples from my own and related work spanning several decades can serve to give an idea of the way in which cultural models affect basic psychological processes such as judgment and inference. The research is illustrative rather than definitive, however, and some of the conclusions given here are controversial.

The first example consists of a simple attempt to assess the degree to which certain kinds of judgments might be affected by or be under the control of contrastive attributes. To return to the paradigmatic analysis of American kin terms, consider the three attributes used to partition the terms — *direct* versus *collateral, ascending* versus *descending,* and *male* versus *female.* Suppose that respondents are presented with pairs of kin terms and asked to select the term that refers to the relative with whom one expects to have the greater *solidarity.* To the extent that respondents are reacting to the prototypic kin as if they were made up of these attributes, it should be possible to predict the degree of solidarity ascribed to each kind of kin solely from knowledge of the degree of solidarity contained in the attributes.

This hypothesis was tested by means of a simple experiment. Nineteen college students were given a questionnaire that consisted of a randomized list of all possible pairs of the fifteen American consanguineal kin terms: *father, mother, son, daughter, brother, sister, grandfather, grandmother, grandson, grandmother, uncle, aunt, nephew, niece* and *cousin.* Respondents were asked to circle in each pair the relative "you would expect to be the warmer, friendlier, and more trustworthy person." Respondents were told that their rating should be based on "how people generally expect kin to be." The solidarity score for each kin term for each respondent was calculated by counting the number of times the term was circled. Mean scores for all respondents are presented in Figure 32.4.

To derive the solidarity weight for each of the attributes, the mean for all terms containing that attribute was computed. The difference between the attribute mean and the grand mean of all the kin terms constitutes the solidarity weight for that feature. To compute the predicted value for each kin from its attributes, the attributes scores are added together with a constant for the grand mean of all the solidarity scores. The predicted score for *nephew,* for example, consists of the sum of the weight for a male (-1.0), *descending* (-1.0), *first generation* ($+1.3$), *collateral* (-3.1), plus the grand mean constant (5.7), yielding a predicted score of 1.9.

The predicted scores for the 15 kin terms are presented under the actual scores in Figure 32.4. The fit between the two sets of scores is relatively good. The Pearson r between the two sets of scores is .91. Even the discrepancies between the observed and predicted-scores appear to be neatly patterned. In every case the ascending female terms and the descending male terms have slightly higher solidarity scores than predicted by the attribute

		Direct		Collateral	
		male	*female*	*male*	*female*
	ascending	grandfather	grandmother		
2nd Generation		5.6	8.3		
		6.1	8.1		
	descending	grandson	granddaughter		
		4.5	5.9		
		4.1	6.1		
	ascending	father	mother	uncle	aunt
1st Generation		9.9	12.7	3.6	6.3
		10.1	12.1	3.9	5.7
	descending	son	daughter	nephew	niece
		8.4	9.7	2.0	3.6
		8.1	10.1	1.9	3.9
		brother	sister	cousin	
Own Generation		9.5	10.8	4.1	
		9.2	10.1	4.0	

r between observed and predicted scores = .92

FIGURE 32.4   Observed and predicted solidarity scores for American kin terms (predicted scores underlined).

weights, while the ascending male terms and the descending female terms have lower solidarity scores than predicted. Respondents seemingly agree that one can expect a little more from senior female kin and junior male kin than either sex or generation alone would predict.

The data above are aggregated, so the degree to which individuals show consistent attribute weightings cannot be determined. To check on the way individuals perform, six respondents were selected randomly and presented the same questionnaire given to the group. The correlation between predicted and observed solidarity scores was still impressive, although slightly lower (r's were .87, .89, .72, .86, .65, and .93). In every case the attribute *female* had a higher solidarity score than the attribute *male; ascending* had a higher weight than *descending*; and *direct* had a higher weight than *collateral.* Only the attribute of *generation* showed large shifts, with considerable variation between *first-* and *second-generation* weights.

The contrastive attributes of a paradigmatic analysis can also be used to predict the ease with which children learn proper definitions of kin terms. Haviland and Clark (1974) studied the degree to which children can appropriately define the 15 American consanguineal kin terms, in a group of 30 children ranging in age from 3 to 10 years. The children were interviewed individually and asked "What is a mother?" "What is an uncle?" and so on. The children's definitions were recorded and then classified by category level: Category 1 consisted of responses in which the child said he or she didn't know, or gave an irrelevant answer; category 2 consisted of responses in which the child used only absolute or nonrelational criteria, such as sex or age, to define the term, category 3 consisted of responses that gave relational criteria; and category 4 consisted of definitions that were relational and also recognized the potential reciprocal nature of the relationship involved in the term.

Figure 32.5 gives the percentages of children whose definitions had reached category 3 or better for each of the 15 kin terms. Using the same procedures to estimate attribute

		Direct		Collateral	
		male	*female*	*male*	*female*
	ascending	grandfather	grandmother		
2nd Generation		30.0%	30.0%		
		38.5%	39.5%		
	descending	grandson	granddaughter		
		30.0%	30.0%		
		27.5%	28.5%		
	ascending	father	mother	uncle	aunt
1st Generation		43.3%	53.3%	30.0%	23.3%
		42.7%	43.7%	22.7%	23.7%
	descending	son	daughter	nephew	niece
		30.0%	33.3%	13.3%	6.7%
		31.7%	32.7%	11.7%	12.7%
		brother	sister	cousin	
Own		36.7%	43.3%	23.3%	
Generation		39.7%	40.7%	20.2%	

r between observed and predicted scores = .89

FIGURE 32.5   Observed and predicted percentage level three or better definitions for American kin terms (predicted scores underlined).

weights, as in the analysis of solidarity scores, the predicted percentages are also presented below the observed scores. The largest difference is between collateral and direct terms; there is a tendency for ascending terms to be learned before descending terms, and for second-generation terms to be more difficult than first or own-generation terms. Overall, the Pearson correlation between observed and predicted frequency is .89.

The results of these two experiments support the hypothesis that the contrastive attributes used to partition kin terms have an effect on how much solidarity one expects from that class of relative, and also on how hard the term is to define, and indicate that there is little interaction between attributes in producing these effects. Although there are undoubtedly cases in which contrastive attributes are not related to various characteristics of a category, or in which there are strong interaction effects between attributes (consider the kin term *mother-in-law,* for example, which would have a much worse observed solidarity score than predicted from the contrastive attributes because the close relation of the mother-in-law to her child is expected to create conflict with the child's spouse), the evidence here is that each attribute acts as an independent force. More generally,

9. Given any category, people can give judgments about it — how much they like it, what it costs, and so on. In many cases these judgments are made by simply summing or averaging the judgments to the various attributes that are distinctive of that category. This makes for cognitive efficiency, in that the judgments about a great many categories can be generated from the combinations of the judgments about a much smaller number of attributes.

32.6   TAXONOMY

Another kind of network between terms created by the attributes of the terms themselves is a *taxonomic* network. A taxonomic relation, in which A is a kind of B, is created whenever A has all the attributes of B, but B also has additional attributes that distinguish it from A (Werner & Schoepfle, 1987). For example, a *cottage* is a kind of *house* (a *cottage* has the attributes of a *house,* plus other attributes involving small size), a *ponderosa* is a kind of *pine* (a *ponderosa* has all the attributes of a *pine,* plus specific attributes involving needle form, size, trunk, etc.), and a *cousin* is a kind of *relative* (a *cousin* has all the attributes of a *relative,* plus specific attributes involving collaterally and generation). In some domains, such as the domain of plant taxa, relatively extensive taxonomic hierarchies can be elicited (Conklin, 1962; Berlin et al., 1966).

Note that the taxonomic relationship, as defined here, is not the same as the subset/superset relationship (D'Andrade, 1976; Werner, 1985). Every taxonomic relationship is a subset/superset relationship, but some subset/superset relationships are not taxonomic relationships. For example, *comic books* are a subset of *stuff I haven't read for years,* but the attributes of the complex term *stuff I haven't read for years* are not included in the term *comic books;* the subset/superset relationship is empiricially or contingently true, but not definitionally true. In some cases it is hard to decide if a true taxonomic relationship holds; for example, is it true by definition that *lamps* are a subset of things that are *furniture!* This question is discussed further in the following paragraphs.

Taxonomies in the plant domain have been investigated extensively, and a series of generalizations about the structure of this kind of hierarchical system have been proposed

(Berlin et al. 1973), along with various modifications (Hunn, 1976, 1985; Randall 1976; Brown, 1977; Wierzbicka, 1984; Dougherty & Keller, 1985). The basic generalizations are as follows:

10. Folk biological taxonomies are based on the identification of generic taxa. Generic taxa correspond approximately to biological genera, which form natural groupings with many more attributes in common. Generics often consist of strongly related species that exhibit a family resemblance, but that cannot be defined by some necessary and sufficient set of attributes. These generics are also called basic-level categories.

   In a recent study of Jivaro folk ornithology, Boster, Berlin, and O'Neill (1986) found that not only do Jivaroan bird generics generally correspond to scientific generics, but also that there is a strong degree of correspondence between folk and scientific systems of classification with respect to the pattern of resemblance between organisms, where resemblance is measured for the scientific systems by taxonomic depth and for the folk system by an information theoretic measure of the degree to which there is specimen overlap in naming.

11. Folk taxonomies rarely exceed five levels. These levels are definable in terms of linguistic and taxonomic criteria. The five levels are labeled unique beginner, life form, generic, specific, and varietal. Unique beginner refers to the largest inclusive grouping of taxa, and is often unlabeled linguistically by a single term. Life form taxa are invariably few in number (5 to 10). The generic taxa are more numerous (approximately 500). Sometimes unusual generics (cacti, cassowary, platypus) are not included in any lexically distinct life form. Specific and varietal taxa are generally less numerous than generics, typically forming small sets of a few members within a single generic. Specific and variental taxa are commonly labeled in binomial (e.g., white pine) or trinomial (e.g., American golden plover) terms.

These generalizations hold not only for folk taxonomies of plants and animals, but also for other domains. Brown et al. (1976) found the same structure for cultural artifacts (American automobiles and Finnish winter vehicles), religious figures (Thai spirits), and partonomies (Huastic body parts).

Using the notion of generics, Rosch (1975) extended Berlin's generalizations to include a wide range of interesting psychological phenomena. Rosch used the term *basic-level category* to refer to genericlike classes, that is, classes composed of "intrinsically separate things" that have many attributes in common, many motor movements in common, and strong similarity in shape. She showed that given three-level taxonomies consisting of a life-form, generics, and specifics (e.g., life-form: *tool;* generics: *hammer, saw, screwdriver;* specifics: *ball-peen hammer, hack hand saw, Phillips screwdriver*) that subjects could list many more attributes and more motor movements for generics than for life-forms, but could not list significantly more attributes and motor movements for specifics than for generics. However, Rosch found that for the categories of *trees, fish,* and *birds,* her subjects could *not* list more attributes for generics than for life-forms. Apparently, for normal urban Americans *tree, fish,* and *bird* are psychologically basic-level objects. With respect to shapes, Rosch found that figure outlines of specifics of the same generic were much more similar in form than generics of the same life-form, and that the basic level is also the most inclusive level at which an average shape of an object can be recognized.

Within the categories of objects, Rosch proposed that where there are different exemplars (different *generics* of some *life-form,* or different *specifics* of some *generic*), that people form a *prototype* (clearest case, best example), which serves to "define" the object, and that nonprototype members can be ordered from better to poorer examples. Rosch (1975) showed that subjects are able to make reliable ratings of "goodness of example" (and that such ratings predict reaction time in categorization tasks), and are also able to predict the order in which subjects list examples of a category. Uyeda and Mandler (1980) replicated Rosch's ratings for 28 categories on a different sample of subjects, and found their ratings correlated with a Spearman's *r* of .867 with Rosch's ratings, a mean Spearman's *r* of .546 with Battig and Montague (1969) norms for production frequency, and a mean Spearman *r* of .199 with the Kucera and Francis (1967) norms of word frequency.

12. People grade examples of some types of categories as good or bad examples of those categories, and are quicker at identifying good examples than bad examples, and generally more likely to think of good examples than bad examples in free recall, and generally more likely to use the good examples when they reason about categories than the bad examples.

Although prototype-related phenomena appear to be robust, there are some limitations to these findings. Rosch (1973) was unable to obtain similar results for certain other types of categories, such as categories of action (*walking, eating,* etc.). The hypothesis, derived from Rosch's work, that people categorize by computing similarity distances between the object to be categorized and various prototypes, and then place the object in the category belonging to the closest prototype, has met with considerable criticism, since there is ample evidence that in some cases a prototype will be most similar to a particular exemplar that is not categorized under the same term as the prototype. For example, most informants judge a *paper cup* to be more generally similar to a *glass* than to a *cup* (Kronenfeld, Armstrong, and Wilmoth, 1985; Ripps, in press; Werner, 1985). However, a number of hypotheses about the *general* process of categorization do use the notion of prototype (Kempton, 1981; Kronenfeld et al., 1985; Lakoff, 1987; Fillmore, 1975).

While Berlin's formulation of folk taxonomy has proven to be valuable to ethnobiological study, and his generalizations about the differences between generics, life-forms, and specifics have been validated in a number of studies, various problems have arisen concerning this formulation. First, it has often been pointed out that folk taxonomies are unlike true scientific taxonomies in that the folk taxonomic relation is not always transitive or mutually exclusive. For example, American informants will say that *strawberries* are a kind of *berry,* and *berries* are kinds of *bushes,* but that *strawberries* are not *bushes* (Randall, 1976), or that although some *oaks* are *bushes, oaks* are really *trees* (D'Andrade, 1976). One response to this criticism is that the folk taxonomic relation is defined on the prototypic forms of the term, not every exemplar. Furthermore, the taxonomic relation does not really hold between *life-forms* and generics, but does hold between generics and specifics (Hunn, 1985). That is, generics like *oak* and specifics like *live oak* are really *natural kinds,* defined by a Kripke-like causal contingency between the name and the objects referred to by the name. We use a variety of attributes to identify the objects, but definition is not accomplished by means of a small number of "arbitrary" necessary and sufficient criteria, as it is in the case of life-forms. According to this view, the terms *tree, grass,* and *bush* are not *taxonomically* related to anything, although some natural kinds do happen to have these attributes, and therefore it is not surprising that various kinds of exception to the taxonomic relation are found between the life-form terms and the generics.

It might also be argued that the problem lies in the application of the concept of taxonomic relation, which should be restricted more than it is at present (Wierzbicka, 1984). According to this view, the taxonomic relation should be limited to cases in which the superordinate category is part of the definition of the subordinate category. Thus an *oak* is really a kind of *tree,* because, in Langacker's terminology, the *tree* domain serves as the *base* for term *oak.* The term *bush,* on the other hand, does not typically serve as a *base* domain for plant terms. A *blackberry* or *lilac* may grow in a bushlike form, but being a *bush* does not happen to be part of their definition. Some supporting evidence for this is that if one asks informants to list kinds of *trees,* informants produce a reasonable set of terms. However, if one asks informants for kinds of *bushes,* one gets primarily confused reactions from informants.

Wierzbicka also extends her analysis to a number of other kinds of superset/subset relations. She distinguishes true taxonomic *kinds of* relations from the relationship found between terms like *bike* and *toy* or *gun* and *weapon,* which she points out are not relations between two kinds of *things,* but relations between a kind of thing and a function. She argues that the superset/subset connection between *functionals* and *things* is not as tight as the taxonomic relation between *things* and *things,* in that *things* like *knives* can be either *weapons* or *toys* or *silverware,* depending on context.

In addition to these two relationships, Wierzbicka distinguishes other types of superset relation. Terms such as *furniture, cutlery, clothing,* and *fruit* are *collections* of objects defined partly by function and partly by unity of place. *Furniture,* for example, is made up of objects used to furnish a house or place of residence, and contrasts with the *fittings* of a house. Other collective terms like *leftovers, groceries,* and *refreshments* are even more ad hoc collections, defined partly by function, place, or common fate. Terms like *vegetable, drugs, medicines,* and *dyes* can be distinguished from the collective terms by the fact that they are not used or treated as a group, but still do not form true taxonomic superclasses, since they refer to *uses* of a certain kind of stuff, not to a *kind of thing.*

13. Basic-level categories are typically kinds of things, but many superordinates (life-forms) are not kinds of things, but rather types of functions, or special collections, or uses of things. This explains Rosch's finding that basic-level terms typically have many more attributes than superordinate terms, since many superordinates are not *things.*

This also explains why Rosch found that in the case of the biological taxonomies (birds, trees, and fish) there was little difference in number of ascribed attributes between the basic-level terms and the superordinates, since here the superordinates were the same kinds of thing as the basic-level objects. In sum, what Rosch found was not that there are intrinsic conceptual differences between different levels of a taxonomy, but rather that there are conceptual differences between terms that refer to kinds of things in the world versus terms that refer to functions of things, or to collections of things. This is not to deny the point made by Dougherty (1978), that the salience of different taxonomic levels varies by culture and subcultural interests.

Other objections to the use of taxonomic models have been made on ethnographic grounds. Randall (1976) points out that just because an ethnographer can, by careful questioning, elicit a large, extensive, taxonomic tree, this does not mean that informants actually use any such cognitive schema. Instead, Randall argues, the available evidence indicates that informants use "dwarf trees" — essentially small networks consisting of a basic object and its attributes. Hunn (1985) points out that biological taxonomies only lexicalize a small portion of the total number of available plant and animal taxa, and that what is lexicalized are the plants and animals that have some special importance to people. For Hunn, terms like *bush* are *residual categories,* constructed to refer to a large number of taxa that are not worth distinguishing further. Hunn, like Wierzbicka, considers the terms at the life-form level to have a different status than the true generics, which he treats as a difference between the multi-attribute, general-purpose definitions of generics and the single-attribute, special-purpose definitions of the life-forms. Hunn argues that the taxonomic system developed by Berlin is a compromise between the Linnean hierarchical model and what Hunn calls the *natural core model,* which treats folk biological domains as "composed of a general purpose, polythetic core of taxa surrounded by special purpose, monothetic concepts in peripheral position" (1985:124). Hunn's position seems right, and suggests a general formulation:

14. Human beings are opportunistic information processors, and in constructing systems of symbols will make use of any kind of structure that will help to communicate information of interest. There are always trade-offs between consistency and generality in categorization. Phenomena such as polysemy and the mixture of terms for kinds of things, functions, and collections within a single hierarchical system represent compromises between the need to have symbols that are defined by simple consistent formulations and the need to organize great varieties of experience by means of a limited number of symbols.

Another kind of semantic network can be isolated by selecting some class of terms and then analyzing the kinds of distinctions utilized by these terms. Talmy (1978), for example, has carried out an extensive analysis of the distinctions conveyed by grammatical particles like *a, the, in, across, -ed* (past tense), *-s* (plural), and so on, in contrast to the distinctions conveyed by lexical items, such as *tree, write,* and *angry.* Talmy finds that grammatical particles are preponderantly *relativistic* or *topological,* and exclude fixed or metrically Euclidean distinctions. For example, many languages inflect nouns to specify the *uniplex* or *multiplex* character of the object, but no language has inflections that specify the particular color or size of a noun. Deitics like *this* or *that* specify the location of an object by setting up a *partition* that divides a space into region, and then *locate* some *entity* at a *point* or *region* that is on the *same* or *different* side as the speaker. The specifications of *this* or *that* appear to be truly topological, in that the partitions and regions set up by using such terms are "rubber-sheet geometry" — they have no metric constraints and may apply to the most concrete or the most abstract "spaces." Prepositions, like verb inflections and various deitics, also have topological rather than metric or absolute specifications:

An illustrative case here are the twenty-odd motion related prepositions in English, such as *through* or *into,* which together subdivide the domain of "paths considered with respect to reference-objects." This domain covers a great and varied range, but any particular "path" falls

FIGURE 32.6

within the purview of one or another preposition, associated there with other "paths." The associations are often language specific and sometimes seem arbitrary or idiosyncratic. Thus, . . . classed together by *through* are such dissimilar cases as a straightforward liquid parting course (walking through water) and a zig-zag obstacle-avoiding course (walking through timber). The question arises why such distinctions should be effaced by the grammatical system, while they are observed by the lexical and other cognitive systems. Why are grammatical elements — say, such prepositions — not a large and open class marking indefinitely many distinctions? One may speculate that the cognitive function of such classification lies in rendering contentful material manipulable — i.e., amenable to transmission, storage, and processing — and that its lack would render content an ineffective agglomeration. (Talmy, 1978:9)

Considerable work has been done on the semantics of English prepositions. Linder (1981), using Langacker's concepts of *landmark* and *trajector,* has analyzed in detail the prepositions *up* and *out.* A similar analysis of *over* has been carried out by Brugman (1981). These analyses support Talmy's hypothesis that grammatical elements are defined by relatively few criteria, and that these criteria are relational and topological in character.

The extensive polysemy of these prepositions is most dramatic. Each of the senses has a specific *image schema,* that is, a schematic pictorial representation, or a metaphoric extension of such an image schema. Lakoff, for example, discusses how one spatial sense of *over,* as in

The plane flew over the hill,
is transformed into the metaphorical sense found in
He was passed over for promotion.

The spatial sense of the first sentence can be represented by the relation between a landmark and a trajector, as in Figure 32.6.

The arrow in the figure represents the path that the trajector is moving along. The trajector has a horizontal path, and is *up* from the landmark, with no contact between them. The metaphorical sense of being "passed over for promotion" is based on the metaphorical equivalences *control is up* and *choosing is touching.* Using these equivalences, the hearer infers that the person was not contacted by whatever is up there, and therefore not chosen for promotion (Lakoff, 1987).

15. Grammatical elements are predominantly relativistic and topological, and can often be represented by simple image schemas. Specific grammatical elements may have a large number of senses, including complex extensions based on metaphoric equivalences.

In another kind of semantic organization, discussed by Fillmore (1977), sets of terms are all based on the same schema (Fillmore sometimes uses the terms *scene* and *scenario* to refer to what are here called *schemas*). Fillmore uses as an example terms that refer to the schema of a commercial event. Elements of the schema are the *buyer,* the *seller,* the *price,* and the transfer of *money* and *goods.* There is a large class of terms that all use this event as part of what Langacker would call the *base* of the term. Thus, *sell, buy, loan, borrow, rent, lease, purchase, charge, embezzle, defraud, haggle, bid, tip, ransom, refund, pension, allowance, tuition, salary, alimony, reward,* and so on, each profile a different aspect of the same underlying commercial transaction.

Fillmore also points out that *base schemas* (defined here as schemas that serve as the *definitional base* of some term) are highly simplified representations of the world, and the application of a particular term to a specific situation that does not reasonably fit the base schema results in odd or inappropriate usage (Fillmore, 1975, 1977). For example, the base schema for the term *widow* does not fit cases in which the woman is a triple bigamist who has lost one of her three husbands. To ask of such a woman whether or not she is a *widow* is inappropriate not because the *profile* of the term does not apply (the profile of *widow* involves the death of a husband), but because the *base* does not have a reasonable fit to the actual situation. As Fillmore (1975) puts it,

> How old does an unmarried man have to be before you can call him a bachelor? Is someone who is professionally committed to the single life properly considered a bachelor? (Is it correct to say of Pope John XXIII that he died a bachelor?) If so, is bachelorhood a state one can enter? That is, if a man leaves the priesthood in middle life, can we say that he became a bachelor at age 47? When we say of a divorced man or a widower that he is a bachelor, are we speaking literally or metaphorically? How can we tell? Would you call a woman a widow who murdered her husband? Would you call a woman a widow whose divorce became final on the day of her husband's death? Would you call a woman a widow if one of her three husbands died but she had two living ones left?
>
> . . . According to the prototype theory of meaning, these concepts are defined in the context of a simple world in which men typically marry around a certain age, they marry once, they marry exclusively, they stay married until one partner dies. Men who are unmarried at the time they could be married are called bachelors. Women whose husbands have died are called widows. (pp. 128–9)

A nice example of the way in which the base schema of a term creates unconscious presuppositions about its meaning has been described by Sweetser (1987), who presents evidence that the way people define the term *lie* is based on simplified schema or folk theory of discourse. The basic assumptions of this folk theory are the maxims

1. Try to help, not harm.
2. Knowledge is a beneficial thing.

   These two maxims entail

3. Try to inform others; don't misinform.

   Further assumptions are

4. Normally people obey the rules.

5. People's beliefs normally have adequate justification.
6. Adequately justified beliefs are normally true.

The result of this set of assumptions — this folk theory of discourse interaction — is that if somebody tells you something, normally that something is true. What then, is a *lie*? Coleman and Kay (1981) found that of the three prototypic conditions of lying,

a. Speaker believes statement is false
b. Speaker intends to deceive hearer by making the statement
c. The statement is false in fact,

when respondents were given various combinations of these statements, condition (a) was strongest in producing a judgment that the speaker was lying, and (c) was weakest. This makes sense given the folk theory Sweetser outlines, for if the speaker believes the statement is false, and if most belief is justified, then the statement would be false in fact. Furthermore, since to be beneficial one should not misinform, one would not give a false statement unless one wanted to deceive. Therefore, (b) and (c) follow from (a) and the folk model. Sweetser also points out that, when the prototypic assumptions do not hold, a special sense of *lie* is created, as in a *white lie,* in which the speaker wants to be beneficial, but believes the truth would not be beneficial, and so says what is intended to be beneficial but not true.

Kay (1987) has carried out a similar type of analysis on linguistic *hedges.* Kay finds that certain hedges are defined relative to schemas or models of language itself. The terms *loosely speaking* and *strictly speaking* are defined with reference to a folk theory of language that portrays words as referring to a world that is independent of our talk, and that can be more or less faithful to the nonlinguistic facts they represent (an intentional theory of reference). In the sentence

Loosely speaking, the first human beings lived in Kenya,

"loosely speaking" serves as a pragmatic hedge, indicating that what is being referred to as the "first human beings" and "Kenya" are only approximate fits to the actual objects. "Loosely speaking" takes a Fregean view of language. In contrast, the hedge *technically speaking,* as in the expression

The movers have come for your furniture, which technically includes TV sets,

assumes a very different theory of language; one in which there is a body of experts who have the power to fix particular words to particular objects and events (a causal theory of reference). This theory is like the baptismal-causal theories of Kripke and Putnam in which a word refers to the things it does because someone stipulated that henceforth this word would designate this particular kind of thing. The point here is that the semantics of English are not frozen, but are manipulate by ordinary speakers using appropriate hedges.

16. Cultural schemas serve as the definitional bases for whole sets of terms. Typically such cultural schemas portray simplified worlds, making the appropriateness of the terms that are based on them dependent on the degree to which these schemas fit the actual worlds of the objects being categorized. Such schemas portray not only the world of physical objects and events, but also more abstract worlds of social interaction, discourse, and even word meaning.

32.7   NONDEFINITIONALLY BASED SEMANTIC NETWORKS

All the types of semantic networks discussed so far are based on relations among definitional attributes of some type. A quite different type of network can be constructed by linking objects with non-definitional, extrinsic relationships. Frake (1964), in advance of the work on semantic networks in artificial intelligence, presented a simple network of relations among the elements for yeast making involving relations of *use, part, source,* and *kind.* Metzger and Williams, in a series of pioneering papers (1963a, 1963b, 1966) demonstrated how ethnographic descriptions could be generated by constructing queries that elicited relationships of various types. The goal of this type of research was to find a method to effectively elicit and display cultural knowledge. The following excerpt is taken from Black and Metzger (1965:151–152) and concerns the administration of justice in the Tzeltal-speaking municipio of Tenejapa in highland Chiapas, Mexico:

Q.	banti ya smuk te ?anima e	Where do they bury the dead person?
A.	ya smuk ta yutna	He is buried inside the house.
A.	ya smuk ta kapasanto	He is buried in the cemetery.
Q.	mas lek bal ya smuk ta yutna mak ya smuk la kapasanto	Is it better to bury a person in the house or in a cemetery?
A.	mas lek la yutna	It is better in the house.
Q.	bi yu?un mak lek ta yutna	Why is it better in the house?
A.	melel k'usobel sba yu?un ha?al	Because otherwise he will feel the rain.
Q.	bi ya spas te hmilawai e te me lom p'ih	What does the killer do if he is smart?
A.	ya s?an	He flees.
A.	ya spakan hilei te ?anima e	He turns the dead man face down.
Q.	bi yu?un ya spakan hilil te ?anima e	Why does he turn the dead man face down?
A.	ma sk'an ta scuhk	He does not wish to be captured.
A.	ma ba ya stak yil sc'ulel ?animal	The soul of the dead man will not be able to see him.

This kind of nonimpressionistic, rigorous ethnography has proved extremely demanding and is rarely used. However, frame-elicitation techniques have been more generally adapted for the systematic study of specific domains as a means of investigating cultural knowledge. For example, D'Andrade, Quinn, Nerlove, and Romney (1972) used a simplified frame-elicitation technique in a study of American and Mexican beliefs about illness. To construct frames, they collected a series of ordinary statements about specific illness from informants. These statements were then put in frame form by replacing the particular illness term with a blank — for example, "It is safer to have _____ as a child and get it over with." From a large collection of such statements, the 30 most general, unambiguous, and semantically independent sentence frames were selected. A list of diseases was also elicited,

	cancer	a cold	polio	stroke	ulcers
_ is caused by germs	no	yes	yes	no	no
_ comes from emotional upset	no	no	no	yes	yes
_ is serious	yes	no	yes	yes	no
_ is a sign of old age	yes	no	no	yes	no
_ runs in the family	no	no	no	yes	yes

FIGURE 32.7

and the 30 best-known and most common diseases were selected. From this collection of sentence frames and disease terms a systematic elicitation task was constructed in which each informant was asked for every sentence frame whether or not the insertion of each disease term into the frame would make the sentence true or false (for the American sample of 10 Stanford undergraduates a five-point scale from "definitely true" to "definitely not true" was used). Thus an informant doing the American-English task would be asked for sentence frame 1. *You catch _____ from other people,* whether that was true for (a) *appendicitis,* (b) *arthritis,* (c) *asthma,* and so on. The modal response was then taken as culturally representative. A small piece of the final matrix is presented in Figure 32.7.

A matrix of this type is an efficient way to store a large network of information. It is unlikely, however, that people actually store information in such a manner. The question is, once one has obtained a large matrix of cultural information how is it cognitively organized? One heuristic method of investigating this question is to use multidimensional scaling (MDSCAL) to uncover clusters or dimensions. A median-based cluster analysis technique (D'Andrade et al., 1972) revealed three major clusters of frames and disease terms for the American data. One cluster consisted of contagious diseases (*colds, mumps, mononucleosis,* etc.) and associated frames; another cluster consisted of serious, life-threatening noncontagious diseases (*stroke, leukemia, heart attack,* etc.) and associated frames; and the third cluster consisted of less severe, old age, inherited, or emotion-caused diseases (*rheumatism, epilepsy, ulcers,* etc.) and associated frames. A MDSCAL dimensional analysis and a principal components factor analysis both produced similar results. The major conclusion of this research was

17. The defining properties of a set of terms are not always the properties that determine how people categorize or react to the objects referred to by these terms.

Thus, the categories discovered by the analysis of how disease terms distribute across beliefs do not seem to be related to the features that define these disease terms. Our informants agree that *cancer is serious, noncontagious,* and not a *childhood* illness. These properties are major foci for how Americans conceive of diseases. But these are neither necessary nor sufficient conditions for making the decision that someone has cancer.

A major drawback of this research is that multidimensional scaling, although an effective means of detecting structure and summarizing data, does not yield results that fit a cognitive processing model. That is, one cannot, from scaling results, construct a computer program that reproduces the original judgments in a manner that even roughly simulates human thinking processes. But, then, how *are* ordinary people able to fill out large matrices of the type used in this research? Perhaps attention to how people actually process cultural information can yield more effective and general models than multidimensional scaling.

32.8   CULTURAL SCHEMAS AND CULTURAL MODELS

To construct a model that has the capacity to reproduce the original judgments in a reasonably human manner, a propositionally based model was developed with some simple rules of inference for the American disease terms and frame data (D'Andrade, 1976). To determine the inferential relations between all pairs of attributes, contingency tables for all pairs of attributes were computed, and those with zero cells or near-zero cells were selected, as indicated in Figure 32.8.

The contingency table shows that there is no disease that is both *catching* and *a sign of old age*. Thus one can infer the absence of the old age property from the presence of the contagion. More generally, whenever there is a zero in any of the four cells of a two-by-two contingency table, one can use the fact that a certain combination of variables does *not* occur to make inferences about what *can* occur. In the example in Figure 32.8,

		_ is a sign of old age	
		yes	no
you can catch _ from other people	yes		whooping cough
			typhoid fever
			tuberculosis
			syphilis
			strep throat
			smallpox
			polio
			poison ivy
			pneumonia
			mumps
			mononucleosis
			measles
			laryngitis
			influenza
			gonorrhea
			a cold
			chicken pox
	no	bronchitis	appendicitis
		cancer	dental cavities
		heart attack	epilepsy
		psychosis	leukemia
		rheumatism	malaria
		stroke	tonsliltis
		ulcers	

FIGURE 32.8

            1. not (*catching* and *a sign of old age*)

therefore   **2.** if *catching* then not (*a sign of old age*)

and therefore   **3.** if *a sign of old age* then not (*catching*).

The next step was to use the fact that inference relations of this sort are transitive to eliminate redundant relationships. For example, if any disease is a *children's* disease then it is a *contagious* disease, and if any disease is a *contagious* disease then it is a *germ-caused* disease. Because implicational relations are transitive, the fact that if any disease is a *children's* disease then it is a *germ* disease does not need to be "remembered" by the system, but can be generated from the separate relationships.

The final result was a model that contained 31 primary relationships, from which 81 further relationships could be generated. Interestingly, three major chains of if–then relationships were found to correspond to the same three clusters just described. Despite some success however, as a more process-oriented generative model, overall, the effort was a failure. Perhaps because the format of the model was closer to a "natural" representation than the scaling analyses were, one could see immediately that some aspects of it were wrong. The model lacked any description of the nature of germs, routes of infection, the development of antibodies, the structure of the human body, the functions of various organs, and the like. It is knowledge of these things that lie behind the inferences that can be made from the zero cells. Without a representation of this knowledge, the inferences appear arbitrary. *Children's* diseases are a subset of *contagious* diseases. This is not some arbitrary cultural formulation, but rather something that makes good sense given the nature of germs, getting older, resistance, and antibodies. The problem was that the model had propositions and inferences, but it did not represent the basic objects and causal events on which the propositions and inferences are based.

Thus, much of the work on cultural models leads to the same kind of result that work on representation of meaning did, and also that work on taxonomies and related semantic networks did. That is to say,

    18. Evaluation of attempts to represent the use of symbols, ranging from the word level to the level of large knowledge systems, indicates that construction of adequate cultural representations requires explication of the basic cognitive schemas that underlie the use of these symbols.

What, precisely, is meant by a *cognitive schema*? A good summary is presented in Casson's (1983) review paper "Schemata in Cognitive Anthropology":

> Schemata are conceptual abstractions that mediate between stimuli received by the sense organs and behavior responses. They are abstractions that serve as the basis for all human information processing, e.g. perception and comprehension, categorization and planning, recognition and recall, and problem solving and decision making. . . . Bartlett, who is generally credited with being the first to use the term schema in its contemporary sense (although Kant used the term in much the same manner in his *Critique of Pure Reason*), argued that "the past operates as an organized mass rather than a group of elements each of which retains its specific character" (1932, 197). Remembering, Bartlett maintained, is constructive. Not all stimuli are stored in memory; rather, schemata are employed to provide a "general impression of the whole" and to construct (or reconstruct) "probable details" (1932, 206). . . .

[S]chemata occur at differing levels of abstraction. At relatively low levels of abstraction there are schemata for perceiving geometrical figures, colors, faces, etc., while at higher levels there are schemata for comprehending complex activities and events. There are no important differences in kind between schemata for perception and comprehension. . . . schemata, unlike associations, are organic wholes comprised of parts that are oriented both to the whole and to other parts. . . . Schemata are autonomous and automatic–once set in motion they proceed to their conclusion. (pp. 430–431)

Consider, for example, the normal schema for a cat that most of us share. It is really a most remarkable device; it can come up with the interpretation *cat!* with a great range of minimal information — the sound of a certain kind of growl, or the sight of a waving tail, or the physical sensation of something rubbing against one's leg, or a crude line picture on a sheet of paper, or a particular combination of letters. The cat schema contains imagistic, acoustic, sensory, and propositional materials at varying levels of abstraction, from highly schematic line figures to detailed images of the mangled ears of an elderly male. The schema is flexible, and can accommodate new forms, such as a blue point Burmese, or even a *dasyure,* the marsupial cat. The schema has a great number of default values — things that get filled in even if they are not observed or stated. This schema is not a picture in the mind, because no picture can be both pure black and pure white, yet the standard schema contains both these possibilities and more. The schema is well organized, both with respect to how a cat is put together physically and what it does, and contains parts and subparts, each of which is a separate schema in its own right. Yet, despite its detail and organization, the cat schema leaves out an enormous amount and is a great simplification of the potential visual, acoustic, sensory, and propositional information that could be experienced about cats. The values that get filled in by default create prototypic cats — the cats we expect when nothing is known except that it is a cat. Thus the cat schema, which is already a simplification, through the operation of default values, creates further simplifications, or senses of what could be a cat. Finally, the cat schema is sensitive to context, so that in certain places and at certain times we are ready to see a cat, and need only minimal cues to make the identification.

To create such a mechanical device would be a remarkable achievement. Recent work on parallel-distributed processing models indicates that such a device may be constructed by a relatively simple network of interconnected neuronlike elements (Rumelhart & McClelland, 1986). The ability of such parallel processing networks to mimic the behavior postulated for schemas is quite impressive. The possibility of constructing flexible, contextually sensitive, default value-filling, accommodating, and assimilating interpretative devices from simple parallel processing networks can be expected to have a large impact on the various subfields of cognitive science.

Schema theory has served as the underlying psychological mechanism for the development of the concept of a *cultural model.* A cultural model is a cognitive schema that is *intersubjectively shared* by a social group. Because cultural models are intersubjectively shared, interpretations made about the world on the basis of a cultural model are experienced as obvious facts of the world. A wild pitch is obviously a *ball,* except to those who do not know baseball. A further consequence of the intersubjectivity of cultural models is that much of the information relevant to a cultural model need not be made explicit, since what is obvious need not be stated. If the announcer says that the pitch was wild, he need not say that it was a ball.

To get around the limits of short-term memory, cognitive schemas tend to be organized *hierarchically,* so that the parts of any one schema can often be unpacked into further complex subparts. One consequence of the hierarchical structure of schemas is that certain cultural models have a wide range of application because they serve as parts of many other cultural models. Thus the cultural model of *money* is found as a part of a great many other cultural models, such as the models of *buying, interest, banking, inflation,* and *salary.* Knowing a culture requires at least knowing the cultural models that are widely used as parts of other cultural models.

An important characteristic of many cultural models is the fact that informants usually cannot produce an organized description of the entire model. They can *use* the model, but they cannot produce a complete *description* of it. The model is like a well-learned set of procedures one knows how to carry out rather than a body of fact one can recount. However, most cultural models do not seem to be purely procedural, since most informants can describe in part how the model operates when asked questions about specific matters.

In psychology one of the best-known examples of a cultural model is the *restaurant script* (Schank & Abelson, 1977). Of course, the restaurant script is dependent on a sociocultural *institution* — that is, the existence of a particular kind of business that sells cooked food, called a "restaurant." The script concept is intended to refer to stereotyped sequences of events. However, event sequences are just one type of organization of elements. As Casson (1983) has pointed out, some schemas are cultural *object* models (plants, animals, manufactured objects, persons, kinsmen, occupations, ethnic identities, personality descriptors, illnesses, and emotions have all been studied, for example), *orientation* models (e.g., cognitive maps for cities, or even spatial mnemonic devices such as the "method of loci"), as well as *event* models, such as scripts (see, e.g., Randall's 1986 study of Samal fishing, and Frake's 1975 study of how to enter a Yakan house). A special kind of cultural model, the *expressive* model, has been studied in detail over the past two decades (Roberts, 1987). These are models "of and for" behavior, ranging from *riddling* to *trap shooting,* which permit people to express strong affective generalized orientations and which can be both conflict reducing and conflict enhancing.

Quinn and Holland (1987) recently reviewed the cultural model approach, placing it within the general framework of cognitive anthropology. They stress the shift in semantic analysis from earlier work toward greater diversity in methodological techniques, more reliance on native intuitions in formulating the model, with subsequent testing of the adequacy of the model using different kinds of data, and greater reliance on the analysis of natural discourse. They also point to the convergence between anthropologists and linguists in the study of cultural models:

> Understandably, linguists are most concerned with the important implications of underlying cultural models for their theories of word definition, metaphor, polysemy, hedging, and other linguistic phenomena. Anthropologists tend to orient their analyses in the opposite direction, treating linguistic usages as clues to the underlying cultural model, and working towards a more satisfactory theory of culture and its role in non-linguistic tasks such as reasoning, problem solving, and evaluating the behavior of others. But the different questions which draw linguists and anthropologists should not obscure the common insight which brought together this particular group of linguists and anthropologists in the first place: that culturally shared knowledge is organized into prototypical event sequences enacted in simplified worlds. That much of such cultural knowledge is presumed by language use is as significant

a realization to anthropologists as to linguists. For the latter, these cultural models promise the key to linguistic use, while for the former, linguistic usage provides the best available data for reconstruction of cultural models. (p. 48)

Quinn and Holland discuss the relation between what they term, following Lakoff (1983), *image-schemas* and *proposition schemas*. Basically, image-schemas are highly abstract visual representations, whereas proposition schemas are abstract language-based representations. They conclude that, although cultural models may be based solely on one or the other kind of representation, most cultural models contain both kinds of representation.

An important process in the construction of schemas of all types, including cultural models, is the use of analogy and metaphor. Lakoff and Johnson (1983), in pointing out the pervasiveness of metaphor in ordinary talk, ask why it is that certain things are used as metaphors and other things are metaphorized. They suggest that metaphors generally carry structure from physical-world models into nonphysical domains, perhaps because physical-world structures are well formed and experientially universal, although this is not always the case (Holland, 1982). Quinn and Holland (1987) point out that physical-world models, since they are things that can be seen and have spatial properties, allow the construction of image-schemas that can be transferred to nonphysical domains. Thus, for example, *marriage* can be conceptualized as a *manufactured object,* and hence more or less likely to *fall apart.* Even more specifically, there is the question of why one kind of physical object rather than another is used as the source of metaphor. Quinn and Holland say that

> the classes from which speakers select metaphors they consider to be appropriate are those which capture aspects of the simplified world, and the prototypical events unfolding in this world, constituted by the cultural model. Chosen metaphors not only highlight particular features of the cultural model; as we have discussed, they also point to entailments among these elements. Thus, one husband's metaphor of marriage as a "do-it yourself project" at once suggests for him the durable quality of something made in this manner — "it was very strong because it was made as we went along" — and implies, additionally, the craft and care and effort which must go into such a thing to make it well. Speakers often favor just such metaphors, which allow two or more related elements of the source domain to be mapped onto a corresponding set of related elements in the cultural model (Quinn 1985), and a comment upon that relation to be made. At the same time, other metaphors which fail to reflect, or even contradict, aspects of the cultural model in the target domain to which they are mapped, are likely to be rejected. Quinn (ibid.) gives an anecdotal example in which marriage was likened to an ice-cream cone which could be eaten up fast or licked slowly to make it last longer — a metaphor in such clear violation of our understanding of marriage as an enduring relationship that it bothered and offended members of the wedding at which it was voiced. (p. 61)

Several detailed analyses of cultural models are presented in Quinn and Holland's *Cultural Models in Language and Thought* (1987). Quinn, for example, summarizes her work on American marriage. Marriage, as a cultural model, is related to the social institution of marriage, which consists of a complex set of formal and informal behavioral norms concerning licenses, co-residence, sexual partnerships, etc. There are numerous studies of marriage as a social institution, but much less work on what marriage *is* to the people who are involved in this institution.

Quinn's data consist of over 350 hours of taped and transcribed interview material from 11 husband-and-wife couples in which each spouse was seen separately. Analysis involved culling hundreds of linguistic usages from the transcripts and sorting and interpreting these usages. These usages include metaphors for marriage (some of the common metaphors are MARRIAGE IS A MANUFACTURED PRODUCT, MARRIAGE IS AN ONGOING JOURNEY, MARRIAGE IS A DURABLE BOND BETWEEN TWO PEOPLE, A SPOUSE IS A FITTING PART, AND MARRIAGE IS AN INVESTMENT), sequences of reasoning about marriage, and key words, such as *commitment, fulfillment,* and *love,* used to talk about marriage. Quinn finds four propositional schemas around which metaphors, key words, and reasoning appear to be organized; these are MARRIAGE IS ENDURING, MARRIAGE IS MUTUALLY BENEFICIAL, MARRIAGE IS DIFFICULT, and MARRIAGE IS EFFORTFUL.

Using these propositions and their specific metaphorical formulations, Quinn (1987) is able to show how particular sections of discourse can be analyzed to present in explicit form the reasoning of her informants about marriage. Her analysis uses the general method developed by Hutchins in his study of inference among Trobriand Islanders (1980). First, a transcribed section of discourse is presented in which an informant is making some point about something. At first glance, the informant's argument may appear rather scattered and even illogical. Next, the cultural model of the object about which the informant was talking is described, typically formulated in terms of a series of interrelated propositions. Then the informant's sentences are reformulated using the cultural model, and the missing material that the informant ignored because it was too obvious to state is filled in. Finally, the logical form of the argument, using some form of sentential or predicate calculus, is displayed. Often, this type of analysis can show that what seemed to be a rather scattered argument on the part of an informant was in fact a neatly and intricately reasoned piece of work.

One of the models Quinn finds embedded within the model of marriage is that of *need satisfaction.* In simple form, this cultural model is based on the notion that each person has certain needs (needs are wants that, in some sense, *must* to be satisfied if the person is to function properly), and that human relationships, which are seen as essentially dyadic, maintain themselves because each partner in the dyad satisfies enough of the needs of the other to keep the relationship going. Marriage relationships are expected to provide a large part of any human's social needs — that is, companionship, sex, affection, communication, intimacy, caring, nurturance, and so on. It is the problem of mutual need fulfillment that makes for the difficulty and needed effort of marriage, and for its failure. This model of need fulfillment is general in American culture; it is found in other cultural models such as models for friendship and family life, and in models of achievement and accomplishment. This model of need satisfaction is thought to be common sense, a truth beyond ordinary questioning. Of course, like most cultural models, it is not always true, but, like most cultural models, it seems so true that exceptions fail to invalidate the model.

Another cultural model that has been described in some detail is the American folk model of the mind (D'Andrade, 1987). Unlike marriage, or the restaurant script, this model is unrelated to any specific social institution, although it is widely used in ordinary talk. It is a *folk* model in that it contrasts with a *scientific* model, which is something experts know about, and which ordinary people don't. This model has six major elements (see Figure 32.9).

a. Perceptions
  i.   simple state — *see, hear, smell, taste, feel*
  ii. achieved state — *spot, sight, notice*
  iii. simple process — *look, observe, watch, listen, touch*

b. Belief/Thought
  i.   simple state — *believe, know, remember, expect, assume, doubt, Imagine, recall*
  ii. achieved state — *understand, realize, infer, learn, discover, guess, conclude, forget*
  iii. simple process — *reason, think*
  iv. accomplished process — *figure out, plan*

c. Feelings/Emotion
  i.   simple state — *love, like, fear, hate, blame, approve, pity, feel sad, feel happy*
  ii. achieved state — *forgive, surprise, scare*
  iii. simple process — *enjoy, be frightened, be angered, be bored, mourn, emote*

d. Desires/Wishes
  i.   simple state — *want to, desire, like to, feel like, need*
  ii. achieved state — *choose, select*
  iii. simple process — *wish, hope for*

e. Intention
  i.   simple state — *intend to, aim to, mean to, plan to*
  ii. achieved state — *decide to*

f. Resolution, Will
  i.   simple state — *determined to*
  ii. achieved state — *resolved to*
  iii. simple process — *strive, make oneself, force oneself*

FIGURE 32.9

    The distinction between states and processes is a basic image-schema difference. A state is the condition of some entity, a uniform condition that exists through time. In general, when talking about the mind as an entity, the specific metaphor used is the *container* metaphor — a person is said to be "full of" *knowledge, fear, desire, resolve.* The mind as an entity does not change whether the person is sleeping or awake — Einstein would still know the theory of relativity whether or not he was thinking about it. But only if Einstein's mind was doing something could we say that he was *figuring out* a unified theory, or *worrying about* nuclear war, and so on. That is, the mind is alternately conceived of as a set of processes that occur repetitively, like the action of walking. Thus all the process verbs can be put in an -ing form; one can say "I am *looking/thinking/enjoying/hoping for/striving*" but outside of idiomatic use we do not say "I am *hearing/believing/loving.*"

    Both the state and process occur in time, but a process is marked by the repetition of some action and thus has continuous tenses. In the model of the mind, states are linked to process. Typically, someone is in a particular state because of the occurrence of some process. Thus, for example, John *hears* Bill because he is *listening* to Bill; Sally *believes* Lisa is her friend because she went through the process of *assessing* her relationship with Lisa and *concluded* she was a real friend; and Roger has been *frightening* his cousin, which is why his cousin *fears* him.

    There is another relevant time distinction in English verbs based on the notion that certain processes and states are defined by a climax or terminal point that marks the end of the state or processes. When such a terminal point defines a state, it is called an *achievement,* and when it defines a process it is called an *accomplishment.* For both achievements and accomplishments, we can ask "How long did it take to. . . .?" but not for simple states or processes. We do not ask "How long did it take you to *think* that?" but we do ask "How long did it take you to *realize* that?" For simple states and processes, events are treated as if they were homogeneous across the entire period through which it occurs, but for achievements and accomplishment, the event is defined by its terminal point. Thus, even if one *thinks* for only an instant, one has *been thinking,* but, no matter how long one has been at it, one does not *realize* something until the exact instant the light dawns (Vendler, 1967).

In the model of the mind, these six major states/processes are linked together in a complex causal chain: Because of what one *perceives,* one *believes* certain things to be true; because of what one *believes* to have happened, one has certain *feelings* or *emotions;* because of what one *feels,* one has certain *wishes;* because of what one *wishes,* one has certain *intentions;* and certain second-order *intentions* to keep to one's *intentions* constitute *resolve.* This is the major causative order, but a reverse order for some of the elements is also thought to happen, although it is considered to be inappropriate. Thus, strong *feelings* can influence what one *thinks* (but it shouldn't), and if one *thinks* certain things are true, it can influence what one *perceives* (but it shouldn't).

Another important type of relation within the model of the mind is the way in which the things that one *intends* to do, or that one *wants,* are created by one's own *thoughts.* One can only *intend to* do something or *want to* do something that one can *think* of doing, and perhaps one is most likely to *want to* do and *intend to* do what one *thinks of* most often — *evil he who evil thinks.* The situation with respect to emotions is complex, since in the folk model sometimes the object that arouses the feeling is purely an object of thought — for example, "John is afraid of nuclear winter" — while sometimes it is an actual object — for example, "Tom thinks he is afraid of flying, but actually he is afraid of traveling away from home."

There are a number of other complex relationships among these elements (see D'Andrade, 1986). One of these concerns the experiential *self* and the things that can affect it. Clearly, things outside the body can affect the self — we say "The rock hit me." However, things inside the body, and even inside the mind can affect the experiential self — we say "The idea struck me," placing the idea outside the self that experienced the idea. We can even say "The feeling struck me" or "The desire to have a cigarette struck me." That is, almost all the elements of mind can be placed metaphorically outside the self. There is one exception here; *intentions* cannot be placed outside the self. We do not say "The intention struck me." Thus the very core of the self is its *intentions,* from which it cannot be separated.

The model of the mind sketched out here and more elaborately described in D'Andrade (1986) was developed from intuition and from the work of various linguistic philosophers such as Anscombe, Vendler, and Searle. In an attempt to validate this model, interviews were carried out with five college and high school students who had never had courses in psychology. In these interviews the informants were systematically queried about each of the major propositions of the model. None of the interview material contradicted the model, although some of the responses made by informants could not be derived from the model.

When this Western cultural model was compared with the model of the mind described by Lutz (1985) for the people of Ifaluk, a small Micronesian atoll, it was found that both models have the same overall framework. *Thoughts, feelings,* and *desires* are distinguished. Feelings are considered a natural response to experience, not under self-control, and are thought to have the power to move the person to action. The emotions arc distinguished from physical sensations. Understanding is considered necessary for appropriate behavior; without the ability to understand, the person is thought to go out of control. The major difference seems to be that on Ifaluk there is no clear distinction between desire and intention, and there is a greater fusion of the categories of thought and feeling. The emotion terms are defined slightly differently on Ifaluk, and the interpersonal role of emotion is more distinctly conceptualized than in the West, as is the role of emotion in causing illness and the therapeutic role of catharsis.

Another interesting question has to do with the way in which children learn a model of the mind. Since mental events are private, the teacher cannot point directly to the learner's mental machinery and say "What you just experienced is a *thought,* not a *feeling,*" or "That is *anger,* not *fear,* which you just experienced." The question is, how, even if everyone's private experience is highly similar, are the words of others matched to the learner's private experience? It appears that the model can be learned because it is not *just* a model of private experience. The model contains systematic links of public events. Thus thinking is like speech, and speech is public. Feelings are defined in part by the public events that are likely to elicit them, and by the actions we are likely to take because of them. Furthermore, human beings have an innate communication system for the emotions, signaled by patterns of facial expression (Ekman, 1971). To understand what wishes and desires are, we have the speech act, which gives them public expression; requests and commands. Wanting is feeling that makes one say "Gimme, gimme." Intentions are related to the speech acts that are based on making commitments; a promise is the public statement of an intention with the assertion that one has the ability to bring about the intention. The tight connection pointed out by Vendler (1972) between verbs for speech acts and verbs for internal states is not fortuitous; speech acts are one of the major classes of public events used as identifying marks of internal states and processes.

The cultural models presented so far have been purely conceptual in nature, but cultural models may also be *physically realized.* Frake (1985) has described the nature and operation of the medieval *compass rose,* the 32-point compass found printed on many maps. Historical research shows that this compass was used in calculating tides, not just in naming directional points.

The operation of the compass rose depends on the knowledge that high and low tides are related to the position of the moon in the sky. Tide times may vary considerably from place to place along any particular sea coast, but the relation between the position of the moon and the high tide for any particular place along the coast will remain constant. Thus, at La Jolla Shores, along the southern coast of California, high tide occurs at a little less than two hours before the moon crosses the meridian (lunar noon) or two hours before the moon crosses the opposite meridian on the other side of the earth (lunar midnight), and low tide occurs approximately four hours after lunar noon or lunar midnight. A sailor or surfer finds it helpful to know when the moon will be at the meridian. However, during the day, and often much of the night, one cannot see the moon.

The compass rose is used to calculate the time of high and low tides from knowledge of the time of the last full moon and the time of high tide relative to the moon's position for specific places along some coast. This is done by treating the compass rose like a clock, with due south as noon, west as 6 p.m., north as midnight, and east as 6 a.m. Each of the 32 points divides the day into 45-minute intervals. Just like sun time, lunar time can also be represented as a compass bearing, with lunar noon as south, moonset as west, lunar midnight as north, and moonrise as east. Medieval sailing directions gave the tide for any given coastal place by giving the lunar time at which there would be high tide — for La Jolla Shores this would be approximately southeast by south — that is, about 9:45 a.m. moon time.

The solar time of the high tide can be calculated from the date of the last full moon by using the compass rose as a counting device. Each day the tides rise and fall approximately 48 minutes later than they did the day before — close to the 45-minute intervals of the compass rose. This means that 5 days after the full moon the high tide at La Jolla Shores would be 5 points past southeast by south, which is south/southwest, corresponding to approximately 1:30 p.m. Of course, to use the compass rose, one must learn the times of day for each of the 32 points. The compass rose is a cultural model that organizes both time and direction and has the capacity to coordinate solar time with lunar time so that tide times can be estimated.

The problem of isolating the basic cognitive operations that are involved in the use of physically realized models has been addressed in a recent paper by Hutchins (n.d.). Even an extremely simple physical device such as the *checklist* can be seen to be an example of a *mediating structure.* In using a checklist, the user does not coordinate his or her behavior directly with the task environment, but rather coordinates with a mediating object that has a structure that is like the task environment in some important way. Suppose one has to perform a complete ordered sequence of actions to do something (say, start an airplane), and one has a printed checklist of these actions.

For the checklist to work, the printed list of actions must correspond to the user's descriptions of the actions that must be taken to actually start the plane. The user must invoke a sequential execution strategy to determine which step is the next step, and possibly determine an index to the next step so that it can be remembered. One simple way to do this is to start reading at the top of the list, and to place a mark next to the item being performed. The user must then read and understand the printed instructions at some level and then construct a representation of the world from what was read that maps onto the relevant task world. To read "engage the clutch" is not helpful if one does not know what in the environment corresponds to the "clutch." Then the user must coordinate his or her actions with this representation and mapping into the task environment. Thus what might at first look like a simple device in fact turns out to be a complex of mediations — that is, of coordinations between structures.

Hutchins points out that the internalization and automatization of a checklist involves the gradual transfer of control from different coordinating structures. First one learns the list, and in doing the task, one remembers an instruction, then creates a representation of the instruction, then coordinates this representation with the task environment, then coordinates an action with this representation and the task environment. After the task has been even more thoroughly learned, one recalls one task representation after another rather than remembering verbal instructions. Finally, when the checklist is fully automated, one directly recalls the actions to be taken and their associated environmental changes. At that point the mediating structure has become unconscious and all that one is aware of is the task environment and the need to do one thing after another. A good example of this kind of learning has been described by Stigler, Chalip, and Miller (1986) for abacus training. They found that children who had learned the abacus had a different representation of numerical calculations based on a "mental abacus" that enabled them to manipulate numbers with remarkable speed.

For Hutchins (n.d.), all cultural models, whether embodied in artifacts or as image and propositional schemas, are mediating structures:

> In this view, what we learn and what we know, and what our culture knows for us in the form of artifacts and social organizations are these hunks of mediating structure. Thinking consists of bringing these structures into coordination with each other such that they can shape (and be shaped by) each other. The thinker in this world is a special medium that provides coordination among many structured media, some internal, some external, some embodied in artifacts, some in ideas, and some in social relationships. (pp. 13–14).

19. Cultural models, constructed out of complex cognitive schemas, are found in a great range of domains, including events, institutions, and physical and mental objects. Some of these cultural models have special computational properties, serving as inferential and orientational devices of considerable complexity.

32.9 CULTURAL IDEA SYSTEMS

Cultural models are not the only form in which cultural knowledge is packaged. There is a long tradition of investigation of cultural world views, or *cultural idea systems* in anthropology. These idea systems appear to be made up of interrelated and intersubjectively shared propositional schemas that form a coherent (if not always perfectly consistent) perspective or ideology about how the world is. There are a large number of excellent ethnographic studies of cultural idea systems, such as Fortes's *Oedipus and Job in West African Religion* (1983), which use standard ethnographic techniques of investigation. The drawback of such studies is that they fail to make clear exactly what individual natives really believe, since these studies focus primarily on collective representations of various kinds, such as myth and ritual.

One of the contributions of cognitive anthropology has been to develop methods of research — sometimes derived from methods already used in psychology — for investigating the beliefs of individual natives. Shweder and Bourne (1984), for example, in their study of the cultural conceptions of the self in India (Orissa) and the United States, constructed a task in which informants were asked to describe a close acquaintance ("How would you describe so-and-so's personality"). The resulting descriptions were then broken into constituent subject-predicate-object phrases (a total of 3,451 phrases were coded). A coding system was developed to determine if the phrase referred primarily to an *abstract trait* ("she is stubborn"), an *action* ("she uses dirty language"), or an *emotive-evaluative term* ("he is a good man"). Contextual qualifications were also coded: *personal reference* ("he gets angry with his father"), *qualification* ("he gets irritated if provoked"), and *no qualification* ("he is irritable").

The results show strong patterned differences in which Oriyas are more likely to use contextual qualifications whereas Americans are more likely to use no qualifications at all. When Americans do use qualifications, they are most likely to use self-referential qualifiers ("she is beginning to accept herself) and inferential qualifiers ("judging from what others say, he is very reserved"). Oriyas are more likely to describe someone by telling you what the person does ("he shouts curses at his neighbors"), whereas Americans are more likely to use traits ("he is friendly").

Since these results could be caused by differences in level of schooling, Shweder and Bourne checked them against individual years of education, but found that the differences could not be accounted for by this variable. Educated Oriyas were as context dependent in their descriptions of the person as illiterate Oriyas. Shweder and Bourne suggest that these results are due not to differences in the development of cognitive skills, but to differences in the metaphorlike idea systems of these two cultures. Indian culture contains a highly developed holistic idea system that makes extensive use of the metaphor of the body for society, whereas American culture contains a highly developed individualistic idea system that treats the person as distinct from his or her social roles and group affiliations. Thus the use of context and action on the part of Indians to describe others is not due to some failure on their part to attain abstract constructs of the person, but to a different system of ideas about how the person is embedded in a social matrix.

In a study of American and Oriya moral conceptions, Shweder, Mahapatra, and Miller (1987) examined 39 cultural practices involving kinship avoidances, forms of address between inferiors and superiors, sleeping arrangements, incest avoidance, dietary practices, forms of dress, marriage and remarriage, personal possessions and private property, begging, nepotism, monogamy, wife beating, physical punishment for children, family division of labor, inheritance of property, and so on. One aim of the study was to determine the degree to which each of these practices is conceived of as a *moral* versus *conventional* versus *personal* matter. A second aim was to investigate the general character of American and Indian moral codes. A third goal was to investigate the course of development over the life cycle of moral ideas in each culture.

The American sample consisted of 180 children and 60 adults from Hyde Park; the children were divided into three age ranges (5–7, 8–10, 11–13). The Indian sample consisted of two subsamples, Brahmans and Untouchables from Bhubaneswar, Orissa. The Brahman subsample had the same size, age, and gender distribution as the American sample. The Untouchable sample included 30 male and 30 female informants in the 8-10 age range and 30 male and 30 female adults. The informants were examined individually using a short standard set of interview questions and probes designed to assess the moral/conventional/personal status of the obligations pertinent to the case. Questions were asked about each of the 39 practices, and informants were instructed to rank the "seriousness" of the perceived breach or transgression in each case. Standard back-translation procedures were used to ensure translation equivalences for all cases.

The results are somewhat surprising. First, there is no correlation between the Indian and the American rankings of the "seriousness" of the transgression involved in each case. One cannot predict from knowing that a particular practice is regarded as a serious moral matter in one culture anything about how seriously the same issue will be considered in the other. Second, both Americans and Indians consider *most* issues to be matters of objective moral law rather than matters of convention. Third, *only* Americans use the notion that some practices are conventional. Fourth, the children in each culture are most like the adults from that culture, and *not* like the children in the other culture. Fifth, American children are less likely to use the notion of convention than American adults. Sixth, there is more consensus on the moral character of the various practices among the adults in each culture than among the children. Seventh, as Americans get older they are more likely to engage in relativistic moral reasoning and less likely to engage in universal moral reasoning, whereas the reverse in true for Indians.

These findings provide no indication of universal age trends — contrary to the predictions from Kohlberg's theory of moral development (Kohlberg, 1981) or Turiel's theory that certain issues are inherently moral in all cultures (Turiel, 1979). Although the particular practices are understood differently with respect to moral issues by the different cultures, the *justifications* for the moral judgments are much the same in both cultures. According to Shweder et al. (1985),

> Under some description, at some abstract level, justice, harm and protection of the vulnerable might qualify as "deep" universal of all moral codes. The rub, and the irony, is that if one merely focuses upon the abstract principles underlying a judgment about a particular, case, then the principles so abstracted do not make it possible to predict informants' judgments about particular cases. . . . If we are to understand our informants' moral judgements about particular cases we are going to have to understand the culture specific aspects of their moral codes, and we are going to have to understand the way those culture-specific aspects interact with the more universal aspects to produce a moral judgment. (p. 97)

One can extrapolate from the work of Shweder and his associates on morality and conceptions of the person to idea systems in general:

20. Cultural idea systems — about morality, aesthetics, science, human nature, and so on — typically have both universal and culturally specific components. There is little evidence that cultures can be characterized as more or less advanced according to stages of cognitive development, or even that children understand the universal components of these systems more easily than the culturally specific components.

32.10   INFERENCE AND CULTURAL MODELS

Another important area of research in the relation between culture and cognition is the study of inference. A classic problem in this area is the so-called Wason problem (Wason, 1969). One presentation of the problem is as follows:

> All labels made at Pica's Custom Label Factory have either the letter A or the letter E printed on the front of the label, and have either the number 2 or the number 3 printed on the back side. The machine never makes a mistake about this — it always puts the letter A or E on the front, and the number 2 or 3 on the back.
>
> As part of your job as a label checker at Pica's, you have the task of making sure that *if a label has an E printed on the front, it has a 2 printed on the back side*. You have to check this, because sometimes the machine makes a mistake and breaks this rule.
>
> Which of the labels would you have to turn over to make sure that the label had been printed following the rule? Mark an X under the labels you would have to turn over.

The results for this problem are universally poor; typically, 85% or more of the subjects in the experiment fail to get the correct answer. The correct answer is that one should turn over the label with an E on it and the label with a 3 on it. The modal incorrect answer is that one should turn over the label with an E on it and the label with a 2 on it.

There have been a great number of studies about why people get this problem wrong. Subjects do not get the problem wrong if told "No label should have both an E and a 3 on it," which is logically equivalent to the first rule. Interestingly, it is also hard to convince subjects that they have made a mistake — they often try to argue that they are following the rule, whatever combination they have chosen. However, these arguments are never coherent (except for the very few who interpret the rule as an "if and only if relation between E and 2). One can demonstrate that one should turn over the label with the 3 on it by making up some real labels, and showing subjects that a misprinted label will have a 3 on its back side, therefore if the 3 is showing, it should be turned over to check its correctness.

Johnson-Laird, Legrenzi, and Legrenzi (1972) discovered an interesting thing about this problem; that is, if the problem is translated into a "realistic" example, subjects will get it right. Here is realistic form that I have found easy for American college students:

> As part of your job as an assistant at Sears, you have the task of checking sales receipts to make sure that any sale of $30.00 or more has been approved by the section manager. The amount of the sale is written on the front of the form, while the section manager's approval is initialed on the back of the form.
>
> Which of the forms would you have to turn over to make sure that the sales clerk had been following the rule? Mark an X under the forms you would have to turn over.

About 70% of American college subjects get the correct answer on the realistic form of the test. A number of realistic forms have been developed, such as the form that uses rules about the drinking age (Cox & Griggs, 1982). It is interesting that subjects who have just gotten the right answer on the realistic form of the test still get the wrong answer on the letter-number form of the test.

One explanation for these results is that the subjects are unfamiliar with the problem and therefore have some difficulty in understanding it, most probably because their misunderstand the logical connective *if-then*. However, subjects understand the rule well enough, since 86% could correctly translate it for the label problem into "No label should have an E on the front and a 3 on the back." However, only 36% could translate the *if-then* for the label problem into the contrapositive: "Every label that has a 3 on the back should have an A on the front." (D'Andrade, in press-b). Note that this is much like the situation in the Wason problem in which the subject has to decide whether or not to turn over the label with the 3 on the back. In fact, those who got the label problem right were significantly more likely to get the contrapositive right; a phi correlation of .41 was found between a correct answer for the contrapositive label rule question and giving the correct answer for the label version of the Wason problem.

It is generally recognized that one's ability to solve the Wason problem is strongly affected by the kind of content that is used to instantiate the problem. There is much less general agreement on what it is about arbitrary content that makes the Wason problem hard. The hypothesis here is that the difficulty with the Wason problem is an example of a more general problem, the difficulty of the contrapositive. The simplest example of a logical problem with the contrapositive is modus tollens which has the form (1) *if p then q,* (2) *not q,* (3) *therefore not p.* To test the hypothesis that subjects would have difficulty with the contrapositive, a simple questionnaire containing a variety of modus tollens problems was administered to college students. Following is an example of a typical modus tollens with arbitrary content:

GIVEN: If Roger is a musician, then Roger is a Bavarian.
SUPPOSE: Roger is not a Bavarian.
THEN: **a.** It must be the case that Roger is a musician.
          b. Maybe Roger is a musician, maybe he isn't.
          c. It must be the case that Roger is not a musician.

No widely shared cultural schema links someone's being a musician with someone's being a Bavarian, which leaves the subject who tries to solve this problem more dependent on logical form alone. Only 53% of a sample of undergraduates gave the correct answer to this problem (D'Andrade, in press-b).

Subjects do much better when the problem contains a well-formed cultural schema linking *p* and *q,* as in the following problem:

GIVEN: If this rock is a garnet, then it is a semiprecious stone.
SUPPOSE: This rock is not a semiprecious stone.
THEN: **a.** It must be the case that this rock is a garnet.
          b. Maybe this rock is a garnet and maybe it isn't.
          c. It must be the case that this rock is not a garnet.

In this instance, 96% of the undergraduate sample gave the correct answer. For this problem there is a well-shared cultural schema linking something being a garnet and something being semiprecious — that is, garnets are semiprecious stones. Here are some other examples of modus tollens problems with well-formed schematic links between *p* and *q* that have been tested on UCSD undergraduates:

If Tom was born is San Diego, then Tom is a native Californian. (86% correct)
If Janet lives in San Cristobal, then Janet lives in Mexico. (80% correct)
If Bill cut himself, then Bill would be bleeding. (77% correct)
If it is raining, then the roof is wet. (68% correct)
If John bought a present, then John spent some money. (65% correct)

The following examples illustrate problems that lack well-formed schematic linkages between *p* and *q* and that subjects had more difficulty solving:

If Janet went to town, then Janet brought home some bread. (57% correct)
If Roger drank Pepsi, then Tom sat down. (53% correct)

If James is a watchman, then James likes candy. (51% correct)
If D is true, then E is true. (E is false). (45% correct)
If Harold is a politician, then Harold is from New York. (40% correct)
If J is true, then K is true (not K is true). (33% correct)

Samples sizes for these results range from 30 to 50.

It is not the case that people always have difficulty reasoning with arbitrary content. People do seem to be able to reason correctly with certain *simple* logical forms irrespective of content. Perhaps the simplest of all logical forms is modus ponens: (1) *if p then q,* (2) *p,* (3) *therefore q,* as in the following modus ponens problem:

GIVEN: If James is a watchman, then James likes candy.
SUPPOSE: James is a watchman.
THEN: **a.** It must be the case that James likes candy.
          b. Maybe James likes candy, maybe he doesn't.
          c. It must be the case that James does not like candy.

Ninety-six percent of an undergraduate sample gave the correct answer. In general, people seem to be able to solve modus ponens problems no matter how bizarre the content. In solving modus ponens problems, people act like true logicians for whom only form counts. Other logical forms besides modus ponens that people seem to be able to use effectively no matter what the content are

Not not *p.* Therefore *p.*
P or *q.* Not *p.* Therefore *q.*

These findings raise the question, "How do people reason when not using logical forms?" Although a long way from a full answer, work on reasoning carried out in natural settings has given some clues. An examination of legal disputes among the Trobriand Islanders (Hutchins, 1980) indicates that connectives such as *and, if-then, not, or,* and so on, are apparently culturally universal and of central importance in reasoning. The conceptual materials that these universal connectives organize into larger structures are typically made up of parts of cultural models. Furthermore, these connectives arc not understood in terms of truth table relations, but rather in terms of various kinds of temporal and causal contingencies (D'Andrade, in press-b; Johnson-Laird, 1983).

21. In reasoning, people use logical form only for the simplest inferences. Most commonly, people use well-learned cognitive models in reasoning, mentally manipulating these models to compute what could or could not happen, or what is likely or unlikely to happen. When these models are well learned, as is usually the case with cultural models, people can do quite complex manipulations, such as the kind of manipulation that is abstractly described as modus tollens. When the models are not so well learned or well structured, as is usually the case for the arbitrary situations given in logic problems, people can do only the simplest manipulations without error.

The representations that are mentally manipulated in reasoning are often surprisingly concrete and particular. For example, in a study of the missionaries and cannibals puzzle, Hutchins and Levin (1979) found that subjects were less likely to detect that they had attempted illegal moves when they imagined events taking place on the river bank away from them compared with imagined events on their side of the river (the subject's point of view with respect to the river was determined by the subject's use of deixis in verbal protocols — for example, "they go to the other side, then I bring them back here"). It is as if events that are imagined to occur on the subject's side of the river are closer and hence easier to see than events that are imagined to occur on the other side of the river. Similarly, it is said that chess players prefer to play with familiar-shaped chess sets, and that they complain if they have to use pieces of unusual shapes because they say such pieces are harder to manipulate mentally. Preferred mental models appear to be those that are most familiar, immediate, and best understood.

One major effect of this limitation in formal reasoning is to make complex reasoning appear context bound. That is, somebody may be able to do a certain problem in one domain, but not be able to do a problem with the same logical or mathematical form in a different domain. However, if the analysis given here is correct, the reason for the differential performance has nothing to do with context per se. One can do some mental manipulation of a well-formed schema in one domain that one cannot do in another domain simply because one lacks a well-formed schema of the relations within that domain.

This means that one cannot know from any test of reasoning ability how well someone is likely to be able to reason about some particular topic, because from a test one does not know how well formed that person's schemas are about that topic. This also means that the ability to reason will be strongly influenced by culture, since many of any person's schemas come from their culture — they are cultural models. To the extent that a culture has good cultural models (*good* in the sense that the representation captures the real world contingencies of interest), one will be able to reason well about the objects and events represented within these models.

32.11   SCHEMAS AND MOTIVATION

Cognition, if sealed off from everything else in the world, would not be very interesting. It is in its relation to action that cognition is of interest to most social scientists. The main relation between cognition and behavior that has been assumed in cognitive anthropology is a competence relation — if you don't have a well-formed cognitive representation of something, you can't identify it, remember it, or make inferences about it. But, if you do have a well-formed representation of that something, then identification, memory, inference, and actions dependent on such processes are possible. According to this view, cognitive schemas and other forms of knowledge representation give one the competence to do certain things — to use kin terms, solve a hard puzzle, be appropriately deferent to a chief, choose the right market, label manioc, go ocean fishing, or predict the time of high tide.

This competence model is useful and powerful. But there is the possibility that cognition is also related to behavior in another even more immediate and direct way. The idea is that some cognitive schemas-and hence some culturally formed schemas or cultural models — have motivational properties.

727

During the 1940s and 1950s motivation was a central concept in psychology and the social sciences. To understand someone's behavior, one had to understand what moved that person — that is, what motives that person had. Although theorists differed on the details, the common notion was that motives acted like a strong stimulus that pushed toward action and was rewarding if relieved, painful if not.

A major problem in the research on motivation, however, has been that it is difficult to determine which motives are "driving" which behaviors at any one time. Second, no consensus has developed on how many kinds of drives there are. Every motivation theorist has presented a different list of drives. Third, drives are difficult to measure. Fantasy measures, such as the TAT, are generally not too reliable and have only moderate correlations to most outcome measures. Finally, the great situational variance that exists among humans has made prediction to any given situation on the basis of motivation uncertain. A very "dependent" child, for example, as measured by whatever motivational measure, might prove to be quite independent in certain situations (say, in school settings) but very dependent in others (say, at home). Mischel's book, *Personality and Assessment,* published in 1968, summarized these problems and thus marked the end of an era of a certain type of motivational research.

However, the question of how people categorize things, make decisions, and infer things is not the question that the early motivational theorists were trying to answer. For example, some students work hard and some don't. Some colleagues like to get involved in collaborative research and some don't, some publish up a storm and others don't. In some places people put much time and effort into religious endeavors, and in some places religion is a minimal concern. These differences cannot be explained by standard cognitive analyses. The problems that motivational theorists have tried to solve have not gone away.

Recent work in cognitive anthropology and cognitive psychology indicates that there is a relatively direct relation between cognitive schemas and action and that it may account for a significant part of the phenomena that the motivational theorists have been studying (Mandler, 1984). The basic idea is that some cognitive schemas are connected to behavior through the activation of goals.

There appear to be large differences among schemas in the degree to which they activate goals *autonomously.* Some schemas have only weak connections to goals, so that goals are triggered only if other schemas also activate these same goals. The schema for dirt, for example, is typically linked to goals concerning cleaning, but the cleaning goal will normally be activated only if the thing that is dirty is one's own responsibility, it is an appropriate time for cleaning, one has a way to dispose of the dirt, and so on. However, some schemas are more mono autonomous and less dependent on contextually related schemas for the activation of their goals. Physical danger would be a simple example of such a schema — given the interpretation that one is in real physical danger, the goal of removing oneself from the danger tends to be strongly activated regardless of other concurrent interpretations.

The hierarchical organization of schemas plays an important part in human motivation. Schemas are hierarchical in the sense that interrelations created by one schema are passed on to higher-level schemas in order to make more general interpretations. It seems reasonable to assume that it is the topmost level of interpretation that is typically linked to the actions by which the organism operates in its environment. This is, of course, not a hard and fast expectation — sometimes one makes a general interpretation just to understand what is going on, as in watching a play and trying to understand why one character is hiding something, or pursuing some issue. However, it seems reasonable to expect that a person's most general interpretation of what is going on will be strongly attached to important goals, since top-level schemas are typically used to guide action at the most general effective level that the organism has learned.

In summary, the argument here goes as follows:

22. To understand people, one needs to understand what leads them to act as they do; to understand what leads them to act as they do, one needs to know their goals; to understand their goals, one must understand the overall interpretive system they have that triggers these goals; and to understand their interpretive system — their schemas — one must understand something about the hierarchical relations among these schemas. When a schema is frequently activated (by whatever drives), functions at a high level of interpretation, and triggers in a relatively context-free way particular goals, we can say such a schema has motivational force.

This account does not replace the drive model. Physiological or psychological drives, in this account, are special sources of activation that energize particular schemas. A complete analysis of motivation would determine not only particular schemas and goals, but also the specific drives that activate these schemas. The network of connections between goals and drives, however, is without doubt extremely complex and can rarely be empirically determined. Perhaps it is this complexity and indeterminacy in the linkage of drive to goal that led Freud to group all the drives together into one motivational source, the libido. The complexity of human drive–goal linkages would seem to be the product of a general evolutionary process in which, as intelligence increases, the connections between instinct and action become more complex, indirect, and modifiable.

Treating motives as activated schemas with embedded goals results is quite different from treating motives as vectors. Basically, a vector is something that has a direction (to get food, to help others, to make money) and an amount — a scale to measure the strength of a drive as indicated by frequency, persistence, emotionality, or fantasy. One might characterize someone with the vector model of motivation by saying that he is very hostile. This is quite different from saying that someone has a top-level schema in which this individual sees himself surrounded by enemies who wish to humiliate him, and whom he must attack to keep himself from being destroyed. And to say something about the nature of the situations that most strongly activate this interpretation, the characteristic feelings that go along with this interpretation, and the more specific goals that are activated whenever this interpretation is regnant presents a picture of a kind of organized complexity that outlines the way in which various goals are organized and activated. One of the important advantages of treating motivation as drive-activated schemas with embedded goals is that such an account not only connects cognition to behavior — it also shows how behavior may be organized through schemas.

A question that has received relatively little attention is how it is that some people learn — come to possess (or be possessed by) — *particular* goal-embedded schemas that organize their behavior. Many of the *general* schemas learned by individuals are culturally learned, shared, and transmitted. Achievement, love, security, recognition, freedom — all these terms refer to intersubjectively shared schemas, or collections of schemas — cultural models — through which events are interpreted and responded to. We assume that these cultural schemas, when internalized, are used extensively to interpret the world and organize sets of goals that deal with the world.

This formulation also rests on the assumption that many general human motives are culturally shaped. Things like achievement, acquisition, affiliation, power, and so on are, from an anthropological point of view, basically cultural models. Not only is what counts as achievement, acquisition, affiliation, and power dependent on the culture, but the very recognition that such things exist is dependent on the culture. With the increasing sophistication in the methods and techniques used to identify and analyze schemas, anthropologists and other social scientists may soon be able to determine the motivational force of cultural models, and thereby link cultural analyses to predictions about action.

32.12   INDIVIDUAL VARIABILITY

One of the persistent problems in cognitive anthropology is individual variability. Cognitive anthropology has emphasized the role of the psychological functioning of the individual as a carrier of culture. The problem is that when human groups are systematically surveyed, there is considerable disagreement about most items (Roberts, 1964).

One way to avoid this problem is to treat the most frequently held items — the *modal* items — as if they were *the* culture of the group. The disadvantage of this approach is that it takes a purely statistical characteristic and treats it as if it had some kind of "reality." A descriptive procedure should do more than just make it easy to say what is in the culture and what is not. It has been argued that characterizing a culture by its modal items is not a bad thing to do because the degree of sharing across items shows an almost bimodal pattern, in which most items are either highly shared or are unique (D'Andrade, in press-a). But the assurance that the modal items are held by large percentages of the population still does not give any special status to the description — it simply says that this strategy catches a lot of what is there. It would be much more satisfying theoretically if there were something about the more highly shared items that indicates that they have some special kinds of psychological or social *reality* — something that marked off these items from the less highly shared items besides frequency. Therefore some attention should be given to the recent work by Boster, Romney, Weller, and others on intracultural variation, which demonstrates that selection of modal items is associated with a special set of social and psychological characteristics (Boster, 1985). These characteristics are, first,

23a. Reliability: Persons who are more likely to give modal responses on a task are more likely to give the same responses if the task is presented at a later time.

For example, Boster (1985) found that Aguaruna Jivaro informants who tended to use the modal names for a set of manioc plants were much more likely to be consistent when asked to name these same plants on a second occasion. The agreement measure was computed by counting the number of plants (out of a total of 90) on which each informant agreed with the majority name for the plant. The reliability measure was computed for each informant by counting the number of plants given the same name on both occasions. Boster found that the correlation between reliability and agreement across six informants was .92.

23b. Consistency: Persons who are more likely to give modal responses on some task are more likely to give responses that are consistent with each other.

For example, Weller (1984) found that rural Mexican women who gave the majority response (when there are only two alternatives, the modal response will also be the majority response) about which of a pair of diseases was the hotter, or more severe, or more contagious, were more likely to be consistent in their choices as measured by the likelihood that they would not fall into the "error" of saying that disease A is hotter than B, and that B is hotter than C, but that A is not hotter than C. Agreement with the majority was measured by computing the number of pairs of diseases for which the informant agreed with the majority choice. Consistency was measured by the number of triples of disease terms for each informant that did not show the "intransitivity error" described earlier. The correlations between consistency and agreement was .57 for contagion, .21 for severity, but only .07 for the hot–cold dimension.

23c. Normality: Persons who are more likely to give modal responses on a task are more likely to have had "normal" experiences with respect to the material symbolized by the task.

For example, Weller, Romney, and Orr (in press) found Orange County high school students who agreed most with the majority response about the truth or falsity of 135 statements about parental sanctions for rule breaking were less likely to have been physically abused by their parents as measured by their response to a question about parental use of physical punishment. It is interesting that the abused children did not have a special pattern of their own — they merely appear to be less knowledgeable about these cultural norms.

23d. Education, intelligence, and experience: Persons who are more likely to give modal responses on a task are more likely to be better educated with respect to that task and judged more intelligent with respect to their ability in that task domain, and tend to have more experience in that task domain.

Weller (1984), in her Mexican study of disease characterisitics, found that literate and educated women were most likely to give modal responses on the contagion and hot–cold dimensions, whereas older women were more likely to give modal responses on the severity and age dimensions. Further evidence for the association of education and intelligence with modal responses can be found in data from word association tests (D'Andrade, 1987). In a study by Moran, Mefferd and Kimble (1964) a standard word list of 125 words was given to subjects on four successive days. After being tested on each set of 25 words, subjects were retested on the same sets of words but were instructed to give the same responses that they had given the first time. From the word association data, Moran et al. constructed a measure of modality they called *commonality*. Commonality was computed by giving a value for each response corresponding to the percentage of times that response was given by the total sample of subjects. Responses were also coded for *reliability* (the number of times the subject gave exactly the same associations to the same stimulus word), *speed* (reaction time), being *blank* (failing to give any response within 20 seconds), and being *distant* (giving a response that has no apparent semantic connection to the stimulus word). The number of years of *education* of each subject, and the subjects' scores on the vocabulary part of the Wexler-Bellvue IQ test were also obtained. Pearson correlations of all variables across subjects were computed. It was found that those who most frequently chose the modal response (measured here by "commonality") had higher IQs ($r = .42$), were somewhat better educated ($r - .29$), were more reliable ($r = .58$), gave their responses faster ($r = .45$), were less likely to give semantically unrelated responses ($r = -.66$), and were less likely to fail to give any response at all ($r = -.33$).

The kind of intelligence postulated here as being associated with modal or majority responses on some task is not *general* intelligence (whatever that may be), but rather a specific ability to do well with the kinds of materials that are involved in the task. The ability to choose good definitions is clearly related to word association tasks, in that both involve the cognitive manipulation of semantic relations. It may seem strange that the "smart" people were more likely to give the "common" response in word association tests. The average respondent gave only 10% common responses across all stimulus words (with the "smart" people tending to give a few percentage points more than this), which still leaves plenty of opportunity for "creative" responses. If Moran et al. had measured the number of different words used by each subject they would likely have found that the subjects with higher IQs used both more common associations *and* a greater number of different word types.

The greater degree of reliability, consistency, normality, education, intelligence, and experience of those who are more likely to give modal or majority responses can only be expected when the conditions that Romney, Weller, and Batchelder (1986) stipulate for a *consensus model* are in effect. For the consensus model to apply, there must first be only one major factor in the person-to-person correlation matrix; that is, the sample must be homogeneous and must not contain major subcultural groupings. Second, the sample must show a reasonable level of agreement on what constitutes "correct" responses — otherwise, it will be impossible to distinguish the data from random "noise."

Assuming that there is evidence to support the propositions presented in the preceding paragraphs, the question is *why* — why should those who give modal or majority responses in doing various tasks tend to be more reliable, consistent, normal, educated, intelligent, and experienced? There are probably a number of related causes at work here, but one possibility is that most cultural domains are characterized by a kind of coherence and substance. Consider a set of questions about algebra. Those people who know algebra well are more likely to give the more highly shared answers — since in most cases the "right" answer will be the most frequent answer because the many possible "wrong" answers will each have only a small number of adherents. Those who know algebra well are also more likely to be more reliable since they are more likely to "compute" the same answer to the same problem every time because they have a more highly practiced set of skills. They arc also more likely to be experienced because learning and domain usually requires practice. And they are more likely to show up as "smart" in domain-related tests because the same kinds of cognitive computations are likely to be involved in both tasks, and, to the extent that they have "natural" ability, they will learn the "correct" procedures better than others with less ability. Thus the pattern that emerges is that *those who give more modal responses display the behavioral characteristics of an expert.*

All of this seems reasonable for algebra. But in what sense is labeling types of manioc (or determining which of two diseases is more contagious, or deciding what are appropriate parental sanctions, or giving word associations) like doing algebra problems? Certainly these domains are less organized and less clearly matters of provable truth than algebra. However, all these domains do involve complex relations and discriminations in which the criteria used to answer one series of questions are likely to recur in answering other series of questions. Once a domain has enough structure so that it is possible to generalize from one thing to another, then expertise becomes possible. To label plants one must use combinations of complex discriminations, and the discriminations needed to label one series of plants are likely to be needed to label another series. Similarly, common word associations are derived from a relatively small set of semantic relationships, such as opposition on a dimension of contrast (dark/light), coordinate members of a contrast set (red/blue), superordinate relations (cabbage/vegetable), subordinate relations (jewel/diamond), and so on, which form a structured field. If one can use these relations effectively with one series of stimulus words, it is more likely that one will be able to use these same relations effectively with another series of stimulus words.

Thus, there is a reasonable sense in which one can speak of being an *expert* in each of these domains, where being an expert means that one not only knows a lot about some domain, but also that one can operate cognitively in an especially effective way, using the internal consistencies within the domain to reason, extrapolate, remember, and discriminate more accurately than ordinary folk. These findings substantiate the intuitive judgment of many ethnographers that some informants are experts on some topics, and that their single judgments can sometimes represent the group consensus more accurately than the judgments of a number of less expert informants.

The fact that one can be an expert in a cultural system implies that such cultural systems are indeed real. There would be no way for people to become experts in some cultural system if the system were just something in the mind of the ethnographer, totally dependent on the ethnographer's classificatory strategies. Further, if becoming adept at understanding a system were just an individual matter (rather than a social matter), there would be no reason to expect an association between being an expert and giving modal responses. Knowledge in most if not all cultural systems is socially distributed — that is, some people know things that others do not (Roberts, 1964). Even with respect to the simplest cultural systems, it is rare for any individual to control all the relevant knowledge. To become an expert, one must gather and integrate knowledge from a number of other people, and this type of communication requires *common* meanings and understandings with respect to the system being learned or used. Since the most general and widely accessible common meanings are those that are modal in the group, the expert gains a large advantage by knowing and using them. Although a developing expert could negotiate separate agreements about the relevant meanings and procedures with each person he or she worked with, this would be extremely costly and inefficient. The expert is more likely to maximize "communicative accuracy" across persons by using modal meanings and understandings.

To return to the issue of individual variability, one can consider the observed disagreement about cultural items to be the cost of the social distribution of knowledge and belief. Given that large numbers of people must each learn at least some part of a system, there are bound to be errors in transmission because of the difficulties inherent in learning and recall. These errors would snowball over time and eventually make the system totally idiosyncratic, were there not other processes continuously pushing people to adopt the more highly shared items. There are probably many processes by which to increase commonality, such as imitating people with high social standing and not sanctioning those who act differently. I suggest that one such force that has not been widely recognized is the communicative advantage of using the most common meanings and understandings in developing expertise in a cultural system. This suggestion is supported by the data discussed earlier, which show that those who perform most consistently and reliably are also most likely to use modal meanings and understandings.

32.13   END REMARKS

The discussion in this chapter points to one general trend, which I call the move from *extension* to *intension*. Early work in cognitive anthropology often assumed that it is possible to work primarily from extensional definitions — that is, from the natives' statements about what things got what labels, or what sentences were true rather than false, or what terms could be filled into what sentence frames. With an extensional approach, the investigator could avoid trying to understand what was in the native's mind, and instead concentrate on finding out how what the native said correlated with what was in the world. Indeed, this kind of approach made it possible to find out a great deal about native systems of knowledge and understanding. At the same time, however, it became difficult to formulate definitions, to account for the properties of classificational and taxonomic systems, to represent the productive capacities of informants, and to formulate the descriptions of complex objects. Consequently, there was greater reliance on models based on the *sense* that the native had of things. The schema notion is an example of this; a schema is an internal mechanism through which interpretations are made — it is a general sense-maker. There probably has been a certain loss of rigor in this trend, since work with extensional meaning is more explicit and directly verifiable than work with sense and intensional meaning, which requires the investigator to develop a cognitive model of how the native represents things that can only be indirectly verified. However, the gain has been worth the loss, in that many of the generalizations about the relationship between culture and cognition described here could not have been discovered without such models of native representation.

REFERENCES

Battig, W. F., & Montague, W. E. (1969). Category norms for verbal behavior in 56 categories: A replication and extension of the Connecticut category norms. *Journal of Experimental Psychology Monographs 80* (3, part 2).

Berlin, B., Breedlove, D. & Raven, P. H. (1966). Folk taxonomies and biological classification. *Science 154*:273–275.

——— (1973). General principle of classification and nomenclature in folk biology. *American Anthropologist 75*:214–242.

Berlin, B., &. Kay, P. (1969). *Basic Color Terms.* Berkeley: University of California Press.

Black, M., & Metzger, D. (1965). Ethnographic description and the study of law. *American Anthropologist 67* (6, part 2):141–165.

Boster, J. S. (1985). Requiem for the omniscient informant: There's life in the old girl yet. In *Directions in Cognitive Anthropology,* J. Dougherty (Ed.), pp. 177–197. Urbana: University of Illinois Press.

Boster. J., Berlin, B., & O'Neill, J. (1986). The correspondence of Jivaroan to scientific ornithology. *American Anthropologist 88*:569–583.

Brown, C. (1977). Folk botanical life-forms: Their universality and growth. *American Anthropologist 79*:317–342.

Brown, C., Kolar, J., Torrey, B., Truon-Quan, T., & Volkman, P. (1976). Some general principles of biological and non-biological folk classification. *American Ethnologist 3*:73–85.

Brown, R., & Lenneberg, E. (1954). A study in language and cognition. *Journal of Abnormal and Social Psychology 49:*73–85.

Brugman, C. (1981). The Story of Over. Master's thesis, University of California, Berkeley.

Casson, R. (1983). Schemata in cognitive anthropology. *Annual Review of Anthropology 72:*429–462.

Coleman, L., & Kay, P. (1981). Prototype semantics: The English verb "lie." *Language 57,* 26–44.

Conklin, H. C. (1962). Lexicographic treatment of folk taxonomies. In *Indiana University Research Center in Anthropology, Folklore, and Linguistics, Publication 21. Problems in Lexicography,* Householder, F. & Saporta, S. (Eds.), pp. 119–141. Bloomington: University of Indiana Press.

Cox, J. R., & Griggs, R. A. (1982). The effects of experience on performance in Wason's selection task. *Memory and Cognition 71:*496–502.

D'Andrade, R. G. (1965). Trait psychology and componential analysis. *American Anthropologist 67:* 215–228.

(1974a). The colors of emotion. *American Ethnologist 1:*49–63.

(1974b). Memory and the assessment of behavior. In *Social Measurement,* Blalock, T. (Ed.), pp. 139–186. Chicago: Aldine-Atherton.

(1976). A propositional analysis of U.S. American beliefs about illness. In *Meaning in Anthropology,* Basso, K. & Selby, H. (Eds.), pp. 155–180. Albuquerque: University of New Mexico Press.

(1985). Character terms and cultural models. In *Directions in Cognitive Anthropology,* Dougherty, J. (Ed.), pp. 88–119. New York: Cambridge University Press.

(1986). Three scientific world views and the covering law model. In *Metatheory in Social Science,* Fiske, D. & Shweder, R. (Eds.), pp. 19–41. Chicago: University of Chicago Press.

(1987). A folk model of the mind. In *Cultural Models in Language and Thought,* Holland, D. & Quinn, N. (Eds.), pp. 112–148. New York: Cambridge University Press.

In press-a. Cultural sharing and diversity. In *Models of Culture: Essays in Honor of John Roberts,* Bolton, R. (Ed.). New Haven: HRAF Press.

In press-b. Culturally based reasoning. In *Cognition and Social Worlds,* Gellatly, A. & Rogers D. (Eds.), Oxford: Clarendon Press.

D'Andrade, R. G., & Egan, M. (1974). The colors of emotion. *American Ethnologist 1:*49–63.

D'Andrade, R. G., Quinn, N., Nerlove, S. B., & Romney, A. K. (1972). Categories of disease in American-English and Mexican-Spanish. In *Multidimensional Scaling, Volume II,* Romney, A. K., Shepard, R. N., & Nerlove, S. B. (Eds.), pp. 11–54. New York: Seminar Press.

Dougherty, J. (1978). Salience and relativity in classification. *American Ethnologist 5:*66–80. Dougherty, J., & Keller, C. 1985. Taskonomy: A practical approach to knowledge structures. In *Directions in Cognitive Anthropology,* Dougherty, J. (Ed.), pp. 161–174. Urbana: University of Illinois Press.

Ekman, P. (1971). Universal and cultural differences in facial expressions of emotion. In *Nebraska Symposium on Motivation,* Cole, J. (Ed.), pp. 207–283. Lincoln: University of Nebraska Press.

Fillmore, C. (1975). An alternative to checklist theories of meaning. In *Proceedings of the First Annual Meeting of the Berkeley Linguistics Society,* Cogen, C., Thomson, H., Thurgood, G., Whilstler, K., & Wright, J. (Eds.), pp. 123–131. Berkeley: Berkeley Linguistic Society.

(1977). Topic in lexical semantics. In *Current Issues in Linguistic Theory,* Cole, R. (Ed.), pp. 76–138. Bloomington: Indiana University Press.

Fortes, M. (1983). *Oedipus and Job in West African Religion.* Cambridge: Cambridge University Press.

Frake, C. (1964). Notes on queries in ethnography. *American Anthropologist 66:*(3, part 2):132–145.

(1975). How to enter a Yakan house. In *Sociocultural Dimensions of Language Use,* Sanches, M., & Blount, B. (Eds.), pp. 25–40. New York: Academic Press.

(1985). Cognitive maps of time and tide among medieval seafarers. *Man 20:*254–270.

Garro, L. (1986). Language, memory, and locality: A reexamination. *American Anthropologist 88:*128–136.

Gerber, E. (1975). The Cultural Patterning of Emotion in Samoa. Ph.D. dissertation. University of California, San Diego.

(1985). Rage and obligation: Samoan emotion in conflict. In *Person, Self, and Experience,* White, G., & Kirkpatrick, J. (Eds.), pp. 121–167. Berkeley: University of California Press.

Goldin-Meadow, S., & Feldman, H. (1977). The development of language-like communication without a language model. *Science 197:*401–403.

Haviland, S., & Clark, E. (1974). "This man's father is my father's son": A study of acquisition of English kin terms. *Journal of Child Language 1:*23–47.

Heider, E. (1972). Universals in color naming and memory. *Journal of Experimental Psychology 93:*10–20.

Holland, D. (1982). Conventional metaphors in human thought and language. *Reviews in Anthropology 9:*287–297.

Hunn, E. (1976). Toward a perceptual model of folk biological classification. *American Ethnologist 3:* 508–524.

(1985). The utilitarian factor in folk biological classification. In *Directions in Cognitive Anthropology,* Dougherty, J. (Ed.), pp. 117–140. Urbana: University of Illinois Press.

Hutchins, E. (1980). *Culture and Inference: A Trobriand Case Study.* Cambridge, MA: Harvard University Press.

n.d. Mediation and automatization. Manuscript, University of California, San Diego.

Hutchins, E., & Levin, J. A. (1979). *Point of View in Problem Solving.* CHIP Technical Report, University of California, San Diego.

Johnson, A., Johnson, O., & Baksh, M. (1986). Cognitive and emotional aspects of Machiguenga color terms. *American Anthropologist 88*:674–681.

Johnson-Laird, P. N. (1983). *Mental Models.* Cambridge, MA: Harvard University Press.

Johnson-Laird, P. N., Legrenzi, P., & Legrenzi, M. (1972). Reasoning and a sense of reality. *British Journal of Psychology 63*:392–400.

Kay, P. (1987). Linguistic competence and folk theories of language: Two English hedges. In *Cultural Models in Language and Thought,* Holland, D., & Quinn, N. (Eds.), pp. 67–77. New York: Cambridge University Press.

Kay, P., & Kempton, W. (1984). What is the Sapir–Whorf hypothesis? *American Anthropologist 86*, 65–79.

Kempton, W. (1981). *The Folk Classification of Ceramics.* New York: Academic Press.

Kieffer, M. (1974). Color and Emotion: Synesthesia in Tzutujil Mayan and Spanish. Ph.D. dissertation, University of California, Irvine.

Kohlberg, L. (1981). The *Philosophy of Moral Development: Moral Stages and the Idea of Justice, Volume 1: Essays on Moral Development.* San Francisco: Harper and Row.

Kronenfeld, D., Armstrong, J., & Wilmoth, S. (1985). Exploring the internal structure of linguistic categories: An extensionist semantic view. In *Directions in Cognitive Anthropology.* Dougherty, J. (Ed.), p. 110. Urbana: University of Illinois Press.

Kucera, H., & Francis, W. N. (1967). *Computational Analysis of Present-day American English.* Providence: Brown University Press.

Lakoff, G. (1987). *Women, Fire, and Dangerous Things: What Categories Reveal about the Mind.* Chicago: University of Chicago Press.

Lakoff, C., & Johnson, M. (1983). *Metaphors We Live By.* Chicago: University of Chicago Press.

Langacker, R. (1986). An introduction to cognitive grammar. *Cognitive Science 10*:1–40.

(1987). *Foundations of Cognitive Grammar.* Stanford, CA: Stanford University Press.

Lantz, D, & Stefflre, V. (1964). Language and cognition revisited. *Journal of Abnormal and Social Psychology 69*:472–481.

Lenneberg, E. (1961). Color naming, color recognition, color discrimination: A reappraisal. *Perceptual and Motor Skills 12*:375–382.

1967. The *Biological Foundations of Language.* New York: Wiley.

Lenneberg, E., & Roberts, J. (1956). The language of experience; A study in methodology. *International Journal of Linguistics,* Memoir no. 13.

LeVine, R. (1984). Properties of culture: An ethnographic view. In *Culture Theory Essays on Mind, Self, and Emotion,* Shweder, R., & LeVine, R. (Eds.), pp. 67–87. New York: Cambridge University Press.

Levy, R. L. (1973). *Tahitians: Mind and Experience in Society Islands.* Chicago: University of Chicago Press.

1985. Emotion, knowing, and culture. In *Culture Theory: Essays on Mind, Self, and Emotion,* Shweder, R. & LeVine, R. (Eds.), 214–237. Cambridge: Cambridge University Press.

Linder, S. (1981). A Lexico-Semantic Analysis of Verb-Particle Constructions with UP and OUT. Ph.D. dissertation. University of California, San Diego.

Lucy, J., & Shweder, R. (1979). Whorf and his critics: Linguistic and non-linguistic influences on color memory. *American Anthropologist 81*:581–615.

(1988). The effect of incidental conversation on memory for focal colors. *American Anthropologist 90*(4):923–931.

Lutz, C. (1982). The domain of emotion words on Ifaluk. *American Ethnologist 9*:113–128.

(1985). Ethnopsychology compared to what: Explaining behavior and consciousness among the Ifaluk. In *Person, Self, and Experience,* White, G. & Kirkpatrick, J. (Eds), pp. 35–79. Berkeley: University of California Press.

(1986). Emotion, thought, and estrangement: Emotion as a cultural category. *Cultural Anthropology 1*:287–309.

Lutz, C, & White, G. (1986). The anthropology of emotions. *Annual Review of Anthropology 15*:405–436.

Mandler, G. (1984). *Mind and Body.* New York: W. W. Norton.

Metzger, D., & Williams, G. (1963a). A formal ethnographic analysis of Tencjapa Ladino weddings. *American Anthropologist 65*:1076–1101.

(1963b). Tenejapa medicine I: The curer. *Southwestern Journal of Anthropology 19*:216–234.

(1966). Some procedures and results in the study of native categories: Tenejapa "firewood." *American Anthropologist 68*:389–407.

Miller, G. A. (1956). The magical number seven plus or minus two: Some limits on your capacity for processing information. *Psychological Review 63*:81–96.

Miller, G. A., & Johnson-Laird, P. N. (1976). *Language and Perception.* Cambridge, MA: Harvard University Press.

Mischel, W. (1968). *Personality and Assessment.* New York: Wiley.

Moran, L. J., Mefferd, R. B., & Kimble, J. P. (1964). Idio-dynamic sets in word association. *Psychological Monographs: General and Applied 78*(2):1–22.

Nerlove, S., & Romney, A. K. (1967). Sibling terminology and cross-sex behavior. *American Anthropologist 74*:1249–1253.

Poole, F. J. P. (1985). Coming into social being: Cultural images of infants in Bimin-Kuskusmin folk psychology. In *Person, Self, and Experience,* White, G. & Kirkpatrick, J. (Eds.), pp. 183–242. Berkeley: University of California Press.

Quinn, N. (1985). American marriage through metaphors: A cultural analysis. *North Carolina Working Papers in Culture and Cognition No. I.* Durham, NC: Duke University Department of Anthropology.

——— (1987). What discourse can tell about culture: Convergent evidence for a cultural model of American marriage. In *Cultural Models in Language and Thought,* Holland, D., & Quinn, N. (Eds.), pp. 173–192. New York: Cambridge University Press.

Quinn, N., & Holland, D. (1987). Introduction. In *Cultural Models in Language and Thought,* Holland, D., & Quinn, N. (Eds), pp. 3–40. New York: Cambridge University Press.

Randall, R. (1976). How tall is a taxonomic tree? Some evidence for dwarfism. *American Ethnologist 3*:543–553.

——— (1986). Steps toward an ethnosemantics of verbs. In *Directions in Cognitive Anthropology,* Dougherty, J. (Ed.), pp. 249–268. Urbana: University of Illinois Press.

Rips, L. In press. Similarity, typicality, and categorization. In *Similarity and Analogical Reasoning,* Vosniadou, S., & Ortony, A. (Eds.). Cambridge: Cambridge University Press.

Roberts, John M. (1987). Within culture variation. *American Behavioral Scientist 31*(2):266–279.

Romney, A. K., & D'Andrade, R. G. (1964). Cognitive aspects of English kin terms. American *Anthropologist 66*:146–170.

Romney, A. K., Weller, S. C. & Batchelder, W. H. 1986. Culture as consensus: A theory of culture and informant accuracy. *American Anthropologist 88*: 313–338.

Rosch, E. (1973). On the internal structure of perceptual and semantic categories. In *Cognitive Development and the Acquisition of Language,* Moore, T. (Ed.), pp. 123–142. New York: Academic Press.

——— (1975). Cognitive representations of semantic categories. *Journal of Experimental Psychology 104*:192–233.

Rumelhart, D., & McClelland, J. (1986). *Parallel Distributed Processing: Explorations in the Microstructure of Cognition. Volume I: Foundations.* Cambridge, MA: MIT Press.

Savage-Rumbaugh, S., Rumbaugh, D. S. Smith, & Lawson, J. (1980). Reference: The linguistic essential. *Science 210*:922–925.

Schank, R., & Abelson, R. (1977). *Scripts, Plans, Coals, and Understanding: An Inquiry into Human Knowledge Structures.* Hillsdale, NJ: Erlbaum.

Schneider, D., & Roberts, J. (1953). Role designating and role classifying aspects of kin terms. *Papers of the Peabody Museum 32*:121–133.

Shweder, R. A. (1972). Semantic Structures and Personality Assessment. Doctoral dissertation. Department of Social Relations, Harvard University.

——— (1977a). Illusory correlation and the M.M.P.I, controversy. *Journal of Consulting and Clinical Psychology 45*:917–924.

——— (1977b). Illusory correlation and the M.M.P.I, controversy: Author's reply to some allusions and elusions in Block's and Edward's commentaries. *Journal of Consulting and Clinical Psychology 45*:936–940.

——— (1977c). Likeness and likelihood in everyday thought: Magical thinking in judgments about personality. *Current Anthropology 18*:637–648.

Shweder, R. A., & D'Andrade, R. G. (1979). Accurate reflection or systematic distortion? A reply to Block, Weiss, and Thorne. *Journal of Personality and Social Psychology 37*:1075–1084.

——— (1980.) The systematic distortion hypothesis. In *New Directions for Methodology of Social and Behavioral Science 4*:37–58. San Francisco: Jossey Bass.

Shweder, R. A., & Bourne, E. J. (1984). Does the concept of the person vary cross-culturally? In *Culture Theory: Essays on Mind, Self, and Emotion,* Shweder, R. & LeVine, R. (Eds.), pp. 158–199. New York: Cambridge University Press.

Shweder, R. A., Mahapatra, M., & Miller, S. G. (1987). Culture and *moral* development. In *The Emergence of Morality in Young Children,* Kagan, J. & Lamb, S. (Eds.), pp. 1–83. Chicago: University of Chicago Press.

Stefflre, V., Castillo, V., & Moreley, L. (1966). Language and cognition in Yucatan: A crosscultural replication. *Journal of Personality and Social Psychology 4*:112–115.

Stigler, J. W., Chalip, L., & Miller, K. F. (1986). Consequences of skill: The case of abacus training in Taiwan. *American Journal of Education 94*:447–479.

Swartz, M. J., & Jordan, D. K. (1976). *Anthropology: Perspective on Humanity.* New York: Wiley.

Sweetser, E. (1987). The definition of *lie:* an examination of the folk models underlying a semantic prototype. In *Cultural Models in Language and Thought,* Holland, D. & Quinn, N. (Eds.), pp. 43–66. New York: Cambridge University Press.

Talmy, L. (1978). The relation of grammar to cognition — a synopsis. In *Proceedings of TINLAP-2 Theoretical Issues in Natural Language Processing,* Waltz, D. (Ed.), pp., 3–23. Champaign: Coordinated Science Laboratory, University of Illinois.

Turiel, E. (1979). Distinct conceptual and developmental domains: Social-convention and morality. In *Nebraska Symposium on Motivation, Volume 25,* Keasy, C. (Ed.). Lincoln: University of Nebraska Press.

Uyeda, K., & Mandler, G. (1980). Prototypicality norms for 28 semantic categories. *Behavioral Research Methods and Instrumentation 12*:587–595.

Vendler, Z. (1967). *Linguistics in Philosophy.* Ithaca, NY: Cornell University Press.

——— (1972). *Res Cognitans: An Essay in Rational Philosophy.* Ithaca, NY: Cornell University Press.

Wallace, A. F. C. (1961). On being just complicated enough. *Proceedings of the National Academy of Sciences 47*:458–464.

Wason, P. (1969). Regression in reasoning. *British Journal of Psychology 60*:471–480.

Weller, S. C. (1984). Consistency and consensus among informants: Disease concepts in a rural Mexican town. *American Anthropologist 56*:966–975.

Weller, S. C, Romney, A. K., & Orr, D. P. (1986). The myth of a sub-culture of corporal punishment. *Human Organization 46*:39–47.

Werner. O. (1985). Folk knowledge without fuzz. In *Directions in Cognitive Anthropology,* Dougherty, J. (Ed.), pp. 73–90. Urbana: University of Illinois Press.

Wexler, K., & Romney, A. K (1972). Individual variations in cognitive structures. In *Multidimensional Scaling Vol. 11,* Shepard, R. & Nerlove, S. (Eds.), pp. 73–92. New York: Seminar Press.

Whorf, B. L. (1956). Science and linguistics. In *Language, Thought, and Reality,* Carrol, J. B. (Ed.). Cambridge, MA: MIT Press.

Wierzbicka, A. (1984). Apples are not a "kind of fruit": The semantics of human categorization. *American Ethnologist 11*:313–328.

——— (1986). Human emotions: Universal or culture specific? *American Anthropologist 88*:584–594.

CHAPTER THIRTY-THREE

DO THE LANGUAGES WE SPEAK SHAPE THE WAY WE THINK?

LERA BORODITSKY

Do the languages we speak shape the way we think? Do they merely express thoughts, or do the structures in languages (without our knowledge or consent) shape the very thoughts we wish to express?

Take "Humpty Dumpty sat on a [. . .]" Even this snippet of a nursery rhyme reveals how much languages can differ from one another. In English, we have to mark the verb for tense; in this case, we say "sat" rather than "sit." In Indonesian you need not (in fact, you can't) change the verb to mark tense.

In Russian, you would have to mark tense and also gender, changing the verb if Mrs. Dumpty did the sitting. You would also have to decide if the sitting event was completed or not. If our ovoid hero sat on the wall for the entire time he was meant to, it would be a different form of the verb than if, say, he had a great fall.

In Turkish, you would have to include in the verb how you acquired this information. For example, if you saw the chubby fellow on the wall with your own eyes, you'd use one form of the verb, but if you had simply read or heard about it, you'd use a different form.

Do English, Indonesian, Russian and Turkish speakers end up attending to, understanding, and remembering their experiences differently simply because they speak different languages?

These questions touch on all the major controversies in the study of mind, with important implications for politics, law and religion. Yet very little empirical work had been done on these questions until recently. The idea that language might shape thought was for a long time considered untestable at best and more often simply crazy and wrong. Now, a flurry of new cognitive science research is showing that in fact, language does profoundly influence how we see the world.

From *The Wall Street Journal*, July 24, 2010, New York.

The question of whether languages shape the way we think goes back centuries; Charle-magne proclaimed that "to have a second language is to have a second soul." But the idea went out of favor with scientists when Noam Chomsky's theories of language gained pop-ularity in the 1960s and '70s. Chomsky proposed that there is a universal grammar for all human languages — essentially, that languages don't really differ from one another in sig-nificant ways. And because languages didn't differ from one another, the theory went, it made no sense to ask whether linguistic differences led to differences in thinking.

The search for linguistic universals yielded interesting data on languages, but after decades of work, whether there are in fact universals remains an open question (Boroditsky & Gaby, in press). Instead, as linguists probed deeper into the world's languages (7,000 or so, only a fraction of them analyzed), innumerable unpredictable differences emerged. Of course, just because people talk differently doesn't necessarily mean they think differently. In the past decade, cognitive scientists have begun to measure not just how people talk, but also how they think, asking whether our understanding of even such fundamental domains of experience as space, time and causality could be constructed by language.

For example, in Pormpuraaw, a remote Aboriginal community in Australia, the indige-nous languages don't use terms like "left" and "right." Instead, everything is talked about in terms of absolute cardinal directions (north, south, east, west), which means you say things like, "There's an ant on your southwest leg." To say hello in Pormpuraaw, one asks, "Where are you going?", and an appropriate response might be, "A long way to the south-southwest. How about you?" If you don't know which way is which, you literally can't get past hello.

About a third of the world's languages (spoken in all kinds of physical environments) rely on absolute directions for space. As a result of this constant linguistic training, speak-ers of such languages are remarkably good at staying oriented and keeping track of where they are, even in unfamiliar landscapes. They perform navigational feats scientists once thought were beyond human capabilities. This is a big difference, a fundamentally different way of conceptualizing space, trained by language (Chan & Bergen, 2005).

Differences in how people think about space don't end there. People rely on their spa-tial knowledge to build many other more complex or abstract representations including time, number, musical pitch, kinship relations, morality and emotions. So if Pormpuraawans think differently about space, do they also think differently about other things, like time?

To find out, my colleague Alice Gaby and I traveled to Australia and gave Pormpu-raawans sets of pictures that showed temporal progressions (for example, pictures of a man at different ages, or a crocodile growing, or a banana being eaten). Their job was to arrange the shuffled photos on the ground to show the correct temporal order. We tested each per-son in two separate sittings, each time facing in a different cardinal direction. When asked to do this, English speakers arrange time from left to right. Hebrew speakers do it from right to left (because Hebrew is written from right to left).

Pormpuraawans, we found, arranged time from east to west (Evans & Levinson, 2009). That is, seated facing south, time went left to right. When facing north, right to left. When facing east, toward the body, and so on. Of course, we never told any of our participants which direction they faced. The Pormpuraawans not only knew that already, but they also sponta-neously used this spatial orientation to construct their representations of time. And many other ways to organize time exist in the world's languages. In Mandarin, the future can be below and the past above (Fausey, Long, & Boroditsky, 2009). In Aymara, spoken in South America, the future is behind and the past in front (Fausey & Boroditsky, 2008).

In addition to space and time, languages also shape how we understand causality. For example, English likes to describe events in terms of agents doing things. English speakers tend to say things like "John broke the vase" even for accidents. Speakers of Spanish or Japanese would be more likely to say "the vase broke itself" or "the vase broke." Such differences between languages have profound consequences for how their speakers understand events, construct notions of causality and agency, what they remember as eyewitnesses and how much they blame and punish others.

In studies conducted by Caitlin Fausey at Stanford, speakers of English, Spanish and Japanese watched videos of two people popping balloons, breaking eggs and spilling drinks either intentionally or accidentally. Later everyone got a surprise memory test: For each event, can you remember who did it? She discovered a striking cross-linguistic difference in eyewitness memory. Spanish and Japanese speakers did not remember the agents of accidental events as well as did English speakers. Mind you, they remembered the agents of intentional events (for which their language would mention the agent) just fine. But for accidental events, when one wouldn't normally mention the agent in Spanish or Japanese, they didn't encode or remember the agent as well (Fausey & Boroditsky, in press; Frank, Everett, Fedorenko, & Gibson, 2008).

In another study, English speakers watched the video of Janet Jackson's infamous "wardrobe malfunction" (a wonderful nonagentive coinage introduced into the English language by Justin Timberlake), accompanied by one of two written reports. The reports were identical except in the last sentence where one used the agentive phrase "ripped the costume" while the other said "the costume ripped." Even though everyone watched the same video and witnessed the ripping with their own eyes, language mattered. Not only did people who read "ripped the costume" blame Justin Timberlake more, they also levied a whopping 53% more in fines (Gordon, 2004).

Beyond space, time and causality, patterns in language have been shown to shape many other domains of thought. Russian speakers, who make an extra distinction between light and dark blues in their language, are better able to visually discriminate shades of blue (Majid & Sweetser, 2006). The Piraha, a tribe in the Amazon in Brazil, whose language eschews number words in favor of terms like few and many, are not able to keep track of exact quantities (Núñez & Sweetser, 2006). And Shakespeare, it turns out, was wrong about roses: Roses by many other names (as told to blindfolded subjects) do not smell as sweet.

Patterns in language offer a window on a culture's dispositions and priorities. For example, English sentence structures focus on agents, and in our criminal-justice system, justice has been done when we've found the transgressor and punished them accordingly (rather than finding the victims and restituting appropriately, an alternative approach to justice). So does the language shape cultural values, or does the influence go the other way, or both?

Languages, of course, are human creations, tools we invent and hone to suit our needs. Simply showing that speakers of different languages think differently doesn't tell us whether it's language that shapes thought or the other way around. To demonstrate the causal role of language, what's needed are studies that directly manipulate language and look for effects in cognition.

One of the key advances in recent years has been the demonstration of precisely this causal link. It turns out that if you change how people talk, that changes how they think.

If people learn another language, they inadvertently also learn a new way of looking at the world. When bilingual people switch from one language to another, they start thinking differently, too. And if you take away people's ability to use language in what should be a simple nonlinguistic task, their performance can change dramatically, sometimes making them look no smarter than rats or infants. (For example, in recent studies, MIT students were shown dots on a screen and asked to say how many there were. If they were allowed to count normally, they did great. If they simultaneously did a nonlinguistic task — like banging out rhythms — they still did great. But if they did a verbal task when shown the dots — like repeating the words spoken in a news report — their counting fell apart. In other words, they needed their language skills to count.) (Winawer, Witthoft, Wu, Frank, Wade, & Boroditsky, 2007)

All this new research shows us that the languages we speak not only reflect or express our thoughts, but also shape the very thoughts we wish to express. The structures that exist in our languages profoundly shape how we construct reality, and help make us as smart and sophisticated as we are.

Language is a uniquely human gift. When we study language, we are uncovering in part what makes us human, getting a peek at the very nature of human nature. As we uncover how languages and their speakers differ from one another, we discover that human natures too can differ dramatically, depending on the languages we speak. The next steps are to understand the mechanisms through which languages help us construct the incredibly complex knowledge systems we have. Understanding how knowledge is built will allow us to create ideas that go beyond the currently thinkable. This research cuts right to the fundamental questions we all ask about ourselves. How do we come to be the way we are? Why do we think the way we do? An important part of the answer, it turns out, is in the languages we speak.

REFERENCES

Boroditsky, L., & Gaby, A. (in press). Absolute spatial representations of time in an Aboriginal Australian community. *Psychological Science.*

Chan, T. T., & Bergen, B. (2005). Writing Direction Influences Spatial Cognition. In Proceedings of the Twenty-Seventh Annual Conference of the Cognitive Science Society.

Evans, N., & Levinson, S. C. (2009). The myth of language universals: Language diversity and its importance for cognitive science. *Behavioral and Brain Sciences, 32(5),* 429–492.

Fausey, C., & Boroditsky, L. (2008). English and Spanish Speakers Remember Causal Agents Differently. *Proceedings of 30th Annual Conference of the Cognitive Science Society.*

Fausey, C., Long, B., Inamori, A., & Boroditsky, L. (2010). Constructing agency: the role of language. *Frontiers in Psychology.* doi: 10.3389/fpsyg .2010.00162

Fausey, C. M., Long, B. L., & Boroditsky, L. (2009). The role of language in eye-witness memory: Remembering who did it in English and Japanese. *Proceedings of the 31st Annual Meeting of the Cognitive Science Society.*

Fausey, C., & Boroditsky, L. (in press). Who dunnit? Cross-linguistic differences in eye-witness memory. *Psychonomic Bulletin & Review.*

Gordon, P. (2004) Numerical Cognition without Words: Evidence from Amazonia. *Science, 306,* 496–499.

Majid, A., Bowerman, M., Kita, S., Haun, D. B. M., & Levinson, S. C. (2004). Can language restructure cognition? The case for space. *Trends in Cognitive Sciences, 8(3),* 108–114.

Núñez, R. E., & Sweetser, E. (2006). With the Future Behind Them: Convergent Evidence From Aymara Language and Gesture in the Crosslinguistic Comparison of Spatial Construals of Time, *Cognitive Science, 30(3),* 401–450.

Winawer, J., Witthoft, N., Wu, L., Frank, M., Wade, A., & Boroditsky, L. (2007). The Russian blues: Effects of language on color discrimination. *Proceedings of the National Academy of Sciences, 104(19),* 7780–7785.

INDEX

Absence of reinforcement (S^Δ), 251–252

Absolute pitch, 264, 267–270, 382, 398

Abstraction, level of, 158

Acquisition utility, 504

Action, attention for, 648–649

Action potential, 660

Activation map, 333

Adaptation, cognitive, 548–563

Adaptation, in evolutionary process, 527–544

Adjustment heuristic, 464–466

Alertness, 320–324, 666

Alignable difference, 502

Ambiguous perception, 82–84, 88–89, 93, 96, 100, 110, 115, 130, 142–145, 188

Ambiguous sentences, 31, 599

American Sign Language (ASL), 162, 166, 575

Ames room, 106–107

Amodal symbols in representations, 194–196

Amusia, 264, 266–267

Amygdala, 665–666, 681

Analysis of variance (ANOVA), 73, 74

Analytic stage of perception, 88

Analyzing data in experimental design, 72–75

Ancestral adaptation, 559–561

Anchoring, 466–467

Animal learning, experimental paradigms in, 231–258

Animal psychophysics, 252–253

Anterior attention system, 645, 652–653

Apparent motion, 99, 133–134, 136–137

Appetitive stimuli, 243

Approach goals, 488

Armstrong, L., 446–448

Arousal, 320, 322–324, 344, 496, 662

Artificial intelligence (AI)
  behaviorism and, 54–55, 59
  brain simulator reply to, 53–54
  combination reply to, 54–55
  computers and, 28–45
  learning and, 225
  Many Mansions reply to, 56–60
  mental-nonmental distinction, 51–52
  other minds reply to, 55–56
  personal location and, 18–27
  present state of technology and, 56–60
  of robots, 52–53
  strong, 46–48, 50–54, 56, 59–60
  systems theory and, 50–52
  technology and, 56–60

Assimilation principle, 290–292

Association area, 193, 201, 214

Atkinson, R., 260

Attention, 319–359
  alertness and arousal and, 322–324
  basics of, 321–322
  controlled, 333
  disorder of (hemineglect), 353–355
  focus of, 90–91
  meanings of, 320
  as mental process, 231
  as mental resource, 322, 344–352
  perceptual, 90–91
  reflexive control and, 326–330
  selective, 90–91
  selective attention and, 333–344
  thalamus and, 665

visual search and, 330–333
  voluntary control and, 326–330, 333–344

Attentional blink, 344

Attention for action, 648–649

Attenuation theory, Treisman's, 338–340

Attraction effect, 476

Auditory agnosia, 267

Auditory scene, 121–154

Auditory streams, 127–137

Autographical memory, 287–288, 450

Automaticity, 345–352

Automatons, 9

Autonomic nervous system (ANS), 661

Autoshaping, 256

Availability heuristic, 461–464

Aversive stimuli, 243

Avoidance goals, 488

Avoidance learning, 241

Background knowledge, 209–210

Baddelley, A., 260

Bartlett, F. C., 278, 279, 290

Basal ganglia, 666

Basic-level categories, 158–162, 168, 701

Basic-level objects, 158–161

Behavioral methods, 669–670

Behaviorism, 5–6, 54–55, 59, 228

Belongingness, 129–130, 139–142

Berkeley, Bishop George., 4

Between-subjects design, 70–71

Biases
  cultural, intelligence and, 608
  due to effectiveness of search set, 462